Contents

Previous Years' Papers (Solved)

Practice Test Papers (Solved)

R. Gupta's®

IIT-JAM

Joint Admission Test for M.Sc.

CHEMISTRY

Previous Years' Papers & Practice Test Papers

(Solved with Explanations)

by

RPH Editorial Board

2027
EDITION

RAMESH PUBLISHING HOUSE, NEW DELHI

Published by
O.P. Gupta *for* Ramesh Publishing House

Admin. Office
12-H, New Daryaganj Road, Opp. Officers' Mess,
New Delhi-110002 ✆ 23275224, 23245124

E-mail: info@rameshpublishinghouse.com
For Online Shopping: www.rameshpublishinghouse.com

Showroom
- Balaji Market, Nai Sarak, Delhi-110006 ✆ 23282525 📱 9354373464
- 4457, Nai Sarak, Delhi-110006

Book Code: R-1281

ISBN: 978-93-5012-129-0

Price: ₹ 445

Printed at: Deepak Offset, Delhi

IIT-JAM

JOINT ADMISSION TEST FOR M.Sc. (CHEMISTRY), 2026

Section A : Multiple Choice Questions (MCQ)

Directions (Qs. No. 1-10): *Carry One mark each.*

1. The molecule that gets inter-converted into its enantiomer, upon ring flipping in its chair conformation, is ________.

A. *cis*-1,2-dimethylcyclohexane
B. *cis*-1,3-dimethylcyclohexane
C. *cis*-1,4-dimethylcyclohexane
D. *trans*-1,2-dimethylcyclohexane

2. In DNA, the number of hydrogen bonds that hold each adenine-thymine base pair and each guanine-cytosine base pair, respectively, are ________.

A. 3 and 3 B. 2 and 2
C. 2 and 3 D. 3 and 2

3. The correct relationship between the molecules X and Y is that, they are _____.

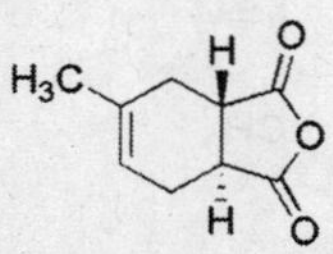

X

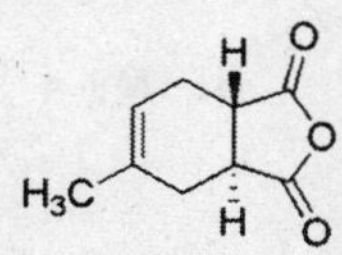

Y

A. regioisomers B. diastereomers
C. enantiomers D. identical molecules

4. The major product **W** formed in the following reaction is

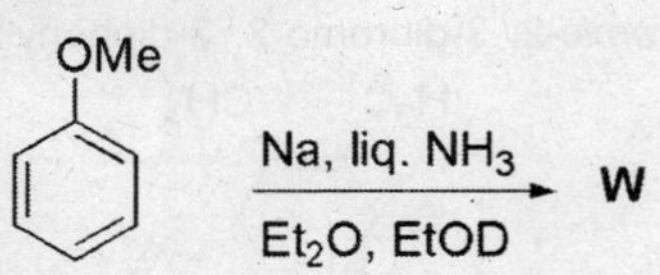

A. 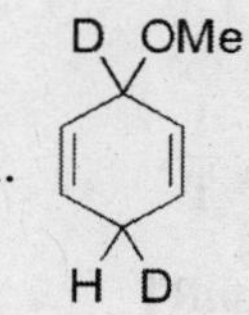

B. 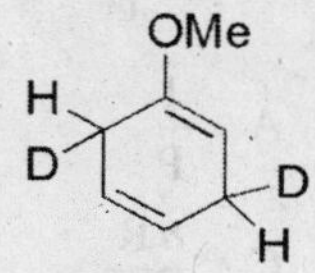

C. 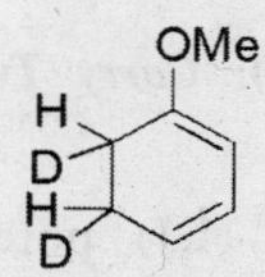

D. 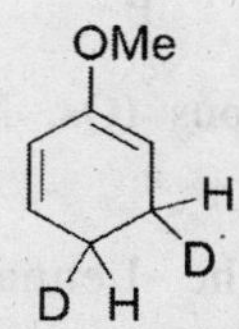

5. Ellingham diagram is a plot of ________.

A. $\Delta_f H^o$ *versus temperature*
B. $\Delta_f G^o$ *versus time*
C. $\Delta_f G^o$ versus temperature
D. $\Delta_f H^o$ versus time

6. The major product formed from the reaction between B_2H_6 and two equivalents of NH_3 at 300° is

A. $BH_3{\cdot}NH_3$
B. $[NH_4]^+ [BH_4]^-$
C. $[(H_3N)_2BH]^{2+} 2[BH_4]^-$
D. $(HBNH)_3$

7. The metal that is used as a catalyst in the synthesis of $(CH_3)_2SiCl_2$ in Rochow-Müller process is

A. Cu B. Zn
C. Sn D. Fe

8. The molecule that has ONLY one lone pair of electrons on xenon is

A. XeF_2 B. XeF_4
C. XeO_2F_2 D. XeO_3F_2

9. For first-order diffraction, the smallest value of d_{hkl} that can be detected with X-ray having a wavelength of 1.54 Å is ____ Å.

A. 0.38 B. 0.77 C. 1.02 D. 2.05

10. For an ideal gas, the isothermal compressibility $\left[k_T = -\frac{1}{V}\left(\frac{\partial V}{\partial P}\right)_T\right]$ is

A. $\frac{1}{P}$ B. $\frac{1}{T}$

C. $\frac{nR}{P}$ D. nRT

Directions (Qs. No. 11-30): *Carry Two marks each.*

11. The Lennard-Jones (LJ) potential of interaction between two molecules as a function of distance (r), is given by $V_{LJ}(r) = 4\epsilon\left[\left(\frac{\sigma}{r}\right)^{12} - \left(\frac{\sigma}{r}\right)^{6}\right]$, where ϵ and σ are constants. The expression of r at which $V_{LJ}(r)$ reaches minimum is

A. $\left(\frac{11}{6}\right)^{1/4}\sigma^{3/2}$ B. $2^{1/6}\sigma$

C. σ D. $4^{1/5}\epsilon^{1/6}$

12. The ^{1}H-NMR spectral data of a compound **X** is as follows: δ(ppm): 11.6 (*s*, 1H, exchangeable with D_2O), 7.60 (*d*, 1H, J = 7.2 Hz), 7.20 (*t*, 1H, J = 7.2 Hz), 6.90 (*d*, 1H, J = 7.2 Hz), 3.70 (*s*, 3H), 3.58 (*s*, 3H). Based on the spectral data, choose the appropriate structure for compound **X**.

A. 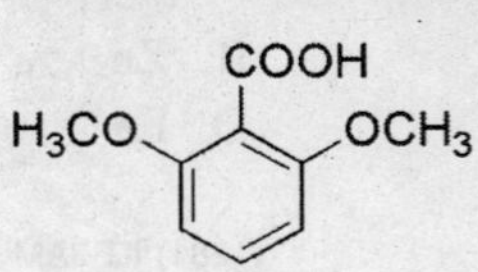

B. 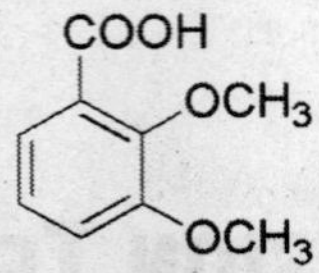

C. 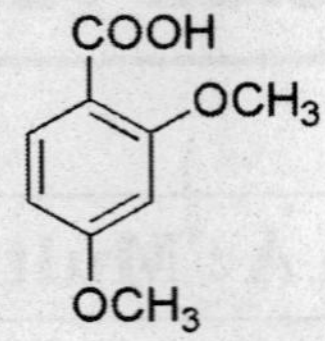

D. 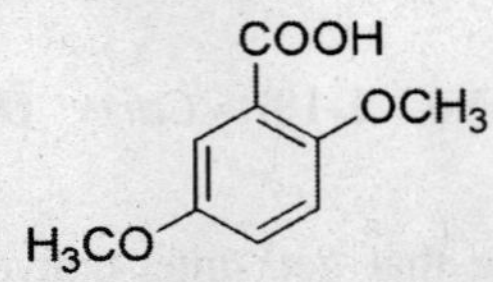

13. The major products **M** and **N** formed in the following reaction sequence are

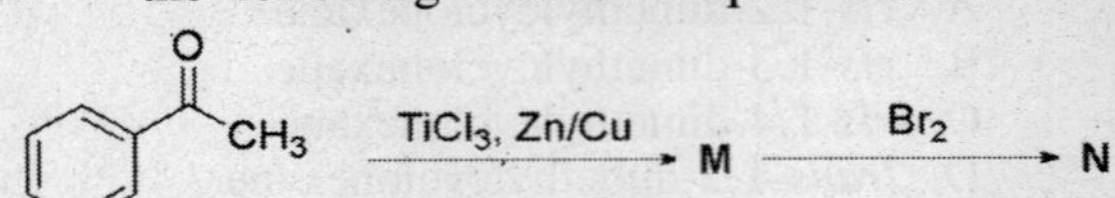

A. **M** = 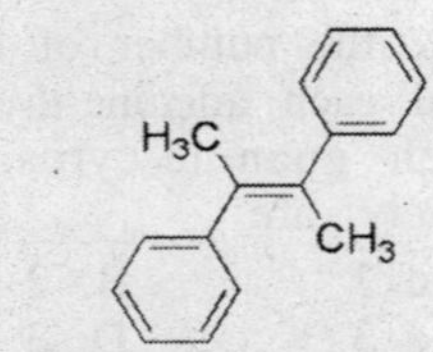

N = *meso*-2, 3-dibromo-2, 3-diphenylbutane

B. **M** = 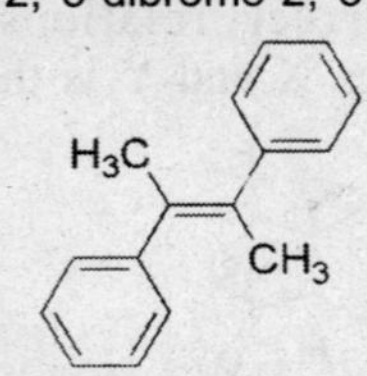

N = *racemic*-2, 3-dibromo-2, 3-diphenylbutane

C. **M** = 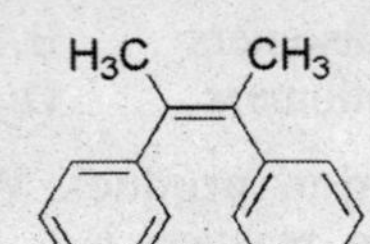

N = *racemic*-2, 3-dibromo-2, 3-diphenylbutane

D. **M** = 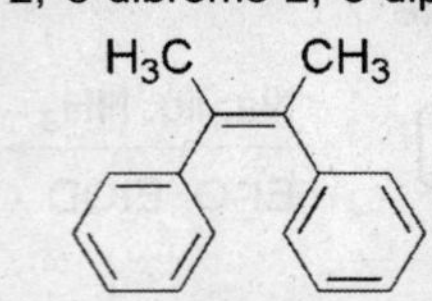

N = *meso*-2, 3-dibromo-2, 3-diphenylbutane

14. The major products **X** and **Y** formed in following reaction sequence are

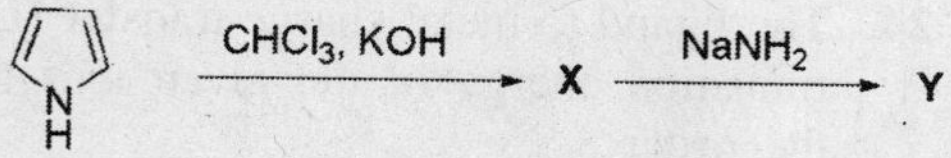

A. X = 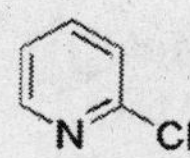 Y = 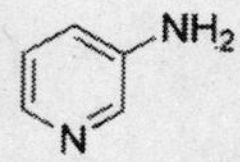

B. X = 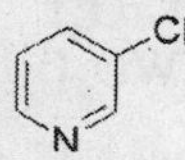 Y = 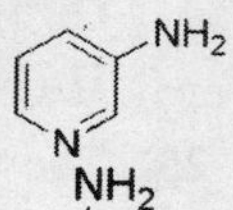

C. X = 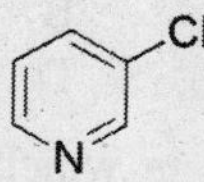 Y = 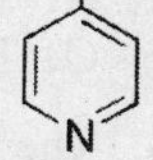

D. X = 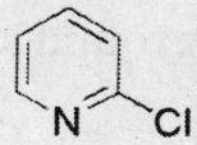 Y = 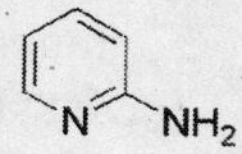

15. A mono-substituted aromatic compound **P** decolourizes bromine water, gives a purple red colour with aqueous $FeCl_3$ and is also soluble in aqueous NaOH. Compound **P** undergoes acetylation with reagent **Q** in the presence of a base to give **R** as the major product. Reagent **Q** displays two characteristic bands at 1830 cm^{-1} and 1750 cm^{-1} in its IR spectrum. P, Q and R are

A. P = 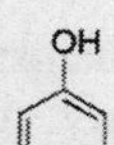 Q = 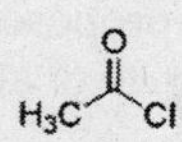 R = 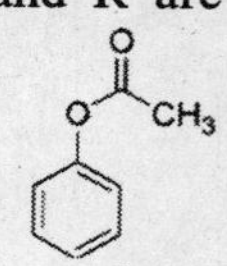

B. P = 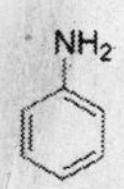 Q = 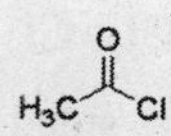 R = 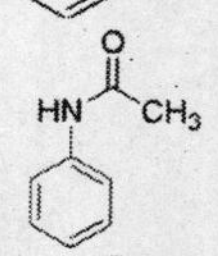

C. P = 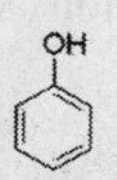 Q = 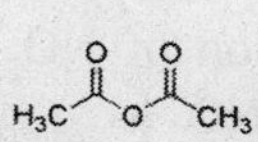 R = 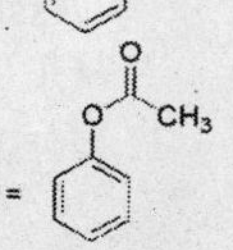

D. P = 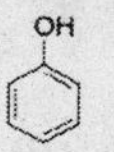 Q = 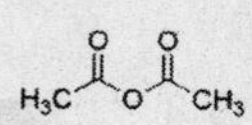 R = 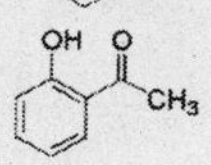

16. The major product **P** formed in the following transformation is

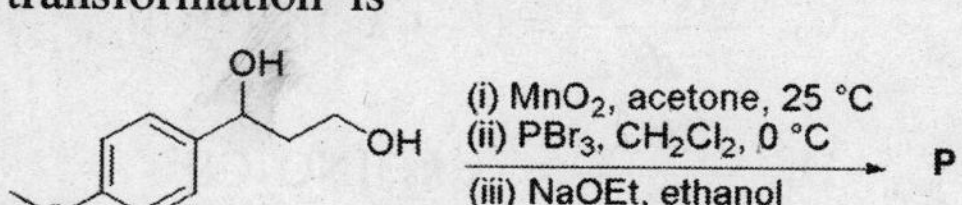

A. 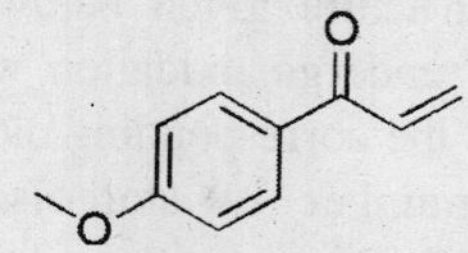

B. 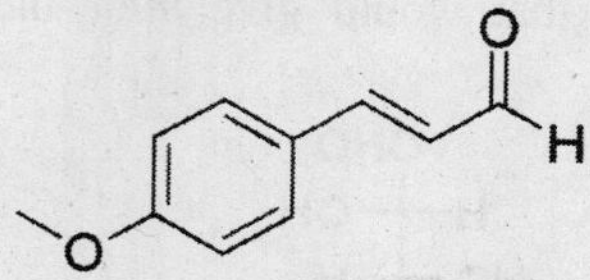

C. 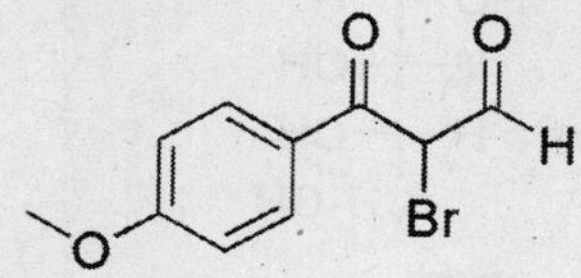

D. 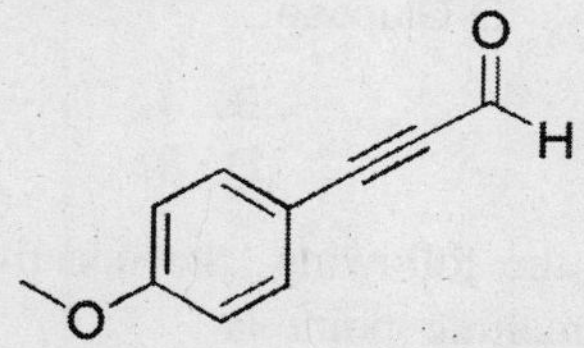

17. The molecules that possess σ (plane of symmetry) as the ONLY element of symmetry are

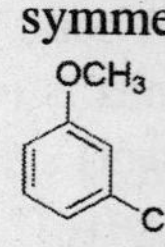 (I)

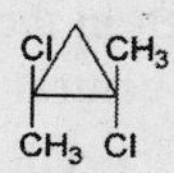 (II)

$(CH_3)_2SO$ (III)

$(CH_3)_2CO$ (IV)

A. II and IV   B. I and IV

C. III and IV   D. I and III

18. Reaction that yields **P** as the major product is

P = 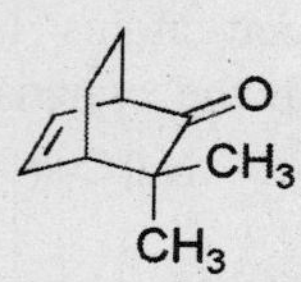

A. 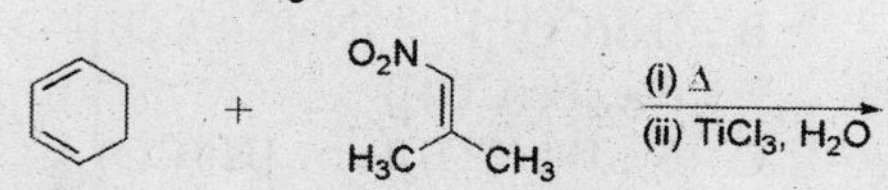

B. 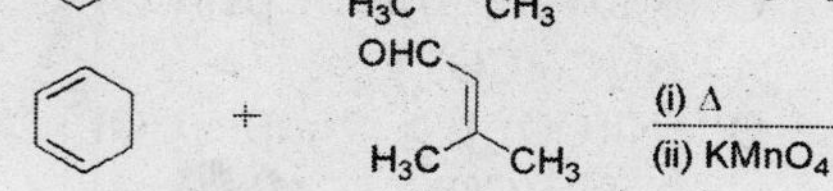

C. 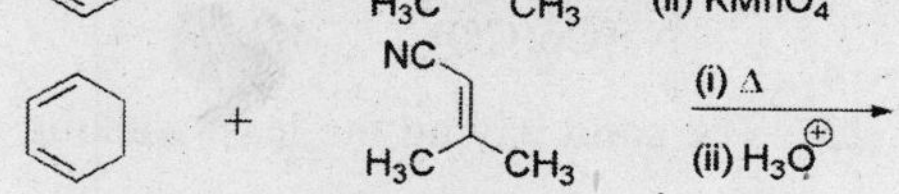

D. 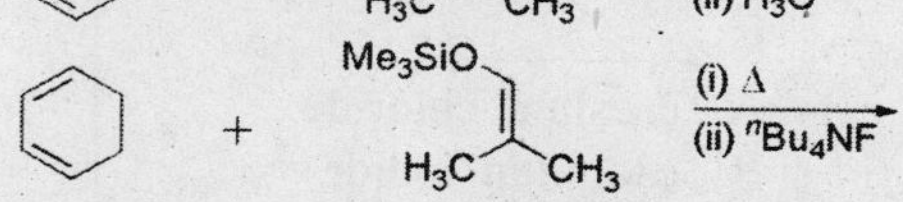

19. D-Glucose (structure given below) and its stereoisomers undergo oxidation with conc. HNO_3 to give the corresponding dicarboxylic acids. The number of stereoisomers of glucose that would give *meso*-dicarboxylic acid is

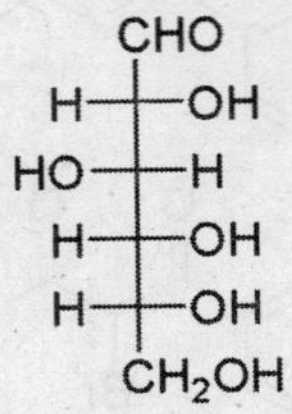

D-Glucose

A. 2 B. 4
C. 6 D. 8

20. Among the following, the one that has the lowest melting point is

A. LiBr B. $AlBr_3$
C. NaBr D. $MgBr_2$

21. The correct order of F—M—F bond angle of compounds given in the options is (where M represents the central element)

A. $XeF_2 > BF_3 > OF_2 > [NF_4]^+$
B. $XeF_2 > BF_3 > [NF_4]^+ > OF_2$
C. $BF_3 > XeF_2 > [NF_4]^+ > OF_2$
D. $XeF_2 > OF_2 > BF_3 > [NF_4]^+$

22. The correct order of bond length between carbon and oxygen atoms in the metal carbonyls given in the options is

A. $Na_2[Fe(CO)_4] > Na[Co(CO)_4] > [Ni(CO)_4]$
B. $[Ni(CO)_4] > Na[Co(CO)_4] > Na_2[Fe(CO)_4]$
C. $Na_2[Fe(CO)_4] > [Ni(CO)_4] > Na[Co(CO)_4]$
D. $[Ni(CO)_4] > Na_2[Fe(CO)_4] > Na[Co(CO)_4]$

23. The solid having the least packing efficiency is ________.

A. caesium chloride
B. cadmium iodide
C. zinc sulfide (wurtzite form)
D. zinc sulfide (zinc blende form)

24. The ligand to metal charge transfer (LMCT) transition energy of the given ions follows the order

A. $[WO_4]^{2-} > [MoO_4]^{2-} > [CrO_4]^{2-}$
B. $[CrO_4]^{2-} > [MoO_4]^{2-} > [WO_4]^{2-}$
C. $[MoO_4]^{2-} > [CrO_4]^{2-} > [WO_4]^{2-}$
D. $[MoO_4]^{2-} > [WO_4]^{2-} > [CrO_4]^{2-}$

25. The species that has 'T' shape is

A. PCl_3 B. $SOCl_2$
C. BrF_3 D. $[IO_3]^-$

26. The correct pair in which both the complex ions show the ground state electronic degeneracy is

A. $[TiF_6]^{2-}$ and $[Ti(H_2O)_6]^{2+}$
B. $[Fe(CN)_6]^{4-}$ and $[Mn(CN)_6]^{3-}$
C. $[Ti(H_2O)_6]^{2+}$ and $[Mn(CN)_6]^{3-}$
D. $[Fe(CN)_6]^{4-}$ and $[TiF_6]^{2-}$

27. The complex having the lowest molar extinction coefficient is

A. $Na_2[Ni(Br)_4]$ B. $[Cr(NH_3)_6]SO_4$
C. $Na_2[Co(Cl)_4]$ D. $[Mn(H_2O)_6]SO_4$

28. For the reaction $NO_2Cl \rightarrow NO_2 + \frac{1}{2}Cl_2$, the proposed mechanism involves the following two elementary steps:

$$NO_2Cl \xrightarrow{k_1} NO_2 + Cl$$

$$NO_2Cl + Cl \xrightarrow{k_2} NO_2 + Cl_2$$

Assuming steady state approximation for Cl, the correct expression for the rate of formation of NO_2 is

A. $\frac{d[NO_2]}{dt} = 2k_1[NO_2Cl]$

B. $\frac{d[NO_2]}{dt} = \left(\frac{k_1}{k_2}\right)[NO_2Cl]$

C. $\frac{d[NO_2]}{dt} = (k_1 + k_2)[NO_2Cl]$

D. $\frac{d[NO_2]}{dt} = (k_1k_2)[NO_2Cl]$

29. In the van der Waals equation of state, the volume correction factor (b) arises from the repulsive interactions between the gas molecules. Considering the molecules to behave as hard spheres of radius r, $b = Y \times V_{molecule} \times N_A$. The value of Y is ______.

[Given: N_A is the Avogadro's Number, $V_{molecule}$ is the volume of a gas molecule]

A. 8
B. 2
C. 16
D. 4

30. For the transformation of 1 mole of an ideal gas from an initial temperature of 27°C and an initial pressure of 1 atm to a final temperature of 327°C and a final pressure of 17 atm, the change in enthalpy, ΔH, is ______ kJ.

[Given: Molar heat capacity of the gas is $C_p(JK^{-1}\ mol^{-1}) = a + bT$, where $a = 20.9\ JK^{-1}\ mol^{-1}$, $b = 0.042\ JK^{-2}\ mol^{-1}$ and T is Temperature].

A. 6.30
B. 8.50
C. 11.94
D. 17.61

Section B : Multiple Select Questions (MSQ)

Directions (Qs. No. 31-40): *Carry Two marks each.*

31. The possible value(s) of energy (E) obtained from setting the following determinant equal to zero is/are

$$\begin{vmatrix} \alpha - E & \beta & 0 \\ \beta & \alpha - E & \beta \\ 0 & \beta & \alpha - E \end{vmatrix}$$

A. $\alpha + \sqrt{2}\beta$
B. $\alpha + \beta$
C. $\alpha - \sqrt{2}\beta$
D. α

32. The reaction(s) that give(s) *tert*-butylbenzene as the major product is/are

A. 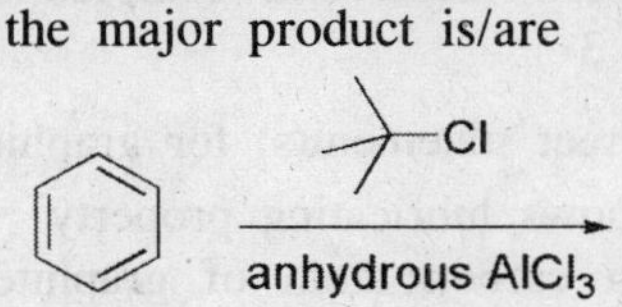

B. 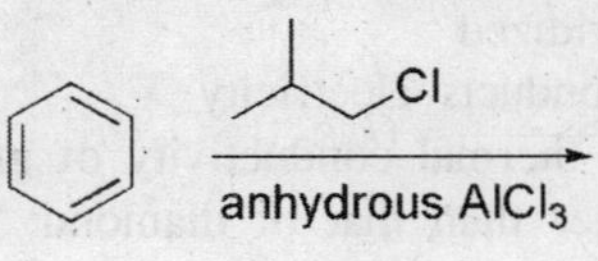

C. 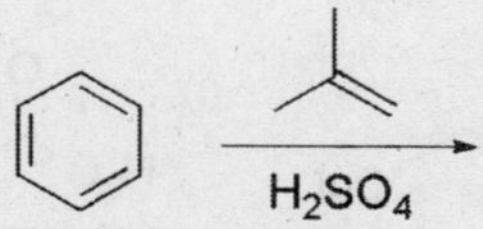

D. 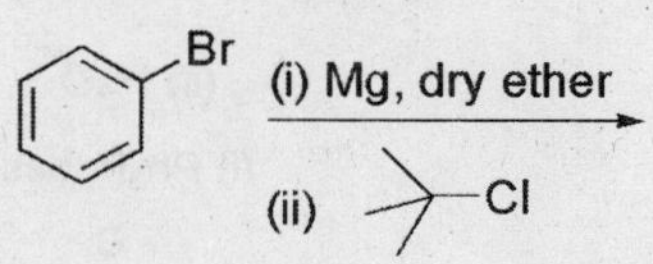

33. Choose the correct statement(s) with regard to the terpenes given below.

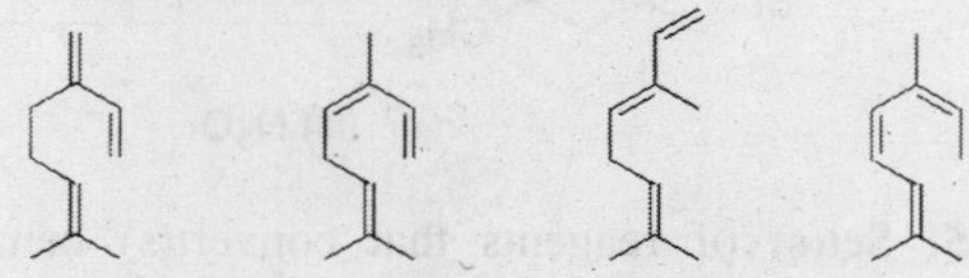

M N O P

A. Upon ozonolysis, all the terpenes would produce at least one identical carbonyl compound
B. Terpenes **N** and **O** are geometrical isomers
C. Terpene **O** cannot undergo Diels-Alder reaction with maleic anhydride
D. Amongst all, λ_{max} for π–π^* absorption is the lowest for terpene **P**

34. The reaction(s) that yield(s) **P** as the major product is/are

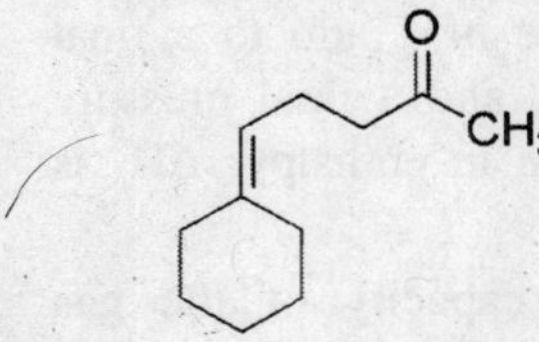

P

A. 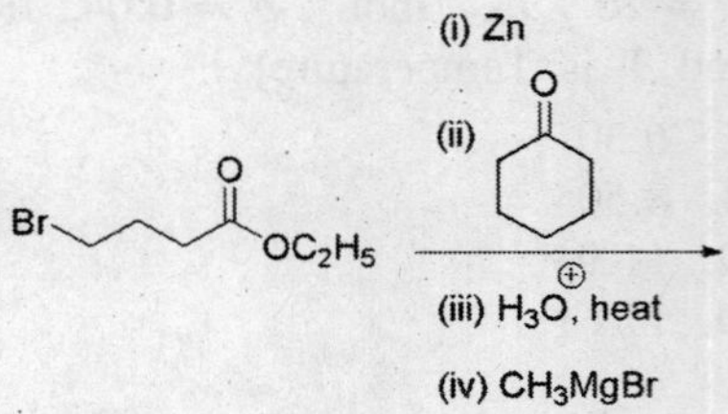

B. 

C. 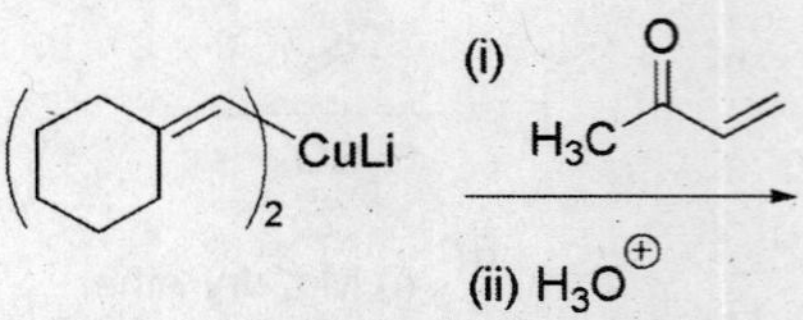

D. 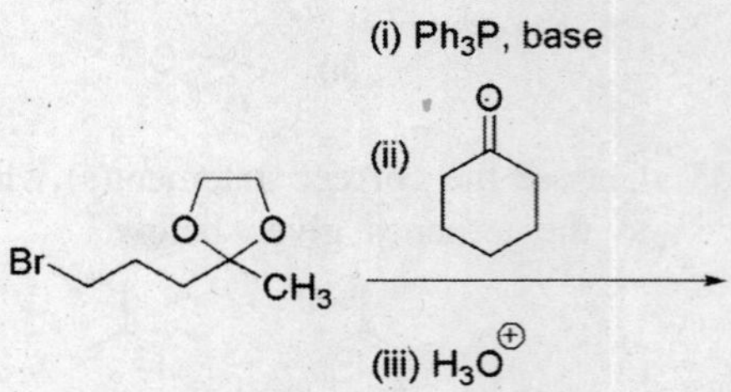

35. Set(s) of reagents that convert(s) benzoyl chloride to aniline is/are

A. (i) NH_3; (ii) Br_2, NaOH; (iii) H_2O
B. (i) CH_2N_2; (ii) H_2O
C. (i) NaN_3; (ii) H_2O
D. (i) NH_2OH; (ii) TsCl, Pyridine; (iii) NaOH, Δ; (iv) H_2O

36. The reactions of Li, Na and K with an excess of oxygen results in the formation of X, Y and Z respectively, as major products. The correct option(s) is/are

A. X is an oxide, Y is a peroxide and Z is a superoxide
B. X and Y are diamagnetic but Z is paramagnetic
C. X is an oxide, Y is a superoxide and Z is a peroxide
D. aqueous solutions of X, Y and Z are basic in nature

37. Choose the correct option(s) with regard to haemoglobin (Hb)

A. Hb binds oxygen in a co-operative process
B. The metal ion in oxy-Hb has a larger size than that in deoxy-Hb
C. Hb takes up more oxygen at pH 7.4 than at pH 6.8
D. The metal ion is paramagnetic in deoxy-Hb

38. Choose the correct statement(s) with regard to the complexometric titration of $[Ni(H_2O)_6]^{2+}$ ion with a complexing agent Na_2H_2EDTA, using a suitable indicator under basic conditions.

A. The correct choice of indicator is phenolphthalein
B. The stoichiometry of nickel and EDTA ions in the metal complex formed between metal and complexing agent is 1:1
C. The binding constant for the complex formed between metal ion and complexing agent is higher than that for the complex formed between metal ion and indicator
D. The stoichiometry of nickel and EDTA ions in the metal complex formed between metal and complexing agent is 1:3

39. The correct statement(s) for graphite is/are

A. It shows lubricating property
B. Each carbon atom of graphite is *sp*-hybridized
C. It conducts electricity
D. The thermal conductivity of graphite is higher than that of diamond

40. The Langmuir isotherm for the adsorption of a gas on a solid surface can be expressed as $\theta = \frac{K_p}{1+K_p}$. The correct statement(s) about this isotherm is/are

[Given: θ is the fractional coverage; p is the pressure of the gas; K is a constant]

A. At very low pressures, plot of θ against p is a straight line passing through the origin with slope equal to K

B. At very high pressures, plot of θ against p is a straight line parallel to the x-axis with the value of the y-intercept equal to 1

C. The Langmuir isotherm can also be expressed as $\frac{1}{\theta} = 1 + \frac{1}{K_p}$

D. The Langmuir isotherm is applicable for multilayer adsorption

Section C : Numerical Answer Type (NAT)

Directions (Qs. No. 41-50): *Carry One mark each.*

41. For the equation $y = 3x^5 + 4x^4 - 3x^3 + x^2 - 2x + 1$, the value of $\frac{d^5y}{dx^5}$ is ____. *(answer in integer)*

42. The number of stereogenic centre(s) present in the given alkaloid is ____. *(answer in integer)*

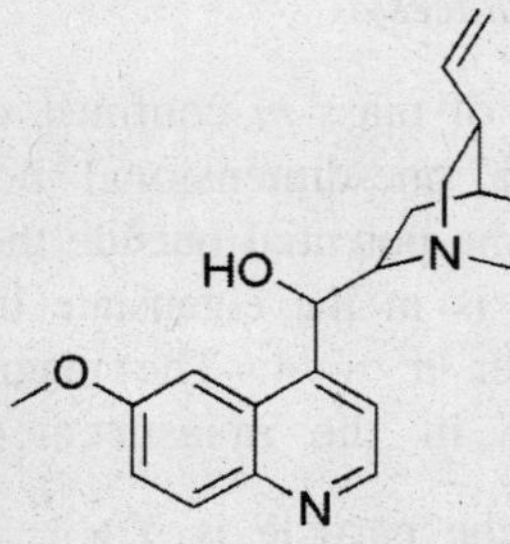

43. The type(s) of chemically non-equivalent protons present in the following molecule is____. *(answer in integer)*

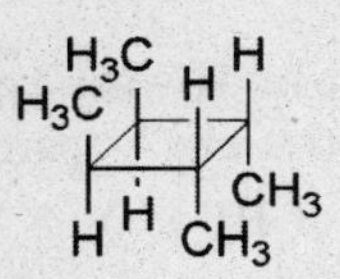

44. The number of unpaired electron(s) of chromium in $[(\eta^6 - C_6H_6)Cr(CO)_3]$ is ____. *(answer in integer)*

45. Consider the following radioactive decay process

$$^{238}_{92}U \longrightarrow {}^{210}_{82}Pb + 7\alpha + m\beta$$

The value of m is ____. *(answer in integer)*

46. The Debye temperatures (θ_D) of diamond and copper are 2230 K and 343 K, respectively. The maximum value of the frequency of the atomic oscillations of diamond is Y times the maximum value of the frequency of the atomic oscillations of copper. The value of Y is ____. *(rounded off to two decimal places)*

47. A system consists of 110 (one hundred and ten) particles. Each particle can have only two non-degenerate energy states ϵ_1 and ϵ_2 (with $\epsilon_1 > \epsilon_2$). The energy difference between these two states is 0.10 eV. The temperature at which only 10 particles of the system will be present in the energy state ϵ_2 is ____ K. *(rounded off to two decimal places)*

[Given: The value of Boltzmann's constant $= 1.38 \times 10^{-23}$ J K^{-1}

1 eV $= 1.6 \times 10^{-19}$ J]

48. When 3.00 g of a substance of molar mass 250 g mol^{-1} is dissolved in 100 g of CCl_4,

the boiling point of the solvent (CCl_4) will be elevated by ________ K.
(rounded off to two decimal places)
[Given: Boiling point constant, K_b, for CCl_4 = 5.00 K kg mol^{-1}]

49. The number of normal modes of vibration in benzene is ________.
(answer in integer)

50. At 30°C, the half-life for the decomposition of a compound is 100 seconds and the value of the half-life is independent of the initial concentration of the reactant.
The time required for 30% of the reactant to be consumed is ________ seconds.
(rounded off to one decimal place)

Directions (Qs. No. 51-60): *Carry Two marks each.*

51. The specific rotation $[\alpha]_D^{25}$ of (S)-2-pentanol is +13.0 degrees. A one molar solution of (S)-2-pentanol is mixed with an equal volume of one molar solution of *racemic* 2-pentanol. The observed rotation, α, of the resulting solution, when measured in a polarimeter tube of path length 10 cm is_____degrees.
(rounded off to three decimal places)
(Given: Molar mass of 2-pentanol is 88 g mol^{-1})

52. The number of iron atom(s) in Fe_3O_4 with an oxidation state of III along with a coordination number of six is ________.
(answer in integer)

53. The total number of P–O–P bridge(s) in the solid state structure of P_4O_8 is________.
(answer in integer)

54. At pH 7, the reaction for the oxidation of NADH at 298 K and a pressure of 1 atm is given below:

$$NADH + H^+ + \frac{1}{2}O_2 \rightarrow NAD^+ + H_2O$$

At 298 K, E°(NAD^+/NADH) = –0.320 V and E°(O_2/H_2O) = 0.816 V
The standard Gibbs free energy change (ΔG°) for this reaction is _____ kJ.
(rounded off to two decimal places)
[Given: Faraday's constant = 96500 C mol^{-1}]

55. The mobility of Na^+ ions in water at 298 K is 5.19×10^{-8} m^2s^{-1} V^{-1}. If the effective radius of a Na^+ ion is $Y \times 10^{-12}$ m, the value of Y is ________.
(rounded off to two decimal places)
[Given: Elementary charge = 1.6×10^{-19}C
Viscosity of water at 298 K is 1 mPa s]

56. For the dissociation reaction,

$$N_2O_3\ (g) \leftrightharpoons NO_2\ (g) + NO\ (g)$$

when 1 mole of N_2O_3 (g) is allowed to reach equilibrium at 27°C and at a total pressure of 1 bar, its degree of dissociation is found to be 0.20. The value of equilibrium constant, K_P, is ______. *(rounded off to three decimal places)*

57. A free particle of mass *m* confined within the walls of a one-dimensional box of length a (with the potential outside the box being infinity), is in the eigenstate having quantum number *n* = 4. The magnitude of uncertainty in the measurement of momentum of the particle is $Y \times \frac{h}{a}$. The value of Y is ________. *(answer in integer)*
[Given: The potential V inside the box is equal to zero and *h* is the Planck's constant]

58. The rotational spectrum of HF has equally spaced lines that are 40.9 cm^{-1} apart.
The moment of inertia of HF is $Y \times 10^{-47}$ kg m^2. The value of Y is ________.
(rounded off to three decimal places)
[Given: Speed of light, $c = 3 \times 10^8$ m s^{-1}
Planck's constant, $h = 6.63 \times 10^{-34}$J s]

59. At a constant pressure, the entropy of mixing of 1 mole of oxygen with 3 moles of nitrogen at 25°C is ______ J K^{-1}. (*rounded off to two decimal places*)

[Given: Universal gas constant, R = 8.314 J mol^{-1} K^{-1} Assume that the gases behave ideally]

60. If the radial wavefunction of the 3*p* orbital of a hydrogen-like atom is

$$R_{31}(r) = \frac{1}{\sqrt{486}}\left(\frac{Z}{a_0}\right)^{3/2}(4-\rho)e^{-\rho/2}$$

then, the radial node of the orbital is located at Y × $\frac{a_0}{Z}$, where Y is equal to ______. (*answer in integer*)

[Given: Z is the atomic number of the hydrogen-like atom a_0 is the Bohr radius $\rho = \left(\frac{2Z}{na_0}\right)r$, *n* is the principal quantum number]

ANSWERS

SECTION A: MCQ (Multiple Choice Questions)

1	2	3	4	5	6	7	8	9	10
A	C	D	B	C	D	A	C	B	A
11	**12**	**13**	**14**	**15**	**16**	**17**	**18**	**19**	**20**
B	B	MTA	C	C	A	D	A	B	B
21	**22**	**23**	**24**	**25**	**26**	**27**	**28**	**29**	**30**
B	A	A	A	C	C	D	A	D	C

SECTION B: MSQ (Multiple Select Questions)

31	32	33	34	35
AC; D	A; B ; C	A; B	B; C; D	A; C; D OR A; D
36	**37**	**38**	**39**	**40**
A; B; D	A; C; D	B; C	A; C	A; B; C

SECTION C: NAT (Numerical Answer Type)

41	42	43	44	45
360 to 360	5 to 5	2 to 2	0 to 0	4 to 4
46	**47**	**48**	**49**	**50**
6.40 to 6.60	500.00 to 505.00	0.60 to 0.60	30 to 30	50.5 to 52.5
51	**52**	**53**	**54**	**55**
0.560 to 0.580	1 to 1	6 to 6	-220.00 to -219.00	162.50 to 164.50
56	**57**	**58**	**59**	**60**
0.040 to 0.044	2 to 2	1.300 to 1.500	18.55 to 18.80	6 to 6

EXPLANATORY ANSWERS

1. In *cis*-1, 2-dimethylcyclohexane, one methyl group is axial and the other is equatorial in a chair conformation. On ring flipping, the axial methyl becomes equatorial and the equatorial methyl becomes axial, while the cis relationship is retained. The two chair forms so produced are non-superimposable mirror-image conformations, so they are conformational enantiomers. In *trans*-1, 2-dimethylcyclohexane, ring flipping mainly interconverts diaxial and diequatorial forms of the same stereoisomer, not its enantiomer; hence option A fits the question correctly.

2. In DNA, adenine pairs specifically with thymine through two hydrogen bonds, while guanine pairs specifically with cytosine through three hydrogen bonds. This difference is important because G–C-rich regions of DNA are more thermally stable than A–T-rich regions. The complementary base-pairing rule is A = T and G ≡ C, where the double and triple bonding pattern shows the number of hydrogen bonds. Therefore, the numbers asked respectively for adenine–thymine and guanine–cytosine are 2 and 3.

3. Molecules X and Y have the same connectivity, the same double-bond position, and the same relative stereochemistry at the fused ring junction. The apparent change in the position of the methyl group is due to the way the molecule is drawn; by rotating one structure in space, the methyl-bearing end of the double bond corresponds exactly to the other drawing. The wedge and dash hydrogens at the ring junction also match after this rotation, so there is no change in configuration. Hence X and Y are not regioisomers, diastereomers or enantiomers; they are identical molecules.

4. The reaction of anisole with Na/liquid NH_3 in the presence of EtOD is a Birch reduction. The methoxy group is an electron-releasing group, so the carbon bearing OMe remains part of a double bond in the major 1,4-cyclohexadiene product. Since EtOD is used as the deuterium donor, deuterium is incorporated at the two reduced/saturated ring carbons formed during the Birch reduction. Option B correctly shows the methoxy-substituted diene with deuterium placed at the proper saturated positions, whereas the other options place deuterium or double bonds in positions inconsistent with the Birch reduction of anisole.

5. Ellingham diagram is a graph showing the variation of standard Gibbs free energy change of formation of metal oxides, sulphides, halides, etc., with temperature. It is mainly used in metallurgy to predict the feasibility of reduction of metal oxides by reducing agents like carbon, carbon monoxide or hydrogen. The lower the ΔG° line on the Ellingham diagram, the more stable is the compound formed. Since the diagram directly compares $\Delta_f G^\circ$ with temperature and not enthalpy or time, option C is the correct answer.

6. The reaction of diborane, B_2H_6, with two equivalents of ammonia at high temperature such as about 300°C gives borazine, whose formula is $B_3N_3H_6$ or $(HBNH)_3$. Borazine is also called inorganic benzene because it has a six-membered ring with alternating boron and nitrogen atoms, similar in arrangement to the carbon ring of benzene. At lower temperature, ammonia–borane type adducts or ionic intermediates may form, but on heating dehydrogenation and ring formation take place. Therefore, under the given heated condition, the major product is $(HBNH)_3$.

7. In the Rochow–Müller process, dimethyl-dichlorosilane, $(CH_3)_2SiCl_2$, is prepared by

the direct reaction of methyl chloride with silicon in the presence of copper as catalyst. Copper activates silicon and promotes the formation of organochlorosilanes, among which dimethyldichlorosilane is the most important product for silicone manufacture. This process is industrially significant because $(CH_3)_2SiCl_2$ is hydrolysed and polymerised to produce silicones. Zinc, tin and iron are not the main catalyst used in this synthesis, so the correct metal is Cu.

8. In XeO_2F_2, xenon is bonded to two oxygen atoms and two fluorine atoms, and it has only one lone pair of electrons on the xenon atom. Its structure is generally described with five electron domains around xenon: four bonding domains and one lone-pair domain. In XeF_2, xenon has three lone pairs, while in XeF_4, xenon has two lone pairs. In XeO_3F_2, xenon has five bonding domains and no lone pair on xenon. Therefore, the molecule having only one lone pair of electrons on xenon is XeO_2F_2.

9. For X-ray diffraction, Bragg's equation is $n\lambda = 2d\sin\theta$. For first-order diffraction, $n=1$, and the smallest detectable value of doccurs when $\sin\theta$ has its maximum possible value, i.e. $\sin\theta = 1$. Therefore, $d_{min} = \lambda/2 = 1.54/2 = 0.77$ Å. A value smaller than this would require $\sin\theta > 1$, which is physically impossible, so the correct value is 0.77 Å.

10. For an ideal gas, PV = nRT, so at constant temperature, $V = \frac{nRT}{P}$. Differentiating with respect to pressure at constant temperature gives $\left(\frac{\partial V}{\partial P}\right)_T = -\frac{nRT}{P^2}$. Since $V = \frac{nRT}{P}$ this derivative becomes $-\frac{V}{P}$. Hence, $k_T = -\frac{1}{V}\left(-\frac{V}{P}\right) = \frac{1}{P}$, so the isothermal compressibility of an ideal gas is $\frac{1}{P}$.

11. For the Lennard-Jones potential,

$$V_{LJ}(r) = 4\varepsilon\left[\left(\frac{\sigma}{r}\right)^{12} - \left(\frac{\sigma}{r}\right)^{6}\right].$$

At minimum potential, $\frac{dV}{dr} = 0$.

Thus, $4\varepsilon[-12\sigma^{12}r^{-13} + 6\sigma^6 r^{-7}] = 0$, so $6\sigma^6\, r^{-7} = 12\sigma^{12}\, r^{-13}$.

Hence, $r^6 = 2\sigma^6$, and therefore $r = 2^{1/6}\sigma$. This is the equilibrium separation where attractive and repulsive forces balance each other, so the correct expression is $2^{1/6}\sigma$.

12. The signal at δ11.6 *ppm*, singlet, 1H, exchangeable with D_2O, confirms the presence of a carboxylic acid proton. The two singlets at δ3.70 and δ3.58, each integrating for 3H, show the presence of two non-equivalent methoxy groups. The aromatic region shows three protons as *d*, *t*, *d*, each with J = 7.2Hz, which indicates three adjacent aromatic hydrogens in a 1,2,3-trisubstituted benzene ring. Option B has COOH at one position and two methoxy groups at adjacent 2,3-positions, leaving three consecutive aromatic hydrogens; hence it matches the given NMR data correctly.

13. Ambiguous question/options:
$TiCl_3$, Zn/Cu brings about McMurry coupling of acetophenone to form 2,3-diphenylbut-2-ene, but the given reaction conditions do not make the stereochemical outcome of M completely unambiguous from the question alone. If M is the trans/E alkene, anti addition of Br_2 gives meso-2,3-dibromo-2,3-diphenylbutane, matching option A. If M is the cis/Z alkene, anti addition of Br_2 gives a racemic 2,3-dibromo-2,3-diphenylbutane product, matching option C. Since both stereochemical paths are chemically reasonable and the question does not provide a condition or statement that fixes only one alkene stereoisomer as the definite major product, the question is ambiguous and should be treated as NONE

rather than having a single 100% correct option.

14. Pyrrole reacts with $CHCl_3$/KOH through dichlorocarbene formation and undergoes ring expansion to give 3-chloropyridine as product X. This transformation is characteristic because the five-membered pyrrole ring is converted into a six-membered pyridine ring with chlorine at the 3-position. On treatment with $NaNH_2$, 3-chloropyridine undergoes strong-base-induced cine substitution through a pyridyne-type intermediate rather than simple direct replacement only at the same carbon. The amino group is introduced predominantly at the adjacent 4-position, giving 4-aminopyridine as Y; therefore option C correctly represents both X and Y.

15. Compound P decolourises bromine water, gives a purple-red colour with aqueous $FeCl_3$, and dissolves in aqueous NaOH, which together identify it as phenol. Phenol is acidic enough to form sodium phenoxide in NaOH and gives coloured complexes with ferric chloride, while aniline would not satisfy the NaOH-solubility condition. Reagent Q shows two characteristic carbonyl stretching bands near 1830 cm^{-1} and 1750 cm^{-1}, which is typical of an acid anhydride, so Q is acetic anhydride and not acetyl chloride. In the presence of a base, phenol undergoes O-acetylation with acetic anhydride to form phenyl acetate as the major product R, so option C is correct.

16. The starting compound contains a benzylic secondary alcohol and a terminal primary alcohol, and MnO_2 selectively oxidises the benzylic alcohol to a ketone under mild conditions while the ordinary primary alcohol remains unchanged. Thus the first step gives *p*-methoxyphenyl-CO-CH_2CH_2OH. In the second step, PBr_3 converts the terminal alcohol group into the corresponding bromide, giving p-methoxyphenyl-CO-CH_2CH_2Br. Treatment with NaOEt then removes an acidic α-hydrogen next to the carbonyl and eliminates HBr to form the conjugated alkene *p*-methoxyphenyl-CO-CH = CH_2. Therefore, option A represents the major product P correctly.

17. Compound I, the unsymmetrically disubstituted benzene derivative shown, is a planar molecule and has only the molecular plane as its symmetry plane; the different substituents destroy any higher rotational symmetry. Compound III, $(CH_3)_2$ SO, has two identical methyl groups and a plane of symmetry passing through the S=O bond, so it also belongs to the type where σ is the only symmetry element apart from identity. Compound IV, acetone, has more symmetry than just one plane, because it possesses a C_2 axis and additional symmetry planes in its ideal structure. Compound II also does not fit the condition as cleanly as I and III because its substituted cyclic framework has additional stereochemical symmetry features beyond only a single mirror plane. Hence the correct set is I and III.

18. cyclopentadiene + the nitroalkene shown in option A; (*i*) Δ, (*ii*) $TiCl_3$, H_2O: The nitroalkene in option A acts as an electron-deficient dienophile and undergoes Diels–Alder reaction with cyclopentadiene on heating to give the corresponding norbornene-type adduct. In this cycloaddition, the carbon bearing the nitro group becomes the carbon that can later be converted into the carbonyl centre, while the adjacent carbon retains the two methyl groups as a gem-dimethyl unit. The second step, $TiCl_3/H_2O$, brings about reductive Nef-type conversion of the nitro group into a carbonyl group. Therefore, the sequence in option A gives the shown bicyclic ketone P as the major product, whereas aldehyde, nitrile or silyl enol ether alternatives do not match this transformation as directly and correctly.

19. On oxidation with concentrated HNO_3, an aldohexose is converted into an aldaric acid because both terminal groups, CHO and CH_2OH, become COOH. After this oxidation, the two ends of the molecule become identical, so a meso dicarboxylic acid will be formed only when the configuration pattern at C_2–C_5 has internal symmetry. Writing the OH-side arrangement as four positions, the *meso*-forming patterns must read the same from both ends: RRRR, RLLR, LRRL and LLLL. Thus, among glucose and its stereoisomers, 4 stereoisomers give meso-dicarboxylic acids on oxidation.

20. Among the given bromides, $AlBr_3$ has the lowest melting point because it has considerable covalent character and exists largely as molecular aluminium bromide rather than as a strongly ionic lattice like NaBr or $MgBr_2$. According to Fajan's rule, the small highly charged Al^{3+} ion strongly polarises the large Br^- ion, increasing covalent character and lowering the melting point. NaBr, LiBr and $MgBr_2$ have stronger ionic lattice interactions and therefore require more heat to melt. Hence $AlBr_3$ is the compound with the lowest melting point.

21. XeF_2 has a linear structure with three equatorial lone pairs on xenon, so its F–Xe–F bond angle is 180°. BF_3 is trigonal planar with no lone pair on boron, giving an F–B–F angle of 120°. In $[NF_4]^+$, nitrogen is tetrahedral and the F–N–F angle is approximately 109.5°. OF_2 has two bond pairs and two lone pairs on oxygen, so lone-pair repulsions reduce the F–O–F angle below the tetrahedral angle, making it the smallest among the given compounds.

22. The C–O bond length in metal carbonyls increases when metal-to-CO π-back bonding increases, because back donation places electron density into the antibonding π^* orbital of CO. In $Na_2[Fe(CO)_4]$, the carbonylate ion has the highest negative charge and Fe is most electron-rich, so back bonding is strongest and the C–O bond is longest. In $Na[Co(CO)_4]$, back bonding is less than in the iron carbonylate but more than in neutral $Ni(CO)_4$. Therefore, the correct decreasing order of C–O bond length is $Na_2[Fe(CO)_4] > Na[Co(CO)_4] > [Ni(CO)_4]$.

23. Caesium chloride has a CsCl-type cubic structure which is less efficiently packed than the close-packed arrangements present in the other listed structures. Cadmium iodide has a layered structure based on close packing of iodide ions, while zinc sulphide in both wurtzite and zinc blende forms is based on close-packed sulphide-ion arrangements with zinc ions occupying tetrahedral voids. Close-packed arrangements generally have higher packing efficiency than the CsCl-type arrangement. Hence, among the given solids, caesium chloride has the least packing efficiency.

24. In these tetrahedral oxoanions, chromium, molybdenum and tungsten are all in the +6 oxidation state and have d^0 configuration, so the observed transition is ligand-to-metal charge transfer from oxygen-based orbitals to empty metal-based orbitals. On moving from $[CrO_4]^{2-}$ to $[MoO_4]^{2-}$ to $[WO_4]^{2-}$, the energy gap involved in the LMCT transition increases, so the wavelength of absorption decreases. Since transition energy is inversely proportional to wavelength, $\Delta E = \frac{hc}{\lambda}$, the LMCT transition energy order becomes $[WO_4]^{2-} > [MoO_4]^{2-} > [CrO_4]^{2-}$. This also agrees with the fact that chromate absorbs at relatively lower energy and is coloured, whereas molybdate and tungstate absorb at higher energy mainly in the ultraviolet region.

25. Three bond pairs and two lone pairs. According to VSEPR theory, these electron pairs are arranged in a trigonal-bipyramidal electron geometry, with the two lone pairs occupying equatorial positions to minimise repulsion. The remaining three fluorine atoms occupy two axial and one equatorial position, giving a T-shaped molecular structure. PCl_3, $SOCl_2$ and $[IO_3]^-$ are not T-shaped; they are mainly trigonal-pyramidal-type species around the central atom.

26. Ground-state electronic degeneracy is shown when the electronic arrangement gives an orbitally degenerate ground state rather than a completely symmetrical non-degenerate state. In $[Ti(H_2O)^{2+}$, titanium is in the +2 oxidation state, giving Ti^{2+} as a d^2 ion; in an octahedral field, the t_2g^2 arrangement possesses orbital degeneracy. In $[Mn(CN)_6]^{3-}$, manganese is in the +3 oxidation state, giving Mn^{3+} as d^4, and with strong-field CN^- ligand it forms a low-spin t_2g^4 configuration that also has electronic degeneracy. In contrast, $[TiF_6]^{2-}$ is Ti^{4+}, d^0, and $[Fe(CN)_6]^{4-}$ is low-spin Fe^{2+}, d^6, t_2g^6, so these do not show such ground-state electronic degeneracy.

27. The molar extinction coefficient is lowest when the electronic transition is highly forbidden. In $[Mn(H_2O)_6]SO_4$, manganese is present as Mn^{2+}, which has a d^5 high-spin configuration in an octahedral field. For high-spin d^5 ions, all *d-d*transitions are spin-forbidden because the ground state has maximum spin multiplicity. They are also Laporte-forbidden in an octahedral complex, so the absorption intensity is extremely weak. Tetrahedral complexes like $[NiBr_4]^{2-}$ and $[CoCl_4]^{2-}$ show comparatively stronger absorptions, while the manganese (II) aqua complex has the lowest molar extinction coefficient.

28. For the given mechanism, the chlorine atom is the reactive intermediate. Applying steady-state approximation to Cl,

$$\frac{d[Cl]}{dt} = k_1\,[NO_2Cl] - k_2[NO_2Cl][Cl] = 0,$$

So $k_1[NO_2Cl] = k_2[NO_2Cl]\,[Cl]$ and $[Cl] = \frac{k_1}{k_2}$. The rate of formation of NO_2 comes from both elementary steps:

$$\frac{d[NO_2]}{dt} = k_1\,[NO_2Cl] + k_2\,[NO_2Cl][Cl].$$

Substituting $[Cl] = \frac{k_1}{k_2}$,

$$\frac{d[NO_2]}{dt} = k_1\,[NO_2Cl] + k_1[NO_2Cl]$$

$$= 2k_1[NO_2Cl].$$

29. For hard-sphere gas molecules, the excluded volume for a pair of molecules is the volume of a sphere of radius $2r$, i.e. $4/3\pi(2r)^3 = 8V_{molecule}$. Since this excluded volume is shared by two molecules, excluded volume per molecule $= \frac{8V_{molecule}}{2} = 4V_{molecule}$.

Therefore, for one mole of gas molecules, $b = 4 \times V_{molecule} \times N_A$. Comparing this with $b = Y \times V_{molecule} \times N_A$, the value of Y is 4.

30. For an ideal gas, enthalpy depends only on temperature, so pressure change does not affect ΔH.

$T_1 = 27°C = 300K,$

$T_2 = 327°\ C = 600K$

$$\Delta H = \int_{T_1}^{T_2} Cp\, dT = \int_{300}^{600} (a + bT)dT$$

$$\Delta H = a(T_2 - T_1) + \frac{b}{2}(T_2^2 - T_1^2)$$

$$\Delta H = 20.9(300) + \frac{0.042}{2}(600^2 - 300^2)$$

$$\Delta H = 6270 + 0.021(270000)$$

$$= 6270 + 5670$$

$$= 11940J = 11.94\,kJ.$$

31. Let $x = \alpha - E$. The determinant becomes

$$\begin{vmatrix} x & \beta & 0 \\ \beta & x & \beta \\ 0 & \beta & x \end{vmatrix} = 0$$

Expanding, $x(x^2 - \beta^2) - \beta(\beta x)$
$= x^3 - 2\beta^2 x$
$= x(x^2 - 2\beta^2) = 0.$

Thus, $x = 0$, $x = \sqrt{2}\beta$,
$x = -\sqrt{2}\beta$.

Since $x = \alpha - E$, the possible values of E are α, $\alpha - \sqrt{2}\beta$, $\alpha + \sqrt{2}\beta$. Hence options A, C and D are correct.

32. In option A, benzene reacts with tert-butyl chloride in the presence of anhydrous $AlCl_3$ through Friedel–Crafts alkylation, directly forming the tert-butyl carbocation and giving tert-butylbenzene. In option B, isobutyl chloride first gives a less stable primary carbocationic species under Friedel–Crafts conditions, which rearranges to the more stable tert-butyl carbocation before electrophilic substitution on benzene, so tert-butylbenzene is the major product. In option C, 2-methylpropene is protonated in the presence of H_2SO_4 to generate the tert-butyl carbocation, which alkylates benzene to form tert-butylbenzene. Option D involves formation of phenylmagnesium bromide, but reaction with tert-butyl chloride is not the normal reliable route for giving tert-butylbenzene as the major product.

33. Upon ozonolysis, all the terpenes would produce at least one identical carbonyl compound; Terpenes N and O are geometrical isomers: Each of the given terpenes contains a common methyl-substituted alkene unit, and cleavage of that part by ozonolysis gives an identical carbonyl fragment, so statement A is correct. Terpenes N and O have the same molecular formula, same carbon skeleton and same positions of double bonds, but they differ in the spatial arrangement around one carbon–carbon double bond; therefore, they are geometrical isomers and statement B is correct. Statement C is incorrect because terpene O contains a conjugated diene system, so it can undergo Diels–Alder reaction with maleic anhydride. Statement D is also incorrect because terpene P is not the structure with the lowest λ_{max} for $\pi - \pi^*$ absorption among the given terpenes.

34. Option B gives P through Claisen rearrangement of the allylic isopropenyl ether; heating shifts the allylic double bond and generates the methyl ketone with the required cyclohexylidene side chain. Option C gives P because the organocuprate undergoes conjugate 1,4-addition to methyl vinyl ketone, followed by protonation to form the same unsaturated methyl ketone. Option D also gives P because the bromo acetal first forms a Wittig ylide, reacts with cyclohexanone to form the exocyclic alkene, and acid hydrolysis of the acetal then regenerates the methyl ketone. Option A does not directly give P as the major product because the ester/Grignard sequence does not stop cleanly at the required methyl ketone.

35. Broad interpretation — (*i*) NH_3; (*ii*) Br_2, NaOH; (*iii*) H_2O; (*i*) NaN_3; (*ii*) H_2O; and (*i*) NH_2OH; (*ii*) TsCl, Pyridine; (*iii*) NaOH, Δ; (*iv*) H_2O/Strict interpretation — A and D only: Option A is definitely correct because benzoyl chloride first forms benzamide with NH_3, and benzamide undergoes Hofmann bromamide degradation with Br_2/NaOH to give aniline. Option D is also definitely correct because benzoyl chloride forms a hydroxamic acid derivative with NH_2OH, which after activation with TsCl/pyridine undergoes Lossen rearrangement under basic heating, and hydrolysis finally gives aniline. Option C may be considered correct in a broad synthetic sense because benzoyl chloride forms benzoyl azide with NaN_3, and benzoyl azide can undergo Curtius rearrangement followed by hydrolysis to give aniline; thus A, C and D can be accepted if Curtius rearrangement is assumed under the given sequence. However, if the reagent set is read strictly as only NaN_3 followed by H_2O, without explicitly mentioning heat or rearrangement conditions, then option C is incomplete and only A and D remain definitely correct.

36. X is an oxide, Y is a peroxide and Z is a superoxide; X and Y are diamagnetic but Z is paramagnetic; aqueous solutions of X, Y and Z are basic in nature: Lithium reacts with excess oxygen mainly to form lithium oxide, Li_2O, sodium forms sodium peroxide, Na_2O_2, and potassium forms potassium superoxide, KO_2, so statement A is correct. Oxide ion, O^{2-}, and peroxide ion, O_2^{2-}, have all electrons paired, hence X and Y are diamagnetic, while superoxide ion, O_2^-, contains one unpaired electron and is paramagnetic, so statement B is also correct. On reaction with water, these products form alkaline solutions because Li_2 Ogives LiOH, Na_2O_2 gives NaOH along with H_2O_2, and KO_2 gives KOH along with peroxide/oxygen products; therefore statement D is also correct.

37. Hb binds oxygen in a co-operative process; Hb takes up more oxygen at pH 7.4 than at pH 6.8; The metal ion is paramagnetic in deoxy-Hb: Haemoglobin binds oxygen cooperatively, meaning the binding of one oxygen molecule increases the affinity of the remaining haem sites for oxygen, so statement A is correct. In oxy-haemoglobin, iron becomes effectively smaller and moves into the porphyrin plane, whereas deoxy-haemoglobin contains high-spin Fe^{2+}, which is larger; hence statement B is incorrect. Due to the Bohr effect, haemoglobin has greater oxygen affinity at physiological pH 7.4 than at the more acidic pH 6.8, so statement C is correct. Deoxy-haemoglobin contains high-spin Fe^{2+} and is paramagnetic, while oxy-haemoglobin is diamagnetic; therefore statement D is also correct.

38. The stoichiometry of nickel and EDTA ions in the metal complex formed between metal and complexing agent is 1:1; The binding constant for the complex formed between metal ion and complexing agent is higher than that for the complex formed between metal ion and indicator:
A is incorrect because phenolphthalein is an acid-base indicator, not the suitable metallochromic indicator for nickel–EDTA complexometric titration. B is correct because EDTA forms a chelate with Ni^{2+} in 1 : 1 metal-to-ligand stoichiometry, irrespective of the charge on the metal ion. C is correct because EDTA must form a more stable complex with Ni^{2+} than the metal-indicator complex, so that EDTA can displace the indicator at the end point. D is incorrect because nickel and EDTA do not combine in 1 : 3 ratio; EDTA is a hexadentate ligand and normally gives a 1 : 1 chelate with nickel ion.

39. A is correct because graphite has a layered structure in which carbon sheets can slide over one another due to weak forces between the layers, giving it lubricating property. B is incorrect because each carbon atom in graphite is sp^2-hybridised, not sp-hybridised; each carbon is bonded to three other carbon atoms in a planar hexagonal sheet. C is correct because graphite has delocalised π-electrons within its layers, and these mobile electrons allow electrical conduction along the layers. D is incorrect because diamond generally has higher thermal conductivity than graphite when compared as a material property; graphite is highly anisotropic and conducts heat especially well along layers, but the given statement is not correct in the usual comparative sense.

40. At very low pressures, plot of θ against p is a straight line passing through the origin with slope equal to K; At very high pressures, plot of θ against p is a straight line parallel to the x-axis with the value of the y-intercept equal to 1; The Langmuir isotherm can also be expressed as $\frac{1}{\theta} = 1 + \frac{1}{K_p}$:

A is correct because at very low pressure, $K_p \ll 1$, so $1 + K_p \approx 1$, and therefore $\theta = \frac{K_p}{1+K_p} \approx K_p$. Hence the plot of θ versus p is linear, passes through the origin, and has slope K.

B is correct because at very high pressure, $K_p \gg 1$, so $\theta = \frac{K_p}{1+K_p} \approx 1$. This means the surface becomes almost completely covered, and the θ versus p plot becomes nearly horizontal, parallel to the x-axis, at $\theta = 1$.

C is correct because rearranging the given equation gives $\frac{1}{\theta} = \frac{1+K_p}{K_p} = 1 + \frac{1}{K_p}$. This is a valid reciprocal form of the Langmuir adsorption isotherm.

D is incorrect because the Langmuir isotherm is based on monolayer adsorption on a surface having a fixed number of equivalent adsorption sites. Multilayer adsorption is explained by BET theory, not by the Langmuir isotherm.

41. $y = 3x^5 + 4x^4 - 3x^3 + x^2 - 2x + 1$

$$\frac{d^5}{dx^5}(3x^5) = 3 \times 5!$$

$$= 3 \times 120 = 360$$

$$\frac{d^5}{dx^5}(4x^4 - 3x^3 + x^2 - 2x + 1) = 0$$

$$\therefore \quad \frac{d^5y}{dx^5} = 360$$

So the required numerical range is 360 to 360.

42. The given alkaloid contains one stereogenic carbinol carbon bearing OH, H, quinoline ring and quinuclidine unit as four different groups. The rigid quinuclidine part contains three stereogenic carbon centres because the substituted bicyclic framework makes the relevant carbon paths non-equivalent. In addition to these four stereogenic carbon centres, the bridgehead tertiary nitrogen is also counted as a stereogenic centre here because nitrogen inversion is prevented in the rigid bicyclic system and the three carbon paths attached to nitrogen are not equivalent. Therefore, the total number of stereogenic centres present in the given alkaloid is 5, so the required range is 5 to 5.

43. The given substituted cubane-type molecule has high symmetry in the arrangement of four methyl groups and four ring hydrogens. All four methyl groups are chemically equivalent by symmetry, and rapid rotation of each methyl group makes the three protons within every methyl group equivalent. Similarly, the four hydrogen atoms directly attached to the cubane framework are also mutually equivalent by the same symmetry operations of the molecule. Therefore, only two types of chemically non-equivalent protons are present: one methyl-proton type and one ring-proton type. Hence the required range is 2 to 2.

44. In $[(\eta^6 - C_6H_6)Cr(CO)_3]$, benzene and carbonyl ligands are neutral, so chromium is in the zero oxidation state. Chromium (O) has a d^6 configuration. Electron count is

$$Cr(0) = 6e^-,\ \eta^6 - C_6H_6 = 6e^-,\ 3CO = 6e^-$$

Total electron count $= 6 + 6 + 6 = 18e^-$

This is an 18-electron low-spin organometallic complex, so all electrons are paired and the number of unpaired electrons is 0.

45. Given radioactive decay process:
U-238 with atomic number 92 gives Pb-210 with atomic number 82 + 7 alpha particles + m beta particles.
Mass number after 7 alpha emissions:
$238 - 7 \times 4 = 238 - 28 = 210$
Atomic number after 7 alpha emissions:
$92 - 7 \times 2 = 92 - 14 = 78$
Each beta-minus emission increases atomic number by 1:
$$78 + m = 82$$
$$m = 82 - 78 = 4$$
So, the required value of m is 4 to 4.

46. $\theta_D = \frac{h\nu_{max}}{k}$

$\nu_{max} \propto \theta_D$

$$Y = \frac{\nu_{max,\,diamond}}{\nu_{max,\,copper}} = \frac{\theta_D,\,diamond}{\theta_D,\,copper}$$

$$Y = \frac{2230}{343} = 6.50$$

Rounded to two decimal places, the value is 6.50, so the acceptable range is 6.40to 6.60.

47. Energy difference = 0.10 eV
$$0.10\ eV = 0.10 \times 1.6 \times 10^{-19}\ J = 1.6 \times 10^{-20}\ J$$
For two non-degenerate states:
Population ratio = 100/10 = 10
Using Boltzmann relation:
$$10 = e^{(\Delta E/kT)}$$
Taking log:
$\ln 10 = \Delta E/kT$
$T = \Delta E/(k \ln 10)$
$T = (1.6 \times 10^{-20})/(1.38 \times 10^{-23} \times 2.303)$
$T = 503.53$ K
So the suitable numerical answer range is 500.00 to 505.00.

48. $\Delta T_b = K_b m$

Moles of solute $= \frac{3.00}{250} = 0.012$ mol

Mass of solvent = 100 g ≐ 0.100 kg

$$m = \frac{0.012}{0.100} = 0.12\ mol\ kg^{-1}$$

$$\Delta T_b = 5.00 \times 0.12 = 0.60 K$$

So, the elevation in boiling point is 0.60 K.

49. Benzene, C_6H_6, contains total
$$6 + 6 = 12 \text{ atoms}$$
Benzene is a non-linear molecule, so the number of normal modes of vibration is
$$3N - 6 = 3(12) - 6 = 36 - 6 = 30$$
Therefore, the number of normal modes of vibration in benzene is 30.

50. Half-life is independent of initial concentration, so the reaction is first order.
Half-life = 100 seconds
For first-order reaction:
$$k = 0.693/100$$
$$k = 0.00693 \text{ per second}$$
30% reactant consumed means 70% reactant remains.
$$t = (2.303/k) \log(100/70)$$
$$t = (2.303/0.00693) \log(10/7)$$
$$t = 51.5 \text{ seconds approximately}$$
So the suitable numerical answer range is 50.5 to 52.5.

51. Equal volume of 1 M (S)-2-pentanol and 1 M *racemic* 2-pentanol are mixed.
From 1 M (S)-2-pentanol solution:
(S)-2-pentanol = 1 mol equivalent
From 1 M *racemic* 2-pentanol solution:
(S)-2-pentanol = 0.5 mol equivalent
(R)-2-pentanol = 0.5 mol equivalent
Net optically active excess:
1 + 0.5 − 0.5 = 1.0 mol equivalent
Final volume becomes double, so effective optically active concentration:
1.0/2 = 0.5 M
Mass concentration:
0.5 × 88 = 44 g/L = 0.044 g/mL
Path length:
10 cm = 1 dm
Observed rotation:
α = specific rotation × path length × concentration
$\alpha = 13.0 \times 1 \times 0.044$
$\alpha = 0.572$ degrees

So the suitable numerical answer range is 0.560 to 0.580.

52. Fe_3O_4 is magnetite and may be written as $FeO.Fe_2O_3$.
Thus, it contains one Fe^{2+} ion and two Fe^{3+} ions per formula unit. Its spinel structure is inverse spinel type: one Fe^{3+} ion occupies tetrahedral sites, while one Fe^{2+} ion and one Fe^{3+} ion occupy octahedral sites. Octahedral sites have coordination number 6. Therefore, the number of Fe atoms having oxidation state +3 and coordination number 6 is 1.
So the required numerical answer range is 1 to 1.

53. The solid-state structure of P_4O_8 is based on a P_4O_8 cage framework.
In this cage framework, oxygen atoms present along the edges act as bridging oxygen atoms between two phosphorus atoms.
Each such bridge is a P–O–P bridge.
The P_4O_6 cage contains 6 bridging oxygen atoms, and in P_4O_8 the additional oxygens are terminal P=O type oxygens, not extra P–O–P bridges.
Therefore, the total number of P–O–P bridges in P_4O_8 is 6.
So the required numerical answer range is 6 to 6.

54. Given reaction:
$NADH + H^+ + 1/2\ O_2 \rightarrow NAD^+ + H_2O$
Reduction potential of $NAD^+/NADH$
$= -0.320$ V
Reduction potential of $O_2/H_2O = 0.816$ V
Cell potential:
$E°cell = 0.816 - (-0.320)$
$E°cell = 1.136$ V
Number of electrons transferred:

$$n = 2$$
$$\Delta G° = -nFE°cell$$
$$\Delta G° = -2 \times 96500 \times 1.136 \text{ J}$$
$$\Delta G° = -219248 \text{ J}$$
$$\Delta G° = -219.248 \text{ kJ}$$

Rounded value $= -219.25$ kJ
So the suitable numerical answer range is −220.00 to −219.00.

55.
$$u = 5.19 \times 10^{-8}\ m^2 s^{-1} V^{-1}$$
$$\eta = 1 \text{ mPa s} = 1 \times 10^{-3} \text{ Pa s}$$
$$e = 1.6 \times 10^{-19} \text{ C}$$
$$u = e/6\pi\eta r$$
$$r = e/6\pi\eta u$$
$$r = 1.6 \times 10^{-19}/(6 \times 3.1416 \times 1 \times 10^{-3} \times 5.19 \times 10^{-8})$$
$$r = 1.6355 \times 10^{-10} \text{ m}$$
$$r = 163.55 \times 10^{-12} \text{ m}$$

So, Y = 163.55, and the suitable numerical range is 162.50 to 164.50.

56. $N_2O_3 \rightleftharpoons NO_2 + NO$
Initial moles of $N_2O_3 = 1$
Degree of dissociation = 0.20
At equilibrium:

$$N_2O_3 = 1 - 0.20 = 0.80$$
$$NO_2 = 0.20$$
$$NO = 0.20$$

Total moles = 0.80 + 0.20 + 0.20 = 1.20

$$p(N_2O_3) = 0.80/1.20 = 0.6667 \text{ bar}$$
$$p(NO_2) = 0.20/1.20 = 0.1667 \text{ bar}$$
$$p(NO) = 0.20/1.20 = 0.1667 \text{ bar}$$
$$K_p = p(NO_2) \times p(NO)/p(N_2O_3)$$
$$K_p = 0.1667 \times 0.1667/0.6667$$
$$= 0.0417$$

So, the suitable numerical range is 0.040 to 0.044.

57. For a particle in a one-dimensional box of length a:
Momentum uncertainty in nth state:

$$\Delta p = nh/2a$$

Given $n = 4$

$$\Delta p = 4h/2a$$
$$\Delta p = 2h/a$$

Given $\Delta p = Y \times h/a$
Therefore, Y = 2 to 2.

58. Spacing between rotational spectral lines $= 40.9 \text{ cm}^{-1}$

$$\text{Spacing} = 2B$$
$$B = 40.9/2 = 20.45 \text{ cm}^{-1}$$
$$B = 2045 \text{ m}^{-1}$$
$$B = h/8\pi^2 cI$$
$$I = h/8\pi^2 cB$$
$$I = 6.63 \times 10^{-34}/(8 \times 3.1416^2 \times 3 \times 10^8 \times 2045)$$
$$I = 1.369 \times 10^{-47} \text{ kg m}^2$$

So, Y = 1.369, and the suitable numerical range is 1.300 to 1.500.

59. Moles of oxygen = 1

Moles of nitrogen = 3

Total moles = 4

Mole fraction of oxygen = 1/4 = 0.25

Mole fraction of nitrogen = 3/4 = 0.75

$$\Delta S \text{ mixing} = -R[n_1 \ln x_1 + n_2 \ln x_2]$$
$$\Delta S \text{ mixing} = -8.314[1 \ln(0.25) + 3 \ln(0.75)]$$
$$\Delta S \text{ mixing} = -8.314[-1.3863 - 0.8630]$$
$$\Delta S \text{ mixing} = 18.70 \text{ JK}^{-1}$$

So, the suitable numerical range is 18.55 to 18.80.

60. Given radial wavefunction contains the factor:

$$(4 - \rho)e^{-\rho/2}$$

Radial node occurs when the radial wavefunction becomes zero:

$$4 - \rho = 0$$
$$\rho = 4$$

Given:

$$\rho = (2Z/na_0)r$$

For $3p$ orbital,

$$n = 3$$
$$4 = (2Z/3a_0)r$$
$$r = 4 \times 3a_0/2Z$$
$$r = 6a_0/Z$$

Given radial node is at Y × a_0/Z, so Y = 6 to 6.

Previous Years' Paper

IIT–JAM

JOINT ADMISSION TEST FOR M.Sc. (CHEMISTRY), 2025

Section A : Multiple Choice Questions (MCQ)

Directions (Qs. No. 1-10): *Carry One mark each.*

1. Maximum value of the function $f(r) = r^2e^{-r}$, when $0 < r < \infty$ is:

A. $4e^{-2}$ B. e^{-1}

C. $2e^{-\sqrt{2}}$ D. $4e^{-\sqrt{2}}$

2. Consider 10 balls each having different colours including a blue ball. If 6 balls are selected randomly, the probability of the blue ball being selected is:

A. 0.3 B. 0.4

C. 0.6 D. 0.8

3. Sulphide ores are concentrated by:

A. froth floatation B. smelting

C. roasting D. reduction

4. Crystal system with the unit cell parameters $a = b \neq c$ and $\alpha = \beta = \gamma = 90°$ is:

A. monoclinic B. orthorhombic

C. tetragonal D. hexagonal

5. The correct trend of acidity of the ions is:

A. $[Fe(H_2O)_6]^{2+} > [Fe(H_2O)_6]^{3+} > [Al(H_2O)_6]^{3+}$

B. $[Al(H_2O)_6]^{3+} > [Fe(H_2O)_6]^{3+} > [Fe(H_2O)_6]^{2+}$

C. $[Fe(H_2O)_6]^{2+} > [Al(H_2O)_6]^{3+} > [Fe(H_2O)_6]^{3+}$

D. $[Fe(H_2O)_6]^{3+} > [Fe(H_2O)_6]^{2+} > [Al(H_2O)_6]^{3+}$

6. Dissolution of SbF_5 in BrF_3 produces:

A. BrF_5 and SbF_3 B. BrF and SbF_7

C. $[BrF_2]^+ [SbF_6]^-$ D. $[SbF_4]^+ [BrF_4]^-$

7. The molecular structure of table sugar is:

A. 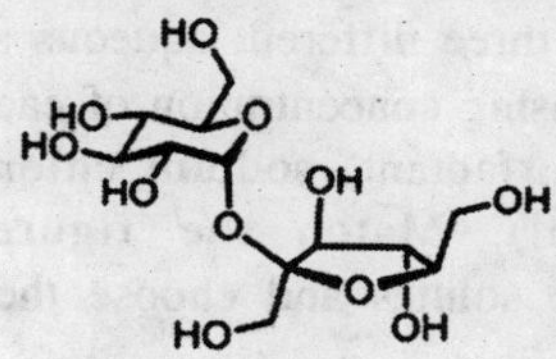

B. 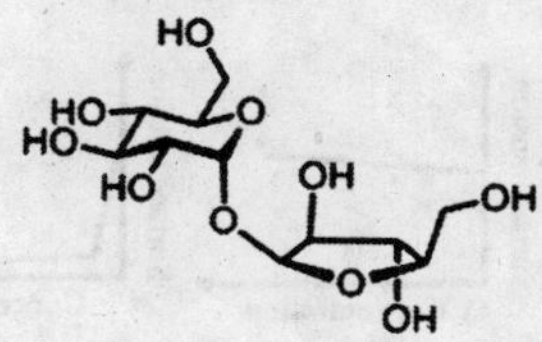

C. 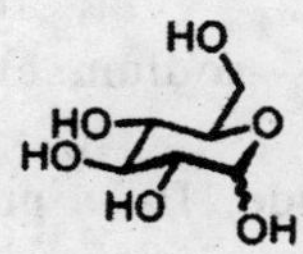

D. 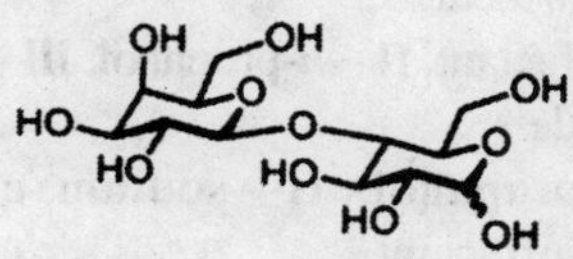

8. The product formed when (R)-2-bromopropionic acid is treated with low concentration of hydroxide ion is:

A. predominantly of S configuration

B. predominantly of R configuration

C. a racemic mixture

D. achiral

9. A system having Hamiltonian $\hat{H}$ follows the eigenvalue equation, $\hat{H}\psi_n = E_n\psi_n$, with $E_n = \left(n+\frac{1}{2}\right)$.

If the state of the system is prepared as,

$\psi = N(\psi_1 + \psi_2 + \psi_3 - \psi_4 - \psi_5)$, where N is the normalization constant, then the expectation value of energy is:

A. –0.5 B. –2.5
C. 3.5 D. 17.5

10. The figures (I, II, III) given below schematically represent variation of surface tension of three different aqueous solutions with increasing concentration of each of the solutes (surfactant, sodium chloride and *n*-propanol). Match the figures with appropriate solutes and choose the correct option.

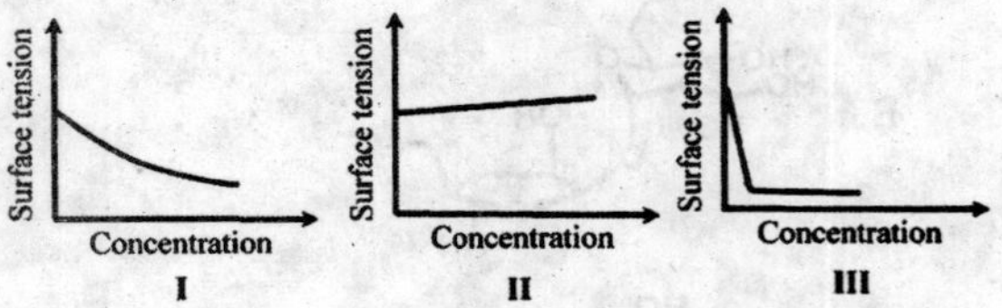

A. I—surfactant, II—sodium chloride, III— *n*-propanol
B. I—sodium chloride, II—*n*-propanol, III—surfactant
C. I—surfactant, II—*n*-propanol, III—sodium chloride
D. I—*n*-propanol, II—sodium chloride, III— surfactant

Directions (Qs. No. 11 to 30): *Carry Two marks each.*

11. The correct option for *x* which satisfies the following equation is

$$\begin{vmatrix} x & 2 & 3 \\ 4 & x & 6 \\ x & 8 & 9 \end{vmatrix} = \begin{vmatrix} 102 & 18 & 36 \\ 1 & 3 & 4 \\ 17 & 3 & 6 \end{vmatrix}$$

A. $3 \pm \sqrt{5}$ B. $\frac{3 \pm \sqrt{5}}{2}$
C. $2\left(3 \pm \sqrt{5}\right)$ D. $3 \pm 2\sqrt{5}$

12. The type of carboxypeptidase metalloenzyme and the metal ion present in it, respectively, are:

A. hydrolase and Zn(II)
B. isomerase and Zn(II)
C. hydrolase and Cu(II)
D. isomerase and Cu(II)

13. The biomolecule that does **NOT** contain iron is:

A. cytochromes B. hemocyanin
C. hydrogenases D. hemerythrin

14. Hydrolysis of P_4O_{10} produces a compound R, which on heating above 320 °C yields a compound S. The compounds R and S, respectively, are:

A. H_3PO_4 and $(HPO_3)_n$
B. H_3PO_3 and $(HPO_3)_n$
C. H_3PO_4 and $H_4P_2O_7$
D. H_3PO_3 and $H_4P_2O_7$

15. Ion-dipole interactions vary with distance (*r*) as:

A. $\frac{1}{r}$ B. $\frac{1}{r^2}$
C. $\frac{1}{r^4}$ D. $\frac{1}{r^6}$

16. In the following transformation, the number of α and β particles emitted, respectively, are:

$$^{223}_{88}Ra \longrightarrow {}^{207}_{82}Pb$$

A. 4, 2 B. 4, 3
C. 2, 4 D. 3, 4

17. Wilkinson's catalyst contains:

A. ruthenium(I) in square planar geometry
B. ruthenium(I) in tetrahedral geometry
C. rhodium(I) in square planar geometry
D. rhodium(I) in tetrahedral geometry

18. The major product of the following transformation is:

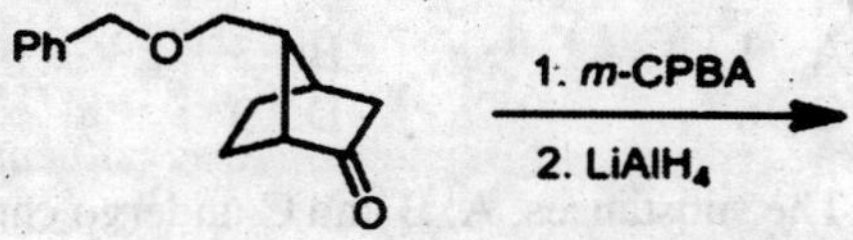

A. 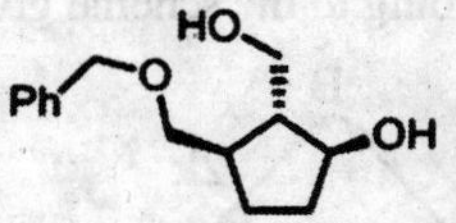

B. 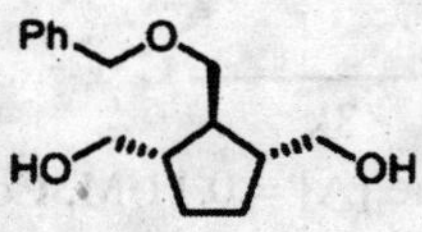

C. 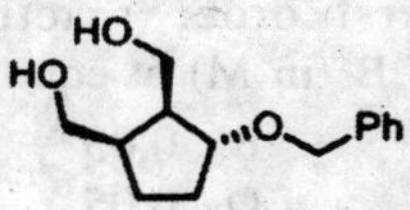

D. 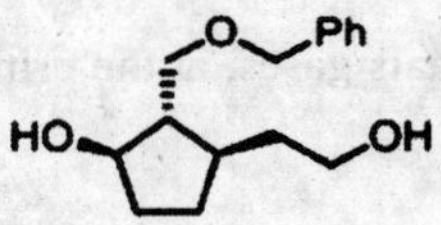

19. The major products P and Q of the following transformations are:

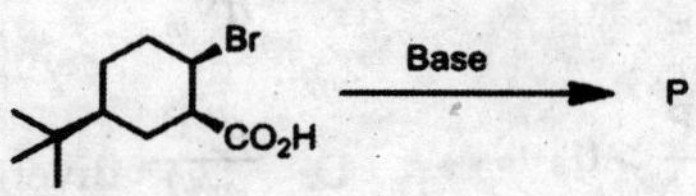

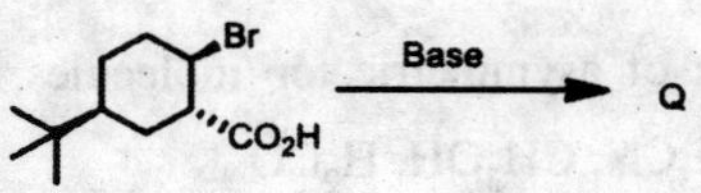

A. P = 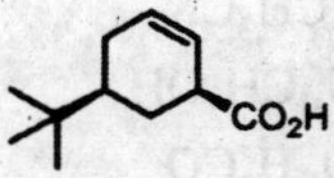 Q = 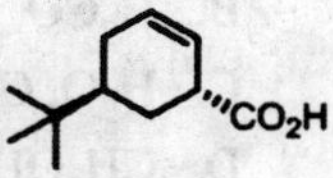

B. P = 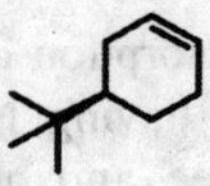 Q = 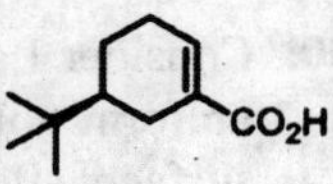

C. P = 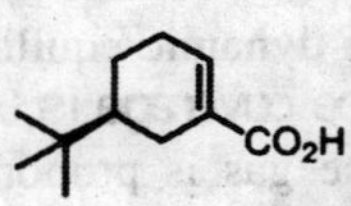 Q = 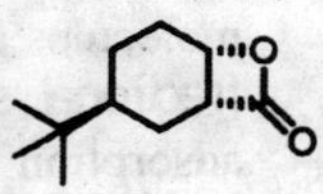

D. P = 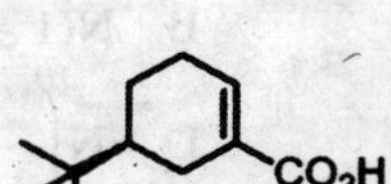 Q = 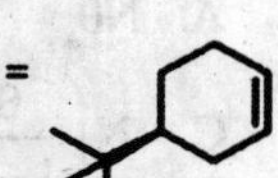

20. The correct order of the rate of mononitration using conc. H_2SO_4/conc. HNO_3 at room temperature is:

A. 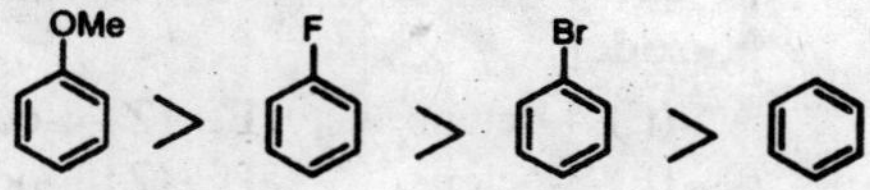

B. 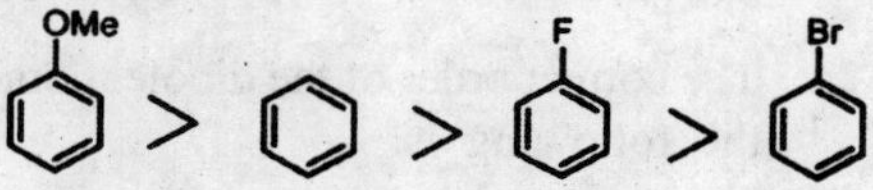

C. 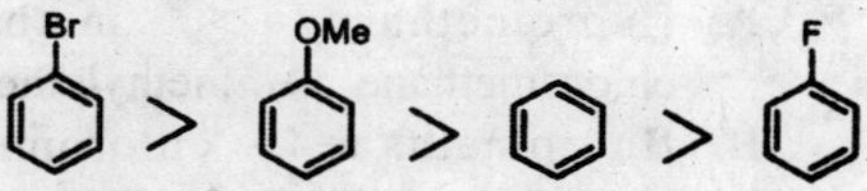

D. 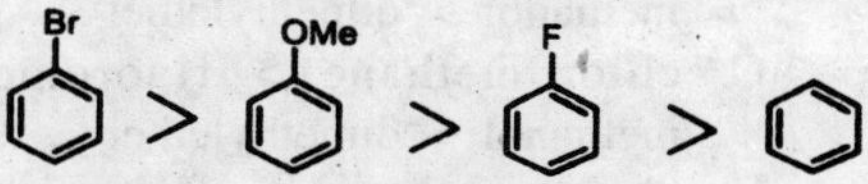

21. Pericyclic reactions involved in the synthesis of Vitamin D_2 from Ergosterol are:

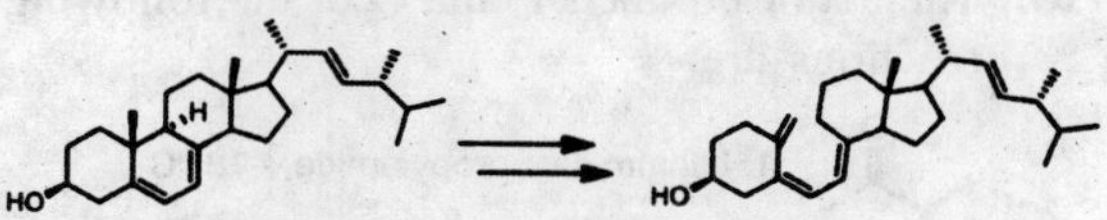

Ergosterol → Vitamin D_2

A. 6 π electrocyclic ring opening followed by [1, 7] sigmatropic shift

B. [1, 5] sigmatropic shift followed by 6π electrocyclic ring opening

C. [3, 3] sigmatropic rearrangement followed by [1, 7] sigmatropic shift

D. 4π electrocyclization followed by 6π electrocyclic ring opening

22. The major product in the following reaction sequence is:

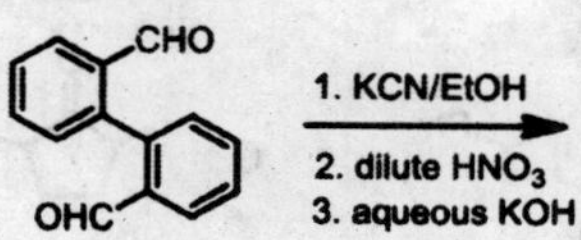

A. 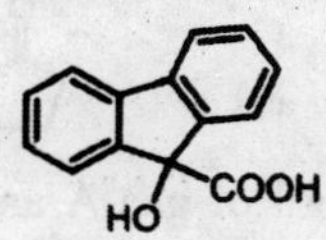

B. 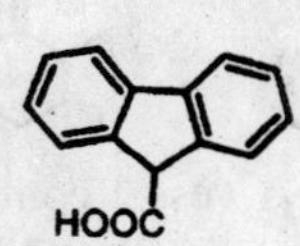

C. 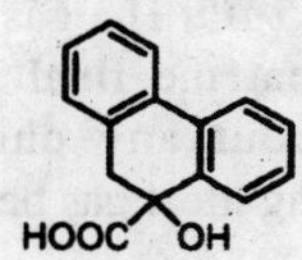

D. 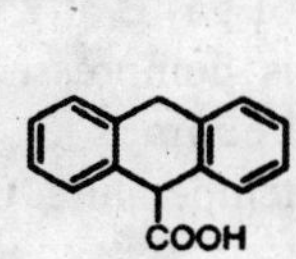

23. An organic compound P (C_8H_{16}) produces a *meso* compound upon oxidation with OsO_4/NMO. The compound P is:
[Where, NMO = N-methylmorpholine N-oxide]

A. (E)-4-octene B. (Z)-4-octene
C. (E)-3-octene D. (Z)-3-octene

24. The correct order of the dipole moment among the following is:

A. fluoromethane > methanol > chloromethane > dimethylether
B. fluoromethane > chloromethane > methanol > dimethylether
C. chloromethane > fluoromethane > methanol > dimethylether
D. chloromethane > fluoromethane > dimethylether > methanol

25. The major products P and Q of the following reactions are:

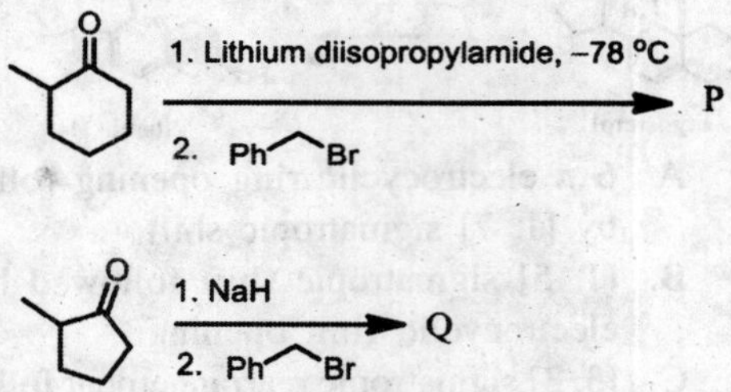

A. P = 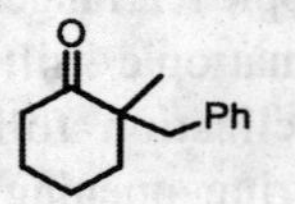 and Q = 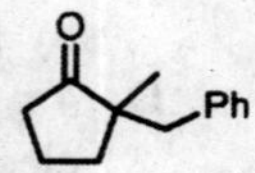

B. P = 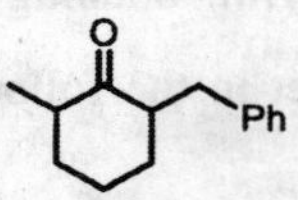 and Q = 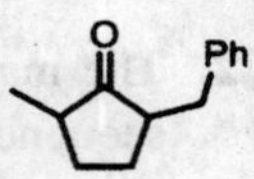

C. P = 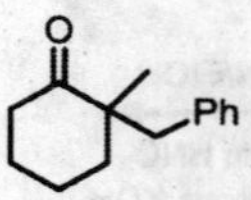 and Q = 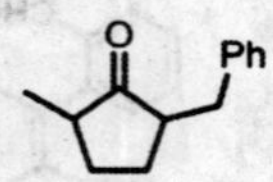

D. P = 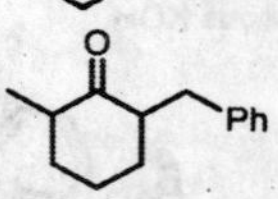 and Q = 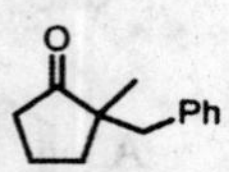

26. A vessel contains 1 mol of gas A and 2 mol of gas B at 2 bar and 25 °C. The gas mixture is compressed such that the final pressure becomes 3 bar without any change in temperature. Considering ideal gas behaviour, the change in Gibbs free energy (in kJ) during the compression is closest to:
[Given: Gas constant, R = 8.314 J mol^{-1} K^{-1}]

A. 1 B. 3
C. 6 D. 9

27. The substances, A, B and C undergo chemical reactions according to the scheme given below.

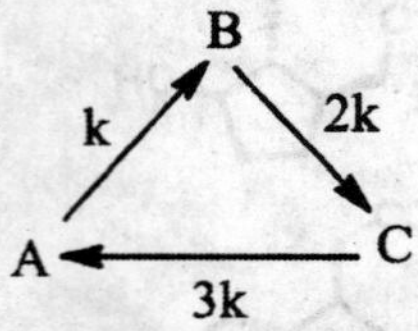

At time t = 0, the [A] = 0.11 M. Considering them to be first order reactions, the concentration of B (in M) at equilibrium is:

A. 0.06 B. 0.03
C. 0.02 D. 0.05

28. For van der Waals gases, at the critical point, $\frac{dP}{dV_m} = 0$ and:

A. $\frac{d^2P}{dV_m^2} = 0$ B. $\frac{d^2P}{dV_m^2} < 0$

C. $\frac{d^2P}{dV_m^2} > 0$ D. $\frac{d^2P}{dV_m^2}$ diverges

29. The set of asymmetric top molecules is:

A. CH_3CN, CH_3OH, H_2CO
B. H_2CO, H_2O, CH_3CN
C. H_2O, CH_3CN, CH_3OH
D. CH_3OH, H_2O, H_2CO

30. Consider Langmuir adsorption of a gas on a uniform solid surface having N number of surface sites. The free and adsorbed gas molecules are in dynamic equilibrium. If the fractional surface coverage is θ, the rate of adsorption of the gas is proportional to:

A. Nθ B. N(1 – θ)

C. $N\left(\frac{\theta}{1-\theta}\right)$ D. $N\left(\frac{1}{1-\theta}\right)$

Section B : Multiple Select Questions (MSQ)

Directions (Qs. No. 31-40): *Carry Two marks each.*

31. According to VSEPR theory, the set(s) of species having trigonal bipyramidal geometry is(are):

A. PCl_5 and SF_4 B. ClF_3 and I^-_3

C. PCl_5 and $Sb(Ph)_5$ D. ClF_3 and BrF_5

32. In alkaline medium, which of the following metal ion(s) form(s) red precipitate/coloration with dimethylglyoxime?

A. Ni(II) B. Bi(III)

C. Zn(II) D. Fe(II)

33. The correct statement(s) about the octahedral Mn-complex with spin only magnetic moment of approximately 6.0 μ_B is(are):

A. possible oxidation state of Mn in the complex is +4

B. possible oxidation state of Mn in the complex is +2

C. ligands associated with the complex is strong field ligand

D. ligands associated with the complex is weak field ligand

34. For $[Mn(CO)_6]^+$ and $[V(CO)_6]^-$ complexes, the correct statement(s) is(are):

A. stretching frequency of the CO is higher in the Mn-complex

B. metal-carbonyl bond is stronger in the V-complex

C. Mn-complex does not obey $18e^-$ rule

D. V-complex obeys $18e^-$ rule

35. The product(s) in the following transformation is(are):

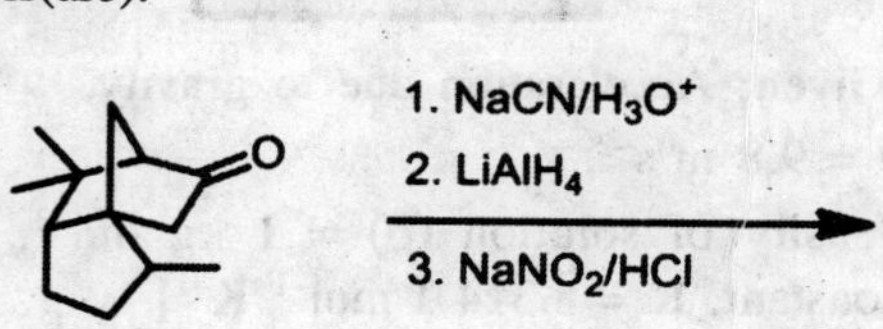

A. 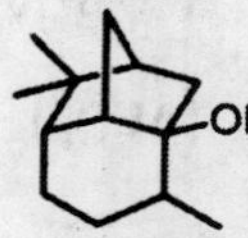

B. 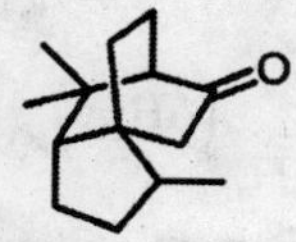

C. 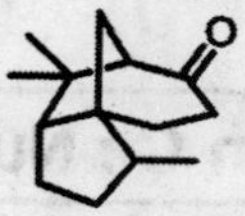

D. 

36. The set(s), in which all the compounds yield *achiral* products upon treatment with CH_3MgBr/ether followed by hydrolysis with dilute mineral acid, is(are):

A. 3,4-epoxyhexane, cyclohexanone and butanone

B. ethyl propionate, phenylacetyl chloride and cyclohexanone

C. butanone, ethyl propionate and cyclohexanone

D. ethyl phenyl ketone, 3,4-epoxyhexane, and phenylacetyl chloride

37. The reaction(s) that will yield cyclic product is(are):

A. (E)-2-hexene with CH_2I_2/Zn-Cu

B. 2-butanone with ethyl 2-chloropropionate with NaOEt/EtOH

C. hexane-2,5-dione with ammonia

D. cyclohexane-1, 2-diol with $NaIO_4$

38. The correct statement(s) among the following is(are):

A. In natural nucleic acids, the nucleosides are linked through phosphodiester bonds

B. Natural nucleic acids have sulphur containing heterocyclic bases

C. The isoelectric point of arginine is higher than that of isoleucine

D. The molecular weight of guanine is higher than that of cytosine

39. Among the following, the correct condition(s) for spontaneity is(are):

A. $\left(\Delta G_{sys}\right)_{P,T} < 0$ B. $\left(\Delta A_{sys}\right)_{V,T} < 0$

C. $\left(\Delta H_{sys}\right)_{P,S} < 0$ D. $\left(\Delta U_{sys}\right)_{V,P} < 0$

40. Correct statement(s) with respect to defects in solids is(are):

A. In Schottky defect, atoms move from interior lattice sites to surface lattice sites

B. Equilibrium concentration of defects remain unchanged with change in temperature

C. A perfect solid is thermodynamically less stable than the solid with defects

D. Common point defects in pure alkali halides are Frenkel-type

Section C : Numerical Answer Type (NAT)

Directions (Qs. No. 41-50): *Carry One mark each.*

41. $\int_0^{\infty} x e^{-x} dx =$ ....

(round off to the nearest integer)

42. Consider $\vec{C} = \vec{A} \times \vec{B}$, where $\vec{A} = 3\hat{i} - 2\hat{j} + 5\hat{k}$ and $\vec{B}$, a unit vector in *xy*-plane, makes an angle of 37° with the *x*-axis. Projection of $\vec{C}$ on the *x*-axis is ....

(round off to one decimal place)

43. A yellow compound X is produced after the reaction of $K_2[Ni(CN)_4]$ with excess of K/liq. NH_3 at −33 °C. The oxidation state of Ni in the compound X is ....

44. Number of spin allowed transition(s) possible for d^2 octahedral configuration is ....

45. Number of ^1H NMR signals observed for the following compound is ....

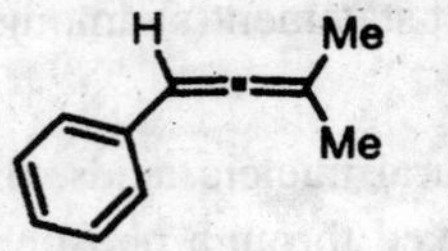

46. The number of stereoisomers possible for the following compound is ....

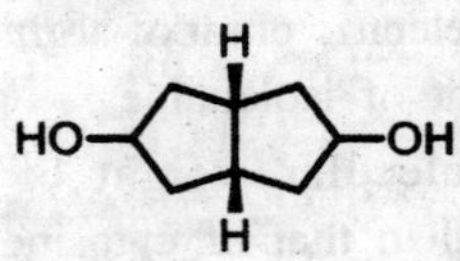

47. An electron at rest is accelerated through 10 kV potential. The de Broglie wavelength (in Å) of the electron is ....

(round off to three decimal places)

[Given: Mass of an electron,

$m_e = 9.11 \times 10^{-31}$ kg;

Planck's constant $(h) = 6.63 \times 10^{-34}$ Js;

1 eV = 1.6×10^{-19} J]

48. A tube fitted with a semipermeable membrane is dipped into 0.001 M NaCl solution at 300 K as shown in the figure. Assume density of the solvent and solution are same. At equilibrium, the height of the liquid column, *h* (in cm) is ....

(round off to one decimal place)

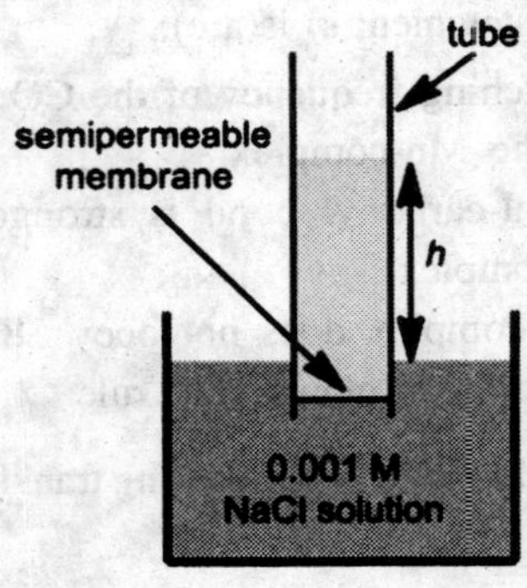

[Given: Acceleration due to gravity, $g = 9.8$ m s^{-2},

density of solution (ρ) = 1 kg dm^{-3}, gas constant, R = 8.314 J mol^{-1} K^{-1}]

49. The resonance frequency of ^{1}H nuclei is 300 MHz in an NMR spectrometer. If the spectrometer is operated at 12 T magnetic field, the resonance frequency (in MHz) of the same ^{1}H nuclei is ....

(round off to one decimal place)

[Given:

Nuclear magneton (β_N) = 5.05×10^{-27} J T^{-1},

Nuclear *g*-factor (g_N) for ^{1}H = 5.586,

Planck's constant (*h*) = 6.63×10^{-34} J s]

50. The first rotational absorption of $^{12}C^{16}O$ molecule is observed at 3.84 cm^{-1}. If an isotopic substitution is made with ^{18}O in the molecule, the frequency (in cm^{-1}) of first rotational absorption is ....

(round off to two decimal places)

Directions (Qs. No. 51-60): *Carry Two marks each.*

51. If $y + x\,e^{y} = \sin x + \tan x$, then the value of $\frac{dy}{dx}$ at $x = 0$ is ....

(round off to the nearest integer)

52. Consider the following matrices A and B.

$$A = \begin{pmatrix} 1 & 2 & 0 & 0 & 0 \\ 3 & 4 & 0 & 0 & 0 \\ 0 & 0 & 5 & 0 & 0 \\ 0 & 0 & 0 & 6 & 7 \\ 0 & 0 & 0 & 8 & 9 \end{pmatrix}$$

$$\text{and } B = \begin{pmatrix} 10 & 11 & 0 & 0 & 0 \\ 12 & 13 & 0 & 0 & 0 \\ 0 & 0 & 4 & 0 & 0 \\ 0 & 0 & 0 & 15 & 16 \\ 0 & 0 & 0 & 17 & 18 \end{pmatrix}$$

If C = AB, sum of the diagonal elements of C is ....

53. The number of species among the following, having bond order of three is ....

N_2, F_2, NO^+, O_2^-, N_2^+, CO, O_2, O_2^{2-}

54. 1.84 g of a mixture of $CaCO_3$ and $MgCO_3$ is heated till no further weight loss. The weight of the residue is 0.96 g. The % composition of $CaCO_3$ in the mixture is ....

(round off to two decimal places)

[Given: Atomic weight of Ca = 40; Mg = 24; C = 12; O = 16]

55. The number of chiral carbon centers in the following molecule is ....

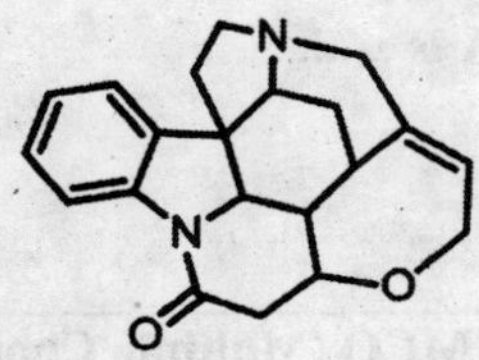

56. One mole of a monoatomic ideal gas starting from state A, goes through B and C to state D, as shown in the figure. Total change in entropy (in J K^{-1}) during this process is ....

(round off to two decimal places)

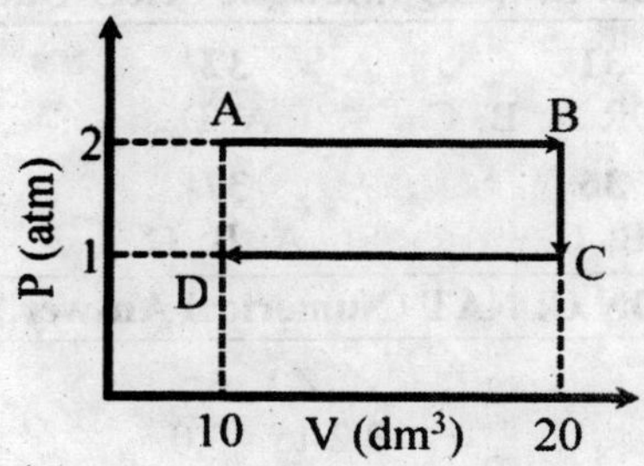

(Not to scale)

[Given: Gas constant, R = 8.314 J mol^{-1} K^{-1}]

57. In one second, 95 moles of He gas particles are hitting a wall of a cubic container of volume 1 dm^3. If the average velocity component of the particles perpendicular to the wall is 1000 m s^{-1}, then the pressure of the gas in the container is $X \times 10^5$ N m^{-2}. The value of X is ....

(round off to two decimal places)

[Given: Avogadro's number, $N_A = 6.02 \times 10^{23}$, mass of He = 4 g mol^{-1}]

58. Solubility of $PbCO_3$ in a buffer of pH 5 is $X \times 10^{-4}$. The value of X is ....

(round off to one decimal place)

[Given: K_{sp} of $PbCO_3 = 1.5 \times 10^{-13}$; for H_2CO_3, $K_{a1} = 4.2 \times 10^{-7}$, $K_{a2} = 4.8 \times 10^{-11}$]

59. The molar conductivity of a 0.02 M weak acid HA is 3.2 mS m^2 mol^{-1} at 298 K. The pK_a of HA is ....

(round off to one decimal place)

[Given: Limiting molar conductivity of HA = 39 mS m^2 mol^{-1} at 298 K]

60. A cell is constructed by $Cl_2/Cl^-(aq)$ and a standard hydrogen electrode half-cells. The standard potential of the complete cell is 1.38 V and $\left(\frac{\partial E^0}{\partial T}\right)_P = -1.24$ mVK^{-1}. The $\Delta S^0_{reaction}$ (in J K^{-1} mol^{-1}) for the following cell reaction is ....

$$H_2\,(gas) + Cl_2(gas) \rightarrow 2\,H^+\,(aq) + 2Cl^-(aq)$$

(round off to one decimal place)

[Given: Faraday constant (F) = 96480 C mol^{-1}]

ANSWERS

SECTION A: MCQ (Multiple Choice Questions)

1	2	3	4	5	6	7	8	9	10
A	C	A	C	B	C	A	MTA	C	D
11	**12**	**13**	**14**	**15**	**16**	**17**	**18**	**19**	**20**
A	A	B	A	B	A	C	D	D	B
21	**22**	**23**	**24**	**25**	**26**	**27**	**28**	**29**	**30**
A	A	B	C	D	B	B	A	D	B

SECTION B: MSQ (Multiple Select Questions)

31	32	33	34	35
A; B OR A; B; C	A; D	B; D	A; B; D	C; D
36	**37**	**38**	**39**	**40**
B; C	A; B; C	A; C; D	A; B; C	A; C

SECTION C: NAT (Numerical Answer Type Questions)

41	42	43	44	45
1	–3.2 to –3.0	0	3	5
46	**47**	**48**	**49**	**50**
3	0.115 to 0.130	MTA	509.0 to 512.0	3.64 to 3.66
51	**52**	**53**	**54**	**55**
1	638	3	53.00 to 56.00	6
56	**57**	**58**	**59**	**60**
–8.80 to –8.50	0.74 to 0.78	8.0 to 9.5	3.6 to 3.9	–240.0 to –238.0

EXPLANATORY ANSWERS

1. (A): To find the maximum of the function $f(r) = r^2e^{-r}$ for $r > 0$, we take the derivative and set it to zero:

$$f'(r) = \frac{d}{dr}(r^2e^{-r})$$
$$= 2re^{-r} - r^2e^{-r}$$
$$= e^{-r}(2r - r^2)$$

Set $f'(r) = 0$:

$$e^{-r}(2r - r^2) = 0$$
$$\Rightarrow \quad 2r - r^2 = 0$$
$$\Rightarrow \quad r(2 - r) = 0$$
$$\Rightarrow \quad r = 0 \text{ or } r = 2$$

Only $r = 2$ lies in the interval $(0, \infty)$, and it gives the maximum.

So, $f(2) = 2^2e^{-2}$
$= 4e^{-2}$.

2. (C): We want the probability that a specific ball (the blue one) is included in a random selection of 6 balls from 10 distinct ones.

Total number of ways to choose 6 balls from $10 = \binom{10}{6}$

Number of favorable outcomes (blue ball is included): choose 5 from remaining $9 = \binom{9}{5}$

$$P(\text{blue included}) = \frac{\binom{9}{5}}{\binom{10}{6}} = \frac{126}{210} = 0.6.$$

3. (A): Sulphide ores such as zinc blende (ZnS) and galena (PbS) are concentrated by froth flotation, a method that exploits the hydrophobic properties of sulphide particles which attach to air bubbles and rise to the surface, separating from gangue.

4. (C). The crystal system defined by the unit cell parameters:

- $a = b \neq c$
- $\alpha = \beta = \gamma = 90°$

is known as tetragonal. It is characterized by two equal axes at right angles and a third, unequal axis also at 90° to the others.

5. (B): The acidity of metal aqua complexes like $[M(H_2O)_6]^{n+}$ depends primarily on the charge-to-radius ratio (also called ionic potential) of the central metal ion. A higher charge and a smaller radius lead to greater polarization of the O–H bond in water molecules, facilitating the release of H^+ ions, thereby increasing acidity.

Among the three ions:

- $[Al(H_2O)_6]^{3+}$: Al^{3+} is small and highly charged, causing strong polarization of coordinated water molecules, leading to higher acidity.
- $[Fe(H_2O)_6]^{3+}$: Fe^{3+} is larger than Al^{3+}, so its charge density is slightly less than Al^{3+}, resulting in somewhat lower acidity.
- $[Fe(H_2O)_6]^{2+}$: Fe^{2+} has a lower charge and larger size, so it has the least polarizing power and lowest acidity.

So, the acidity trend is:

$[Al(H_2O)_6]^{3+} > [Fe(H_2O)_6]^{3+} > [Fe(H_2O)_6]^{2+}$.

6. (C): When antimony pentafluoride (SbF_5) dissolves in bromine trifluoride (BrF_3), it acts as a Lewis acid, while BrF_3 acts as a Lewis base. SbF_5 accepts a fluoride ion, while BrF_3 donates one. This results in the formation of ionic species:

- $[BrF_2]^+$: A cation formed from BrF_3 losing a fluoride ion.
- $[SbF_6]^-$: An anion formed when SbF_5 gains a fluoride ion to become hexafluoro-antimonate(V).

This type of reaction demonstrates the strong fluorinating and ionizing ability of SbF_5 in non-aqueous media like BrF_3.

7. (A): Table sugar, chemically known as sucrose, is a disaccharide composed of glucose and fructose units. In sucrose:

- The glucose unit is in its α-D-gluco-pyranose form.
- The fructose unit is in its β-D-fructo-furanose form.
- They are linked through a glycosidic bond between C1 of glucose and C2 of fructose, i.e., an α(1 → 2)β glycosidic linkage.

This means:

- The anomeric carbon (C1) of glucose is involved in bonding in the α-position.
- The anomeric carbon (C2) of fructose is involved in bonding in the β-position.
- Neither glucose nor fructose has a free anomeric carbon, which makes sucrose a non-reducing sugar.

Only Option A correctly shows:

- Glucose on the left in the α-pyranose form.
- Fructose on the right in the β-furanose form.
- A glycosidic linkage from C1 of glucose to C2 of fructose.

A: [Structure showing α(1 → 2)β linkage between glucose and fructose].

8. (*): When (R)-2-bromopropionic acid is treated with low concentration of hydroxide ion, the type of substitution mechanism that operates needs careful reconsideration, because the product's configuration depends on both the mechanism and the nature of the substrate.

The molecule is (R)-2-bromopropionic acid, which has a chiral center at the α-carbon (the carbon bonded to –Br and –COOH).

Now analyze the key points:

- If the reaction strictly followed SN2 (as typically expected for a primary or unhindered secondary carbon with strong nucleophile like OH^-), then inversion of configuration would occur, and the product would be (S)-2-hydroxypropionic acid.
- However, carboxylic acid group is strongly electron-withdrawing, and under aqueous basic conditions, it stabilizes the carbanion-like transition state of the SN1 mechanism in some cases, especially when OH^- is present in low concentration.
- At low $[OH^-]$, the rate of substitution may be slow enough to allow partial racemization through a partial SN1-like mechanism, especially in aqueous solution where the leaving group Br^- can leave, forming a planar intermediate (though carbocation stability is moderate here).

Hence, under these mild conditions, the product formed may not be predominantly of either R or S configuration, but rather a mixture, tending toward partial racemization.

Given that none of the given options correctly describe a racemized but non-equal mixture (which would require more specific stereochemical data), and assuming low concentration of OH^- allows partial racemization, the product is not necessarily predominantly S, nor fully racemic, nor achiral.

Therefore, the best and most accurate answer under the given conditions is:
NONE: mixture of R and S isomers with partial racemization not predominantly S.

9. (C): The Hamiltonian operator $\hat{H}$ satisfies the eigenvalue equation $\hat{H}\psi_n = E_n\psi_n$, with eigenvalues given as $E_n = \left(n+\frac{1}{2}\right)$, which matches the form of the quantum harmonic oscillator (in units where $\hbar\omega = 1$). The wavefunction is expressed as a linear combination:

$$\langle\psi\rangle = N(\psi_1 + \psi_2 + \psi_3 - \psi_4 - \psi_5)$$

To find the expectation value of energy $\langle E \rangle$, compute:

$$\langle E \rangle = \Sigma \, | c_n |^2 E_n$$

The coefficients c_n are the amplitudes of ψ_n in the linear combination:

$$c_1 = 1, \quad c_2 = 1, \quad c_3 = 1, \quad c_4 = -1, \quad c_5 = -1$$

Now, compute the normalization constant:

$N^2(1^2 + 1^2 + 1^2 + (-1)^2 + (-1)^2) = 1$

$\Rightarrow \quad N^2(5) = 1$

$\Rightarrow \quad N = \dfrac{1}{\sqrt{5}}$

So each coefficient squared becomes:

$$| c_n |^2 = \left(\frac{1}{\sqrt{5}}\right)^2 = \frac{1}{5}$$

Now list the corresponding energy eigenvalues using $E_n = n + \dfrac{1}{2}$, where n = 1 to 5:

- $E_1 = 1 + \dfrac{1}{2} = 1.5$
- $E_2 = 2 + \dfrac{1}{2} = 2.5$
- $E_3 = 3 + \dfrac{1}{2} = 3.5$
- $E_4 = 4 + \dfrac{1}{2} = 4.5$
- $E_5 = 5 + \dfrac{1}{2} = 5.5$

Now compute the expectation value:

$$\langle E \rangle = \frac{1}{5}(1.5 + 2.5 + 3.5 + 4.5 + 5.5)$$

$$= \frac{1}{5}(17.5) = 3.5.$$

10. (D): The question involves identifying the correct trend of surface tension with concentration for three types of solutes: surfactant, sodium chloride, and n-propanol.

- Surfactants significantly reduce surface tension initially and then level off as micelles form. This results in a sharp initial decrease, forming a curve like Figure III.
- Sodium chloride, being an ionic salt, tends to increase surface tension slightly with concentration due to structure-making effect on water molecules. This matches Figure II (a gentle upward slope).
- *n*-Propanol is an alcohol with moderate surface activity. It reduces surface tension, but gradually, not as sharply as surfactants. This corresponds to Figure I, showing a mild decrease.

Therefore:

- I — *n-propanol*
- II — *sodium chloride*
- III — *surfactant.*

11. (A): We are given the determinant equation involving a variable x:

$$\begin{vmatrix} x & 2 & 3 \\ 4 & x & 6 \\ x & 8 & 9 \end{vmatrix} = \begin{vmatrix} 102 & 18 & 36 \\ 1 & 3 & 4 \\ 17 & 3 & 6 \end{vmatrix}$$

First compute the right-hand side determinant:

Let the RHS matrix be:

$$= \begin{vmatrix} 102 & 18 & 36 \\ 1 & 3 & 4 \\ 17 & 3 & 6 \end{vmatrix}$$

Expand along the first row:

$= 102 \cdot (3 \cdot 6 - 4 \cdot 3) - 18 \cdot (1 \cdot 6 - 4 \cdot 17) + 36 \cdot (1 \cdot 3 - 3 \cdot 17)$

$= 102 \cdot (18 - 12) - 18 \cdot (6 - 68) + 36 \cdot (3 - 51)$

$= 102 \cdot 6 + 18 \cdot 62 - 36 \cdot 48$

$= 612 + 1116 - 1728 = 0$

So the RHS determinant is 0.

Now compute the LHS determinant:

$$= \begin{vmatrix} x & 2 & 3 \\ 4 & x & 6 \\ x & 8 & 9 \end{vmatrix}$$

Expand along the first row:

$$= x \cdot \begin{vmatrix} x & 6 \\ 8 & 9 \end{vmatrix} - 2 \cdot \begin{vmatrix} 4 & 6 \\ x & 9 \end{vmatrix} + 3 \cdot \begin{vmatrix} 4 & x \\ x & 8 \end{vmatrix}$$

Compute each of the 2 × 2 minors:

- $\begin{vmatrix} x & 6 \\ 8 & 9 \end{vmatrix} = 9x - 48$
- $\begin{vmatrix} 4 & 6 \\ x & 9 \end{vmatrix} = 36 - 6x$
- $\begin{vmatrix} 4 & x \\ x & 8 \end{vmatrix} = 32 - x^2$

Now substitute:

$= x(9x - 48) - 2(36 - 6x) + 3(32 - x^2)$

$= 9x^2 - 48x - 72 + 12x + 96 - 3x^2$

$= (9x^2 - 3x^2) + (-48x + 12x) + (-72 + 96)$

$= 6x^2 - 36x + 24$

Now equate to zero:

$6x^2 - 36x + 24 = 0$

$\Rightarrow \quad x^2 - 6x + 4 = 0$

$$\Rightarrow \quad x = \frac{6 \pm \sqrt{36-16}}{2} = \frac{6 \pm \sqrt{20}}{2}$$

$$= \frac{6 \pm 2\sqrt{5}}{2} = 3 \pm 5.$$

12. (A): Carboxypeptidase is an enzyme that catalyzes the hydrolysis of peptide bonds at the carboxy-terminal (C-terminal) end of proteins. It functions by cleaving amino acids from this end and is thus classified as a hydrolase. It requires a metal ion, typically Zn(II), in its active site to polarize the carbonyl group of the substrate, making the peptide bond more susceptible to nucleophilic attack by water.

13. (B): The biomolecule hemocyanin is an oxygen-carrying protein found in some arthropods and mollusks. It uses copper (Cu), not iron, to bind oxygen. In contrast, cytochromes, hydrogenases, and hemerythrin all contain iron (Fe) in various oxidation states and coordination environments.

14. (A): Tetraphosphorus decoxide P_4O_{10} undergoes hydrolysis to form phosphoric acid (H_3PO_4):

$P_4O_{10} + 6H_2O \rightarrow 4H_3PO_4$

On heating above 320 °C, phosphoric acid undergoes condensation (dehydration) to form metaphosphoric acid, a cyclic or linear polymer represented as $(HPO_3)_n$.

15. (B): Ion-dipole interactions are forces between an ion and a polar molecule. These interactions arise due to the electrostatic attraction between the ion and the partial charges on the dipole. The potential energy U of ion-dipole interaction varies inversely with the square of the distance:

$$U \propto \frac{1}{r^2}.$$

16. (A): In this nuclear transformation, we are given:

$$^{223}_{88}\text{Ra} \rightarrow {}^{207}_{82}\text{Pb}$$

We need to find how many α-particles (helium nuclei: $^{4}_{2}\text{He}$) and β-particles (electrons: $^{0}_{-1}\text{e}$) are emitted during this decay sequence.

Step 1: Use conservation of mass number (A)

Each α-particle reduces the mass number by 4. So if n α-particles are emitted:

$$223 - 4n = 207$$

$$\Rightarrow \quad 4n = 16 \Rightarrow n = 4$$

Step 2: Use conservation of atomic number (Z)

Each α-particle reduces atomic number by 2, and each β-particle increases it by 1 (because a neutron converts to a proton during β-decay). So if m β-particles are emitted:

$$88 - 2n + m = 82$$

$$\Rightarrow \quad 88 - 8 + m = 82$$

$$\Rightarrow \quad m = 2$$

So the transformation involves 4 α-particles and 2 β-particles.

17. (C): Wilkinson's catalyst is widely used in homogeneous hydrogenation reactions of alkenes. Its chemical formula is:

$$[RhCl(PPh_3)_3]$$

This complex contains rhodium in the +1 oxidation state, and the geometry around rhodium is square planar due to its d^8 electron configuration, which favors such geometry in low-spin complexes.

Thus, Wilkinson's catalyst contains rhodium(I) in a square planar geometry.

18. (D): The given transformation consists of two sequential steps:

Step 1: Treatment with m-CPBA (meta-chloroperbenzoic acid)

This is a Baeyer-Villiger oxidation, which inserts an oxygen atom adjacent to the carbonyl carbon, forming an ester or lactone, depending on whether the carbonyl is in an open or ring structure.

- In Baeyer-Villiger reactions, the migratory aptitude follows the order:
  tertiary > secondary > aryl > primary > methyl
- In this molecule, the carbon adjacent to the carbonyl that bears the phenyl group is more substituted, so that side migrates, leading to formation of a bridged lactone where the oxygen is inserted between the carbonyl carbon and the benzylic carbon.

Step 2: Treatment with $LiAlH_4$

This step reduces the lactone to a diol:

- Specifically, $LiAlH_4$ cleaves the ester/lactone, reducing:
  The carbonyl carbon to a primary alcohol, and
  The alkoxy side to a secondary alcohol.

This yields a 1,4-diol, with the oxygen and hydroxyl groups on opposite sides of the ring system.

Now examine the stereochemistry:

- The hydride attack in the lactone ring opening typically happens from the less hindered side, leading to trans or anti orientation in the final product.
- The phenyl ether (Ph-O–) ends up on one carbon and the OH group on another, with the new hydroxyls formed anti to each other due to stereoelectronic factors and approach of the hydride.

Now match this transformation with the options:

Option D shows:

- The PhO group on one carbon,
- A trans-diol configuration,
- Matches the expected outcome of Baeyer–Villiger followed by $LiAlH_4$ reduction.

Therefore, the correct and more accurate answer is (D): [Product with anti-diol configuration and PhO substituent as expected from BV + LAH].

19. (D): Let's reanalyze both transformations step by step, paying special attention to stereochemistry and reaction conditions.

First Transformation (Formation of P):

The given compound is a cis-1-bromo-2-carboxylic acid substituted cyclohexane, with both Br and COOH in axial-equatorial positions, making them not anti-periplanar — i.e., E2 elimination is not stereochemically allowed.

However, a chair flip can place both groups in axial positions (Br axial up, COOH axial down), allowing for E2 elimination.

In E2 reactions:

- The base abstracts a β-H anti to the Br,

- Elimination of Br leads to formation of a double bond,
- The resulting product is an alkene with COOH retained.

This is a standard E2 reaction, leading to a monosubstituted cyclohexene with a COOH group at the allylic position.

This matches the structure shown in Option D (P) — a cyclohexene with isopropyl and COOH groups.

Second Transformation (Formation of Q):

The starting compound has the Br and COOH group in a different relative configuration (opposite wedge/dash), which makes anti-periplanar arrangement impossible even after chair flipping.

In this case:

- E2 elimination is blocked due to stereo-chemistry.
- Under basic conditions, elimination does not occur.
- Instead, base promotes simple debromination (Br^- leaves), or proton abstraction might lead to non-eliminated product.
- The most likely product is the unreacted cyclohexane carboxylic acid, with Br replaced by H (or no change if reaction stalls).

This matches the structure shown in Option D (Q) — a saturated ring with COOH and isopropyl substituents.

Final Answer:

- P = Elimination gives cyclohexene with COOH group
- Q = No elimination, product remains saturated

(D): P = alkene-COOH product, Q = saturated COOH compound.

20. (B): The rate of mononitration of aromatic compounds using conc. H_2SO_4 / HNO_3 depends on the electron-donating or withdrawing nature of substituents on the benzene ring:

Electron Donating Groups (EDGs) like–OMe:

- Increase electron density on the ring.
- Strongly activate the ring towards electrophilic substitution (like nitration).
- Greatly increase the rate.

Halogens (–F, –Br):

- Are electron-withdrawing via induction, but electron-donating via resonance.
- Net effect: mild deactivation, but still direct ortho/para.
- Among halogens, F is more electronegative and deactivates more than Br.

H (benzene without substituents):

- Serves as reference point.

Order of activation:

- –OMe (strong EDG) > –Br (mildly deactivating) > –F (more deactivating) > H (no substituent)

Now compare the options:

- Option A: –OMe > –F > –Br > H *(Wrong)* (–F cannot be faster than –Br)
- Option B: –OMe > –Br > –F > H *(Correct)*
- Option C and D place –Br ahead of –OMe *(Wrong)*

21. (A): The transformation of Ergosterol to Vitamin D_2 is a classic example of pericyclic reactions, particularly involving photo-chemical activation followed by thermal rearrangement.

Here's what happens mechanistically:

Step 1: 6π Electrocyclic Ring Opening

- The cyclohexadiene ring in the B-ring of Ergosterol undergoes a 6π conrotatory electrocyclic ring opening under photochemical conditions, forming a triene system.
- This reaction breaks the C–C bond in the B-ring, converting it into a conjugated triene.

Step 2: [1,7] Sigmatropic Shift

- Once the triene system is formed, a [1,7] sigmatropic hydrogen shift occurs,
- This rearranges the π system and places the hydrogen at a new location along the conjugated chain,
- Leading to the open-ring product known as Vitamin D_2.

These two transformations are classic pericyclic processes:

- One is an electrocyclic ring opening, and
- The other is a sigmatropic shift.

22. (A): The reaction sequence involves three classical organic transformations applied to an ortho-dialdehyde aromatic compound:

Step 1: KCN/EtOH

This promotes an intramolecular benzoin condensation, where one aldehyde carbonyl attacks the other via nucleophilic cyanide catalysis. This leads to formation of a fused ring system featuring an α-hydroxy ketone intermediate.

Step 2: Dilute HNO_3

This oxidizes the α-hydroxy ketone to a 1,2-diketone (benzil-type compound). Both carbonyl groups now sit adjacent to each other on a fused ring structure.

Step 3: Aqueous KOH

Under basic conditions, a benzilic acid rearrangement takes place. One aromatic ring migrates from one carbonyl carbon to the adjacent one, and a carboxylic acid group and hydroxyl group appear on the new carbon framework. The resulting structure retains the aromaticity and includes the characteristic COOH and OH groups positioned on adjacent carbons, on a shifted ring system.

Among the options, this transformation is correctly represented by (A): Product with fused ring one ring migration and COOH OH substitution.

23. (B): The molecular formula given is C_8H_{16}, indicating an alkene (1 degree of unsaturation). The reaction condition involves OsO_4/NMO, which performs syn dihydroxylation of alkenes to give vicinal diols.

We are told that the product is a meso compound. A meso compound:

- Has two or more chiral centers,
- But also possesses an internal plane of symmetry making it achiral overall.

Let's examine the options:

- **(E)-4-octene:** Gives enantiomers, not meso.
- **(Z)-4-octene:** Substitution around the double bond is symmetric (two ethyl groups on both sides). Upon syn addition of OH, the product becomes meso-4,5-octanediol because the molecule has a plane of symmetry through the central bond.
- **(E)-3-octene and (Z)-3-octene:** The alkyl chains differ (n-propyl vs. butyl), so the products are not meso.

Only (Z)-4-octene leads to a meso compound after syn dihydroxylation.

24. (C): Dipole moment depends on:

- Bond polarity (electronegativity difference),
- Bond direction and geometry,
- Vector sum of dipoles.

Now analyze each compound:

- **Fluoromethane (CH_3F):** High electronegativity of F, but small bond length.
- **Chloromethane (CH_3Cl):** Lower EN than F but longer bond length → net dipole may be comparable or even greater.
- **Methanol (CH_3OH):** Has a strong O–H dipole, but the geometry reduces net dipole compared to halomethanes.
- **Dimethylether (CH_3OCH_3):** Two dipoles partially cancel due to bent geometry; lowest dipole.

Experimental dipole moments support:

- CH_3Cl: ~1.87 D
- CH_3F: ~1.85 D
- CH_3OH: ~1.70 D
- CH_3OCH_3: ~1.30 D

So, the correct order is (C): chloromethane > fluoromethane > methanol > dimethylether.

25. (D): In the first reaction, lithium diisopropylamide (LDA) at –78 °C is used, which typically gives the kinetic enolate by deprotonation at the less substituted α-position. When this enolate reacts with benzyl bromide ($PhCH_2Br$), the alkylation occurs at the less hindered α-carbon, resulting in a product where the phenylmethyl group is added adjacent to the methyl group already present on the ring.

In the second reaction, sodium hydride (NaH) is used, which favors the formation of the more substituted, thermodynamic enolate under equilibrium conditions. The resulting enolate alkylates at the more substituted α-position, giving a product where the phenylmethyl group is introduced away from the methyl side of the ring.

Comparing with the options, the product P has $PhCH_2$ at the methyl-bearing α-position (kinetic site), and product Q has $PhCH_2$ at the more substituted α-position (thermodynamic site).

(D): P = kinetic alkylation at less substituted α-position,

Q = thermodynamic alkylation at more substituted α-position.

26. (B): Given:

- $n = 3$ mol
- $P_1 = 2$ bar, $P_2 = 3$ bar
- T = 298 K
- R = 8.314 J mol^{-1} K^{-1}

Use: $$\Delta G = nRT\ln\left(\frac{P_2}{P_1}\right)$$

Substitute:

$$\Delta G = 3\times 8.314\times 298\times \ln\left(\frac{3}{2}\right)$$

$$\ln\left(\frac{3}{2}\right) \approx 0.405$$

$$\Delta G = 3 \times 8.314 \times 298 \times 0.405$$
$$= 3 \times 2478.57 \times 0.405$$
$$= 3 \times 1003.72 = 3011.16 \text{ J}$$
$$\Delta G \approx 3.01 \text{ kJ}.$$

27. (B): The reaction involves three first-order steps:

- A → B with rate constant k
- B → C with rate constant $2k$
- A → C with rate constant $3k$

Let the equilibrium concentrations be:

- $[A] = a$, $[B] = b$, $[C] = c$

From conservation of mass:

$$a + b + c = 0.11 \quad ...(1)$$

From equilibrium condition for B:

Rate of formation of B from A

= Rate of loss of B to C

$$k \cdot a = 2k \cdot b$$

$$\Rightarrow \quad a = 2b \quad ...(2)$$

Substituting (2) into (1):

$$2b + b + c = 0.11$$

$$\Rightarrow \quad 3b + c = 0.11 \quad ...(3)$$

Try option B: $b = 0.03$

Then: $a = 2.0.03$
$= 0.06,$
$c = 0.11 - 0.06 - 0.03$
$= 0.02$

Check:

- $a + b + c = 0.11$ *(Correct)*
- $a = 2b$ *(Correct)*

Other options give invalid (negative) or inconsistent values.

Thus, the most consistent value for [B] at equilibrium is (B): 0.03.

28. (A): For a van der Waals gas, at the critical point, the isotherm has a point of inflection on the P vs V_m curve.

This means both the first derivative and the second derivative of pressure with respect to molar volume vanish:

$$\left(\frac{dP}{dV_m}\right)_T = 0 \text{ and}$$

$$\left(\frac{d^2P}{dV_m^2}\right)_T = 0$$

This condition is used to derive expressions for the critical constants P_c, V_c, T_c of a van der Waals gas.

Thus, the correct condition is (A): $\frac{d^2P}{dV_m^2} = 0$.

29. (D): An asymmetric top molecule has all three principal moments of inertia (I_a, I_b, I_c) different.

Let's analyze each molecule:

- **CH_3CN (methyl cyanide):** Linear CN group + methyl = asymmetric distribution → asymmetric top
- **CH_3OH (methanol):** Has a bent OH and asymmetric methyl = asymmetric top
- **H_2CO (formaldehyde):** Planar but not symmetric along all axes = asymmetric top
- **H_2O:** Bent structure, two Hs unequal along axes = asymmetric top

The correct set where all three molecules are asymmetric tops is (D): CH_3OH, H_2O, H_2CO.

30. (B): In Langmuir adsorption, the rate of adsorption is proportional to:

- The number of available vacant sites, which is N(1 – θ), where:
- N = total sites,
- θ = fraction of sites already occupied.

So, more vacant sites ⇒ more adsorption.

(B) N(1 – θ).

31. (C): According to VSEPR theory, the set(s) of species having trigonal bipyramidal geometry is(are):

We are looking for actual molecular geometry as per VSEPR — not just electron pair geometry.

Option A: PCl_5 and SF_4

- **PCl_5 :** AX_5 → 5 bond pairs → Trigonal bipyramidal *(Correct)*
- **SF_4 :** AX_4E → 4 bond pairs + 1 lone pair → Seesaw *(Inorrect)*

So this set is not fully correct.

Option B: ClF_3 and I_3^-

- **ClF_3 :** AX_3E_2 → T-shape *(Inorrect)*
- **I_3^- :** AX_2E_3 → Linear *(Inorrect)*

So both are not trigonal bipyramidal *(Inorrect)*

Option C: PCl_5 and $Sb(Ph)_5$

- **PCl_5 :** AX_5 → Trigonal bipyramidal *(Correct)*
- **$Sb(Ph)_5$:** Has 5 phenyl ligands → AX_5 → Trigonal bipyramidal *(Correct)*

This is a correct set *(Correct)*

Option D: ClF_3 and BrF_5

- **ClF_3 :** AX_3E_2 → T-shape *(Inorrect)*
- **BrF_5 :** AX_5E → Square pyramidal *(Inorrect)*

Only Option C is fully correct

Thus, final answer is (C): PCl_5 and $Sb(Ph)_5$

32. (A): In alkaline medium, which metal ion(s) form red precipitate/coloration with dimethylglyoxime?

Ni(II): Forms a cherry red precipitate with dimethylglyoxime in alkaline medium *(Correct)*

Bi(III): Does not form any characteristic red complex *(Incorrect)*

Zn(II): Does not form red precipitate with DMG *(Incorrect)*

Fe(II): Does not form a red complex with DMG *(Incorrect)*

Only Ni(II) gives the red complex.

Thus, final answer is (A): Ni(II).

33. (B, D): A spin-only magnetic moment of ~6.0 μB corresponds to 5 unpaired electrons.

$$\mu_{\text{spin-only}} = \sqrt{n(n+2)} \approx \sqrt{35} \approx 6.0$$

$$\Rightarrow \quad n = 5$$

For Mn (Z = 25):

- Mn^{2+} : $3d^5$ → 5 unpaired electrons *(Correct)*
- Mn^{4+} : $3d^3$ → 3 unpaired *(Incorrect)*
- Weak field ligands do not pair electrons → high-spin → supports 5 unpaired *(Correct)*
- Strong field ligands would reduce number of unpaired electrons *(Incorrect)*

B and D: Mn^{2+} oxidation state, weak field ligands.

34. (A, B, D): Electron counts:

- $[Mn(CO)_6]^+$: Mn^+ (d^6), 6 CO (2e each) → 6 + 12 = 18e⁻ *(Correct)*
- $[V(CO)_6]^-$: V^- (d^6), 6 CO → 6 + 12 = 18e⁻ *(Correct)*
- CO stretching frequency increases with less backbonding. Mn^+ is more positive than V^- → less backbonding → higher V(CO) in Mn-complex *(Correct)*
- Stronger backbonding → stronger metal–carbon bond → V-complex has stronger M–CO bond *(Correct)*.

35. (C, D): Starting compound: A bicyclic ketone (norbornone derivative).

Step 1: NaCN / H_3O^+

This is a cyanohydrin formation:

- The carbonyl (C=O) reacts with NaCN, forming a new OH and CN on the same carbon.
- Stereochemically, this addition can occur from either face of the planar carbonyl group, generating diastereomers (due to a new stereocenter).

So, two stereoisomeric cyanohydrins are formed.

Step 2: $LiAlH_4$

- Reduces the –CN group to $-CH_2NH_2$ (primary amine).
- The OH group is unchanged.
- We now have two possible stereoisomeric amino alcohols.

Step 3: $NaNO_2$ / HCl

- This step performs diazotization of the primary amine ($-NH_2$) to form a diazonium salt ($-N_2^+$).
- However, in aliphatic amines, this leads to formation of a carbocation, which is then replaced by OH or C=O depending on the structure and stability.

Now consider the bridgehead position:

- At bridgeheads in bicyclic systems, formation of planar intermediates like carbocations or diazonium is disfavored, especially if they would require violating Bredt's rule.
- The result is rearrangement or elimination, typically leading to oxidation back to a ketone.

Since two stereoisomeric amino alcohols were formed in step 2, both can give two different ketones upon deamination, due to different stereochemistry of the leaving group.

Now examine the given options:

- Option C and D represent two different ketones — they are stereoisomers at the carbon that originally bore the OH/NH_2 group.
- These arise from the two different diastereomers formed during cyanohydrin addition.

Hence, both C and D are formed.

Final Answer: C and D.

36. (B, C): Let's caref"'y re-evaluate each set (A to D) for whether all the compounds in a given set produce achiral products or racemic mixtures (which are optically inactive, hence achiral as a mixture) when treated with CH_3MgBr/ether followed by hydrolysis.

Set A: 3,4-epoxyhexane, cyclohexanone, and butanone

1. **3,4-Epoxyhexane**

- Epoxides open under nucleophilic attack by CH_3MgBr.
- Regioselective opening will lead to addition of a methyl and OH at adjacent carbons → forms a chiral center.
- Product is chiral, and unless a racemic mixture is confirmed, it's not guaranteed to be achiral overall.

2. **Cyclohexanone**

- Attack at carbonyl by CH_3MgBr forms a tertiary alcohol on cyclohexane, which is symmetrical and achiral.

3. **Butanone ($CH_3COCH_2CH_3$)**

- Attack by CH_3MgBr forms 3-pentanol ($CH_3CH(OH)CH_2CH_3$), a chiral compound, but racemic mixture forms → optically inactive ⇒ overall achiral.

Due to 3,4-epoxyhexane possibly giving non-racemic chiral product, Set A is not correct.

Set B: Ethyl propionate, phenylacetyl chloride, and cyclohexanone

1. **Ethyl propionate ($CH_3CH_2COOCH_2CH_3$)**

- Undergoes two additions of CH_3MgBr (Grignard cannot stop at ketone) → forms a tertiary alcohol, $CH_3CH_2C(CH_3)_2OH$
- This alcohol has no chiral center ⇒ achiral product

2. **Phenylacetyl chloride ($C_6H_5CH_2COCl$)**

- Two CH_3MgBr add to acid chloride → gives $C_6H_5CH_2C(CH_3)_2OH$
- Again, no chiral center ⇒ achiral product

3. **Cyclohexanone**

- CH_3MgBr adds → gives a tertiary alcohol at a ring carbon
- The product is symmetrical ⇒ achiral

All three give achiral products ⇒ Set B is correct

Set C: Butanone, ethyl propionate, and cyclohexanone

1. **Butanone ($CH_3COCH_2CH_3$)**

- Addition of CH_3MgBr → gives 3-pentanol
- 3-pentanol is chiral, but the reaction forms racemic mixture, which is optically inactive ⇒ overall achiral

2. **Ethyl propionate**

- Forms $CH_3CH_2C(CH_3)_2OH$ → achiral

3. **Cyclohexanone**

- Forms tertiary ring alcohol → achiral

All products are achiral or racemic ⇒ Set C is correct

Set D: Ethyl phenyl ketone, 3,4-epoxyhexane, phenylacetyl chloride

1. **Ethyl phenyl ketone ($C_6H_5COCH_2CH_3$)**

- CH_3MgBr adds to carbonyl → forms $C_6H_5C(OH)(CH_3)(CH_2CH_3)$
- This has a chiral center, but forms racemic mixture ⇒ achiral overall

2. **3,4-Epoxyhexane**

- Opens with CH_3MgBr attack → depending on regioselectivity and chain orientation, may or may not be racemic
- Likely chiral, and unless symmetry exists, it may not be achiral overall.

3. **Phenylacetyl chloride**

- As shown in Set B, forms achiral alcohol

Due to uncertainty in 3,4-epoxyhexane product being racemic, Set D is not guaranteed to be achiral overall.

Final Answer: B and C.

37. (A, B, C): The reaction of (E)-2-hexene with CH_2I_2/Zn-Cu is a Simmons–Smith cyclopropanation, where the carbene generated from CH_2I_2 adds across the double bond to form a three-membered cyclopropane ring. Since a ring is formed as part of the product, it is considered a cyclic compound, even though the starting material is acyclic.

The reaction of 2-butanone with ethyl 2-chloropropionate in the presence of NaOEt/EtOH involves a Dieckmann condensation. This is an intramolecular Claisen-type reaction that forms a cyclic β-keto ester.

The nucleophile generated from ethyl 2-chloropropionate attacks the carbonyl carbon of 2-butanone, resulting in ring closure and formation of a five- or six-membered ring, thus yielding a cyclic product.

Hexane-2,5-dione reacts with ammonia to form a cyclic compound through condensation. The 1,4-dicarbonyl system undergoes cyclization with ammonia, leading to the formation of a five-membered heterocycle, such as a dihydropyrrole derivative. This is a classic method for synthesizing nitrogen-containing cyclic compounds.

The reaction of cyclohexane-1,2-diol with $NaIO_4$ involves periodate-mediated oxidative cleavage of the vicinal diol. Instead of forming a ring, this reaction breaks the C–C bond between the diol carbons, forming two separate carbonyl compounds, which are not cyclic products.

38. **(A, C, D):** In natural nucleic acids, nucleosides are linked through phosphodiester bonds. This involves the phosphate group forming ester bonds with the 3'-OH of one sugar and the 5'-OH of the next, creating the sugar-phosphate backbone of DNA and RNA. Hence, this statement is correct.

Natural nucleic acids do not contain sulphur-containing heterocyclic bases. The bases found in DNA and RNA—adenine, guanine, cytosine, thymine, and uracil—are composed of carbon, hydrogen, nitrogen, and oxygen only. Therefore, this statement is incorrect.

The isoelectric point (pI) of arginine is higher than that of isoleucine. Arginine has a basic guanidinium side chain, which raises its pI to around 10.8, while isoleucine, a neutral nonpolar amino acid, has a pI around 6.0. Therefore, this statement is correct.

The molecular weight of guanine is higher than that of cytosine. Guanine has the molecular formula $C_5H_5N_5O$, with a molar mass of approximately 151 g/mol, while cytosine has the formula $C_4H_5N_3O$, with a molar mass of around 111 g/mol. Therefore, this statement is correct.

39. **(A, B, C):** For a process at constant pressure and temperature, a negative change in Gibbs free energy ($\Delta G < 0$) indicates spontaneity. This is the most general and widely accepted criterion for spontaneity, so statement A is correct.

For a process at constant volume and temperature, a negative change in Helmholtz free energy ($\Delta A < 0$) also indicates spontaneity. Helmholtz free energy is relevant in thermodynamic systems held at constant V and T, making statement B correct.

For a process at constant pressure and entropy, a decrease in enthalpy ($\Delta H < 0$) can favor spontaneity, though entropy is rarely held constant in practice.

Nevertheless, under isentropic conditions, minimizing enthalpy can correspond to a spontaneous direction, making statement C conditionally acceptable.

For a process at constant volume and pressure, internal energy (ΔU) does not determine spontaneity. In fact, V and P are not conjugate thermodynamic variables, so this thermodynamic condition is invalid for determining spontaneity. Hence, statement D is incorrect.

40. **(A, C):** In Schottky defects, atoms or ions (both cations and anions) leave their lattice sites and move to the surface or out of the crystal entirely, creating a pair of vacancies. This movement contributes to the formation of a vacancy-type point defect and is correctly described in statement A.

The equilibrium concentration of defects increases with temperature, due to the exponential dependence on thermal energy in the Arrhenius-type expression for defect formation.

Hence, it is incorrect to say that defect concentration remains unchanged with temperature. Therefore, statement B is incorrect.

A perfect solid, with zero configurational entropy due to lack of defects, is thermodynamically less stable than a real solid that contains defects. The presence of defects increases entropy and can reduce free energy, making the solid more stable. Therefore, statement C is correct.

In pure alkali halides such as NaCl, Schottky defects are more common. Frenkel defects are observed in crystals with large anion-to-cation size ratio or low coordination number, such as AgCl. Hence, the common defect in pure alkali halides is not of the Frenkel type, making statement D incorrect.

41. (1): The given integral is $\int_0^\infty xe^{-x}dx$

This is a standard integral that arises frequently in problems involving exponential decay and probability distributions. It can be evaluated using the Gamma function, defined as:

$$\Gamma(n) = \int_0^\infty x^{n-1}e^{-x}dx$$

In this case, we can write $x = x^{2-1}$, so the integral becomes:

$$\int_0^\infty xe^{-x}dx = \Gamma(2)$$

Using the identity $\Gamma(n) = (n-1)!$ for positive integers, we have:

$$\Gamma(2) = 1! = 1$$

Hence, the value of the given integral is 1. Rounding off to the nearest integer, the final answer remains: 1.

42. (–3.0): We are given two vectors:

$$\vec{A} = 3\hat{i} - 2\hat{j} + 5\hat{k},$$

$$\vec{B} = \cos(37°)\hat{i} + \sin(37°)\hat{j}$$

Here, $\vec{B}$ is a unit vector in the *xy*-plane making a 37° angle with the *x*-axis, so it has no *z*-component. We are to compute:

$$\vec{C} = \vec{A} \times \vec{B}$$

Then, we need to find the projection of $\vec{C}$ on the *x*-axis, i.e., the *x*-component of $\vec{C}$.

Let's compute the cross product $\vec{C} = \vec{A} \times \vec{B}$ using the determinant:

$$\vec{C} = \begin{vmatrix} \hat{i} & \hat{j} & \hat{k} \\ 3 & -2 & 5 \\ \cos(37°) & \sin(37°) & 0 \end{vmatrix}$$

Now expand the determinant:

$$\vec{C} = \hat{i}(-2.0 - 5.\sin(37°)) - \hat{j}(3.0 - 5.\cos(37°)) + k(3.\sin(37°) + 2.\cos(37°))$$

$$\vec{C} = -5\sin(37°)\hat{i} + 5\cos(37°)\hat{j} + (3\sin(37°) + 2\cos(37°))\hat{k}$$

Now extract the *x*-component of $\vec{C}$, which is the coefficient of $\hat{i}$:

$$C_x = -5\ \sin(37°)$$

Use $\sin(37°) \approx 0.6018$:

$$C_x = -5 \times 0.6018 = -3.009$$

Rounded to one decimal place, the projection of $\vec{C}$ on the *x*-axis is –3.0.

43. (0): The compound $K_2[Ni(CN)_4]$ contains Ni in the +2 oxidation state, as cyanide (CN^-) is *a* – 1 ligand and the complex has *a* – 2 charge overall. When this complex is treated with excess potassium in liquid ammonia at –33 °C, it undergoes a Birch-type reduction, where solvated electrons from K/NH_3 reduce the metal center.

The yellow compound X formed is typically a Ni(0) complex — that is, Ni is reduced from +2 to 0 oxidation state. The tetrahedral $[Ni(CN)_4]^{2-}$ complex accepts electrons, and Ni^{2+} is reduced by 2 units:

$$Ni^{2+} \xrightarrow{+2e^-} Ni^0$$

Thus, the oxidation state of Ni in compound X is 0.

44. **(3):** For a d^2 octahedral configuration, the electrons occupy the lower-energy t_2g orbitals in a crystal field.

Now, spin-allowed transitions are those in which there is no change in the total spin multiplicity, meaning the spin quantum number (S) remains the same. In a d^2 configuration, with both electrons unpaired in t_2g orbitals, the total spin is S = 1 → spin multiplicity = 2S + 1 = 3 (a triplet ground state).

Transitions to excited states must also result in triplet states for the transitions to be spin-allowed.

Electronic configurations for excited states in octahedral fields can be calculated based on terms from the Tanabe–Sugano diagram for a d^2 system.

The term symbols for d^2 in an octahedral field yield three spin-allowed transitions:

From the ground state ^3T_1g, allowed transitions go to:

- $^3T_{2}g$
- $^3A_{2}g$
- $^3T_{1}g$ (P)

These transitions preserve spin multiplicity (triplet → triplet), hence are allowed.

Therefore, the number of spin-allowed transitions is 3.

45. **(5):** In the given structure $Ph–CH=C(CH_3)_2$:

- The phenyl ring, being monosubstituted, gives three distinct signals for the aromatic protons (ortho, meta, and para).
- The vinylic proton adjacent to the phenyl ring is in a unique environment and gives one signal.
- The two methyl groups attached to the same sp^2 carbon are in equivalent environments due to symmetry around that carbon, and hence give one signal.

So the total number of distinct ^1H NMR signals is:

3 (aromatic) + 1 (vinylic) + 1 (methyls) = 5 answer is 5.

46. **(3):** The given compound is a bicyclic system based on the norbornane framework, with two hydroxyl substituents on adjacent bridge carbons and two explicitly shown hydrogen atoms on the bridgehead positions. The only stereocenters in this structure are the two carbon atoms bearing the –OH groups. The bridgehead positions are not stereogenic, as their configuration is fixed by the rigid bicyclic structure.

With two stereogenic centers, the maximum number of stereoisomers is 2^2 = 4. These correspond to the configurations: (R, R), (S, S), (R, S), and (S, R).

However, in this system, the (R, S) and (S, R) configurations result in a compound with an internal plane of symmetry, making it a meso form. Hence, they are not optically active and are considered a single achiral stereoisomer.

The remaining (R, R) and (S, S) forms are non-superimposable mirror images and thus constitute one pair of enantiomers.

Therefore, the total number of stereoisomers possible is 3.

47. **(0.123 Å):** An electron at rest is accelerated through a potential difference of 10 kV = 10,000 V. The kinetic energy gained by the electron is:

$$K.E. = eV = 1.6 \times 10^{-19} \times 10^4$$
$$= 1.6 \times 10^{-15} \text{ J}$$

This energy is converted into kinetic energy:

$$\frac{1}{2}mv^2 = 1.6 \times 10^{-15}$$

Solving for v:

$$v = \sqrt{\frac{2\times1.6\times10^{-15}}{9.11\times10^{-31}}}$$

$$v = \sqrt{\frac{3.2\times10^{-15}}{9.11\times10^{-31}}}$$

$$= \sqrt{3.5137\times10^{15}}$$

$$\approx 5.928 \times 10^7 \text{ m/s}$$

Now, the de Broglie wavelength λ is given by:

$$\lambda = \frac{h}{mv}$$

$$\lambda = \frac{6.63\times10^{-34}}{9.11\times10^{-31}\times5.928\times10^7}$$

$$= \frac{6.63\times10^{-34}}{5.401\times10^{-23}}$$

$$\approx 1.227 \times 10^{-11} \text{ m}$$

Converting to Ångströms (1 Å = 10^{-10} m):

$$\lambda = 0.1227 \text{ Å}$$

Rounded off to three decimal places, the de Broglie wavelength is 0.123 Å.

48. (*): There is a subtle ambiguity in Question 48, and it lies in the interpretation of the concentration (C) and the system described. Here's the reasoning behind the ambiguity:

Key facts given:

- The solution is 0.001 M NaCl.
- The setup describes a semipermeable membrane allowing only solvent (not solute) to pass.
- We are to compute the osmotic pressure and the corresponding height of the liquid column h.
- The equation used is: $\pi = iCRT$
  Where: i = van't Hoff factor = 2 for NaCl
  C = molar concentration of solute particles

Potential ambiguity:

The term "0.001 M NaCl" may be interpreted in two ways:

1. **As the concentration of NaCl units (molecules)**
   → This would be C = 0.001 mol/L, and since NaCl dissociates into 2 particles (Na^+ + Cl^-), the effective particle concentration is:
   $iC = 2 \times 0.001 = 0.002$ mol/L
2. **As the total concentration of solute particles (after dissociation)**
   → If the examiner intended that "0.001 M" refers to the total effective particle concentration (after considering dissociation), then we should not multiply by $i = 2$ again, and just use C = 0.001.

But in standard chemistry practice, when a solution is said to be "0.001 M NaCl", it usually means 0.001 mol/L of NaCl units before dissociation.

Therefore, multiplying by $i = 2$ is appropriate.

Conclusion:

- The correct assumption is to use $i = 2$ and C = 0.001 mol/L, leading to the final answer: 50.9 cm
- But the lack of clarity on whether the concentration refers to NaCl units or total particles after dissociation introduces a potential ambiguity.

49. (510.0 MHz): The resonance (Larmor) frequency ν of a nucleus in an NMR spectrometer is given by:

$$\nu = \frac{g_N \beta_N B}{h}$$

Where:

- g_N = 5.586 (nuclear g-factor for ^{1}H)
- $\beta_N = 5.05 \times 10^{-27}$ J/T (nuclear magneton)
- B = 12 T (magnetic field strength)
- $h = 6.63 \times 10^{-34}$ J\cdotps

Substitute the values:

$$\nu = \frac{5.586\times5.05\times10^{-27}\times12}{6.63\times10^{-34}}$$

$$\nu = \frac{338.21\times10^{-27}}{6.63\times10^{-34}}$$

$$= \frac{3.3821\times10^{-25}}{6.63\times10^{-34}}$$

$$\approx 5.1 \times 10^{8} \text{ Hz} = 510 \text{ MHz}.$$

50. (3.66 cm^{-1}): The rotational transition frequency of a diatomic molecule depends inversely on its moment of inertia, and hence on the reduced mass μ. The rotational constant B ∝ 1/μ, so the ratio of frequencies is:

$$\frac{\nu'}{\nu} = \frac{B'}{B} = \frac{\mu}{\mu'}$$

Given:

- Original molecule: $^{12}C^{16}O$
- Isotopically substituted: $^{12}C^{18}O$
- Frequency for $^{12}C^{16}O$: $\nu = 3.84$ cm^{-1}

Reduced mass (in atomic mass units):

$$\mu = \frac{12\times16}{12+16} = \frac{192}{28} = 6.8571$$

$$\mu' = \frac{12\times18}{12+18} = \frac{216}{30} = 7.2$$

Now: $$\mu' = \nu\times\frac{\mu}{\mu'} = 3.84\times\frac{6.8571}{7.2}$$

$$\approx 3.84 \times 0.9521$$

$$= 3.658 \text{ cm}^{-1}.$$

Answer: 3.66 cm^{-1}.

51. (1): Given the equation:

$$y + xe^{y} = \sin x + \tan x$$

We are to find $\frac{dy}{dx}$ at $x = 0$.

Step 1: Differentiate both sides with respect to *x*

Use implicit differentiation:

Left-hand side:

$$\frac{d}{dx}(y)+\frac{d}{dx}(xe^{y}) = \frac{dy}{dx}+\left(e^{y}+xe^{y}\frac{dy}{dx}\right)$$

Right-hand side:

$$\frac{d}{dx}(\sin x+\tan x) = \cos x + \sec^2 x$$

Now combine both:

$$\frac{dy}{dx}+e^{y}+xe^{y}\frac{dy}{dx} = \cos x + \sec^2 x$$

Group $\frac{dy}{dx}$ terms:

$$(1+xe^{y})\frac{dy}{dx} = \cos x + \sec^2 x - e^{y}$$

Solve for $\frac{dy}{dx}$:

$$\frac{dy}{dx} = \frac{\cos x+\sec^2 x-e^{y}}{1+xe^{y}}$$

Step 2: Evaluate at $x = 0$

First, find the value of y at $x = 0$:

From the original equation:

$$y + 0 \cdot e^{y} = \sin 0 + \tan 0$$

$$\Rightarrow \quad y = 0$$

Now plug $x = 0$, $y = 0$, into the derivative expression:

$$\frac{dy}{dx} = \frac{\cos(0)+\sec^2(0)-e^{0}}{1+0\cdot e^{0}}$$

$$= \frac{1+1-1}{1} = \frac{1}{1} = 1.$$

52. (638): We are given matrices A and B, and we are to compute the sum of the diagonal elements (i.e., the trace) of matrix C = AB. The trace of a matrix product C = AB can be calculated using:

$$\text{Tr(C)} = \sum_{i=1}^{n}(\text{AB})_{ii}$$

This means we compute the sum of the diagonal entries of the product matrix, each of which is:

$$(AB)_{ii} = \sum_{k=1}^{n} A_{ik}B_{ki}$$

We will calculate each diagonal element of C step by step.

Step 1: Dimensions and diagonal entries

Matrices A and B are both 5 × 5, so C is also 5 × 5.

We compute:

$$Tr(C) = C_{11} + C_{22} + C_{33} + C_{44} + C_{55}$$

Step 2: Compute C_{11}

$$C_{11} = A_{11} \cdot B_{11} + A_{12} \cdot B_{21} = 1 \cdot 10 + 2 \cdot 12 = 10 + 24 = 34$$

Step 3: Compute C_{22}

$$C_{22} = A_{21} \cdot B_{12} + A_{22} \cdot B_{22} = 3 \cdot 11 + 4 \cdot 13 = 33 + 52 = 85$$

Step 4: Compute C_{33}

$$C_{33} = A_{33} \cdot B_{33} = 5 \cdot 4 = 20$$

Step 5: Compute C_{44}

$$C_{44} = A_{44} \cdot B_{44} + A_{45} \cdot B_{54} = 6 \cdot 15 + 7 \cdot 17 = 90 + 119 = 209$$

Step 6: Compute C_{55}

$$C_{55} = A_{54} \cdot B_{45} + A_{55} \cdot B_{55} = 8 \cdot 16 + 9 \cdot 18 = 128 + 162 = 290$$

Step 7: Add all diagonal elements

$$Tr(C) = 34 + 85 + 20 + 209 + 290 = 638.$$

53. **(3):** We are to find how many species among the following have a bond order of 3:

Species given:

N_2, F_2, NO^+, O_2^-, N_2^+, CO, O_2, O_2^{2-}

To determine the bond order, we refer to Molecular Orbital Theory for diatomic species. The bond order is calculated as:

$$\text{Bond Order} = \frac{1}{2}(\text{Number of bonding electrons} - \text{Number of antibonding electrons})$$

Let's evaluate each:

1. **N_2** : Total electrons = 14 → Bond order = 3 (✔)
2. **F_2** : Total electrons = 18 → Bond order = 1 (✗)
3. **NO^+** : Total electrons = 14 (N = 7, O = 8, minus 1) → Bond order = 3 (✔)
4. **O_2^-** : Total electrons = 17 → Bond order = 1.5 (✗)
5. **N_2^+** : Total electrons = 13 → Bond order = 2.5 (✗)
6. **CO** : Total electrons = 14 → Isovalent to N_2 → Bond order = 3 (✔)
7. **O_2** : Total electrons = 16 → Bond order = 2 (✗)
8. **O_2^{2-}** : Total electrons = 18 → Bond order = 1 (✗)

Species with bond order = 3:

N_2, NO^+, CO.

54. **(54.35%):** Given: A mixture of $CaCO_3$ and $MgCO_3$ weighs 1.84 g before heating. After heating (decomposition to CaO and MgO), the residue weighs 0.96 g.

Reactions:

- $CaCO_3 \rightarrow CaO + CO_2$
- $MgCO_3 \rightarrow MgO + CO_2$

Let the mass of $CaCO_3 = x\ g$, and $MgCO_3 = 1.84 - x\ g$

From molar masses:

- Molar mass of $CaCO_3$ = 40 + 12 + 3 × 16 = 100 g/mol → residue CaO = 56 g/mol
- Molar mass of $MgCO_3$ = 24 + 12 + 3 × 16 = 84 g/mol → residue MgO = 40 g/mol

$$\text{Mass of CaO obtained} = \frac{56}{100} \times x = 0.56x$$

$$\text{Mass of MgO obtained} = \frac{40}{84} \times (1.84 - x)$$

Total residue = 0.96 g

$$0.56x+\frac{40}{84}(1.84-x) = 0.96$$

Multiply through by 84 to eliminate denominators:

$47.04x + 40(1.84 - x) = 80.64$

$47.04x + 73.6 - 40x = 80.64$

$7.04x = 80.64 - 73.6 = 7.04$

$\Rightarrow \quad x = 1.00$ g

So, mass of $CaCO_3$ = 1.00 g

% of $CaCO_3$ in the original mixture:

$$\frac{1.00}{1.84}\times 100 = 54.35\%.$$

55. (6): To determine the number of chiral carbon centers in the given complex tetracyclic molecule, we must carefully examine each tetrahedral (sp^3-hybridized) carbon and check whether it is attached to four different groups, making it chiral.

Key Criteria for a Chiral Carbon:

- It must be sp^3-hybridized (i.e., have 4 single bonds).
- It must be bonded to four different atoms or groups.
- It must not lie in a plane (i.e., not part of an aromatic ring or be sp^2-hybridized).
- Carbons at the fusion points of multiple rings, especially in rigid fused bicyclic systems, are likely chiral if asymmetry exists around them.

Step-by-Step Analysis of the Given Structure:

- This is a complex fused ring system with multiple ring junctions and heteroatoms (two nitrogens and a carbonyl group).
- The aromatic rings (like benzene) are excluded, as their carbons are sp^2 and not chiral.
- We focus on the bridgehead and junction carbon atoms in the fused aliphatic ring system.

Let's count the sp^3-hybridized carbon atoms in the non-aromatic part of the molecule:

1. The carbon connected to the indole ring system and the N atom of the six-membered ring is sp^3 and connected to four different groups → chiral
2. The next carbon at the junction with the lactam ring and the six-membered ring is chiral
3. The carbon connecting the central nitrogen to the fused six-membered ring also meets the chiral criteria
4. The carbon at the bottom ring junction in the fused six-membered system is chiral
5. The carbon between the nitrogen and the fused ring opposite to the carbonyl shows asymmetry
6. Another carbon in the fused ring system near the top-right junction also satisfies the condition for chirality

All these centers are stereocenters due to the rigid, non-planar geometry and the presence of different ring systems and substituents attached at each junction.

Final Count: A total of 6 carbon atoms in the rigid ring system satisfy the conditions of being sp^3-hybridized and bonded to four different groups, making them chiral centers.

56. (–8.64 J/K): The process shown is:

$A \rightarrow B \rightarrow C \rightarrow D$ for 1 mole of a monoatomic ideal gas.

We are to find the total change in entropy, which is a state function. So, we only need to consider the initial state A and the final state D, not the path.

Step 1: Use the entropy change formula for an ideal gas

$$\Delta S = nR\left[\ln\left(\frac{V_f}{V_i}\right)+\frac{3}{2}\ln\left(\frac{T_f}{T_i}\right)\right]$$

Where:

- $V_i = 10\ dm^3$, $V_f = 10\ dm^3$
  → No change in volume

- P_i = 2 atm, P_f = 1 atm
- n = 1 mole
- R = 8.314 J/mol\cdotpK

From the ideal gas law:

$$PV = nRT$$

$$\Rightarrow \quad T \propto PV \text{ (for fixed } n, R)$$

So, $$\frac{T_f}{T_i} = \frac{P_f V_f}{P_i V_i} = \frac{1 \times 10}{2 \times 10} = \frac{1}{2}$$

Now, since $V_f = V_i$, the volume term becomes zero, so:

$$\Delta S = nR\left[0 + \frac{3}{2}\ln\left(\frac{1}{2}\right)\right]$$

$$= 1 \times 8.314 \times \frac{3}{2}\ln\left(\frac{1}{2}\right)$$

$$\Delta S = 12.471 \times \ln(0.5)$$

$$= 12.471 \times (-0.6931)$$

$$\approx -8.64 \text{ J/K.}$$

57. **(X = 0.76):** We are given:

- Number of moles of He atoms hitting wall per second = 95 mol/s
- Volume of the container = 1 dm³ = 10^{-3} m³
- Average perpendicular velocity = 1000 m/s
- Molar mass of He = 4 g/mol = 4 × 10^{-3} kg/mol
- Avogadro's number $N_A = 6.02 \times 10^{23}$

Step 1: Find mass per He atom

$$m = \frac{4 \times 10^{-3}}{6.02 \times 10^{23}}$$

$$= 6.6445 \times 10^{-27} \text{ kg}$$

Step 2: Total number of atoms hitting wall per second

$$n = 95 \text{ mol/s}$$

$$\Rightarrow \quad N = 95 \times 6.02 \times 10^{23}$$

$$= 5.719 \times 10^{25} \text{ particles/s}$$

Step 3: Momentum change per particle

Since each particle hits and rebounds elastically, the momentum change per particle:

$$\Delta p = 2mv$$

$$= 2 \times 6.6445 \times 10^{-27} \times 1000$$

$$= 1.3289 \times 10^{-23} \text{ kg\cdotpm/s}$$

Step 4: Total force on wall

$$F = \text{rate of change of momentum}$$

$$N \times \Delta p = 5.719 \times 10^{25} \times 1.3289 \times 10^{-23}$$

$$= 760.1 \text{ N}$$

Step 5: Area of the wall

For a cube of volume V = 10^{-3} m³,

side length L = $(10^{-3})^{1/3}$ = 0.1 m

So, wall area = A = 0.1^2 = 0.01 m²

Step 6: Pressure on wall

$$P = \frac{F}{A} = \frac{760.1}{0.01}$$

$$= 7.601 \times 10^4 \text{ N/m}^2$$

$$= 0.7601 \times 10^5$$

Final Answer: X = 0.76.

58. **(8.8):** The solubility equilibrium of lead(II) carbonate is:

$$PbCO_3(s) \rightleftharpoons Pb^{2+}(aq) + CO_3^{2-}(aq)$$

with the solubility product:

$$K_{sp} = \left[Pb^{2+}\right]\left[CO_3^{2-}\right]$$

$$= 1.5 \times 10^{-13}$$

Let the solubility be s. Then,

$$\left[Pb^{2+}\right] = s, \left[CO_3^{2-}\right] = s.\alpha_{CO_3^{2-}}$$

where $\alpha_{CO_3^{2-}}$ is the fraction of carbonate species present as CO_3^{2-} at pH 5.

Using the dissociation equilibria:

$$H_2CO_3 \xrightleftharpoons{K_{a1}} H^+ + HCO_3^-$$

$$K_{a1} = 4.2 \times 10^{-7}$$

$$HCO_3^- \underset{}{\overset{K_{a2}}{\rightleftharpoons}} H^+ + CO_3^{2-}$$

$$K_{a2} = 4.8 \times 10^{-11}$$

Total carbonate species

$$= [H_2CO_3]+[HCO_3^-]+[CO_3^{2-}]$$

Then, $\alpha_{CO_3^{2-}} = \dfrac{[CO_3^{2-}]}{\text{Total carbonate}}$

$$= \frac{K_{a1}K_{a2}}{[H^+]^2 + K_{a1}[H^+] + K_{a1}K_{a2}}$$

Substituting values with $[H^+] = 10^{-5}$:

$$\alpha_{CO_3^{2-}} = \frac{4.2\times10^{-7}\cdot4.8\times10^{-11}}{(10^{-5})^2 + 4.2\times10^{-7}\cdot10^{-5} + 4.2\times10^{-7}\cdot4.8\times10^{-11}}$$

$$= \frac{2.016\times10^{-17}}{1.042\times10^{-10}}$$

$$\alpha_{CO_3^{2-}} = 1.934 \times 10^{-7}$$

Now, $K_{sp} = s^2 \,.\, \alpha_{CO_3^{2-}}$

$$\Rightarrow \quad s^2 = \frac{K_{sp}}{\alpha_{CO_3^{2-}}} = \frac{1.5\times10^{-13}}{1.934\times10^{-7}}$$

$$= 7.759 \times 10^{-7}$$

$$s = \sqrt{7.759\times10^{-7}}$$

$$\approx 8.81 \times 10^{-4}$$

This corresponds to:

$$X \times 10^{-4} = 8.81 \times 10^{-4}$$

$$\Rightarrow \quad X = 8.8.$$

59. (3.8): The molar conductivity Λ_M of a 0.02 M solution of a weak acid HA is given as 3.2 mS·m²·mol⁻¹, and the limiting molar conductivity Λ_m° is 39 mS.m².mol⁻¹ at 298 K. The degree of dissociation α of the weak acid is calculated using the relation:

$$\alpha = \frac{\Lambda_m}{\Lambda_m^\circ} = \frac{3.2}{39} \approx 0.08205$$

Using the expression for the dissociation constant of a weak acid:

$$K_a = \frac{c\alpha^2}{1-\alpha} = \frac{0.02\times(0.08205)^2}{1-0.08205}$$

$$K_a = \frac{0.02\times0.006733}{0.91795}$$

$$= \frac{1.3466\times10^{-4}}{0.91795}$$

$$\approx 1.467 \times 10^{-4}$$

Now, the pK_a is:

$$pK_a = -\log_{10}(1.467 \times 10^{-4})$$

$$\approx 3.8.$$

60. (–239.3 J.K⁻¹.mol⁻¹): The given cell reaction is:

$H_2(g) + Cl_2(g) \rightarrow 2H^+(aq) + 2Cl^-(aq)$

To determine the standard entropy change ΔS° for the reaction, the relation between entropy and the temperature dependence of the standard cell potential is used:

$$\Delta S^\circ = nF\left(\frac{\partial E^\circ}{\partial T}\right)_P$$

Here:

- $n = 2$ (number of electrons transferred),
- F = 96480 C\cdotp mol⁻¹
- $\dfrac{\partial E^\circ}{\partial T} \approx -1.24 \times 10^{-3}$ V\cdotpK⁻¹, based on standard literature values for the Cl_2/Cl^- half-cell.

Substituting into the equation:

ΔS° = 2 × 96480 × (–0.00124)

= –239.32928 J\cdotpK⁻¹\cdotpmol⁻¹

Rounding to one decimal place is:

–239.3 J.K⁻¹.mol⁻¹.

Previous Years' Paper

IIT–JAM

JOINT ADMISSION TEST FOR M.Sc. (CHEMISTRY), 2024

Section A : Multiple Choice Questions (MCQ)

Directions: (Q. No. 1 to 10) *Carry **One** mark each.*

1. The following dipeptide derivative is used as an artificial sweetener:

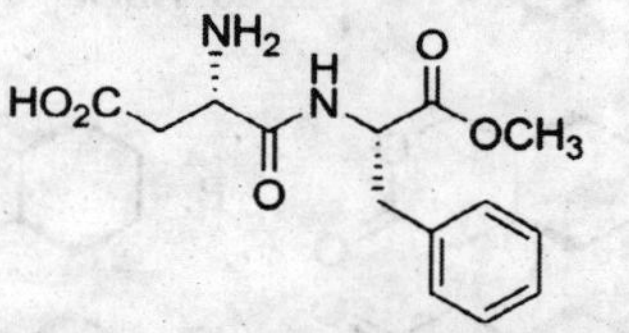

The constituent α-amino acids of this dipeptide are:

A. phenylalanine and glutamic acid.
B. phenylalanine and aspartic acid.
C. tyrosine and aspartic acid.
D. tyrosine and glutamic acid.

2. The suitable reagent combination for the following transformation is:

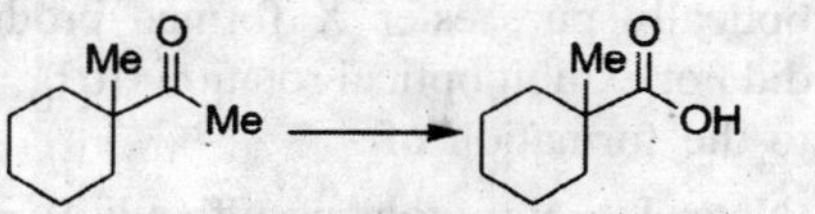

A. (*i*) *meta*-chloroperbenzoic acid (*m*-CPBA); (*ii*) NaOH; (*iii*) aq. HCl
B. (*i*) OsO_4; (*ii*) aq. HCl
C. (*i*) I_2/NaOH; (*ii*) aq. HCl
D. (*i*) dimethyldioxirane (DMDO); (*ii*) aq. HCl

3. For the reaction

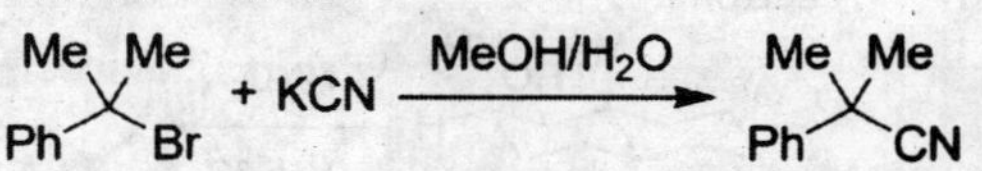

if the concentration of KCN is increased four times, then the rate of the reaction would be

A. unaffected.
B. increased by two times.
C. decreased by four times.
D. increased by four times.

4. Consider the wavefunction $\psi(x) = N[\exp(ikx) + \exp(-ikx)]$. The complex conjugate $\psi^*(x)$ is

[Given: N is the normalization constant; $i = \sqrt{-1}$]

A. $N[\exp(-ikx) - \exp(ikx)]$
B. $N^*[\exp(-ikx) - \exp(ikx)]$
C. $N^*[\exp(ikx) + \exp(-ikx)]$
D. $2N[\sin(kx)]$

5. Wavelength of X-rays used in a diffraction experiment is 1.54 Å. X-rays are diffracted from a set of planes with an interplanar spacing of 1.54 Å. Then the angle θ (in degrees) corresponding to the first-order Bragg diffraction is

A. 30°
B. 15°
C. 45°
D. 90°

6. Identify the reaction for which, at equilibrium, a change in the volume of the closed reaction vessel at a constant temperature will not affect the extent of the reaction.

A. $CaCO_3(s) \rightleftharpoons CaO(s) + CO_2(g)$
B. $H_2(g) + I_2(g) \rightleftharpoons 2HI(g)$
C. $2NO_2(g) \rightleftharpoons N_2O_4(g)$
D. $CO_2(s) \rightleftharpoons CO_2(g)$

7. Among $[Ti(H_2O)_6]^{3+}$, $[NiCl_4]^{2-}$, $[CrO_4]^{2-}$, and $[Mn(H_2O)_6]^{2+}$, the complex that exhibits the largest molar absorptivity in the visible region of the electronic absorption spectrum is:

A. $[Ti(H_2O)_6]^{3+}$ B. $[NiCl_4]^{2-}$
C. $[CrO_4]^{2-}$ D. $[Mn(H_2O)_6]^{2+}$

8. $[Co(NH_3)_5(SO_4)]Br$ and $[Co(NH_3)_5Br]SO_4$ are examples of:

A. ionization isomers.
B. linkage isomers.
C. optical isomers.
D. coordination isomers.

9. The pair of proteins having heme core is:

A. hemoglobin and myoglobin.
B. hemerythrin and myoglobin.
C. hemoglobin and hemocyanin.
D. hemocyanin and hemerythrin.

10. The shape of SCN^- is:

A. linear. B. bent.
C. pyramidal. D. trigonal planar.

Directions: (Q. No. 11 to 30) *Carry Two marks each.*

11. The major product formed in the following reaction

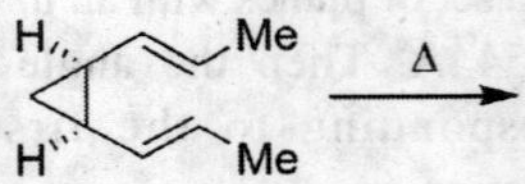

is:

A. 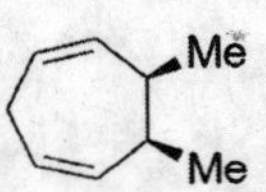 B. 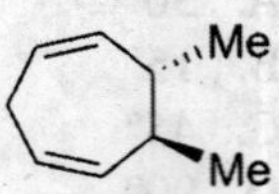

C. 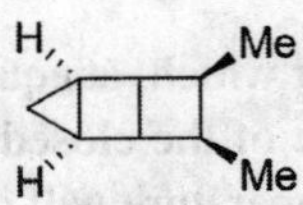 D. 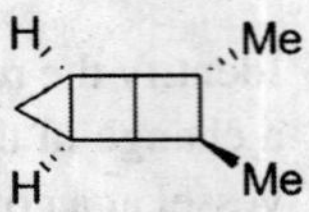

12. The major product formed in the following reaction

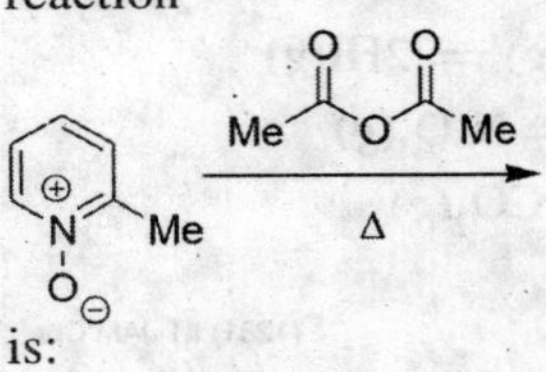

is:

A. 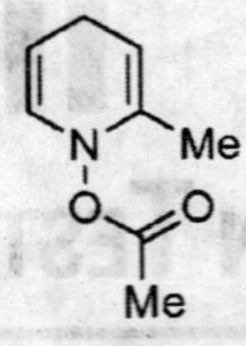 B. 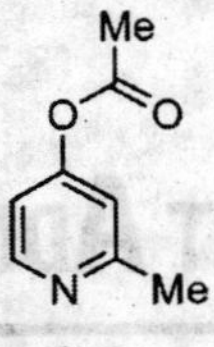

C. 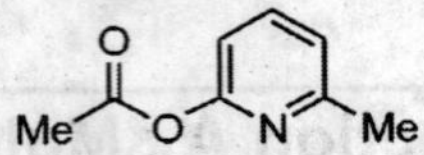 D. 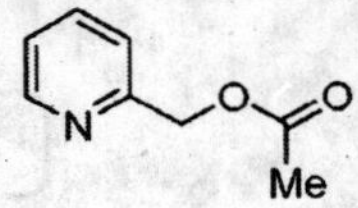

13. The major product formed in the following reaction

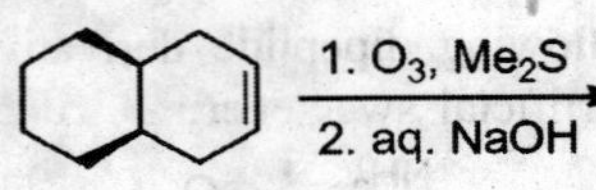

is:

A. 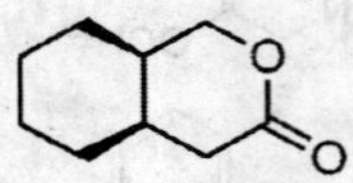 B. 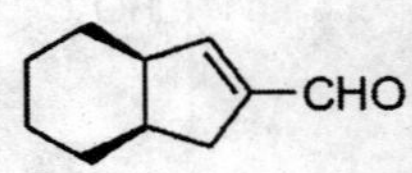

C. 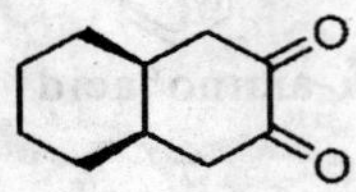 D. 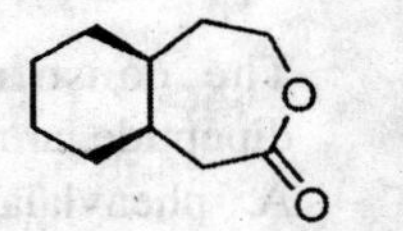

14. In the following reaction

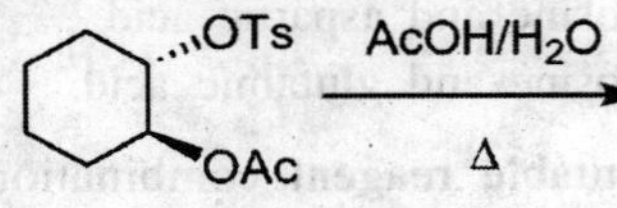

X

optically pure ester X formed product that did not exhibit optical rotation ($[\alpha]_D = 0$) due to the formation of

(Note: Ts = *para*-toluenesulfonyl; Ac = acetyl)

A. *cis*-1,2-diacetoxycyclohexane.
B. a racemic mixture of *trans*-1, 2-diacetoxycyclohexane.
C. cyclohexene.
D. cyclohexene oxide.

15. The major products X and Y in the following reactions

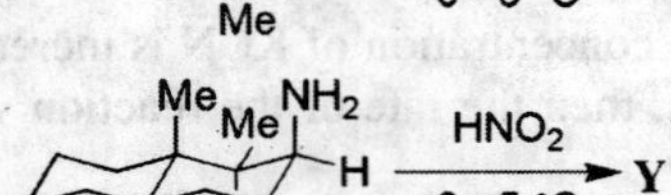

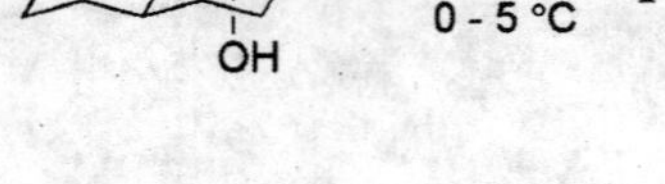

respectively, are:

A. 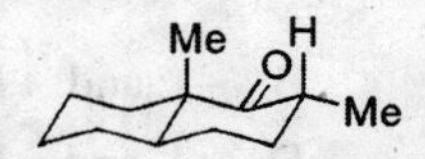 and 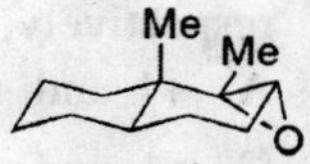

B. 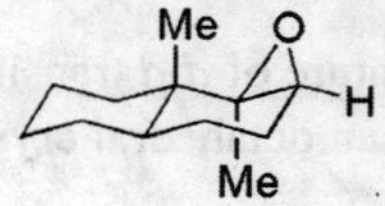 and 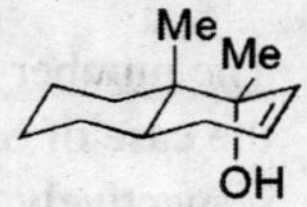

C. 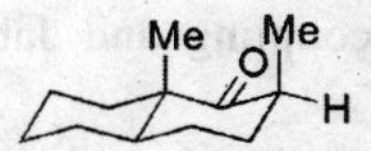 and 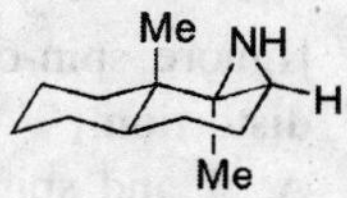

D. 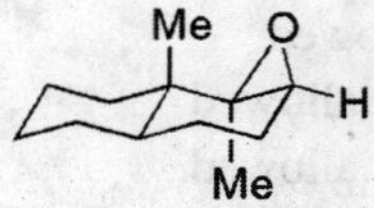 and 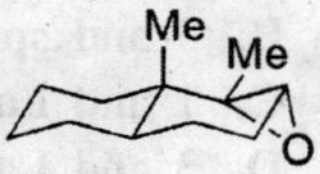

16. The major product formed in the following reaction

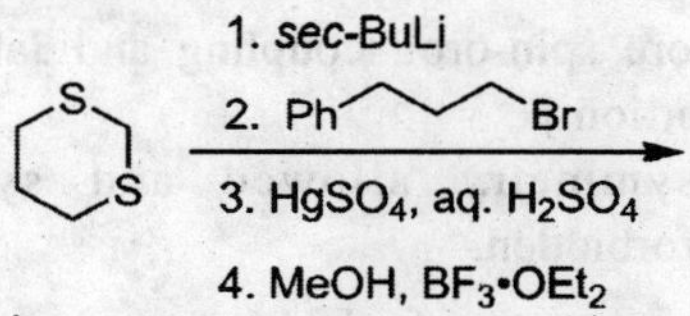

is:

A. 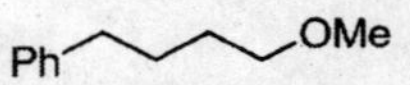

B. 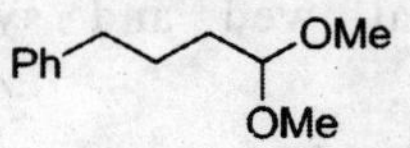

C. 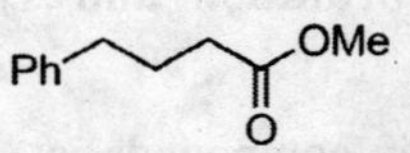

D. 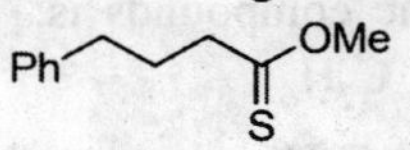

17. The acidity of the compounds shown below

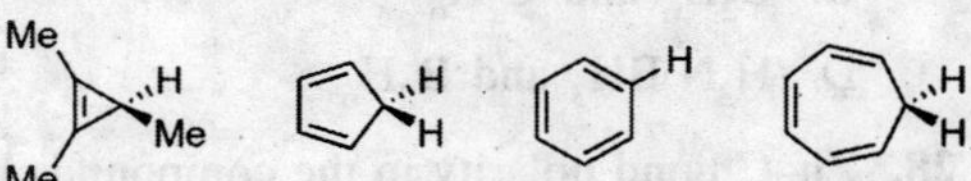

I II III IV

follows the order:

A. II > I > III > IV B. II > IV > III > I

C. I > II > IV > III D. III > IV > II > I

18. The major product formed in the following reaction

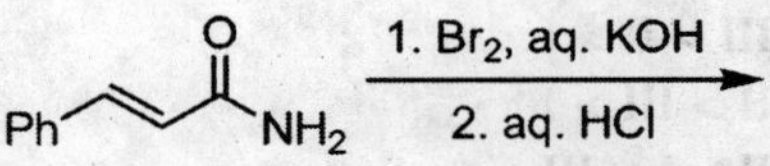

is:

A. 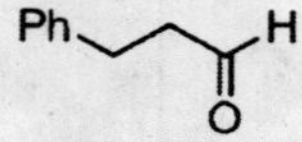 B. 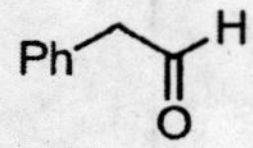

C. 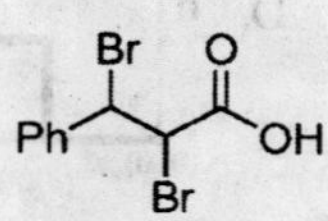 D. 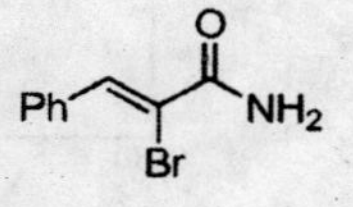

19. The ratio of osmotic pressures of aqueous solutions of 0.01 M $BaCl_2$ to 0.005 M NaCl is

[Given: Both compounds dissociate completely in water]

A. 3:1

B. 1:4

C. 1:1

D. 3:2

20. In the cell reaction

$P^+(aq) + Q(s) \rightarrow P(s) + Q^+(aq)$

the EMF of the cell, E_{cell} is zero. The standard EMF of the cell, E°_{cell} is:

[Given: Activities of all solids are unity.

Activity of $P^+(aq)$ is 2 M. Activity of $Q^+(aq)$ is 1 M.

R = universal gas constant; T = temperature; F = Faraday constant]

A. $\frac{RT}{F}$ B. $\frac{RT}{2F}$

C. $-\frac{RT}{F}\ln(2)$ D. $\frac{RT}{F}\ln(2)$

21. Consider photoelectric effect. The number of incident photons is the same for all frequencies. The plot that best describes the dependence of the number of photoelectrons (n) emitted as a function of the incident light frequency (ν) is:

A. 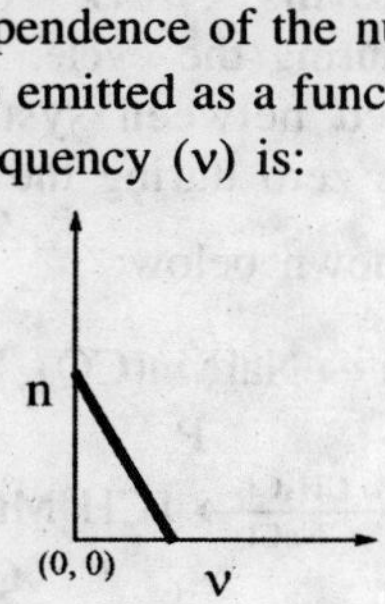

B. 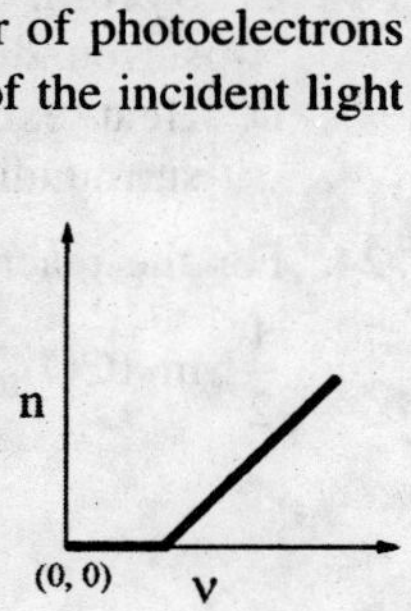

C. 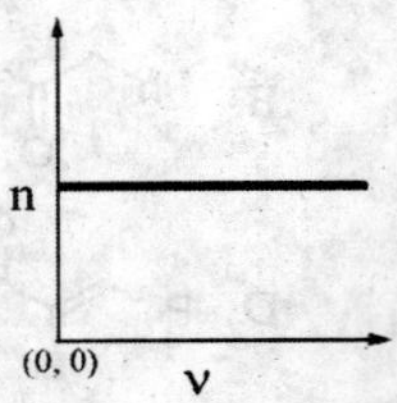

D. 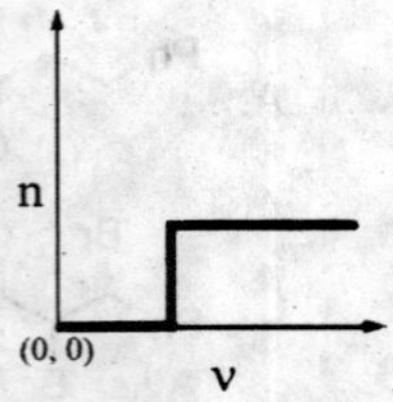

22. If nitrogen and oxygen gases are at the same temperature, the correct statement according to the kinetic theory of gases is:
A. Average kinetic energy of nitrogen and oxygen molecules is inversely proportional to temperature.
B. For nitrogen and oxygen molecules, the root mean square speed is equal to the most probable speed.
C. Average speed of nitrogen molecules is less than the average speed of oxygen molecules.
D. Average kinetic energies of nitrogen and oxygen molecules are equal.

23. A system undergoes one clockwise cycle from point X back to point X as shown in the figure below:

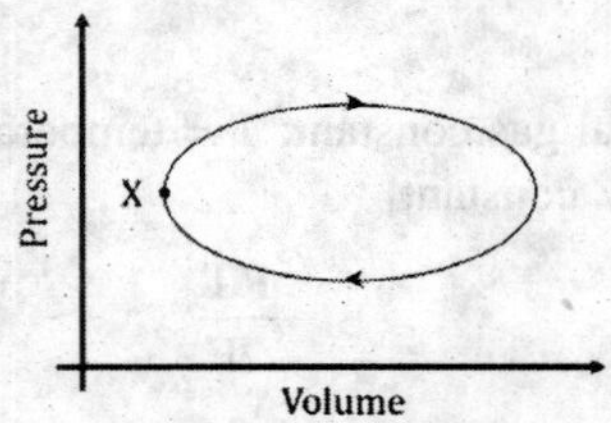

The correct statement about this process is
A. Internal energy of the system decreases at the end of the cycle.
B. Entropy of the system increases at the end of the cycle.
C. System performs work on the surroundings during the cycle.
D. Heat exchanged between system and surroundings is zero during the cycle.

24. For the reaction shown below:

$$\frac{1}{2}Mn_2(CO)_{10} + Na \rightarrow \underset{P}{Na[Mn(CO)_5]} \xrightarrow[-NaCl]{CH_3Cl} \underset{Q}{[CH_3Mn(CO)_5]}$$

the oxidation states of Mn in P and Q, respectively, are:
A. +1 and +1 B. −1 and +1
C. −1 and −1 D. +1 and −1

25. The number and nature of *d-d* transition(s) in the case of Sc^{2+} in an octahedral crystal field, respectively, are
[Ignore spin-orbit coupling and Jahn-Teller distortion.]
A. 1 and spin allowed.
B. 3 and spin allowed.
C. 1 and Laporte allowed.
D. 3 and Laporte allowed.

26. The *d-d* transitions in $[Mn(H_2O)_6]^{2+}$ and $[Ti(H_2O)_4]^{3+}$, respectively, are
[Ignore spin-orbit coupling and Jahn-Teller distortion.]
A. symmetry allowed and symmetry forbidden.
B. symmetry forbidden and symmetry allowed.
C. symmetry allowed and symmetry allowed.
D. symmetry forbidden and symmetry forbidden.

27. A pair of isosteric compounds is:
A. H_2NBH_2 and C_2H_6
B. $H_3N{\cdot}BH_3$ and C_2H_6
C. B_2H_6 and C_2H_6
D. $H_3N{\cdot}BH_3$ and B_2H_6

28. Zn–C bond polarity in the compounds below

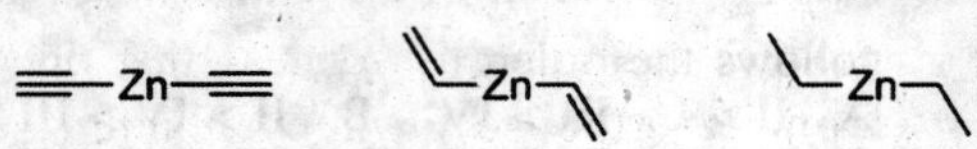

I II III

follows the order
A. I > II > III
B. III > II > I
C. II > III > I
D. II > I > III

29. B_2 and C_2, respectively, are:

A. paramagnetic and diamagnetic.
B. diamagnetic and paramagnetic.
C. paramagnetic and paramagnetic.
D. diamagnetic and diamagnetic.

30. Mobility of ions
Li^+, Na^+, K^+, Ag^+
in water at 298 K follows the order

A. $K^+ < Ag^+ < Na^+ < Li^+$
B. $Li^+ < K^+ < Na^+ < Ag^+$
C. $Ag^+ < Li^+ < K^+ < Na^+$
D. $Li^+ < Na^+ < Ag^+ < K^+$

Section B : Multiple Select Questions (MSQ)

Q. 31 – Q. 40 carry two marks each.

31. The suitable synthetic route(s) for the following transformation

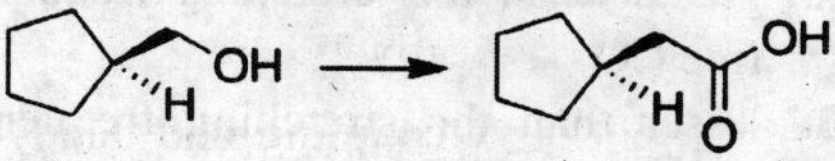

is/are:

A. (*i*) *para*-toluenesulfonyl chloride (TsCl), pyridine; (*ii*) KI; (*iii*) Mg/Et_2O; (*iv*) CO_2; (*v*) aq. HCl
B. (*i*) *para*-toluenesulfonyl chloride (TsCl), pyridine; (*ii*) KCN; (*iii*) conc. aq. NaOH, reflux; (*iv*) aq. HCl
C. (*i*) CrO_3, H_2SO_4; (*ii*) $SOCl_2$; (*iii*) CH_2N_2; (*iv*) Ag_2O, H_2O
D. (*i*) CrO_3, H_2SO_4; (*ii*) CH_2N_2

32. The compound(s) which on reaction with CH_3MgBr followed by treatment with aqueous NH_4Cl would produce 1-methyl-1-phenylethanol as the major product is/are:

A. methyl benzoate. B. phenyl acetate.
C. acetaldehyde. D. acetophenone.

33. Among the following, the compound(s) which produce the same osazone as that obtained from D-glucose, when reacted with phenylhydrazine, is/are:

A. 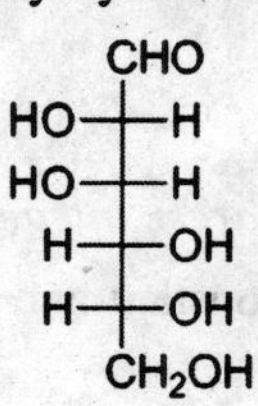

B. 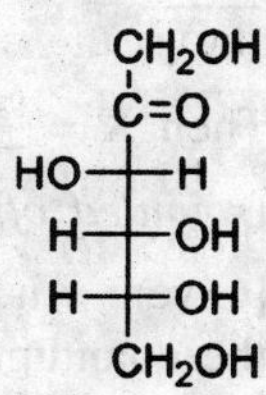

C. 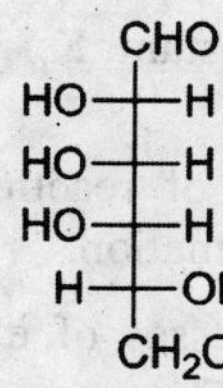

D. 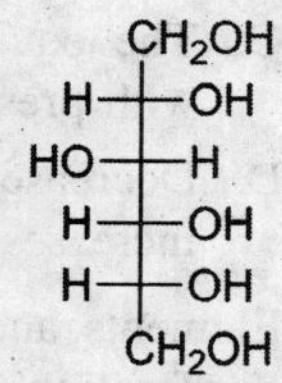

34. Among the following, the chiral molecule(s) is/are

A. 

B. 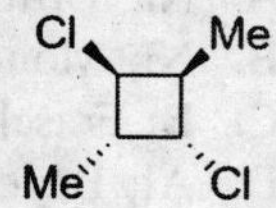

C. 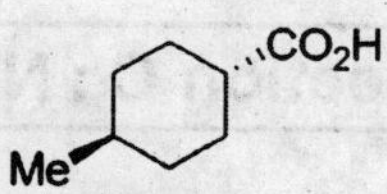

D. 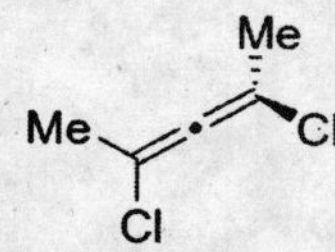

35. The correct assumption(s) required to derive Langmuir adsorption isotherm is/are:

A. Adsorption is limited to a monolayer on adsorbing surface.
B. All binding sites on adsorbing surface are identical.
C. Adsorption of a molecule on a site enhances binding of other molecules on neighboring sites.
D. Rate of adsorption and rate of desorption are equal at equilibrium.

36. For one mole of an ideal gas, the correct statement(s) is/are

[U = internal energy; V = volume; T = temperature; P = pressure]

A. $\left(\dfrac{\partial U}{\partial V}\right)_T = 0$ B. $\left(\dfrac{\partial U}{\partial T}\right)_V > 0$

C. $\left(\frac{\partial P}{\partial T}\right)_V > 0$ D. $\left(\frac{\partial V}{\partial P}\right)_T > 0$

37. Consider the exothermic chemical reaction $O_2(g) + 2H_2(g) \rightleftharpoons 2H_2O(g)$ at equilibrium in a closed container. The correct statement(s) is/are:

A. At equilibrium, introduction of catalyst increases product formation.

B. Equilibrium constant decreases with increase in temperature.

C. The equilibrium constant K_P increases with pressure.

D. Decrease in volume of reaction vessel increases product formation.

38. Elements and their processes of extraction/purification are given. The correct pair(s) is/are:

A. Na; Downs process

B. Ni; Mond process

C. B; Frasch process

D. Al; Bayer process

39. The correct statement(s) about the ligand substitution/exchange reaction is/are:

A. The rate is faster in the case of SF_6 than in $[AlF_6]^{3-}$.

B. The rate is faster in the case of $[Mg(H_2O)_6]^{2+}$ than in $[Sr(H_2O)_6]^{2+}$.

C. The rate of water exchange is faster in the case of $[Ni(H_2O)_6]^{2+}$ than in $[Co(NH_3)_5(H_2O)]^{3+}$.

D. The rate is faster in case of $[Cr(H_2O)_6]^{2+}$ than in $[Cr(H_2O)_6]^{3+}$.

40. The stretching frequency of CO in $H_3B.CO$ is:

A. greater than the stretching frequency in free CO.

B. lesser than the stretching frequency in free CO.

C. lesser than the stretching frequency of CO in $Fe(CO)_5$.

D. greater than the stretching frequency of CO in $Fe(CO)_5$.

Section C : Numerical Answer Type (NAT)

Q. 41 – Q. 50 carry one mark each.

41. For the following compound

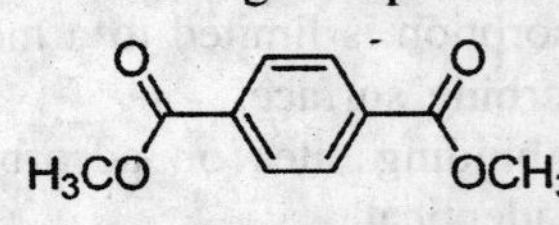

the number of signals expected in the ^{1}H NMR spectrum is ______.

42. Exhaustive hydrogenation of the following compound

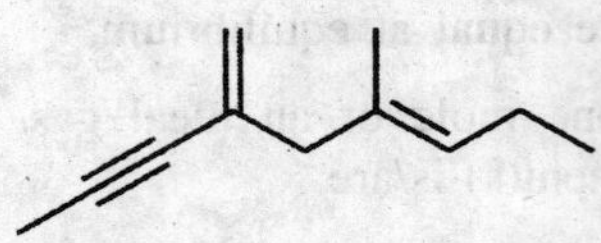

under Pd/C generates a saturated hydrocarbon as the product.

The number of stereoisomers possible for this product is ______.

43. For a zero-order reaction P → Q, the concentration of P becomes half of its initial concentration in 30 minutes after starting the reaction.

The concentration of P becomes zero at ______ minutes. (*rounded off to the nearest integer*)

44. The magnitude of energy difference between the energy levels $n = 3$ and $n = 2$ of a quantum particle of mass m in a box of length L is $\frac{Xh^2}{8mL^2}$.

Then X = ______.

(*rounded off to the nearest integer*)

[Given: h is Planck's constant and n denotes the quantum number]

45. The function $\exp(-2(x - 1)^2)$ attains a maximum at x = ______.
(rounded off to the nearest integer)

46. 0.1 M aqueous solution of a weak monobasic acid has pH 2.0. The pK_a of the monobasic acid is ______. *(rounded off to one decimal place)*

47. The enthalpy change for the reaction

$C(g) + \frac{1}{2}O_2(g) \rightarrow CO(g)$ is ______ kJ per mole of CO(*g*) produced. *(rounded off to one decimal place)*

[Given:
$C(g) + O_2(g) \rightarrow CO_2(g)$, $\Delta H_{rxn} = -393.5$ kJ per mole of $CO_2(g)$ produced

$CO_2(g) \rightarrow CO(g) + \frac{1}{2}O_2(g)$, $\Delta H_{rxn} = 283.0$ kJ per mole of CO(*g*) produced]

48. The N–O bond order in $[NO]^-$ is ....

49. The bond length of CO is 113 pm and its dipole moment ($\bar{\mu}$) is 0.1 D. The charge (in units of electronic charge) on carbon in the CO molecule *including its sign* is ______.
(rounded off to three decimal places)

[Given: charge of electron = 1.602×10^{-19} C; 1 D = 3.336×10^{-30} C m]

50. The magnetic moment of O_3 molecule is ______ Bohr magneton (B.M.).

(rounded off to the nearest integer)

Q. 51 – Q. 60 carry two marks each.

51. A reaction of 10.50 g of 1,2-diphenyl -ethane-1,2-dione with conc. NaOH followed by aqueous acidic work-up furnished 8.55 g of a carboxylic acid.

The yield of the carboxylic acid in this reaction is ______ %.

(rounded off to the nearest integer)

52. The specific rotation of an optically pure compound is +75.3 (*c* 1.0 in $CHCl_3$) at 20°C. A synthetic sample of the same compound showed a specific rotation of +66.3 (*c* 1.0 in $CHCl_3$) at 20°C. The enantiomeric excess (*ee*) of the synthetic sample is ______ %.

(rounded off to the nearest integer)

53. A salt QCl of a certain metal Q is electrolyzed to its elements. 40 g of metal Q is formed at an electrode. The volume of Cl_2 formed at the other electrode at 1 atm pressure and 298 K is ______ litres. *(rounded off to one decimal place)*

[Given: The gas constant R = 0.082 L atm mol^{-1} K^{-1}, the molar mass of Q is 40 g mol^{-1} and Cl_2 is assumed to be an ideal gas]

54. If 1 M of a dye in water transmits 50% of incident light at 400 nm, then 2 M of the dye in water transmits ______ % of the incident light at 400 nm.

(rounded off to the nearest integer)

[Given: Both experiments are performed in the same spectrophotometric cell.]

55. A 1.0 L solution is prepared by dissolving 2.0 g of benzoic acid and 4.0 g of sodium benzoate in water. The pH of the resulting solution is ______.

(rounded off to one decimal place)

Given:

Molar mass of benzoic acid is 122 g mol^{-1}

Molar mass of sodium benzoate is 144 g mol^{-1}

pK_a of benzoic acid is 4.2

56. The total vapour pressure of an ideal binary liquid mixture of benzene and toluene is 0.3 bar. The vapour pressure of pure benzene is 0.5 bar and that of toluene is 0.2 bar. The mole fraction of benzene in this mixture is ______.

(rounded off to two decimal places)

57. The unit cell of a two-dimensional square lattice with lattice parameter **a** is indicated by the dashed lines as shown below:

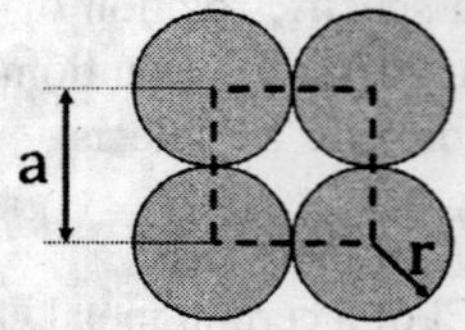

The percentage (%) area occupied by the grey circles (of radius r) inside the unit cell is ________. (*rounded off to the nearest integer*)

58. In the oxidation of phosphorus with oxygen, 0.2 mol of P_4 produces ________ g of P_4O_{10}. (*rounded off to one decimal place*)

[Given: Atomic weight of P = 31; Atomic weight of O = 16]

59. An element E has three isotopes:

$^{28}_{14}E$ (abundance 92.21%, atomic mass: 27.977 a.m.u.),

$^{29}_{14}E$ (abundance 4.70%, atomic mass: 28.976 a.m.u.), and

$^{30}_{14}E$ (abundance 3.09%, atomic mass: 29.974 a.m.u).

The atomic mass of E is ______ a.m.u. (*rounded off to three decimal places*)

60. The wavelength of the γ-ray emitted in

$$^{137m}_{56}Ba \rightsquigarrow {}^{137}_{56}Ba + \gamma\text{-ray (0.66 MeV)}$$

is ______ Å. (*rounded off to three decimal places*)

[Given: $h = 6.626 \times 10^{-34}$ J s; $c = 2.998 \times 10^{8}$ m s^{-1}; 1 MeV = 1.602×10^{-13} J]

ANSWERS

SECTION A: MCQ (Multiple Choice Questions)

1	2	3	4	5	6	7	8	9	10
B	C	A	C	A	B	C	A	A	A
11	**12**	**13**	**14**	**15**	**16**	**17**	**18**	**19**	**20**
A	D	*	B	A	B	B	B	A	C
21	**22**	**23**	**24**	**25**	**26**	**27**	**28**	**29**	**30**
D	D	C	B	A	B	B	A	A	D

SECTION B: MSQ (Multiple Select Questions)

31	32	33	34	35
A, B, C	A, D	A, B	A, D	A, B, D
36	**37**	**38**	**39**	**40**
A, B, C	B, D	A, B	C, D	A, D

SECTION C: NAT (Numerical Answer Type Questions)

41	42	43	44	45
2	3	60	5	1
46	**47**	**48**	**49**	**50**
2.9 to 3.0	–111.0	2	–0.019 to –0.017	0
51	**52**	**53**	**54**	**55**
74 to 76	88	12.1 to 12.3	25	4.4 to 4.5
56	**57**	**58**	**59**	**60**
0.32 to 0.34	77 to 79	56.7 to 56.9	28.082 to 28.089	0.017 to 0.021

EXPLANATORY ANSWERS

1. (B):

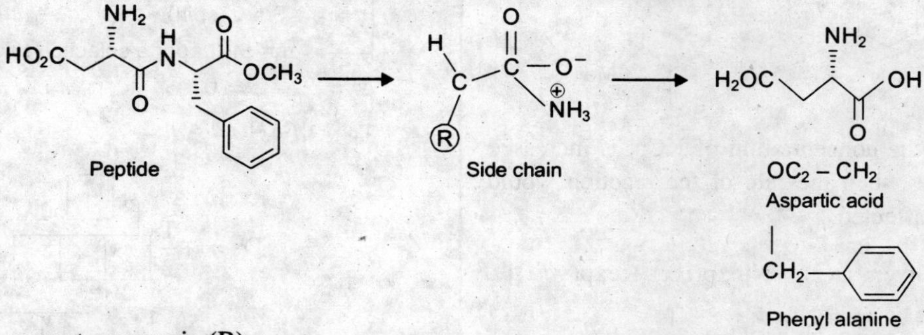

Thus, correct answer is (B).

2. (C):

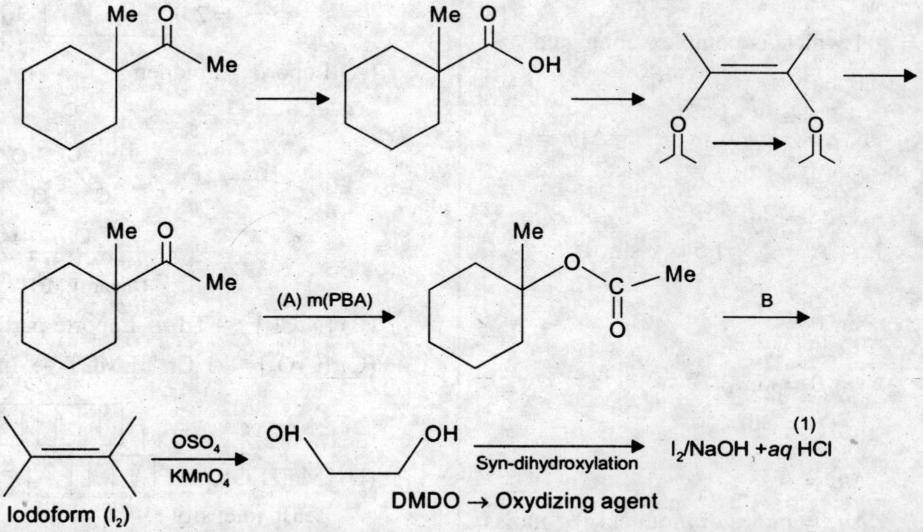

Thus, the suitable reagent combination for the transformation is I_2/NaOH and aqueous HCl. Hence, correct answer is (C)

3. (A):

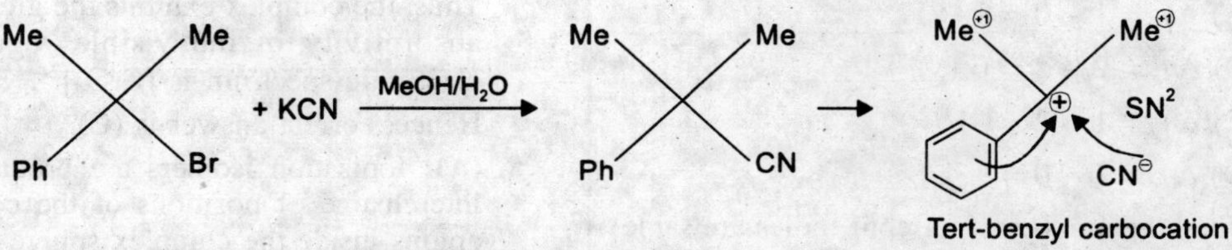

$SN^1 \rightarrow$ Rate = k[R – X] → slow → RDS (unaffected)

KCN increased four times

SN^2, Rate = k[R – X] [$Nu^{\ominus}$]

KCN → conc. 4 times.

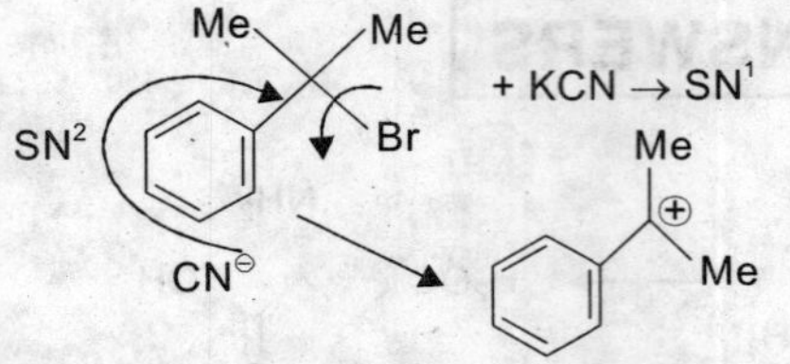

Since the concentration of KCN is increased 4 times, then the rate of the reaction would be unaffected.

4. (C): Given, $\psi(x) = N[\exp(ikx) + \exp(-ikx)]$

$$\psi = N[e^{ikx} + e^{-ikx}]$$
$$\psi^* = N^*[e^{ikx} + e^{-ikx}]^*$$
$$\psi^* = N^*[e^{-ikx} + e^{ikx}]$$

[$\because i = -1$] which is complex conjugate.

$$\therefore \quad \psi^* = N^*(e^{ikx} + e^{-ikx}]$$

5. (A): Given, $\lambda = 1.54$ Å, $d = 1.54$Å, $n = 1$

From Bragg's law

$$n\lambda = 2d \sin\theta$$
$$\Rightarrow 1 \times 1.54 \text{ Å} = 2 \times 1.54 \text{ Å} \sin\theta$$
$$\Rightarrow \quad \sin\theta = \frac{1}{2}$$
$$\sin\theta = \sin 30°$$
$$\therefore \quad \theta = 30°$$

6. (B): $\Delta n_g = 0$

Δn_g = moles of product (g) – moles of gaseous reactant (g)

$= 0$

(A) $\Delta n_g = 1 - 0 = 1$ (×)

(B) $\Delta n_g = 2 - 2 = 0$ (√)

(C) $\Delta n_g = 1 - 2 = -1$ (×)

(D) $\Delta n_g = 1 - 0 = +1$ (×)

When the number of gaseous moles are same on the both sides.

2 gaseous moles of reactant = 2 moles of product $\Delta n_g = 0$

Hence, correct answer is (B).

7. (C): Co-ordination complex:

→ ΔS = 0 (spin)

→ Δl = ±1 (Laporte selection rule)

$\Delta l = 2 - 2 = 0$

Ti : $3d^2 4s^2 \rightarrow 3d^1$

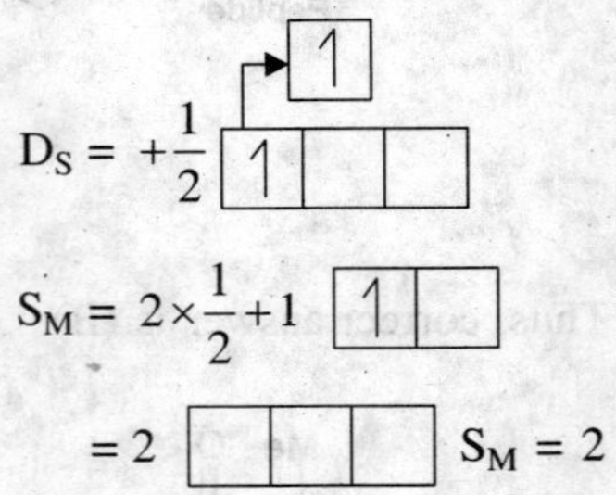

(A) Laporte forbidden

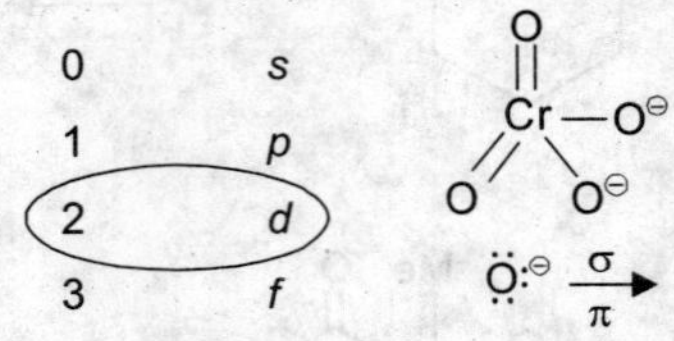

Donar LMCT.

(B) $[NiCl_4]^{2-}$ – Td → Laporte partly allowed.

(C) $[CrO_4]^{2-} \rightarrow Cr^{+6}$ LMCT → Intensity I.

(D) $[Mn(H_2O)_6]^{2+}$ d^5 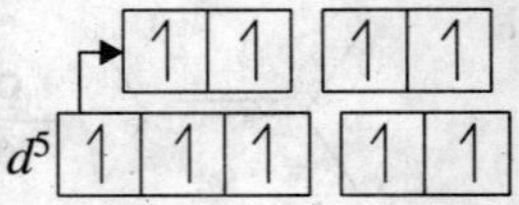 SF,

Least intensity

$d^5 = \frac{5}{2}$.

Thus, the complex exhibits the greatest molar absorptivity in the visible region of the electronic spectrum is $[CrO_4]^{2-}$.

Hence, correct answer is (C).

8. (A): Ionisation isomers are produced by an interchange of positions of the coordination anions inside the complex sphere and anions outside the complex sphere. In the complexes $[Co(NH_3)_5Br]SO_4$ and $[Co(NH_3)_5SO_4]Br$, the ligands bromide and sulphate exchange their positions. The two isomers are thus ionisation isomers. $[Co(NH_3)_5Br]SO_4$ isomer gives a while ppt. with $BaCl_2$ solution, confirming the presence of free sulphate ions. The complex $[Co(NH_3]_5SO_4]Br$, does not respond to this test. The structure of complex $[Co(NH_3)_5SO_4]Br$ is

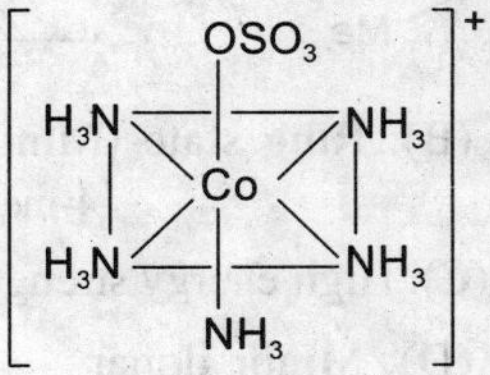

9. (A): Haemoglobin functions as an oxygen carrier from the lungs to the entire body, and myoglobin functions as a storer of oxygen in the muscle cells. Heme plays multiple roles in cellular processes. The strong affinity of heme toward oxygen makes it possible for hemoglobin and myoglobin, two heme-containing proteins, to function as major oxygen transporters. Heme also participates in respirations, sensing of diatomic gases, drug detoxification, signal transduction and regulation of transcription, translation, microRNA processing, mitochondrial protein import, protein stability, and differentiation. While most cells synthesize heme, differentiating erythrocytes represent the major site of heme production in humans due to the synthesis of hemoglobin, which accounts for 85% of the total heme. Malfunction of heme synthesis can lead to disorders such as anemia and porphyrias.

Heme is not a protein. Heme is a cofactor and is composed of a molecule called protoporphyrin complexed with Iron. Cofactors are like helper molecules which help the protein to perform their function. The iron (Fe) in the heme cofactor, helps in coordination of oxygen molecules with the protein so that, the oxygen can be transported across the circulatory system. A molecule of heme looks like this.

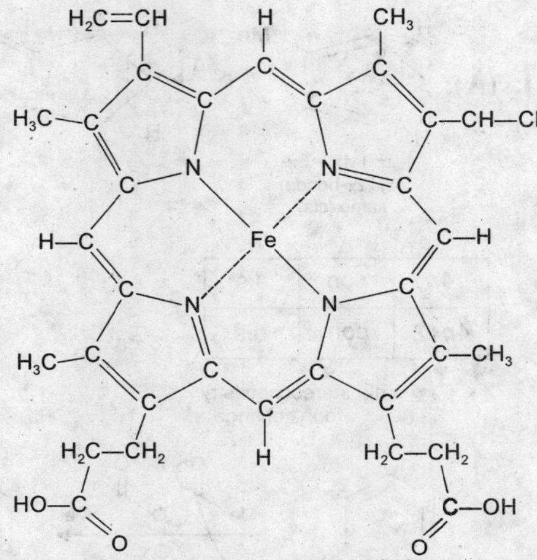

Proteins are made of amino acids as their basic subunits. The name 'globin' comes from the fact that hemoglobin is a globular protein belonging to the globin superfamily. Hemoglobin is composed of 4 subunits-2 alpha subunits and 2 beta subunits which differ by their amino acid sequence. Each of the 4 subunits have 1 molecule of heme bound to them.

1-subunit → Myoglobin

4-subunits → Hemoglobin

10. (A): The molecular shape of the thiocyanate anion (SCN^-), when carbon is the central atom, as predicted by VSEPR theory, is linear. This linear structure occurs because the SCN^- has a total of 16 valence electrons which are used to form triple bonds between the central carbon atom, the nitrogen and sulphur atoms. As a result, both the central carbon and the terminal atoms are surrounded by groups that form a straight line, and the C-N and C-S bonds align end-to-end, creating a 180° angle between them.

The SCN^- has the same molecular geometry as the electron geometry of the ion because the central atom has only bond pair of electrons. The molecular geometry of SCN^- ion is linear.

11. (A):

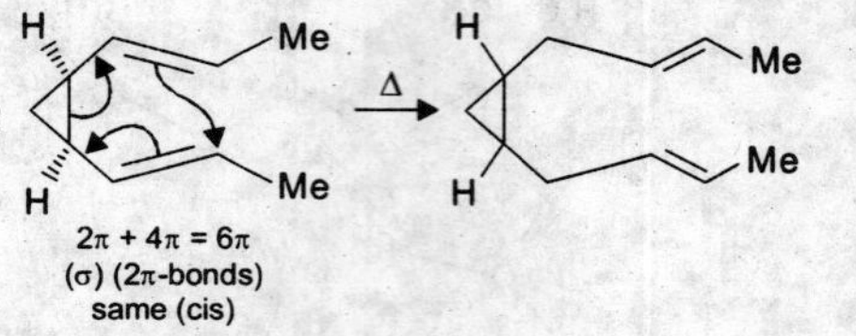

	Δ	hν
4n	con	dis
4n+2	con	dis

4 × 1 + 2 = 6π stereochemistry don't change

Option (A):

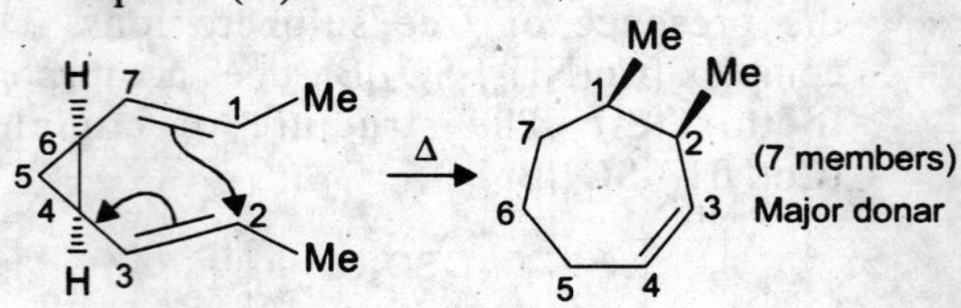

Option (B): Ring state (Minor donar 4-members)

Option (C): High energy strength (Minor donar)

Option (D): Minor donar

12. (D):

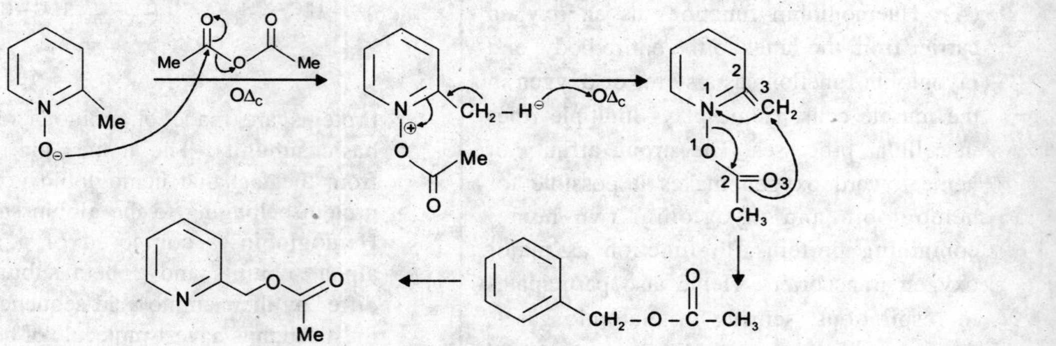

14. (B):

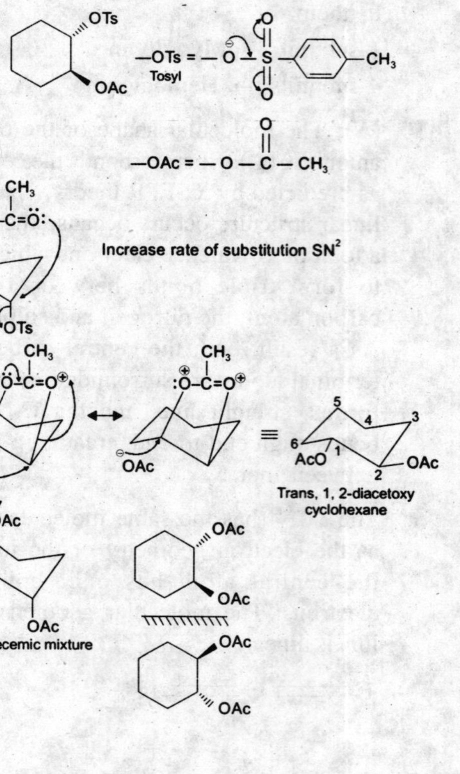

15. (A): 1. Semi Pinacol-Pinacolone rearrangement

2. Epoxide Formation Reaction

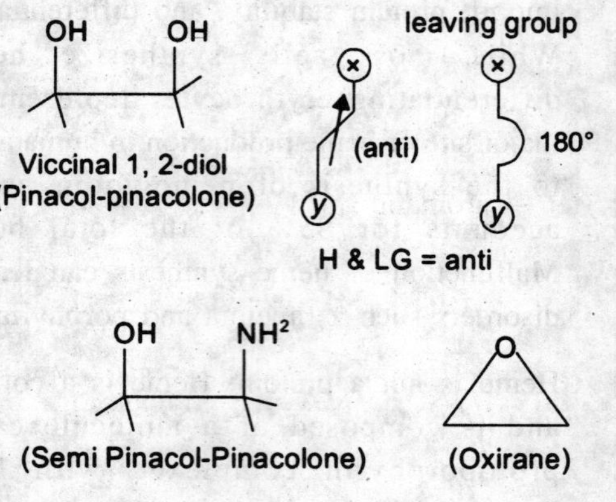

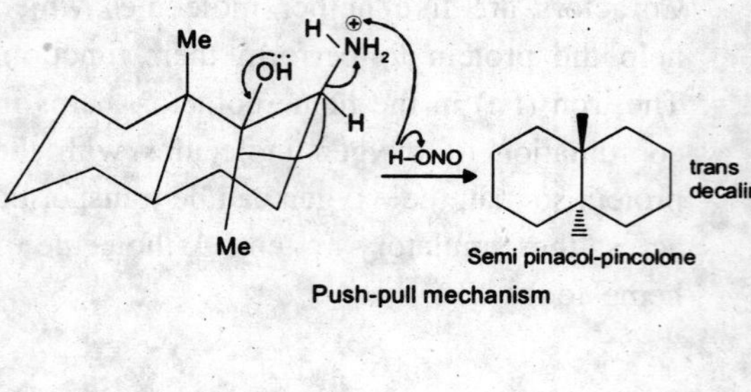

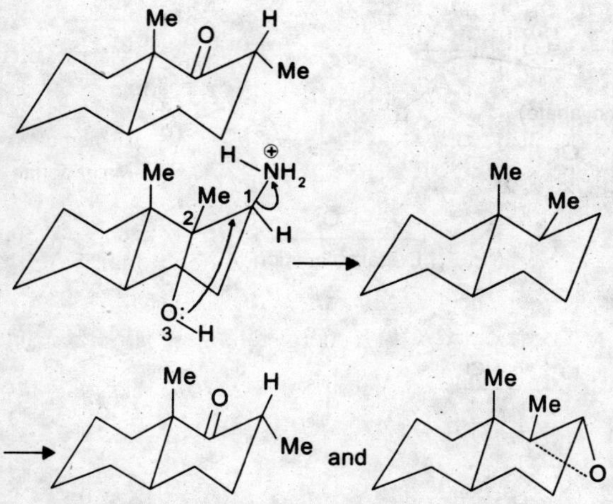

Hence, correct answer is (A).

16. (B): We have,

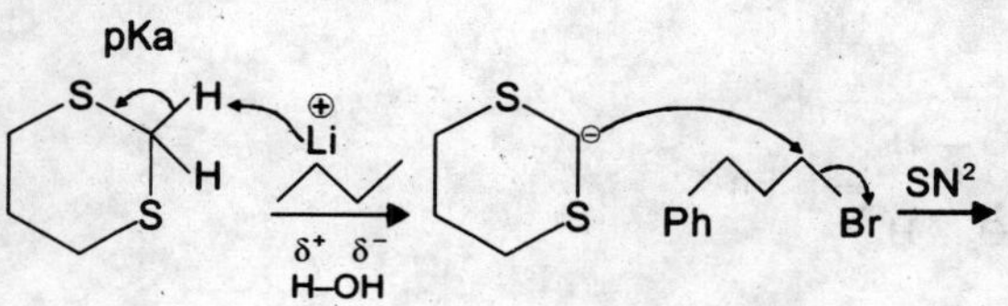

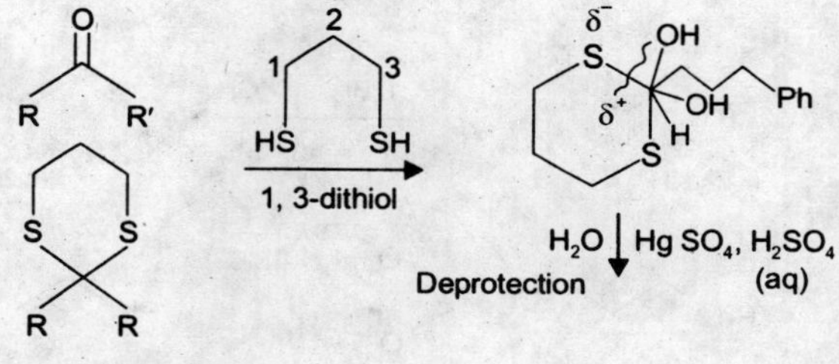

Now,

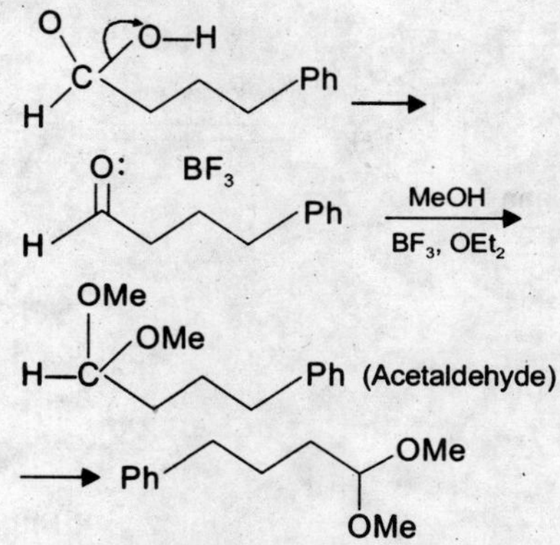

Hence, correct answer is (B).

17. (B): ↑ Acidity α stability of C.B. ↑ (species formed)

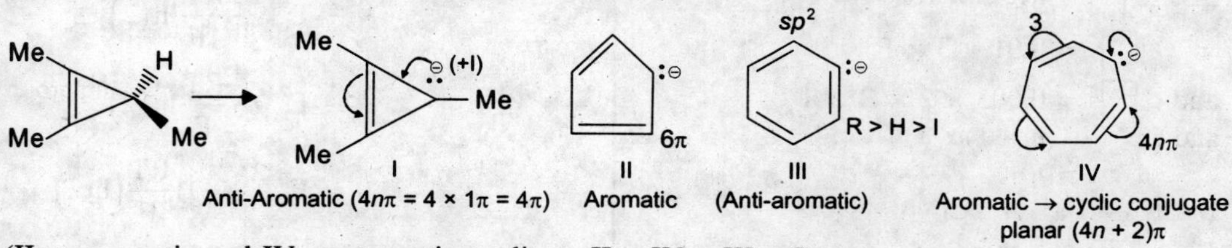

(II → aromatic and IV → aromatic cyclic ∴ II > IV > III > I)

∴ Correct answer is (B).

18. (B): 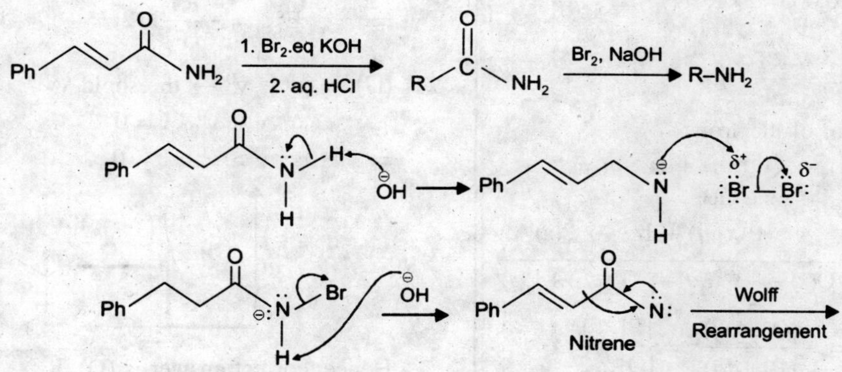

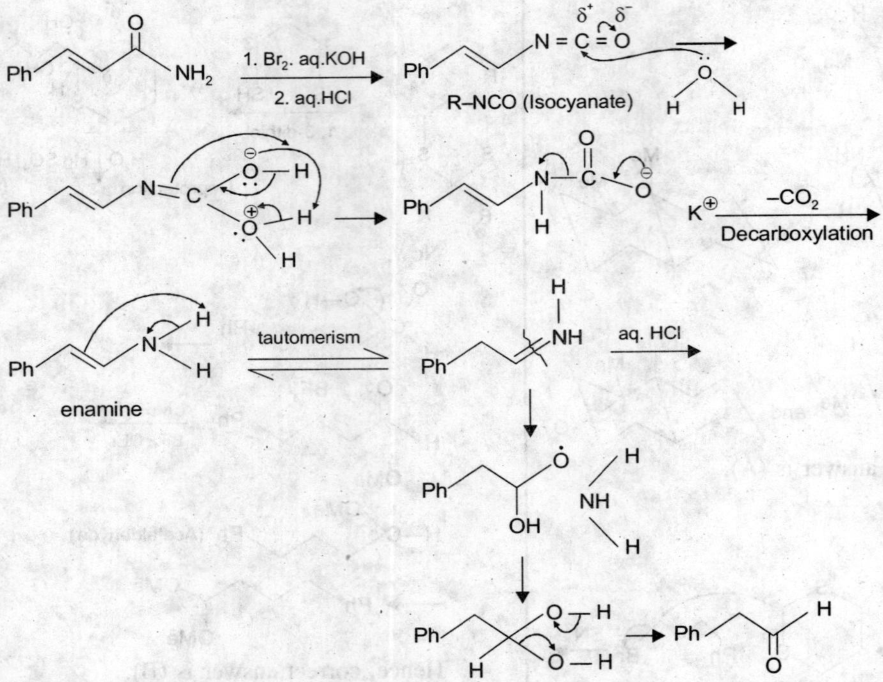

Hence, correct answer is (B).

19. (A): $\Pi = i \times C \times R \times T$

$\Rightarrow \quad \Pi_1 = 0.01 \times 3 \times R \times T$

and $\Pi_2 = 0.005 \times 2 \times R \times T$

and $i = 1 + (n - 1)\alpha$

$i = n$

$BaCl_2 \rightarrow Ba^{2+} + 2Cl^-$

$\therefore \quad i = 3$

$$\therefore \quad \frac{\Pi_1}{\Pi_2} = \frac{0.01 \times 3 \times R \times T}{0.005 \times 2 \times R \times T} = \frac{3}{1} = 3:1$$

20. (C): $E_{cell} = E^\circ_{cell} - \frac{RT}{nF}\log k$

where $n \rightarrow$ no. of electrons

At anode, $Q(s) \rightarrow Q^+(aq) + 1e^- \quad n = 1$

oxidation

At cathode, $P^+(aq) + 1e^- \rightarrow P(s)$

$$Q(s) \rightarrow P^+(aq) \rightarrow Q^+(aq) + P(s)$$

$$k = \frac{a(Q^+)(aq)}{a(P^+)(aq)} = \frac{[P]}{[Q]} = \frac{1}{2}$$

$$0 = E^\circ_{cell} - \frac{RT}{1F}\ln(2)$$

$$= E^\circ_{cell} - \frac{RT}{F}\ln(2)$$

$$0 = E^\circ_{cell} - (-1)\frac{RT}{F}(\ln 2)$$

$$0 = E^\circ_{cell} + \frac{RT}{F}\ln 2$$

$$\Rightarrow \quad E^\circ_{cell} = -\frac{RT}{F}\ln 2$$

21. (D): $n \propto I \quad \nu^0 \rightarrow$ threshold ν

$\nu < \nu^0 \quad I = 0$

$\Rightarrow \quad \nu > \nu^0 \quad I \neq 0$

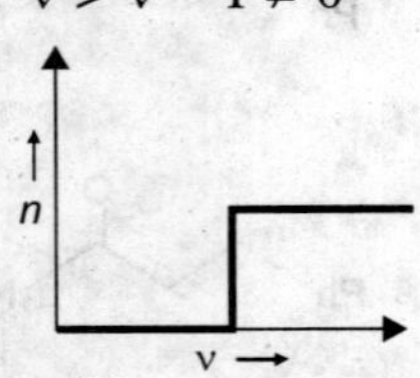

Hence, correct answer is (D).

22. (D): We have, N_2 and O_2 are gases.

(A) $T_{KE} = \frac{3}{2}KT \Rightarrow T_{KE} \propto T$

(where $T_{KE} \rightarrow$ translational (KE))

Hence, option (A) is false.

(B) $v_{rms} = \sqrt{\frac{3RT}{M}}$, $v_{rms} \propto \frac{1}{\sqrt{M}}$ ($v_{rms} \rightarrow$ root mean square)

Hence, option (B) is false.

(C) $v_{av} = \sqrt{\frac{8RT}{\pi M}}$, $v_{av} \propto \frac{1}{\sqrt{M}} \uparrow$ (O_2 is less) (and N_2 high)

Hence, option (C) is false.

Thus, KE_{av} of N_2 and O_2 molecules are equal.

Hence, correct answer is (D).

23. (C): If a system does work on the surroundings, it means that the system is losing energy to perform work. In this case, the internal energy of the system is expected to decrease rather than increase. This is because the work done by the system is a form of energy leaving the system, resulting in a decrease in the internal energy of the system.

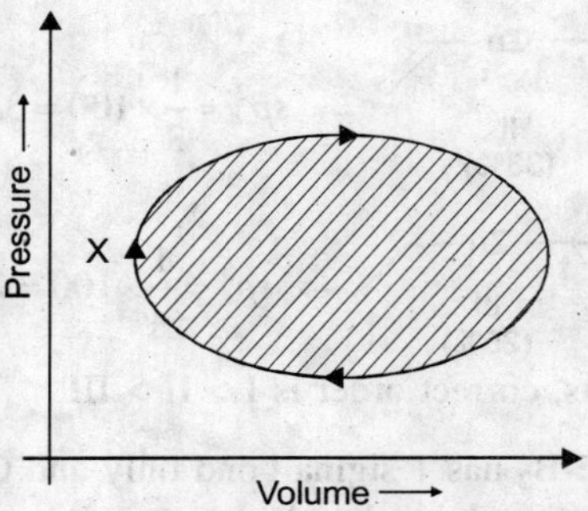

According to the first law of thermodynamics, the change in internal energy of a system is equal to the heat added to the system minus the work done by the system:

$$\Delta U = Q - W$$

Where ΔU is the change in internal energy, Q is the heat added to the system, and W is the work done by the system.

If the system is doing work on the surroundings ($W > 0$), the work term in the equation is positive, indicating that the internal energy of the system is decreasing. This means that the energy is being transferred from the system to the surroundings during the cycle in the form of work.

24. (B): We have,

$$\frac{1}{2}Mn_2(CO)_{10} + Na \rightarrow \underset{P}{Na^+[Mn(CO)_5]}$$

$$\xrightarrow[-NaCl]{CH_3Cl} \underset{Q}{[CH_3Mn(CO)_5]}$$

$[Mn(O)_5]^-$

$\downarrow$

$x + 0(5) = -1$

$x = -1$

$CH_3Mn(CO)_5]^0$

$\uparrow$ $\uparrow$ Neutral

$-1 + x + 5(0) = 0$

$\Rightarrow x - 1 = 0$

$x = +1$

Hence, oxidation states of Mn in P and Q are -1 and $+1$.

25. (A): In order to understand clearly the crystal field interactions in transition metal complexes, it is necessary to have knowledge of the geometrical or spatial disposition of *d* orbitals. The *d*-orbitals are five fold degenerate in a free gaseous metal ion. If a spherically symmetric field of negative ligand field charge is imposed on a central metal ion, the *d-d* transitions will remain degenerate but followed by some changes in the energy of the free ion.

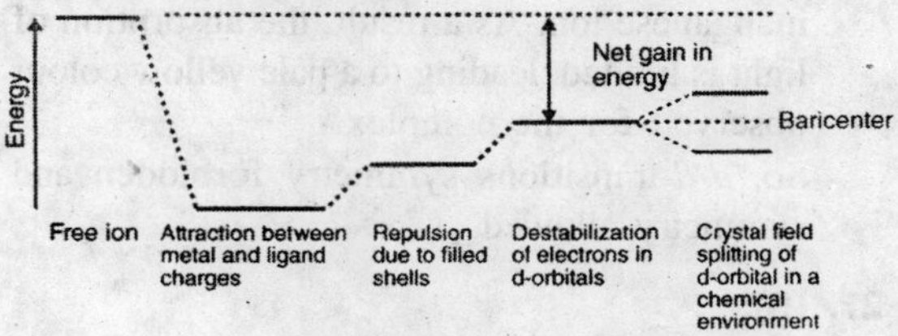

Crystal Field Splitting

Crystal field theory was proposed which described the metal-ligand bond as an ionic bond arising purely from the electrostatic interactions between the metal ions and ligands. Crystal field theory considers anions as point charges and neutral molecules as dipoles.

When transition metals are not bonded to any ligand, their *d*-orbitals degenerate that is they have the same energy. When they start bonding with other ligands, due to different symmetries of the *d*-orbitals and the inductive effect of the ligands on the electrons, the *d*-orbitals split apart and become non-degenerate.

$Sc^{2+} \rightarrow d^1$. JTD

⇒ 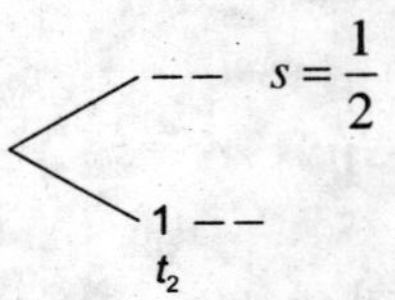

SM = 1 + 1 = 2 (Spin allowed)

Hence, the number and nature of *d*-*d* transitions of Sc^{2+} in an octahedral crystal field are 1 and spin allowed.

26. (B): The pale yellow colour of $[Mn(H_2O)_6]^{2+}$ is due to a spin forbidden *d*-*d* transition. This means that the transition between the *d* orbitals involves a change in the spin state of the electrons. According to the selection rules, a transition that involves a change in spin is unlikely to occur, leading to a low probability of absorption of light in this case.

The pale yellow colour of $[Mn(H_2O)_6]^{2+}$ is due to a spin forbidden *d*-*d* transition. This transition involves a change in the spin state of the electrons in the *d* orbitals of the manganese ion. As a result, the absorption of light is limited, leading to a pale yellow colour observed for the complex.

So, *d*-*d*-transitions symmetry forbidden and symmetry allowed.

27. (B):

(A) H_2NBH_2 and C_2H_6
(6) (8)
Hence, (A) is false.

(B) H_3N . BH_3 and C_2H_6
8 8

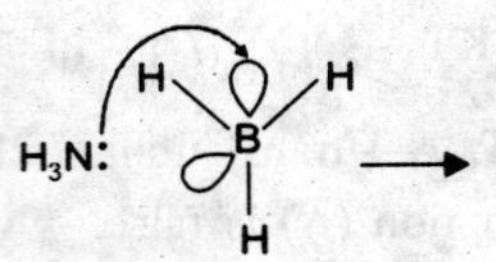

C_nH_{2n+2} (Alkane)
5 + 3 + 6 = 14
$H_3N \rightarrow BH_3$ linear
$H_3C - CH_3 \rightarrow$ linear
4 × 2 + 6 = 14

Hence, correct option is (B).

(C) B_2H_6 and C_2H_6

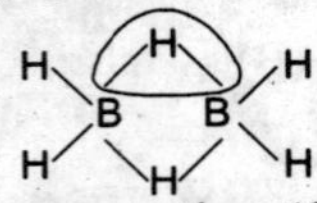

$H_3C - CH_3$

Hence, option (C) is false.

(D) $H_3N - BH_3$ and B_2H_6
14 8

Hence, the pair of isosteric compounds is $H_3N.BH_3$ and C_2H_6.

Thus, option (D) is false.

28. (A): Polarity α electronegativity difference between A and B increases.

EN = α% character
σ bonds

$2\pi \equiv\!-\overset{sp}{Zn}-\!\equiv \rightarrow sp = \frac{1}{3} \times 100 = 50\%$
50%
I

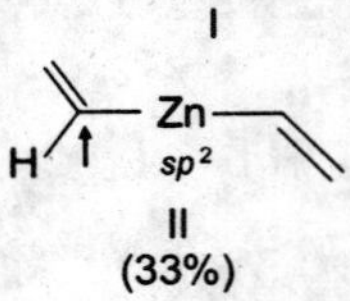

$\rightarrow sp^2 = \frac{1}{3} \times 100 = 33.33\%$

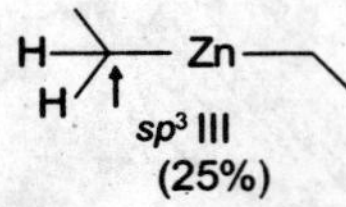

$\rightarrow sp^3 = \frac{1}{4} \times 100 = 25\%$

Thus, correct order is I > II > III.

29. (A): B_2 has 1 sigma bond only and C_2 has 1 sigma and 1 π bond.

B_2 and C_2 have different bond orders. Hence, they have different bond lengths.

The bond orders of B_2 and C_2 are 1 and 2 respectively.

B_2 has 2 unpaired electrons and is para-magnetic in nature where C_2 has all paired electrons and is diamagnetic in nature.

Thus, correct answer is (A).

30. (D): The order of ionic mobilities for these ions in aqueous solution at 298 K is as follows: Li^+ (Lithium), Na^+ (Sodium), Ag^+ (Silver) and K^+ (Potassium).

The trend arises from a combination of factors, including the degree of hydration and the size of the cations. Smaller cations like Lithium (Li) are heavily hydrated, resulting in lower mobility, while larger cations like Potassium (K) exhibit higher mobility due to less extensive hydration.

Thus, the order is $Li^+ < Na^+ < Ag^+ < K^+$.

31. (A, B, C):

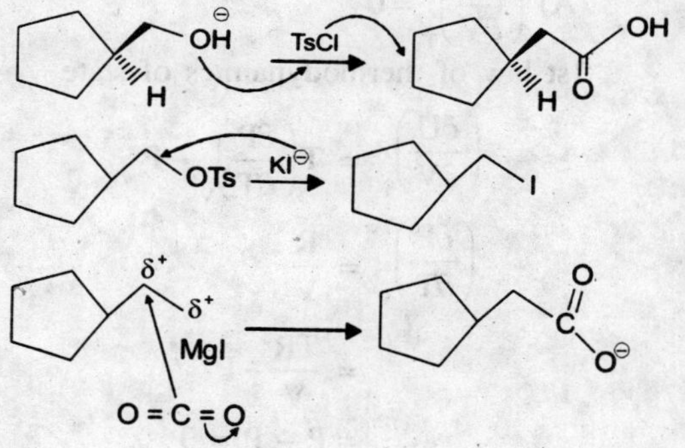

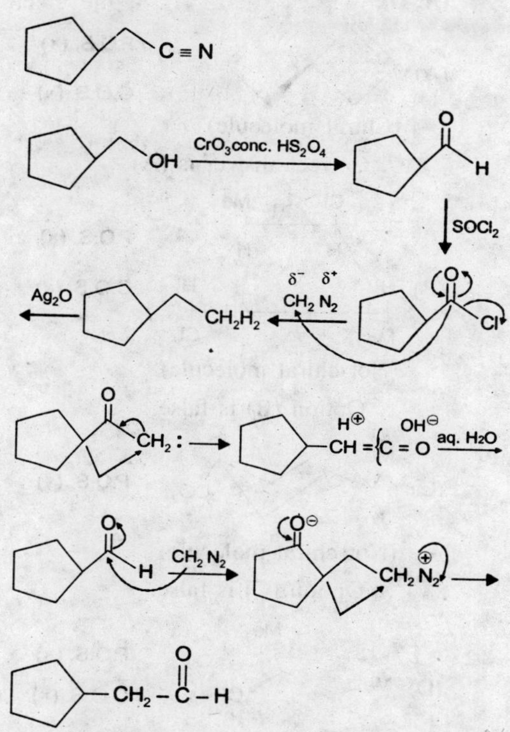

Hence, correct answers are (A), (B) and (C).

32. (A, D):

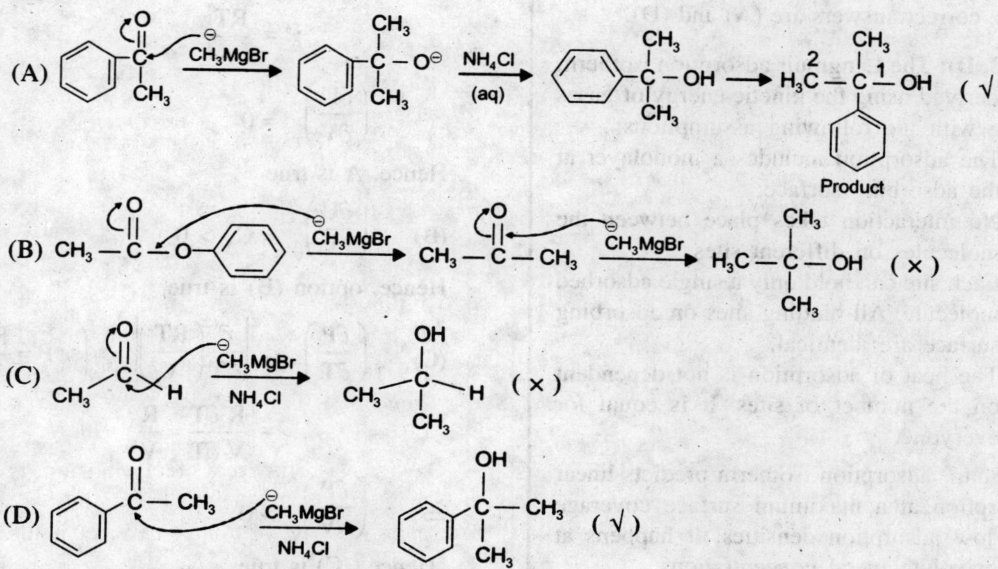

Hence, correct options are (A) and (D).

34. (A, D):

(A) 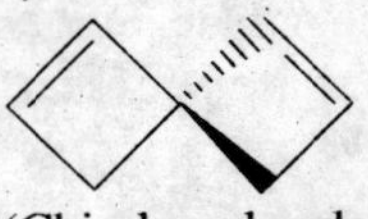 P.O.S. (×) C.O.S. (√)

(Chiral molecule)

∴ Correct answer is (A)

(B) 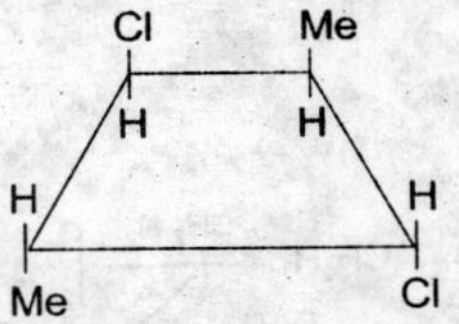 P.O.S. (×) C.O.S. (√)

(Not chiral molecule)

∴ Option (B) is false.

(C)  P.O.S. (√)

(Not chiral molecule)

∴ Option (C) is false.

(D) 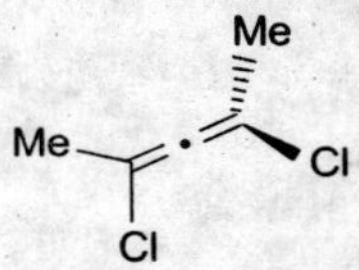 P.O.S. (×) C.O.S. (×)

(Chiral molecule)

∴ Option (D) is true.

Thus, correct answers are (A) and (D).

35. (A, B, D): The Langmuir adsorption isotherm was derived using the kinetic energy of gases along with the following assumptions:

1. The adsorption includes a monolayer at the adsorbing surface.
2. No interaction takes place between the molecules on different sites.
3. Each site can hold only a single adsorbed molecule. All binding sites on adsorbing surface are identical.
4. The heat of adsorption is not dependent on the number of sites. It is equal for everyone.

Langmuir adsorption isotherm predicts linear adsorption at a maximum surface coverage and low adsorption densities. It happens at higher solute metal concentrations.

This isotherm takes the following form in the process:

$$K_aCe\,(1-\theta) = K_a\theta$$

Here,

K_a refers to the respective rate constant required for adsorption,

K_d refers to the respective rate constant required for desorption.

θ stands for the fraction of the surface covered by an adsorbed molecule

Hence correct answers are (A, B, D).

36. (A, B, C)

(A) $\left(\frac{\partial U}{\partial V}\right)_T = 0$

1st law of thermodynamics of state

$$\left(\frac{\partial U}{\partial V}\right)_T = T\left(\frac{\partial P}{\partial T}\right)_V - P$$

$$\left(\frac{\partial P}{\partial T}\right)_V = \frac{R}{V}$$

$$= \frac{TR}{V} - P$$

$$= P - P = 0$$

$$\because \quad PV = RT$$

$$P = \frac{RT}{V}$$

$$\therefore \quad \left(\frac{\partial U}{\partial V}\right)_T = 0$$

Hence, A is true.

(B) $\left(\frac{\partial U}{\partial V}\right)_V = C_V > 0$

Hence, option (B) is true.

(C) $\left(\frac{\partial P}{\partial T}\right)_V = \left|\frac{\partial}{\partial T}\left(\frac{RT}{V}\right)\right|_V \quad \left(\because P = \frac{RT}{V}\right)$

$$= \frac{R}{V}\frac{\partial T}{\partial T} = \frac{R}{V}$$

$$\Rightarrow \quad \left(\frac{\partial P}{\partial V}\right)_V > 0$$

Hence, (C) is true.

(D) $\left(\frac{\partial V}{\partial P}\right)_T = \left[\frac{\partial}{\partial T} RTP^{-1}\right]_T$

$$= RT\left[\frac{\partial}{\partial P} P^{-1}\right] = -\frac{RT}{P^2}$$

$\therefore \quad \left(\frac{\partial V}{\partial P}\right)_T > 0$

Hence, option (D) is false.

38. (A, B):

1. **Extraction of Metals from Ores:**
   - *Concentration of the Ore:* Before extracting a metal, we concentrate the ore. This step involves removing impurities and increasing the metal content.
   - *Isolation of the metal:* Once concentrated, we extract the metal from the ore, Reduction reactions are commonly used to convert metal oxides to the corresponding metals.
   - *Purification of the metal:* The isolated metal may still contain impurities. Purification methods like distillation, crystallization, and chromatography help remove these impurities.
2. **Occurrence of metals:**
   - Aluminum (Al) is the most abundant metal in the Earth's crust, making up about 8.3% of its weight. It occurs in minerals like mica and clays.
   - Iron (Fe) is the second most abundant metal. It forms various compounds and has diverse applications.
3. **Specific Processes:**
   - *Down's Process:* Used for extracting sodium (Na) from sodium chloride (NaCl) or common salt.
   - *Mond Process:* Used for refining nickel (Ni) by convering impure nickel carbonyl gas into pure nickel metal.

39. (C, D): Ligand Substitution Rates:

- The dynamic range of ligand substitution rates spans at least 15 orders of magnitude. Some complexes exchange water molecules on a nanosecond time scale, while others take much longer.

  The ratio of water exchange is faster in case of $[Ni(H_2O)_6]^{2+}$ than in $[Co(NH_3)_5(H_2O)]^{3+}$.
- For example, $[Co(NH_3)_6]^{3+}$ is thermodynamically unstable but kinetically inert. Its hydrolysis reaction with concentrated HCl takes about a week to complete at room temperature:

$$[Co(NH_3)_6]^{3+}(aq) + 6H_3O^+(aq) \rightarrow [Co(H_2O)_6]^{3+}(aq) + 6NH_4^+(aq)$$

The rate is faster in case of $[Cr(H_2O)_6]^+$ than in $[Cr(H_2O)_6]^{3+}$

40. (A, D):

1. **Free CO (Uncoordinated):** The stretching frequency of uncoordinated or "free" CO is approximately 2143 cm^{-1}.
2. **CO in $H_3B.CO$ (Borane-Carbonyl Complex):** In the borane-carbonyl complex, the CO stretching frequency is greater than that of free CO. This is due to the backbonding effect, where the metal centre donates electron density back to the ligand (CO). As a result, the C–O bond order in the complex is lower than that of free CO, leading to a reduced stretching frequency.
3. **CO in $Fe(CO)_5$ (Iron Pentacarbonyl):**
   - The infrared spectrum of $Fe(CO)_5$ shows four CO stretching bands. These bands correspond to different vibrational modes of CO in the complex.
   - Despite the presence of five CO ligands, the stretching frequency of CO in $Fe(CO)_5$ is lower than that of free CO. Again, this is attributed to backbonding, which weakens the C–O bond in the complex.

41. (2): 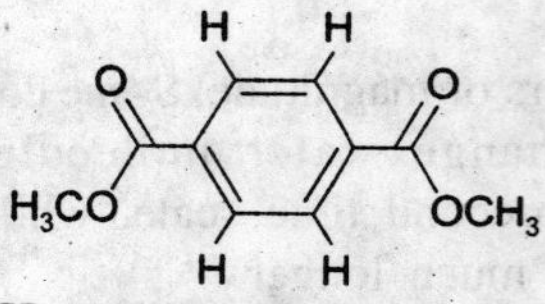

$\therefore$ 6H → (1) and 4H → 1

Thus, the number of signals expected in the ^{1}HNMR spectrum = 1 + 1 = 2.

42. (3):

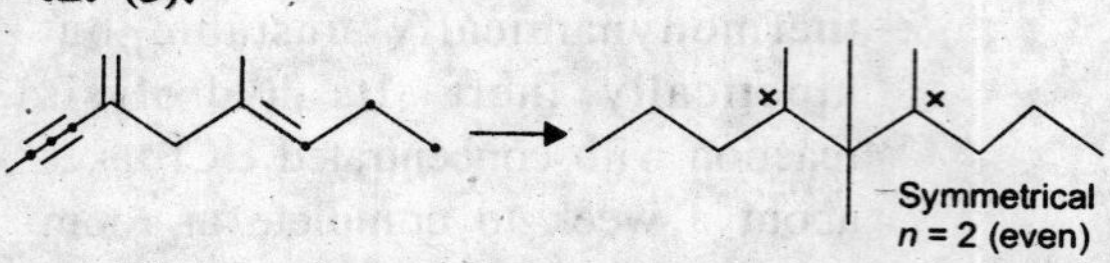

The number of stereoisomers possible for this product

i.e., $SI = 2^{\frac{n}{2}} + 2^{\frac{n}{2}-1}$

$= 2^{\frac{2}{2}} + 2^{\frac{2}{2}-1} = 2^1 + 2^{1-1}$

$= 2 + 1 = 3$

43. (60): We have, P → Q

$t_{\frac{1}{2}} = 30$ min

$\therefore \quad t_{100\%} = 2 \times t_{\frac{1}{2}}$

$= 2 \times 30 \times 60$ minutes

44. (5): As, $E_n(1 - D \text{ Box}) = \dfrac{n^2h^2}{8mL^2}$

For $n = 3$, $\quad E_3 = \dfrac{3^2h^2}{8mL^2} = \dfrac{9h^2}{8mL}$

$n = 2$, $\quad E_2 = \dfrac{2^2h^2}{8mL^2} = \dfrac{4h^2}{8mL^2}$

$\therefore \quad E_3 - E_2 = \dfrac{9h^2}{8mL^2} - \dfrac{4h^2}{8mL^2}$

$= \dfrac{h^2}{8mL^2}(9-4)$

$\therefore \quad E_3 - E_2 = \dfrac{5h^2}{8mL^2}$ ...(*i*)

Since, $\quad L = \dfrac{Xh^2}{8mL^2}$ ...(*ii*)

Comparing equations (*i*) and (*ii*), we get, the value of X = 5.

45. (1): $\psi(x) = f(x) = e^{-2(x-1)^2}$

$= e^{-2(x^2+1-2x)}$

$= e^{-2x^2-2+4x}$

At maxima,

$$\frac{d\psi(x)}{dx} = 0 \quad \Big| \quad \frac{d}{dx}e^{-2x^2-2+4x} = 0$$

$\Rightarrow \quad e^{-2x^2-2+4x}\dfrac{d}{dx}(-2x^2-2-4x) = 0$

$\Rightarrow \quad -4x + 0 + 4 = 0$

$\Rightarrow \quad -4x = -4$

$x = 1$

46. (3): $HA \rightleftharpoons H^+ + A^-$

	HA	H^+	A^-
Initially,	0.1	0	0
$t = t$	$(0.1 - n)$	n	n

$pH = 2$

$-\log [H^+] = 2$

$\log[H^+] = -2$

$[H^+ = 10^{-2}$

$K_a = \dfrac{n.n}{(0.1-n)}$

$= \dfrac{n^2}{(0.1-n)}$

$\Rightarrow \quad K_a = \dfrac{(10^{-2})^2}{0.1+10^{-2}}$

$= \dfrac{10^{-4}}{0.1-0.01}$

$= \dfrac{10^{-4}}{0.09}$

$= \dfrac{10^{-2} \times 10^{-2}}{9 \times 10^{-2}}$

$= \dfrac{10^{-2}}{9} = \dfrac{1}{9} \times 10^{-2}$

$\because \quad K_a = 0.111 \times 10^{-2}$

$= 1.11 \times 10^{-3}$

$\therefore \quad pK_a = -\log K_a$

$= -\log [1.11 \times 10^{-3}]$

$= -\log 1.11 - \log 10^{-3}$
$= -0.0414 + 3$
$= 2.958 = 3.0$

47. (–110.5):

$C(g) + O_2(g) \rightarrow CO_2(g)$ ...(1)

$CO_2(g) \rightarrow CO(g) + \frac{1}{2}O_2(g)$ ...(2)

$C(g) + \frac{1}{2}O_2(g) \rightarrow CO(g)$

The required value = eqn. (1) + eqn. (2)

$= (-393.5 + 283.0)$ kJ

$= -110.5$ kJ

48. (2): Electronic configuration of N : $1s^2 2s^2 2p^3$

Electronic configuration of O : $1s^2 2s^2 2p^4$

The molecular orbital (MO) electronic configuration of NO:

$\sigma^1 s^2 \sigma^* 1s^2, \sigma 2s^2 \sigma^* 2s^2, \sigma^2 p_x^2,\ \pi 2p_y^2,\ \pi 2p_z^2,$
$\pi^* 2px^1$

$[\because$ Bond order $= \frac{1}{2}(n_{Be} - n_B)]$

$\therefore$ Bond order of NO = 2.5

Bond order of N–O, in $[NO]^- = 2.0$

49. (–0.0184): We have,

$\mu = 0.1$ D

$d = 113$ pm $= 113 \times 10^{-12}$ m

$= 0.1 \times 3.336 \times 10^{-30}$ Cm

$= 3.336 \times 10^{-11}$ Cm

$\mu = q \times d$

$\Rightarrow \quad q = \frac{\mu}{de}$

$= \frac{3.336 \times 10^{-31} \text{ Cm}}{113 \times 10^{-12} \text{ m} \times 1.602 \times 10^{-19} \text{C}}$

$= -0.0184$

50. (0): Magnetic Moment (μ): Ozone (O_3) is an unstable, blue gas with a characteristic pungent odor. It consists of three oxygen atoms (O_3). It diamagnetic, which means it does not exhibit a net magnetic moment. Diamagnetic substances have all their electrons paired, resulting in no overall magnetic behaviour. The magnetic moment (μ) of O_3 is zero in terms of Bohr magnetons (BM).

51. (75):

Benzyl → Benzoic acid
10.5 g   8.55 g

210 g → 228 g

$10.5 \text{ g} \rightarrow \frac{228 \times 10.5}{10.5} = 11.4$ g

$\%$ yield $= \frac{\text{Obs}}{\text{Ths}} \times 100$

$= \frac{8.55}{11.4} \times 100$

$= 75\%$

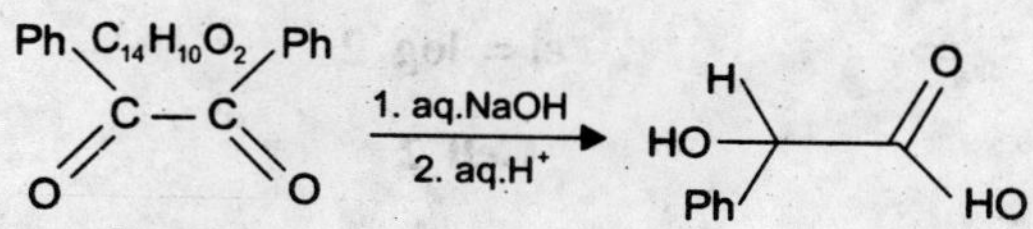

Benzyl

52. (88): $[\alpha] = 75.3 \rightarrow$ specific rotation of an optically pure compound

$[\alpha_{Obs}] = 66.3 \rightarrow$ specific rotation of synthetic sample of same compound

$ee = \frac{\alpha_{Obs}}{\alpha_{pure}}$

$= \frac{66.3}{75.3} \times 100$

$= 88.04$

$\simeq 88$

53. (12.1):

Anode　　Cathode

$Cl^- \rightarrow \frac{1}{2}Cl + e^-$　　$Q^+ + e^- \rightarrow Q$

1 mol → 0.5 mol Cl^-　1 mol　1 mol

$NCl_2 = 0.05$

$PV = nRT$

$V = \frac{nRT}{P}$

$$= \frac{0.5 \text{ mol} \times 0.082 \text{ L atm. mol}^{-1} \text{ K}^{-1} \times 298 \text{ K}}{1 \text{ atm}}$$

$= 0.5 \times 0.082 \times 298$

= 12.12 litres.

54. (25):

Cell I

$$A = -\log\left(\frac{I}{I_0}\right) = \varepsilon Cl$$

$$\Rightarrow -\log\left(\frac{50}{100}\right) = \varepsilon l$$

$$\Rightarrow \log\left(\frac{100}{50}\right) = \varepsilon l$$

$$\Rightarrow \varepsilon l = \log 2$$

Cell 2

$$\varepsilon Cl = -\log\left(\frac{I}{I_0}\right)$$

$$2 \log 2 = \log\left(\frac{I_0}{I}\right)$$

$$\log 2^2 = \log\left(\frac{100}{I}\right)$$

$$\Rightarrow 2^2 = \frac{100}{I}$$

$$\Rightarrow I = \frac{100}{4} = 25$$

55. (4.4):

$$pH = pK_a + \log\frac{[\text{Composite}]}{[\text{Acid}]}$$

$$= 4.2 + \log\left[\frac{\frac{4}{144}}{\frac{2}{122}}\right]$$

$$= 4.2 + \log\left[\frac{61}{36}\right]$$

$= 4.2 + 0.2 = 4.4$

56. (0.33):

$$p_A = p^\circ_A\, x_A$$

Benzene → x

Toluene = $(1 - x)$

Pressure of whole box

$p_{total} = p_B + p_T$

$= p^\circ_B\, x_B + p^\circ_T(1 - x_B)$

$\Rightarrow 0.3 = 0.5 \times x_B + 0.2\,(1 - x_B)$

$\Rightarrow 0.3 = 0.5 \times x_B + 0.2 - 0.2\, x_B$

$\Rightarrow 0.3 = 0.5\, x_B - 0.2\, x_B + 0.2$

$\Rightarrow 0.1 = 0.3\, x_B$

$\therefore x_B = \frac{1}{3} = 0.33$

57. (78.5): Angle approach

$$Z = 4 \times \frac{1}{4} = 1$$

$$PE = \frac{1 \times 22r^2}{7 \times 4r^2}$$

$$= \frac{22}{28} = 0.785$$

% area occupied by the grey circle

$= 0.785 \times 100\%$

$= 78.5\%$

58. (56.8): We have,

$P_4 + 5O_2$ (Excess) → P_4O_{10}

1 mol　　1 mol

0.2 mol　　0.2 mol

Molecular weight (MW) of P_4O_{10}

$$= (31 \times 4) + (16 \times 10)$$
$$= 124 + 160 = 284$$

$\therefore$ $MW = 284 \times 0.2 = 56.8$ g

59. (28.084):

Mol. weight $= \Sigma f_1 m_1$

$$= \frac{92.21}{100} \times 27.97 + \frac{4.7}{100} \times 28.966 + \frac{309}{100} \times 29.974$$

$$= \frac{1}{100}(92.21 \times 27.97 + 4.7 \times 28.966 + 309 \times 29.974)$$

$= 28.084$

60. (0.0189): Given,

γ-ray = 0.66 MeV

As, $E = \frac{hc}{\lambda} \Rightarrow \lambda = \frac{hc}{E}$

$$= \frac{6.626 \times 10^{-34} \times 2.998 \times 10^{8}}{0.66 \times 1.602 \times 10^{-31}}$$

$= 18.78 \times 10^{-13}$

$= 18.78 \times 10^{-3} \times 10^{-10}$

$= 0.0189 \times 10^{-10}$ m

$= 0.0189$ Å

YOUR SPACE

Previous Years Paper

IIT-JAM

Joint Admission Test for M.Sc. (Chemistry), 2023

Section A : Multiple Choice Questions (MCQ)

Directions: (Q. No. 1 to 10) *Carry One mark each.*

1. The structure of **Q** in the following reaction scheme is:

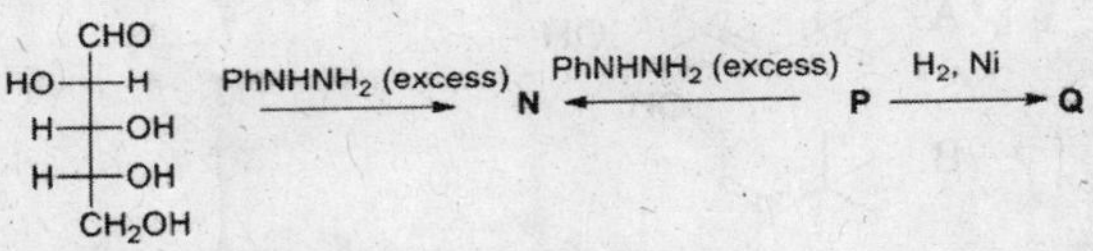

M (enantiopure)

A. 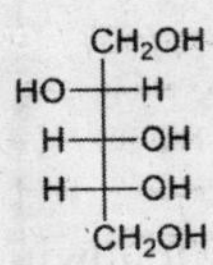

B. 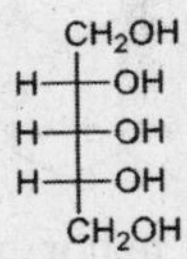

C. 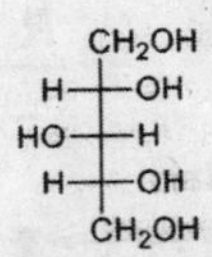

D. 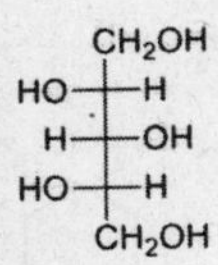

2. The major product of the reaction is:

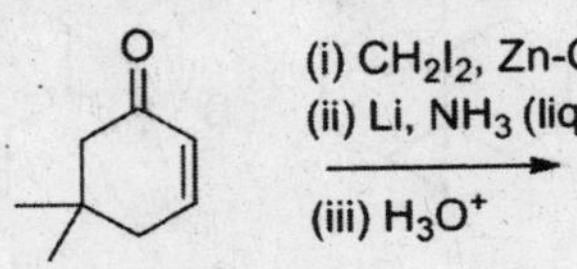

A. 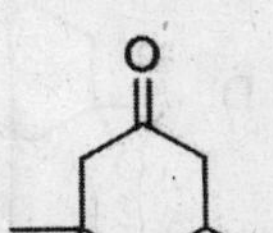

B. 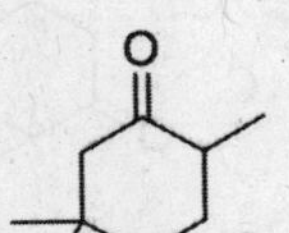

C. 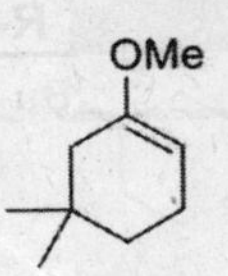

D. 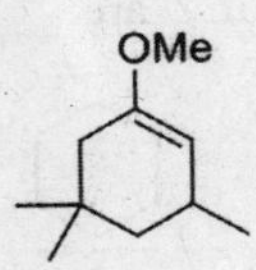

3. The rate of addition of 1-hexyl radical to the given molecules follows the order:

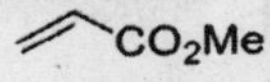
P

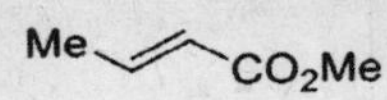
Q

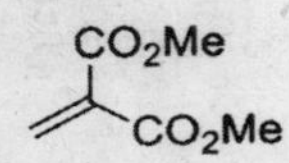
R

A. P > R > Q B. Q > P > R

C. R > P > Q D. P > Q > R

4. The major product of the reaction is:

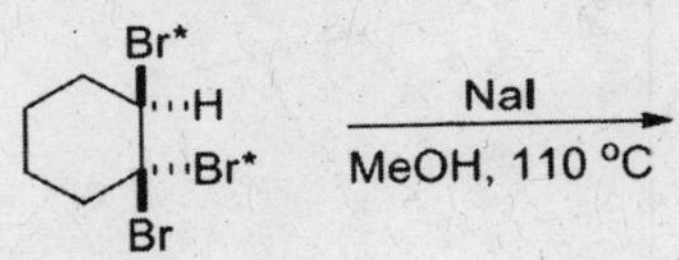

$Br^* = {}^{82}Br$

A. 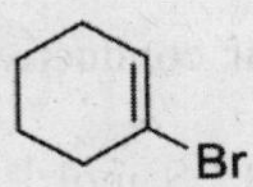

B. 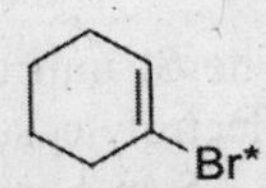

C. 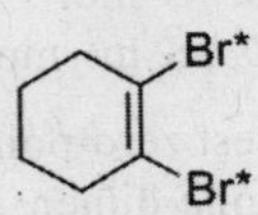

D. 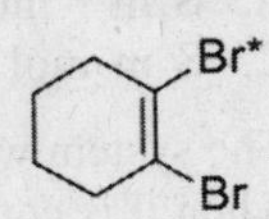

5. The diagram that best describes the variation of viscosity (η) of water with temperature at 1 atm is

A. 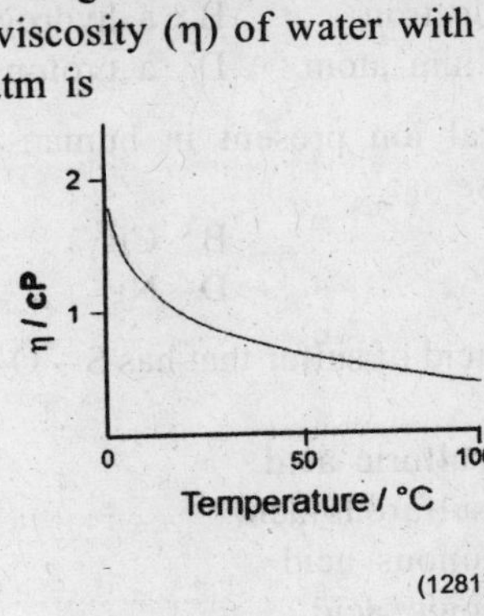

B. 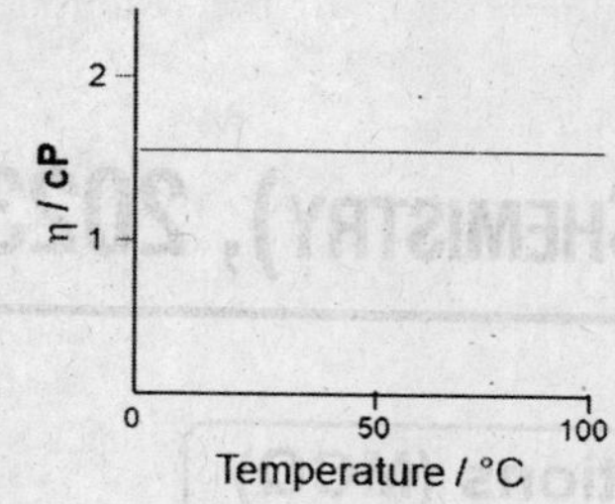

C. 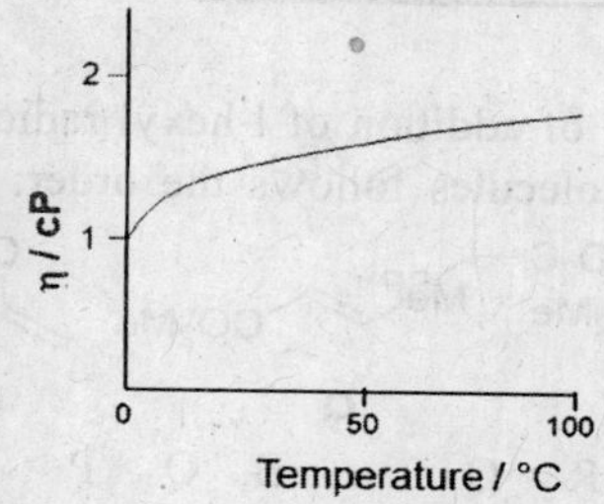

D. 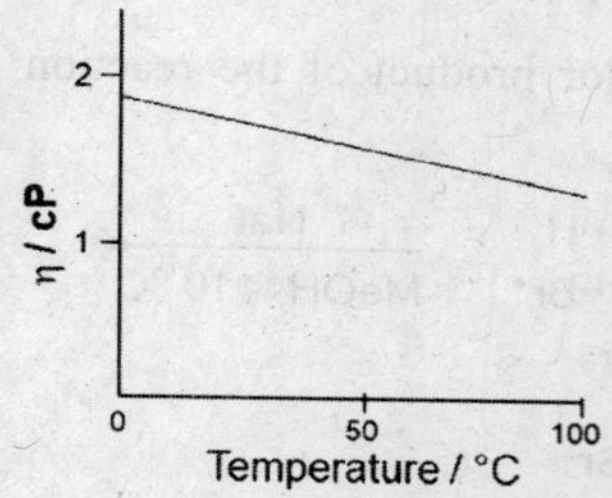

6. The SI unit of the molar conductivity of an electrolyte solution is:

A. $S\ m^{-1}\ mol^{-1}$ B. $S\ mol^{-1}$
C. $S\ m\ mol^{-1}$ D. $S\ m^2\ mol^{-1}$

7. The system with the lowest zero-point energy when it is confined to a one-dimensional box of length L is:

A. an electron B. a hydrogen atom
C. a helium atom D. a proton

8. The metal ion present in human *carbonic anhydrase* is:

A. Fe^{3+} B. Cu^{2+}
C. Zn^{2+} D. Ni^{2+}

9. The oxoacid of sulfur that has S – O – S bond is

A. Pyrosulfuric acid
B. Pyrosulfurous acid
C. Dithionous acid
D. Dithionic acid

10. An alkaline (NaOH) solution of a compound produces a yellow colored solution on addition of $NaBO_3$. The compound is:

A. $Mn(OH)_2$ B. $Pb(OH)_2$
C. $Cr(OH)_3$ D. $Fe(OH)_3$

Directions: (Q. No. 11 to 30) *Carry* ***Two*** *marks each.*

11. The major product of the reaction is:

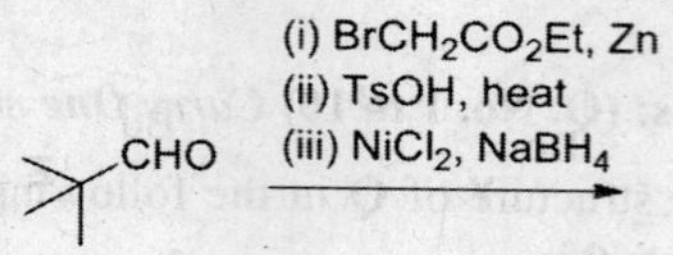

A. 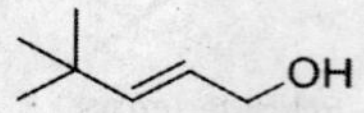

B. 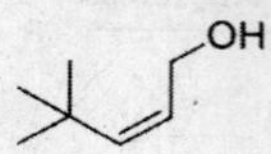

C. 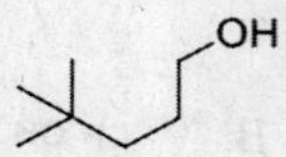

D. 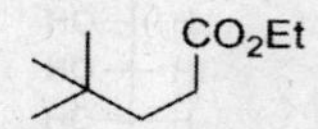

12. The major product in the following reaction is:

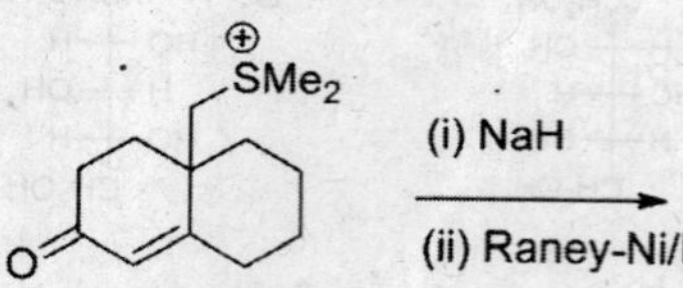

A. 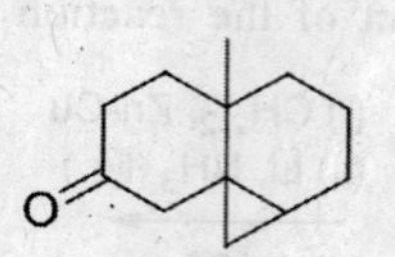

B. 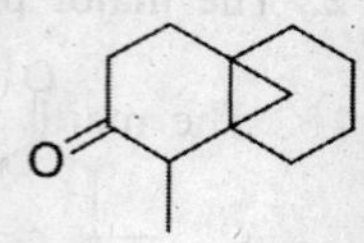

C. 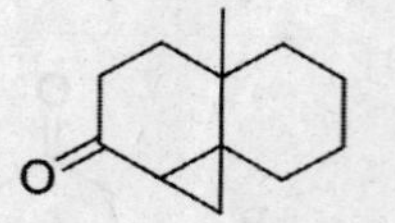

D. 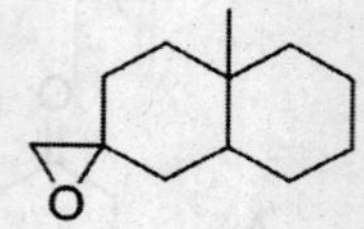

13. The most stable conformation of **Y** and that of Z are:

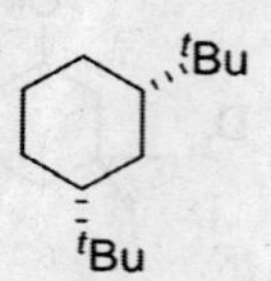

Y

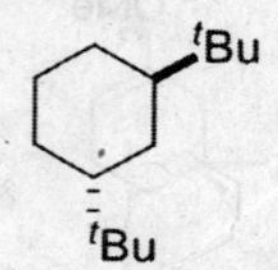

Z

A. 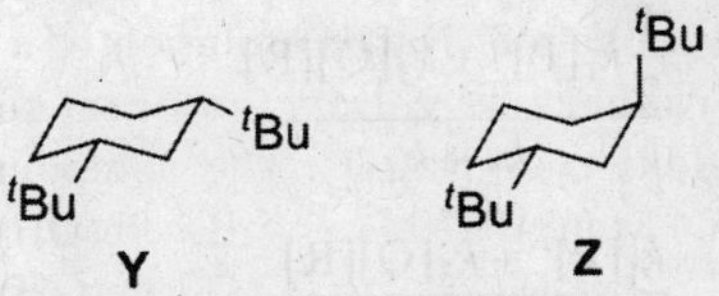

B. 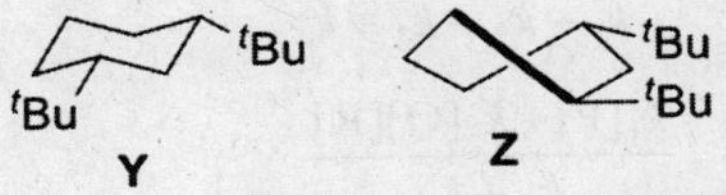

C. 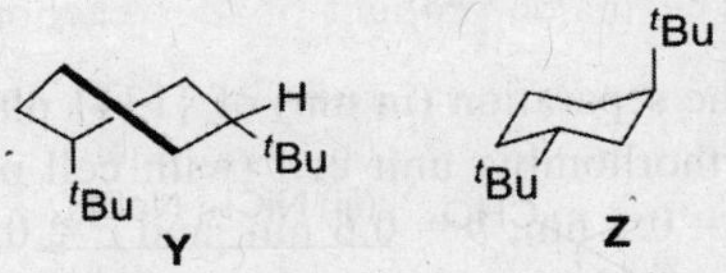

D. 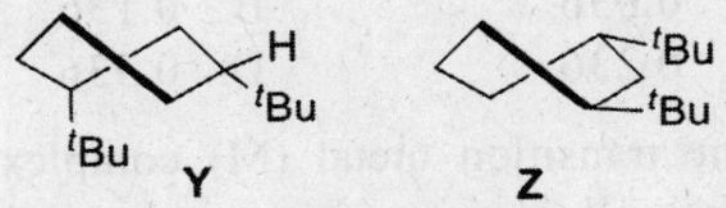

14. The major product **Y** in the following reaction scheme is:

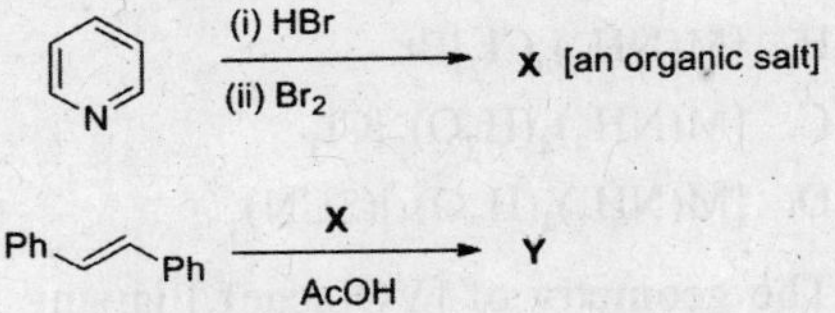

A. 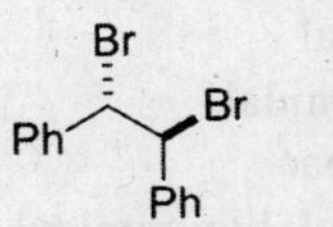
B. 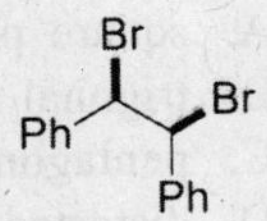

C. 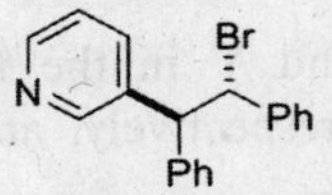
D. 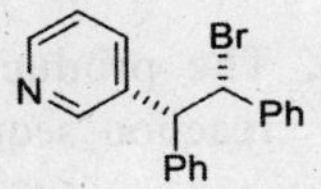

15. The major product of the reaction is:

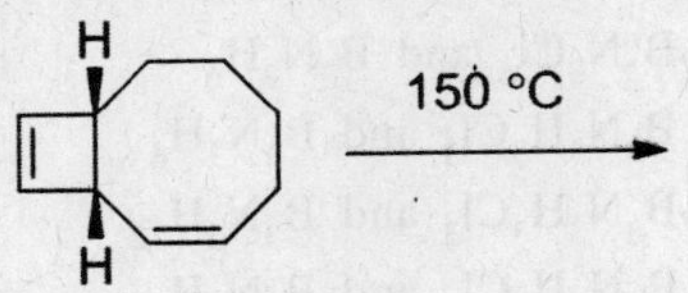

A. 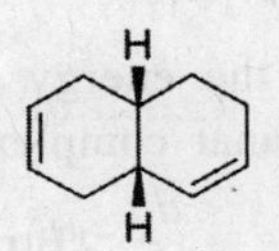
B. 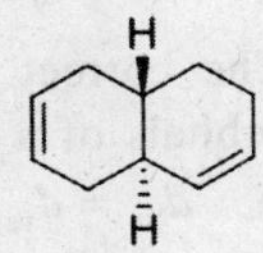

C. 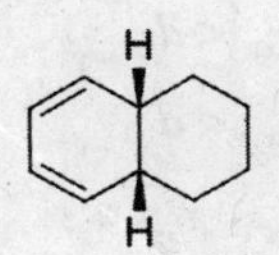
D. 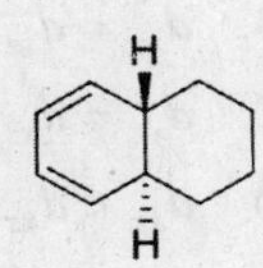

16. The major product of the reaction is:

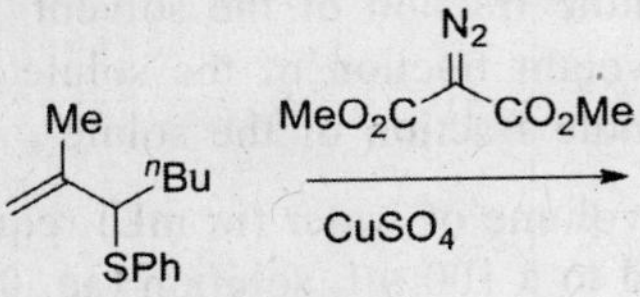

A. 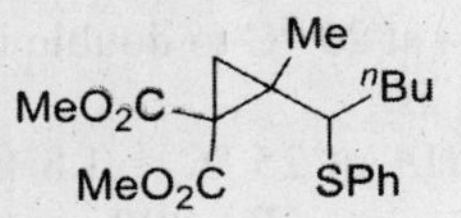

B. 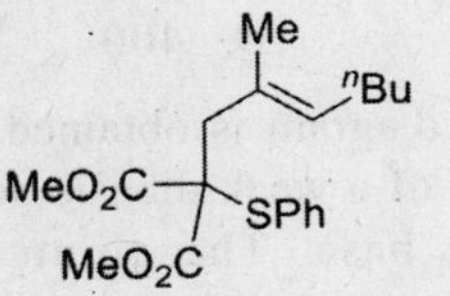

C. 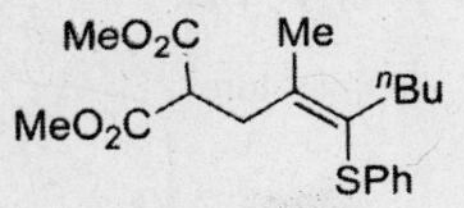

D. 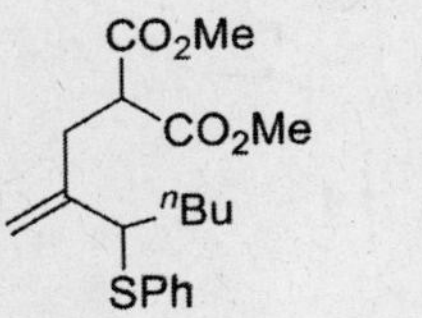

17. Adsorption of a gas on a solid surface follows the Langmuir isotherm. If $k_a/k_d = 1.0 \text{ bar}^{-1}$, the fraction of adsorption sites occupied by the gas at equilibrium under 2.0 bar pressure of the gas at 25 °C is:

(k_a and k_d are the rate constants for adsorption and desorption processes, respectively, at 25 °C)

A. $\frac{1}{4}$
B. $\frac{1}{3}$

C. $\frac{1}{2}$
D. $\frac{2}{3}$

18. The vapour pressure of a dilute solution of a non-volatile solute and the vapour pressure of the pure solvent at the same temperature are P and P*, respectively.

$\frac{P^* - P}{P^*}$ is equal to

(Assume that the vapour phase behaves as an ideal gas)

A. molality of the solution
B. mole fraction of the solvent
C. weight fraction of the solute
D. mole fraction of the solute

19. The volume of water (in mL) required to be added to a 100 mL solution (aq. 0.1 M) of a weak acid (HA) at 25 °C to double its degree of dissociation is:
[Given: K_a of HA at 25 °C = 1.8×10^{-5}]

A. 100   B. 200
C. 300   D. 400

20. The following diagram is obtained in a pH-metric titration of a weak dibasic acid (H_2A) with a strong base. The point that best represents $[HA^-] = [A^{-2}]$ is:

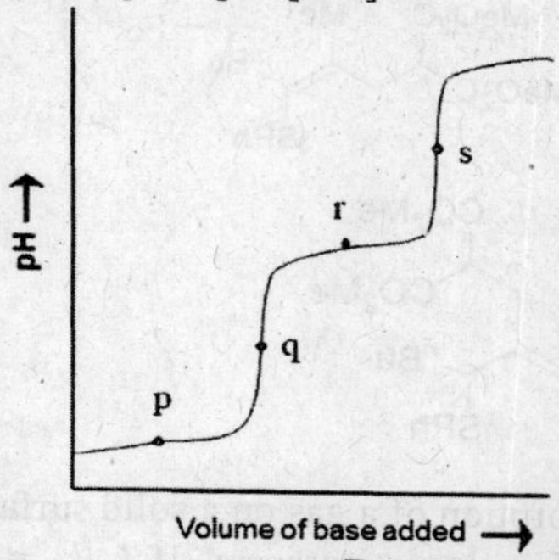

A. p   B. q
C. r   D. s

21. Equal number of gas molecules A (mass m and radius r) and B (mass $2m$ and radius $2r$) are placed in two separate containers of equal volume. At a given temperature, the ratio of the collision frequency of B to that of A is (Assume the gas molecules as hard spheres)

A. $\sqrt{2}:1$ B. $2\sqrt{2}:1$
C. $1:\sqrt{2}$ D. $1:2\sqrt{2}$

22. For the given elementary reactions, the steady-state concentration of X is:

$$2P \xrightarrow{k_1} X \underset{k_3}{\overset{k_2}{\rightleftharpoons}} Q + R, \quad X \xrightarrow{k_4} S$$

A. $\dfrac{k_1[P]^2 + k_3[Q][R]}{k_2 + k_4}$

B. $\dfrac{\frac{1}{2}k_1[P]^2 + k_3[Q][R]}{k_2 + k_4}$

C. $\dfrac{k_1[P]^2 + k_3[Q][R]}{-k_1 + k_2 - k_3 + k_4}$

D. $\dfrac{k_1[P] + k_3[Q][R]}{k_2 + k_4}$

23. The separation (in nm) of {134} planes of an orthorhombic unit cell (with cell parameters a = 0.5 nm, b = 0.6 nm, and c = 0.8 nm) is:

A. 0.036   B. 0.136
C. 0.236   D. 0.336

24. The transition metal (M) complex that can have all isomers (geometric, linkage, and ionization) is:

A. $[M(NH_3)_4Br_2]SCN$
B. $[M(NH_3)_4Cl_2]Br$
C. $[M(NH_3)_4(H_2O)_2]Cl_3$
D. $[M(NH_3)_4(H_2O)_2](SCN)_3$

25. The geometry of $[VO(acac)_2]$ is:

A. square pyramidal
B. trigonal bipyramidal
C. pentagonal planar
D. distorted trigonal bipyramidal

26. The products X and Y in the following reaction sequence, respectively, are:

$$BCl_3 \xrightarrow[150\ °C]{NH_4Cl \text{ in } C_6H_5Cl} X \xrightarrow{NaBH_4} Y$$

A. $B_3N_3Cl_6$ and $B_3N_3H_6$
B. $B_3N_3H_3Cl_3$ and $B_3N_3H_6$
C. $B_3N_3H_3Cl_3$ and $B_3N_3H_{12}$
D. $B_3N_3H_9Cl_3$ and $B_3N_3H_{12}$

27. The correct order of the energy of the d orbitals of a square planar complex is:

A. $d_{xz} = d_{yz} < d_{xy} < d_{z^2} < d_{x^2-y^2}$
B. $d_{xz} = d_{yz} < d_{z^2} < d_{xy} < d_{x^2-y^2}$
C. $d_{yz} = d_{xz} < d_{z^2} < d_{xy} < d_{x^2-y^2}$
D. $d_{xy} < d_{xz} < d_{yz} < d_{x^2-y^2} < d_{z^2}$

28. X and Y in the following reactions, respectively, are:

$EtOH + 2H_2SO_4 \rightarrow X + H_3O^+ + HSO_4^-$

$HNO_3 + 2H_2SO_4 \rightarrow Y + H_3O^+ + 2HSO_4^-$

A. CH_3COOH and NO^+

B. CH_3CHO and NO_2^+

C. $EtOSO_3H$ and NO_2^+

D. $EtOSO_3H$ and NO^+

29. The correct order of energy levels of the molecular orbitals of N_2 is:

A. $1\sigma_g < 1\sigma_u < 2\sigma_g < 2\sigma_u < 1\pi_x < 3\sigma_g < 1\pi_g < 3\sigma_u$

B. $1\sigma_g < 1\sigma_u < 2\sigma_g < 2\sigma_u < 3\sigma_g < 3\sigma_u < 1\pi_u < 1\pi_g$

C. $1\sigma_g < 1\sigma_u < 2\sigma_g < 2\sigma_u < 1\pi_g < 3\sigma_g < 1\pi_u < 3\sigma_u$

D. $1\sigma_g < 1\sigma_u < 2\sigma_g < 2\sigma_u < 3\sigma_g < 1\pi_u < 1\pi_g < 3\sigma_u$

30. Free heme in aqueous solution when exposed to dioxygen is finally converted to (circle around iron in the given choices represents the protoporphyrin IX)

A. 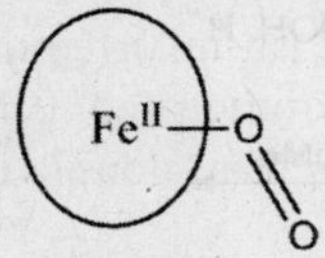

B. 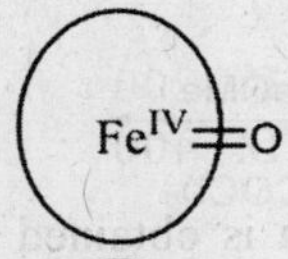

C. 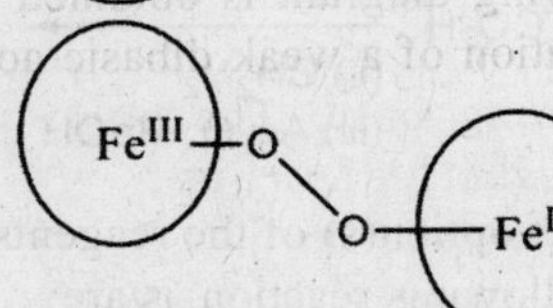

D. 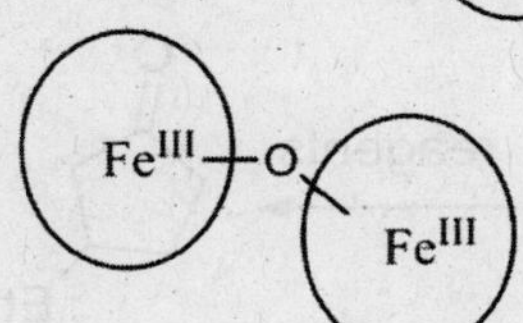

Section B : Multiple Select Questions (MSQ)

Q. 31 – Q. 40 carry two marks each.

31. Correct statement(s) about Q and R is/are:

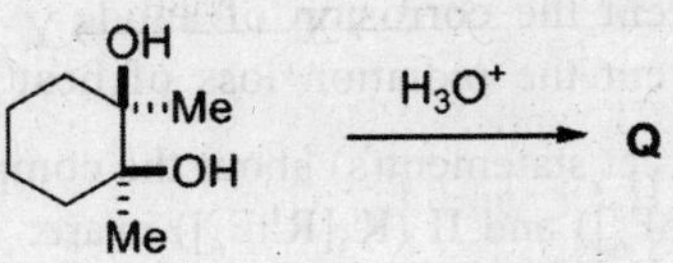

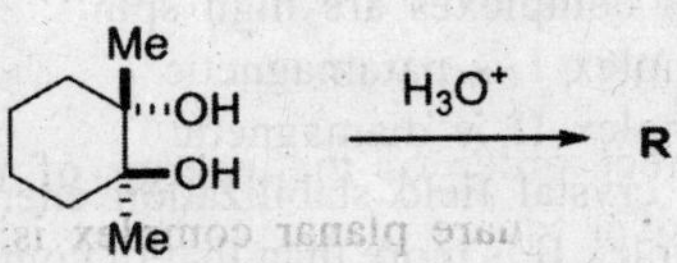

A. Both Q and R give positive Fehling's test

B. Q gives positive iodoform test and its ^1H NMR spectrum shows singlets at 1.0 ppm (3H) and at 1.3 ppm (3H)

C. R gives positive iodoform test and its ^1H NMR spectrum shows singlets at 1.0 ppm (3H) and at 2.2 ppm (3H)

D. A bright yellow precipitate is formed when Q and R treated separately with 2,4-dinitrophenyl hydrazine

32. The correct statement(s) is/are:

A. The pK_{a1} of *cis*-cyclohexane 1,3-diol is greater than that of the *trans* isomer

B. The *trans*-4-(*tert*-butyl) cyclohexanamine is more basic than its *cis* isomer

C. 2,6-Dihydroxybenzoic acid is more acidic than salicylic acid

D. 2,4,6-Trinitrophenol is more acidic than 2,4,6-trinitrobenzoic acid

33. The reaction(s) that yield(s) Ph-CH_2-CH_2-CO_2Me as the major product is/are:

A. 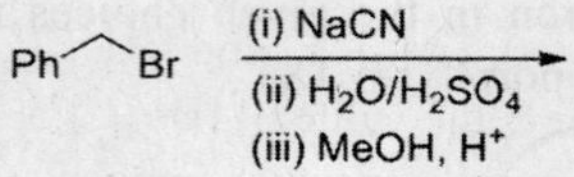

B. 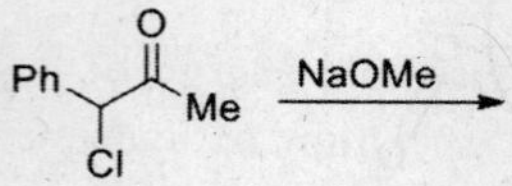

C. 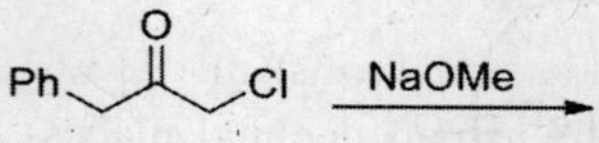

D. 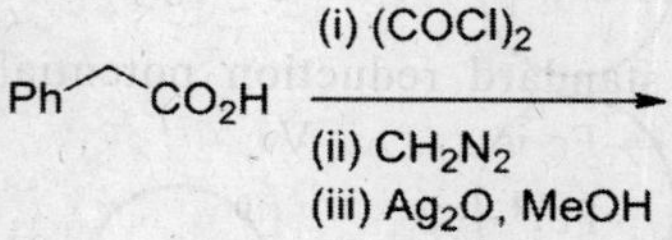

34. The correct option(s) of the reagents required for the following reaction is/are:

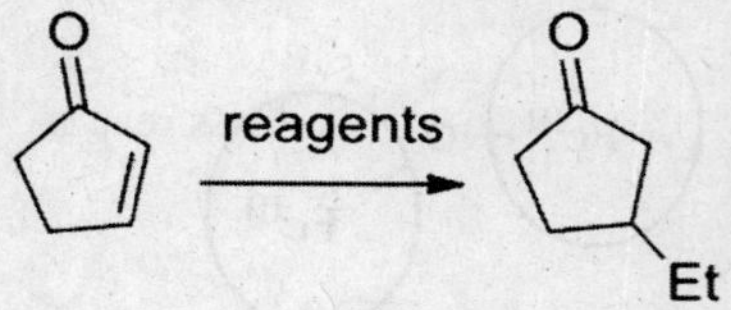

A. (i) Et_3B, O_2 (cat), THF; (ii) H_2O

B. (i) Et_2CuLi, Me_3SiCl; (ii) H_3O^+

C. (i) EtMgBr, Et_2O; (ii) H_2O

D. (i) ^nBuLi, THF; (ii) EtI

35. The reaction(s) that yield(s) 1-naphthol as the major product is/are:

A. 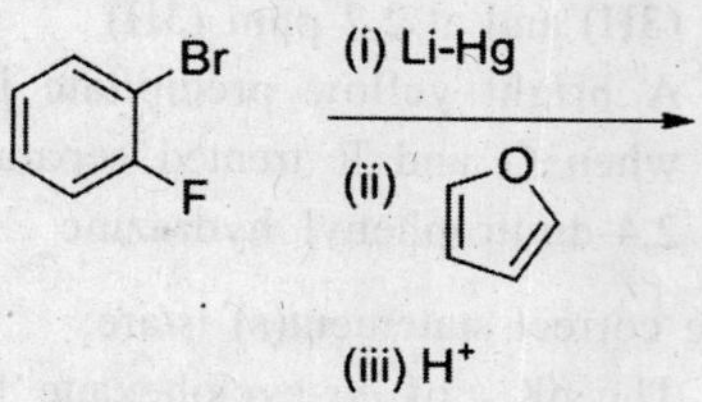

B. 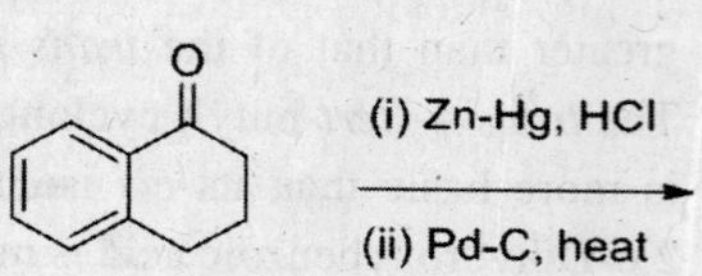

C. 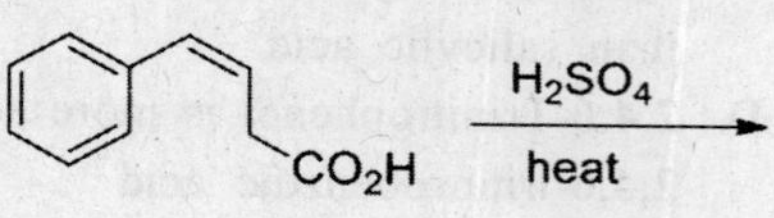

D. 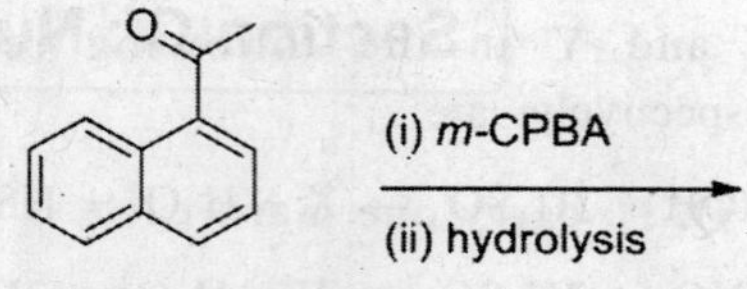

36. The correct relation(s) for an ideal gas in a closed system is/are:

A. $\left(\frac{\partial H}{\partial V}\right)_T = 0$

B. $\left(\frac{\partial T}{\partial P}\right)_H = 0$

C. $\left(\frac{\partial H}{\partial P}\right)_T = 0$

D. $\left(\frac{\partial H}{\partial T}\right)_P = 0$

37. The molecule(s) that follow(s) $I_a < I_b = I_c$ (I_a, I_b, and I_c are the principal moments of inertia) is/are

A. HCN

B. CH_3Cl

C. $CH_3C \equiv CH$

D. C_6H_6

38. The role(s) of fluorspar in the electrolytic reduction of Al_2O_3 is/are to:

A. decrease the melting point of Al_2O_3

B. improve the electrical conductivity of the melt

C. prevent the corrosion of anode

D. prevent the radiation loss of heat

39. The correct statement(s) about the complexes I ($K_3[CoF_6]$) and II ($K_3[RhF_6]$) is/are:

A. Both complexes are high spin

B. Complex I is paramagnetic

C. Complex II is diamagnetic

D. The crystal field stabilization energy of complex II is more than that of complex I

40. The diatomic molecule(s) that has/have bond order of one is/are:

A. B_2 B. N_2^{2-}

C. Li_2 D. O_2^{2-}

Section C : Numerical Answer Type (NAT)

Q. 41 – Q. 50 carry one mark each.

41. The molecular weight of the major product of the reaction is .... (in integer).

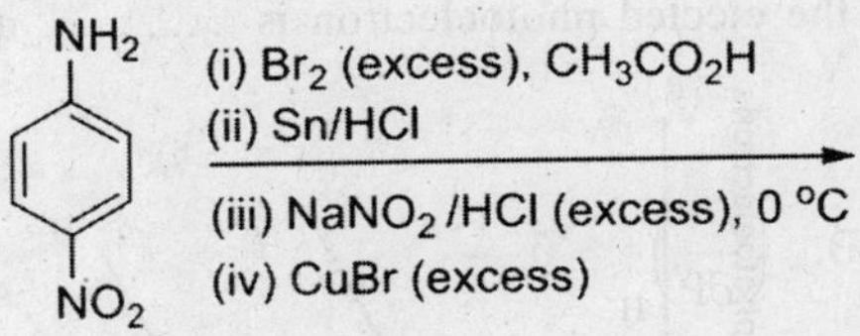

[Given: atomic weight of H = 1, C = 12, N = 14, and Br = 80]

42. A 0.06 g/mL solution of (S)-1-phenylethanol placed in a 5 cm long polarimeter tube shows an optical rotation of 1.2°. The specific rotation is ....°.
(round off to the nearest integer)

43. The isoelectric point of glutamic acid is ....

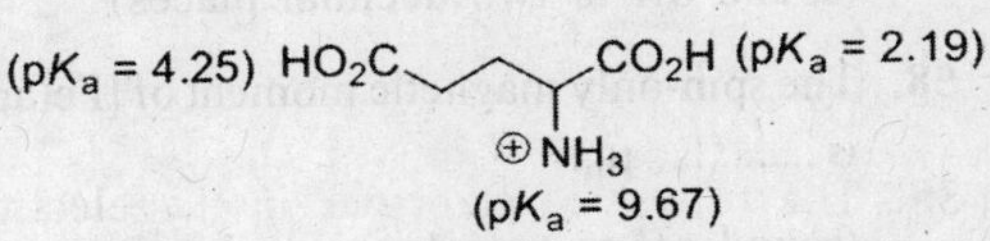

(round off to two decimal places)

44. Consider the following reaction:

$2\ C_6H_6 + 15\ O_2 \rightarrow 12\ CO_2 + 6\ H_2O$

$\Delta_r H^0_{298} = -3120$ kJ mol^{-1}.

A closed system initially contains 5 moles of benzene and 25 moles of oxygen under standard conditions at 298 K. The reaction was stopped when 17.5 moles of oxygen is left. The amount of heat evolved during the reaction is .... kJ.
(round off to the nearest integer)

45. For the elementary reaction

$C \xleftarrow{k_2} A \xrightarrow{k_1} B,\ k_1 = 2k_2.$

At time $t = 0$, [A] = A_0 and [B] = [C] = 0. At a later time t, the value of [B]/[C] is ....
(round off to the nearest integer)

46. The highest possible energy of a photon in the emission spectrum of hydrogen atom is .... eV.
[Given: Rydberg constant = 13.61 eV]
(round off to two decimal places)

47. The standard reduction potential (E^0) of $Fe^{3+} \rightarrow Fe$ is .... V.
[Given: $Fe^{3+} \rightarrow Fe^{2+}$ E^0 = 0.77 V and
$Fe^{2+} \rightarrow Fe$ E^0 = –0.44 V]
(round off to three decimal places)

48. The number of valence electrons in $Na_2[Fe(CO)_4]$ (the Colman's reagent) is ....

49. In the Born-Haber cycle, the heat of formation of CuCl is _______ kJ/mol.
[Given:
Heat of atomization of Cu = +338 kJ/mol,
Ionization energy of Cu = +746 kJ/mol,
Heat of atomization of Cl_2 = +121 kJ/mol,
Electron affinity of Cl = –349 kJ/mol, and
Lattice energy of CuCl = –973 kJ/mol]
(round off to the nearest integer)

50. The spin-only magnetic moment of B_2 molecule is .... μ_B.
(round off to two decimal places)

Q. 51 – Q. 60 carry two marks each.

51. The sum of the total number of stereoisomers (including enantiomers) present in the following molecules is ....

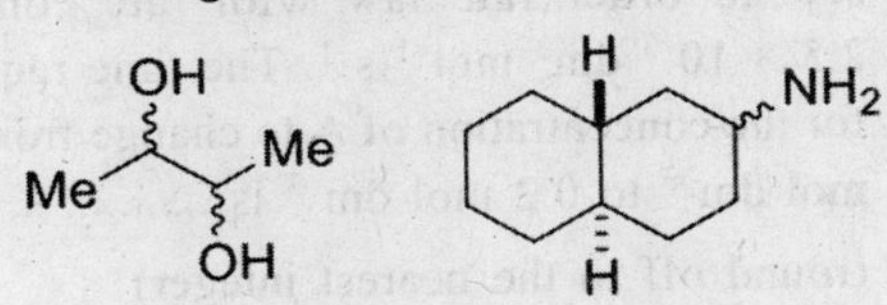

52. The number of singlets observed in the ^{1}H NMR spectrum of P is ....

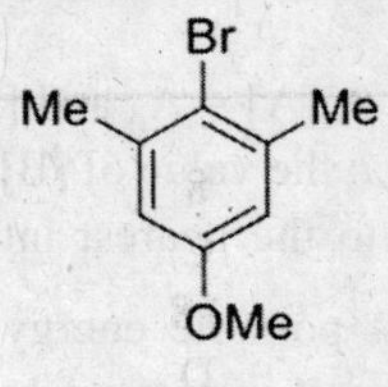

P

53. When a glass capillary tube is dipped in water, a 1.0 cm rise in the water level is observed at 18 °C. The internal radius of the capillary is .... cm.

[Given: Surface tension of water at 18 °C = 73.2 dyne cm^{-1}; difference in the densities of water and air at 18 °C = 0.996 g cm^{-3}; gravitational acceleration constant, g = 980 cm s^{-2}.

Assume that water completely wets the glass capillary and the interface between the water and the air phase inside the capillary is a hemisphere.]

(round off to two decimal places)

54. The volume of 2.0 mol of an ideal gas is reduced to half isothermally at 300 K in a closed system. The value of ΔG is .... kJ.
[Given: R = 8.314 J mol^{-1} K^{-1}]
(round off to two decimal places)

55. The harmonic vibrational frequency of a diatomic molecule is 2000 cm^{-1}. Its zeropoint energy is .... eV.

[Given: Planck's constant = 6.62×10^{-34} J s; 1 eV = 1.6×10^{-19} J]

(round off to two decimal places)

56. An elementary reaction $2A \rightarrow P$ follows a second order rate law with rate constant 2.5×10^{-3} dm^3 mol^{-1} s^{-1}. The time required for the concentration of A to change from 0.4 mol dm^{-3} to 0.2 mol dm^{-3} is .... s.

(round off to the nearest integer)

57. The following diagram shows the kinetic energy of the ejected photoelectrons against the energy of incident radiation for two metal surfaces M_1 and M_2. If the energy of the incident radiation on M_1 is equal to the work function of M_2, the de Broglie wavelength of the ejected photoelectron is .... nm.

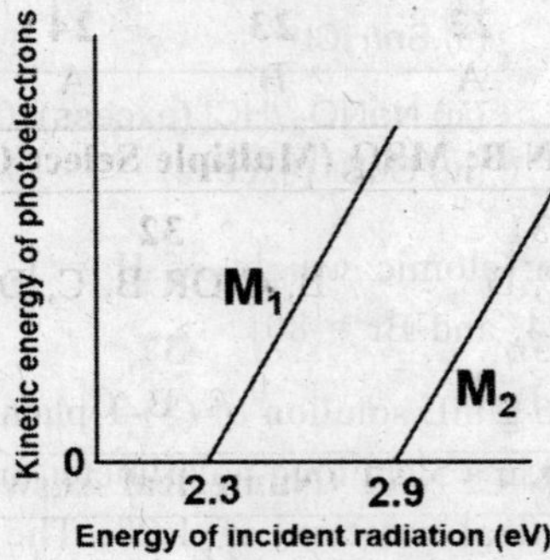

[Given: Mass of electron = 9.11×10^{-31} kg; Planck's constant = 6.62×10^{-34} J s; 1 eV = 1.6×10^{-19} J.]

(round off to two decimal places)

58. The spin-only magnetic moment of $[Fe(acac)_3]$ is .... μ_B.

(round off to two decimal places)

59. The amount of ethane produced in the following reaction is .... kg.

$$C_2H_4(2\ kg) + H_2(2\ kg) \xrightarrow{\text{Wilkinson's Catalyst}} C_2H_6\ (90\%\ \text{catalytic conversion})$$

(round off to two decimal places)

60. In a gravimetric estimation of Al, a sample of 0.1000 g $AlCl_3$ is precipitated with 8-hydroxyquinoline. The weight of the precipitate is .... g.

[Given: atomic weight of Al is 26.98; molecular weight of $AlCl_3$ is 133.34; and molecular weight of 8-hydroxyquinoline is 145.16]

(round off to 4 decimal places)

ANSWERS

SECTION A: MCQ (Multiple Choise Questions)

1	2	3	4	5	6	7	8	9	10
B	A	C	A	A	D	C	C	A	C
11	**12**	**13**	**14**	**15**	**16**	**17**	**18**	**19**	**20**
D	C	B	B	D	C	D	D	C	C
21	**22**	**23**	**24**	**25**	**26**	**27**	**28**	**29**	**30**
B	A	B	A	A	B	B	C	A	D

SECTION B: MSQ (Multiple Select Questions)

31	32	33	34	35
C, D	B, C OR B, C, D	B, C, D	A, B	A, C, D
36	**37**	**38**	**39**	**40**
A, B, C	A, B, C	A, B	B, C, D	A, C, D

SECTION C: NAT (Numerical Answer Type Questions)

41	42	43	44	45
394	39 to 41	3.21 to 3.23	1560	2
46	**47**	**48**	**49**	**50**
13.60 to 13.62	–0.037 to –0.036	18	–117 or –178 to –177	2.82 to 2.83
51	**52**	**53**	**54**	**55**
5 or 7	3	0.148 to 0.151	3.44 to 3.46	0.12 to 0.13
56	**57**	**58**	**59**	**60**
500	1.58 to 1.59	5.91 to 5.92	1.92 to 1.93	0.3440 to 0.3452

EXPLANATORY ANSWERS

1.

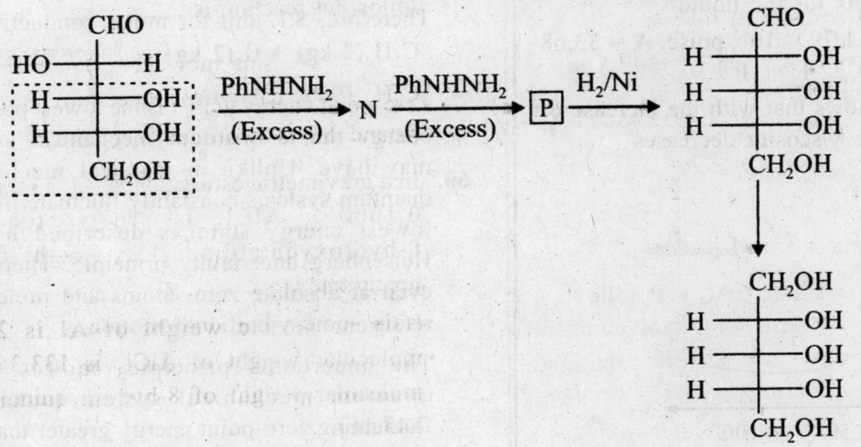

Hence, correct answer is (B).

2.

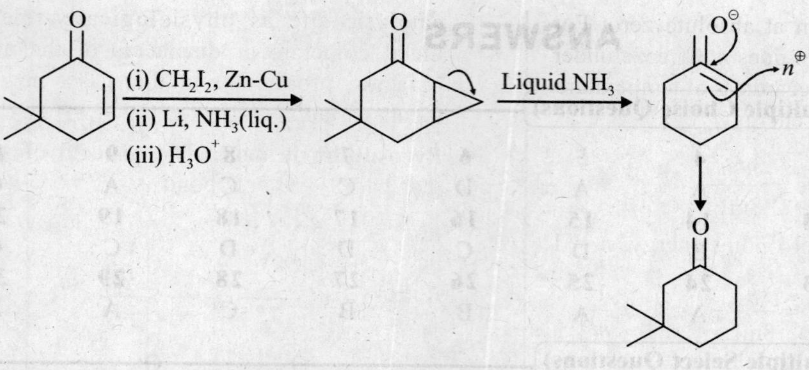

5. Variation of Viscosity with Temperature:

The viscosity of liquids decreases when the temperature increases, while the viscosity of gases increases with the increase in temperature. This is due to the reason that the viscous forces in a fluid are due to cohesive forces and molecular momentum transfer.

In liquids the cohesive forces are more important than the molecular momentum transfer, due to closely packed molecules, and with the increase in temperature, the cohesive forces decrease with the result of decreasing viscosity.

For liquid (water)

$\mu = \mu_0 \ (1/1 + At + Bt^2)$

where μ = Viscosity of liquids at t °C, in poise

μ_0 = Viscosity of liquids at 0 °C, in poise

A, B = Cosntants for the liquid

For water, $\mu_0 = 1.79 \times 10^{-3}$ poise, $A = 33.68 \times 10^{-3}$ and $B = 22.1 \times 10^{-3}$

The equation shows that with the increase of temperature, the viscosity decreases

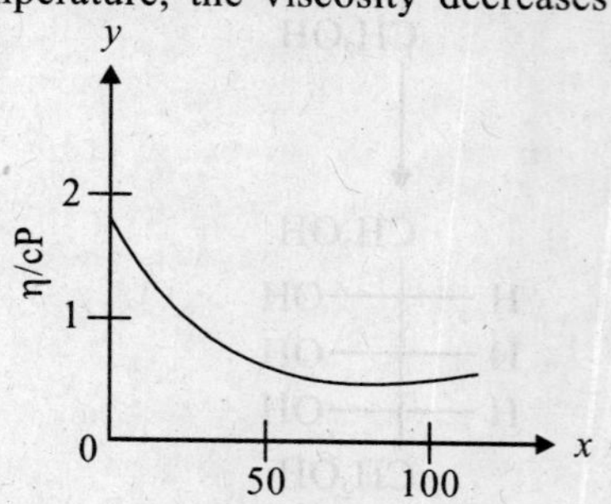

6. It is basically a scientific method which is used for the expressing of magnitudes as well as the quantities. Molar conductivity is actually the conductivity of the electrolyte solution which is divided by the molar concentration of the electrolyte which actually measures the efficiency with which the given electrolyte will conduct the electricity in the solution.

So, Molar conductivity

$$= \frac{\text{Conductivity of electrolytic solution}}{\text{Molar concentration of electrolyte}}$$

Hence, S.I. unit of Molar conductivity:

$$\frac{S.m^3}{m^1.mol^1} = S.m^2.mol^{-1}$$

Therefore, S.I. unit for molar conductivity:

$S.m^2.mol^{-1}$.

7. Zero-point energy (ZPE) is the lowest possible energy that a quantum mechanical system may have. Unlike in classical mechanics, quantum systems constantly fluctuate in their lowest energy state as described by the Heisenberg uncertainty principle. Therefore, even at absolute zero, atoms and molecules retain some vibrational motion.

The uncertainty principle requires every quantum mechanical system to have a fluctuating zero-point energy greater than the minimum of its classical potential well. This results in motion even at absolute zero. For example, liquid helium does not freeze under atmospheric pressure regardless of temperature due to its zero-point energy.

(A) $1e^{\ominus}$ $\quad E_n = \dfrac{n^2h^2}{8mL^2}$

(B) $1p + 1e^-$ $\quad$ Zero point energy, $n = 1$

(C) $2p\ 2n\ 2e^{\ominus}$ $\quad E = \dfrac{h^2}{8mL^2}\ \therefore\ E \propto \dfrac{1}{m}$

(D) 1p

Hence, mass order

$\therefore C > B > D > A$

and correct energy order

$C < B < D < A$

Hence, correct answer is (C).

8. The metal (M) in the carbonic anhydrase metal-hydroxide $[Lig^3M^{2+}(OH)^-]$ mechanism is Zn^{2+} for all classes, but other transition metals have been demonstrated to bind to the catalytic site as physiologically-relevant metal cofactors or displacers of the native cofactor, producing, in this case, new CA metal variants.

9. Pyrosulphuric acid: The oxoacid of sulfur that has S – O – S bond is:

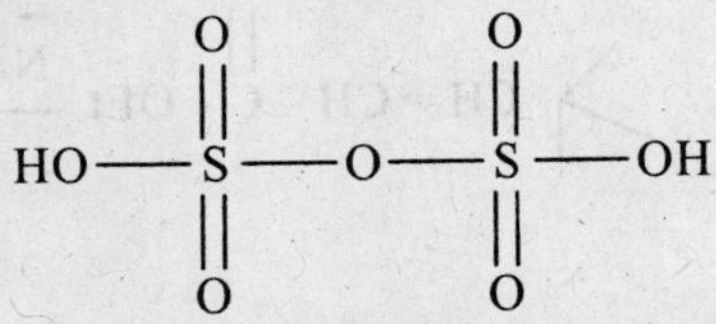

Pyrosulphuric acid

10. Yellow colour due to the formation of CrO_4^{2-} ion

$\therefore 2\,Cr(OH)_3 + 3(O) + 4\,NaOH$
↓
(from $NaBO_3$)
$\rightarrow 2Na_2CrO_4 + 5H_2O$

Hence, correct answer (C).

11. 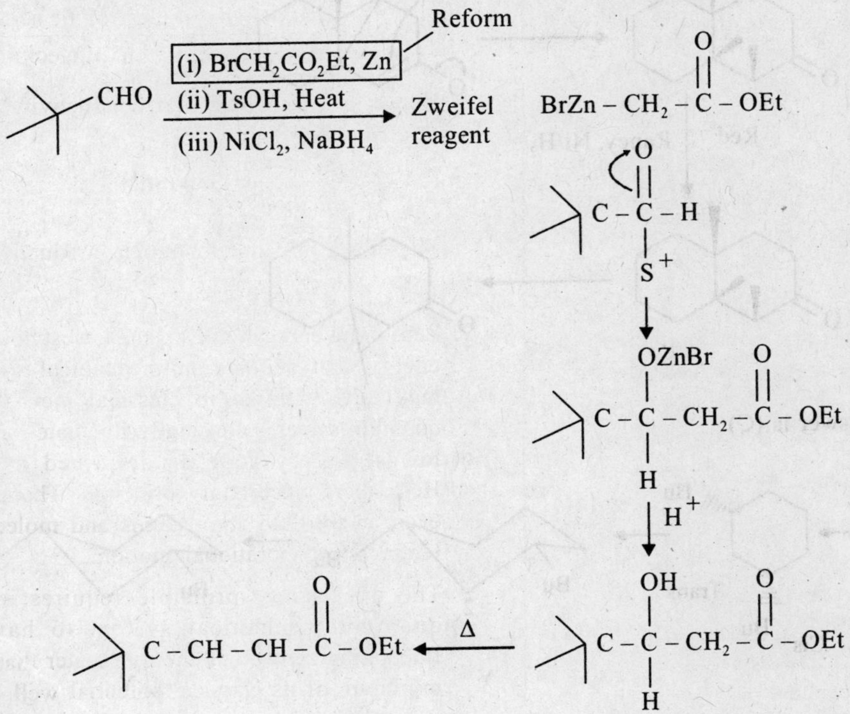

Now,

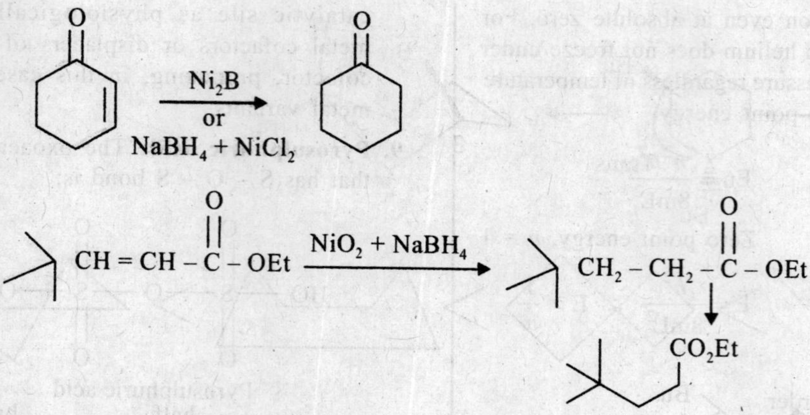

12.

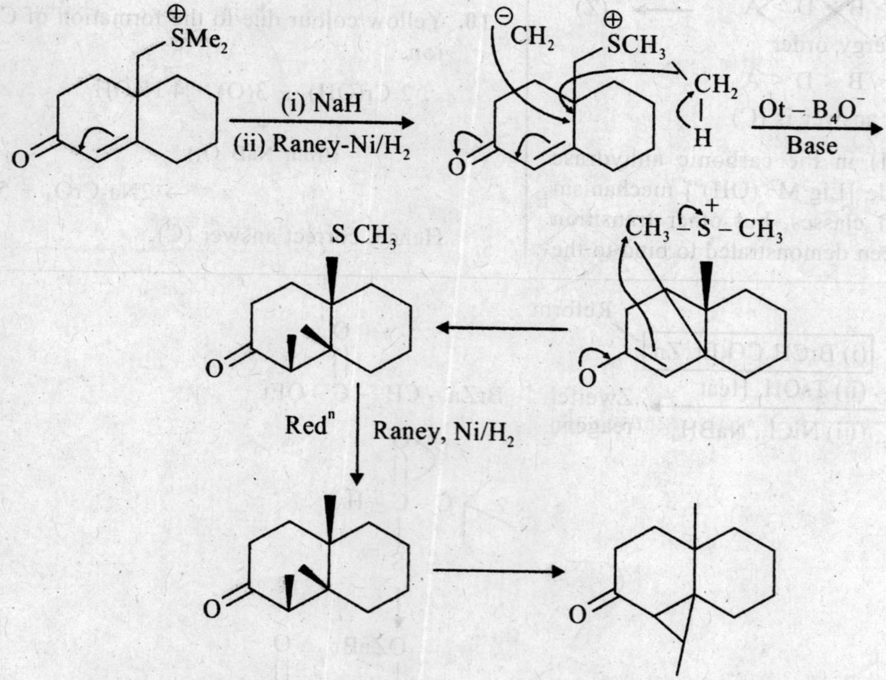

Hence, correct answer is (C).

13.

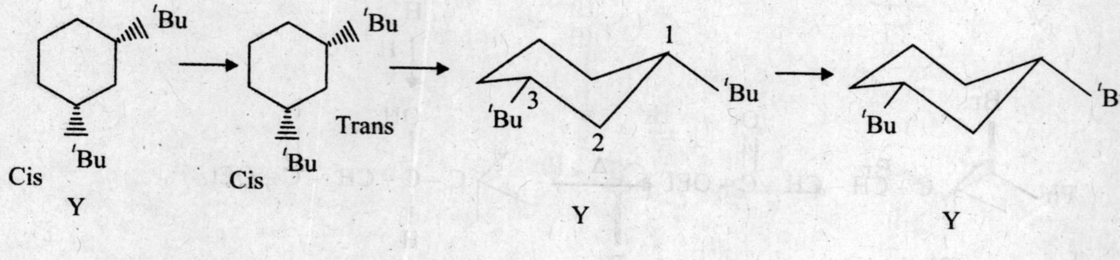

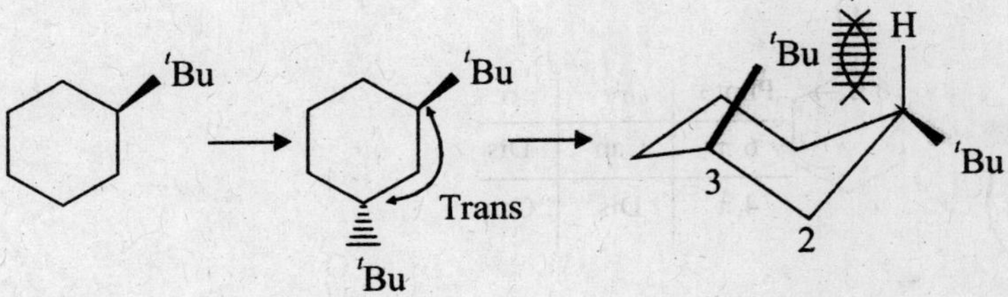

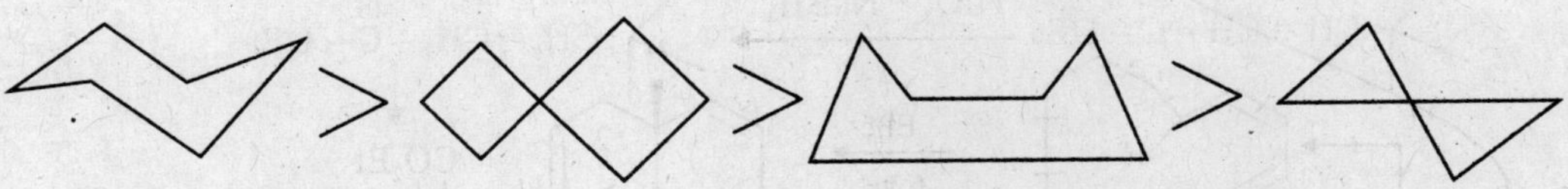

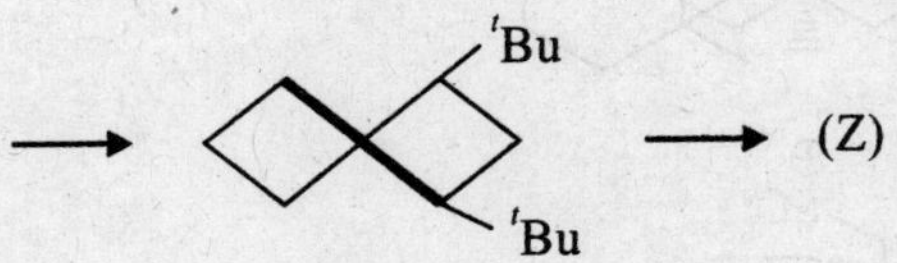

Z

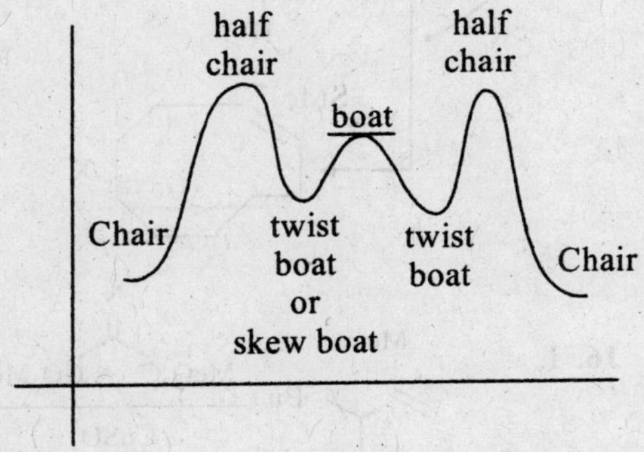

From (Y) and (Z), we get,

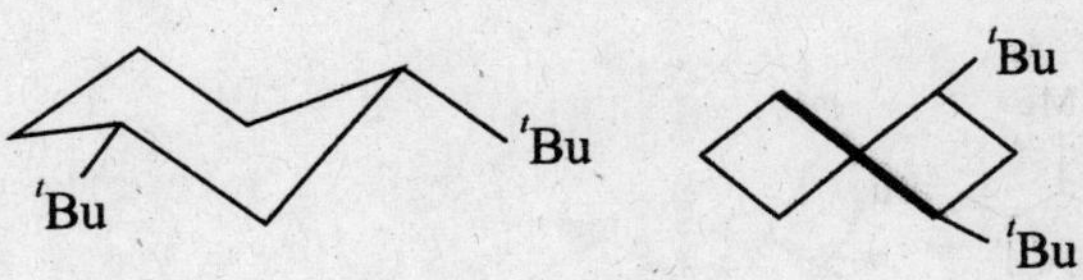

Y Z

14.

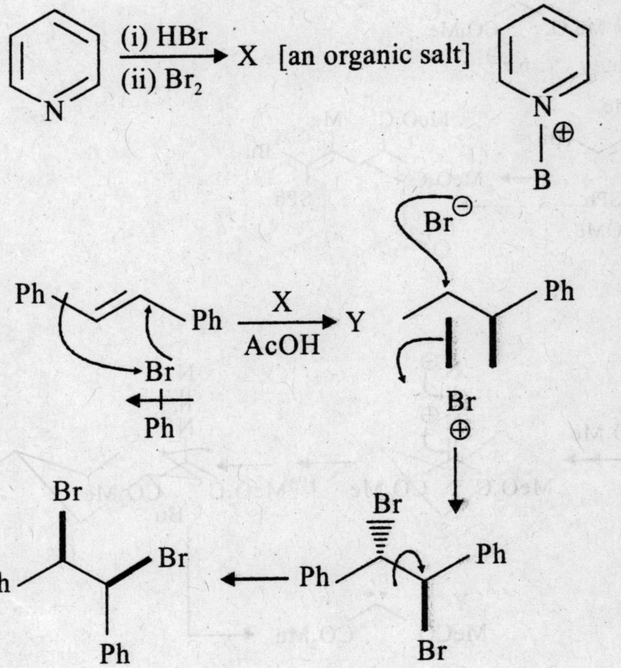

15.

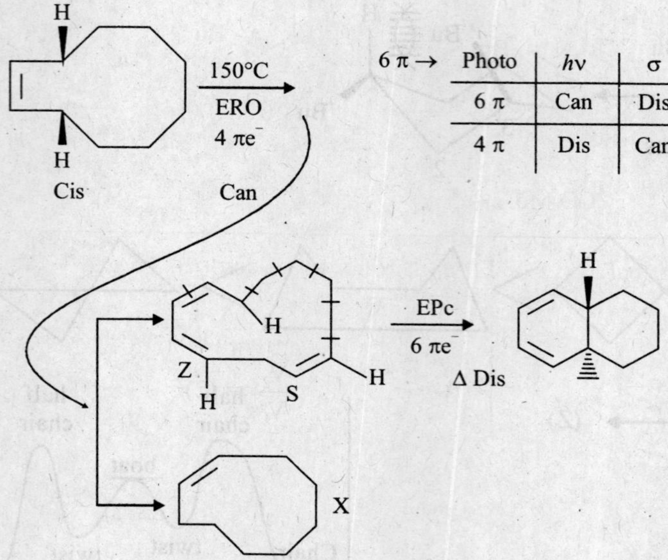

6 π → Photo	hν	σ
6 π	Can	Dis
4 π	Dis	Can

16. I.

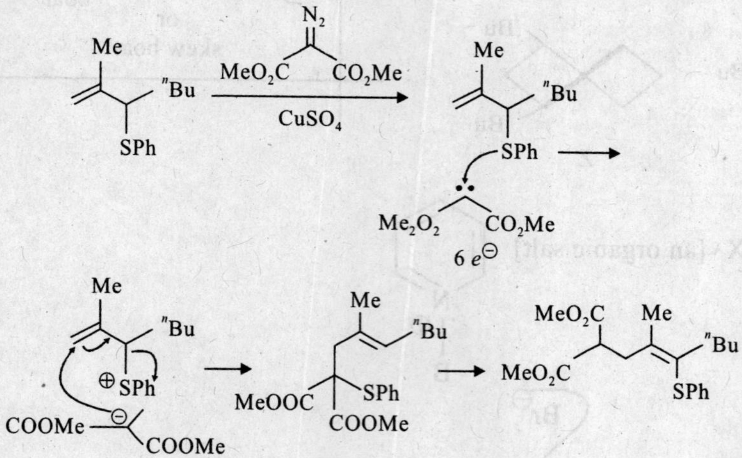

Hence, correct answer is (C).

II.

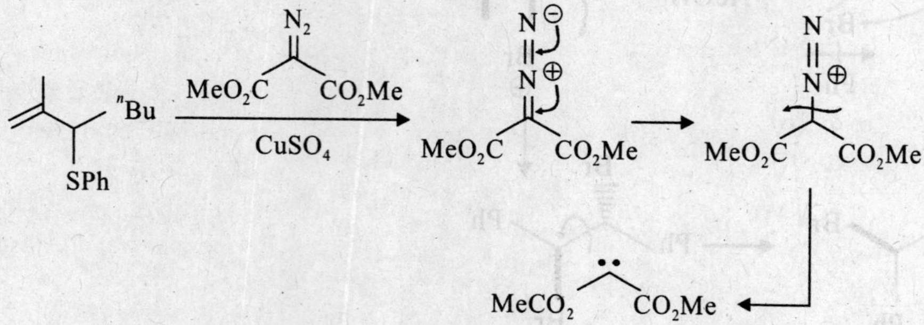

15.

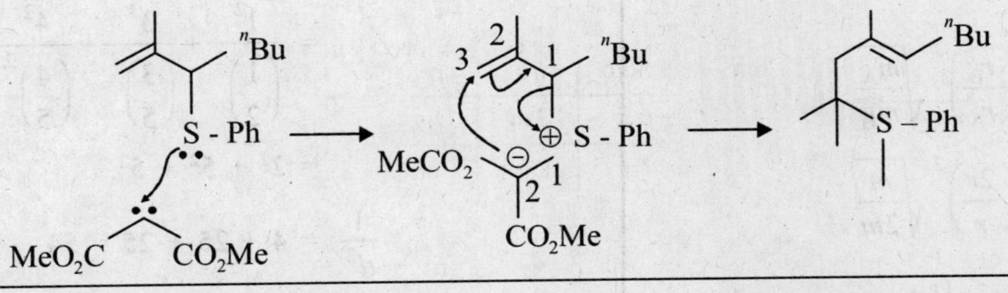

17. Given, $k_a/k_d = 1.0\ \text{bar}^{-1}$ $P = 2.0$ bar

As, $$Q = \frac{kP}{1+kP}$$

$$= \frac{1\text{bar}\times 2\text{bar}}{1+1\text{bar}\times 2\text{bar}}$$

$$= \frac{2}{1+2}$$

$$= \frac{2}{3}$$

18. Relative lowering of vapour pressure

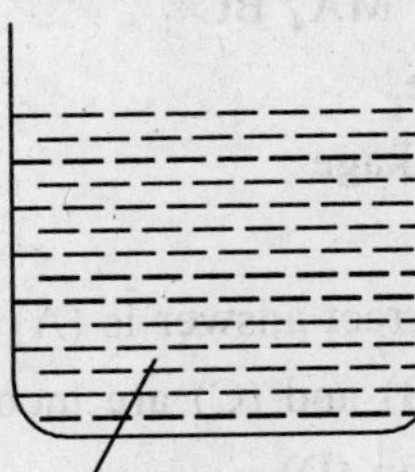

$$\frac{P_{solvent} - P_{sol}}{P_{solvent}} = X_{solute}$$

= Mole fraction of solute.

19. Given, $V_1 = 100$ mL

Degree of dissociation (α) $= \sqrt{\frac{k_a}{c}}$

$$= \sqrt{\frac{k_a \times V}{4}}$$

$\Rightarrow$ $\alpha \propto \sqrt{V}$

$\therefore$ $$\frac{\alpha_2}{\alpha_1} = \sqrt{\frac{V_2}{V_1}} \quad ...(i)$$

$\because$ $\alpha_2 = 2\alpha_1$

$\therefore$ $$\frac{\alpha_2}{\alpha_1} = 2 \quad ...(ii)$$

From eqn (*i*) and (*ii*), we get,

$$\frac{\alpha_2}{\alpha_1} = \sqrt{\frac{V_2}{V_1}} = 2$$

$\therefore$ $\frac{V_2}{V_1} = (2)^2$

$\Rightarrow$ $\frac{V_2}{V_1} = 4$

$\Rightarrow$ $V_2 = 4\ V_1 = 4 \times 100$

$= 400$ mL

$\therefore$ Volume of water = 400 mL

Hence, the volume of water required to be added

$= V_2 - V_1$

$= 400$ mL $- 100$ mL

$= 300$ mL

Hence, correct answer is (C).

20.

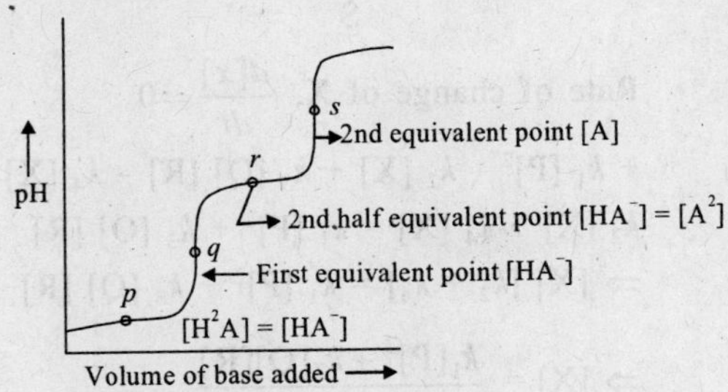

From the figure,

q $\rightarrow$ First equivalent point = $[HA^-]$

s $\rightarrow$ Second equivalent point = $[A^{2-}]$

r $\rightarrow$ Second-half equivalent point $= [HA^-] = [A^{2-}]$

p $\rightarrow$ $[H_2A] = [HA^-]$

Thus, the point that best represents $[HA^-] = [A^{2-}]$ is r.

Hence, correct answer is (C).

21. We have,

$$\frac{Z_B}{Z_A} = \left(\frac{r_B}{r_A}\right)^2 \sqrt{\frac{m_A}{m_B}}$$

$$= \left(\frac{2r}{r}\right)^2 \sqrt{\frac{m}{2m}}$$

$$= 4 \times \sqrt{\frac{1}{2}}$$

$$= 4 \times \frac{1}{\sqrt{2}}$$

$$= \frac{2 \times 2}{\sqrt{2}}$$

$$= \frac{2 \times \sqrt{2} \times \sqrt{2}}{\sqrt{2}}$$

$$= \frac{2\sqrt{2}}{1}$$

$\therefore Z_B : Z_A = 2\sqrt{2} : 1.$

22.

$$2P \xrightarrow{k_1} X \underset{k_3}{\overset{k_2}{\rightleftharpoons}} Q + R$$
$$X \xrightarrow{k_4} S$$

Rate of change of X, $\frac{d[x]}{dt} \simeq 0$

$+ k_1 [P]^2 - k_2 [X] + k_3 [Q] [R] - k_4 [X] \simeq 0$

$k_2 [X] + k_4 [X] = k_1 [P]^2 + k_3 [Q] [R]$

$\Rightarrow [X] [k_2 + k_4] = k_1 [P]^2 + k_3 [Q] [R]$

$$\Rightarrow [X] = \frac{k_1[P]^2 + k_3[Q][R]}{k_2 + k_4}.$$

23. Given, {134}

$a = 0.5$ nm, $b = 0.6$ nm and $c = 0.8$ nm

As, $$\frac{1}{d_{hkl}^2} = \frac{h^2}{a^2} + \frac{k^2}{b^2} + \frac{l^2}{c^2}$$

$$= \frac{1^2}{(0.5)^2} + \frac{3^2}{(0.6)^2} + \frac{4^2}{(0.8)^2}$$

$$= \frac{1^2}{\left(\frac{1}{2}\right)^2} + \frac{3^2}{\left(\frac{3}{5}\right)^2} + \frac{4^2}{\left(\frac{4}{5}\right)^2}$$

$$= 2^2 + 5^2 + 5^2$$

$$\frac{1}{d^2} = 4 + 25 + 25 = 54$$

$$\Rightarrow \quad d^2 = \frac{1}{54}$$

$$\Rightarrow \quad d = \frac{1}{\sqrt{54}}$$

$$= \frac{1}{7.348}$$

$$= 0.136 \text{ nm.}$$

24. We have, $[M(NH_3)_4Br_2]SCN$

MA_4B_2 or MA_4 BC

GI linkage,

Isomer linkage

Ionization

Hence, correct answer is (A)

Options (B) and (C) are incorrect

Now, option (D),

$[M(NH_3)_4(H_2O)_2](SCN)_3 \rightarrow$ GI $\rightarrow$ GI

MA_4B_2 or MA_4 BC

GI linkage

Hydration

Hence, option is incorrect.

Thus correct option is (A).

25. Geometry of $[VO(acac)^2]$

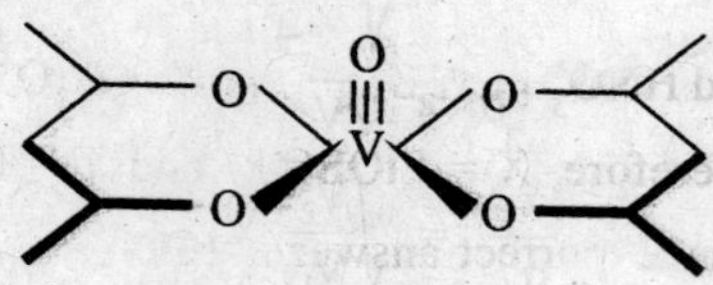

bis (acetylacetonato oxperoxovendium (iv))

It is square pyramidal with a short V - O band.

26.

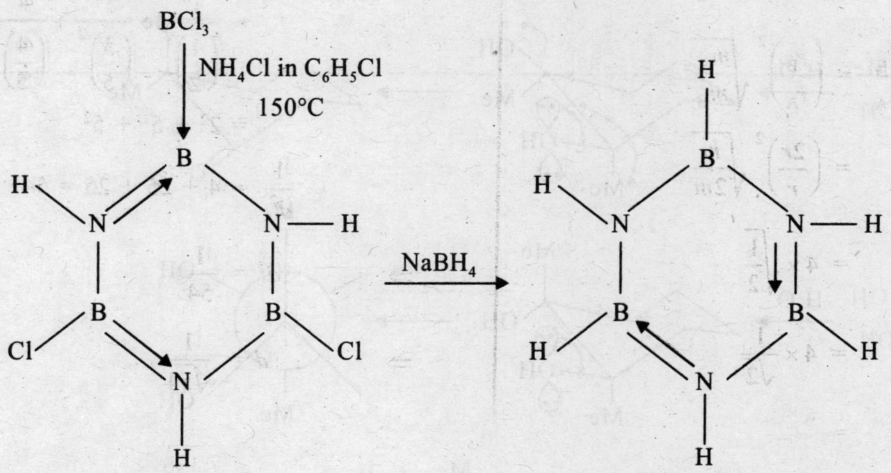

($B_3N_3H_3Cl_3$) ($B_3N_3H_6$)

∴ Products of X and Y are:

$B_3N_3H_3Cl_3$ and $B_3H_3H_6$.

---

27. Highest energy — $d_{x^2-y^2}$

— d_{xy}

— d_{z^2}

— — d_{xz} d_{yz}

Correct order of energy of the orbitals of square planar complex is

$d_{xz} = d_{yz} < d_{z^2} < d_{xy} < d_{x^2-y^2}$

Hence, correct answer is (A).

28. $Et^+OH^\ominus + 2H_2SO_4 \rightarrow X + H_3O^+ + HSO_4^-$

$HNO_3 + 2H_2SO_4 \rightarrow Y + H_3O^+ + 2HSO_4^-$

$EtOH + 2H_2SO_4 \rightarrow Et^+OSO_3^- H + H_3O^+ + HSO_4^-$

and $HNO_3 + 2H_2SO_4 \rightarrow NO_2^+ + H_3O^+ + 2HSO_4^-$

Therefore, X = $EtOSO_3H$ and Y = NO_2^+

Hence, correct answer is (C).

29. $N_2 \rightarrow$ sp mixing

$\sigma_g \rightarrow \sigma_g$ (bonding)

$\sigma_u \rightarrow \sigma_u^*$ (antibonding)

$\pi_u \rightarrow \pi_u$

$\pi_g \rightarrow \pi_g^*$

Now, we have

Before mixing

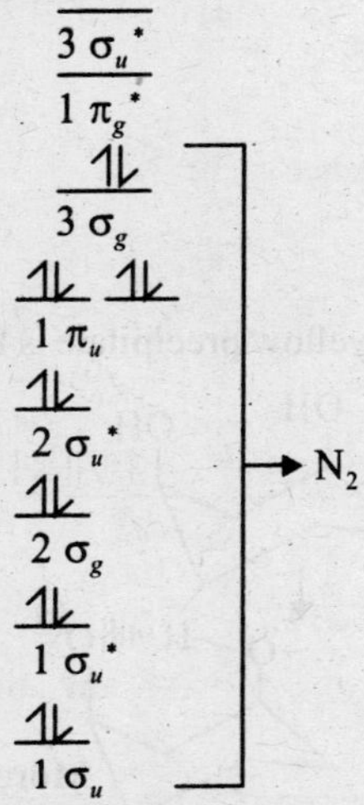

Hence, correct order of energy levels of the molecular orbitals of N_2 is:

$1\sigma_g < 1\sigma_u < 2\sigma_g < 2\sigma_u < 1\pi_u < 3\sigma_g < 1\pi_g < 3\sigma_u$.

31. 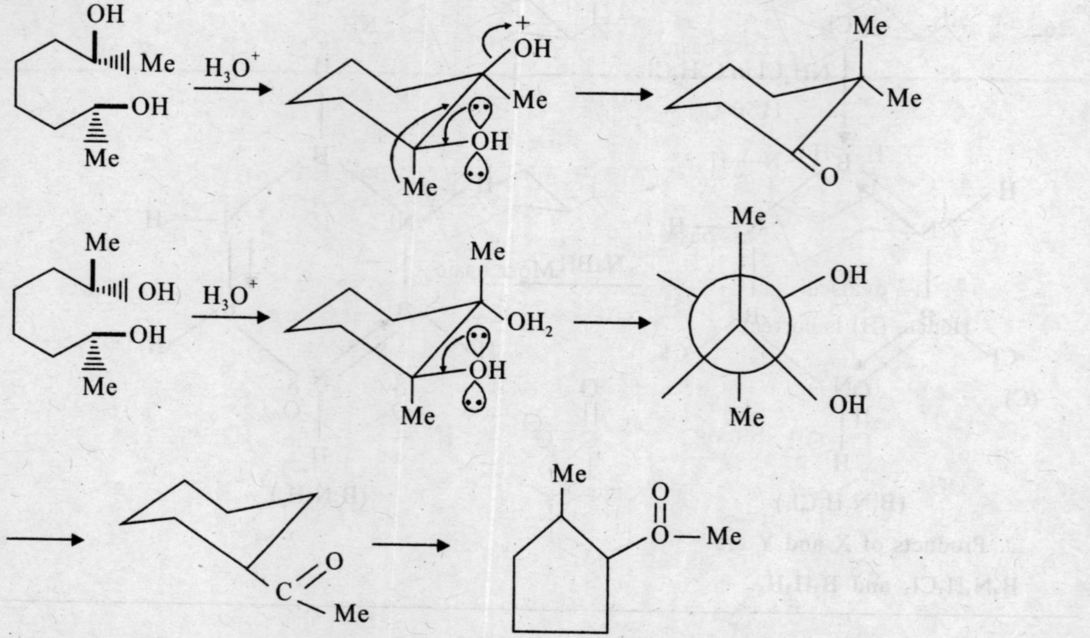

R gives positive iodoform test and its ^{1}H-NMR spectrum shows singlets at 1.0 ppm (3H) and at 2.2 ppm (3H)

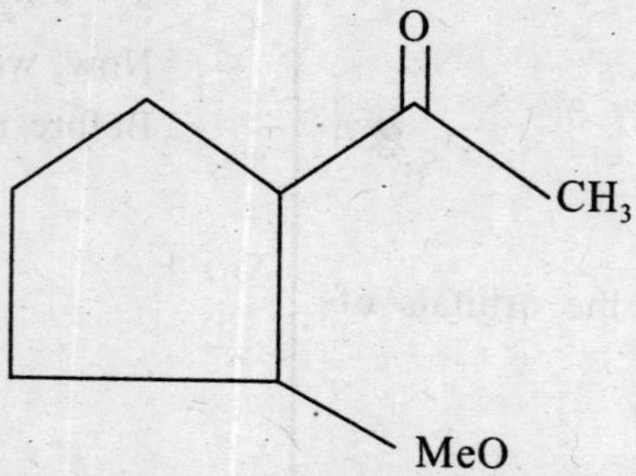

A bright yellow precipitate is formed when Q and R treated separately with 2,4-dinitrophenyl hydrazine.

32. (A)

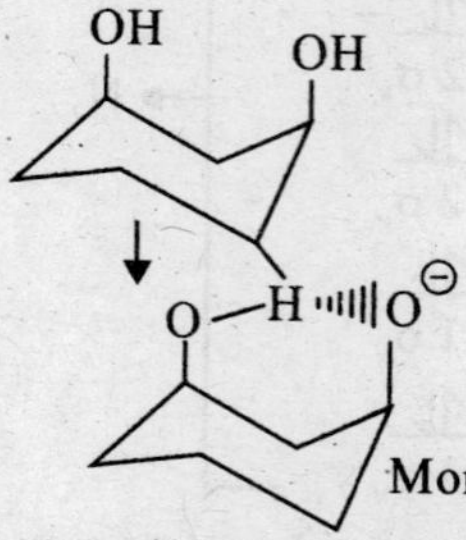

More stable

k_1 for cis > k_1 for trans

pk_1 for cis < pk_1 for trans

Hence, (A) is incorrect.

(B)

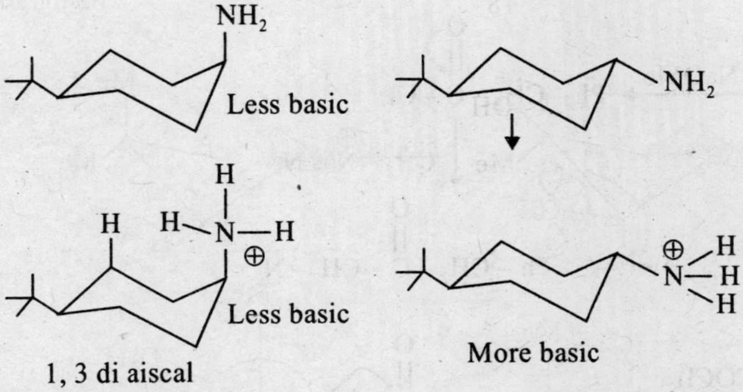

Hence, (B) is correct.

(C)

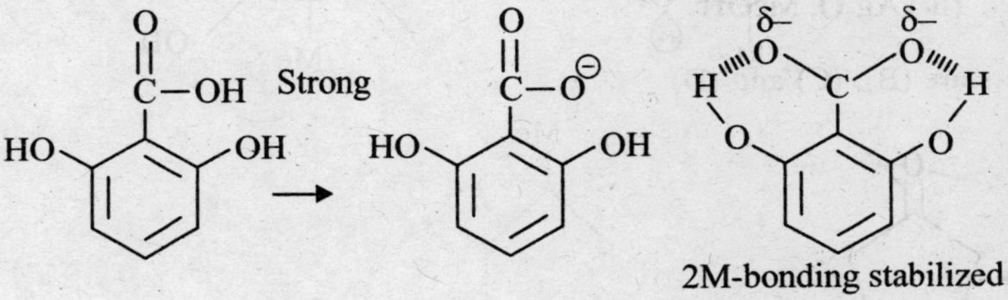

Hence, (C) is correct.

(D)

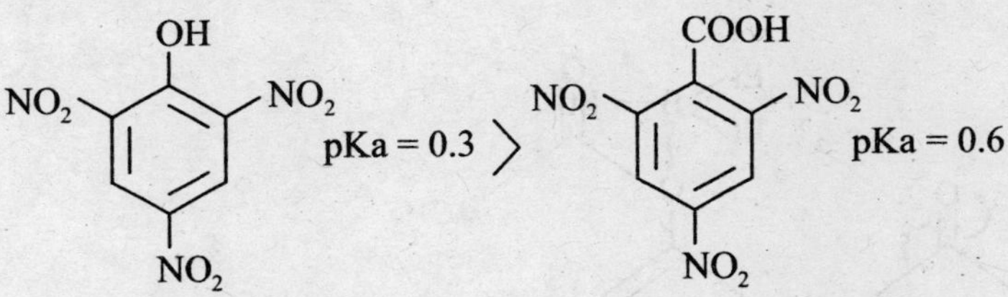

Hence, (D) is correct.

33. Given, Ph-CH_2-CH_2-CO_2Me

(A)

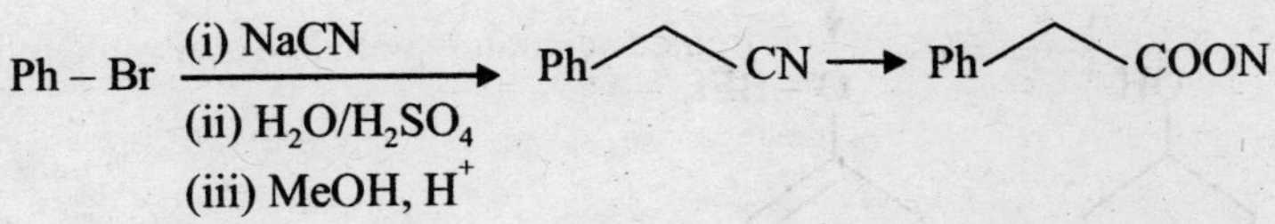

Hence, (A) is incorrect.

(B)

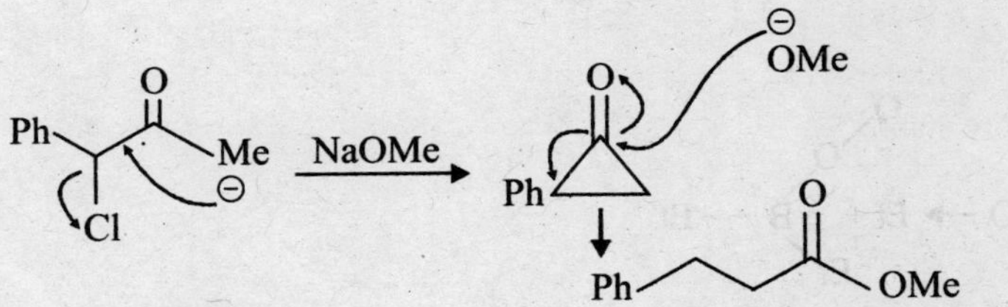

(C) 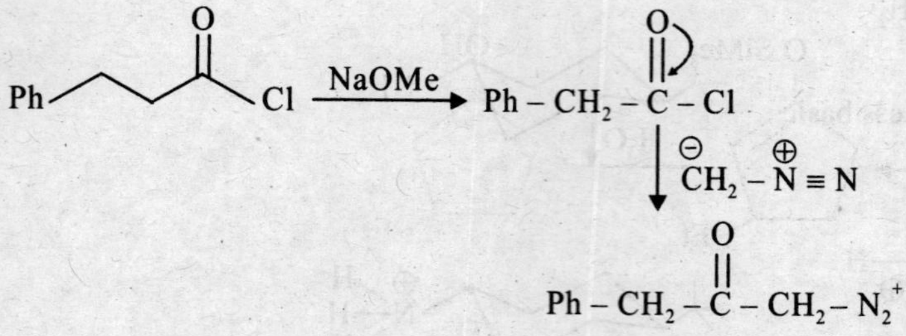

(D) 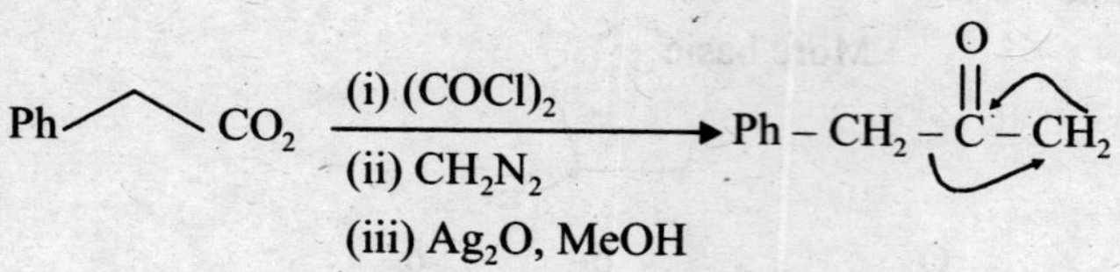

Hence, correct answers are (B), (C) and (D).

34.

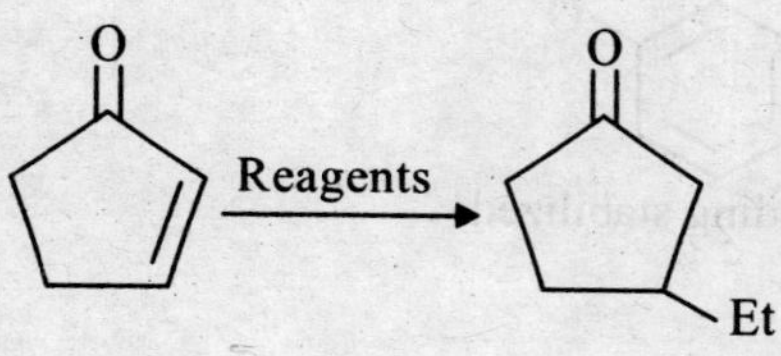

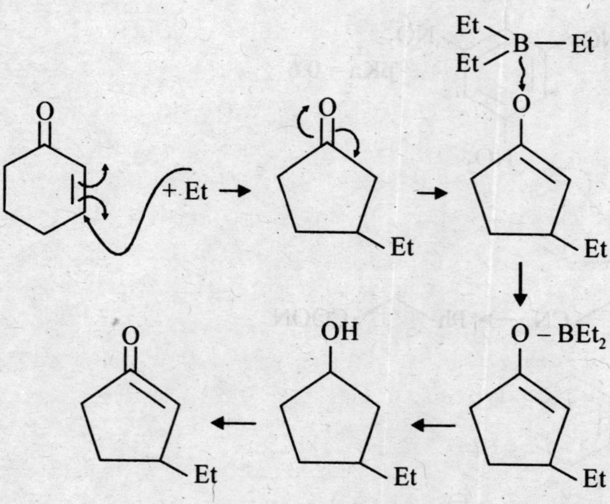

(A) 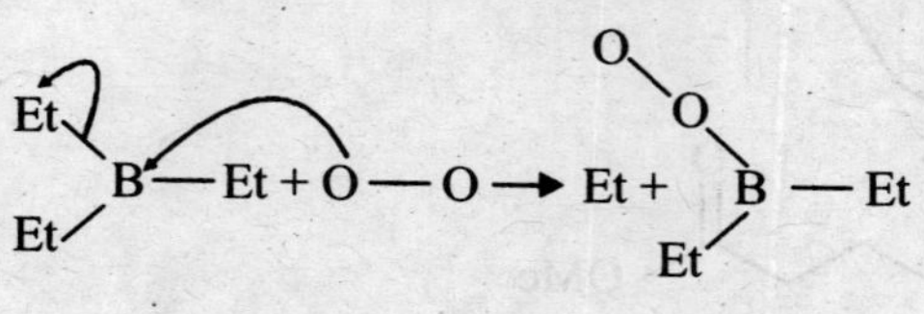

(B) 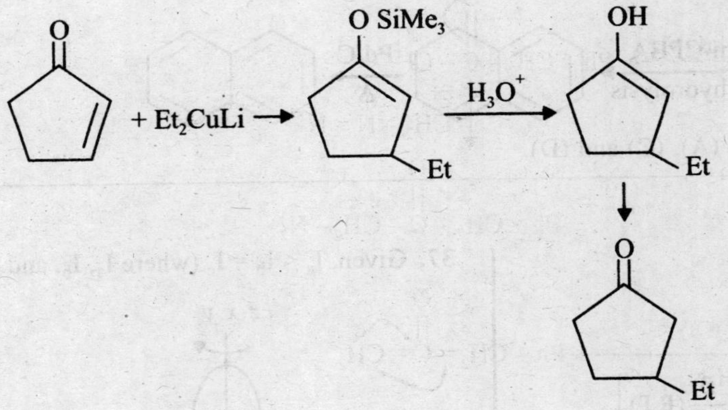

(C) (C) is incorrect.

(D) 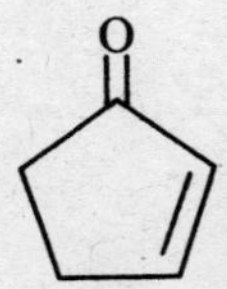 hard

So, (D) is incorrect.

Thus, correct answers are (A) and (B).

35. (A) 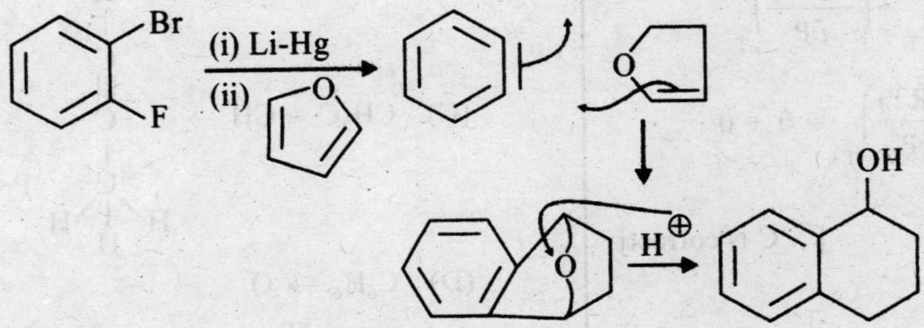

(B) 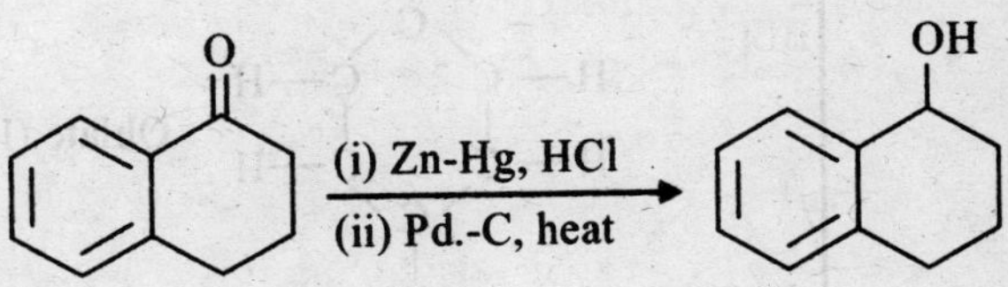

(C) 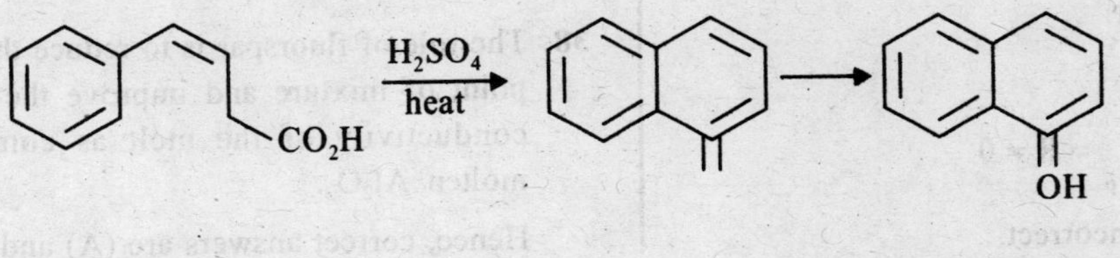

(D) 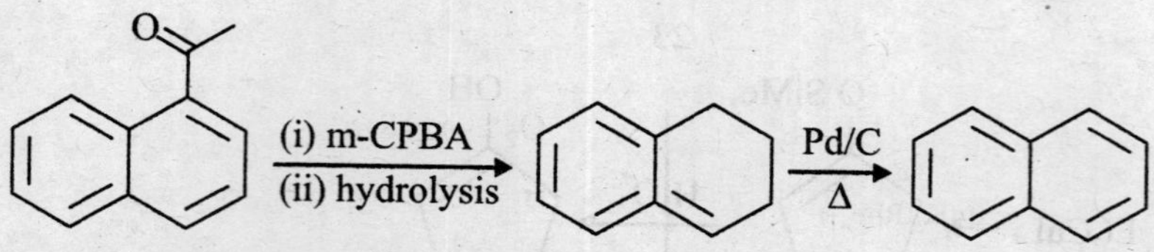

Hence, correct answers are (A), (C) and (D).

---

36. We know that, $PV = RT$

$H = U + PV = U + RT$

We have,

(A) $\left(\frac{\partial H}{\partial V}\right)_T = \left(\frac{\partial U}{\partial V}\right)_T + \left[\frac{\partial}{\partial V}(RT)\right]_T$

$= 0 + 0 = 0$

$\therefore \left(\frac{\partial H}{\partial V}\right)_T = 0$ [∴ A is correct]

(B) $\left(\frac{\partial T}{\partial P}\right)_H = \mu_{JT} = 0$ (For ideal gas)

[∴ B is correct]

(C) $\left(\frac{\partial H}{\partial P}\right)_T = \left(\frac{\partial U}{\partial P}\right)_T + \left(\frac{\partial (PV)}{\partial P}\right)_T$

$= \left(\frac{\partial U}{\partial P}\right)_T + \left(\frac{\partial (RT)}{\partial P}\right)_T = 0 + 0$

$\therefore \left(\frac{\partial H}{\partial P}\right)_T = 0$ [∴ C is correct]

(D) $\left(\frac{\partial H}{\partial T}\right)_P = \left[\frac{\partial}{\partial T}(U + RT)\right]$

$= \left(\frac{\partial U}{\partial T}\right)_P + \left(\frac{\partial (RT)}{\partial T}\right)_P$

$= \left(\frac{\partial U}{\partial T}\right)_P + R$

$= 0 + R$

$\therefore \left(\frac{\partial H}{\partial T}\right)_P = R \neq 0$

Hence, (D) is incorrect.

37. Given, $I_a < I_b = I_c$ (where I_a, I_b, and I_c are Mt)

Prolate

(A) HCN → linear

(B) CH_3Cl → 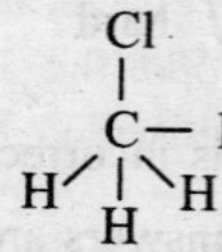 Prolate

(C) $CH_3C \equiv CH$ →  Prolate

(D) C_6H_6 → O

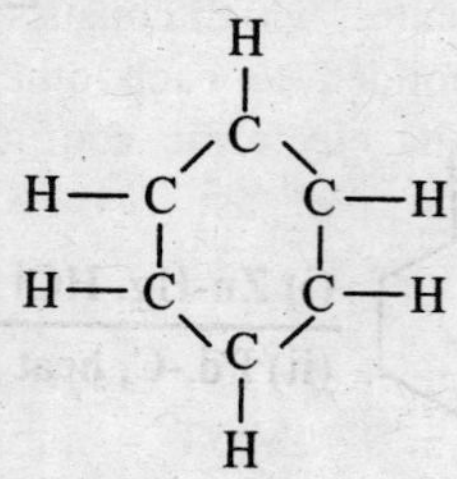 Oblate ($I_a = I_b < I_c$)

38. The role of fluorspar is to reduce the melting point of mixture and improve the electrical conductivity of the melt as compared to molten Al_2O_3.

Hence, correct answers are (A) and (B).

39. We have,

3d	4d
I ($K_3[CoF_6]$)	II ($K_3[RhF_6]$)
Co^{+3} d^6, High spin	d^6, low spin

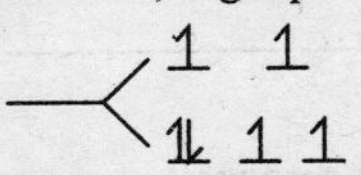

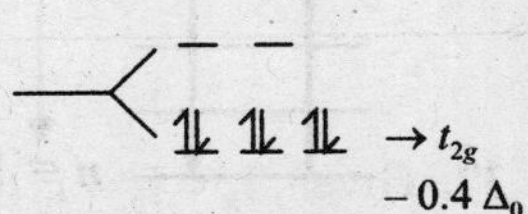

Paramagnetic	Diamagnetic
Low CFSE	High CFSE
(3d) – 0.4 Δ_0	(4d) – 2.4 Δ_0

Complex I → Paramagnetic   Complex II → Diamagnetic

CFSE of complex II > complex I

Hence, correct answers are (B), (C) and (D).

40. $1.B_2 = 10e^-$

The molecule's bond order is 1. The ground state electron configuration of B is $1s^22s^22p^1$. This means that the B^2 molecule has 10 electrons organised in MOs.

$$(\sigma_{1s})^2(\sigma_{1s})^2(\sigma_{2s})^2(\sigma_{2s})^2\left(\pi_{2p_y^1} = \pi_{2p_y^1}\right)$$

Bond order = $\frac{1}{2}$ (Number of bonding electrons – number of anti-bonding electrons)

$$= \frac{1}{2}(6-4) = 1$$

Lithium (Li_2) molecule belongs to the family of diatomic molecules, which consists of two lithium atoms, bonded to each other by a covalent bond. The electronic configuration of Li_2 molecule is given as:

Li_2 $(\sigma_{1s})^2$ $(\sigma^*_{1s})^2$ $(\sigma_{2s})^2$

Bond order = (number of electrons in bonding MOT – number of electrons in antibonding MOT)/2

$$\text{Bond order} = \frac{4-2}{2} = 1$$

Thus the Li_2 molecule is stable and is diamagnetic in nature due to the absence of unpaired electrons.

$O_2^{2-} \rightarrow 18\ e^-$

$\sigma_{1s}^2\ \sigma^{*2}_{1s}\ \sigma_{2s}^2\ \sigma^{*2}_{2s}\ \sigma_{pz}^2\ \pi_{2px}^2$

$= \pi_2^2\ py.$

For O_2^{2-} molecule, two electrons are added to $2px^1$ and $*2py^1$ orbitals.

$$\therefore \text{ Bond order} = \frac{10-8}{2} = 1$$

41.

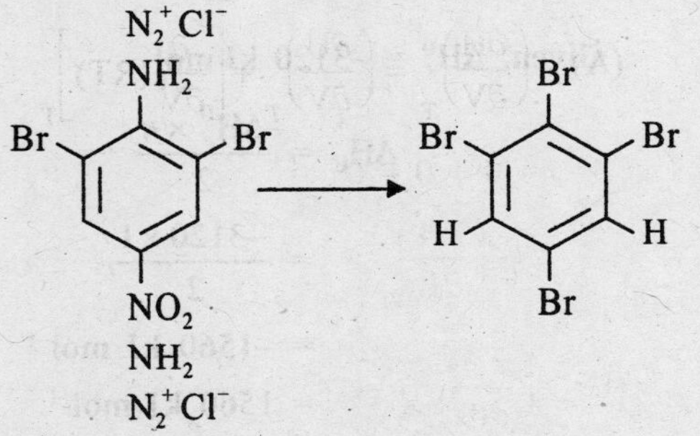

$= 6 \times 12 + 1 \times 2 + 4 \times 80$

$= 48 + 2 + 320$

$= 394.$

42. Given, $\rho = 0.06$ g/mL, $\alpha = 1.2°$, $b = 5$ cm $= 0.5$ mm

$$\therefore \text{ Specific rotation, } [\alpha]° = \frac{\alpha}{b+\rho}$$

$$= \frac{1.2°}{0.5 \times 0.06} - \frac{1.2}{0.030}$$

$$= \frac{1200}{30}$$

$= 40.$

43. Given, pka, = 2.19 and pka_2 = 4.25

$$\therefore \quad PI = \frac{pka_1 + pka_2}{2}$$

$$= \frac{2.19 + 4.25}{2}$$

$$= \frac{6.44}{2}$$

$= 3.22$

The isoelectric point of glutamic acid is 3.22.

44. We have, $\Delta(O_2) = 25 - 17.5 = 7.5$ mol

2 moles of $C_6H_6 = 15O_2$

$\therefore$ 15 moles of $O_2 \rightarrow$ 2 moles of C_6H_6

$\therefore$ 1 mole of $O_2 = \dfrac{2 \text{ moles of } C_6H_6}{15}$

7.5 moles of $O_2 = \dfrac{2 \times 7.5}{15}$ 1 mol (= n)

Given, $\Delta H_r^0 = -3120$ kJ/mol

$$\therefore \quad \Delta H_C = \frac{\Delta H_r^0 \times n}{2}$$

$$= \frac{-3120 \times 1}{2}$$

$$= -1560 \text{ kJ mol}^{-1}$$

$$= 1560 \text{ kJ mol}^{-1}.$$

45. Given, $C \xleftarrow{k_2} A \xrightarrow{k_1} B,\ k_1 = 2k_2$

We have, $[B_t] = \dfrac{k_1}{k_1 + k_2}\left[1 - e^{-(k_1+k_2)t}\right]$ –

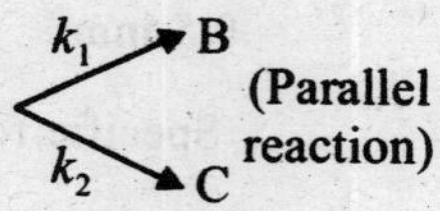

and $[C_t] = \dfrac{k_2}{k_1 + k_2}\left[1 - e^{-(k_1+k_2)t}\right]$

$$\therefore \quad \frac{[B_t]}{[C_t]} = \frac{[B]}{[C]} = \frac{\dfrac{k_1}{k_1+k_2}\left[1 - e^{-(k_1+k_2)t}\right]}{\dfrac{k_2}{k_1+k_2}\left[1 - e^{-(k_1+k_2)t}\right]}$$

$$\frac{[B_t]}{[C_t]} = \frac{[B]}{[C]} = \frac{k_1}{k_2}$$

$$\therefore \quad \frac{[B]}{[C]} = \frac{k_1}{k_2} = \frac{2k_1}{k_2} = 2$$

$$\therefore \quad \frac{[B]}{[C]} = 2.$$

46.

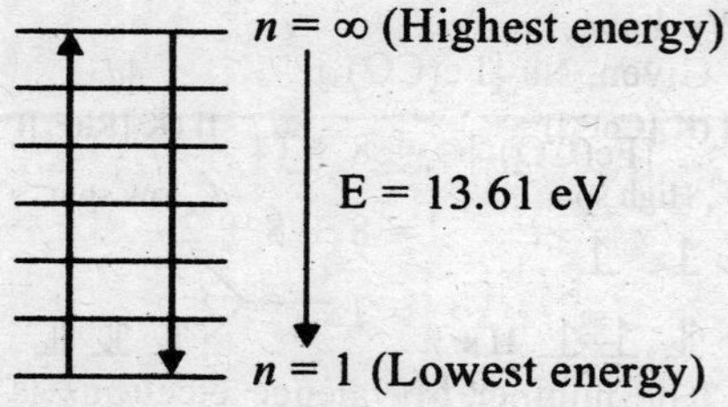

As, $\dfrac{1}{\lambda} = R_H\left(\dfrac{1}{n_1^2} - \dfrac{1}{n_2^2}\right)$

$n_1 = 1$ and $n_2 = \infty$

$$\therefore \quad \Delta E = R_H\left(\frac{1}{n_1^2} - \frac{1}{n_2^2}\right)$$

$$= 13.61\left(\frac{1}{1^2} - \frac{1}{0^2}\right)$$

$$= 13.61 \times \left(\frac{1}{1}\right)$$

$$= 13.61 \text{ eV}.$$

47. Given, $Fe^{3+} \rightarrow Fe^{2+}\ E_1^0 = 0.77$ V

$Fe^{2+} \rightarrow Fe\ E_2^0 = -0.44$ V

We have,

$Fe^{3+} \rightarrow Fe^{2+}$

$Fe^{2+} \rightarrow Fe$

$Fe^{3+} \rightarrow Fe$

$[n_1 = 1,\ n_2 = 2,\ n = n_1 + n_2 = 1 + 2 = 3]$

$$\therefore \quad E^0 = \frac{n_1E_1^0 + n_2E_2^0}{n}$$

$$= \frac{1 \times 0.77 + 2 \times (-0.44)}{3}$$

$$= \frac{0.77 - 0.88}{3}$$

$$= -0.0366$$

$$= -0.037.$$

48. Given, $Na_2[Fe(CO)_4]$

$\therefore\ [Fe(CO)_4]^{2-} = 8 + (4 \times 2) + 2$

$= 8 + 8 + 2$

$= 18\ e^{\ominus}$

The number of valence electrons is

$Na_2\ [Fe(CO)_4]$ is 18.

49. Given:

Heat of atomization of Cu = +338 kJ/mol^{-1},

Ionization energy of Cu = +746 kJ/mol^{-1},

Heat of atomization of Cl_2 = +121 kJ/mol^{-1},

Electron affinity of Cl = –349 kJ/mol^{-1},

Lattice energy of CuCl = –973 kJ/mol^{-1}]

Here, CuCl(s)

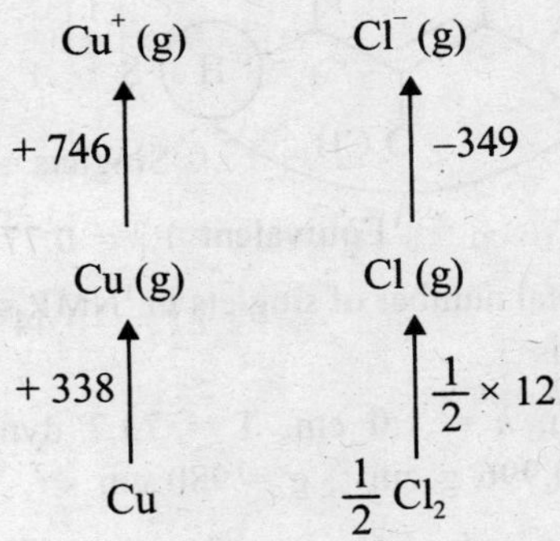

Now, $Cu^+(g) + Cl^-(g) \xrightarrow{-973} CuCl(s)$

$$Cu^+(g) + \frac{1}{2}Cl_2(g) \longrightarrow CuCl(s)$$

$\Delta°Hr$ = Heat of atomisation of Cu + Ionization energy T

Heat of atomisation of $\frac{1}{2}Cl_2$ + Electron affinity T

Lattice energy of CuCl

$= 338 + 746 + \frac{1}{2} \times 121 - 349 - 973$

$= 338 + 746 + 60.5 - 349 - 973$

$= -177.5$ kJ mol^{-1}

$\simeq -177.0$ kJ mol^{-1}

Hence, in the Born-Haber cycle, the heat of formation of CuCl is – 177 kJ/mol.

50. $\mu = \sqrt{n(n+2)}$

$B_2 \rightarrow 10\ e^-$

$\sigma_{1s}^2\ \sigma^*{}_{1s}^2\ \sigma_{2s}^2\ \sigma^*{}_{2s}^2\ \pi^*{}_{2px}^1 = \pi_{2py}^1$

$n = 2$

$\therefore \quad \mu = \sqrt{2(2+2)}$

$= \sqrt{2 \times 4}$

$= \sqrt{8}$

$= 2.83$ BM.

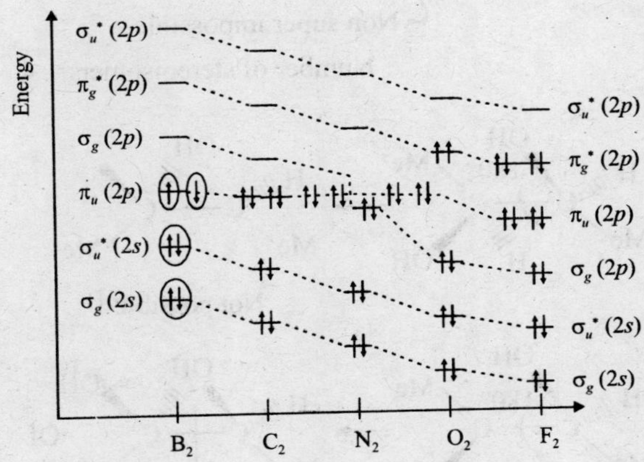

51. We have,

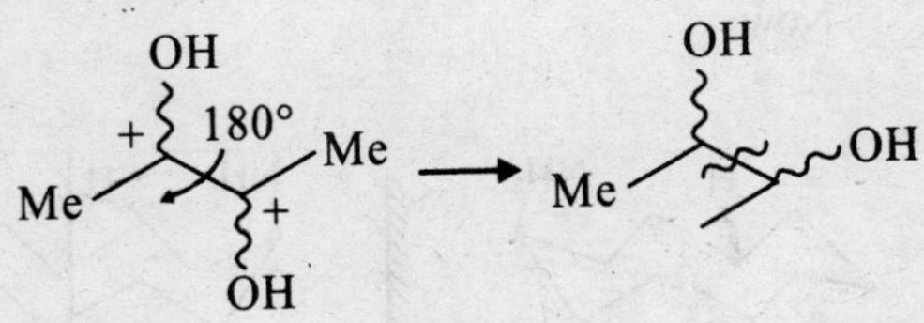

(A) So, $\quad SI = 2^{n-1} + 2^{\frac{n}{2}-1}$

$= 2^{2-1} + 2^{\frac{2}{2}-1}$

$= 2 + 2°$

$= 2 + 1$

$= 3$

$\therefore$ No. of stereoisomers in A = 3

Now,

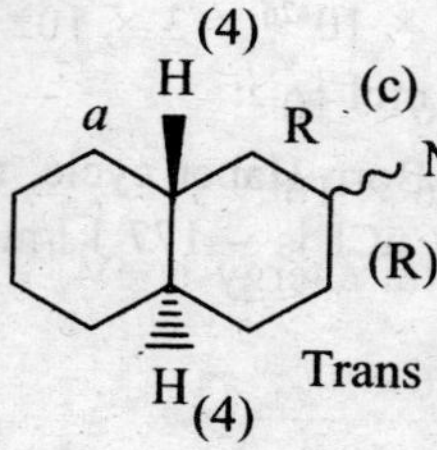

(a)	(b)	(c) NH$_2$
R	R	R → OA
R	R	S → OA

SSR

SSR

↳ Non super impossible

∴ Number of stereoisomers = 4

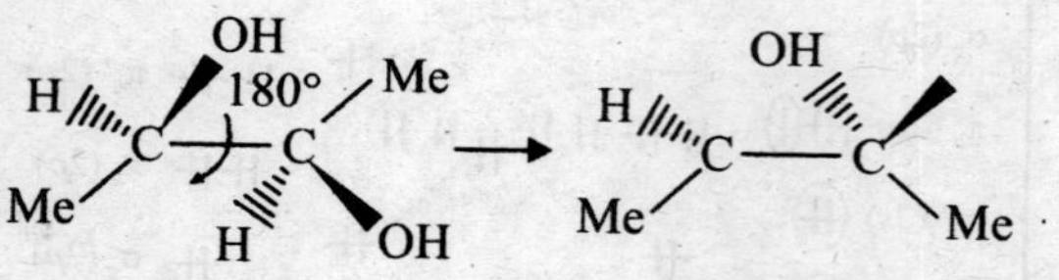

Not possible

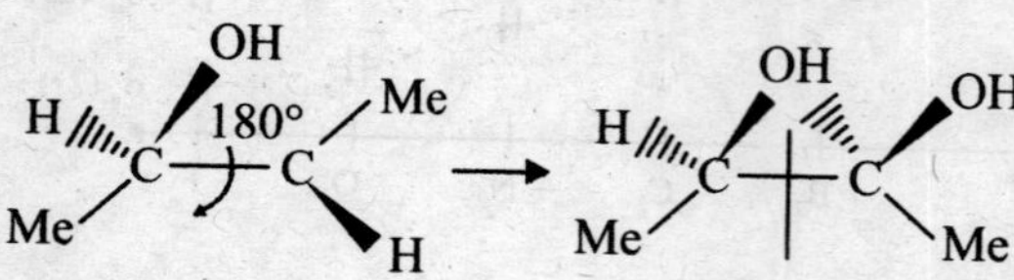

OI

Now,

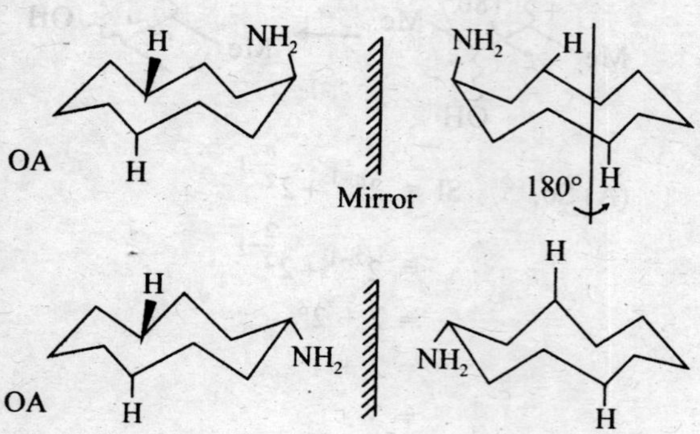

∴ Sum of the total number of stereoisomers

$$= 3 + 4$$

$$= 7$$

52. Given,

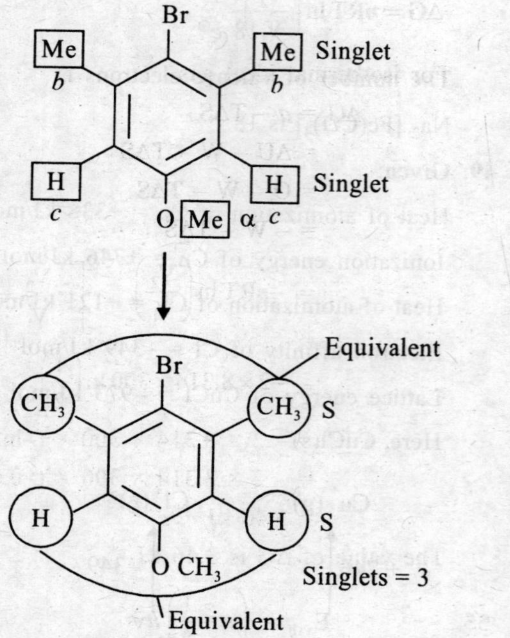

∴ Total number of singlets in [1]NMR spectrum of P is 3.

53. Given, h = 1.0 cm, T = 73.2 dyne cm^{-1}, ρ = 0.996 g cm^{-3}, g = 980 cm s^{-2}.

Where surface tension of water = T

As, $$T = \frac{h\rho g r_c}{2}$$

where $r_c \rightarrow$ radius of capillary tube

$$\therefore \quad r_c = \frac{2T}{h\rho g}$$

$$= \frac{2 \times 73.2}{1.0 \times 0.996 \times 980}$$

$$= \frac{146.4}{976.08}$$

$$= 0.150 \text{ cm.}$$

54. We know that

$$\Delta G = nRT \ln\left(\frac{P_2}{P_1}\right), \quad \Delta G = nRT \ln\left(\frac{V_2}{V_1}\right)$$

$$\Delta G = nRT \ln\left(\frac{V_2}{V_1}\right)$$

For isothermal ideal gas

$$\Delta G = q - T\Delta S$$

$$= \Delta U - W - T\Delta S$$

$$= O - W - T\Delta S$$

$$= -W - T\Delta S$$

$$= -nRT \ln\left(\frac{V_2}{V_1}\right) \qquad \left[\because \frac{V_2}{V_1} = \frac{1}{2}\right]$$

$$= -2 \times 8.314 \times 300 \ln\left(\frac{1}{2}\right)$$

$$= -2 \times 8.314 \times 300 \times (-\ln 2)$$

$$= -2 \times 8.314 \times 300 \times (-0.693)$$

$$= 3.46 \text{ kJ}$$

The value of ΔG is 3.46 kJ.

55.

$$E_{vib} = \left(n + \frac{1}{2}\right) h\nu$$

$$= \left(n + \frac{1}{2}\right) hc\bar{\nu}$$

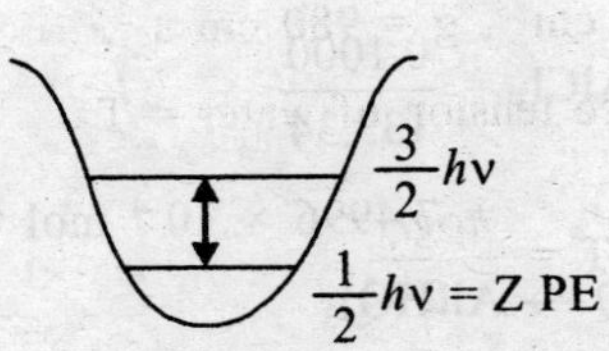

$$\bar{\nu} = 2000 \text{ cm}^{-1}$$

$$= 2 \times 10^3 \times 10^2 \text{ m}^{-1}$$

$$= 2 \times 10^5$$

ZPE $\Rightarrow n = 0$

$$E_{vib} = \frac{1}{2} hc\bar{\nu}$$

$$= \frac{1}{2} \times 6.62 \times 10^{-34} \times 3 \times 10^8 \times 2 \times 10^5$$

$$= 6.62 \times 10^{-26} \times 3 \times 10^5$$

$$= 19.86 \times 10^{-21}$$

$$= 1.986 \times 10^{-20} \text{ J}$$

Now, zero point energy is eV

$$= \frac{1.986 \times 10^{-20}}{1.6 \times 10^{-19}} \text{ eV}$$

$$= 1.2 \times 10^{-1} \text{ eV}$$

$$= 0.12 \text{ eV.}$$

56. Given, $k = 2.5 \times 10^{-3}$ dm^3 mol^{-1} s^{-1}

At = 0.2 mol dm^{-3}

A_0 = 0.4 mol dm^{-3}

Here, $2A \rightarrow P$

$$\text{As, } \frac{1}{A_t} = \frac{1}{A_0} + 2kt$$

$$\Rightarrow \frac{1}{0.2} = \frac{1}{0.4} + 2kt$$

$$\Rightarrow \frac{10}{2} = \frac{10}{4} + 2kt$$

$$\Rightarrow \frac{10}{2} - \frac{10}{4} = 2kt$$

$$\Rightarrow \frac{20 - 10}{4} = 2kt$$

$$\Rightarrow \frac{10}{4} = 2kt$$

$$\Rightarrow 2.5 = 2kt$$

$$\therefore \quad t = \frac{2.5}{2 \times 2.5 \times 10^{-3}}$$

$$= \frac{1}{2 \times 10^{-3}}$$

$$= \frac{10^3}{2}$$

$$= \frac{1000}{2}$$

$$= 500 \text{ s}$$

Thus, time required for the concentration is 500 s.

57. Given, $h\nu = h\nu_0 + \frac{1}{2}mV^2$

For metal M_2, $h\nu = 2.9$

M_1 $h\nu_0 = 2.3$

$\therefore 2.9 = 2.3 + \frac{1}{2}mV^2$

$\Rightarrow \frac{1}{2}mV^2 = 2.9 - 2.3 = 0.6$ eV

$\Rightarrow$ E = 0.6 eV

As, $\lambda = \frac{h}{\sqrt{2mE}}$

$$= \frac{6.62 \times 10^{-34}}{\sqrt{2 \times 9.11 \times 10^{-31} \times 0.6\,\text{eV}}}$$

$$= \frac{6.62 \times 10^{-34}}{\sqrt{2 \times 9.11 \times 10^{-31} \times 0.6 \times 1.6 \times 10^{-19}}}$$

$$= \frac{6.62 \times 10^{-34}}{\sqrt{2 \times 9.11 \times 0.6 \times 1.9 \times 10^{-50}}}$$

$$= \frac{6.62 \times 10^{-34} \times 10^{25}}{\sqrt{20.77}}$$

$$= \frac{6.62 \times 10^{-9}}{4.56}$$

$= 1.583 \times 10^{-9}$ m

= 1.58 nm.

58. We have,

$Fe^{+3} \longrightarrow d^5$ (LHS)

↿ ↿ e_g

↿ ↿ ↿ t_{2g}

$n = 5$

$\therefore \quad \mu = \sqrt{n(n+2)}$

$= \sqrt{5(5+2)}$

$= \sqrt{5 \times 7}$

$= \sqrt{35}$

= 5.92 BM

Thus, the spin magnetic moment of $[Fe(acac)_3]$ is 5.92 BM.

59. $C_2H_4 + H_2 \rightarrow C_2H_6$

Molar mass 28 2 30

Moles $\frac{2}{28}k$ mol $\left(\frac{2}{2}\right)k$ mol

Less More

So, limiting reagents decides amount of products.

CH_4	C_2H_6
1 mol	30
$\frac{2}{28}k$ mol	$\frac{2}{28} \times 30$ kg

$100\% \rightarrow \frac{30}{14}$ kg

$1\% \rightarrow \frac{30}{14 \times 100}$

$\therefore 90\% \rightarrow \frac{90 \times 30}{14 \times 100}$

$= \frac{27}{14} = 1.93$

Therefore amount of ethane (C_2H_6) produced in reaction is 1.93 kg.

60. Given, weight of sample = 0.1000 g

Mol of $AlCl_3 = \frac{0.1000}{133.34}$

$= 7.4996 \times 10^{-4}$ mol

$AlCl_3 + 3HQ \rightarrow Al(HQ)_3$

$= 26.98 + 3 \times 145.16$

$= 26.98 + 435.48$

$= 462.46$ g mol^{-1}

$\therefore$ Mass of ppt $= 7.4996 \times 10^{-4} \times 462.46$

= 0.3468 g

$\simeq$ 0.3452

Hence, the weight of the precipitate is 0.3468 g.

Previous Years Paper

IIT–JAM

JOINT ADMISSION TEST FOR M.Sc. (CHEMISTRY), 2022

Section A : Multiple Choice Questions (MCQ)

Directions: (Q. No. 1 to 10) *Carry **One** mark each.*

1. The reagent required for the following transformation

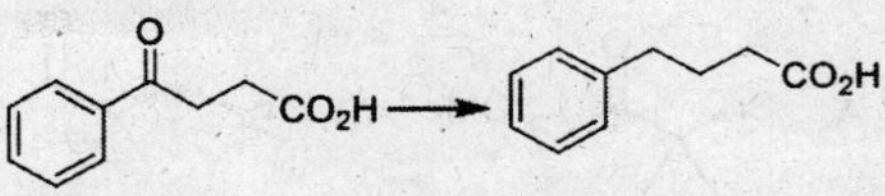 is:

A. $NaBH_4$
B. $LiAlH_4$
C. $H_3B{\cdot}THF$
D. Zn(Hg)/HCl

2. The major product formed in the following reaction

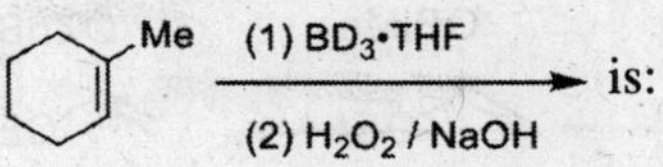 is:

A. 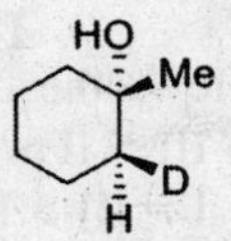
(±)

B. 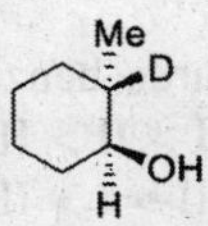
(±)

C. 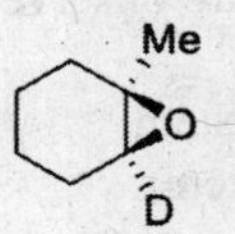
(±)

D. 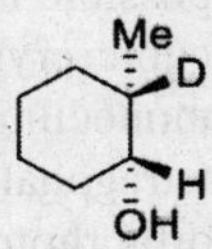
(±)

3. The major product formed in the following reaction

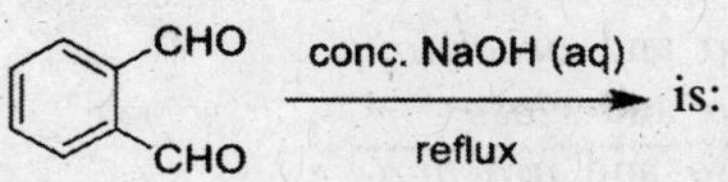 is:

A. 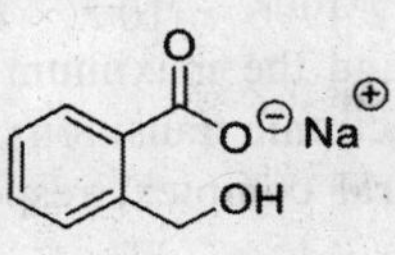

B. 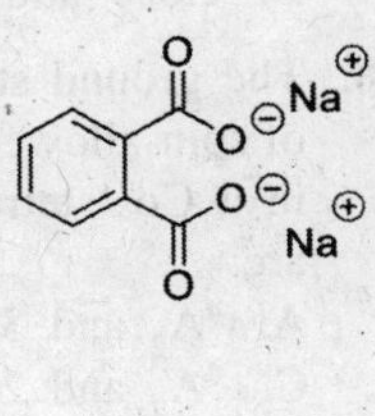

C. 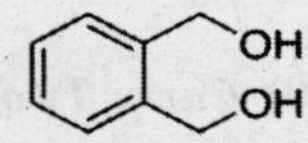

D. 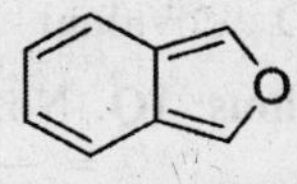

4. The major product formed in the following reaction $K + O_2 \rightarrow$ is:

A. K_2O
B. K_2O_2
C. KO_2
D. K_2O_3

5. Which one of the following options is best suited for effecting the transformation?

A. MnO_2
B. DMSO, $(COCl)_2$, Et_3N
C. $Al(Oi\text{-}Pr)_3$
D. Ag_2O/NH_4OH

6. The structure of $[XeF_8]^{2-}$ is:

A. cubic
B. hexagonal bipyramid
C. square antiprism
D. octagonal

7. Among the following, the compound that forms the strongest hydrogen bond is:

A. HF
B. HCl
C. HBr
D. HI

8. Among the following, the biomolecule with a direct metal-carbon bond is:

A. coenzyme B_{12}
B. nitrogenase
C. chlorophyll
D. hemoglobin

9. For the reaction

$H_2PO_2^-\,(aq) + OH^-\,(aq) \rightarrow HPO_3^{2-}\,(aq) + H_2(g)$

the rate expression is $k[H_2PO_2^-][OH^-]^2$. If the

concentration of $H_2PO_2^-$ is doubled, the rate is:

A. tripled B. halved

C. doubled D. unchanged

10. The nature of interaction involved at the gas-solid interface in physisorption is:

A. ionic

B. van der Waals

C. hydrogen bonding

D. covalent

Directions: (Q. No. 11 to 30) *Carry* ***Two*** *marks each.*

11. The major product formed in the following reaction

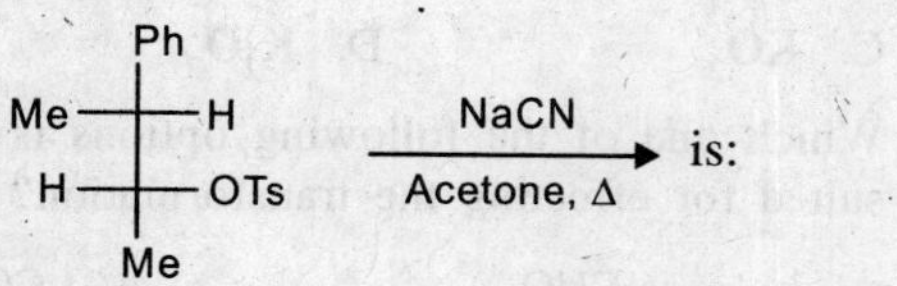

A. 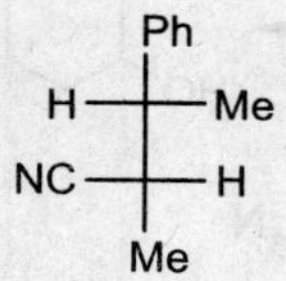 B. 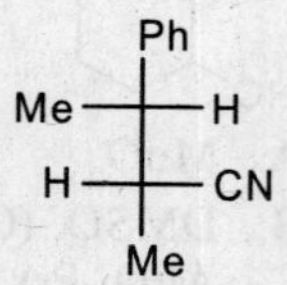

C. 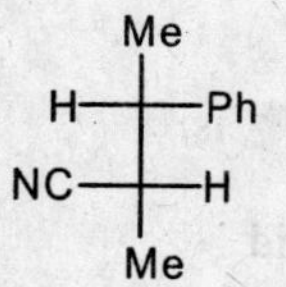 D. 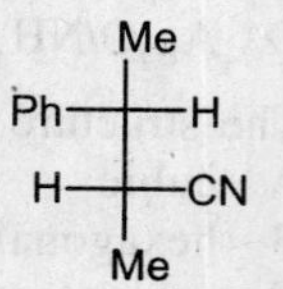

12. An organic compound having molecular formula $C_9H_{10}O_2$ exhibits the following spectral characteristics:

^{1}H NMR: δ 9.72 (*t*, 1H), 7.1 (*d*, 2H), 6.7 (*d*, 2H), 3.8 (*s*, 3H), 3.6 (*d*, 2H)

IR: ~1720 cm^{-1}

The most probable structure of the compound is:

A. 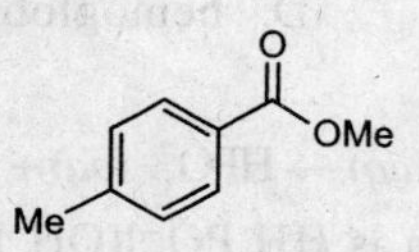 B. 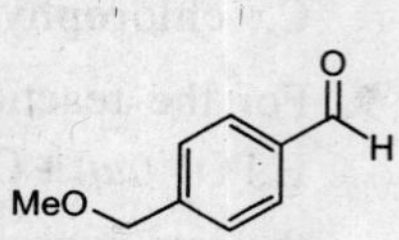

C. 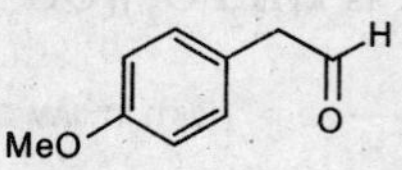 D. 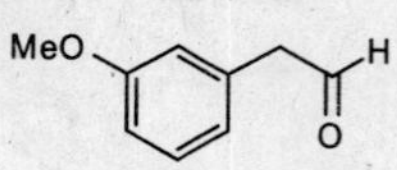

13. The major product formed in the reaction of (2S, 3R)-2-chloro-3-phenylbutane with NaOEt in EtOH is:

A. (E)-2-phenyl-but-2-ene

B. (Z)-2-phenyl-but-2-ene

C. 3-phenyl-but-1-ene

D. (2R,3R)-2-ethoxy-3-phenylbutane

14. The major product formed in the following reaction

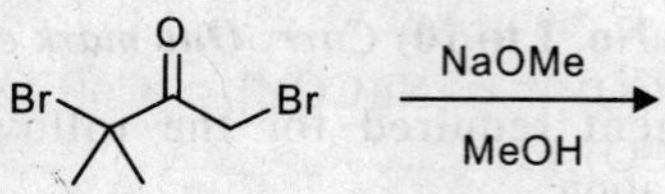 is:

A. 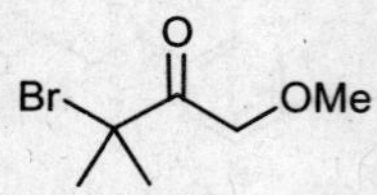 B. 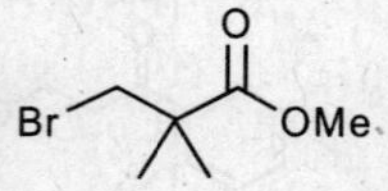

C. 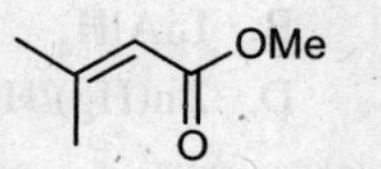 D. 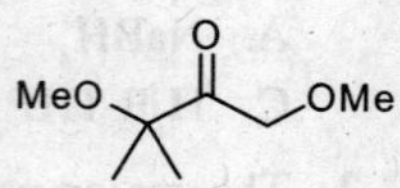

15. The reactivity of the enol derivatives

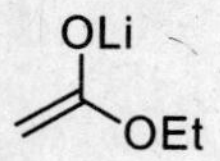 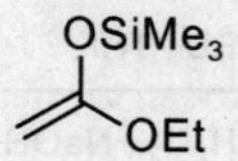 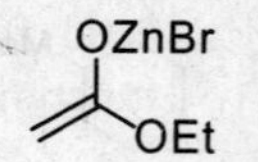

I II III

towards benzaldehyde follows the order:

A. I > II > III B. III > II > I

C. II > I > III D. I > III > II

16. All possible lattice types are observed in the:

A. cubic crystal system

B. monoclinic crystal system

C. tetragonal crystal system

D. orthorhombic crystal system

17. The structure types of [$B_{10}H_{10}^{2-}$] and [$B_{10}H_{14}$], respectively, are:

A. *closo* and *nido*

B. *nido* and *arachno*

C. *nido* and *closo*

D. *closo* and *arachno*

18. The ground state and the maximum number of spin-allowed electronic transitions possible in a Co^{2+} tetrahedral complex, respectively, are:

A. $^4A_2$ and 3 B. $^4T_1$ and 2

C. $^4A_2$ and 2 D. $^4T_1$ and 3

19. The correct statement about the geometries of BH_2^+ and NH_2^+ based on valence shell electron pair repulsion (VSEPR) theory is
A. both BH_2^+ and NH_2^+ are trigonal planar
B. BH_2^+ is linear and NH_2^+ is trigonal planar
C. BH_2^+ is trigonal planar and NH_2^+ is linear
D. both BH_2^+ and NH_2^+ are linear

20. The order of increasing CO stretching frequencies in $[Co(CO)_4]^-$, $[Cu(CO)_4]^+$, $[Fe(CO)_4]^{2-}$ and $[Ni(CO)_4]$ is:
A. $[Cu(CO)_4]^+ < [Ni(CO)_4] < [Co(CO)_4]^- < [Fe(CO)_4]^{2-}$
B. $[Fe(CO)_4]^{2-} < [Co(CO)_4]^- < [Ni(CO)_4] < [Cu(CO)_4]^+$
C. $[Co(CO)_4]^- < [Fe(CO)_4]^{2-} < [Cu(CO)_4]^+ < [Ni(CO)_4]$
D. $[Ni(CO)_4] < [Cu(CO)_4]^+ < [Co(CO)_4]^- < [Fe(CO)_4]^{2-}$

21. The reaction of 2,4-dinitrofluorobenzene with hydrazine produces a yellow orange solid **X** used for the identification of an organic functional group **G**. **X** and **G**, respectively, are:

A. 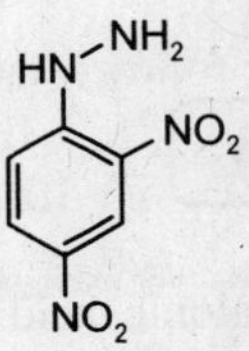

and carboxylic acid

B. 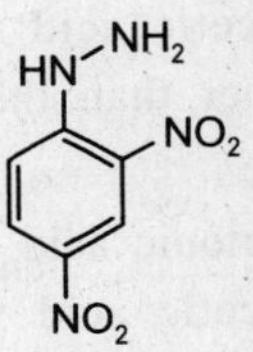

and aldehyde

C. 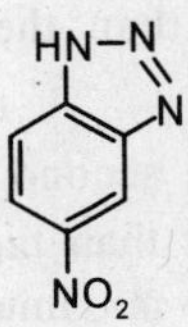

and aldehyde

D. 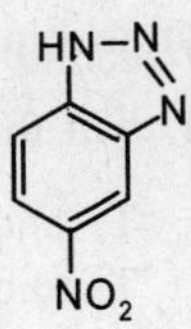

and carboxylic acid

22. The stability of adducts $H_3B·PF_3$, $H_3B·NMe_3$, $H_3B·CO$, $H_3B·OMe_2$ follows the order:
A. $H_3B·OMe_2 < H_3B·CO < H_3B·PF_3 < H_3B·NMe_3$
B. $H_3B·PF_3 < H_3B·CO < H_3B·NMe_3 < H_3B·OMe_2$
C. $H_3B·CO < H_3B·PF_3 < H_3B·NMe_3 < H_3B·OMe_2$
D. $H_3B·PF_3 < H_3B·CO < H_3B·OMe_2 < H_3B·NMe_3$

23. The spacing between successive rotational energy levels of a diatomic molecule XY and its heavier isotopic analogue X′Y′ varies with the rotational quantum number, J, as:

A. 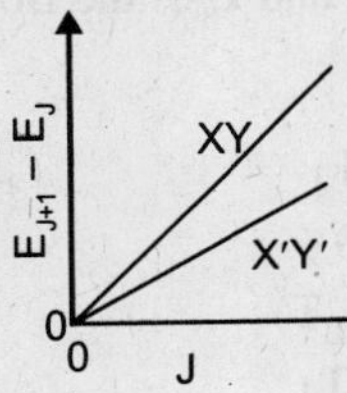

B. 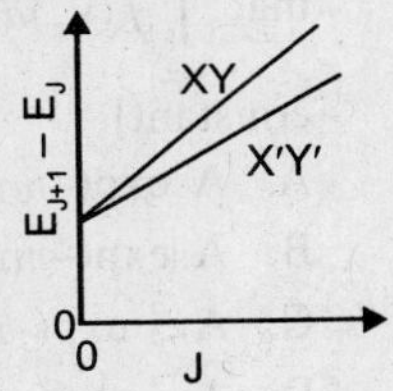

C. 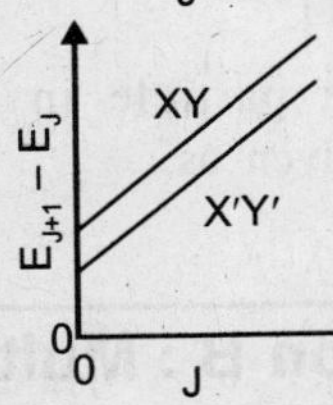

D. 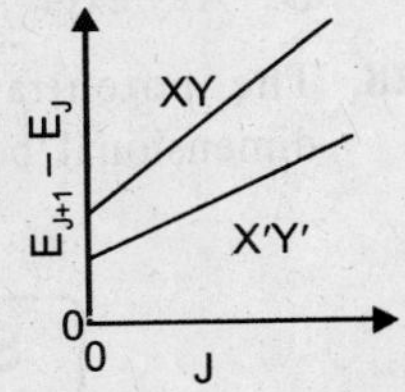

24. The ratio of the $2p \rightarrow 1s$ transition energy in He^+ to that in the H atom is closest to:
A. 1
B. 2
C. 4
D. 8

25. The phase diagram of water is best represented by:

A. 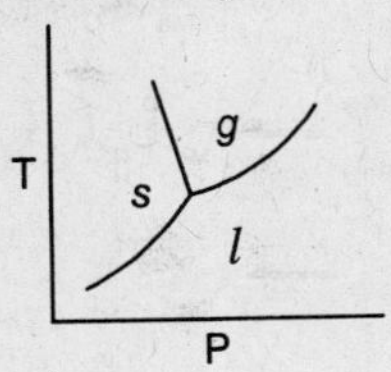

B. 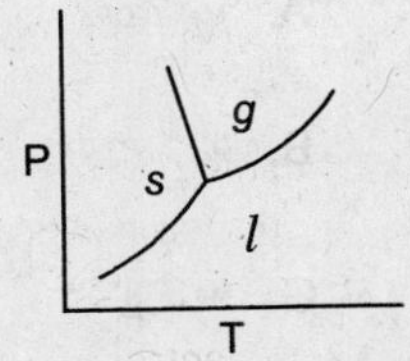

C. 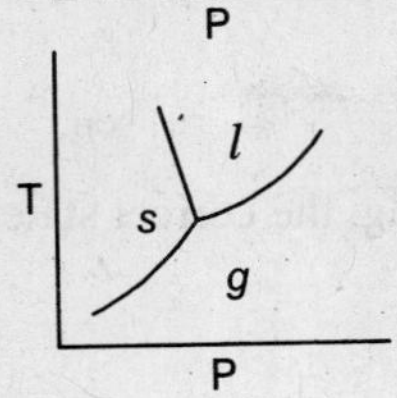

D. 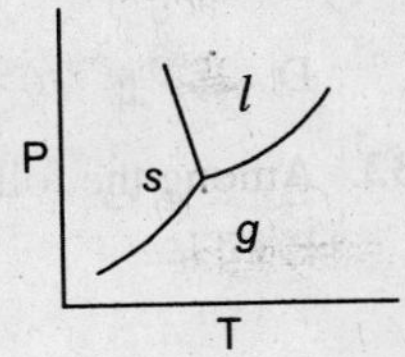

26. Capillary W contains water and capillary M contains mercury. The contact angles between the capillary wall and the edge of the meniscus at the air-liquid interface in W and M are θ_W and θ_M, respectively.

The contact angles satisfy the conditions

A. $\theta_W > 90°$ and $\theta_M > 90°$
B. $\theta_W > 90°$ and $\theta_M < 90°$
C. $\theta_W < 90°$ and $\theta_M > 90°$
D. $\theta_W < 90°$ and $\theta_M < 90°$

27. The Maxwell-Boltzmann distribution $f(v_x)$ of one-dimensional velocities v_x at temperature T is

[Given: A is a normalization constant such that $\int_{-\infty}^{\infty} f(v_x)dv_x = 1$, and k_B is the Boltzmann constant]

A. $A \exp(-mv_x^2/2k_BT)$
B. $A \exp(-mv_x^2/k_BT)$
C. $Av_x^2 \exp(-mv_x^2/2k_BT)$
D. $Av_x^2 \exp(-mv_x^2/k_BT)$

28. The potential for a particle in a one-dimensional box is given as:

$V(x) = 0$ for $0 \le x \le L$, and $V(x) = \infty$ elsewhere.

The locations of the internal nodes of the eigenfunctions $\psi_n(x)$, $n \ge 2$, are:

[Given: m is an integer such that $0 < m < n$]

A. $x = \frac{m+\frac{1}{2}}{n}L$ B. $x = \frac{m}{n}L$
C. $x = \frac{m}{n+1}L$ D. $x = \frac{m+1}{n+1}L$

29. The number of CO stretching bands in the infrared spectrum of $Fe(CO)_5$ is:

A. 1 B. 2
C. 3 D. 4

30. The standard Gibbs free energy change for the reaction

$$H_2O(g) \rightarrow H_2(g) + \frac{1}{2} O_2(g)$$

at 2500 K is +118 kJ mol^{-1}.

The equilibrium constant for the reaction is

[Given: R = 8.314 J K^{-1} mol^{-1}]

A. 0.994 B. 1.006
C. 3.42×10^{-3} D. 292.12

Section B : Multiple Select Questions (MSQ)

Q. 31 – Q. 40 carry two marks each.

31. Among the following, the reaction(s) that favor(s) the formation of the products at 25°C is/are:

A. 

B. 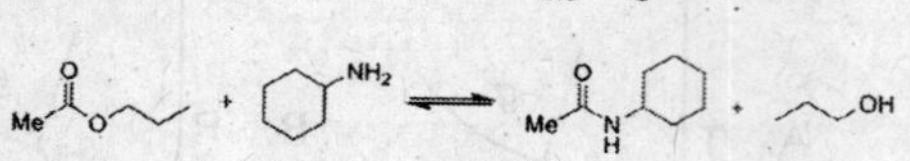

C. 

D. 

32. Among the following, the correct statement(s) is/are:

A. The first pK_a of malonic acid is lower than the pK_a of acetic acid while its second pK_a is higher than the pK_a of acetic acid.

B. The first pK_a of malonic acid is higher than the pK_a of acetic acid while its second pK_a is lower than the pK_a of acetic acid.

C. Both the first and the second pK_as of malonic acid are lower than the pK_a of acetic acid.

D. Both the first and the second pK_as of malonic acid are higher than the pK_a of acetic acid.

33. The compound(s) that participate(s) in Diels-Alder reaction with maleic anhydride is/are:

A. 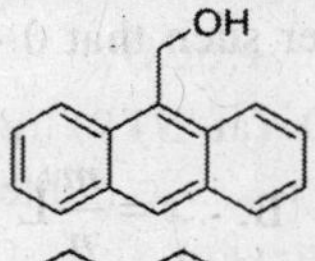
B. 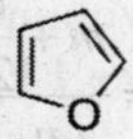
C. 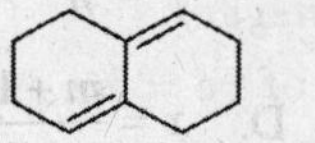
D. 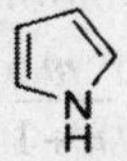

34. Among the following, the suitable route(s) for the conversion of benzaldehyde to acetophenone is/are:
A. CH_3COCl, anhydrous $AlCl_3$
B. (*i*) $HS(CH_2)_3SH$, $F_3B{\cdot}OEt_2$; (*ii*) n-BuLi; (*iii*) MeI; (*iv*) $HgCl_2$, $CdCO_3$, H_2O
C. $NaNH_2$, MeI
D. (*i*) MeMgBr; (*ii*) aq. acid; (*iii*) pyridinium chlorochromate (PCC)

35. The reaction

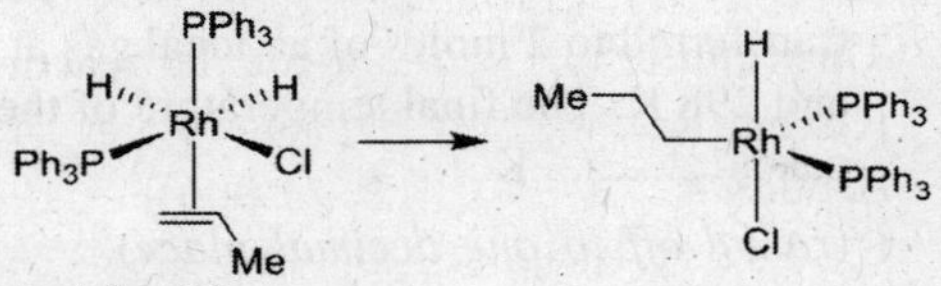

involve(s)
A. migratory insertion
B. change in electron count of Rh from 18 to 16
C. oxidative addition
D. change in electron count of Rh from 16 to 18

36. The reason(s) for the lower stability of Si_2H_6 compared to C_2H_6 is/are:
A. silicon is more electronegative than hydrogen
B. Si—Si bond is weaker than C—C bond
C. Si—H bond is weaker than C—H bond
D. the presence of low-lying *d*-orbitals in silicon

37. For an N-atom nonlinear polyatomic gas, the constant volume molar heat capacity $C_{v,m}$ has the expected value of 3(N – 1)R, based on the principle of equipartition of energy. The correct statement(s) about the measured value of $C_{v,m}$ is/are:
A. The measured $C_{v,m}$ is independent of temperature.
B. The measured $C_{v,m}$ is dependent on temperature.
C. The measured $C_{v,m}$ is typically lower than the expected value.
D. The measured $C_{v,m}$ is typically higher than the expected value.

38. Zinc containing enzyme(s) is/are:
A. carboxypeptidase
B. hydrogenase
C. carbonic anhydrase
D. urease

39. The conversion of ICl to ICl^+ involve(s)
A. the removal of an electron from a π^* molecular orbital of ICl
B. an increase in the bond order from 1 in ICl to 1.5 in ICl^+
C. the formation of a paramagnetic species
D. the removal of an electron from a molecular orbital localized predominantly on Cl

40. The common point defect(s) in a solid is/are:
A. Wadsley defect B. Schottky defect
C. Suzuki defect D. Frenkel defect

Section C : Numerical Answer Type (NAT)

Q. 41 – Q. 50 carry one mark each.

41. Among the following

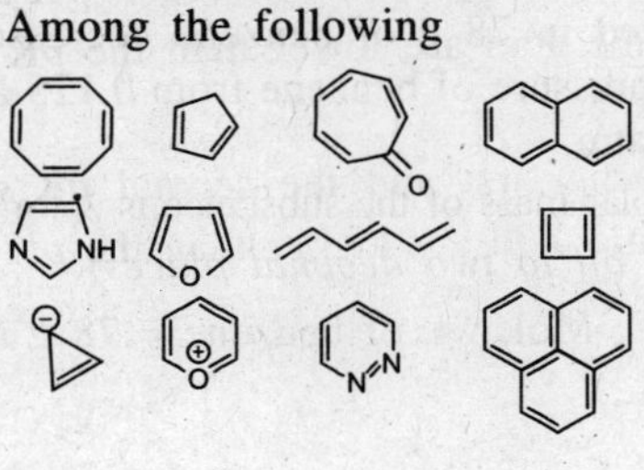

the number of aromatic compounds is ....

42. The number of stereoisomers possible for the major product formed in the reaction

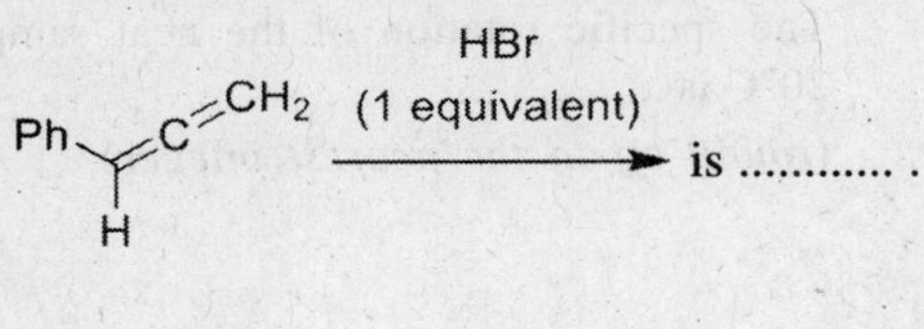

is ....

43. The number of signals observed in the ^1H NMR spectrum of the compound

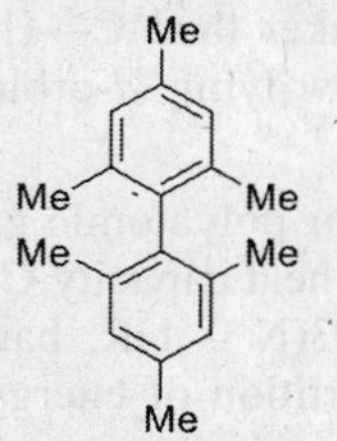

is ....

44. The reaction of 122 g of benzaldehyde with 108 g of phenylhydrazine gave 157 g of the product

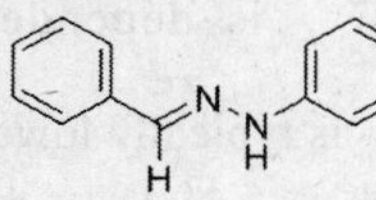

The yield of the product is .... %. *(round off to the nearest integer)*

45. The B–B bond order in B_2 is ....

46. The number of unpaired electrons in $[Co(H_2O)_6]^{2+}$ is ....

47. The number of significant figures in 5.0820×10^2 is ....

48. The *d* spacing for the first-order X-ray ($\lambda = 1.54$ Å) diffraction event of metallic iron (*fcc*) at $2\theta = 20.2°$ is .... Å. *(round off to three decimal places)*.

49. The volume fraction for an element in an *fcc* lattice is ..... . *(round off to two decimal places)*

50. A steady current of 1.25 A is passed through an electrochemical cell for 1.5 h using a 12 V battery. The total charge, Q, drawn during this process is .... Coulombs. *(round off to the nearest integer)*

Q. 51 – Q. 60 carry two marks each.

51. The specific rotation of optically pure (R)-1-phenylethylamine is +40 (neat, 20°C). A synthetic sample of the same compound is shown to contain 4:1 mixture of (S)- and (R)-enantiomers.

The specific rotation of the neat sample at 20°C is ....

(round off to the nearest integer)

52. The number of β particles emitted in the nuclear reaction $^{238}_{92}U \rightarrow \,^{206}_{82}Pb$ is ....

53. Iron is extracted from its ore via the reaction.

$Fe_2O_3 + 3CO \rightarrow 2Fe + 3CO_2$

The volume of CO (at STP) required to produce 1 kg of iron is .... liters. *(round off to the nearest integer)*

[Given : Atomic wt. of Fe = 56; assume STP to be 0°C and 1 atm]

54. Total degeneracy (number of microstates) for a Ti^{3+} ion in spherical symmetry is ....

55. A galvanic electrochemical cell made of Zn^{2+}/Zn and Cu^{2+}/Cu half-cells produces 1.10 V at 25°C. The ratio of $[Zn^{2+}]$ to $[Cu^{2+}]$ is maintained at 1.0. The $\Delta G°$ for the reaction when 1.0 mol of Zn gets dissolved is .... kJ. *(round off to the nearest integer)*

[Given : Faraday's constant = 96485 C mol^{-1}]

56. At constant volume, 1.0 kJ of heat is transferred to 2 moles of an ideal gas at 1 atm and 298 K. The final temperature of the ideal gas is .... K.

(round off to one decimal place)

[Given; R = 8.314 J K^{-1} mol^{-1}]

57. Two close lying bands in a UV spectrum occur at 274 nm and 269 nm. The magnitude of the energy gap between the two bands is .... cm^{-1}

(round off to the nearest integer)

58. The pH of an aqueous buffer prepared using CH_3COOH and $CH_3COO^-Na^+$ is 4.80. The quantity $\frac{[CH_3COO^-]-[CH_3COOH]}{[CH_3COOH]}$ is ....

(round off to three decimal places)

[Given : pK_a of CH_3COOH in water is 4.75]

59. At constant temperature, 6.40 g of a substance dissolved in 78 g of benzene decreases the vapor pressure of benzene from 0.125 atm to 0.119 atm.

The molar mass of the substance is ..... g mol^{-1}. *(round off to two decimal places)*

[Given : Mol. wt. of benzene = 78 g mol^{-1}]

60. For a van der Waals gas, the critical temperature is 150 K and the critical pressure is 5×10^6 Pa. The volume occupied by each gas molecule is .... Å^3.

(round off to two decimal places)

[Given: $R = 8.314$ J mol^{-1} K^{-1}, $N_A = 6.023 \times 10^{23}$].

ANSWERS

SECTION A: MCQ (Multiple Choise Questions)

1	2	3	4	5	6	7	8	9	10
D	B	A	C	D	C	A	A	C	B
11	**12**	**13**	**14**	**15**	**16**	**17**	**18**	**19**	**20**
C	C	B	C	D	D	A	A	B	B
21	**22**	**23**	**24**	**25**	**26**	**27**	**28**	**29**	**30**
B	D	D	C	D	C	A	B	B	C

SECTION B: MSQ (Multiple Select Questions)

31	32	33	34	35
A, B	A	A, B	B, D	A, B
36	**37**	**38**	**39**	**40**
B, C, D	B, C	A, C	A, B, C	B, D

SECTION C: NAT (Numerical Answer Type Questions)

41	42	43	44	45
5 to 5	2 to 2	3 to 3	80 to 80	1 to 1
46	**47**	**48**	**49**	**50**
3 to 3	5 to 5	4.390 to 4.400	0.73 to 0.75	6750 to 6750
51	**52**	**53**	**54**	**55**
– 24 to – 24	6 to 6	599 to 602	10 to 10	– 212 to – 212
56	**57**	**58**	**59**	**60**
338.0 to 338.2	670 to 685	0.121 to 0.123	126.0 to 128.0	*

EXPLANATORY ANSWERS

1. 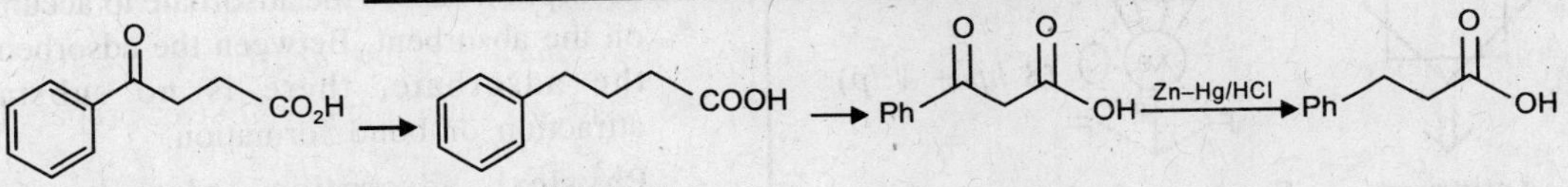

Hence, the transformation is Zn(Hg)/HCl.

2. 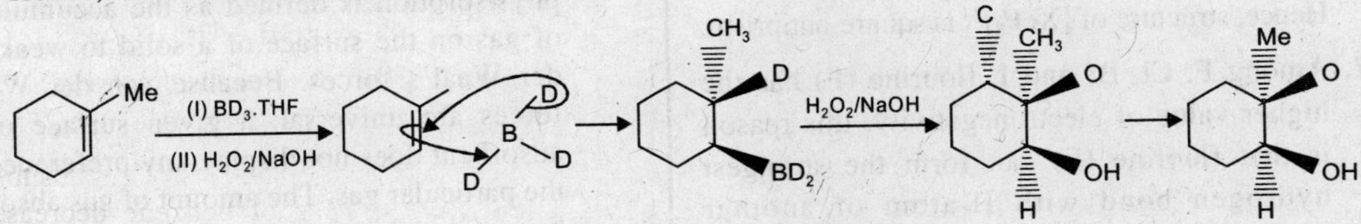

3. 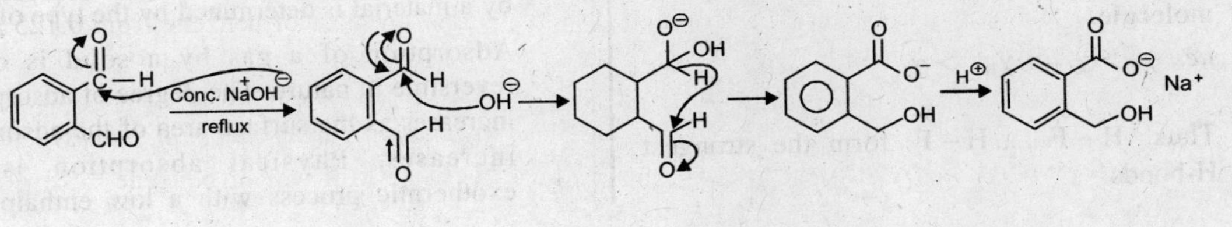

4. K + O_2 $\rightarrow$ KO_2

$K^+ O_2^-$ Superoxide Alkali

Superoxide Na_2O_2 Li

Na

(K) $\rightarrow$ Superoxide

Rb

Cs

5. Given,

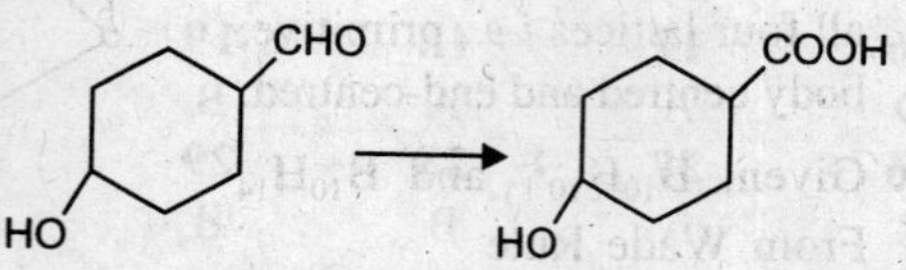

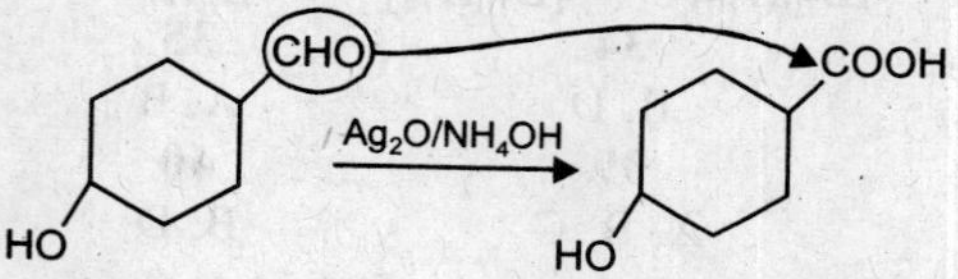

Ag_2O/NH_4OH is Tollent's reagent.

Hence, Ag_2O/NH_4OH is suited for effecting the transformation.

6. Given, $[XeF_8]^{2-}$

VSER Theory Hybridisation (H)

$$= \frac{1}{2}(8+8+2-0) = \frac{18}{2} = 9$$

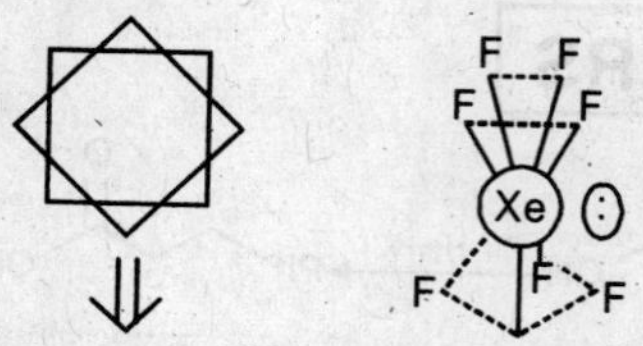

(8 *hp* + 1 *lp*)

Antiprism Square-antiprism

Hence, structure of $[XeF_8]^{2-}$ is square-antiprism.

7. Among F, Cl, Br and I, flourine (F) has the higher value of electronegativity, this reason is that fluorine (F) can form the strongest hydrogen bond with H-atom of another molecule.

i.e., $\chi_F > \chi_{Cl} > \chi_{Br} > \chi_I$

Thus, $H-\overset{\delta-}{F}$ ..... $H-\overset{\delta-}{F}$ form the strongest H-bonds.

8.

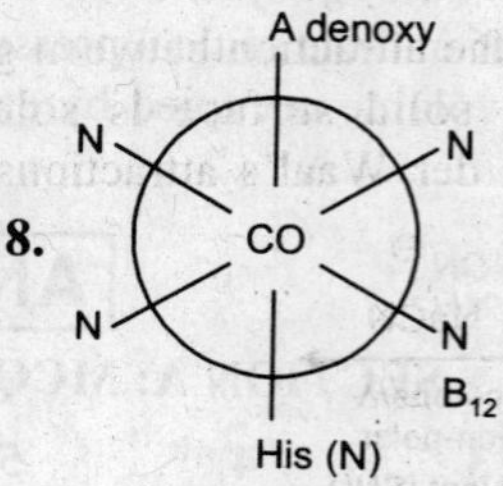

$\Rightarrow$ M–C Bond

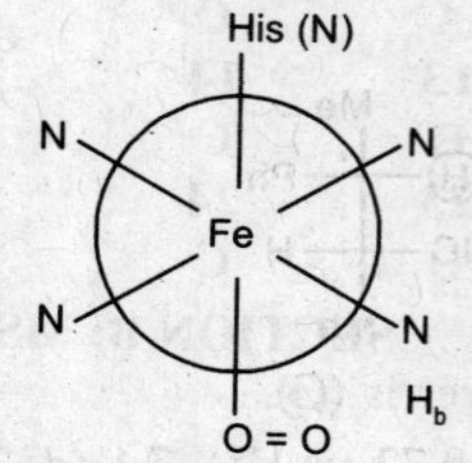

$\Rightarrow$ No M–C Bond

Nitrogenase and Chlorophyll has no M-C bonds

Thus, coenzyme B_{12} has metal carbon bond.

9. Given, $H_2PO_2^-$ (*aq*) + OH^- (*aq*) $\rightarrow$ HPO_3^{2-} (*aq*) + H_2(*g*)

We have, $R_2 = K[2(H_2PO_2)^-][OH^-]^2$

$= 2K [H_2 PO_2]^- [OH^-]^2$

But $K[H_2PO_2^-][OH^-]^2 = R_1$

$\therefore \quad R_2 = 2R_1$

Therefore, the concentration of $H_2PO_2^-$ is doubled, the rate is also doubled.

10. Due to weak van der Waal's forces, physical adsorption causes the adsorbate to accumulate on the absorbent. Between the adsorbent and the adsorbate, there is no substantial attraction or bond formation.

Physical adsorption, also known as physisorption is defined as the accumulation of gas on the surface of a solid to weak van der Waal's forces. Because van der Waal's forces are universal, a given surface of an adsorbent does not display any preference for the particular gas. The amount of gas absorbed by a material is determined by the type of gas.

Adsorption of a gas by a solid is often reversible in nature. The degree of adsorption increases as the surface area of the adsorbent increases. Physical absorption is an exothermic process with a low enthalpy of adsorption because the attraction between gas molecules and the solid surface is solely owing to weak van der Waal's attractions.

11.

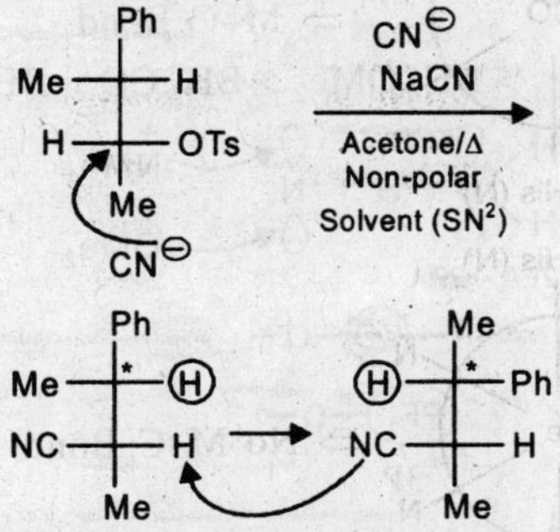

Hence, correct answer is (C).

12. Given, ^1H NMR: δ 9.72 (*t*, 1H), 7.1 (*d*, 2H), 6.7 (*d*, 2H), 3.8 (*s*, 3H), 3.6 (*d*, 2H)

IR: ~1720 cm^{-1}

9.72 (1) H(*t*)

⇒ aldehyde group →

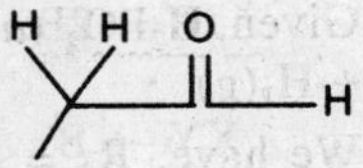

7.1	(2H)	(*d*)
6.7	(2H)	(*d*)
3.8	(*s*)	3H
3.6	(*d*)	2H

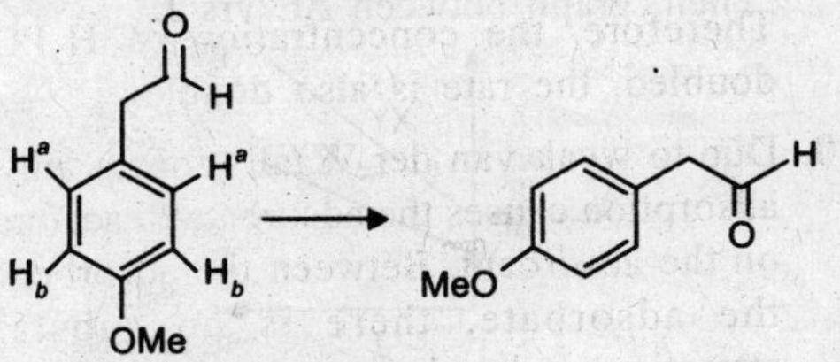

∴ Correct answer is (C)

14.

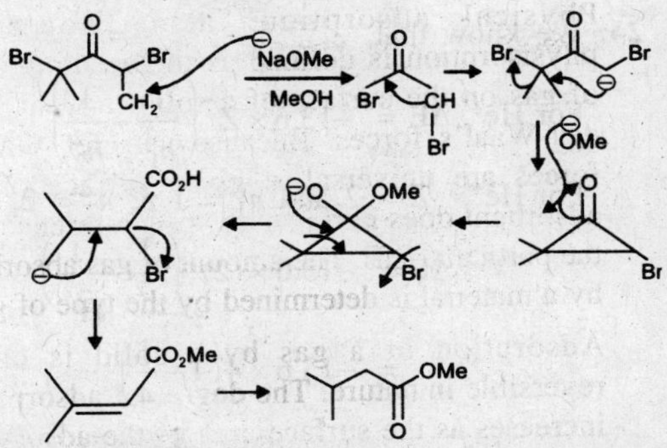

16. Orthorhombic system, one of the structural categories systems to which crystalline solids can be assigned. Crystals in this system are referred to three mutually perpendicular axes that are unequal in length.

In orthorhombic system, all three axes are unequal in length, and all are perpendicular to another. Orthorhombic crystal system has all four lattices *i.e.*, primitive, body centred and end-centred.

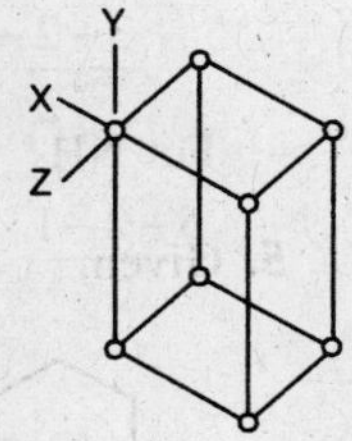

17. Given, $B_{10}H_{10}^{2-}$ and $B_{10}H_{14}$

From Wade Rule

$[B_{10}H_{10}]^{2-}$	$[B_{10}H_{14}]$	B_nH_6
$[B_nH_n]^{2-}$	$[B_{10}H_{10}]H_4$	Arachno
Closo	$[B_{10}H_{10}]^{4-}$	
	Nido $[B_{10}H_{14}]$	

Hence, structure types of $[B_{10}H_{10}^{2-}]$ and $[B_{10}H_{14}]$ are closo and nido.

18. $Co^{2+} \rightarrow 3d^7\ 4s^2$

d^1	d^2	d^3	d^4	d^5	d^6	d^7	d^8	d^9
2_D	3_F	4_F	5_D	6_S	5_D	4_F	3_F	2_D

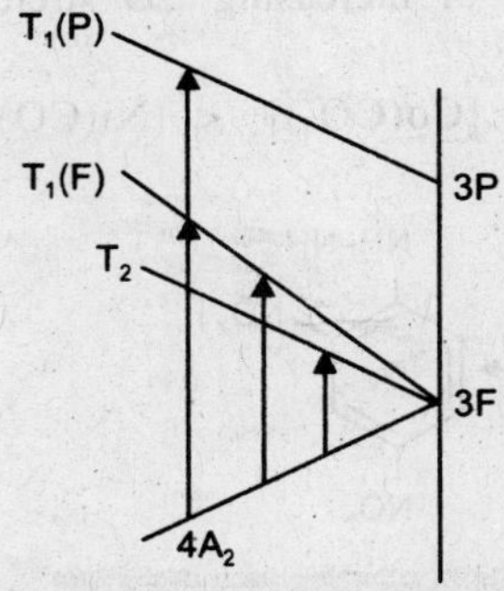

i.e., $4A_2$ and 3

Therefore, the ground state and the maximum number of spin allowed electronic transitions possible in a Co^{2+} tetrahedral complex are $^4A_2$ and 3.

19. We have,

No. of valence electron of central metal atom +

$$\text{No. of } \frac{\text{Monovalent metal} \pm \text{charge}}{2}$$

— CH_3
— H
— X (F, Cl, Br)

or

$$\frac{\text{No. of VE of CMA + No. of monovalent metal} \pm \text{Charge}}{2}$$

$\therefore$ For BH_2^+ :

$$\frac{3+2-1}{2} = 2(sp) \Rightarrow \text{linear}$$

For NH_2^+ :

$$\frac{5+2-1}{2} = \frac{6}{2} = 3\ (sp^2) \Rightarrow \text{trigonal planar.}$$

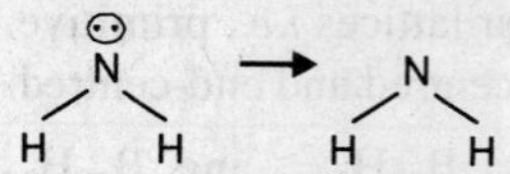

Bent shape

Hence, BH_2^+ is linear and NH_2^+ is trigonal planar.

20. The stretching frequencies order:

$[Co(CO_4)]^-$, $[Cu(CO)_4]^+$, $[Fe(CO)_4]^{-2}$, $[Ni(CO)_4]^-$
(*a*) (*b*) (*c*) (*d*)

The metal has more positive oxidation state means less back bonding.

Less back bonding means more negative frequency. Thus, the stretching frequencies order with

$$b > d > a > c$$

i.e., The order of increasing CO stretching frequencies is

$[Fe(CO)_4]^{-2} < [Co(CO_4)]^- < [Ni(CO)_4] < [Cu(CO)_4]^+$

21. 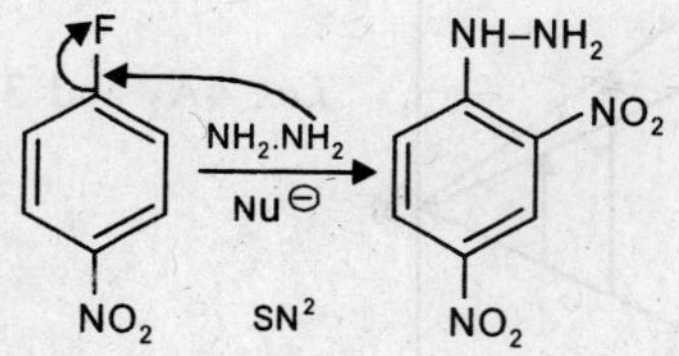

(2,4 – DNP)

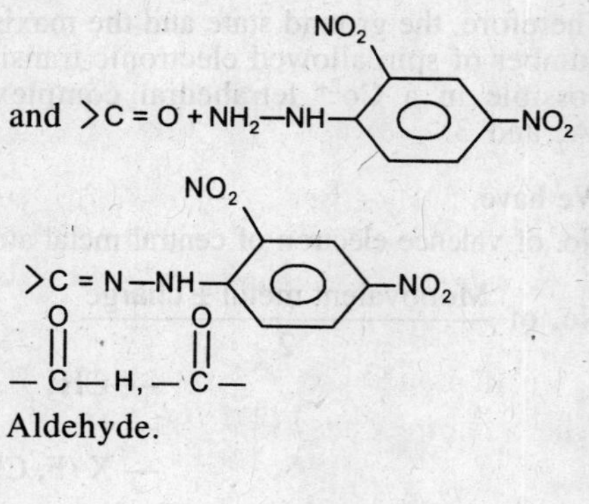

Aldehyde.

22. More LB (Lewis base) and more LA (Lewis acid) will form adducts.

$NMe_3 < OMe_2 < CO > PF_3$

Stability : $BH_3 \rightarrow$ electrons deficient $\rightarrow$ Lewis Acid.

$BH_3.NMe_3 > BH_3.OMe_2 > BH_3.CO > BH_3.PF_3$

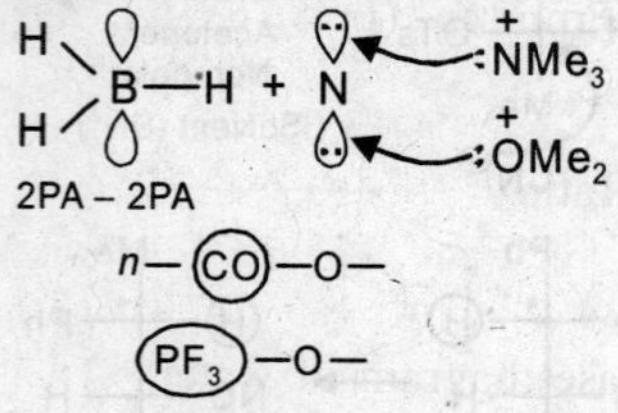

3P

23. Graph ΔE vrs J

$\Delta E = 2B\ (J + 1)$, $\Delta E = 2BJ + 2B$

$y = mx + C$

$\downarrow$

Slope + 2B

$\therefore \quad C = 2B, \ B \propto \frac{1}{\mu}$

So, $\frac{XY \rightarrow B'}{\mu}$ and $\frac{X'Y' \rightarrow B'}{\mu'}$ $\therefore B > B'$

The slope XY $\rightarrow$ increasing (heavy isotope) and slope X′Y′ $\rightarrow$ decreasing

Then, graph between ΔE vrs J.

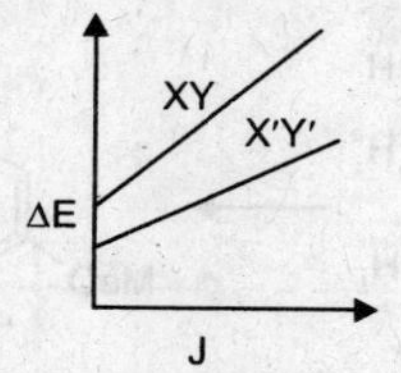

Hence, correct answer is D.

24. We know that,

For He^+, $\Delta E = -13.6 \times Z^2 \left(\frac{1}{n_1^2} - \frac{1}{n_2^2}\right)$

For He^+, $Z = 2$ and $n_1 = 1$ & $n_2 = 2$

$$\therefore \quad \Delta E = -13.6 \times (2)^2 \left(\frac{1}{1^2} - \frac{1}{2^2}\right)$$

$$= -13.6 \times 4\left(1 - \frac{1}{4}\right)$$

$$= -13.6 \times 4 \times \frac{3}{4} \quad \text{....}(i)$$

Now, for H-atom, $n_1 = 1$, $n_2 = 2$ and Z = 1

$$\Delta E = -13.6 \times (1)^2\left(\frac{1}{1^2}-\frac{1}{2^2}\right)$$

$$= -13.6 \times \left(1-\frac{1}{4}\right) = -13.6 \times \frac{3}{4} \quad ....(ii)$$

∴ From eq. (*i*) & (*ii*), we get

$$\text{Ratio} = \frac{-13.6 \times 4 \times \frac{3}{4}}{-13.6 \times \frac{3}{4}} = 4$$

25. Phase diagram of water

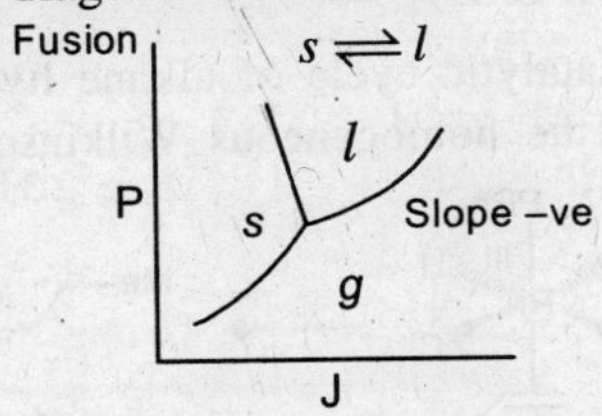

$$\frac{dP}{dT} = -\text{ve}$$

$$\frac{dP}{dT} = \frac{\Delta H}{T\Delta V} \Rightarrow \Delta V = V_l - V_s$$

For H_2O : $V_s > V_e$ ∴ $\Delta V = -\text{ve}$

Hence correct answer is (D).

26. For water:

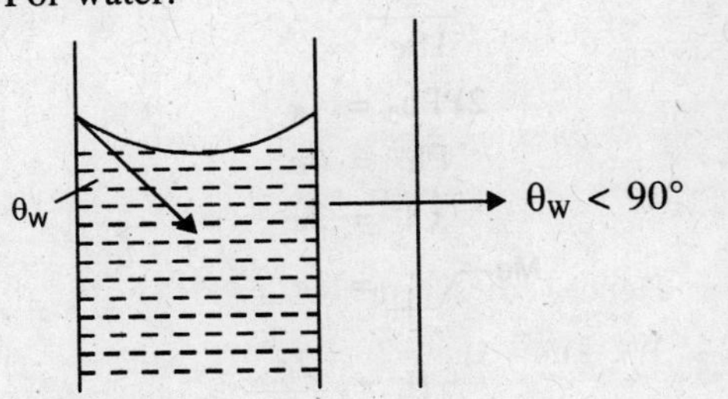

For mercury:

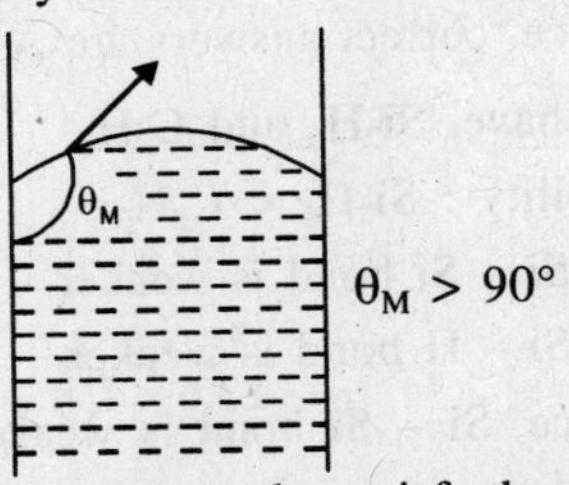

Hence, the contact angles satisfy the conditions $\theta_w < 90°$ and $\theta_M > 90°$

28. Given, the potential for a particle in a one-dimensional box:

$V(x) = 0$ for $0 \le x \le L$ and $V(x) = \infty$

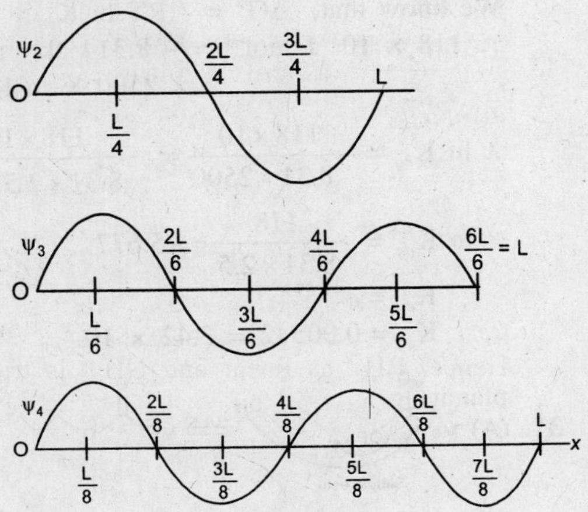

$$n = 2 \Rightarrow m = 1$$

$$\text{Modes } (n) = \frac{mL}{n}$$

$$n = 3 \Rightarrow m = 1, 2$$

$$x = \frac{1}{3}L \text{ and } x = \frac{2}{3}L$$

$$n = 4 \Rightarrow m = 1, 2, 3$$

$$x = \frac{1}{4}L,\ x = \frac{2}{4}L,\ x = \frac{3}{4}L, ...$$

$$\therefore \quad x = \frac{m}{n}L$$

29. Given, $Fe(CO)_5 \rightarrow$ No. of CO bond (Infrared spectrum)

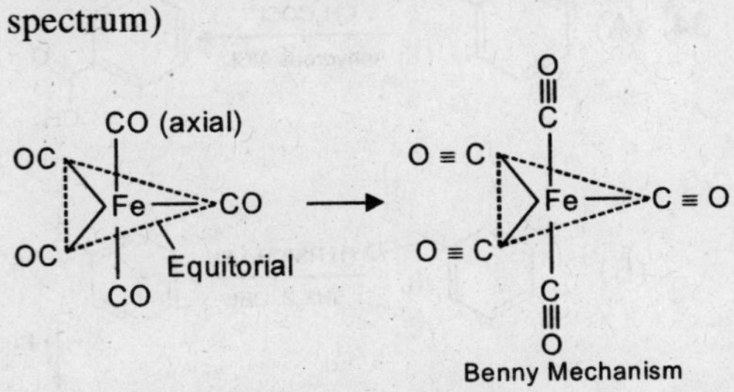

Low rate of inter change between axial and equitorial CO-ligands.

Two IR bonds [2034 cm^{-1} and 2014 cm^{-1}].

Hence, correct answer is (B).

30. Given, $T = 2500$ K, $\Delta G° = 118$ kJ mol^{-1}

$= 118 \times 10^3$ J mol^{-1}.

We know that, $\Delta G° = -RT \ln K_{eq}$

$\therefore$ 118×10^3 J mol^{-1} $= -8.314$ Jk^{-1} mol^{-1} $\times 2500$ K $\ln K_{eq}$.

$$\therefore \ln K_{eq} = -\frac{118\times10^3}{8.31\times2500} = -\frac{118\times10^3}{8.31\times2.5\times10^3}$$

$$\ln K_{eq} = -\frac{118}{8.31\times2.5} = -5.677$$

$$K_{eq} = e^{-5.677}$$

$$\therefore K_{eq} = 0.00342 = 3.42 \times 10^{-3}$$

31. (A) 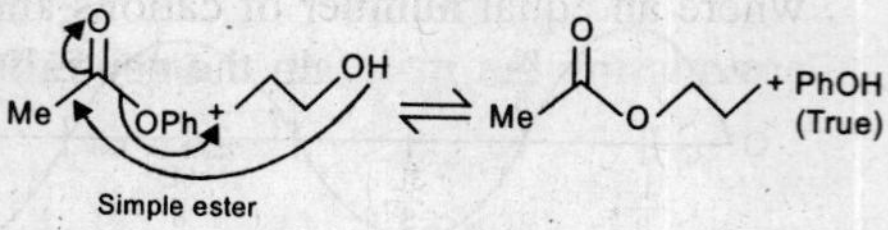

(B) 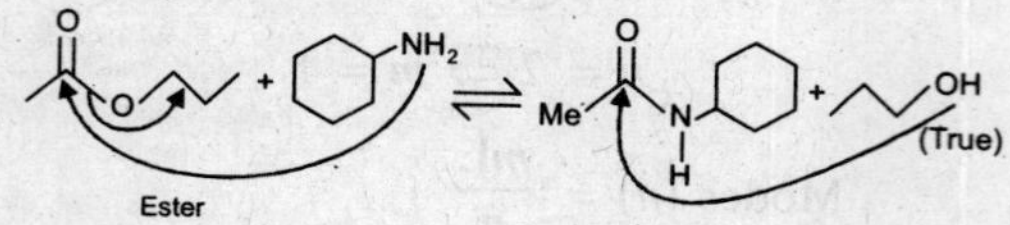

(C) 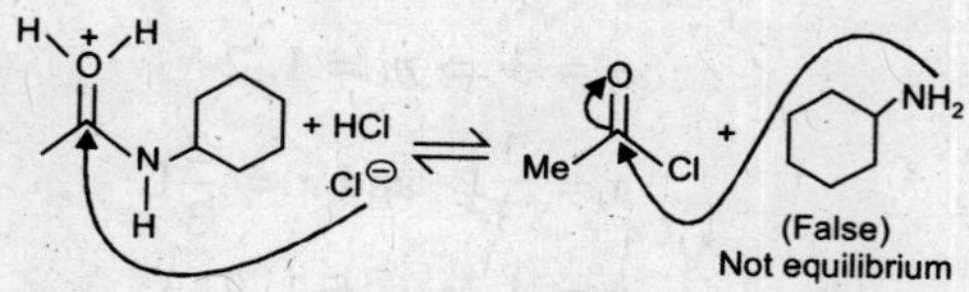

(D) 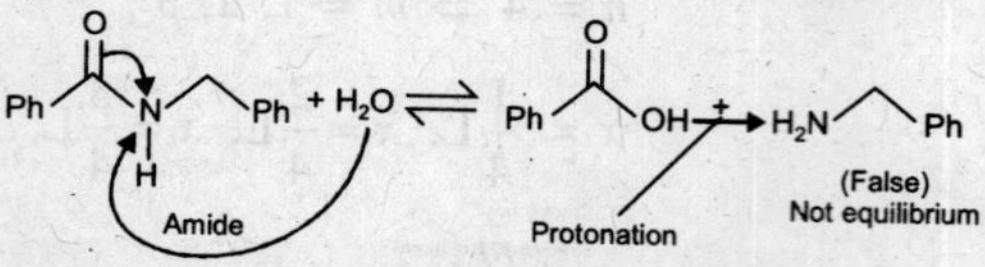

Hence, correct answers are A and B.

34. (A) 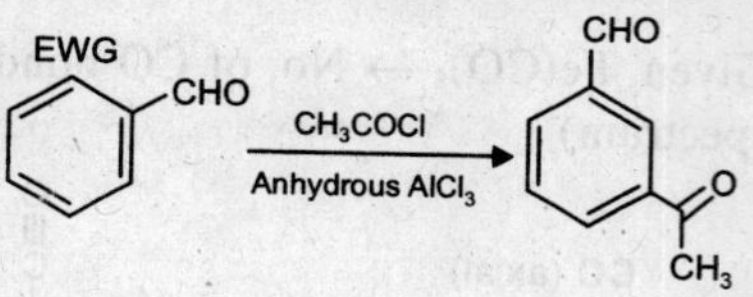

(B) 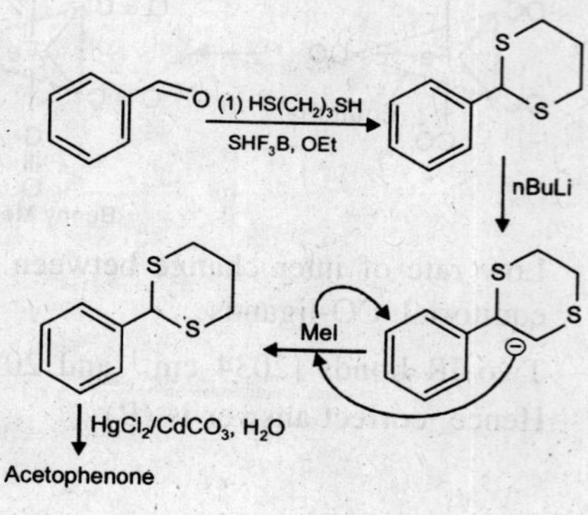

(C) 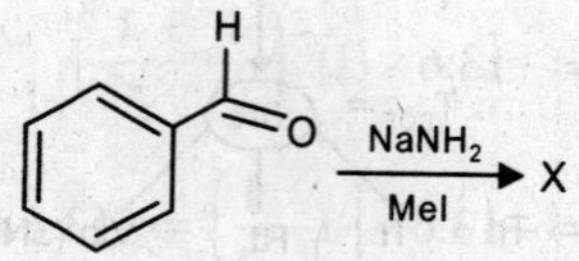

(D) 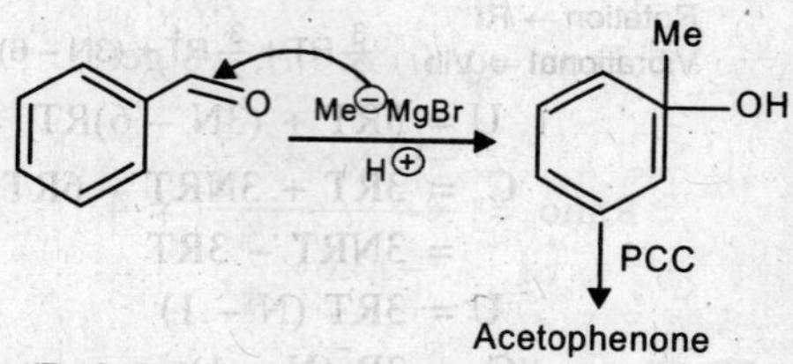

Ans. (B & D)

35. The catalytic cycle of alkane hydrogenation using the homogeneous Wilkinson catalyst.

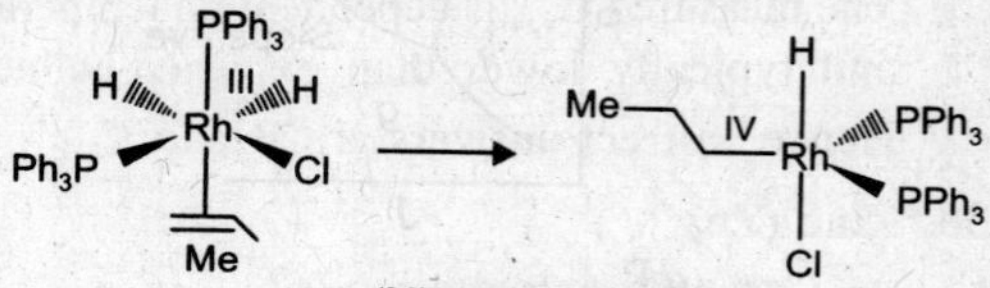

(Migratory insertion)

Electron count

R P

$8e^-$

$2H^-$ $4e^-$

Cl^- $2e^-$

$2PPh_3$ $4e^-$

$18e^-$

$2PPh_3 = 4e^-$

$Ph^m = 6e^-$

$Cl^- = 2e^-$

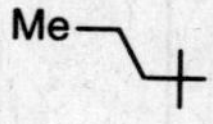 $= 2e^-$

$H^- = 2e^-$

$16e^-$

Hence, correct answers are A and B.

36. We have, Si_2H_6 and C_2H_6

Stability : $Si_2H_6 < C_2H_6$

(B) Si – Si bond is weaker

(C) Si – H bond is weaker

Hence, Si – Si bond is weaker than C – C bond

Si – H bond is weaker than C – H bond and presence of lowlying *d*-orbitals in the silicon.

37.

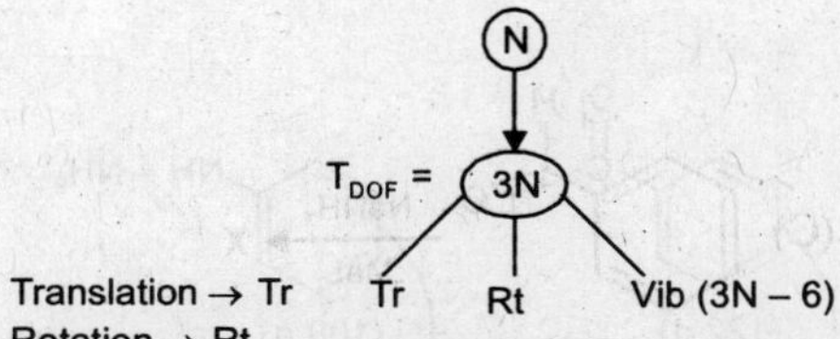

$$\frac{3}{2}RT + \frac{3}{2}RT + (3N - 6)\ RT$$

$$U = 3RT + (3N - 6)RT$$

$$C_v = 3RT + 3NRT - 6RT$$

$$= 3NRT - 3RT$$

$$U = 3RT\ (N - 1)$$

$$\therefore \quad C_v = 3R\ (N - 1)$$

Experiment $3(N - 1)R$

$$C_{v,\,m} = 3RT\ (3N - 6)R$$

The measured $C_{v,m}$ is dependent on temperature and typically lower than expected value.

Hence, correct answers are B and C.

38. Zinc (Zn)

→ Carbonic anhydrase

→ Carboxy peptidase

→ Carbonic enzyme

→ LADH

Hence, Zn containing carboxypeptidase and carbonic anhydrase.

Hence, correct answer are A and C.

39. $ICl \xrightarrow{-e} ICl^+$

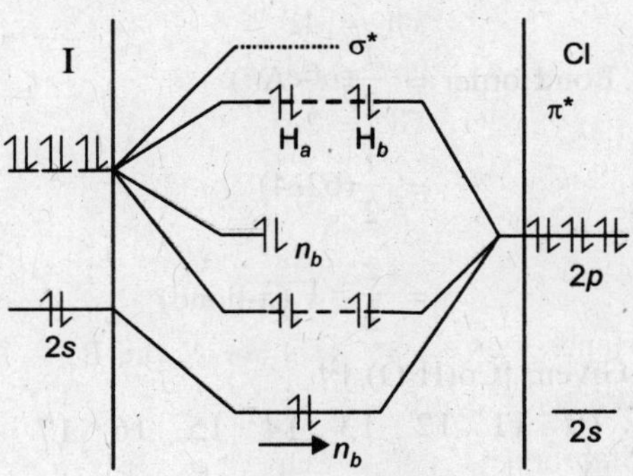

$$BO = \frac{1}{2}(6-4) = \frac{2}{2} = 1$$

$$BO = \frac{1}{2}(6-3) = \frac{3}{2} = 1.5$$

Hence, correct answers are (A), (B) and (C).

40. Solids are formed from many small crystals. The defect in solid occurs due to the fast or moderate rate of formation of crystals. The common point defects in solids are: Schottky and Frenkel defects.

Schottky Defects: This defects occur due to the missing the same number of cations and anions from the lattice site. This type of defect is shown by the substance having the higher coordination number. Schottky defect generally occurs in ionic compounds in which the radius of cation and anion $[r^+/r^-]$ is not for below unity. It is kind of vacancy defect where an equal number of cations and anions are missing but maintain the neutrality of the crystal. Example, NaCl, CsCl, KCl, AgBr etc.

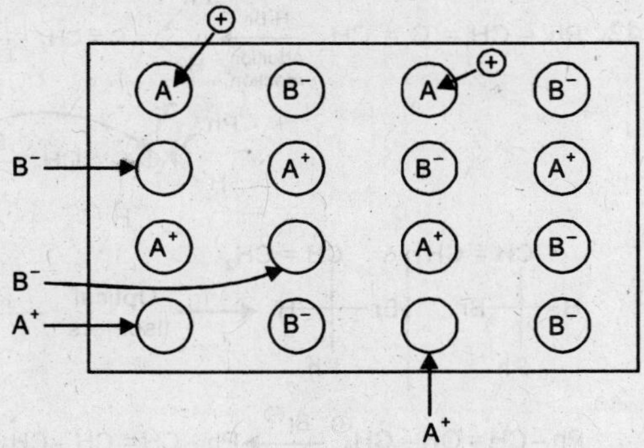

Frenkel Defect: In this type of defect, some cations are missing from their lattice site and occupy the interstitial site of the lattice. This type of defect is shown by the substances which have low coordination number. The closeness of like charges tends to increase the dielectric constant of the crystal. Frenkel defect is a kind of dissociation defect in which smaller ion generally cation dislocate

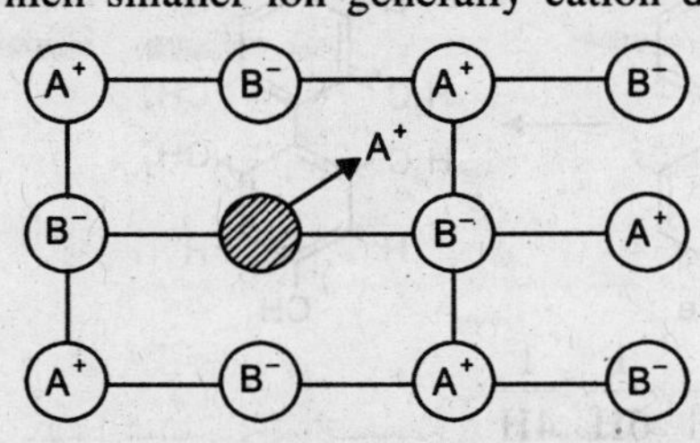

from their position to occupy the interstitial site of the lattice crystal. This defect is exhibited in those ionic compounds in which the radius $[r^+/r^-]$ is low. Example, ZnS, AgBr, AgCl, AgI.

41. 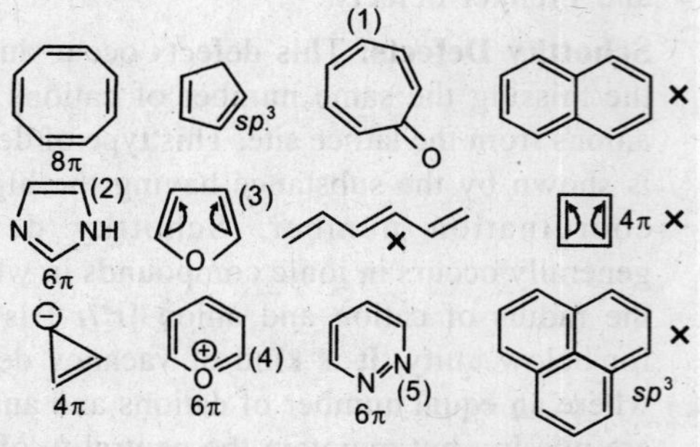

Hence number of aromatic compounds is 5.

42. 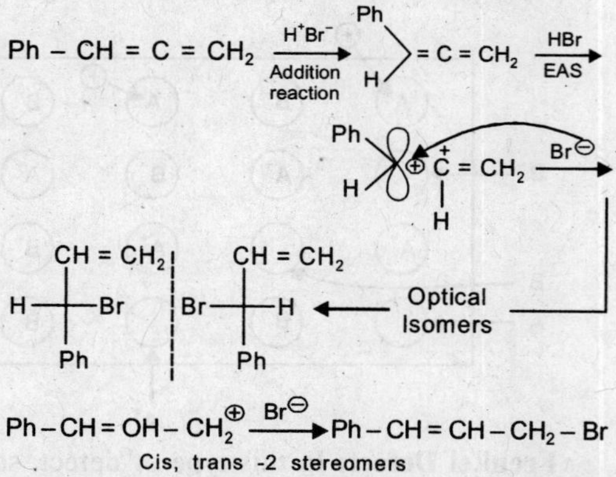

Hence, number of stereomers possible in the reaction is 2.

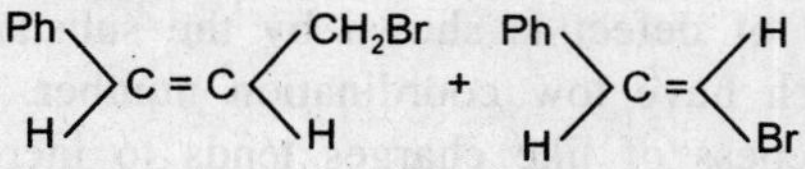

43. 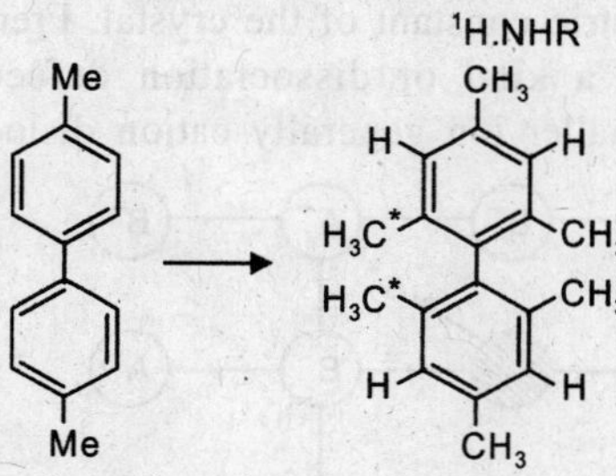

$\frac{1}{12H}, \frac{1}{6H}, \frac{1}{4H}$

Total 12 : 6 : 4

6 : 3 : 2

Hence, Total number of signals = 3.

44. 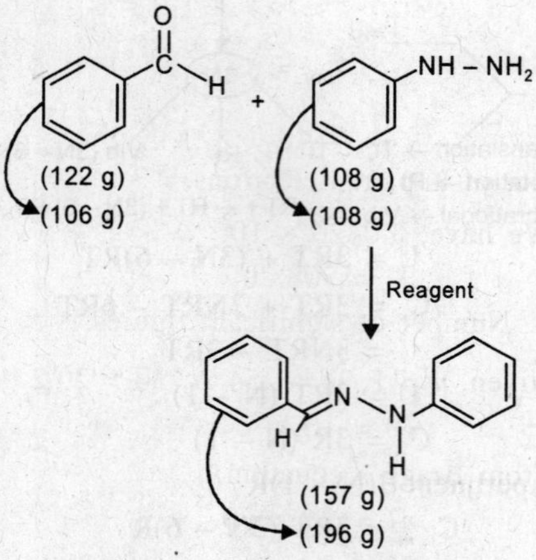

$\therefore$ Yield $= \frac{157}{196} \times 100 = 80.70\% \simeq 80\%$

45. 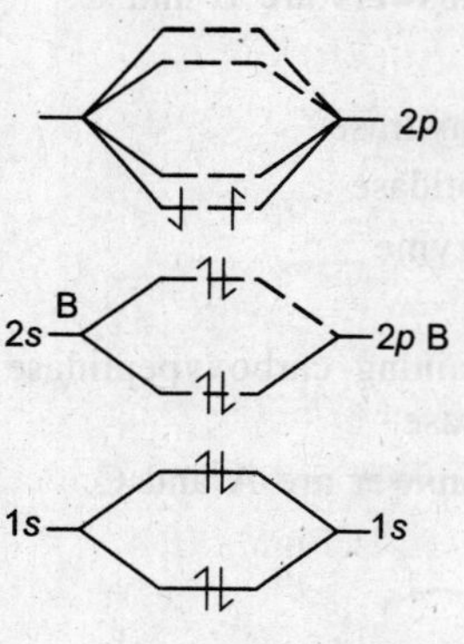

$$\text{Bond order} = \frac{1}{2}(b - \text{A}b)$$

$$= \frac{1}{2}(6-4)$$

$$= \frac{2}{2} = 1\ (\pi\text{-bond})$$

46. Given, $[Co(H_2O)_6]^{2+}$

10	11	12	13	14	15	16	17	18
↓	↓	↓		↓	↓	↓	↓	↓
1	15	2	25	3	2.5	2	1.7	1

Co^{2+}

↓

d^7 (octa hedral)

↓

High spin complexes

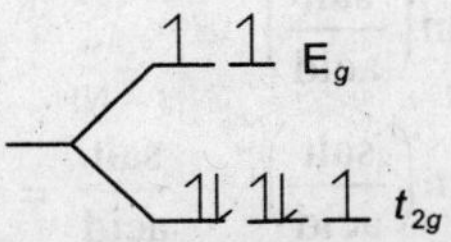

No. of unpaired electrons = 3.

47. We have, 5.0820×10^2

$$= 508.20$$

$\therefore$ Number of significant figures is 5.

48. Given, $n = 1$, $\lambda = 1.54$ Å, $2\theta = 20.2$

$$\Rightarrow \quad \theta = 10.1°$$

From Bragg's equation,

$$n\lambda = 2d \sin\theta$$

$$\Rightarrow 1 \times 1.54 = 2 \times d \times \sin(10.1)$$

$$\Rightarrow \quad 1.54 = 2d \sin(10.1)$$

$$\therefore \quad d = \frac{1.54}{2\sin(10.1)}$$

$$= 4.39079 = 4.391 \text{ Å}$$

49. For fcc, $a\sqrt{2} = 4r$

$$\Rightarrow \quad a = \frac{4}{\sqrt{2}}r = 2\sqrt{2}r$$

Volume fraction or packing fraction

$$= \frac{\text{Volume occupied by atoms its unit cell}}{\text{Volume of unit cell}}$$

$$= 4 \times \frac{\frac{4}{3}\pi r^3}{a^3} = \frac{\frac{16}{3}\pi r^3}{(2\sqrt{2}r)^3}$$

$$= \frac{16\pi r^3}{16\sqrt{2}r^3 \times 3} = \frac{\pi}{3\sqrt{2}} = 0.74$$

50. Given, $i = 1.25$A, $t = 1.5\ hr = 1.5 \times 60 \times 60$ seconds

We know that,

$$Q = i \times t$$

$$= 1.25 \times 1.5 \times 3600$$

$$= 6750 \text{ C.}$$

Thus, total charge is 6750 C.

51. Specific rotation: $\%(S) = \frac{4}{5} \times 100 = 80\%$

$$\%(R) = \frac{1}{5} \times 100 = 20\%$$

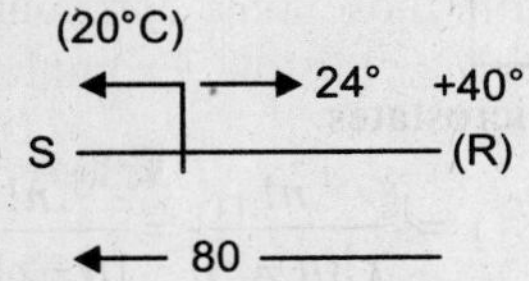

$\therefore$ $ee = 60\%$ in (S)

S : R
4 : 1

$$\Rightarrow \quad 60 = \frac{?}{-40} \times 100$$

$$\therefore \quad ? = -\frac{60 \times 40}{200} = -24$$

52. $^{238}_{92}U \rightarrow ^{206}_{82}Pb$

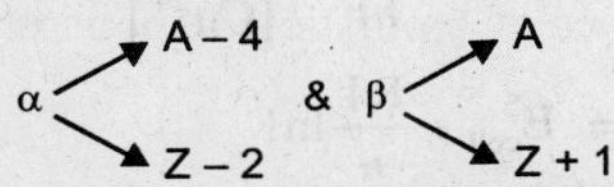

$$238 = 206 + 4x$$

$$4x = 238 - 206$$

$$4x = 32$$

$$\therefore \quad x = 8$$

$$92 = 82 + 2x - y$$

$$\Rightarrow \quad 92 = 82 - 16$$

$$4\alpha = 238 - 206 = 32 \quad ...(i)$$

$$\therefore \quad \alpha = 8$$

$$\therefore \quad 2\alpha - \beta = 92 - 82 \quad ...(ii)$$

or $\quad 2\alpha - \beta = 10$

or $\quad 2 \times 8 - \beta = 10$ (putting $\alpha = 8$)

or $\quad 16 - \beta = 10 \Rightarrow \beta = 16 - 10 = 6$

$\therefore \quad \beta = 6$

Hence, $\alpha = 8$ and $\beta = 6$

Therefore, the number of β-particles emitted = 6.

53. 2 mol. Fe $\rightarrow$ 3 mol CO

$$\therefore \text{ 1 mol Fe} = \frac{3}{2} \text{ mol CO} = 1.5 \text{ mol CO}$$

$$\because \quad 1 \text{ kg} = 1000 \text{ g}$$

$$= \frac{1000}{56} = 17.86 \text{ mol}$$

17.86 mol of Fe = 26.79 mol of CO

At STP, 1 mol gas = 22.4 L

$\therefore \quad$ 26.79 mol = (22.4 × 22.79)L

$= 600.096$ L $= 600$ L

54. Ti : $3s^2\ 3d^2$

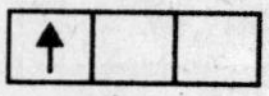

No. of microstates

$$= \frac{n!}{r!(n-r)!} = \frac{n!}{(n-r)!r!}$$

$$= \frac{10!}{(10-1)!\,1!} = \frac{10!}{9!\,1!} = 10$$

55. $Zn \rightarrow Zn^{2+} + 2e^-$

$$\frac{Cu^{2+} + 2e^- \rightarrow Cu}{Cu^{2+} + Zn \rightarrow Cu + Zn^{2+}}$$

$$E_{cell} = E^\circ_{cell} - \frac{RT}{nF} \ln \frac{[Zn^{2+}]}{[Cu^{2+}]}$$

$$= E^\circ_{cell} - \frac{RT}{n} \ln 1$$

$\therefore$ $E_{cell} = E^\circ_{cell} - 1$

$E^\circ_{cell} = 1.10$ V

$\therefore$ $\Delta G^\circ = -nF\,E^\circ_{cell}$

$= -\ 2 \times 96500 \times 1.10$

$= -\ 2 \times 96485 \times 10$

$= -\ 212267$ J $= -\ 212.67$ kJ.

$\simeq -\ 212$ kJ

57. As, $\Delta E = \dfrac{hc}{\lambda}$

$\Rightarrow$ $\dfrac{\Delta E}{hc} = \dfrac{1}{\lambda}$ (length)$^{-1}$

$$\Delta E = \frac{1 \times 10^{-9}\,m^{-1}}{274} - \frac{10^{-9}\,m^{-1}}{269}$$

$$= 10^{-7}\left[\frac{1}{274} - \frac{1}{269}\right] cm^{-1}$$

$= 678\ cm^{-1}$

Hence, the magnitude of the energy gap between two bonds is 678 cm^{-1}.

58. Given, pH = 4.80 and $pK_a = 4.75$

We know that,

$$pH = pK_a + \ln\left(\frac{salt}{acid}\right)$$

$$\Rightarrow \quad 4.80 = 4.75 + \ln\left(\frac{salt}{acid}\right)$$

$$\Rightarrow 4.80 - 4.75 = \ln\left(\frac{salt}{acid}\right)$$

$$\Rightarrow \quad 0.05 = \ln\left(\frac{salt}{acid}\right) \therefore \frac{salt}{acid} = 1.12$$

The quantity $\dfrac{[CH_3COO^-] - [CH_3COOH]}{[CH_3COOH]}$

$$= \frac{[CH_3COO^-]}{[CH_3COOH]} - 1$$

$= 1.12 - 1 = 0.12$

Hence, the quantity $\dfrac{[CH_3COO^-] - [CH_3COOH]}{[CH_3COOH]}$ is 0.120.

59. Given,

We have, $\dfrac{\Delta P}{P} = x_B = \dfrac{W_B / M_B}{\dfrac{W_A}{M_A} + \dfrac{W_B}{M_B}}$

$$\Rightarrow \quad \frac{0.125 - 0.119}{0.125} = \frac{\frac{6.4}{x}}{1 + \frac{6.4}{x}}$$

$$\Rightarrow \quad 0.048 = \frac{\frac{6.4}{x}}{1 + \frac{6.4}{x}}$$

$$\Rightarrow \quad \frac{6.4}{x} = 0.048 + \frac{0.048 \times 6.4}{x}$$

$$\Rightarrow \quad \frac{6.4}{x} = 0.048 + \frac{0.3072}{x}$$

$$\Rightarrow \quad \frac{6.4}{x} - \frac{0.3072}{x} = 0.048$$

$$\Rightarrow \frac{1}{x}[6.4 - 0.3072] = 0.048$$

$$\Rightarrow \quad \frac{1}{x} \times 6.0928 = 0.048$$

$$\Rightarrow \quad x = \frac{6.0928}{0.048}$$

$\therefore$ $x = 126.9 \simeq 127$

Hence, molar mass of substance is 127 g mol^{-1}.

Previous Years Paper

IIT–JAM

JOINT ADMISSION TEST FOR M.Sc. (CHEMISTRY), 2021

Section A : Multiple Choice Questions (MCQ)

Directions: (Q. No. 1 to 10) *Carry **One** mark each.*

1. The CORRECT order of pK_a for the compounds I to IV in water at 298 K is

$HCo(CO)_4$	$HCo(CO)_3(PPh_3)$
I	**II**
$HCo(CO)_3(P(OPh)_3)$	$HCo(CO)_2(PPh_3)_2$
III	**IV**

A. I > II > III > IV B. IV > III > II > I
C. IV > II > III > I D. I > III > II > IV

2. For Na^+, Mg^{2+}, Al^{3+} and F^-, the CORRECT order of ionic radii is
A. $Al^{3+} > Mg^{2+} > Na^+ > F^-$
B. $Al^{3+} > Na^+ > Mg^{2+} > F^-$
C. $F^- > Na^+ > Mg^{2+} > Al^{3+}$
D. $Na^+ > F^- > Mg^{2+} > Al^{3+}$

3. Spin-only magnetic moments (in BM) of $[NiCl_2(PPh_3)_2]$ and $[Mn(NCS)_6]^{4-}$, respectively, are
A. 0.00 and 5.92
B. 2.83 and 1.89
C. 0.00 and 1.89
D. 2.83 and 5.92

4. Two sets of quantum numbers with the same number of radial nodes are
A. $n = 3$; $l = 0$; $m_l = 0$ and $n = 2$; $l = 0$; $m_l = 0$
B. $n = 3$; $l = 1$; $m_l = 1$ and $n = 2$; $l = 1$; $m_l = 0$
C. $n = 3$; $l = 2$; $m_l = 0$ and $n = 2$; $l = 1$; $m_l = 0$
D. $n = 3$; $l = 1$; $m_l = -1$ and $n = 2$; $l = 1$; $m_l = 0$

5. The major product formed in the following reaction is

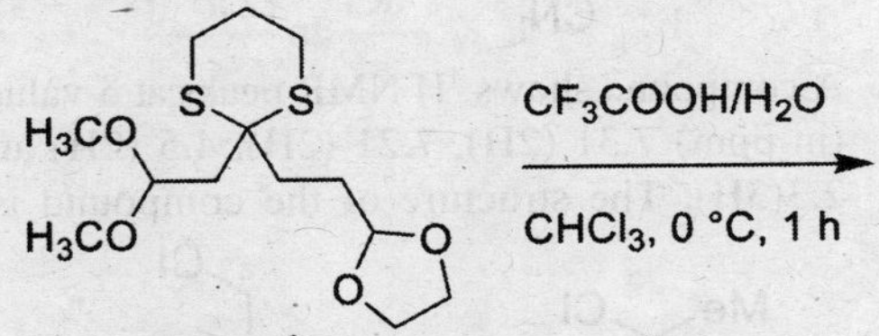

A. 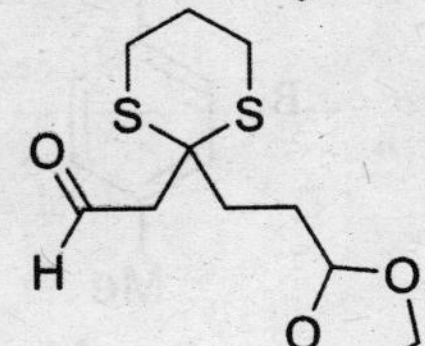

B. 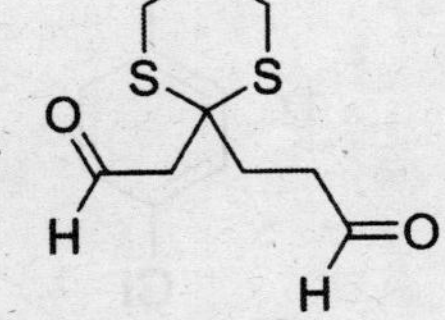

C. 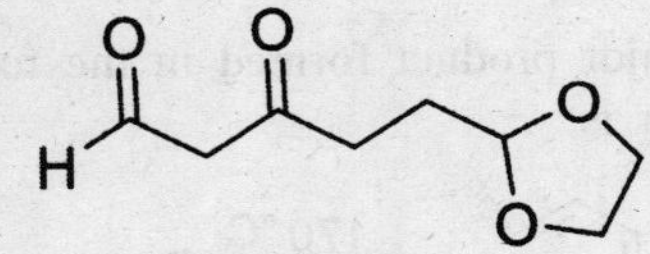

D. 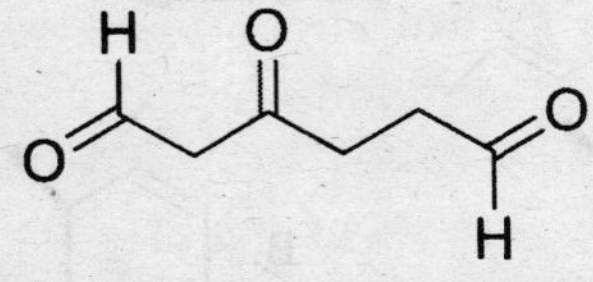

6. The major product formed in the following reaction is

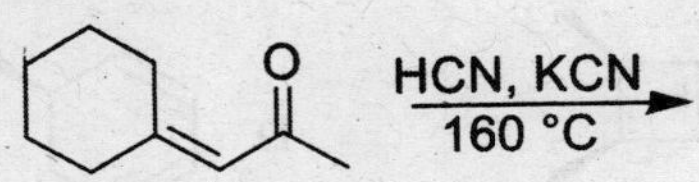

A. 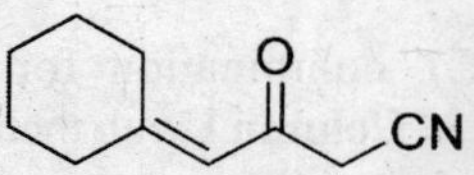

B. 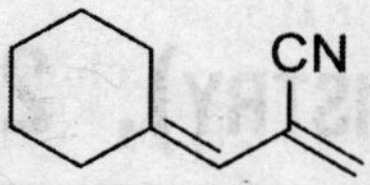

C. 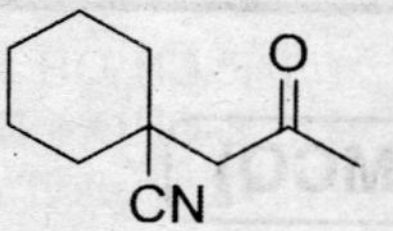

D. 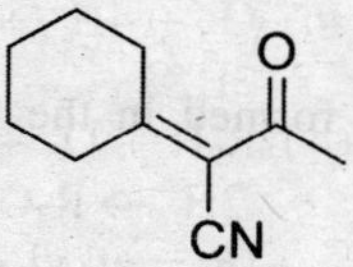

7. A compound shows ^1H NMR peaks at δ-values (in ppm) 7.31 (2H), 7.21 (2H), 4.5 (2H) and 2.3(3H). The structure of the compound is

A. 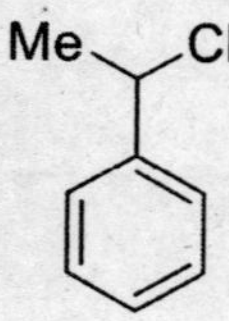

B. 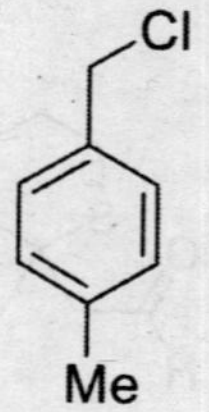

C. 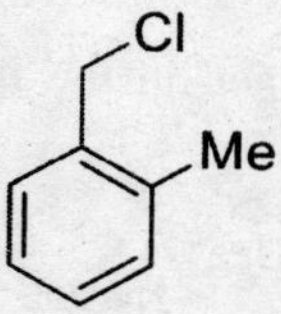

D. 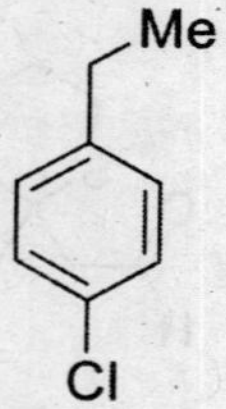

8. The major product formed in the following reaction is

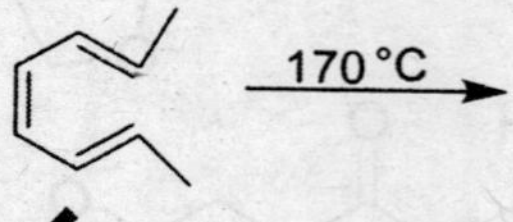

A. 

B. 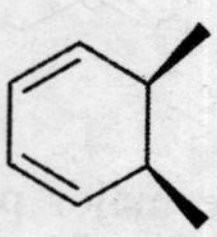

C. 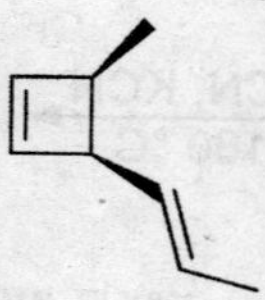

D. 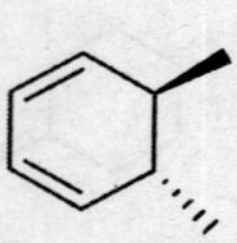

9. A pure substance **M** has lesser density in solid state than in liquid state. The ΔS_{fusion} of **M** is +25 J K^{-1}. The CORRECT representative Pressure-Temperature diagram for the fusion of **M** is

A. 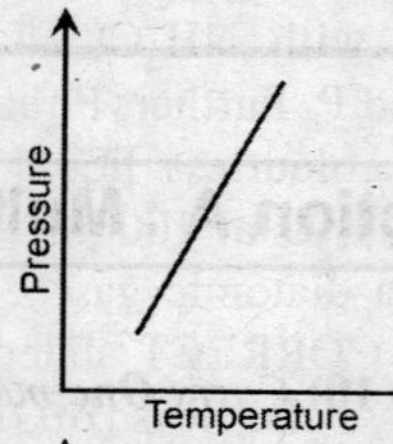

B. 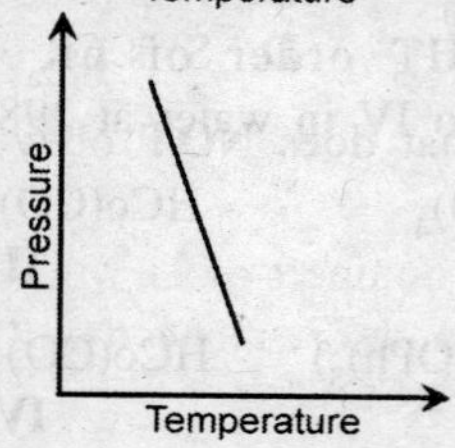

C. 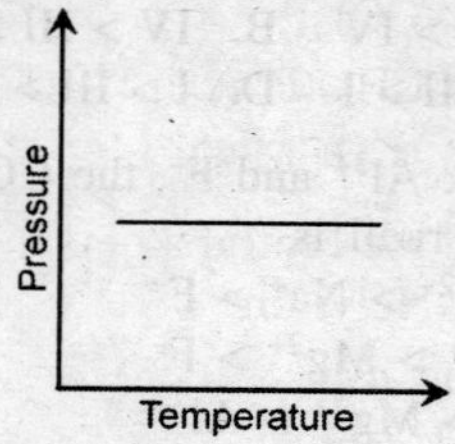

D. 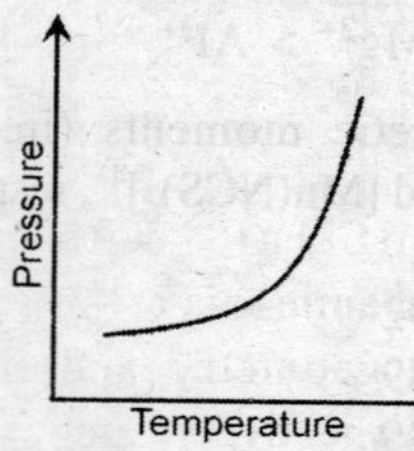

10. Among the following, the matrices with non-zero determinant are

$$P = \begin{bmatrix} 1 & 0 & 0 & 0 \\ 0 & 1 & 0 & 0 \\ 0 & 0 & 1 & 0 \\ 0 & 0 & 0 & 1 \end{bmatrix} \quad Q = \begin{bmatrix} 1 & 0 & 0 & 0 \\ 0 & 2 & 0 & 0 \\ 0 & 0 & 3 & 0 \\ 0 & 0 & 0 & 4 \end{bmatrix}$$

$$R = \begin{bmatrix} 1 & 0 & 0 & 0 \\ 2 & 2 & 0 & 0 \\ 3 & 1 & 3 & 0 \\ 4 & 3 & 1 & 4 \end{bmatrix} \quad S = \begin{bmatrix} 1 & 2 & 3 & 1 \\ 2 & 3 & 4 & 2 \\ 3 & 4 & 1 & 3 \\ 4 & 1 & 2 & 4 \end{bmatrix}$$

A. P, Q and R B. P, R and S
C. P, Q and S D. Q, R and S

Directions: (Q. No. 11 to 30) *Carry Two marks each.*

11. Reaction of BCl_3 with NH_4Cl at 140 °C produced compound P. Further, P reacts with $NaBH_4$ to give a colourless liquid Q. The reaction of Q with H_2O at 100 °C produces compound R and a diatomic gas S. Among the following, the CORRECT statement is
A. P is $B_3N_3H_6$ B. R is $[B(OH)NH]_3$
C. Q is $[BClNH]_3$ D. S is Cl_2

12. The complex that does **NOT** obey the 18-electron rule is
(*Given:* Atomic numbers of Ti, Mn, Ta and Ir are 22, 25, 73 and 77, respectively)
A. $[(\eta^5\text{–}C_5H_5)Ti(CO)_4]^-$
B. $[Mn(SnPh_3)_2(CO)_4]^-$
C. $[(\eta^5\text{–}C_5H_5)Ir(CH_2)(PMe_3)]$
D. $[TaCl_3(PEt_3)_2(CHCMe_3)]$

13. Hybridization of the central atoms in I_3^-, ClF_3 and SF_4, respectively, are
A. sp^3d, sp^2 and dsp^2
B. sp, sp^3d and dsp^2
C. sp^3d, sp^3d and sp^3d
D. sp, sp^2 and sp^3d

14. Reaction of $[Ni(CN)_4]^{2-}$ with metallic potassium in liquid ammonia at –33 °C yields complex E. The geometry and magnetic behaviour of E, respectively, are
A. Square planar and diamagnetic
B. Tetrahedral and diamagnetic
C. Octahedral and paramagnetic
D. Square pyramidal and paramagnetic

15. The decreasing order of C=C bond length in the following complexes is

$[Cl_3Pt(CH_2{=}CH_2)]^-$ (I) $[Cl_3Pt(C(CN)_2{=}C(CN)_2)]^-$ (II)

$[Cl_3Pt(CF_2{=}CH_2)]^-$ (III) $[Cl_3Pt(CF_2{=}CF_2)]^-$ (IV)

A. II > III > IV > I B. IV > II > III > I
C. II > IV > III > I D. IV > II > I > III

16. The CORRECT combination for metallo-enzymes given in **Column I** with their catalytic reactions in **Column II** is

Column I	Column II
(*a*) Cytochrome P-450	(*i*) $2H_2O_2 \rightarrow 2H_2O + O_2$
(*b*) Catalase	(*ii*) $R\text{-}CH_2OH + O_2 \rightarrow R\text{-}CHO + H_2O_2$ (R = alkyl or aryl)
(*c*) Galactose oxidase	(*iii*) $O_2 + 4H^+ + 4e^- \rightarrow 2H_2O$
(*d*) Cytochrome c oxidase	(*iv*) $R\text{-}H + O_2 + 2e^- + 2H^+ \rightarrow R\text{-}OH + H_2O$ (R = alkyl or aryl)

	(*a*)	(*b*)	(*c*)	(*d*)
A.	(*iii*)	(*iv*)	(*i*)	(*ii*)
B.	(*iv*)	(*ii*)	(*i*)	(*iii*)
C.	(*iv*)	(*i*)	(*ii*)	(*iii*)
D.	(*iii*)	(*i*)	(*ii*)	(*iv*)

17. According to the crystal field theory, d-d transition observed in $[Ti(H_2O)_6]^{3+}$ is
A. Laporte forbidden and spin forbidden
B. Laporte allowed and spin forbidden
C. Laporte allowed and spin allowed
D. Laporte forbidden and spin allowed

18. The major product formed in the following reaction sequence is

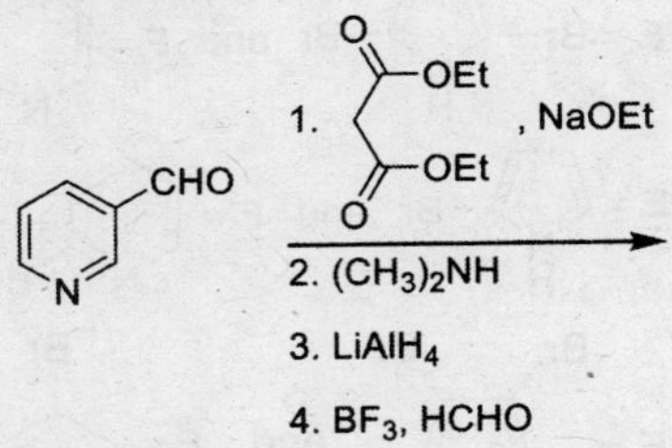

A. 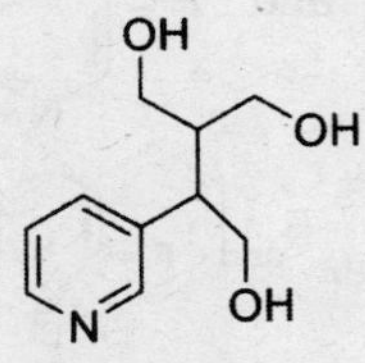

B. 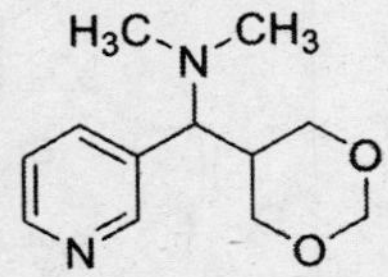

C. 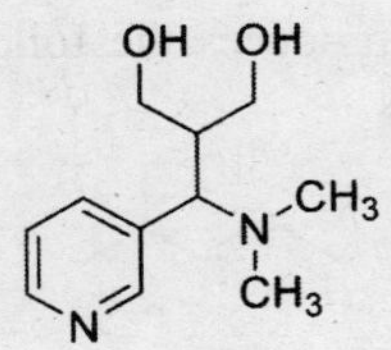

D. 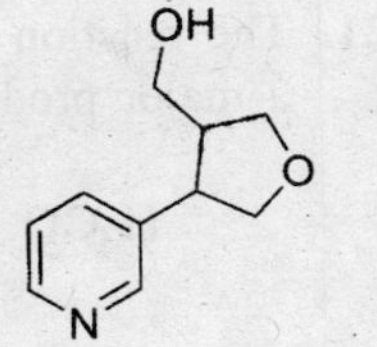

19. The products P, Q, R and S formed in the following reactions are

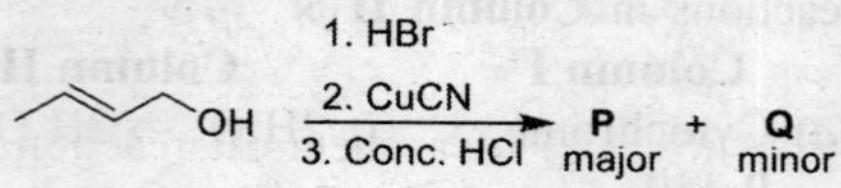

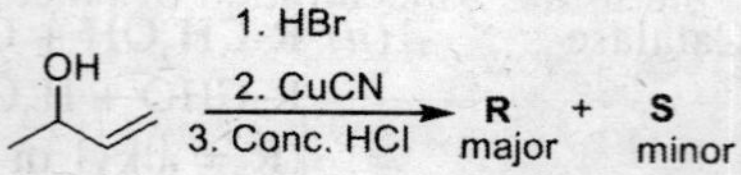

A. 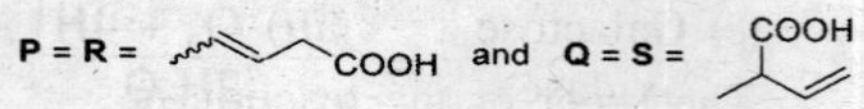

B. 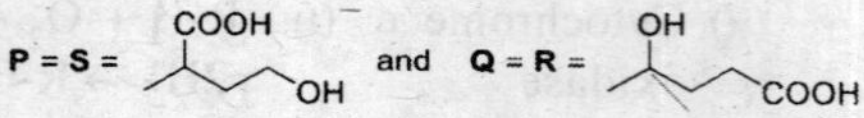

C. 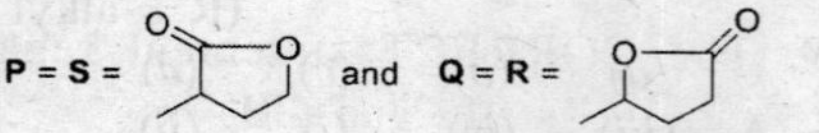

D. 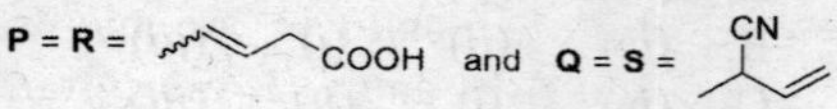

20. The major products E and F formed in the following reactions are

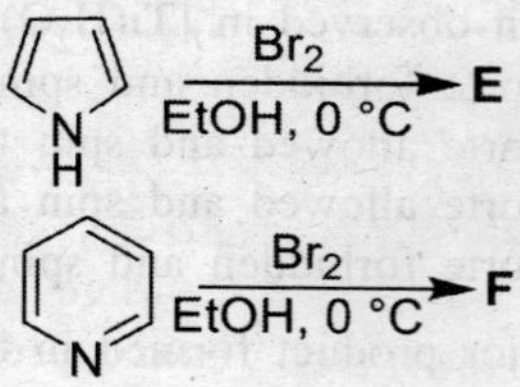

A. 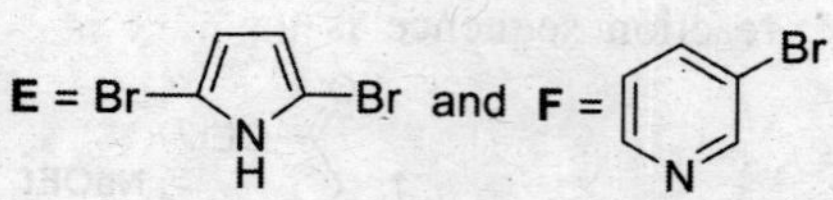

B. 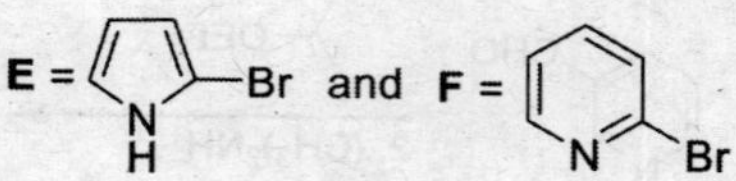

C. 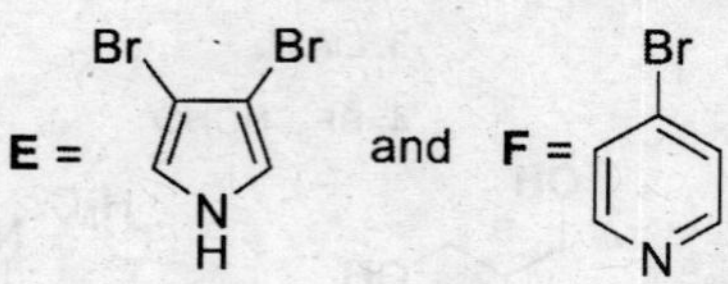

D. 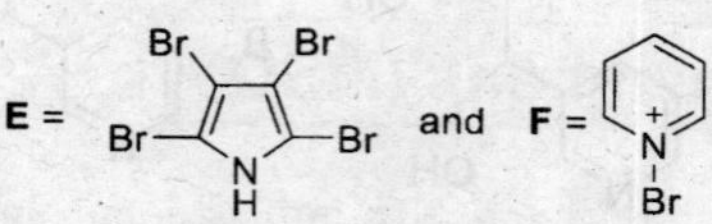

21. The reaction that produces the following as a major product is

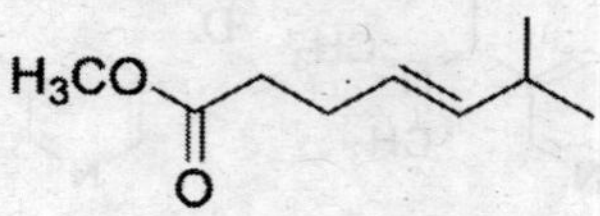

A. 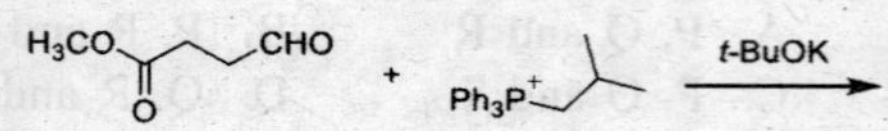

B. 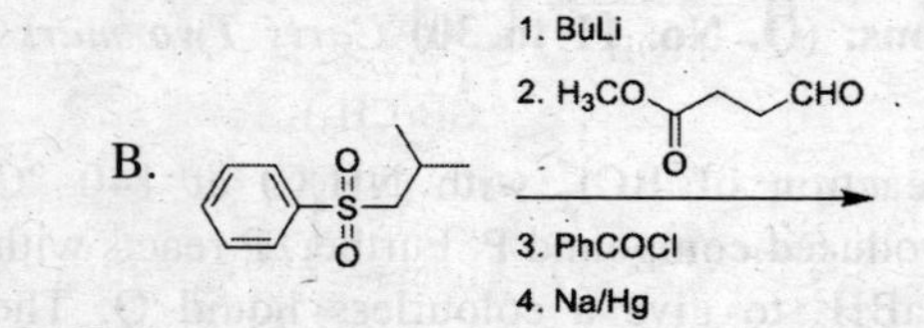

C. 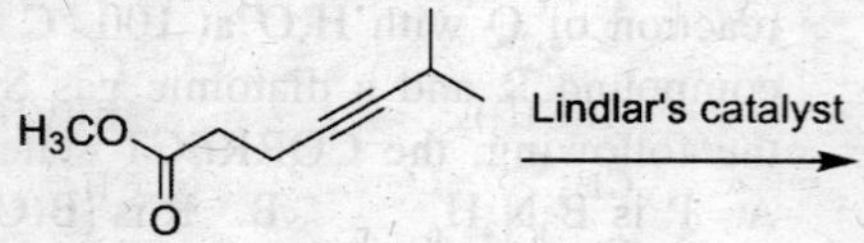

D. 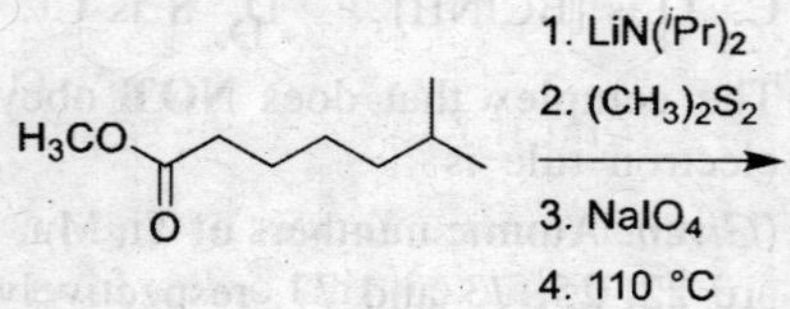

22. The major product formed in the following reaction is

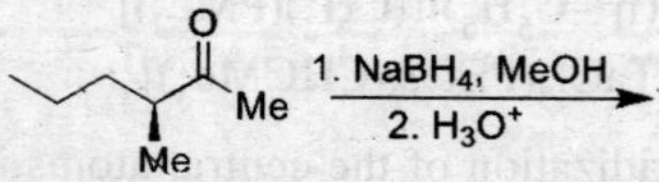

A. 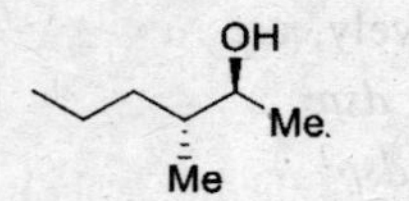

B. 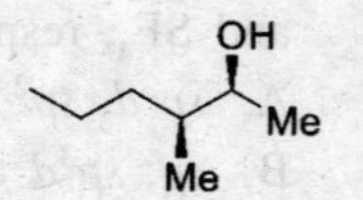

C. 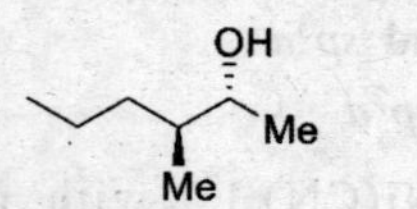

D. 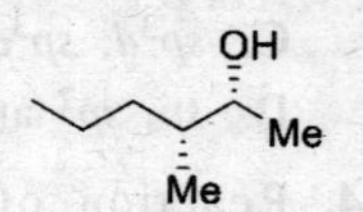

23. The major product formed in the following reaction is

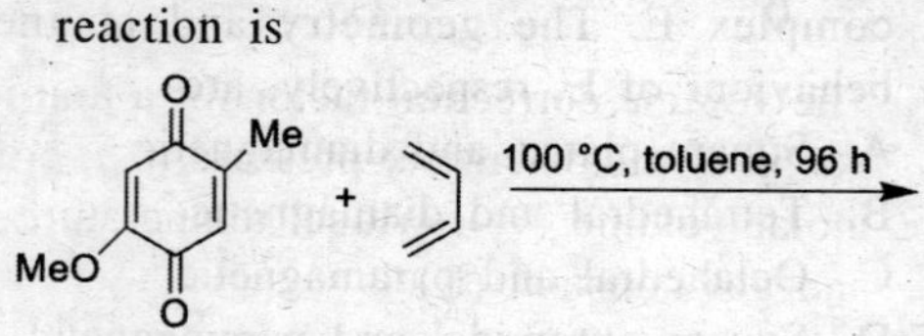

A. 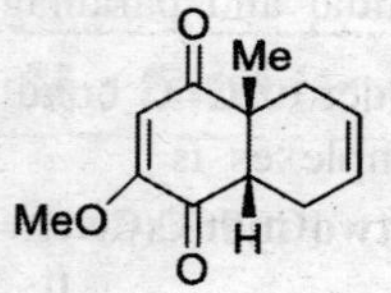

B. 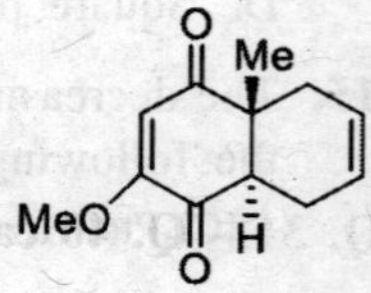

C. 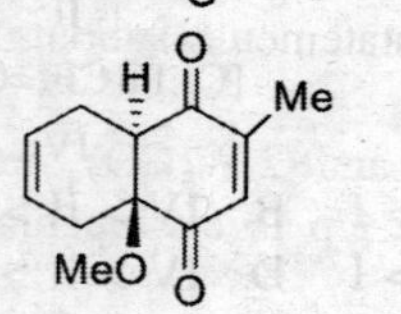

D. 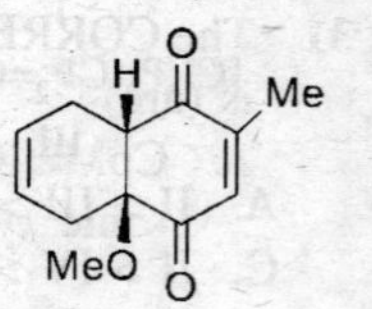

24. In the following reaction, compound Q is

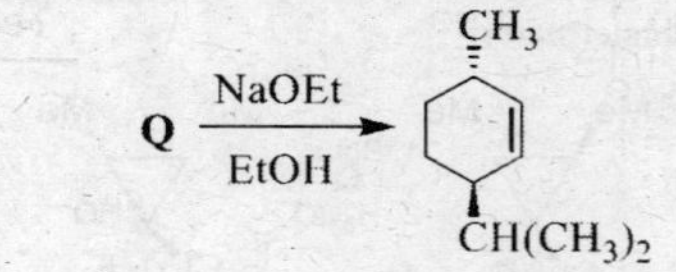

(only product)

A. 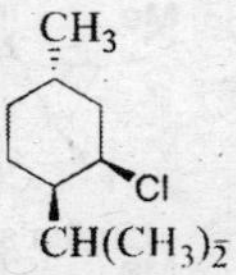

B. 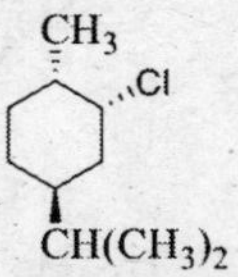

C. 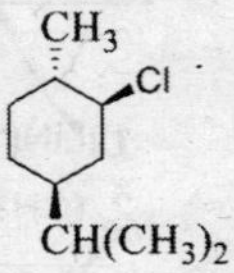

D. 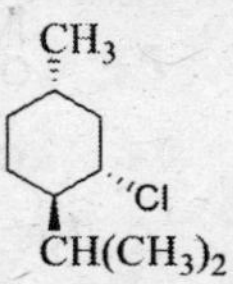

25. Monochromatic X-rays having energy 2.8×10^{-15} J diffracted (first order) from 200) plane of a cubic crystal at an angle 8.5°. The length of unit cell in Å of the crystal (*rounded off to one decimal place*) is
(*Given:* Planck's constant, $h = 6.626 \times 10^{-34}$ J s; $c = 3.0 \times 10^8$ m s^{-1})

A. 2.4 B. 3.4
C. 4.8 D. 9.8

26. For $\alpha > 0$, the value of the integral $\int_{-\infty}^{+\infty} xe^{-\alpha x^2}\,dx$ is

A. $\sqrt{\frac{\pi}{\alpha}}$ B. ∞
C. 0 D. 1

27. The volume correction factor for a non-ideal gas in terms of critical pressure (p_c), critical molar volume (V_c), critical temperature (T_c) and gas constant (R) is

A. $\frac{RT_c}{8p_c}$ B. $\frac{27R^2T_c^2}{64p_c}$
C. $\frac{8p_cV_c}{3T_c}$ D. $3p_cV_c^2$

28. Half-life ($t_{1/2}$) of a chemical reaction varies with the initial concentration of reactant (A_o) as given below:

A_o (mol L^{-1})	5×10^{-2}	4×10^{-2}	3×10^{-2}
$t_{1/2}$ (s)	360	450	600

The order of the reaction is

A. 0 B. 1
C. 2 D. 3

29. The CORRECT statement regarding the molecules BF_3 and CH_4 is

A. Both BF_3 and CH_4 are microwave active
B. Both BF_3 and CH_4 are infrared active
C. CH_4 is microwave active and infrared inactive
D. BF_3 is microwave active and infrared active

30. For the consecutive reaction,

$$X \xrightarrow{k_X} Y \xrightarrow{k_Y} Z$$

C_0 is the initial concentration of X. The concentration of X, Y and Z at time t are C_X, C_Y and C_Z, respectively. The expression for the concentration of Y at time t is

A. $\frac{k_X C_0}{k_Y - k_X}(e^{-k_X t} - e^{-k_Y t})$
B. $\frac{k_X C_X}{k_Y - k_X}(e^{-k_X t} - e^{-k_Y t})$
C. $\frac{k_X C_0}{k_Y - k_X}(e^{-k_Y t} - e^{-k_X t})$
D. $\frac{k_X C_X}{k_Y - k_X}(e^{-k_Y t} - e^{-k_X t})$

Section B : Multiple Select Questions (MSQ)

Q. 31 – Q. 40 carry two marks each.

31. The CORRECT statement(s) about the species is (are)

A. $CpMO(CO)_3$ and $C_pW(CO)_3$ are isoelectronic (where Cp is cyclopentadienyl)
B. CH_2^- and NH_2 are isolobal and isoelectronic
C. BH and CH are isolobal and isoelectronic
D. CH_3 and $Mn(CO)_5$ are isolobal

32. The complex(es) that show(s) Jahn-Teller distortion is (are)

A. $[Co(CN)_5(H_2O)]^{3-}$

B. $[NiF_6]^{2-}$

C. $[Mn(CNMe)_6]^{2+}$

D. $[Co(en)_2F_2]^+$

33. The CORRECT statement(s) about sodium nitroprusside is (are)

A. It is a paramagnetic complex

B. Nitroprusside ion is formed in the brown ring test for nitrates

C. It is used for the detection of S^{2-} in aqueous solution

D. It contains nitrosyl ligand as NO^+

34. The pigment responsible for red colour in tomato has one functional group. The CORRECT statement(s) about this functional group is (are)

A. It decolourizes bromine water

B. It gives hydrazone derivative on reaction with 2, 4-dinitrophenylhydrazine

C. It gets cleaved on reaction with ozone

D. It gives positive silver mirror test

35. Hantzsch pyridine synthesis involves several steps. Some of those are

A. Aldol reaction

B. Darzens reaction

C. Mannich reaction

D. Michael addition

36. The compound(s), which give(s) benzoic acid on oxidation with $KMnO_4$, is (are)

A. 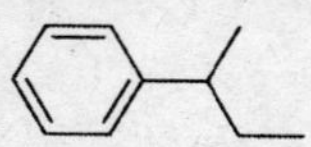

B. 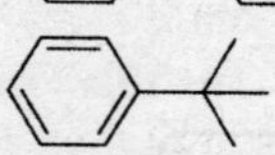

C. 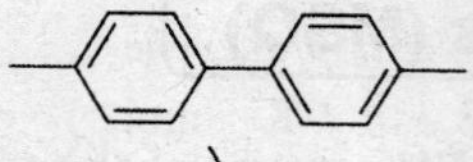

D. 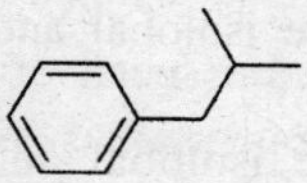

37. The products **P** and **Q** formed in the reaction are

A. **P** = 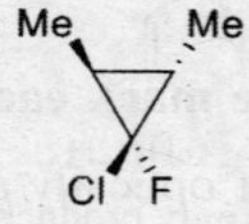 **Q** = 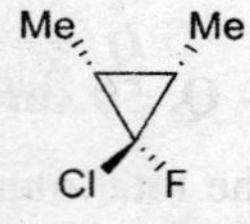

B. **P** = 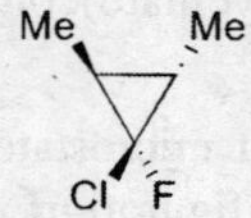 **Q** = 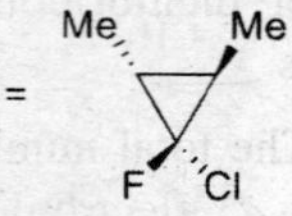

C. **P** = 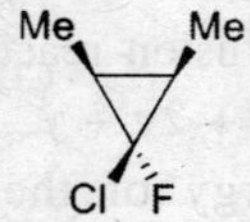 **Q** = 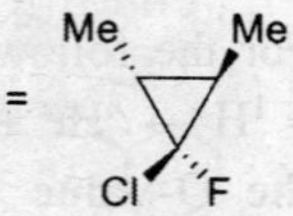

D. **P** = 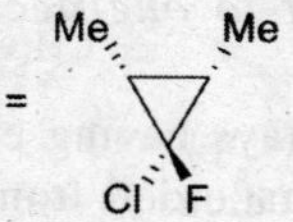 **Q** = 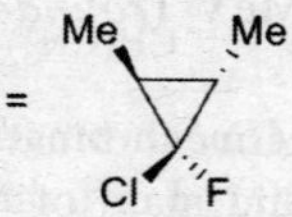

38. The functional group(s) in reducing sugar that test positive with Tollen's reagent is (are)

A. Aldehyde B. Ketone

C. Hemi-acetal D. Acetal

39. Among the following, the anti-aromatic compound(s) is (are)

A.  B. 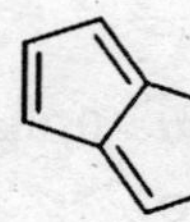

C.  D. 

40. The CORRECT Maxwell relation(s) derived from the fundamental equations of thermodynamics is (are)

A. $\left(\frac{\partial S}{\partial p}\right)_T = -\left(\frac{\partial V}{\partial T}\right)_p$

B. $\left(\frac{\partial S}{\partial V}\right)_T = \left(\frac{\partial p}{\partial T}\right)_V$

C. $\left(\frac{\partial T}{\partial V}\right)_S = \left(\frac{\partial p}{\partial S}\right)_V$

D. $\left(\frac{\partial T}{\partial p}\right)_S = \left(\frac{\partial V}{\partial S}\right)_p$

Section C : Numerical Answer Type (NAT)

Q. 41 – Q. 50 carry one mark each.

41. The total number of optically active isomers of dichloridobis(glycinato)cobaltate(III) ion is ____.

42. The total number of microstates possible for a d^8 electronic configuration is ____.

43. For the following fusion reaction,

$4\ {}^{1}H \rightarrow {}^{4}He + 2\beta^{+} + 2\nu + \gamma$

the Q-value (energy of the reaction) in MeV (*rounded off to one decimal place*) is ____.

(*Given:* Mass of ${}^{1}H$ nucleus is 1.007825 *u* and mass of ${}^{4}He$ nucleus is 4.002604 *u*)

44. MgO crystallizes as rock salt structure with unit cell length 2.12 Å. From electrostatic model, the calculated lattice energy in kJ mol^{-1} (*rounded off to the nearest integer*) is ____.

(*Given:* $N_A = 6.022 \times 10^{23}\ mol^{-1}$; Madelung constant = 1.748; $\varepsilon_0 = 8.854 \times 10^{-12}\ J^{-1}\ C^2\ m^{-1}$; charge of an electron = 1.602×10^{-19} C)

45. Calcium crystallizes in *fcc* lattice of unit cell length 5.56 Å and density 1.4848 g cm^{-3}. The percentage of Schottky defects (rounded off to one decimal place) in the crystal is ____.

(*Given*: Atmoic mass of Ca is 40 g mol^{-1}; $N_A = 6.022 \times 10^{23}\ mol^{-1}$)

46. Among the following, the total number of terpenes(terpenoids) is ____.

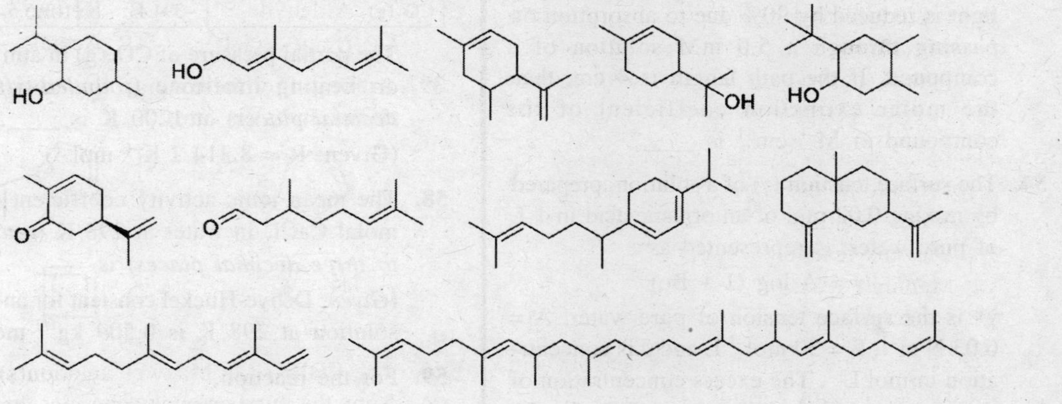

47. A buffer solution is prepared by mixing 0.3 M NH_3 and 0.1 M NH_4NO_3. If K_b of NH_3 is 1.6×10^{-5} at 25 °C, then the pH (*rounded off to one decimal place*) of the buffer solution at 25 °C is ____.

48. The dissociation constant of a weak monoprotic acid is 1.6×10^{-5} and its molar conductance at infinite dilution is 360.5×10^{-4} mho m^2 mol^{-1}. For 0.01 M solution of this acid, the specific conductance is $n \times 10^{-2}$ mho m^{-1}. The value of *n* (*rounded off to two decimal places*) is ____.

49. Adsorption of a toxic gas on 1.0 g activated charcoal is 0.75 cm^3 both at 2.5 atm, 140 K and at 30.0 atm, 280 K. The isosteric enthalpy for adsorption of the gas in kJ mol–1 (*rounded off to two decimal places*) is ____.

(*Given:* R = 8.314 J K^{-1} mol^{-1})

50. If the root mean square speed of hydrogen gas at a particular temperature is 1900 m s^{-1}, then the root mean square speed of nitrogen gas at the same temperature, in m s^{-1} (*rounded off to the nearest integer*), is ____.

(*Given:* atomic mass of H is 1 g mol^{-1}; atomic mass of N is 14 g mol^{-1})

Q. 51 – Q. 60 carry two marks each.

51. If the crystal field splitting energy of $[Co(NH_3)_4]^{2+}$ is 5900 cm^{-1}, then the magnitude of its crystal field stabilization energy, in kJ mol^{-1} (*rounded off to one decimal place*), is ____.

52. A salt mixture (1.0 g) contains 25 wt% of $MgSO_4$ and 75 wt% of $\mathbf{M}_2SO_4$. Aqueous solution of this salt mixture on treating with excess $BaCl_2$ solution results in the precipitation of 1.49 g of $BaSO_4$. The atomic mass of **M** in g mol^{-1} (*rounded off to two decimal places*) is ____.
(*Given:* the atomic masses of Mg, S, O, Ba and Cl are 24.31, 32.06, 16.00, 137.33 and 35.45 g mol^{-1}, respectively)

53. The intensity of a monochromatic visible light is reduced by 90% due to absorption on passing through a 5.0 mM solution of a compound. If the path length is 4 cm, then the molar extinction coefficient of the compound in M^{-1} cm^{-1} is ____.

54. The surface tension (γ) of a solution, prepared by mixing 0.02 mol of an organic acid in 1 L of pure water, is represented as

$$\gamma^* - \gamma = A \log (1 + Bc)$$

γ^* is the surface tension of pure water, A = 0.03 N m^{-1}, B = 50 mol^{-1} L and c is concentration in mol L^{-1}. The excess concentration of the organic acid at the surface of the liquid, determined by Gibbs adsorption equation at 300 K is $n \times 10^{-6}$ mol m^{-2}. The value of n (*rounded off to two decimal places*) is ____.
(*Given:* R 8.314 J K^{-1} mol–^{1})

55. The separation of energy levels in the rotational spectrum of CO is 3.8626 cm^{-1}. The bond length (assume it does not change during rotation of CO in Å (*rounded off to two decimal places*) is ____.
(*Given:* Planck's constant h = 6.626 × 10^{-34} J s; NA = 6.022 × 10^{23} mol^{-1}; atomic mass of C is 12 g mol^{-1}; atomic mass of O is 16 g mol^{-1}; c = 3 × 10^{8} m s^{-1})

56. A dilute solution prepared by dissolving a nonvolatile solute in one litre water shows a depression in freezing point of 0.186 K. This solute neither dissociates nor associates in water. The boiling point of the solution in K (*rounded off to three decimal places*) is ____.
(*Given:* For pure water, boiling point = 373.15 K; cryoscopic constant = 1.86 K (mol kg^{-1})$^{-1}$; ebullioscopic constant = 0.51 K (mol kg^{-1})$^{-1}$)

57. The thermodynamic data at 298 K for the decomposition reaction of limestone at equilibrium is given below

$$CaCO_3(s) \rightleftharpoons CaO(s) + CO_2(g)$$

Thermodynamic quantity	$\mu°$(kJ mol^{-1})	ΔH_f°(kJ mol^{-1})
$CaCO_3(s)$	–1128.8	–1206.9
CaO(s)	–604.0	–635.1
$CO_2(g)$	–394.4	–393.5

The partial pressure of CO_2(g) in atm evolved on heating limestone (*rounded off to two decimal places*) at 1200 K is ____.
(Given: R = 8.314 J K^{-1} mol^{-1})

58. The mean ionic activity coefficient of 0.004 molal $CaCl_2$ in water at 298 K (*rounded off to three decimal places*) is ____.
(*Given:* Debye-Hückel constant for an aqueous solution at 298 K is 0.509 kg$^{1/2}$ mol$^{-1/2}$)

59. For the reaction,

$$\mathbf{Q} + \mathbf{R} \underset{k_{-1}}{\overset{k_1}{\rightleftharpoons}} \mathbf{X} \xrightarrow{k_2} \mathbf{P}$$

k_1 = 2.5 × 10^{5} L mol^{-1} s^{-1}, k_{-1} = 1.0 × 10^{4} s^{-1} and k_2 = 10 s^{-1}. Under steady state approximation, the rate constant for the overall reaction in L mol^{-1} s^{-1} (*rounded off to the nearest integer*) is ____.

60. For the molecule,
$CH_3–CH=CH–CH(OH)–CH=CH–CH=C(CH_3)_2$
the number of all possible stereoisomers is ____.

ANSWERS

SECTION A: MCQ (Multiple Choise Questions)

1	2	3	4	5	6	7	8	9	10
C	C	D	C	A	C	B	B	B	A
11	**12**	**13**	**14**	**15**	**16**	**17**	**18**	**19**	**20**
B	D	C	B	C	C	D	B	D	D
21	**22**	**23**	**24**	**25**	**26**	**27**	**28**	**29**	**30**
B	C	A	C	C	C	A	C	B	A

SECTION B: MSQ (Multiple Select Questions)

31	32	33	34	35
A, B, D	A, C	C, D	A, C	A, D
36	**37**	**38**	**39**	**40**
A, D	B	A, B, C	B, C, D	A, B, D

SECTION C: NAT (Numerical Answer Type Questions)

41	42	43	44	45
6	45	26.7 to 26.8	−7880 to −6150 or 6150 to 7880	3.9 to 4.1
46	**47**	**48**	**49**	**50**
7	9.7	1.44 to 1.47	−5.81 to −5.75	507 to 510
51	**52**	**53**	**54**	**55**
−84.8 to −84.2 or 84.2 to 84.8	39.98 to 39.25	50	2.60 to 2.62	1.12 to 1.14
56	**57**	**58**	**59**	**60**
373.201	4320 to 4.35	0.772 to 0.775	250	8

EXPLANATORY ANSWERS

1. We have,

I. $$HCO(CO)_4 \xrightarrow{at\ 298K} \underset{\text{Conjugate base}}{{}^{+}CO(CO)_4} + H^+$$

II. $$HCO(CO)_3(PPh_3) \xrightarrow{298K} \underset{\text{Conjugate base}}{{}^{\ominus}CO(CO)_3(PPh_3)} + H^{\oplus}$$

III. $$HCO(CO)_3(P(OPh)_3) \xrightarrow{298K} \underset{\text{Conjugate base}}{{}^{\ominus}CO(CO)_3P(OPh)_3} + H^{\oplus}$$

Hence,

π = acceptor tendency

$CO > P(OPh)_3 > PPh_3$

Since, stability of base conjugate

= Acidity of compounds

$$= \frac{1}{pK_a}$$

Therefore, correct order of pK_a for the compounds I to IV in water at 298K.

IV > II > III > I.

2. For isoelectronic species

Ionic radius = Negative charge

$$= \frac{1}{\text{Positive charge}}$$

Therefore, the correct order of ionic radii are:

$F^{\ominus} > Na^+ > Mg^{2+} > Al^{3+}$.

3. We have, $[NiCl_2(PPh_3)_2]$

Oxidation state of Ni = +2

At room temperature, pairing does not occur, then

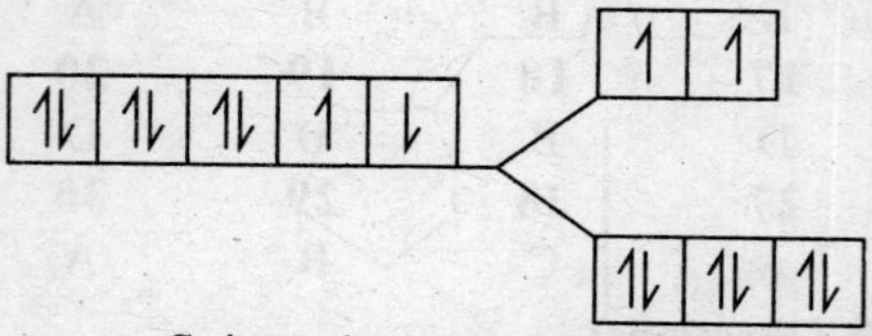

$\therefore n = 2$

$\therefore$ Spin only magnetic moment

$= \sqrt{n(n+2)}$

$= \sqrt{2(2+2)} = \sqrt{8} = 2.83$ BM

Now, $[Mn(NCS)_6]^{4-}$

Oxidation state of Mn = +2

NCS in weak field ligand, so pairing does not occur. Then,

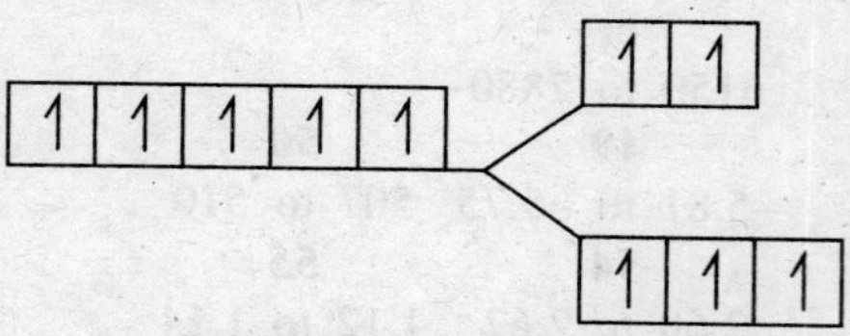

$\therefore n = 5$

$\therefore$ Spin only magnetic moment

$= \sqrt{n(n+2)}$

$= \sqrt{5(5+2)}$

$= \sqrt{5 \times 7}$

$= \sqrt{35} = 5.92$ BM.

4. We have, Radial node = $n - l - 1$

For option,

A. $n = 3,\ l = 0,\ m_l = 0$

$\therefore$ Radial node = 3 − 0 − 1 = 2

$n = 2,\ l = 0,\ m_l = 0$

= 2 − 0 − 1 = 1.

Since, the radial nodes of two sets of quantum numbers are not equal.

Hence, option (A) is false.

B. $n = 3,\ l = 1,\ m_l = 1$

$\therefore$ Radial node = 3 − 1 − 1 = 1

$n = 2,\ l = 1,\ m_l = 0$

= 2 − 1 − 1 = 0

Since, the radial nodes of two sets of quantium numbers are not equal.

Hence, option (B) is false.

C. $n = 3,\ l = 2,\ m_l = 0$

$\therefore$ Radial node = 3 − 2 − 1 = 0

$n = 2,\ l = 1,\ m_l = 0$

= 2 − 1 − 1 = 0

Since, the radial nodes of two sets of quantum numbers are same.

Hence, option (C) is true.

D. $n = 3,\ l = 1,\ m_l = -1$

$\therefore$ Radial node = 3 − 1 − 1 = 2

$n = 2,\ l = 1,\ m_l = 0$

= 2 − 1 − 1 = 0.

Since, the radial nodes of two sets of quantum numbers are not equal, then option (D) is false.

Therefore, correct option is (C).

5.

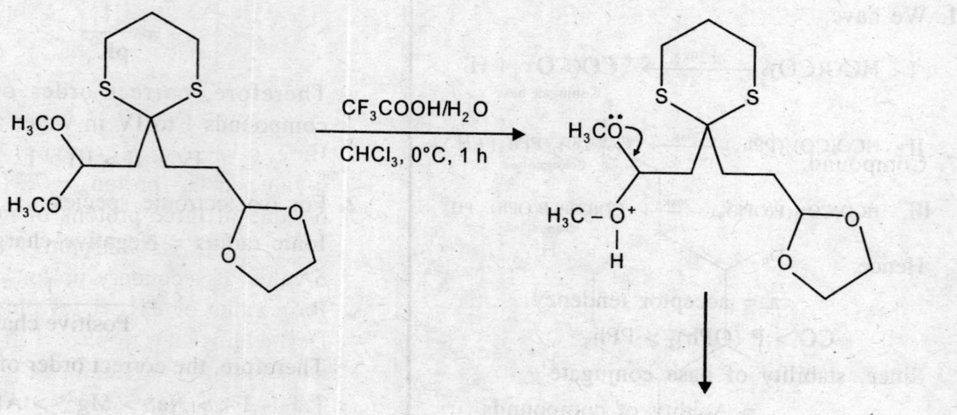

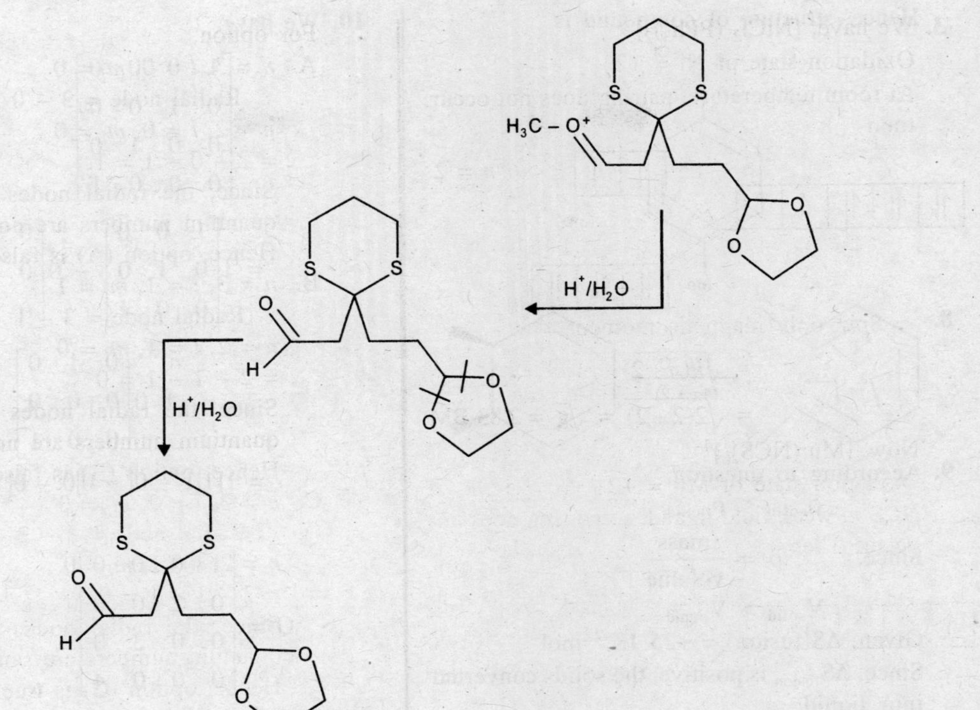

6.

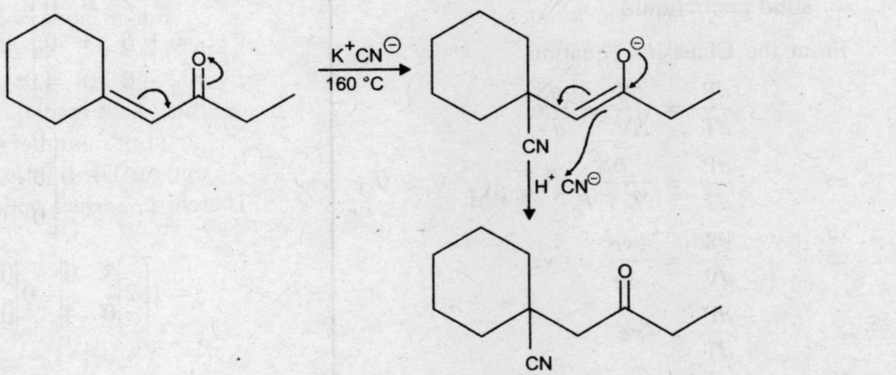

7. Compound:

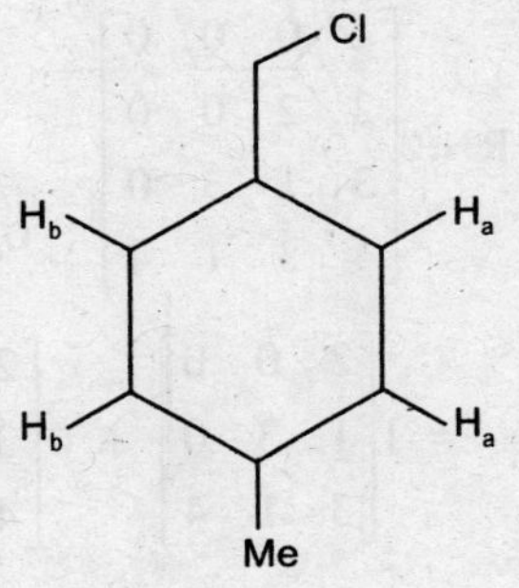

Here, δ-value of H_a (proton) = 7.21 ppm

δ-value of H_b (proton) = 7.31 ppm

δ-value of three protons of methyl group = 2.3 ppm

δ-value of secondary proton of CH_2 group

Base value of CH_2 = 1.3 ppm

Deshielding due to phenyl group = 1.5 ppm

Deshielding due to chloride group = 2.0 ppm

Total = 4.8 ppm

Hence, structure of compound is

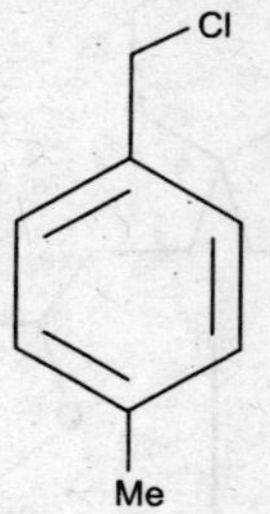

8.

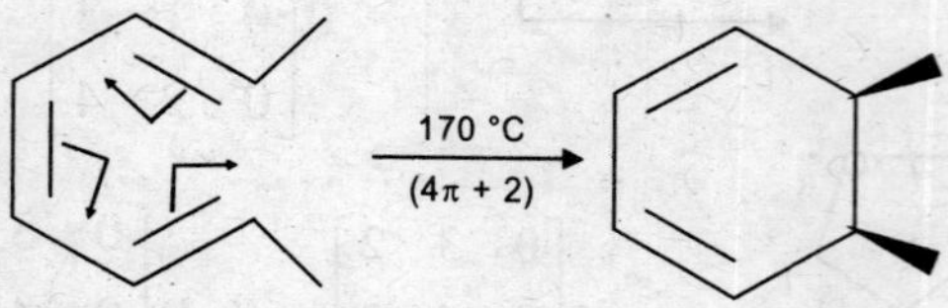

9. According to question,

$$\rho_{solid} < \rho_{liquid}$$

Since, $\rho = \dfrac{\text{mass}}{\text{volume}}$

$\therefore \quad V_{solid} > V_{liquid}$

Given, $\Delta S(\text{fusion}) = +25 \text{ JK}^{-1} \text{ mol}^{-1}$

Since, ΔS_{fusion} is positive, the solids converted into liquid

$\therefore$ solid $\rightleftharpoons$ liquid

From the Claussius equation,

$$\frac{dP}{dT} = \frac{\Delta S}{\Delta V} = \frac{dS}{dV}$$

$$\Rightarrow \frac{dP}{dT} = \frac{\Delta S}{V_l - V_s} \qquad (\because V_l < V_s)$$

$$\Rightarrow \frac{dS}{dV} = \frac{+ve}{-ve} = -\text{ve}$$

$$\therefore \frac{dP}{dT} = -\text{ve}$$

Hence, slope has negative value.

Therefore, pressure-temperature diagram for the fusion of M is given as

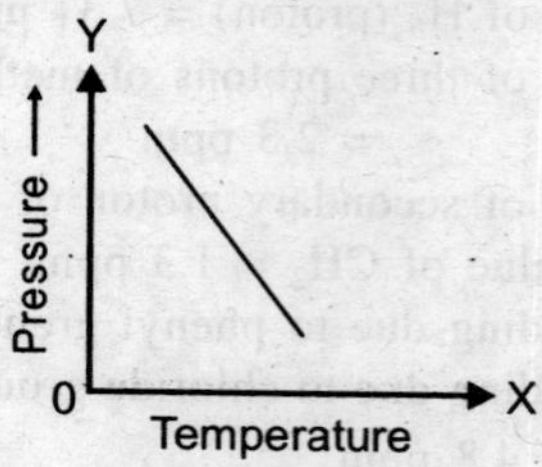

10. We have,

$$P = \begin{bmatrix} 1 & 0 & 0 & 0 \\ 0 & 1 & 0 & 0 \\ 0 & 0 & 1 & 0 \\ 0 & 0 & 0 & 1 \end{bmatrix}$$

$$= 1\begin{bmatrix} 1 & 0 & 0 \\ 0 & 1 & 0 \\ 0 & 0 & 1 \end{bmatrix} - 0\begin{bmatrix} 0 & 0 & 0 \\ 0 & 1 & 0 \\ 0 & 0 & 1 \end{bmatrix}$$

$$+ 0\begin{bmatrix} 0 & 1 & 0 \\ 0 & 0 & 0 \\ 0 & 0 & 1 \end{bmatrix} - 0\begin{bmatrix} 0 & 1 & 0 \\ 0 & 0 & 1 \\ 0 & 0 & 0 \end{bmatrix}$$

$$= 1[1|1 - 0| - 0|0 - 0| + 0|0 - 0|]$$
$$- 0 + 0 - 0 = 1$$

$$Q = \begin{bmatrix} 1 & 0 & 0 & 0 \\ 0 & 2 & 0 & 0 \\ 0 & 0 & 3 & 0 \\ 0 & 0 & 0 & 4 \end{bmatrix}$$

$$= 1\begin{bmatrix} 2 & 0 & 0 \\ 0 & 3 & 0 \\ 0 & 0 & 4 \end{bmatrix} - 0\begin{bmatrix} 0 & 0 & 0 \\ 0 & 3 & 0 \\ 0 & 0 & 4 \end{bmatrix}$$

$$+ 0\begin{bmatrix} 0 & 2 & 0 \\ 0 & 0 & 0 \\ 0 & 0 & 4 \end{bmatrix} - 0\begin{bmatrix} 0 & 2 & 0 \\ 0 & 0 & 3 \\ 0 & 0 & 0 \end{bmatrix}$$

$$= 1\left[2\begin{vmatrix} 3 & 0 \\ 0 & 4 \end{vmatrix} - 0\begin{vmatrix} 0 & 0 \\ 0 & 4 \end{vmatrix} + 0\begin{vmatrix} 0 & 3 \\ 0 & 0 \end{vmatrix}\right]$$
$$+ 0 + 0 + 0$$

$$= 1[2[12 - 0]] + 0 + 0 + 0 + 0 + 0 = 24$$

$$R = \begin{bmatrix} 1 & 0 & 0 & 0 \\ 2 & 2 & 0 & 0 \\ 3 & 1 & 3 & 0 \\ 4 & 3 & 1 & 4 \end{bmatrix}$$

$$= 1\begin{bmatrix} 2 & 0 & 0 \\ 1 & 3 & 0 \\ 3 & 1 & 4 \end{bmatrix} + 0\begin{bmatrix} 2 & 0 & 0 \\ 3 & 3 & 0 \\ 4 & 1 & 4 \end{bmatrix}$$

$$+\,0\begin{bmatrix}2&2&0\\3&1&0\\4&3&4\end{bmatrix} - 0\begin{bmatrix}2&2&0\\3&1&3\\4&3&1\end{bmatrix}$$

$$=1\left[2\begin{vmatrix}3&0\\1&4\end{vmatrix} - 0\begin{vmatrix}1&0\\3&4\end{vmatrix} + 0\begin{vmatrix}1&3\\3&1\end{vmatrix}\right] + 0 + 0 + 0$$

$$= 1[2(12 - 0) - 0 + 0] + 0 + 0 + 0 = 24$$

$$S = \begin{array}{c} \\ R_1 \\ R_2 \\ R_3 \\ R_4 \end{array}\begin{array}{c} \begin{matrix}C_1 & C_2 & C_3 & C_4\end{matrix} \\ \begin{bmatrix}1&2&3&1\\2&3&4&2\\3&4&1&3\\4&1&2&4\end{bmatrix}\end{array} \xleftarrow{C_1 + C_2 + C_4}$$

$$\begin{array}{c} \\ R_1 \\ R_2 \\ R_3 \\ R_4 \end{array}\begin{array}{c} \begin{matrix}C_1 & C_2 & C_3 & C_4\end{matrix} \\ \begin{bmatrix}0&2&3&1\\0&3&4&2\\0&4&1&3\\0&1&2&4\end{bmatrix}\end{array} \xrightarrow{R_1 \to 2R_2 \to R_3}$$

$$\begin{bmatrix}0&0&5&-1\\0&3&4&2\\0&4&1&3\\0&1&2&4\end{bmatrix}$$

$$= 0\begin{bmatrix}3&4&2\\4&1&3\\1&2&4\end{bmatrix} - 0\begin{bmatrix}0&4&2\\0&1&3\\0&2&4\end{bmatrix}$$

$$+\,5\begin{bmatrix}0&3&2\\0&4&3\\0&1&4\end{bmatrix} - (-1)\begin{bmatrix}0&3&4\\0&4&1\\0&1&2\end{bmatrix}$$

$$= 0 - 0 + 5[0(16 - 3) - 3(0 - 0) + 2(0 - 0)]$$
$$+ 1[0(8 - 1) - 3(0 - 0) + 4(0 - 0)] = 0$$

Hence, the matrices with non-zero determinant are: P, Q and R.

11.

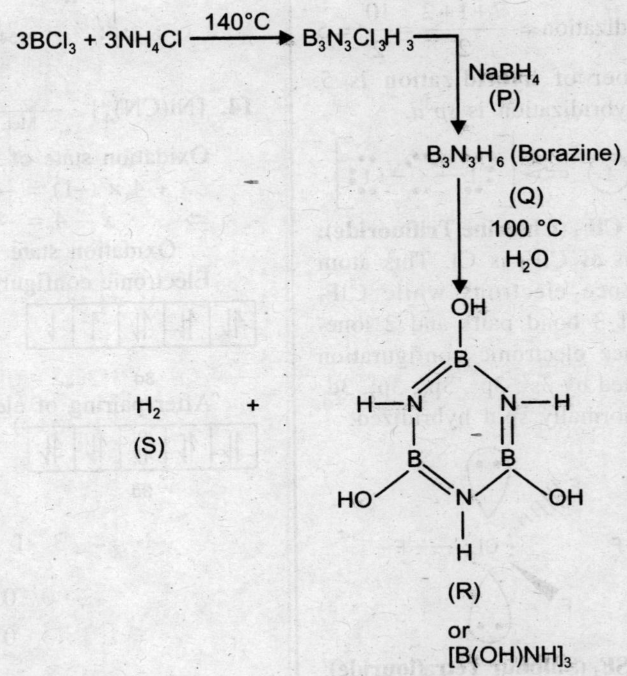

Hence, the value of R is $[B(OH)NH]_3$.

12. We have, $[TaCl_3(PEt_3)_2(CHCMe_3)]$

Count number of electrons

$$Ta = 5e^{\ominus}$$
$$Cl = 1e^{\ominus}$$
$$[PEt_3] = 2e^{\ominus}$$
$$(CHCMe_3) = 2e^{\ominus}$$
$$\therefore 5 + (1 \times 3) + (2 \times 2) + 2$$
$$= 5 + 3 + 4 + 2 = 14e^{\ominus}.$$

13. Hybridization of I_3^- (Triiodide ion)

We have,

Numer of hybridization = Valence electron + Monovalent + (Negative charge) – (Positive charge)/2

There are 7 valence electrons in its outer shell and 2 monovalent atoms are also present. Further during the combination of iodine with the two other iodine atoms, the central atom gains a negative charge whose value will be taken as 1.

We substitute the values according to formula,

We get,

$$\text{Number of hybridization} = \frac{7+1+2}{2} = \frac{10}{2} = 5$$

Thus, the number of hybridization is 5. Therefore, the hybridization is sp^3d.

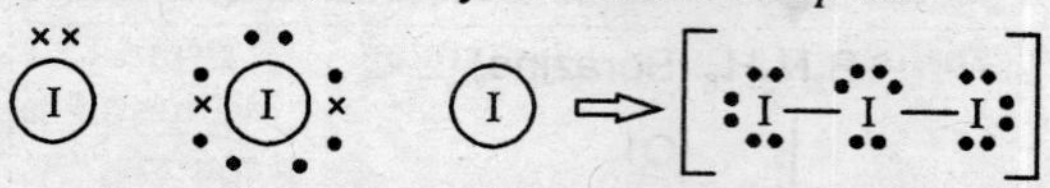

Hybridization of ClF_3 (Chlorine Trifluoride): The central atom of ClF_3 is Cl. This atom contains 7 valence electrons while ClF_3 should consist of 3 bond pairs and 2 lone-pairs. The valence electronic configuration of Cl is represented by $3s^2$, $3p_x^2$, $3p_y^2$, $3p_z^1$, 3d. Hence, ClF_3 is normally sp^3d hybridized.

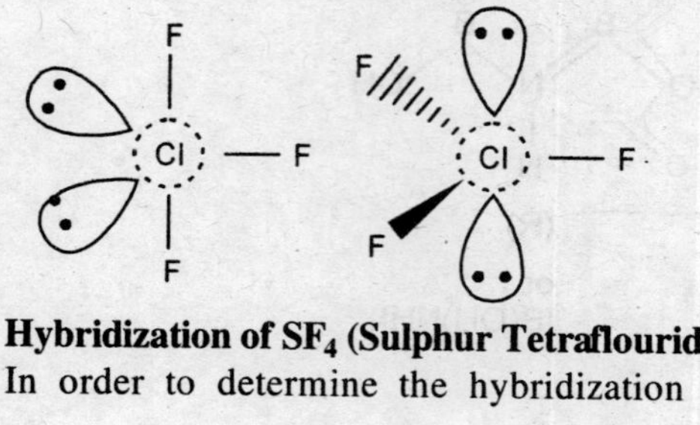

Hybridization of SF_4 (Sulphur Tetraflouride): In order to determine the hybridization on SF_4, first we understand Lewis structure and number of valence electrons that are present. The SF_4 molecule consists of a total number of 34 valence electrons. Here, 6 will come from sulphur (S) and each of the flourine (F) atoms will have 7 valence electrons.

During the formation of SF_4, the sulphur (S) atom will form bonds with each F atoms, where 8 of valence electrons are used. Mean while, 4 flourine atoms will have 3 lone pair of electrons in it octet, which will further utilize 24 valence electrons. In addition 2 electrons will be kept as lone pair in S atom. When bonding takes place, there is a formation of 4 single bonds in S and it has 1 lone pair. So number of regions of electron density is 5.

The central atom S containing 5 valence atomic orbitals is basically hybridized to form five sp^3d hybrid orbitals.

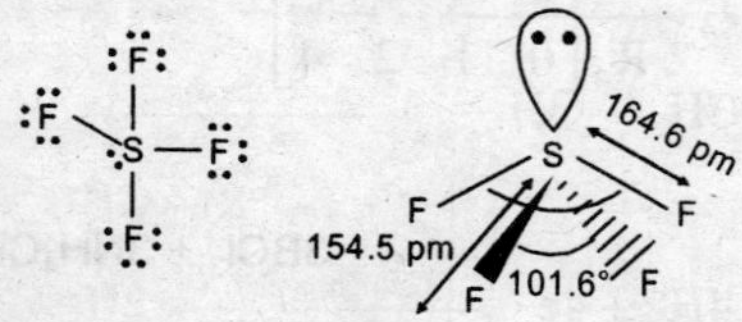

14. $[Ni(CN)_4]^{2-} \xrightarrow[\text{Met. K, liq. NH}_3]{-33°C} [Ni(CN)_4]^{4-}$

Oxidation state of Ni in $[Ni(CN)_4]^{4-}$

$$x + 4 \times (-1) = -4$$
$$\Rightarrow \quad x - 4 = -4 \Rightarrow x = 4 - 4 = 0$$

$\therefore$ Oxidation state of Ni = 0

Electronic configuration of Ni = [Ar] $3d^8\,4s^2$

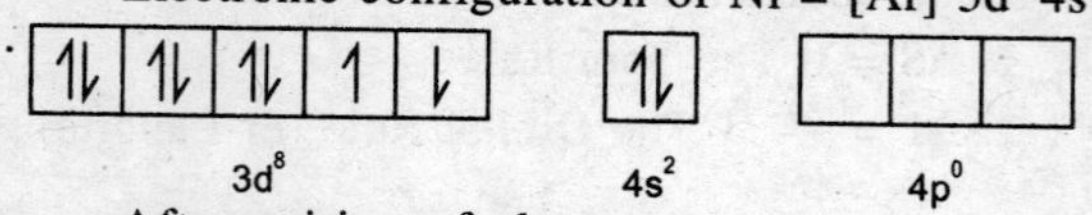

After pairing of electrons

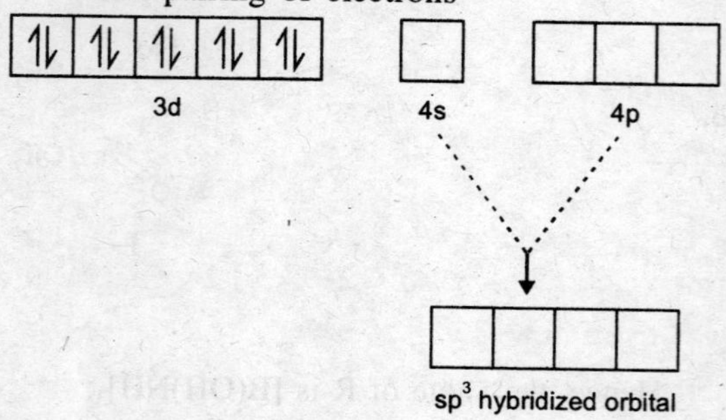

After pairing of electrons, there is no unpaired electron, therefore, the complex E is diamagnetic.

∴ Hybridization of complex E is sp^3. It is tetrahedral.

Thus, the geometric and magnetic behaviour of E are:

Tetrahedral and diamagnetic.

15. Back donation order in $CH_2 = CH_2$ from metal

$$CN > F > H$$

Back donation from metal ∝ Bond length of

$$CH_2 = CH_2$$

∴ The decreasing order of complexes are:

$$II > IV > III > I.$$

16. We have,

$$R - OH + H_2O \xrightarrow{\text{Cytochrome P-450}} R - OH + H_2O + 2e^{\ominus} + 2H^+$$

$$2H_2O_2 \xrightarrow{\text{Catalase}} 2H_2O + O_2$$

$$R - CH_2 - OH + O_2 \xrightarrow[\text{oxidase}]{\text{Galactose}} R - CHO + H_2O_2$$

$$O_2 + 4H^{\oplus} + 4e^{\ominus} \xrightarrow[\text{oxidase}]{\text{Cytochrome c}} 2H_2O$$

Hence, correct answer is (C).

17. From the crystal field theory, *d-d* transition is observed in $[Ti(H_2O)_6]^{3+}$.

The selection rules governing transitions between electronic energy levels of transition metal complexes are:

1. $\Delta S = 0$ The Spin Rule
2. $\Delta l = +/- 1$ The Orbital Rule (or Laporte)

The first rule says that allowed transitions must involve the promotion of electrons without a change in their spin. The second rule says that if the molecule has a center of symmetry, transitions within a given set of *p* or *d* orbitals (*i.e.*, those which only involve a redistribution of electrons within a given subshell) are forbidden.

Relaxation of these rules can occur through:

- **Spin-Orbit coupling:** this gives rise to weak spin forbidden bands.
- **Vibronic coupling:** an octahedral complex may have allowed vibrations where the molecule is asymmetric. Absorption of light at that moment is then possible.
- **Mixing:** π-acceptor and π-donor ligands can mix with the *d*-orbitals so transitions are no longer purely *d-d*.

Transition Types

1. **Charge transfer,** either ligand to metal or metal to ligand. These are often extremely intense and are generally found in the UV but they may have a tail into the visible.
2. *d-d*, these can occur in both the UV and visible region but since they are forbidden transitions have small intensities.

Expected intensities of electronic transitions

Transition type	Example	Typical values of ε/m^2mol^{-1}
Spin forbidden, Laporte forbidden	$[Mn(H_2O)_6]^{2+}$	0.1
Spin allowed (octahedral complex), Laporte forbidden	$[Ti(H_2O)_6]^{3+}$	1 – 10

18.

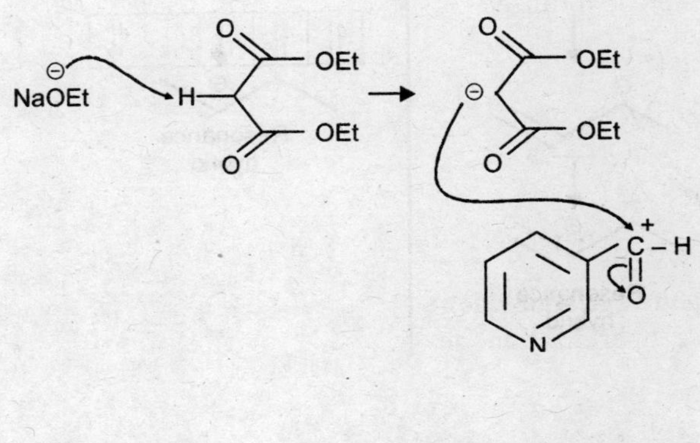

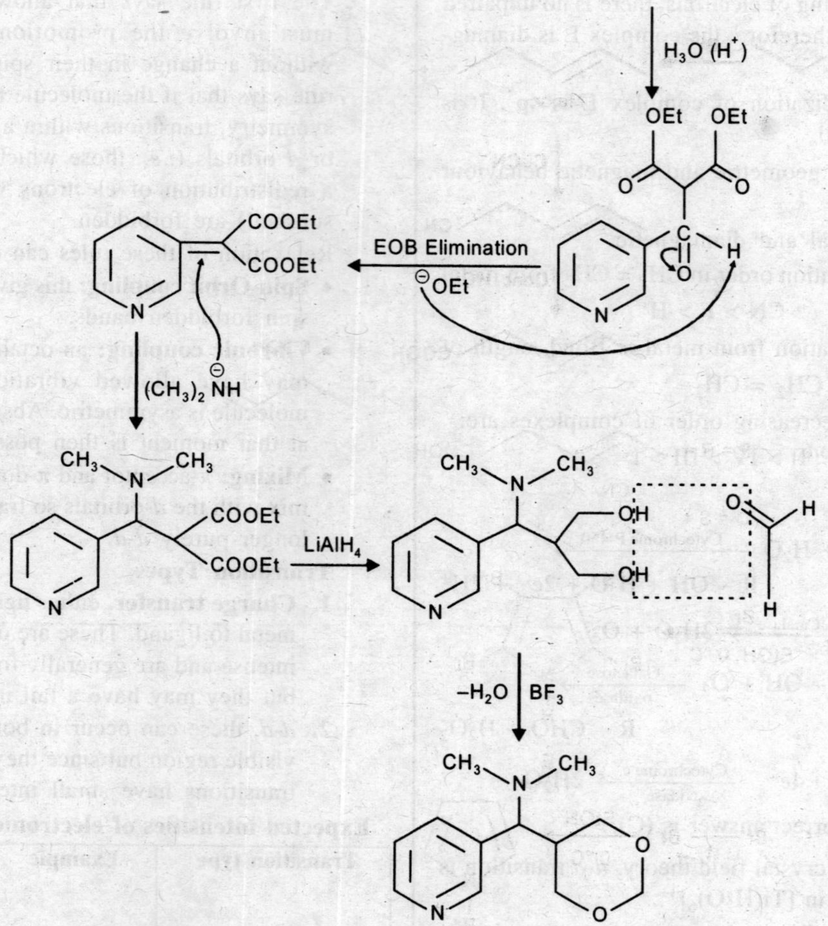
H3O (H+)
OEt
OEt
EOB Elimination
COOEt
COOEt
OEt
(CH3)2 NH
CH3
CH3
LiAlH4
OH
OH
−H2O
BF3

19.

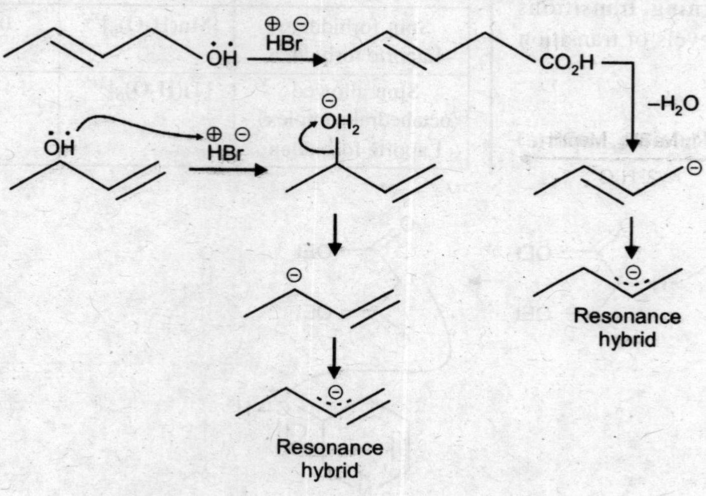
HBr
CO2H
−H2O
OH2
Resonance hybrid
Resonance hybrid

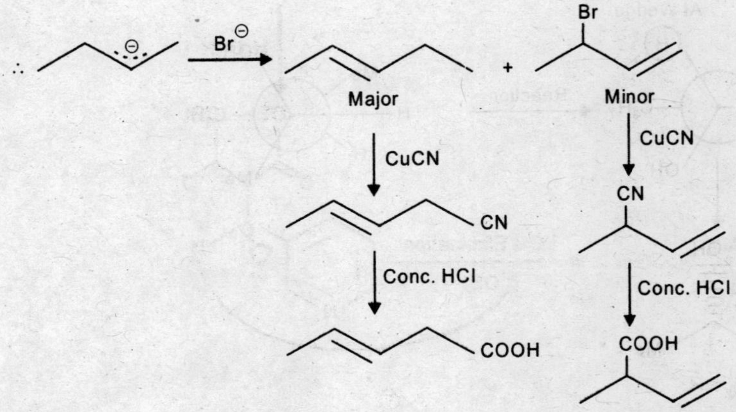

Therefore, P = R = 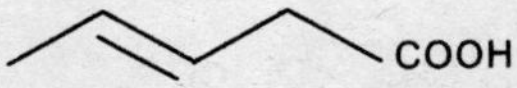 and

Q = S = 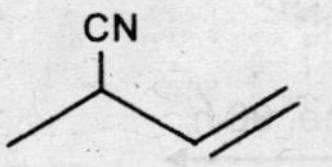

20. 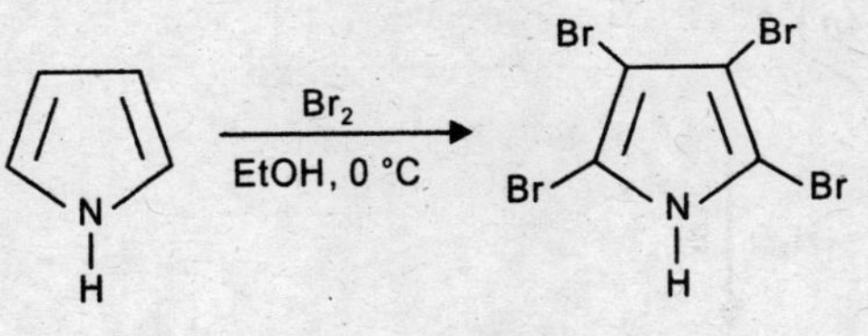

E

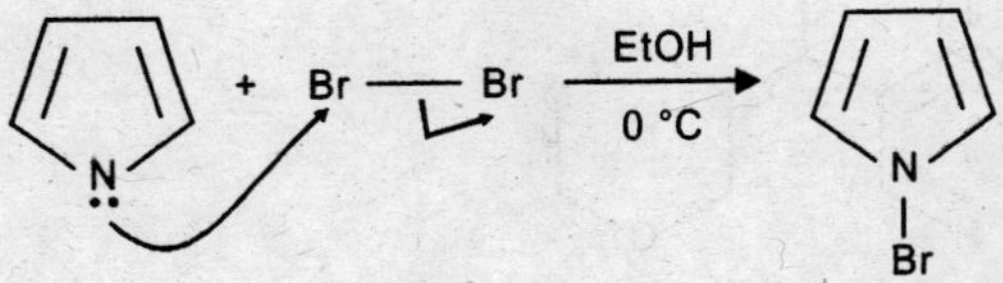

F

22. 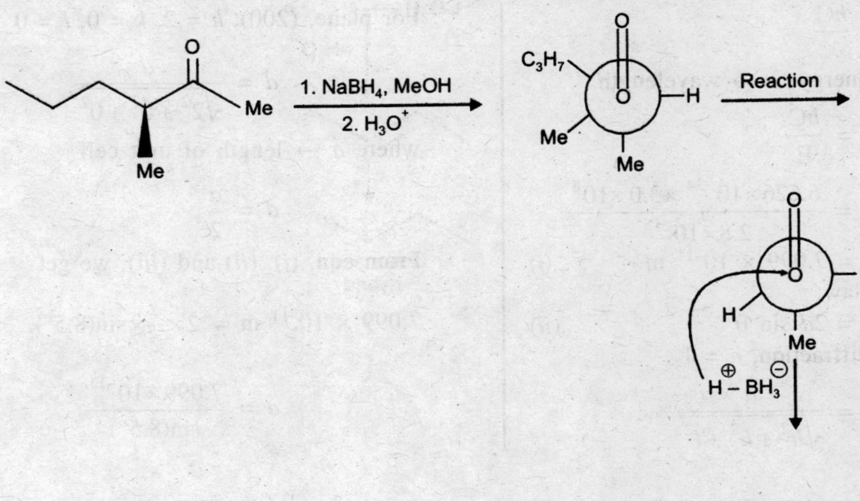

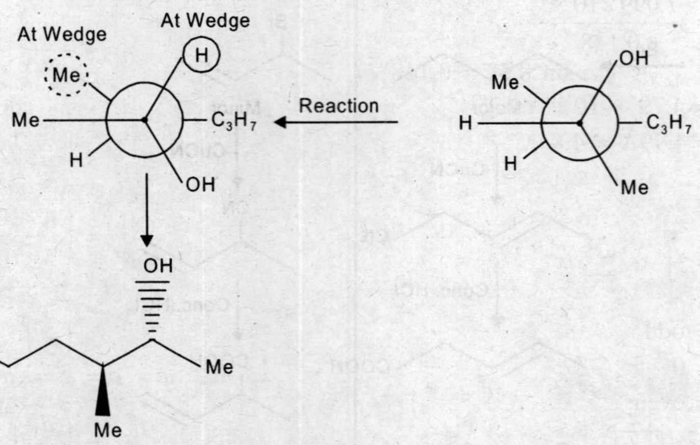

23.

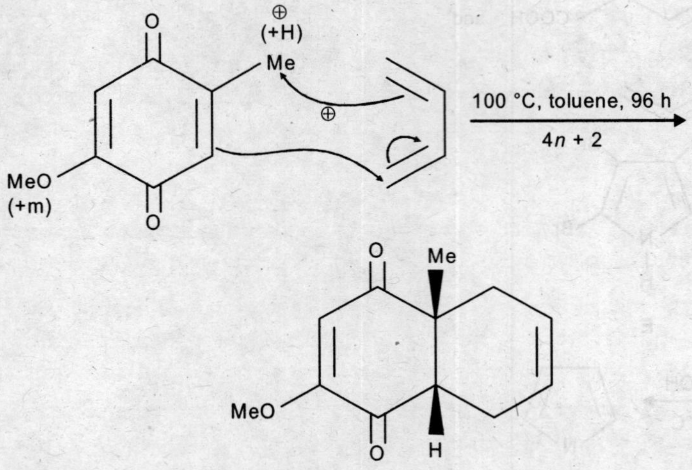

Hence, correct answer is (A).

25. We have, $E = \dfrac{hC}{\lambda}$

Where, E → energy, λ → wavelength

$$\therefore \quad \lambda = \frac{hC}{E}$$

$$= \frac{6.626\times10^{-34}\times3.0\times10^{8}}{2.8\times10^{-15}}$$

$$= 7.099 \times 10^{-11} \text{ m} \quad ...(i)$$

From Bragg's law,

$$n\lambda = 2d \sin\theta \quad ...(ii)$$

For Ist order diffraction, $n = 1$

$$d = \frac{a}{\sqrt{h^2+k^2+l^2}}$$

For plane, (200), $h = 2$, $k = 0$, $l = 0$

$$\therefore \quad d = \frac{a}{\sqrt{2^2+0^2+0^2}}$$

where a → length of unit cell

$$d = \frac{a}{2} \quad ...(iii)$$

From eqn. (*i*), (*ii*) and (*iii*), we get

$$7.099 \times 10^{-11} \text{ m} = 2\times\frac{a}{2}\times\sin(8.5°)$$

$$\therefore \quad a = \frac{7.099\times10^{-11}}{\sin(8.5°)}$$

$$= \frac{7.099 \times 10^{-11}}{0.148}$$
$$(\because \sin 8.5° = 0.148)$$
$$\therefore \quad a = 4.79 \times 10^{-10} \text{ m}$$
$$\therefore \quad a = 4.79 Å = 4.8 Å.$$

26. We have,

$$I = \int_{-\infty}^{+\infty} xe^{-\alpha x^2}\, dx$$

If n = odd
then $I = 0$
If n = even

then, $$I = \frac{\sqrt{\frac{n+1}{2}}}{\beta \frac{n+1}{2}}$$

$$\therefore \int_{-\infty}^{+\infty} x^1 e^{-\alpha x^2}\, dx$$

$n = 1$ *i.e.*, odd
Therefore, the integration becomes zero.

27. We know that,

$$T_c = \frac{8a}{27Rb}$$

$$\therefore \quad 27b = \frac{8a}{T_c R} \quad ...(i)$$

and $$P_c = \frac{a}{27b^2} \quad ...(ii)$$

From eqn. (*i*) and (*ii*), we get

$$P_c = \frac{a \times T_c \times R}{b \times 8a}$$

$$\therefore \quad b = \frac{T_c R}{8P_c}.$$

28. Given, $t'_{1/2} = 360$s
$t''_{1/2} = 450$s
$t'''_{1/2} = 600$ s
$a_1 = 5 \times 10^{-2}$ mol L^{-1}
$a_2 = 4 \times 10^{-2}$ mol L^{-1}
and $a_3 = 3 \times 10^{-2}$ mol L^{-1}

We know that

$$t_{1/2} \propto \frac{1}{a^{n-1}}$$

$$\therefore \quad \frac{t'_{1/2}}{t''_{1/2}} = \left(\frac{a_2}{a_1}\right)^{n-1}$$

$$\Rightarrow \quad \frac{360}{450} = \left(\frac{4 \times 10^{-2}}{5 \times 10^{-2}}\right)^{n-1}$$

$$\Rightarrow \quad \frac{4}{5} = \left(\frac{4}{5}\right)^{n-1}$$

$$\Rightarrow \quad n - 1 = 1 \Rightarrow n = 2$$

Again, $$\frac{t''_{1/2}}{t'''_{1/2}} = \left(\frac{a_3}{a_2}\right)^{n-1}$$

$$\therefore \quad \frac{450}{600} = \left(\frac{3 \times 10^{-2}}{4 \times 10^{-2}}\right)^{n-1}$$

$$\Rightarrow \quad \frac{3}{4} = \left(\frac{3}{4}\right)^{n-1}$$

$$\Rightarrow \quad n = 1 = 1 \Rightarrow n = 2.$$

29. The molecule is microwave active when molecule have permanent dipole moment:

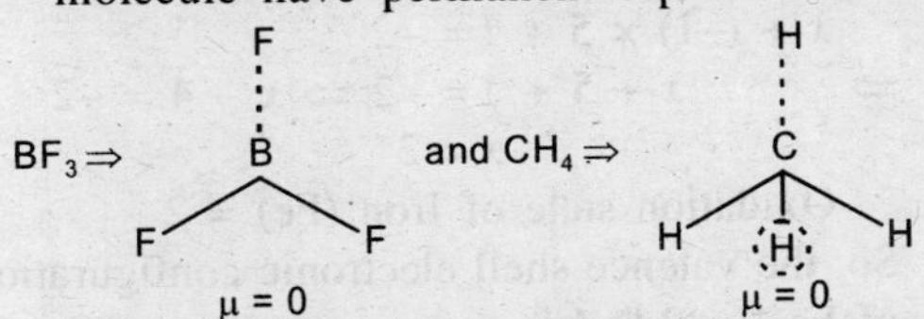

BF_3 and CH_4 have no permanent dipole moment, so they are not microwave active. During the transition in IR, bond length will change which causes dipole moment $\mu \neq 0$. Hence BF_3 and CH_4 are IR active.

30. For consecutive reaction:

$$A \xrightarrow{K_1} B \xrightarrow{K_2} C$$

$$[B] = \frac{K_1[A]_0}{K_2 - K_1}(e^{-K_1 t} - e^{-t_2 t})$$

Similarly, we can write the consecutive reaction.

$$X \xrightarrow{K_x} Y \xrightarrow{K_y} Z$$

$$[Y] = \frac{K_x C_0}{K_y - K_x}(e^{-K_x t} - e^{-K_y t})$$

32. We have, $[CO(CN)_5(H_2O)]^{3-}$

Oxidation state of CO = +2

Valence shell electronic configuration of CO^{2+} = $3d^2$

CN, H_2O is strong field ligand so pairing occur.

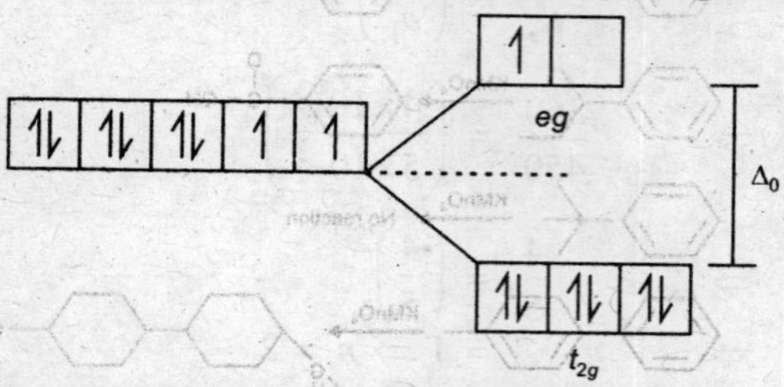

⇒ unsymmetric filling of electrons in t_{2g} and eg.

Therefore, Jahn-Teller distortion is occur.

Similarly also $[Mn(CNMe)_6]^{2+}$ have unsymmetrical filling of electrons.

Thus, Jahn-Teller distortion occurs.

Hence, correct options are (A) and (C).

33. Sodium nitroprusside: $Na_2[Fe(CN)_5NO]$

It contains NO^+ ligand oxidation

Oxidation state of Fe

$[Fe(CN)_5NO]^{2-}$

$$x + (-1) \times 5 + 1 = -2$$

$$\Rightarrow \quad x - 5 + 1 = -2 \Rightarrow x - 4 = -2$$

$$\therefore \quad x = 2$$

∴ Oxidation state of Iron (Fe) = 2

So, the valence shell electronic configuration of Fe^{2+} = $3d^6\,4s^0$

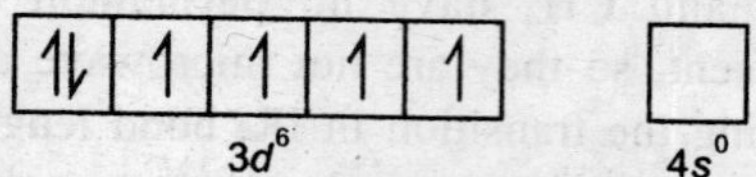

CN^- is strong field ligand, then it causes pairing of electrons in Fe^{2+} ion

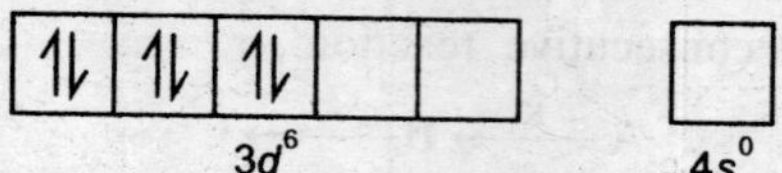

Thus, compound becomes low spin and it is dimagnetic in nature.

It is used to detect S^{2-} in aqueous medium.

$$Na_2S + Na_2[Fe(CN)_5NO] \rightarrow Na_4[Fe(CN)_5NOS]$$

Purple colour

In brown ring test $[Fe(H_2O)_5NO]SO_4$ is complex form.

34. The tomato changes colour from green to yellow and ultimately turns to red as it ripens. This gradual colour change is due to a chlorophyll breakdown. Lycopene, the red carotenoid, is synthesised as a result of breakdown of chlorophyll and it is reason for the red colour in ripe tomatoes.

Red colour of tomato contains alkene as functional group

→ alkene gives ozonolysis reaction

→ It gives anti addition of Br_2

Ozonolysis

$$R-CH=CH_2 + O_3 \xrightarrow{Zn/H_2O} R-\underset{H}{C}=O + O=CH_2$$

Addition of Br_2

$$R-CH=CH_2 + Br_2 \longrightarrow R-\underset{Br}{CH}-\underset{Br}{CH_2}$$

Hence, Both statements (A) and (C) are correct.

35. Hantzsch Dihydropyridine (Pyridine) Synthesis

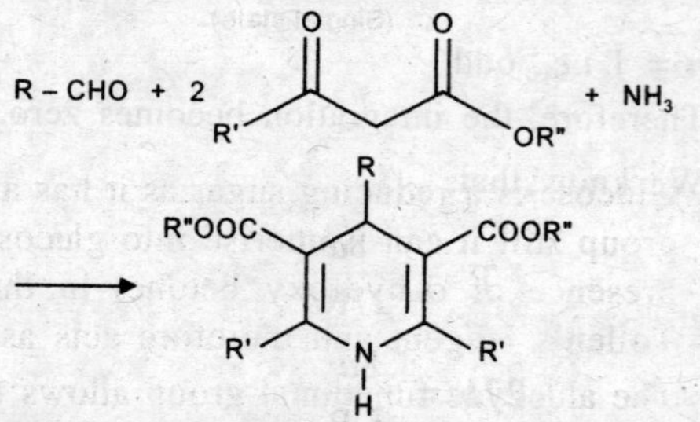

This reaction allows the preparation of dihydropyridine derivatives by condensation of an aldehyde with two equivalents of a β–ketoester in the presence of ammonia. Subsequent oxidation (or dehydrogenation) gives pyridine-3, 5-dicarboxylates, which may also be decarboxylated to yield the corresponding pyridines.

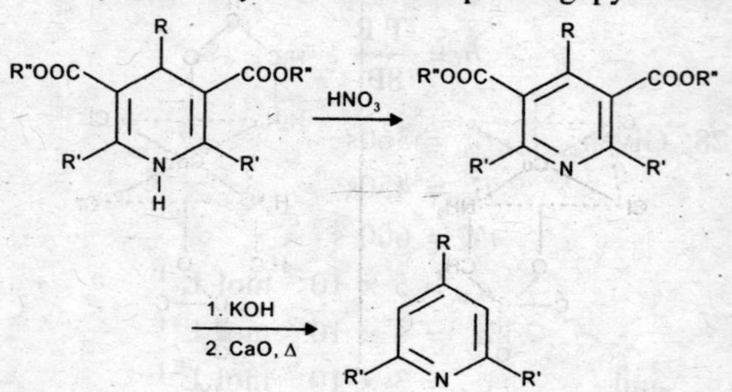

Mechanism of the Hantzsch Dihydropyridine Synthesis

The reaction can be visualized as proceeding through a Knoevenagel Condensation product as a key intermediate.

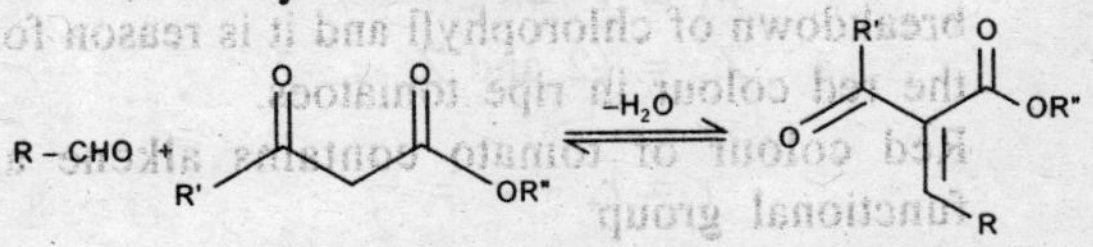

A second key intermediate is an ester enamine, which is produced by condensation of the second equivalent of the β-ketoester with ammonia:

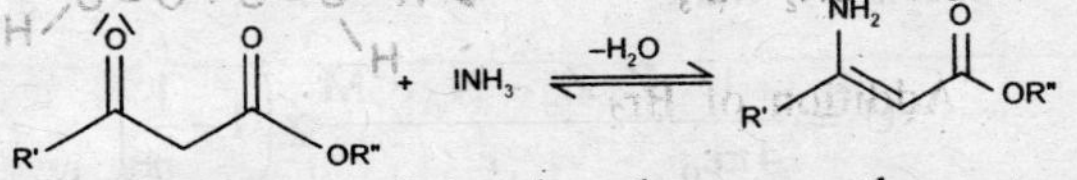

Further condensation between these two fragments gives the dihydropyridine derivative.

Hence, Hantzsch pyridine synthesis involves the steps:

Aldol reaction and Michael addition.

36. 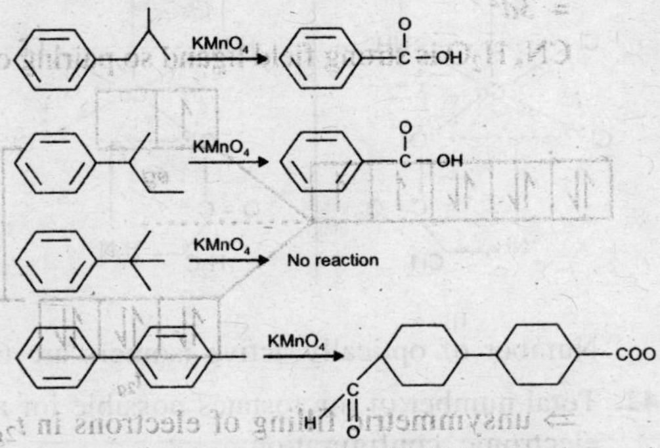

For the oxidation with $KMNO_4$, at least 1 hydrogen must be present at α-position of phenyl ring

Hence, correct answers are (A) and (D).

37. 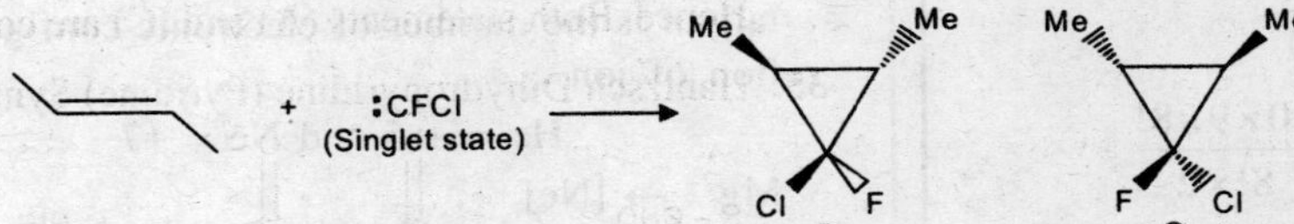

P *Trans* Q *Trans*

38. Glucose is a reducing sugar as it has a free aldehyde group. Fructose does not have any aldehyde group still it can isomerise into glucose and manmose (by Keto-enol tautomerism because of the presence of α-hydroxy ketone) in the alkaline medium, therefore giving a positive test with Tollen's reagent and therefore acts as a reducing sugar.

The aldehyde functional group allows the sugar to act as a reducing agent, for example, in the the Tollens' test. The cyclic hemiacetal forms of aldoses can open to reveal an aldehyde and certain ketoses can undergo tautomerization to become aldoses.

41. Dichloridobis (glycinato) cobaltate (III) ion

$= [COCl_2\ (gly)_2]^{-1}$

The number of optically active isomers are:

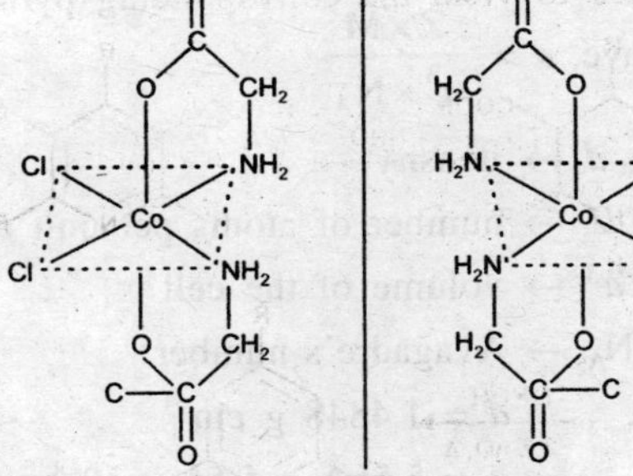

I IV

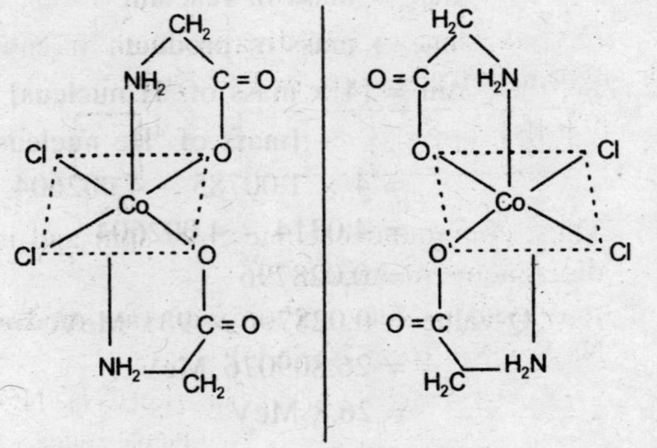

II V

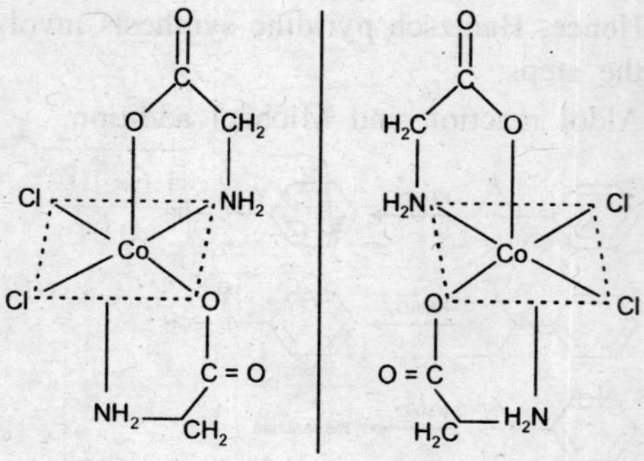

III VI

Number of optically active isomers are 6.

42. Total number of microstates possible for a d^8 electronic configuration

$\because$ Microstate $= \dfrac{n!}{R!(n-R!)}$

$= \dfrac{10!}{8!(10-8!)}$

$= \dfrac{10!}{8!\,2!} = \dfrac{10\times9\times8!}{8!\times2}$

$= \dfrac{10\times9}{2} = 45$

Hence, total number of microstates possible for a d^8 electronic configuration is 45.

43. For the fusion reaction,

$$4\ {}^1H \rightarrow {}^4He + 2\beta^+ + 2\nu + \gamma$$

$\because$ Q-value $= \Delta m \times 931$ MeV

Where $\Delta m = m_R - m_P$

$m_R \rightarrow$ mass of reactant

$m_P \rightarrow$ mass of product

$\therefore$ Δm = [4 × mass of ${}^1H$ nucleus] – [mass of ${}^4He$ nucleus]

$= 4 \times 1.00785 - 4.002604$

$= 4.0314 - 4.002604$

$= 0.028796$

$\therefore$ Q-value $= 0.028796 \times 931$ MeV

$= 26.809076$ MeV

$= 26.8$ MeV

44. We have,

$$MgO \rightarrow Mg^{2+} + O^{2-}$$

Given, $a = 2.12$ Å

$N_A = 6.022 \times 10^{23}$ mol^{-1}

$\varepsilon_0 = 8.854 \times 10^{-12}$ J^{-1} C^2 m^{-1}

$e = 1.602 \times 10^{-19}$ C

$M = 1.748$

$Z_+ = +2$ and $Z_- = -2$

$\because$ $r = r_+ + r_- = \dfrac{a}{2}$

$\therefore$ $r = \dfrac{2.12}{2} = 1.06$ Å

$= 1.06 \times 10^{-10}$ m

We know that,

$$U = \frac{1}{4\pi\varepsilon_0}\,\frac{Z_+Z_- - N_A e^2 M}{r} \times \left(1 - \frac{1}{n}\right)$$

where n is the Born exponent *i.e.*, typically between 5 and 12 and determined experimentally n is the number of electronic configuration of ion.

He = + 5 and Ne = +7

$Mg^{2+} \rightarrow$ [Ne]

$O^{2-} \rightarrow$ [Ne]

For MgO, $n = \dfrac{7+7}{2} = 7$

$$\therefore U = \frac{1\times(+2)\times(-2)\times6.022\times10^{23}\times(1.602\times10^{-19})^2\times1.748}{4\times3.14\times8.854\times10^{-12}\times1.06\times10^{-10}} \times \left(1 - \frac{1}{7}\right)$$

$$= \frac{-6.022\times2.567\times1.748\times6\times10^{-15}}{3.14\times8.854\times1.06\times7\times10^{-22}}$$

$= -0.7859$ KJ mol^{-1}.

45. We have, $d = \dfrac{Z\times M}{a^3\times N_A}$

where, $d \rightarrow$ density

$Z \rightarrow$ number of atoms per unit cell

$a^3 \rightarrow$ volume of the cell

$N_A \rightarrow$ Avagadre's number

Given, $d = 1.4848$ g cm^{-3}

$a = 5.56$Å $= 5.56 \times 10^{-8}$ cm

$$M = 40 \text{ g mol}^{-1}$$
$$N_A = 6.022 \times 10^{23} \text{ mol}^{-1}$$

$\because$ Z defects

$$Z = \frac{d \times a^3 \times N_A}{M}$$
$$= \frac{1.4848 \times (5.56 \times 10^{-8})^3 \times 6.022 \times 10^{23}}{40}$$
$$= \frac{1.4848 \times (5.56)^3 \times 10^{-24} \times 6.022 \times 10^{23}}{40}$$
$$= 3.842$$

For *fcc* lattice, Z = 4

$$\therefore \quad \text{Defect} = Z_{acc} - Z_{def}$$
$$= 4 - 3.842 = 0.158$$

$\therefore$ The percentage of Schottky defects

$$= \frac{\text{defect}}{Z_{acc}} \times 100$$
$$= \frac{0.158}{4} \times 100 = 3.95.$$

47. We know that,

$$pOH = pK_b + \log\frac{[\text{Salt}]}{[\text{Base}]}$$

and
$$pOH = -\log K_b + \log\frac{[\text{Salt}]}{[\text{Base}]}$$
$$[\because pK_a = -\log K_b]$$
$$= -\log(1.6 \times 10^{-5}) + \log\frac{(0.1)}{(0.3)}$$
$$= 4.795 + (-0.477)$$
$$= 4.795 - 0.477 = 4.318$$
$$\therefore \quad pOH = 4.318$$

Therefore, *p*H of the buffer solution

$$pH = 14 - pOH$$
$$= 14 - 4.318$$
$$= 9.682 \simeq 9.7.$$

48. Given, $K_a = 1.6 \times 10^{-5}$

$$\lambda_m^\circ = 360.5 \times 10^{-4} \text{ mho m}^2 \text{ mol}^{-1}$$

and $C = 0.0$ M

We know that,

$$K_a = C\,\alpha^2$$
$$\Rightarrow \quad \alpha^2 = \frac{K_a}{C}$$
$$\therefore \quad \alpha = \sqrt{\frac{K_a}{C}} = \sqrt{\frac{1.6 \times 10^{-5}}{0.01}}$$
$$= \sqrt{16 \times 10^{-4}} = 4 \times 10^{-2}$$

Now,
$$\alpha = \frac{\lambda_m}{\lambda_m^\circ}$$
$$\Rightarrow \quad \lambda_m = \lambda_m^\circ \times \alpha$$
$$= 360.5 \times 10^{-4} \times 4 \times 10^{-2}$$
$$= 1.442 \times 10^{-3}$$

But
$$\lambda_m = \frac{K}{C}$$
$$\Rightarrow \quad K = \lambda_m C$$
$$= 1.442 \times 10^{-3} \times 0.01 \times 10^3$$
$$= 1.442 \times 10^{-2} \text{ mho m}^{-1}$$
$$\left[\because 1\text{L} = \frac{1 \text{ m}^3}{1000}\right]$$

Given, $K = n \times 10^{-2}$

$$\therefore \quad 1.442 \times 10^{-2} = n \times 10^{-2}$$
$$\therefore \quad n = 1.442 \simeq 1.44.$$

50. Let rms value of nitrogen gas at particular temperature be *x*.

i.e., rms $(N_2) = x$

Given, rms $(H_2) = 1900 \text{ ms}^{-1}$

We know that

$$\text{rms} = \sqrt{\frac{3RT}{M}}$$

For hydrogen gas, rms (H_2)

$$= \sqrt{\frac{3RT}{M(H_2)}}$$

or
$$1900 = \sqrt{\frac{3RT}{M(H_2)}} \quad ...(i)$$

For nitrogen gas, rms (N_2)

$$= \sqrt{\frac{3RT}{M(N_2)}}$$

or
$$x = \sqrt{\frac{3RT}{M(N_2)}} \quad ...(ii)$$

On dividing eqn. (*i*) by (*ii*), we get

$$\frac{1900 = \sqrt{\dfrac{3RT}{M(H_2)}}}{x = \sqrt{\dfrac{3RT}{M(N_2)}}}$$

$$\Rightarrow \quad \frac{1900}{x} = \sqrt{\frac{M(N_2)}{M(H_2)}}$$

$$\left[\begin{array}{l} \text{Mol. mass of } H_2 = 2 \\ \text{Mol. mass of } N_2 = 28 \end{array}\right]$$

$$\Rightarrow \quad \frac{1900}{x} = \sqrt{\frac{28}{2}} = \sqrt{14}$$

$$\Rightarrow \quad x = \frac{1900}{\sqrt{14}}$$

$$= \frac{1900}{3.74} = 508$$

Thus, rms of nitrogen gas is 508 ms^{-1}.

51. Given, $\Delta_0 = 5900\ cm^{-1}$

We have,

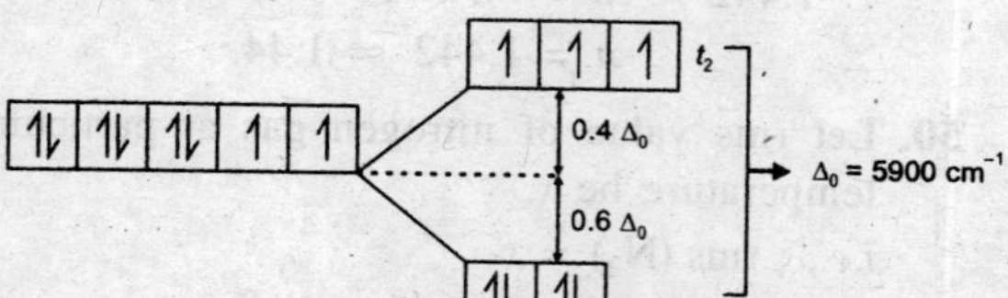

Now, crystal field splitting energy *i.e.*,

$$\text{CFSE} = (-0.6 \times 4)\Delta_0 - (-0.4 \times 3)\Delta_0$$
$$= -2.4\Delta_0 + 1.2\Delta_0$$
$$= -1.2\Delta_0$$
$$= -12 \times 5900\ cm^{-1} = -7080$$

$\therefore$ Magnitude of $[CO(NH_3)_4]^{2+}$

$$\text{CFSE} = -7080 \times hc \times N_A$$
$$= -7080 \times 6.626 \times 10^{-34} \times 3 \times 10^{10} \times 6.022 \times 10^{23}$$
$$[\because C = 3 \times 10^{10}\ cms^{-1}]$$
$$= -7080 \times 6.626 \times 3 \times 6.022 \times 10^{-34} \times 10^{33}$$
$$= -847513.6 \times 10^{-1}\ \text{J/mol}$$
$$= -84751.3\ \text{J/mol}$$
$$= -84.75\ \text{kJ/mol.}$$

52. Mass of $MgSO_4$ in mixture

$$= 1 \times \frac{25}{100} = 0.25g$$

$$\text{Aqueous solution} + \underset{\text{(Excess)}}{BaCl_2} \longrightarrow \underset{(1.49g)}{BaSO_4}$$

Molar mass of $BaSO_4$ = 233.39 g/mol

$\therefore$ 233.39*g* of $BaSO_4 \xrightarrow{\text{Contains}}$ 96.06*g* of SO_4^{2-}

$\therefore$ 1*g* of $BaSO_4 \longrightarrow \dfrac{96.06}{233.39}$ *g* of SO_4^{2-}

$\therefore$ 1.46*g* of $BaSO_4 \longrightarrow \dfrac{96.06}{233.39} \times 1.46$ *g* of SO_4^{2-}

$$= 0.6133g \text{ of } SO_4^{2-}$$

Now, Molar mass of $MgSO_4$ = 120.37 *g*/mol

$\therefore$ 120.37*g* of $MgSO_4$ contains 96.06*g* of SO_4^{2-}

$\therefore$ 1*g* of $MgSO_4$ contains

$$= \frac{96.06}{120.37} g \text{ of } SO_4^{2-}$$

$\therefore$ 0.25*g* of $MgSO_4$ contains

$$= \frac{96.06}{120.37} \times 0.25g \text{ of } SO_4^{2-}$$
$$= 0.1995g \text{ of } SO_4^{2-}$$

Amount of SO_4^{2-} in $MgSO_4$

= Amount of SO_4^{2-} in $BaSO_4$ – Amount of SO_4^{2-} in $MgSO_4$

$$= 0.6133 - 0.19951$$
$$= 0.413798$$

$\therefore$ 0.41379*g* of SO_4^{2-} present in 0.75g of $MgSO_4$

$\therefore$ 1*g* of $SO_4^{2-} \rightarrow \dfrac{0.75}{0.41379}$ *g* of $MgSO_4$

$\therefore$ 96.06*g* of $SO_4^{2-} = \dfrac{0.75}{0.41379} \times 96.06$*g of* $MgSO_4$

$$= 174.11001g \text{ of } MgSO_4$$

$\therefore$ Mass of metal (M)

$$= 174.11001 - 96.06 = 78.05001$$

$$\therefore \quad M = \frac{78.05001}{2} = 39.03g.$$

53. Since, monochromatic visible light is reduced by 90% due to absorption

$\therefore$ Transmittance (T) = 10% $= \dfrac{10}{100} = 0.1$

Given, $l = 4$ cm, $c = 5$ mM $= 5 \times 10^{-3}$ M

Since, $A = \Sigma d$ ...(i)

and $A = -ln T$ ...(ii)

From eqn. (i) & (ii), we get

$$-ln T = \Sigma d$$

$$\Rightarrow -ln(0.1) = \Sigma \times 4 \times 5 \times 10^{-3}$$

$$\Rightarrow -ln(10^{-1}) = \Sigma \times 20 \times 10^{-3}$$

$$\Rightarrow 1 = \Sigma \times 20 \times 10^{-3}$$

$$\therefore \Sigma = \frac{1}{20 \times 10^{-3}}$$

$$= 0.05 \times 10^{3}$$

$$= 50 \text{ M}^{-1} \text{ cm}^{-1}$$

Hence, the molar extinction coefficient of the compound is $50 M^{-1} cm^{-1}$.

55. We have,

$$B = \frac{h}{8\pi^2 Ic} = \frac{h}{8\pi^2 \mu r^2 c}$$

$$\Rightarrow r^2 = \frac{h}{8\pi^2 \mu Bc}$$

Now, $\mu = \dfrac{m_1 \times m_2}{m_1 + m_2}$

$$= \frac{12 \times 16}{12 + 16} = \frac{192}{28} \text{ g/mol}$$

$$= \frac{192}{28} \times \frac{10^{-3}}{6.022 \times 10^{23}} \text{ kg}$$

$$= 11.45 \times 10^{-27} \text{ kg}$$

Given, $2B = 3.8626$

$$\therefore B = \frac{3.8626}{2}$$

$$\therefore r^2 = \frac{2 \times 6.626 \times 10^{-34}}{8 \times (3.14)^2 \times 11.45 \times 10^{-27} \times 3.8626 \times 3 \times 10^{10}}$$

$$= \frac{13.252}{10465.398} \times 10^{-17}$$

$$= 0.00126626813 \times 10^{-17}$$

$$= 1.267 \times 10^{-20}$$

$$\therefore r = 1.12 \times 10^{-10} = 1.12 \text{Å}.$$

56. Given,

$$\Delta T_f = 0.186 \text{K}$$

$$T_b^\circ = 373.15 \text{ K}$$

$$K_f = 1.86 \text{K (mol kg}^{-1})^{-1}$$

$$K_e = 0.51 \text{K (mol kg}^{-1})^{-1}$$

We know that

$$\Delta T_f = K_f \times m$$

or $m = \dfrac{\Delta T_f}{K_f}$

$$= \frac{0.186}{1.86} = 0.1 \text{ mol kg}^{-1}$$

Now, $\Delta T_b = K_e \times m$

$$= 0.51 \times 0.1 = 0.051 \text{ K}$$

$$\because \Delta T_b = T_b - T_b^\circ$$

$$\therefore T_b = \Delta T_b + T_b^\circ$$

$$= 0.051 + 373.15$$

$$= 373.201 \text{K}.$$

57. Given, $CaCO_3(s) \rightleftharpoons CaO(s) + CO_2(g)$

As, $\mu = \mu_0 + RT\, ln\left(\dfrac{P}{P^0}\right)$

Where, $P^0 \rightarrow$ atmospheric partial pressure of CO_2

Now, $\mu_0 = \mu_{CaCO_3} - \mu_{CaO} - \mu_{CO_2}$

$$= -1128.8 - (-604.0) - (-394.4)$$

$$= -1128.8 + 604.0 + 394.4$$

$$= -130.4 \text{ KJ/mol}$$

Since, $\mu = \mu_0 + \alpha\, \Delta T$

where $\alpha \rightarrow$ temp. coeff. of $CO_2 = 0.772$

$$\therefore \mu = -130.4 + 0.0772\,(1200 - 298)$$

$$= -130.4 + 0.0772 \times 902$$

$$= -130.4 + 69.63 = -60.77 \text{ KJ}$$

From eqn. (i), we have

$$\frac{\mu - \mu_0}{RT} = ln\left(\frac{P}{P^0}\right)$$

$$\Rightarrow \frac{(-60.77) - (130.4)}{8.314 \times 10^3 \text{ KJ} \times 1200} = ln\left(\frac{P}{P^0}\right)$$

$$\Rightarrow \frac{69.63}{8.314 \times 10^3 \times 1200} = ln\left(\frac{P}{P^0}\right)$$

Taking antilog on both sides, we get

$$1075 = \frac{P}{P^0} \quad [\because P^0 = 0.004 \text{ atm}]$$

$$\therefore P = 1075 \times 0.004 \text{ atm}$$

$$= 4.30 \text{ atm}.$$

58. We know that

$$CaCl_2 \longrightarrow \underset{(0.004)}{Ca^{2+}} + \underset{(2\times0.004)=0.008}{2Cl^{\ominus}}$$

Now, $I = \frac{1}{2}\Sigma m_i z_i^2$

$= \frac{1}{2}[0.004\times(2)^2 + 0.008(-1)^2]$

$= \frac{1}{2}[0.004\times4 + 0.008]$

$= \frac{1}{2}[0.016 + 0.008]$

$= \frac{1}{2}\times0.024 = 0.012$

Hence, mean ionic activity coefficient,

$\log \gamma_{\pm} = -A|z_+ z_-|\sqrt{I}$

$= -(0.509)(2\times-1)\sqrt{0.012}$

$= 1.018 \times 0.1095445$

$= 0.111516$

$\therefore \quad \gamma_{\pm} = 0.774.$

59. Given $K_l = 2.5 \times 10^5$ L mol^{-1} s^{-1}

$K_{-l} = 1.0 \times 10^4$ s^{-1}

and $K_2 = 10$s^{-1}

We have, $Q + R \underset{K_{-l}}{\overset{K_l}{\rightleftharpoons}} X \xrightarrow{K_2} P$

Now, $Q + R \xrightarrow{K_l} X$

$X \xrightarrow{K_{-l}} Q + R$

and $X \xrightarrow{K_2} P$

$\therefore \quad$ Rate $= K_2[X]$ ...(*i*)

From SSA on [X], we get

$\frac{d[X]}{dt} \Rightarrow K_l[Q][R] - K_{-l}[X] - K_2[X] = 0$

$\Rightarrow \quad K_l[Q][R] = +K_{-l}[X] + K_2[X]$

$\therefore \quad [X] = \frac{K_l[Q][R]}{K_{-l} + K_2}$ ...(*ii*)

From eqn. (*i*) and (*ii*), we get

Rate $= \frac{K_2K_l[Q][R]}{K_{-l} + K_2}$

$\therefore \quad K_{overall} = \frac{K_2K_l}{K_{-l} + K_2} = \frac{10\times2.5\times10^5}{1.0\times10^4 + 10}$

$= \frac{2.5\times10^{-6}}{10010}$

$= 0.00024975 \times 10^6$

$= 249.75$L mol^{-1} s^{-1}

$\simeq 250$L mol^{-1} s^{-1}.

60. 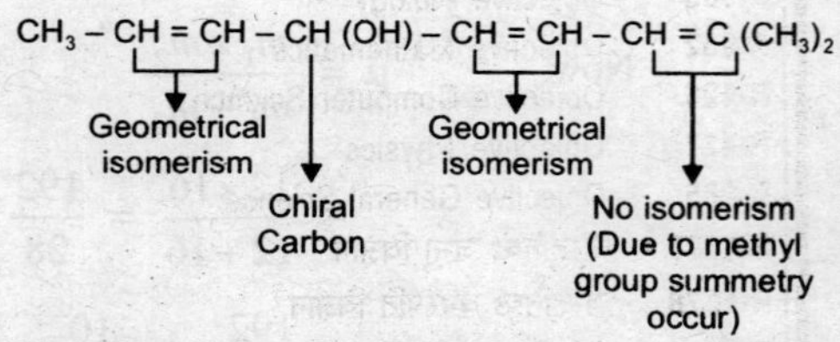

Therefore, the terminal of alkene is different. Hence, the total number of stereoisomers $= 2^n = 2^3 = 8$.

Previous Years Paper

IIT–JAM

JOINT ADMISSION TEST FOR M.SC. (CHEMISTRY), 2020

Section A : Multiple Choice Questions (MCQ)

Directions: (Q. No. 1 to 10) *Carry One mark each.*

1. The graph that represents the temperature (T) – entropy (S) variation of a Carnot cycle is

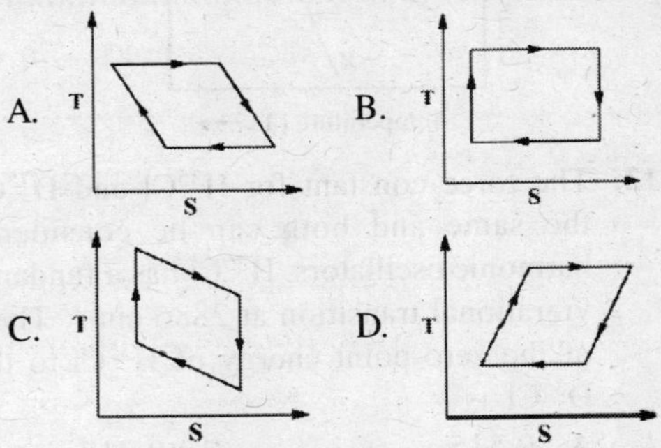

2. For the radical chain reaction below, the correct classification for step 2 and step 3 is, respectively,

Step 1 : $Br_2 + M \longrightarrow 2Br^{\bullet} + M$

Step 2 : $Br^{\bullet} + H_2 \rightleftharpoons HBr + H^{\bullet}$

Step 3 : $H^{\bullet} + Br_2 \longrightarrow HBr + Br^{\bullet}$

A. chain propagating, chain terminating
B. chain branching, chain terminating
C. chain propagating, chain propagating
D. chain propagating, chain branching

3. The salt bridge in a galvanic cell allows the flow of

A. ions but NOT electrons
B. BOTH ions and electrons
C. electrons but NOT ions
D. NEITHER ions NOR electrons

4. The nucleobase NOT found in DNA is

A. Thymine B. Uracil
C. Guanine D. Adenine

5. The correct statement for the following structures is

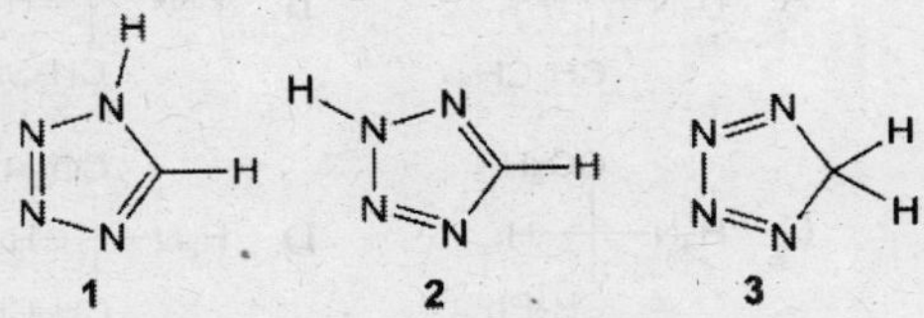

A. 1, 2 and 3 are resonance structures
B. 1 and 2 are resonance structures, whereas 3 is an isomer of 1 and 2
C. 1 and 3 are resonance structures, whereas 2 is an isomer of 1 and 3
D. 1, 2 and 3 are constitutional isomers

6. The correct order of boiling points of compounds I–IV is

I II III IV

A. II > I > III > IV
B. II > III > I > IV
C. I > III > IV > II
D. I > IV > III > II

7. One of the products of the hydrolysis of calcium phosphide at 25° C is

A. phosphine
B. phosphoric acid
C. phosphorus pentoxide
D. white phosphorus

8. Treatment of formic acid with concentrated sulphuric acid gives

A. $CO + H_2O$

B. $CO_2 + H_2$

C. $HCHO + ½ O_2$

D. no product (no reaction)

9. The *d*-orbitals involved in the hybridization to form square planar and trigonal bipyramidal geometries are, respectively,

A. d_{z^2} and d_{z^2} B. d_{yz} and d_{z^2}

C. $d_{x^2-y^2}$ and d_{z^2} D. $d_{x^2-y^2}$ and d_{yz}

10. The amino acid with R configuration is

A. 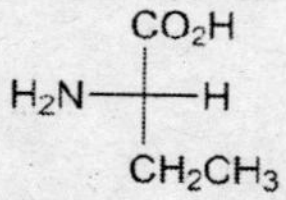

B. 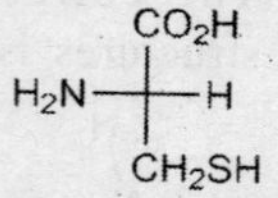

C. 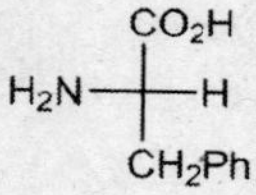

D. 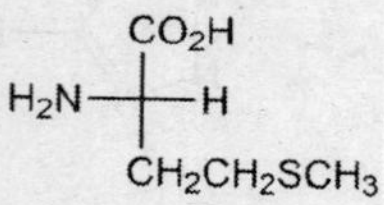

Directions: (Q. No. 11 to 30) ***Carry Two marks each.***

11. At constant pressure, the μ – T diagram for a pure substance that sublimes is (*s* = solid, *l* = liquid and *g* = gas)

A. 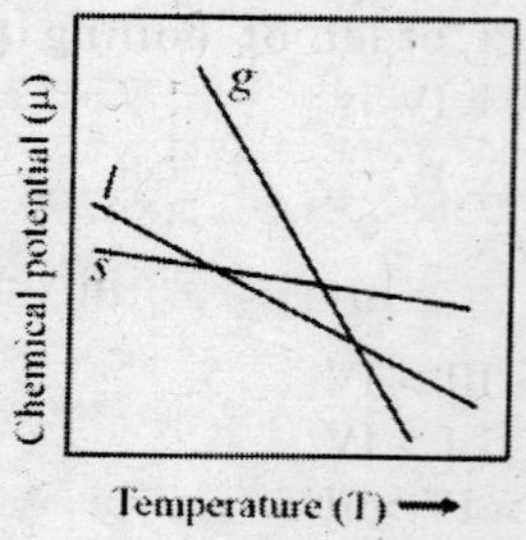

B. 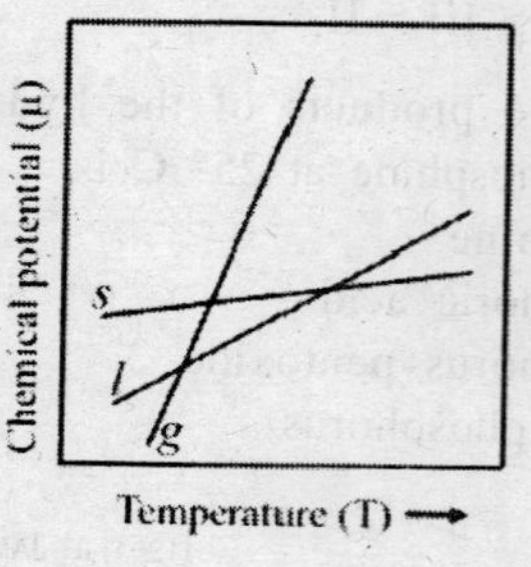

C. 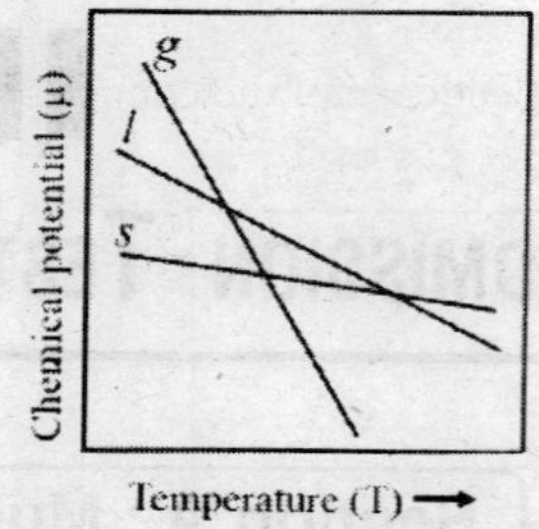

D. 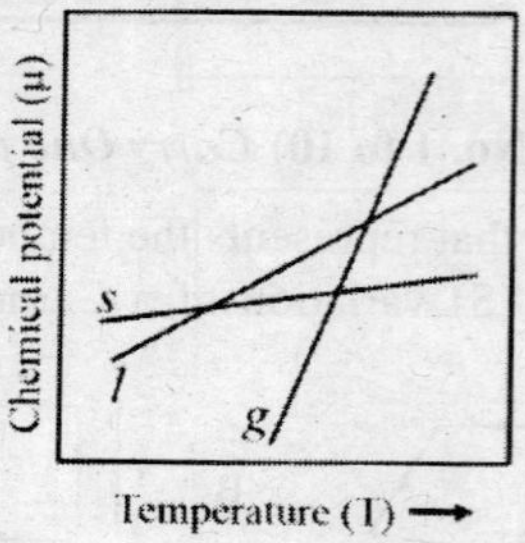

12. The force constant for $H^{35}Cl$ and $D^{35}Cl$ are the same and both can be considered as harmonic oscillators. $H^{35}Cl$ has a fundamental vibrational transition at 2886 cm^{-1}. The ratio of the zero-point energy of $H^{35}Cl$ to that of $D^{35}Cl$ is

A. 0.515 B. 0.717

C. 1.395 D. 1.946

13. The correct statement regarding the determinants (Det) of matrices R, S and T is

$$R = \begin{bmatrix} 3 & 2 & 4 \\ 4 & 5 & 7 \\ 1 & 3 & 8 \end{bmatrix} \quad S = \begin{bmatrix} 2 & 3 & 4 \\ 5 & 4 & 7 \\ 3 & 1 & 8 \end{bmatrix}$$

$$T = \begin{bmatrix} 3 & 4 & 1 \\ 2 & 5 & 3 \\ 4 & 7 & 8 \end{bmatrix}$$

A. Det(R) = Det(S) ≠ Det(T)

B. Det(R) = Det(T) ≠ Det(S)

C. Det(R) = Det(S) = Det(T)

D. Det(R), Det(S), Det(T) are all different

14. The Boyle temperature (T_B) is defined as the temperature at which the properties of a real gas coincide with those of an ideal gas in the low pressure limit. The graph that shows the pressure dependence of the compression factor (Z) for a real gas at T_B is

A. 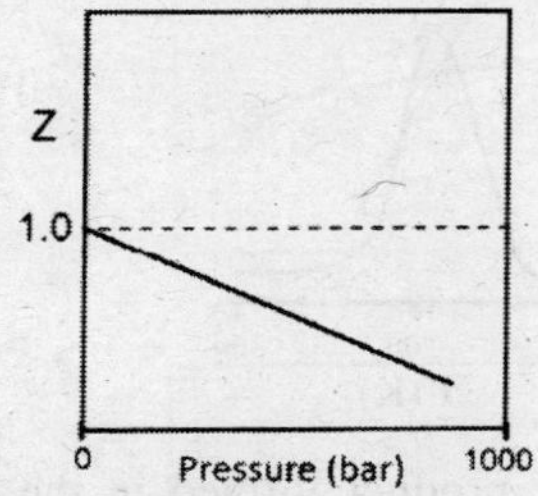

B. 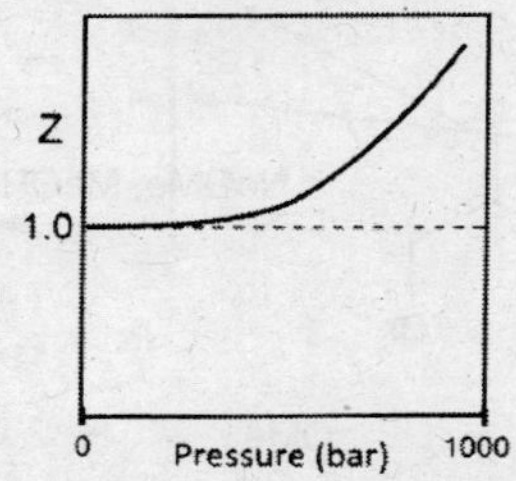

C. 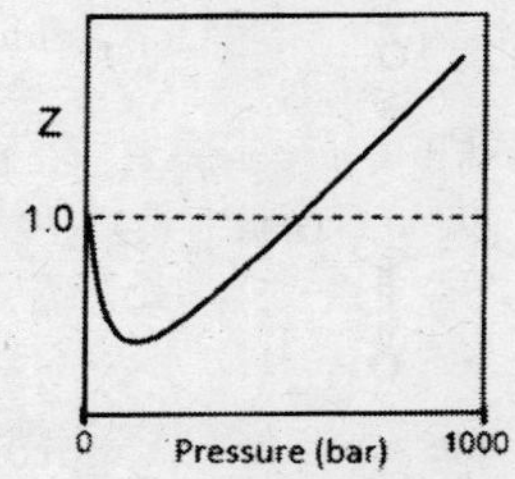

D. 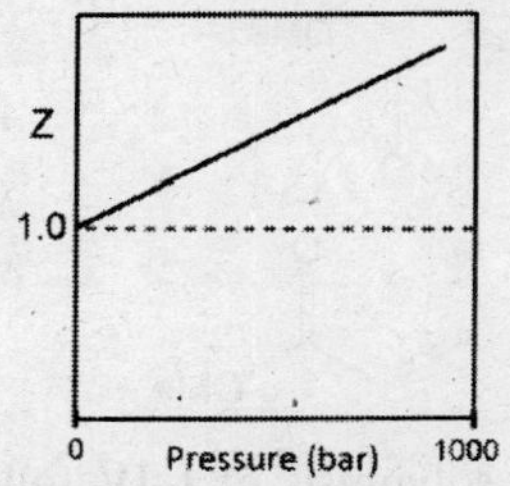

15. The major product formed in the following reaction sequence is

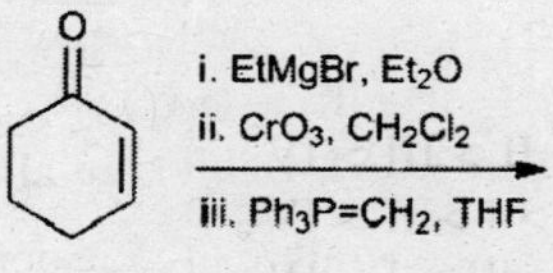

A. 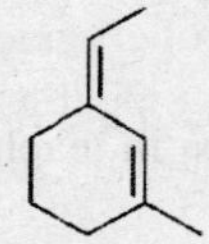

B. 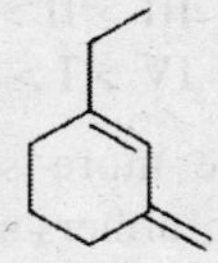

C. 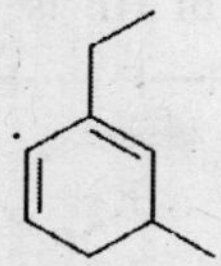

D. 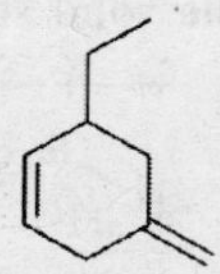

16. The geometries of the species $[Br_3]^+$, $[Br_3]^-$ and $[BrF_3]$ are, respectively,

A. linear, trigonal bipyramidal and trigonal bipyramidal
B. linear, linear and trigonal planar
C. tetrahedral, trigonal bipyramidal and trigonal bipyramidal
D. tetrahedral, trigonal pyramidal and trigonal planar

17. The cage – type structure adopted by boron hydride, $[B_5H_{11}]$, is

A. *closo* B. *nido*
C. *hypo* D. *arachno*

18. The order of the M–C bond strength in the following species is
(Atomic number for Cr = 24, Mn = 25, Ti = 22, Co = 27)

$[Cr(CO)_6]$ (I) $[Mn(CO)_6]^+$ (II) $[Ti(CO)_6]^{2-}$ (III) $[Co(CO)_4]^-$ (IV)

A. II > I > IV > III B. I > III > II > IV
C. III > IV > I > II D. III > I > II > IV

19. The number of non-bonding electrons present in the frontier molecular orbitals of HF is

A. 10 B. 4
C. 6 D. 8

20. The coordination number of aluminum ion and the number of bridging hydrogen atoms in $[Al(BH_4)_4]^-$ are, respectively,

A. 8 and 8 B. 6 and 6
C. 4 and 6 D. 8 and 12

21. The complex which does NOT obey 18-electron rule is
(atomic number for Mn = 25, Fe = 26, Co = 27, Ru = 44)

A. $[Co_2(CO)_8]$
B. $[Fe(CO)_4]^{2-}$
C. $[HMn(CO)_5]$
D. $[(\eta^5-C_5H_5)RuCl(CO)(PPh_2)]$

22. The solid state structure of HF is

A. H—F·····H—F·····H—F·····H—F·····

B. 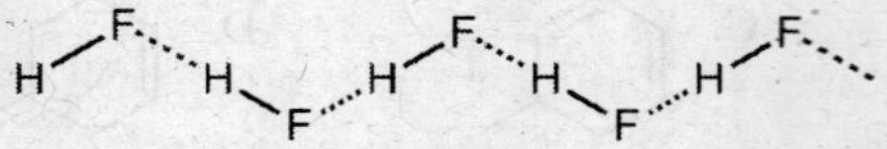

C. 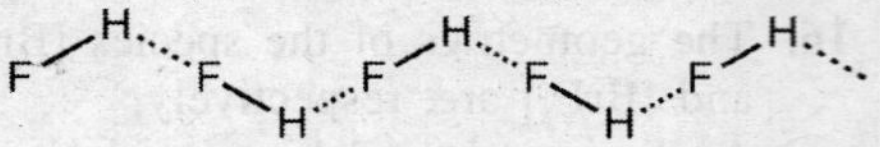

D. 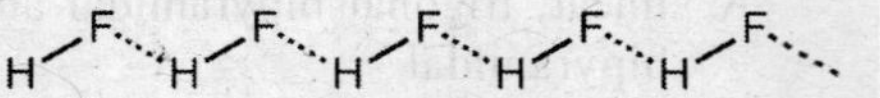

23. The number of *d-d* transition(s) expected for the complex $[Cu(NH_3)_2(H_2O)_4]^{2+}$ is

A. 1 B. 2

C. 3 D. 4

24. The plot showing the magnetic behaviour of oxy- (solid line) and deoxy-haemoglobin (dashed line) is

(χ_M = molar magnetic susceptibility, T = temperature)

A. 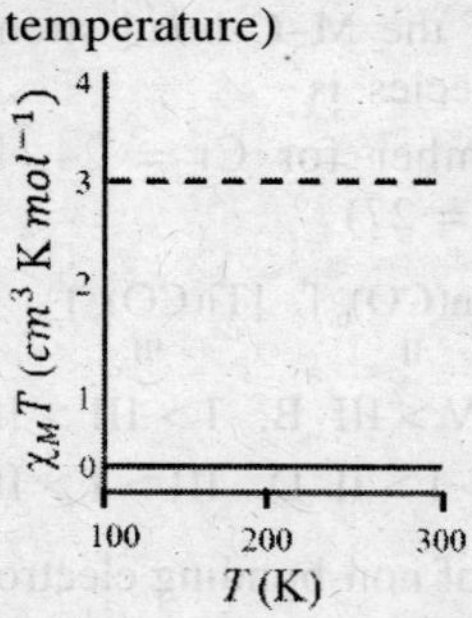

B. 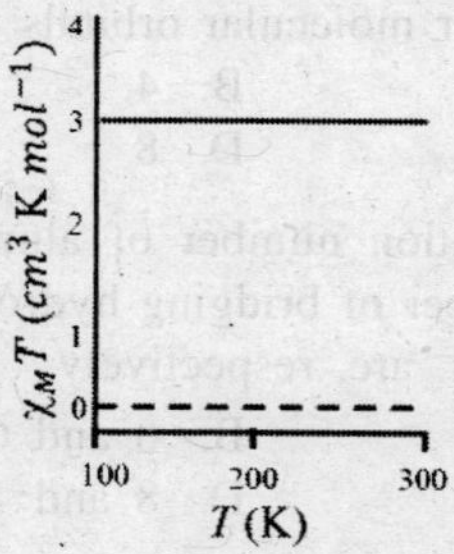

C. 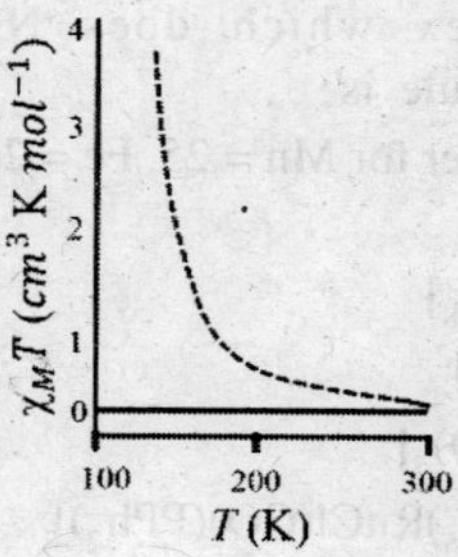

D. 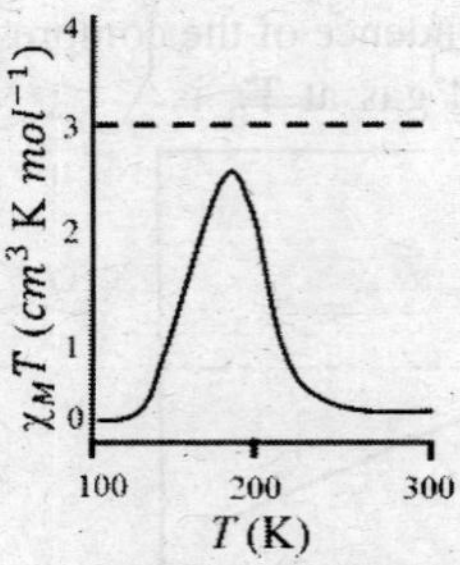

25. The major product formed in the following reaction is

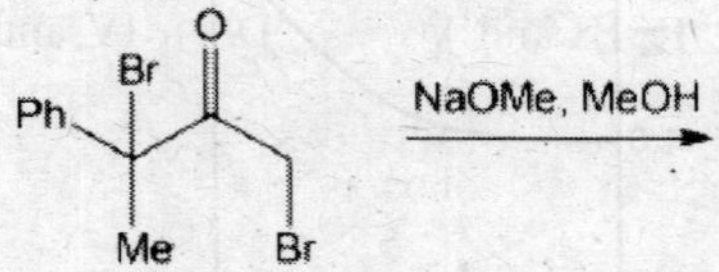

A. 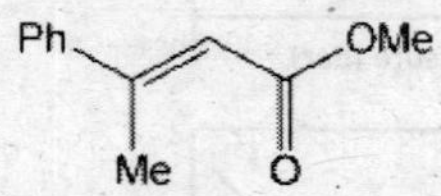

B. 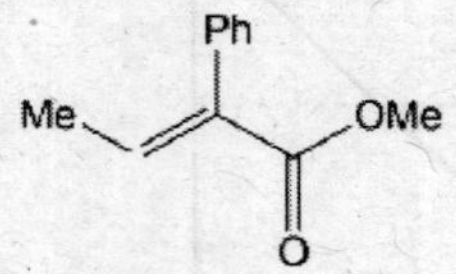

C. 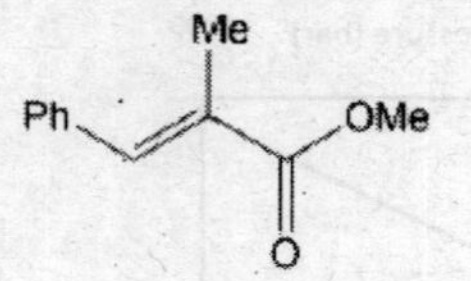

D. 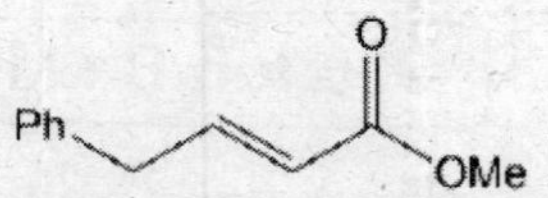

26. The rate of solvolysis of I–IV follows

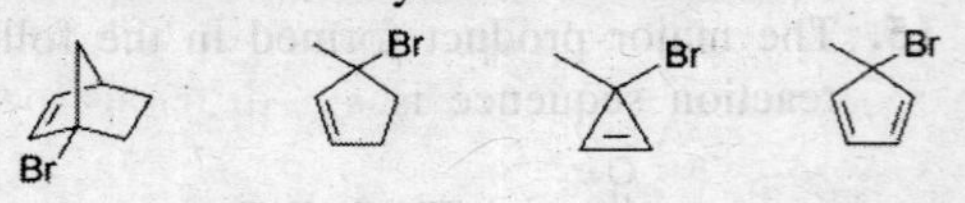

I II III IV

A. I > II > III > IV

B. III > I > II > IV

C. III > II > I > IV

D. IV > I > II > III

27. The more stable species in each pair of conformers are

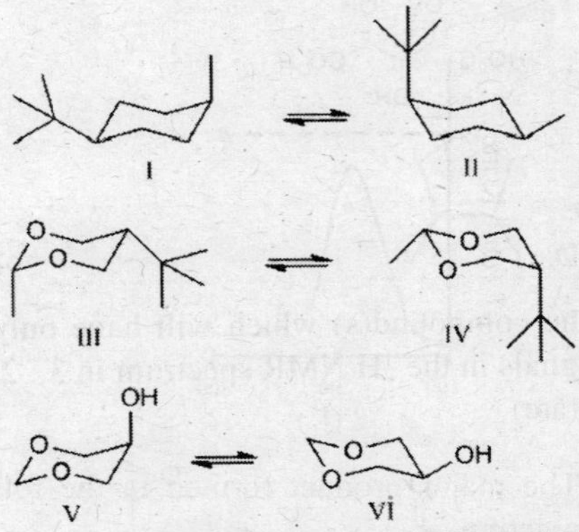

A. II, IV and V B. I, IV and V
C. II, III and V D. I, IV and VI

28. The major product formed in the following reaction sequence is

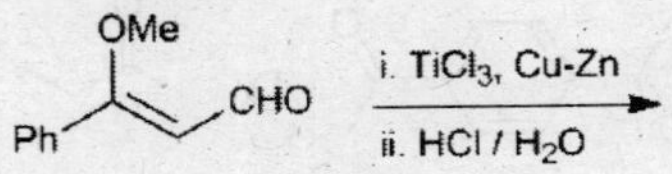

A. 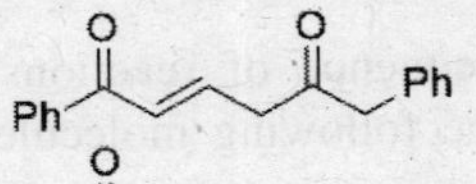

B. 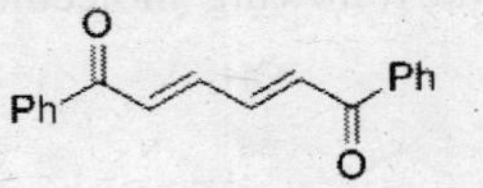

C. 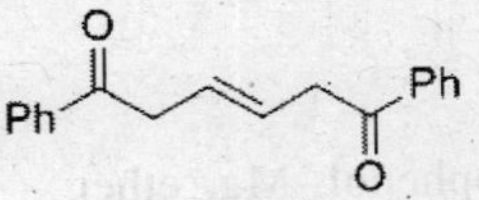

D. 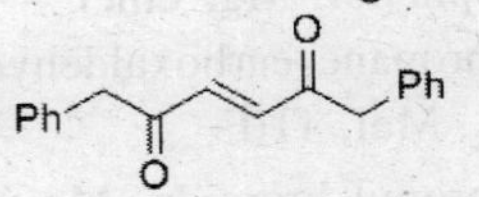

29. For the Diels-Alder reactions I–IV, the activation barriers follow the order

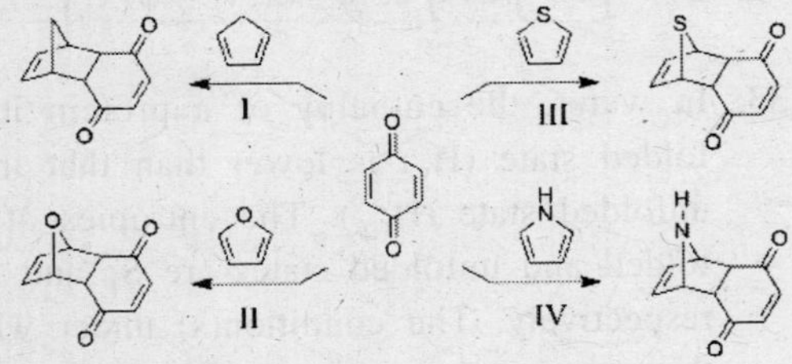

A. II > I > III > IV
B. I > III > IV > II
C. III > IV > II > I
D. IV > III > II > I

30. The major product formed in the following reaction is

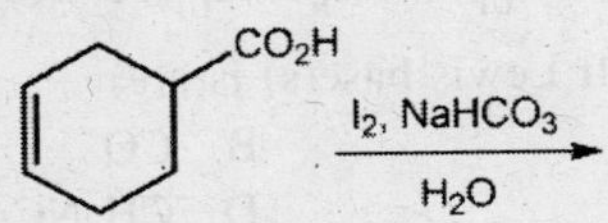

A. 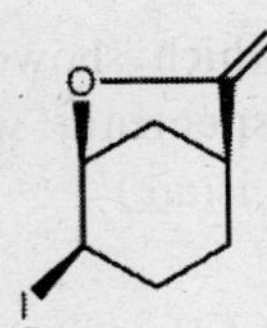

B. 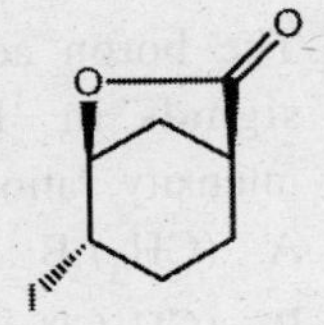

C. 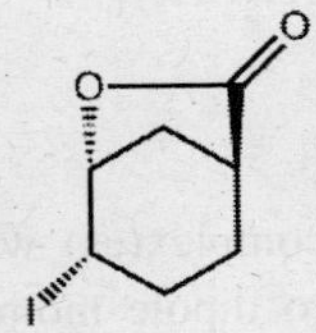

D. 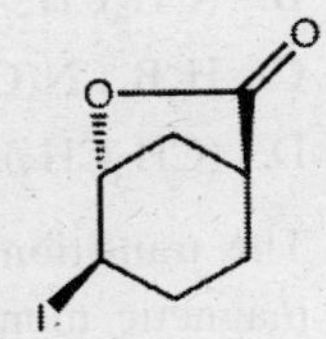

Section B : Multiple Select Questions (MSQ)

Q. 31 – Q. 40 carry two marks each.

31. For the reaction shown in Scheme 1, the concentration profiles of different species are provided.

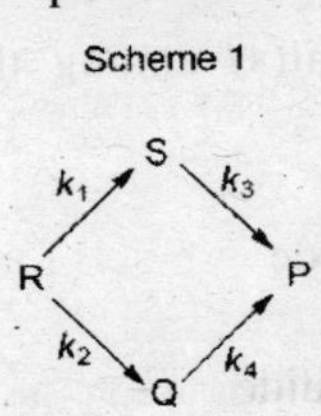

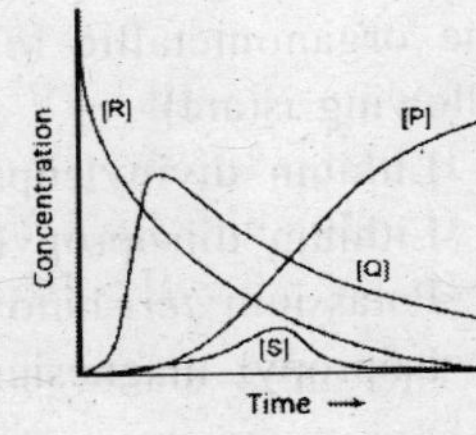

Based on this graph, the correct condition(s) regarding the rate constants is(are)

A. $k_2 > k_4$ B. $k_3 > k_1$
C. $k_2 > k_1$ D. $k_1 = k_2$

32. $\psi(x, y, z)$ describes the wavefunction of a particle. The probability of finding the particle between x and $x + dx$, y and $y + dy$, z and $z + dz$, can be expressed as

A. $\psi^*(x, y, z)\ \psi(x, y, z)$
B. $|\psi(x, y, z)|^2\ dx\ dy\ dz$

C. $\psi^*(x, y, z)\, \psi(x, y, z)\, dx\, dy\, dz$

D. $\int_{-\infty}^{\infty} dx \int_{-\infty}^{\infty} dy \int_{-\infty}^{\infty} dz\, \psi^*(x,y,z)\, \psi(x,y,z)$

33. In water, the enthalpy of a protein in its folded state (H_F) is lower than that in its unfolded state (H_{UF}). The entropies of the folded and unfolded states are S_F and S_{UF}, respectively. The condition(s) under which this protein spontaneously folds in water at a temperature T, is(are)

A. $S_{UF} < S_F$

B. $S_{UF} = 0$

C. $S_{UF} = S_F$

D. $(S_F - S_{UF}) > (H_F - H_{UF})/T$

34. The soft Lewis base(s) is(are)

A. I^- B. CO

C. H^- D. CH_3NC

35. The boron adduct(s), which show(s) three signals in ^{1}H NMR spectrum with the intensity ratio 1 : 2 : 3 is(are)

A. $(CH_3)_3B : N(CH_3)_3$

B. $(CH_3CH_2)_3B : N(CH_2CH_3)_3$

C. $H_3B : N(CH_2CH_3)_3$

D. $(CH_3CH_2)_3B : NH_3$

36. The transition metal complex(es) with zero magnetic moment, zero dipole moment and CFSE of $-2.4\ \Delta^o$ is(are)

A. $[Mn(CO)_5(CH_3)]$

B. [*trans*-Ni(ethylene diamine)$_2$Cl$_2$]

C. [*trans*-Co(CN)$_4$(H$_2$O)$_2$]$^-$

D. [*trans*-Fe(CN)$_4$Cl$_2$]$^{4-}$

37. Achiral stereoisomer(s) is(are) possible for

A. 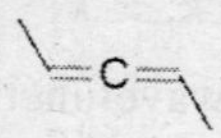

B. 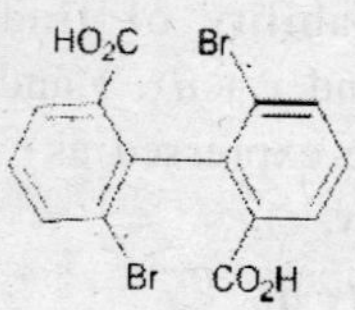

C. 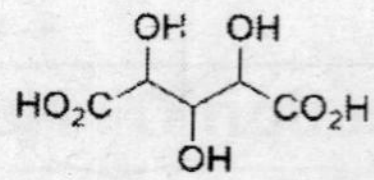

D. 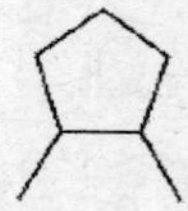

38. The compound(s) which will have only two signals in the ^{1}H NMR spectrum in 3 : 2 ratio is(are)

A. 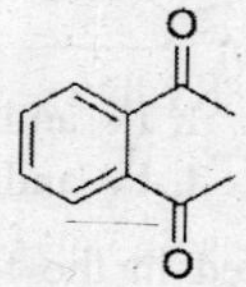

B. 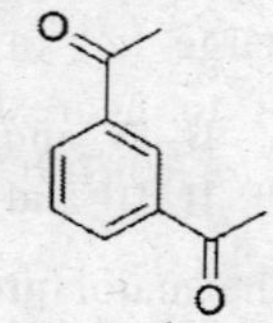

C. 

D. 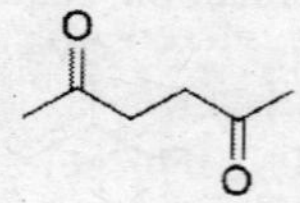

39. The correct sequence of reactions for the synthesis of the following molecule is(are)

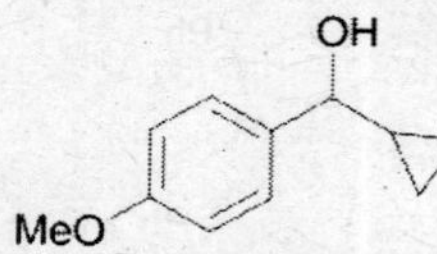

A. (*i*) 4-Iodophenol, Mg, ether
(*ii*) Cyclopropane carboxaldehyde, THF
(*iii*) $CsCO_3$, MeI, THF

B. (*i*) Cyclopropyl bromide, Mg, ether
(*ii*) 4-Hydroxybenzaldehyde, THF.
(*iii*) $CsCO_3$, MeI, THF

C. (*i*) 4-Iodophenol, $CsCO_3$, MeI, THF
(*ii*) Mg, ether
(*iii*) Cyclopropane carboxaldehyde, THF

D. (*i*) Cyclopropyl bromide, Mg, ether
(*ii*) Methyl 4-methoxybenzoate, THF

40. The organometallic reagent(s) among the following is(are)

A. Lithium divinylcuprate

B. Lithium diisopropylamide

C. Potassium *tert*-butoxide

D. Isopropyl magnesiumiodide

Section C : Numerical Answer Type (NAT)

Q. 41 – Q. 50 carry one mark each.

41. The function $x^4e^{-2x/3}$ (for $x > 0$) has a maximum at a value of x equal to ______ (Round off to two decimal places)

42. The longest wavelength of light absorbed by a hydrogen-like atom is 2.48 nm. The nuclear charge (Z) of the atom is ______ (Round off to nearest integer) (Rydberg constant R_H = 109700 cm^{-1})

43. Fullerene (C_{60}) crystallizes in an FCC unit cell (edge length = 14.14 Å) with one C_{60} centered at each lattice point. The smallest distance (in Å) between the centers of two C_{60} molecules is ______ (Round off to two decimal places)

44. A film of stearic acid partially covers the water surface in a container. The work needed to decrease this coverage by 1 cm^2 is 25.0×10^{-7} J. The surface tension (in N/m) of the film is ______ (Round off to three decimal places) (Surface tension of pure water is 0.072 N/m)

45. The value of 'n' in $[P_nO_{18}]^{6-}$ is ______

46. The total number of all possible isomers of $[Co(H_2NCH_2CH_2NH_2)_2Cl_2]^+$ and $[Co(H_2NCH_2CH_2NH_2)_3]^{3+}$ together is ______

47. The number of lone pairs present in phosphonic acid (phosphorus acid) is ______

48. Total number of constitutional isomers possible for trimethyl cyclohexane is ______

49. The dihedral (torsional) angle (in degrees) between the two methyl groups in the most stable conformation of n-butane is ______ (Round off to nearest integer)

50. The degree of unsaturation (double bond equivalent) for a compound with molecular formula $C_{14}H_{12}O_2$ is ______

Q. 51 – Q. 60 carry two marks each.

51. The heat of formation of MgO at 300 K and 1 bar pressure is –600.60 kJ mol^{-1}. The free energy (in kJ mol^{-1}) of formation of MgO at 280 K is ______ (Round off to nearest integer)

Given: In the range 280-300 K, the constant pressure heat capacities (C_P) and molar entropies (S_m) are:

	Mg	O_2	MgO
C_P (in J mol^{-1} K^{-1})	24.9	29.4	27.0
S_m (in J mol^{-1} K^{-1})	0	205.2	0

52. Sea water containing 1 M NaCl has to be desalinated at 300 K using a membrane permeable only to water. The minimum pressure (in bars) required on the sea-water side of the membrane is ______ (Round off to one decimal place) (R = 8.3 J mol^{-1} K^{-1}, 1 bar = 10^5 N/m^2)

53. A bacterial colony grows via cell division where each mother bacterium independently produces two daughter cells in 20 minutes. If the concentration of bacteria is 10^4 cm^{-3}, the colony becomes harmful. Starting from a colony with an initial concentration of 5 cm^{-3}, the time taken (in minutes) for the colony to become harmful is ______ (Round off to nearest integer)

54. The Maxwell distribution of speeds of a gas at 300 K is given below

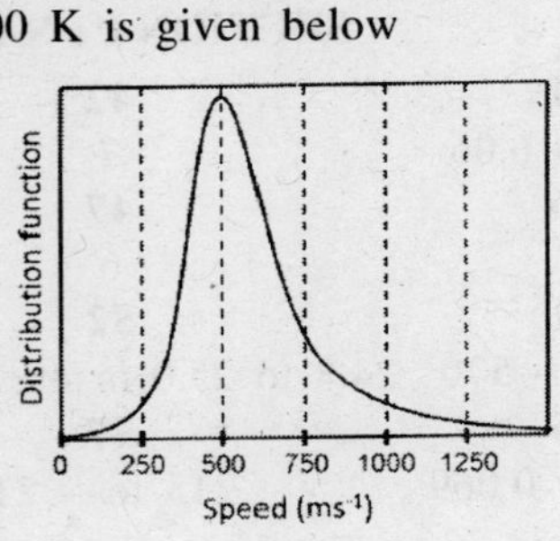

The molar mass (in g mol^{-1}) of this gas is ________ (Round off to one decimal place) (R = 8.3 J mol^{-1} K^{-1})

55. At a certain wavelength, liquid P transmits 70%, whereas liquid Q transmits 30% of the incident light when separately placed in a spectrophotometric cell (path length = 1 cm). In a binary mixture of liquids P and Q (assume non-interacting liquids), the absorbance in the same cell is 0.25. The volume fraction of liquid P in the binary mixture is ______ (Round off to two decimal places)

56. The mean ionic activity coefficient for a 0.01 M aqueous solution of $Ca_3(PO_4)_2$ is ______ (Round off to three decimal places)

(Given: $\log_{10} \gamma_{\pm} = -0.509\, z_+ \,|z_-|\, \sqrt{I}$)

57. For the reaction, $CuSO_4(aq) + Zn(s) \rightarrow ZnSO_4(aq) + Cu(s)$, the value of $\Delta G°$ (in kJ mol^{-1}) is ________ (Round off to the nearest integer) (Reduction potential: $Cu^{2+}(aq)/Cu(s)$ = +0.34 V; $Zn^{2+}(aq)/Zn(s)$ = – 0.76 V) (Faraday constant = 96485 C mol^{-1})

58. Titanium tetrachloride ($TiCl_4$) reacts with THF to form an octahedral complex X under inert atmosphere at 25 °C. If 5.0 g of $TiCl_4$ is used and the yield is 80%, the amount of X (in grams) formed is ______ (Round off to one decimal place) (Use atomic weights: Ti = 48, Cl = 35.5, O = 16, C = 12, and H = 1)

59. The total number of tautomers possible for I and II together is ______

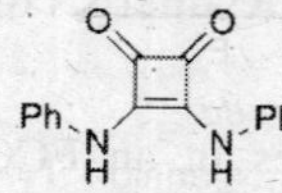

I

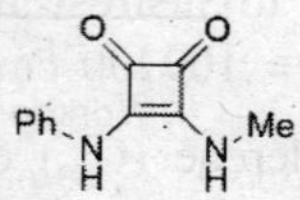

II

60. The total number of head to tail isoprene linkages in the following molecule is ______

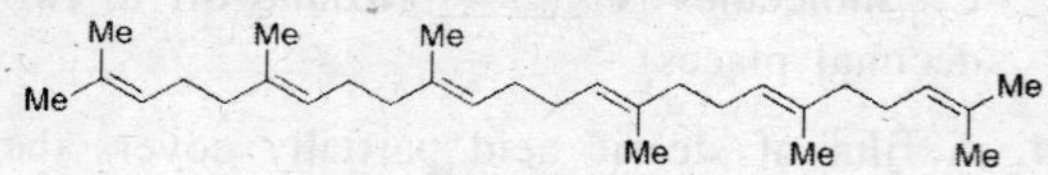

ANSWERS

SECTION A: MCQ (Multiple Choise Questions)

1	2	3	4	5	6	7	8	9	10
B	C	A	B	D	C	A	A	C	B
11	**12**	**13**	**14**	**15**	**16**	**17**	**18**	**19**	**20**
C	C	B	B	B	C	D	C	B	A
21	**22**	**23**	**24**	**25**	**26**	**27**	**28**	**29**	**30**
D	B	C	A	A	C	B	C	C	B

SECTION B: MSQ (Multiple Select Questions)

31	32	33	34	35
A, B, C	B, C	A, B, C, D	A, B, C, D	C, D
36	**37**	**38**	**39**	**40**
C, D	C, D	C, D	C	A, D

SECTION C: NAT (Numerical Answer Type Questions)

41	42	43	44	45
5.97 to 6.06	7	9.90 to 10.10	0.040 to 0.050	6
46	**47**	**48**	**49**	**50**
5	6	6	180	9
51	**52**	**53**	**54**	**55**
–574 to –570	24.8 to 25.0 or 49.7 to 49.9	210 to 225	19.8 to 20.2	0.73 to 0.75
56	**57**	**58**	**59**	**60**
0.063 to 0.069	–213 to – 211	6.9 to 7.1	13	4

EXPLANATORY ANSWERS

1. TS diagram:

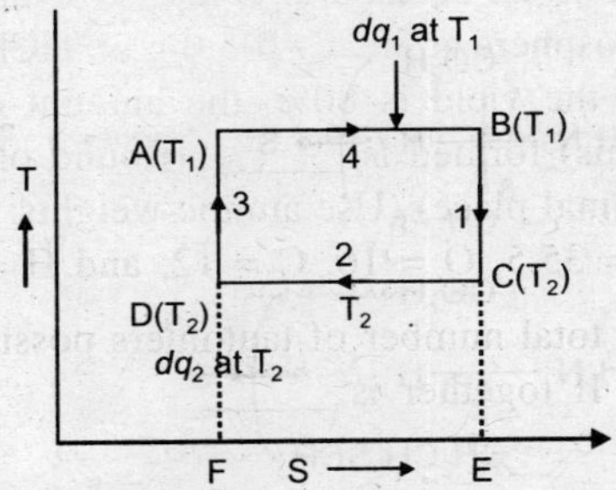

Workdone = $dq_1 - dq_2$

1. Adiabatic, reversible and expansion $T_1 > T_2$
2. Isothermal, reversible and compression.
3. Adiabatic, reversible and compression.
4. Isothermal, reversible and expansion.

Hence, correct option is (B).

2. $Br_2 \xrightarrow{k_1} 2Br^{\bullet}$

$Br^{\bullet} + H_2 \xrightarrow{k_2} HBr + H^{\bullet}$

$H^{\bullet} + Br \xrightarrow{k_3} HBr + Br^{\bullet}$

$HBr + H^{\bullet} \xrightarrow{k-2} Br^{\bullet} + H_2$

$Br^{\bullet} + Br^{\bullet} \xrightarrow{k-1} Br_2$

Initiate reaction (Create radicals)
Propagate cycle (Conserve radicals)
Inhibit – reverse 2nd step
Terminate – reverse 1st step
Therefore, the correct classification for step 2 and step 3 are both chain propagating.
Hence, correct option is (C).

3. Salt Bridge: Salt bridge is a U-shaped glass-tube containing Agar-Agar Jelly and a salt that having nearly same mobility of cation and anion. For example, KCl, NH_4Cl, NH_3NO_3, KNO_3 etc.
This is shown as:

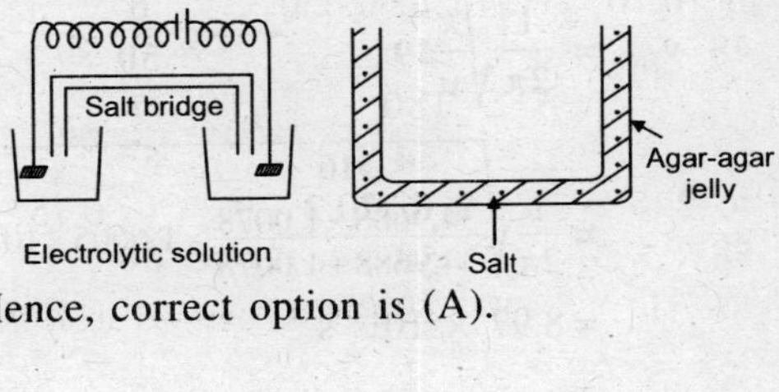

Hence, correct option is (A).

4. In case of RNA, the nucleosides obtained as D-nibase as their sugar component and adenine, guanine, cytosine, uracil as their heterocyclic.

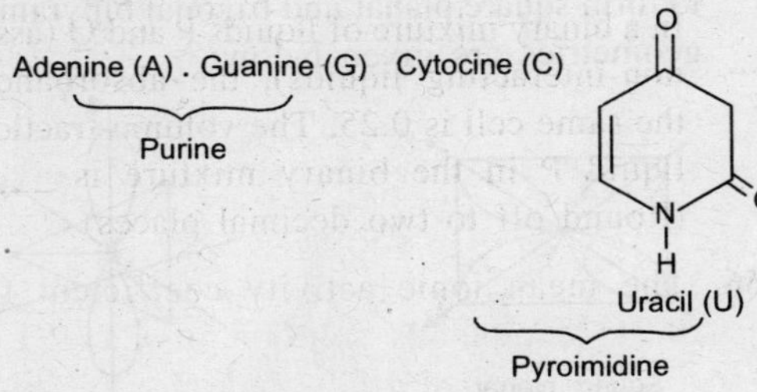

5. We can't shift H atom as in the case of resonance, only I_p or π (pi) bond deiocalise. They all have same bonding connectivity and that's why these are constitutional isomors.
Hence, correct option is (D).

6.

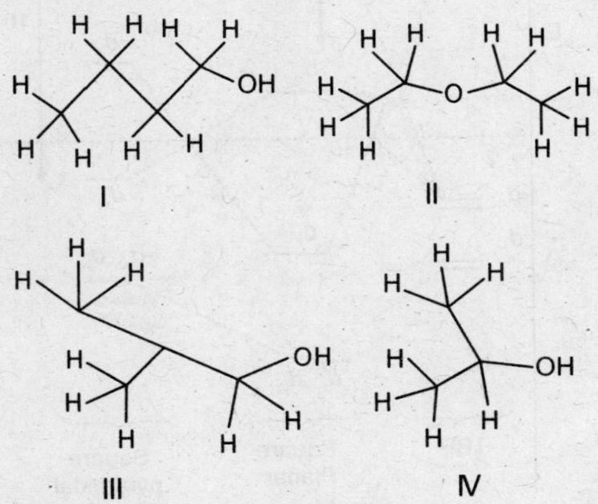

Surface area boiling point
BP of alcohols > ether
and Linear alcohols > branched alcohols
Larger surface area ⇒ greater intermolecular forces ⇒ higher boiling point
∴ I > III > IV > II.

7. Calcium phosphide reacts with water to produce calcium hydroxide and phosphine.

i.e., $\underset{\text{calcium phosphide}}{Ca_3P_3} + 6H_2O \rightarrow 3Ca(OH)_2 \downarrow + \underset{\text{phosphine gas}}{2PH_3(\uparrow)}$

8. We have,

$$H_2SO_4 + HCOOH \rightarrow CO + H_2O$$

Sulphuric acid (H_2SO_4) reacts with formic acid (HCOOH) to produce carbon monoxide and hydrate sulphuric acid.

9. The *d*-orbitals involved in the hybridisation to form square planar and trigonal bipyramidal geometries are given below:

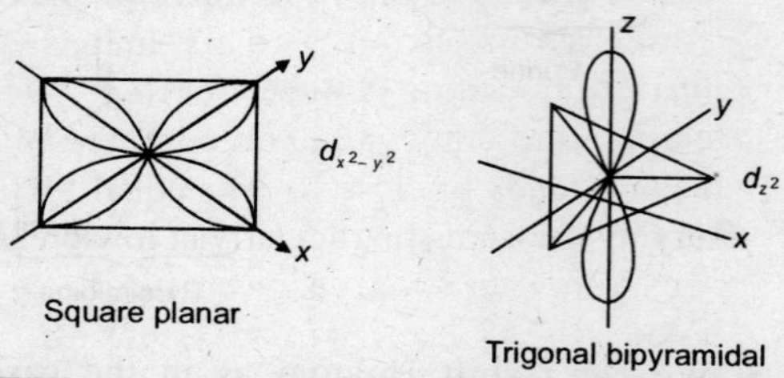

TBP → square planar → square pyramidal:

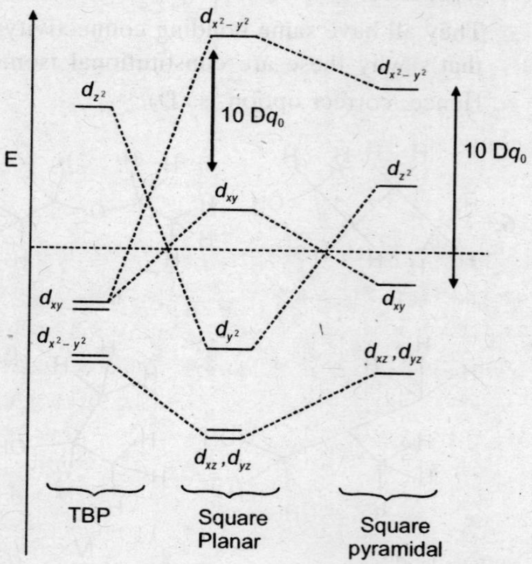

10. Amino acids are organic compounds that combine to form proteins. Amino acids and proteins are building blocks of life. When proteins are digested or broken down, amino acids are left. The human body uses amino acids to make proteins to help the body, break down food.

(A) 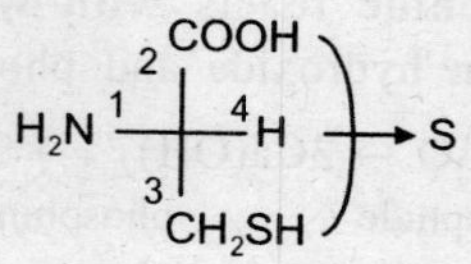

(B) 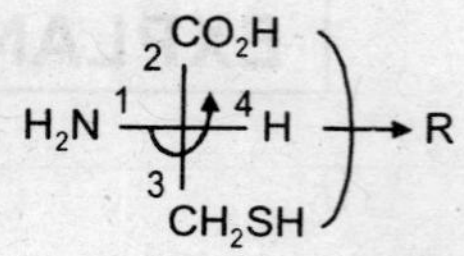

(C) 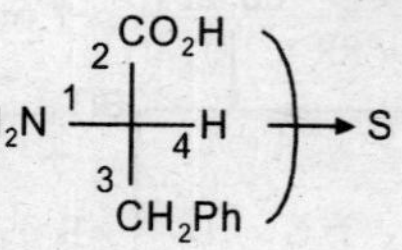

(D) 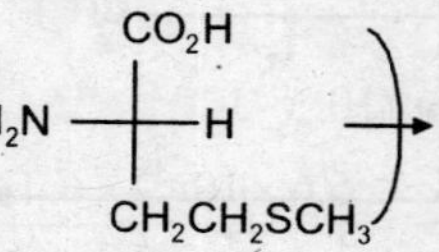

Hence, correct option is (B).

11. At constant pressure, μ Vs T

Since,

$$dG = UdP - SdT$$

and

$$dU = U_mP - S_m dT$$

$$\therefore \quad \left(\frac{dU}{dT}\right)_p = -S_m$$

$$S_{m,s} < S_{m,l} << S_{m,g}$$

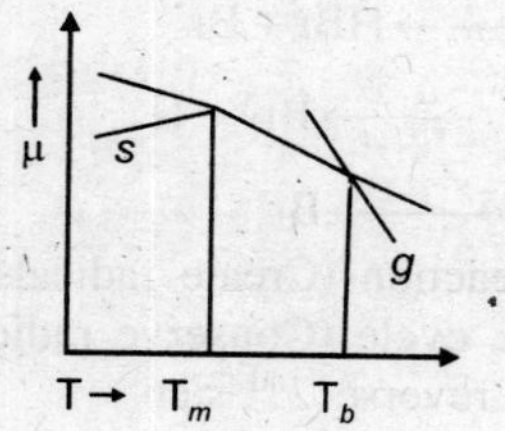

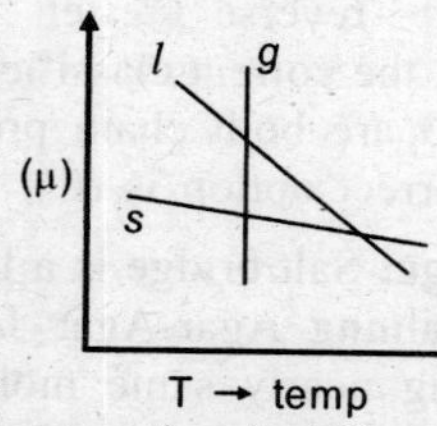

Hence, correct option is (C).

12. We have,

$$\nu_{HCl} = \frac{1}{2\pi}\sqrt{\frac{k}{\mu}}$$

$$= \frac{1}{2\pi}\sqrt{\frac{516}{\frac{34.9688 \times 1.0078}{34.9688 + 1.0078} \times 1.6605 \times 10^{-27}}}$$

$$= 8.97 \times 10^{13}\ s^{-1}$$

$$\nu_{DCl} = \frac{1}{2\pi}\sqrt{\frac{k}{\mu}}$$

$$= \frac{1}{2\pi}\sqrt{\frac{516}{\frac{34.9688 \times 2.0140}{34.9688 + 2.0140} \times 1.6605 \times 10^{-27}}}$$

$$= 6.43 \times 10^{13}\ s^{-1}$$

$$\therefore\ E_0^{HCl} = \frac{h\nu_{HCl}}{2} = \frac{6.6 \times 10^{-34} \times 8.97 \times 10^{13}}{2}$$

$$= 2.96 \times 10^{-20}\ J$$

$$E_0^{DCl} = \frac{h\nu_{DCl}}{2} = \frac{6.6 \times 10^{-34} \times 6.43 \times 10^{13}}{2}$$

$$= 2.12 \times 10^{-20}$$

$$\therefore\ \frac{E_0^{HCl}}{E_0^{DCl}} = \frac{2.97 \times 10^{-20}}{2.13 \times 10^{-20}} = 1.395$$

Hence, the ratio of the zero point energy of $H^{35}Cl$ to that of $D^{35}Cl$ is 1.395.

13. We have, $R = \begin{vmatrix} 3 & 2 & 4 \\ 4 & 5 & 7 \\ 1 & 3 & 8 \end{vmatrix}$

$$\therefore\ |R| = 3(5 \times 8 - 7 \times 3) - 2(4 \times 8 - 1 \times 7) + 4(4 \times 3 - 5 \times 1)$$

$$= 57 - 50 + 28 = 35$$

$$|S| = \begin{vmatrix} 2 & 3 & 4 \\ 5 & 4 & 7 \\ 3 & 1 & 8 \end{vmatrix}$$

$$= 2(4 \times 8 - 1 \times 7) - 3(5 \times 8 - 7 \times 3) + 4(5 \times 1 - 4 \times 3)$$

$$= 2(32 - 7) - 3(40 - 21) + 4(5 - 12)$$

$$= 2 \times 25 - 3 \times 19 + 4 \times -7$$

$$= 50 - 57 - 28 = -35$$

$$T = \begin{vmatrix} 3 & 4 & 1 \\ 2 & 5 & 3 \\ 4 & 7 & 8 \end{vmatrix}$$

$$= 3(5 \times 8 - 3 \times 7) - 4(2 \times 8 - 3 \times 4) + 1(2 \times 7 - 5 \times 4)$$

$$= 3(40 - 21) - 4(16 - 12) + 1(14 - 20)$$

$$= 3 \times 19 - 4 \times 4 + 1 \times -6$$

$$= 57 - 16 - 6 = 35$$

14. Boyle's temperature is formally as the temperature for which the second viral coefficient becomes zero. It is at this temperature that the attractive forces and the repulsive forces acting on the gas particles balance out. This is the viral equation of state describes as a real gas.

The temperature at which a real gas behaves like an ideal gas for wide range of pressure (low pressure values). This means at a particular temperature called Boyle temperature, the value of compressibility factor z tends to close to 1 or equal to 1 for varying pressures [particularly at low pressure range). For gas has a characteristic T_B eg. 23 K for He, 347 K for air and 715 K for CO_2.

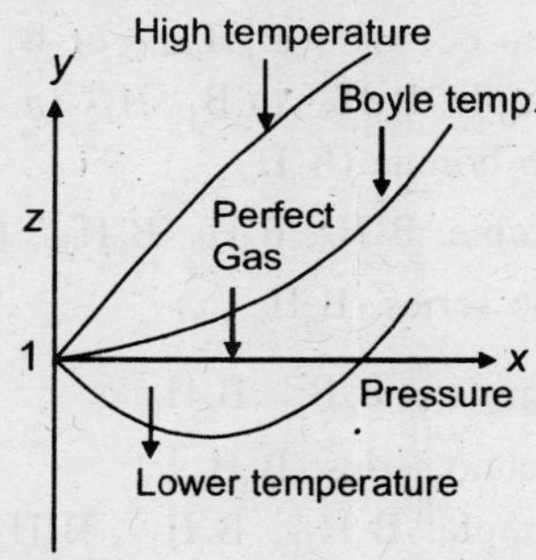

The compression factor approaches 1 at low pressures, but does show with different slopes. For perfect gas, the slope is zero, but real gases may have either positive or negative slopes and the slope may vary with temperature. At the Boyle temperature, the slope is zero and the gas behaves perfectly over a wider range of conditions than at other temperatures.

15. Given,

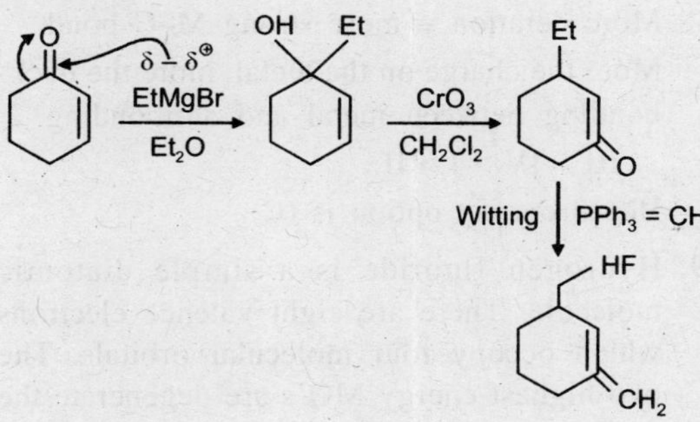

16. From, VSEPR,

$Br_3^{\oplus} \Rightarrow Br \rightarrow \ddot{Br}:-Br \Rightarrow$ 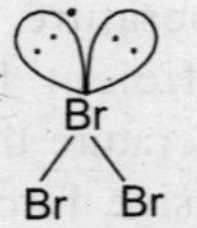

Central atom ($6e^-$)

$Br_3^{\ominus} \Rightarrow Br \rightarrow \ddot{Br}: \rightarrow Br^- \Rightarrow$ 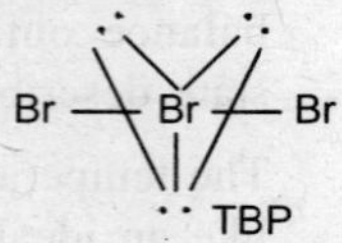

Central atom $6e^-$

and $BrF_3 \Rightarrow$ 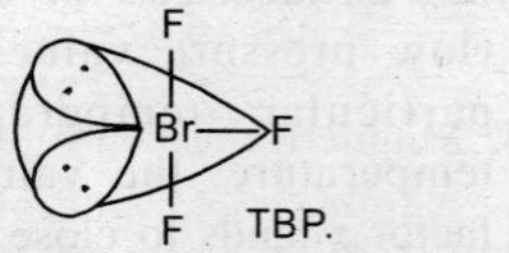

Central atom $7e^-$

Hence, the geometries: tetrahedral, trigonal, bipyramidal and trigonal bipyramidal.

17. Classification of different class of Borane:

(A) Close borane : (B_nH_{n+2} or $B_nH_n^{2-}$)

For example, $B_5H_5^{2-}$ to $B_{12}H_{12}^{2-}$ (n = 5 to 12)

(B) Nido borane (B_nH_{n+4})

For example, B_2H_6, B_5H_9, B_6H_{10}, $B_{10}B_{13}^{\ominus}$ etc.

(C) Hypo series (B_nH_{n+8})

For example : $B_5B_{12}^{\ominus}$, $B_5H_{11}^{2-}$

(D) Arachno series (B_nH_{n+6})

For example, B_4H_{10}, B_5H_{11}, B_6H_{12}, B_8H_{14}, B_9H_{15} etc.

Hence, correct option is (D).

18. $\underset{\text{III}}{[Ti(CO)_6]^{2-}} > \underset{\text{IV}}{[CO(CO)_4]^{-}} > \underset{\text{I}}{[Cr(CO)_6]} > \underset{\text{II}}{[Mn(CO)_6]^{+}}$

M → CO 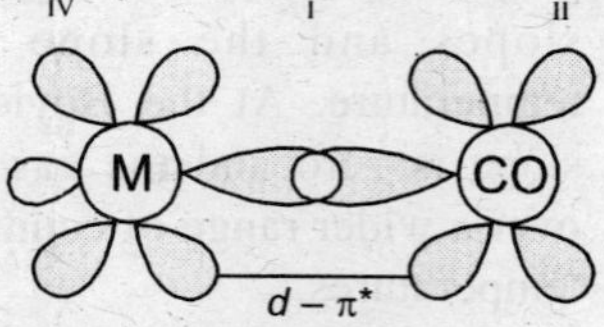

More negative charge density ≡

More deration ≡ more strong M–C bond.

More the charge on the metal, more the back-bonding between metal and antibonding.

∴ III > IV > I > II.

Hence correct option is (C).

19. Hydrogen fluoride is a simple diatomic molecule. There are eight valence electrons which occupy four molecular orbitals. The two highest energy MO's are degenerate the *p*-type and have no electron density associated with the hydrogen atom, i.e., they are non-bonding orbitals (NBO) and in Lewis theory are represented as two lone pairs. Another important difference between hydrogen fluoride and previous molecules is that the electron density is not equally distributed about the molecule. There is much greater electron density around the fluorine atom. This is because fluorine is an extremely electronegative elements, in each bonding molecular orbital, fluorine will take a greater share of the electron density.

For the energy diagram of the orbitals given below.

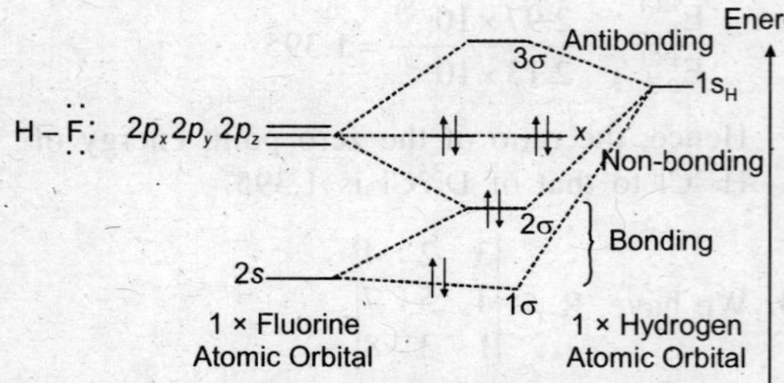

Hydrogen Fluoride Molecular Orbital

Therefore, number of non-bonding electrons present in the trontier molecular orbitals of HF is 6.

20. Given, $[Al(BH_4)_4]^-$

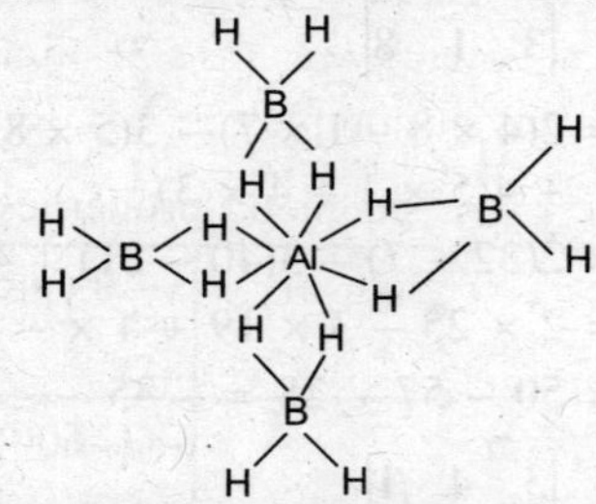

The coordination number of aluminum ion and the number of bridging hydrogen atoms in $[Al(BH_4)_4]^-$ are 8 and 8.

21. We have,

(A) $CO_2(CO)_8 = \frac{1}{2}(9 \times 2 + 16 + 2)$

$= \frac{1}{2}(18 + 16 + 2) = \frac{1}{2} \times 36 = 18e^{\ominus}$

(B) $[Fe(CO)_4]^{2-} = 8 + 8 + 2 = 18e^-$

(C) $[HMn(CO)_5] = 1 + 7 + 10 = 18e^-$

(D) $[(\eta^5 - C_5H_5)RuCl(CO)(PPh_2)]$

$-1 + x + 1 + 0 - 1 = 0$

$\Rightarrow x = +3$

$\eta^5 - C_5H_5^{\ominus}$	:	6
Ru^{3+}	:	5
Cl^-	:	2
CO	:	2
$\overset{\ominus}{PPh_2}$	:	2

Total electrons $17e^{\ominus}$

Hence, correct option is (D).

22. H – F : 95 PM

H ---- F : 155 PM [Zig-Zag]

HF → strong hydrogen bonding.

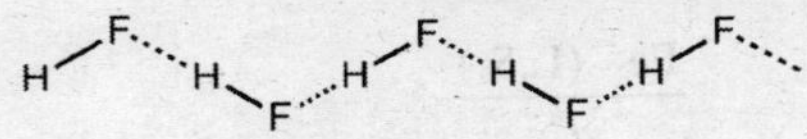

23. We have,

Case I: (d^1, d^4, d^6, d^9)

[The degeneracy of these orbitals are 5 and thus D-atom].

As, d^1, d^4, d^6, d^9 systems have D(state) configuration. Then, all would have corresponding splitting pattern in the tetrahedral field as well as octahedral field.

Thus, the number of *d-d* transitions expected for the given complex is 3.

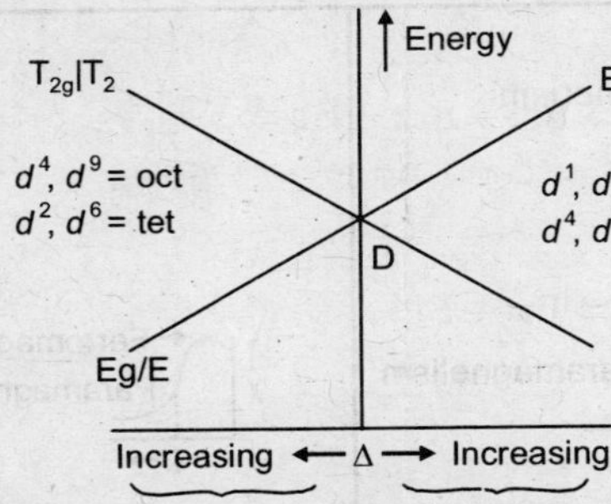

24. Magnetic susceptibility vs temperature: Applied field interplay and thermal randomization leads to temperature dependence described by the Curie law,

$$\chi = C/T$$

where C → Curie constant and T is in Kelvin. Paramagnetic substances with localized, weakly interacting electrons obey the Curie-Weiss law,

$$\chi_m = C/T-\theta$$

where χ_m → molar magnetic susceptibility, C = Curie constant and θ = Weiss constant.

A graph of $\frac{1}{\chi_m}$ vs temperature is known as a curie meiss plot. It should be linear, when the C – W law is obeyed. From such graph, we see that the extract the curie constant from the inverse of the slope and the weiss constant from the *y*-intercept.

Characteristics of magnetic properties:

Type	Sign of χ	Typical χ	Dependence of χ on H field dependence	Change of χ. W/in C temp.	Origin
Diamagnetism	–	$-(1–600) \times 10^{-5}$	Independent	None	Charge on electrons
Paramagnetism	+	0.001 – 0.1	– do –	Dec	Spin and orbital motion of electrons on atoms
Ferromagnetism	+	$0.1 - 5 \times 10^3$	Dependent	Dec	Cooperative interaction between magnetic properties of individnal atoms
Antiferro-magnetism	+	0 – 0.1	May be dependent	Inc	

Pauli Paramagnetism	+	1×10^{-5}	Independent	None	Spin and orbital motion of delocalized electrons
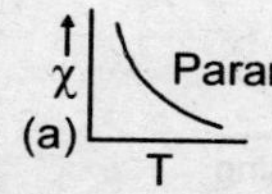	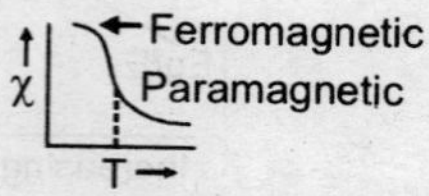			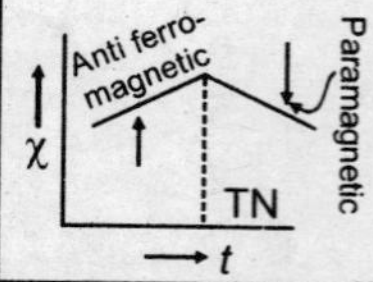	

Hb

Deoxy Hb → High spin → Paramagnetic

Oxy-Hb → Low spin → Diamagnetic

Deoxy-haemoglobin

Fe^{2+} (H.S.)

d^6

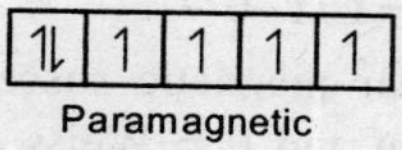

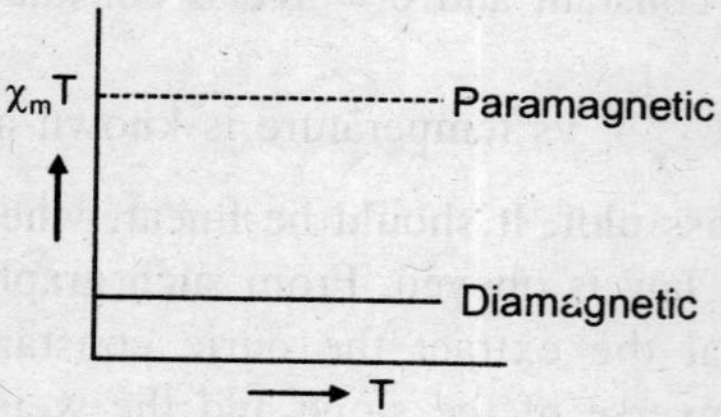

Oxy-haemoglobin

Fe^{2+} (L.S.)

d^6

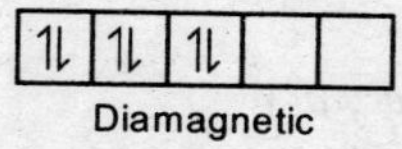

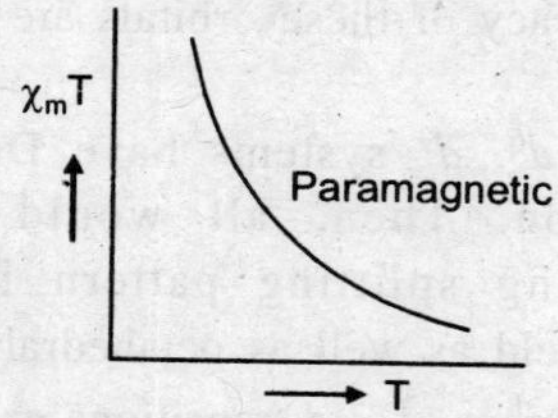

25. We have,

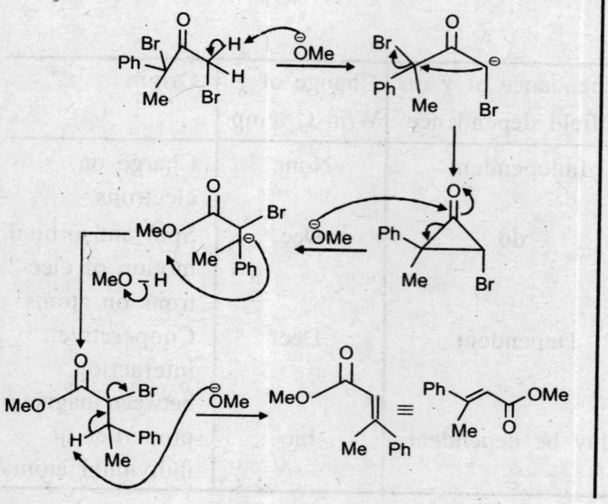

26. We have,

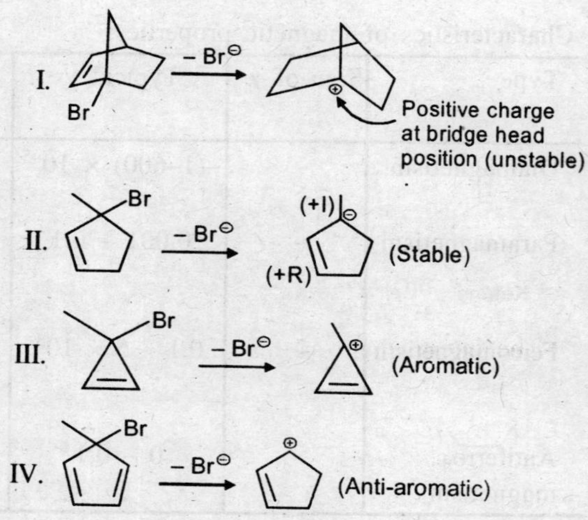

∵ Stability α rate of solvolysis.

Hence, the rate of solvolysis of I-IV of order:

III > II > I > IV

Hence, correct option is (C).

27. From the elimination method:

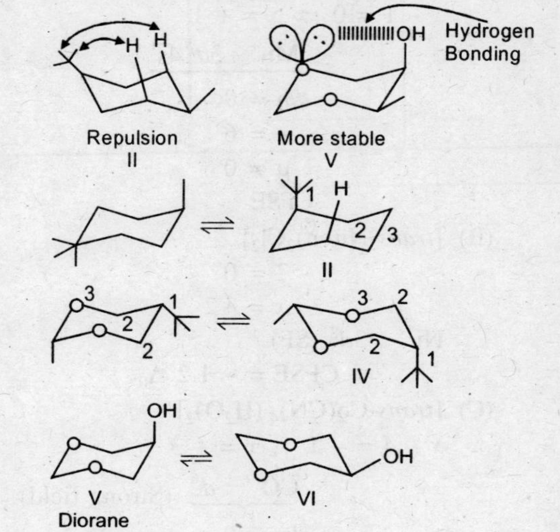

i.e., I > IV

Hence, correct option is (B).

28.

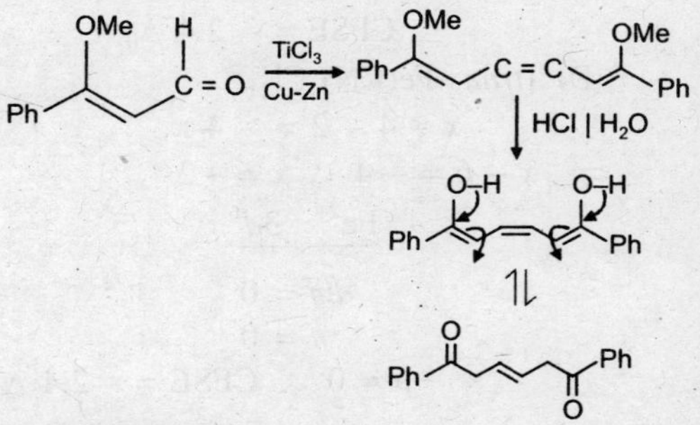

For example,

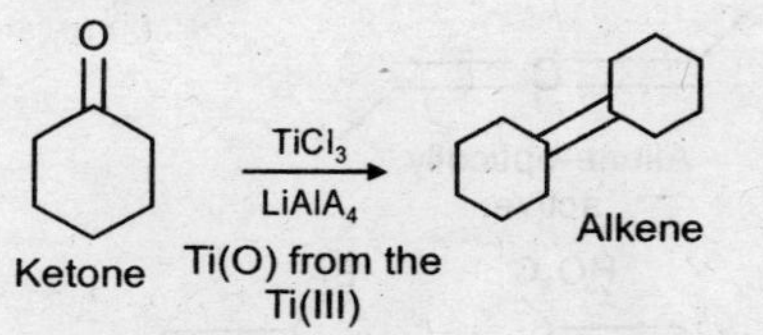

The intermediate in this reaction is:

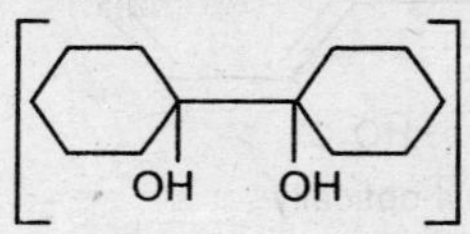 → It can be observed by the low temp.

Mechanism:

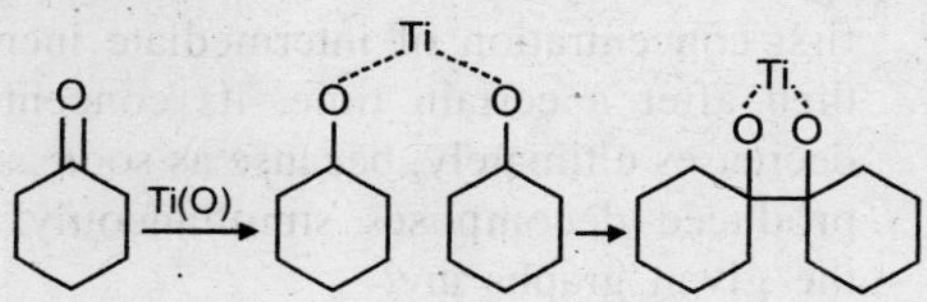

29. We have,

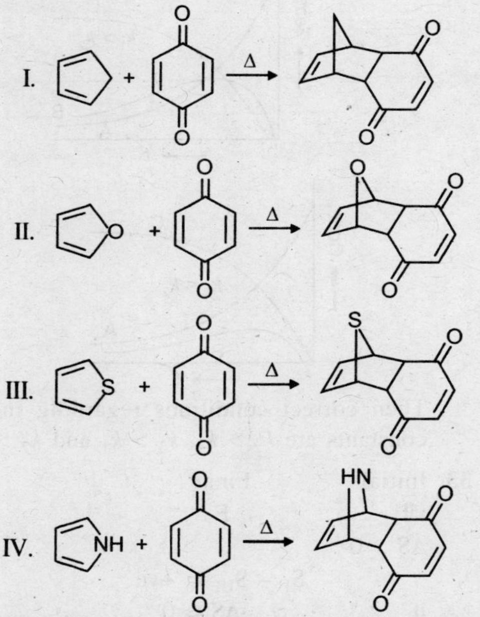

The diels Alder reactions I-IV, the activation barriers of the order: III > IV > II > I

Less delocatization ∝ less energy barrier.

Hence, correct option is (C).

30. Based on iodolocalization:

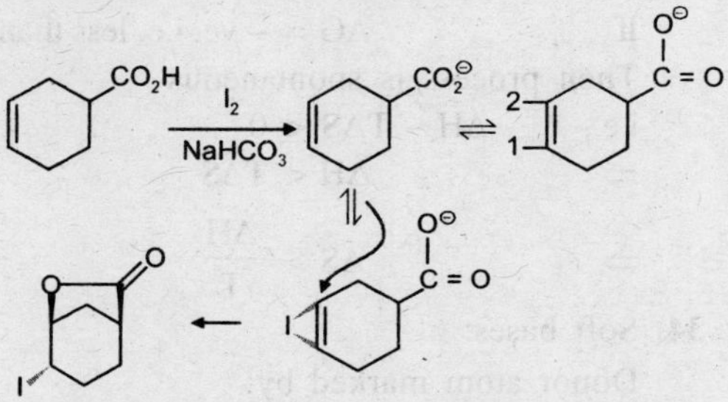

31. Consider a reaction $A \xrightarrow{k_1} B \xrightarrow{k_2} C$

If $k_1 > k_2$: In this reaction, with progress of reaction concentration of reaction decreases with time. The product increases with time spontaneously, but in the case of intermediate, first concentration of intermediate increases, then after a certain time, its concentration decreases ultimately, because as soon as, they produced decomposes simultaneouly. Then the given graphs are:

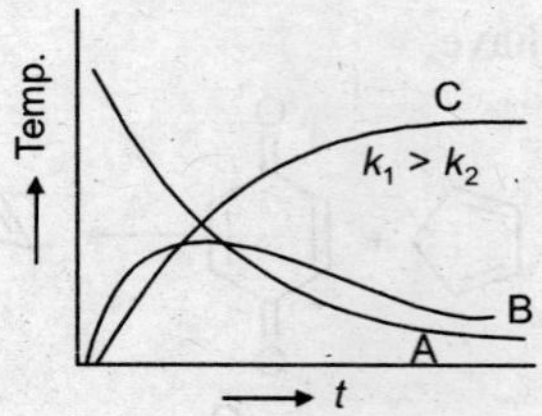

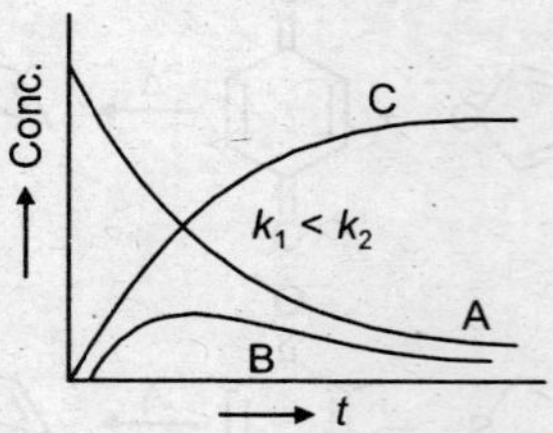

Then correct conditions regarding the rate constants are $k_2 > k_4$, $k_3 > k_1$ and $k_2 > k$.

33. Initial Final

UF F

$\Delta S > 0$

$S_F - S_{UF} = +ve$

If $\Delta S = 0$

$\because \Delta G = \Delta H - T\Delta S = \Delta H - T \times 0$

$= \Delta H$

$\Rightarrow \Delta G = H_F - H_{UF} = -ve$

Given, $H_{UF} > H_F$

Now, $\Delta G = \Delta H - T\Delta S$

If $\Delta G = -$ ve. i.e. less than zero.

Then process is spontaneous

i.e., $\Delta H - T\Delta S < 0$

$\Rightarrow \Delta H < T\Delta S$

$$\Rightarrow \Delta S > \frac{\Delta H}{T}$$

34. Soft bases:

Donor atom marked by:

(*i*) low electronegativity

(*ii*) high polarizability

(*iii*) partially filled orbitals: empty orbitals are low lying.

Examples:

H^-, I^-, SCN^-, CN^-, $S_2O_3^{2-}$, CO, C_2H_4, C_6H_6, R_2S, RSH, RS^-, R_3P, R_3As.

36. We have,

(A) $[Mn(CO)_5(CH_3)]$

$x - 1 = 0 \Rightarrow x = +1$

$\underbrace{Mn^+ : 3d^5 4s^1}$

$dm \neq 0$

$n = 6$

$\mu \neq 0$

CFSE

(B) $[trans\text{-}Ni(en)_2Cl_2]$

$x - 2 = 0$

$x = +2$

$Ni^{2+} : 3d^8$ (SF)

$\text{CFSE} = -1.2\ \Delta_0$

(C) $[trans\text{-}Co(CN)_4(H_2O)_2]$

$x - 4 = -1 \therefore x = +3$

$\underbrace{CO^{3+} : d^6}$ (Strong field)

$dm = 0$

$n = 0$

$\mu = 0$

$\text{CFSE} = -2.4\ \Delta_0$

(D) $[trans\text{-}Fe(CN)_4Cl_2]^{4-}$

$x - 4 - 2 = -4$

$\Rightarrow x - 6 = -4 \therefore x = +2$

$\underbrace{Fe^{2+} : 3d^6}$

$dm = 0$

$n = 0$

$\mu = 0 \therefore \text{CFSE} = -2.4\ \Delta_0$

37. Chirality → Absence of symmetry elements:

(A)

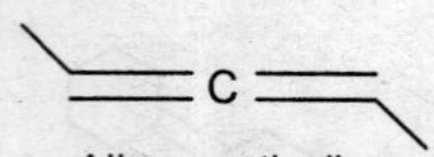

Allene-optically active

(B)

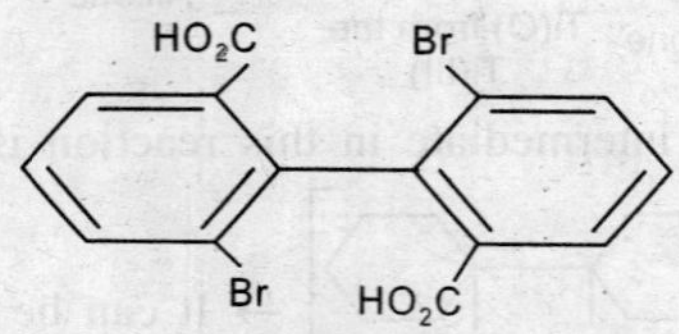

Biphenyl-optically active

(C) 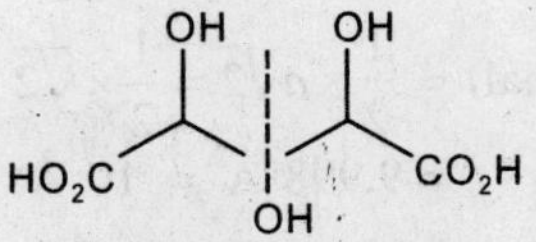

Plane of symmetry (σ)
Achiral optically inactive

(D) 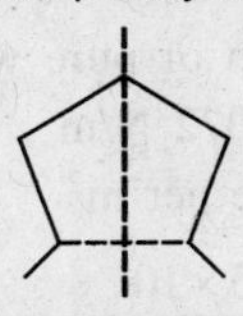

Plane of symmetry (σ)
Achiral Optically inactive

38. (A) 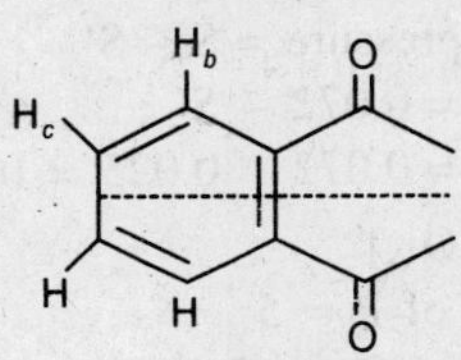

3-signals

(B) 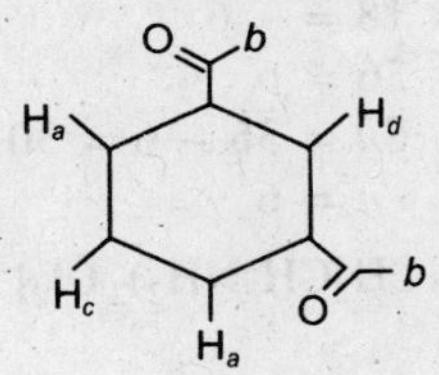

4-signals

(C) 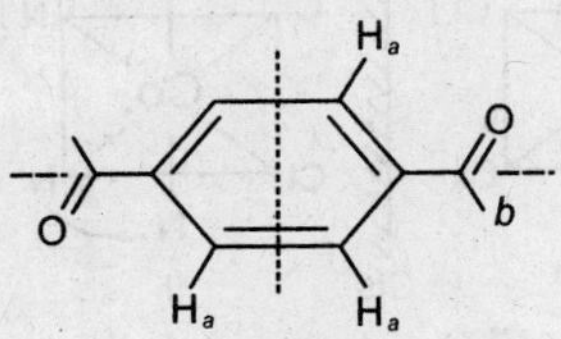

2-signals

(D) 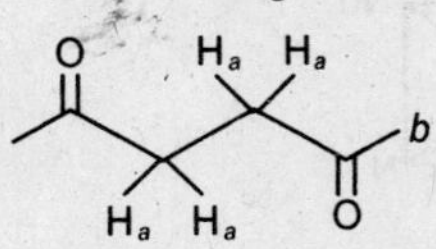

Symmetrical

Two →	6 : 4	Aromatic
CH_3	⇓	H_a
$6H_b$	3 : 2	
$6H_b$	6 : 4	$4H_b$
(CH_3)	⇓	(CH_2)
	3 : 2	

Hence, correct options are (C) and (D).

39. We have,

(A) 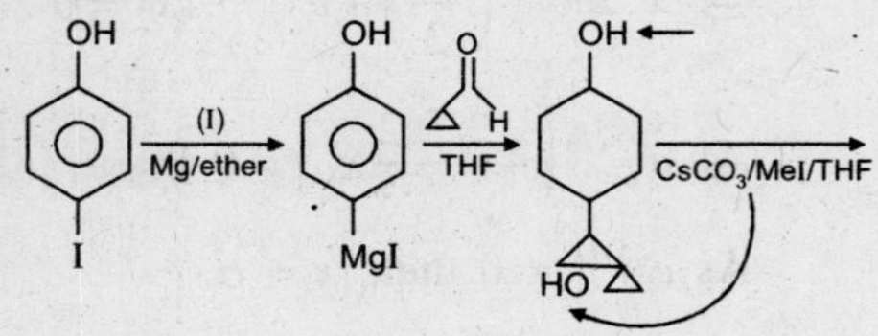

(B) 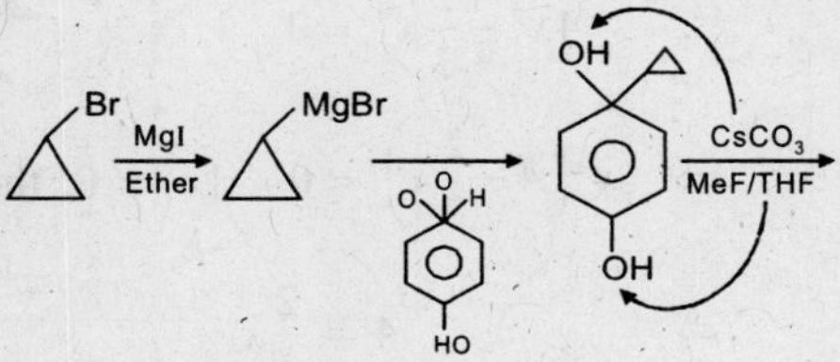

(C) 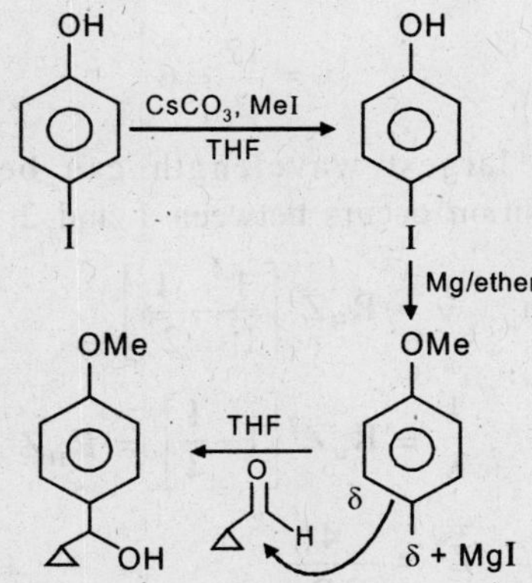

(D) 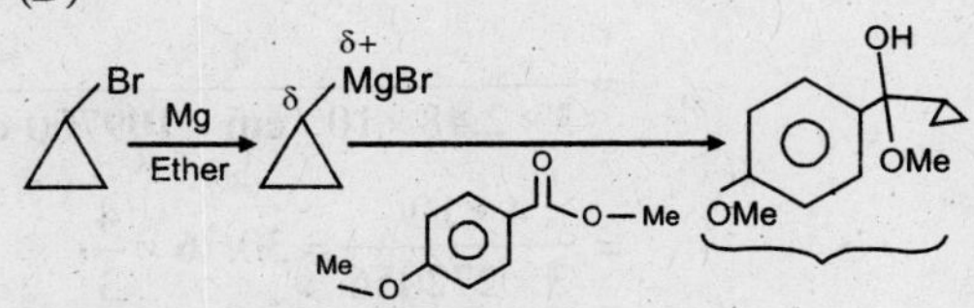

Hence, correct option is (C).

40. (A) 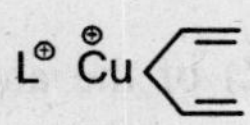 (B) 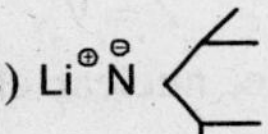

(C) 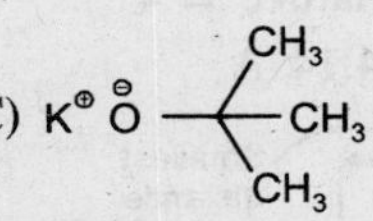 (D) 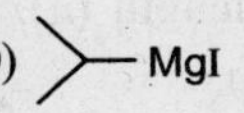

Hence, the organometallic reagents are lithium divinylcuprate and isopropyl magnesium iodide.

41. Given, $f(x) = x^4e^{-2x/3}$ [for $x > 0$]

$$\therefore \quad \frac{d}{dx}f(x) = 0 \Rightarrow \frac{d}{dx}\left\{x^4e^{-2x/3}\right\} = 0$$

$$\Rightarrow x^4.e^{-2x/3}\left(\frac{-2}{3}\right)+e^{-2x/3}.4x^3=0$$

$$\Rightarrow e^{-2x/3}\left(4x^3-\frac{2}{3}x^4\right)=0$$

As $e^{-2x/3} \neq 0$ then, $x = \alpha$

$$\therefore \quad 4x^3-\frac{2}{3}x^4=0$$

$$\Rightarrow x^3\left(4-\frac{2}{3}x\right)=0 \quad [x^3 \neq 0, \text{ then } x = 0]$$

$$\Rightarrow \quad 4=\frac{2}{3}x$$

$$\Rightarrow \quad x=\frac{12}{2}=6$$

42. The largest wavelength can be got, if transition occurs between 1 and 2.

Then, $\bar{\nu} = R_H Z^2\left[\frac{1}{1^2}-\frac{1}{2^2}\right]$

$$\Rightarrow \frac{1}{\lambda} = R_H Z^2\left[1-\frac{1}{4}\right] = R_H Z^2\left[\frac{3}{4}\right]$$

$$\Rightarrow Z^2 = \frac{4}{3\lambda R_H}$$

$$= \frac{4}{3\times 2.48\times 10^{-7}\text{ cm}\times 109700\text{ cm}^{-1}}$$

$$= \frac{4\times 10^7}{3\times 272056} = 30.76\times\frac{4}{3}$$

$$= 49.0 \simeq 49$$

$\therefore \quad Z = 7$

Hence, nuclear charge (Z) of the atom is 7.

43. FCC unit cell, total lattice = 4

Edge length (a) = 14.14 Å

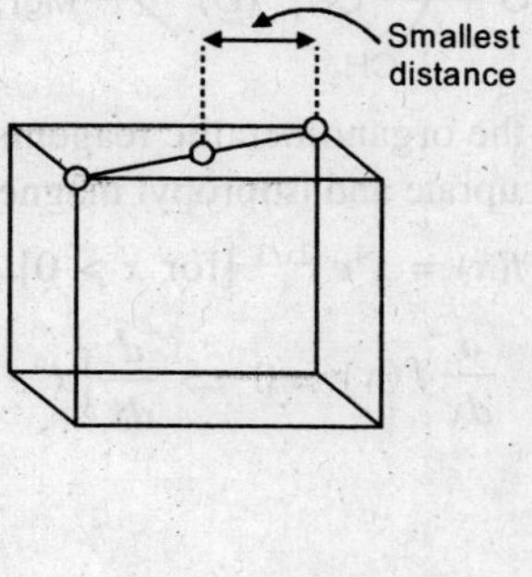

$$\frac{1}{2}\text{ (diagonal)} = \frac{1}{2}\times a\sqrt{2} = \frac{1}{2}\times\sqrt{2}\times 14.14\text{ Å}$$

$$= 9.998\text{ Å} \simeq 10\text{ Å}$$

44. Given surface pressure per cm^2

$$= 25 \times 10^{-7}\text{ J}$$

and surface tension of pure water

$$S = 0.072\text{ N/m}$$

$\therefore$ Surface pressure per m^2

$$= \frac{25\times 10^{-7}}{10^{-4}} = 25\times 10^{-3}\text{ J}$$

$$S = 0.072\text{ N/m}$$

Now, surface pressure = S – S′

$\Rightarrow 25 \times 10^{-3} = 0.072 - S'$

$\therefore \quad S' = 0.072 - 0.025 = 0.047$

45. We have, $[P_n O_{18}]^{6-}$

Valency of P = 5

Valency of O = –2

$\therefore \quad 5n - 2 \times 18 = -6$

$\Rightarrow \quad 5n - 36 = 6$

$5n = 36 - 6 = 30$

$\therefore \quad n = 6$

46. Given, $[Co(H_2NCH_2CH_2NH_2)_2Cl_2]^+$

$(Co(en)_2Cl_2]^+$

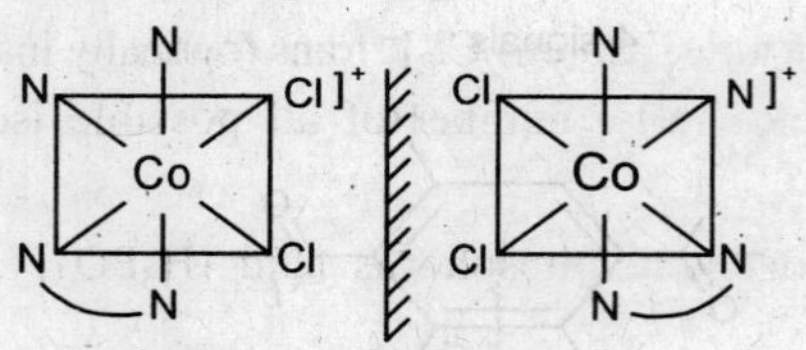

I Cis II

and

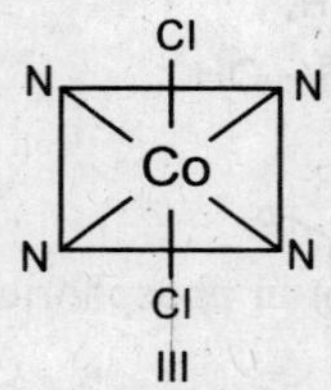

III

Trans

and $[Co(H_2NCH_2CH_2NH_2)_3]^{3+} \Rightarrow (Co(en)_3]^{3+}$

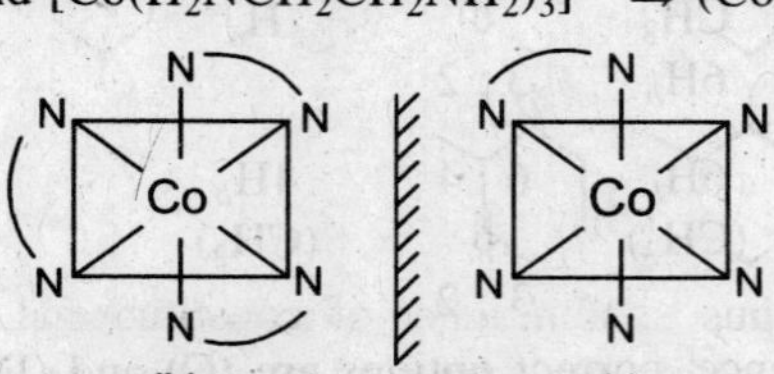

IV V

∴ Total = 5.

(I) $M(AA)_3$: (2 isomers)

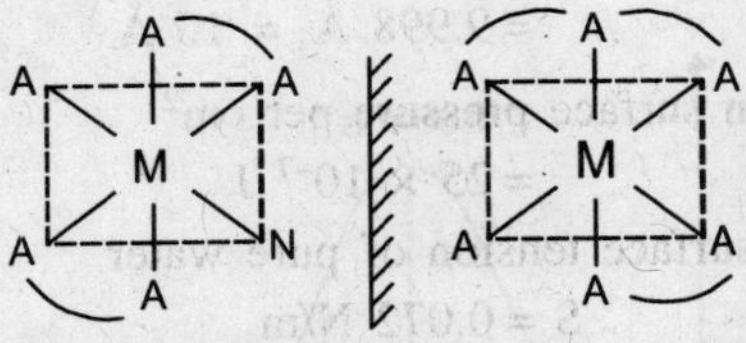

Two optical isomers: A pair of enantiomers optically active

Example: $[Co(en)_3]^{3+}$, $[Cr(OX)_3]^{3-}$

(I) $M(AA)_2\ b_2$: (3 isomers)

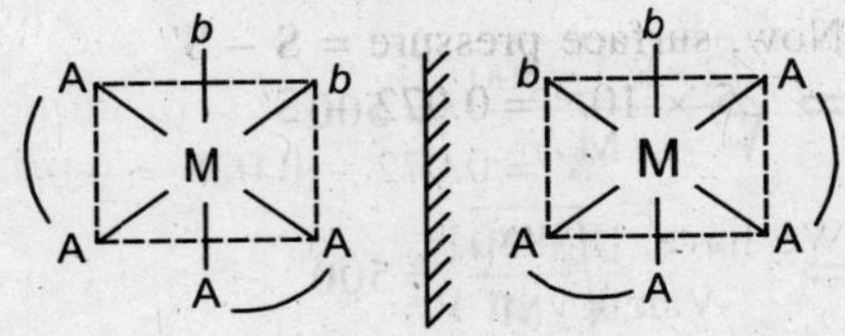

(Cis – isomer) : A pair of enantiomers (optically active)

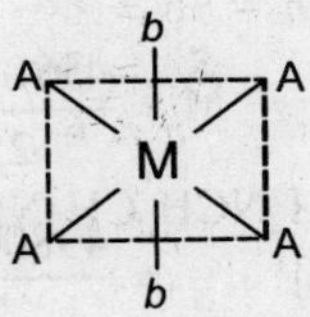

Example: $[Co(en)_2Cl_2]^+$ trans (optically inactive)

Hence, total number of all possible isomers is 5.

47. Phosphonic/phosphorus acid $[H_3PO_3]$

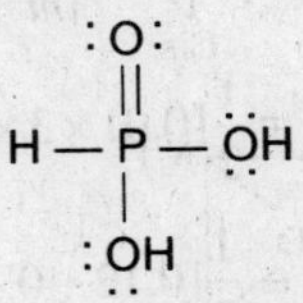

∴ Lone pairs present in phosphoric acid is 6.

48.

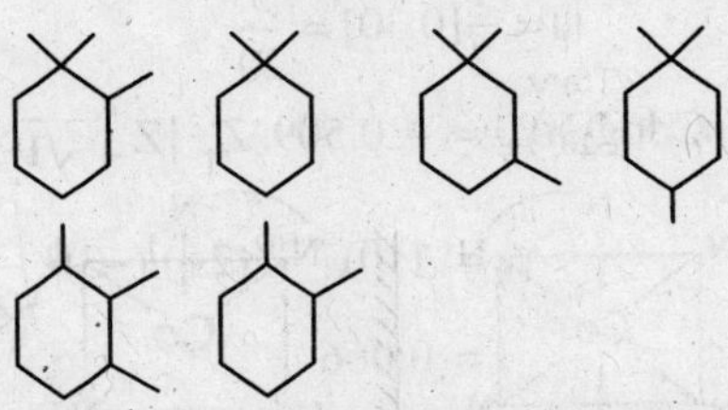

Thus total number of constitutional isomers possible for trimethyl cyclohexane is 6.

49.

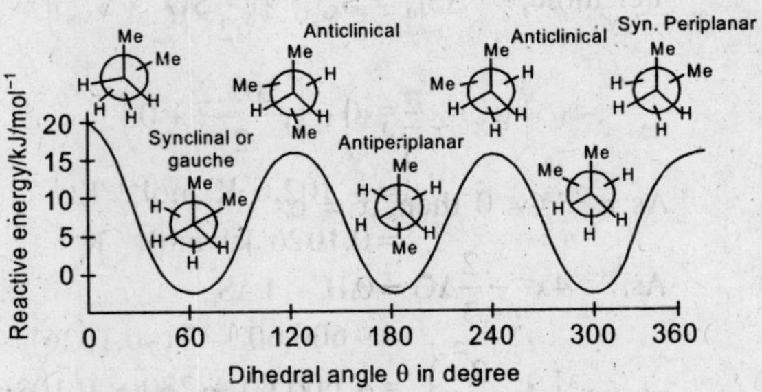

n-butane:

$CH_3–CH_2–CH_2–CH_3$

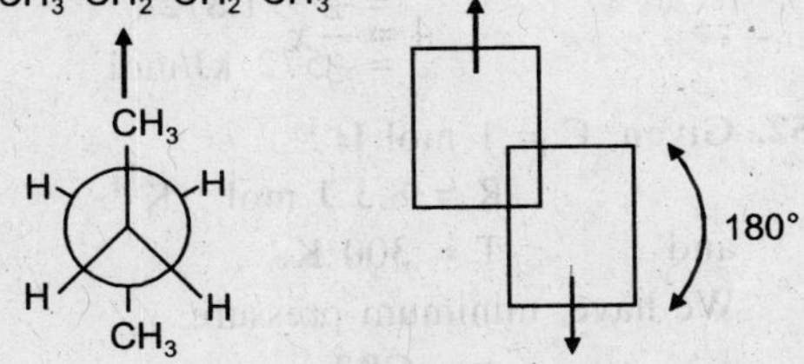

Hence, the dihedral angle between the two methyl groups is the most stable configuration of *n*-butane is 180°.

50. The double bond equivalency 180° (DBE) or index of hydrogen deficiency of a system (molecular formula) determines the row structure of a systems.

$$DBE = \frac{1}{2}[2c + 2 + n - (h + x)]$$

Where, $c \rightarrow$ no. of carbon atom

$n \rightarrow$ no. of nitrogen atom

$h \rightarrow$ no. of hydrogen atom

$x \rightarrow$ no. of halogen atom

∴ Double bond equivalent (DBE)

$$= \frac{1}{2}[2c + 2 + n - (h - x)]$$

$$= \frac{1}{2}[2 \times 14 + 2 + 0 - (12 - 0)]$$

$$= \frac{1}{2}[28 + 2 - 12] = \frac{1}{2} \times 18 = 9$$

51. $Mg(s) + \frac{1}{2}O_2(g) \rightarrow MgO(s) > \Delta H^\circ_f$

$= -\ 600.60$ kJ/mol

Per mole, $\Delta S_m = S_{MgO} - \left(\frac{1}{2}SO_2 + S_{Mg}\right)$

$$= 0 - \left(\frac{205.2}{2} + 0\right)$$

$$= -102.6 \text{ K mol}^{-1} \text{ K}^{-1}$$

$$= 0.1026 \text{ kJ mol}^{-1} \text{ K}^{-1}$$

As, $\Delta G = \Delta H - T\Delta S$

$$= -600.60 - T(-0.1026)$$

$$= -600.60 + 280 \times 0.1026$$

$$= 600.60 + 28.728$$

$$= -571.872$$

$$\approx -572 \text{ kJ/mol}$$

52. Given, $C = 1 \text{ mol L}^{-1}$

$R = 8.3 \text{ J mol}^{-1} \text{ K}^{-1}$

and $T = 300 \text{ K}$.

We have, minimum pressure,

$$\pi = CRT$$

$$= 1 \times 8.3 \times 300 \text{ NmL}^{-1}$$

$$= 8.3 \times 300 \text{ Nm } (10^3 \text{ m}^{-3})$$

$[\because 1 \text{ bar} = 10^5 \text{ Nm}^{-2}]$

$$= 8.3 \times 300 \times 10^3 \text{ Nm}^{-2}$$

$$= 8.3 \times 300 \times 10^3 \times 10^{-5} \text{ bar}$$

$$= 24.9 \text{ bar}$$

53. Bacterial growth is a first order kinetics.

Mother cell < Two daughter cell / 20 minutes — conc ≡ number

As, $\lambda = \frac{2.303}{20} \log \frac{N_o}{N_t}$

$$= \frac{2.303}{t} \log \frac{1}{2} \text{ min}^{-1}$$

$$= -0.035 \text{ min}^{-1}$$

Now, $t = \frac{2.303}{\lambda} \log \frac{C_o}{C_t}$

$$= \frac{2.303}{(-0.035)} \log \frac{5}{10^4} \text{ min}$$

$$= 217 \text{ min}$$

54. Most probable velocity, $v = \sqrt{\frac{2RT}{M}} = 500$

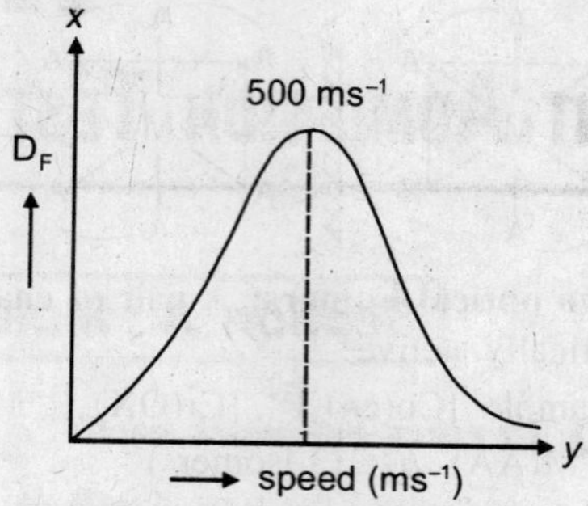

$$\Rightarrow \sqrt{\frac{2 \times 8.3 \times 300}{M}} = 500$$

$$\Rightarrow \sqrt{\frac{4980}{M}} = 500$$

$$\Rightarrow \frac{4980}{M} = (500)^2$$

$$\therefore \quad M = \frac{4980 \text{ kg m/s}^{-2} \text{ mol}^{-1}}{250000 \text{ m/s}^{-2}}$$

$$= \frac{4980000 \text{ g mol}^{-1}}{250000}$$

$$= 19.92 \text{ g/mol.}$$

56. The ionic strength (I) $= \frac{1}{2}\sum_i M_i Z_i^2$

$[m = \text{conc.} = 0.01 \text{ M}]$

$$= \frac{1}{2}[0.01 \times 3 \times 2^2 + 0.01 \times 2 \times 3^2]$$

$$= \frac{1}{2}[0.12 + 0.18]$$

$$= \frac{1}{2}[0.30] = \frac{3}{20}$$

Given, $\log_{10} \gamma_\pm = -0.509\, Z_+ \,|Z_-|\, \sqrt{I}$

$$\Rightarrow \quad \gamma_\pm = (10)^{-0.509}(2+)|(-3)|\sqrt{\frac{3}{20}}$$

$$= 0.066$$

Previous Years Paper

IIT–JAM

JOINT ADMISSION TEST FOR M.Sc. (CHEMISTRY), 2019

Section A : Multiple Choice Questions (MCQ)

Q. 1 – Q. 10 carry one mark each.

1. For a reaction of the type A + B $\rightarrow$ Products, the unit of the rate constant is mol L^{-1} s^{-1}. The overall order of the reaction is:

A. 0 B. 1
C. 2 D. 3

2. The thermodynamic criterion for spontaneity of a process in a system under constant volume and temperature and in the absence of any work other than expansion work (if any) is:

A. change in entropy is positive
B. change in enthalpy is negative
C. change in Helmholtz free energy is negative
D. change in Gibbs free energy is negative

3. The number of vibrational mode(s) of a carbon dioxide molecule that can be detected using infrared spectroscopy is:

A. 1 B. 2
C. 3 D. 4

4. For three non-coplanar vectors **a**, **b** and **c**, the expression **a** . (**b** × **c**) can be written as:

A. (**a** × **b**) . **c**
B. (**a** × **b**) . (**a** × **c**)
C. (**a** . **b**) × (**a** . **c**)
D. (**a** . **b**) × **c**

5. Correct trend in the bond order is:

A. $O_2^+ > O_2^{2-} > O_2^-$
B. $O_2^- > O_2^+ > O_2^{2-}$
C. $O_2^{2-} > O_2^- > O_2^+$
D. $O_2^+ > O_2^- > O_2^{2-}$

6. The correct option for the metal ion present in the active site of myoglobin, hemocyanin and vitamin B_{12}, respectively, is:

A. iron, iron and zinc
B. molybdenum, iron and copper
C. iron, copper and cobalt
D. molybdenum, copper and cobalt

7. The correct order of wavelength (λ_{max}) of the halide to metal charge-transfer band of $[Co(NH_3)_5Cl]^{2+}$ (I), $[Co(NH_3)_5Br]^{2+}$ (II) and $[Co(NH_3)_5I]^{2+}$ (III), is:

A. III < II < I B. I < II < III
C. II < III < I D. I < III < II

8. The correct option for the major products of the following reaction is:

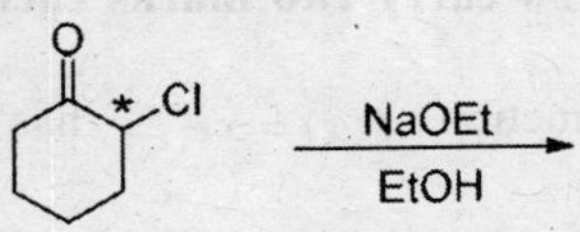

(* represents isotopically labelled carbon atom)

A. 

B. 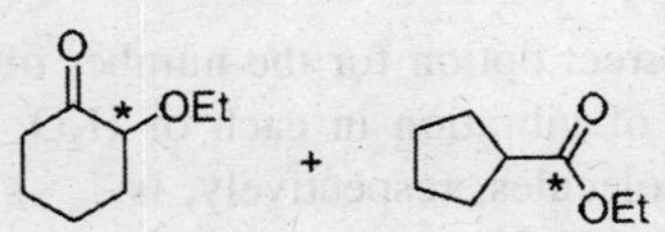

C. 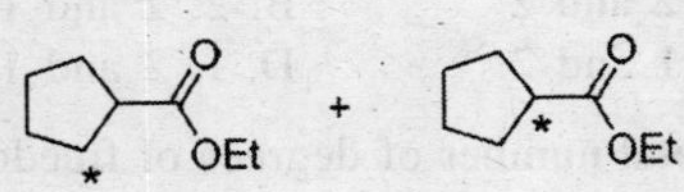

D. 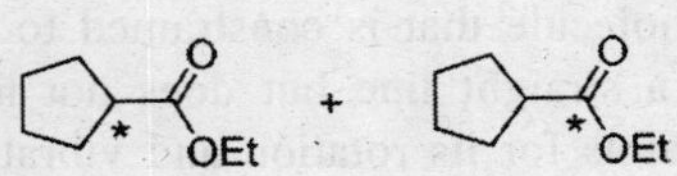

9. The major product formed in the following reaction is:

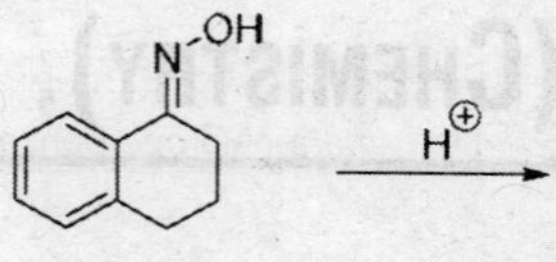

A. 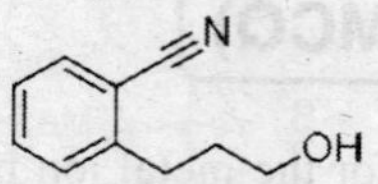 B. 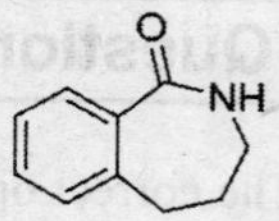

C. 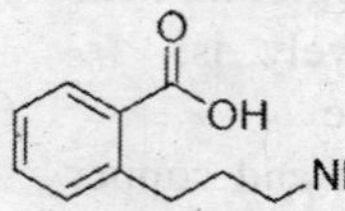 D. 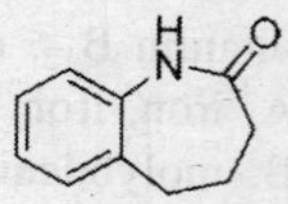

10. The complementary strand for the following single strand of DNA is:

5' ← A — T — G — C — T → 3'

A. 3' ← T — A — C — G — A → 5'

B. 3' ← A — T — G — C — T → 5'

C. 5' ← T — A — C — G — A → 3'

D. 5' ← A — A — C — G — T → 3'

Q. 11 – Q. 30 carry two marks each.

11. The function $f(x) = x e^{-x^2}$ has a minimum at:

A. $x = \sqrt{2}$ B. $x = -\sqrt{2}$

C. $x = \frac{1}{\sqrt{2}}$ D. $x = -\frac{1}{\sqrt{2}}$

12. The correct option for the number of bending modes of vibration in each of H_2O, CS_2 and SO_2 molecules, respectively, is:

A. 1, 2 and 2 B. 2, 2 and 1

C. 2, 1 and 2 D. 1, 2 and 1

13. The total number of degrees of freedom of an HBr molecule that is constrained to translate along a straight line but does not have any constraints for its rotation and vibration is:

A. 6 B. 5

C. 4 D. 3

14. According to the kinetic theory of gases, the ratio of the root mean square velocity of molecular oxygen and molecular hydrogen at 300 K is:

A. 1 : 1 B. $1 : 2\sqrt{2}$

C. 1 : 4 D. 1 : 16

15. The half-life of the chemical reaction, A → Product, for initial reactant concentrations of 0.1 and 0.4 mol L^{-1} are 200 and 50 s, respectively. The order of the reaction is:

A. 0 B. 1

C. 2 D. 3

16. The ratio of the nearest neighbour atomic distances in body-centered cubic (bcc) and face centered cubic (fcc) crystals with the same unit cell edge length is:

A. $\sqrt{\frac{3}{2}}$ B. $\frac{\sqrt{3}}{2}$

C. $\frac{1}{\sqrt{2}}$ D. $\frac{1}{2}$

17. The correct trend in the rate of substitution of Cl^- by pyridine in the following complexes is:

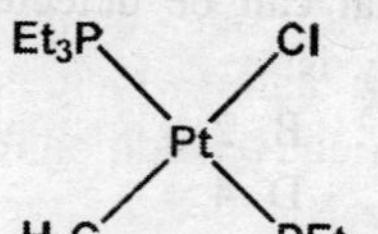

I

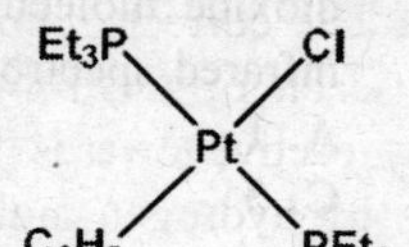

II

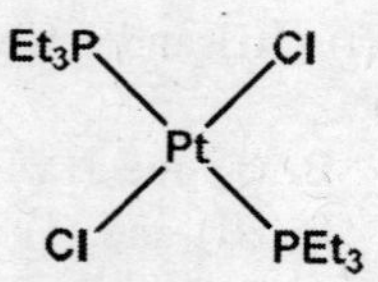

III

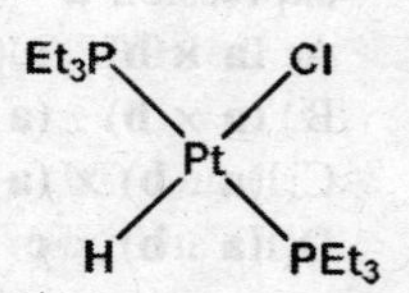

IV

A. III < II < I < IV B. II < III < I < IV

C. I < II < III < IV D. III < II < IV < I

18. In qualitative inorganic analysis of metal ions, the ion which precipitates as sulphide in the presence of H_2S in warm dilute HCl is:

A. Cr^{3+} B. Al^{3+}

C. Co^{2+} D. Bi^{3+}

19. The correct statement regarding the observed magnetic properties of NO, O_2, B_2, and C_2 in their ground state is:

A. NO, B_2, and C_2 are paramagnetic

B. B_2, O_2 and NO are paramagnetic

C. O_2, C_2 and NO are paramagnetic

D. O_2, B_2 and C_2 are paramagnetic

20. The observed magnetic moments of octahedral Mn^{3+}, Fe^{3+} and Co^{3+} complexes are 4.95, 6.06 and 0.00 BM, respectively. The correct option for the electronic configuration of Mn^{3+}, Fe^{3+} and Co^{3+} metal ions in these complexes, respectively, is:

A. $t_{2g}^4e_g^0$, $t_{2g}^3e_g^2$ and $t_{2g}^4e_g^2$

B. $t_{2g}^3e_g^1$, $t_{2g}^5e_g^0$ and $t_{2g}^6e_g^0$

C. $t_{2g}^3e_g^1$, $t_{2g}^3e_g^2$ and $t_{2g}^6e_g^0$

D. $t_{2g}^3e_g^1$, $t_{2g}^3e_g^2$ and $t_{2g}^4e_g^2$

21. Among the following compounds, the one having the lowest boiling point is:

A. $SnCl_4$ B. $GeCl_4$

C. $SiCl_4$ D. CCl_4

22. The correct option having one complex from each of the following pairs which is more reactive towards the oxidative addition reaction by hydrogen molecule is:

Pair 1: $IrCl(PMe_3)_3$ (I) and $IrCl(CO)(PMe_3)_2$ (II)

Pair 2: $IrCl(CO)(PPh_3)_2$ (III) and $IrCl_3(PPh_3)$ (IV)

A. (I) and (III) B. (I) and (IV)

C. (II) and (III) D. (II) and (IV)

23. Among the following, the correct statement is:

A. The density follows the order, Cs > Rb > Li > Na.

B. The solubility in water follows the order, $Cs_2CO_3 > K_2CO_3 > Na_2CO_3 > Li_2CO_3$.

C. The first ionization potential follows the order, Li > K > Na > Cs.

D. The melting point follows the order, $MgCl_2 > BeCl_2 > CaCl_2 > SrCl_2$.

24. The major product of the following reaction is:

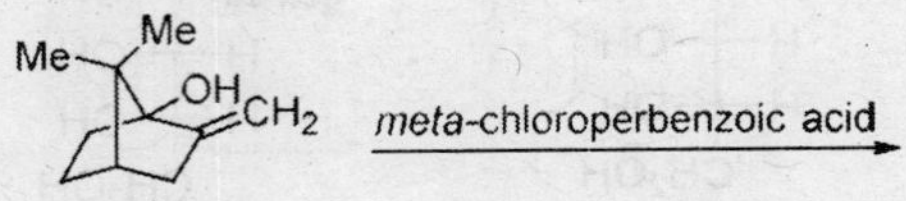

A. 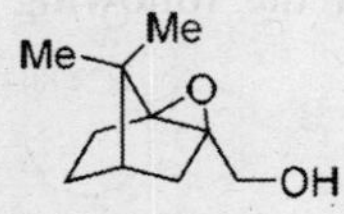

B. 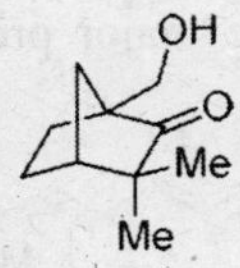

C. 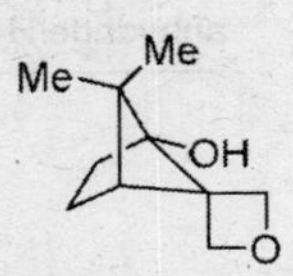

D. 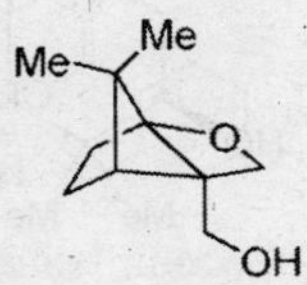

25. In ^1H NMR spectrum of the given molecule, the correct order of chemical shifts of the labelled protons (H^X, H^Y, H^Z) is:

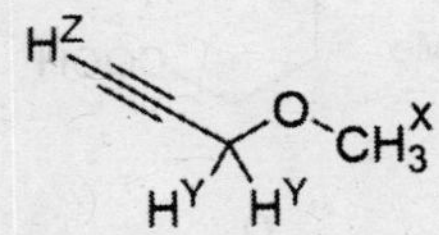

A. $H^Z > H^X > H^Y$

B. $H^Z > H^Y > H^X$

C. $H^X > H^Y > H^Z$

D. $H^Y > H^X > H^Z$

26. In the following reaction of (D)-Glucose, a product P is formed.

$$\text{(D)-Glucose} \xrightarrow[\text{2. } H_2O_2,\ Fe_2(SO_4)_3]{\text{1. } Br_2/H_2O} P$$

Among the following compounds, the one which will give the same product (P) under identical reaction conditions is:

A. 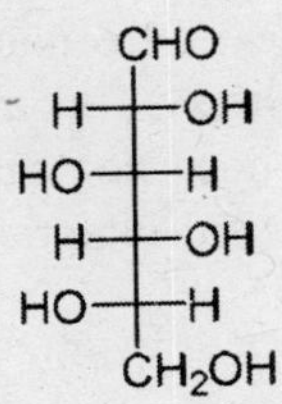

B. 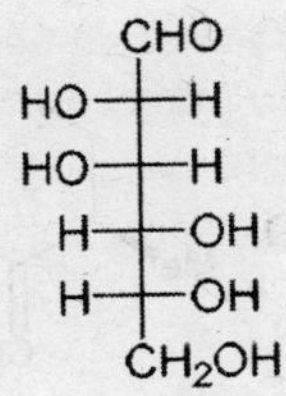

C.

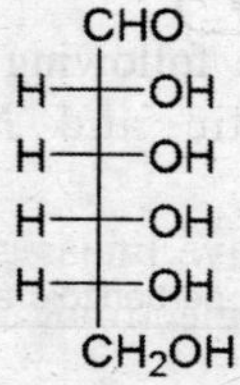

D.

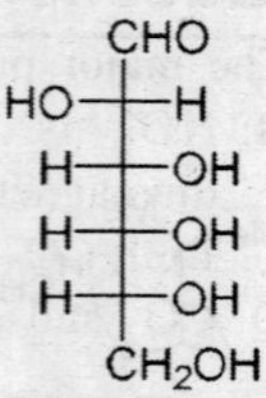

27. The major product of the following reaction is:

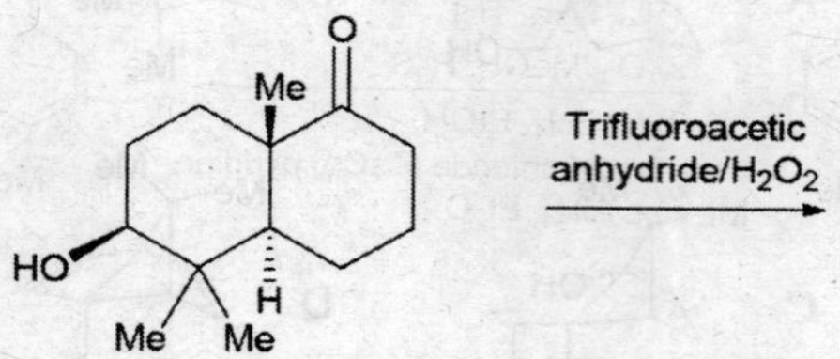

A.

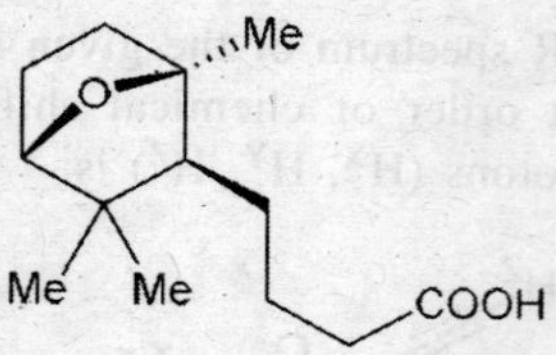

B.

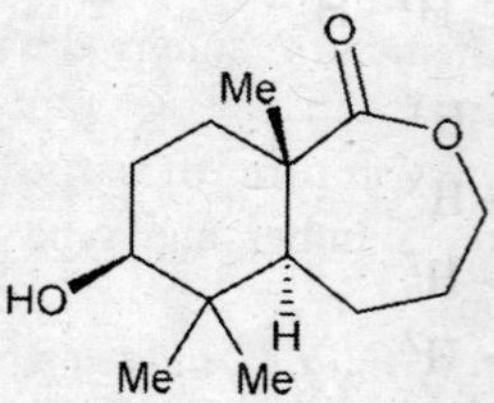

C.

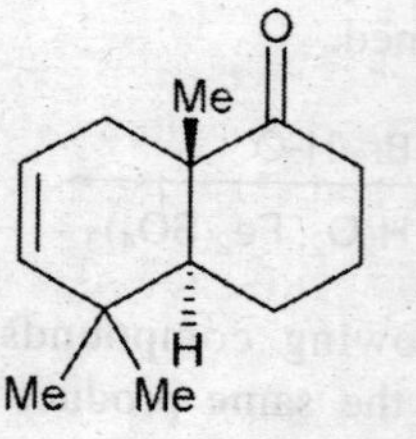

D.

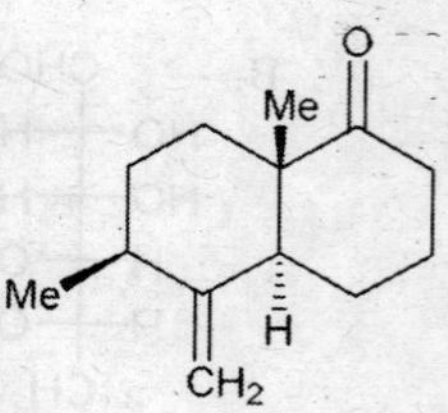

28. The correct option for the product(s) of the following reaction is:

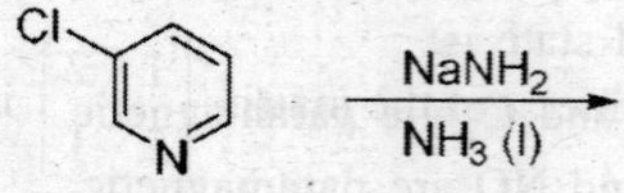

A.

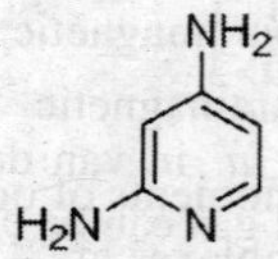

B.

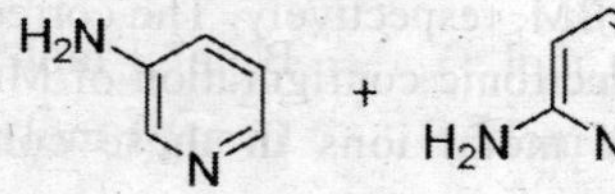

C.

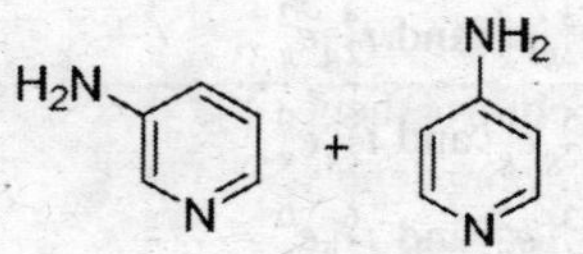

D.

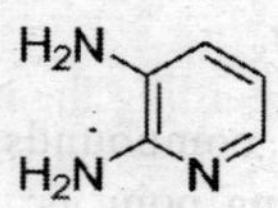

29. The increasing order of acidity of the given molecules in aqueous media is:

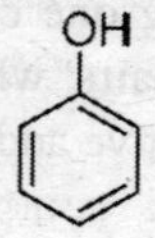

I

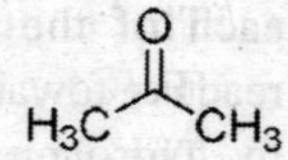

II

FCH_2COOH
III

CH_3OH
IV

A. IV < I < II < III

B. II < I < IV < III

C. II < IV < I < III

D. IV < II < I < III

30. The compound formed upon subjecting an aliphatic amine to Lassaigne's test is:

A. $NaNH_2$

B. $NaNO_2$

C. NaCN

D. NaN_3

Section B : Multiple Select Questions (MSQ)

Q. 31 – Q. 40 carry two marks each.

31. The eigenvalue(s) of the matrix $\begin{bmatrix} 1 & 2 \\ 2 & 1 \end{bmatrix}$ is/are:

A. –1 B. 1
C. 2 D. 3

32. The unit of the constant '*a*' in van der Waals equation of state of a real gas can be expressed as:

A. m^6 Pa mol^{-2} B. m^6 J mol^{-2}
C. m^3 Pa mol^{-2} D. m^3 J mol^{-2}

33. Among the following, microwave active molecule(s) is/are:

A. *trans*-dichloroethene
B. 1,2-dinitrobenzene
C. 3-methylphenol
D. *para*-aminophenol

34. The true statement(s) regarding the brown ring test carried out in the laboratory for the detection of NO_3^- is/are:

A. Brown ring is due to the formation of the iron nitrosyl complex.
B. Concentrated nitric acid is used for the test.
C. The complex formed in the reaction is $[Fe(CN)_5NO]^{2-}$.
D. The brown coloured complex is paramagnetic in nature.

35. The true statement(s) regarding the carbonic anhydrase enzyme is/are:

A. It is involved in peptide bond cleavage.
B. Redox inactive Zn^{2+} ion is involved in the catalytic activity of this enzyme.
C. Activated M-OH_2 (M = metal ion) acts as the nucleophile in the enzyme.
D. The metal ion is coordinated to the side chain of histidine residues.

36. The correct statement(s) about NO_2, NO_2^+ and CO_2 is/are:

A. Both NO_2 and CO_2 are paramagnetic.
B. NO_2 is paramagnetic and NO_2^+ is diamagnetic
C. Both CO_2 and NO_2^+ have linear geometry.
D. CO_2 and NO_2^+ are isoelectronic

37. The compound(s) formed as intermediate(s) in the following reaction sequence is/are:

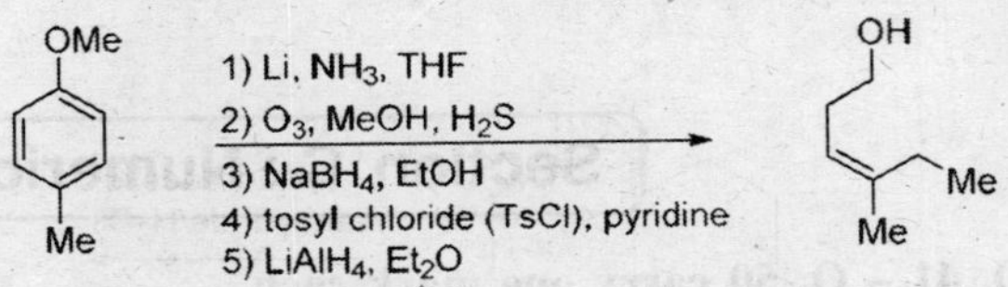

A. 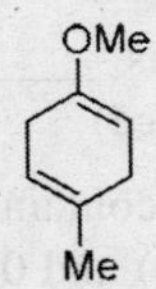

B. 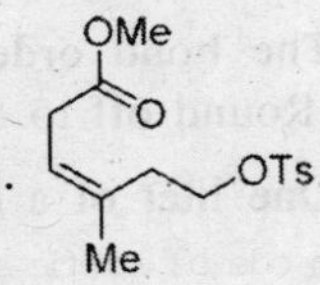

C. 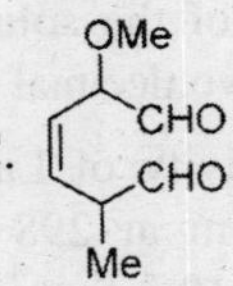

D. 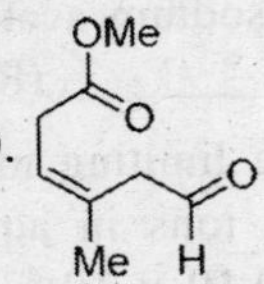

38. The correct statement(s) among the following is/are:

A. Secondary structure of a polypeptide describes the number and type of amino acid residues.
B. Uracil is a pyrimidine nucleobase.
C. Natural fatty acids have odd number of carbon atoms.
D. Reaction of (D)-glucose with $Ca(OH)_2$ gives a product mixture containing (D)-fructose, (D)-mannose, and (D)-glucose.

39. The diastereomeric pair(s) among the following option(s) is/are:

A. 

B. 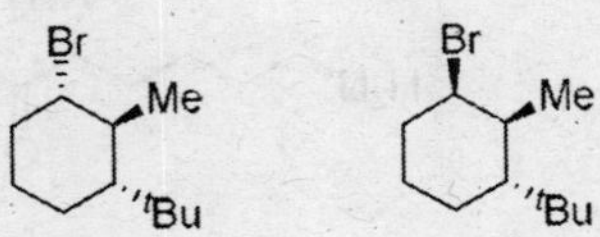

C. 

D. 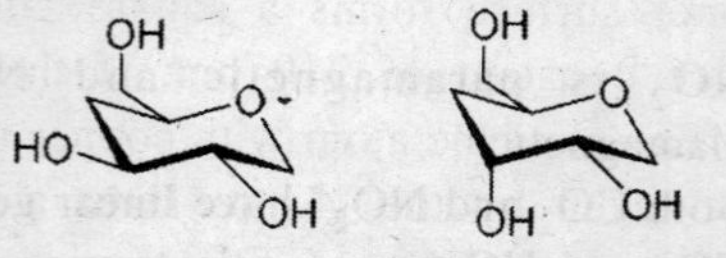

40. The reaction(s) that result(s) in the formation of aromatic species is/are

A. 

B. 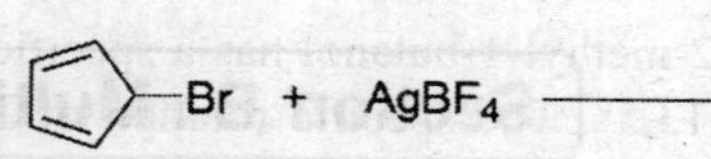

C. 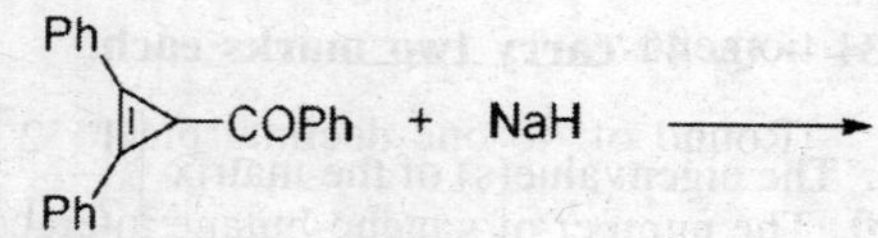

D. 

Section C : Numerical Answer Type (NAT)

Q. 41 – Q. 50 carry one mark each.

41. The bond order of N_2^+ ion is __________. (Round off to one decimal place)

42. One liter of a buffer solution contains 0.004 mole of acetic acid (pK_a = 4.76) and 0.4 mole of sodium acetate. The pH of the solution is __________. (Round off to two decimal places)

43. The limiting molar conductivity of La^{3+} and Cl^- ions in aqueous medium at 298 K are 209.10×10^{-4} and 76.35×10^{-4} S m² mol⁻¹, respectively. The transport number of Cl^- in an infinitely dilute aqueous solution of $LaCl_3$ at 298 K is ________. (Round off to two decimal places)

44. The magnetic field strength required to excite an isolated proton to its higher spin state with an electromagnetic radiation of 300 MHz is __________ Tesla (T). (Round off to two decimal places)
[Magnetogyric ratio of proton is 26.75×10^7 rad T^{-1} s^{-1}]

45. The value of n for the complex $[Fe(CO)_4(SiMe_3)]^n$ satisfying the 18-electron rule is ________.

46. In the structure of P_4O_{10}, the number of P-O-P bond(s) is ________.

47. Number of vertices in an icosahedral closo-borane is ______.

48. Based on the information given below, the isoelectric point (pI) of lysine is __________. (Round off to one decimal place)

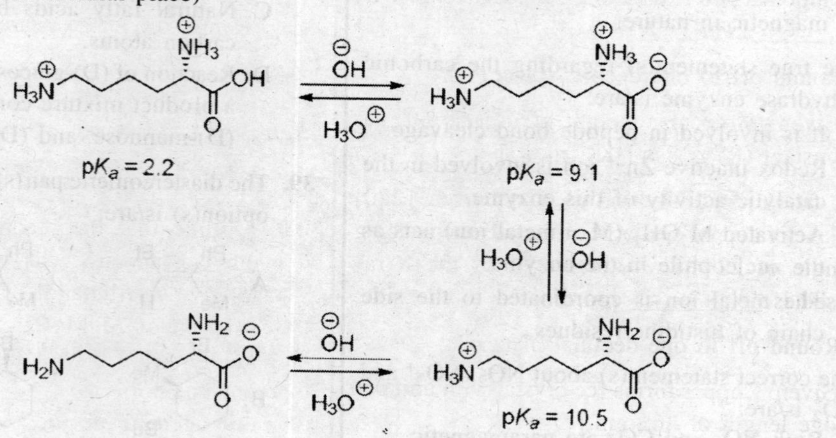

49. (R)-2-methyl-1-butanol has a specific rotation of +13.5°. The specific rotation of 2-methyl-1-butanol containing 40% of the (S)-enantiomer is __________°.

(Round off to one decimal place)

50. The number of gauche-butane interaction(s) in the following compound is__________.

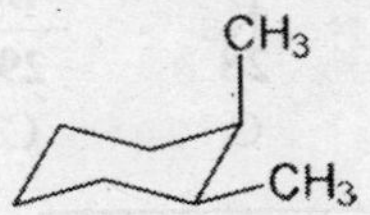

Q. 51 – Q. 60 carry two marks each.

51. The ionization energy of hydrogen atom is 13.6 eV and the first ionization energy of sodium atom is 5.1 eV. The effective nuclear charge experienced by the valance electron of sodium atom is ______.

(Round off to one decimal place)

52. One mole of an ideal gas is subjected to an isothermal increase in pressure from 100 kPa to 1000 kPa at 300 K. The change in Gibbs free energy of the system is ______ kJ mol^{-1}.

(Round off to one decimal place)

[Given: Gas constant (R) = 8.3 J K^{-1} mol^{-1}]

53. One liter of an aqueous urea solution contains 6 g of urea. The osmotic pressure of the solution at 300 K (assuming an ideal behaviour) is ______ kPa.

(Round off to one decimal place)

[Given: Molecular weight of urea is 60, gas constant (R) is 8.3 J K^{-1} mol^{-1}]

54. A first order reflection of X-ray from {220} plane of copper crystal is observed at a glancing angle of 22°. The wavelength of the X-ray used is __________ pm.

(Round off to one decimal place)

[Given: Copper forms fcc crystal with unit cell edge length of 361 pm.]

55. The collision flux of a monoatomic gas on copper surface is 3.0×10^{18} m^{-2} s^{-1}. Note that copper surface forms a square lattice with lattice constant of 210 pm. If the sticking coefficient of the atom with copper is 1.0, the time taken by the gas to form a complete monolayer on the surface is __________ s.

(Round off to one decimal place)

56. The turnover frequency (TOF) for the catalytic reaction,

$$\text{A (1 mol)} \xrightarrow[\text{5 hours}]{\text{Catalyst (0.01 mol)}} \text{B}$$

with 90% yield of the product is __________ $hour^{-1}$

(Round off to the nearest integer)

57. A radioactive sample decays to 10% of its initial amount in 4600 minutes. The rate constant of this process is ________ $hour^{-1}$.

(Round off to two decimal places)

58. Given that the radius of the first Bohr orbit of hydrogen atom is 53 pm, the radius of its third Bohr orbit is __________ pm.

(Round off to the nearest integer)

59. 5.3 g of benzaldehyde was reacted with an excess of acetophenone to produce 5.2 g of the enone product as per the reaction shown below. The yield of the reaction is ______ %.

(Round off to the nearest integer)

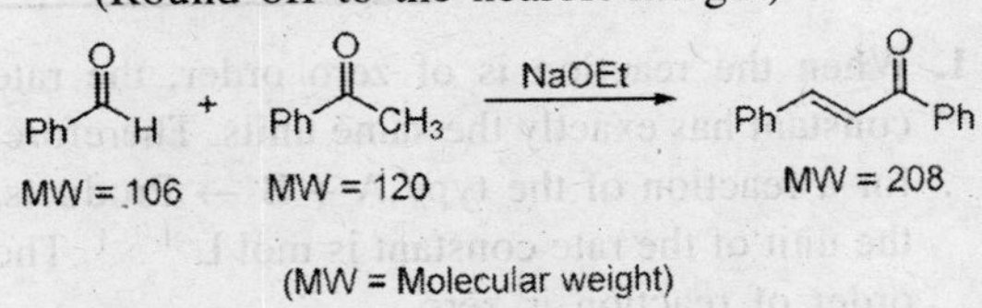

60. Assume that the reaction of MeMgBr with ethylacetate proceeds with 100% conversion to give *tert*-butanol. The volume of 0.2 M solution of MeMgBr required to convert 10 mL of a 0.025 M solution of ethylacetate to *tert*-butanol is __________ mL. (Round off to one decimal place)

ANSWERS

SECTION A: MCQ (Multiple Choice Questions)

1	2	3	4	5	6	7	8	9	10
A	C	C	A	D	C	B	C	D	A
11	**12**	**13**	**14**	**15**	**16**	**17**	**18**	**19**	**20**
C	D	C	C	C	A	A	D	B	C
21	**22**	**23**	**24**	**25**	**26**	**27**	**28**	**29**	**30**
C	A	B	B	D	B	A	C	C	C

SECTION B: MSQ (Multiple Select Questions)

31	32	33	34	35
A, D	A, D	B, C, D	A, D	B, C, D
36	**37**	**38**	**39**	**40**
B, C, D	A, B, D	B, D	A, B, D	A, D

SECTION C: NAT (Numerical Answer Type Questions)

41	42	43	44	45
2.5	6.67 to 6.86	0.51 to 0.53	7.00 to 7.10	–1
46	**47**	**48**	**49**	**50**
6	12	9.8	2.7	3
51	**52**	**53**	**54**	**55**
1.7 to 1.9	5.6 to 5.8	247.0 to 250	95.0 to 96.0	7.5 to 7.7
56	**57**	**58**	**59**	**60**
18	0.02 to 0.04	477	50	2.5

EXPLANATORY ANSWERS

1. When the reaction is of zero order, the rate constant has exactly the same units. Therefore, for a reaction of the type A + B → Products, the unit of the rate constant is mol L^{-1} s^{-1}. The order of reaction is zero.

2. The criterion for spontaneity is

$(\Delta H)_{S,\,P < 0}$, $(\Delta G)_{B,\,T < 0}$

$(\Delta V)_{V,\,T < 0}$, $(\Delta U)_{S,\,V < 0}$

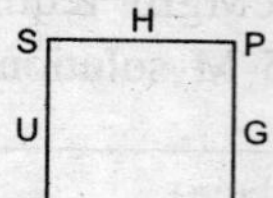

Therefore, the change in Helmholtz free energy is negative for the thermodynamic criterion of spontaneity of a process in a system under contact volume and temperature and in the absence of any work other than expansion work.

3. Carbon dioxide (CO_2) can be detecting using the IR spectroscopy is 3 modes. It is a linear molecule have normal mode of vibration even through it does not have permanent dipole moment, the dipole moment changes during 3 of the 4 modes.

O=C=O (CO_2)

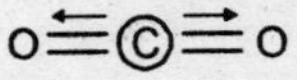

Symmetric stretch IR

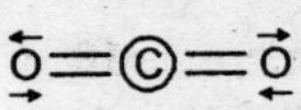

A symmetric stretch in plane.

4. a . (b × c) can be written as (a × b) . c.

5. We have,

Number of electron	**Bond order**
10	1
11	1.5
12	2.0
13	2.5
14	3.0
15	2.5
16	2.0
17	1.5
18	1.0
19	0.5
20	0.0

Therefore, the correct trend in the bond order is:

$O_2^+ > O_2^- > O_2^{2-}$

2.5 > 1.5 > 1.0.

6. We have,

Myoglobin – Iron (Fe)

Hemocyanin – Copper (Cu)

Vitamin B_{12} – Cobalt (Co)

Hence, the metal ion present in the active site of myoglobin, hemocyanin and vitamin B_{12} is iron (Fe), copper (Cu) and cobalt (Co).

7. We have, $[Co(NH_3)_5I]^{2+}$ – III

$[Co(NH_3)_5Br]^{2+}$ – II

$[Co(NH_3)_5Cl]^{2+}$ – I

There, the correct order of wavelength (λ_{max}) of halide (*i.e.*, Cl < Br < I) to metal charge transfer band is

$[Co(NH_3)_5Cl]^{2+}$ < $[Co(NH_3)_5Br]^{2+}$ < $[Co(NH_3)_5I]^{2+}$, *i.e.*, I < II < III.

8. We have,

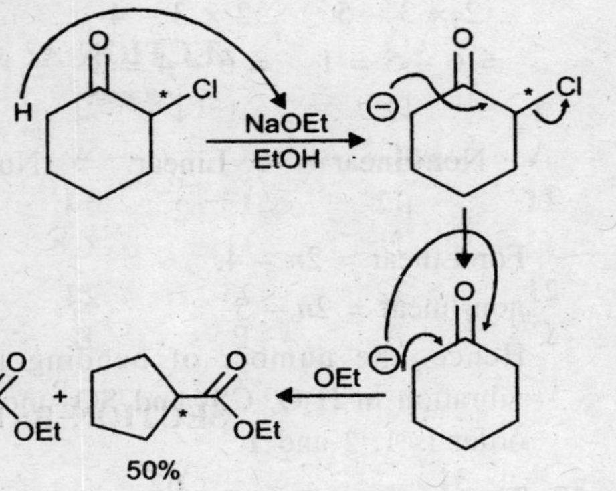

Hence, (C) is correct option.

9. The major product formed in reaction is:

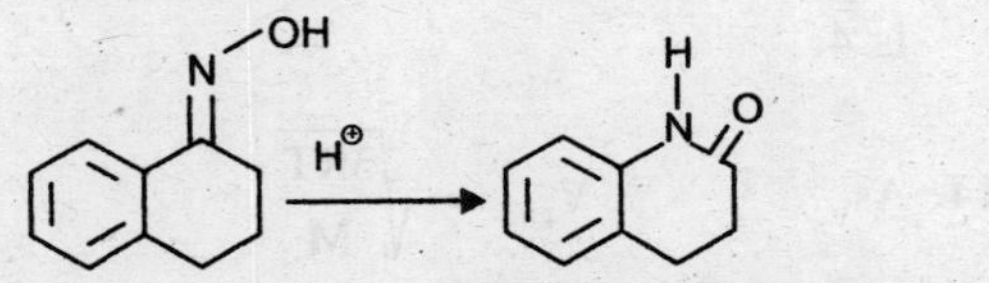

Beckmann reaction

10. Here, the complementary strand for the given single strand of DNA,

5′ ← A — T — G — C — T → 3′

Since the DNA is replication through 5′ — 3′

So, 3′ ← T — A — C — G — A → 5′ is correct answer.

11. We have, $f(x) = xe^{-x^2}$

$\therefore \quad f'(x) = xe^{-x^2}(-2x) + e^{-x^2}$

$\Rightarrow \quad 0 = e^{-x^2}(-2x^2+1)$

$\therefore \quad -2x^2 + 1 = 0$

$\Rightarrow \quad 2x^2 = 1$

$\therefore \quad x = \frac{1}{\sqrt{2}}$

Hence, the function $f(x) = xe^{-x^2}$ has a minimum at $x = \frac{1}{\sqrt{2}}$.

12. We have,

H_2O	CS_2	SO_2
$2 \times 3 - 5$	$2 \times 3 - 4$	
$= 6 - 5 = 1$	$= 6 - 4 = 2$	
↓	↓	↓
Non-linear	Linear	Non-linear
1	2	1

For Linear = $2n - 4$,

non-linear = $2n - 5$

Hence, the number of bending modes of vibration in H_2O, CS_2 and SO_2 molecules of order is 1, 2 and 1.

13. The total number of degree of freedom of an HBr molecule *i.e.,* constrained to translate along the straight line but does not have any constraints for its rotation and vibration is 4.

14. As, $$V_{rms} = \sqrt{\frac{3RT}{M}}$$

For Oxygen, $$V_{O_2} = \sqrt{\frac{3RT}{32}} \quad ...(i)$$

For Hydrogen, $$V_{H_2} = \sqrt{\frac{3RT}{2}} \quad ...(ii)$$

From equations (*i*) and (*ii*),

we get,

$$\therefore \quad \text{Ratio} = \frac{V_{O_2}}{V_{H_2}}$$

$$= \frac{\sqrt{\frac{3RT}{32}}}{\sqrt{\frac{3RT}{2}}}$$

$$= \sqrt{\frac{1}{16}}$$

$$= \frac{1}{4}$$

$$= 1 : 4.$$

15. Here, $[A_0] = 0.1 \rightarrow t_{1/2} = 200$ s

$[A_0] = 0.4 \rightarrow (t_{1/2})_2 = 50$ s

$\therefore$ Zero order = $\frac{t_{1/2}}{A_0}$ = constant

First Order $\rightarrow t_{1/2}$ = constant

Second Order $\rightarrow (t_{1/2})\,A_0$ = constant

Hence, $(t_{1/2})(A_0)_3 = 20$, $(t_{1/2})(A_0)_2 = 20$ — constant

i.e., IInd order

Hence, the order of the reaction is 2.

16. For BCC, $4r = \sqrt{3}a$

$$\therefore \quad r^+ + r^- = \frac{\sqrt{3}}{2}a$$

For FCC, $4r = \sqrt{2}a$

$$\Rightarrow \quad r^+ + r^- = \frac{\sqrt{2}}{2}a$$

Now, the ratio of BCC to FCC is

$$\frac{BCC}{FCC} = \frac{\frac{\sqrt{3}}{2}a}{\frac{\sqrt{2}}{2}a}$$

$$= \sqrt{\frac{3}{2}}$$

17. We have,

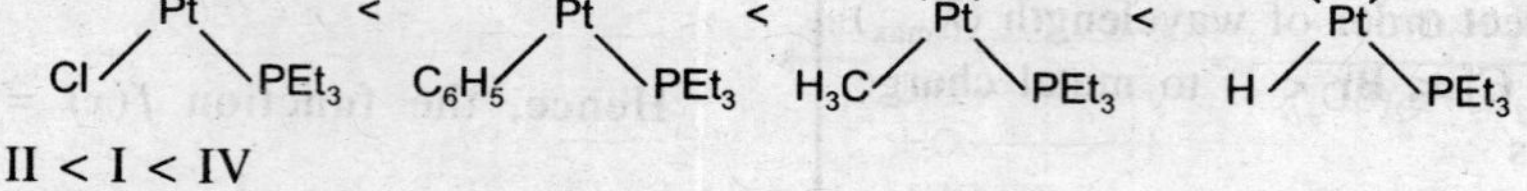

i.e., III < II < I < IV

Therefore, the correct option is (A).

18. In the qualitative inorganic analysis of metal ions, the ion which precipitates sulphide in the presence of H_2S in warm dil. HCl is Bi^{3+}.

19. We have,

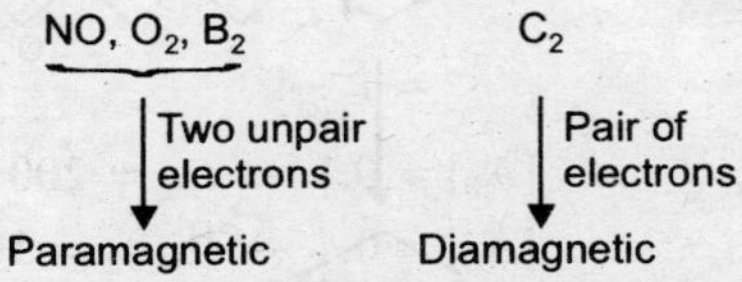

The magnetic properties of NO, O_2, B_2 and C_2 in their group state is diatomic molecules as paramagnetic a diamagnetic. The magnetism origin lies in the spin motion and orbital of the electrons and also be the interaction of electrons with each other. Therefore, NO, O_2 and B_2 have two unpair electrons, hence these are paramagnetic whereas C_2 has only pair electrons. So, it is diamagnetic.

20. We have,

$Mn^{3+} \Rightarrow 4.95 \rightarrow 4 \rightarrow Mn^{3+} \rightarrow d^4$

$_{25}Mn = d^5s^2$

$Mn^{3+} = d^4$

$\therefore\ t_{2g}^3 e_g^1$

$Fe^{3+} \Rightarrow 6.06 \rightarrow 6 \rightarrow Fe^{3+} \rightarrow d^5$

$_{26}Fe = d^6s^2$

$Fe^{3+} = d^5$

$\therefore\ t_{2g}^3 e_g^2$

$Co^{3+} \Rightarrow O \rightarrow O \rightarrow Co^{3+} \rightarrow d^6$

$_{27}Co = d^7s^2$

$Co^{3+} = d^6$

$\therefore\ t_{2g}^6 e_g^0$

Therefore, correct option is (C).

21. Here, $SnCl_4$ has more boiling point as $SiCl_4 < CCl_4$ due to the size of Si being greater than C, Ge is a metalloid while Sn is a metal. Therefore, this metal plays a role as well.

22. The pair $IrCl(PMe_3)_2$ and $IrCl(CO)(PPh_3)_2$ is more reactive towards the oxidative addition reaction by hydrogen molecule. Hence, correct option is (A).

23. When we move down the group, the solubility of alkali metal carbonates increases, when we move down the group, the ionic radii increase. Therefore, it is the ionic character of carbonates.

$\therefore$ Correct order of the water solubility would be $Li_2CO_3 < Na_2CO_3 < K_2CO_3 < Cs_2CO_3$.

24. We have,

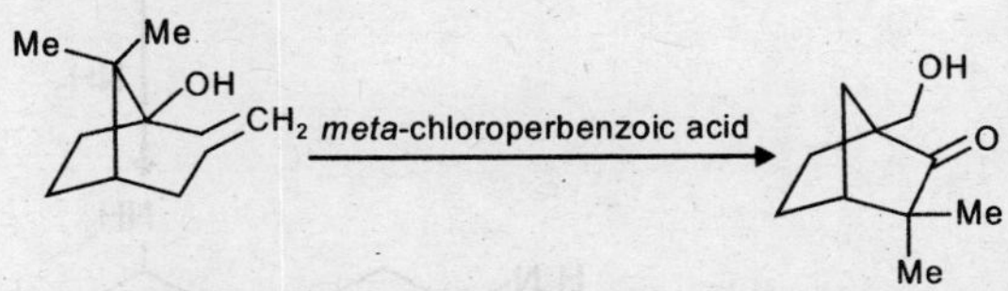

Hence, correct option is (B).

25. We have,

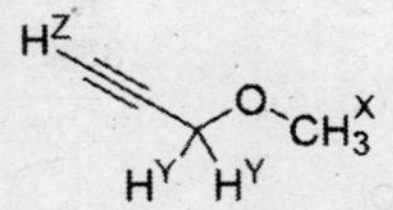

then,

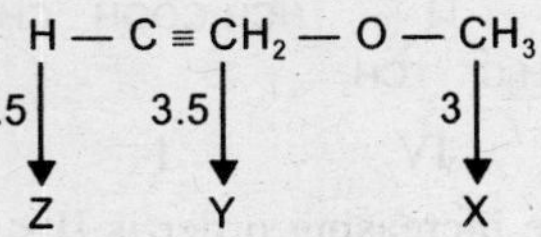

i.e., 3.5 > 3 > 2.5.

Therefore, $H^Y > H^X > H^Z$.

26.

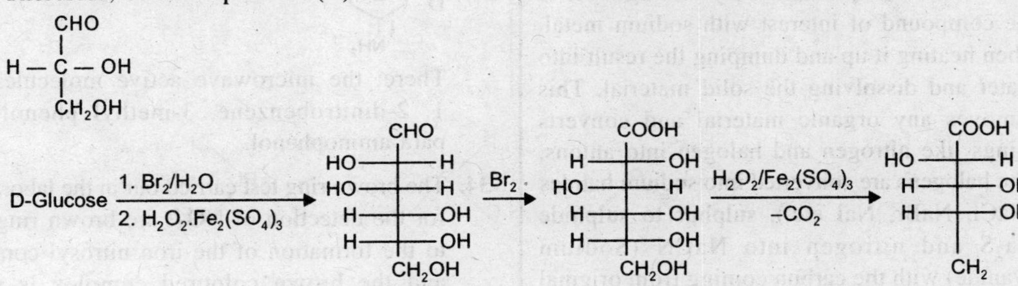

Mannose

27.

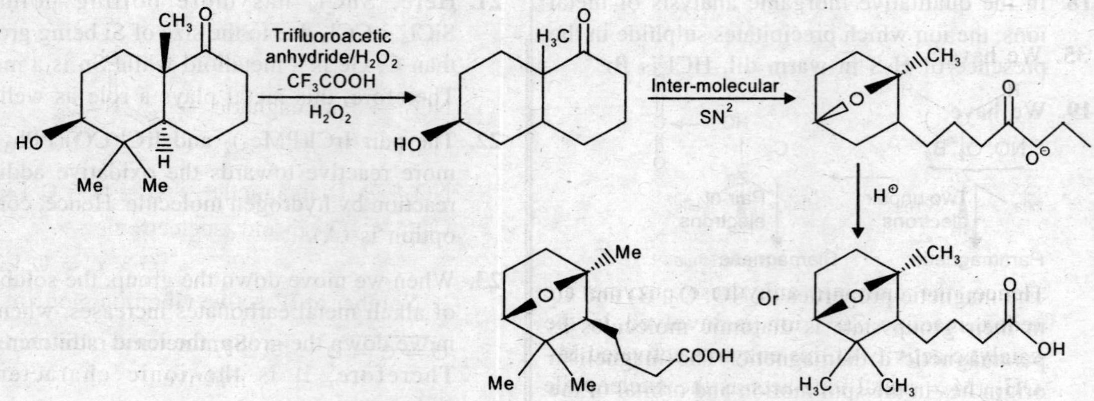

28.

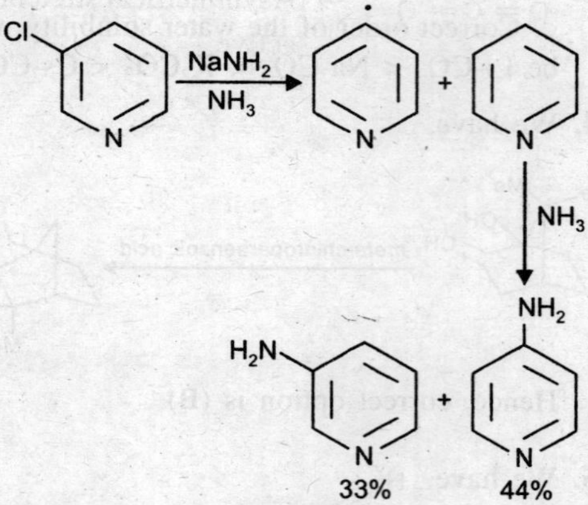

29. We have,

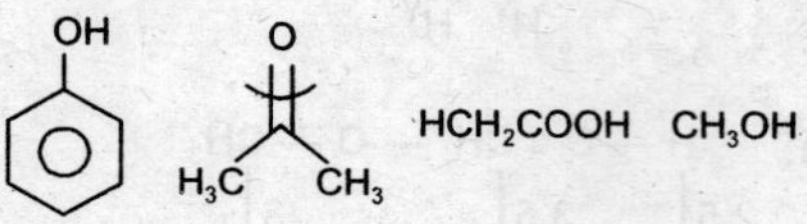

II IV I III

Thus, the increasing order is II < IV < I < III.

30. The Lassaigne's test is known as the Sodium fusion test. It is performed by mixing a bit of the compound of interest with sodium metal. Then heating it up and dumping the result into water and dissolving the solid material. This removes any organic material and converts things like nitrogen and halogen into anions. The halogens are converted into sodium halides (NaCl, NaBr, NaI etc.), sulphur to sulphide Na_2S and nitrogen into NaCN (Sodium cyanide) with the carbon coming from original compound.

31. The eigenvalues of the given matrix $\begin{bmatrix} 1 & 2 \\ 2 & 1 \end{bmatrix}$ are –1 and 3.

32. We know that the van der Waals equation $(P + a/v^2)(v - b) = RT$ is an equation similar to the real gas law.

The unit of a real gas can be expressed as m^6 Pa mol^{-2} and m^3 J mol^{-2}.

33. A. 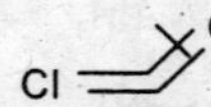 $\mu = O(X)$

B. 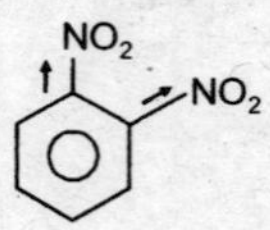 ($\mu \neq O$) (✓)

C. 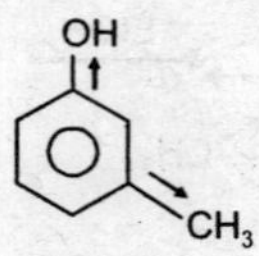 ($\mu \neq O$) (✓)

D. 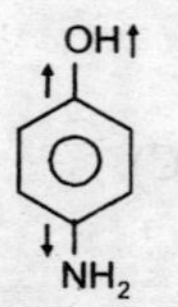 ($\mu \neq O$) (✓)

There, the microwave active molecules are 1, 2-dinitrobenzene, 3-methyl phenol and para-aminophenol.

34. The brown ring test carried out in the laboratory for the detection of NO_3^- are brown ring due to the formation of the iron nitrosyl complex and the brown coloured complex is para-magnetic in the nature.

35. We have,

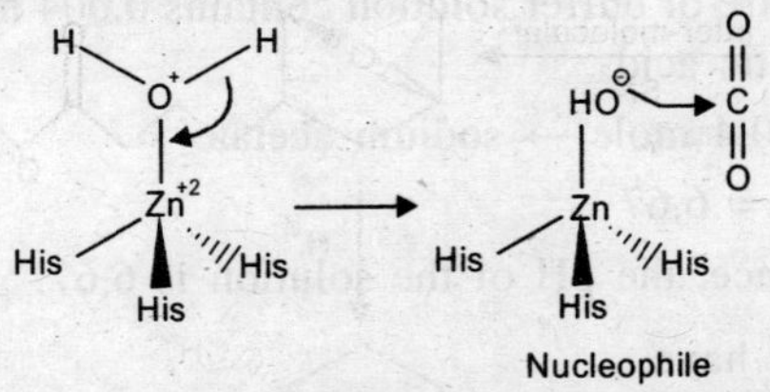

Hence, the carbonic anhydrase enzyme are redox inactive Zn^{2+} ion is involved in the catalytic activity of this enzyme, activated M–OH_2 (M = metal ion) acts as the nucleophile in the enzyme and metal ions is coordinated to the side chain of the histidine residues.

36.

NO_2	NO_2^+	CO_2
↓	↓	↓
7 + 16 = 23	7 + 16 – 1 = 23 – 1 = 22	6 + 16 = 22

NO_2 → Paramagnetic →

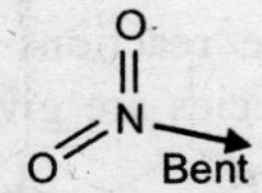

NO_2^+ → Diamagnetic → O = $\overset{\oplus}{N}$ = O Linear

CO_2 → Linear and isoelectronic → O = C = O Linear

∴ Number of IR active vibration mode of CO_2

O = C = O → Symmetrical stretching IR inactive

O = C = O → Asymmetrical stretching IR active

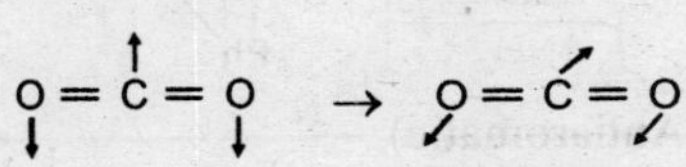

Bending IR active.

37. We have,

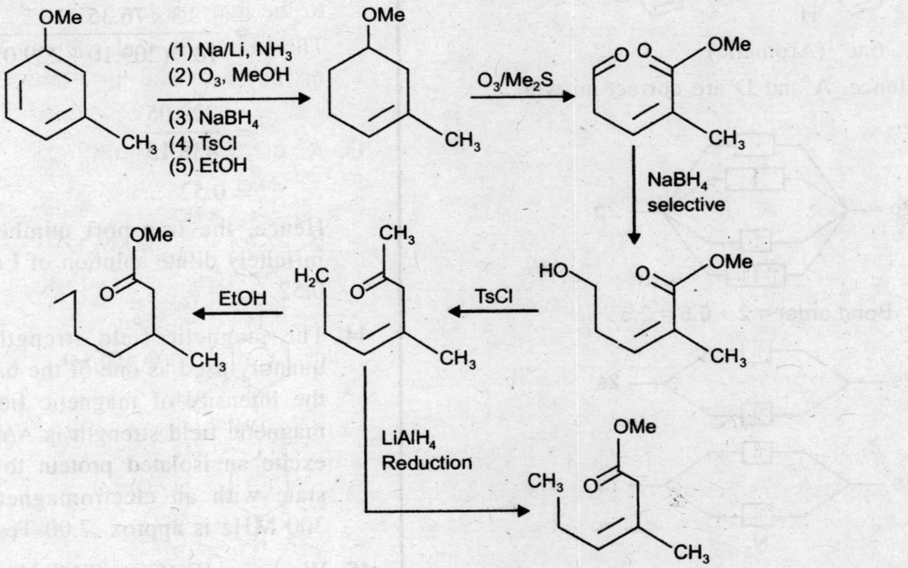

38.

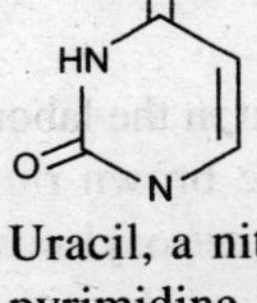

Uracil, a nitrogenous base in RNA, uracil is a pyrimidine. Two other pyrimidines are cytosine and thymine (RNA) and natural fatty acids have odd number of carbon atoms.

39. The diastereomeric pairs are:

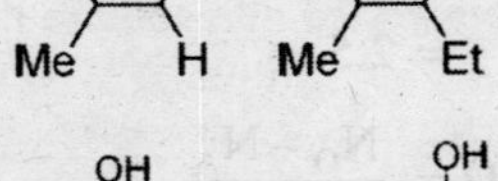

and

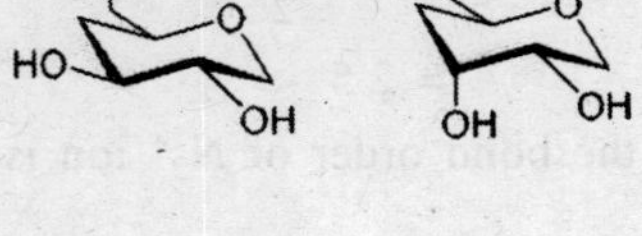

40. The reactions in the formation of aromatic species are given as:

A. 

$2\pi e^-$ (Aromatic)

B. 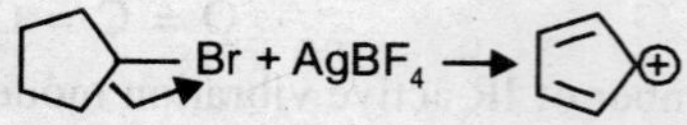

$4\pi e^-$ (Antiaromatic)

C. 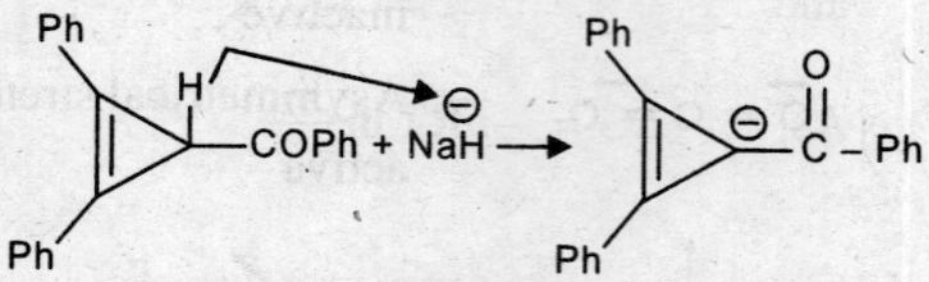

$4\pi e^-$ (Antiaromatic)

D. 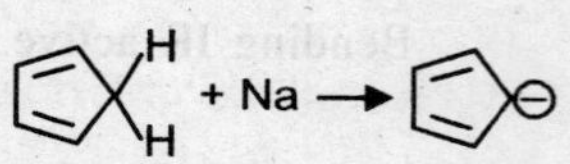

$6\pi e^-$ (Aromatic)

Hence, A and D are correct answer.

41.

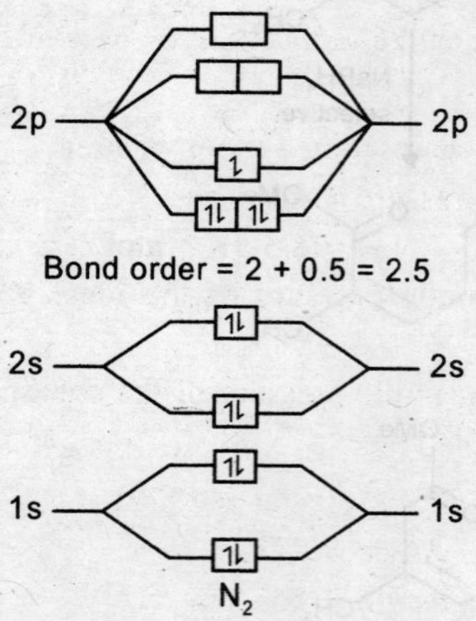

The atomic mass of $N_2^+ = 14 - 13$

$\therefore$ The bond order of N_2^+

$$= 2 + 0.5$$

$$= 2.5$$

$$\therefore \qquad BO = \frac{N_O - N_A}{2}$$

$$= 2.5$$

Therefore, the bond order of N_2^+ ion is 2.5.

42. 1 litre of buffer solution contains 0.004 mol of acetic acid

$\therefore$ 0.4 mole → sodium acetate

pH = 6.67

Hence, the pH of the solution is 6.67.

43. We have,

$$T_{Cl^-} = \frac{(n_{Cl^-})(\lambda_{Cl^-})}{A^*_m}$$

$$= \frac{(\lambda_{Cl^-})(\lambda^\circ_{Cl^-})}{\left(n^3_{La^+}\right)\lambda^*_{La^{3+}} + \left(n_{Cl^-}\right)\lambda_{Cl}}$$

$$= \frac{3 \times 76.35 \times 10^{-4}}{(1)(209.10 \times 10^{-4}) + 3 \times 76.35 \times 10^{-4}}$$

$$= \frac{3 \times 76.35 \times 10^{-4}}{10^{-4}(209.10 + 229.05)}$$

$$= \frac{229.05}{438.15}$$

$$= 0.52$$

Hence, the transport number of Cl^- in an infinitely dilute solution of $LaCl_3$ at 298 K is 0.52.

44. The magnetic field strength is a physical quantity used as one of the basic measures of the intensity of magnetic field. The unit of magnetic field strength is A/m. It required to excite an isolated protein to its higher spin state with an electromagnetic radiation of 300 MHz is approx. 7.00 Tesla (T).

45. We have, $[Fe(CO)_4(SiMe_3)]^n$

Fe → 8 $\qquad 3d^6 4s^2$

Co → 8

$\therefore \qquad (SiMe)_3 \rightarrow 1$

$\Rightarrow \qquad 17e^- + 1 = 18e^-$

$\therefore \qquad n = -1$

Thus, the value of n for the complex $[Fe(CO)_4(SiMe_3)]^n$ satisfying the 18 electrons rule is −1.

46. We have, P_4O_{10} has P – O – P bonds
Structure of P_4O_{10}:

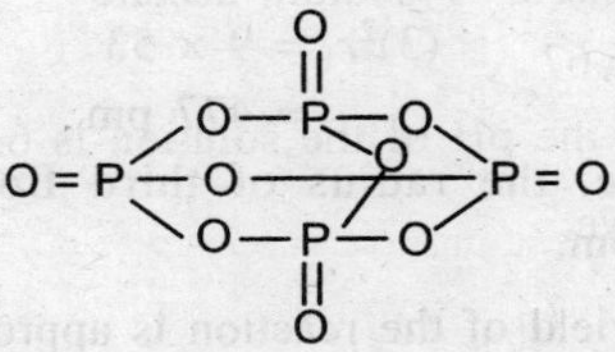

Therefore, the number of P – O – P bonds are 6.

47. The single bond B – OH vertex of the icosahedral clorane (*Closo* – $B_{12}(OH)_{12}^{2-}$) was derivatized to prepared [*Closo*–$B_{12}(OR)(OH)_{11}]^{2-}$ using optimized alkylation condition and purification procedures several representatives vertex differentiated icosahedral *closo*-boranes were prepared by utilizing carbonane ester and azide-alkyne click chemistries on the surface of the *closo*-B_{12}^{2-}.

Hence, the number of vertices are 12.

48.

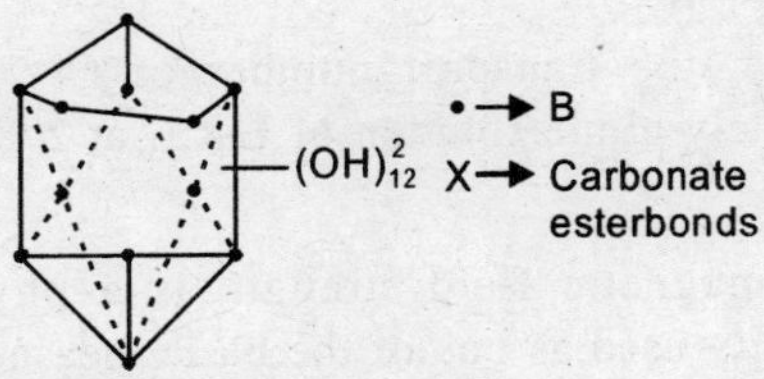

[Closo-B_{12} (OH)]

Therefore, the isoelectric point of lysine is 9.8.

49. The specific rotation of 2-methyl-1 butanol containing 40% of the (s) enantiomer is 2.7.

50. We have,

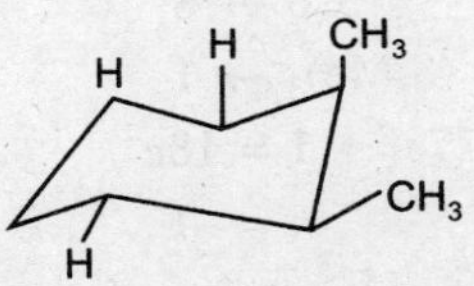

∴ The number of gauche-butane interaction(s) in the above compound is 3.

51. We have, H → 13.6 eV

Na → 5.1 eV

$z_{eff} = 1.8$

Hence, the effective nuclear charge experienced by the valence electrons of sodium atom is 1.8.

52. Given, $P_1 = 100$ kPa,

$P_2 = 1000$ kPa

and $T = 300$ K

As, $\Delta G = -nRT \ln \frac{V_2}{V_1}$

$= -nRT(2.303) \log \frac{P_2}{P_1}$

$= -(1)(8.3)(300)(2.303) \log \frac{100}{1000}$

$= 8.3 \times 300 \times 2.303$

$= 5734.47$ J mol^{-1}

$= 5.7$ kJ mol^{-1}

Hence, the change in Gibbs free energy of the system is 5.7 kJ mol^{-1}.

53. Here, in Urea solution → 6 g of urea

Osmotic pressure = ideal gas

$R = 8.3$ JK^{-1} mol^{-1}

∴ The Osmotic pressure of the ideal gas is 5.7 kJ mol^{-1}.

Hence, the osmotic pressure of the solution at 300 K is 250 kPa.

54. Here, plane of Cu crystal = {220}

Angle = 22%

Edge length = 361 pm

Wavelength (λ) = 95 pm

∴ The wavelength of the X-ray used is 95 pm.

55. If the sticking coefficient of atom with copper is 1.0, the time taken by the gas to form a complete monolayer on surface is 7.6 s.

56. $\text{A (1 mol)} \xrightarrow[\text{5 hours}]{\text{Catalyst (0.01 mol)}} \text{B}$

$$\text{TON} = \frac{1 \text{ mol}}{0.01 \text{ mol}} \times \frac{90}{100}$$

$$\text{TOF} = \frac{\text{TON}}{\text{Time}}$$

$$= \frac{1}{0.01} \times \frac{90}{100} \times \frac{1}{5}$$

$\therefore$ TOF = 18 hours.

57. As, $$K = \frac{2.303}{t} \log \frac{a}{a.x}$$

$$= \frac{2.303}{4600} \times 60 \log \frac{a}{100/100}$$

On solving, we get, the rate constant is 0.03 hour^{-1}.

58. Given, $r_1 = 53$ pm

As, $r_n = n^2 r_1$

$\therefore$ Radius of 3rd Bohr orbit

$$(3)^2 r_1 = 9 \times 53$$
$$= 477 \text{ pm}$$

Hence, the radius of third Bohr orbit is 477 pm.

59. The yield of the reaction is approx. 50%.

60. $\because$ 0.2 M solution of MeMgBr

$\therefore$ 0.10 mol of 0.025 M of ethylacetate $\rightarrow$ *tert*-butanol = 2.5 mL

Hence, the volume of 0.2 M solution of MeMgBr required to convert 10 mL of a 0.025 M solution of ethylacetate to *tert*-butanol is 2.5 mL.

Previous Years Paper

IIT–JAM

JOINT ADMISSION TEST FOR M.Sc. (CHEMISTRY), 2018

Section A : Multiple Choice Questions (MCQ)

Q. 1 – Q. 10 carry one mark each.

1. On hydrolysis, aluminium carbide produces:
A. CH_4 B. C_2H_6
C. C_2H_4 D. C_2H_2

2. Carbonic anhydrase is an example of:
A. Hydrolysis enzyme B. Redox enzyme
C. O_2 transport protein D. Heme protein

3. The CORRECT order of melting points of group 15 trifluorides is:
A. $PF_3 < AsF_3 < SbF_3 < BiF_3$
B. $BiF_3 < SbF_3 < PF_3 < AsF_3$
C. $PF_3 < SbF_3 < AsF_3 < BiF_3$
D. $BiF_3 < AsF_3 < SbF_3 < PF_3$

4. NaF, KF, MgO and CaO are crystalline solids. They have NaCl structure. Their lattice energies vary in the order:
A. NaF < KF < MgO < CaO
B. KF < NaF < CaO < MgO
C. MgO < CaO < NaF < KF
D. CaO < MgO < KF < NaF

5. The major product formed in the following reaction is:

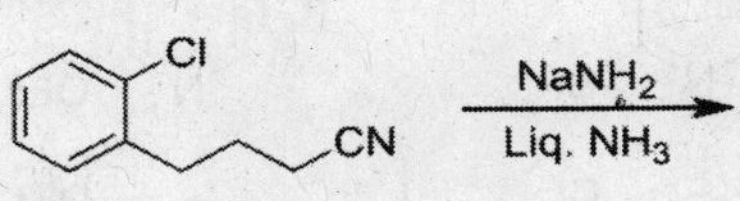

A. 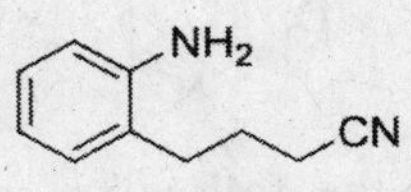

B. 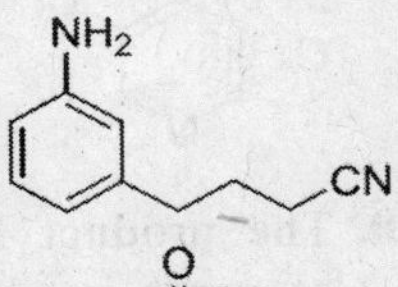

C. 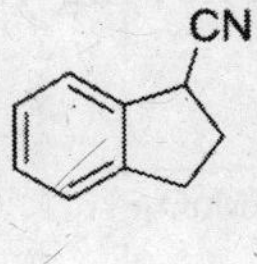

D. 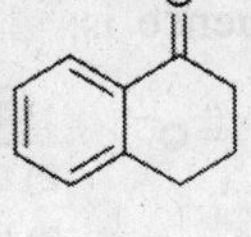

6. The compound that contains the most acidic hydrogen is:
A. $H_2C = CH_2$ B. $HC \equiv CH$
C. $H_2C = C = CH_2$ D. $H_3C - CH_3$

7. The C-2 epimer of D-glucose is:
A. D-Mannose B. D-Fructose
C. D-Galactose D. D-Glucose

8. The value of integral $\int_{-2}^{+2} x e^{-2x^2} dx$ is:
A. 0 B. $\frac{1}{2}$
C. 1 D. 2

9. The number of crystal systems and the number of Bravais lattices are, respectively:
A. 14 and 7 B. 7 and 32
C. 32 and 14 D. 7 and 14

10. For adsorption of a gas on a solid surface, the plot that represents Freundlich isotherm is (x = mass of gas, m = mass of adsorbent, P = pressure)

A. 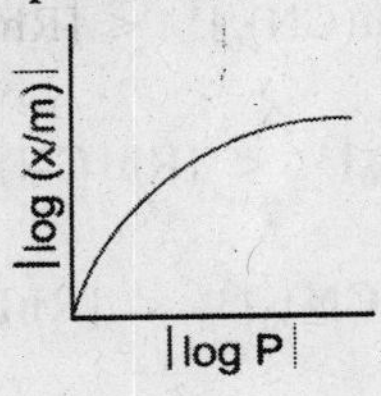

B. 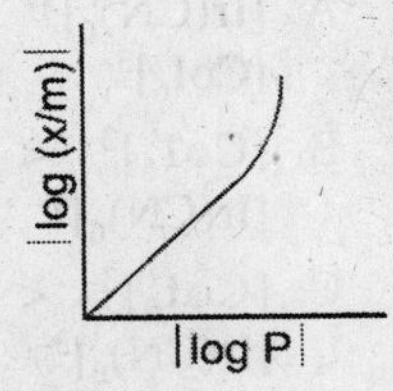

C. 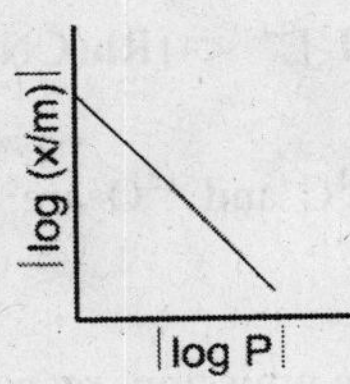

D. 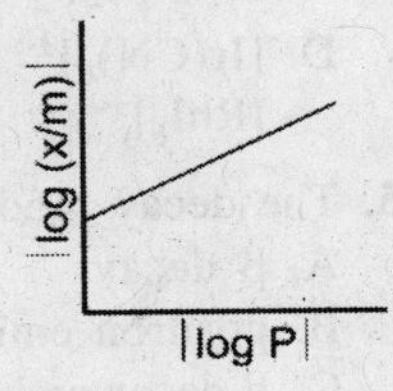

Q. 11 – Q. 30 carry two marks each.

11. With respect to periodic properties, the CORRECT statement is:

A. Electron affinity order is F > O > Cl

B. First ionisation energy order is Al > Mg > K

C. Atomic radius order is N > P > As

D. Ionic radius order is $K^+ > Ca^{2+} > Mg^{2+}$

12. Which plot represents a spectrophotometric titration, where the titrant alone absorbs light in the visible region?

A. 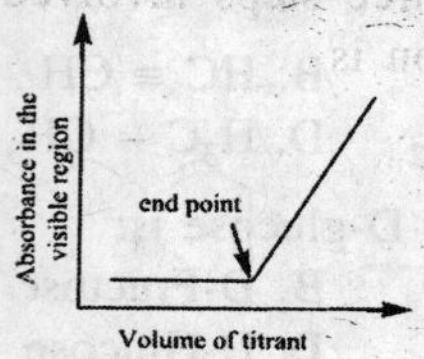

B. 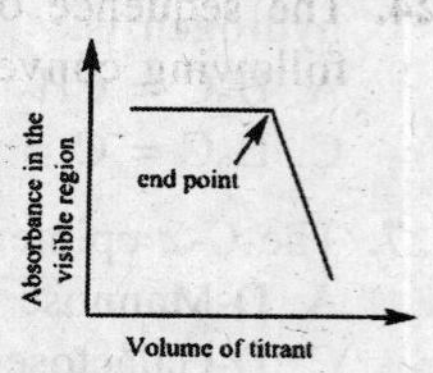

C. 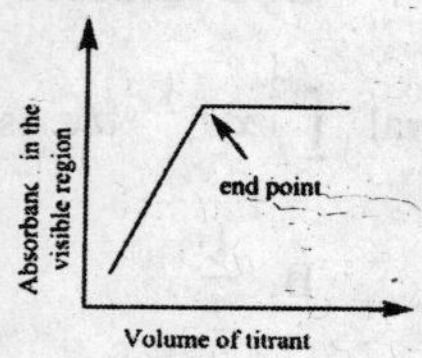

D. 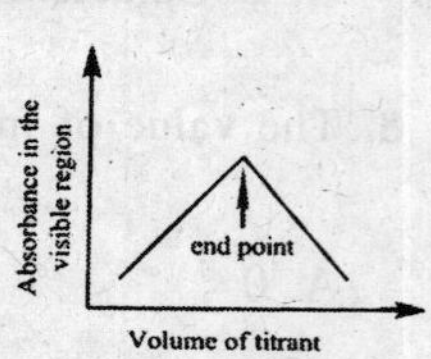

13. Among the following metal carbonyl species, the one with the highest metal-carbon back bonding is:

A. $[Ti(CO)_6]^{2-}$ B. $[V(CO)_6]^-$

C. $Cr(CO)_6$ D. $[Mn(CO)_6]^+$

14. The CORRECT order of Δ_o (the octahedral crystal field splitting of *d*-orbitals) values for the following anionic metal complexes is:

A. $[Ir(CN)_6]^{3-} < [Rh(CN)_6]^{3-} < [RhI_6]^{3-} < [CoI_6]^{3-}$

B. $[CoI_6]^{3-} < [RhI_6]^{3-} < [Rh(CN)_6]^{3-} < [Ir(CN)_6]^{3-}$

C. $[CoI_6]^{3-} < [Rh(CN)_6]^{3-} < [RhI_6]^{3-} < [Ir(CN)_6]^{3-}$

D. $[Ir(CN)_6]^{3-} < [CoI_6]^{3-} < [Rh(CN)_6]^{3-} < [RhI_6]^{3-}$

15. The decay modes of ^{14}C and ^{14}O are:

A. β decay

B. positron emission

C. β decay and positron emission, respectively

D. positron emission and β decay, respectively

16. Consider the following four xenon compounds: XeF_2, XeF_4, XeF_6 and XeO_3.

The pair of xenon compounds expected to have non-zero dipole moment is:

A. XeF_4 and XeF_6 B. XeF_2 and XeF_4

C. XeF_2 and XeO_3 D. XeF_6 and XeO_3

17. The CORRECT order of stability for the following carbocations is

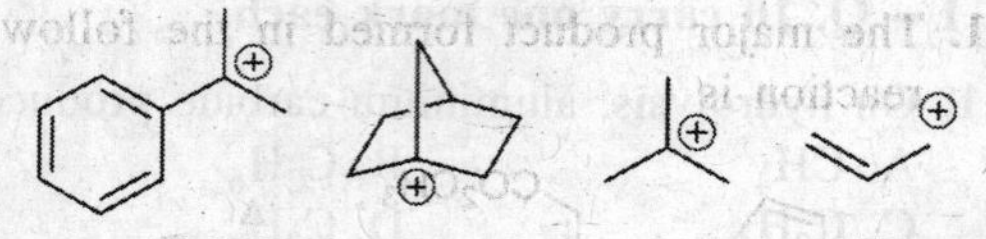

I II III IV

A. I < III < IV < II B. III < II < IV < I

C. II < IV < III < I D. IV < III < I < II

18. Among the dimethylcyclohexanes, which one can be obtained in enantiopure form?

A. 

B. 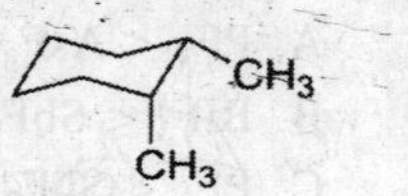

C. 

D. 

19. The major product formed in the following reaction is:

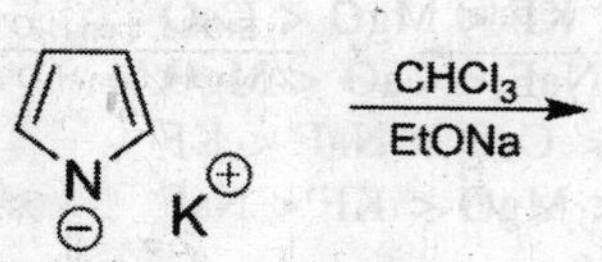

A. 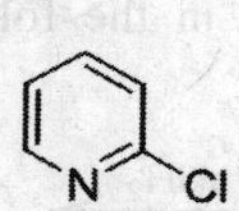

B. 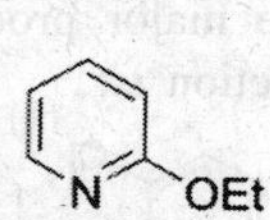

C. 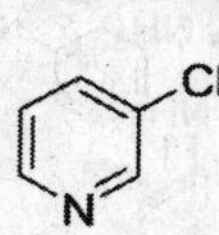

D. 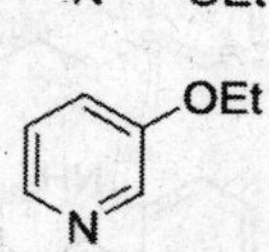

20. The product X in the following reaction sequence is:

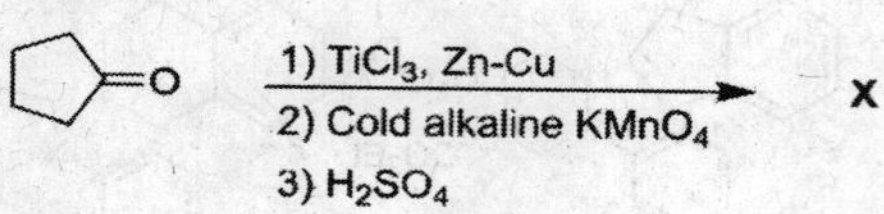

A. 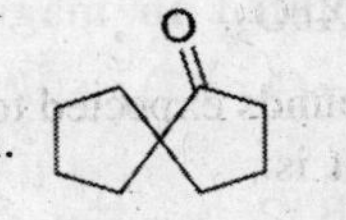 B. 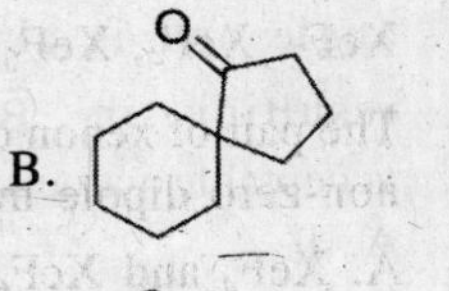

C. 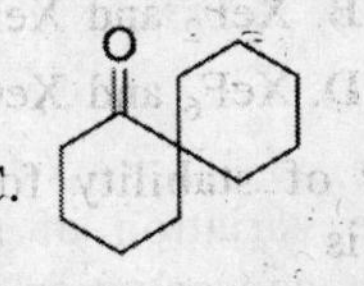 D. 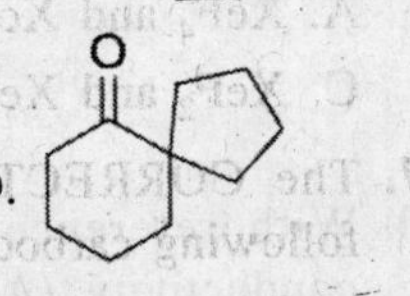

21. The major product formed in the following reaction is

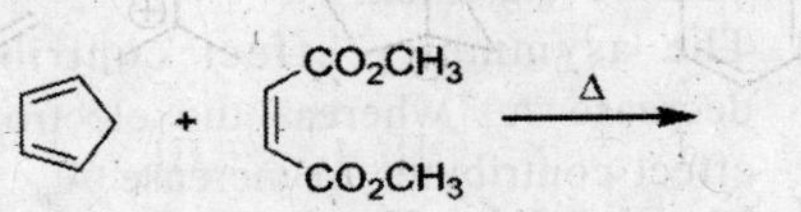

A. 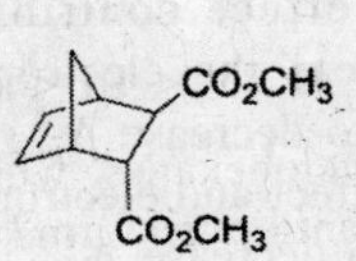 B. 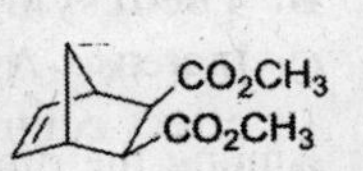

C. 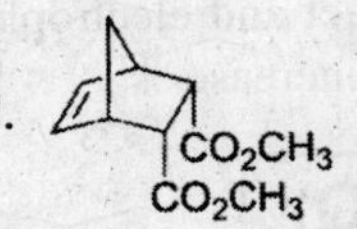 D. 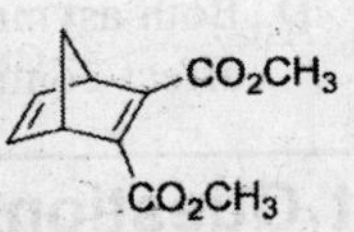

22. The major products **Y** and **Z** in the following reaction sequence are

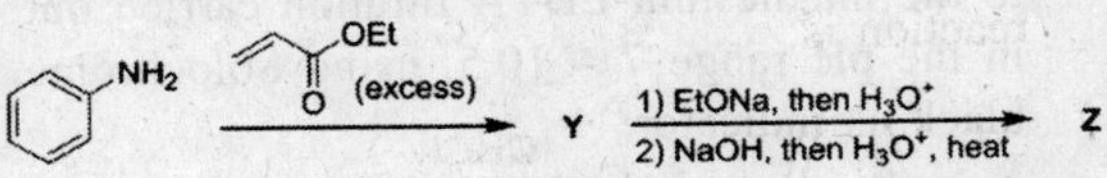

A. Y = 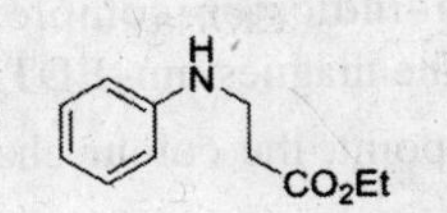 Z = 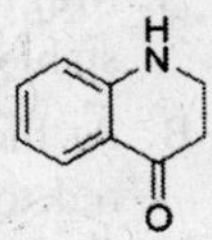

B. Y = 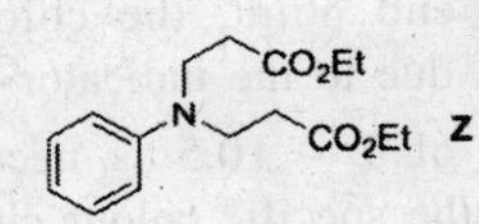 Z = 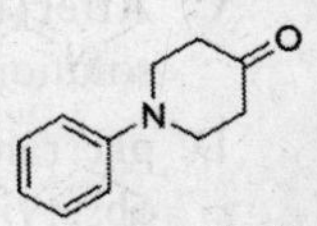

C. Y = 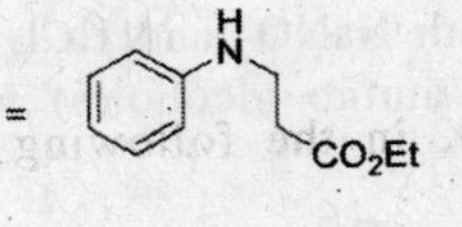 Z = 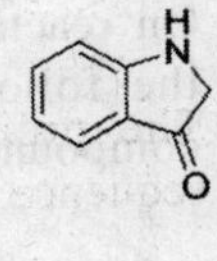

D. Y = 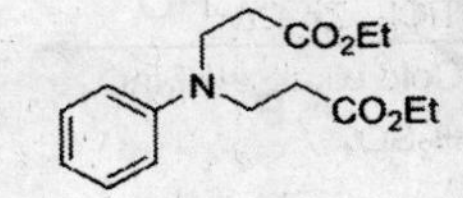 Z = 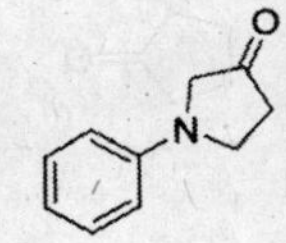

23. The **CORRECT** order of carbonyl stretching frequencies for the following compounds is:

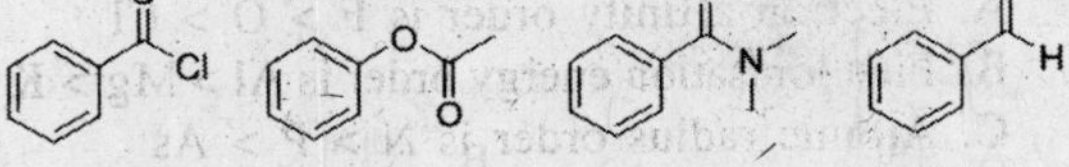

I II III IV

A. II < I < III < IV B. I < III < II < IV

C. IV < II < III < I D. III < IV < II < I

24. The sequence of three steps involved in the following conversion is

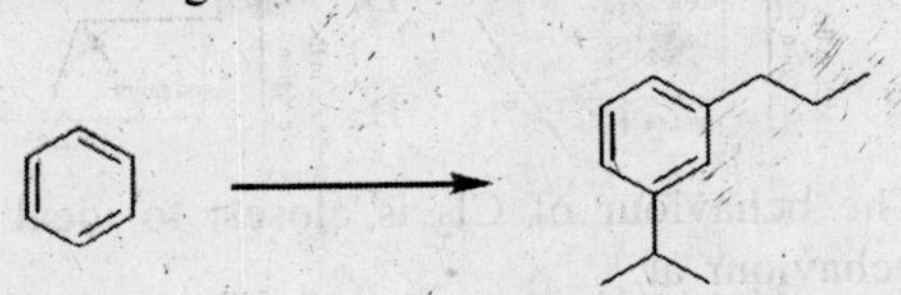

A. (*i*) Friedel-Crafts alkylation;
(*ii*) Reduction;
(*iii*) Friedel-Crafts acylation

B. (*i*) Friedel-Crafts acylation;
(*ii*) Friedel-Crafts alkylation;
(*iii*) Reduction

C. (*i*) Friedel-Crafts acylation;
(*ii*) Reduction;
(*iii*) Friedel-Crafts alkylation

D. (*i*) Friedel-Crafts alkylation;
(*ii*) Friedel-Crafts acylation;
(*iii*) Reduction

25. The **CORRECT** expression that corresponds to reversible and adiabatic expansion of an ideal gas is:

A. $\Delta U = 0$ B. $\Delta H = 0$

C. $\Delta S = 0$ D. $\Delta G = 0$

26. The electrolyte AB_2 ionises in water as

$$AB_2 \rightleftharpoons A^{2+} + 2B^-$$

The mean ionic activity coefficient ($\gamma_\pm$) is:

A. $\gamma_{A^{2+}}^{\frac{1}{2}} \gamma_{B^-}$ B. $\gamma_{A^{2+}}^{\frac{1}{2}} \gamma_{B^-}^{\frac{2}{3}}$

C. $\gamma_{A^{2+}}^{\frac{2}{3}} \gamma_{B^-}^{\frac{1}{3}}$ D. $\left(\gamma_{A^{2+}} + 2\gamma_{B^-}\right)^{\frac{1}{2}}$

27. The reaction, **A → Products**, follows first-order kinetics. If [A] represents the concentration of reactant at time t, the INCORRECT variation is shown in:

A. 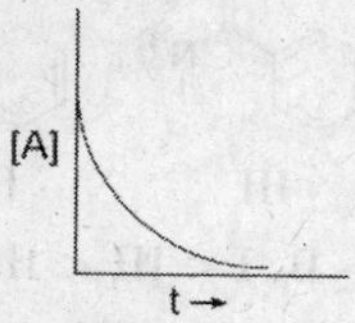

B. 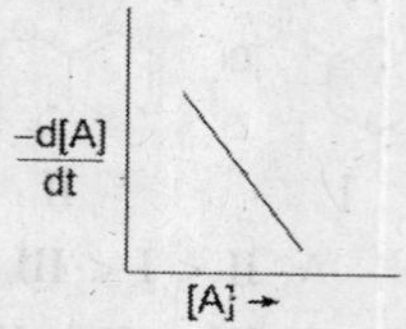

C. 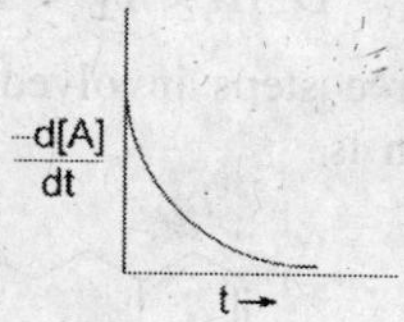

D. 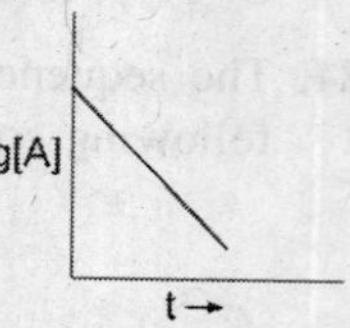

28. The behaviour of Cl_2 is closest to ideal gas behaviour at:

A. 100 °C and 10.0 atm

B. 0 °C and 0.50 atm

C. 200 °C and 0.50 atm

D. –100 °C and 10.0 atm

29. A vector $\vec{A} = \vec{i} + x\vec{j} + 3\vec{k}$ is rotated through an angle and is also doubled in magnitude resulting in $\vec{B} = 4\vec{i} + (4x-2)\vec{j} + 2\vec{k}$. An acceptable value of x is:

A. 1 B. 2

C. 3 D. $\frac{4}{3}$

30. With reference to the variation of molar conductivity (Λ_m) with concentration for a strong electrolyte in an aqueous solution, the CORRECT statement is:

A. The asymmetry effect contributes to decrease Λ_m whereas the electrophoretic effect contributes to increase Λ_m

B. The asymmetry effect contributes to increase Λ_m whereas the electrophoretic effect contributes to decrease Λ_m

C. Both asymmetry effect and electrophoretic effect contribute to decrease Λ_m

D. Both asymmetry effect and electrophoretic effect contribute to increase Λ_m

Section B : Multiple Select Questions (MSQ)

Q. 31 – Q. 40 carry two marks each.

31. Which of the following metal(s) is(are) extracted from its(their) sulphide ore(s) by self-reduction/air reduction method?

A. Cu B. Al

C. Au D. Pb

32. In a saturated calomel electrode, the saturation is with respect to:

A. KCl B. Hg_2Cl_2

C. $HgCl_2$ D. AgCl

33. Consider the following six solid binary oxides: CaO, Al_2O_3, PbO, Cs_2O, SiO_2 and Sb_2O_3. The pair(s) of ionic oxides is(are):

A. CaO and Al_2O_3

B. CaO and PbO

C. Cs_2O and Al_2O_3

D. SiO_2 and Sb_2O_3

34. Choose the CORRECT answer(s) with respect to the magnesium-EDTA titration carried out in the pH range 7 – 10.5, using Solochrome black as indicator:

A. Magnesium–indicator complex is more stable than the magnesium–EDTA complex

B. At the end point, the colour changes from red to blue

C. After the end point, the colour of the solution is due to the indicator

D. pH range of 7 – 10.5 is necessary for observing the specific colour change

35. On reaction with $NaNO_2$ and HCl, which of the following amino alcohol(s) will yield compound P?

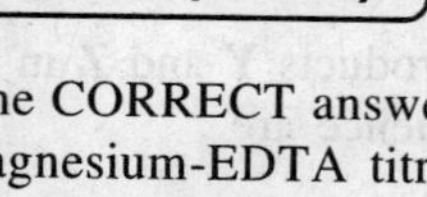

P

A. 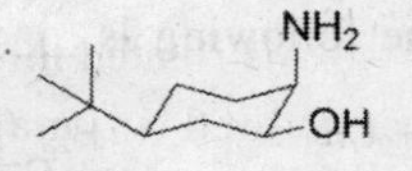 B. 

C. 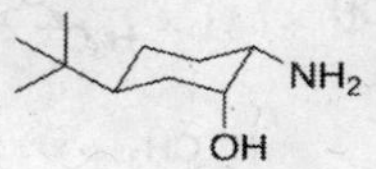 D. 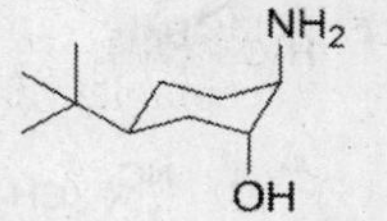

36. The CORRECT statement(s) about carbene is (are):

A. Carbene is a neutral species
B. Carbene is an intermediate in the Curtius rearrangement
C. Carbene can insert into both σ and π-bonds
D. Carbene is generated from amines on reaction with nitrous acid

37. The compound(s) that shows(show) positive haloform test is(are):

A. 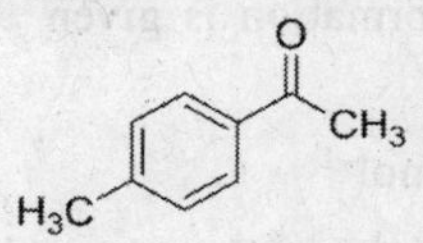 B. 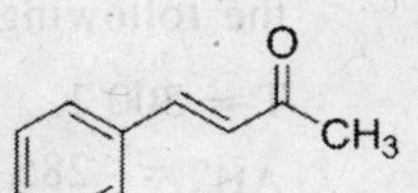

C. 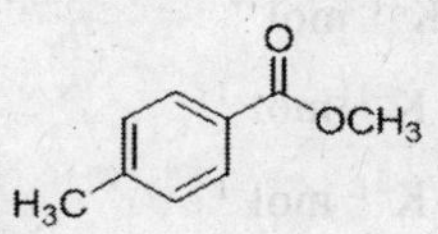 D. 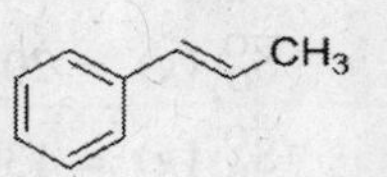

38. Tetrapeptide(s) that gives(give) the following product on reaction with Sanger's reagent followed by hydrolysis is(are):

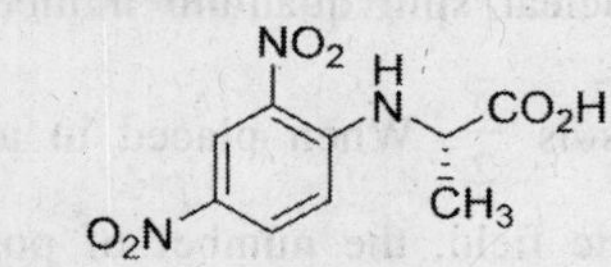

A. Ala-Gly-Leu-Phe B. Asp-Phe-Leu-Pro
C. Asp-Gly-Tyr-Phe D. Ala-Phe-Tyr-Pro

39. Which of the following set(s) of quantum numbers is(are) NOT allowed?

A. $n = 3,\ l = 2,\ m_l = -1$
B. $n = 4,\ l = 0,\ m_l = -1$
C. $n = 3,\ l = 3,\ m_l = -3$
D. $n = 5,\ l = 3,\ m_l = +2$

40. The CORRECT expression(s) for isothermal expansion of 1 mol of an ideal gas is(are):

A. $\Delta A = RT\ln\dfrac{V_{initial}}{V_{final}}$ B. $\Delta G = RT\ln\dfrac{V_{initial}}{V_{final}}$

C. $\Delta H = RT\ln\dfrac{V_{final}}{V_{initial}}$ D. $\Delta S = RT\ln\dfrac{V_{final}}{V_{initial}}$

Section C : Numerical Answer Type (NAT)

Q. 41 – Q. 50 carry one mark each.

41. The number of possible isomers for $[Pt(py)(NH_3)BrCl]$ is ________. (py is pyridine)

42. The volume of 0.3 M ferrous ammonium sulphate solution required for the completion of redox titration with 20 mL of 0.1 M potassium dichromate solution is ________ mL.

43. Among the following hydrocarbon(s), how many of them would give rise to three groups of proton NMR peaks with 2:2:3 integration ratio?

  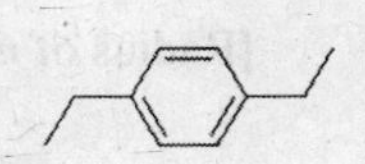

44. The number of stereoisomers possible for the following compound is ______.

Ph–CH(OH)–CH(OH)–Ph

45. The number of hydrogen bond(s) present in a guanine-cytosine base pair is ______.

46. The time for 50% completion of a zero order reaction is 30 min. Time for 80% completion of this reaction is ______ min.

47. Consider the reaction

$$CO(g) + \frac{1}{2}O_2(g) \longrightarrow CO_2(g)$$

The value of ΔU for the reaction at 300 K is –281.8 kJ mol^{-1}. The value of ΔH at same temperature is ______ kJ mol^{-1} (rounded up to the first decimal place).

[$R = 8.3\ J\ K^{-1}\ mol^{-1}$]

48. The nuclear spin quantum number (I) of a nucleus is $\frac{3}{2}$. When placed in an external magnetic field, the number of possible spin energy states it can occupy is ______.

49. The value of C_v for 1 mol of N_2 gas predicted from the principle of equipartition of energy, ignoring vibrational contribution, is ______ $J\ K^{-1}\ mol^{-1}$ (rounded up to two decimal places).

[$R = 8.3\ J\ K^{-1}\ mol^{-1}$]

50. Assuming ideal gas behaviour, the density of O_2 gas at 300 K and 1.0 atm is ______ g L^{-1} (rounded up to two decimal places).

[$R = 0.082$ L atm mol^{-1} K^{-1}, molar mass of $O_2 = 32$]

Q. 51 – Q. 60 carry two marks each.

51. How many of the following interhalogen species have 2 lone pairs of electrons on the central atom?

ClF_3, ClF_2^-, ClF_5 and ICl_2^+

52. ^{24}Na decays to one-fourth of its initial amount in 29.8 hours. Its decay constant is______ $hour^{-1}$ (rounded up to four decimal places).

53. The magnitude of crystal field stabilization energy (CFSE) of octahedral $[Ti(H_2O)_6]^{3+}$ complex is 7680 cm^{-1}. The wavelength at the maximum absorption (λ_{max}) of this complex is ______ nm (rounded up to the nearest integer).

54. Elemental analysis of an organic compound containing C, H and O gives percentage composition: C: 39.9 % and H: 6.7 %. If the molecular weight of the compound is 180, the number of carbon atoms present in the molecule is______.

55. The number of compounds having S-configuration among the following is ______.

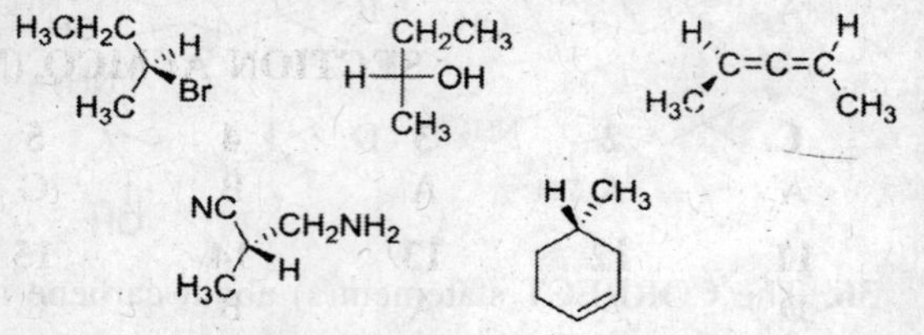

56. The *emf* of a standard cadmium cell is 1.02 V at 300 K. The temperature coefficient of the cell is -5.0×10^{-5} V K^{-1}. The value of $\Delta H°$ for the cell is ______ kJ mol^{-1} (rounded up to two decimal places).

[$1\ F = 96500\ C\ mol^{-1}$]

57. For the reaction $H_2(g) + \frac{1}{2}O_2(g) \rightarrow H_2O(l)$, the following information is given

T = 300 K

$\Delta \bar{H}° = -285$ kJ mol^{-1}

$\bar{S}^{o}_{H_2O}(l) = 70\ J\ K^{-1}\ mol^{-1}$

$\bar{S}^{o}_{O_2}(g) = 204\ J\ K^{-1}\ mol^{-1}$

$\bar{S}^{o}_{H_2}(g) = 130\ J\ K^{-1}\ mol^{-1}$

$\Delta \bar{S}^{o}_{universe}$ for the reaction is ___ $J\ K^{-1}\ mol^{-1}$.

58. For H_2 molecule, the fundamental vibrational frequency $(\bar{\upsilon}_e)$ can be taken as 4400 cm^{-1}. The zero-point energy of the molecule is ______ kJ mol^{-1} (rounded up to two decimal places).

[$h = 6.6 \times 10^{-34}$ J s, $c = 3 \times 10^{8}$ m s^{-1}, $N_A = 6 \times 10^{23}$ mol^{-1}]

59. The solubility of PbI_2 in 0.10 M KI(aq) is ______ $\times 10^{-7}$ M (rounded up to two decimal places).

[The solubility product, $K_{sp} = 7.1 \times 10^{-9}$].

60. The electron of a hydrogen atom is in its nth Bohr orbit having de-Broglie wavelength of 13.4 Å. The value of n is ______ (rounded up to the nearest integer).

[Radius of nth Bohr orbit = $0.53n^2$ Å, $\pi = 3.14$].

ANSWERS

SECTION A: MCQ (Multiple Choice Questions)

1	2	3	4	5	6	7	8	9	10
A	A	A	B	C	B	A	A	D	D
11	**12**	**13**	**14**	**15**	**16**	**17**	**18**	**19**	**20**
D	A	A	B	C	D	C	A	C	D
21	**22**	**23**	**24**	**25**	**26**	**27**	**28**	**29**	**30**
C	B	D	B	C	*	B	C	B	C

SECTION B: MSQ (Multiple Select Questions)

31	32	33	34	35
A, D	A, B	A, C	B, C, D	B, C
36	**37**	**38**	**39**	**40**
A, C	A, B	A, D	B, C	A, B, D

SECTION C: NAT (Numerical Answer Type Questions)

41	42	43	44	45
3	40	2	3	3
46	**47**	**48**	**49**	**50**
48	–286.0 to –282.0	4	20.00 to 21.00	1.29 to 1.31
51	**52**	**53**	**54**	**55**
2	0.0460 to 0.0470	520 to 521	6	4
56	**57**	**58**	**59**	**60**
–201.00 to –198.00	786 to 790	25.80 to 26.40	7.0 to 7.2	4

* Error in question/option

EXPLANATORY ANSWERS

1. Aluminium carbide is quite a hard substance, and is often used as an abrasive material.

Hydrolysis is a reaction that takes place between a substance and water, as a result of which the substance and water break down, and new compounds form. Al_3C_4 is a salt-like carbide, which is essentially the product of the displacement of the hydrogen atom in methane by metal atoms. So in its hydrolysis, reverse displacement takes place easily, and methane forms.

Equation of the hydrolysis of aluminium carbide:

$$Al_4C_3 + 12H_2O \rightarrow 4Al(OH)_3 \downarrow + 3CH_4 \uparrow$$

The hydrolysis of aluminium carbide is an irreversible reaction.

2. The **carbonic anhydrases** (or carbonate dehydratases) form a family of enzymes that catalyze the interconversion between carbon dioxide and water and the dissociated ions of carbonic acid (*i.e.*, bicarbonate and protons). This interconversion is a reversible reaction and the enzyme catalyzes both reactions, forward and reverse.

The reaction catalyzed by carbonic anhydrase is:

$$CO_2 + H_2O \xrightarrow{\text{Carbonic anhydrase}} H^+ + HCO_3^-$$

(in tissues – high CO_2 concentration)

The reaction rate of carbonic anhydrase is one of the fastest of all enzymes, and its rate is typically limited by the diffusion-rate of its substrates. Typical catalytic rates of the different forms of this enzyme ranging between 10^4 and 10^6 reactions per second.

3. PF_3 colourless gas

- Melting point: –152° C
- Boiling point: –102° C

AsF_3 colourless liquid

- Melting point: –6° C
- Boiling point: 63° C

SbF_3 colourless crystalline solid

- Melting point: 290° C
- Boiling point: 345° C

BiF_3 grey-white crystalline solid

- Melting point: 649° C
- Boiling point: 900° C

4. Lattice energy of an ionic crystal is the energy released when the required number of gaseous cations and anions are brought together from an infinite distance to form one gm mole of the solid crystal. The energy required to separate ions of one gm mole of solid ionic crystal from their equilibrium position in the crystal to infinity is also known as lattice energy.

The magnitude of lattice energy depends upon (*a*) Ionic charges (*b*) Distance between the ions (*c*) Size of the ions and (*d*) Crystal structure. As the charge on the ions increases, the lattice energy also increases.

Table: *Lattice Energies*

Compound	*Lattice Energy (kJ/mol)*
LiF	1036
LiCl	853
LiBr	807
LiI	757
NaF	923
NaCl	786
NaBr	747
NaI	704
KF	821
KCl	715
KBr	682
KI	649
CsCl	657
MgF_2	2957
$MgCl_2$	2526
$MgBr_2$	2440
MgI_2	2327
$CaCl_2$	2258
Na_2O	2481
MgO	3791
CaO	3401

6. The compound that contains the most acidic hydrogen is Acetylene.

Acetylene has two acidic hydrogen this is because in acetylene two carbons bonded by a triple bond. Three electron pairs exactly in middle of two carbon atoms. Being more electronegative Carbon try to gain the electron pair which is shared between hydrogen and carbon by the dissociation of bond which results the elimination of proton.

7.

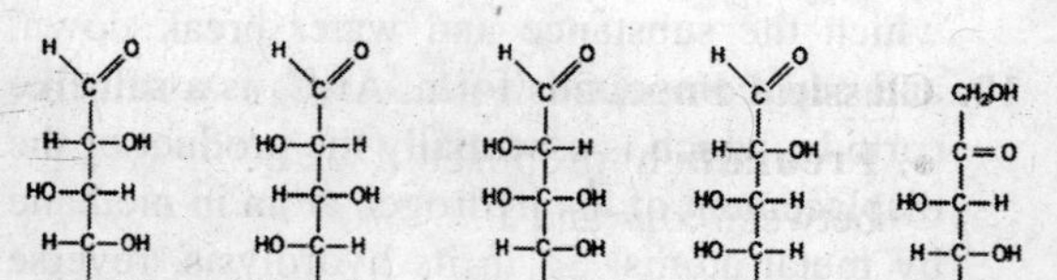

D-Glucose L-Glucose D-Mannose D-Galactose D-Fructose

Structures of hexoses: D- and L-glucose, D-mannose, D-galactose and D-fructose. The D and L designations are based on the configuration at the highest numbered asymmetric center, C-5 in the case of hexoses. Note that L-glucose is the mirror image of D-glucose, *i.e.*, the geometry at all of the asymmetric centers is reversed. Mannose is the C-2 epimer, and galactose the C-4 epimer of glucose. These linear projections of carbohydrate structures are known as Fischer projections.

9. Crystal System: There are seven types of crystals depending upon the axial ratio ($a : b : c$) and angles between them (α, β, γ). In the element crystals, each lattice point of the lattice is occupied by an atom; while in the case of compound, each lattice point is occupied by an assembly of atoms which is repeated according to the translation vector T. The unit assembly of atom is called the basis. The crystal structure may be considered to be formed by the addition of a unit assembly or basis of atoms to every lattice of the space-lattice.

Obviously lattice + basis = Crystal structure.

Bravais Lattices: Bravais showed that there could be only 14 different lattices under the seven system of the crystals. These lattices are called Bravais lattices.

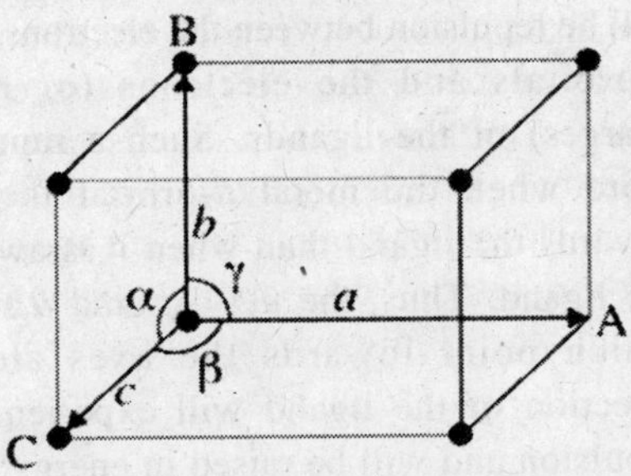

10. Classical Freundlich Adsorption Isotherm

- **Freundlich** proposed following relation between x/m and P.

$$\frac{x}{m} = KP^{1/n}$$

($n > 1$) and T being constant

Here K and n are parameters depending upon nature of gas and solid.

- $\frac{x}{m}$ increases as P increases but since $n > 1$, the $\frac{x}{m}$ does not increase as rapidly as P as is clear from the following isotherm:
- In case of solution, the equation takes the form

$$\frac{x}{m} = KC^{1/n}$$

(C = conc. of solute in gm mole per litre).

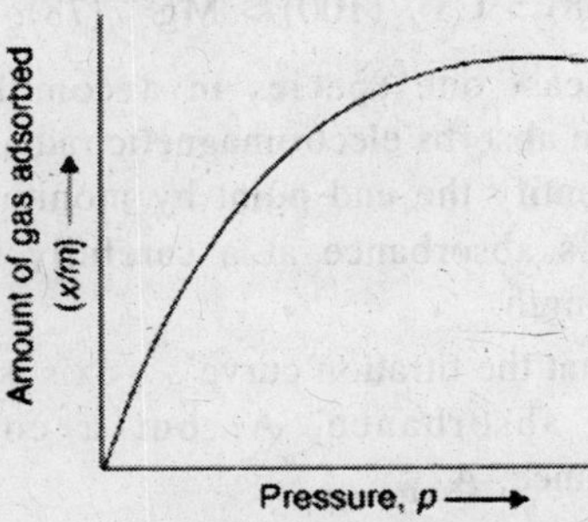

Fig. : *Freundlich adsorption isotherm*

- Taking the log on both sides of equation, we get,

$$\log\frac{x}{m} = \log K + \frac{1}{n}\log p$$

If $\log\frac{x}{m}$ is plotted against $\log p$ or $\log C$, a straight line is obtained giving slope $= \frac{1}{n}$ and intercept = log K.

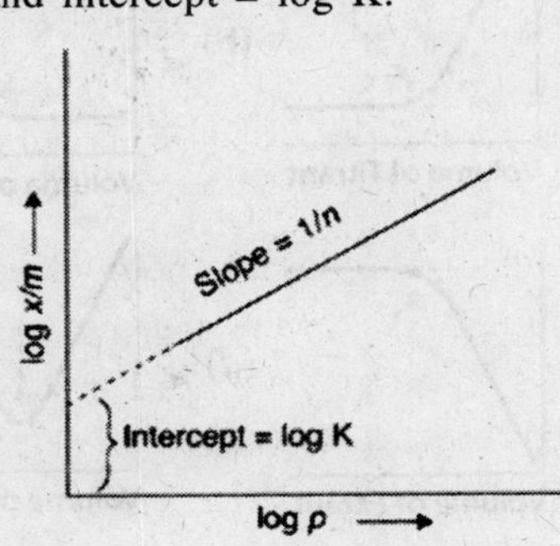

- Limitation of Freundlich isotherm is that it fails at high pressure of gas. Secondly Freundlich isotherm equation is an empirical equation without any theoretical background.

11. The ionic radius in general

- increases moving down a group
- decreases moving along a period from left to right.

Thus, $Na^+ > Li^+ > Mg^{2+} > Be^{2+}$

Ionic radius *r* (in pm):

K^+ (138) > Ca^{2+} (100) > Mg^{2+} (78).

12. If at least one species in a complexation titration absorbs electromagnetic radiation, we can identify the end point by monitoring the titrand's absorbance at a carefully selected wavelength.

Note that the titration curve's *y*-axis is not the actual absorbance, A, but a corrected absorbance, A_{corr}

$A_{corr} = A \times (V_{EDTA} + V_{Cu})/V_{cu}$

where V_{EDTA} and V_{Cu} are, respectively, the volumes of EDTA and Cu. Correcting the absorbance for the titrand's dilution ensures that the spectrophotometric titration curve consists of linear segments that we can extrapolate to find the end point.

Other common spectrophotometric titration curves are shown in panels *b-f*.

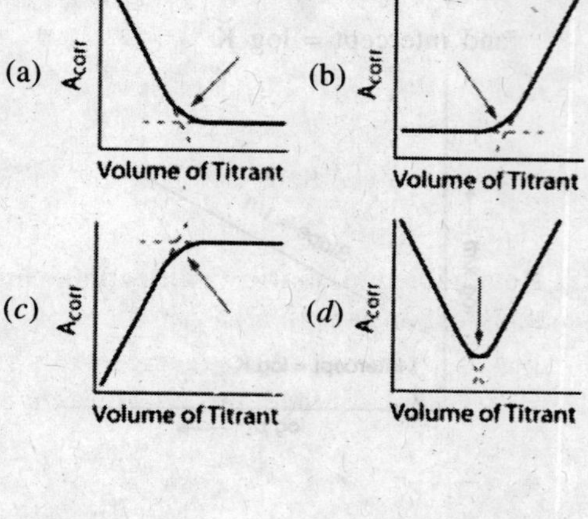

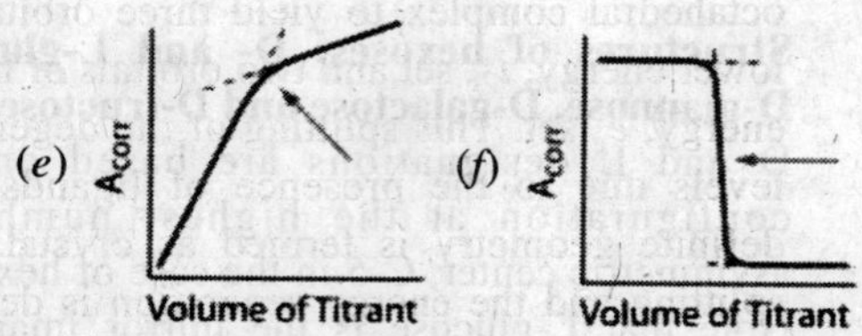

Examples of spectrophotometric titration curves:

(*a*) only the titrand absorbs;

(*b*) only the titrant absorbs;

(*c*) only the product of the titration reaction absorbs;

(*d*) both the titrand and the titrant absorb;

(*e*) both the titration reaction's product and the titrant absorb;

(*f*) only the indicator absorbs. The red arrows indicate the end points for each titration curve.

13. Metal carbonyls are coordination complexes of transition metals with carbon monoxide ligands. Among the given species the one with the highest metal-carbon back bonding is $[Ti(CO)_6]^{2-}$.

14. Crystal field splitting in octahedral coordination entities

In an octahedral coordination entity with six ligands surrounding the metal atom/ion, there will be repulsion between the electrons in metal *d*-orbitals and the electrons (or negative charges) of the ligands. Such a repulsion is more when the metal *d*-orbital is directed towards the ligand than when it is away from the ligand. Thus, the $d_{x^2-y^2}$ and d_{z^2} orbitals which point towards the axes along the direction of the ligand will experience more repulsion and will be raised in energy: and the d_{xy}, d_{yx} and d_{xz} orbitals which are directed between the axes will be lowered in energy relative to the average energy in the spherical crystal field. Thus, the degeneracy of the *d* orbitals has been removed due to ligand electron-metal electron repulsions in the octahedral complex to yield three orbitals of lower energy, t_{2g} set and two orbitals of higher energy, e_g set. This splitting of the degenerate levels due to the presence of ligands in a definite geometry is termed as crystal field splitting and the energy separation is denoted by Δ_o (the subscript o is for octahedral). Thus, the energy of the two e_g orbitals will increase by (3/5) Δ_o and that of the three t_{2g} will decrease by $(2/5)\Delta_o$.

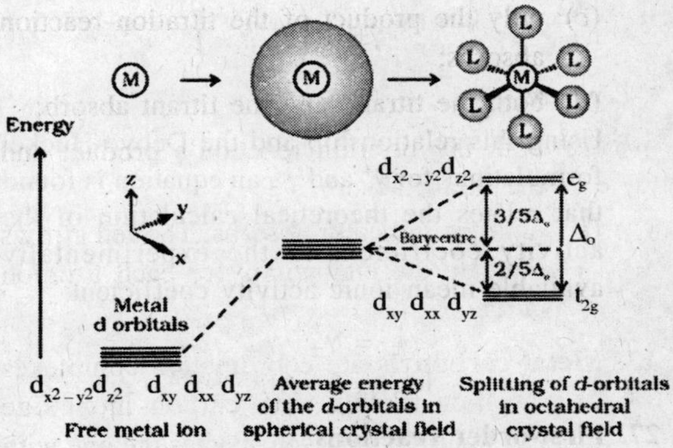

Fig.: *d-orbital splitting in an octahedral crystal field.*

The crystal field splitting, Δ_o, depends upon the field produced by the ligand and charge on the metal ion. Some ligands are able to produce strong fields in which case, the splitting will be large whereas others produce weak fields and consequently result in small splitting of *d*-orbitals. In general, ligands can be arranged in a series in the order of increasing field strength as given below:

$I^- < Br^- < SCN^- < Cl^- < S^{2-} < F^- < OH^- < C_2O_4^{2-} < H_2O < NCS^- < edta^{4-} < NH_3 < en < CN^- < CO$

CORRECT order of Δ_o (the octahedral crystal field splitting of *d*-orbitals) values for the following anionic metal complexes is

$[CoI_6]^{3-} < [RhI_6]^{3-} < [Rh(CN)_6]^{3-} < [Ir(CN)_6]^{3-}$.

15. In general, radioactive decays can be divided into alpha, beta and gamma decays. However, other process may also be considered as types of decay.

Beta decay: The emission of a negative electron, a positive electron (positron), or the capture of an atomic orbital electron (EC) is called a beta decay process.

- Negative electron emission: A free neutron (n) outside a nucleus is unstable, and it emits an electron and becomes a proton (p). The proton and the electron are the components of a hydrogen atom. A company particle in the emission of electron is the **antineutrino** ν^*.

  $n \rightarrow p^+ + e^- + \nu^*$

  The antineutrino is the antiparticle of neutrino.

  When a nuclide $^M p^Z$ emits an electron, we may consider one of the neutron in the nucleus being converted to a proton. For example,

  $^{14}C^6 \rightarrow {}^{14}N^7 + e^- + \nu^*$

  $^{40}Ca^{19} \rightarrow {}^{40}Ca^{20} + e^- + \nu^*$

  $^{50}V^{23} \rightarrow {}^{50}Cr^{24} + e^- + \nu^*$

  $^{87}Rb^{37} \rightarrow {}^{87}Sr^{38} + e^- + \nu^*$

- Positive electron (positron) emission

  A positive electron is called positron, which is the antiparticle of electron. The company particle for positron emission is an neutrino (ν). Some examples are given here to illustrate the process.

  $^{22}Na^{11} \rightarrow {}^{22}Ne^{10} + e^+ + \nu$

  $^{21}Na^{11} \rightarrow {}^{21}Ne^{10} + e^+ + \nu$

  $^{30}P^{15} \rightarrow {}^{30}Si^{14} + e^+ + \nu$

  $^{34}Cl^{17} \rightarrow {}^{34}S^{16} + e^+ + \nu$

  $^{116}Sb^{51} \rightarrow {}^{116}Sn^{50} + e^+ + \nu$

  $^{14}O_8 \rightarrow {}^{14}N_7 + e^+ + \nu$.

25. Reversible adiabatic (isentropic) compression/expansion of real gas

For a reversible adiabatic process, we have $Q^{rev} = 0$ and since the entropy change is

$dS = dQ^{rev}/T$, it follows that $dS = 0$, *i.e.*, the entropy is constant ("isentropic process") and $S_1 = S_2$. The shaft work is then from the energy balance

Real gas: $W_s^{rev} = (H_2 - H_1)_S$

For a real gas multicomponent mixture, we normally use an equation of state, together with data for ideal gas heat capacity, to compute the enthalpy change at constant entropy. For a pure component, it is practical and insightful to use thermodynamic diagrams as shown in Figure. From a given value for p_1 and $T_1 = T_0$, we read off H_1. We then follow a line for constant entropy until we arrive at p_2, where we can read H_2 (and T_2) for the outlet stream (denoted 2″ in figure).

We consider two important cases:

1. Reversible isothermal process, and
2. Reversible adiabatic process.

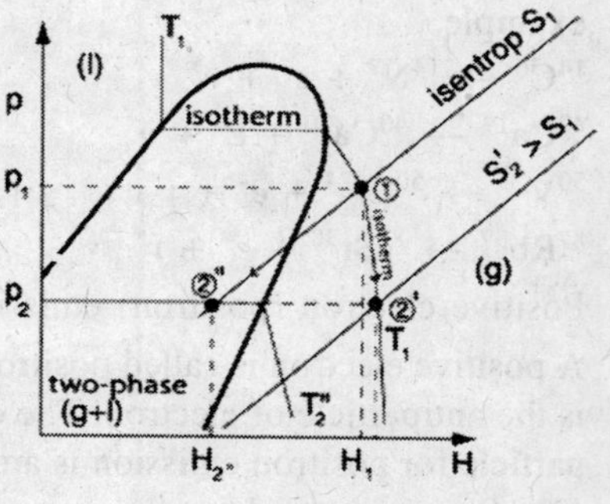

(*a*) Expansion in pH-diagram
② ′ : after isotherm
② ″ : after isentrop (rev. adiabatic process)

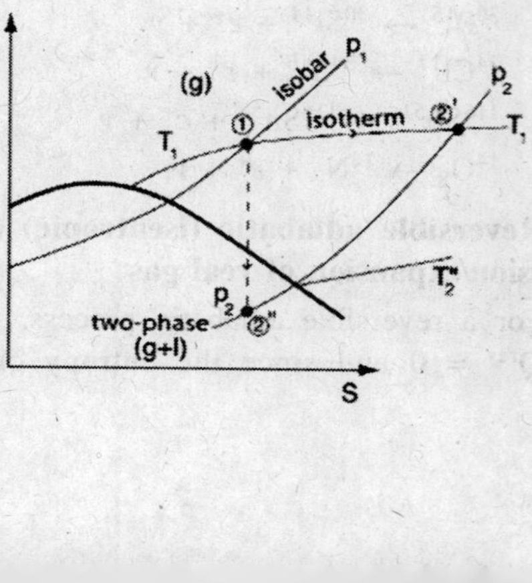

(*b*) Same expansion in HS-diagram
② ′ : after isotherm
② ″ : after isentrop (rev. adiabatic process)

Fig.: *Use of thermodynamic diagram to calculate reversible expansion work for real gas: (a) pH diagram. (b) HS diagram.*

26. The general formula relating the measurable mean ionic activity coefficient to the activity coefficient for each individual ion is

$$\gamma\pm = \left(\gamma^{v^+}\gamma^{v^-}\right)^{1/v}$$

where, $\quad v = v^+ + v^-$

Using this relationship and the Debye-Huckel formulations for γ^+ and γ^-, an equation is found that relates the theoretical calculation of the activity coefficient to the experimentally available mean ionic activity coefficient:

$$\gamma_\pm^v = \gamma_\pm^{v_+} \cdot \gamma_-^{v_-}$$

$$\log \gamma_\pm = -\Lambda(z_+ z_-)^{1/2}.$$

27. First-order reactions

First-order reactions appear to be the most commonly encountered in pharmaceutical stability studies. The rate of a first-order reaction is proportional to the concentration of the reactant:

$$\text{Rate} = -\frac{d[A]}{dt} = k[A]$$

The concentration-time profile of the reactant for a first-order reaction follows an exponential decay to a limiting value, while that of the product follows an exponential increase to a different limiting value:

$$A \rightarrow C$$

$$[A]_t = [A]_0\exp(-kt)$$

$$[C]_t = [A]_0[1 - \exp(-kt)]$$

The half-life, $t_{1/2}$, of the reaction is the time required for the reactant concentration to decrease to 50% of its original value; similarly, the times for the reactant concentration to decrease to 95% and 90% of its original values are designated as t_{95}, and t_{90}, respectively. These quantities can be obtained readily for a first-order reaction if the rate constant is known:

$$t_{1/2} = \frac{\ln 2}{k};$$

$$t_{95} = \frac{\ln 0.95}{k};$$

$$t_{90} = \frac{\ln 0.9}{k}$$

A characteristic feature of first-order reactions is that the time required to lose the first 50% of the material ($t_{1/2}$) is the same as the time required to drop from 50% remaining to 25% remaining, from 25% remaining to 12.5% remaining, and so on.

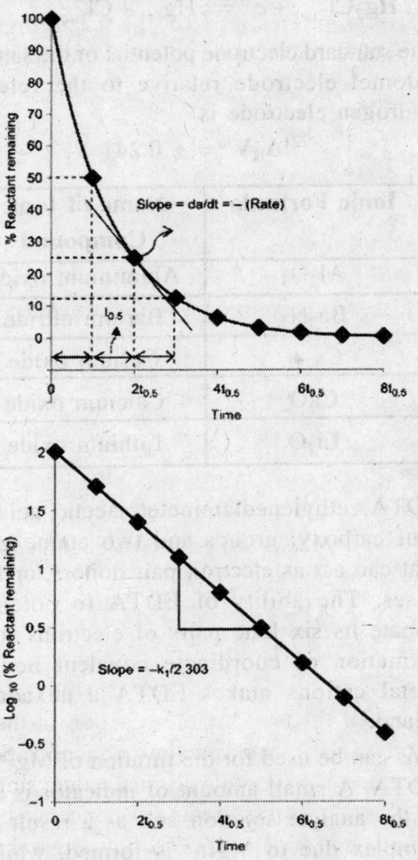

Fig.: *First-order reaction progress. The time-axis has been scaled as multiples of the half-life ($t_{0.5}$).*

30. Molar conductivity of a solution at a given concentration is the conductance of the volume V of solution containing one mole of electrolyte kept between two electrodes with area of cross section A and distance of unit length.

$$\Lambda_m = \frac{K}{c}$$

Here,

c = concentration in moles per volume

K = specific conductivity

Λ_m = molar conductivity

As the solution contains only one mole of electrolyte, the above equation can be modified as:

$$\Lambda_m = KV$$

Molar conductivity increases with decrease in concentration as the total volume, V, of solution containing one mole of electrolyte also increases. Upon dilution the concentration decreases. When the concentration approaches zero, molar conductivity of the solution is known as limiting molar conductivity, Λ_m°. Variation of molar conductivity with concentration is different for strong and weak electrolytes.

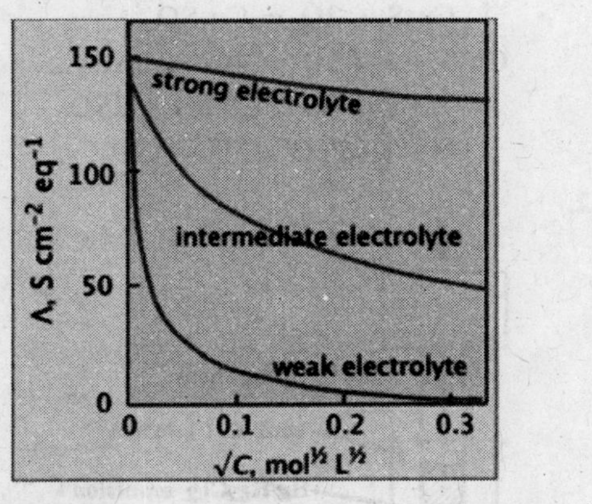

Variation of molar conductivity with concentration for strong electrolytes: For strong electrolytes the molar conductivity increases slowly with the dilution. The plot between the molar conductivity and $\frac{c_1}{2}$ is a straight line having y-intercept equal to $\ddot{E}^{\circ}_{m}$. The value of limiting molar conductivity, $\ddot{E}^{\circ}_{m}$ can be determined from the graph or with the help of Kohlrausch law. The general equation for the plot is given as:

$$\Lambda_m = \ddot{E}^{\circ}_{m} - \frac{Ac_1}{2}$$

Where, –A is a constant equal to the slope of the line. For a given solvent, the value of "A" depends on type of electrolyte at a particular temperature.

31. Self-reduction: This process of extraction of metals is employed in case of the sulphide ores of lead and copper. The sulphide ore is first roasted in a controlled supply of air when a part of the sulphide is oxidized by air to form oxide and sulphate of the metal. The oxide and sulphate thus formed react with the unchanged sulphide at high temperature in absence of air to produce metal. As no external reducing agent is used in this process, the process is called self-reduction process.

$$2Cu_2S + 3O_2 = 2Cu_2O + 2SO_2,$$
$$Cu_2S + 2Cu_2O = 6Cu + SO_2$$
$$Cu_2S + 2O_2 = Cu_2SO_4,$$
$$Cu_2S + Cu_2SO_4 = 4Cu + 2SO_2$$
$$2PS + 3O_2 = 2PbO + 2SO_2,$$
$$PbS + 2PbO = 3Pb + SO_2.$$

32.

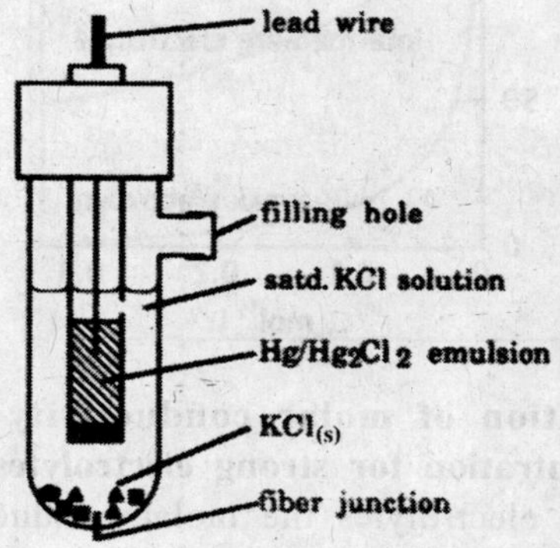

Fig.: *Saturated Calomel electrode.*

The saturated calomel electrode corresponds to the half-cell.

$Hg_{(\ell)} \mid Hg^{+}_{(aq)}, K^{+}_{(aq)}, Cl^{-}_{(aq)}$ $(KCl_{(s)}, Hg_2Cl_{2(s)}$ ~ Hg $|Hg_2Cl_2$ [Sat'd], KCl[Sat'd]|

for which the half reaction is:

$$Hg_2Cl_2 + 2e^- \rightleftharpoons 2Hg(l) + 2Cl^-$$

The presence of KCl_s in equilibrium indicates that the aqueous solution is saturated in KCl. The presence of $Hg_2Cl_{2(s)}$ in equilibrium indicates that the concentration of $Hg^{+}_{(aq)}$ is fixed, as dictated by the small solubility product of Hg_2Cl_2 (calomel) and the saturation of the solution in $Cl^{-}_{(aq)}$. The corresponding reduction reaction can formally be written

$$1/2\, Hg_2Cl_{2(s)} + e^- \rightleftharpoons Hg_{(\ell)} + Cl^{-}_{(aq)}.$$

The standard electrode potential of the saturated calomel electrode relative to the reference hydrogen electrode is

$$^{221}\Delta_H V^\circ = +\ 0.241\ V.$$

33.

Ionic Formula	Name of Ionic Compound
Al_2O_3	Aluminium oxide
Ba_3N_2	Barium nitride
Cs_2O	Cesium oxide
CaO	Calcium oxide
Li_2O	Lithium oxide

34. EDTA, ethylenediaminetetraacetic acid, has four carboxyl groups and two amine groups that can act as electron pair donors, or Lewis bases. The ability of EDTA to potentially donate its six lone pairs of electrons for the formation of coordinate covalent bonds to metal cations makes EDTA a hexadentate ligand.

This can be used for the titration of Mg^{2+} with EDTA. A small amount of indicator is added to the analyte solution and as a result a red complex due to $MgIn^-$ is formed, while the colour of uncomplexed indicator is blue. During titration of EDTA, the following reaction occurs at the end point.

$$Mg^{2+} + H_2In^{2-} \rightarrow MgIn^{-} + H^{+}$$

$$\underset{\text{Red}}{MgIn^{-}} + H_2Y^{2-} \rightarrow \underset{\text{Colourless}}{MgY^{2-}} + \underset{\text{Blue}}{HIn^{2-}} + H^{+}$$

It is therefore recommend to carry out EDTA titration at pH range 8-10 while using Eriochrome Black T as indicator.

36. A species in which a carbon is bivalent is called 'carbene'. These are classified into two categories.

Triplet Carbene: Two unpaired electrons are present in two *p*-orbitals of a carbon which is *sp*-hybridized.

$$H-\dot{\underset{\cdot}{C}}-H$$

Singlet Carbene: A carbon connected to two atoms has a lone pair and a vacant orbital. It can act as an electrophile.

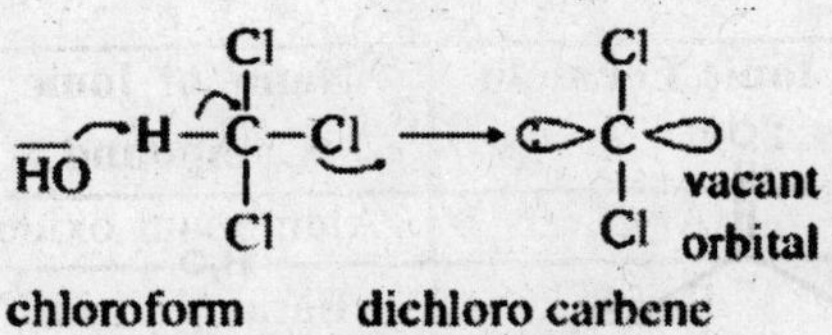

The carbon is sp^2-hybridized

$$:CH_2-N=N: \xrightarrow{\Delta} \underset{\text{methylene carbene}}{:CH_2} + N_2$$

Lone pair is in sp^2 *h-o p*-orbital is vacant.

- **Carbenes are neutral species containing a carbon atom with only six valence electrons.**

  The six electrons of a carbene are located two in each bond, plus two non-bonding electrons often represented as $:CR_2$ (as though they were a lone pair). As you will see later, this can be misleading, but $:CR_2$ is a widely used symbol for a carbene. In the case of $:CH_2$ generated from diazomethane, the carbene is trapped by the alcohol to make an ether.

  Like the radicals, carbenes are extremely reactive species. More important than their reaction with alcohols to make ethers are their reactions with alkenes to make cyclopropanes and their insertion into C–H bonds.

- **Typical carbene reactions**

  The carbene inserts itself into a σ bond or a π bond.

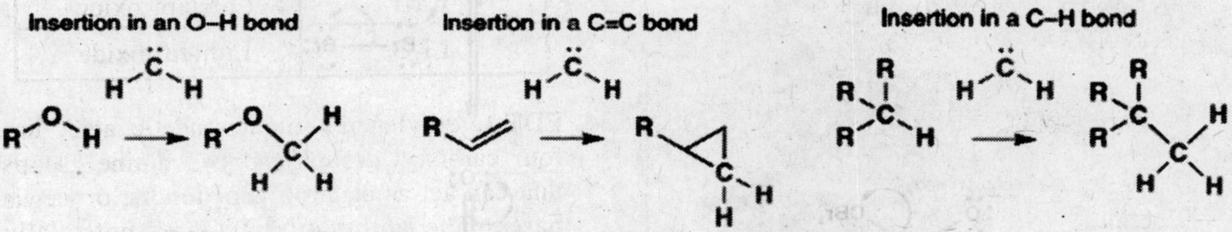

37. The haloform reaction is the reaction of a methyl ketone with chlorine, bromine, or iodine in the presence of hydroxide ions to give a carboxylate ion and a haloform. There is one aldehyde that undergoes the haloform reaction, which is acetaldehyde.

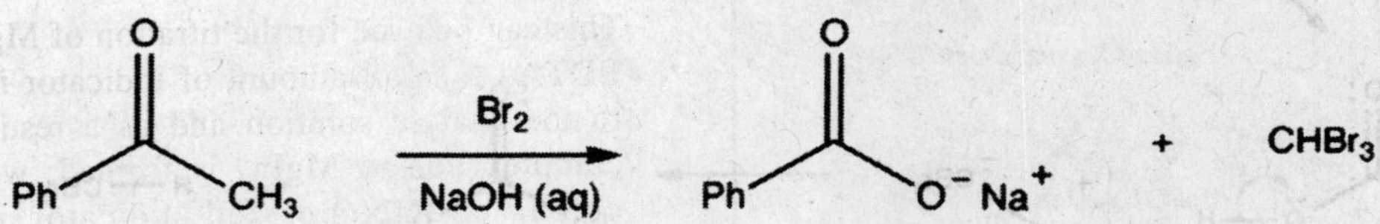

Mechanism:

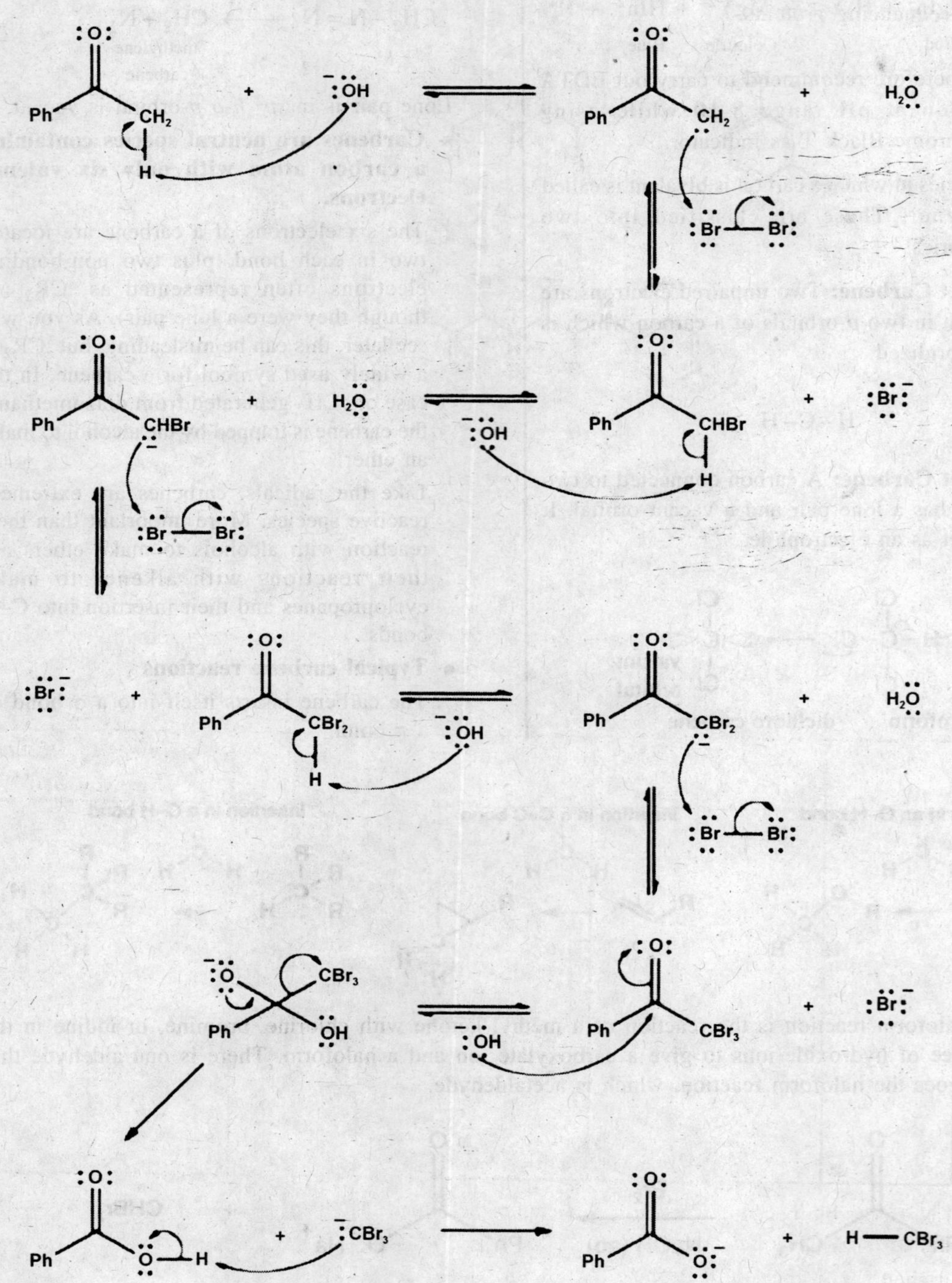

38. 1-Fluoro-2,4-dinitrobenzene (commonly called Sanger's reagent, dinitrofluorobenzene, DNFB or FDNB) is a chemical that reacts with the N-terminal amino acid of polypeptides. This can be helpful for sequencing proteins.

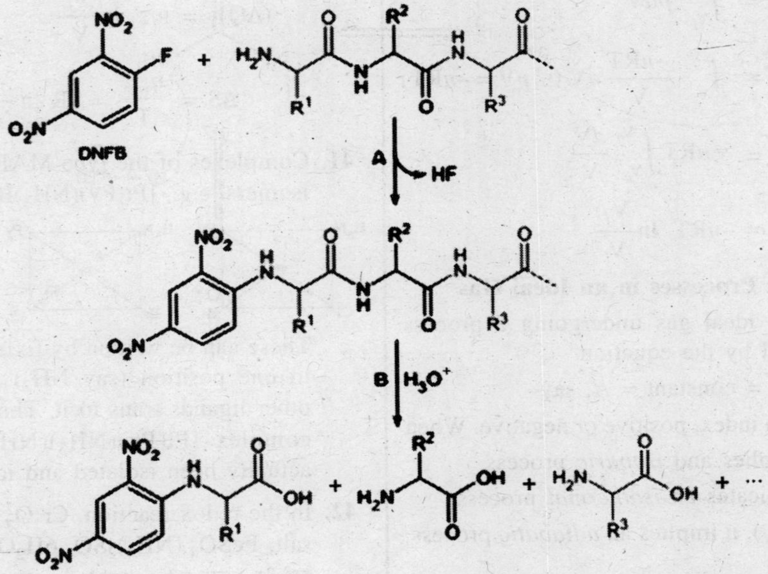

Sanger's method of peptide end-group analysis: (A) derivatization of N-terminal end with Sanger's reagent (DNFB), (B) total acid hydrolysis of the dinitrophenyl peptide.

39. Table: *Allowed Combinations of the n, ℓ and m_ℓ Quantum Numbers*

Shell, n	*Subshell ℓ (label)*	*Orbital, m_ℓ*	*Number of Orbitals in Subshell*
1	0 (1*s*)	0	1
2	0 (2*s*)	0	1
	1 (2*p*)	−1, 0, +1	3
3	0 (3*s*)	0	1
	1 (3*p*)	−1, 0, +1	3
	2 (3*d*)	−2, −1, 0, +1, +2	5
4	0 (4*s*)	0	1
	1 (4*p*)	−1, 0, +1	3
	2 (4*d*)	−2, −1, 0, +1, +2	5
	3 (4*f*)	−3, −2, −1, 0, +1, +2, +3	7

(*a*) Not possible because when $n = 3$, l cannot be equal to 3. The value of l cannot be numerically equal to the value of n.

(*b*) when $l = 0$, then $m_l = 0$ only.

40. Isothermal expansion or compression of an ideal gas, the initial volume V_i changing finally to V_f. The work

$$W_{iso} = \int_{V_i}^{V_f} pdV$$

$$= \int_{V_i}^{V_f} \frac{-nRT}{V} dV \; (\because pV = -nRT)$$

$$= -nRT \int_{V_i}^{V_f} \frac{dV}{V}$$

$$= -nRT \; \ln \frac{V_f}{V_i}$$

Quasi-static Processes in an Ideal Gas

Consider an ideal gas undergoing a process characterised by the equation

$$pV^n = \text{constant} = A, \text{ say}$$

where n is an index, positive or negative. When $n = 0$, it implies and *isobaric* process

$n = 1$, it indicates an *isothermal* process

$n = \gamma(=C_P/C_V)$, it implies an *adiabatic* process, and

$n \to \infty$, it means that the process is *isochoric.*

To obtain an *expression for the heat absorbed* in such a process (A = const.), by an ideal gas, we write

$$\bar{d}Q = C_V dT + pdV$$

$$\therefore \; (\Delta Q)_A = \int_i^f C_V dT + \int_i^f \frac{A}{V^n} dV;$$

i = initial state, f = final state

$$= C_V(T_f - T_i) + \frac{p_i V_i - p_f V_f}{n-1} (n \neq 1)$$

$$= C_V(T_f - T_i) + R\frac{T_i - T_f}{n-1} V \quad ...(1)$$

$$= C_V(T_f - T_i) + PT_i \ln \frac{V_f}{V_i} \quad (n \neq 1)$$

...(2)

For an *isobaric process,* we get from equ. (1)

$$(\Delta Q)_p = C_V(T_f - T_i) + R\frac{T_i - T_f}{-1} \quad (\because n = 0)$$

$$= (T_f - T_i)(C_V + C_p - C_V)$$

$$= c_p(T_f - T_i) \quad ...(3)$$

For an isothermal process $T_i = T_f$. So, from equ. (2)

$$(\Delta Q)_T = RT_i \ln \frac{V_f}{V_i} \quad ...(4)$$

$$\Delta S = \frac{q_{rev}}{T} = nR \ln \frac{V_f}{V_i}.$$

41. Complexes of the type MABCD exhibit three isomers. *e.g.*, [Pt(Py)(NH_3)BrCl] can exist as:

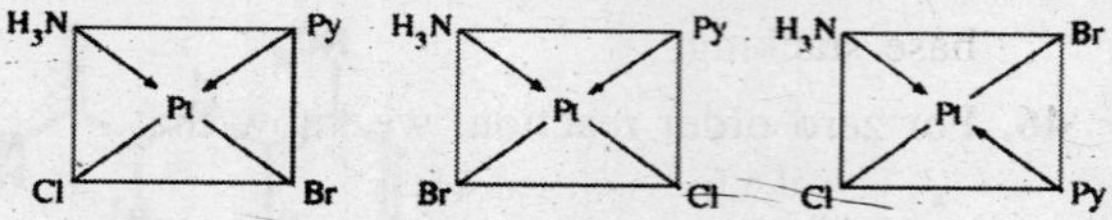

These can be written by fixing any one ligand to one position (say NH_3) and then placing other ligands trans to it. Three isomers of the complex [Pt(Py)(NH_3)(NH_2OH)NO_2] have actually been isolated and identified.

42. In the redox reaction, $Cr_2O_7^{2-}$ oxidises Mohr's salt, $FeSO_4.(NH_4)_2SO_4.6H_2O$

$$6Fe^{2+} + Cr_2O_7^{2-} + 14H^+ \to 6Fe^{3+} + 2Cr^{3+} + 7H_2O$$

Mohr's salt [$FeSO_4.(NH_4)_2SO_4.6H_2O$] and dichromate reacts in 6 : 1 molar ratio, or one more of $Cr_2O_7^{2-}$ will require six moles of Fe^{2+} ions.

Number of mole of $Cr_2O_7^{2-}$ = 20 × 0.1
= 2 mole

Number of mole of Mohr's salt = 6 × 2
= 12 mole

So, Volume of Mohr's salt = 12/0.3 = 40 mL.

45. In molecular biology and genetics, GC-content (or guanine-cytosine content) is the percentage of nitrogenous bases on a DNA or RNA molecule that are either guanine or cytosine.

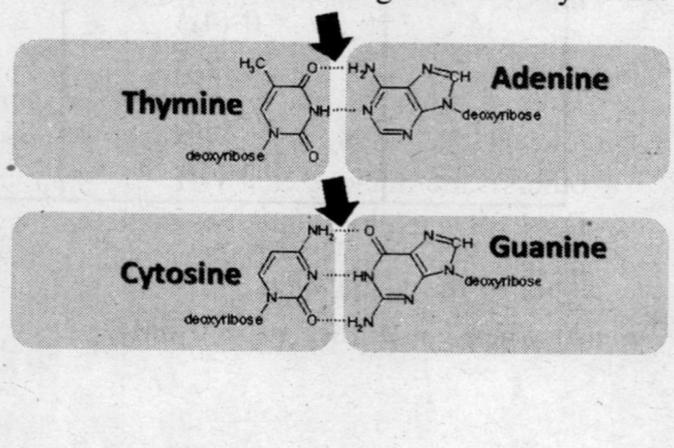

The GC pair is bound by three hydrogen bonds, while AT and AU pairs are bound by two hydrogen bonds. To emphasize this difference in the number of hydrogen bonds, the base pairings can be represented as respectively G ≡ C versus A = T and A = U. DNA with low GC-content is less stable than DNA with high GC-content; however, the hydrogen bonds themselves do not have a particularly significant impact on stabilization, the stabilization is due mainly to interactions of base stacking.

46. For zero order reaction, we know that

$$[A] = -kt + [A]_0$$

$$k = \frac{[A]_0 - [A]}{t}$$

Here, or t = 30 min, A = 0.5 $[A]_0$

So, $\{[A]_0 - 0.5[A]_0\}/2 = 0.8\ [A]_0/t$

$\Rightarrow$ T = 48 min.

47. For following reaction

$$CO_{(g)} + \frac{1}{2}\ O_{2(g)} \rightarrow CO_{2(g)}$$

ΔG° can be calculated as follows:

$$\Delta G^\circ = \Delta G_p^\circ - \Delta G_R^\circ$$
$$= [\Delta G^\circ CO_2 - (\Delta G^\circ CO + 1/2\Delta G^\circ O_2)]$$
$$= -394.4 - (-137.2 + 1/2*0)$$
$$= -257.2 \text{ kj mol}^{-1}$$

Since,

$$\Delta G^\circ = \Delta H^\circ - T\Delta S^\circ$$

or $-257.2 = \Delta H - 300(0.094)$

$\therefore$ $\Delta H^\circ = -285.4$ kj/mol.

48. In the quantum approach, the spin quantum number I defines the number of stationary spin states that the nucleus may occupy in an imposed magnetic field as follows:

#levels = (2**I** + 1) ...(1)

Thus, for I = 1/2 nuclei (this group includes ^1H, ^3H, ^{13}C, ^{15}N, ^{19}F, ^{29}Si and ^{31}P, among others), the nucleus can have two spin states. For I = 1 nuclei (^2H and ^{14}N, for example), the nucleus has three possible spin states, while I = 3/2 nuclei (this includes ^{11}B, ^7Li and ^{23}Na) can have four. Besides the spin quantum number I, each individual spin state also has a quantum number **m** associated with it. Allowed values of **m** are given by:

m = –I, –I + 1, ..., I – 1, I ...(2)

Therefore, the allowable spin states for I = 1/2 nuclei are **m** = –1/2, +1/2, for I = 1 nuclei, m = –1, 0, 1, and for I = 3/2 nuclei, **m** = –3/2, –1/2, 1/2, and 3/2, and so on.

49. In classical statistical mechanics, the equipartition theorem relates the temperature of a system to its average energies. The equipartition theorem is also known as the law of equipartition, equipartition of energy, or simply equipartition. The original idea of equipartition was that, in thermal equilibrium, energy is shared equally among all of its various forms; for example, the average kinetic energy per degree of freedom in translational motion of a molecule should equal that in rotational motion.

At room temperature, the internal energy is due to only the five degrees of freedom associated with the three translational and two rotational degrees of freedom,

$$E_{internal} = N\frac{5}{2}kT.$$

So $E = 1\times\frac{5}{2}\times 8.3 = 20.75\ JK^{-1}mol^{-1}.$

50. Density at T K & 1 atm. is calculated as = (Pressure * Molecular Weight) / (R * Temp.) [where R = .08206 atm.liter/mol/°K]

Density of Oxygen = (1 * 32) / (.08206 * 300) = 1.300 g/l.

51. Interhalogen Compounds:

- Halogens react with each other to form interhalogen compounds of four kinds, AX, AX_3, AX_5 and AX_7 where A is less electronegative halogen and X is more electronegative one.
- Halogen having large atomic size (A) always serves as a central atom and is always written first in the formula. The highest interhalogen compound is IF_7, *i.e.*, the largest halogen (I) attached to smallest (F).

• The structural aspects of interhalogen compounds are summarised in the following table:

Molecule	Type hybridi-zation	No. of lone pairs of electrons on 'A'	No. of bond pairs of electrons on 'A'	Electron pair geometry
AX	—	3	1	Linear
AX_3	sp^3d	2	3	Trigonal bipyramidal (T shape)
AX_5	sp^3d^2	1	5	Square pyramidal
AX_7	sp^3d^3	0	7	Pentagonal bipyramidal

52. From radioactive decay equation, $N = N_0(e^{at})$

$$N/N_0 = e^{(at)}$$

Taking log both sides, $\ln(N/N_0) = at$

$$\ln(1/4)/29.8 = a$$

$$A = 0.0464 \text{ hour}^{-1}$$

Note: Negative sign avoided as the concentration decreases with time.

53. The Octahedral Site Preference Energy (OSPE) is defined as the difference of CFSE energies for a non-octahedral complex and the octahedral complex. For comparing the preference of forming an octahedral ligand field vs. a tetrahedral ligand field, the OSPE is thus:

$$OSPE = CFSE_{(oct)} - CFSE_{(tet)}$$

The OSPE quantifies the preference of a complex to exhibit an octahedral geometry vs. a tetrahedral geometry.

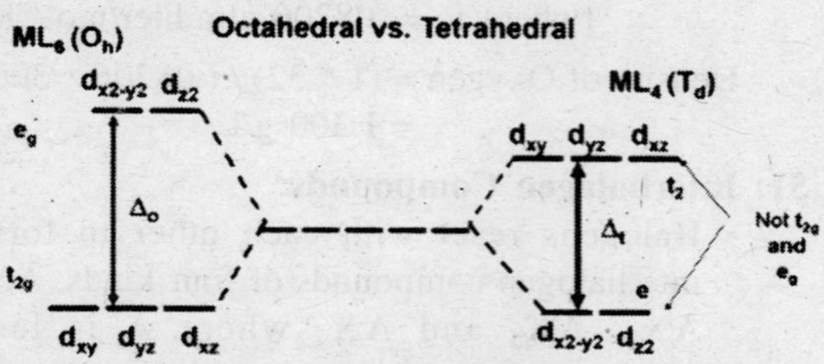

Note: The conversion between Δ_o and Δ_t used for these calculation is:

$$\Delta_t \approx \frac{4}{9}\Delta_o$$

$$= 4/9 \ (1/7680)$$

$$= 520.8 \text{ nm.}$$

55. To name the enantiomers of a compound unambiguously, their names must include the "handedness" of the molecule. The method for this is formally known as R/S nomenclature.

Stereocenters are labeled R or S

The "right hand" and "left hand" nomenclature is used to name the enantiomers of a chiral compound. The stereocenters are labeled as R or S.

Consider the first picture: A curved arrow is drawn from the highest priority (1) substituent to the lowest priority (4) substituent. If the arrow points in a counterclockwise direction (left when leaving the 12 O' clock position), the configuration at stereocenter is considered S ("Sinister" → Latin = "left"). If, however, the arrow points clockwise, (Right when leaving the 12 O' clock position) then the stereocenter is labeled R ("Rectus" → Latin = "right"). The R or S is then added as a prefix, in parenthesis, to the name of the enantiomer of interest.

59. The ICE table is:

$$PbI_2(s) \rightleftharpoons Pb^{2+}(aq) + 2I^-(aq)$$

	Pb^{2+}	I^-
Initial concns, M:		0.10
From PbI_2, M:	s	$2s$
Equil concns, M:	s	$(0.10 + 2s)$

The usual K_{sp} relationship must be satisfied.

$$K_{sp} = [Pb^{2+}][I^-]^2$$

$$= (s)(0.10 + 2s)^2$$

$$= 7.1 \times 10^{-9}$$

To simplify the solution to this equation, let's assume that s is much smaller than 0.10 M, so that $0.10 + 2s \approx 0.10$.

$$s(0.10)^2 = 7.1 \times 10^{-9}$$

$$= \frac{7.1 \times 10^{-9}}{(0.10)^2}$$

$$s = 7.1 \times 10^{-7} \text{ M}$$

$$= \text{molar solubility of } PbI_2.$$

Previous Paper (Solved)

IIT–JAM

JOINT ADMISSION TEST FOR M.Sc. (CHEMISTRY), 2017

Section A: Multiple Choice Questions

Q. 1 – Q. 10 carry one mark each.

1. The correct order of the boiling points of the compounds is:

A. $CH_4 > SiH_4 > SnH_4 > GeH_4$
B. $SiH_4 > CH_4 > GeH_4 > SnH_4$
C. $SnH_4 > GeH_4 > CH_4 > SiH_4$
D. $SnH_4 > GeH_4 > SiH_4 > CH_4$

2. In the following Latimer diagram, the species that undergoes disproportionation reaction is:

$$MnO_4^- \xrightarrow{+0.56} MnO_4^{2-} \xrightarrow{+0.27} MnO_4^{3-} \xrightarrow{+0.93}$$

$$MnO_2 \xrightarrow{+0.15} Mn_2O_3 \xrightarrow{-0.25} Mn(OH)_2 \xrightarrow{-1.56} Mn$$

A. MnO_4^{2-} B. MnO_4^{3-}
C. Mn_2O_3 D. $Mn(OH)_2$

3. A yellow precipitate is formed upon addition of aqueous $AgNO_3$ to a solution of:

A. phosphite B. pyrophosphate
C. metaphosphate D. orthophosphate

4. The compounds having C_3-axis of symmetry are:

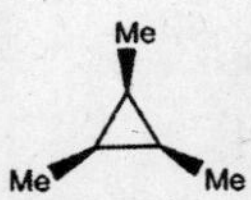
(I)

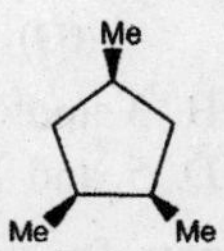
(II)

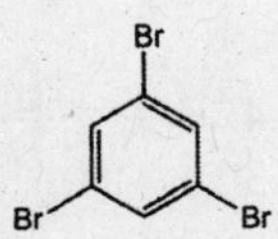
(III)

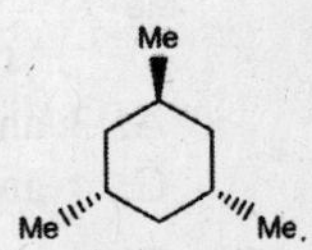
(IV)

A. I, III and IV B. I, II and III
C. I and III D. III and IV

5. The correct order of rate of solvolysis for the following compounds is:

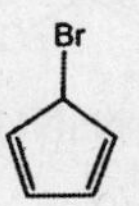
(I)

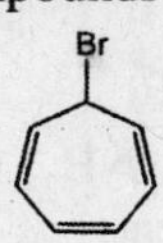
(II)

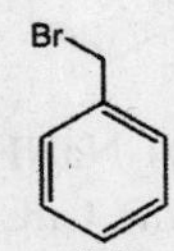
(III)

A. III > II > I B. II > I > III
C. III > I > II D. II > III > I

6. In the following sequence of reactions, the overall yield (%) of O is:

$$L \xrightarrow{92\%\ \text{yield}} M \xrightarrow{78\%\ \text{yield}} N \xrightarrow{85\%\ \text{yield}} O$$

A. 61 B. 85
C. 74 D. 68

7. Catalytic hydrogenation of the following compound produces saturated hydrocarbon(s). The number of stereoisomer(s) formed is:

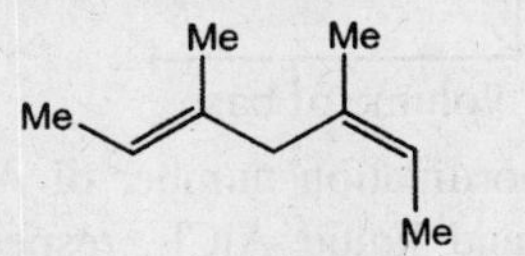

A. 1 B. 2
C. 3 D. 4

8. The number of normal modes of vibration in naphthalene is:

A. 55 B. 54
C. 48 D. 49

9. The number of degrees of freedom of liquid water in equilibrium with ice is:

A. 0 B. 1
C. 2 D. 3

10. A straight line having a slope of $\frac{-\Delta U^0}{R}$ is obtained in a plot between:

A. ln K_p versus T B. ln K_c versus T
C. ln K_p versus 1/T D. ln K_c versus 1/T

Q. 11 – Q. 30 carry two marks each.

11. In a typical conductometric titration of a strong acid with a weak base, the curve resembles:

A. 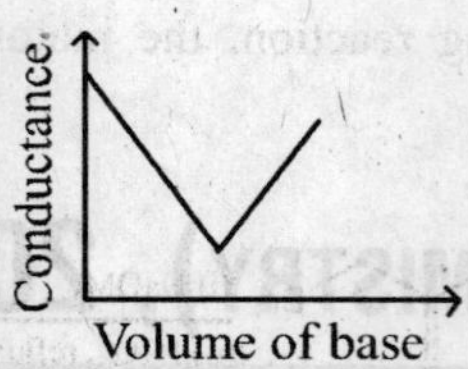

B. 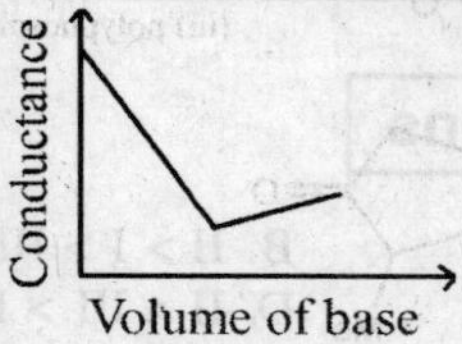

C. 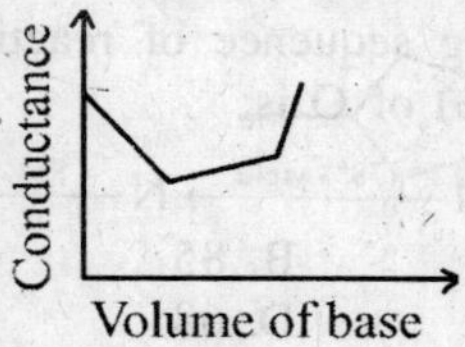

D. 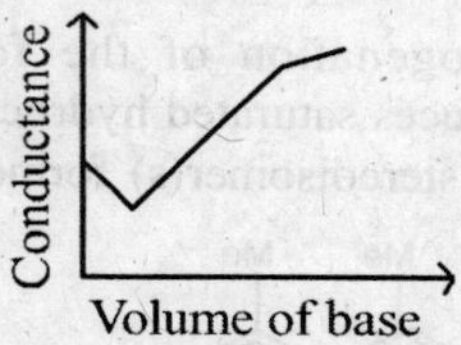

12. The coordination number of Al in crystalline $AlCl_3$ and liquid $AlCl_3$, respectively, is:

A. 4 and 4　　B. 6 and 6
C. 6 and 4　　D. 3 and 6

13. The homogeneous catalyst used in water-gas shift reaction is:

A. $PdCl_2$　　B. Cr_2O_3
C. $[RhCl(PPh_3)_3]$　　D. $[RuCl_2(bipyridyl)_2]$

14. Nitrosyl ligand binds to *d*-metal atoms in linear and bent fashion and behaves, respectively, as:

A. NO^+ and NO^+　　B. NO^+ and NO^-
C. NO^- and NO^-　　D. NO^- and NO^+

15. The metal ion (M^{2+}) in the following reaction is:

$$M^{2+} + S^{2-} \longrightarrow \text{Black precipitate} \xrightarrow{\text{hot conc. HNO}_3} \text{White precipitate}$$

A. Mn^{2+}　　B. Fe^{2+}
C. Cd^{2+}　　D. Cu^{2+}

16. The correct order of wavelength of absorption (λ_{max}) of the Cr-complexes is (en = ethylenediamine)

A. $[CrF_6]^{3-} > [Cr(H_2O)_6]^{3+} > [Cr(en)_3]^{3+} > [Cr(CN)_6]^{3-}$
B. $[Cr(H_2O)_6]^{3+} > [CrF_6]^{3-} > [Cr(en)_3]^{3+} > [Cr(CN)_6]^{3-}$
C. $[Cr(CN)_6]^{3-} > [Cr(en)_3]^{3+} > [Cr(H_2O)_6]^{3+} > [CrF_6]^{3-}$
D. $[Cr(en)_3]^{3+} > [Cr(CN)_6]^{3-} > [Cr(H_2O)_6]^{3+} > [CrF_6]^{3-}$

17. The correct order of enthalpy of hydration for the transition metal ions is:

A. $Cr^{2+} > Mn^{2+} > Co^{2+} > Ni^{2+}$
B. $Ni^{2+} > Co^{2+} > Mn^{2+} > Cr^{2+}$
C. $Ni^{2+} > Co^{2+} > Cr^{2+} > Mn^{2+}$
D. $Cr^{2+} > Mn^{2+} > Ni^{2+} > Co^{2+}$

18. Among the following compounds, the pair of enantiomers is:

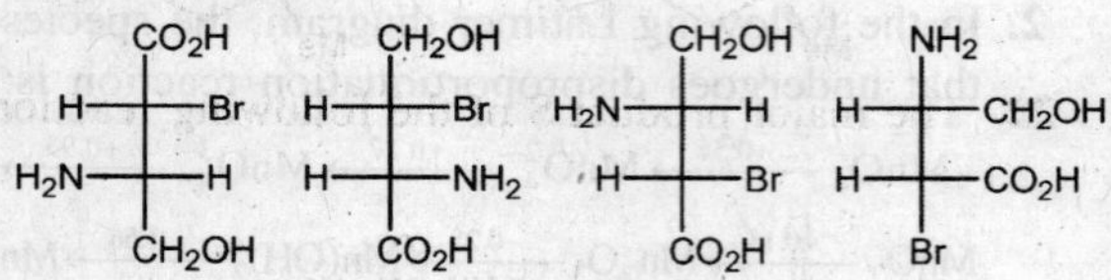

(I)　(II)　(III)　(IV)

A. I and IV　　B. I and III
C. II and III　　D. III and IV

19. The number of proton NMR signals for the compounds **P** and **Q**, respectively, is:

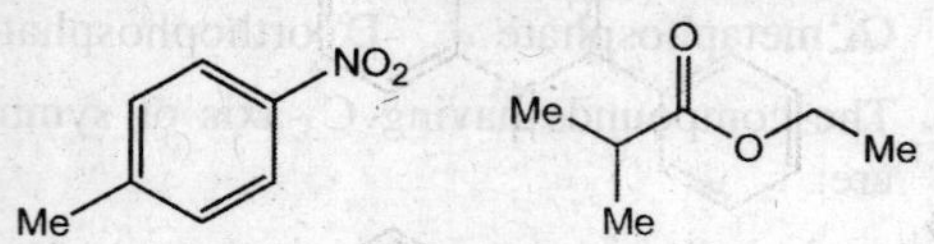

(P)　(Q)

A. 3 and 4　　B. 3 and 5
C. 4 and 3　　D. 5 and 4

20. The correct set of reagents for the following conversion is:

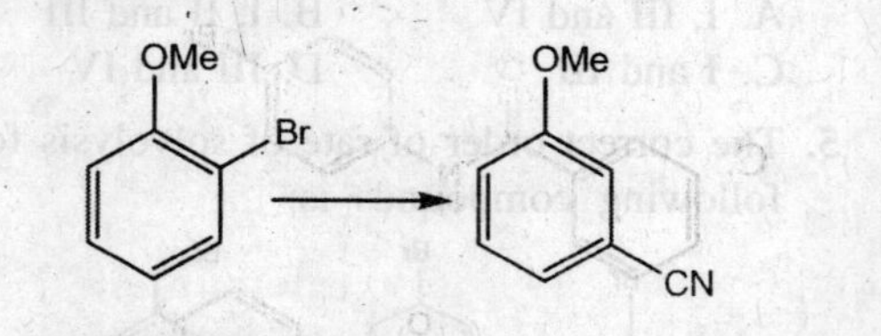

A. (*i*) $NaNH_2$/liq. NH_3; (*ii*) $NaNO_2$/dil. HCl; (*iii*) CuCN, heat
B. (*i*) HNO_3/H_2SO_4; (*ii*) Zn/HCl; (*iii*) $NaNO_2$/dil. HCl; (*iv*) CuCN, heat

C. (*i*) Mg/ether, H_3O^+; (*ii*) $(EtO)_2CO$; (*iii*) NH_4OH; (*iv*) PCl_5

D. (*i*) Mg/ether, H_3O^+; (*ii*) HNO_3/H_2SO_4; (*iii*) $NaNO_2$/dil. HCl; (*iv*) CuCN, heat

21. The product R in the following reaction is:

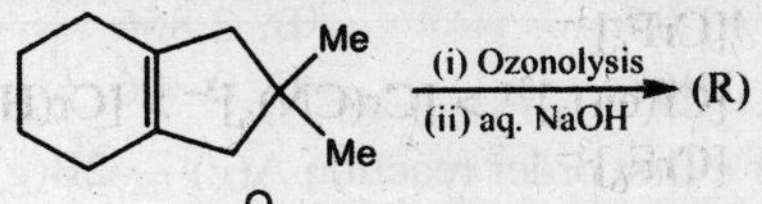

A.

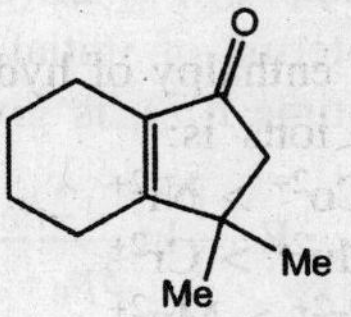

B.

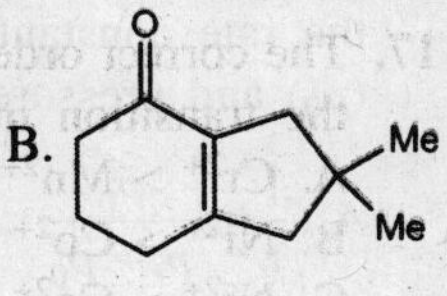

C.

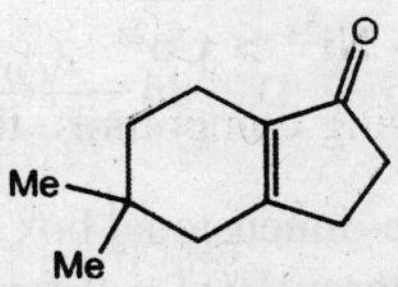

D.

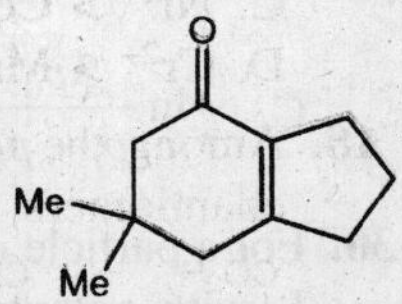

22. The major product S of the following reaction is:

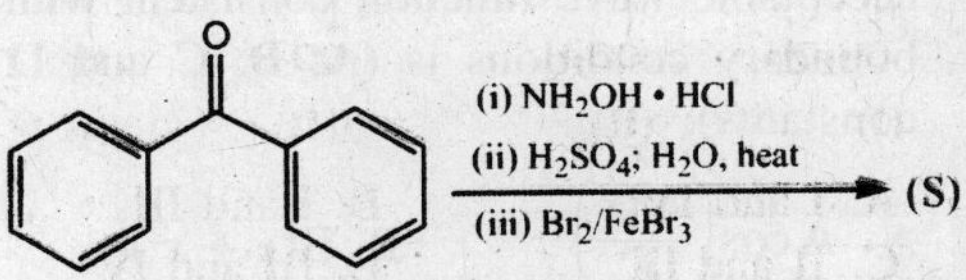

A.

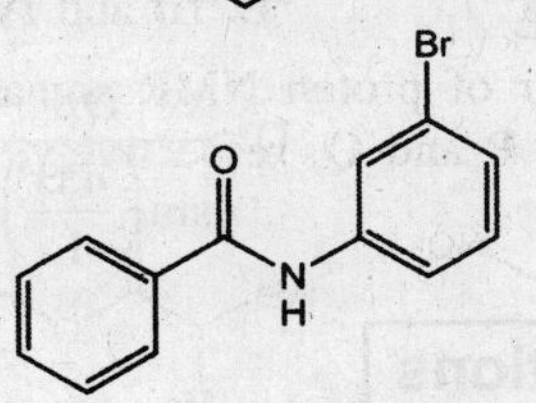

B.

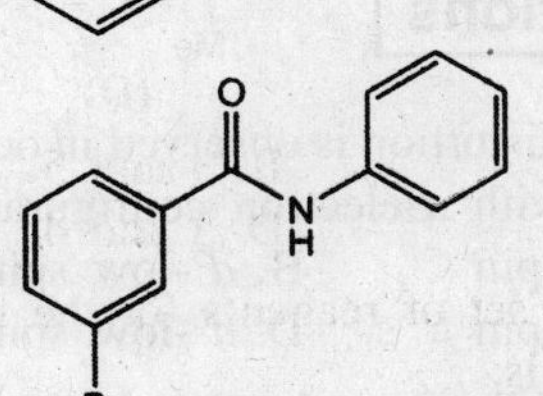

C.

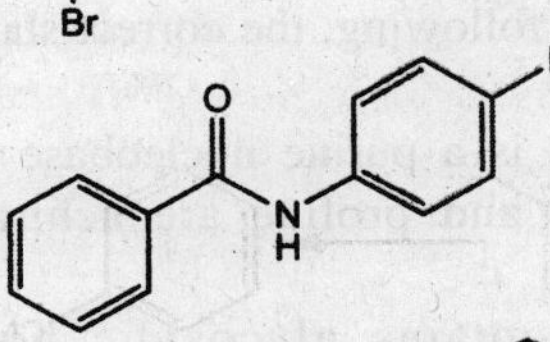

D.

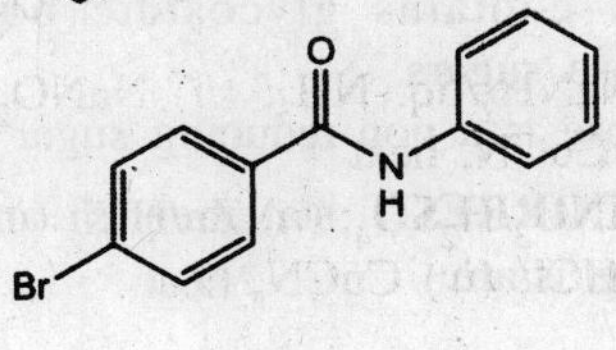

23. In the following reaction, the major product T is:

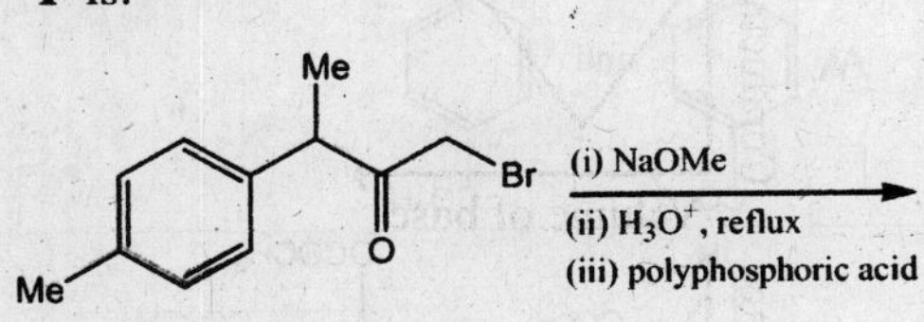

A.

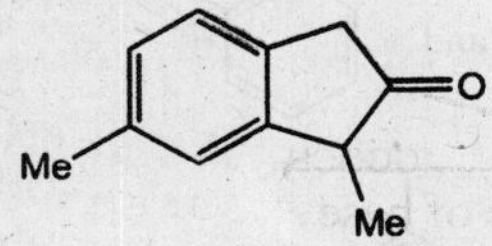

B.

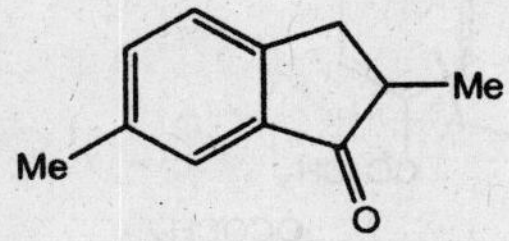

C.

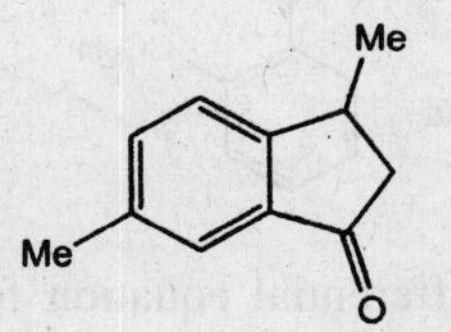

D.

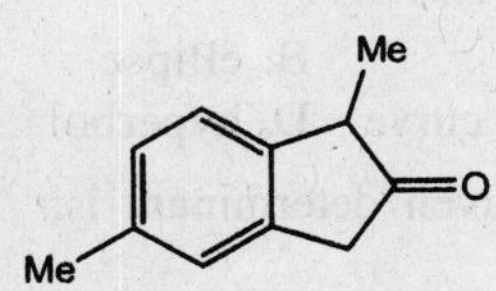

24. The following conversion is carried out using:

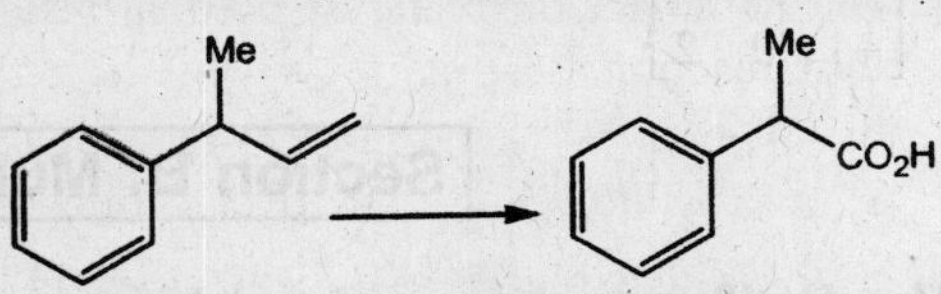

A. hydroboration-oxidation followed by Jones oxidation

B. Wacker oxidation followed by haloform reaction

C. oxymercuration-demercuration followed by Jones oxidation

D. ozonolysis followed by haloform reaction

25. In the following reactions, the major products E and F, respectively, are:

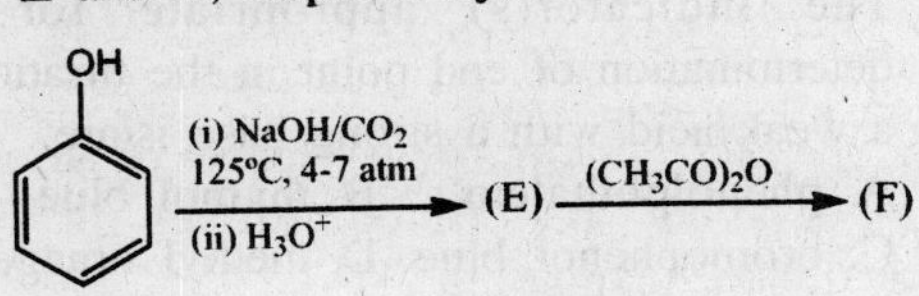

A. 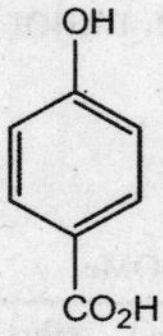 and 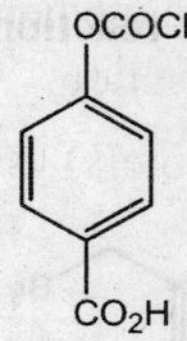

B. 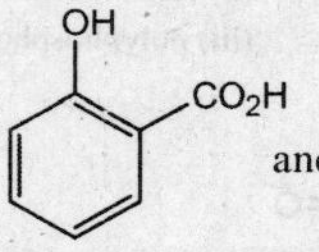 and 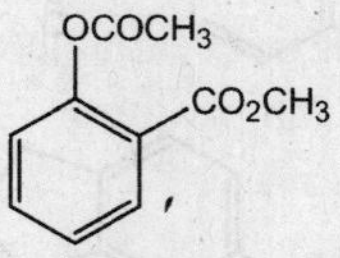

C. 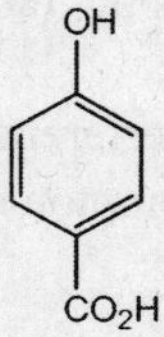 and 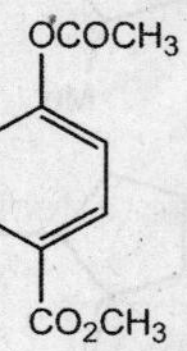

D. 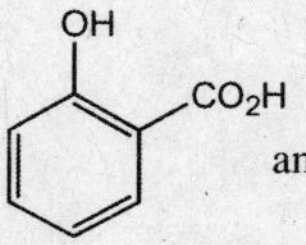 and 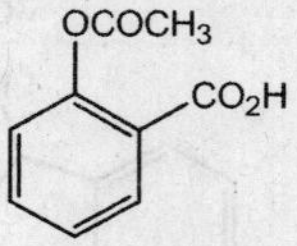

26. $\frac{dy}{dx} = -\frac{y}{x}$ is a differential equation for a/an:

A. circle B. ellipse
C. bell-shaped curve D. hyperbola

27. Value of the given determinant is:

$$\begin{bmatrix} 1 & 3 & 0 \\ 2 & 6 & 4 \\ -1 & 0 & 2 \end{bmatrix}$$

A. −12 B. 0
C. 6 D. 12

28. Ionisation energy of hydrogen atom in ground state is 13.6 eV. The energy released (in eV) for third member of Balmer series is:

A. 13.056 B. 2.856
C. 0.967 D. 0.306

29. For a first order reaction $A(g) \rightarrow 2B(g) + C(g)$, the rate constant in terms of initial pressure (p_0) and pressure at time $t(p_t)$, is given by:

A. $\frac{1}{t}\ln\frac{p_0}{p_t - p_0}$ B. $\frac{1}{t}\ln\frac{2p_0}{3p_0 - p_t}$

C. $\frac{1}{t}\ln\frac{3p_0}{p_t - p_0}$ D. $\frac{1}{t}\ln\frac{3p_0}{3p_t - p_0}$

30. For a particle in one-dimensional box of length L with potential energy $V(x) = 0$ for $L > x > 0$ and $V(x) = \infty$ for $x \geq L$ and $x \leq 0$, an acceptable wave function consistent with the boundary conditions is (A, B, C and D are constants):

A. $A\cos\left(\frac{n\pi x}{L}\right)$ B. $B(x + x^2)$

C. $Cx^3(x - L)$ D. $\frac{D}{\sin\left(\frac{n\pi x}{L}\right)}$

Section B: Multiple Select Questions

Q. 31 – Q. 40 carry two marks each.

31. The "heme" containing protein(s) is/are:

A. cytochrome C B. hemocyanin
C. hemerythrin D. myoglobin

32. Among the following, the species having See-saw shape is/are:

A. SF_4 B. XeF_4
C. ClF_4^+ D. ClF_4^-

33. The indicator(s) appropriate for the determination of end point in the titration of a weak acid with a strong base is/are:

A. phenolphthalein B. thymol blue
C. bromophenol blue D. methyl orange

34. Jahn-Teller distortion is observed in octahedral complexes with *d*-electron configuration of:

A. d^5-high spin B. d^5-low spin
C. d^6-high spin D. d^6-low spin

35. Among the following, the correct statement(s) is/are:

A. Guanine is a purine nucleobase
B. Glycine and proline are achiral amino acids
C. DNA contains glycosidic bonds and pentose sugars
D. Sucrose is a non-reducing sugar

36. The **INCORRECT** statement(s) among the following is/are:

A. $[4\pi + 2\pi]$ cycloaddition reactions are carried out in presence of light

B. $[2\pi + 2\pi]$ cycloaddition reaction between a keto group and an alkene is photo chemically allowed

C. $[4\pi + 2\pi]$ cycloaddition reactions are thermally allowed

D. Transoid dienes undergo Diels-Alder reactions

37. The following conversion is an example of:

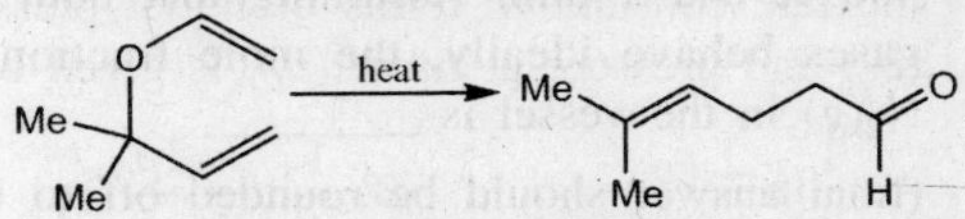

A. oxy-cope rearrangement

B. sigmatropic rearrangement

C. Claisen rearrangement

D. pericyclic reaction

38. IR active molecule(s) is/are:

A. CO_2 B. CS_2

C. OCS D. N_2

39. Intensive variable(s) is/are:

A. Temperature B. Volume

C. Pressure D. Density

40. Wave nature of electromagnetic radiation is observed in:

A. diffraction B. interference

C. photoelectric effect D. Compton scattering

Section C: Numerical Answer Type

Q. 41 – Q. 50 carry one mark each.

41. The number of isomeric structures of di-substituted borazine ($B_3N_3H_4X_2$) is ______

42. The number of S–S bond(s) in tetrathionate ion is ______

43. The number of unpaired electron(s) in K_2NiF_6 is ______

44. The number of reducing sugars among the following is ______

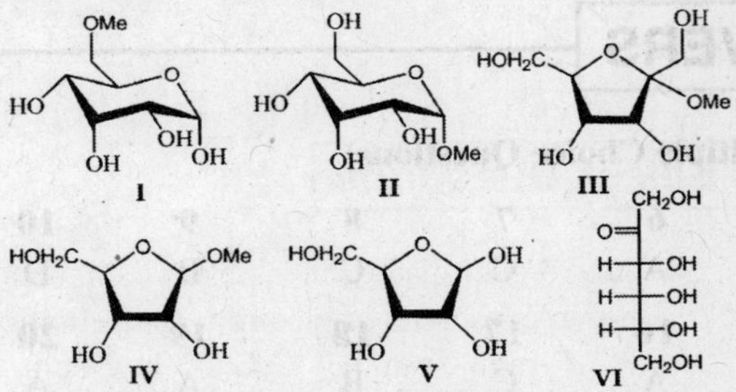

45. The maximum number of dipeptides that could be obtained by reaction of phenylalanine with leucine is ______

46. Among the following, the number of aromatic compound(s) is______

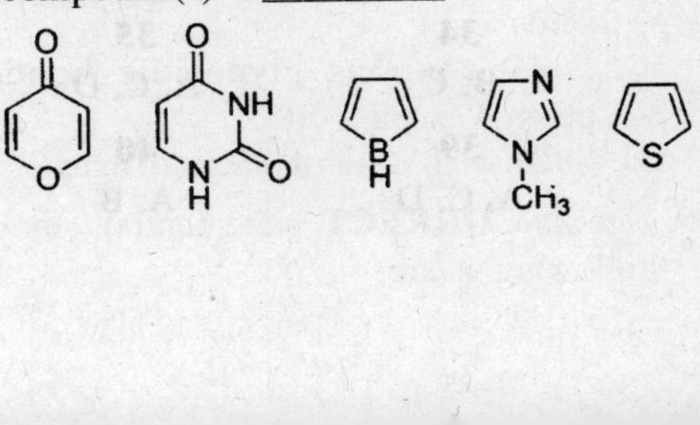

47. At an operating frequency of 350 MHz, the shift (in Hz) of resonance from TMS (tetramethylsilane) of a proton with chemical shift of 2 ppm is ______

48. At 298 K and 1 atm, the molar enthalpies of combustion of cyclopropane and propene are -2091 kJ mol^{-1} and -2058 kJ mol^{-1}, respectively. The enthalpy change (in kJ mol^{-1}) for the conversion of one mole of propene to one mole of cyclopropane is ______

49. For a cell reaction, $Pb(s) + Hg_2Cl_2(s) \rightarrow PbCl_2(s) + 2Hg(l)$, $\left(\frac{\partial E^0}{\partial T}\right)_p$ is 1.45×10^{-4} VK^{-1}. The entropy change (in J mol^{-1} K^{-1}) for the reaction is ______

[Given: 1 F = 96500 C mol^{-1}]

50. For a reaction $2A + B \rightarrow C + D$, if rate of consumption of A is 0.1 mol $L^{-1}s^{-1}$, the rate of production of C (in mol $L^{-1}s^{-1}$) is ______

Q. 51 – Q. 60 carry two marks each.

51. The standard reduction potentials of Ce^{4+}/Ce^{3+} and Fe^{3+}/Fe^{2+} are 1.44 and 0.77 V, respectively. The $\log_{10}K$ (K is the equilibrium constant) value for the following reaction is ______ (final answer should be rounded off to two decimal places)

$$Ce^{4+} + Fe^{2+} \rightleftharpoons Ce^{3+} + Fe^{3+}$$

[Given: RT/F = 0.0257 V]

52. A radioactive element undergoes 80% radioactive decay in 300 min. The half-life for this species in minutes is ________

53. Silver crystallizes in a face-centered cubic lattice. The lattice parameter of silver (in picometer) is ________

[Given: Avogadro's number = 6.023×10^{23} mol^{-1}, molar mass of silver = 107.87 g mol^{-1} and density of crystal = 10.5 g cm^{-3}]

54. The amount of bromine (atomic wt. = 80) required (in gram) for the estimation of 42.3 g of phenol (molecular wt. = 94 g mol^{-1}) is ________

55. The total number of pair of enantiomers possible with molecular formula $C_5H_{12}O$ is ________

56. In 200 g of water, 0.01 mole of NaCl and 0.02 mole of sucrose are dissolved. Assuming solution to be ideal, the depression in freezing point of water (in °C) will be ________ (final answer should be rounded off to two decimal places)

[Given: K_f (H_2O) = 1.86 K kg mol^{-1}]

57. The adsorption of a gas follows the Langmuir isotherm with K = 1.25 kPa^{-1} at 25°C. The pressure (in Pa) at which surface coverage is 0.2 is ________

58. The separation of 123 planes (in nm) in an orthorhombic cell with a = 0.25 nm, b = 0.5 nm and c = 0.75 nm is ________

(final answer should be rounded off to two decimal places)

59. A vessel contains a mixture of H_2 and N_2 gas. The density of this gas mixture is 0.2 g L^{-1} at 300 K and 1 atm. Assuming that both the gases behave ideally, the mole fraction of $N_2(g)$ in the vessel is ________

(final answer should be rounded off to two decimal places)

[Given: R = 0.082 L atm mol^{-1} K^{-1}, atomic wt. of hydrogen = 1.0 and atomic wt. of nitrogen = 14.0]

60. Consider an isothermal reversible compression of one mole of an ideal gas in which the pressure of the system is increased from 5 atm to 30 atm at 300 K. The entropy change of the surroundings (in J K^{-1}) is ________

(final answer should be rounded off to two decimal places)

[Given: R = 8.314 J mol^{-1} K^{-1}]

ANSWERS

SECTION A: MCQ (Multiple Choice Questions)

1	2	3	4	5	6	7	8	9	10
D	B	D	C	D	A	C	C	B	D
11	**12**	**13**	**14**	**15**	**16**	**17**	**18**	**19**	**20**
B	C	D	B	D	A	C	B	A	A
21	**22**	**23**	**24**	**25**	**26**	**27**	**28**	**29**	**30**
D	C	C	B	D	D	A	B	B	C

SECTION B: MSQ (Multiple Select Questions)

31	32	33	34	35
A, D	A, C	A, B	B, C	A, C, D
36	**37**	**38**	**39**	**40**
A, D	B, C, D	A, B, C	A, C, D	A, B

SECTION C: NAT (Numerical Answer Type Questions)

41	42	43	44	45
4	3	0	3	2 or 4
46	**47**	**48**	**49**	**50**
4	700	33	27.90 to 28.10	0.05
51	**52**	**53**	**54**	**55**
11.30 to 11.38	128 to 130	408 to 409	216	4
56	**57**	**58**	**59**	**60**
0.35 to 0.39	200	0.14 to 0.15	0.10 to 0.12	14.80 to 15.00

EXPLANATORY ANSWERS

SECTION-A

1. More the molecular mass of hydrides, stronger the van der Waal force of attraction. Hence, higher the boiling point. Hence, option (D) is correct

$$SnH_4 > GeH_4 > SiH_4 > CH_4$$

2. For disproportionation to happen the species should get oxidized as well as reduced.

Here, suppose

$$MnO_4^- \xrightarrow[E^{0\,anode}_{red}]{0.56} MnO_4^{2-} \xrightarrow[E^{0\,cathode}_{red}]{0.27} MnO_4^{3-}$$

$$\text{So, } E^0_{cell} = E^{0\,cathode}_{red} - E^{0\,anode}_{red}$$
$$= 0.27 - 0.56$$
$$= -0.29$$

Similarly,

$$MnO_4^{2-} \xrightarrow[E^{0\,anode}_{red}]{0.27} MnO_4^{3-} \xrightarrow[E^{0\,cathode}_{red}]{0.93} MnO_2$$

$$\text{So, } E^0_{cell} = E^{0\,cathode}_{red} - E^{0\,anode}_{red}$$
$$= 0.93 - 0.27$$
$$= 0.66$$

$$E^0_{cell} > 0.$$

So, disproportionation takes place.

3. $3Ag^+ + PO_4^{3-} \longrightarrow Ag_3PO_4\downarrow$

from aq. $AgNO_3$ yellow ppt.

4.

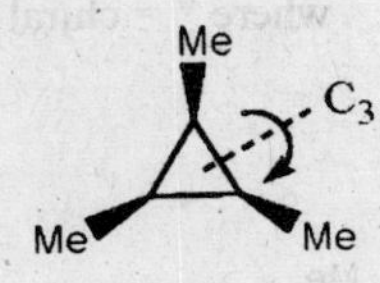

(I)

One C_3 axis, $3C_2$ axis $3\sigma_v$ one σ_h D_{3h} point group

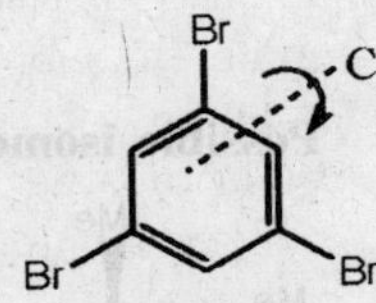

(III)

One C_3 axis, $3C_2$ axis $3\sigma_v$ one σ_h D_{3h} point group

5. Rate of solvolysis $\propto$ stability of intermediate.

Order of stability of carbocation formed will be

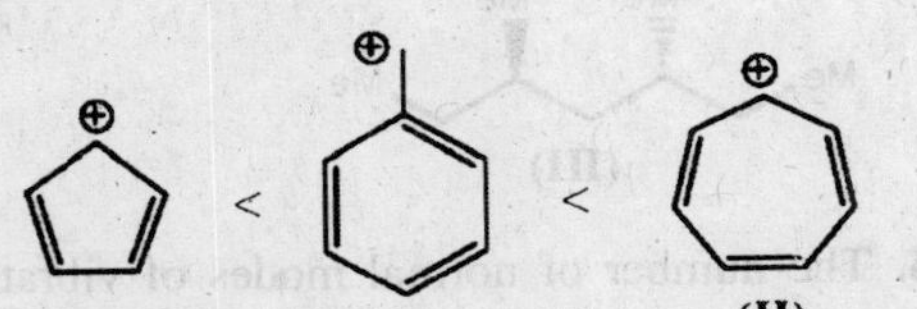

(I) Anti-aromatic < (III) Resonance stabilized carbocation < (II) Aromatic stabilized intermediate

Thus, rate of solvolysis order will be II > III > I

6. $L \xrightarrow{92\%} M \xrightarrow{78\%} N \xrightarrow{85\%} O$

If $L = 100$, $M = \dfrac{92}{100} = 0.92$

$$N = \frac{0.92 \times 78}{100}$$
$$= 71.76 = 0.7176$$

$$O = 0.7176 \times \frac{85}{100}$$
$$= 60.996 = 61\%$$

7. 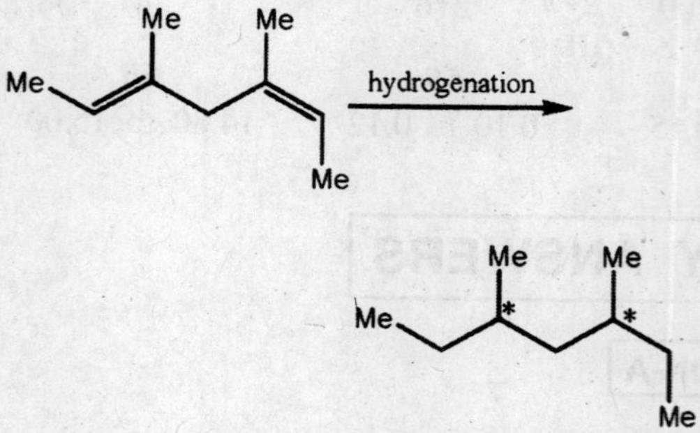

where * = chiral centre

Possible isomers:

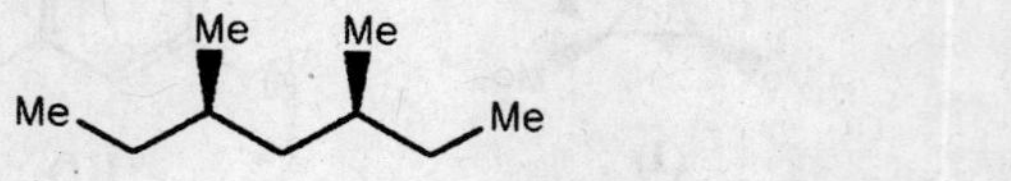

(I)

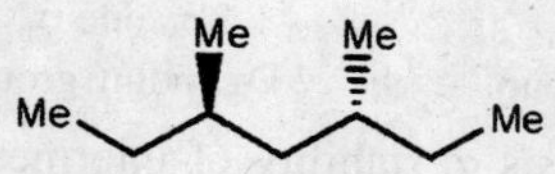

(II)

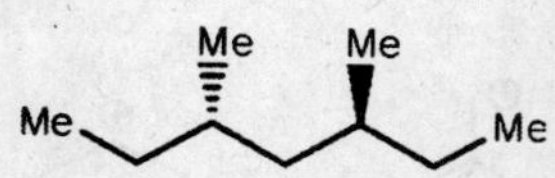

(III)

8. The number of normal modes of vibration in naphthalene is 48

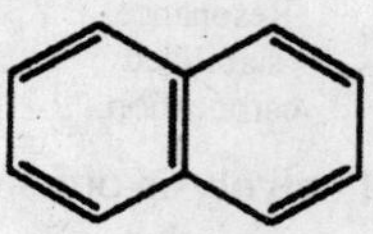

$C_{10}H_8$

For non-linear compounds, the number of normal modes of vibration is given by 3N–6, where N is number of atoms. Thus, per naphthalene, it will be 3 × 18 – 6 = 48.

9. 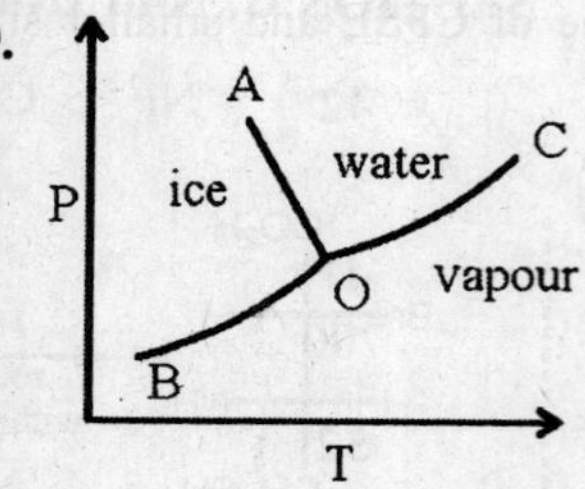

Liquid water (ℓ) $\rightleftharpoons$ ice solid

Number of P = 2

Component = 1

$$F = C - P + 2$$
$$= 1 - 2 + 2 = 1$$

11. Strong acid with weak base have first sharp decreases then almost constant or slight increase.

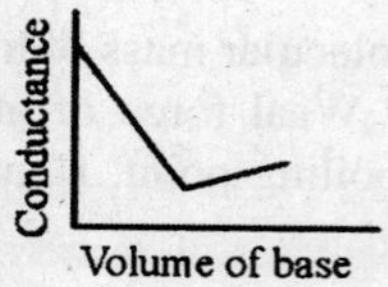

12. In solid state $AlCl_3$ exist as polymer and each Al is hexa co-ordinate. In liquid state $AlCl_3$ exist in dimeric form as Al_2Cl_6.

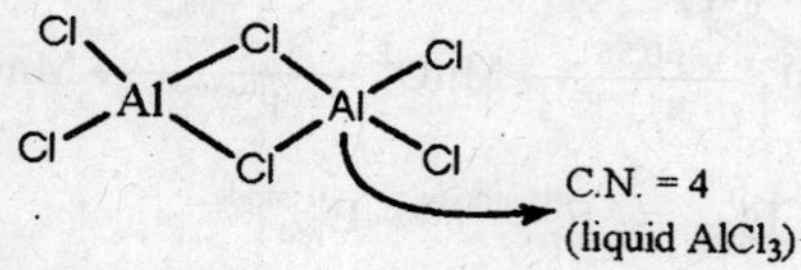

13. Water Gas Shift Reaction:

$$CO + H_2O \longrightarrow CO_2 + H_2$$

Catalyst $[RuCl_2(bpy)_2]$

14. Nitrosyl ligand in linear and bent mode behave as NO^+ and NO^- according to ionic model.

15. $3CuS\downarrow + 8HNO_3 \rightarrow 3Cu(NO_3)_2 + \underset{\text{(white ppt.)}}{3S\downarrow} + 2NO + 4H_2O$

A metal is Cu^{2+}.

16. Stronger the ligand, more the splitting hence more energy gap hence smaller the wavelength of light absorbed.

$$[CrF_6]^{3-} > [Cr(H_2O)_6]^{3+} > [Cr(en)_3]^{3+} > [Cr(CN)_6]^{3-}$$

17. Higher the value of CFSE and smaller size of metal more the hydration energy.

$$Ni^{2+} > Co^{2+} > Cr^{2+} > Mn^{2+}$$

18.

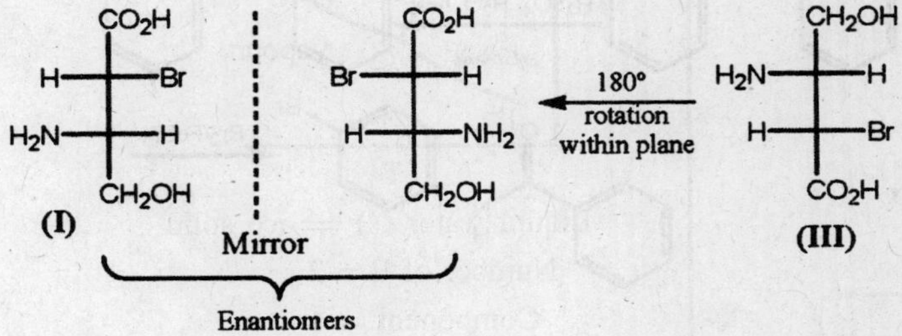

Structure I and III are enantiomer.

19.

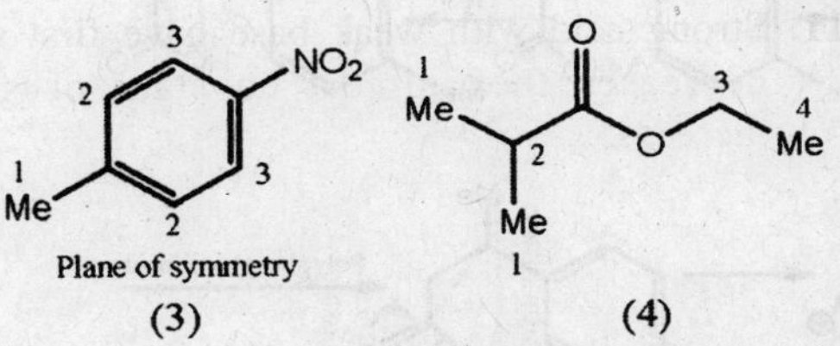

Non-equivalent set of proton = Number of NMR signals.

20.

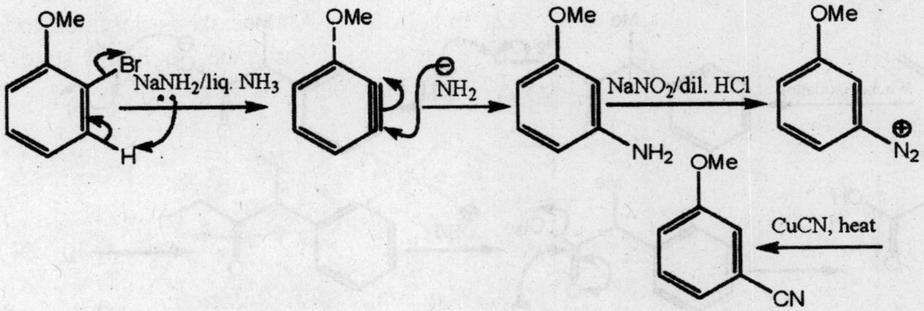

21.

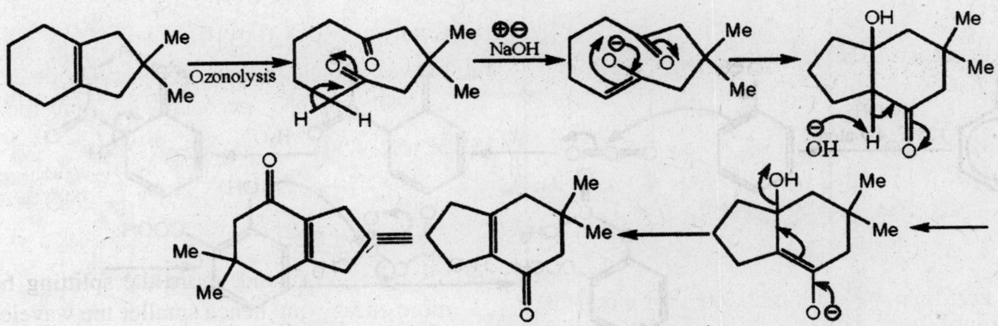

22.

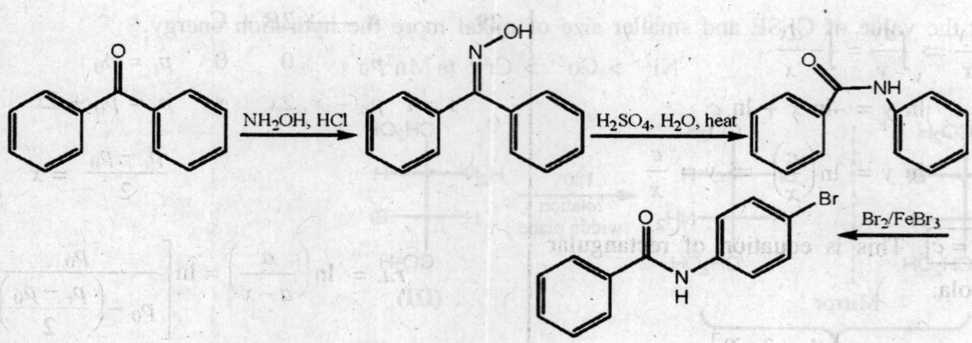
NH2OH, HCl
H2SO4, H2O, heat
Br2/FeBr3

23.

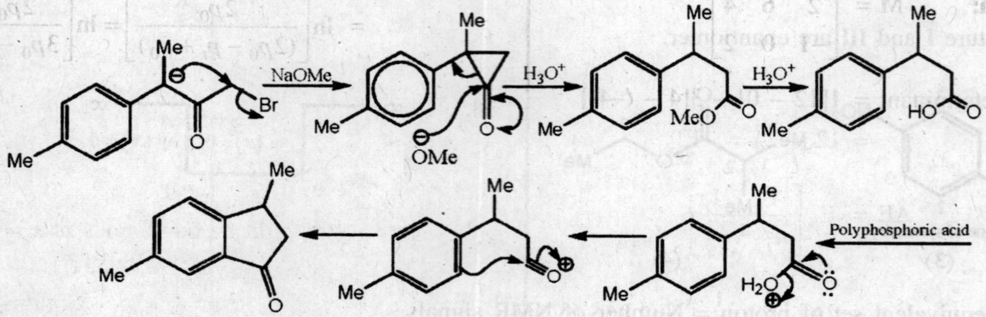
NaOMe
H3O+
H3O+
Polyphosphoric acid

24.

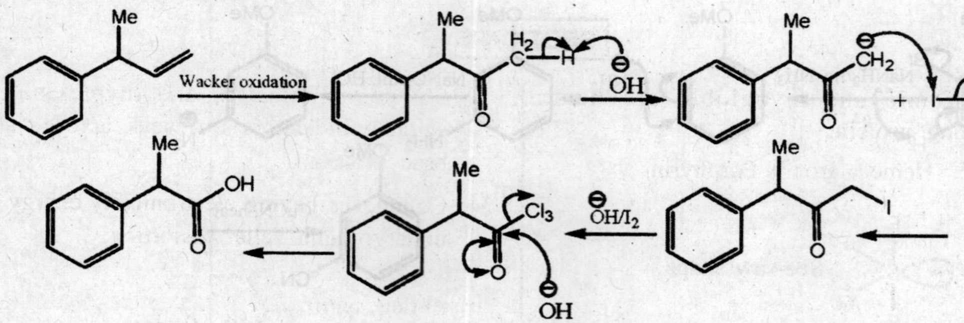
Wacker oxidation
OH
OH/I2

25.

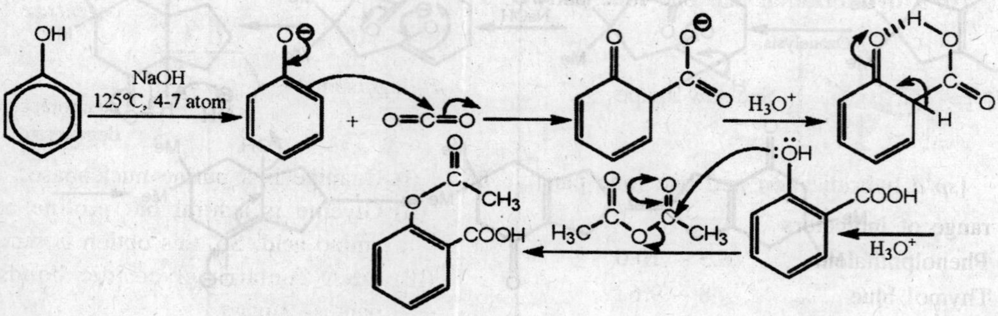
NaOH
125°C, 4-7 atom
H3O+
H3O+

26. $\frac{dy}{dx}=\frac{-y}{x}\Rightarrow\int\frac{dy}{y}=\int-\frac{dx}{x}$

$$\ln y=-\ln x+\ln c$$

$$\ln y=\ln\left(\frac{c}{x}\right)\Rightarrow y=\frac{c}{x}$$

$\Rightarrow$ $\boxed{xy=c}$. This is equation of rectangular hyperbola.

27. Given: $M=\begin{bmatrix}1&3&0\\2&6&4\\-1&0&2\end{bmatrix}$

$$\text{Determinant}=1[12-0]-3[4-(-4)]$$
$$=12-24=-12$$

28. $\Delta E=E_0\left[\frac{1}{n_f^2}-\frac{1}{n_i^2}\right]$

$$=13.6\left[\frac{1}{4}-\frac{1}{25}\right]=2.856\text{ eV}$$

29. $A\longrightarrow 2B+C$

	A	2B	C	
t_0	p_0	0	0	$p_t=p_0$
$t=t$	p_0-x	$2x$	x	$p_t=p_0+2x$

$$\frac{p_t-p_0}{2}=x$$

$$r.t.=\ln\left(\frac{a}{a-x}\right)=\ln\left[\frac{p_0}{p_0-\left(\frac{p_t-p_0}{2}\right)}\right]$$

$$=\ln\left[\frac{2p_0}{(2p_0-p_t+p_0)}\right]=\ln\left[\frac{2p_0}{3p_0-p_t}\right]$$

30. 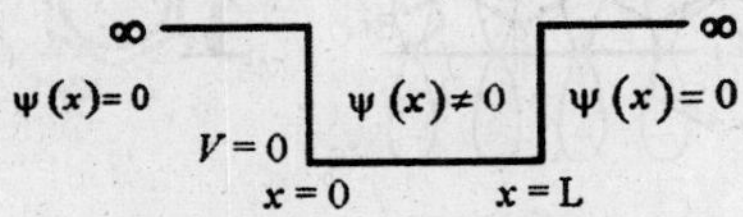

Since, $\psi(x)$ should be continuous at $x=0$, L

So, $\psi(x=0)=0$ and $\psi(x=L)=0$

Only option (C) satisfies both conditions.

SECTION-B

31. Cytochromic and myoglobin are heme containing protein.

Heme = Iron + Porphyrin

32. $SF_4\Rightarrow$ 

See-saw shape

[sp^3d hybridization and one lone pair]

$ClF_4^+\Rightarrow$ 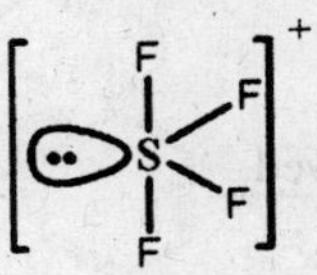

See-saw shape

[sp^3d hybridization and one lone pair]

33. pH range of indicators

(1) Phenolphthalein	8.3 – 10.0
(2) Thymol blue	8 – 9.6
(3) Bromophenol blue	3 – 4.6
(4) Methyl orange	3.2 – 4.4

So, phenolphthalein and thymol blue are suitable indicators for weak acid *vs* strong base titration.

34. Complexes having electronically energy level undergo Jahn-Teller distortion.

d^5-(low spin) 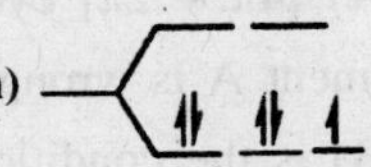 electronically degenerate

d^6-(high spin) 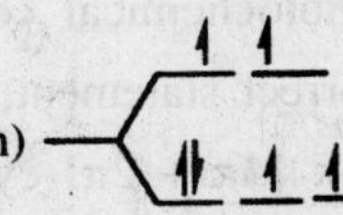 electronically degenerate

35. (I) Guanine is a purine nucleobase.

(II) Glycine is achiral but proline achiral amino acid. So, this option is incorrect.

(III) DNA contains glycosidic bonds and pentose sugars.

(IV) Sucrose is non-reducing sugar.

36. [$4\pi + 2\pi$]

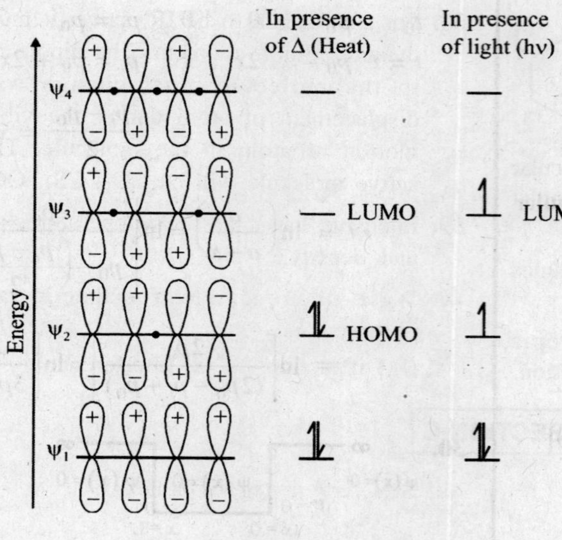

4π system

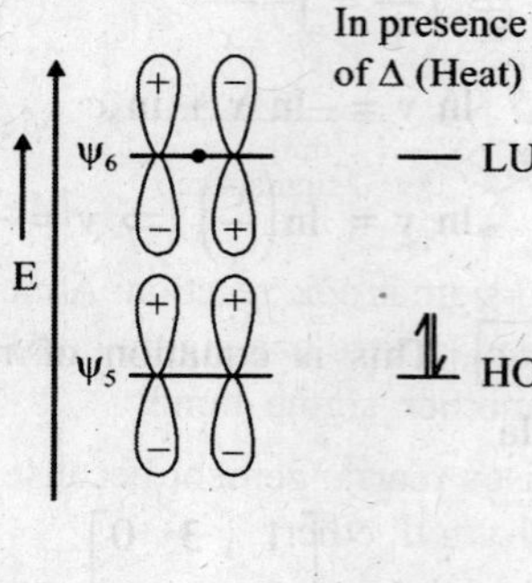

2π system

Since reaction occurs between HOMO & LUMO

$\Rightarrow$ HOMO of 4π & LUMO of 2π

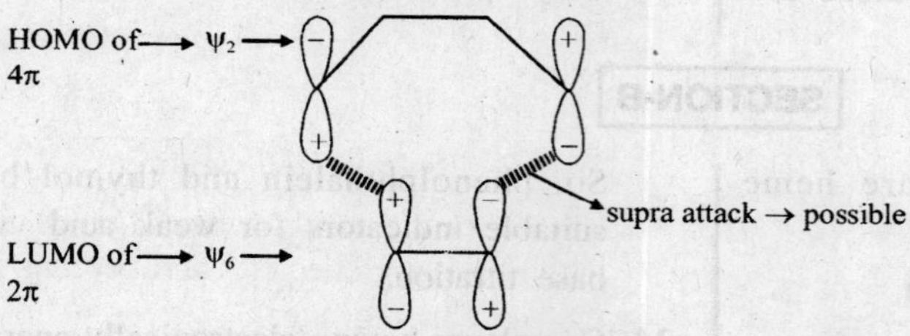

Hence [$4\pi + 2\pi$] is thermally Δ allowed

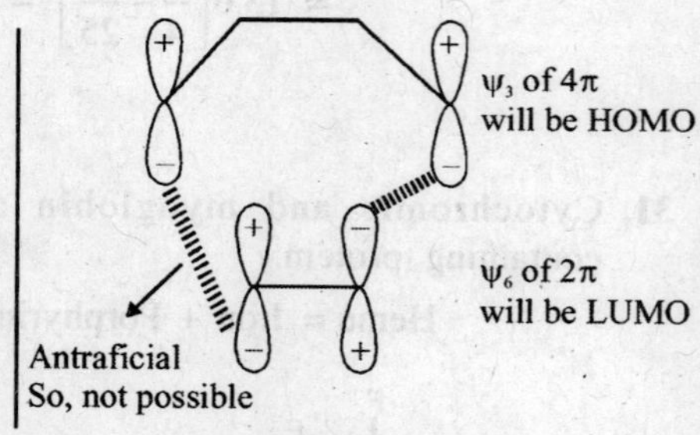

Statement (A) [$4\pi + 2\pi$] cycloaddition is not carried out in photochemically condition.

Hence, statement A is wrong.

Statement (B) is the condition for Patrno Buchi reaction in which a keto group and an alkene is reacted in photochemical condition.

So, it is a correct statement.

Statement (C): [$4\pi + 2\pi$] cycloaddition reactions are thermally allowed.

So it is a correct statement.

Statement (D): Transoid dienes undergo Diels-Alder Reaction.

So it is a incorrect statement.

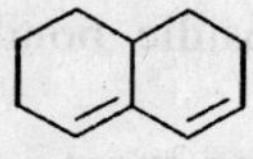

e.g. of transoid dienes

Here, cycloaddition can't possible because overlapping will not be effective.

37. 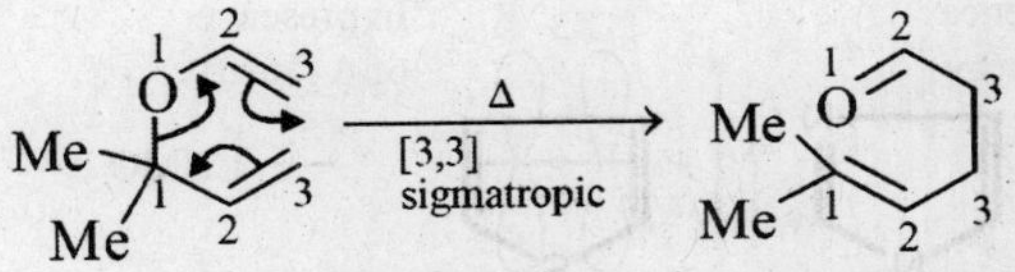

(B) [3,3]-sigmatropic reaction: A intramolecular process where one sigma bond is changed to another sigma bond.

(C) Claisen rearrangement because it includes allyl-vinyl ether.

(D) Pericyclic reaction since sigmatropic reaction is a type of pericyclic reaction.

38. For a molecule to be IR active, it must have dynamic dipole moment. The dipole moment in the molecule must change with the displacement of atom during the vibrational motion of atom in the molecule. Thus, IR active molecule will be CO_2, CS_2, OCS.

39. Intensive variables are temperature, pressure and density.

40. Wave nature of electromagnetic radiation observed in

(1) Diffraction (2) Interference

SECTION-C

41. Isomeric structure of $B_3N_3H_4X_2$

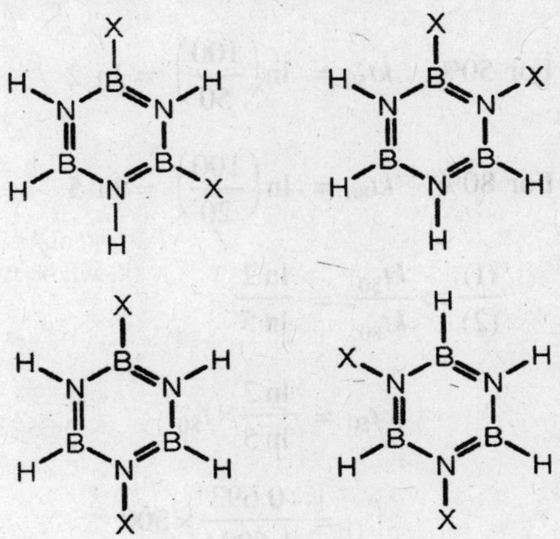

42. Structure of tetrathionate

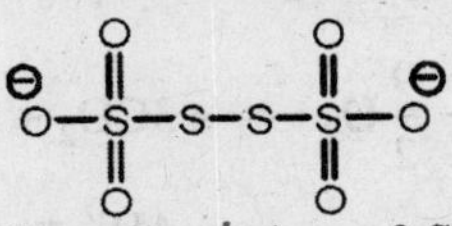

Hence, number of S–S bond is equal to 3.

43. $K_2NiF_6 \Rightarrow [NiF_6]^{2-}$

Ni^{+4} (d^6) low spin 

Hence, zero unpaired electron.

44. Those compound, which gives positive Tollen's test, Benedict's and Fehling's test are called reducing sugar.

Structure I, V and VI are reducing sugar.

45. 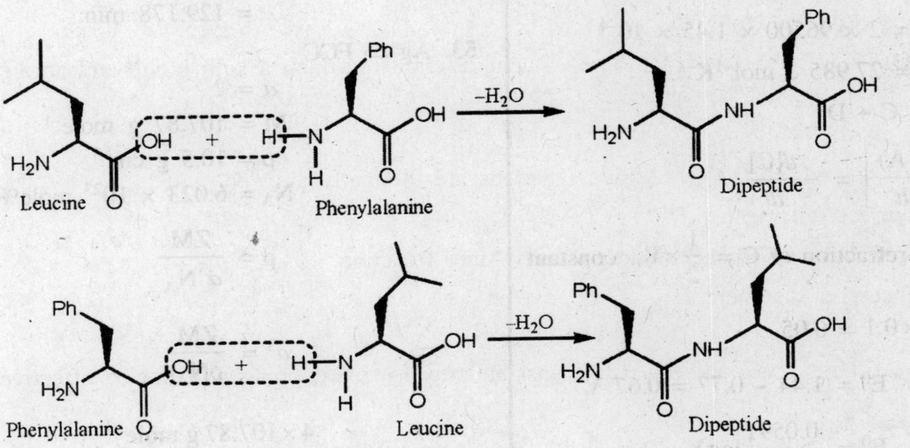

46.

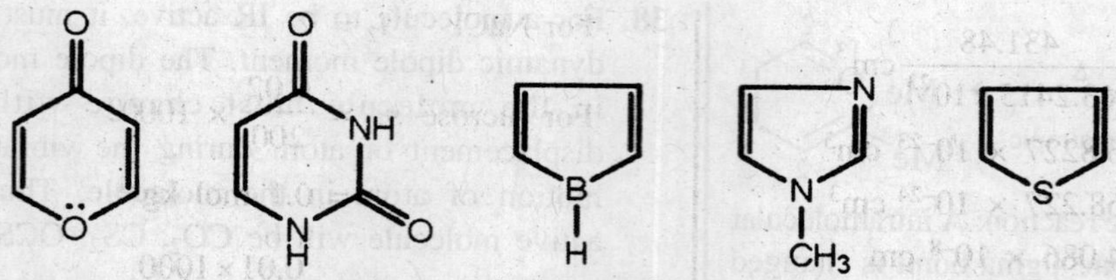

Aromatic Aromatic Anti-aromatic Aromatic Aromatic

The number of aromatic compounds are 4.

47. Chemical shift = 2 ppm

Operating frequency at 350 MHz

So, shift in Hertz = $350 \times 10^6 \times \frac{2}{10^6} = 700$ Hz

48. $\Delta + \frac{9}{2}O_2 \longrightarrow 3CO_2 + 3H_2O \quad \Delta H_1^0 = -2091$

$$CH_2 - CH = CH_2 + \frac{9}{2}O_2 \longrightarrow 3CO_2 + 3H_2O$$

$$\Delta H_2^0 = -2058$$

For reaction,

$$CH_3 - CH = CH_2 \longrightarrow \Delta \qquad \Delta H_3^0 = ?$$

$$\Delta H_3^0 = \Delta H_2^0 - \Delta H_1^0 = -2058 - (-2091)$$

$$\boxed{\Delta H_3^0 = 33 \text{ kJ mol}^{-1}}$$

49.

$$\Delta S^0 = nF\left(\frac{\partial E}{\partial T}\right)$$

$$n = 2,\ F = 90500 \text{ cm}^{-1}$$

$$\Delta S^0 = 2 \times 96500 \times 1.45 \times 10^{-4}$$

$$\Delta S^0 = 27.985 \text{ J mol}^{-1}\text{K}^{-1}.$$

50. 2A + B → C + D

$$-\frac{1}{2}\left[\frac{d(A)}{dt}\right] = -\frac{d[C]}{dt}$$

Therefore, refraction of C = $\frac{1}{2} \times R_0$ constant

of A = $\frac{1}{2} \times 0.1 = 0.05$.

51.

$$E^0 = 1.44 - 0.77 = 0.67 \text{ V}$$

$$E^0 = \frac{0.0591}{1}\log K$$

$$\log K = \frac{0.67}{0.059} = 11.36.$$

52.

$$t_{80} = 300 \text{ min},\ t_{50} = ?$$

$$kt = \ln\left(\frac{C_0}{C_t}\right)$$

For 50%, $kt_{50} = \ln\left(\frac{100}{50}\right) = \ln 2$ ...(1)

For 80%, $kt_{80} = \ln\left(\frac{100}{20}\right) = \ln 5$ ...(2)

$$\frac{(1)}{(2)} \Rightarrow \frac{kt_{50}}{kt_{80}} = \frac{\ln 2}{\ln 5}$$

$$t_{50} = \frac{\ln 2}{\ln 5} \times t_{80}$$

$$= \frac{0.693}{1.6094} \times 300$$

$$= 129.178 \text{ min.}$$

53. Ag ⇒ FCC

$$a = ?$$

$$M = 107.87 \text{ g mole}^{-1}$$

$$\rho = 10.5 \text{ g cm}^{-3}$$

$$N_A = 6.023 \times 10^{23} \text{ mole\%}$$

$$\rho = \frac{ZM}{a^3 N_A}$$

$$\Rightarrow a^3 = \frac{ZM}{\rho N_A}$$

$$\Rightarrow \frac{4 \times 107.87 \text{ g mole}^{-1}}{10.5 \text{ g cm}^{-3} \times 6.023 \times 10^{23} \text{ mole}^{-1}}$$

$$I = \frac{431.48}{63.2415 \times 10^{23}} \text{cm}^3$$
$$= 6.8227 \times 10^{-23} \text{ cm}^3$$
$$a^3 = 68.227 \times 10^{-24} \text{ cm}^3$$
$$a = 4.086 \times 10^{-8} \text{ cm}$$
$$= 408.6 \times 10^{-10} \text{ cm}$$
$$= 408.6 \text{ cm}$$
$$= 408.6 \text{ pm}$$

54. 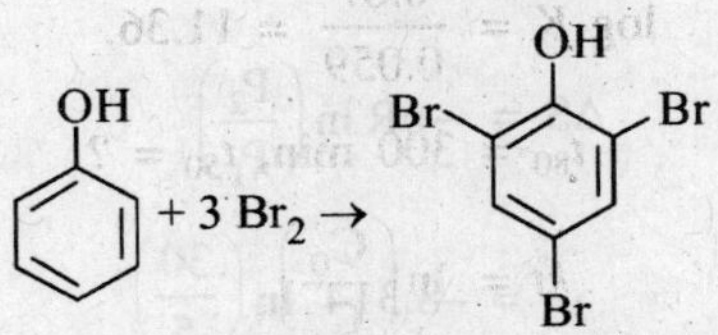

3 moles of bromine is required for one mol phenol.

$$\text{Number of moles of phenol} = \frac{42.3}{94}$$
$$= 0.45 \text{ mol}$$

Hence number of moles of Br_2 required
$$= 3 \times 0.45 \text{ mol}$$

Amount of bromine required
$$= 3 \times 0.45 \times 160 \text{ g} = 216 \text{ g}$$

55. (1) $CH_3-CH_2-CH_2-\overset{*}{C}H(OH)-CH_3$

(2) $CH_3-CH(CH_3)-\overset{*}{C}H(OH)-CH_3$

(3) $CH_3-O-\underset{*}{C}H(CH_3)-C_2H_5$

(4) $HO-CH_2-\underset{*}{C}H(CH_3)-C_2H_5$

Four pair of enantiomers are possible.

56. $$\Delta T_f = (i_1 m_1 + i_2 m_2)k_f$$

For sucrose $i_1 = 1$

For NaCl $i_2 = 2$

$$\text{For sucrose } m_1 = \frac{0.02}{200} \times 1000$$
$$= 0.1 \text{ mol kg}^{-1}$$

$$\text{For NaCl } m_2 = \frac{0.01 \times 1000}{200}$$
$$= 0.05 \text{ mol kg}^{-1}$$
$$\Delta T_f = (1 \times 0.1 + 2 \times 0.05)1.86$$
$$\Rightarrow 0.372$$

57. Given: $\theta = 0.2$, $K = 1.25 \text{ kPa}^{-1}$, $P = \rho\text{Pa}$

$$KP = \frac{\theta}{1-\theta} \Rightarrow P = \frac{1}{k}\left[\frac{\theta}{1-\theta}\right]$$
$$= \frac{1}{1.25(kPa^{-1})}\left[\frac{0.2}{1-0.2}\right]$$
$$= 0.2 \text{ kPa}$$
$$= 0.2 \times 1000 \text{ Pa}$$
$$= 200 \text{ Pa.}$$

58. $$\frac{1}{d^2} = \frac{1}{\frac{h^2}{a^2}+\frac{k^2}{b^2}+\frac{\ell}{c^2}}$$

$$\Rightarrow \quad d = \sqrt{\frac{a^2}{h^2}+\frac{b^2}{k^2}+\frac{c^2}{\ell^2}}$$

$$\frac{1}{d_{123}^2} = \frac{1}{(0.25)^2}+\frac{4}{(0.50)^2}+\frac{9}{(0.75)^2}$$

$$\frac{1}{d_{123}^2} = 0.16 + 0.16 + 0.16$$

$$= 0.48 \Rightarrow d_{123}^2 = \frac{1}{0.48}$$

$$d_{123} = \sqrt{\frac{1}{0.48}}$$
$$= \sqrt{2.0833}$$
$$= 1.44 \text{ nm.}$$

59. Suppose the volume of mixture is 1L. So, according to ideal gas equation.

$$PV = nRT$$

$$n = \frac{PV}{RT} = \frac{1 \times 1}{0.0821 \times 300}$$

$$= \frac{1}{24.6} = 0.04$$

$$n = n_{H_2} + n_{N_2}$$

$$\Rightarrow \quad n = \frac{w_{H_2}}{\mu_{H_2}} + \frac{w_{N_2}}{\mu_{N_2}}$$

$$\Rightarrow \quad 0.04 = \frac{x}{2} + \frac{(0.2 - x)}{28}$$

$$= \frac{14x + 0.2 - x}{28}$$

$$\Rightarrow \quad 28 \times 0.04 = 13x + 0.2$$

$$\Rightarrow \quad 1.12 - 0.2 = 13x = 0.07 = x$$

$$\Rightarrow \quad w_{H_2} = 0.07$$

$$\Rightarrow \quad w_{N_2} = 0.2 - 0.07 = 0.13$$

$$\Rightarrow \quad X_{H_2} = \frac{\frac{w_{H_2}}{\mu_{H_2}}}{n} = \frac{\frac{0.07}{2}}{0.04}$$

$$= \frac{0.07}{0.08} = 0.875$$

$$\Rightarrow \quad X_{N_2} = 1 - 0.875 = 0.125.$$

60. $$\Delta S = -nR \ln\left(\frac{P_2}{P_1}\right)$$

$$= -8.314 \ \ln\left(\frac{30}{5}\right)$$

$$= -14.89 \ JK^{-1}mol^{-1}.$$

Previous Paper (Solved)

IIT–JAM

JOINT ADMISSION TEST FOR M.Sc. (CHEMISTRY), 2016

Section A : Multiple Choice Questions

Q. 1 – Q. 10 carry one mark each.

1. The correct order of pK_a for the following compounds is

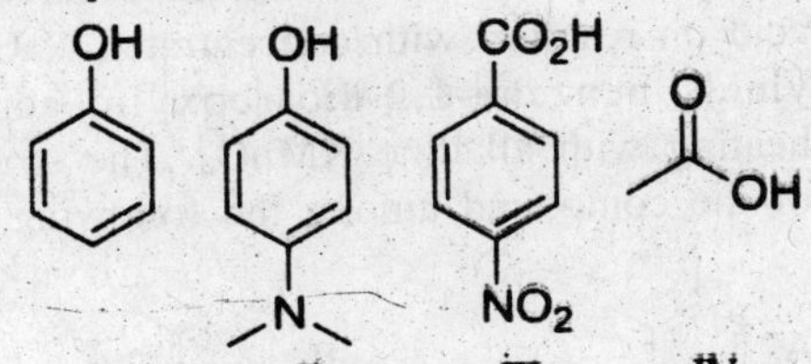

I II III IV

A. II > I > III > IV
B. II > I > IV > III
C. III > IV > I > II
D. IV > II > I > III

2. The major product formed in the following reaction is

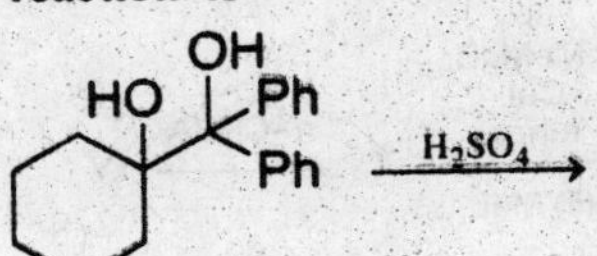

A. 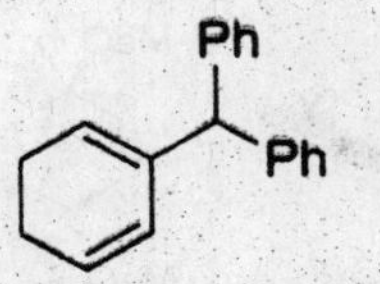

B. 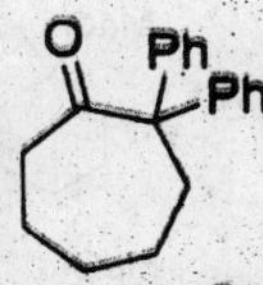

C. 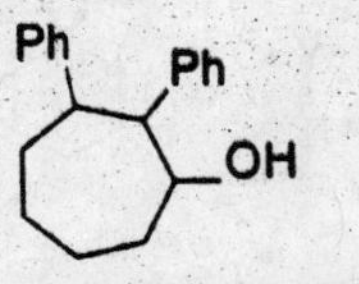

D. 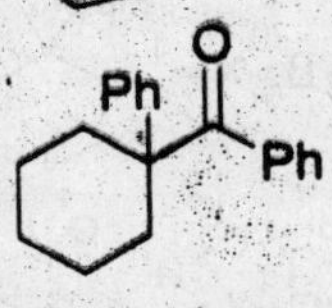

3. The mechanism of the following transformation involves

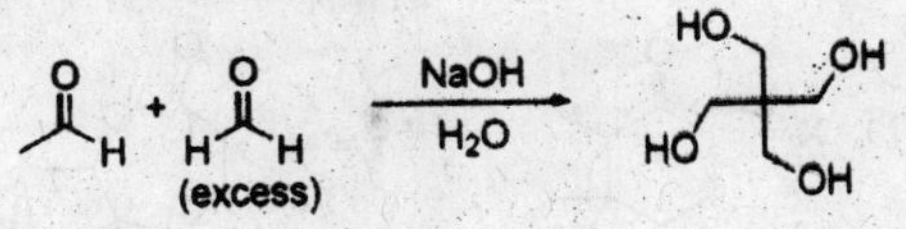

A. Aldol reaction and Cannizzaro reaction
B. Aldol reaction and Claisen-Schmidt reaction
C. Knoevenagel condensation and Cannizzaro reaction
D. Stobbe condensation and Cannizzaro reaction

4. The most basic amino acid among the following is

A. tyrosine B. methionine
C. arginine D. glutamine

5. The crystal field stabilization energy (CFSE) in $[Mn(H_2O)_6]^{2+}$ is

A. $0\ \Delta_0$ B. $2.0\ \Delta_0 - 2P$
C. $0.4\ \Delta_0 - 2P$ D. $2.0\ \Delta_0$

6. Indicator used in redox titration is

A. Eriochrome black T
B. Methyl orange
C. Phenolphthalein
D. Methylene blue

7. Among the following, the compound that has the lowest degree of ionic character is

A. NaCl B. $MgCl_2$
C. $AlCl_3$ D. $CaCl_2$

8. The correct order of entropy for various states of CO_2 is

A. $CO_2(s) > CO_2(l) > CO_2(g)$
B. $CO_2(l) > CO_2(s) > CO_2(g)$
C. $CO_2(g) > CO_2(l) > CO_2(s)$
D. $CO_2(g) > CO_2(s) > CO_2(l)$

9. The coordination numbers of Cs^+ and Cl^- ions in the CsCl structure, respectively, are

A. 4,4 B. 4,8
C. 6,6 D. 8,8

10. Determinant of a square matrix is always

A. a square matrix B. a column matrix
C. a row matrix D. a number

Q. 11 – Q. 30 carry two marks each.

11. The correct order of ^{1}H NMR chemical shift (δ) values for the labelled methyl groups in the following compound is

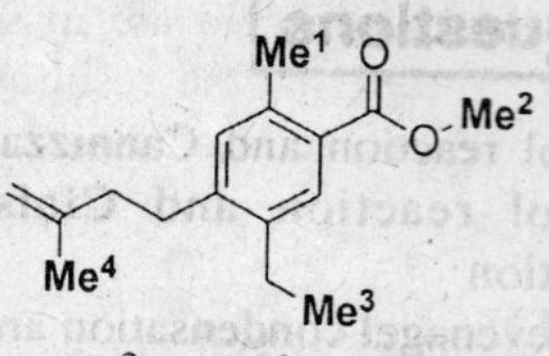

A. $Me^1 < Me^2 < Me^3 < Me^4$
B. $Me^3 < Me^4 < Me^1 < Me^2$
C. $Me^3 < Me^1 < Me^4 < Me^2$
D. $Me^2 < Me^4 < Me^3 < Me^1$

12. Among the following, the most stable conformation of *meso*-2,3-dibromobutane is

A. 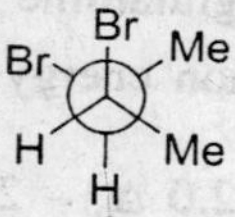
B. 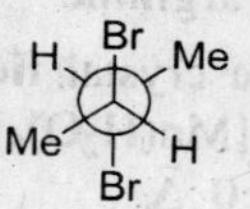
C. 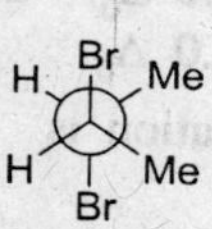
D. 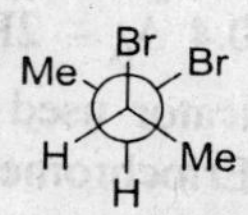

13. The major products **X** and **Y** in the following reaction sequence are

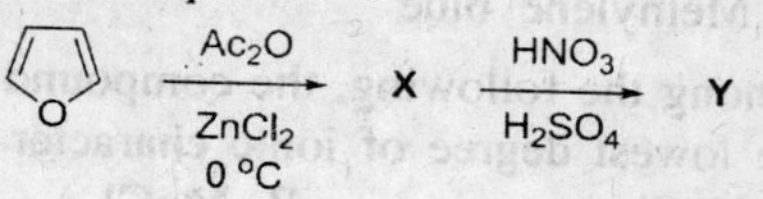

A. **X** = 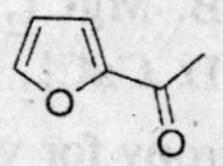 **Y** = 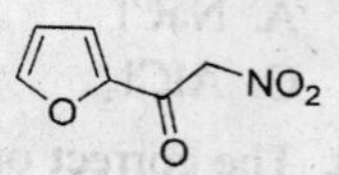

B. **X** = 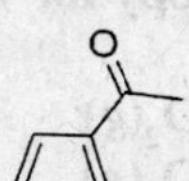 **Y** = 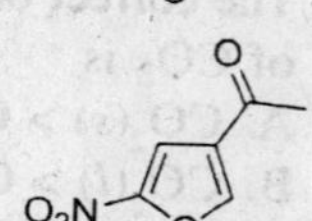

C. **X** =  **Y** = 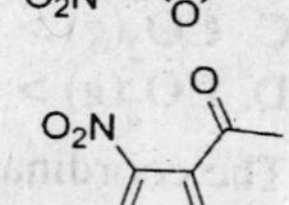

D. **X** = 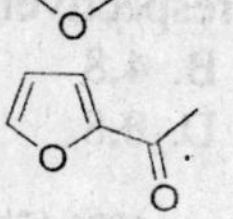 **Y** = 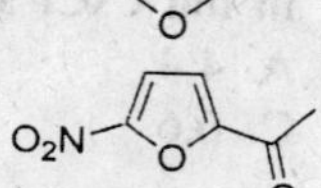

14. The major product formed in the reaction of butanenitrile with phenylmagnesium bromide followed by acidification is

A. 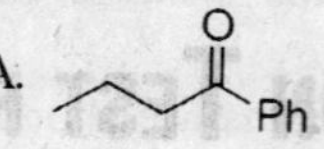
B. 
C. 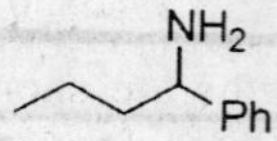
D. 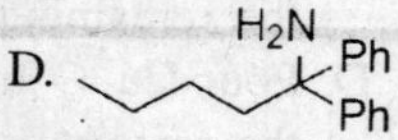

15. An organic compound on reaction with 2,4-dinitrophenylhydrazine (2,4-DNP) gives a yellow precipitate. It also gives silver mirror on reaction with ammoniacal $AgNO_3$. It gives an alcohol and sodium salt of a carboxylic acid on reaction with concentrated NaOH. It yields benzene-1,2-dicarboxylic acid on heating with alkaline $KMnO_4$. The structure of the compound among the following is

A. 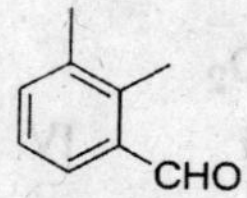
B. 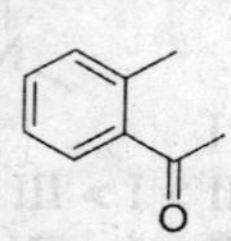
C. 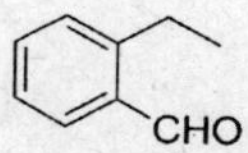
D. 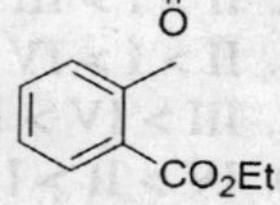

16. The major products **X** and **Y** in the following reaction sequence are

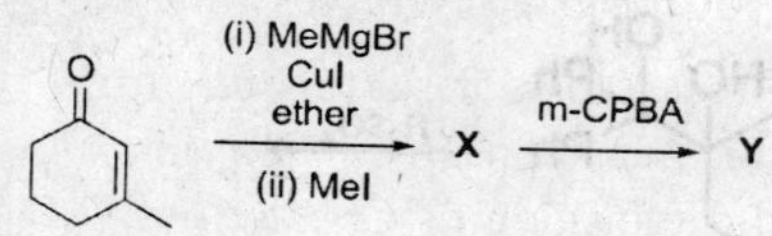

A. **X** = 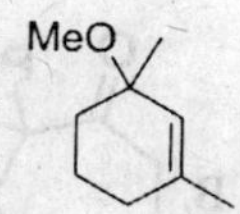 **Y** = 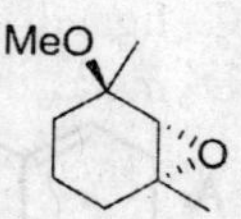

B. **X** = 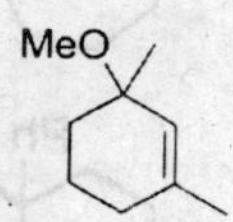 **Y** = 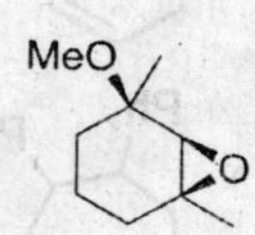

C. **X** = 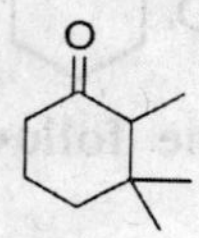 **Y** = 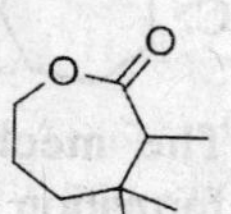

D. **X** = 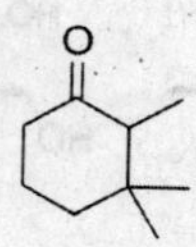 **Y** = 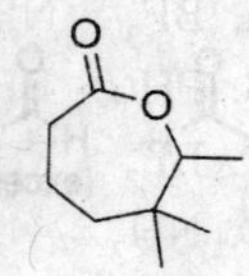

17. The TRUE statement about $[Cu(H_2O)_6]^{2+}$ is
A. All Cu–O bond lengths are equal
B. One Cu–O bond lengths is shorter than the remaining five
C. Three Cu–O bond lengths are shorter than the remaining three
D. Four Cu–O bond lengths are shorter than the remaining two

18. The complexes $[Pt(CN)_4]^{2-}$ and $[NiCl_4]^{2-}$, respectively, are
A. paramagnetic, paramagnetic
B. diamagnetic, diamagnetic
C. paramagnetic, diamagnetic
D. diamagnetic, paramagnetic

19. The value of 'x' in $[Cu(CO)_x]^+$ such that it obeys the 18 electron rule is
A. 6 B. 5
C. 4 D. 3

20. The correct order of ν_{NO} (cm^{-1}) in the following compounds is
A. $NO^+ > NO > [NiCp(NO)] > [Cr(Cp)_2(NO)_4]$
B. $[Cr(Cp)_2(NO)_4] > [NiCp(NO)] > NO^+ > NO$
C. $NO^+ > [Cr(Cp)_2(NO)_4] > NO > [NiCp(NO)]$
D. $[NiCp(NO)] > NO > [Cr(Cp)_2(NO)_4] > NO^+$

21. The red colour of ruby is due to
A. d-d transition of Cr^{3+} ion in Cr_2O_3 lattice
B. d-d transition of Cr^{3+} ion in Al_2O_3 lattice
C. ligand to metal charge transfer transition
D. metal to metal charge transfer transition

22. The final products in the reaction of BF_3 with water are
A. $B(OH)_3$ and OF_2
B. H_3BO_3 and HBF_4
C. B_2O_3 and HBF_4
D. B_2H_6 and HF

23. The correct order of bond angles in BF_3, NH_3, NF_3 and PH_3 is
A. $BF_3 > NH_3 > NF_3 > PH_3$
B. $PH_3 > BF_3 > NF_3 > NH_3$
C. $BF_3 > PH_3 > NH_3 > NF_3$
D. $NH_3 > NF_3 > BF_3 > PH_3$

24. The maximum of a function Ae^{-ax^2} (A > 0; $a > 0$) is at $x =$
A. 0 B. $+\infty$
C. $-\infty$ D. $\frac{1}{\sqrt{a}}$

25. At 298 K, 0.1 mol of ammonium acetate and 0.14 mol of acetic acid are dissolved in 1 L of water. The pH of the resulting solution is [Given: pK_a of acetic acid is 4.75]
A. 4.9 B. 4.6
C. 4.3 D. 2.3

26. An electrochemical cell consists of two half-cell reactions
$AgCl(s) + e^- \rightarrow Ag(s) + Cl^-(aq)$
$Cu(s) \rightarrow Cu^{2+}(aq) + 2e^-$
The mass of copper (in grams) dissolved on passing 0.5 A current for 1 hour is
[Given: atomic mass of Cu is 63.6; F = 96500 C mol^{-1}]
A. 0.88 B. 1.18
C. 0.29 D. 0.59

27. For a zero order reaction, the half-life depends on the initial concentration $[C_0]$ of the reactant as
A. $[C_0]$ B. $[C_0]^0$
C. $[C_0]^{-1}$ D. $[C_0]^{1/2}$

28. The effective nuclear charge of helium atom is 1.7. The first ionization energy of helium atom in eV is
A. 13.6 B. 23.1
C. 39.3 D. 27.2

29. The relationship between the van der Waals 'b' coefficient of N_2 and O_2 is
A. $b(N_2) = b(O_2) = 0$ B. $b(N_2) = b(O_2) \neq 0$
C. $b(N_2) > b(O_2)$ D. $b(N_2) < b(O_2)$

30. From the kinetic theory of gases, the ratio of most probable speed (C_{mp}) to root mean square speed (C_{rms}) is
A. $\sqrt{3}$ B. $\frac{\sqrt{2}}{\sqrt{3}}$
C. $\frac{\sqrt{3}}{\sqrt{2}}$ D. $\frac{3}{\sqrt{2}}$

Section B : Multiple Select Questions

Q. 31 – Q. 40 carry two marks each.

31. The correct statement(s) about the following species is(are)

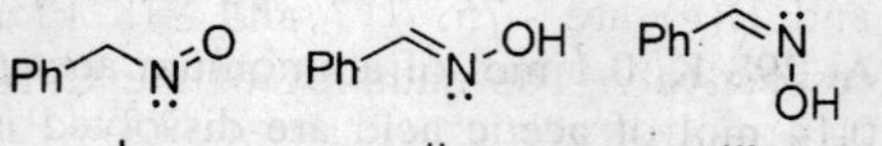

I II III

A. I and II are resonance structures
B. II and III are resonance structures
C. II and III are diastereomers
D. III is a tautomer of I

32. Consider the following reaction:

$$(D)\text{-glucose} \xrightarrow[\text{cat. } H^+]{\text{Ph-NH-NH}_2 \text{ (3 equiv)}} X$$

Among the following, the compound(s) whose osazone derivative(s) will have the same melting point as that of **X** is(are)

A. 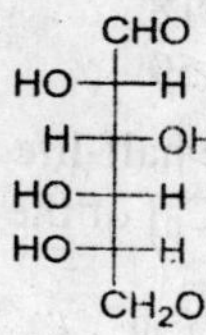

B. 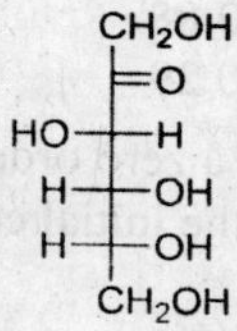

C. 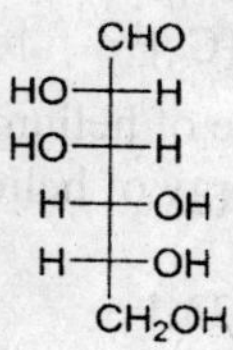

D. 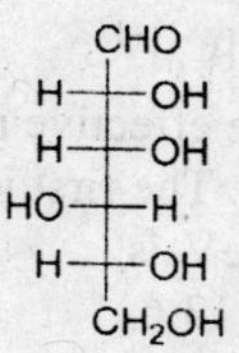

33. The appropriate reagents required for carrying out the following transformation are

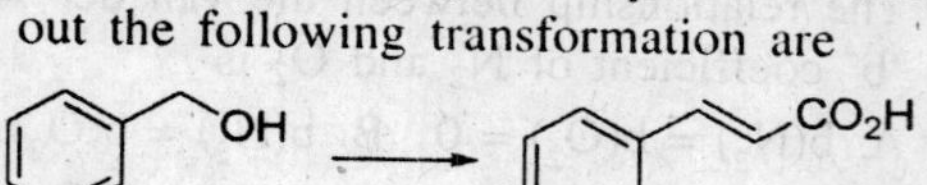

A. (i) PCC, CH_2Cl_2; (ii) $Ph_3P = CHCO_2Et$; (iii) aq. NaOH, heat, then acidify
B. (i) CrO_3, H_2SO_4, aq. acetone (ii) Ac_2O, NaOAc
C. (i) MnO_2; (ii) $CH_2(CO_2H)_2$, piperidine, pyridine
D. (i) PCC, CH_2Cl_2; (ii) $BrCH_2CO_2C(CH_3)_3$, Zn (iii) H_3O^+, heat

34. The appropriate reagents required for carrying out the following transformation are

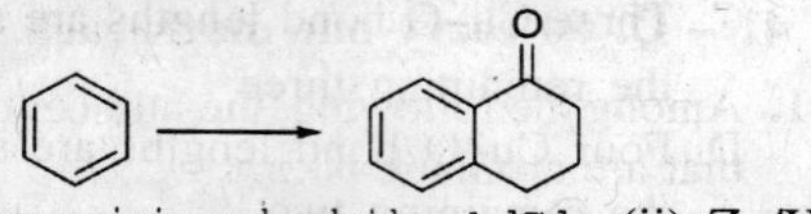

A. (i) succinic anhydride. $AlCl_3$; (ii) Zn/Hg, HCl; (iii) polyphosphoric acid
B. (i) maleic anhydride, $AlCl_3$; (ii) $H_2N\text{-}NH_2$, KOH; (iii) H_2SO_4
C. (i) succinic anhydride, $FeCl_3$; (ii) $LiAlH_4$; (iii) H_2SO_4
D. (i) phthalic anhydride, $F_3B{\cdot}OEt_2$; (ii) $HS(CH_2)_2SH$, H^+; (iii) Raney Ni; (iv) polyphosphoric acid

35. The protein(s) that belong to the class of blue copper proteins is(are)

A. ceruloplasmin B. superoxide dismutase
C. hemocyanin D. azurin

36. The ion(s) that exhibit only charge transfer bands in the absorption spectra (UV-visible region) is(are)

A. $[Cr(C_2O_4)_3]^{3-}$ B. $[CrO_4]^{2-}$
C. $[ReO_4]^-$ D. $[NiO_2]^{2-}$

37. The type(s) of interaction(s) that hold layers of graphite together is(are)

A. π-π stacking B. van der Waals
C. hydrogen bonding D. Coulombic

38. TRUE statement(s) about Langmuir isotherm is(are)

A. valid for monolayer coverage
B. all adsorption sites are equivalent
C. there is dynamic equilibrium between free gas and adsorbed gas
D. adsorption probability is independent of occupancy at the neighbouring sites

39. The $3p_z$ orbital has

A. one radial node B. two radial nodes
C. one angular node D. two angular nodes

40. The diatomic molecule(s) that has(have) two π-type bonds is(are)

A. B_2 B. C_2
C. N_2 D. O_2

Section C : Numerical Answer Type (NAT)

Q. 41 – Q. 50 carry one mark each.

41. Among the following, the number of molecules that are aromatic is ....

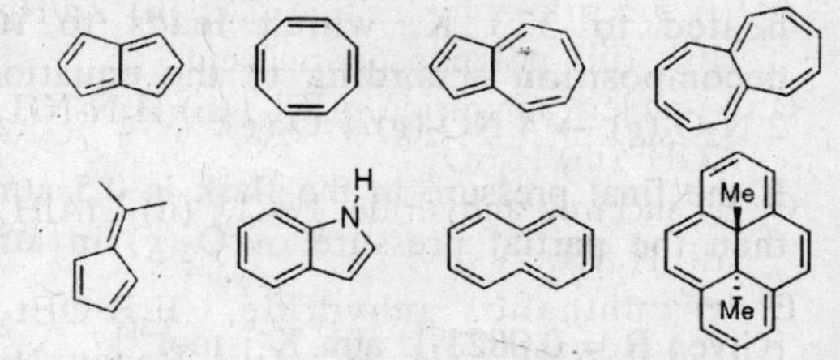

42. The number of all possible isomers for the molecular formula C_6H_{14} is ....

43. Hydrolysis of 15.45 g of benzonitrile produced 10.98 g of benzoic acid. The percentage yield of acid formed is ....

44. Acetic acid content in commercial vinegar was analyzed by titrating against 1.5 M NaOH solution. A 20 mL vinegar sample required 18 mL of titrant to give endpoint. The concentration of acetic acid in the vinegar (in mol L^{-1}) is ....

45. The bond order of Be_2 molecule is ....

46. The number of P–H bonds in hypophosphorus acid is ....

47. The isotope $^{214}_{84}Po$ undergoes one alpha and one beta particle emission sequentially to form an isotope "X". The number of neutrons in "X" is ....

48. In a diffraction experiment with X-rays of wavelength 1.54 Å, a diffraction line corresponding to $2\theta = 20.8°$ is observed. The inter-planar separation in Å is ....

49. The potential energy of interaction between two ions in an ionic compound is given by $U = 1389.4 \left[\frac{Z_1Z_2}{r/Å}\right]$ kJ mol^{-1}. Assuming that $CaCl_2$ is linear molecule of length 5.6 Å, the potential energy for $CaCl_2$ molecule in kJ mol^{-1} is ....

50. The enthalpy of formation for $CH_4(g)$, $C(g)$ and $H(g)$ are –75, 717 and 218 kJ mol^{-1}, respectively. The enthalpy of the C–H bond in kJ mol^{-1} is ....

Q. 51 – Q. 60 carry two marks each.

51. Specific rotation of the (*R*)-enantiomer of a chiral compound is 48. The specific rotation of a sample of this compound which contains 25% of (*S*)-enantiomer is ....

52. Among the following, the number of compounds, which can participate as **'diene'** component in a Diels-Alder reaction is ....

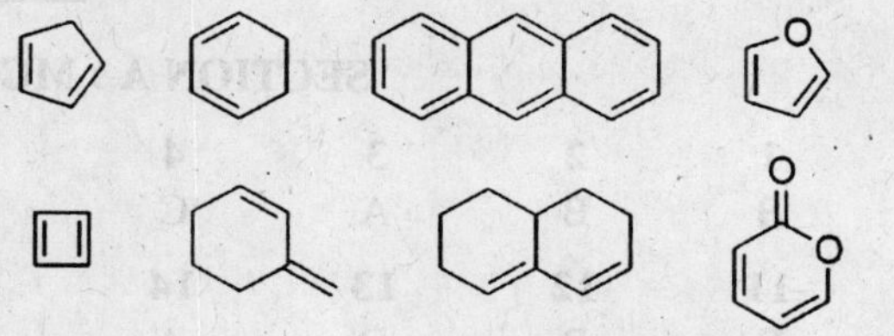

53. Among the following, the number of molecules that possess C_2 axis of symmetry is ....

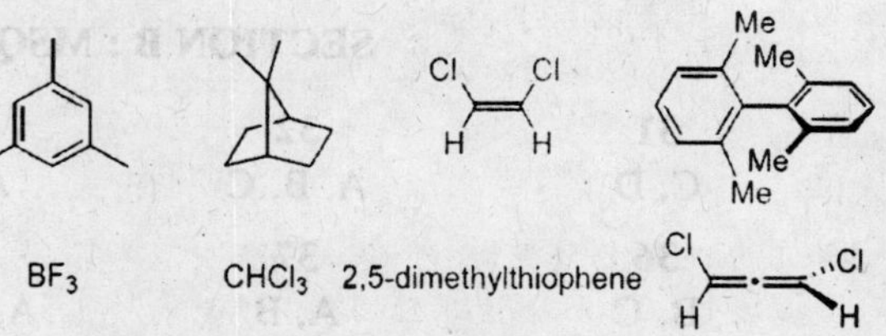

54. Effective nuclear charge for 3d electron in vanadium (atomic number = 23) according to Slater's rule is ....

55. The total number of isomers possible for the molecule $[Co(NH_3)_4Cl(NO_2)]^+$ is ....

56. The bond angle in PBr_3 is 101°. The percent 's' character of the central atom is ....

57. $Cu(s) + 4H^+(aq) + 2NO_3^-(aq) \rightarrow 2NO_2(g) + Cu^{2+}(aq) + 2H_2O(l)$

In the above reaction at 1 atm and 298 K, if 6.36 g of copper is used. Assuming ideal gas

behaviour, the volume of NO_2 produced in liters is ....
[Given: atomic mass of Cu is 63.6; R = 0.0821 L atm K^{-1} mol^{-1}]

58. The ΔH° for the reaction $CO(g) + \frac{1}{2}O_2(g) \rightarrow CO_2(g)$ at 400 K in kJ mol^{-1} is ....
Given at 298 K:

	ΔH_f^0	C_p^0
	kJ mol^{-1}	J mol^{-1} K^{-1}
O_2	0	29.4
CO	–110	29.1
CO_2	–394	37.1

59. The rate constants for a reaction at 300 and 350 K are 8 and 160 L mol^{-1} s^{-1}, respectively. The activation energy of the reaction in kJ mol^{-1} is ....
[Given R = 8.314 J K^{-1} mol^{-1}]

60. A 10 L flask containing 10.8 g of N_2O_5 is heated to 373 K, which leads to its decomposition according to the equation $2\ N_2O_5(g) \rightarrow 4\ NO_2(g) + O_2(g)$.

If the final pressure in the flask is 0.5 atm, then the partial pressure of $O_2(g)$ in atm is ....
[Given R = 0.0821 L atm K^{-1} mol^{-1}]

ANSWERS

SECTION A : MCQ (Multiple Choice Questions)

1	2	3	4	5	6	7	8	9	10
B	B	A	C	A	D	C	C	D	D
11	**12**	**13**	**14**	**15**	**16**	**17**	**18**	**19**	**20**
B	B	D	A	C	D	D	D	C	*
21	**22**	**23**	**24**	**25**	**26**	**27**	**28**	**29**	**30**
B	B	A	A	B	D	A	C	C	B

SECTION B : MSQ (Multiple Select Questions)

31	32	33	34	35
C, D	A, B, C	A, C, D	A	A, D
36	**37**	**38**	**39**	**40**
B, C	A, B	A, B, C, D	A, C	B, C

SECTION C : NAT (Numerical Answer Type Questions)

41	42	43	44	45
3.0 to 3.0	5.0 to 5.0	60.0 to 60.0	1.3 to 1.4	0.0 to 0.0
46	**47**	**48**	**49**	**50**
2.0 to 2.0	127.0 to 127.0	4.2 to 4.3	–1738 to –1734	–417.0 to –415.0
51	**52**	**53**	**54**	**55**
24.0 to 24.0	6.0 to 6.0	7.0 to 7.0	4.2 to 4.4	4.0 to 4.0
56	**57**	**58**	**59**	**60**
*	4.8 to 5.0	–284.70 to –284.65	52.0 to 53.0	0.06 to 0.07

EXPLANATORY ANSWERS

SECTION-A

1. 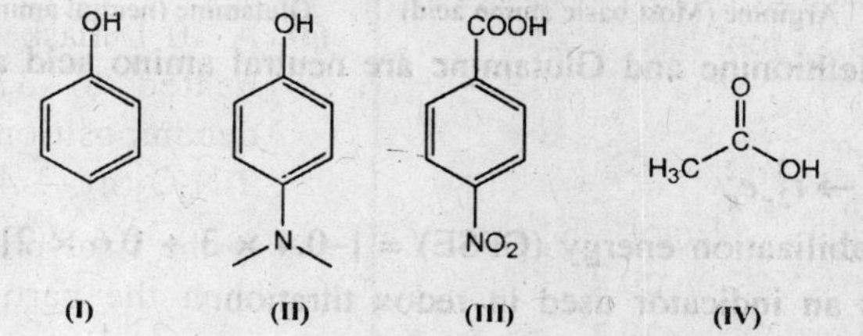

We know that:

- Electron withdrawing group increases the acidic character
- Electron donating group decreases the acidic behaviour and, Acid $\rightleftharpoons$ Conjugate Base + H^+

For higher the K_a, lower will be pK_a, higher will be acidity $\Rightarrow$ acidic behaviour $\propto \frac{1}{pK_a}$

- Benzoic acid is more acidic as compared to acetic acid, which in turn is more acidic as compared to phenol.

Thus order of acidic behaviour will be III > IV > I > II

Hence, correct order of pK_a will be III < IV < I < II.

2. 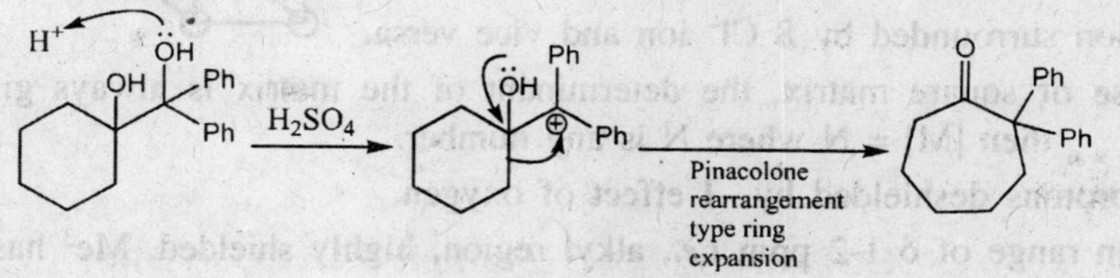

3. 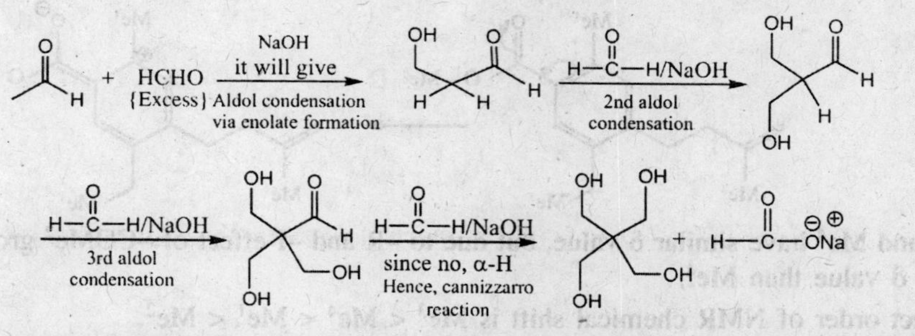

4. If the number of amine (basic) groups are more than caroxylic (acidic) groups then the amino acid will be basic in nature.

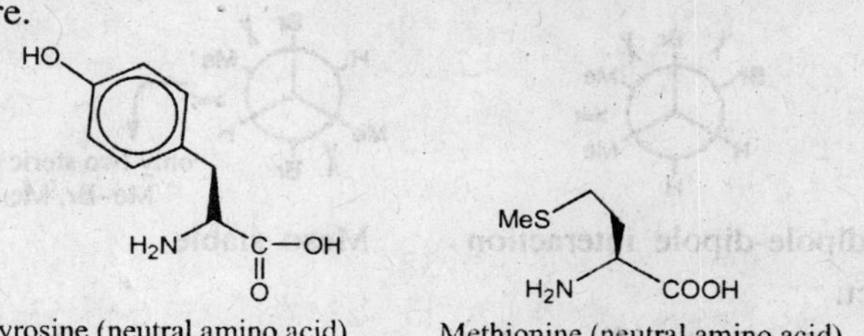

Tyrosine (neutral amino acid) Methionine (neutral amino acid)

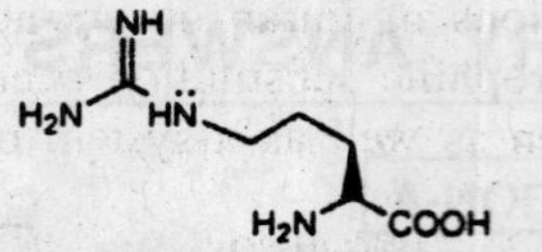

Arginine (Most basic amino acid)

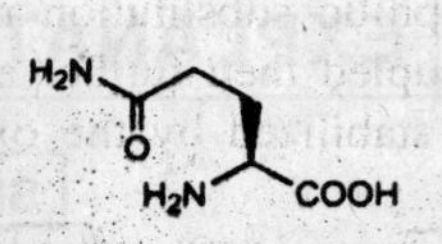

Glutamine (neutral amino acid)

Here, Tyrosine, Methionine and Glutamine are neutral amino acid and Arginine is the most basic amino acid.

5. $Mn^{2+} \rightarrow 3d^5 (HS) \rightarrow t_{2g}^3 e_g^2$

$\therefore$ Crystal field stabilization energy (CFSE) = $[-0.4 \times 3 + 0.6 \times 2]\ \Delta_0 = 0\Delta_0$.

6. Methylene blue is an indicator used in redox titration.

7. More the polarisation, lesser will be ionic character.

NaCl	$MgCl_2$ $CaCl_2$	$AlCl_3$

Ionic character $\longrightarrow$

From Fajan rule, we know that as positive charge on cation increases, size of cation decreases, and its polarisation increases. Its covalent character increases and so, its ionic character decreases.

9. CsCl is packed in body-centre cubic (bcc) structure.

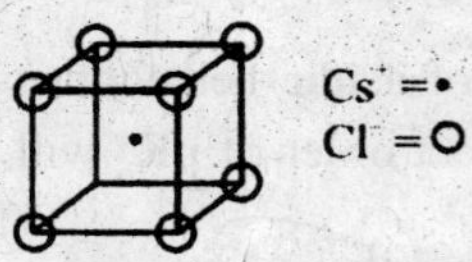

Cs^+ = at body centre

Cl^- = At corners

One Cs^+ ion surrounded by 8 Cl^- ion and vice versa.

10. In the case of square matrix, the determinant of the matrix is always gives out a number *i.e.*, $M = [a_{ij}]_{n \times n}$ then $|M| = N$ where N is any number.

11. $-O-Me^2$ protons deshielded by $-I$ effect of oxygen.

Me^3 lies in range of δ 1-2 ppm *i.e.*, alkyl region, highly shielded. Me^3 has lower δ value.

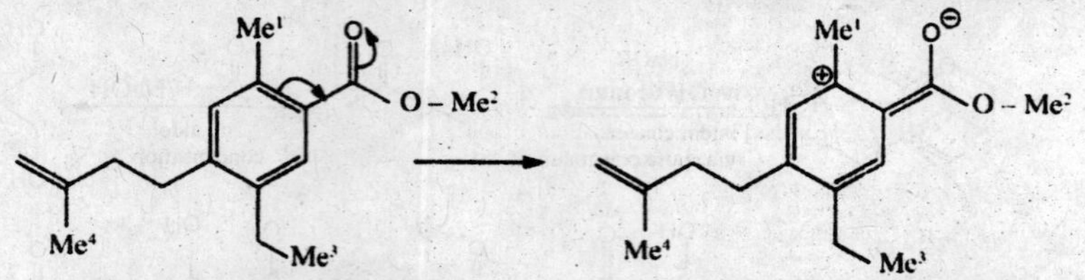

Me^1 and Me^4 have similar δ value, but due to $-R$ and $-I$ effect of $-COMe^2$ group, Me^1 has slightly more δ value than Me^4.

Correct order of NMR chemical shift is $Me^3 < Me^4 < Me^1 < Me^2$.

12. Only (A) and (B) represents meso form

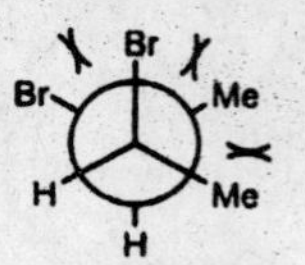

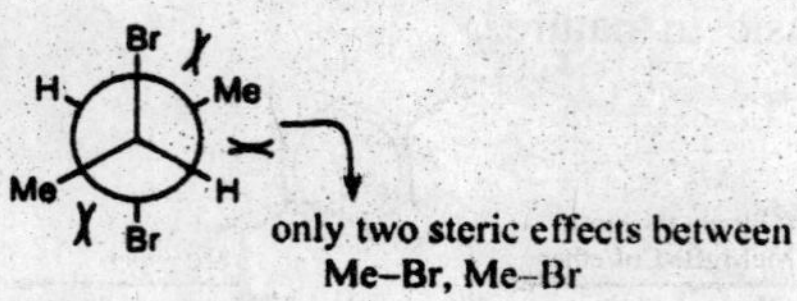

Br–Br steric and dipole-dipole interaction

Me–Br steric effect.

Steric effect in Me-Me bond is less stable.

Meso stable

13. We know that electrophilic substitution reactions of Furan occurs at second position and if the second position is occupied then further electrophilic substitution occurs at fifth position, because the positive charge is stabilized by the oxygen as well as π-system of the ring.

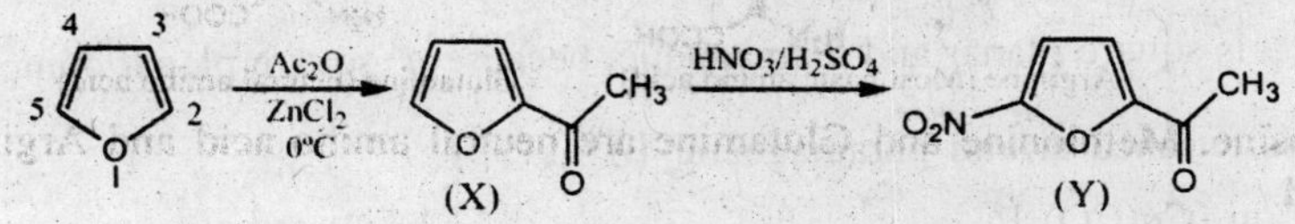

14.

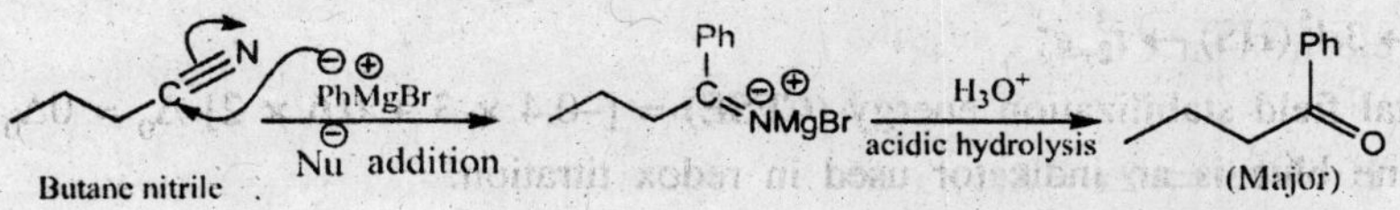

15.

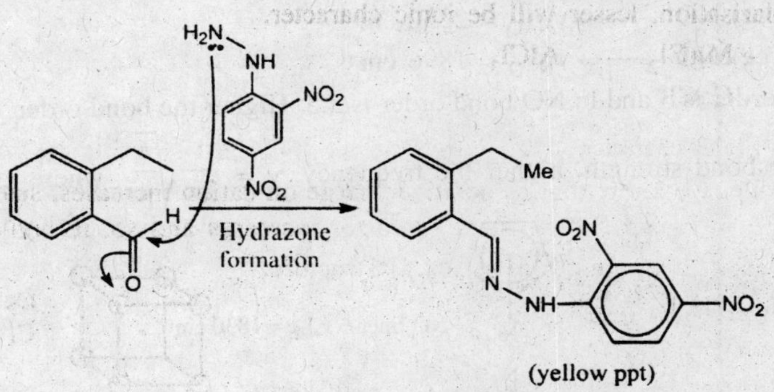

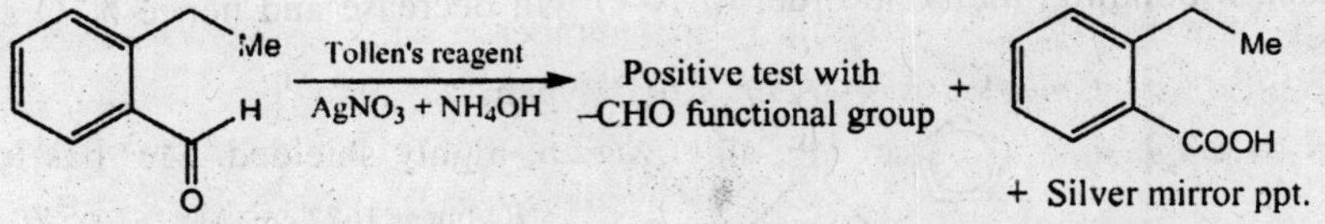

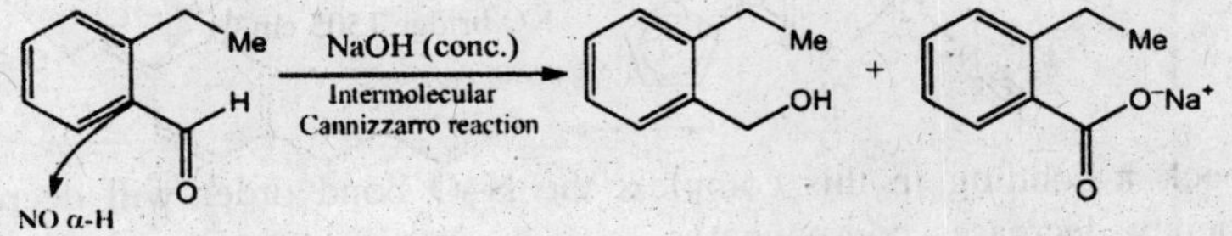

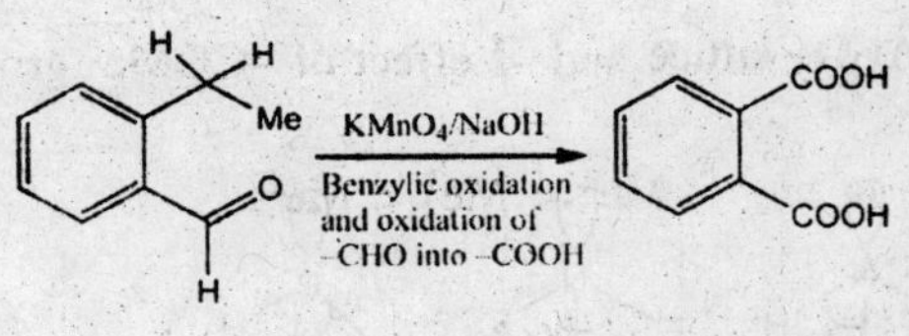

16.

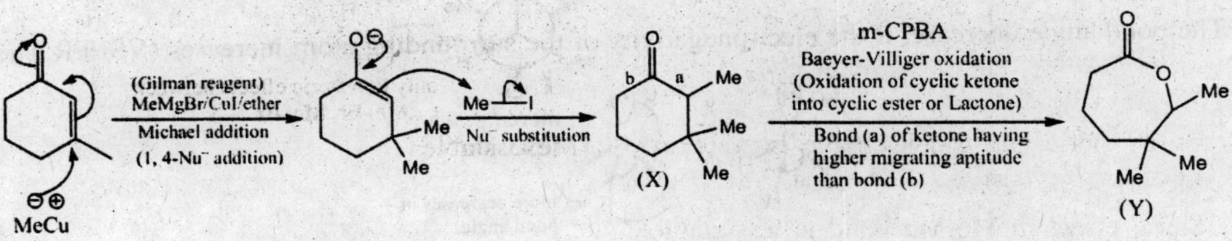

17. $[Cu(H_2O)_6]^{2+} \longrightarrow 3d^9 \rightarrow t_{2g}^6 eg^3$

The *eg* orbitals are unsymmetrically filled. Thus, due to John-Teller distortion four Cu–O bond lengths are shorter than the remaining two.

18. $[Pt(CN)_4]^{2-}$ is square planar and diamagnetic, because d^8 square planar complexes are diamagnetic.

$[NiCl_4]^{2-}$ is tetrahedral and paramagnetic $\left(d^8 : e^4 t_2^4\right)$.

19. Value of '*x*' in $[Cu(CO)_x]^+$

Valence electron in Cu = $3d^{10}4s^1$

$Cu^+ = 3d^{10}$

So, $2x + 10 = 18 \Rightarrow 2x = 8 \therefore x = 4$.

20. From (Free) $NO^+ \longrightarrow \nu_{N-O} = 2250\ cm^{-1}$

and (Free) $NO \longrightarrow \nu_{N-O} = 1896\ cm^{-1}$

In NO^+ bond order is 3 and in NO bond order is 2.5. Higher the bond order, higher the bond strength.

so, higher the bond strength, higher the frequency, $\nu = \dfrac{1}{2\pi}\sqrt{\dfrac{k}{\mu}}$, where *k* is bond strength.

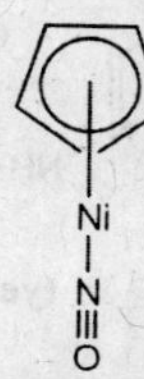

NO linear $\nu_{N-O} = 1830\ cm^{-1}$

Due to back π-bonding, the bond order of N–O will decrease and hence N–O stretching frequency decreases.

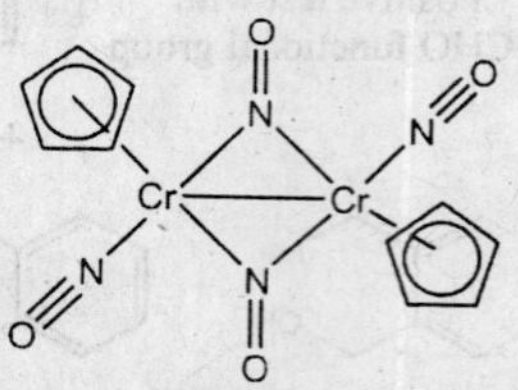

NO linear 1672 cm^{-1}

NO bridge 1505 cm^{-1}

Due to more back π-bonding in this complex, the N–O bond order will decreases and its ν_{N-O} stretching frequency decreases consequently.

21. Due to d–d transition of Cr^{3+} ion in Al_2O_3 lattice.

23. BF_3 is trigonal planar hence

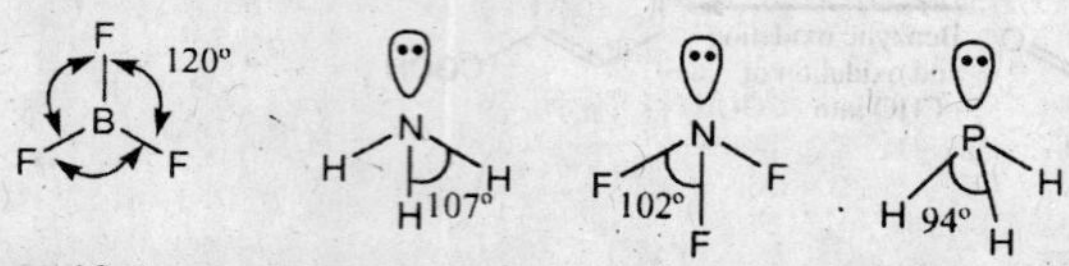

The bond angle decrease, if the electronegativity of the surrounding atom increases (VSEPR Theory)

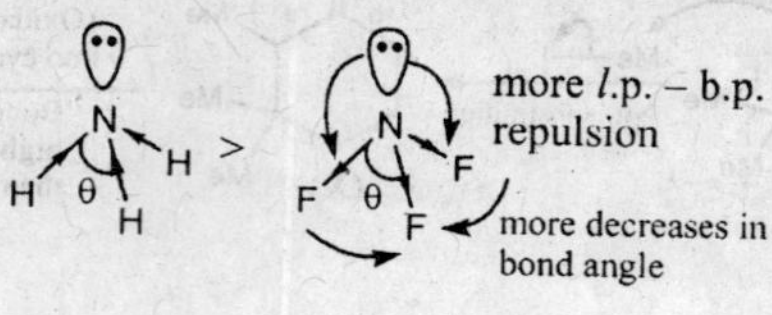

If the electronegativity of central atom decreases, bond angle decreases (VSEPR Theory)

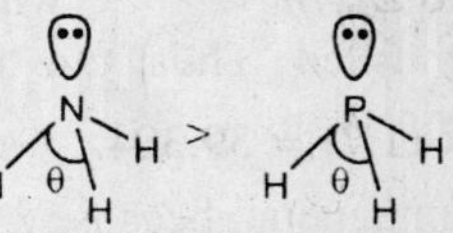

The correct bond order, $BF_3(120°) > NH_3\ (107°) > NF_3(102°) > PH_3(94°)$.

24. $\frac{d}{dx}(Ae^{-ax^2}) = A(-2ax)\cdot e^{-ax^2} = -A\cdot 2ax\cdot e^{-ax^2}$

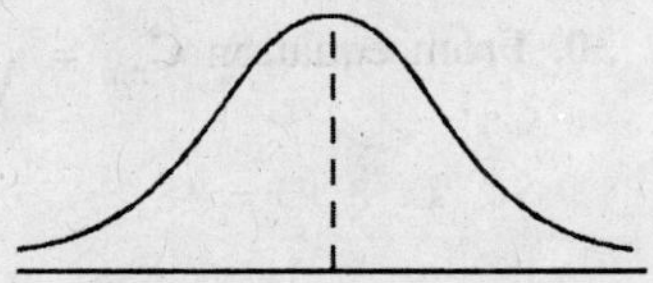

0

At maximum value, $\frac{d}{dx}(Ae^{ax^2}) = 0$

$x\cdot e^{-ax^2} = 0 \Rightarrow x = 0, \infty$

Now, $\frac{d}{dx}(-2Aax\cdot e^{-ax^2}) = -2A\cdot ae^{-ax^2} + 4Aa^2x^2\cdot e^{-ax^2}$

at $x = 0,\ \frac{d}{dx}(-2Aaxe^{-ax^2}) < 0$

$\therefore$ Function is maximum at $x = 0$.

25. 0.1 mole of ammonium acetate in 1L of water, $[\text{salt}] = \frac{0.1}{1} = 0.1$ mole/L

0.14 mole of acetic acid in 1L of water, $[\text{acid}] = \frac{0.14 \text{ mol}}{1} = 0.14$ mol/L

As it is a buffer solution,

We know that, $\text{pH} = \text{pK}_a + \log\frac{[\text{salt}]}{[\text{acid}]} = 4.75 + \log\frac{[0.1]}{[0.14]} = 4.75 + \log\frac{10}{14}$

$= 4.75 + (\log 10 - \log 14) = 4.60.$

26. Amount of charge passed $= i \times t = 0.5 \times 60 \times 60$ coulomb.

Number of Faraday passed $= \frac{0.5\times 60\times 60}{96500} = 0.01865$

Since, two Faraday dissolves 1 mole of Cu.

Therefore, so,

0.01865 Faraday's will dissolve $= \frac{1\times 0.01865}{2}$ moles of Cu

So, weight of Cu dissolved $= \frac{0.01865}{2}\times 63.6 = 0.59$ gm.

27. For '0' order reaction, $t_{1/2} = \frac{C_0}{2k};\ t_{1/2} \propto \frac{1}{C_0^{n-1}}$

for zero order reaction $n = 0$

$t_{1/2} \propto \frac{1}{C_0^{n-1}}\ \therefore\ t_{1/2} \propto C_0$ where C_0 is concentration.

28. He $\longrightarrow He^+ + e^-$ $\quad E_n = 13.6\, Z_{eff}^2/n^2$ $\quad$ where, Z_{eff} is effective nuclear charge

$$\frac{+13.6 \times (1.7)^2 eV}{1} = (13.6) \times (1.7) \times (1.7) = 39.304.$$

29. As '*b*' represents (4 × molecular volume per mole)

$b(N_2) > b(O_2)$ $\quad$ As molecular of N_2 is larger than O_2.

30. From equation $C_{mp} = \sqrt{\frac{2RT}{M}} \Rightarrow C_{rms} = \sqrt{\frac{3RT}{M}} \Rightarrow$ *i.e.* required ratio $\frac{C_{mp}}{C_{rms}} = \frac{\sqrt{2}}{\sqrt{3}}$.

SECTION-B

31.

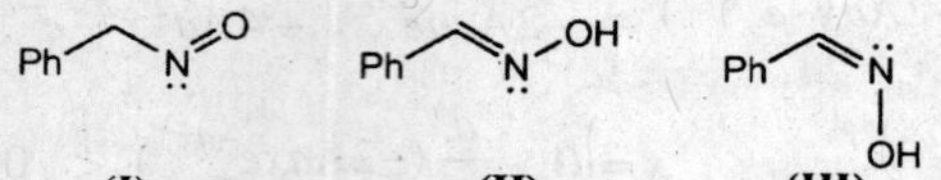

(I) $\quad$ (II) $\quad$ (III)

As we know that in resonating structure there is no shift of atom takes place.

cis and *trans* stereoisomer are a pair of diastereoisomers.

Hence, III and II are diastereoisomer and III is also a tautomeric form of I.

32. We know that, all C_2 epimers form same osazone moiety. During osazone formation the chirality of C_2 carbon is lost.

As for example: D-glucose, D-mannose are C_2-epimers and they form same osazone. Fructose also form the same osazone like that of D-glucose.

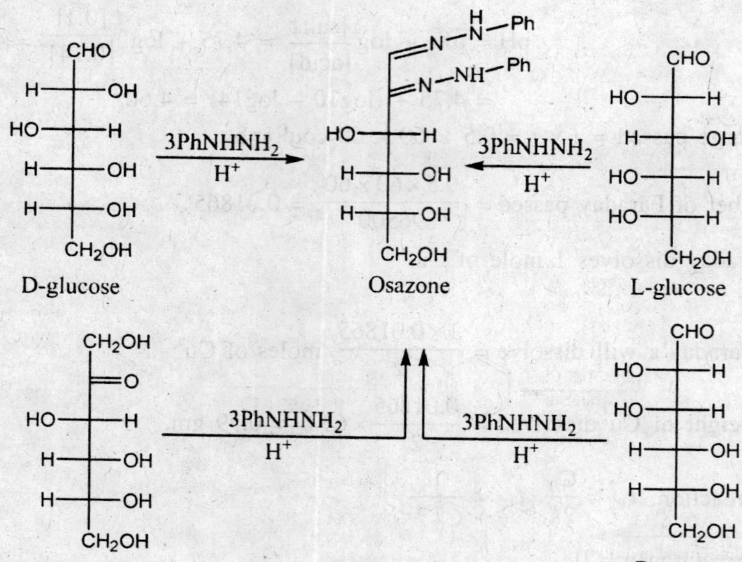

D-glucose $\quad$ Osazone $\quad$ L-glucose

D-fructose $\quad$ D-mannose

The osazone formed by D-glucose, L-glucose, D-mannose and D-fractose are structurally similar. Hence, they have the same melting point.

33.

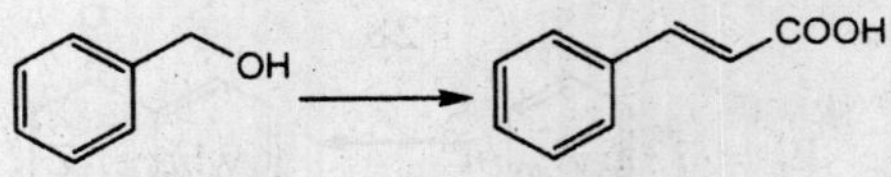

Reaction (A):

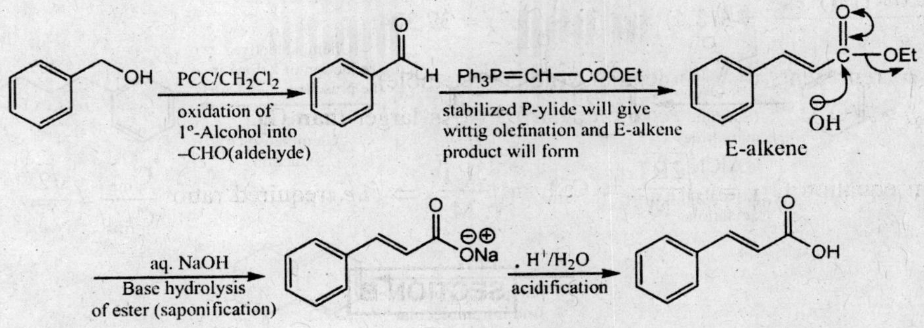

Reaction (C):

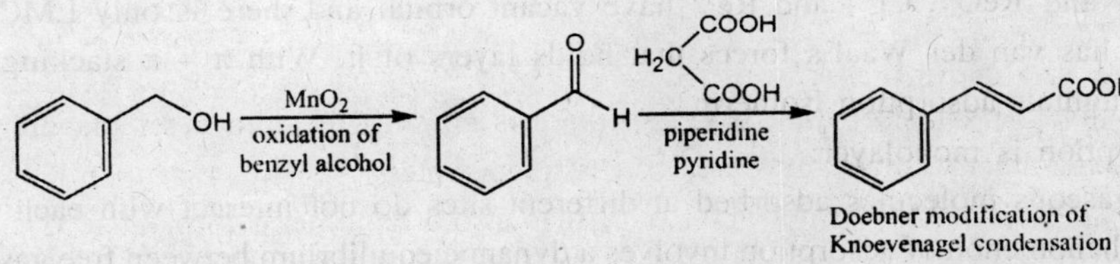

Mechanism:

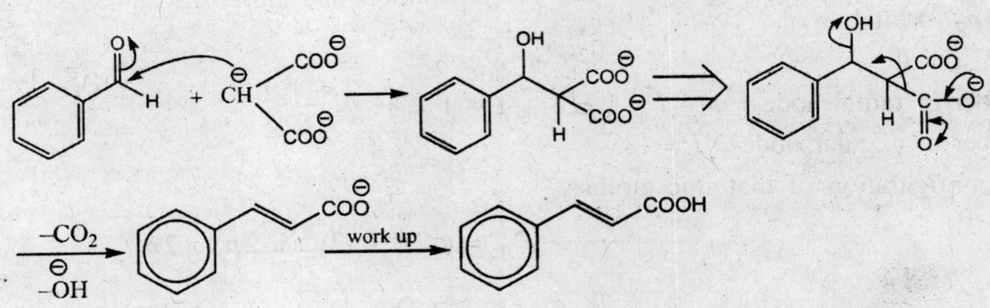

Reaction (D):

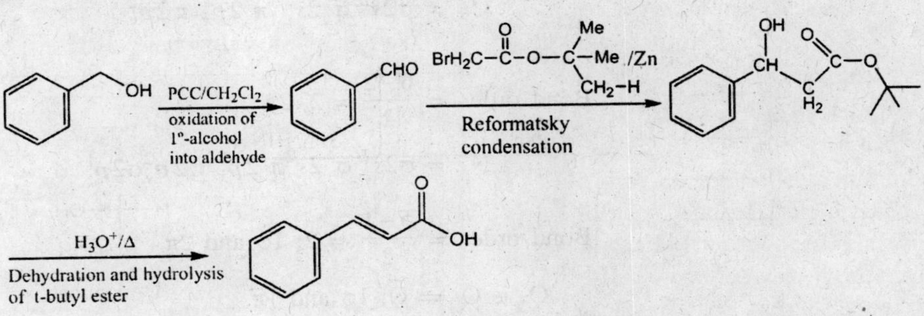

34.

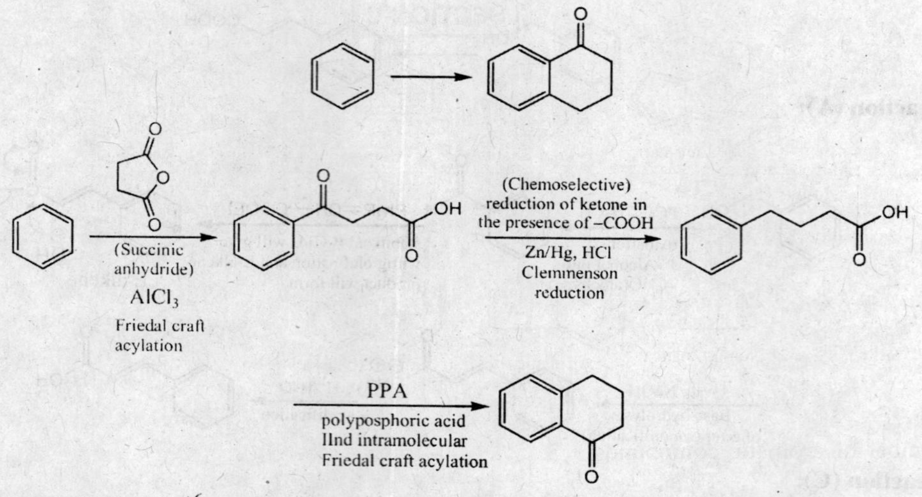

36. In CrO_4^{2-} and ReO_4^-, Cr^{+6} and Re^{+7} have vacant orbital and there is only LMCT.

37. Graphite has van der Waal's forces that holds layers of it. With $\pi - \pi$ stackings

38. From Langmuir adsorption isotherm

- Adsorption is monolayer.
- The gaseous molecules adsorbed at different sites do not interact with each other.
- The phenomenon of adsorption involves a dynamic equilibrium between free gas and adsorbed gas.
- Each site can hold only one gaseous molecule and involves a constant heat of adsorption. The latter is identical for all adsorption sites.

39. For $3p_z$ orbital

$n = 3, l = 1$

Number of radial node $= n - l - 1 = 3 - 1 - 1 = 1$

Number of angular node $= l = 1$.

40. The configuration of diatomic atoms:

$$B_2 = \sigma 2s^2\, \sigma^* 2s^2,\, \pi\, 2p_x^1\, \pi 2p_y^1 \quad \text{(one } \pi)$$

$$\text{Bond order} = \frac{4-2}{2} = 1,\ 1\pi$$

$$C_2 = \sigma 2s^2\, \sigma^* 2s^2\, \pi\, 2p_x^2\, \pi 2p_y^2 \quad \text{(two } \pi)$$

$$\text{Bond order} = \frac{6-2}{2} = 2,\ 2\pi$$

$$N_2 = \sigma 2s^2\, \sigma^* 2s^2 \pi\, 2p_x^2\, \pi 2p_y^2 \sigma 2p_z^1$$

$$\text{Bond order} = \frac{5-1}{2} = 2;\ 1\sigma \text{ and } 2\pi$$

O_2 is $O = O$; 1σ and 1π.

SECTION-C

41.

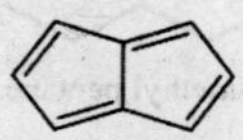

Non-aromatic (A)

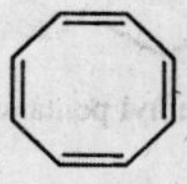

Non-aromatic (B)

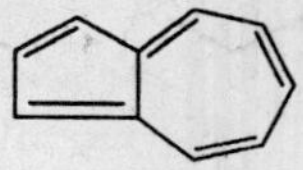

Aromatic (C)

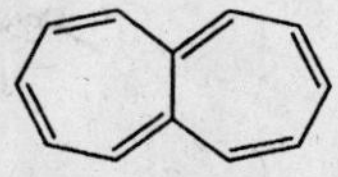

Non-aromatic (D)

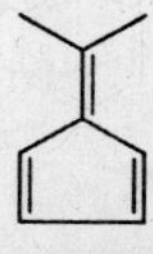

Non-aromatic (E)

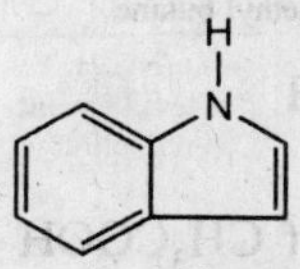

Aromatic (F)

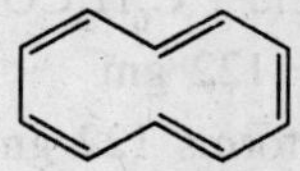

Non-aromatic (G)

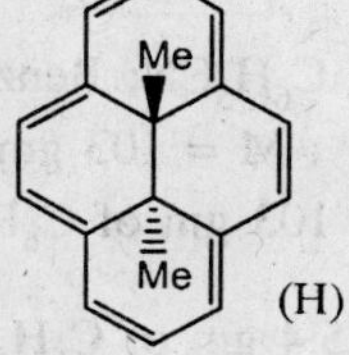

(H) Aromatic

Number of aromatic compounds = 3

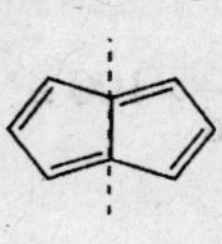

(A)

$n-1 = 3 \Rightarrow$ odd

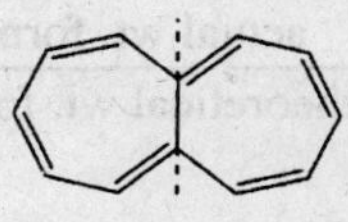

(D)

$n-1 = 5 \Rightarrow$ odd

According to Craig's Rule: in non-benzenoid compound containing C_2 axis of symmetry

If $n-1$ = even; compound is aromatic

If $n-1$ = odd; compound is non-aromatic

Therefore, hence A and D are not aromatic. [Where n = number of double bond]

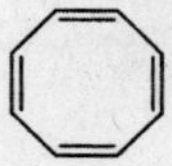

(B)

exist in non-planar tub shape

Since compound is not planar. Thus, it is non-aromatic.

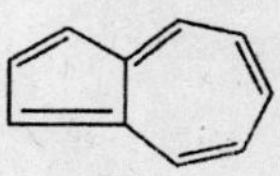

(C)

Azulene is aromatic[via Craig's rule also]

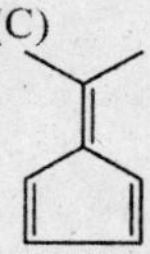

(E)

Dimethyl fulvene

Localized, structure and variable bond length, proves that it is non-aromatic

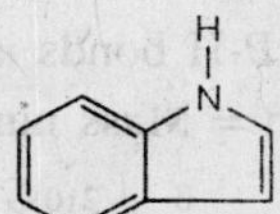

(F)

10 π electron system; aromatic

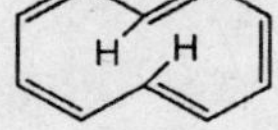

(G)

Transannular interaction non-planer structure; non-aromatic

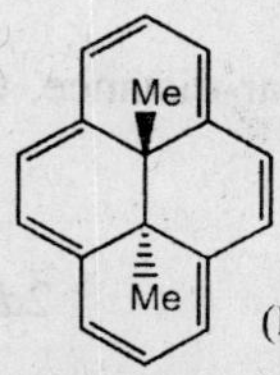

(H)

14 π electron system, aromatic

The number of aromatic compound = 3.

42. Possible isomers for hexane (C_6H_{14})

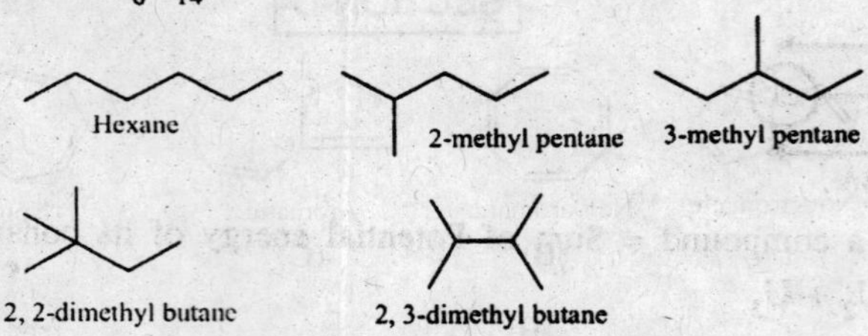

43. Benzonitrite : C_6H_5CN; Benzoic acid : C_6H_5COOH

Molecular wt. : M = 103 gm; M = 122 gm

Since, ideally 103 gm of C_6H_5CN forms 122 gm of CH_3COOH

Therefore, 15.4 gm of C_6H_5CN will form $= \dfrac{122 \times 15.45}{103} = 18.3$ gm of CH_3COOH

But actual CH_3COOH formed = 10.98 gm

So, percentage yield $= \dfrac{\text{actual wt. formed}}{\text{theoretical wt. formed}} \times 100 = \dfrac{10.98}{18.3} \times 100 = 60$

44. At equilibrium point,

Millimoles of CH_3COOH = millimoles of NaOH

$$M_1V_1 = M_2V_2; \quad M_1(20) = 1.5(18)$$

$$M_1 = \frac{1.5 \times 18}{20}, \quad M_1 = 1.35 \text{ mol L}^{-1}.$$

45. The configuration of $Be_2 = \sigma 1s^2\ \sigma^* 1s^2\ \sigma 2s^2\ \sigma^* 2s^2$

$\therefore$ Bond order $= \dfrac{4-4}{2} = 0$ (zero).

46. Hypophosphorus acid is H_3PO_2.

Its structure is 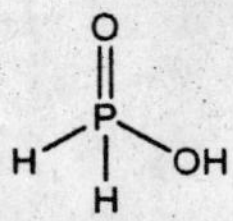

Hence, number of P-H bonds is **two.**

47. Number of neutron = Mass number – Number of proton

$$^{214}_{84}P_0 \xrightarrow{-\alpha} {}^{210}_{82}X \xrightarrow{-\beta} {}^{210}_{83}X$$

$\therefore$ Number of neutron = 210 – 83 = 127.

48. From, Bragg's law, $2d \sin\theta = n\lambda$

where, d = interplanar distance, θ = angle of diffraction, n = order of reflection

$$2\theta = 20.8$$

$\therefore$ $\theta = 10.4$

$$2d \sin 10.4° = 1 \times 1.54 \text{ Å}$$

$\therefore$ $d = \dfrac{1.54 \text{ Å}}{2 \sin 10.4°} = \dfrac{1.54}{0.1805 \times 2} = 4.266$ Å.

49.

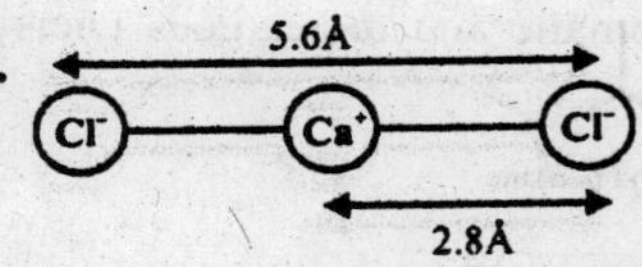

Potential energy of a compound = Sum of Potential energy of its constituents

$$U = U_1 + U_2 + U_3$$

$$= U_{(Ca^{2+}-Cl^-)} + U_{Ca^{2+}-Cl^-} + U_{(Cl^--Cl^-)}$$

$$= 1389.4\left(\frac{2\times(-1)}{2.8}\right) \text{kJmol}^{-1} + 1389.4\left(\frac{2\times(-1)}{2.8}\right) \text{kJmol}^{-1} + 1389.4\left(\frac{(-1)\times(-1)}{5.6}\right) \text{kJmol}^{-1}$$

$$= 1389.4\left[-\frac{2}{2.8} - \frac{2}{2.8} + \frac{1}{5.6}\right] = 1389.4\left[\frac{-4}{2.8} + \frac{1}{5.6}\right] = 1389.4\left(\frac{-7}{5.6}\right)$$

$$\therefore \quad U = -1736.7 \text{ kJ mol}^{-1}.$$

50. $C(g) + 4H(g) \rightarrow CH_4(g)$

$$\Delta H_r = \Sigma\Delta H_f (P) - \Sigma\Delta H_f (R)$$

$$= -75 - (717 + 4 \times 218)$$

$$\Delta H_r = -1664 \text{ kJmol}^{-1} \quad ...(i)$$

$$\Delta H_r = \Sigma(B.E.)_R - \Sigma(B.E.)_P$$

$$\Delta H_r = 0 - 4E_{(C-H)} \quad ...(ii)$$

From equations (*i*) and (*ii*),

$$-4E_{(C-H)} = -1664 \text{ kJ mol}^{-1}$$

$$E_{(C-H)} = \frac{1664}{4} = 416 \text{ kJ mol}^{-1}.$$

51. From question, we have specific rotation of R enantiomer = 48°

Sample = 25% S enantiomer with 75% R enantiomer

R-isomer is in excess.

So, specific rotation of mixture will have +ve sign.

Enantiomeric excess (e.e.) = 75% R – 25% S = 50%

$$\text{e.e.} = \frac{\text{specific rotation of sample } (x)}{\text{specific rotation of pure R-isomer}} \times 100$$

$$50 = \frac{x}{48°} \times 100 \Rightarrow x = \frac{48° \times 50}{100} = 24°.$$

52. Only cisoid form of Dienes undergoes Dields-Alder reaction.

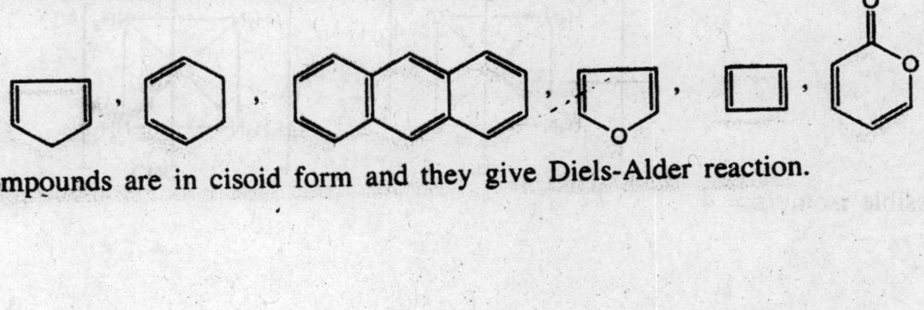

All these compounds are in cisoid form and they give Diels-Alder reaction.

Among the given compounds Furan and anthracene are less aromatic and under goes Diels-Alder reaction.

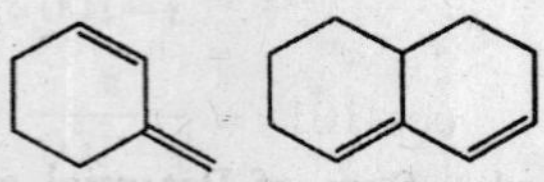

These two Dienes are in transoid form and they will not give the Diels-Alder reaction.

53.

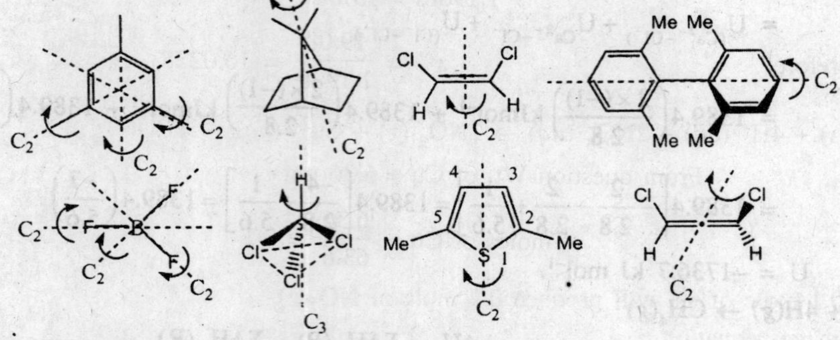

54. Configuration of vanadium, atomic number

$z = 23 = 1s^2 2s^2 2p^6 3s^2 3p^6\ 4s^2 3d^3$

or $(1s^2)\ (2s2p)^8\ (3s3p)^8\ (3d)^3\ (4s)^2$

$\underline{n-3 \quad n-2 \quad n-1} \quad n$

$S = [18 \times 1] + [2 \times 0.35] = 18 + 0.7 = 18.7$

Therefore, $z_{eff} = 23 - 18.7 = 4.3$

55. Given molecule: $[Co(NH_3)_4\ Cl(NO_2)]^+$

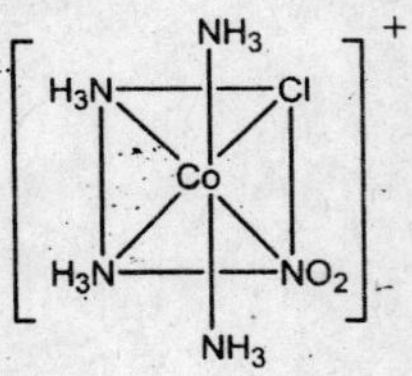

there is plane of symmetry optically inactive.

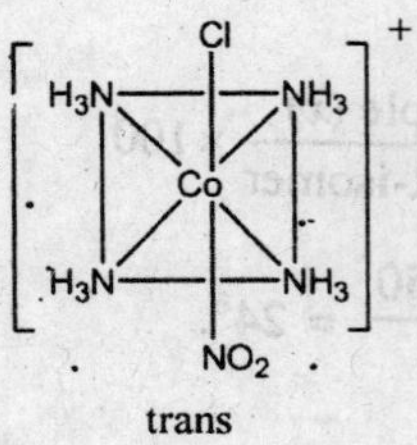

there is plane of symmetry, therefore, optically inactive.

trans

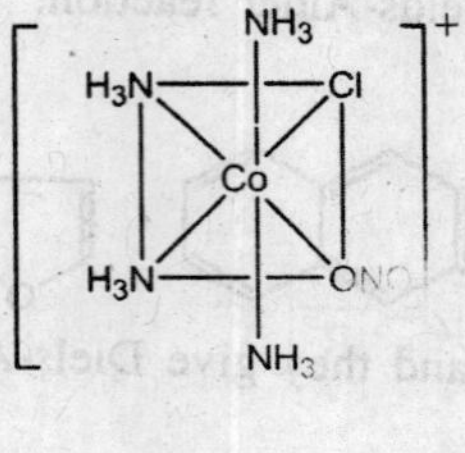

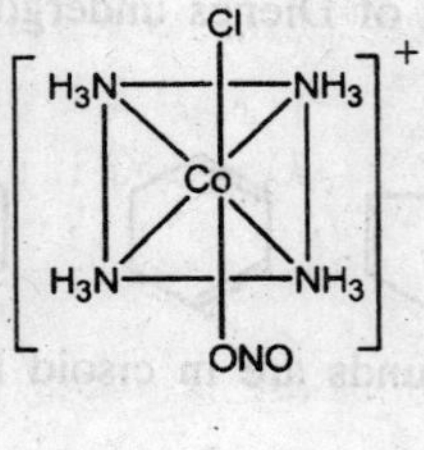

Possible isomers = 4.

56. From question $\theta = 101°$

$$\cos\theta = \frac{s}{s-100}$$

$$\cos 101° = \frac{s}{s-100} = -0.1908$$

Or, $s = -0.1908s + 19.08$

Or, $1.1908s = 19.08$

Therefore, $s\% = \frac{19.08}{1.1908} = 16.0228$

57. $Cu(s) + 4H^+ (aq) + 2NO_3^- (aq) \rightarrow 2NO_2 (g) + Cu^{2+} (aq) + 2H_2O(\ell)$

From question Wt. of Cu = 6.36 gm.

So, moles of Cu $= \frac{6.36}{63.6} = 0.1$

$\therefore$ 0.1 mole of Cu will produce 0.2 mole of $NO_2(g)$.

From gas equation $PV = nRT$

$$V = \frac{nRT}{P} = \frac{(0.2)(0.0821)\times(298)}{1} = 4.89 \text{ L.}$$

58. ΔH^0 at 298

$$\Delta H^0 = \Sigma\Delta H^0_{f(\text{products})} - \Sigma\Delta H^0_{f(\text{reactants})} = (-394)\text{ kJmol}^{-1} - \left(-110 + 0\times\frac{1}{2}\right)\text{kJmol}^{-1}$$

$$= -394 \text{ kJmol}^{-1} + 110 \text{ kJmol}^{-1} = -284 \text{ kJmol}^{-1} = -284 \times 10^3 \text{ Jmol}^{-1}$$

$$\int_{\Delta H_1^0}^{\Delta H_2^0} d(\Delta H^0) = \int_{T_1}^{T_2} \Delta C_P dT$$

$$\Delta C_P = \Sigma C_{P(\text{products})} - \Sigma C_{P(\text{reactants})} = 37.1 - \left(29.1 + \frac{1}{2}\times 29.4\right)$$

$$= 37.1 - (43.8) = -6.7 \text{ J mol}^{-1} \text{ K}^{-1}$$

$$\Delta H_2^0 - \Delta H_1^0 = \Delta C_P (T_2 - T_1);\ \Delta H_2^0 - \Delta H_1^0 = -6.7\ (400 - 298)$$

$$\Delta H_2^0 = \Delta H_1^0 - 6.7\ (102) = -284 \times 10^3 - 683.4 = (-284 \times 10^3 - 0.68 \times 10^3) \text{ kJ mol}^{-1}$$

$$= -284.68 \text{ kJmol}^{-1}.$$

59. From Temperature

$T_1 = 300$ K, $k_1 = 8$ L mole^{-1} s^{-1}

$T_2 = 350$ K, $k_2 = 160$ L mole^{-1} s^{-1}

$$\ln\left(\frac{k_2}{k_1}\right) = \frac{E_a}{R}\left[\frac{1}{T_1} - \frac{1}{T_2}\right] = \frac{E_a}{R}\left[\frac{T_2 - T_1}{T_1 T_2}\right]$$

$$E_a = \frac{RT_1T_2}{T_2 - T_1}\ln\left(\frac{k_2}{k_1}\right)$$

$$= \frac{8.314\ JK^{-1}mole^{-1} \times 300\ K \times 350\ K}{(350-300)K}\ln\left(\frac{160}{8}\right)$$

$$= 52.30368\ kJmole^{-1}.$$

60. Decomposition equation, $2N_2O_5\ (g) \longrightarrow 4NO_2(g) + O_2\ (g)$

$$\text{Numeber of moles of } N_2O_5 = \frac{10.8}{M_{N_2O_5}}$$

$$M_{N_2O_5} = 10.5$$

$$\Rightarrow \quad n_{N_2O_5} = \frac{10.8}{108} = 0.1$$

From question, at 373 K temperature, pressure is 0.5 atm

$$V = 10\ L,$$

From gas equation $PV = nRT$

$$\text{Total number of moles } (n) = \frac{PV}{RT} = \frac{0.5 \times 10}{0.0821 \times 373} = 0.1632$$

After decomposition, let x moles of N_2O_5 decomposed

$$2N_2O_5 \longrightarrow 4NO_2(g) + O_2(g)$$

$$0.1 - x \quad 2x \quad \frac{x}{2}$$

$$\text{Total number of moles} = 0.1 - x + 2x + \frac{x}{2}$$

$$= 0.1 + x + \frac{x}{2} = 0.1 + \frac{3x}{2}$$

$$0.1 + \frac{3x}{2} = 0.1632 \text{ (total number of moles)}$$

$$\frac{3x}{2} = 0.1632 - 0.1 = 0.0632$$

$$\Rightarrow \quad \frac{x}{2} = \frac{0.0632}{3} = 0.0210$$

$$\frac{x}{2} = \text{number of moles of } O_2 = 0.021$$

$$P_{O_2} = \frac{\text{nubmer of moles of } O_2}{\text{total number of moles}} \times \text{total pressure}$$

$$= \frac{0.021}{0.1632} \times 0.5 = 0.0643 \text{ atm.}$$

Previous Paper (Solved)

IIT–JAM

JOINT ADMISSION TEST FOR M.Sc. (CHEMISTRY)-2015

Section A : Multiple Choice Questions

Qs. 1 to 10 carry one mark each.

1. The first row transition metal complexes having tetrahedral geometry are high-spin due to

A. $\Delta_t > P$ B. $\Delta_t < P$

C. $\Delta_t = P$ D. $\Delta_t > \Delta_0$

2. The species responsible for the superacidity of SbF_5-HSO_3F system is

A. HSO_3F B. SbF_5

C. HF D. $H_2SO_3F^+$

3. A filter paper moistened with cadmium acetate solution turns yellow upon exposure to H_2S. The transition responsible for the yellow colour is

A. d–d

B. metal-to-ligand charge transfer

C. ligand-to-metal charge transfer

D. σ–σ^*

4. Low-spin iron(III) center is present in

A. deoxy form of hemoglobin

B. oxy form of hemoglobin

C. hemocyanin

D. carbonic anhydrase

5. The major product formed in the following reaction is

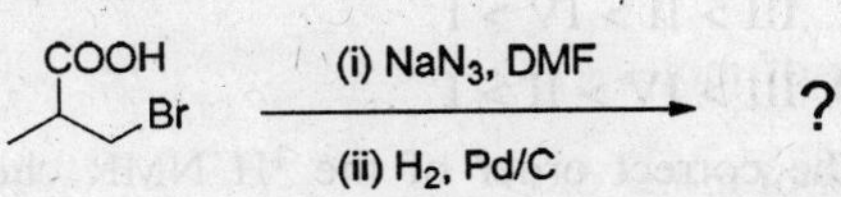

A. 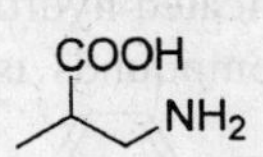

B. 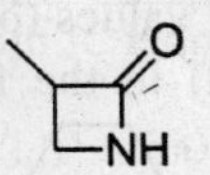

C. 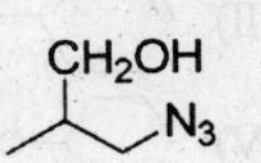

D. 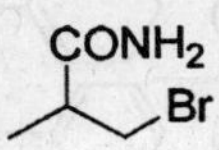

6. The structure of (2S,3R)-2-amino-3-hydroxy butanoic acid is

A. 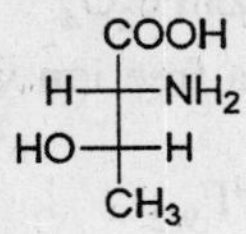

B. 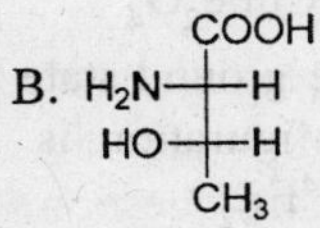

C. 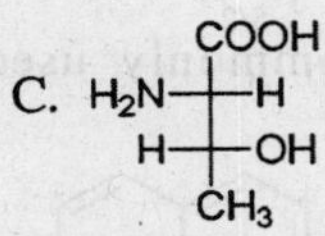

D. 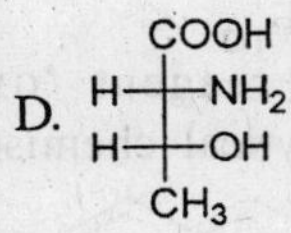

7. The ene-yne that produces a chiral compound upon treatment with Lindlar's catalyst is

A. 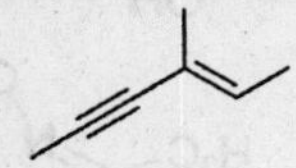

B. 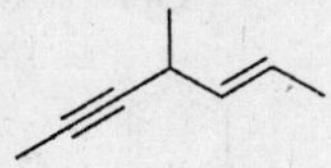

C. 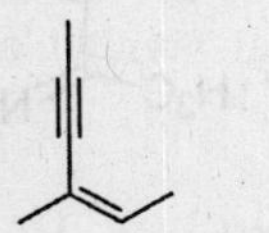

D. 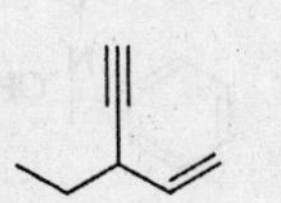

8. An organic compound **P** (C_4H_8O) is positive to Bayer's test, but inert to sodium metal. On treatment with conc. HCl, **P** gives CH_3CH_2Cl and CH_3CHO. The structure of **P** is

A. 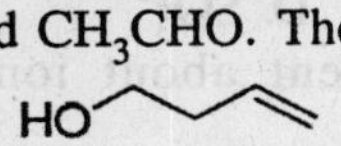

B. 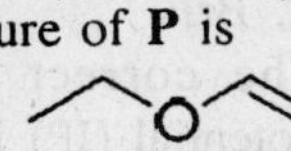

C. 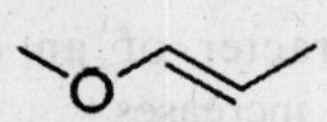

D. 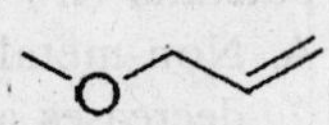

9. Which one of the following is an identity matrix?

A. $\begin{pmatrix} 0 & 0 \\ 0 & 0 \end{pmatrix}$ B. $\begin{pmatrix} 1 & 0 \\ 0 & 1 \end{pmatrix}$

C. $\begin{pmatrix} 0 & 1 \\ 1 & 0 \end{pmatrix}$ D. $\begin{pmatrix} 1 & 1 \\ 1 & 1 \end{pmatrix}$

10. The intermolecular van der Waals potential is inversely proportional to r^6. The corresponding force is proportional to

A. $\frac{1}{r^5}$ B. $\frac{1}{r^6}$

C. $\frac{1}{r^7}$ D. $\frac{1}{r^{12}}$

Qs. 11 to 30 carry two marks each.

11. The normal spinel among the following mixed metal-oxides is

A. $CoFe_2O_4$ B. $NiFe_2O_4$

C. $CuFe_2O_4$ D. $ZnFe_2O_4$

12. The ground state term for a free ion with $3d^7$ configuration is

A. $^4F_{3/2}$ B. $^4F_{9/2}$

C. $^4F_{1/2}$ D. $^4F_{5/2}$

13. The reagent 'oxine' commonly used in analytical chemistry is

A. 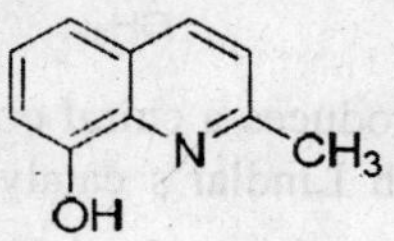 B. 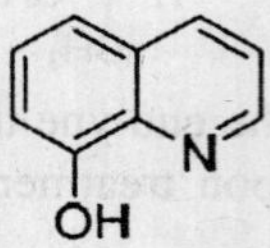

C. 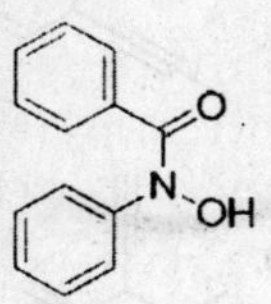 D. 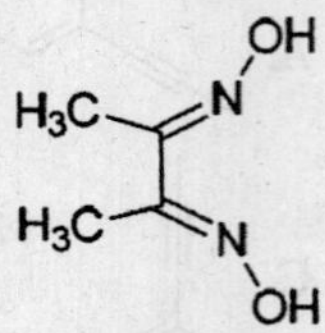

14. The species having trigonal pyramidal shape is

A. NO_3^- B. CO_3^{2-}

C. BrF_3 D. SO_3^{2-}

15. The correct statement about ionization potential (IP) is

A. Non-metallic character of an element decreases as the IP increases

B. IP decreases down the group in the periodic table

C. Second IP of Ca is larger than second IP of K

D. IP decreases on going from left to right in the periodic table

16. The Volhard method is used for the estimation of

A. cyanide ion by titration with silver nitrate

B. silver ion directly

C. oxygen in water

D. glucose in blood

17. The set of products formed in the following reaction is

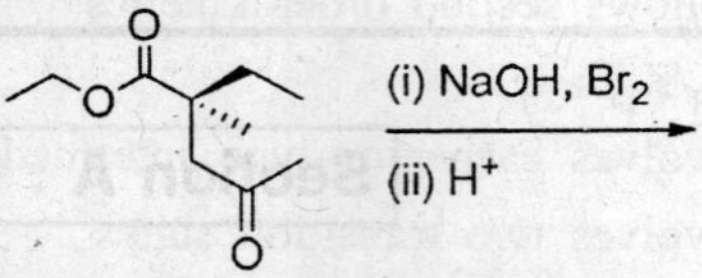

A. $CHBr_3$ and a racemic acid

B. $CHBr_3$ and a chiral acid

C. $CHBr_3$ and a racemic ester

D. CH_2Br_2 and a chiral ester

18. The correct set of reagents required for the following transformation is

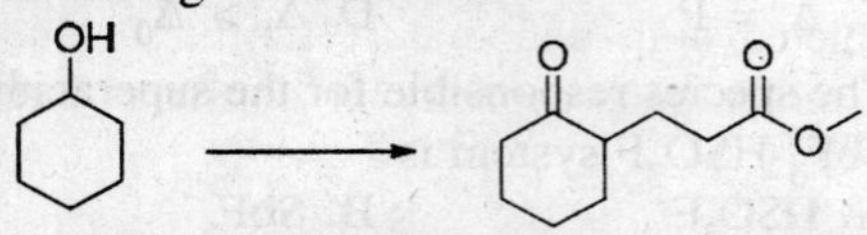

A. (i) CrO_3; (ii) acrylonitrile; (iii) H_3O^+

B. (i) O_2; (ii) methyl acrylate

C. (i) CrO_3; (ii) NaOMe/MeOH, methyl acrylate; (iii) H_3O^+

D. (i) H_2O; (ii) methyl acrylate

19. The correct order of the pKa values for the conjugate acids of heterocyclic compounds given below is

(I)  (II) 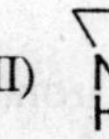

(III)  (IV) 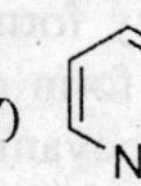

A. II > III > I > IV

B. IV > II > III > I

C. III > II > IV > I

D. III > IV > II > I

20. The correct order of the ^1H NMR chemical shift values (δ) for the indicated hydrogens (in bold) in the following compounds is

(I) 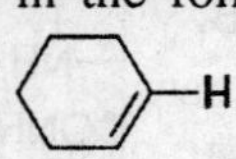 (II) 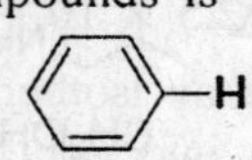

(III) 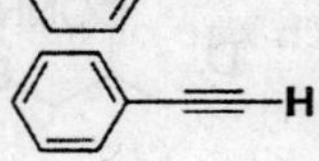 (IV) 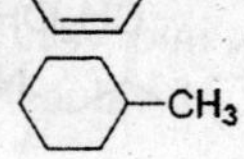

A. I > II > III > IV
B. II > I > III > IV
C. III > II > I > IV
D. II > III > IV > I

21. Which of the following statements are correct for S_NAr reaction?

(*i*) Follows second order kinetics

(*ii*) $K_H/K_D > 1$

(*iii*) Involves carbanion-type intermediate

(*iv*) Involves two transition states

A. (*i*) and (*ii*) only
B. (*ii*) and (*iii*) only
C. (*i*), (*iii*) and (*iv*) only
D. (*i*) and (*iii*) only

22. According to the equipartition principle, the predicted high temperature limiting value of the molar heat capacity at constant volume for C_2H_2 is

A. 5.5R   B. 6.0R
C. 9.0R   D. 9.5R

23. The major product formed in the following reaction is

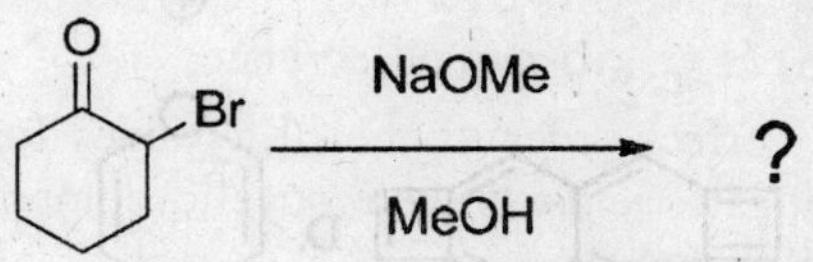

A. 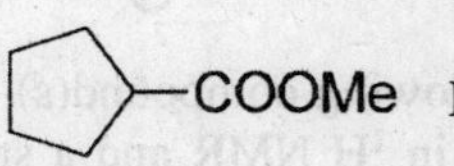

B. 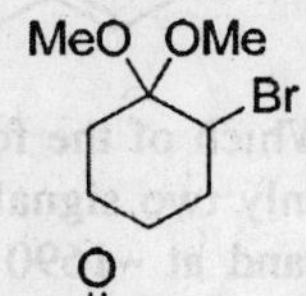

C. 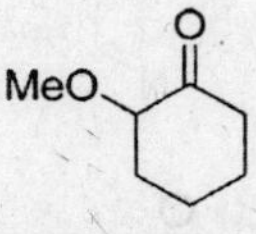

D. 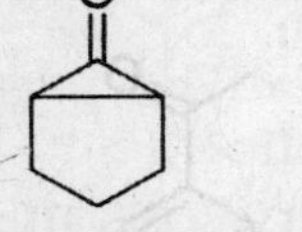

24. At 25°C, the solubility product (K_{sp}) of CaF_2 in water is 3.2×10^{-11}. The solubility (in mole per kg of water) of the salt at the same temperature (ignore ion pairing) is

A. 4.0×10^{-6} B. 3.2×10^{-4}
C. 2.5×10^{-4} D. 2.0×10^{-4}

25. For an isothermal free expansion of an ideal gas into vacuum, which one of the following set of values is correct?

A. $\Delta U = 0, q > 0, w < 0$
B. $\Delta U > 0, q > 0, w = 0$
C. $\Delta U = 0, q = 0, w = 0$
D. $\Delta U < 0, q = 0, w < 0$

26. The kinetics of the reaction $2N_2O_5 \rightarrow 4NO_2 + O_2$ in liquid bromine medium was measured independently for three different initial concentrations of N_2O_5: 0.11, 0.07 and 0.05 mol L^{-1}. The half-life of the reaction was found to be 4.5 hours for all these concentrations. The order of the reaction is

A. 0   B. 1
C. 2   D. 0.5

27. The concentration of K^+ ion inside a biological cell is 20 times higher than outside. The magnitude of potential difference between the two sides is [Given: 2.303 RT/F = 59 mV]

A. 0 mV   B. 26 mV
C. 77 mV   D. 177 mV

28. The correct order of the fundamental vibrational frequencies of the following diatomic molecules is

A. $^1H^{35}Cl > {}^1H^{37}Cl > {}^2D^{35}Cl$
B. $^2D^{35}Cl > {}^1H^{37}Cl > {}^1H^{35}Cl$
C. $^1H^{37}Cl > {}^1H^{35}Cl > {}^2D^{35}Cl$
D. $^1H^{37}Cl > {}^2D^{35}Cl > {}^1H^{35}Cl$

29. Identify the correct reagents required for the following transformation

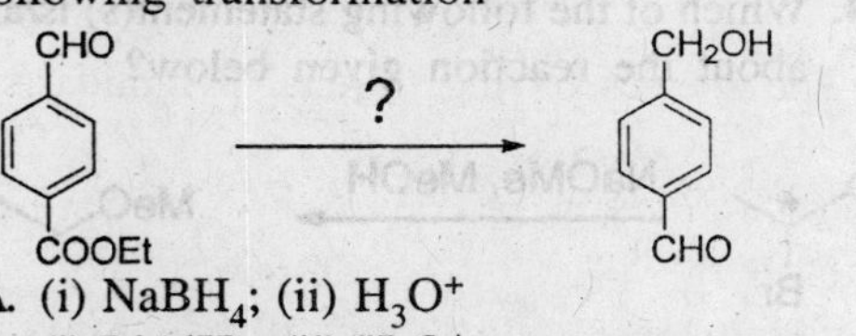

A. (i) $NaBH_4$; (ii) H_3O^+
B. (i) $LiAlH_4$; (ii) H_3O^+
C. (i) $HOCH_2CH_2OH, H^+$; (ii) $LiAlH_4$; (iii) H_3O^+
D. (i) $HSCH_2CH_2SH, H^+$; (ii) $LiAlH_4$; (iii) H_3O^+

30. The complex that is expected to show orbital contribution to the overall magnetic moment is

A. $[Cr(CN)_6]^{3-}$ B. $[Co(H_2O)_6]^{2+}$
C. $[Ni(en)_3]^{2+}$ D. $[Cu(NH_3)_6]^{2+}$

SECTION B : MULTIPLE SELECT QUESTIONS

Qs. 1 to 10 carry two marks each.

1. The common feature(s) of Rb^+, Kr and Br^- is/are that they

A. have same number of valence electrons

B. have same magnitude of effective nuclear charge

C. have same magnitude of first ionization potential

D. are isoelectronic species

2. The characteristics of the blue solution of sodium in liquid ammonia is/are

A. diamagnetic

B. paramagnetic

C. reducing in nature

D. conducts electricity

3. Which of the following statement(s) is/are true about the transition metal-alkene complexes?

A. Back-bonding weakens the double bond of the alkene

B. σ-Bonding and back-bonding synergistically strengthen metal-alkene interaction

C. Electron-withdrawing substituents on alkene reduce back-bonding

D. π-Acidic co-ligands on metal strengthen back-bonding

4. Which of the following statement(s) is/are true about the reaction given below?

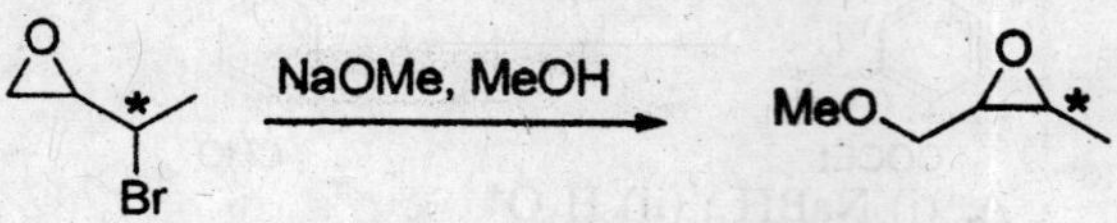

A. It involves a carbocation intermediate

B. Rearrangement is due to S_N1 reaction mechanism

C. It proceeds via a concerted S_N2 pathway

D. It involves neighbouring group participation

5. The reaction(s) which give(s) phenol is/are

A. 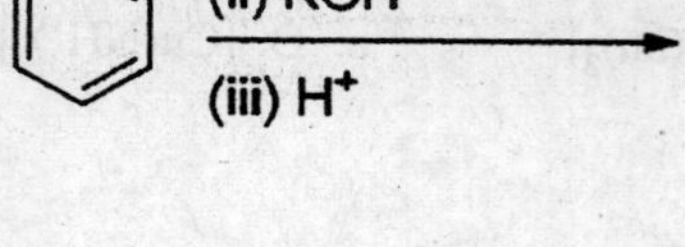

B. 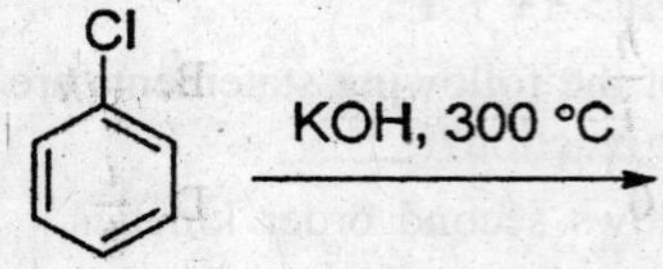

C. 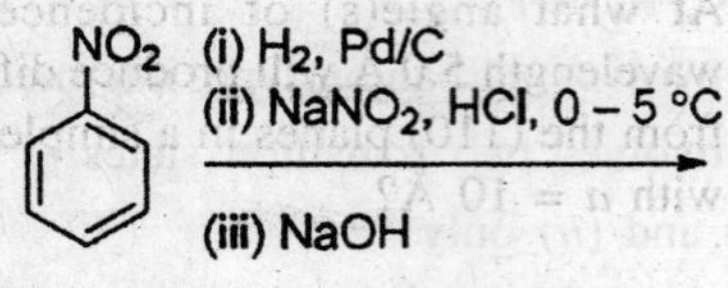

D. 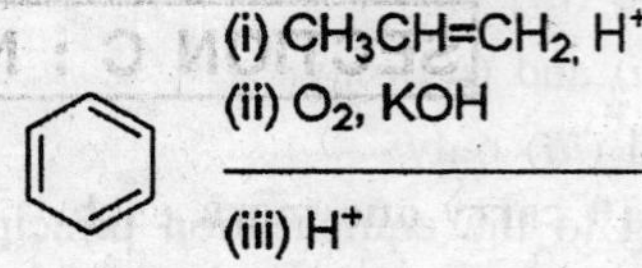

6. Which of the following species is/are aromatic in nature?

A. 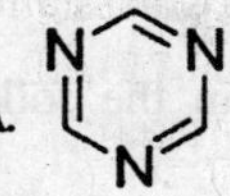

B. 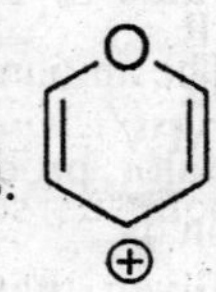

C. 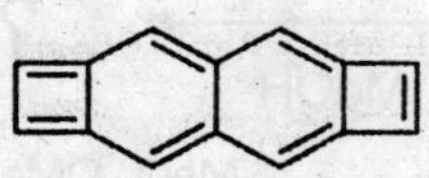

D. 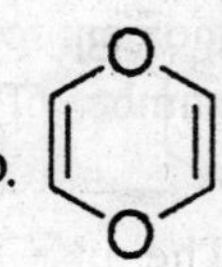

7. Which of the following compound(s) show(s) only two signals in ^1H NMR and a strong IR band at ~1690 cm^{-1}?

A. 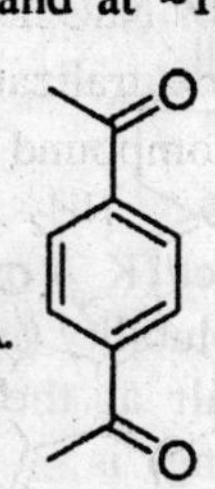

B. 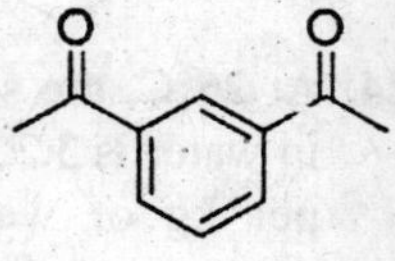

C. 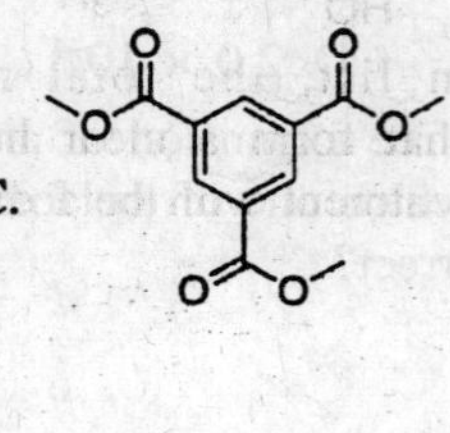

D. 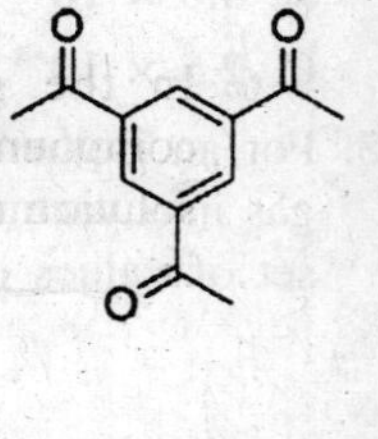

8. If $\hat{x} = x$ and $\hat{p}_x = \frac{h}{2\pi i}\frac{d}{dx}$, then the value(s) of $\hat{p}_x\hat{x} - \hat{x}\hat{p}_x$ is/are

A. $\frac{\hbar}{i}$ B. $-i\hbar$

C. 0 D. $\frac{i}{\hbar}$

9. At what angle(s) of incidence, X-rays of wavelength 5.0 Å will produce diffracted beam from the (110) planes in a simple cubic lattice with a = 10 Å?

A. 6.8° B. 10.2°

C. 20.7° D. 45.0°

10. Which of the following thermodynamic relation(s) is/are correct?

A. $\left(\frac{\partial T}{\partial V}\right)_S = \left(\frac{\partial P}{\partial S}\right)_V$ B. $\left(\frac{\partial T}{\partial P}\right)_S = \left(\frac{\partial V}{\partial S}\right)_P$

C. $\left(\frac{\partial S}{\partial V}\right)_T = \left(\frac{\partial P}{\partial T}\right)_V$ D. $\left(\frac{\partial S}{\partial P}\right)_T = \left(\frac{\partial V}{\partial T}\right)_P$

SECTION C : NUMERICAL ANSWER TYPE (NAT)

Qs. 1 to 10 carry one mark each.

1. Given that the crystal field stabilization energy for $[Co(H_2O)_6]^{2+}$ is 7360 cm^{-1}, the calculated value of Δ_0 in kJ mol^{-1} is _______

2. The amount (in grams) of potassium dichromate (MW = 294) present in 75 mL of 0.16 M aqueous solution is _______

3. Given that the expected spin-only magnetic moment for $(Et_4N)_2[NiCl_4]$ is 2.83 μ_B, the total number of unpaired electrons in this complex is _______

4. The pK_a values of lysine are 2.18, 8.95 and 10.79. The isoelectric point of lysine is _______

5. The amount (in grams) of NaOH (MW = 40) required for complete neutralization of one mole of the following compound is _______

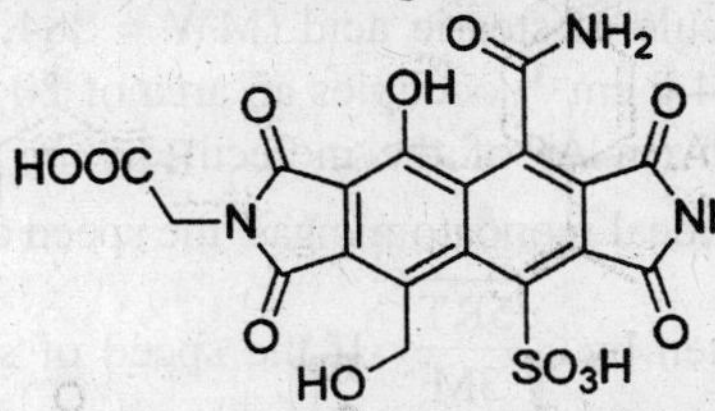

6. In the given list, the total number of compounds that form a clear homogenous solution on treatment with cold dilute H_2SO_4 is _______

1-propyne
cyclohexanone
cyclohexane
1-propene
propan-1-amine
propoxypropane
tetrahydropyran
ethyl butanoate
pyridine

7. In the gas phase, the ratio of excluded volume to molecular volume for a spherical molecule is _______

8. The pK_a values of H_3PO_4 are 2.12, 7.21 and 12.67. The pH of a phosphate buffer containing 0.2 M NaH_2PO_4 and 0.1 M Na_2HPO_4 is _______

9. For the reaction, $2SO_2 + O_2 \rightleftharpoons 2SO_3$, the equilibrium constant K_p = 5.0 at 207°C. If the partial pressures of SO_2, O_2 and SO_3 are 1.0 × 10^{-3}, 0.20 and 1.0 × 10^{-4}, respectively, then the Gibbs free energy of the reaction ($\Delta_r G$) in kJ mol^{-1} at 207°C is _______

[Given: R = 8.314 J K^{-1} mol^{-1}]

10. Two moles of an ideal gas is expanded isothermally and reversibly from 5 to 1 bar at 298 K. The change in the entropy (in J K^{-1}) of the system is _______

Qs. 11 to 20 carry two marks each.

11. The ionic radii of Cs^+ and Cl^- ions are 181 and 167 pm, respectively. The Born exponents for the He, Ne, Ar, Kr and Xe configurations are 5, 7, 9, 10 and 12, respectively. If the value of $\frac{ANe^2}{4\pi\varepsilon_0}$ is 2.45×10^{-4} J m, the lattice energy (in kJ mol^{-1}) of CsCl according to Born-Landé equation is ________

12. A 2.5×10^{-4} M solution of a complex exhibits an absorption maximum at 625 nm with an absorbance of 0.90 when measured in a cuvette with a path length of 1.5 cm. The absorbance of 1.5×10^{-3} M solution of the same complex recorded in a cuvette with a path length of 0.2 cm is ________

13. A wood specimen containing ^{14}C taken from an ancient palace showed 24 counts in 3 minutes per gram of carbon in a detector. However, a fresh wood showed 52 counts in 2 minutes per gram of carbon. Assuming no background signal in the detector and half life of ^{14}C as 5730 years, the age (in years) of the wood specimen is ________

14. The magnetic field (in Tesla) required for flipping a ^{1}H nucleus in an NMR spectrometer operating at 400 MHz is ________

[Given: $\gamma = 2.67 \times 10^8\ T^{-1}\ s^{-1}$, $\pi = 3.14$]

15. The total number of compounds (shown below) that form phenylhydrazone derivatives under acidic conditions is ________

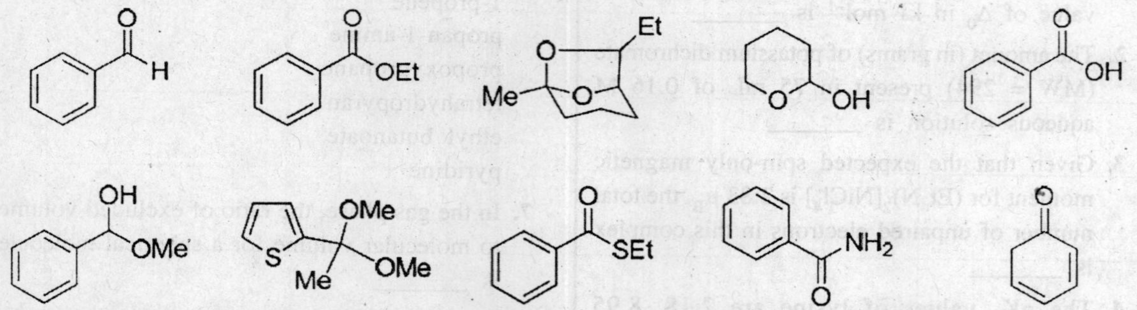

16. The number of possible monoalkylated products formed in the Friedel-Crafts reaction of anisole with 2-chloro-3-methylbutane in the presence of anhydrous $AlCl_3$ at 50°C is ________

17. For a reaction, the rate constant at 25°C is doubled when the temperature is raised to 45°C. The activation energy (in kJ mol^{-1}) of the reaction is ________ [Given: ln2 = 0.693]

18. The standard reduction potentials of the Fe^{3+}/Fe^{2+} and Fe^{2+}/Fe couples are 0.77 and –0.44 V, respectively. The standard reduction potential (in V) for the Fe^{3+}/Fe couple is ________

19. When a perfect monolayer of stearic acid is formed at the air-water interface, each molecule of stearic acid (MW = 284, density = 0.94 g cm^{-3}) occupies an area of 20 Å^2. The length (in Å) of the molecule is ________

20. In an ideal monoatomic gas, the speed of sound is given by $\sqrt{\frac{5RT}{3M}}$. If the speed of sound in argon at 25°C is 1245 km h^{-1}, the root mean square velocity in m s^{-1} is ________

ANSWERS

SECTION A : MCQ (Multiple Choice Questions)

1	2	3	4	5	6	7	8	9	10
B	D	C	B	A	C	B	B	B	C
11	**12**	**13**	**14**	**15**	**16**	**17**	**18**	**19**	**20**
D	B	B	D	B	X	B	C	C	B
21	**22**	**23**	**24**	**25**	**26**	**27**	**28**	**29**	**30**
C	D	A	D	C	B	C	A	C	B

SECTION B : MSQ (Multiple Select Questions)

1	2	3	4	5
A, D	B, C, D	A, B	C, D	A, B, C, D
6	**7**	**8**	**9**	**10**
A, B, C	A, D	A, B	C, D	B, C

SECTION C : NAT (Numerical Answer Type Questions)

1	2	3	4	5
109.0 to 111.0	3.52 to 3.54	2	9.0 to 10.0	160
6	**7**	**8**	**9**	**10**
4	8	6.9 to 7.0	–18.5 to –18.3	26.5 to 27.0
11	**12**	**13**	**14**	**15**
–638.0 to –636.0	0.70 to 0.74	9600 to 9900	9.0 to 10.0	5
16	**17**	**18**	**19**	**20**
4	27.0 to 27.6	–0.04 to –0.03	24 to 26	462 to 465

SOME SELECTED EXPLANATORY ANSWERS

SECTION-A

2. A superacid is defined as a substance that is a more efficient proton donor than 100% H_2SO_4. In practice, it can be up to 10^{18} times better than H_2SO_4. The physical features of superacids is that they are typically viscous, highly corrosive (as one might expect) liquids.

When SbF_5 is added, HSO_3F reacts with itself to produce a molecule of $H_2SO_3F^+$, containing a fluorine atom with a formal charge of +1. The F-H bond in this case is highly unstable, making this species a very strong acid.

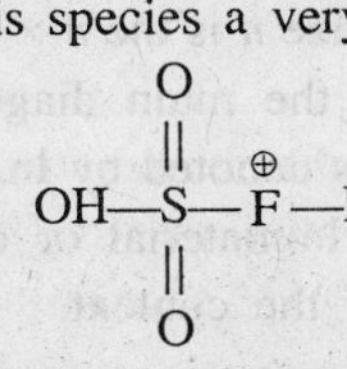

$$SbF_5 + 2HSO_3F \rightarrow H_2SO_3F^+ + SbF_5SO_3F^-$$

4. In hemoglobin, a high-spin Fe(II) is coordinated to four N atoms of porphyrin ring. The fifth coordination site is occupied by a histidine group. In this condition the protein containing four heme compartments is in stain condition and called tense (T) state. After binding to molecular oxygen high-spin Fe(II) changes to low-spin Fe(III) and molecular oxygen is transferred to superoxide.

6. Structure of (2S, 3R)-2-amino-3-hydroxy butanoic acid:

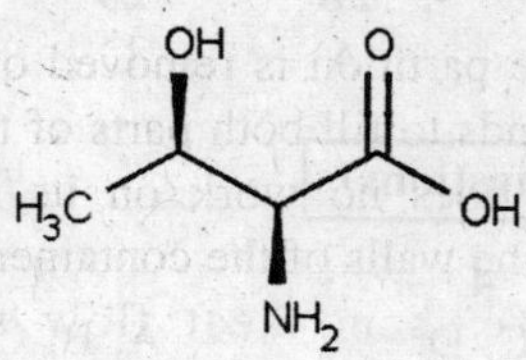

Threonine (abbreviated as Thr or T) is an α-amino acid with the chemical formula $HO_2CCH(NH_2)CH(OH)CH_3$. Its codons are ACU, ACA, ACC, and ACG. This essential amino acid is classified as polar. Together with serine, threonine is one of two proteinogenic amino acids bearing an alcohol group. It is also one of two common amino acids that bear a chiral side chain, along with isoleucine.

8. Ethoxyethene (C_4H_8O): This compound belongs to the class of organic compounds known as organooxygen compounds. These are organic compounds containing a bond between a carbon atom and an oxygen atom. This show positive result with Bayer's test.

9. In linear algebra, the identity matrix or unitmatrix of size n is the $n \times n$ square matrix with ones on the main diagonal and zeros elsewhere. It is denoted by In, or simply by I if the size is immaterial or can be trivially determined by the context.

The potential energy representing the dipole-induced dipole interaction is:

$$V = -\frac{\alpha\mu^2}{4\pi\epsilon_0 r^6}$$

α = polarizability of the non-polar molecule. Polarizability defines how easy the electron density of an atom or a molecule can be distorted by an external electric field and force

$$F = \frac{dv}{dr}$$

$$\Rightarrow \qquad F \propto \frac{1}{r^7}$$

11. **Mixed Metal Oxide Pigments**. Mixed metal oxides refer to pigments that crystallize in a stable oxide lattice. The colour is due to coloured cations incorporated in the lattice. The number of possible mixed metal oxides obtainable from different substituent elements and oxide lattices is very large, but only a limited number of structures, principally spinel, rutile, and hematite structures, have the stability and optical properties necessary for pigment applications. In a normal spinel (*e.g.*, $NiCr_2O_4$ and $ZnFe_2O_4$) the tetrahedral and octahedral sites are occupied by divalent and trivalent cations, respectively. If tetrahedral sites are completely occupied by trivalent cations and the octahedral sites are shared by both divalent and trivalent cations, it is an inverse spinel (*e.g.*, $NiFe_2O_4$ and γ-Fe_2O_3).

12. The ground state electron configuration of ground state gaseous neutral cobalt is [Ar] . $3d^7$. $4s^2$ and the term symbol is $^4F_{9/2}$.

13. 8-Hydroxyquinoline, usually known as oxine, was introduced into analytical chemistry by Berg and Hahn. With the majority of cations it forms chelate salts insoluble in water but soluble in various organic solvents. The analytical conversion factors of the oxine complexes are low and therefore favour their gravimetric use.

8-Hydroxyquinoline (oxine, 8-quinolinol)

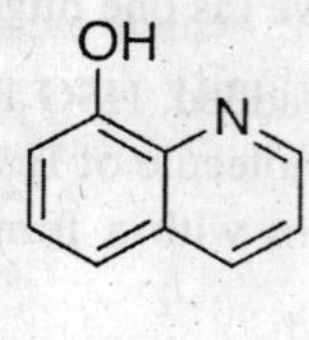

14.

Example	Bond electron pairs	Lone pairs	Geometry of molecule or composite ion
NO_3^-; 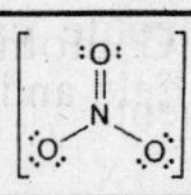	3	0	Trigonal planar
BrF_3; 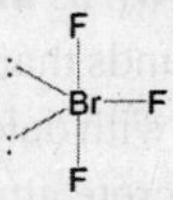	3	2	Trigonal bipyramidal
CO_3^{2-}; 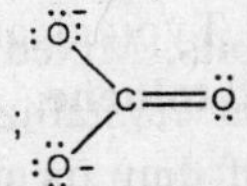	3	0	Trigonal planar
SO_3^{2-}; 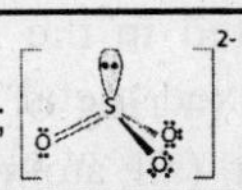	3	1	Trigonal Pyramidal

15. Ionization potential—In a period ionisation potential generally increases with increase in atomic number because the atomic size decreases as one moves from left to right in a period.

I.P. values for second period elements are

	Li	Be	B	C	N	O	F	Ne
I.P. (eV)	5.4	9.32	8.3	11.3	14.5	13.6	17.4	21.5

IP-gradually increases from Li to Ne except Be and N. The IP of Be and N are exceptionally high because of extra stability of fully filled *s*-orbital in Be and half filled 2*p*-orbital in N.

In the 3rd period trend of I.P. is same as that of in 2nd period.

I.P. values decrease as one descend down the group of the periodic table.

Highest I.P. is shown by inert gases in respective periods.

21. The kinetics of the reaction provide some insight into the rate-determining step of the mechanism. S_NAr reaction follows second-order kinetics. The rate of the reaction depends on the concentration of both the aryl halide and the nucleophile, which means that both must be mechanistically involved in the rate-determining step of the reaction.

Rate = k[aryl halide] [nucleophile]

S_NAr reaction involves carbanion type intermediate and also involves in two transition states.

25. For an ideal gas, the internal energy *U* depends only on temperature, not on pressure or volume. A thermally insulated container with rigid walls is divided into two compartments by a partition. One compartment has a quantity of an ideal gas and the other is evacuated.

When the partition is removed or broken, the gas expands to fill both parts of the container. The gas does no work on its surroundings because the walls of the container don't move, and there is no heat flow through the insulation. So both *Q* and *W* are zero and change in internal energy *U* is zero, this is an isothermal process.

27. The relationship between the concentration gradient across the membrane of any given ion and the membrane potential which will just balance it at electrochemical equilibrium is given by the physiochemical relationship known as the Nernst equation. It represents the equilibrium potential for that particular ionic type.

$$E = RT/zF \ \ln C_1/C_2$$

$$E = 59.\log(20)$$

$$= 59 \times 1.301$$

$$= 76.8$$

$$\cong 77 \text{ mV}.$$

30. Orbital contribution to magnetic moments: From a quantum mechanics viewpoint, the magnetic moment is dependent on both spin and orbital angular momentum contributions. The spin-only formula used given as:

$$\mu_{s.o.} = \sqrt{4S(S+1)}$$

and this can be modified to include the orbital angular momentum

$$\mu_{S+L} = \sqrt{4S(S+1) + L(L+1)}$$

An orbital angular momentum contribution is expected when the ground term is triply degenerate (*i.e.*, a triplet state). These show temperature dependence as well.
Based on above formula complexes $[Co(H_2O)_6]^{2+}$ show orbital contribution to the overall magnetic moment.

SECTION-B

1.

Sym.	Electrons per Shell	Electron Configuration	Valence Electrons
Br^-	2, 8, 8, 10, 8	[Ar] $3d^{10}\ 4s^2 4p^6$	$4s^2 4p^6$
Kr	2, 8, 18, 8	[Ar] $3d^{10}\ 4s^2 4p^6$	$4s^2 4p^6$
Rb^+	2, 8, 18, 8	[Ar] $3d^{10}\ 4s^2 4p^6$	$4s^2 4p^6$

Hence, Rb^+, Kr and Br^- are isoelectronic species and having same number of valence electrons.

2. Alkali metals dissolve in liquid ammonia to produce blue coloured solutions which conduct electricity.
The alkali metals dissolve in liquid ammonia to give blue to bronze colour. The colour is attributed to the presence of solvated electrons *e.g.*, $[e(NH_3)_4]^-$ in dilute solution.

$M^+ (x + y)\ NH_3 \rightarrow [M(NH_3)_x]^+ + [e(NH_3)y]^-$

However in concentrated solutions, the ammoniated metal ions are bound by the free unpaired electrons which give bronze colour. The blue solutions are paramagnetic, whereas the bronze coloured solutions are diamagnetic.

3. According to this bonding model, the resulting σ-forward bond is additionally strengthened by π-back bonding of electrons from an occupied metal orbital of suitable symmetry (d_{xy} or d_{yz} and p_x or p_y, AOs) into an empty π* – MO of the alkene. Because electrical neutrality must be preserved, the contributions of the σ-forward and π-back bonding are not independent (synergism): as one bond component increases, the other must also. The π-back bonding, in particular, weakens the CC bond and causes it to stretch. As the electron flow increases, the *alkene complex* undergoes successive lengthening of the CC bond and decreases in the interplanar angle (increases in α) until it forms a *metallacyclopropane complex* with the C atoms in a distorted tetrahedral arrangement.

6. Aromatic compounds, also known as **arenes** or aromatics, are chemical compounds that contain **conjugated** planar ring systems with delocalized π electron clouds instead of discrete alternating single and double bonds. Typical aromatic compounds are **benzene** and **toluene**.

A compound is aromatic, if they meet all the following criteria:

1. The molecule is cyclic (a ring of atoms)
2. The molecule is planar (all atoms in the molecule lie in the same plane)
3. The molecule is fully conjugated (*p* orbitals at every atom in the ring)
4. The molecule has $4n + 2$ π electrons (n = 0 or any positive integer)

8. $$\hat{p}_x\hat{x} - \hat{x}\hat{p}_x = \frac{h}{2\pi i}\frac{d}{dx}x - x\frac{h}{2\pi i}\frac{d}{dx}(1)$$

[∵ given as]

$$= \frac{h}{2\pi i}\times 1 - x\frac{h}{2\pi i}\times 0 \quad \left[\because \frac{d}{dx}x = 1 \text{ and } \frac{d}{dx}(1) = 0\right]$$

$$= \frac{h}{2\pi i} - 0 = \frac{h}{2\pi}\times\frac{1}{i} = \hbar\times\frac{1}{i} \quad \left[\because \hbar = \frac{h}{2\pi}\right]$$

$$= \frac{\hbar}{i} \text{ (A)}$$

$$= \frac{\hbar\times i}{i\times i} = \frac{\hbar i}{i^2}$$

$$= \frac{\hbar i}{-1} \quad [\because i^2 = -1]$$

$$= -\hbar i \text{ (B)}$$

Hence, A and B both options are true.

9. From $n\lambda = 2d \sin\theta$

n is an integer and is the order of the reflection (*i.e.*, how many wavelengths of the X-ray go on to make the path difference between planes).

And

$$d_{hkl}^{cubic\,crystal} = \frac{a}{\sqrt{h^2+k^2+l^2}}$$

$$= \frac{10}{\sqrt{1^2+1^2+0}}$$

$$= \frac{10}{\sqrt{2}} = 5\sqrt{2}$$

For $n = 1$

$$\lambda = 2d \sin \theta$$

$$5 \times 10^{-10} = 2 \times 5\sqrt{2} \times 10^{-10} \times \sin\theta$$

$$\sin \theta = \frac{5\times10^{-10}}{2\times5\sqrt{2}\times10^{-10}} = 0.3535$$

$\therefore$ $\theta = 20.7°$.

For $n = 2$,

$$2\lambda = 2d \sin \theta$$

$$\lambda = d \sin \theta$$

$$\Rightarrow \quad \sin \theta = \frac{\lambda}{d}$$

$$= \frac{5\times10^{-10}}{5\sqrt{2}\times10^{-10}} = \frac{1}{\sqrt{2}}$$

$\therefore$ $\theta = 45°$.

10. According to first and second law of thermodynamics, we have

$$dQ = dU + pdV \quad [\because dW = pdV]$$

and $$dQ = TdS$$

where all symbols have their usual meanings.

We can write as,

$$TdS = dU + pdV$$

or $$dU = Tds - pdV \quad ...(i)$$

Let, U, S and V are the functions of two independent variable x and y, then, we have

$$dU = \frac{\partial U}{\partial x}dx + \frac{\partial U}{\partial y}dy$$

$$dS = \frac{\partial S}{\partial x}dx + \frac{\partial S}{\partial y}dy$$

and $$dV = \frac{\partial V}{\partial x}dx + \frac{\partial V}{\partial y}dy$$

Putting these values in equation (*i*), we get

$$\frac{\partial U}{\partial x}dx + \frac{\partial U}{\partial y}dy = T\left(\frac{\partial S}{\partial x}dx + \frac{\partial S}{\partial y}dy\right) - p\left(\frac{\partial V}{\partial x}dx + \frac{\partial V}{\partial y}dy\right)$$

Equating the coefficient of dx and dy on both sides, we get

$$\frac{\partial U}{\partial x} = T\frac{\partial S}{\partial x} - p\frac{\partial V}{\partial x} \quad ...(ii)$$

and $$\frac{\partial U}{\partial y} = T\frac{\partial S}{\partial y} - p\frac{\partial V}{\partial y} \quad ...(iii)$$

Differentiating equation (*ii*) w.r.t. y and equation (*iii*) w.r.t. x, we get

$$\frac{\partial^2 U}{\partial y \partial x} = \frac{\partial T}{\partial y}\frac{\partial S}{\partial x} + T\frac{\partial^2 S}{\partial y \partial x} - \frac{\partial p}{\partial y}\frac{\partial V}{\partial x} - p\frac{\partial^2 V}{\partial y \partial x}$$

and $$\frac{\partial^2 U}{\partial x \partial y} = \frac{\partial T}{\partial x}\frac{\partial S}{\partial y} + T\frac{\partial^2 S}{\partial x \partial y} - \frac{\partial p}{\partial x}\frac{\partial V}{\partial y} - p\frac{\partial^2 V}{\partial x \partial y}$$

Since dU, dS and dV are all perfect differentials. So,

$$\frac{\partial^2 U}{\partial y \partial x} = \frac{\partial^2 U}{\partial x \partial y}, \frac{\partial^2 S}{\partial y \partial x} = \frac{\partial^2 S}{\partial x \partial y} \text{ and } \frac{\partial^2 V}{\partial y \partial x} = \frac{\partial^2 V}{\partial x \partial y}$$

Hence, we get

$$\frac{\partial T}{\partial y}\frac{\partial S}{\partial x} - \frac{\partial p}{\partial y}\frac{\partial V}{\partial x} = \frac{\partial T}{\partial x}\frac{\partial S}{\partial y} - \frac{\partial p}{\partial x}\frac{\partial V}{\partial y} \quad ...(iv)$$

This is the general Maxwell's thermodynamic equation. Now, we put $x = T$ and $y = V$, then we have

$$\frac{\partial T}{\partial x} = 1, \frac{\partial V}{\partial y} = 1 \text{ and } \frac{\partial T}{\partial y} = 0, \frac{\partial V}{\partial x} = 0$$

Therefore, equation (*iv*) becomes,

$$\frac{\partial S}{\partial y} - \frac{\partial p}{\partial x} = 0$$

or $$\left(\frac{\partial S}{\partial V}\right)_T = \left(\frac{\partial P}{\partial T}\right)_V \quad [\because x = \text{T and } y = \text{V}]$$

This is the required relation.

From Maxwell relation, the change in the value of a property between two states is independent of the *path*. Mathematically, this means that the order in taking the second derivative does not matter.

Applying this condition gives

$$\left[\frac{\partial T}{\partial V}\right]_S = \left[\frac{\partial}{\partial V}\left(\frac{\partial U}{\partial S}\right)_V\right]_S$$

$$= \left[\frac{\partial}{\partial S}\left(\frac{\partial U}{\partial V}\right)_S\right]_V$$

$$= -\left(\frac{\partial p}{\partial S}\right)_V$$

Usually the above second derivatives are more loosely written as $\left(\frac{\partial^2 U}{\partial V \partial S}\right)$ and $\left(\frac{\partial^2 U}{\partial S \partial V}\right)$. The complete list of these equations, called Maxwell's relations, is given below:

$$\left(\frac{\partial T}{\partial V}\right)_S = -\left(\frac{\partial p}{\partial S}\right)_V$$

$$\left(\frac{\partial T}{\partial p}\right)_S = \left(\frac{\partial V}{\partial S}\right)_P$$

SECTION-C

2. Molar mass of $K_2Cr_2O_7$ is 294 g/mol.

Amount of $K_2Cr_2O_7$ present

$= 0.16 \times 0.075 \times 294$

$= 3.528$ grams

3. The formula used to calculate the spin-only magnetic moment can be written in two forms; the first based on the number of unpaired electrons, *n*, and the second based on the electron spin quantum number, *S*. Since for each unpaired electron, $n = 1$ and $S = 1/2$ then the two formulae are clearly related and the answer obtained must be identical.

$$\mu_{so} = \sqrt{n(n+2)}$$

$$\mu_{so} = 2.83$$

$$2.83 = \sqrt{n(n+2)}$$

squaring both sides,

$$(2.83)^2 = n(n+2)$$

$$8 = n^2 + 2n$$

$$n^2 + 2n - 8 = 0$$

$$(n-2)(n+4) = 0$$

$$n = 2$$

Hence, number of unpaired electrons $n = 2$.

4. The pI of lysine is the average of the pK_a values of the two groups that are positively charged in their acidic form and uncharged in their basic form. The pI of glutamic acid, on the other hand, is the average of the pK_a values of the two groups that are uncharged in their acidic form and negatively charged in their basic form.

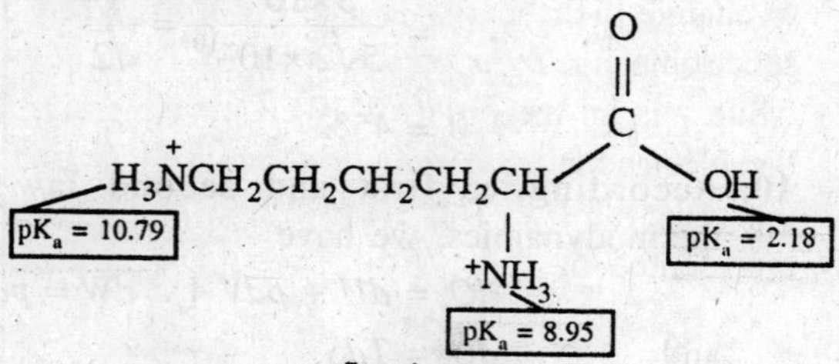

Lysine

$$\text{pI} = \frac{8.95 + 10.79}{2} = \frac{19.74}{2} = 9.87.$$

10. T.W. Richards and W. Nernst studied the entropy changes of certain isothermal chemical reactions and found that the change in entropy approached zero as the temperature was reduced. The entropy change for a chemical reaction can be determined calorimetrically using $\Delta S = q_{rev}/T$ because reactions occur reversibly.

$$\Delta S = \frac{\Delta \theta}{T}$$

$$= nR.\ln\left(\frac{P_1}{P_2}\right)$$

$$= 2\times8.314\times\ln\left(\frac{5}{1}\right)$$

$$= 2 \times 8.314 \times 1.61$$

$$= 26.77 \text{ J/k.}$$

11. The Born-Lande equation is given below:

$$\Delta U = \frac{AN_A Z_+ Z_- e^2}{4\pi\varepsilon_0 r}\left(1-\frac{1}{n}\right)$$

Cs^+ and Cl^- both have the electronic configuration [Ar]. Both have Born exponents $n = 9$, $Z_+ = 1$ and $Z_- = 1$, $r = 181 + 167 = 348$ pm. Putting these value into equation we have

$$= \frac{2.45\times10^{-4}\times1}{348\times10^{-12}}\times\left(1-\frac{1}{9}\right) \cong -625.8 \text{ KJ/mol.}$$

14. In order for the NMR experiment to work, a spin flip between the energy levels must occur. The energy difference between the two states corresponds to the energy of the electromagnetic radiation that causes the nuclei to change their energy levels. For most NMR spectrometers, B_0 is on the order of Tesla (T) while γ is on the order of 10^7. Consequently, the electromagnetic radiation required is on the order of Hz. The energy of a photon is represented by

$$E = h\nu$$

and thus the frequency necessary for absorption to occur is represented as:

$$\nu = \frac{\gamma B_0}{2\pi}$$

$$\Rightarrow \quad B_0 = \frac{2\pi\nu}{\gamma}$$

here $\nu = 400$ MHz

$\pi = 3.14$

$\gamma = 2.67 \times 10^8 \text{ T}^{-1}\text{S}^{-1}$

$$\therefore \quad B_0 = \frac{2\times3.14\times400\times10^6}{2.67\times10^8}$$

$$= 9.4 \text{ T.}$$

17. $T_1 = 298$ K, $T_2 = 318$ K

$$\ln\left(\frac{k_2}{k_1}\right) = \left(\frac{E_a}{R}\right)\left(\frac{1}{T_1}-\frac{1}{T_2}\right)$$

T_1 = initial Kelvin temp. = 298 K

T_2 = final Kelvin temp. = 318 K

R = 8.314 J/mol K

E_a = activation energy in joules

$\frac{k_2}{k_1}$ = ratio of rate constants

= 2 (reaction rate doubles, k doubles)

$$\ln 2 = \frac{E_a}{8.314}\left[\frac{1}{298}-\frac{1}{318}\right]$$

$$0.693 = \frac{E_a}{8.314}\left[\frac{20}{298\times318}\right]$$

$$\Rightarrow \quad E_a = \frac{0.693\times298\times318\times8.314}{20}$$

$$= 27299.6 \text{ J/mol}$$

$$= 27.3 \text{ KJ/mol.}$$

18. The Nernst Equation for an arbitrary reaction $Ox + z\,.\,e^- \rightleftharpoons$ Red:

$$E = E^{\ominus}\left(\frac{Red}{Ox}\right) - z^{-1}.RTF^{-1}\ln\frac{Red}{Ox}$$

For our given system that boils down to the following reaction and their potentials:

$Fe^{2+} + 2.e^- \rightarrow Fe$

$$E_1 = E^{\ominus}\left(\frac{Fe^{2+}}{Fe}\right) - \frac{1}{2}.RTF^{-1}\ln\left(\frac{Fe^{2+}}{Fe}\right) \quad ...(i)$$

$Fe^{3+} + 1.e^- \rightarrow Fe^{2+}$

$$E_2 = E^{\ominus}\left(\frac{Fe^{3+}}{Fe^{2+}}\right) - \frac{1}{1}.RTF^{-1}\ln\left(\frac{Fe^{3+}}{Fe^{2+}}\right) \quad ...(ii)$$

$Fe^{3+} + 3.e^- \rightarrow Fe$

$$E_3 = E^{\ominus}\left(\frac{Fe^{3+}}{Fe}\right) - \frac{1}{3}.RTF^{-1}\ln\left(\frac{Fe^{3+}}{Fe}\right) \quad ...(iii)$$

Consider the potential E_3, which can be build from E_1 and E_2:

$$E_3 = a \cdot E_1 + b \cdot E_2$$

Here,

$$a = \frac{2}{3},$$

$$b = \frac{1}{3},$$

Therefore resulting in

$$E\left(\frac{Fe^{3+}}{Fe}\right) = \frac{2.E^{\ominus}\left(\frac{Fe^{2+}}{Fe}\right) + E^{\ominus}\left(\frac{Fe^{3+}}{Fe^{2+}}\right)}{3}$$

$$= \frac{2\times(-0.44)+0.77}{3}$$

$$= \frac{-0.88+0.77}{3}$$

$$= -\frac{0.11}{3} = -0.037 \text{ V.}$$

20. Speed of sound in m/sec $= \frac{1245\times 5}{18}$

$= 345.833$ m/sec.

R.M.S. speed of sound in monoatomic gas

$$= \sqrt{\frac{3RT}{M}}$$

From question speed of sound $= \sqrt{\frac{5RT}{3M}}$

$= 345.833$

$$\frac{\sqrt{5}}{3}\sqrt{\frac{3RT}{M}} = 345.833$$

$$\frac{2.24}{3} V_{rms} = 345.833$$

$$\therefore \quad V_{rms} = \frac{345.833\times 3}{2.24}$$

$$\cong 463 \text{ m/sec.}$$

Previous Paper (Solved)

IIT–JAM

JOINT ADMISSION TEST FOR M.SC. (CHEMISTRY)-2014

Part-I : Objective Questions

Directions (Qs. 1-35): *Part-I consists of 35 objective type questions. The first ten questions carry* ***one*** *mark each and the rest of the objective questions carry* ***two*** *marks each.*

1. For square matrices M and N, if MN = M and NM = N, then:

A. $M^2 = M$ and $N^2 = N$

B. $N^2 \neq N$ and $M^2 = M$

C. $M^2 \neq M$ and $N^2 \neq N$

D. $M^2 \neq M$ and $N^2 = N$

2. The energy of an electron in a hydrogenic atom with nuclear charge Z varies as:

A. Z B. Z^2

C. 1/Z D. $1/Z^2$

3. The carbonyl stretching frequency ($V_{C=O}$) is highest for:

A. 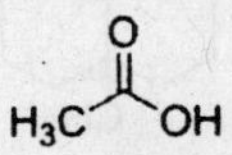 B. 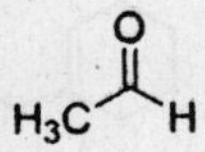

C. 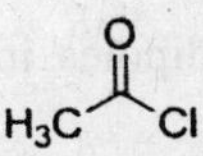 D. 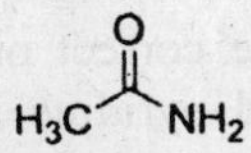

4. The homolytic breaking of the $C_a - C_b$ bond is easiest in:

A. 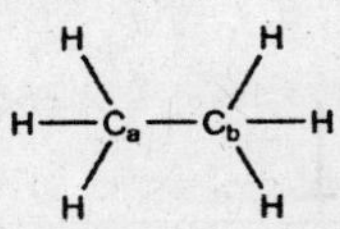 B. 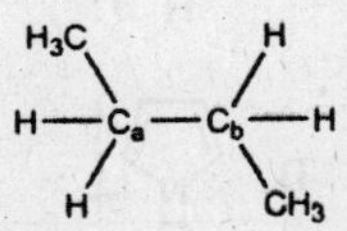

C. 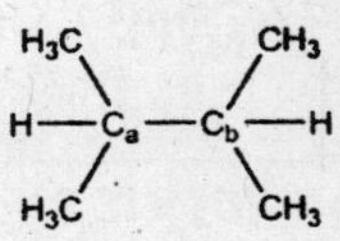 D. 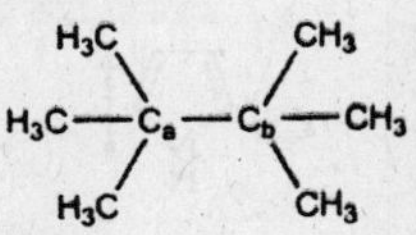

5. Tollen's test will be negative for:

A. Glucose B. Mannose

C. Sucrose D. Galactose

6. Which one among the following is a sesquiterpene?

A. 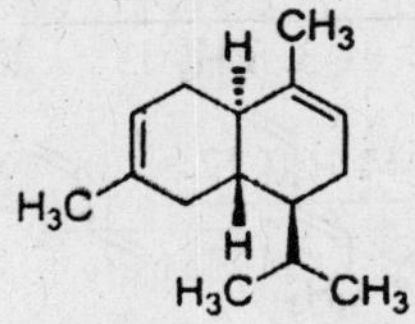

B. 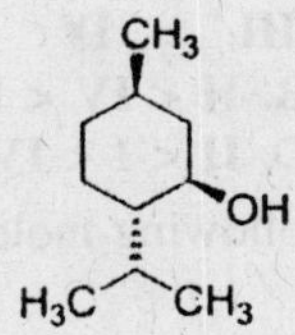

C. 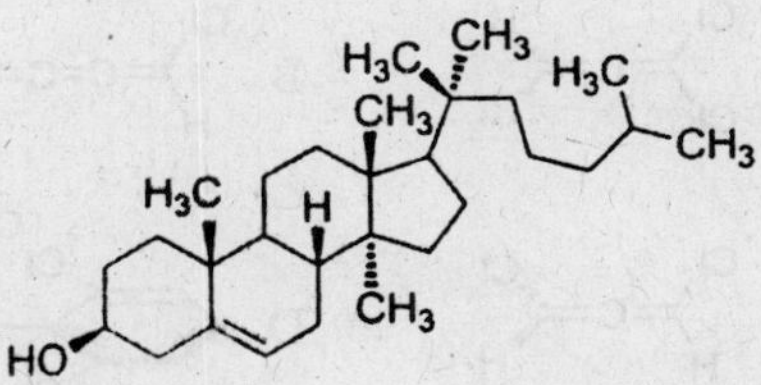

D. 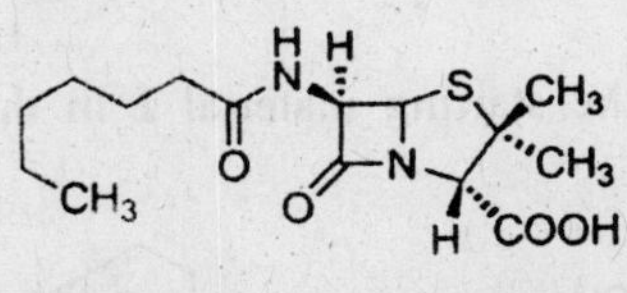

7. The predicted geometry of TeF_4 by **VSEPR theory** is:

A. Octahedral

B. Square planar

C. Tetrahedral

D. Trigonal bipyramidal

8. Among the following, the isoelectronic pair is:

A. NO and CO

B. O_2^- (superoxide anion) and NO^-

C. NO^+ and CO

D. O_2^- (superoxide anion) and NO^+

9. The metal ion of an enzyme involved in hydration of CO_2 is:

A. Cu (II) B. Fe (II)
C. Mg (II) D. Zn (II)

10. Among the following, the element having maximum inert pair effect is:

[Given : Atomic number of Ge = 30, Pb = 82, Si = 14 and Sn = 50]

A. Ge B. Pb
C. Si D. Sn

11. The reactivity of compounds **I-IV** with maleic anhydride (**V**) follows the order:

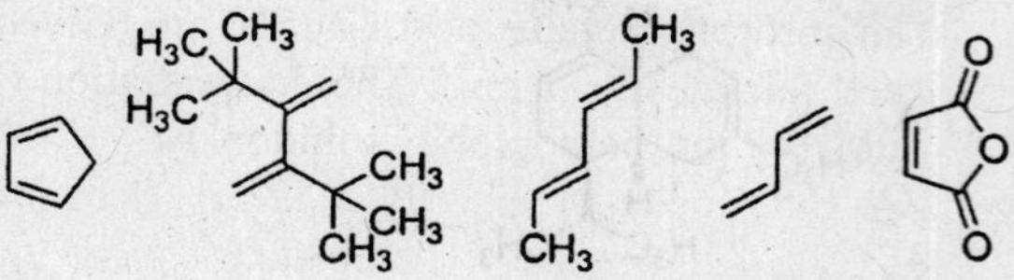

I **II** **III** **IV** **V**

A. **I < II < III < IV** B. **II < IV < III < I**
C. **II < I < III < IV** D. **II < I < IV < III**

12. Which one among the following molecules is chiral?

A. 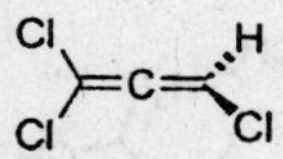 B. 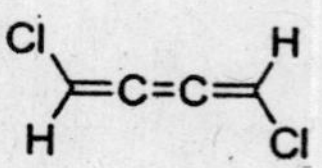

C. 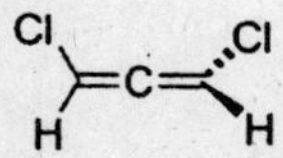 D. 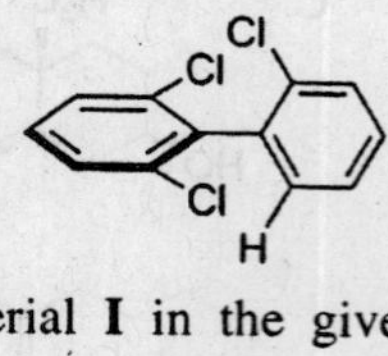

13. Identify the starting material I in the given reaction:

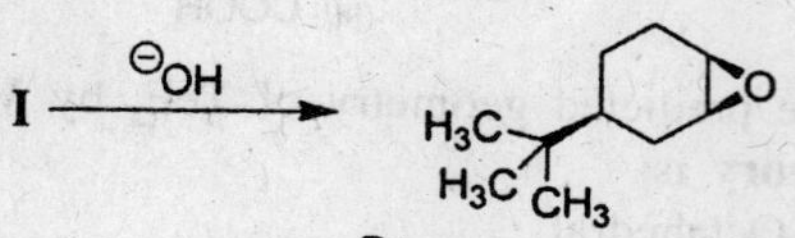

A. 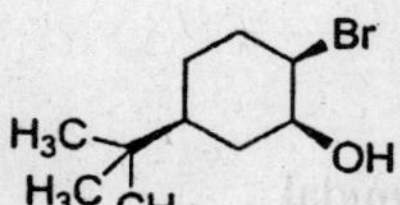 B. 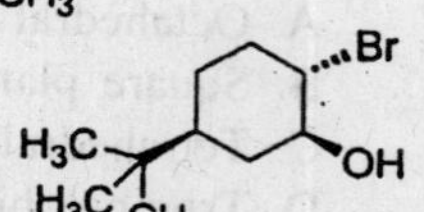

C. 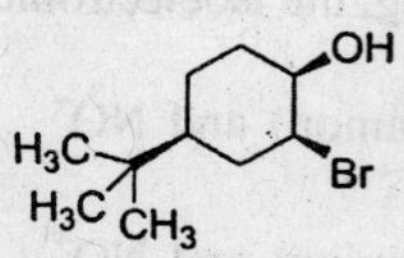 D. 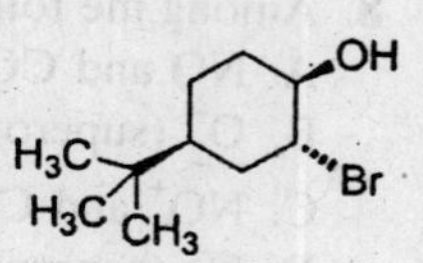

14. The major product for the following reaction is:

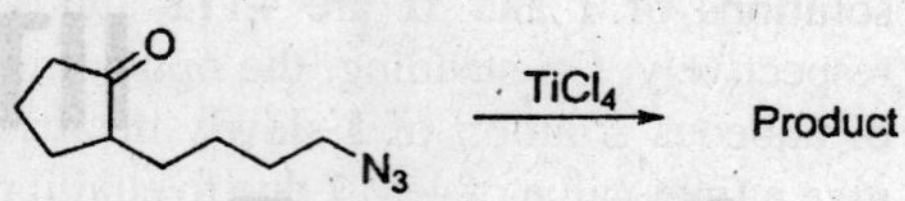

A. 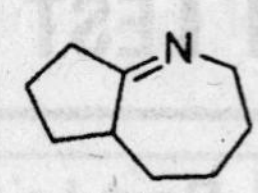 B. 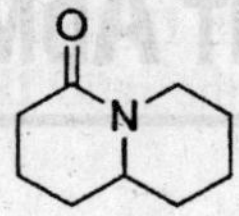

C. 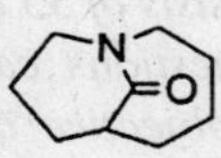 D. 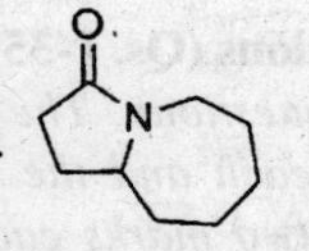

15. The structure of the major product in the following reaction is:

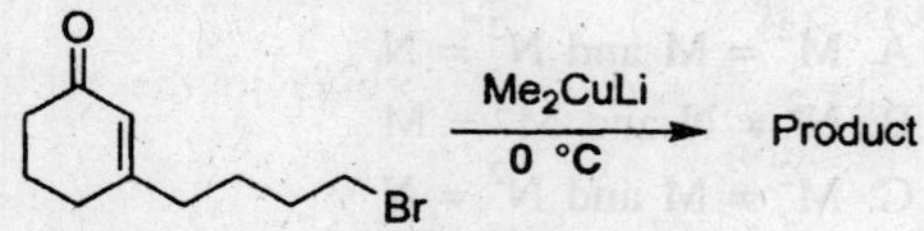

A. 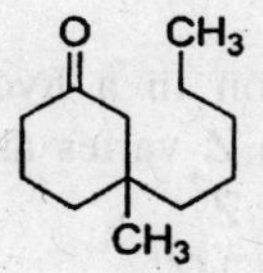 B. 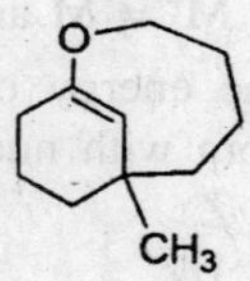

C. 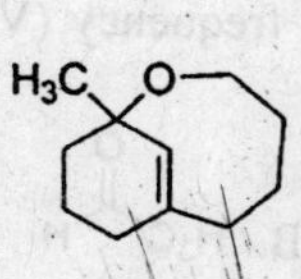 D. 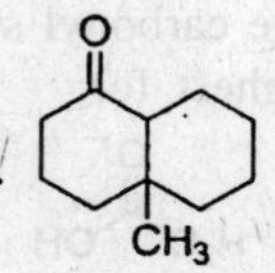

16. The correct orientation of dipoles in pyrrole and pyridine is:

A. 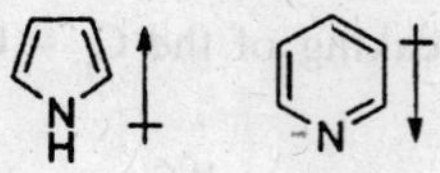

B. 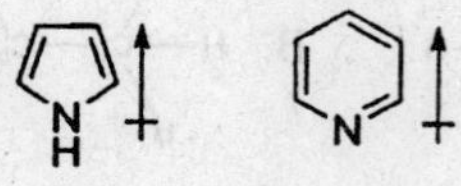

C. 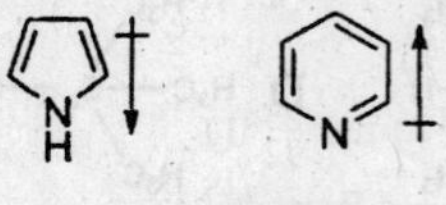

D. 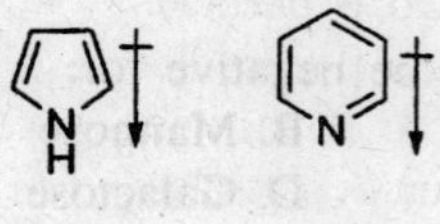

17. Specific rotations of freshly prepared aqueous solutions of **I** and **II** are +112 and +18.7, respectively. On standing, the optical rotation of aqueous solution of **I** slowly decreases to give a final value of +52.7 due to equilibration with **II**. Under this state of equilibrium, what is the ratio **II** : **I**?

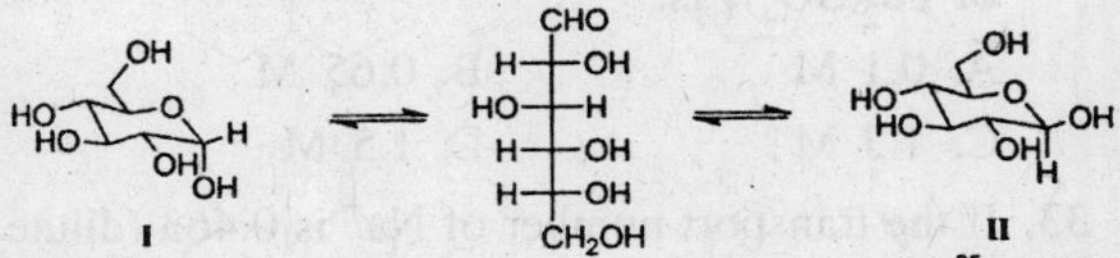

I $[\alpha]_D^{25} = +112$ II $[\alpha]_D^{25} = +18.7$

A. 0.57
B. 1.00
C. 1.75
D. 5.9

18. The major product formed in the following reaction is :

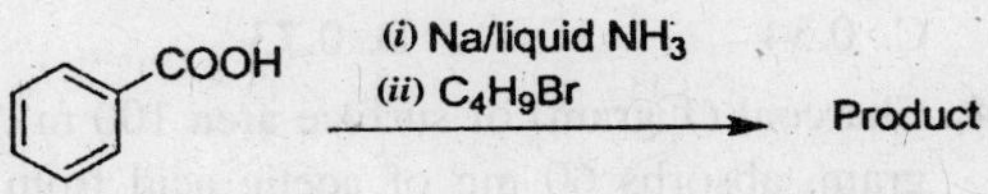

A. 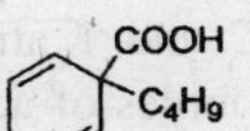

B. 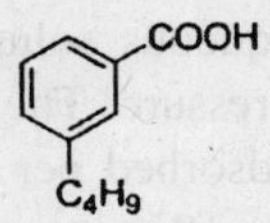

C. 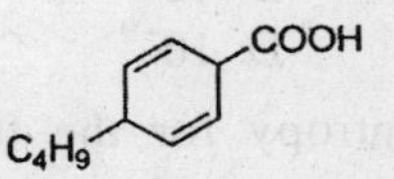

D. 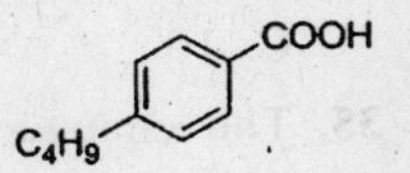

19. In boron neutron capture therapy, the initial boron isotope used and the particle generated after neutron capture respectively are:

A. ^{11}B and α particle
B. ^{10}B and α particle
C. ^{11}B and β particle
D. ^{10}B and β particle

20. The number of α and β particle(s), generated in the following radioactive decay process, are:

$$^{238}_{92}U \rightarrow ^{234}_{92}U$$

A. one α and two β particles
B. two α and one β particles
C. one α and four β particles
D. no α and four β particles

21. In the measurement of hardness of water by complexometric titration, identify **P** and **Q** in the following equation.

$$[P]^- + [H_2Y]^{2-} \rightarrow [Q]^{2-} + [HIn]^{2-} + H^+$$

red colourless colourless blue

A. **P** = MgY; **Q** = MgIn
B. **P** = MgY_2; **Q** = $MgIn_2$
C. **P** = $MgIn_2$; **Q** = MgY_2
D. **P** = MgIn; **Q** = MgY

22. An aqueous solution of hemoglobin has a molar absorptivity value of 18,600 L mol^{-1} cm^{-1} for an absorbance value of 0.1 at 540 nm (Given : cell thickness = 1 cm). The concentration (in μM) of the hemoglobin solution is:

A. 0.537 B. 5.37
C. 53.7 D. 537.0

23. The electronic transitions responsible for the colour of $K_2Cr_2O_7$ and porphine in their solid state respectively are:

A. $d \rightarrow d$; $\pi \rightarrow \pi^*$
B. M → L charge transfer; $\pi \rightarrow \pi^*$
C. L → M charge transfer; $\pi \rightarrow \pi^*$
D. L → M charge transfer; $d \rightarrow d$

24. The correct order of M – C (M = Ti, V, Cr and Mn) bond stretching frequency is:
(Given : Atomic number of Ti = 22, V = 23, Cr = 24 and Mn = 25)

A. $[V(CO)_6]^- < Cr(CO)_6 < [Mn(CO)_6]^+ < [Ti(CO)_6]^{2-}$
B. $[Ti(CO)_6]^{2-} < [V(CO)_6]^- < Cr(CO)_6 < [Mn(CO)_6]^+$
C. $[Mn(CO)_6]^+ < Cr(CO)_6 < [V(CO)_6]^- < [Ti(CO)_6]^{2-}$
D. $[Mn(CO)_6]^+ < [V(CO)_6]^- < Cr(CO)_6 < [Ti(CO)_6]^{2-}$

25. For the following reactions, the metal complexes **X** and **Y** are:

(i) $Ni(s) \xrightarrow[1\,atm\,/\,25°C]{CO(g)} X$

(ii) $FeCl_2 \xrightarrow{2\,NaC_5H_5} Y$

A. **X** = $Ni(CO)_4$; **Y** = $Fe(\eta^5\text{–}C_5H_5)_2$
B. **X** = $Ni(CO)_4$; **Y** = $Fe(\eta^1\text{–}C_5H_5)_2$
C. **X** = $Ni(CO)_5$; **Y** = $Fe(\eta^5\text{–}C_5H_5)_2$
D. **X** = $Ni(CO)_6$; **Y** = $Fe(\eta^1\text{–}C_5H_5)_2$

26. The correct order of crystal field strength is:
(Given: en = ethylenediamine)
A. $Cl^- < H_2O <$ en $< (\eta^5\text{–}C_5H_5)^-$
B. $H_2O < Cl^- < (\eta^5\text{–}C_5H_5)^- <$ en
C. $H_2O < (\eta^5\text{–}C_5H_5)^- <$ en $< Cl^-$
D. en $< Cl^- < H_2O < (\eta^5\text{–}C_5H_5)^-$

27. The carbon-oxygen bond in an organic compound absorbs electromagnetic radiation of frequency 6×10^{13} Hz. This frequency corresponds to the region:
A. Infrared
B. Microwave
C. Ultraviolet
D. Visible

28. According to the equipartition principle of energy, the molar heat capacity at constant volume for $CO_2(g)$, $SO_2(g)$ and $H_2O(g)$ follows the trend:
A. $CO_2 = SO_2 = H_2O$
B. $CO_2 > SO_2 = H_2O$
C. $H_2O > SO_2 = CO_2$
D. $CO_2 = SO_2 > H_2O$

29. $$\left[\frac{-h^2}{(8\pi^2 m)}\frac{d^2}{dx^2}+\frac{h^2\alpha^2 x^2}{(2\pi^2 m)}\right]\exp(-\alpha x^2)$$

$$= C\frac{h^2}{(4\pi^2)}\exp(-\alpha x^2)$$, where h, π, m and α are constants. Then C is:
A. $2\alpha/m$
B. $\alpha/2m$
C. α/m
D. α^2/m

30. Among Ar, NH_4Cl, HF and HCl, the strength of interatomic/intermolecular forces follows the order:
A. $NH_4Cl >$ HF $>$ HCl $>$ Ar
B. HF $>$ HCl $>$ Ar $> NH_4Cl$
C. HCl $>$ Ar $> NH_4Cl >$ HF
D. Ar $> NH_4Cl >$ HF $>$ HCl

31. The number of degrees of freedom in the homogeneous liquid region of a two component system with a eutectic point, at one atmosphere pressure, is:
A. 0 B. 1
C. 2 D. 3

32. The ionic strength of 0.1 M aqueous solution of $Fe_2(SO_4)_3$ is:
A. 0.1 M B. 0.65 M
C. 1.3 M D. 1.5 M

33. If the transport number of Na^+ is 0.463 (dilute solution of NaCl in methanol), the transport number of H^+ (dilute solution of HCl in methanol) is:
(Given, Λ^∞ (NaCl in methanol) = 96.9 ohm^{-1} cm^2 mol^{-1} and Λ^∞ (HCl in methanol) = 192 ohm^{-1} cm^2 mol^{-1})
A. 0.27 B. 0.46
C. 0.54 D. 0.73

34. Charcoal (1 gram) of surface area 100 m^2 per gram, absorbs 60 mg of acetic acid from an aqueous solution at 25°C and 1 atmosphere pressure. The number of moles of acetic acid adsorbed per cm^2 of charcoal surface is:
A. 10^{-2} B. 10^{-6}
C. 10^{-5} D. 10^{-9}

35. The change in entropy for the following transformations is respectively:
(+ indicates increase, – indicates decrease and 0 indicates no change)

(*i*) $SO_2Cl_2(g) \xrightarrow{\Delta} SO_2(g) + Cl_2(g)$

(*ii*) $n\,CH_2{=}CH_2(g) \xrightarrow{\text{Catalyst}} \text{[}CH_2\text{–}CH_2\text{]}_n(s)$

(*iii*) $I_2(s) \xrightarrow[\text{1 atmosphere}]{\Delta} I_2(v)$

(*iv*) Adiabatic reversible expansion of an ideal gas

A. +, –, 0, +
B. +, –, 0, 0
C. –, +, +, 0
D. +, –, +, 0

Part-II : Descriptive Questions

Directions (Qs. 36-43): *Each question carry five marks.*

36. Using crystal field theory (CFT), for the $[Co(NH_3)_6]^{3+}$ ion

(*a*) draw the *d*-orbital splitting including their orbital labels (designations) and show their electron occupancy.

(*b*) calculate the crystal field stabilization energy (ignore pairing energy) and spin-only magnetic moment values.

(Given : atomic number of Co = 27)

37. (*a*) Write the correct order of lattice energy for LiX, X = F, Cl, Br and I.

(*b*) A first order reflection from (111) plane is observed for LiX with $2\theta = 24.6°$ (X-ray of wavelength 1.54 Å). Assuming LiX to be a cubic crystal system, calculate the length of the side of the unit cell in Å.

38. For the reaction:

$$2NO + 2H_2 \xrightarrow{700°C} N_2 + 2H_2O$$

(*i*) Write the expression for the rate of the reaction in terms of the change in concentrations of NO and H_2O.

(*ii*) Given the following data for the above reaction, find the order of the reaction with respect to (*a*) NO and (*b*) H_2 and the rate constant of the reaction along with the proper unit.

	$[NO]_{t=0}$ (mol dm^{-3})	$[H_2]_{t=0}$ (mol dm^{-3})	Initial rate (mol dm^{-3} s^{-1})
Experiment 1	0.025	0.01	2.4×10^{-6}
Experiment 2	0.025	0.005	1.2×10^{-6}
Experiment 3	0.0125	0.01	0.6×10^{-6}

39. The vapour pressure of benzene is 5333 Pa at 7.6°C and 53330 Pa at 60.6°C. Calculate the heat of vapourization of benzene and the normal boiling point of benzene.

40. The following graph represents the dependence of certain properties **I to V** (given below) as a function of temperature.

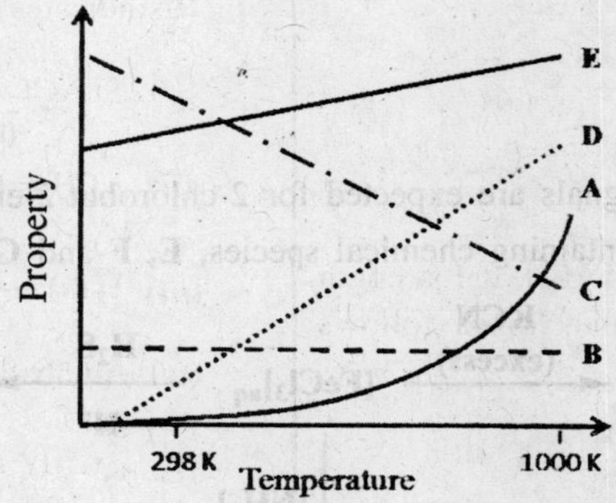

Property

I. The enthalpy change of a gas phase reaction in which the sum of the number of moles of products is greater than the sum of the number of moles of reactants.

II. The osmotic pressure of an ideal solution at a given concentration.
III. The standard Gibbs free energy of formation of metal oxides.
IV. The molar heat capacity at constant volume for an ideal gas, as predicted by the equipartition of energy.
V. The rate constant of a reaction with E_a = 100 kJ mol^{-1}.

The lines/curves **A**, **B**, **C**, **D** and **E** corresponding to the appropriate property are:

Answer :

Property	*Line/Curve*
I	
II	
III	
IV	
V	

41. Draw the structures **A-E** for the given transformation.

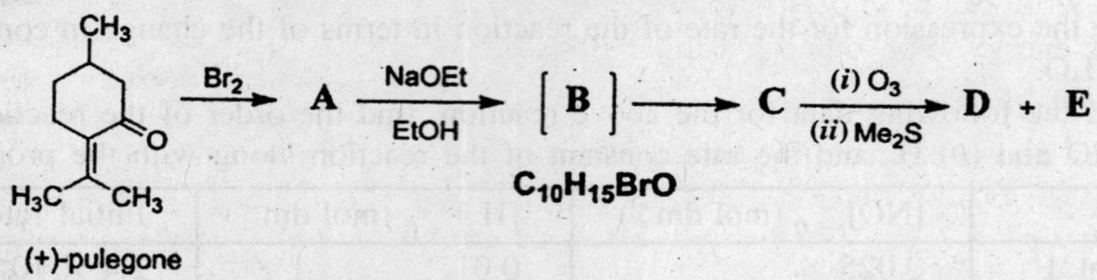

42. In the reaction sequence given below, draw the structures of **A**, **C**, **D** and reagent **B**.

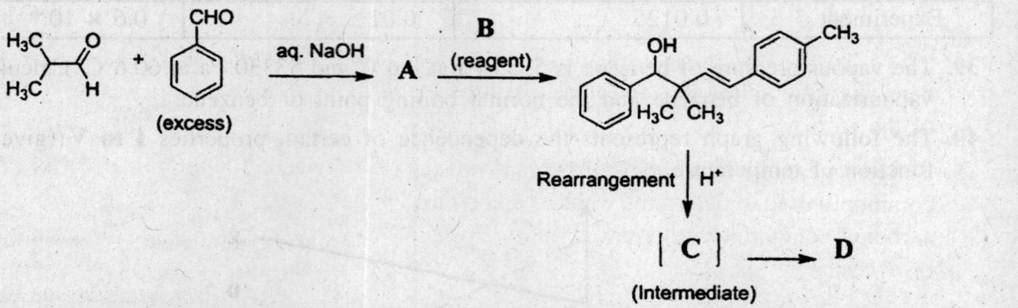

43. (*a*) How many ^{1}H NMR signals are expected for 2-chlorobut-2-ene? (ignore spin-spin coupling)

(*b*) Write down the iron containing chemical species, **E**, **F** and **G** in the following reactions.

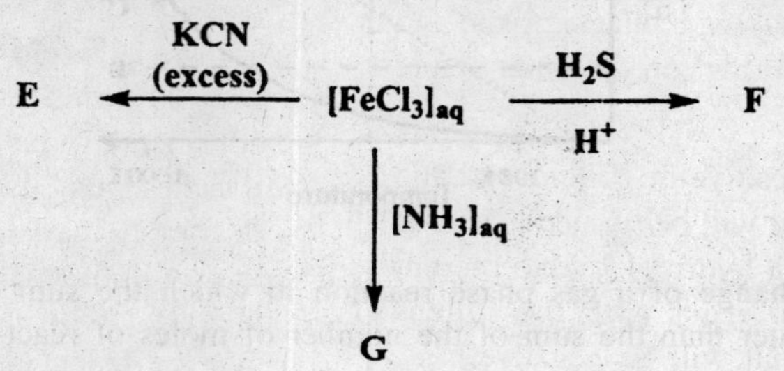

ANSWERS

1	2	3	4	5	6	7	8	9	10
A	B	C	D	C	A	D	C	D	B
11	**12**	**13**	**14**	**15**	**16**	**17**	**18**	**19**	**20**
B	C	D	B	D	A	C	A	B	A
21	**22**	**23**	**24**	**25**	**26**	**27**	**28**	**29**	**30**
D	B	C	C	A	A	A	B	C	A
31	**32**	**33**	**34**	**35**					
C	D	D	D	D					

SOME SELECTED EXPLANATORY ANSWERS

2. Expression of energy for hydrogen like ions. Hydrogen atom can have only certain specific values of energy. For other hydrogen like species such as He^+, Li^{2+} etc.

The energy of the electron in various energy level is given by the relation

$$E_n = -k^2 . \frac{2\pi^2 me^4 z^2}{n^2 h^2}$$

or, $\qquad E_n \propto z^2.$

here z is the nuclear charge (atomic number) of the atom.

5. Tollens' reagent is a chemical reagent most commonly used to determine whether a known carbonyl-containing compound is an *aldehyde* or a *ketone.*

A positive test with Tollens' reagent results in elemental silver precipitating out of solution, occasionally onto the inner surface of the reaction vessel, producing a characteristic and memorable "silver mirror" on the inner vessel surface.

Aldehydes will be positive in Tollen's test and a mirror-like material will be formed. There is no aldehyde or alpha hydroxy ketone present in sucrose for it to react with the tollens reagent. So, test result will be negative.

7. TeF_4

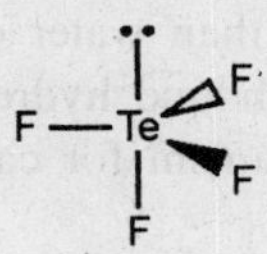

lp-bp

3 at 120°

1 at 180°

bp-bp

3 at 120°

3 at 90°

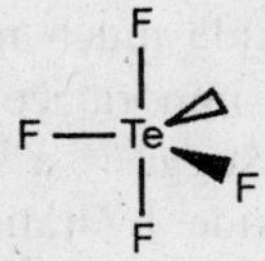

lp-bp

2 at 120°

2 at 90°

bp-bp

4 at 90°

1 at 120°

1 at 180°

Trigonal bipyramid hybridization : dsp^3.

8. Two or more molecular entities (atoms, molecules, or ions) are described as being **isoelectronic** with each other if they have the same number of electrons or a similar electron configuration and the same structure (number and connectivity of atoms), regardless of the nature of the elements involved. CO and NO^+ are isoelectronic because each has two nuclei and 10 valence electrons, with each atom considered to have 5 of them (a lone-pair and a triple-bond). Isoelectronicity does not relate to formal charge on the atoms in a structure: these all have the same configuration even though carbon monoxide has formal charges that are balanced ($^-$:C≡O:$^+$).

9. A major clue comes from the pH profile of enzymatically catalyzed carbon dioxide hydration. At pH 8, the reaction proceeds near its maximal rate. As the pH decreases, the rate of the reaction drops. The midpoint of this transition is near pH 7, suggesting that a group with $pK_a = 7$ plays an important role in the activity of carbonic anhydrase and that the deprotonated (high pH) form of this group participates more effectively in catalysis. Thus, the binding of a water molecule to the positively charged zinc center reduces the pK_a of the water molecule from 15.7 to 7. With the lowered pK_a, a substantial concentration of hydroxide ion (bound to zinc) is generated at neutral pH. A zinc-bound hydroxide ion is sufficiently nucleophilic to attack carbon dioxide much more readily than water does. The importance of the zinc-bound hydroxide ion suggests a simple mechanism for carbon dioxide hydration.

1. Zinc facilitates the release of a proton from a water molecule, which generates a hydroxide ion.
2. The carbon dioxide substrate binds to the enzyme's active site and is positioned to react with the hydroxide ion.
3. The hydroxide ion attacks the carbon dioxide, converting it into bicarbonate ion.
4. The catalytic site is regenerated with the release of the bicarbonate ion and the binding of another molecule of water.

12. A **chiral molecule** is a type of molecule that has a non-superposable mirror image. The presence of an asymmetric carbon atom is often the feature that causes chirality in molecules. **Achiral** objects, such as atoms, are symmetrical, identical to their mirror image.

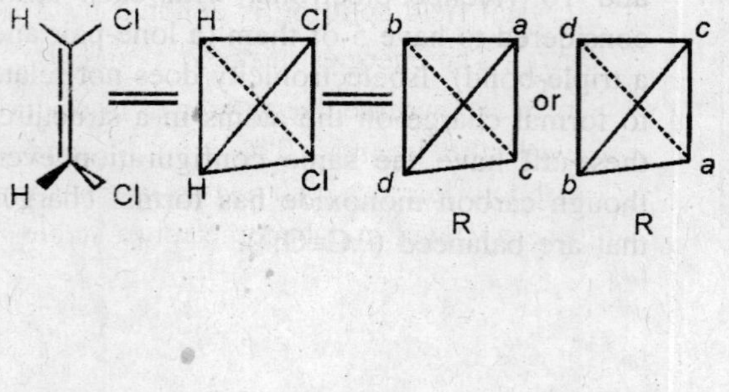

16.

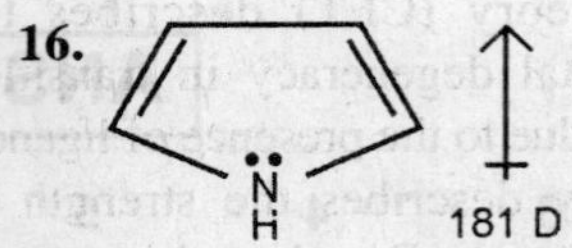

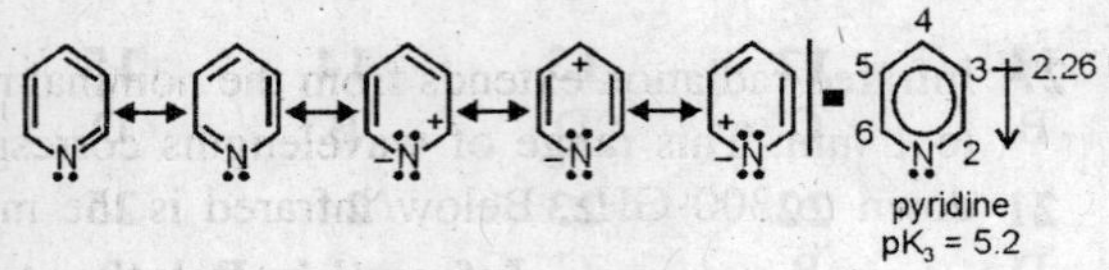

20. The alpha decay process may be represented as

$${}^{A}_{Z}X \rightarrow {}^{A-4}_{Z-2}X + {}^{4}_{2}He$$

The beta decay process may be represented by

$${}^{A}_{Z}X \rightarrow {}^{A}_{Z+1}X + e + \bar{v}$$

One alpha particle emission:

$${}^{238}_{92}U \rightarrow {}^{234}_{90}U + {}^{4}_{2}He$$

Two beta particle emission:

$${}^{238}_{90}U \rightarrow {}^{234}_{92}U + 2e + \bar{v}$$

21. As a sample is titrated with EDTA, the calcium ions in the sample are preferentially complexed by the EDTA, while magnesium complexes with the indicator. EDTA-metal complexes are generally uncoloured; however, metallochromic indicators change colour depending on whether they are bound or unbound. After all the free calcium and magnesium are bound by EDTA, additional EDTA extracts the magnesium ions from the Eriochrome Black T indicator, restoring it to its uncomplexed blue colour, and an endpoint is observed.

$MgIn^-$ (PURPLE-RED) + H_2Y^{2-}(CLEAR) $\rightarrow$ MgY^{2-} (CLEAR) + HIn^{2-}(BLUE) + H^+

Eriochrome Black T does not give a sharp colour change for water containing calcium, but no magnesium. To make sure that there is some magnesium present in your sample, we add a small amount of Mg-EDTA (Magnesium already complexed with EDTA). Since we add the same amont of EDTA as Mg^{2+}, the addition of Mg-EDTA to the sample has no net effect on the subsequent titration.

26. Crystal field theory (CFT) describes the breaking of orbital degeneracy in transition metal complexes due to the presence of ligands. CFT qualitatively describes the strength of the metal-ligand bonds. Based on the strength of the metal-ligand bonds, the energy of the system is altered. This may lead to a change in magnetic properties as well as colour. The correct order of CFT is $Cl^- < H_2O <$ en $< (\eta^5\text{–}C_5H_5)^-$.

27. Infrared radiation extends from the nominal red edge of the visible spectrum at 700 nanometers (nm) to 1 mm. This range of wavelengths corresponds to a frequency range of approximately 430 THz down to 300 GHz. Below infrared is the microwave portion of the electromagnetic spectrum.

Infrared in Relation to Electromagnetic Spectrum

Light Comparison

Name	Wavelength	Frequency (Hz)	Photon Energy (eV)
Gamma ray	less than 0.01 mm	more than 30 EHz	124 keV – 300 + GeV
X-Ray	0.01 nm – 10 nm	30 EHz – 30 PHz	124 eV – 124 keV
Ultraviolet	10 nm – 380 nm	30 PHz – 790 THz	3.3 eV – 124 keV
Visible	380 nm – 700 nm	790 THz – 430 THz	1.7 eV – 3.3 keV
Infrared	**700 nm – 1 mm**	**430 THz – 300 GHz**	**1.24 meV – 1.7 eV**
Microwave	1 mm – 1 meter	300 GHz – 300 MHz	1.24 μeV – 1.24 meV
Radio	1 mm – 100,000 km	300 GHz – 3 Hz	12.4 feV – 1.24 meV

30. Intermolecular forces allow us to determine which substances are likely to dissolve in which other substances and what the melting and boiling points of substances are. Without intermolecular forces holding molecules together we would not exist.

The strength of intermolecular forces are as follows: $NH_4Cl > HF > HCl > Ar$.

32. Ionic strength of $Fe_2(SO_4)_3$

$= 0.1 \times 2 \times (2)^2 + 0.1 \times (2)^3$

$= 0.8 + 0.8 = 1.6$

$\cong 1.5$ M.

36. (*a*) Crystal field theory (CFT) describes the breaking of orbital degeneracy in transition metal complexes due to the presence of ligands. CFT qualitatively describes the strength of the metal-ligand bonds. Based on the strength of the metal-ligand bonds, the energy of the system is altered. This may lead to a change in magnetic properties as well as colour.

For example, consider a molecule with octahedral geometry. Ligands approach the metal ion along the *x*, *y*, and *z* axes. Therefore, the electrons in the d_{z^2} and $d_{x^2-y^2}$ orbitals (which lie along these axes) experience greater repulsion. It requires more energy to have an electron in these orbitals than it would to put an electron in one of the other orbitals. This causes a splitting in the energy levels of the *d*-orbitals. This is known as crystal **field splitting.** For octahedral complexes, crystal field splitting is denoted by Δ_o (or Δ_{oct}). The energies of the d_{z^2} and $d_{x^2-y^2}$ orbitals increase due to greater interactions with the ligands. The d_{xy}, d_{xz}, and d_{yz} orbitals decrease with respect to this normal energy level and become more stable.

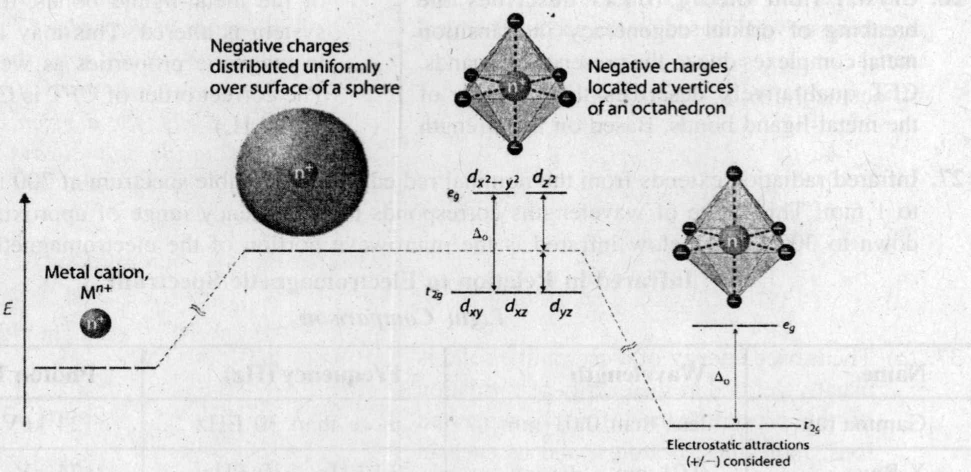

Fig. : *Distributing a charge of –6 uniformly over a spherical surface surrounding a metal ion causes the energy of all five d-orbitals to increase due to electrostatic repulsions, but the five d-orbitals remain degenerate.*

Electrons in Orbitals

According to the Aufbau principle, electrons are filled from lower to higher energy orbitals. For the octahedral case above, this corresponds to the d_{xy}, d_{xz} and d_{yz} orbitals. Following Hund's rule, electrons are filled in order to have the highest number of unpaired electrons. For example, if one had a d^3 complex, there would be three unpaired electrons. If one were to add an electron, however, it has the ability to fill a higher energy orbital $\left(d_{z^2} \text{ or } d_{x^2-y^2}\right)$ or pair with an electron residing in the d_{xy}, d_{xz}, or d_{yz} orbitals. This pairing of the electrons requires energy (spin pairing energy). If the pairing energy is less than the crystal field splitting energy, Δ_o, then the next electron will go into the d_{xy}, d_{xz} or d_{yz} orbitals due to stability. This situation allows for the least amount of unpaired electrons, and is known as low spin. If the pairing energy is greater than Δ_o, then the next electron will go into the d_{z^2} or $d_{x^2-y^2}$ orbitals as an unpaired electron. This situation allows for the most number of unpaired electrons and is known as high spin. Ligands that cause a transition metal to have a small crystal field splitting, which leads to high spin, are called weak-field ligands. Ligands that produce a large crystal field splitting, which leads to low spin, are called strong field ligands.

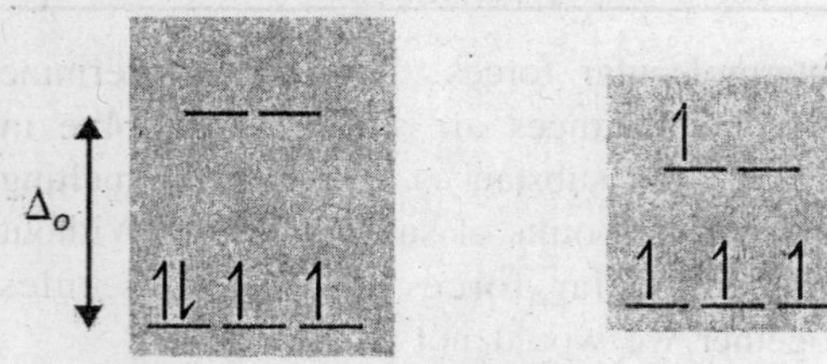

Low Spin, Strong field ($\Delta_O P$) *High Spin, Weak field ($\Delta_O P$)*

As mentioned above, CFT is based primarily on symmetry of ligands around a central metal/ion and how this an isotropic (properties depending on direction) ligand field affects the metal's atomic orbitals; the energies of which may increase, decrease or not be affected at all. Once the ligands' electrons interact with the electrons of the *d*-orbitals, the electrostatic interactions cause the energy levels of the d-orbital to fluctuate depending on the orientation and the nature of the ligands. For example, the oxidation state and the strength of the ligands determine splitting; the higher the oxidation state or the stronger the ligand, the larger the splitting. Ligands are classified as strong or weak based on the spectrochemical series.

4. octahedra, 6, 0, diamagnetic, low, spin

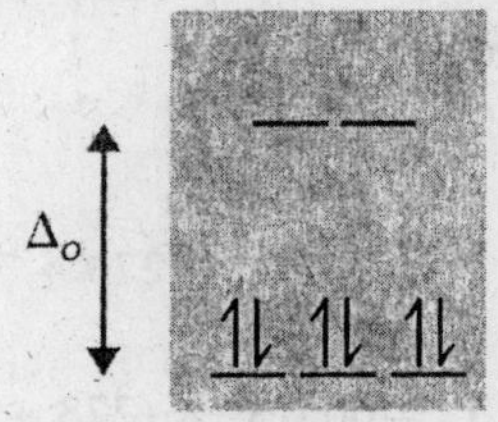

37. (*a*) The **lattice energy** of a crystalline solid is usually defined as the energy of formation of the crystal from infinitely-separated ions, molecules, oratoms, and as such in invariably negative.

The lattice energy of nearly any ionic solid can be calculated rather accurately using a modified form

$$U = -k.\frac{Q_1Q_2}{T_0}, \text{where } U > 0$$

U, which is always a positive number, represents the amount of energy required to dissociate 1 mol of an ionic solid into the gaseous ions. If we assume that $\Delta V = 0$, then the lattice energy, U, is approximately equal to the change in enthalpy, ΔH.

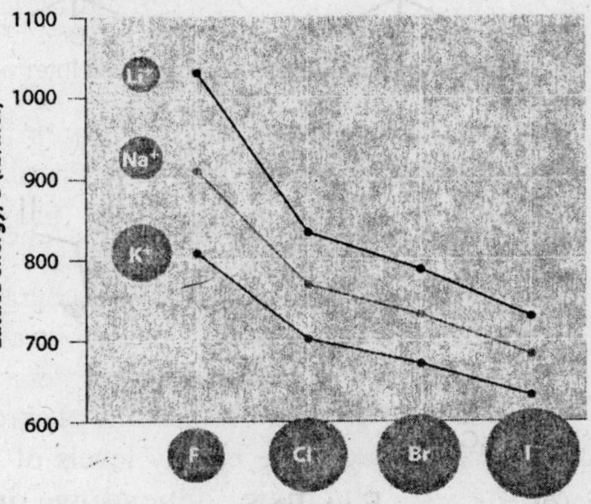

Fig.: *A Plot of Lattice Energy versus the Identity of the Halide for the Lithium, Sodium, and Potassium Halides*

Because the ionic radii of the cations decrease in the order $K^+ > Na^+ > Li^+$ for a given halide ion, the lattice energy decreases smoothly from Li^+ to K^+. Conversely, for a given alkali metal ion, the fluoride salt always has the highest lattice energy and the iodide salt the lowest.

37. (*b*) $n.\lambda = 2d \sin\theta, \theta = 12.3°$,

$$\lambda = 1.54 \text{ Å}, n = 1$$

$$1.54 \times 10^{-10} = 2.d.\sin(12.3°)$$

$$d = \frac{1.54 \times 10^{-10}}{2\sin(12.3°)}$$

$$= \frac{1.54 \times 10^{-10}}{0.426}$$

$$= 3.61 \times 10^{-10} \text{ m}$$

$$= 3.61 \text{ Å}.$$

38. (*i*) The speed of the reaction is called Rate of the reaction.

Rate = time rate of change of the molar concentration of a reactant or product.

For the reaction

$$2NO(g) + 2H_2(g) \rightarrow N_2(g) + 2H_2O(g)$$

$$\text{Rate} = \frac{\Delta[H_2O]}{\Delta t} = -\frac{\Delta[NO]}{\Delta t} = -\frac{\Delta[H_2]}{\Delta t} = 2\frac{\Delta[N_2]}{\Delta t}$$

Dimensions = mol/Ls or Ms^{-1}

Rate is always a positive number.

Instantaneous rate = rate at a given instant in time = slope of the concentration vs. time plot at that time.

If for the reaction $2NO(g) + 2H_2(g) \rightarrow N_2(g) + 2H_2O(g)$ the rate was measured by following the appearance of H_2O, then the instantaneous rate at a particular time will be the slope of the $[H_2O]$ vs. time plot at that time.

$$\lim_{\Delta t \to 0} \frac{\Delta[H_2O]}{\Delta t} = \frac{d[H_2O]}{dt}$$

$$\text{Instantaneous Rate} = \frac{d[H_2O]}{dt}$$

Variation of rate with concentration – Rate low.

1. Rate Law = mathematical equation that gives the rate as a function of concentration. Must be determined experimentally.
2. In many cases the rate law for a reaction such as $aA + bB \rightarrow dD + eE$ is of the rather simple form

   Rate = $k[A]^x[B]^y$

(*a*) x = the order of the reaction in A

y = the order of the reaction in B

$x + y$ = overall order of the reaction.

(*b*) x and y are usually small positive integers, they must be determined experimentally.

(*c*) *Example:* Suppose the rate law was found to be of the form Rate = $k[A]^2[B]$

$x = 2$ ∴ the reaction is said to be second order in A.

$y = 1$ ∴ the reaction is said to be first order in B.

$x + y = 3$ ∴ the reaction is overall third. This is a 3rd order reaction that is 2nd order in A and 1st order in B.

3. k = Specific rate constant = The proportionality constant between the rate and concentrations.

38. (*ii*) The rate law is of the form,

Rate = $k[H_2]^x[NO]^y$.

Order in NO (value of y)

From experiment 1 and 3,

Rate ∝ $[NO]^y$ when the [NO] was halfed, the rate constant decreased by a factor of 4. Therefore, the reaction rate is proportional to the concentration of NO square.

The value of $y = 2$, the reaction is 2nd order in NO.

Again, the reaction rate is directly proportional to $[H_2]$ that is, when the $[H_2]$ was halfed the rate. Rate law is then Rate = $k[H_2]\ [NO]^2$ and its unit is mol/Ls.

39. Let use the Clausius–Clapeyron equation:

$$\ln\left(\frac{P_2}{P_1}\right) = \frac{\Delta H}{R}\left(\frac{1}{T_1}-\frac{1}{T_2}\right)$$

Given datas:

$P_1 = 5333$ Pa

$P_2 = 53330$ Pa

$T_1 = 7.6°C = (273 + 7.6)$ K $= 280.6$ K.

$T_2 = 60.6°C = (273 + 60.6)$ K $= 333.6$K

$R = 8.31447$

$\Delta H = ?$

$$\ln\left(\frac{53330}{5333}\right) = \frac{\Delta H}{8.31447}\left(\frac{1}{280.6}-\frac{1}{333.6}\right)$$

$$2.3026 = \frac{\Delta H}{8.31447}(0.003564 - 0.002998)$$

$$\Delta H\ (0.000566) = 19.14489$$

$$\therefore \quad \Delta H = 33824.909 \text{ J/mol.} = 33.825 \text{ kJ/mol.}$$

41. A. 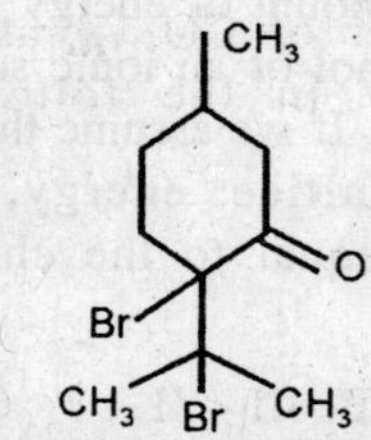

Pulegone dibromide

B. 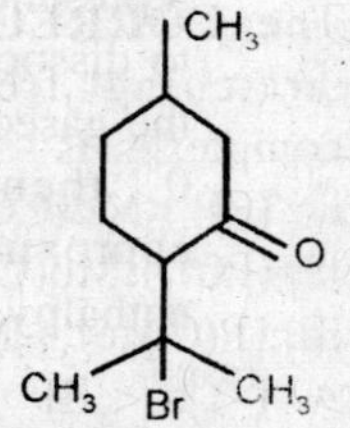

Favorskii Intermediate

C. 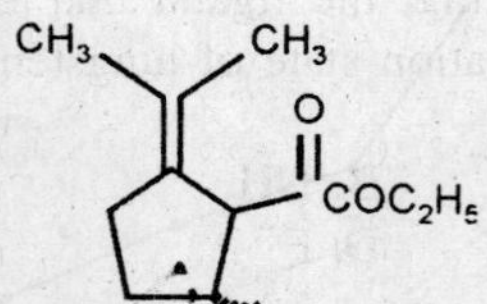

D. 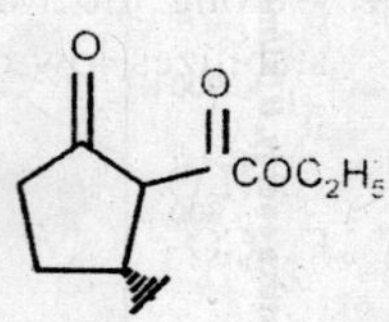

E. $CH_3\overset{O}{\overset{\|}{C}}-CH_3$

43. (*b*) $F \rightarrow Fe_2S_3$

$G \rightarrow FeCl_2$ or Fe.

Previous Paper (Solved)

IIT–JAM

JOINT ADMISSION TEST FOR M.Sc. (CHEMISTRY)-2013

Directions (Qs. 1-30): *(Objective questions) carry two marks each, questions* **(Qs. 11-20)** *(Subjective questions) carry* ***three*** *marks each and questions* **(Qs. 21-30)** *(descriptive questions) carry* ***five*** *marks each.*

1. The most polar compound among the following is

A. SF_4 B. BF_3

C. XeF_4 D. SO_3

2. Which one of the following order of the carbonates is **CORRECT** for their decomposition temperature?

A. $BaCO_3 > CaCO_3 > SrCO_3 > MgCO_3$

B. $BaCO_3 > SrCO_3 > CaCO_3 > MgCO_3$

C. $MgCO_3 > CaCO_3 > SrCO_3 > BaCO_3$

D. $MgCO_3 > CaCO_3 > BaCO_3 > SrCO_3$

3. The **CORRECT** order of CO vibrational stretching frequency in the following complexes is

I. $(PF_3)_3Mo(CO)_3$

II. $(PCl_3)_3Mo(CO)_3$

III. $\{P(OMe)_3\}_3Mo(CO)_3$

A. I < II < III B. III < II < I

C. II < I < III D. III < I < II

4. Among the following, the ligand that BEST stabilizes low oxidation state of tungsten (W) is

A. H_2O B. NH_3

C. CO D. F^-

5. The function $y = x\exp(-x^2)$ has a minimum at $x = -\frac{1}{\sqrt{2}}$. The second derivative of the function at the minimum is

A. $2\sqrt{2}\exp\left(-\frac{1}{2}\right)$ B. $-2\sqrt{2}\exp\left(-\frac{1}{2}\right)$

C. 0 D. $-\sqrt{2}\exp\left(-\frac{1}{2}\right)$

6. For a particular reaction at constant temperature, a plot of inverse of reactant concentration $\left(\frac{1}{[A]}\right)$ versus time is a straight line with a slope of 4.0×10^{-2} L mol^{-1} s^{-1}. The time required (in seconds) for 1.0 M of reactant to decrease to 0.25 M is

A. 18.8 B. 34.7

C. 75.0 D. 187.5

7. For a physisorption process, which one of the following statements is **NOT** correct?

A. There are van der Waals' interactions between the adsorbate and the adsorbent.

B. The process predominates at low temperature.

C. The process cannot proceed beyond a monolayer.

D. The process is reversible.

8. The product of the following reaction is

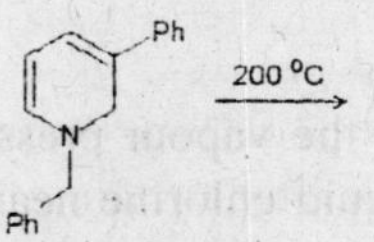

A. 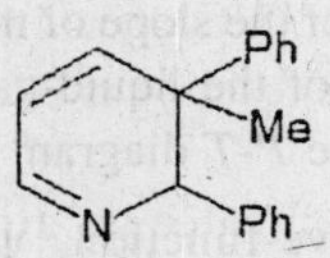

B. 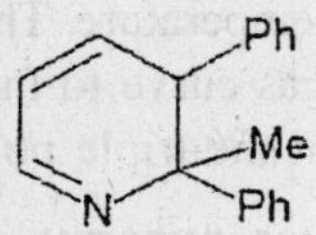

C. 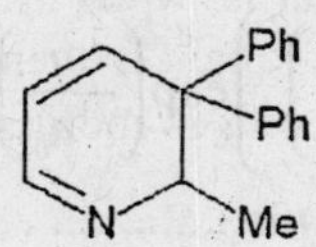

D. 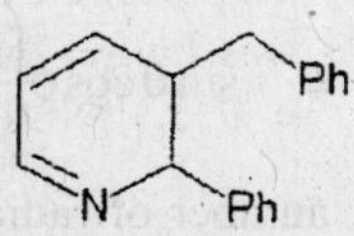

9. The **CORRECT** order of stability of the following carbonium ions is

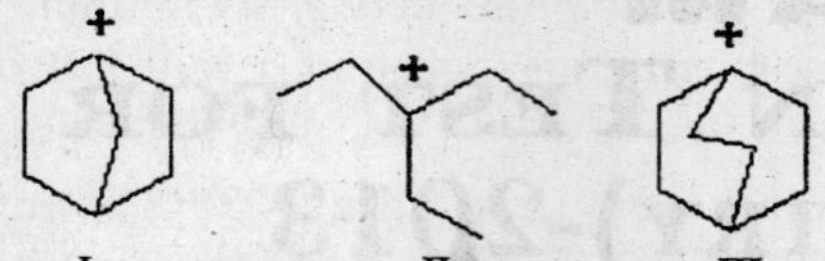

I II III

A. II > I > III B. III > II > I

C. I > III > II D. II > III > I

10. Which one of the following statements is **CORRECT**?

A. Naturally occurring DNA has B-configuration

B. Nucleic acids are derived from proteins

C. Proteins store genetic information

D. Vitamins generally act as enzymes

11. The reaction of anhydrous $FeCl_2$ with sodium-pentadienyl in ether gives an air-stable diamagnetic orange solid, which on oxidation gives an air-sensitive paramagnetic blue-green compound in solution. The blue green compound is ....

12. CaO, VO and MnO have octahedral coordination of the metal ions in a rock-salt structure. The correct increasing order of their lattice enthalpies is ....

13. The shape of the interhalide IF_8^- is ....

14. The vapour pressures of solid and liquid chlorine are given by

$$\log_e P^{solid} = 24 - \frac{3900}{T} \text{ and}$$

$$\log_e P^{liq} = 18 - \frac{2600}{T},$$

Where P^{solid} and P^{liq} are the vapour pressures (in Torr) of solid and liquid chlorine near the triple point, respectively and T is the absolute temperature. The ratio of the slope of the solid-gas curve to the slope of the liquid-gas curve at the triple point in the *P-T* diagram is ....

15. For unnormalized wave-function, $\psi(r,\theta,\phi)$

$$= \sin\theta\cos\phi\left(\frac{2r}{a_0} - \left(\frac{r}{a_0}\right)^2\right)\exp\left(-\frac{r}{a_0}\right), \text{ the}$$

number of radial node(s) is ....

16. A hypothetical element (atomic weight = 300) crystallizes in a simple cubic lattice. For this crystal, the first order X-ray diffraction with wavelength of 5Å appears at an angle of 30°. The density of the crystal is .... g cm^{-3}. [Avogadro number, $N_A = 6.02 \times 10^{23}$]

17. $MnO_4^-(aq) + Zn(s) + H_3O^+(aq) \rightarrow Mn^{2+}(aq) + Zn^{2+}(aq) + H_2O(l)$

For the above reaction if the equilibrium constant at 298 K is represented by 10^X, then the value of X is ....

[Given : The standard cell potential $E^0 = 2.4$V and $\frac{2.303RT}{F} = 0.06$ V at 298 K]

18. The rotational energy barrier between the most stable and the least stable conformations of 2, 3-dimethylbutane along $C_2 - C_3$ bond is .... kcal mol^{-1}.

[Given : The energies (kcal mol^{-1}) for H/CH_3 eclipsing = 1.8, CH_3/CH_3 eclipsing = 2.9 and CH_3/CH_3 gauche = 0.9]

19. The number of peaks or signals in ^{1}H NMR of N, N-dimethylformamide (DMF) at 25°C is ....

20. 

calixene

Calixene is a polar hydrocarbon with a high dipole moment. The most stable dipolar canonical structure is ....

21. A mixture of C_3H_8 and oxygen in 1L closed vessel has an internal pressure of 4 atm at 100°C. When the mixture is ignited, the reaction produces CO_2(g) and H_2O(g) until all the oxygen is consumed. After the reaction, pressure of the vessel is 4.2 atm at the same temperature. Calculate the weight of oxygen present before the reaction. [Gas constant, R = 0.082 L atm mol^{-1} K^{-1}]

22. The following reaction is carried out at 1 atm and 300 K.

$2H_2\ (g) + O_2\ (g) \rightarrow 2H_2O\ (l)$

ΔU for the above reaction is 550 kJ. Assuming ideal gas behaviour for H_2 and O_2, calculate the value of ΔH. The value of gas constant, $R = 0.082$ L atm $mol^{-1}\ K^{-1} = 8.314$ J $mol^{-1}\ K^{-1}$.

[Given : The volume of 1 mol of liquid water is 18 mL under the above reaction condition]

23. At 298 K, calculate the solubility of metal sulfide, MS(s), in a saturated solution of H_2S where the concentration of H_2S and pH are maintained at 0.1 M and 3.0, respectively.

Given at 298 K,

$$H_2S\ (aq) + H_2O\ (l) \rightleftharpoons H_3O^+\ (aq) + HS^-\ (aq) \qquad K = 10^{-7}$$

$$MS\ (s) + H_2O\ (l) \rightleftharpoons M^{2+}\ (aq + HS^-\ (aq) + {}^-OH\ (aq) \qquad K = 5 \times 10^{-19}$$

24. For each of the following metallo-proteins identify the metal-ion at the active-site and the function of the proteins :

deoxy-hemoglobin, deoxy-myoglobin, oxy-hemocyanin, cytochrome-c and carbonic anhydrase.

25. A solution containing 250 ppm of $CuSO_4.5H_2O$ (formula weight = 250) has an absorbance of 0.1 measured in 1 cm cell at 600 nm. Calculate the molar absorptivity (ε) of $CuSO_4.5H_2O$ in L M^{-1} cm^{-1}. When 25 mL of the above solution is titrated against Na_2EDTA (aq) solution, it consumes 50 mL of Na_2EDTA (aq) solution. Calculate the concentration of Na_2EDTA (aq) solution in moles L^{-1}.

26. Assume the complex $[Ni(PPh_3)_2(SCN)_2]$ is paramagnetic. The analogous complex of Pd(II) is diamagnetic. Draw all the probable isomers for both the complexes considering SCN^- is an ambidentate ligand.

27. Write the structures of **A** to **E** in the following reaction sequence :

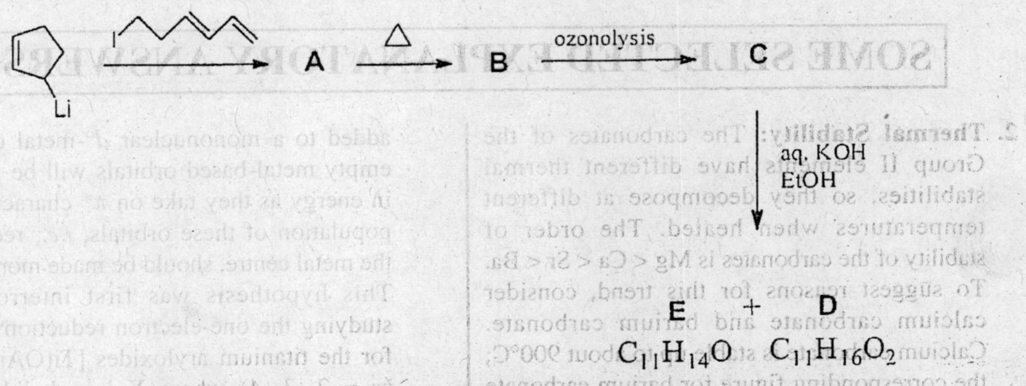

28. Write the structures of F to J in the following reaction scheme :

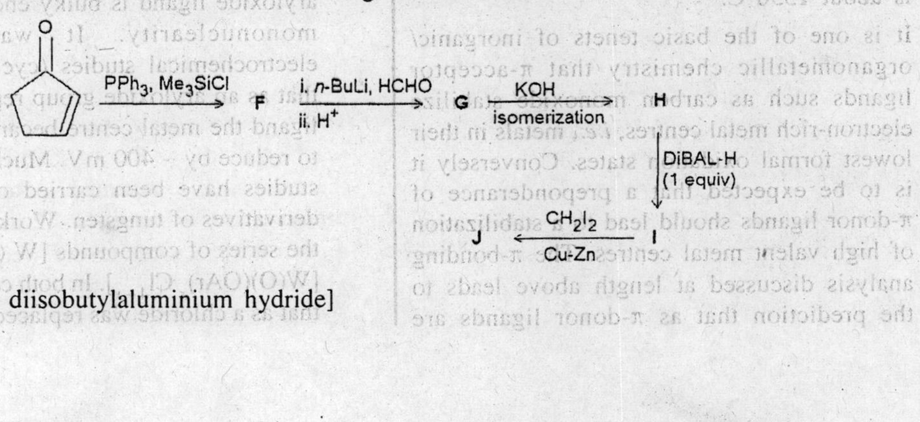

[DiBAL-H = diisobutylaluminium hydride]

29. Propose a mechanism for the following reaction. Show stepwise correct reactive intermediates.

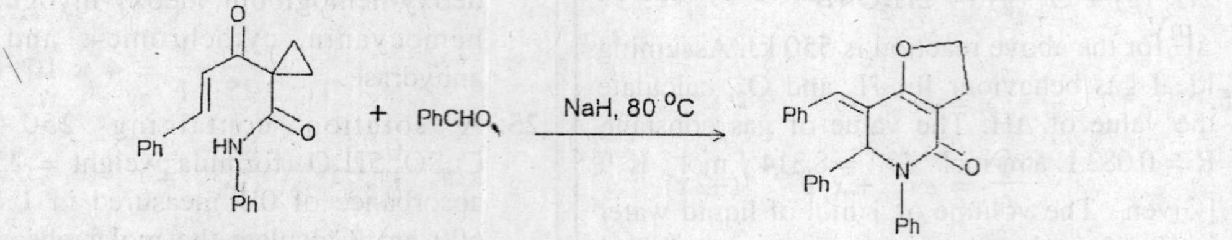

30. Complete the following reaction sequence and write structures of **K** to **O**.

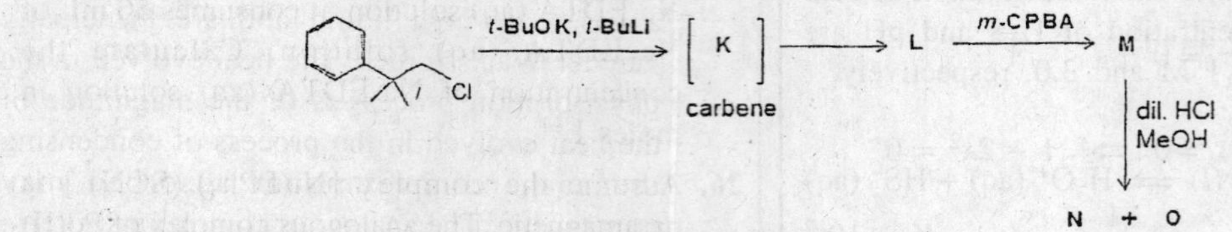

ANSWERS

1	2	3	4	5	6	7	8	9	10
A	B	B	C	A	C	C	*	C	A

SOME SELECTED EXPLANATORY ANSWERS

2. Thermal Stability: The carbonates of the Group II elements have different thermal stabilities, so they decompose at different temperatures when heated. The order of stability of the carbonates is Mg < Ca < Sr < Ba. To suggest reasons for this trend, consider calcium carbonate and barium carbonate. Calcium carbonate is stable up to about 900°C; the corresponding figure for barium carbonate is about 1350°C.

4. It is one of the basic tenets of inorganic/organometallic chemistry that π-acceptor ligands such as carbon monoxide stabilize electron-rich metal centres, *i.e.*, metals in their lowest formal oxidation states. Conversely it is to be expected that a preponderance of π-donor ligands should lead to a stabilization of high valent metal centres. The π-bonding analysis discussed at length above leads to the prediction that as π-donor ligands are added to a mononuclear d°-metal centre any empty metal-based orbitals will be pushed up in energy as they take on π* character. Hence population of these orbitals, *i.e.*, reduction of the metal centre, should be made more difficult. This hypothesis was first interrogated by studying the one-electron reduction potentials for the titanium aryloxides $[Ti(OAr)_x(X)_{4-x}]$ (x = 2, 3, 4) where X is a halide and the aryloxide ligand is bulky enough to maintain mononuclearity. It was shown by electrochemical studies (cyclic voltammetry) that as an aryloxide group replaced a chloride ligand the metal centre became more difficult to reduce by ~ 400 mV. Much more extensive studies have been carried out on aryloxide derivatives of tungsten. Work has focussed on the series of compounds $[W(OAr)_x Cl_{6-x}]$ and $[W(O)(OAr)_x Cl_{4-x}]$. In both cases it was shown that as a chloride was replaced by an aryloxide the reduction potential for formation of the d^1-anion became more negative by 200-300 mV.

5. $$y = xe^{-x^2}$$

$$\frac{dy}{dx} = e^{-x^2} + x \cdot e^{-x^2} \cdot (-2x)$$

$$= e^{-x^2} \cdot (1-2x^2)$$

For minimum or maximum,

$$\frac{dy}{dx} = 0$$

$$e^{-x^2}(1-2x^2) = 0 \Rightarrow 1 - 2x^2 = 0$$

$$x = \pm\frac{1}{\sqrt{2}}$$

Given that, at $x = -\frac{1}{\sqrt{2}}$, function has a minimum.

again, $\frac{d^2y}{dx^2} = (1-2x^2)e^{-x^2} \cdot (-2x) - 4x \cdot e^{-x^2}$

$$= 2x(2x^2-3) \cdot e^{-x^2}$$

At $x = -\frac{1}{\sqrt{2}}$

$$\frac{d^2y}{dx^2} = 2 \cdot \left(-\frac{1}{\sqrt{2}}\right)\left(2 \cdot \frac{1}{2} - 3\right) \cdot e^{-\frac{1}{2}}$$

$$= 2\sqrt{2}\exp\left(-\frac{1}{2}\right).$$

6. As the graph of $\frac{1}{[A]}$ versus time is straight line, so its equation

$$y = mx + c$$

where, $y = \frac{1}{[A]}$ and x = time (t)

m = Slope = 4×10^{-2} L/mol. sec (given)

At time t, $y = 0$, $\Rightarrow$ $c = 0$

equation reduced to

$$y = 4 \times 10^{-2}(x)$$

According to the question,

$$\frac{1}{0.25} - \frac{1}{1} = 4 \times 10^{-2}(t)$$

or, $$\frac{0.75}{0.25} \times \frac{1}{4 \times 10^{-2}} = t$$

time (t) = 75 sec.

7. The forces causing physisorption are the same type as those that cause the condensation of a gas to form a liquid and are principally van der Waals forces. The heal evolved in the physisorption process is of the magnitude of the heat evolved in the process of condensing the gas and the amount adsorbed may correspond to several monolayers. Physisorption can usually be easily reversed by lowering the pressure of the gas or the concentration of the solute and the extent of physisorption is smaller at higher temperatures. There is normally no change in the electron density in either the adsorbate or at the substrate surface, which would correspond to a chemical bond being formed.

Chemisorption involves the formation of chemical bonds. It is therefore more specific than physisorption, but there are borderline cases in which it is not possible to make a sharp distinction between two kinds of adsorption. Usually the enthalpy change in chemisorption is much larger than for physisorption, lying in the range of 40-200 kJ mol^{-1}. Surfaces of most adsorbents are not uniform. The energy of adsorption is different at various sites because of the arrangement of atoms and molecules in the surface. There is substantial change in the electron density of both the adsorbate and the substrate that corresponds to the chemical bond formation.

11. Reaction of alkali metal cyclo pentadienides with metal complexes: A solution of the alkali metal cyclo pentadienide is prepared by the action of dispersed alkali metal on cyclo pentadinene in tetrahydrop furan.

$$2C_5H_5 + 2Na \rightarrow 2C_5H_5^-Na^+ + H_2$$

Now this solution is used for the preparation of number of organometallic compounds of transition metals as:

By reacting freshly prepared solution of sodium or potassium cyclo pentadienide in tetrahydro furan or in a poly-ether like ethylene glycol dimethyl ether and anhydrous metal halides.

$$2C_5H_5^-Na^+ + FeCl_2 \rightarrow (C_5H_5)_2Fe + 2NaCl$$

All are crystalline solids which are generally coloured *e.g.*, $(\pi\text{-}C_5H_5)_2Ni$ is bright green $(\pi\text{-}C_5H_5)_2$ TiCl has bright red crystals $(\pi\text{-}C_5H_5)_2Fe$ has orange crystals. The neutral compounds of Ti, Cr, Fe, Co, Ni are soluble in hydrocarbon solvents. They readily sublime in vaccum. Most of the sandwich complexes are thermally stable and melt without decomposition at about 173°C. The titanium compounds is thermally unstable and decomposes at about 140°C before melting.

The stability of the cyclo Pentadienyl towards oxygen has been found to vary widely. Ferrocene is stable toward molecular oxygen at room temperature while π-cyclo Pentadienyl metal oxide derivatives are found if these complexes are put to controlled oxidation.

Practically all the compounds reacts in acid solution with a variety of oxidising agents to yield cations.

$$(\pi\text{-}C_5H_5)_2M \rightarrow (\pi C_5H_5)_2M^+ + e^-$$

These cations can be isolated by precipitation with suitable anions.

The V^{2+}, Fe^{2+}, Ni^{2+}, Co^{2+} compounds are not affected by water. However, they are merely oxidised to $M(C_5H_5)^+_2$ by 3M – HNO_3. The hydrogen atoms of π-cyclo pentadienyl ligands are normally not replaceable and do not exchange with D_2O. However at higher temperatures $Ca(OD)_2$ reacts with $(\pi\text{-}C_5H_5)_2Fe$ to form deutoro ferrocenes.

$$(\pi - C_5H_5)_2Fe + 5VCa(OD)_2 \rightarrow \underset{\text{Deutero ferrocene}}{(C_5H_5)_2Fe} + 5Ca(OH)_2$$

The di π-cyclo pentadienyl complexes have been found to be even resistant to catalytic hydrogenation. Ferrocene is even more resistant to hydrogenation then benzene.

12. Rocksalt Structure: The rocksalt structure consists in two interpenetrating fcc lattices of anions and cations, in which all atoms are in an octahedral environment. It is met in alkaline-earth oxides (MgO, CaO, SrO, BaO) and in some transition metal oxides like TiO, VO, MnO, FeO, CoO, NiO, etc, with cations in a+2 oxidation state. The non-polar surfaces of lowest Miller indices are (100) and (110) surfaces: they have neutral layers, with as many cations as oxygen ions, and their outermost atoms are 5- and 4-fold coordinated, respectively. Actually, *planar* surfaces can only be produced along the (100) orientation. The polar direction of lowest indices in (111): it has an hexagonal 2D unit cell, three-fold coordinated surface atoms and equidistant layers of either metal or oxygen composition.

The lattice enthalpy increases with increasing atomic number because of the general (V2+ is an exception) decrease in ionic radius of M^{2+} — the smaller the ion, the stronger the ionic bonding to the oxide lattice. Superimposed on this trend, the lattice enthalpy parallels the CFSE of the metal ion in an octahedral oxide (high-spin) environment. A larger CFSE leads to a larger lattice enthalpy, i.e., a stronger metal oxide lattice.

Oxide	d^n	CFSE	Ionic radius M^{2+} (pm)	Lattice enthalpy (kJ/mol)
CaO	0	0	114	3460
VO	3	$-1.2\Delta_0$	93	3913
MnO	5	$0\Delta_0$	97.0	3810

13. IF_8^-, which are regular square-antiprismatic.

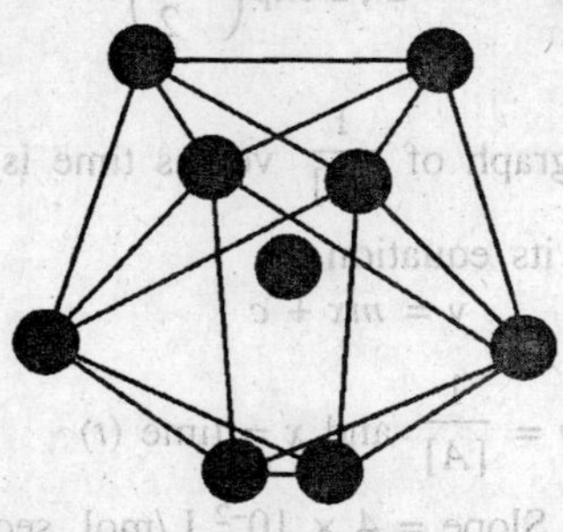

Square antiprism

14. P_{vap} = Vapour Pressure (torr)

ΔH_{vap} = Heat of Vaporization (J/mol)

T = Temperature in K

R = Gas constant (8.31 J/(K• mol)

A = Constant Factor relating to Vapour Pressure of a Particular Liquid

$$P_{vap} = Ae^{\frac{-\Delta H_{vep}}{RT}}$$

(P_{vap} is an exponential function of the reciprical of T)

$$\ln (P_{vap}) = \ln\left(Ae^{\frac{-\Delta H_{vep}}{RT}}\right)$$

(Natural Log [ln] both sides of the equation can bring the exponent of the natural number down)

$$\ln(P_{vap}) = \ln(A) + \ln\left(e^{\frac{-\Delta H_{vep}}{RT}}\right)$$

[Using Logarithm Law:
ln(MN) = ln(M) + ln (N)]

$$\ln(P_{vap}) = \ln(A) + \frac{-\Delta H_{vep}}{RT}$$

[ln (e^x) = x] and let ln(A) = C

$$\ln (P_{vap}) = \frac{-\Delta H_{vep}}{RT}\left(\frac{1}{T}\right)+C$$

[Now, ln (P_{vap}) has a linear relationship with (1/T)]

When $y = \ln(P_{vap})$ is plotted against x = (1/T), the graphs turned linear

$$\ln(P_{vap}) = \frac{-\Delta H_{vap}}{RT}\left(\frac{1}{T}\right)+C$$

with *slope* = $\frac{-\Delta H_{vap}}{R}$ any *y*-intercept

= C = ln(A)

hence ratio of the slope of two curve = $\frac{3900}{2600}$

$$= \frac{3}{2} = 3 : 2.$$

15. According to wave mechanics, atomic orbitals are described by wave function $\psi(r, \theta, \phi)$ obtained from the solution of the schrodinger wave equation. It is a mathematical function of the three co-ordinates of the electron (r, θ, ϕ) and can be represented as a product of three parts each of which is a function of only one co-ordinate as:

$$\psi(r, \theta, \phi) = R(r)\ \Theta(\theta)\ \Phi(\phi)$$

$R(r)$ depends upon the distance r alone, $\Theta(\theta)$ depends upon angle θ alone and $\Phi(\phi)$ depends upon angle Φ alone.

Radial wave function $R(r)$ gives the distribution of the electron as a function of the distance (r) from the nucleus.

All points for which $r = 0$, gives radial nodes.

When, $R(r) = 0$

$$\left(\frac{2r}{a_0} - \left(\frac{r}{a_0}\right)^2\right)e^{-\left(\frac{r}{a_0}\right)} = 0$$

or

$$\frac{r}{a_0}\left(2 - \frac{r}{a_0}\right) = 0$$

$\Rightarrow$ $r = a_0$

and $r = 2a_0$

Hence, number of radial nodes = 2.

16. From Bragg's equation

$$2d \sin \theta = n\lambda$$

here $n = 1,\quad \lambda = 5Å,\quad \theta = 30°$

$$\therefore \quad d = \frac{1*5}{2*\sin 30°} = 5Å$$

For simple cubic lattice, nearest neighbour distance (d) is related to the edge (a) as

$$d = a = 5Å$$

For S.C.C., $z = 1$

and atomic weight = 300.

$$\therefore \quad \text{density } (\rho) = \frac{z \times m}{a^3 \times N_A}$$

$$= \frac{1 \times 300}{(5 \times 10^{-8})^3 \times 6.02 \times 10^{23}}$$

$$= 4 \text{ g/cm}^3.$$

17. From, the Nernst equation,

$$E_{cell} = E^\circ_{cell} - \frac{2.303\,RT}{nF}\log\frac{[zn^+(aq)]}{[Mno_4^-(aq)]}$$

In equilibrium state, the concentration of substances oxidised and reduced will be in equilibrium concentration and emf of the cell will be zero.

$$0 = E^\circ_{cell} - \frac{0.06}{n}\log(10)^x$$

$$E^\circ_{cell} = \frac{0.06}{n}(x)$$

$$2.4 = \frac{0.06}{n}(x)$$

$$x = \frac{2.4\times n}{0.06}$$

$$x = 40n.$$

18.

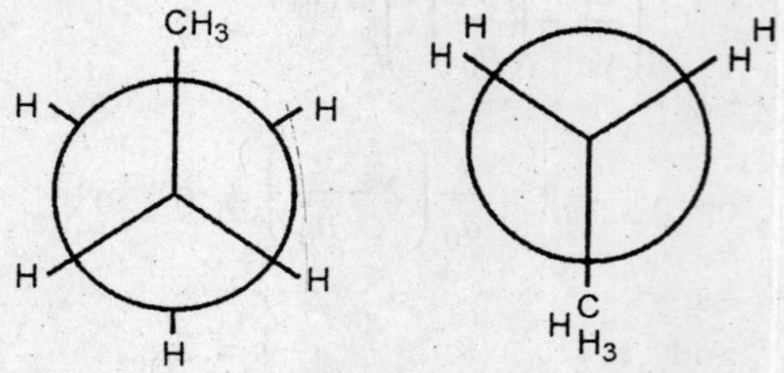

Most stable Least stable

Rotate from

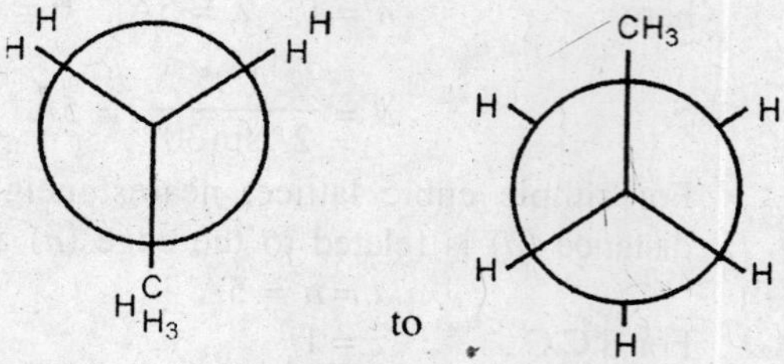

The energy will be 2.9 – 0.9 = 2 kcal/mol

19. Due to the contribution of the two major resonance structures of an amide, the bond order of the carbonyl C = O bond is reduced and that of the carbon-nitrogen bond is increased. Thus the infrared spectrum of DMF shows a lower C = O stretching frequency at 1675 cm^{-1} than an unsubstituted C = O bond. Also, because of the partial double bond character, the rotation about the C-N axis is slow at room temperature, making the two methyl groups inequivalent on the NMR time scale, giving rise to two singlets of 3 protons each at δ 2.97 and 2.88, instead of one singlet of 6 protons in the proton NMR spectrum.

DMF is miscible with water in all proportions. The vapour pressure at 20°C is 3.5hPa. A Henry's law constant of 7.47 × 10^{-5} hPa.m^3/mol can be deduced from an experimentally determined equilibrium constant at 25°C. The partition coefficient logPOW is measured to –0.85. Since the density of DMF (0.95 g/cm^3 at 20°C) is very similar to that of water, significant flotation or stratification in surface waters in case of accidental losses is not expected.

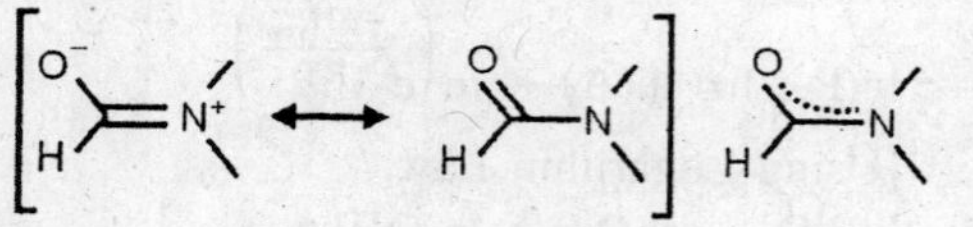

The two resonance forms of DMF

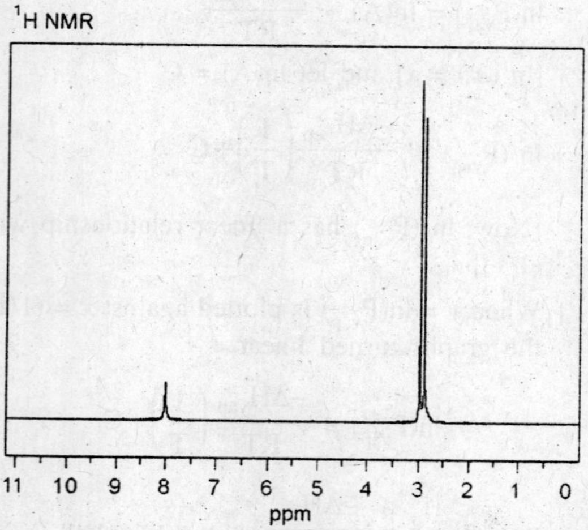

NMR of DMF

20. Resorcarenes are very closely related to calixarenes and are sometimes referred to as calixresorcarenes. They are prepared from the acid-catalysed condensation of resorcinol (1, 3-dihydroxybenzene) with aldehydes, a reaction first carried out by Baeyr. This macrocycle is arguably one of the most important molecules in the field, as resorcarenes serve as the basic building blocks for many cavitands and (hemi) carcerands. Both calixarenes and resorcarences posses a shallow bowl-shaped conformation in their most stable forms. However, [4]resorcarenes (the [4] prefix refers to the number of resorcinol units that make up the molecule, just as in calix[n] arenes) tend to produce a more shallow bowl compared to calix[4]arenes. This is because intramolecular hydrogen bonding interactions between the peripheral hydroxyl groups stabilise the molecule in a more splayed conformation.

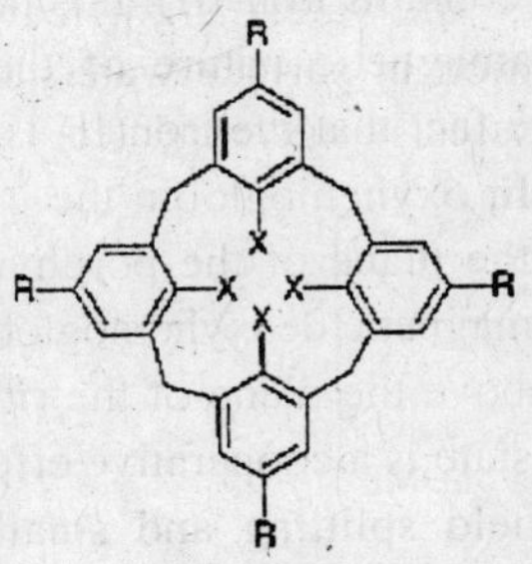

Calix[4]arene
X = OH
R = H, CH_3, t-Bu

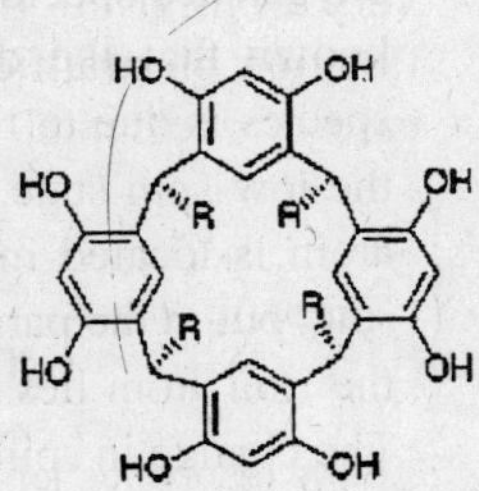

R = alkyl
Calix[4]resorcarene

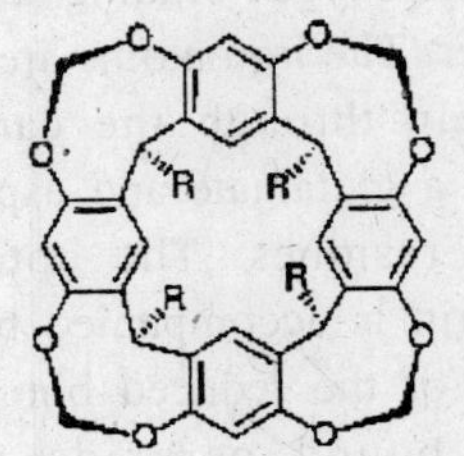

A bridged resorcarene

21. $\frac{1}{5}C_3H_8 + O_2 \rightarrow \frac{3}{5}CO_2(g) + \frac{4}{5}H_2O(g)$

Initial conc. (in moles)	n_1	n_2		
Final conc.	$\left(n_1 - \frac{n_2}{5}\right)$	0	$\frac{3n_2}{5}$	$\frac{4n_2}{5}$

From Ideal gas equation,

$$PV = nRT$$

Initial pressure P_1 = 4 atm.

$$4 \times 1 = (n_1 + n_2)\ R \times (273 + 100)$$

{R = gas constant}

$$\text{or,} \quad (n_1 + n_2) = \frac{4}{373R} \quad ...(1)$$

when pressure P_2 = 4.2 atm

$$n = n_1 - \frac{n_2}{5} + \frac{3n_2}{5} + \frac{4n_2}{5}$$

$$= n_1 + \frac{6n_2}{5}$$

$$\text{so,} \quad 4.2 \times 1 = \left(n_1 + \frac{6n_2}{5}\right) \cdot R \cdot 375$$

$$\text{or,} \quad n_1 + \frac{6n_2}{5} = \frac{4.2}{373R} \quad ...(2)$$

from (1) and (2), we get

$$\frac{n_2}{5} = \frac{0.2}{373R}$$

$$n_2 = \frac{1}{373R}$$

wt. of oxygen at start of the titration

$$= \frac{32}{373 \times 0.082}$$

$$= 1.046 \text{ gm.}$$

22. $2H_2(g) + O_2(g) \rightarrow 2H_2O(l)$

Change in internal energy

$$\Delta U = 550 \text{ kj}$$

As ΔU is positive, so heat is absorbed

$$\Delta n_g = (n_p - n_r)_{\text{gaseous}}$$

$$= (0 - 1 - 2) = -3.$$

From the equation,

Enthalpy of the reaction

$$\Delta H = \Delta U + \Delta nRT$$

$$= 550 + (-3) \times 0.08314 \times 300$$

$$= 550 - 7.4826$$

$$= 542.5174 \text{ kj}$$

24. Metalloprotein: Metalloprotein is a generic term for a protein that contains a metal ion cofactor. A large fraction of all proteins are members of this category, so the area is very large.

Metalloenzymes are widespread and diverse in function: It is estimated that approximately half of all proteins contain a metal. In another estimate, about one quarter to one third of all proteins are proposed require metals to carry out their functions. Thus, metalloproteins have many different functions in cells, such as enzymes, transport and storage proteins and signal transduction proteins.

Coordination chemistry principles: In metalloproteins, metal ions are usually coordinated by nitrogen, oxygen or sulphur centres belonging to amino acid residues of the protein. These donor groups are often provided by side-chains on the amino acid residues. Especially important are the imidazole substituent in histidine residues, thiolate substituents in cysteinyl residues and carboxylate groups provided by aspartate. Given the diversity of the metalloproteome, virtually all amino acid residues have been shown to bind metal centres. The peptide backbone also provides donor groups, these include deprotonated amides and the amide carbonyl oxygen centres.

In addition to donor groups that are provided by amino acid residues, a large number of organic cofactors function as ligands. Perhaps most famous are the tetradentate N4 macrocyclic ligands incorporated into the hemeprotein. Inorganic ligands such as sulfide and oxide are also common.

Storage and transport metalloprotein

Oxygen carriers: Hemoglobin, which is the principal oxygen carrier in humans has four sub-units in which the iron(II) ion is coordinated by the planar, macrocyclic ligand protoporphyrin IX (PIX) and the imidazole nitrogen atom of a histidine residue. The sixth coordination site contains a water molecule or a dioxygen molecule, myoglobin has only one such unit. The active site is located in an hydrophobic pocket. This is important as, without it, the iron(II) would be irreversibly oxidised to iron(III). The equilibrium constant for the formation of HbO_2 is such that oxygen is taken up or released depending on the partial pressure of oxygen in the lungs or in muscle. In hemoglobin the four sub-units show a cooperativity effect which allows for easy oxygen transfer from hemoglobin to myoglobin.

In both hemoglobin and myoglobin it is sometimes incorrectly stated that the oxygenated species contains iron(III). It is now known that the diamagnetic nature of these species is due to the fact that the iron(II) is in the low-spin state. In oxyhemoglobin the iron atom is located in the plane of the porphyrin ring, but in the paramagnetic deoxyhemoglobin the iron atom lies above the plane of the ring. The change in spin state is a cooperative effect of higher crystal field splitting and smaller ionic radius of Fe^{2+} in the oxy-moiety.

Hemerythrin is another iron-containing oxygen carrier. The oxygen binding site is a binuclear iron center. The iron atoms are coordinated to the protein through the carboxylate side chains of a glutamate and aspartate and five histidine residues. The uptake of O_2 by hemerythrin is accompanied by two-electron oxidation of the reduced binuclear center to produce bound peroxide (OOH^-). The mechanism of oxygen uptake and release have been worked out in detail.

Hemocyanins carry oxygen in the blood of most molluses and some arthropods such as the horseshoe crab. They are second only to hemoglobin in biological popularity of use in oxygen transport. On oxygenation the two copper(I) atoms at the active site are oxidised to copper(II) and the dioxygen molecules is reduced to peroxide, O_2^{2-}.

Cytochromes: Oxidation and reduction reactions are not common in organic chemistry as few organic molecules can act as oxidizing or reducing agents. Iron(II), on the other hand, can easily be oxidized to iron(III). This functionality is used in cytochromes which function as electron-transfer vectors. The presence of the metal ion allows metalloenzymes to perform functions such as redox reactions that cannot easily be performed by the limited set of functional groups found in amino acids. The iron atom in most cytochromes is contained in a heme group. The differences between those cytochromes lies in the different side-chains. For instance Cytochrome a has a heme a prosthetic group and cytochrome b has a heme b prosthetic group. These differences result in different Fe^{2+}/Fe^{3+} redox potentials such that various cytochromes are involved in the mitochondrial electron transport chain.

Cytochrome P450 enzymes perform the function of inserting an oxygen atom into a C—H bond, an oxidation reaction.

Carbonic anhydrase:

Active site of carbonic anhydrase. The three coordinating histidine residues are shown in green, hydroxide in red and white, and the zinc in gray.

$$CO_2 + H_2O \rightleftharpoons H_2CO_3$$

This reaction is very slow in the absence of a catalyst, but quite fast in the presence of the hydroxide ion

$$CO_2 + OH^- \rightleftharpoons HCO_3^-$$

A reaction similar to this is almost instantaneous with carbonic anhydrase. The structure of the active site in carbonic anhydrases is well-known from a number of crystal structures. It consists of a zinc ion coordinated by three imidazole nitrogen atoms from three histidine units.

Previous Paper (Solved)

IIT–JAM

JOINT ADMISSION TEST FOR M.Sc. (CHEMISTRY)-2012

Directions (Qs. 1-30): *(Objective questions) carry three marks each and questions* **(Qs. 31-44)** *(Subjective questions) carry **fifteen** marks each.*

1. Molecular shape of $SOCl_2$ is

A. square planar
B. trigonal pyramidal
C. triangular planar
D. T-shaped

2. Number of three-centre two-electron (3c–2e) bonds present in diborane is

A. 2 B. 4
C. 6 D. 8

3. The lattice energy of LiF calculated from Born-Lande equation is –1000 kJ mol^{-1}. Assume that for both LiF and MgO the Madelung constants, interionic distances and Born exponents have the same value. The lattice energy of MgO in kJ mol^{-1} is

A. –4000 B. –2000
C. 2000 D. 4000

4. The compound formed by dissolving elemental gold in aqua regia is

A. AuCl B. $AuNO_3$
C. $H[AuCl_4]$ D. $H[Au(NO_3)_4]$

5. Number of moles of ions produced by complete dissociation of one mole of Mohr's salt in water is

A. 3 B. 4
C. 5 D. 6

6. The tetrachloro complexes of Ni(II) and Pd(II) respectively, are (atomic numbers of Ni and Pd are 28 and 46 respectively)

A. diamagnetic and diamagnetic
B. paramagnetic and paramagnetic
C. diamagnetic and paramagnetic
D. paramagnetic and diamagnetic

7. The total number of steps involved and number of beta particles emitted in the spontaneous decay of ${}^{238}_{92}U \rightarrow {}^{208}_{82}Pb$ respectively, are

A. 8 and 6 B. 14 and 6
C. 6 and 8 D. 14 and 8

8. A filter paper moistened with ammoniacal sodium nitroprusside solution turns violet on contact with a drop of alkaline Na_2S solution. The violet colour is due to the formation of

A. $[Fe(SCN)_5(NO)]^{1-}$ B. $[Fe(SCN)_5(NO)]^{2-}$
C. $[Fe(CN)_5(NOS)]^{3-}$ D. $[Fe(CN)_5(NOS)]^{4-}$

9. The species/compounds that are aromatic among the following are

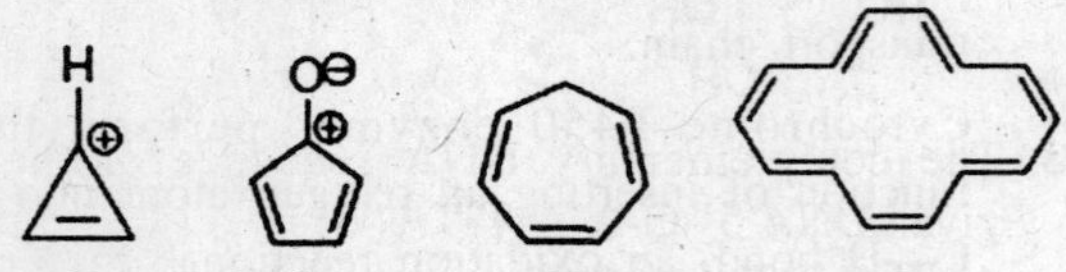

P Q R S

A. R and S B. P and Q
C. Q and S D. P and S

10. The major product obtained in the reaction below is

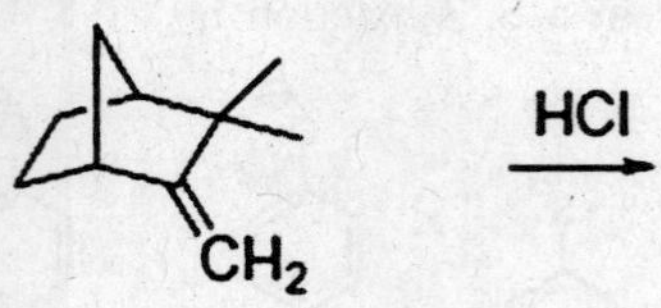

A. 

B. 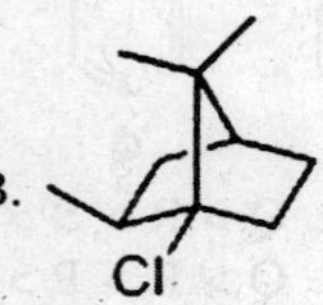

C. 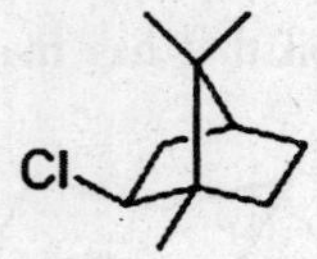

D. 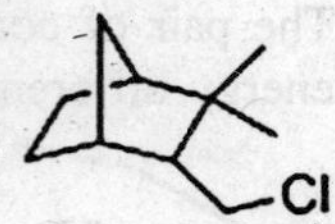

11. The rates of acetolysis for the following norbornyl derivatives are in the order

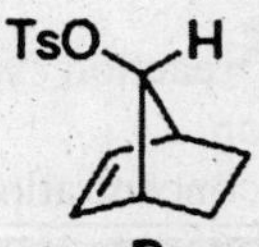
P

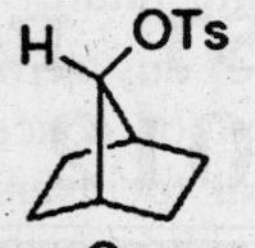
Q

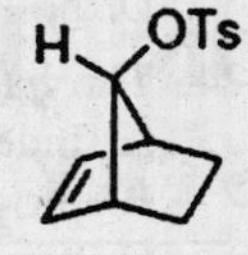
R

A. R > Q > P B. Q > R > P
C. P > R > Q D. R > P > Q

12. The Haworth projection for α-anomer of D-glucose is

A. 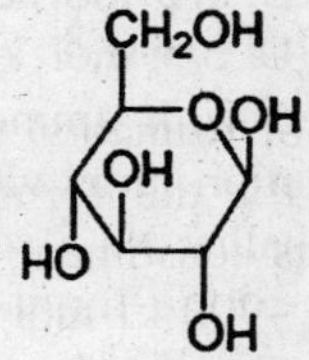

B. 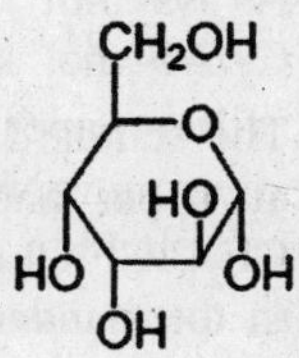

C. 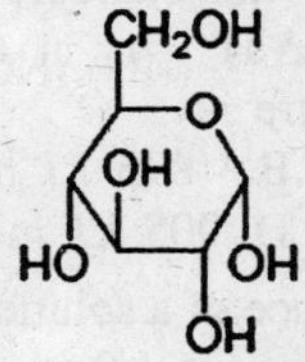

D. 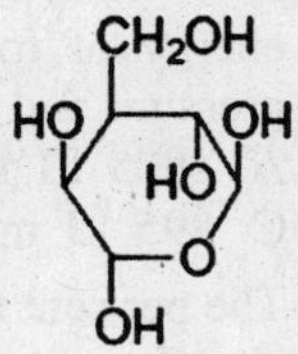

13. The complementary DNA sequence of the given DNA 5'-G-A-A-T-T-C-3' is
A. 5'-C-T-T-A-A-G-3'
B. 5'-C-U-U-A-A-G-3'
C. 3'-C-T-T-A-A-G-5'
D. 3'-G-A-A-T-T-C-5'

14. The order of nucleophilicity of the following anions in a S_N2 reaction is

P

Q

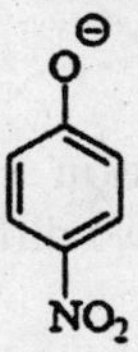
R

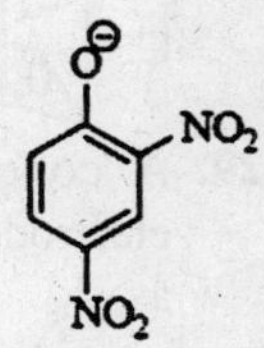
S

A. Q > R > S > P B. Q > P > R > S
C. Q > R > P > S D. P > S > R > Q

15. The pair of conformation that has maximum energy difference is

A.  and 

B.  and 

C.  and 

D.  and 

16. The major mono-sulfonation product of α-tetralone is

A. 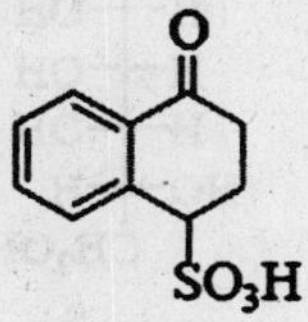

B. 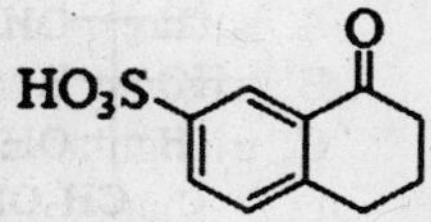

C. 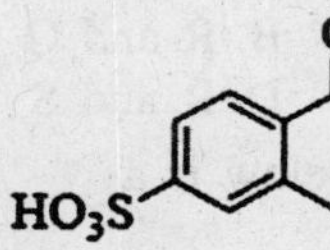

D. 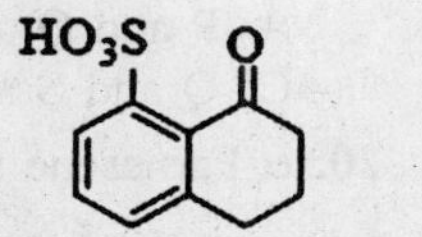

17. Electrophilic nitrations of the following compounds follow the trend

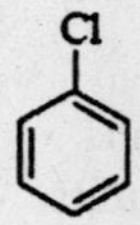
P

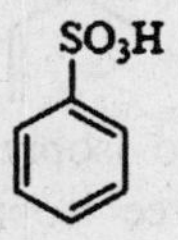
Q

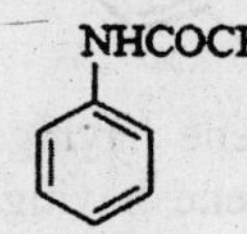
R

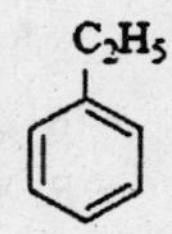
S

A. S > R > P > Q B. R > S > P > Q
C. R > P > S > Q D. P > S > R > Q

18. The compounds those would not respond to tests of both nitrogen and sulphur with sodium fusion extracts are

$H_2N-\overset{\oplus}{N}H_3\cdot HSO_4^{\ominus}$
I

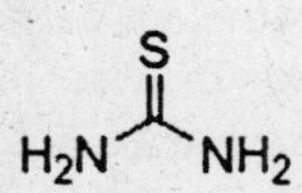
II

$H_2N-\overset{\oplus}{N}H_3\cdot HCO_3^{\ominus}$
III

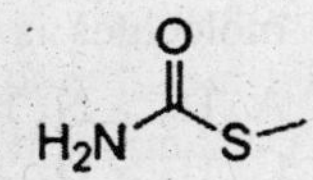
IV

A. I and III B. III and IV
C. I and IV D. II and IV

19. The correct epimeric pair of the following is

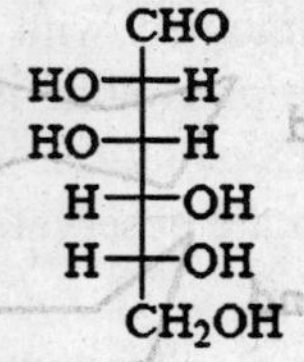

P

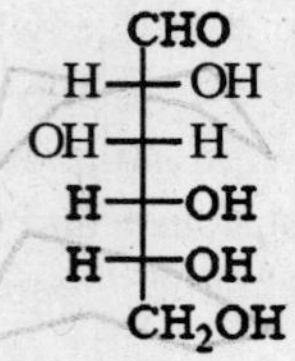

Q

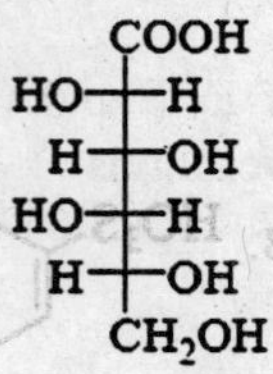

R

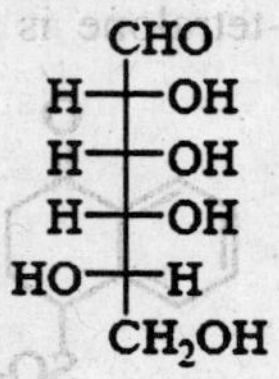

S

A. P and Q B. R and Q

C. Q and S D. R and S

20. α-Farnesene shown below is a

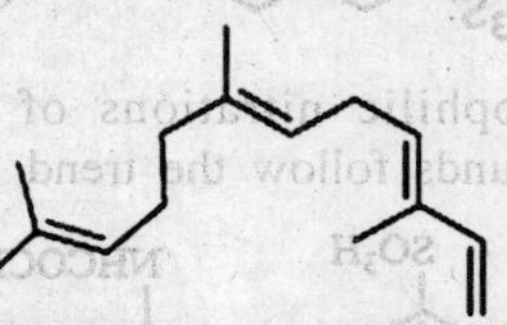

A. diterpene having two isoprene units

B. triterpene having three isoprene units

C. triterpene having four isoprene units

D. sesquiterpene having three isoprene units

21. For the equilibrium $N_2 + 3H_2 \rightleftharpoons 2NH_3$, the equilibrium constant, K_p is expressed as

A. $3^3 K_p = \frac{p_{NH_3}}{p^2_{N_2}}$ B. $3^3 K_p = \frac{p^2_{NH_3}}{p_{N_2} p^3_{H_2}}$

C. $3^3 K_p = \frac{p^2_{NH_3}}{p^4_{N_2}}$ D. $3^{3/2} K_p^{1/2} = \frac{p^2_{NH_3}}{p^4_{N_2}}$

22. The average speed of H_2, N_2 and O_2 gas molecules is in the order

A. $H_2 > N_2 > O_2$ B. $O_2 > N_2 > H_2$

C. $H_2 > O_2 > N_2$ D. $N_2 > O_2 > H_2$

23. The enthalpy of vaporization ($\Delta_{vap}H$) is zero at

A. Boyle temperature

B. critical temperature

C. inversion temperature

D. boiling temperature

24. The half-life of any zero-order reaction is

A. independent of concentration

B. proportional to inverse of concentration

C. proportional to concentration

D. proportional to square of the concentration

25. The molality of $(NH_4)2SO_4$ solution that has the same ionic strength as 1 mol kg^{-1} solution of KCl is

A. 1/3 mol kg^{-1} B. 1/2 mol kg^{-1}

C. 2/5 mol kg^{-1} D. 3/5 mol kg^{-1}

26. The standard enthalpy of formation ($\Delta_f H^0_{300}$) at 1 bar and 300 K for the formation of CF_2ClCF_2Cl (g) from its constituent elements in the standard state is –900 kJ mol^{-1}. Given R = 8.3 J K^{-1} mol^{-1}, the standard internal energy of formation ($\Delta_f H^0_{300}$) at the same pressure and temperature is

A. –905 kJ mol^{-1} B. –895 kJ mol^{-1}

C. 895 kJ mol^{-1} D. 905 kJ mol^{-1}

27. The per cent transmittance of a solution having absorbance (optical density) 1.0 is

A. 1 B. 10

C. 50 D. 99

28. The matrix which transforms $\begin{pmatrix} x \\ y \end{pmatrix}$ to $\begin{pmatrix} -y \\ -x \end{pmatrix}$ is

A. $(-1 \ -1)$ B. $\begin{pmatrix} -1 \\ -1 \end{pmatrix}$

C. $\begin{pmatrix} -1 & 0 \\ 0 & -1 \end{pmatrix}$ D. $\begin{pmatrix} 0 & -1 \\ -1 & 0 \end{pmatrix}$

29. A concentration cell with two hydrogen electrodes at two different pressures is depicted as

$$\begin{array}{c|c|c} H_2(g)(Pt) & HCl(aq) & H_2(g)(Pt) \\ p_{H_2} = p_1 & & p_{H_2} = p_2 \end{array}$$

The potential (E_{cell}) of the cell is

A. $\frac{RT}{F} \ln \frac{p_2}{p_1}$ B. $\frac{RT}{F} \ln \frac{p_1}{p_2}$

C. $\frac{RT}{2F} \ln \frac{p_2}{p_1}$ D. $\frac{RT}{2F} \ln \frac{p_1}{p_2}$

30. An aqueous solution containing $1 gL^{-1}$ of a polymer exerts osmotic pressure of 4 torr at 300 K. Given R = 0.082 L atm, the molar mass ($g mol^{-1}$) of the polymer is

A. 4500 B. 4564
C. 4674 D. 4800

31. A. Identify the most acidic compound from the following: $CH_3{-}CH_3$, $CH_2{=}CH_2$ and $CH{\equiv}CH$, and justify your answer. Draw overlap of the orbitals to show bonding in the most acidic compound using the concept of hybridization

B. Write a balanced chemical equation to represent acid-base reaction of orthoboric acid in water.

Addition of ethylene glycol to aqueous orthoboric acid enhances its acidity. Explain the above statement using appropriate chemical equation.

32. A. Draw the unit cell structure of NaCl. Calculate the limiting radius ratio of any ionic solid having NaCl like structure.

B. Give molecular formula and structure of the compound formed by reaction of $Be(OH)_2$ with acetic acid.

33. A. The spin-only magnetic moments of $K_3[Fe(oxalate)_3]$ and $K_3[Ru(oxalate)_3]$ are 5.91 μ_B and 1.73 μ_B, respectively. Write down their ligand field electronic configurations. Justify your answer. Atomic numbers of Fe and Ru are 26 and 44 respectively.

B. Draw the structures of NO_2^+, NO_2 and NO_2^-. Arrange them in the increasing order of O–N–O bond angles.

34. A. Show with labels the splitting of *d*-orbitals in an octahedral ligand field. Calculate the CFSE of (i) high spin d^6 and (ii) low spin d^6 metal ions in octahedral field.

B. Schematically represent orbital overlaps in metal carbonyls. Show the correct signs of the lobes.

35. A. A coordination compound is composed of one Co(III), one chloride, one sulphate and four molecules of ammonia. The aqueous solution of the compound gives no precipitate when combined with aqueous $BaCl_2$, while a white precipitate is formed with aqueous $AgNO_3$ solution. Draw its structure and explain the observations with chemical equations.

B. Draw the structures of dimethylglyoxime ($DMGH_2$) and its Ni(II) complex formed in aqueous ammonia.

36. A. Write the structures of **E**, **F** and **G** in the following scheme of reactions

CHO
|
CHOH
|
$(CHOH)_2$
|
CH_2OH

$\xrightarrow{NH_2OH} E \xrightarrow[(CH_3CO)_2O]{\text{excess}} F \xrightarrow[\text{aq. AgOH}]{\text{excess}} G$ ($C_4H_8O_4$)

B. Identify the structures of **H** and **I** in the following synthetic transformation

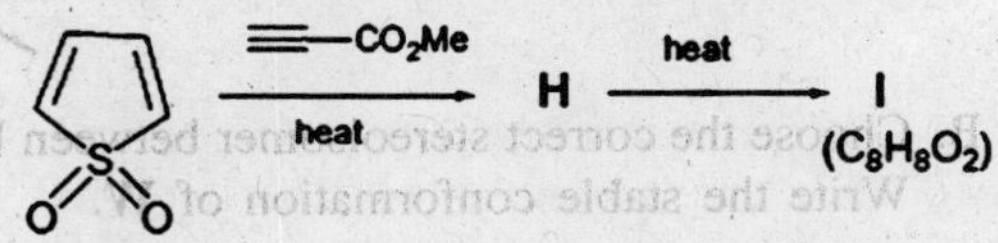

37. A. Complete the following reaction sequence with appropriate structures of **J**, **K** and **L**.

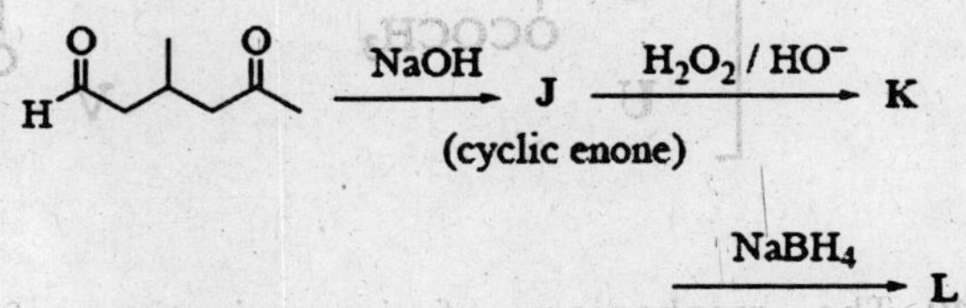

B. Identify the structures of **M** and **N** in the following synthetic transformation

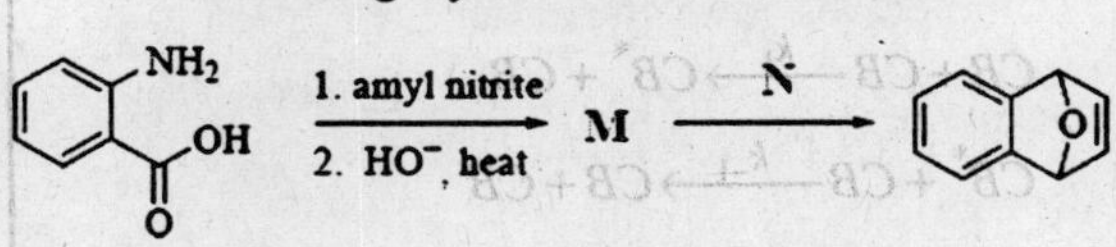

38. A. In the following reaction scheme, write the structures of **O**, **P** and **Q**.

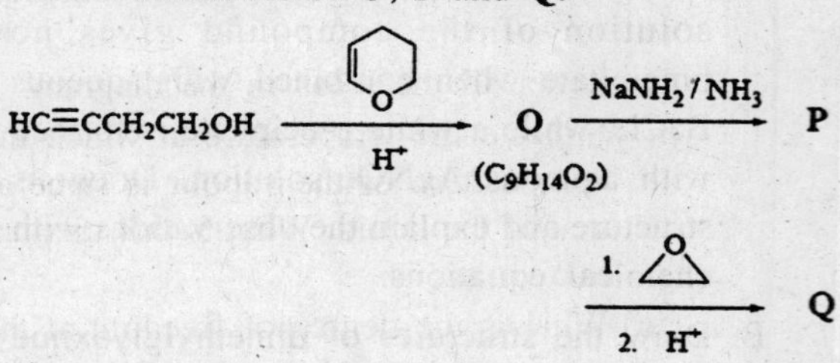

B. Given below are structures of some natural products. Identify them as vitamin A, B_6, C, and D and classify them according to their classes (*isoprenoid, alkaloid, carbohydrate and steroid*).

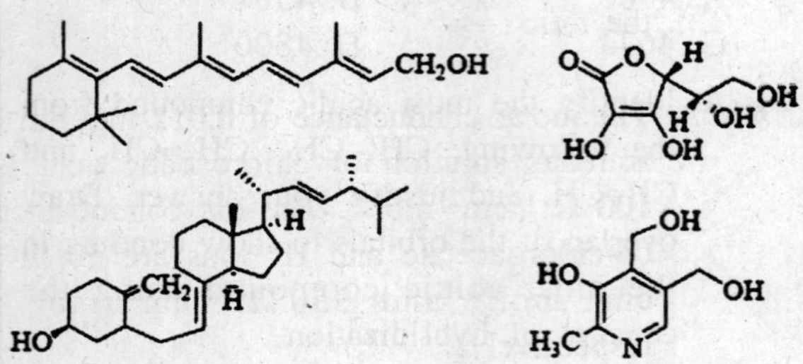

39. A. Write the appropriate structures for **R**, **S** and **T** in the following scheme.

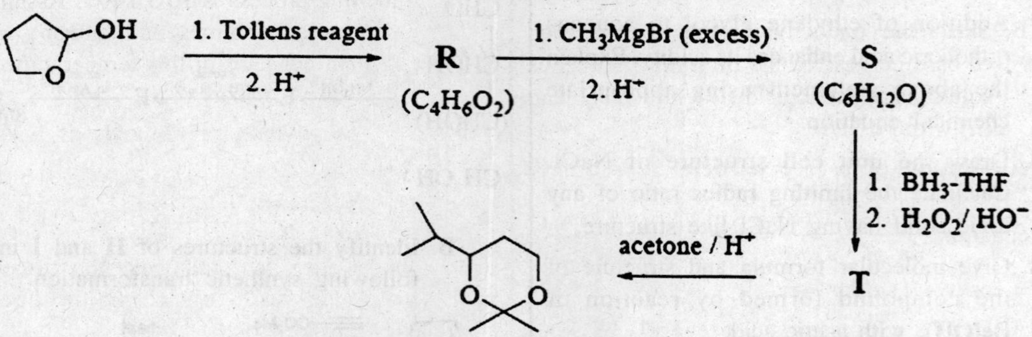

B. Choose the correct stereoisomer between **U** and **V** that would furnish **W** on controlled hydrolysis. Write the stable conformation of **W**.

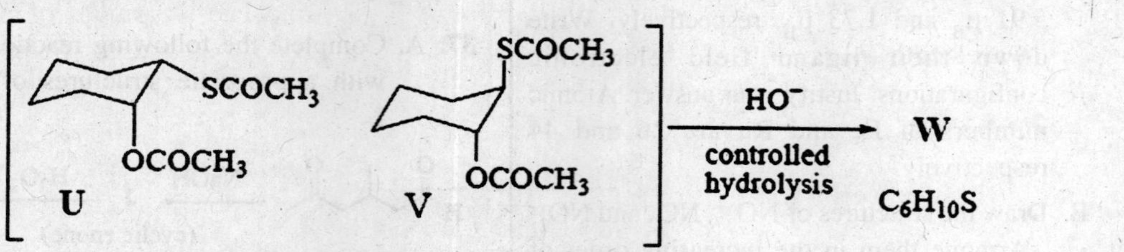

40. The mechanism of isomerization of cyclobutene (*CB*) to 1,3-butadiene (*BD*) is as follows.

$$CB + CB \xrightarrow{k_1} CB^* + CB$$

$$CB^* + CB \xrightarrow{k_{-1}} CB + CB$$

$$CB^* \xrightarrow{k_2} BD$$

A. Show that the rate law is

$$\frac{d[DB]}{dt} = \frac{k_2 \cdot k_1 \cdot [CB]^2}{k_{-1} \cdot [CB] + k_2}.$$

B. The apparent first-order rate constant, $k_{app} = \frac{k_2 \cdot k_1 \cdot [CB]}{k_{-1} \cdot [CB] + k_2}$. At the *CB* concentration of 1×10^{-5} mol dm^{-3}. the value of k_{app} reaches 50% of its limiting value obtained at very high concentrations of *CB*. Evaluate the ratio $\frac{k_2}{k_{-1}}$.

41. A. The molar conductance of 0.012 mol dm^{-3} aqueous solution of chloroacetic acid is 100 Ω^{-1} cm^2 mol^{-1}. The ion conductance of chloroacetate and H^+ ions are 50 Ω^{-1} cm^2 mol^{-1} and 350 Ω^{-1} cm^2 mol^{-1}, respectively.

Calculate (*i*) degree of dissociation and pK_a of chloroacetic acid, and (*ii*) H^+ ion concentration in the solution.

B. Sketch the conductivity versus concentration of base curves for the titration of aqueous solutions of acetic acid (*i*) with NaOH, and (*ii*) with NH_4OH.

42. A solution of a free particle Schrödinger equation $\frac{-h^2}{8\pi^2 m}\frac{d^2\psi(x)}{dx^2} = E\psi(x)$ is $\psi(x) = e^{ikx}$ $= \cos kx + i \sin kx$

A. Derive expressions for energy '*E*' and momentum '*p*' of the particle.

B. Using the above relations, show that the wavelength (λ) is $\frac{h}{p}$.

43. A. Sketch the temperature-composition phase diagram at 1 atm pressure for the ethanol-water system.

(*i*) Label all the areas in the diagram.

(*ii*) Indicate the temperature at which the composition of the vapour is same as that of the liquid. What is this mixture known as?

(*iii*) What is the degree of freedom at the corresponding composition?

B. Estimate the pressure necessary to melt ice at –10°C if the molar volume of liquid water is 18.01 mL and molar volume of ice is 19.64 mL. The entropy change for the melting process is 16.3 J K^{-1}. Assume that the molar volumes and entropy change remain constant in this temperature range. [100 J = 1 L bar]

44. A. (*i*) Show that for *n* moles of a van der Waals gas, $\left(\frac{\partial U}{\partial V}\right)_T = \frac{n^2 a}{V^2}$.

(*ii*) Can a gas that obeys the equation of state $p(V - nb) = nRT$ be liquefied? Explain.

B. Consider ideal mixing of 2 moles of toluene and 2 moles of benzene at 1 atm and 300 K. Calculate the values of $\Delta_{mix}V$, $\Delta_{mix}U$, $\Delta_{mix}H$, $\Delta_{mix}G$, and $\Delta_{mix}S$ for the process. (ln 2 = 0.69)

ANSWERS

1	2	3	4	5	6	7	8	9	10
B	A	*	C	D	A	C	C	D	A
11	**12**	**13**	**14**	**15**	**16**	**17**	**18**	**19**	**20**
D	C	C	D	A	B	B	D	A	D
21	**22**	**23**	**24**	**25**	**26**	**27**	**28**	**29**	**30**
B	A	B	A	A	A	B	D	C.	B

SOME SELECTED EXPLANATORY ANSWERS

1.

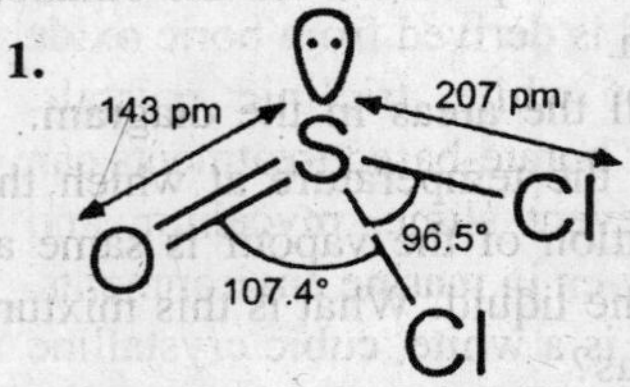

The molecule $SOCl_2$ is trigonal pyramidal, indicating the presence of a lone pair of electrons on the sulphur(IV) center.

2.

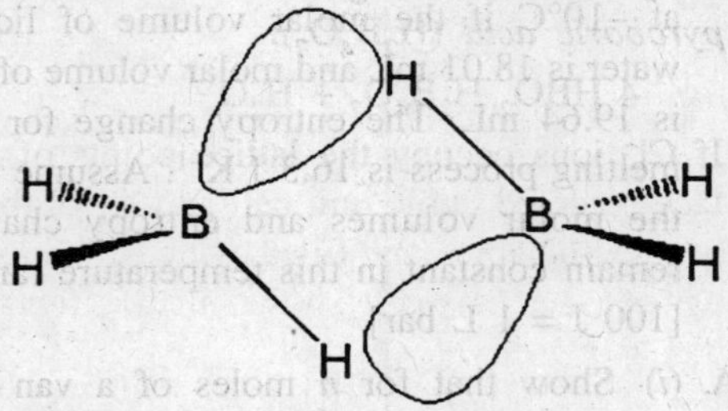

The B_2H_2 ring is held together by four electrons of 3-centre 2-electron bonding. It is sometimes called a 'banana bond'.

4. Chloroauric acid is the inorganic compound with the formula $HAuCl_4$. It is obtained by dissolving gold in aqua regia.

$Au + HNO_3 + 4\,HCl \rightarrow HAuCl_4 + NO + 2\,H_2O.$

5. Mohr's salt is a double salt, ferrous ammonium sulphate (hexahydrate), $FeSO_4.(NH_4)_2SO_4.6H_2O$, so it contains Fe^{++}, NH_4^+ and $SO_4^{=}$ ions.

6. Ni(n) is d^8 and both trigonal bipyramidal and square-based pyramidal complexes which is diamagnetic and Pd is also diamagnetic.

8. Sodium sulphide (ionic form of sulphur in the extract) reacts with sodium nitroprusside to give sodium sulphonitroprusside which is violet in colour.

$Na_2S + Na_2[Fe(CN)_5NO]$ (sodium nitroprusside) $\rightarrow Na_4[Fe(CN)_5NOS]$.

9. P and S, the cyclopropenyl cation $C_3H_3^+$ has 4_{n+2} electrons in the π electron loop, where $n = 0$ and is aromatic.

12. In an open-chain, the glucose molecule has an open and unbranched backbone of six carbon atoms, where C–1 is part of H(C = 0)–, and each of the other five carbons bears one hydroxyl group –OH. The remaining bonds of the backbone carbons are satisfied by hydrogen atoms –H.

13. The DNA sequence is double stranded, so we read the base pairs, not just the bases on one strand to determine a palindrome. Many restriction endonucleases recognize specific palindromic sequences and cut them. The restriction enzyme $E_{co}R1$ recognizes the palindromic sequence as stated.

17.

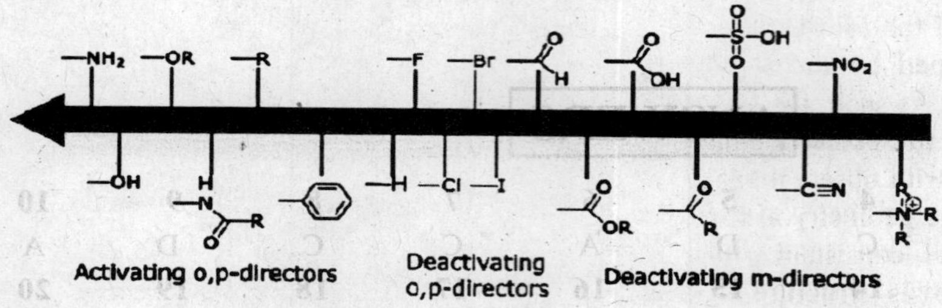

18. Since these compounds do not contain carbon.

20. Sesquiterpenes are of lower volatility than monoterpenes and can be isolated from their natural sources by extraction. Purification of these compounds involves either vacuum fractional distillation or chromatography.

23. The heat of vaporization is zero at the critical temperature because above the critical temperature the liquid and vapour phase doesn't exist.

24. In a zero-order reactions, the half-life depends on the initial concentration of reactant.

27.
$$A = 1 = \log I_0/I$$
$$I_0/I = 1$$
$$\%\ T = 10\%$$

28. $\begin{pmatrix} 0 & -1 \\ -1 & 0 \end{pmatrix} \begin{pmatrix} x \\ y \end{pmatrix}$

$$\begin{pmatrix} 0x & -1y \\ -1x & 0y \end{pmatrix}$$

$$\begin{pmatrix} -y \\ -x \end{pmatrix}$$

31. A. $HC \equiv CH > CH_2 = CH_2 > CH_3 - CH_3$

The overlap of each sp^3-hybridized orbital in figure shows that with the 1s orbital of a hydrogen atom leads to a methane molecule shown in fig.

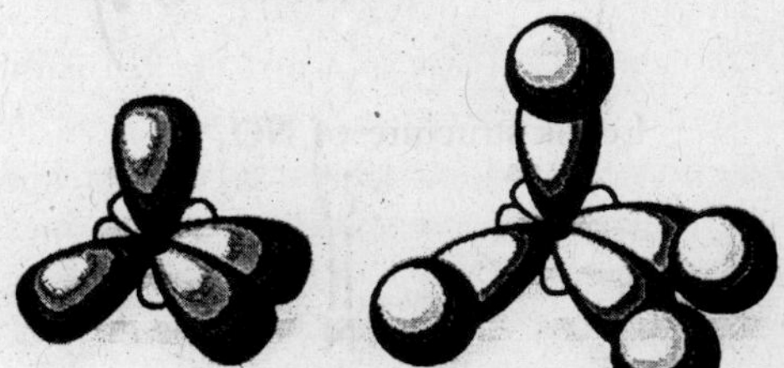

In second figure, each of the four carbon-hydrogen bonds is formed by the same overlap: sp^3 (C)–1s (H). As such, the four carbon-hydrogen bonds in second figure are identical, consistent with observations. Also in second figure, the geometry at the carbon atom is tetrahedral, consistent with VSEPR theory. The Lewis structure of acetylene as shown indicates that there are one carbon-carbon bond and two carbon-hydrogen bonds in the acetylene molecule.

$$H-C \equiv C-H$$

B. Ethylene glycol is an organic compound widely used as automotive antifreeze and a precursor to polymers. It is odourless, colourless, syrupy, sweet-tasting liquid. Orthoboric acid is derived from boric oxide in the form of white, triclinic crystals. Concentrates of borate-based treatments can be used to prevent slime, mycelium and algae growth, even in marine environments. Metaboric acid is a white, cubic crystalline solid and is only slightly soluble in water. Metaboric acid melts at about 236 C, and when heated above about 300 C further dehydrates, forming *tetraboric acid* or *pyroboric acid* ($H_2B_4O_7$):

$$4\ HBO_2\ H_2B_4O_7 + H_2O$$

32. A. If Cl^- ions occupy the lattice points of a face-centered cubic unit cell and all of the octahedral holes are filled with Na^+ ions, we get the unit cell shown in the figure below.

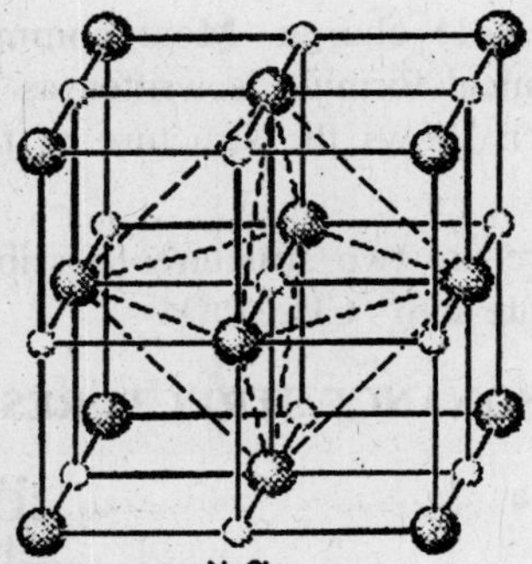

NaCl

CsCl Cesium Chloride

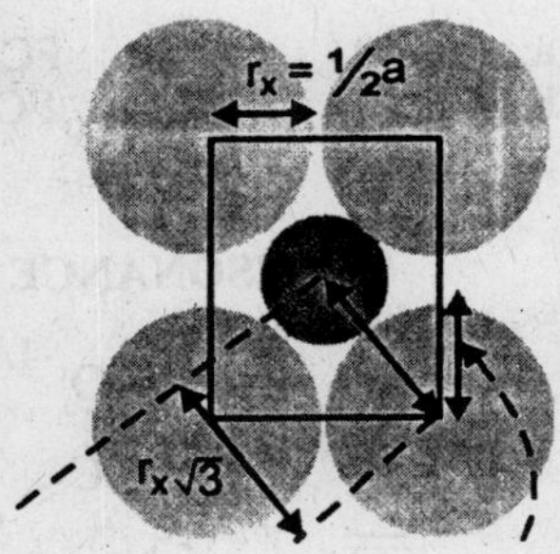

- *Motif:* Cl at (0,0,0); Cs at $\left(\frac{1}{2}, \frac{1}{2}, \frac{1}{2}\right)$
- 1CsCl in unit cell

- *Coordination:* 8:8 (cubic)
- Adoption by chlorides, bromides and iodides of larger cations,

$$\tfrac{1}{2}a\sqrt{2} = r_x\sqrt{2}$$

$$r_x + r_x = r_x\sqrt{3}$$

$$r_x/r_x = \sqrt{3}-1$$

$$1 > r_+/r_- > 0.732$$

B. $Be(OH)_{2(s)} + 2CH_3COOH_{(aq)} \rightarrow Be^{2+}_{(aq)} + 2H_2O_{(l)} + 2CH_3COO^-_{(aq)}$

Acetate (CH_3COO^-) is the conjugate base of acetic acid (CH_3COOH), the acid associated with vinegar. The acetate ion is composed of two carbon (C) atoms, three hydrogen (H) atoms, and two oxygen (O) atoms.

Acetate is a polyatomic ion with a minus one (–1) charge. Most commonly, the chemical formula is written as CH_3COO^- which shows the structure of the acetate ion.

There are two structures possible for the acetate ion: CH_3COO^-.

RESONANCE STRUCTURES

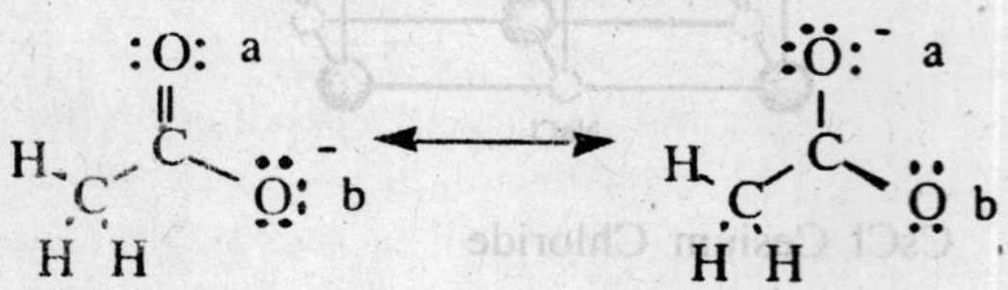

For Oxygen a: FC = 0   FC = –1
For Oxygen b: FC = –1   FC = 0

RESONANCE HYBRID

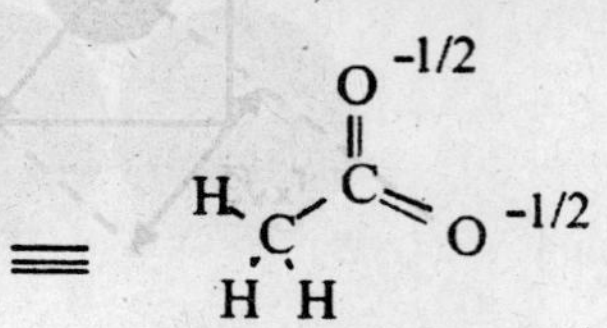

Each Oxygen has a –1/2 Formal Charge. The one double bond is shared.

33. A. Ligands are species (neutral or anionic) bonded to the metal ion. Since the oxalate ligand is fairly low in the series, a weak field ligand at this point will be considered which explains why it is a weak ligand. Since it is a weak field ligand it is likely to cause quite a small *d*(oct) splitting energy, so is likely to give rise to a high spin compound.

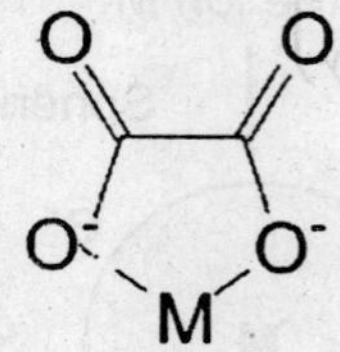

In case of $K_3[Fe(C_2O_4)_3]$, the electron configuration is by considering *d*5. Fe in the compound is Fe (III) so 23 electrons are there in *d*5.

B. Lewis structure of NO_2^+

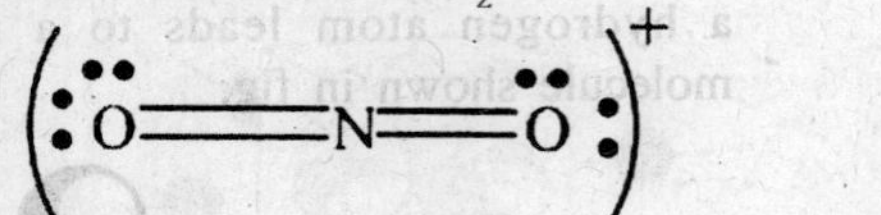

Lewis structure of NO_2^-

Lewis structure of NO_2

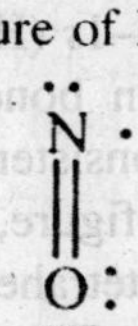

In case of NO_2, there will be 1 unpaired electron on Nitrogen, so the total valence electrons is odd = 17. The molecule is in fact bent. In this, the unpaired electron will be 1 plus 2 bonds, which will have total of 3 electrons. Therefore the hybrid for Nitrogen is sp2, and the ideal bond angle is 120.

In case of NO_2^-, the molecule is bent with the ideal of 120. In this, there will be 1 lone pair on nitrogen which takes more space than 1 unpaired electron. So that all makes the bond angle of 115.

Now for NO_2^+, the molecule is linear. The total valences are 16. In this, the ideal angle will be 180.

So NO_2^- (115) < NO_2 (120) < NO_2^+ (180)

34. A. The five d-orbitals are given the symbols dxy, dzx, dyz, $dx^2 - y^2$ and dz^2.

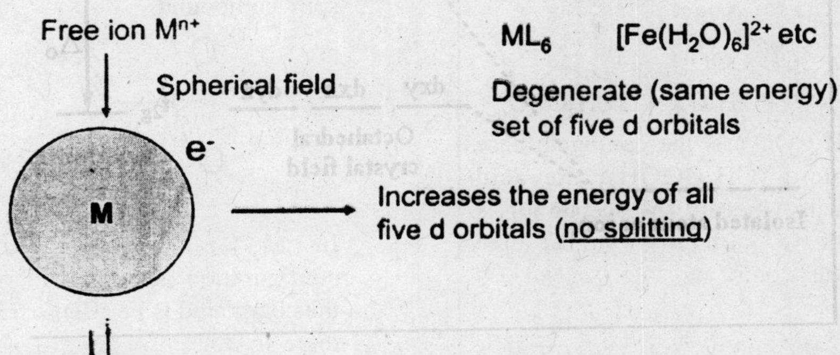

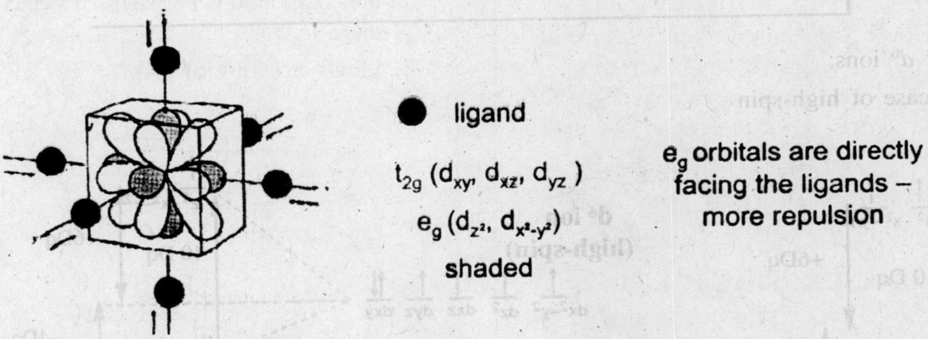

In a complex, they are all differently aligned relative to the incoming charge. Depending on the geometry of the complex, some of the *d*-orbitals will point directly towards the ligands, while some will point between them. Thus the orbitals pointing at the ligands will be less stable and higher in energy. Now all the *d*-orbitals are no longer equivalent, giving rise to the phenomenon of orbital splitting, and the difference in energy between the more and less repelled orbitals is called the crystal field splitting parameter. The electrons can go into either a high spin or low spin arrangement depending on the magnitude of the crystal field splitting energy.

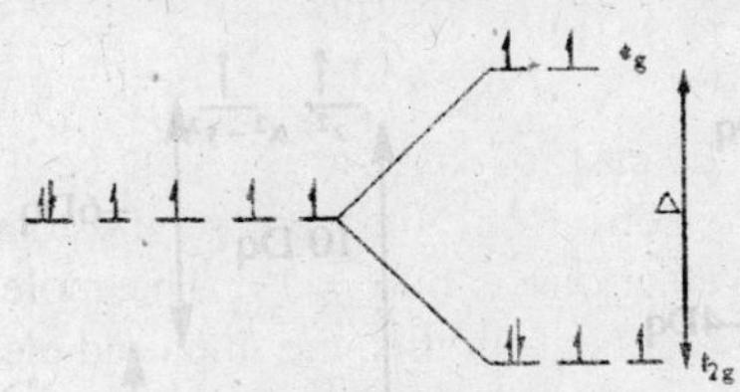

High Spin

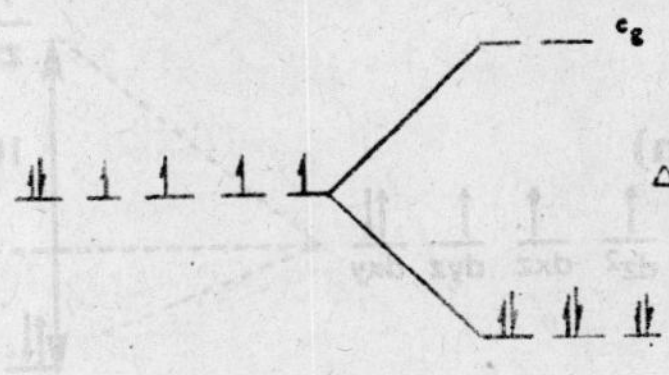

Low Spin

As a result, the approach of six ligands along the *x*, *y*, *z*, –*x*, –*y* and –*z* directions will increase the energy of $dx^2 - y^2$ and dz^2 orbitals much more than that it increases the energy of *dxy*, *dzx* and *dyz* orbitals. Thus, under the influence of an octahedral field, the *d*-orbitals split into triply degenerate orbitals with less energy and another as doubly degenerate orbitals with higher energy. The main energy level between these two sets of orbitals is taken as zero, which is called *bari centre*. The splitting between these two orbitals is called crystal field splitting. The magnitude of stabilization will be 0.4 Δ_0 and the magnitude of destabilization will be 0.6 Δ_0.

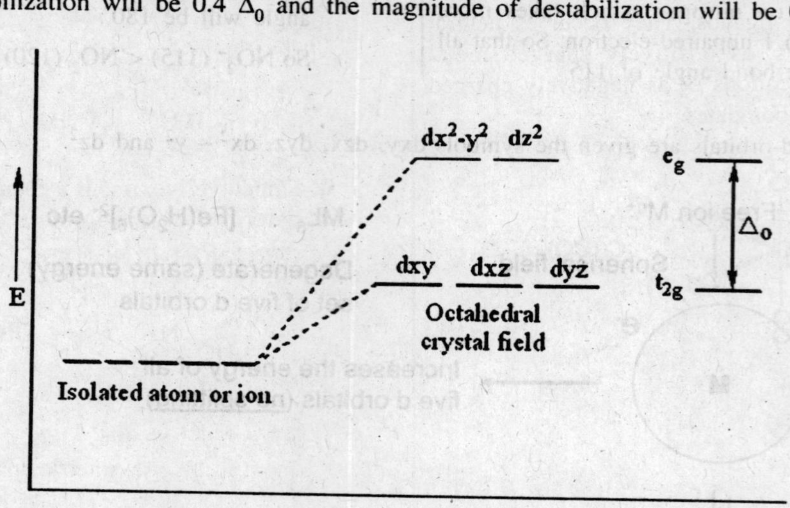

For d^6 ions:

In case of high-spin

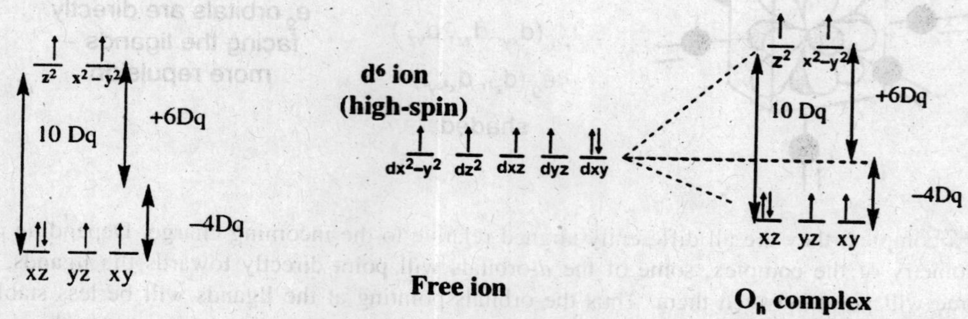

$$CFSE = 4(-4Dq) - 2(6Dq) = -4Dq$$

In case of low-spin

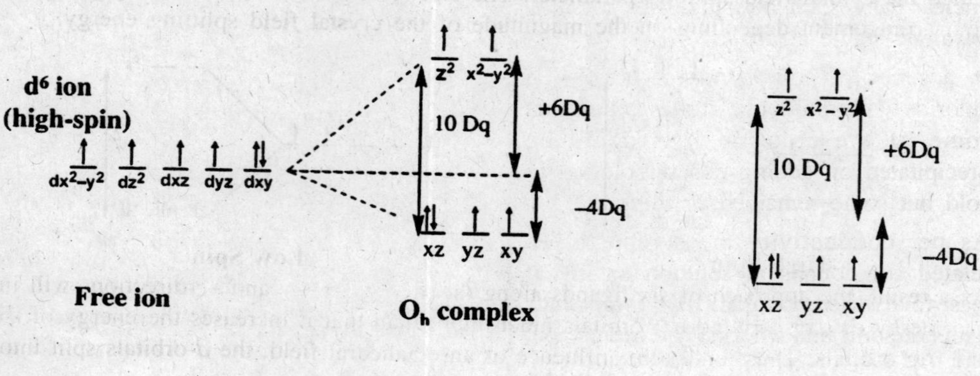

$CFSE = 6(-4Dq) + 2P = -24Dq + 2P$

B. Metal carbonyls are coordination complexes of transition metals with carbon monoxide ligands. They occur as neutral complexes, as positively charged metal carbonyl cations or as negatively charged metal carbonylates.

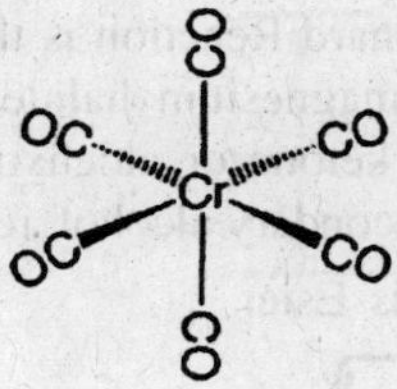

$Cr(CO)_6$ O_h

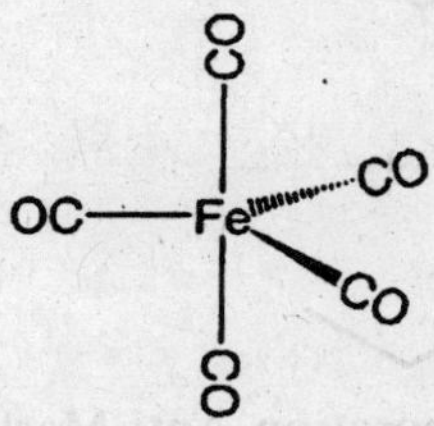

$Fe(CO)_5$ D_{3h}

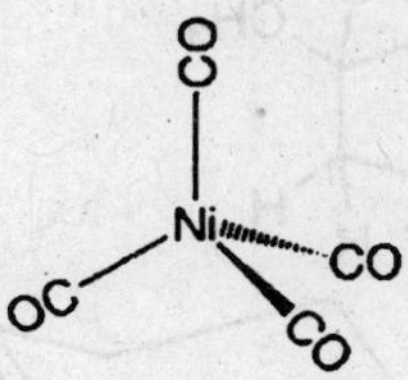

$Ni(CO)_4$ T_d

A metal carbonyl compound consists of carbon monoxide coordinated to a zero valent metal. For a long time, it had been unclear why such bonding was possible, let alone stable at all.

35. A. In a series of compounds of cobalt(III) chloride with ammonia, it was found that some of the chloride ions could be precipitated on adding excess solution in cold but some remained in solution.

As per conductivity measurements on related compounds in solution having at least four different cobalt(III) compounds with ammonia and chloride had been made, all with different colours. The total number of ions per mole of $CoCl_3 \cdot 4NH_3$ in solution was two moles.

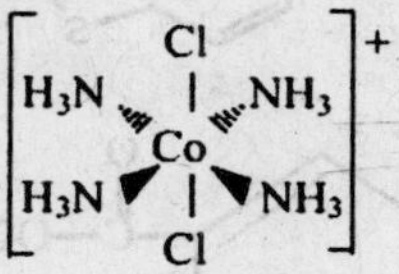

B. Dimethylglyoxime is a chemical compound described by the formula $CH_3C(NOH)C(NOH)CH_3$.

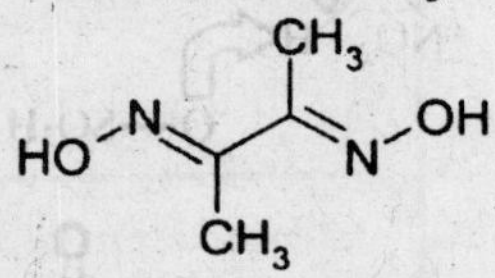

Dimethylglyoxime is used as a chelating agent in the gravimetric analysis of nickel:

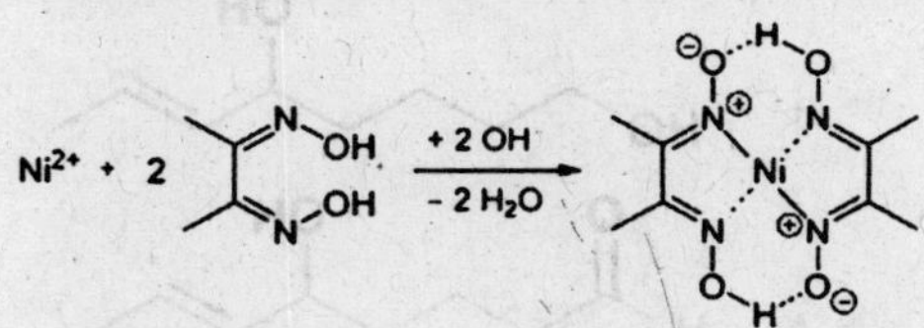

The most famous complex is the bright red $Ni(dmgH)_2$, formed by treatment of Ni(II) sources with $dmgH_2$.

36. A.

$$\begin{array}{l} CH = NOH \\ | \\ E = CHOH \\ | \\ (CHOH)_3 \\ | \\ CH_2OH \end{array}$$

$$\begin{array}{l} CN \\ | \\ F = CHO.CO.CH_3 \\ | \\ (CH.O.CO.CH_3)_3 \\ | \\ CH_2O.CO.CH_3 \end{array}$$

$$\begin{array}{l} CHO \\ | \\ G = (CHOH)_3 + AgCN \\ | \\ CH_2OH \end{array}$$

B. H = 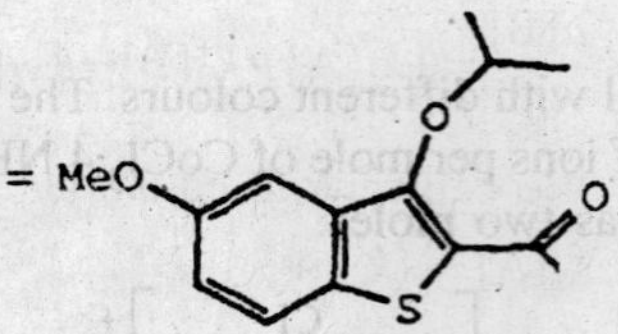

I = 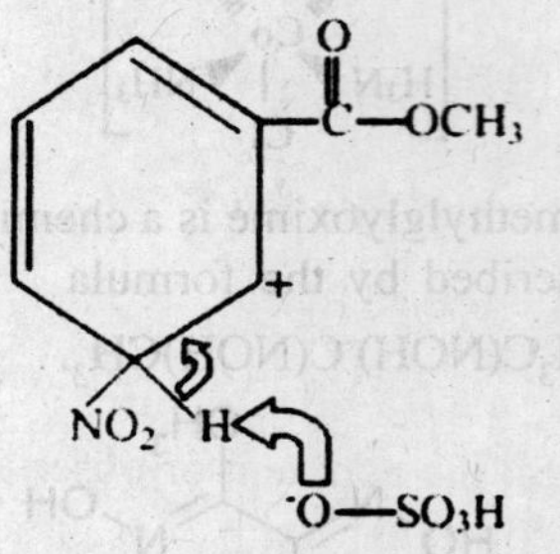

37. A. J = 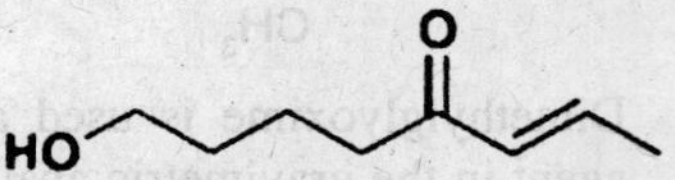

K = 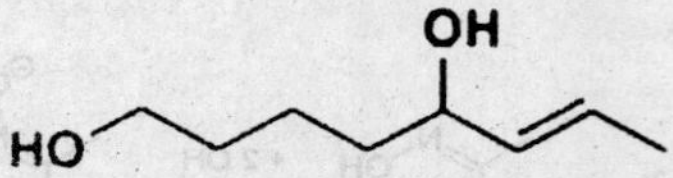

L = 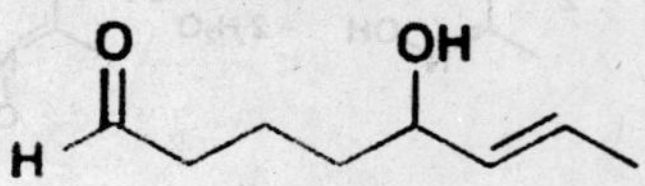

B. M = 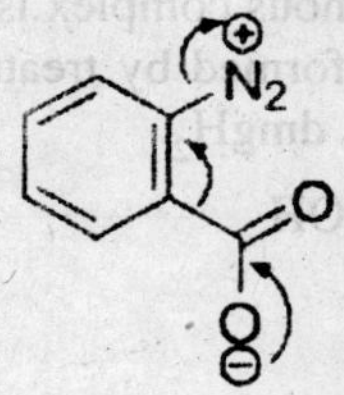

In this reaction pentyle nitrite (amyl nitrite) is used to prepare the diazonium salt N = $NaNO_3$, HCl.

38. A. O = 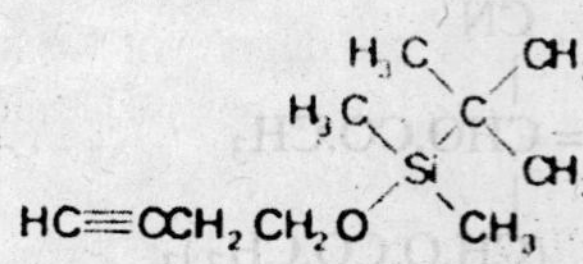

P = 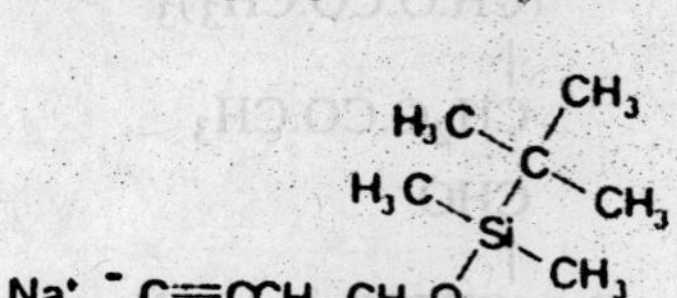

Q = 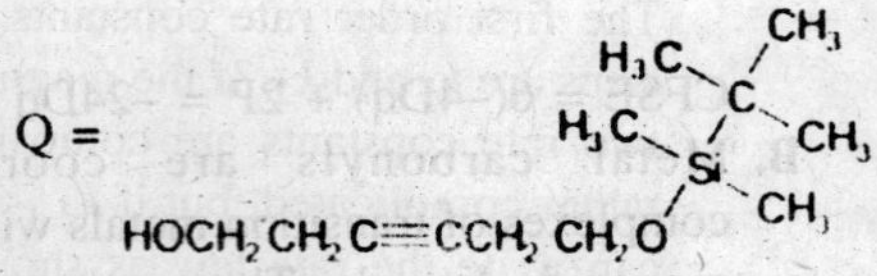

B. a. Vitamin A — *isoprenoid*
b. Vitamin C — carbohydrates
c. Vitamin D — steroids
d. Vitamin B6 — alkaloids

39. A. R = The Grignard Reaction is the addition of an organomagnesium halide (Grignard reagent) to a ketone or aldehyde, to form a tertiary or secondary alcohol, respectively. The product is Ester

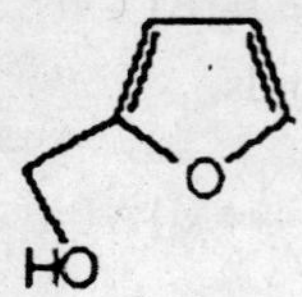

S = 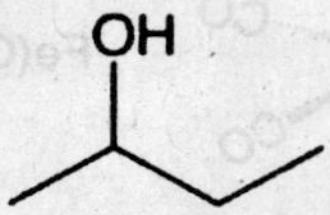

T = Hydroboration-Anti-Markovnikov addition of H-OH, Syn addition of H-OH

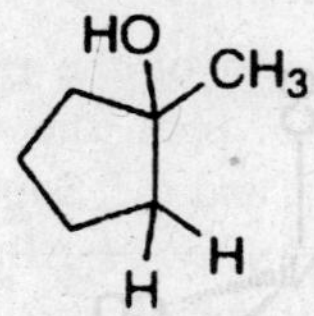

B. $SCOCH_3$

The product obtained at W is of Alkynes group

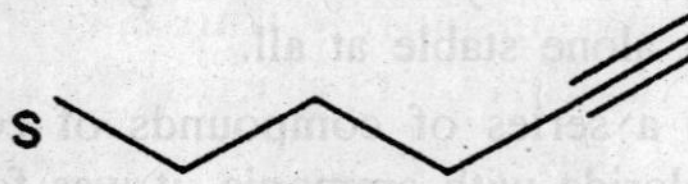

40. A. Let us suppose that in the conversion of reactant A to product C occurs through the formation of an intermediate, B

$$A \xrightarrow{k_1} B$$

$$B \xrightarrow{k_2} C$$

The first order rate constants for the two steps are k_1 and k_2. If the magnitudes of the two rate constants are comparable, this is rather complicated, but if $k_2 >> k_1$, then we can write the rate law as shown below in equation.

$$v = -\frac{d[A]}{dt} = +\frac{d[C]}{dt} = k_1[A]$$

Since $k_2 >> k_1$, $d[B]/dt = 0$. This is the steady state approximation, equation

$$\frac{d[B]}{dt} = k_1[A] - k_2[B] = 0$$

So, $k_1[A] = k_2[B]$

In other words,

$$v = \frac{d[C]}{dt} = k_1[A] = k_2[B]$$

Now let's make the situation more complex, and more realistic too, by making the first step reversible

$$A \underset{k_{-1}}{\overset{k_1}{\rightleftharpoons}} B$$

$$B \xrightarrow{k_2} C$$

The form of the rate law for Scheme II depends upon the relative magnitudes of k_1, k_{-1}, and k_2. Suppose that $k_1 >> k_2$ and that $k_{-1}, >> k_2$. In this case, the second step, in which B is converted to C is rate-determining.

$$v = k_2[B]$$

However, since $k_1 >> k_2$ and that $k_{-1} >> k_2$, B is a transient intermediate (think of the carbocation in the reaction shown above, for instance), whose concentration is constant, *i.e.* it exists in a steady state. That is,

$$\frac{d[B]}{dt} = 0$$

The intermediate can form by one pathway, but it can disappear by two pathways. The rate law for the formation and disappearance of B is given by equation

$$\frac{d[B]}{dt} = +k_1[A] - k_2[B] - k_{-1}[B] = 0$$

We can rewrite equation

$k_1[A] = (k_{-1} + k_2)[B]$

Solving for B gives

$$[B] = \frac{k_1[A]}{(k_{-1} + k_2)}$$

So the rate law

$$= \frac{k_1 k_2 [CB]}{(k_{-1} + k_2)}$$

So the apparent or observed first order rate constant

$$k_{observed} = \frac{k_1 k_2}{(k_{-1} + k_2)}$$

B. If we pick two reactants say A and B, and make the initial concentration greater than the concentration of B, then, the reaction experimentally works with above 1% of B. At this time the concentration of A will scarcely have changed at all. So the rate law reduces to

$v = k_2[Ao]([B] - x)$

also

$k_{app} = k_2[Ao]$

$k_{app} / [Ao] = k_2$

$0.5 / 1 \times 10^{-5} = k_2$

41. A. The classical method for determining the dissociation constant of an acid or a base is to measure the electrical conductivity of solutions of varying concentrations. From these the degree of dissociation α can be determined and K_a calculated from the equation

$$K_a = \frac{a^2 c}{1 - a}$$

$$\alpha_1 = \frac{[A^-]}{[HA] + [A^-]} = \frac{[A^-]}{c_{HA}}$$

where c_{HA} = [HA] + [A⁻] is the total, analytical concentration of the weak acid and [HA] and [A⁻] are the equilibrium concentrations of the acid and its conjugate base respectively. Obviously one can also define a_0, the fraction of the weak acid that is not dissociated

$$\alpha_0 = \frac{[HA]}{[HA]+[A^-]} = \frac{[HA]}{c_{HA}}$$

from which it is clear that since the acid must be present either in the acid or base form :

$\alpha_0 + \alpha_1 = 1$

This leads to the following simplifications :

$$K_a = [H^+]\frac{\alpha_1}{\alpha_2}$$

$$\alpha_0 = \frac{[H^+]}{[H^+]+K_a}$$

$$\alpha_1 = \frac{K_a}{[H^+]+K_a}$$

In *'p'* notation, becomes

$$\log\frac{\alpha_1}{\alpha_0} = pH - pK_a$$

B. (*i*) The neutralization reaction of acetic acid (CH_3COOH) and sodium hydroxide solution occurs as

$CH_3COOH(aq) + NaOH(aq) \;\_\_\_\_\_\; CH_3COONa(aq) + H_2O(l)$ ...(1)

$CH_3COOH(aq) + Na^+(aq) + OH^-(aq) \;\_\_\_\_\_\; Na+(aq) + CH_3COO^-(aq) + H^2O$ ...(2)

$CH_3COOH(aq) + OH^-(aq) \;\_\_\_\_\_\; CH_3COO^-(aq) + H_2O$ ...(3)

A typical curve for the titration of acetic acid with sodium hydroxide solution is given. The equivalence point is found by determining the steepest portion of the curve, but as seen from Figure, the equivalence point does not occur at pH 7, as it would for a strong acid strong base titration.

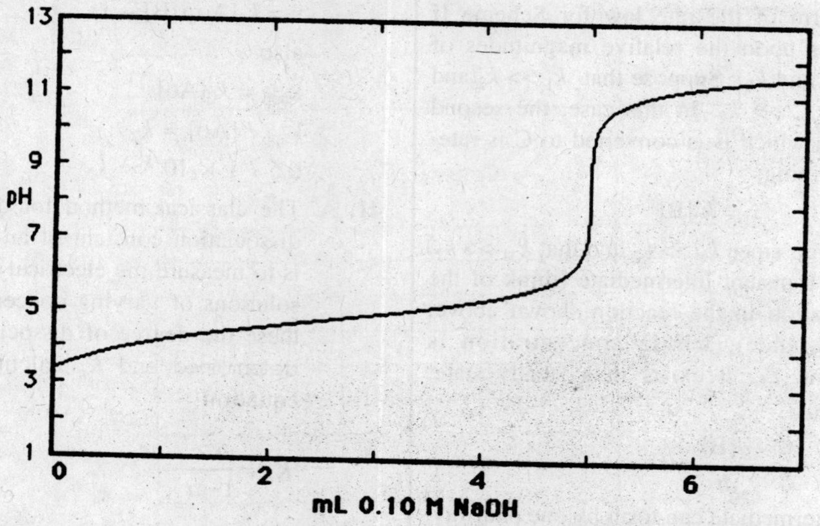

At the equivalence point in the titration, equimolar quantities of acetic acid and hydroxide ions have reacted, so that all of the H⁺ ions available from the acetic acid have combined with all of the OH ions available from the sodium hydroxide solution.

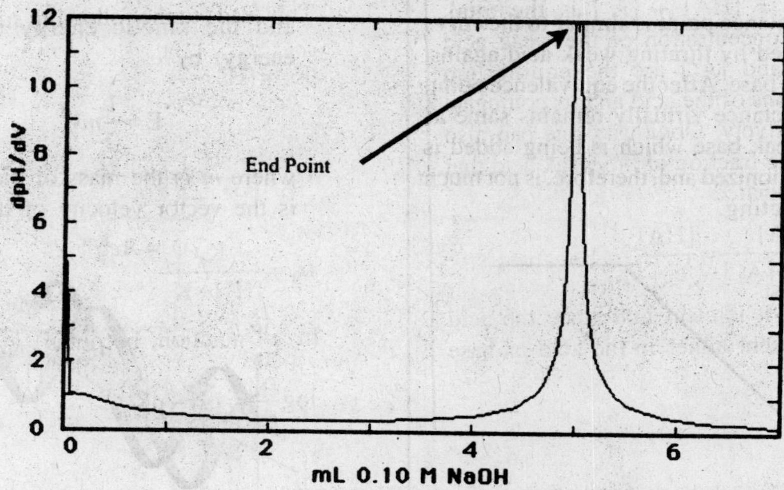
dpH/dV
End Point
mL 0.10 M NaOH
0
2
4
6
8
10
12

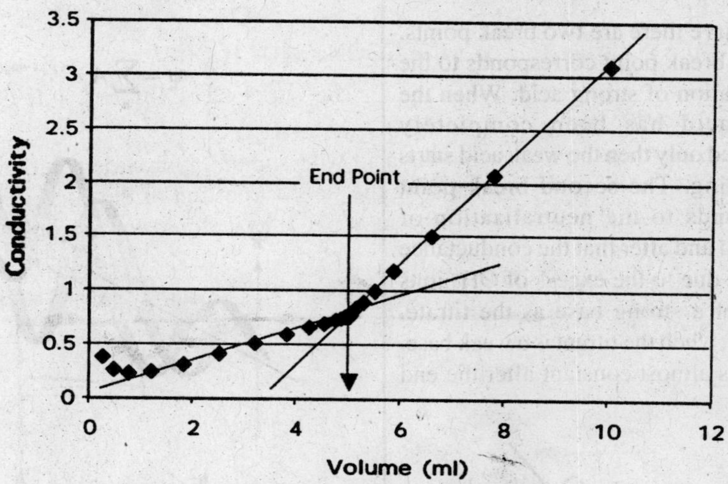
Conductivity
End Point
Volume (ml)
0
0.5
1
1.5
2
2.5
3
3.5
2
4
6
8
10
12

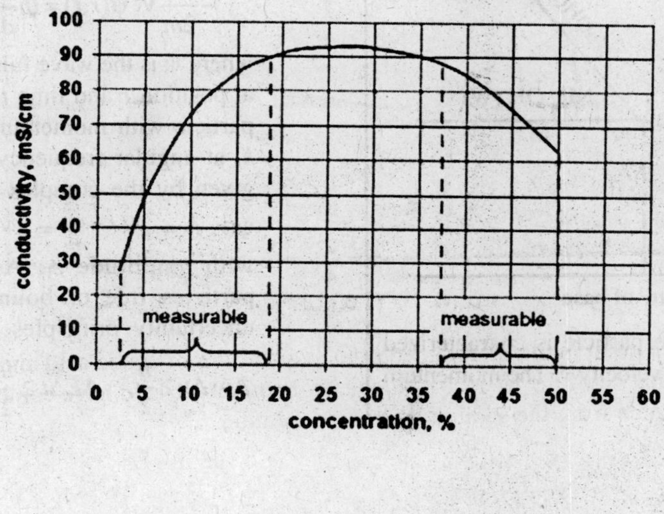
conductivity, mS/cm
measurable
measurable
concentration, %
0
10
20
30
40
50
60
70
80
90
100
5
15
25
35
45
55

(*ii*) The nature of curve before the equivalence point is similar to the curve obtained by titrating weak acid against strong base. After the equivalence point, conductance virtually remains same as the weak base which is being added is feebly ionized and, therefore, is not much conducting.

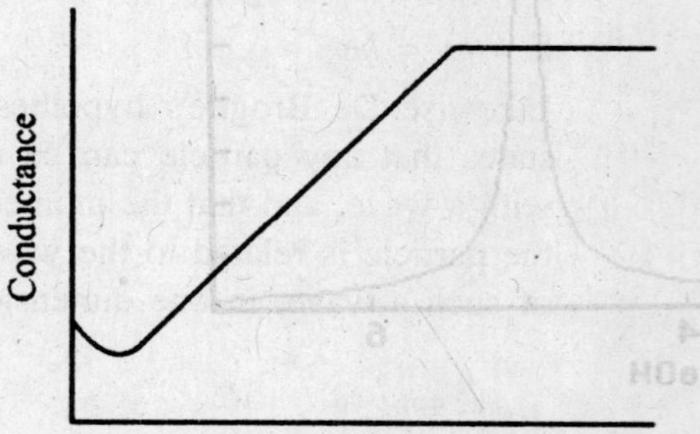

In this curve there are two break points. The first break point corresponds to the neutralization of strong acid. When the strong acid has been completely neutralized only then the weak acid starts neutralizing. The second break point corresponds to the neutralization of weak acid and after that the conductance increases due to the excess of OH^- ions in case of a strong base as the titrate. However, when the titrant is a weak base, it remains almost constant after the end point.

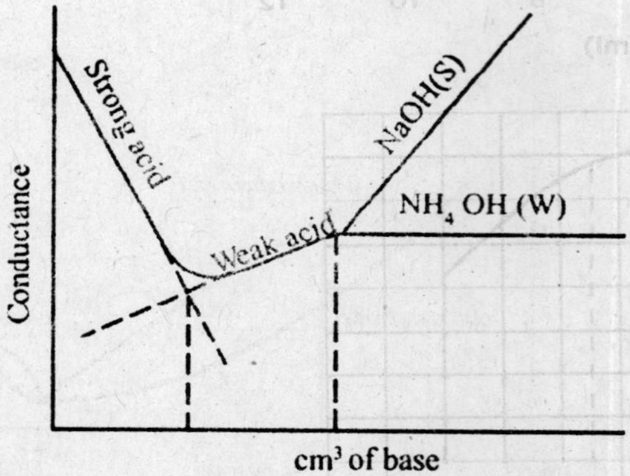

42. A. The classical free particle is characterized simply by a fixed velocity *v*. The momentum is given by

$$P = mv$$

and the kinetic energy (equal to total energy) by

$$E = \frac{1}{2}mv^2$$

where *m* is the mass of the particle and *v* is the vector velocity of the particle.

$$\psi = Ae^{i(px - \omega t)}$$

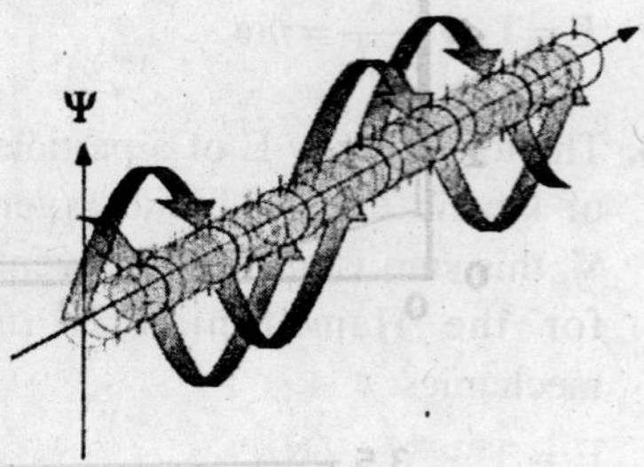

$$\psi = \sum_n A_n e^{i(p_n x - \omega_n t)}$$

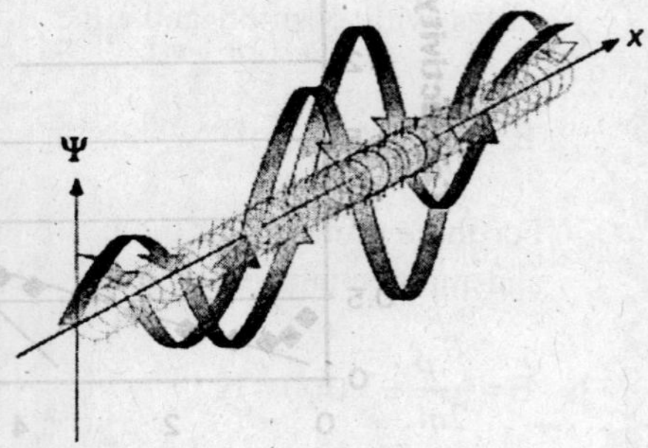

$$-\frac{\hbar^2}{2m}\nabla^2\psi(r,t) = i\hbar\frac{\partial}{\partial t}\psi(r,t)$$

where ψ is the wave function of the particle at position *r* and time *t*. The solution for a particle with momentum *p* or wave vector *k*, at angular frequency ω or energy E, is given by the complex plane wave:

$\psi(r, t) = e^{i(k.r - \omega t)} = e^{i(p.r - Et)/\hbar}$

with amplitude *A*. As for all quantum particles free or bound, the Heisenberg uncertainty principles

$$\Delta px \Delta x \geq \frac{\hbar}{2}, \quad \Delta E \Delta t \geq \frac{\hbar}{2}$$

(similarly for the y and z directions), and the De Broglie relations:

$p = \hbar k$, $E = \hbar\omega$

apply. Since the potential energy is (set to) zero, the total energy E is equal to the kinetic energy, which has the same form as in classical physics

$$E = T \rightarrow \frac{\hbar^2 k^2}{2m} = \hbar\omega$$

B. The total energy E of a particle is the sum of kinetic energy T and potential energy V, this sum is also the frequent expression for the Hamiltonian H in classical mechanics:

$E = T + V = H$

Explicitly, for a particle in one dimension with position x, mass m and momentum p, and potential energy V which generally varies with position and time t:

$$E = \frac{p^2}{2m} + V(x,t) = H$$

For three dimensions, the position vector r and momentum vector p must be used:

$$E = \frac{p.p}{2m} + V(r,t) = H$$

This formalism can be extended to any fixed number of particles: the total energy of the system is then the total kinetic energies of the particles, plus the total potential energy, again the Hamiltonian. However, there can be interactions between the particles, so the potential energy V can change as the spatial configuration of particles changes, and possibly with time. The potential energy, in general, is not the sum of the separate potential energies for each particle, it is a function of all the spatial positions of the particles. Explicitly:

$$E = \sum_{n=1}^{N} \frac{p_n \cdot p_n}{2m_n} + V(r_1, r_2 ... r_N, t) = H$$

Einstein's light quanta hypothesis states that the energy E of a photon is proportional to the frequency v (or angular frequency, $\omega = 2\pi v$) of the corresponding quantum wavepacket of light:

$E = hv = \hbar\omega$

Likewise De Broglie's hypothesis (1924) states that any particle can be associated with a wave, and that the momentum p of the particle is related to the wavelength λ of such a wave, in one dimension, by:

$$p = \frac{h}{\lambda} = \hbar k,$$

in three dimensions:

$$p = \frac{h}{\lambda} = \hbar k.$$

where k is the wave vector (wavelength is related to the magnitude of k)

43. A. (i) Suppose you are going to distil a mixture of ethanol and water with composition C_1 as shown on the next diagram. It will boil at a temperature given by the liquid curve and produce a vapour with composition C_2.

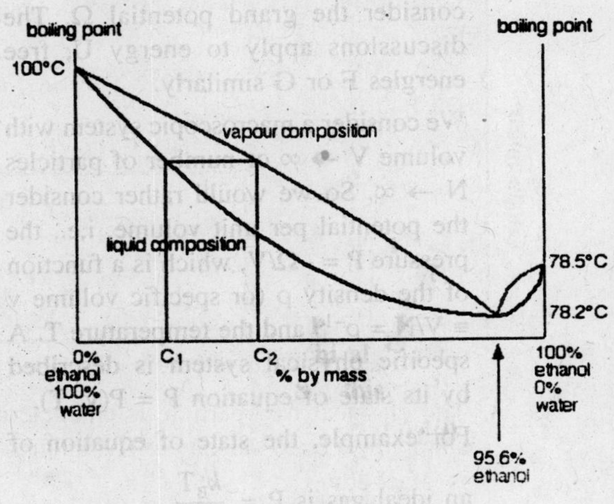

(*ii*)

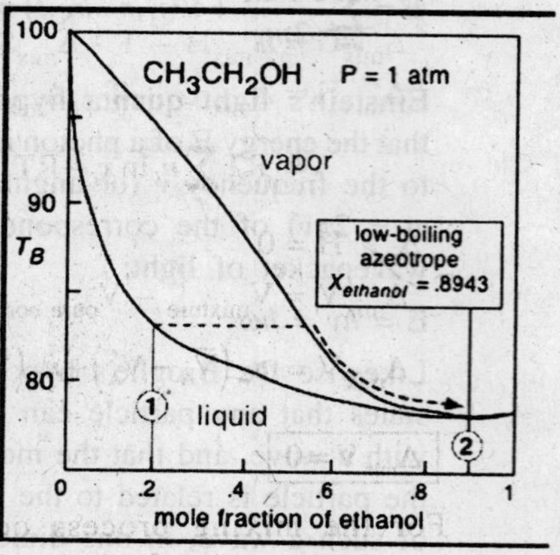

At 78.3°C. The mixture is known as azeotrope.

(*iii*) The degree of freedom of a system is defined as the number of independent parameters of state such as temperature, pressure and concentration, which must be specified in order to define the system completely.

44. A. (*i*) The energy, free energy, and grand potential of a system are always continuous with varying the temperature, volume, magnetic field, etc. But their differentials may not. Phase transitions can be classified according to which order of the diggerentials is discontinuous. Now consider the grand potential Ω. The discussions apply to energy U, free energies F or G similarly.

We consider a macroscopic system with volume $V \to \infty$ or number of particles $N \to \infty$. So we would rather consider the potential per unit volume, i,e., the pressure $P = -\Omega/V$, which is a function of the density ρ (or specific volume v $\equiv V/N = \rho^{-1}$) and the temperature T. A specific physical system is described by its state of equation P = P(v, T).

For example, the state of equation of an ideal gas is $P = \dfrac{k_B T}{v}$.

For an ideal gas, P is analytical for temperature and volume as real numbers, so there is no phase transition. When the nth order differential of P regarding T or V is discontinuous and all the lower order differentials are continuous, the phase transition is called an nth order one.

For example, the nth order differential of the isothermal curve $\left[\dfrac{\partial^n P(v,T)}{\partial v^n}\right]$ is discontinuous for the nth order phase transition. Examples of first-order phase transitions are melting of ice and condensation of vapour.

We know that

$$P_{ideal} = P_{real} + p = \left(P + \alpha\frac{n^2}{V^2}\right)$$

$$\left[\frac{\partial^n P(v,T)}{\partial v^n}\right] = \left(P + \alpha\frac{n^2}{V^2}\right)$$

(*ii*) Real gases do not obey ideal gas equation under all conditions. They nearly obey ideal gas equation at higher temperatures and very low pressures. However they show deviations from ideality at low temperatures and high pressures. The isotherms obtained by plotting pressure, P against volume, V for real gases do not coincide with that of ideal gas, as shown below.

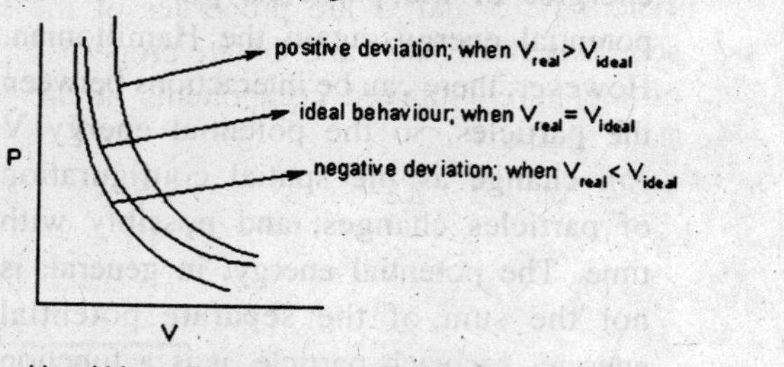

V_{real} = Volume of the real gas at given pressure.
V_{ideal} = Volume of the gas calculated by ideal gas equation at given pressure.

It is clear from above graphs that the volume of real gas is more than or less than expected in certain cases. The deviation from ideal gas behaviour can also be expressed by compressibility factor, Z.

The ratio of volume of real gas, V_{real} to the ideal volume of that gas, $V_{perfect}$ calculated by ideal gas equation is known as compressibility factor.

$$Z = \frac{PV_{real}}{nRT}$$

But from ideal gas equation:

$$PV_{perfect} = nRT \text{ or } V_{perfect} = \frac{nRT}{P}$$

So, $$\boxed{Z = \frac{PV_{real}}{nRT} = \frac{V_{real}}{V_{perfect}}}$$

* For ideal or perfect gases, the compressibility factor, Z = 1.
* But for real gases, $Z \neq 1$.

If Z < 1

* $V_{real} < V_{ideal}$
* The attractive forces are more significant than the repulsive forces.
* The gas can be liquefied easily.
* Z < 1 for gases such as NH_3, CO_2, SO_2.

B. $\Delta_{mix}H \equiv H - H^*$

$\Delta_{mix}S \equiv S - S^* = -R\ n\ \ln x$

$\Delta_{mix}G \equiv G - G^* = n\ RT\ \ln x$

Where H, S and G are properties of the solutions and H*, S* and G* are properties of the pure unmixed components at the same T and P

$\Delta G = \Delta H - T \cdot \Delta S$

We have that

$$\Delta_{mix}G = \Delta_{mix}H - T \cdot \Delta_{mix}S$$

$$\Delta_{mix}H = \Delta_{mix}G + T \cdot \Delta_{mix}S$$

$$= RT\sum_i n_i \ln x_i - RT\sum_i n_i \ln x_i$$

$$\Delta_{mix}H = 0$$

$$\Delta_{mix}V = V_{mixture} - V_{pure\ components}$$

$$\Delta_{mix}V = n_A\left(\bar{V}_A - V_A^*\right) + n_B\left(\bar{V}_B - V_B^*\right) + \ldots$$

$$\boxed{\Delta_{mix}V = 0}$$

For the mixing process occurring at constant pressure, from the definition of enthalpy

$$\Delta_{mix}H = \Delta_{mix}U + \Delta_{mix}(pV)$$

$$\Delta_{mix}H = \Delta_{mix}U + p\,(\Delta_{mix}V)$$

$$\Delta_{mix}U = \Delta_{mix}H - p\,(\Delta_{mix}V)$$

$$= 0 - p(0)$$

$$\boxed{\Delta_{mix}U = 0}$$

We know that:

$$\Delta_{mix}S = -R\sum_i n_i \ln x_i$$

$$\Delta_{mix}G = \sum_i n_i RT \ln x_i$$

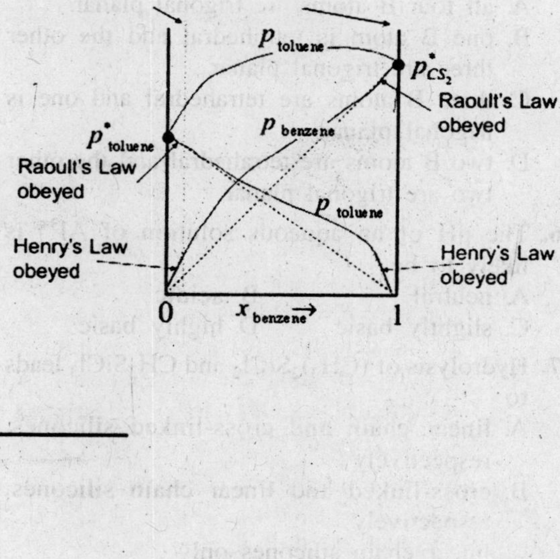

Previous Paper (Solved)

IIT—JAM

JOINT ADMISSION TEST FOR M.SC. (CHEMISTRY)-2011

Directions (Qs. 1-30): *(Objective questions) carry three marks each and questions* **(Qs. 31-44)** *(Subjective questions) carry fifteen marks each.*

1. The pair of semimetals in the following is

A. Al, Si B. Ge, As
C. Sb, Te D. Ca, B

2. The most probable oxidation states for both Cr and Mo are

A. +2, +3, +4 B. +2, +3, +5
C. +2, +3, +6 D. +3, +4, +5

3. The correct order of acidic character is

A. $Al_2O_3 > MgO > SiO_2 > P_4O_{10}$
B. $P_4O_{10} > Al_2O_3 > MgO > SiO_2$
C. $P_4O_{10} > SiO_2 > Al_2O_3 > MgO$
D. $SiO_2 > P_4O_{10} > Al_2O_3 > MgO$

4. The pair of amphoteric oxides is

A. VO, Cr_2O_3 B. V_2O_3, Cr_2O_3
C. VO_2, Cr_2O_3 D. V_2O_5, CrO_3

5. In the structure of $B_4O_5(OH)_4^{2-}$

A. all four B atoms are trigonal planar
B. one B atom is tetrahedral and the other three are trigonal planar
C. three B atoms are tetrahedral and one is trigonal planar
D. two B atoms are tetrahedral and the other two are trigonal planar

6. The pH of an aqueous solution of Al^{3+} is likely to be

A. neutral B. acidic
C. slightly basic D. highly basic

7. Hydrolysis of $(CH_3)_2SiCl_2$ and CH_3SiCl_3 leads to

A. linear chain and cross-linked silicones, respectively
B. cross-linked and linear chain silicones, respectively
C. linear chain silicones only
D. cross-linked silicones only

8. The oxide that has the inverse spinel structure is

A. $FeCr_2O_4$ B. $MnCr_2O_4$
C. $CoAl_2O_4$ D. Fe_2CoO_4

9. The transition metal monoxide that shows metallic conductivity is

A. NiO B. MnO
C. TiO D. CoO

10. The metal that is extracted by the reduction method is

A. Al B. Au
C. Hg D. Mg

11. The most viscous liquid is

A. water B. methanol
C. ethylene glycol D. glycerol

12. In ammonical buffer, oxine (8-hydroxy-quinoline) forms yellow precipitate with

A. Mg(II) B. Ca(II)
C. Ba(II) D. Sr(II)

13. Addition of an aqueous solution of Fe(II) to potassium hexacyanochromate(III) produces a brick-red coloured complex, which turns dark green at 100°C. The dark green complex is

A. $Fe_4[Cr(CN)_6]_3$ B. $KFe[Cr(CN)_6]$
C. $KCr[Fe(CN)_6]$ D. $Fe[Cr(CN)_6]$

14. In the following equation X is

$$^{241}_{95}Am + \alpha \rightarrow {}^{243}_{97}Bk + X$$

A. $2\,^{1}_{0}n$ B. $^{1}_{0}n$
C. $2\,^{1}_{1}H$ D. $^{4}_{2}He$

15. Based on the principle of equipartition of energy, the molar heat capacity of CO_2 at constant volume $C_{v,m}$ is

A. 3.5R B. 6R
C. 6.5R D. 9R

16. One mole of a van der Waals gas undergoes reversible isothermal transformation from an initial volume V_1 to a final volume V_2. The expression for the work done is

A. $RT \ln \frac{V_2}{V_1} + a(V_2 - V_1)$

B. $-RT \ln \frac{V_2 - b}{V_1 - b} + a\left(\frac{1}{V_1} - \frac{1}{V_2}\right)$

C. $RT \ln \frac{P_2}{P_1}$

D. $RT \ln \frac{V_2 - b}{V_1 - b} - a\left(\frac{1}{V_1} - \frac{1}{V_2}\right)$

17. The scalar product of two vectors u and v, where $u = 2i + 3j - 5k$ and $v = i + j + 3k$, is

A. −10 B. $2i + 3j - 15k$
C. $3i + 4j - 2k$ D. 10

18. The minimum concentration of silver ions that is required to start the precipitation of Ag_2S ($K_{sp} = 1 \times 10^{-51}$) in a 0.1 M solution of S^{2-} is

A. 1×10^{-49} M B. 1×10^{-50} M
C. 1×10^{-26} M D. 1×10^{-25} M

19. Identify the correct statement regarding Einstein's photoelectric effect

A. The number of electrons ejected depends on the wavelength of incident radiation.
B. Electron ejection can occur at any wavelength of incident radiation.
C. The number of electrons ejected at a given incident wavelength depends on the intensity of the radiation.
D. The kinetic energy of the ejected electrons is independent of the wavelength of incident radiation.

20. The hydrolysis constant (K_h) of NH_4Cl is 5.6×10^{-10}. The concentration of H_3O^+ in a 0.1 M solution of NH_4Cl at equilibrium is

A. $\sqrt{5.6 \times 10^{-11}}$ B. $\sqrt{5.6 \times 10^{-10}}$
C. 5.6×10^{-10} D. 2.8×10^{-5}

21. The acid dissociation constant (K_a) for HCOOH, CH_3COOH, $CH_2ClCOOH$ and HCN at 25°C are 1.8×10^{-4}, 1.8×10^{-5}, 1.4×10^{-3} and 4.8×10^{-10}, respectively. The acid that gives highest pH at the equivalence point when 0.2 M solution of each acid is titrated with a 0.2 M solution of sodium hydroxide is

A. HCOOH B. CH_3COOH
C. $CH_2ClCOOH$ D. HCN

22. For an ideal gas undergoing reversible Carnot Cycle, the plot of enthalpy (H) versus entropy (S) is

A.
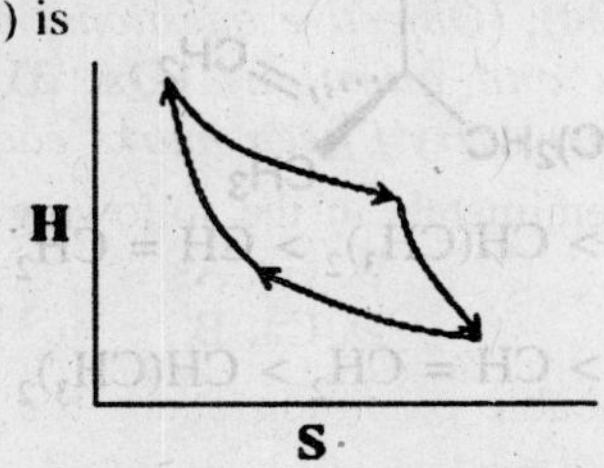

B.
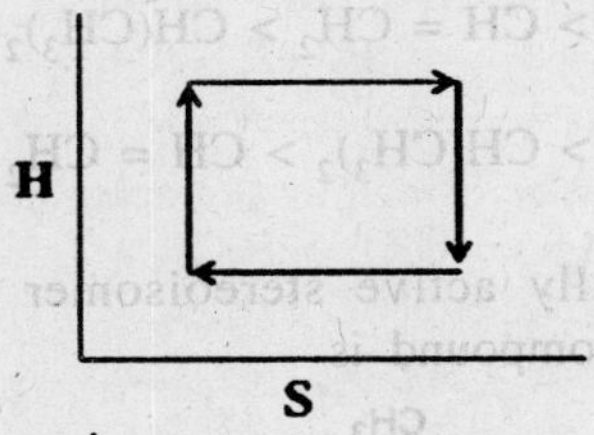

C.
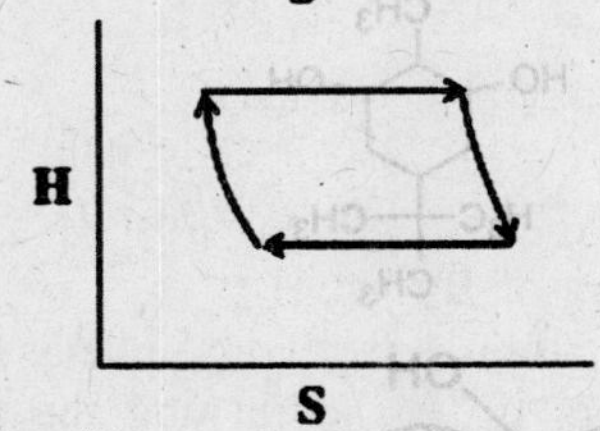

D.
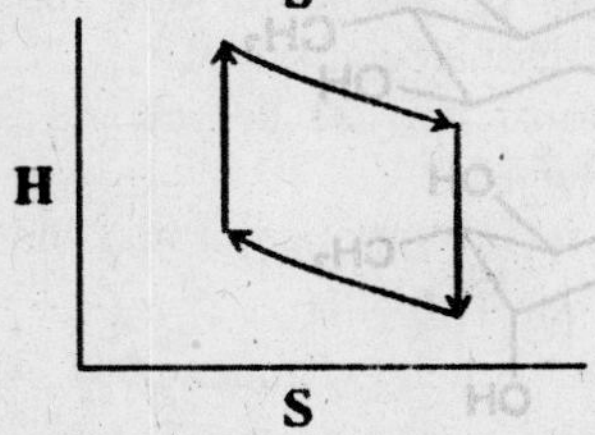

23. Hybridization of the atoms indicated with the asterisk (*) in the following compounds sequentially are

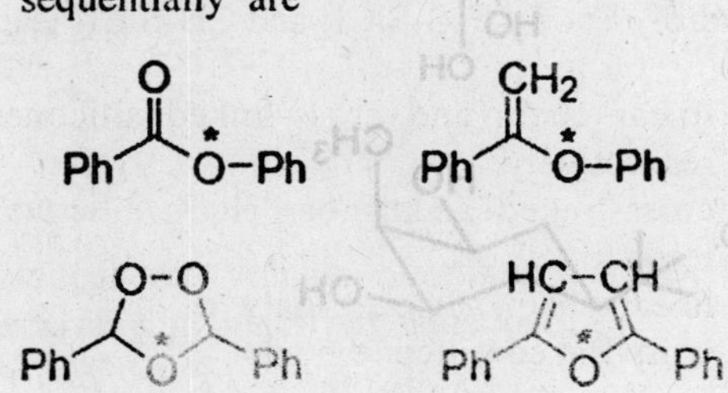

A. sp^2, sp^2, sp^3, sp^2
B. sp^2, sp^3, sp^3, sp^2
C. sp^3, sp^3, sp^3, sp^2
D. sp^2, sp^2, sp^3, sp^3

24. The Cahn-Ingold-Prelog (CIP) priorities of the groups and the absolute configuration (R/S) of the following compound are

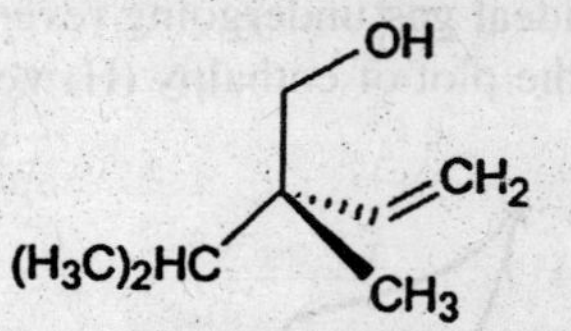

A. $CH_2OH > CH(CH_3)_2 > CH = CH_2 > CH_3$ and S
B. $CH_2OH > CH = CH_2 > CH(CH_3)_2 > CH_3$ and S
C. $CH_2OH > CH = CH_2 > CH(CH_3)_2 > CH_3$ and R
D. $CH_2OH > CH(CH_3)_2 > CH = CH_2 > CH_3$ and R

25. The optically active stereoisomer of the following compound is

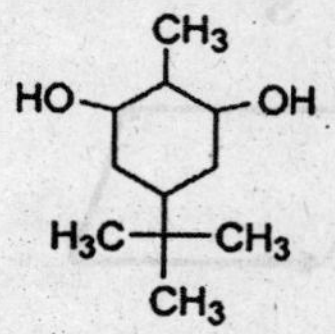

A. 

B. 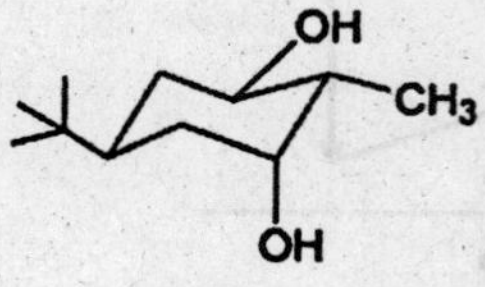

C. 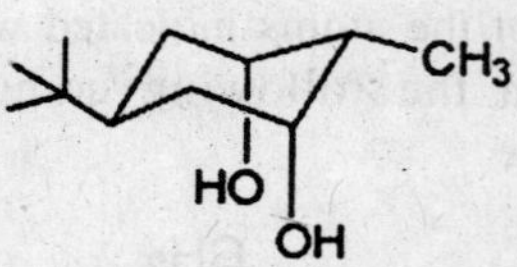

D. 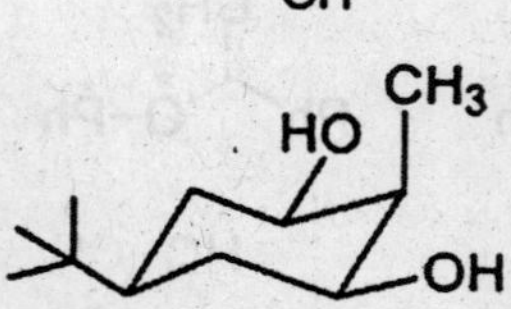

26. The correct relationship within each pair of the natural products is
A. camphor–terpene; insulin–protein; nicotine –alkaloid; streptomycin–carbohydrate
B. camphor–terpene; insulin–carbohydrate; nicotine–alkaloid; streptomycin–lipid
C. camphor–alkaloid; insulin–protein; nicotine –terpene; streptomycin–carbohydrate;
D. camphor–carbohydrate; insulin–protein; nicotine–alkaloid; streptomycin–terpene

27. The correct sequence of relationships between the compounds of the following pairs *i-iv* is

(*i*) 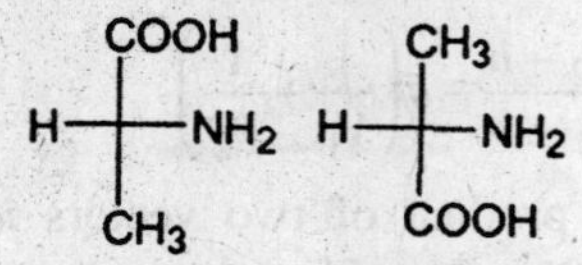

(*ii*) 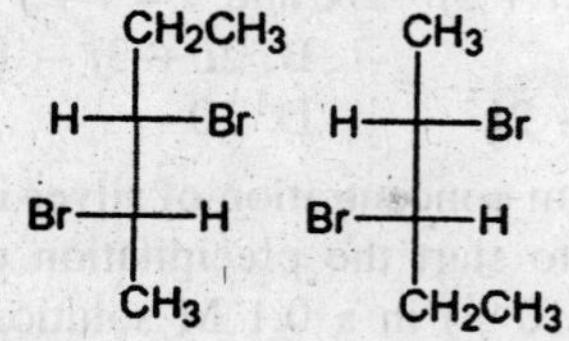

(*iii*) 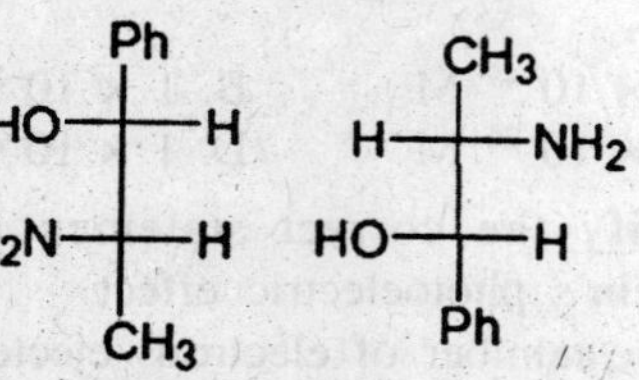

(*iv*) 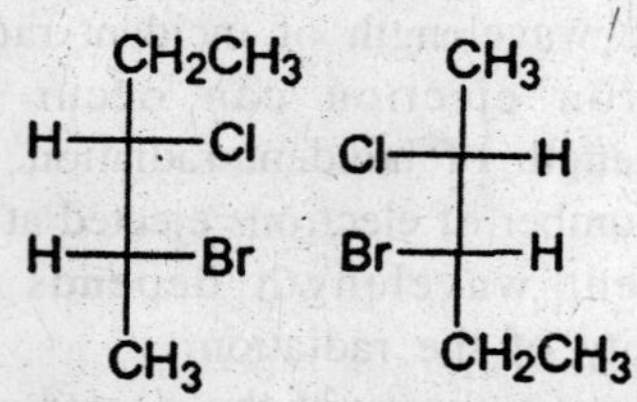

A. identical, enantiomers, diastereomers and structural isomers
B. enantiomers, identical, structural isomers and diastereomers
C. enantiomers, identical, diastereomers and structural isomers
D. identical, identical, diastereomers and structural isomers

28. The INCORRECT statement in the following is
A. the nucleobase pairs are aligned perpendicular to the helical axis in DNA

B. RNA contains uracil and thymine, but DNA contains only thymine

C. all naturally occurring amino acids with the exception of glycine are chiral

D. all enzymes are proteins, but all proteins are not necessarily enzymes

29. The products P and Q in the following reactions, respectively, are

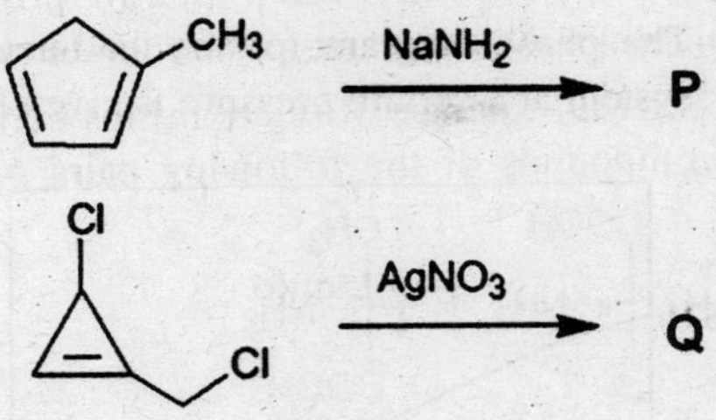

A. 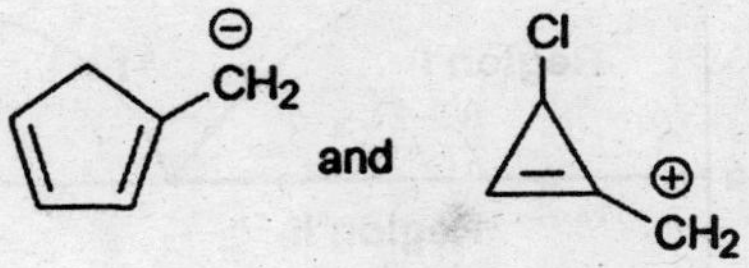

B. 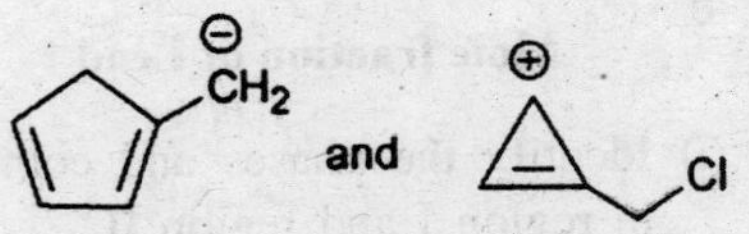

C. 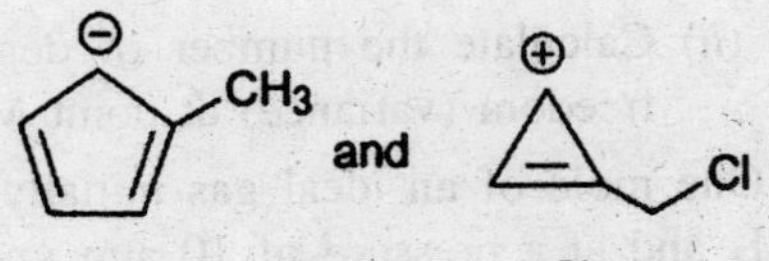

D. 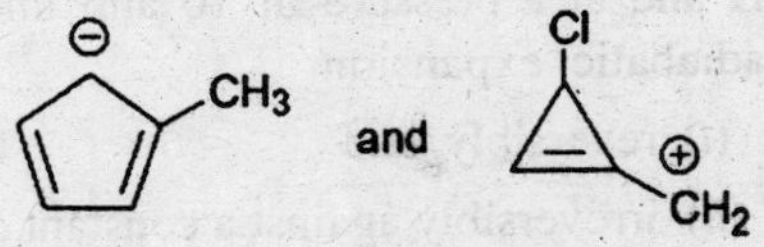

30. The major product in the following reaction is

A. 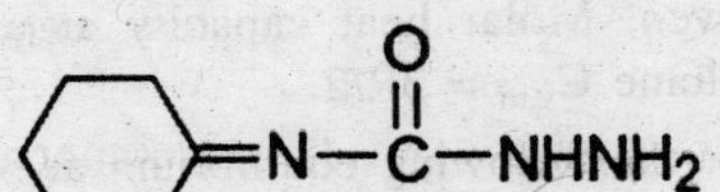

B. 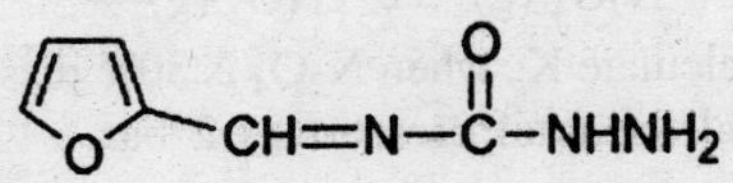

C. 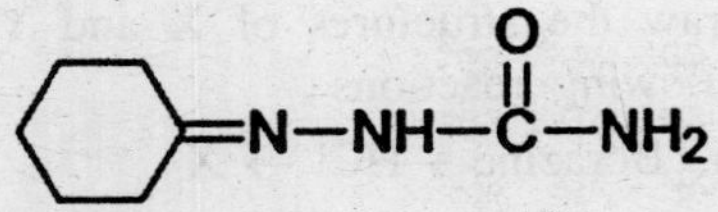

D. 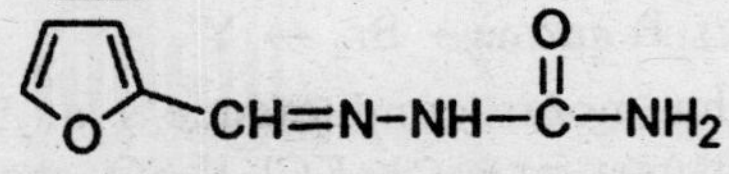

31. A. In the following reactions, identify X, Y and Z.

$$Na_2SO_3 + S \xrightarrow{\text{boiling water}} X(\text{colourless solid})$$

$$AgBr \xrightarrow{\text{excess X}} Y(\text{soluble complex})$$

$$X + Cl_2 + H_2O \xrightarrow{\text{boiling water}} Z + HCl$$

B. Draw the structures of $S_4N_4H_4$ and $N_4S_4F_4$.

32. A. The magnetic moment of $[Fe(phen)_2(NCS)_2]$ varies with temperature. The magnetic moments at 200 K and 50 K are 4.9 BM and 0 BM, respectively. Write the *d*-electron configurations of Fe at both temperatures and give reason for the observed change in the magnetic moment. (phen = 1,10-phenanthroline)

B. PCl_5 exists as a discrete covalent molecule in the gaseous state, but is ionic in the solid state. Draw the structures of PCl_5 in gaseous and solid states.

33. A. A carbonyl compound P, which gives positive iodoform test, undergoes reaction with MeMgBr followed by dehydration to give an olefin Q. Ozonolysis of Q leads to a dicarbonyl compound R, which undergoes intramolecular aldol reaction to give predominantly S.

$$P \xrightarrow[\text{2.}H^+,H_2O \;\; \text{3.}H_2SO_4,\Delta]{\text{1.MeMgBr}} Q \xrightarrow[\text{2.Zn},H_2O]{\text{1. }O_3} R \xrightarrow[\text{2.}\Delta]{\text{1. }OH^-} S$$

B. Fill in the blanks

(*i*) $^{235}U_{92} + {}_0n^1 \rightarrow {}^{137}A_{52} + {}^{97}B_{40} + ...$

(*ii*) $^{82}Se_{34} \rightarrow 2\,{}_{-1}e^0 + ...$

34. A. The edge length of unit cell of a metal having molecular weight 75 g/mol is 5 Å which crystallizes in cubic lattice. If the density is 2 g/cc then find the radius of metal atom. ($N_A = 6 \times 10^{23}$). Give the answer in pm.

B. Draw the structures of X and Y in the following reactions

(*i*) Borazine + HCl → X

(*ii*) Borazine + Br_2 → Y

35. A. The molar conductance's at infinite dilution for $BaCl_2$, KCl, K_2SO_4 and Cl^- are 280, 150, 300 and 76 Ω^{-1} m^2 mol^{-1}, respectively. Calculate the transport number of Ba^{2+} in $BaSO_4$ solution at infinite dilution.

B. Find the heat of formation of ethyl alcohol.

$$C(S) + O_2(g) = CO_2(g)\ \Delta H = -94\ k\ cal$$

$$H_2(g) + \frac{1}{2}O_2(g) = H_2O(g)\ \Delta H = -68\ k\ cal$$

$$C_2H_5OH(l) + 3O_2(g) = 2CO_2(g) + 3H_2O(l)$$

$$\Delta H = -327\ k\ cal$$

36. A. For the reaction R → P, the plot of ln[R] versus time (*t*) gives a straight line with a negative slope. The half life for the reaction is 3 minutes.

(ln 2 = 0.693, ln 0.1 = –2.303)

(*i*) Derive the expression for $t_{1/2}$.

(*ii*) Calculate the slope of the straight line.

(*iii*) Calculate the time required for the concentration of R to decrease to 10% of its initial value.

B. Shown below is the Jablonski diagram that describes various photophysical processes. The solid arrows represent radiative transitions and the wavy arrow represents a non-radiative transition.

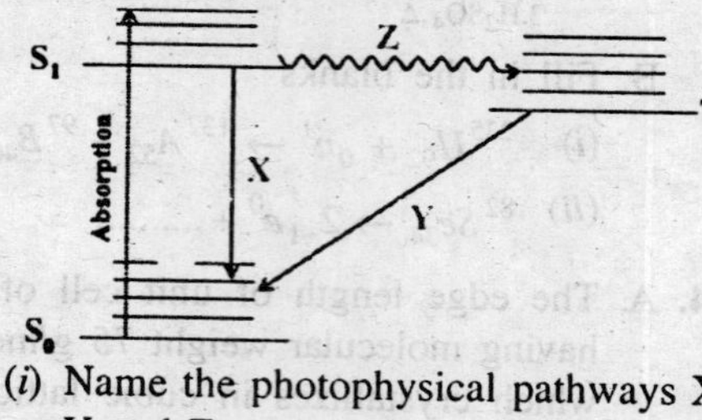

(*i*) Name the photophysical pathways X, Y and Z.

(*ii*) Which of the radiative decays is faster?

37. A. (*i*) Given that ΔG = –*n*FE, derive the expression for the temperature dependence of the cell potential (E) in terms of the change in entropy (ΔS).

(*ii*) For a cell reaction, E (at 25 °C) = 1.26 V, n = 2 and ΔS = –96.5 J K^{-1} mol^{-1}. Calculate E at 85°C by assuming ΔS to be independent of temperature.

(F = 96500 C mol^{-1})

B. The phase diagram for the lead-antimony system at a certain pressure is given below.

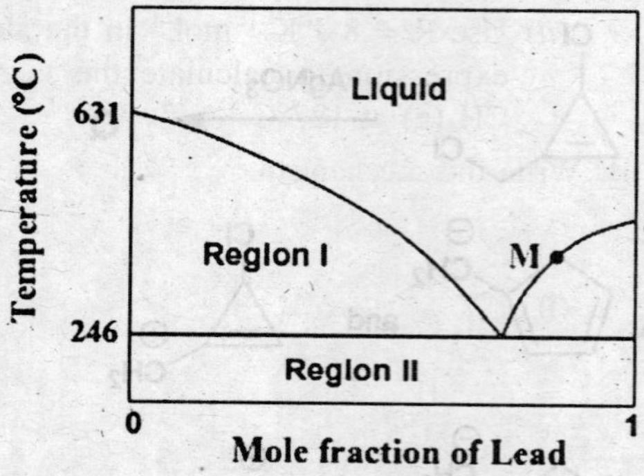

(*i*) Identify the phases and components in region I and region II.

(*ii*) Calculate the number of degrees of freedom (variance) at point M.

38. A. One mole of an ideal gas initially at 300 K and at a pressure of 10 atm undergoes adiabatic expansion

(*i*) reversibly and

(*ii*) irreversibly against a constant external pressure of 2 atm until the final pressure becomes equal to the external pressure.

Calculate ΔS_{system} for (*i*) and (*ii*). For (*ii*), express the final answer in terms of R.

Given: Molar heat capacity at constant volume $C_{v,m}$ = 3R/2.

B. For the following equilibrium at 300°C,

$$N_2O_4\ (g) \rightleftharpoons 2NO_2\ (g)$$

Calculate K_p when N_2O_4 is 30% dissociated and the total pressure is 2 bar.

39. A. The Maxwell probability distribution of molecular speeds for a gas is

$$F(v)dv = 4\pi v^2\left(\frac{m}{2\pi kT}\right)^{3/2}\exp\left(-\frac{mv^2}{2kT}\right)dv$$

where v is the speed, m the mass of a gas molecule and k the Boltzmann constant.

(*i*) Use $F(v)$ to show that the most probable speed v_{mp} is given by the expression $v_{mp} = \left(\frac{2RT}{M}\right)^{1/2}$.

(*ii*) Use R = 8 J K^{-1} mol^{-1} in the above expression to calculate the v_{mp} for $CH_4(g)$ at 127°C.

B. Write the mechanism.

(i) 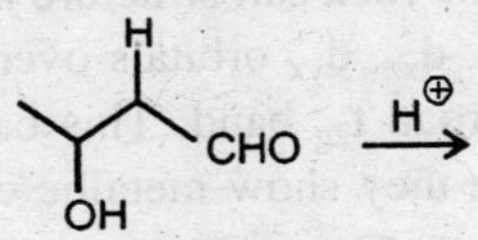

(ii) 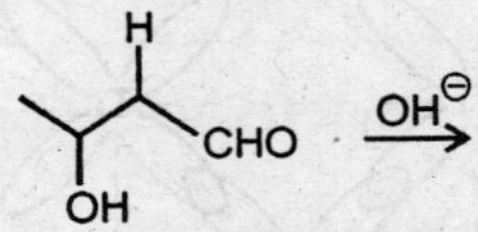

40. A. Write the possible substitution products in the following reactions.

Indicate the type/s of mechanism/s (S_N1/S_N2/S_N2') that is/are operative in each reaction.

(*i*) 

(*ii*) 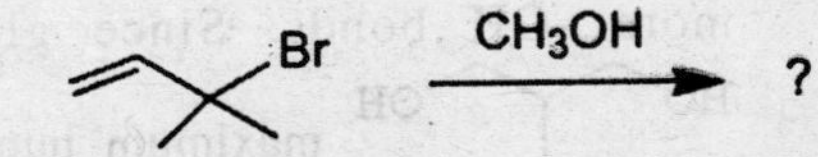

B. Carry out the following transformation.

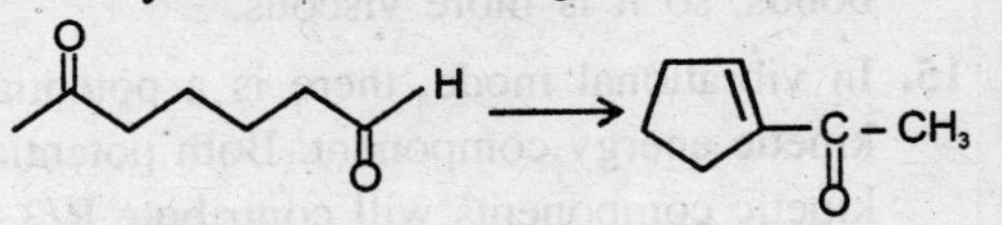

41. A. Write the structures of A to C in the following reaction sequence.

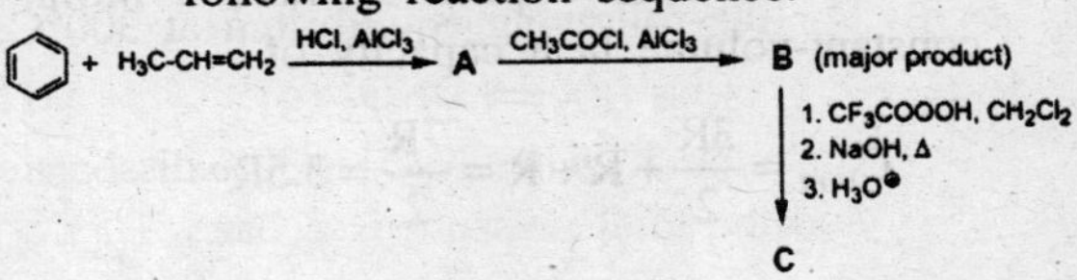

B. Write the structures of D and E in the reactions given below.

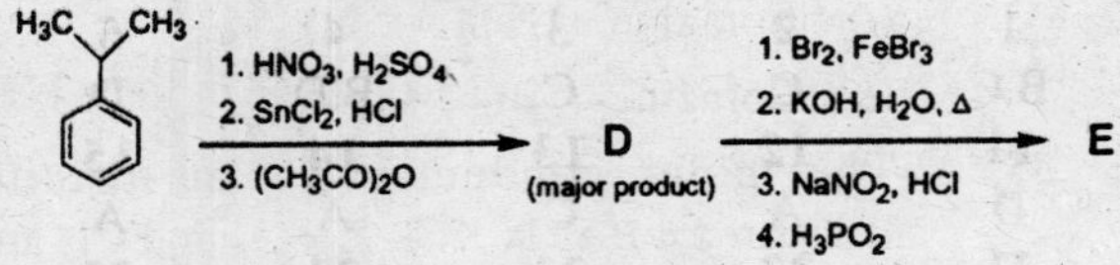

42. A. Identify A, B, C, D and E in the following scheme and write their structures.

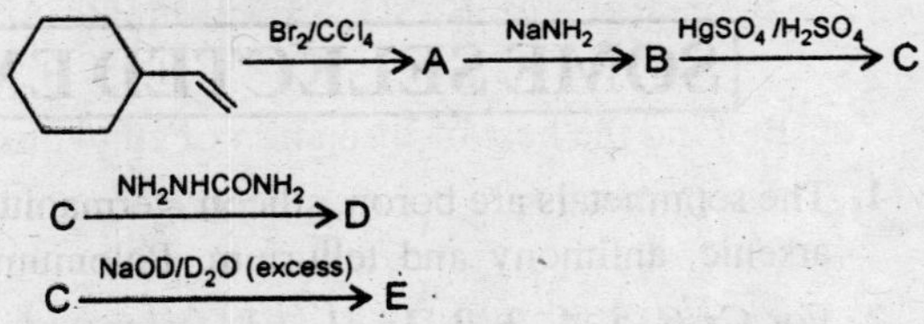

B. Write the structures of D and E in the following reaction.

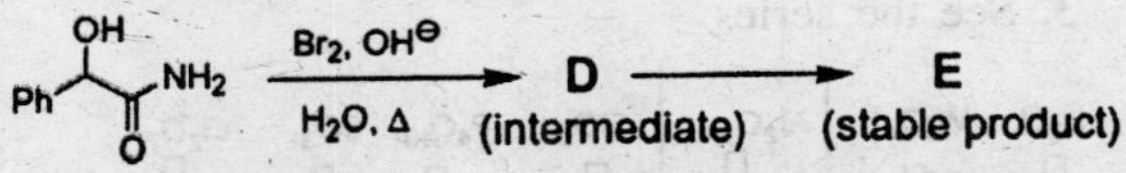

43. A. Identify X, Y and Z in the following reactions

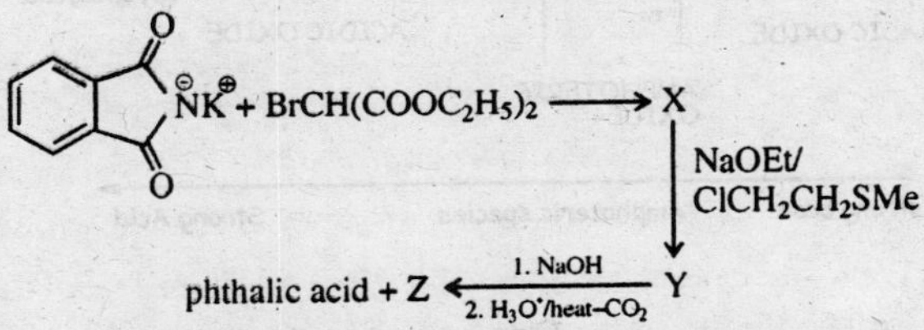

B. Suggest a suitable mechanism for the following reaction.

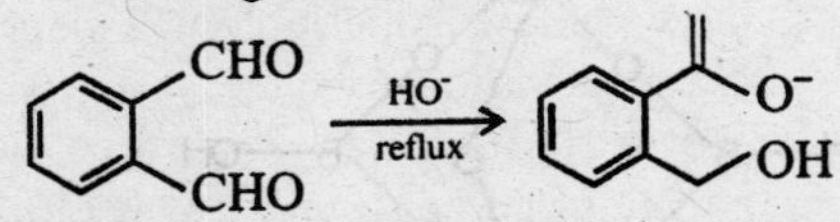

44. Oxanamide O, a tranquilizer, is synthesized according to the following reaction Scheme. Write the missing structures and reagent/s K to O.

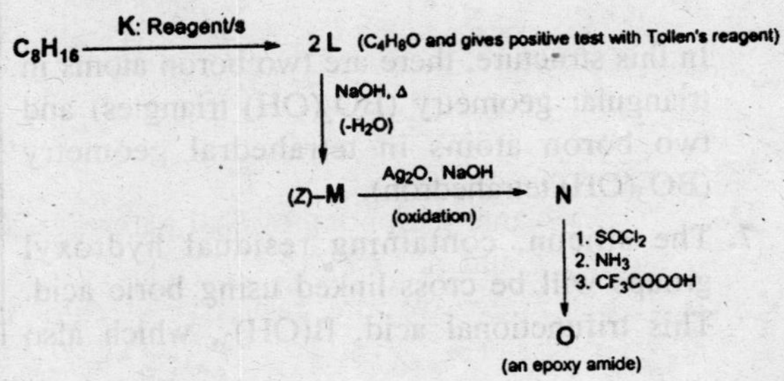

ANSWERS

1	2	3	4	5	6	7	8	9	10
B,C	C	C	B,D	D	C	D	D	A,C	A
11	12	13	14	15	16	17	18	19	20
D	A	C	A	A	B	A	D	D	A
21	22	23	24	25	26	27	28	29	30
C	B	C	B	C,D	A	D	B	B,C	B,A

SOME SELECTED EXPLANATORY ANSWERS

1. The semimetals are boron, silicon, germanium, arsenic, antimony and tellurium. Polonium.

2. For Cr 6, 5, 4, 3, 2, 1, –1, –2
For Mo 6, 5, 4, 3, 2, 1, –1, –2

3. See the series

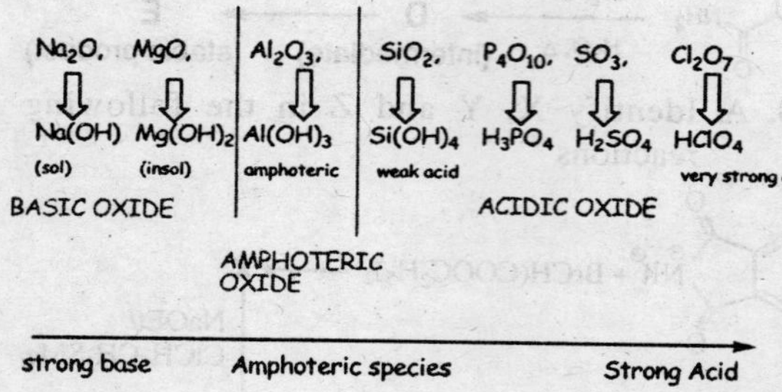

5.

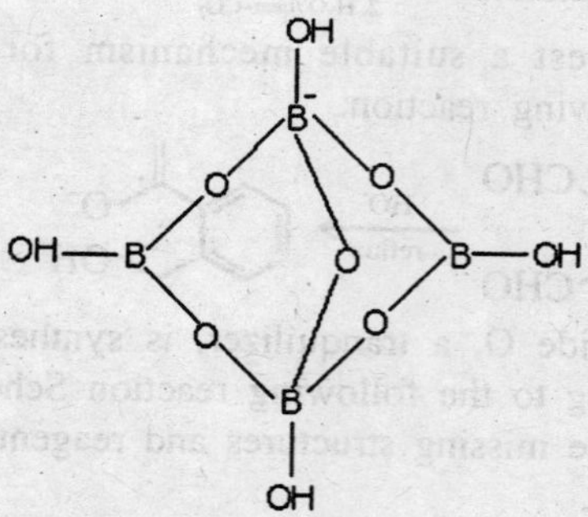

In this structure, there are two boron atoms in triangular geometry ($BO_2(OH)$ triangles) and two boron atoms in tetrahedral geometry ($BO_3(OH)$ tetrahedron).

7. The silicon, containing residual hydroxyl groups will be cross-linked using boric acid. This trifunctional acid, $B(OH)_3$, which also contains hydroxyl groups, forms -Si-O-B- linkages between the siloxane chains, so no linear chain.

8. It can also be written as $Fe^{III}(Co^{II}Fe^{III})O_4$.

9. They have the rock salt structure like NiO, but here the d_{xy}, d_{xz}, d_{yx} orbitals overlap strongly to form a broad t_{2g} band. This band is partly filled, hence they show metallic conductivity.

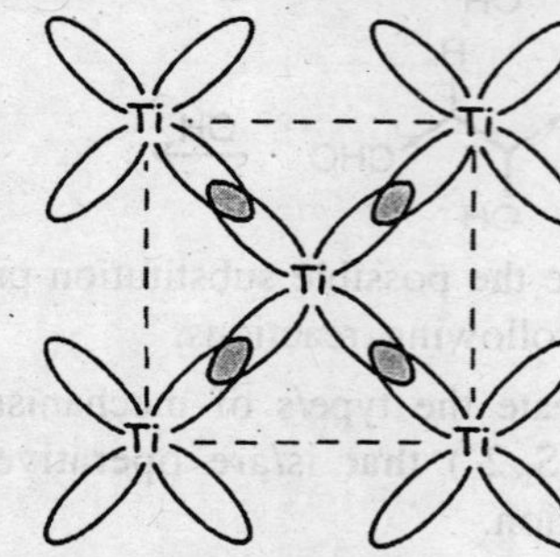

11. The viscosity depends on the amount of hydrogen bonding between molecules, and the more -OH bonds. Since glycerol has

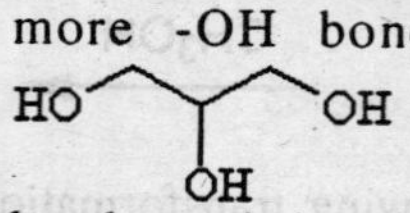

maximum number of OH bonds, so it is more viscous.

15. In vibrational mode, there is a potential and kinetic energy component. Both potential and kinetic components will contribute R/2 to the total molar heat capacity of the gas. So, a molecule would expect to have a molar constant-volume heat capacity of

$$C_{v,m} = \frac{3R}{2} + R + R = \frac{7R}{2} = 3.5R$$

16. For the van der Walls gas

$$w = -\int_{V_i}^{V_f} P_{external}\,dV = -\int_{V_i}^{V_f}\left(\frac{RT}{V_m - b} - \frac{a}{V_m^2}\right)dV$$

$$= -\int_{V_i}^{V_f}\left(\frac{RT}{V_m - b}\right)dV + \int_{V_i}^{V_f}\left(\frac{a}{V_m^2}\right)dV$$

The first integral is solved by making the substitution $y = V_m - b$.

$$-\int_{V_i}^{V_f}\left(\frac{RT}{V_m - b}\right)dV = -\int_{y_i}^{y_f}\left(\frac{RT}{y}\right)dy$$

$$= -RT\left[\ln(V_f + b) - \ln(V_i + b)\right]$$

Therefore, the work is given by

$$w = -nRT\ln\frac{(V_f - b)}{(V_i - b)} + a\left(\frac{1}{V_i} - \frac{1}{V_f}\right).$$

17. Let $u = (2, 3, -5)$ and $v = (1, 1, 3)$.

Then $u \bullet v = (2)(1) + (3)(1) + (-5)(3)$

$= 2 + 3 - 15 = -10.$

18. $Sp_{Ag2S} = [Ag^+]^2\,[S]$

$1 \times 10^{-51} = [Ag^+]^2\,[10^{-1}]$

$\therefore \quad [Ag^+] \approx 1 \times 10^{-50}$

$A^2 = 1 \times 10^{-50}$

$= 1 \times 10^{-25}$ M.

20. Assume that $[NH_3] = x$, then $[H_3O^+] = x$, and you write the concentration as the formula in the reaction:

$NH^{4+} + H_2O \leftrightarrow NH_3 + H_3O^+$

$0.1-x \qquad\qquad x \qquad x$

$K_h = 5.6 \times 10^{-10}$

$$= \frac{x^2}{0.1 - x}$$

We may use

$x = (0.1 \times 5.6 \times 10^{-10})^{1/2}$

$x = (5.6 \times 10^{-11})^{1/2}$.

24.

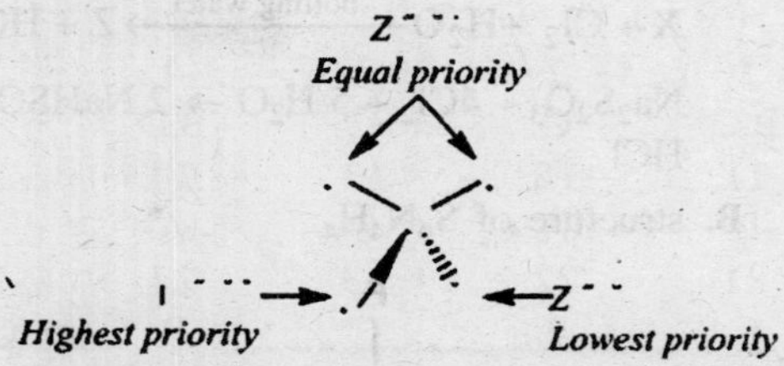

The priority number of a ligand is based on the atomic number of the element in the ligand that bonds the ligand to the chiral center. The higher the atomic number, the higher the priority.

25.

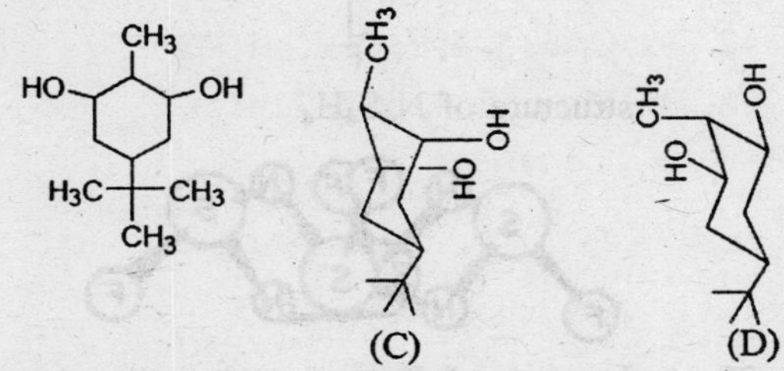

27. Rotate upside down and see whether they are mirror image.

28. RNA has the nucleobase uracil while DNA contains thymine. In RNA thymine is replaced by uracil as the base complementary to adenine.

29. The first step is an acid-base reaction which produces the alkyne conjugate base, or alkynide ion (a nucleophile)

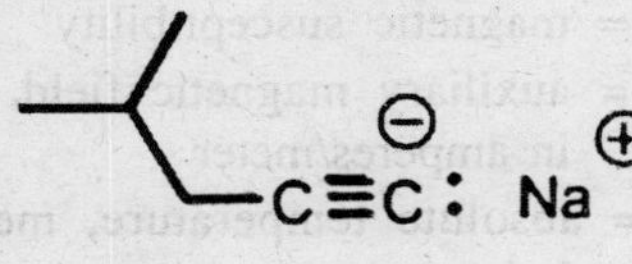

31. A. $Na_2SO_3 + S \xrightarrow{\text{boiling water}}$ X (colourless solid)

A method of preparing sodium thiosulphate is to react sodium sulphite with sulphur.

$Na_2SO_3\ (s) + 1/8\ S_8\ (s) \rightarrow H_2O/100°C \rightarrow Na_2S_2O_3\ (s)$

$AgBr \xrightarrow{\text{excess X}}$ Y(soluble complex)

$AgBr + 2\,Na_2S_2O_3 \rightarrow Na_3[Ag(S_2O_3)_2] + NaBr$

Soluble complex

$$X + Cl_2 + H_2O \xrightarrow{\text{boiling water}} Z + HCl$$

$Na_2S_2O_3 + 4Cl_2 + 5\ H_2O \rightarrow 2\ NaHSO_4 + 8\ HCl$

B. structure of $S_4N_4H_4$

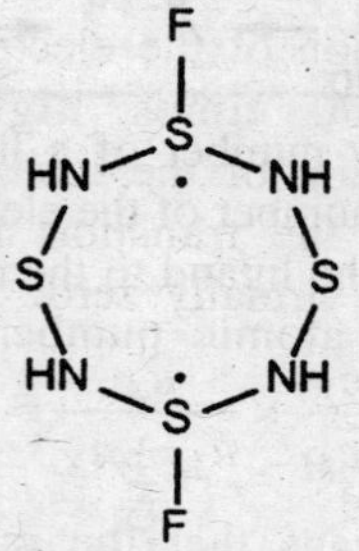

structure of $N_4S_4H_4$

32. A. In case of Fe^{+2} complex, the magnetic moment of $[Fe(phen)_2(NCS)_2]$ varies with temperature. The magnetic moments at 200 K and 50 K are 4.9 BM and 0 BM respectively as because when temperature decreases magnetic moment decreases.

It was observed that as per Curie's law

$M = (C/T)*H = \chi H$

where:

M = resulting magnetization

χ = magnetic susceptibility

H = auxiliary magnetic field, measured in amperes/meter

T = absolute temperature, measured in kelvins

C = material-specific Curie constant

M proportional to 1/T, "d"

Since M = (N/V)m,

where:

M = represents magnetization

m = vector that defines the magnetic moment

V = represents volume

N = number of magnetic moments in the sample.

so

$M = (C/T)*H = \chi H = (N/V)m$

or

m is proportional to 1/T according to Curie's law.

B. Phosphorus pentachloride is the chemical compound with the formula PCl_5. It is one of the most important phosphorus chlorides, others being PCl_3 and $POCl_3$.

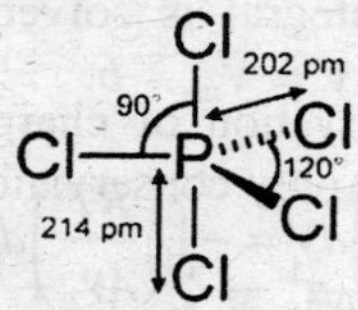

Gaseous and molten PCl_5 is a neutral molecule with trigonal bipyramidal (D_{3h}) symmetry.

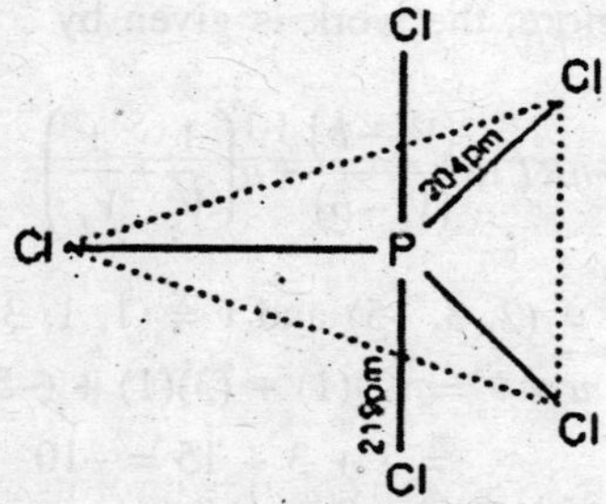

In the solid state PCl_5 is ionic, formulated $PCl_4^+ PCl_6^-$. In solutions of polar solvents, PCl_5 undergoes "autoionization".

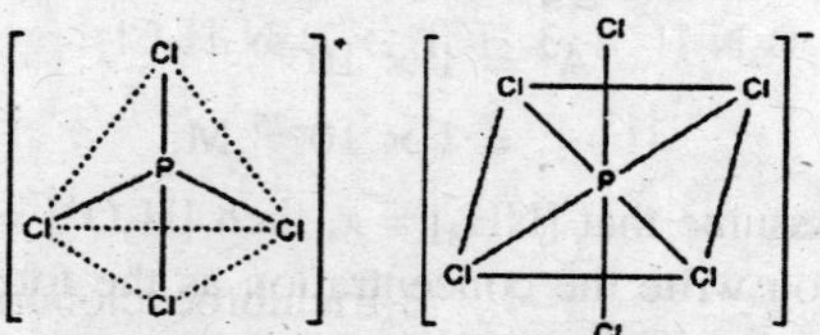

Tetrahedral shape of cation $[PCl_4]^+$ Octahedral shape of $[PCl_6]^-$ anion

33. A. Iodoform test means compounds have

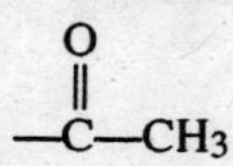

Structure

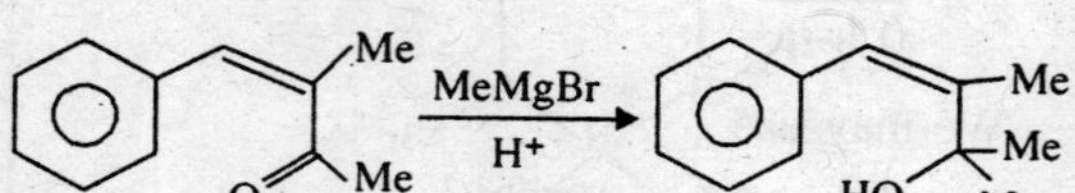

(P)

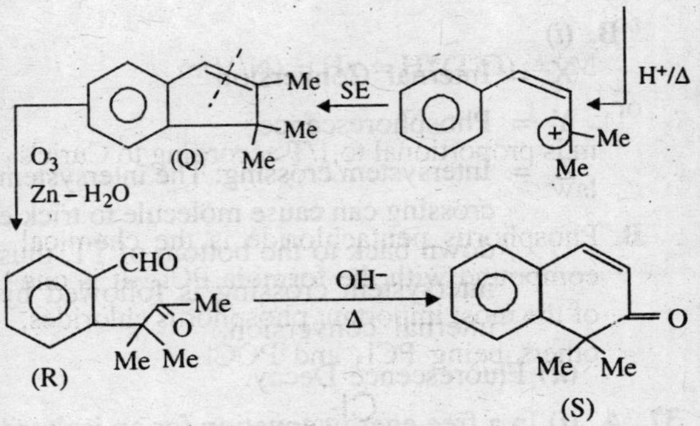

B. Apply conservation of charge and mass to get answer. Apply conservation of mass first.

(i) $^{235}U_{92} + {}_0n^1 \rightarrow {}^{137}A_{52} + {}^{97}B_{40} + 2\,{}_0n^1$

(ii) $^{82}Se_{34} \rightarrow 2\,{}_{-1}e^0 + {}^{82}Kr_{36}$

34. A. $\rho = \dfrac{ZA}{NV}$

$$Z = \frac{\rho NV}{A} = \frac{2\times 6\times 10^{23}\times(5\times 10^{-8})^3}{75}$$

$n = 2$

$$r = \frac{\sqrt{3}}{4}a = \frac{\sqrt{3}}{4}\times 5 = 2.165 \text{ Å} = 216.5 \text{ pm}$$

B. With hydrogen chloride it forms an adduct, whereas benzene is unreactive toward HCl. Addition reaction of borazine with hydrogen chloride.

$B_3N_3H_6 + 3\ HCl \rightarrow B_3N_3H_9Cl_3$

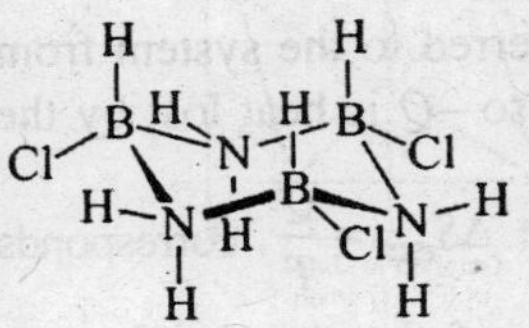

B-trichlorocycloborazine

$B_3N_3H_6 + Br_2 \rightarrow B_3N_3H_6Br_6$

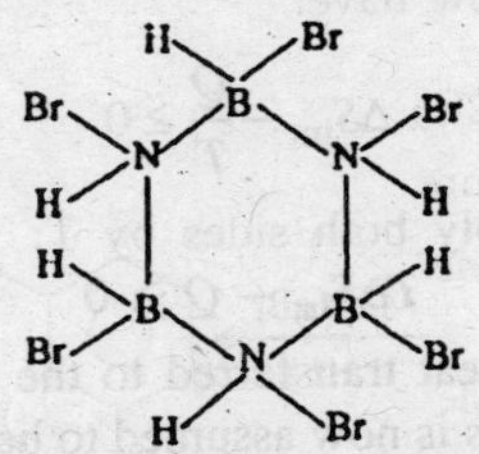

B-hexabromocyclotriborazine.

35. A. The transport number depends on the relative concentration of the respective ion. In electro analytical chemistry, the electrochemical reaction of an analyte ion A^{z+} is measured in the presence of a supporting electrolyte MX. Usually, the concentration of the electrolyte MX is at least 1000 times higher than the concentration of the ion A^{z+}. Under this condition the transport number of the analyte is virtually zero:

$$t_A \approx \frac{z_A c_Z}{z_M c_M} \times \frac{u_A}{u_M + u_X} \approx 10^{-3}$$

which means that the migration of the analyte ion A^{z+} can be neglected.

B. $2C(s) + 3H_2(g) + \frac{1}{2}O_2(g) = C_2H_5OH\ (l)$

$\Delta H_f = ?$

Given

$2C(s) + 2O_2(g) = 2CO_2(g)$

$\Delta H = -\ 188\ k$ cal ...(*i*)

$3H_2 + \frac{3}{2}O_2(g) = 3H_2O(l)\ k$ cal

$\Delta H = -\ 204\ k$ cal ...(*ii*)

$2CO_2 + 3H_2O(l) = C_2H_5OH + 3O_2(g)$

$\Delta H = +327\ k$ cal ...(*iii*)

On adding

$2C(s) + 3H_2(g) + \frac{1}{2}O_2(g) = C_2H_5OH(l)$

$\Delta H = -\ 65\ k$ cal

36. A. (*i*) For the first order reaction

$k = 2.303/t\ x\ \log[R]0[R]$

Half life of the reaction is considered when $[R] = 1/2[R]0$

$$k = \frac{2.303}{t_{\frac{1}{2}}}\log\frac{[R]_0}{\frac{1}{2}[R]_0}$$

so $$t_{\frac{1}{2}} = \frac{2.303}{k}\log_2$$

$$t_{\frac{1}{2}} = \frac{2.303*0.3310}{k}$$

$$t_{\frac{1}{2}} = \frac{0.693}{k}$$

(ii) ln[R] = $-kt$ + C -------(4)

Where C is the integration constant, C the integration constant can be determined by using the following assumption.

When the $t = 0$, the reaction has not started to proceed so [R] = [R]0

so $kt = 0$ and then ln[R] = ln[R]0

then

ln[R] = $-kt$ + C will become ln[R]0= C

So, the equation can be rewritten as

ln[R] = $-kt$ + ln[R]0

This equation is just like $y = mx + c$ where y = ln[R], m is the slope which is equal to $-k$ and intercept is ln[R]0.

So, the plot of ln[R] vs time gives a straight line with a negative slope of $-k$. Rearranging the equation. We get

ln[R][R]0 = $-kt$

Or upon rearranging we get

k = 2.303t log[R]0[R]

At time t_1 fro

(iii) According to the integrated rate equation for a zero order reaction:

$[R] = [R]^\circ - kt$

Where k is the rate constant and t is the time at which the concentration is [R]

At half time

$$[R]=1/2[R]^\circ$$

and time t will become $t^{1/2}$

So,

$$½[R]^\circ = [R]^\circ - kt^{1/2}$$

or

$$kt^{1/2} = [R]^\circ - ½[R]^\circ$$
$$kt^{1/2} = ½[R]^\circ$$
$$t^{1/2} = ½[R]^\circ k$$
$$t^{1/2} = [R]^\circ/2k$$

B. *(i)*

X = Internal Conversion

Y = Phosphorescence

Z = Intersystem crossing: The intersystem crossing can cause molecule to trickle down back to the bottom of T1, thus intersystem crossing is followed by internal conversion.

(ii) Fluorescence Decay.

37. A. *(i)* In a free energy equation for an isolated system, S_{tot} be the total entropy of the isolated system. According to the second law of thermodynamics:

$$\Delta S_{tot} \geq 0$$

if $\Delta S_{tot} = 0$ then the process is reversible. The heat transfer Q vanishes for an adiabatic system. Any adiabatic process that is also reversible is called an isentropic $\left(\frac{Q}{T} = \Delta S = 0\right)$ process.

Now consider systems, having internal entropy S_{int}. Such a system is thermally connected to its surroundings, which have entropy S_{ext}. The entropy form of the second law applies only to the closed system formed by both the system and its surroundings. Therefore a process is possible if

$$\Delta S_{int} + \Delta S_{ext} \geq 0.$$

If Q is heat transferred to the system from the surroundings, so $-Q$ is heat lost by the surroundings so that $\Delta S_{ext} = \frac{Q}{T}$, corresponds to entropy change of the surroundings.

We now have:

$$\Delta S_{int} - \frac{Q}{T} \geq 0$$

Multiply both sides by T:

$$T\Delta S_{int} - Q \geq 0$$

Q is heat transferred to the system; if the process is now assumed to be isobaric, then $Q_p = \Delta H$:

$$T\Delta S_{int} - \Delta H \geq 0$$

ΔH is the enthalpy change of reaction, then

$$\Delta H - T\Delta S_{int} \leq 0d$$

for a possible process. Let the change ΔG in Gibbs free energy be defined as

$$\Delta G = \Delta H - T\Delta S_{int} \text{ (eq. 1)}$$

Notice that it is not defined in terms of any external state functions, such as ΔS_{ext} or ΔS_{tot}. Then the second law becomes, which also tells us about the spontaneity of the reaction:

$\Delta G < 0$ favoured reaction (Spontaneous)

$\Delta G = 0$ Neither the forward nor the reverse reaction prevails (Equilibrium)

$\Delta G >$ disfavoured reaction (Non-spontaneous)

Gibbs free energy G itself is defined as $G = H - TS_{int}$ (eq. 2)

but notice that to obtain equation (2) from equation (1) we must assume that T is constant. Thus, thermodynamic processes are not confined to the two dimensional *P-V* diagram. There is a third dimension for *n*, the quantity of gas. For the study of explosive chemicals, the processes are not necessarily isothermal and isobaric.

If an isolated system ($Q = 0$) is at constant pressure ($Q = \Delta H$), then

$$\Delta H = 0$$

Therefore the Gibbs free energy of an isolated system is:

$$\Delta G = -T\,\Delta S$$

and if $\Delta G \leq 0$ then this implies that $\Delta S \geq 0$, back to where we started the derivation of ΔG

$\Delta G = \Delta H - T\Delta S$ for constant temperature

$\Delta_r G° = -RT \ln K$

$\Delta_r G = \Delta_r G° + RT \ln Q_r$

$$\Delta G = -nFE$$

$$\Delta G° = -nFE°$$

and rearranging gives

$$nFE° = RT \ln K$$

$$nFE = nFE° - RT \ln Q_r$$

$$E = E° - \frac{RT}{nF} \ln Q_r$$

which relates the electrical potential of a reaction to the equilibrium coefficient for that reaction (Nernst equation).

where

ΔG = change in Gibbs free energy, ΔH = change in enthalpy, T = absolute temperature, ΔS = change in entropy, R = gas constant, ln = natural logarithm, $\Delta_r G$ = change of reaction in Gibbs free energy, $\Delta_r G°$ = standard change of reaction in Gibbs free energy, K = equilibrium constant, Q_r = reaction quotient, n = number of electrons per mole product, F = Faraday constant (coulombs per mole), and E = electrode potential of the reaction. Moreover, we also have:

$$K_{eq} = e^{-\frac{\Delta rG°}{RT}}$$

$$\Delta_r G° = -RT\,(\ln K_{eq})$$

$$= -2.303RT\,(\log K_{eq})$$

which relates the equilibrium constant with Gibbs free energy.

(*ii*) $E = E° - \frac{RT}{nF} \ln Q_r$

E = 1.28 V – RT / 2 × 96500 C/mol

E = 1.28 V – (8.314 J $K^{-1}mol^{-1}$)(25 + 85)/ 2 × 96500 C/mol

E = 1.28 V –0.00473 = 1.275.

B. (*i*) In systems such as lead-antimony which form alloys, the grains of A and B are much smaller, yet the two phases remain. In aqueous systems, this eutectic mixture is called a cryohydrate and the eutectic point is called the cryohydric point.

Region 1 contains Sb + liquid and Region II contains Pb + liquid

(ii) $f = c - p + 1 = 2 - 3 + 1 = 0$

In liquid area above curve, two end points exist as homologous liquid solution as temperature is above melting point. By considering only 1 phase:

$f = c - p + 1 = 2 - 1 + 1 = 2$

In the area above curve, the temperature difference needs to define.

38. A. $W_{ad} = -\Delta U = n(C_{v,m} - R)\Delta T$

$W_{reversible} = -1(3/2R - R)300K$

$= -1/2 \times 8.314$ J/molK $\times$ 300K $- 1.247 \times 10^3$J

$$-nRT\ln\frac{P_i}{P_f};\ \ln\frac{P_i}{P_f} = \frac{-w_{reversible}}{nRT}$$

$$\ln\frac{P_i}{P_f} = \frac{nRT}{w_{reversible}}$$

$$= \frac{1.247\times10^5\,\text{J}}{1\text{mol}\times8.314\text{Jmol}^{-1}K^{-1}\times300K}$$

$= P_f = 0.5002P_i$

Since for irreversibity the pressure is 2 atm, so = 1 atm .

B. $K_p = K_c\,(RT)^{\Delta n}$

$K_p = K_c\,[(0.0821)(300\text{ K})]^1$

$$K_c = \frac{[N_2O_4)}{[NO_2]^2}$$

$$K_c = \frac{0.3M}{[NO_2]^2}$$

$K_c = 1.714$

Now

$K_p = K_c\,[(0.0821)(300\text{ K})]^1$

$K_p = 1.714\,[(0.0821)(300\text{ K})]^1 = 42.22.$

39. A. *(i)* Each component of the velocity vector has a normal distribution with mean $\mu_{vx} = \mu_{vy} = \mu_{vz} = 0$ and standard deviation $\sigma_{vx} = \sigma_{vy} = \sigma_{vz} = \sqrt{\frac{kT}{m}}$, so the vector has a 3-dimensional normal distribution, also called a "multinormal" distribution, with mean and standard deviation $\sigma_v = \sqrt{\frac{3kT}{m}}$

The Maxwell-Boltzmann distribution for the speed follows immediately from the distribution of the velocity vector, above. Note that the speed is

$$v = \sqrt{v_x^2 + v_y^2 + v_z^2}$$

$\mu_v = 0$ and the increment of volume is $dv_x\,dv_y dv_z = v^2 \sin\phi dv d\theta d\phi$

where θ and ϕ are the "course" (azimuth of the velocity vector) and "path angle" (elevation angle of the velocity vector). Integration of the normal probability density function of the velocity, above, over the course (from 0 to 2π) and path angle (from 0 to π), with substitution of the speed for the sum of the squares of the vector components, yields the probability density function

$$f(v) = \sqrt{\frac{2}{\pi}\left(\frac{m}{kT}\right)^3}\, v^2 \exp\left(\frac{-mv^2}{2kT}\right)$$

for the speed. This equation is simply the Maxwell distribution with distribution parameter $a = \sqrt{\frac{kT}{m}}$.

We are often more interested in quantities such as the average speed of the particles rather than the actual distribution. The mean speed, most probable speed (mode), and root-mean-square can be obtained from properties of the Maxwell distribution.

Relative speed is defined as $u = \frac{v}{v_p}$, where

$v_p = \sqrt{\frac{2kT}{m}} = \sqrt{\frac{2RT}{M}}$ is the most probable speed. The distribution of relative speeds allows comparison of dissimilar gasses, independent of temperature and molecular weight.

(*ii*) $v_{mp} = \left(\frac{2kT}{m}\right)^{1/2}$

Molar Mass m of CH_4 = 16.04 mol^{-1}

On applying, we get = 15.91 m/s.

B. (*i*)

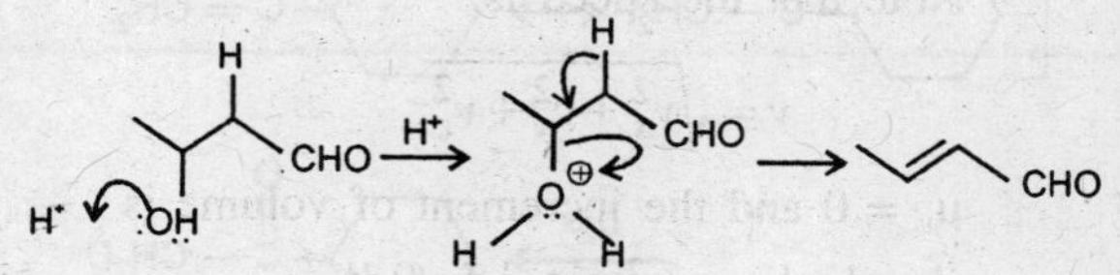

(*ii*)

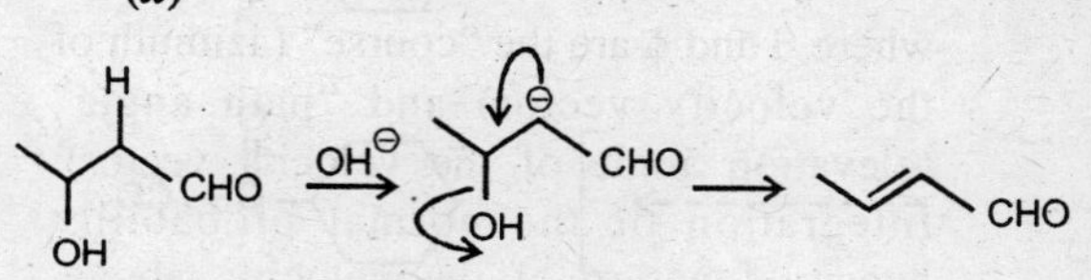

40. A. (*i*) Sn2

SN2 will be faster if:

~Reagent is a strong base.

~C connected to the LG is primary or a methyl group (sometimes secondary)

~The solvent used is polar aprotic (DMF, DMSO, etc.)

(*ii*) Sn1

SN1 will be faster if:

~Reagent is weak base.

~C connected to the Leaving Group is tertiary (sometimes secondary) *i.e.*, the leaving group must be a better leaving group. The leaving ability is inversely proportional to the basisity of the compound (its basic character)

~The solvent used is polar protic (water and alcohols, etc.)

B.

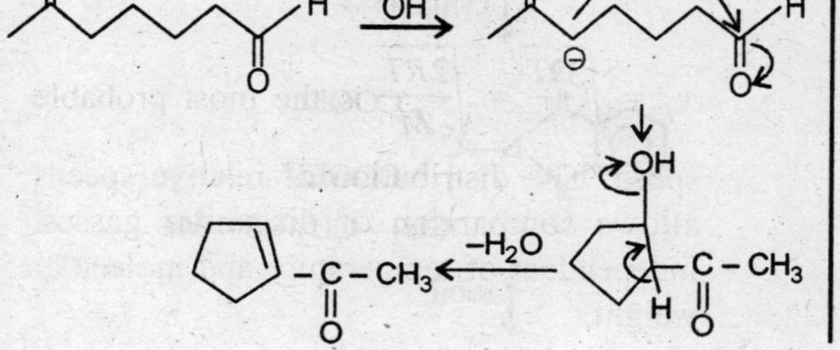

41. A. A = The propyl group becomes attached to the ring via its middle carbon atom — and not its end one. The hydrogen is removed by the $AlCl^{4-}$ ion. The aluminium chloride and hydrogen chloride catalysts are regenerated in this.

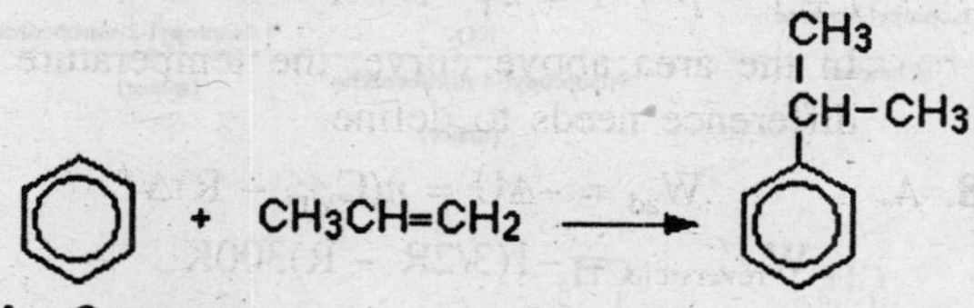

A = Cumene

When the propene reacts with the HCl, the hydrogen becomes attached to the end carbon atom. A secondary carbocation is formed because it is more stable than the primary one which would have been formed if the addition was the other way. Round.

B = 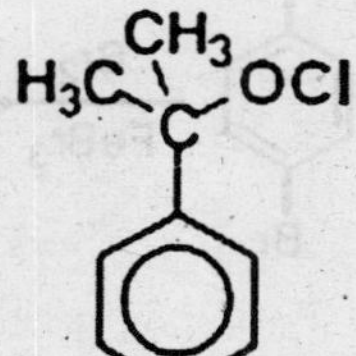

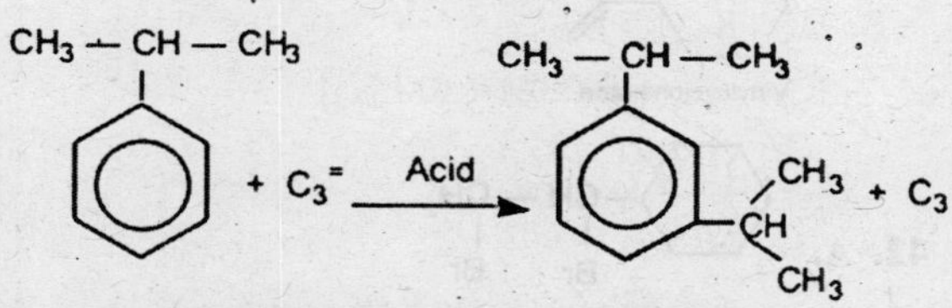

Cumene Propylene DIPB

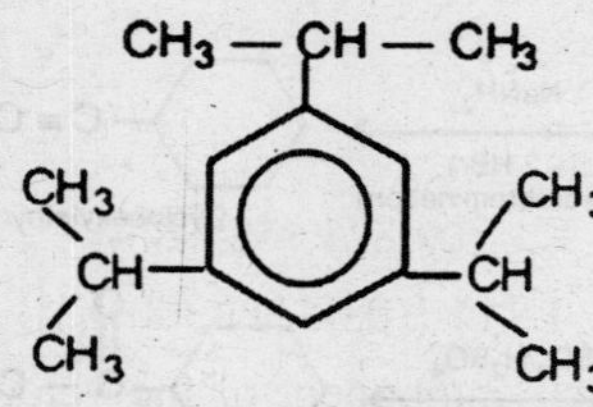

TIPB

C = 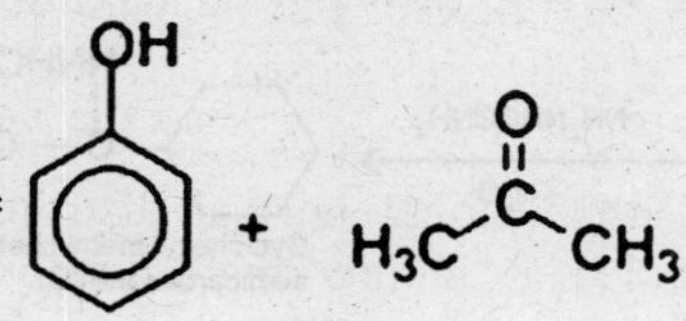

B. D =

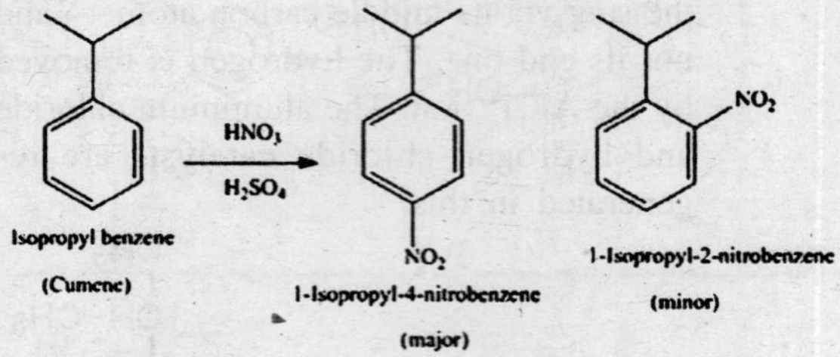

E =

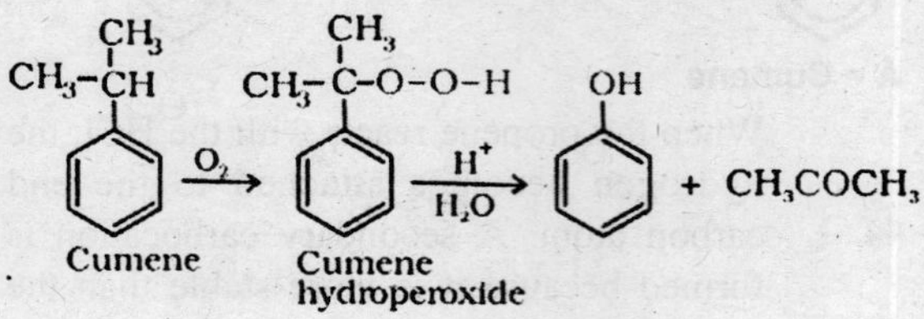

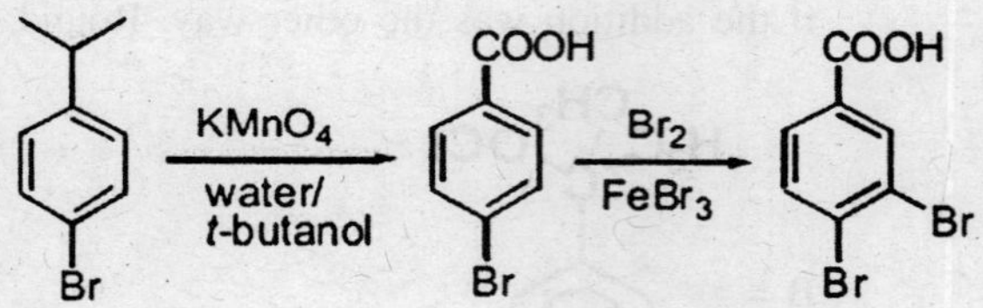

42. A.

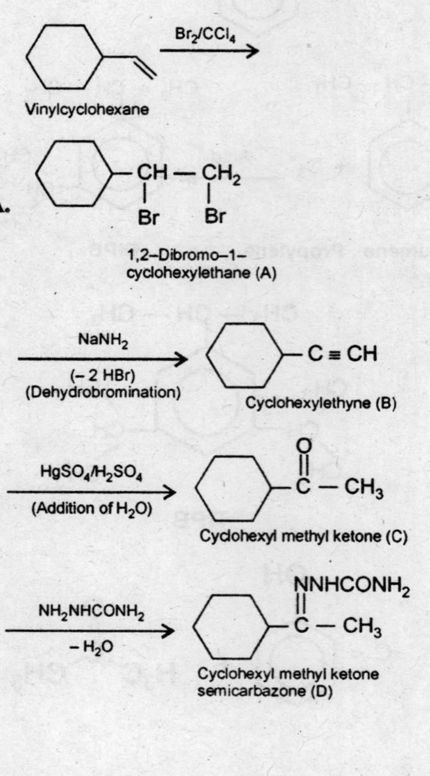

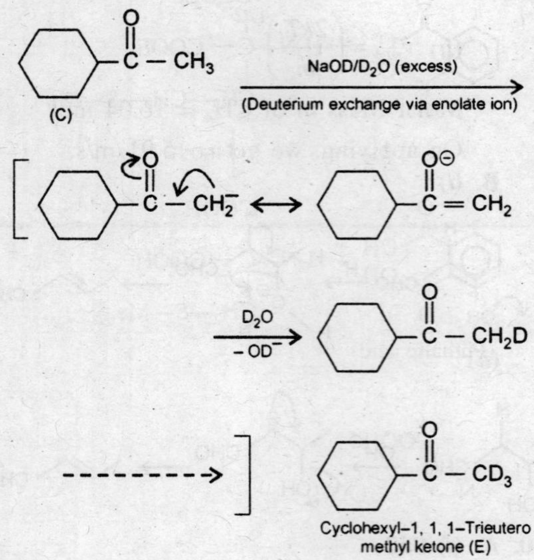

B. D =

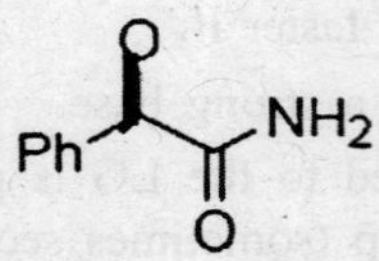

E =

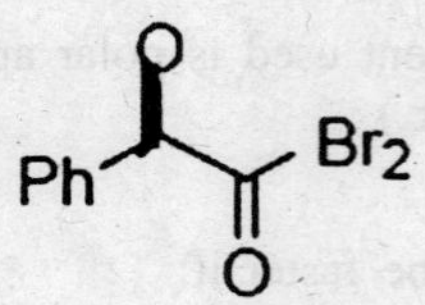

43. A.

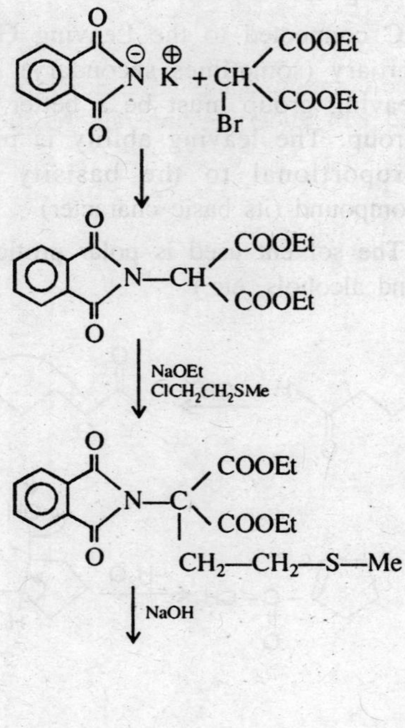

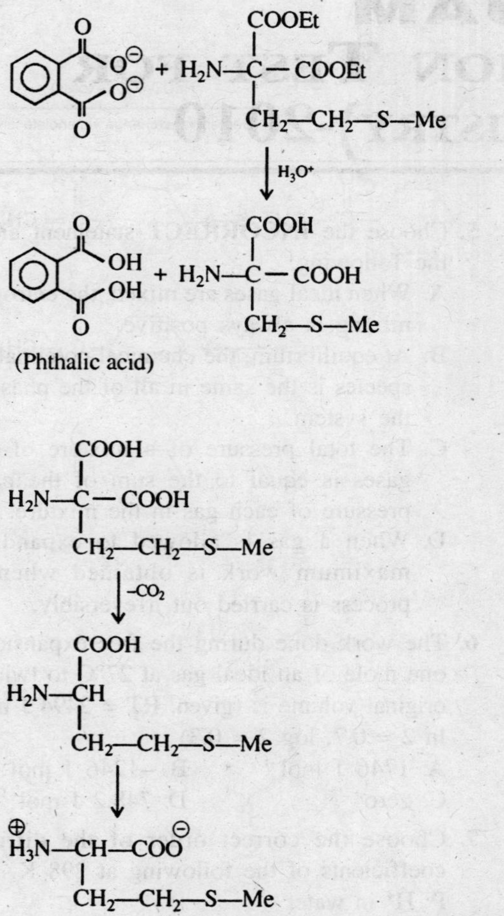

B. The compound has no α acidic hydrogen and will undergo cannizaro reaction.

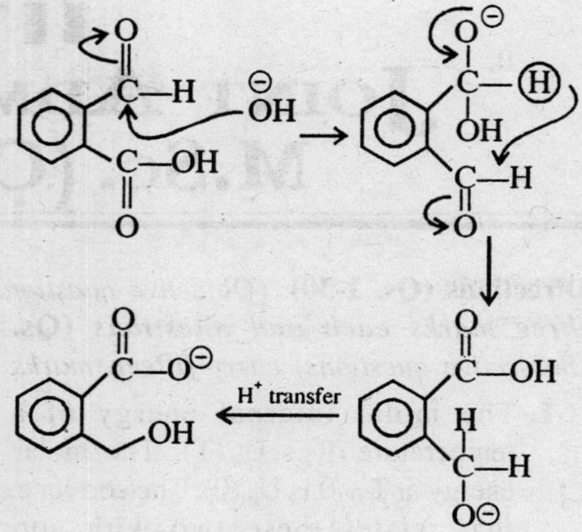

44.

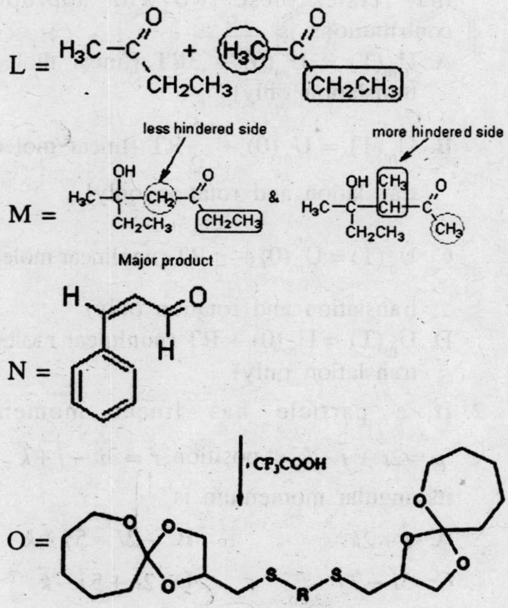

Previous Paper (Solved)

IIT–JAM

JOINT ADMISSION TEST FOR M.SC. (CHEMISTRY)-2010

Directions (Qs. 1-30): *(Objective questions) carry* ***three*** *marks each and questions* **(Qs. 31-44)** *(Subjective questions) carry* ***fifteen*** *marks each.*

1. The molar internal energy of a gas at temperature T is $U_m(T)$. The molar internal energy at T = 0 is $U_m(0)$. The correct expression that relates these two with appropriate contributions is

A. $U_m(T) = U_m(0) + 3RT$ [linear molecule; translation only]

B. $U_m(T) = U_m(0) + \frac{5}{2}RT$ [linear molecule; translation and rotation only]

C. $U_m(T) = U_m(0) + \frac{3}{2}RT$ (nonlinear molecule; translation and rotation only)

D. $U_m(T) = U_m(0) + RT$ (nonlinear molecule; translation only)

2. If a particle has linear momentum $\vec{p} = 2\vec{i} + \vec{j} + \vec{k}$ at position $\vec{r} = 3\vec{i} - \vec{j} + \vec{k}$, then its angular momentum is

A. $\vec{i} + 2\vec{k}$ B. $-2\vec{i} - 5\vec{j} + \vec{k}$

C. $5\vec{i} - 2\vec{j}$ D. $2\vec{i} + 5\vec{j} - \vec{k}$

3. If ψ is the eigenfunction to the Hamiltonian operator with α as the eigenvalue, then α **MUST** be

A. positive B. negative

C. an integer D. real

4. A quantum mechanical particle of mass *m* free to rotate on the surface of a sphere of radius *r* is in the state with energy $\frac{10h^2}{mr^2}$. The degeneracy of this state is

A. 20 B. 10

C. 9 D. 4

5. Choose the **INCORRECT** statement among the following:

A. When ideal gases are mixed, the entropy of mixing is always positive.

B. At equilibrium, the chemical potential of a species is the same in all of the phases of the system.

C. The total pressure of a mixture of ideal gases is equal to the sum of the partial pressure of each gas in the mixture.

D. When a gas is allowed to expand, the maximum work is obtained when the process is carried out irreversibly.

6. The work done during the free expansion of one mole of an ideal gas at 27°C to twice its original volume is (given: RT = 2494 J mol^{-1}, ln 2 = 0.7, log 2 = 0.3)

A. 1746 J mol^{-1} B. –1746 J mol^{-1}

C. zero D. 748.2 J mol^{-1}

7. Choose the correct order of the diffusion coefficients of the following at 298 K.

P: H^+ in water

Q: OH^- in water

R: H_2O in water

S: Sucrose in water

A. P > Q > R > S B. S > R > Q > P

C. S > Q > R > P D. P > R > Q > S

8. Two matrices are given as $X = \begin{pmatrix} 1 & 5 \\ 3 & 7 \end{pmatrix}$ and $Y = \begin{pmatrix} 2 & 4 \\ 6 & 0 \end{pmatrix}$. If X^T is the transpose of X then what would be X^TY?

A. $\begin{pmatrix} 20 & 52 \\ 4 & 20 \end{pmatrix}$ B. $\begin{pmatrix} 20 & 4 \\ 52 & 20 \end{pmatrix}$

C. $\begin{pmatrix} 32 & 4 \\ 48 & 12 \end{pmatrix}$ D. $\begin{pmatrix} 44 & 28 \\ 12 & 12 \end{pmatrix}$

9. Addition of 1.0 g of a compound to 10 g of water increases the boiling point by 0.3°C. The amount of compound needed to prepare a 500 ml or 0.1 M solution is (given: assume negligible dissociation or association of the compound, boiling point constant K_b of water = 0.513 K kg mol^{-1})
A. 0.855 g B. 17.1 g
C. 8.55 g D. 85.5 g

10. The molar conductivity of 0.009 M aqueous solution of a weak acid (HA) is 0.005 S m^2 mol^{-1} and the limiting molar conductivity of HA is 0.05 Sm^2 mol^{-1} at 298 K. Assuming activity coefficients to be unity, the acid dissociation constant (K_a) of HA at this temperature is
A. 1×10^{-4} B. 0.1
C. 9×10^{-4} D. 1.1×10^{-5}

11. The colour of potassium dichromate is due to
A. d-d transition
B. transition in K^+ ion
C. ligand-to-metal charge transfer
D. metal-to-ligand charge transfer

12. Which one of the following configuration will show John-Teller distortion in an octahedral field?
A. high spin d^8 B. high spin d^4
C. high spin d^5 D. low spin d^6

13. B_2H_6 and B_4H_{10}, respectively, are examples of
A. *nido* and *arachno* boranes
B. *nido* and *closo* boranes
C. *closo* and *arachno* boranes
D. *nido* boranes

14. Which of the following has a square planar geometry according to the VSEPR theory?
A. XeO_2F_2 B. SF_4
C. BF_4^- D. XeF_4

15. The structure of rock salt consists of
A. a cubic close-packed array of anions with cations in all the octahedral sites
B. a cubic close-packed array of cations with anions in all the tetrahedral sites
C. a hexagonal close-packed array of anions with cations in all the octahedral sites
D. a cubic close-packed array of anions with cations in all the tetrahedral sites

16. Among lithium, nitrogen, carbon and oxygen, which element has the highest first ionization potential?
A. lithium B. nitrogen
C. carbon D. oxygen

17. In which of the following C-H bond has the highest 's' character?
A. acetylene B. ethylene
C. methane D. CH radical

18. Which one of the following is an electron-deficient molecule according to the octet rule?
A. CH_4 B. $H_3N{:}BH_3$
C. AlH_3 D. GeH_4

19. Which one of the following has the highest lattice energy?
A. LiCl B. $CaCl_2$
C. LiF D. KCl

20. At room temperature, HCl is a gas while HF is a liquid because
A. of a strong bond between H and F in HF
B. HF is less acidic as compared to HCl
C. of strong intermolecular H-bonding in HF
D. HCl is less acidic as compared to HF

21. Benzene and Dewar benzene are

benzene Dewar benzene

A. canonical forms
B. structural isomers
C. tautomers
D. conformational isomers

22. The IUPAC name of the following compound is

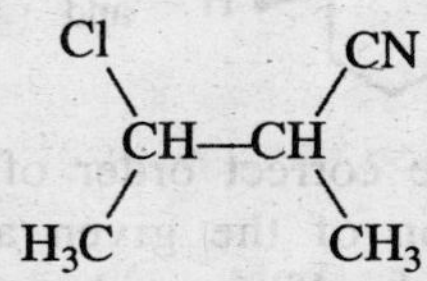

A. 2-cyano-3-chlorobutane
B. 2-chloro-3-cyanobutane
C. 2-methyl-3-chlorobutanenitrile
D. 3-chloro-2-methylbutanenitrile

23. Which chemical test will distinguish the compounds shown below?

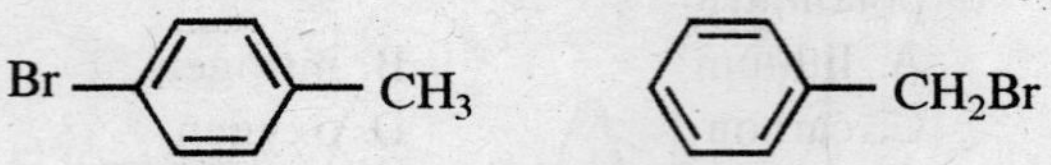

A. Beilstein's flame test
B. Ethanolic silver nitrate test
C. Sodium fusion test
D. Fehling's test

24. The reaction of the bromo compound shown below with sodium ethoxide gives predominantly

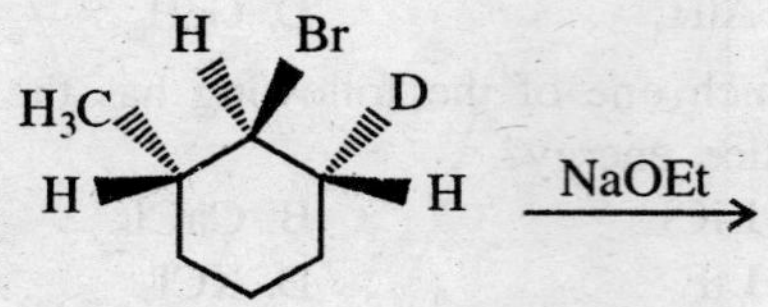

A. 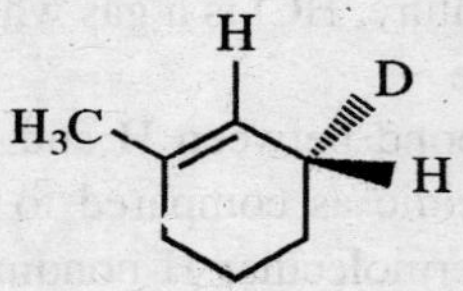

B. 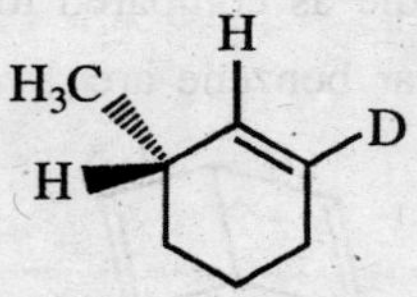

C. 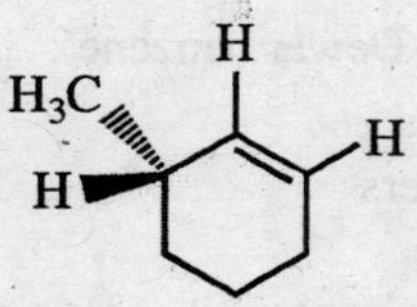

D. 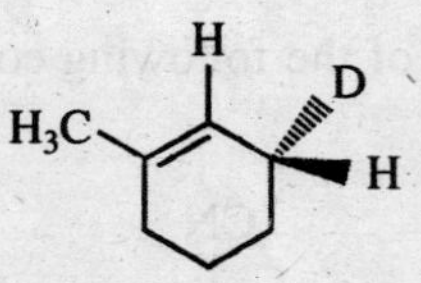 and 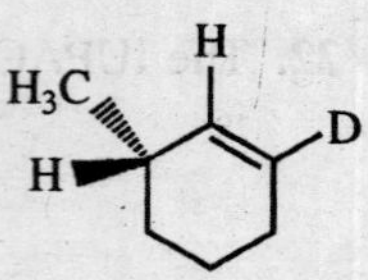

25. Choose the correct order of reactivity for dehydration of the given alcohols using concentrated sulfuric acid.

A. 2-methylpropan-2-ol > 2-butanol > 1-butanol
B. 2-methylpropan-2-ol > 1-butanol > 2-butanol
C. 2-butanol > 2-methylpropan-2-ol > 1-butanol
D. 1-butanol > 2-butanol > 2-methylpropan-2-ol

26. The titration curve of alanine hydrochloride is given below.

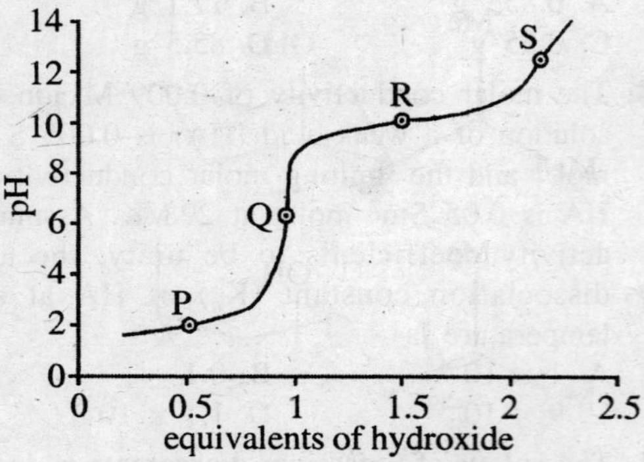

The position in the graph that corresponds to the isoelectric point of alanine is

A. P B. Q
C. R D. S

27. The absolute configurations at the two chiral centers in D-Ribulose are

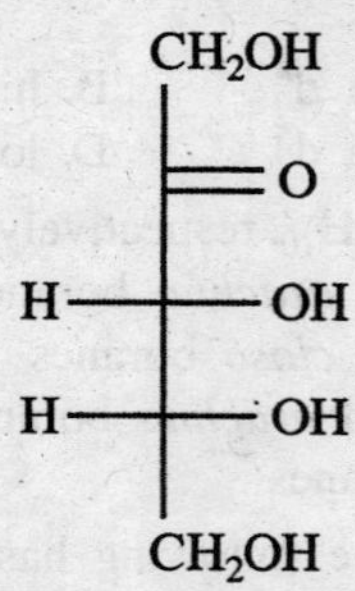

D-Ribulose

A. 3R, 4R B. 3R, 4S
C. 3S, 4R D. 3S, 4S

28. The most stable conformation of the molecule shown below is correctly represented by

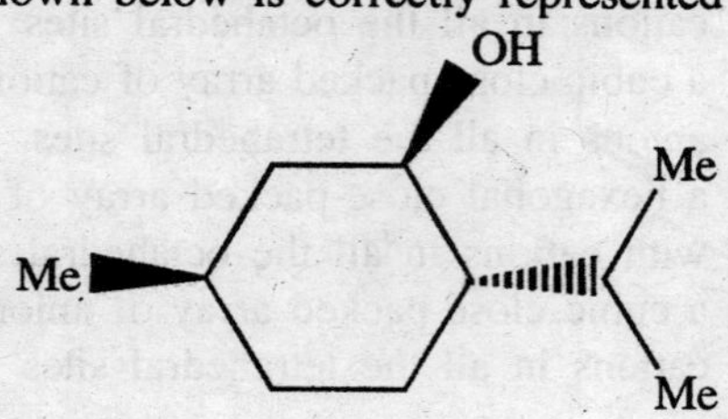

A. 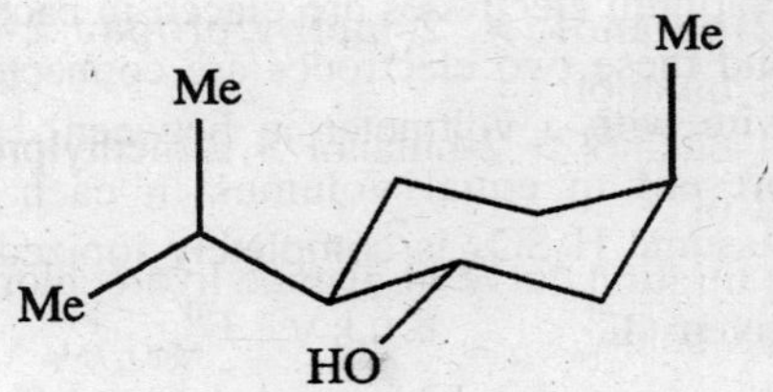

B. 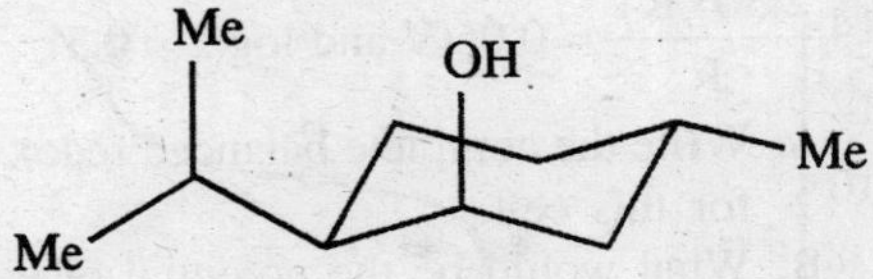

C. 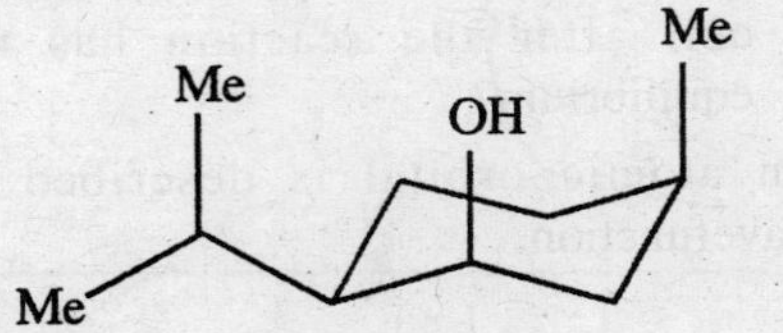

D. 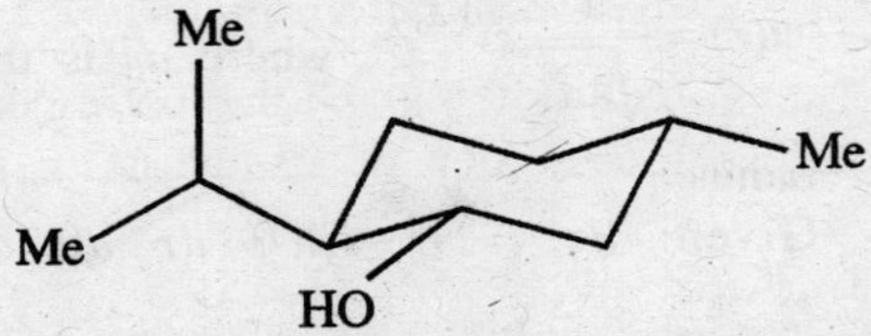

29. Thermal rearrangement of the following compound would give

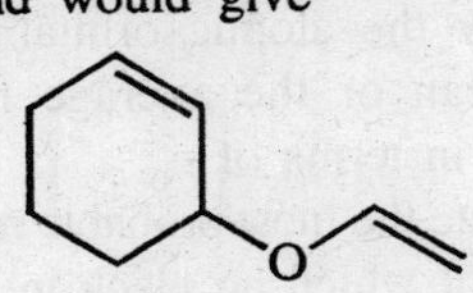

A. 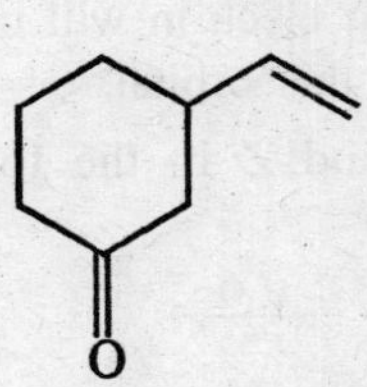

B. 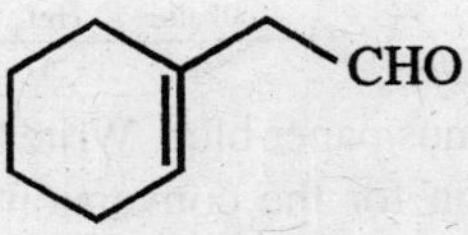

C. 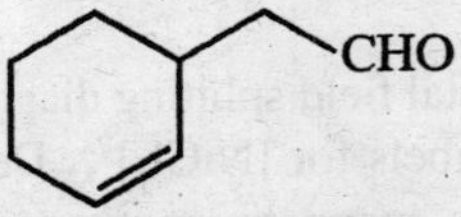

D. 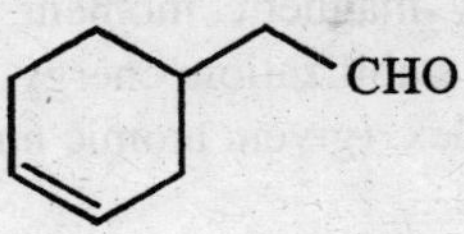

30. The energy profile diagram that corresponds to 1, 2-dihydroxyethane for rotation around the C-C bond is

A. 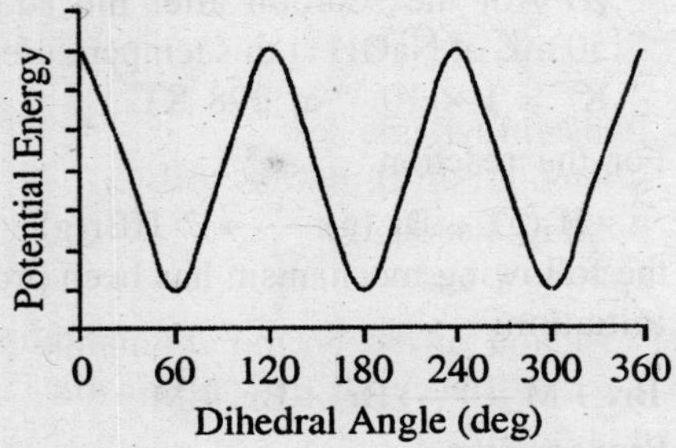

B. 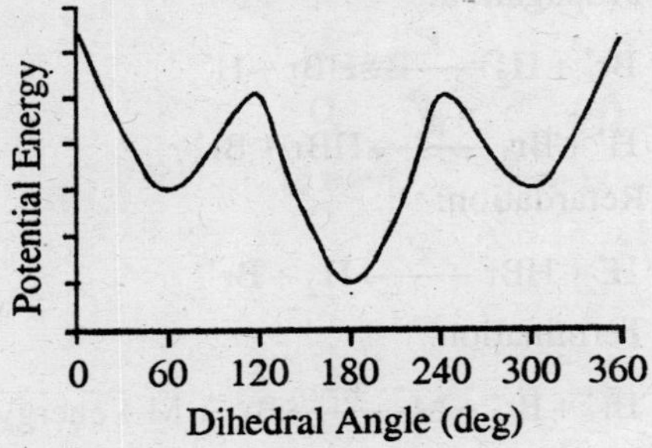

C. 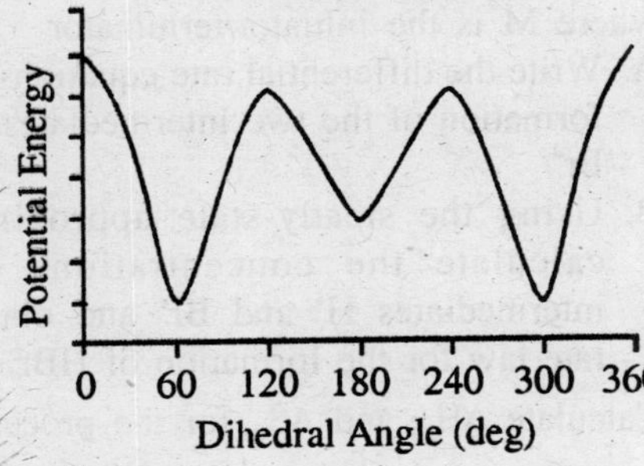

D. 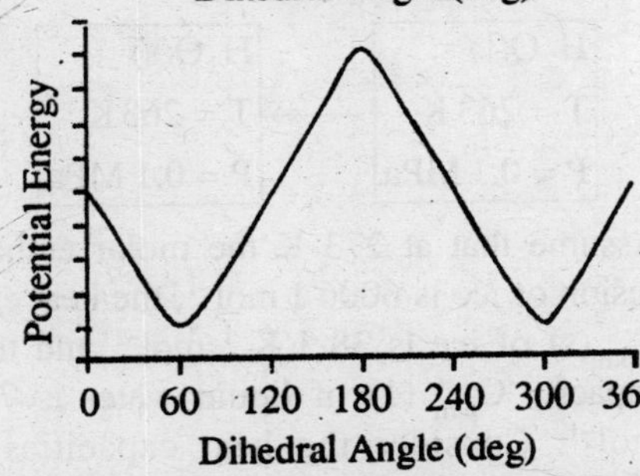

31. A. Equilibrium constant for a reaction doubles as the temperature is increased from 300 K to 600 K. Calculate the standard reaction enthalpy (in kJ mol^{-1}) assuming it to be constant in this temperature range. (given: $R = 8.3\ JK^{-1}\ mol^{-1}$, $\ln 2 = 0.7$).

B. A 50 mL solution of 0.1 M monoprotic acid ($K_a = 1 \times 10^{-5}$ at 298 K) is titrated with 0.1 M NaOH at 298 K. Calculate the (H^+) of the solution after the addition of 50 mL of NaOH at this temperature. (given: $K_w = 1 \times 10^{-14}$ at 298 K).

32. For the reaction

$$H_2(g) + Br_2(g) \longrightarrow 2\ HBr(g)$$

the following mechanism has been proposed.

Initiation:

$$Br_2 + M \xrightarrow{K_i} Br^{\bullet} + Br^{\bullet} + M$$

Propagation:

$$Br^{\bullet} + H_2 \xrightarrow{K_p} HBr + H^{\bullet}$$

$$H^{\bullet} + Br_2 \xrightarrow{K_p} HBr + Br^{\bullet}$$

Retardation:

$$H^{\bullet} + HBr \xrightarrow{K_r} H_2 + Br^{\bullet}$$

Termination:

$$Br^{\bullet} + Br^{\bullet} + M \xrightarrow{K_t} Br_2 + M + \text{energy}$$

where M is the initiator/terminator

A. Write the differential rate equations for the formation of the two intermediates $H^{\bullet}$ and $Br^{\bullet}$.

B. Using the steady-state approximation, calculate the concentrations of the intermediates $H^{\bullet}$ and $Br^{\bullet}$ and obtain the rate law for the formation of HBr.

33. Calculate ΔH_m and ΔS_m for the process

$H_2O(l)$		$H_2O(s)$
T = 263 K	$\longrightarrow$	T = 263 K
P = 0.1 MPa		P = 0.1 MPa

Assume that at 273 K the molar enthalpy of fusion of ice is 6006 J mol^{-1}, the heat capacity $C_{p,m}(s)$ of ice is 38 J K^{-1} mol^{-1} and the heat capacity $C_{p,m}$ (l) of liquid water is 76 JK^{-1} mol^{-1}. Consider the heat capacities to be constants. (given: ln 263 = 5.57 and ln 273 = 5.61)

34. Two beakers, one containing 0.02 M $KMnO_4$, 0.2 M $MnSO_4$ and 0.5 M H_2SO_4, and another containing 0.15 M $FeSO_4$ and 0.05 M $Fe_2(SO_4)_3$, are connected by a salt-bridge. Platinum electrodes are placed in each beaker and these two electrodes are connected via a wire with a voltmeter in between. H_2SO_4 is present in equal volumes in each beaker. Assume H_2SO_4 is completely ionized.

given: $E^0_{Fe^{3+}/Fe^{2+}} = 0.8$ V, $E^0_{MnO_4/Mn^{2+}} = 1.5$ V,

$$\frac{2.303\ RT}{F} = 0.06 \text{ V and } \log 2 = 0.3$$

A. Write the complete balanced redox reaction for this cell.

B. What would be the potential of each half-cell after the reaction has reached equilibrium?

35. An atomic orbital is described by the wavefunction

$$\psi(r) = \frac{1}{\sqrt{\pi a_0^3}} e^{-\left(\frac{r}{a_0}\right)}$$, where a_0 is the Bohr radius.

Given: $d\tau = r^2 \sin\theta\ dr\ d\theta\ d\phi$ and

$$\int_0^{\infty} r^n e^{-\beta r} dr = \frac{n!}{\beta^{n+1}}$$ (n is a positive integer)

A. Identify the atomic orbital and calculate the mean or the average radius of this orbital in terms of a_0.

B. Calculate the most probable radius (in terms of a_0) at which an electron will be found when it occupies this orbital.

36. Identify W, X, Y and Z in the following sequence.

$$Li + W(g) \xrightarrow{\text{heat}} \underset{\text{(red)}}{X} \xrightarrow{H_2O}$$

$$Y(g) \xrightarrow{\text{alkaline } K_2HgI_4} \underset{\text{(brown)}}{Z}$$

Y turns moist litmus paper blue. Write balanced chemical equation for the conversion of Y to Z.

37. A. Draw the crystal field splitting diagram with appropriate labels for $[NiCl_4]^{2-}$. Determine the spin only magnetic moment and the crystal field stabilization energy (CFSE) for this complex. (given: atomic number of Ni = 28).

B. Write the balanced equations for the reactions involved in the iodometric estimation of Cu^{2+} using thiosulphate.

38. A. In the reaction sequence given below P is an anionic Fe(II) complex.

$$P \xrightarrow{\text{aq. } NO_2^-} \underset{\text{(brown)}}{Q} \xrightarrow{\text{aq. } S^{2-}} \underset{\text{(purple)}}{R}$$

Identify P, Q and R.

B. Draw a properly labeled unit cell diagram of CsCl. Show through calculations that there is only one CsCl per unit cell.

39. A. Write the balanced chemical equations for the reactions involved in the synthesis of borazine using ammonium chloride as one of the starting materials. Write the structure of borazine.

B. Draw Lewis structures of SF_4 and NO_3^-.

40. A. Complete the following sequence by identifying E, F and G.

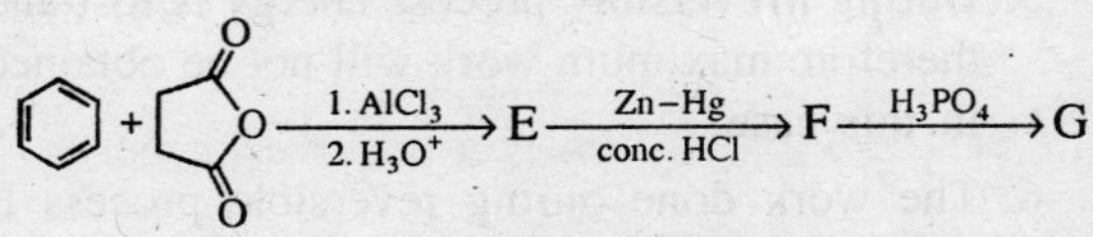

B. Identify H and I in the reactions below.

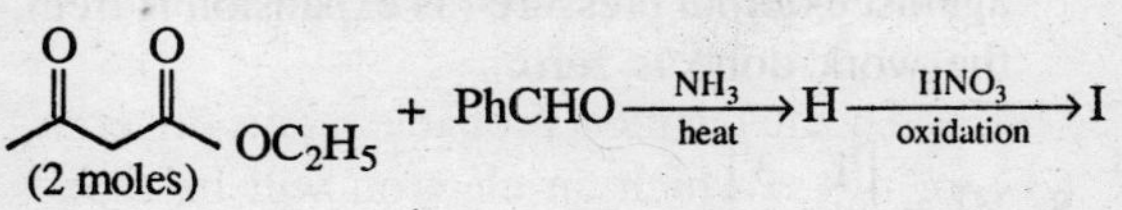

41. A. Identify the products J, K and L in the following reactions. Lassigne's test for L shows the presence of nitrogen only.

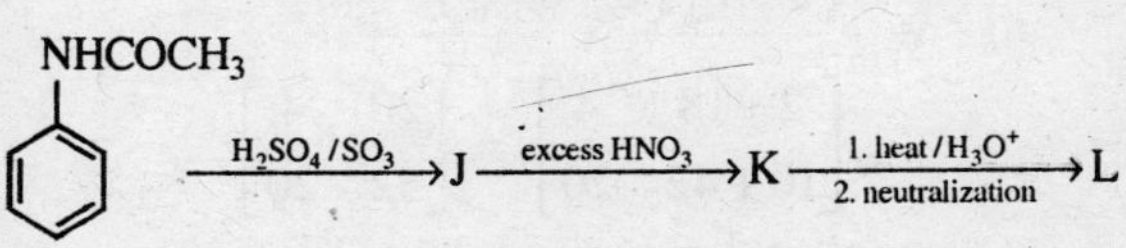

B. Write the structures of M and N in the following reactions.

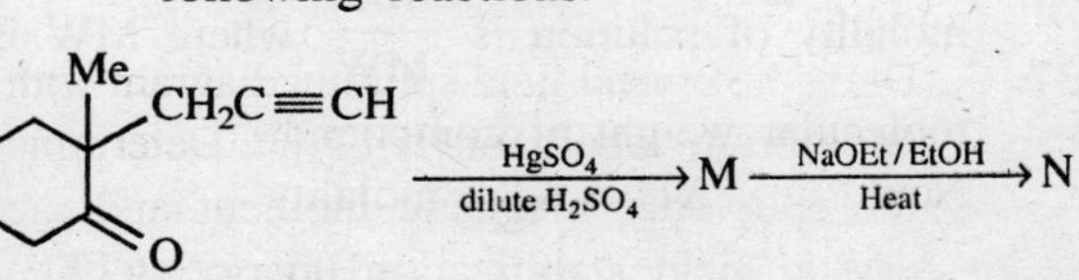

42. A. Write the structures of P, Q and R in the given reaction sequence.

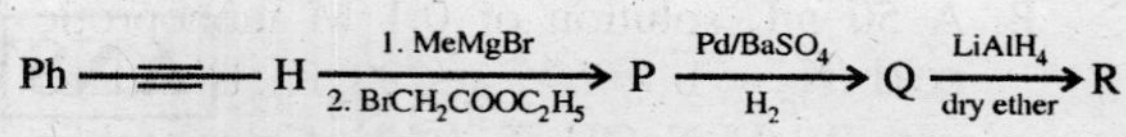

B. Identify S and T in the reactions given below.

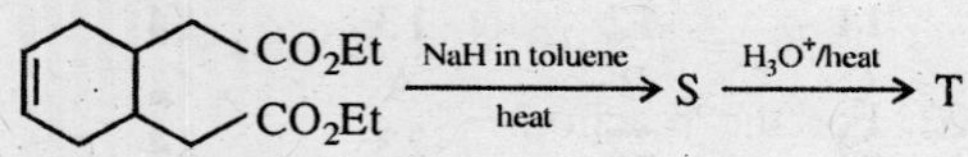

43. A. Identify X, Y and Z in the following reactions

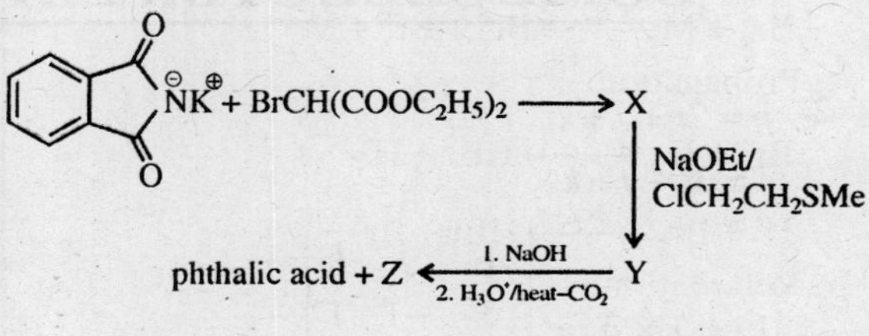

B. Suggest a suitable mechanism for the following reaction.

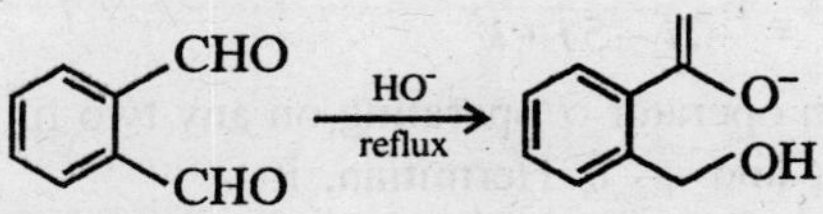

44. Consider the following reactions for a compound with molecular formula $C_{10}H_{16}$.

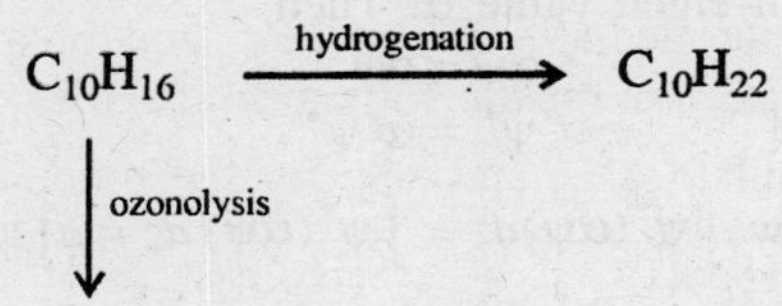

2 moles of HCHO + 1 mole of acetone + 1 mole of

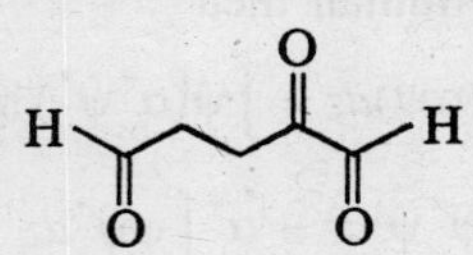

A. Write structures that are consistent with the above data for the formula $C_{10}H_{16}$.

B. Given that *myrcene* is a terpene and has the molecular formula $C_{10}H_{16}$, using the isoprene rule identify the correct structure of *myrcene* among the structures elucidated in part (A).

ANSWERS

1	2	3	4	5	6	7	8	9	10
B	B	D	C	D	C	A	B	B	A
11	**12**	**13**	**14**	**15**	**16**	**17**	**18**	**19**	**20**
C	B	A	C	A	B	A	C	C	C
21	**22**	**23**	**24**	**25**	**26**	**27**	**28**	**29**	**30**
A	D	B	C	A	B	A	D	C	C

SOME SELECTED EXPLANATORY ANSWERS

2. $\vec{p} = 2\hat{i} + \hat{j} + \hat{k}$

$\vec{r} = 3\hat{i} - \hat{j} + \hat{k}$

$$L = \vec{r} \times \vec{p} = \begin{vmatrix} i & j & \hat{k} \\ 3 & -1 & 1 \\ -2 & 1 & 1 \end{vmatrix}$$

$$= \hat{i}(-2) - \hat{j}(5) + \hat{k}(1)$$

$$= -2\hat{i} - 5\hat{j} + \hat{k}$$

3. An operator α operating on any two functions ψ_1 and ψ_2 is Hermitian, it

$$\int \psi_2^*(\alpha\psi_1)dz = \int \psi_1(\alpha^*\psi_2^*)\, dz$$

Let ψ be an eigen function of an operator α with eigen value α. Then

$$\alpha\psi = \alpha\psi$$

and $$\alpha^*\psi^* = \alpha^*\psi^*$$

Now $\int \psi^*(\alpha\psi)dz = \int \psi^*(\alpha\psi)\, dz = a\int \psi^*\psi dz$

and $\int \psi(\alpha^*\psi^*)dz = \int \psi(\alpha^*\psi^*)\, dz = a^*\int \psi\psi^* dz$

If α is Hermitian then

$$\int \psi^*(\alpha\psi)dz = \int \psi(\alpha^*\psi^*)\, dz$$

$$\therefore \quad \alpha\int \psi^*\psi\, dz = \alpha^*\int \psi\psi^* dz$$

or $$\alpha = \alpha^*$$

which is true only when α is real.

4. $J = \sqrt{J(J+1)}\ \hbar$

$$E = \frac{J^2}{2I} = \frac{J(J+1)\,\hbar^2}{2I}$$

$$= \frac{J(J+1)}{2mr^2}\hbar^2 \qquad (\because\ I = mr^2)$$

The above is equal to $\dfrac{10\hbar^2}{mr^2}$

Solving we get J = 4

∴ Degeneracy of state = 2J + 1

= 2 × 4 + 1 = 9

5. During irreversibly process energy is lost and therefore maximum work will not be obtained in this case.

6. The work done during reversible process is given by ∫Pdv. Since here no work is done against external pressure (as expansion is free), the work done is zero.

8. $X^T = \begin{bmatrix} 1 & 3 \\ 5 & 7 \end{bmatrix}$

$$X^TY = \begin{bmatrix} 1 & 3 \\ 5 & 7 \end{bmatrix}\begin{bmatrix} 2 & 4 \\ 6 & 0 \end{bmatrix}$$

$$= \begin{bmatrix} 2+18 & 4 \\ 10+42 & 20 \end{bmatrix} = \begin{bmatrix} 20 & 4 \\ 52 & 20 \end{bmatrix}$$

9. 1 gm of compound to 10 gm of water mean molality of solution is $\dfrac{100}{MW}$ where MW is molecular weight of compound.

Now $\Delta T_b = K_b \times$ molality

$$.3 = .513 \times \frac{100}{MW}$$

$\Rightarrow$ MW = 171

$\therefore$ For .1 M solution 17.1 gm has to be added to 1000 ml. For 500 ml divide it by 2.

10. $\Lambda_m = .005 \text{ Sm}^2 \text{ mol}^{-1}$
C = .009 M.

$$\text{Degree of dissociation} = \frac{\Lambda_m}{\Lambda_m^\circ}$$

$$= \frac{.005}{.05} = .1$$

$$HA \rightleftharpoons H^+ + A^{-1}$$

$$(1-\alpha)C \quad \alpha C \quad \alpha C$$

$$K_a = \frac{\alpha^2 C}{1-\alpha} = \frac{.1^2 \times .009}{.9} = 10^{-4}$$

12. 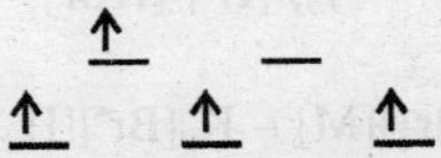

In this high spin d^4 configuration, the symmetry is absent and therefore it will show John – Teller distortion.

13. Nido borane = $B_n H_{n+4}$
$\Rightarrow$ B_2H_6 is nido borane
Arachno borane = $B_n H_{n+6}$
$\Rightarrow$ B_4H_{10} is arachno borane

16. Nitrogen has half filled orbital and therefore it is very stable.

22. –CN has higher priority than Halo groups.

23. 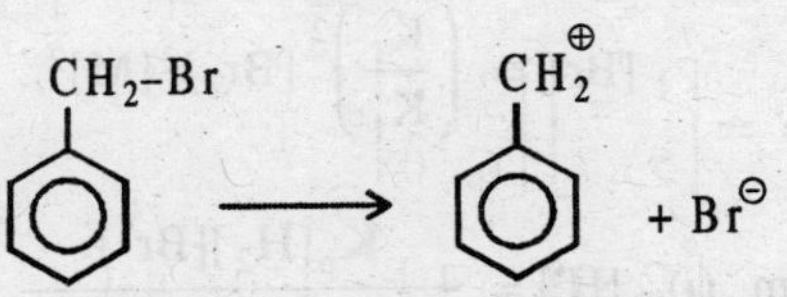

Carbocation is resonance stabilized and Br^- react with Ag to give AgBr ppt. But other compound will not give this test as the bond between C and Br has some double bond character and therefore it is strong. The double bond character is acquired as shown below.

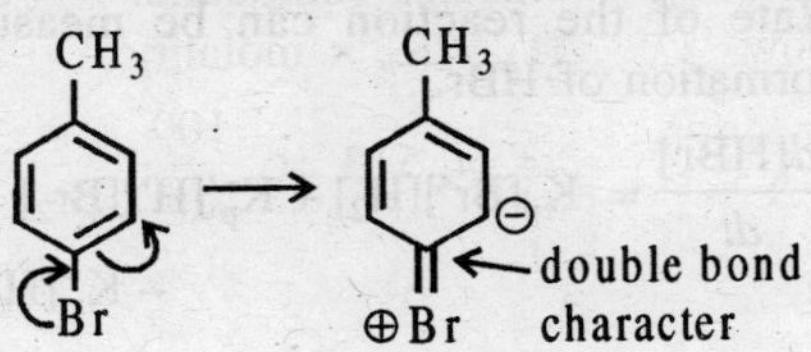

24. E-2 elimination required anti periplanar structure formation. Since D is opposite to Br, its elimination only ensure above condition.

25. 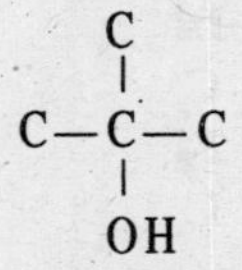

(2-methyl propan-2-ol)

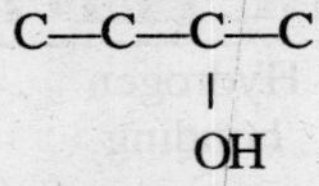

(2 butanol)

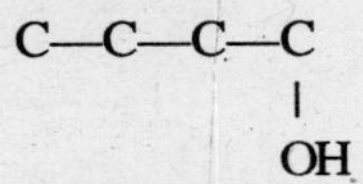

(1 butanol)

2-methyl propan-2-ol will give tertiary carbocation which undergo dehydration readily. While primary undergo dehydration less readily.

26. The isoelectric point of amino acid is the pH at which it has no net charge. In case of alanine pI is average of pK_a values of carbonyl group and the protonated amino group as it does not have an ionisable side chain.

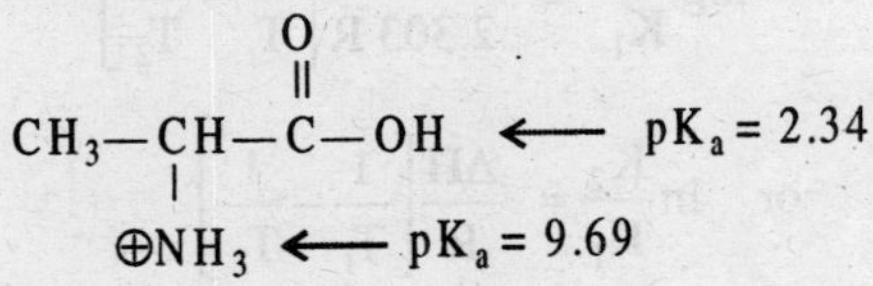

$$pI = \frac{2.34 + 9.69}{2} = 6.02$$

28. All groups occupy equatorial positions and therefore it gives most stable conformation.

29. 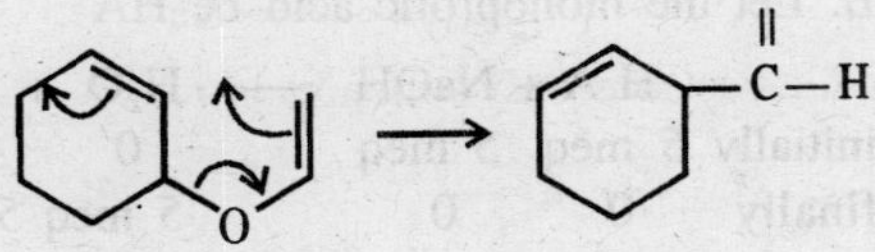

30. 1-2 dihydroxyethane

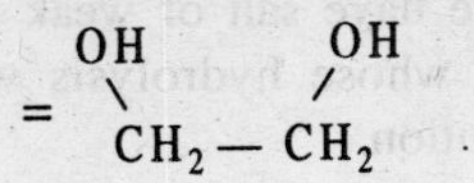

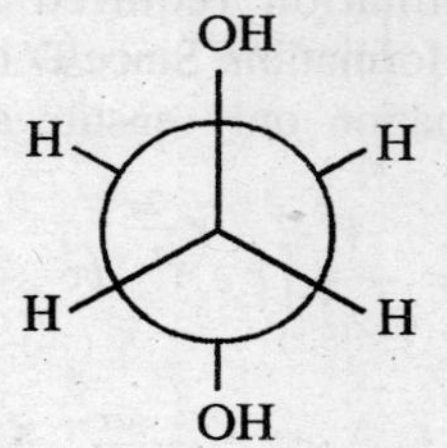

(one of conformation)

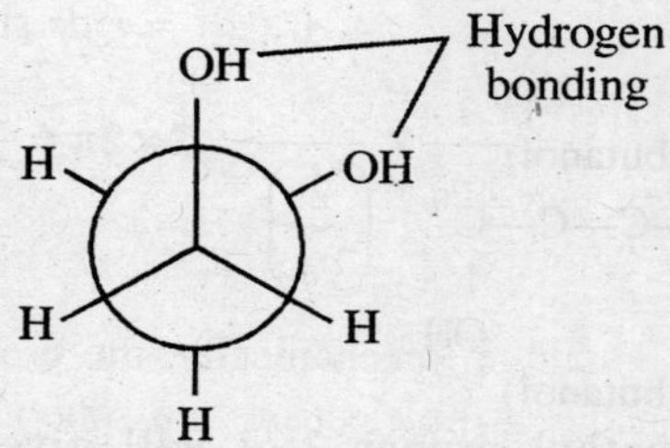

Such conformation will be stable due to possible hydrogen bonding. Therefore, a potential energy of such conformer will be less at 60° and 300°.

31. A. The equilibrium constant dependence upon temperature is given by equation

$$\log\frac{K_2}{K_1} = \frac{\Delta H}{2.303\,R}\left[\frac{1}{T_1}-\frac{1}{T_2}\right]$$

or $$\ln\frac{K_2}{K_1} = \frac{\Delta H}{R}\left[\frac{1}{T_1}-\frac{1}{T_2}\right]$$

$$0.7 = \frac{\Delta H}{R}\left[\frac{1}{T_1}-\frac{1}{T_2}\right]$$

Here $T_2 = 600K$, $T_1 = 300$ K

and $R = 8.3\ JK^{-1}\ mol^{-1}$

B. Let the monoprotic acid be HA

	H A	+ NaOH	⟶ H_2O	+ NaA
initially	5 meq	5 meq	0	0
finally	0	0	5 meq	5 meq

$K_a = 10^{-5}$ indicate that acid is weak. Therefore we have salt of weak acid and strong base whose hydrolysis will give alkaline solution.

Since the volume has been double, the concentration of salt will be reduced to half i.e. .1/2 = .05

The pH of the solution after hydrolysis will be given by

$$pH = 7 + \frac{1}{2}\ PK_a + \frac{1}{2}\ \log C$$

$$= 7 + \frac{1}{2}[PK_a + \log C]$$

$$= 7 + \frac{1}{2}\ [5 + \log .05]$$

$$= 8.85$$

32. A. $$\frac{d[H^\bullet]}{dt} = K_p[Br^\bullet][H_2] - K_p'[H^\bullet][Br_2] - K_r\,[H^\bullet]\,[HBr] \quad ...\ (i)$$

$$\frac{d[Br^\bullet]}{dt} = 2K_1[Br_2][M] - K_p[Br^\bullet][H_2] + K_p'\,[H^\bullet]\,[Br_2] + K_r\,[H^\bullet][HBr] - 2\,K_t\,[Br^\bullet]^2\ ...\ (ii)$$

B. Under steady state $\frac{d[H^\bullet]}{dt}$ and $\frac{d[Br^\bullet]}{dt}$ will be zero (i.e. their concentration will not change with respect to time)

Adding equation (*i*) and (*ii*) we get

$$2K_1[Br_2][M] = 2K_t\,[Br^\bullet]^2$$

$$\Rightarrow \quad [Br^\bullet] = \left(\frac{K_1}{K_t}\right)^{\frac{1}{2}}[Br_2]^{\frac{1}{2}}[M]^{\frac{1}{2}} \quad ...(iii)$$

From (*i*) $$[H^\bullet] = \frac{K_p[H_2][Br^\bullet]}{K_p'[Br_2]+K_r[HBr]} \quad ...(iv)$$

$$= \frac{K_p[H_2]}{K_p'[Br_2]+K_r[HBr]}\times\left(\frac{K_1}{K_t}\right)^{\frac{1}{2}}[Br_2]^{\frac{1}{2}}[M]^{\frac{1}{2}} \quad ...(v)$$

Rate of the reaction can be measured by tormation of HBr.

$$\frac{d[HBr]}{dt} = K_p[Br^\bullet][H_2] + K_p'[H^\bullet][Br_2] - K_r\,[H^\bullet]\,[HBr]$$

$$= K_p[Br^\bullet][H_2] + \frac{\{K_p'[Br_2] - K_r[HBr]\}K_p[H_2][Br^\bullet]}{K_p'[Br_2] + K_r[HBr]}$$

$$= K_p[H_2][Br^\bullet]\left[\frac{2K_p'[Br_2]}{K_p'[Br_2] + K_r[HBr]}\right]$$

$$= \frac{2K_p'K_p[H_2][Br_2]}{K_p'[Br_2] + K_r[HBr]} \times \left(\frac{K_1}{K_t}\right)^{\frac{1}{2}} [Br_2]^{\frac{1}{2}}[M]^{\frac{1}{2}}$$

33. To calculate the ΔH_m for the above process, the process can be broken into

$H_2O(l)$, T = 263 K, P = 0.1 MPa	$\xrightarrow{1}$	$H_2O(l)$, T = 273 K, P = 0.1 MPa	$\xrightarrow{2}$	$H_2O(s)$, T = 273 K, P = 0.1 MPa
				$\downarrow 3$
				$H_2O(s)$, T = 263 K, P = 0.1 MPa

Process 1

$$\Delta H_{m_1} = C_p\Delta T = 76 \times 10 = 760$$

$$\Delta S_{m_1} = \int_{263}^{273} C_p \frac{dT}{T} = 76 \ln \frac{273}{263}$$

Process 2

$$\Delta H_{m_2} = L = 6006 \text{ J mol}^{-1}$$

$$\Delta S_{m_2} = \frac{L}{T} = \frac{6006}{273} = 22$$

Process 3

$$\Delta H_{m_3} = C_p\Delta T = 38 \times (-10) = -380$$

$$\Delta S_{m_3} = C_p \ln \frac{T_2}{T_1} = C_p \ln \frac{263}{273} = 38 \times \ln \frac{263}{273}$$

$\therefore$ ΔH_m for process = $\Delta H_{m_1} + \Delta H_{m_2} + \Delta H_{m_3}$

and $\Delta S_m = \Delta S_{m_1} + \Delta S_{m_2} + \Delta S_{m_3}$

35. A. $\langle r \rangle = \int_0^\infty \psi^* r \psi \, d\tau$ $\quad$ ($\because$ ψ is normalised)

$$= \frac{1}{\pi a_0^3}\int_0^\infty r\, e^{-\frac{2r}{a_0}} d\tau$$

$$= \frac{1}{\pi a_0^3}\int_0^\infty r^3 e^{-\frac{2r}{a_0}} dr \int_0^\pi \sin\theta \, d\theta \int_0^{2\pi} d\phi$$

($\because$ $d\tau = r^2 dr \sin\theta \, d\theta \, d\phi$)

$$= \frac{1}{\pi a_0^3} \times \frac{3!}{\left(\frac{2}{a_0}\right)^4} \times 2 \times 2\pi = \frac{3}{2} a_0$$

B. Quantum mechanically, the probability of finding the electron in a spherical shell of thickness dr at a distance r from the nucleus is given by

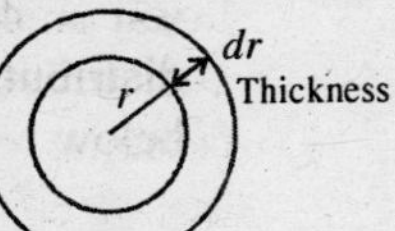

$$P(r)\, dr = 4\pi |\psi|^2 r^2 dr$$

$$= 4\pi r^2 \left(\frac{1}{\pi a_0^3}\right) e^{-\frac{2r}{a_0}} dr$$

For the probability to be maximum

$$\frac{dP(r)}{dr} = \frac{4}{a_0^3}\left(\frac{-2r^2}{a_0} + 2r\right) e^{-\frac{2r}{a_0}} = 0$$

Since the Bohr radius $a_0 \neq 0$ and the exponential is also $\neq 0$ hence

$$\frac{-2r^2}{a_0} + 2r = 0 \Rightarrow r = a_0$$

According to Bohr's theory of hydrogen atom, the distance of the electron from the nucleus in ground state is exactly equal to a_0. But according to Heisenberg's uncertainty principle, the electron cannot be exactly located in its orbit. Hence quantum mechanically, while the most probable distance is a_0, the average distance is $3a_0/2$ i.e., average distance is 50% greater than the Bohr result.

36. $6\,Li + N_2 \longrightarrow 2\,Li_3N$
(W) (X)

$Li_3N + 3H_2O \longrightarrow 3\,LiOH + NH_3$
Y(g)

$2\,K_2HgI_4 + NH_3 + 3KOH \longrightarrow$ 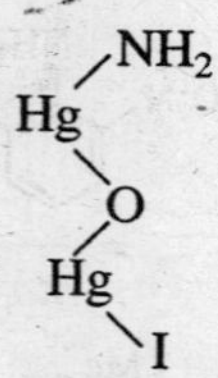 $+ 7\,KI + 2\,H_2O$

Iodide of million's base (Brown PPt)

Y i.e. NH_3 is basic in nature and therefore turn moist litmus paper blue.

37. A. This ion has Ni^{2+} ion which has $3d^8$ configuration. Since Cl^- ion is a weak ligand, $[NiCl_4]^{2-}$ ion in which C.N of Ni^{2+} ion = 4 has tetrahedral geometry. The distribution of electron has been shown below.

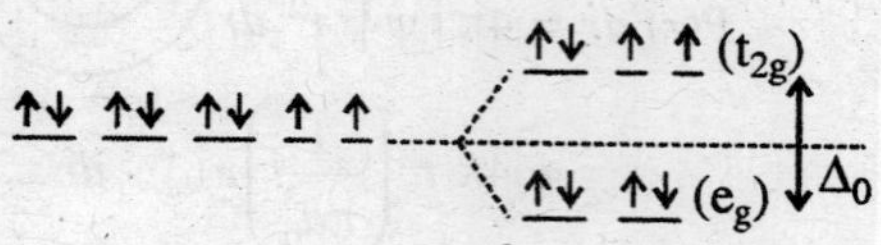

$$CFSF = \left(4\times\frac{3}{5} - 4\times\frac{2}{5}\right)\Delta_0$$

$$= \frac{4}{5}\Delta_0$$

$$S = \frac{1}{2} + \frac{1}{2} = 1 \text{ (rest others are paired)}$$

∴ Magnetic moment due to spin

$$= \sqrt{S(S+1)}\,\hbar$$

Here we have two unpaired electron

$$\therefore \quad \mu = \sqrt{n(n+2)} \text{ B.M.}$$

$$= \sqrt{2\times 4} \text{ B.M.} = 2.83 \text{ B.M.}$$

B. In iodometric titrations, an oxidising agent is allowed to react in neutral or acidic medium, with excess of potassium iodide to liberate free iodine. Free iodine is titrated against a standard reducing agent usually with sodium thiosulphate.

$$2CuSO_4 + 4KI \longrightarrow Cu_2I_2 + 2K_2SO_4 + I_2$$

$$I_2 + Na_2S_2O_3 \longrightarrow 2NaI + Na_2S_4O_6$$

38. A. The famous ring test for nitrate and nitrite ions is based on the fact that NO gas is first generated by the action of H_2SO_4 on nitrate or nitrite ion. The gas then combines with Fe^{2+} ion to yield a brown complex $[Fe(H_2O)_5NO]^{2+}$. (ring test)

The second part of reaction is used in the qualitative analysis in the detection of soluble sulphides with which it gives deep purple colouration

$$Na_2S + Na_2[Fe(CN)_5NO] \rightarrow Na_4[Fe(CN)_5NOS]$$
Purple colour(R)

∴ P is $[Fe(CN)_6]^{3-}$

$$[Fe(CN)_6]^{3-} + NO \rightarrow [Fe(CN)_5NO]$$
(P) (Q)

B.

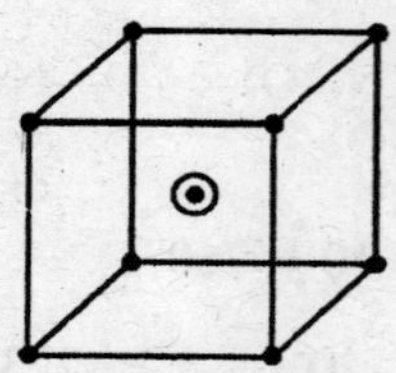

(Unit cell representation of CsCl)

Cs is at the centre and therefore does not contribute to any other unit cell. Therefore CsCl has one Cs atom per unit cell.

Cl^- ions form the simple cubic arrangement. They are eight in numbers in unit cell. But each Cl^- ion contribute to eight other unit cell. Therefore contribution of Cl^- in each unit cell is $\frac{1}{8}$. Total number of Cl^- is eight in unit cell, therefore, Cl^- ion per unit cell $= \frac{1}{8}\times 8 = 1$.

39. A. Borazine can be prepared by heating together BCl_3 and NH_4Cl. The initial product formed is trichloroborazine which on reduction with $NaBH_4$ yields borazine. It can also be prepared by treating $NaBH_4$ with NH_4Cl.

$3BCl_3 + 3NH_4Cl \rightarrow Cl_3B_3N_3H_3 + 9HCl.$

The B—Cl bond is subsequently converted to B—H bond.

$2Cl_3B_3H_3N_3 + 6\ NaBH_4 \rightarrow 2B_3H_6N_3 + 3B_2H_6 + 6NaCl.$

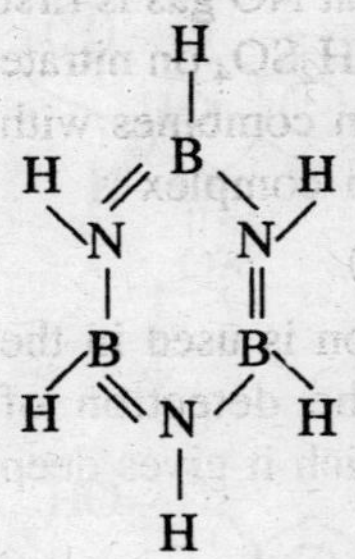

In this structure, the valence shell orbitals of both boron and nitrogen atoms are Sp^2 hybridised. Each nitrogen atom has a lone pair of electrons while each boron atom has an empty *p* orbital. The bonding in borazine is dative and it arises from the sidewise overlapping of fully filled *p* orbitals of nitrogen and empty *p* orbitals of boron. Because of similarity of the structures of borazine and benzene, borazine is also known as inorganic benzene. However, in case of borazine, electrons are only partially delocalised.

B. NO_3^-

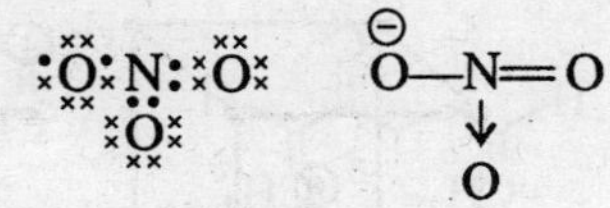

SF_4

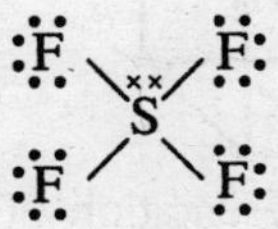

40. A.

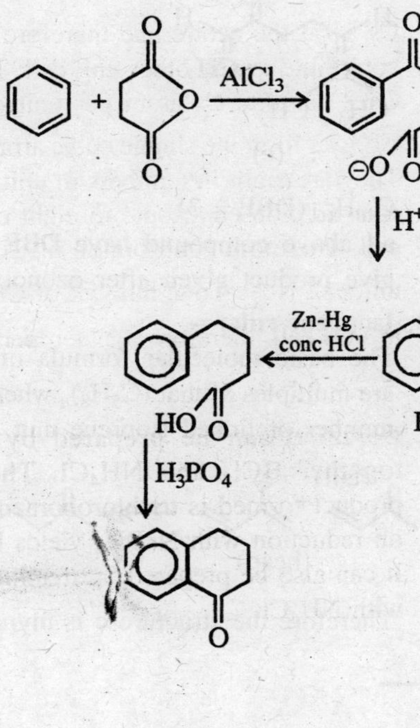

41. A.

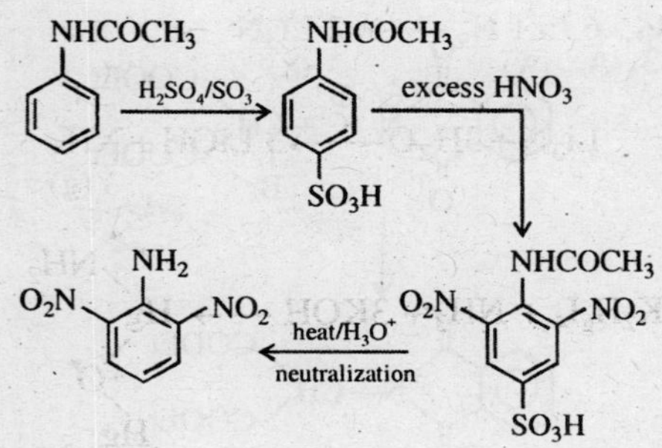

B.

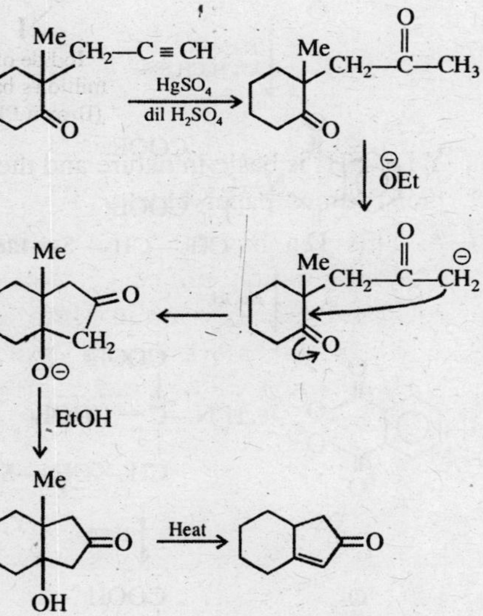

42. A.

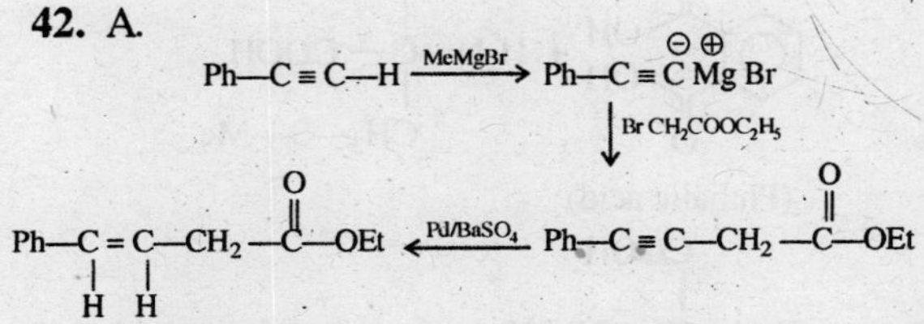

B.

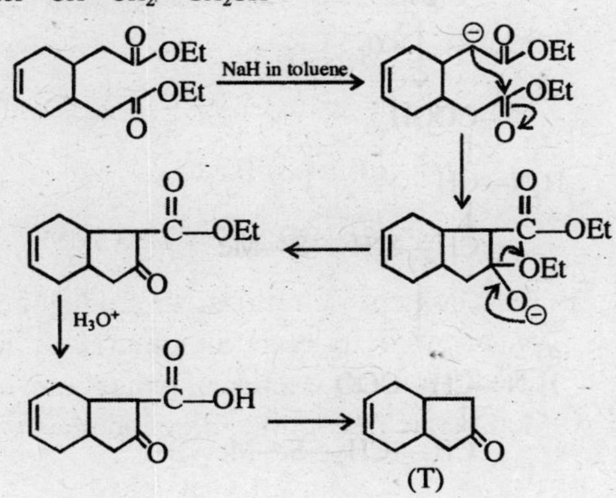

43. A.

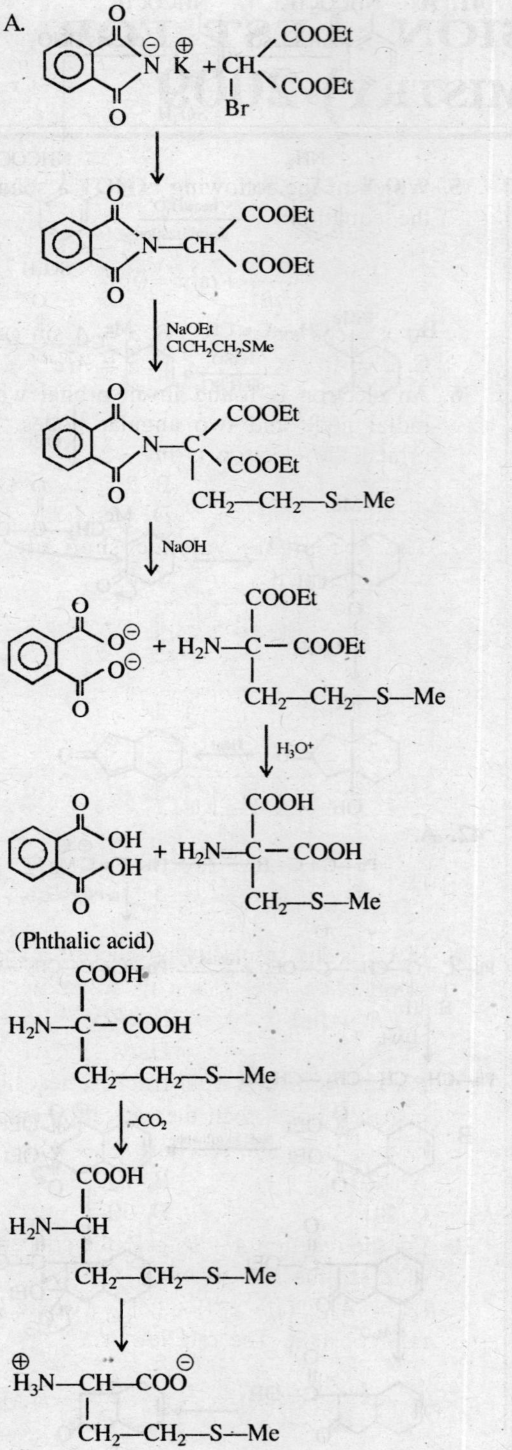

B. The compound has no α acidic hydrogen and will undergo cannizaro reaction.

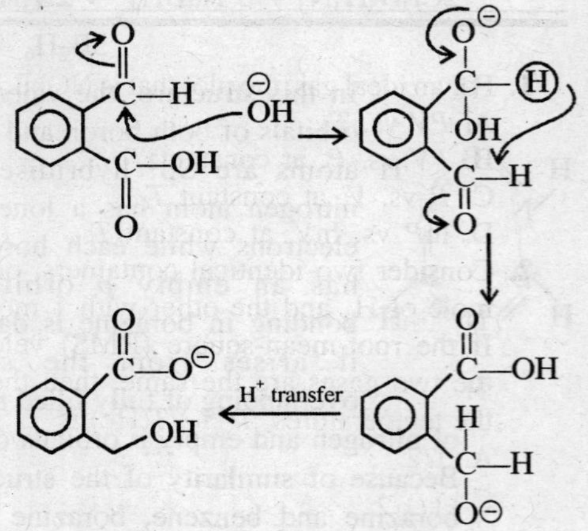

44. A.

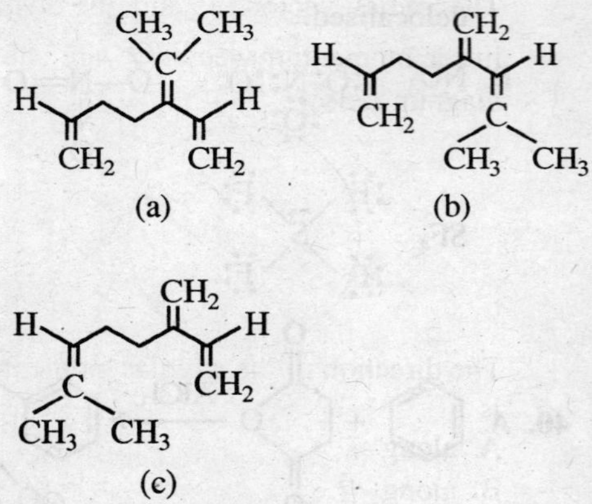

$C_{10}H_{16}$ (DBE = 3)

all above compound have DBE = 3 and give product given after ozonolysis.

B. **Isoprene rule:—**

The basic molecular formula of terpenes are multiples of that $(C_5H_8)_n$ where n is the number of linked isoprene unit.

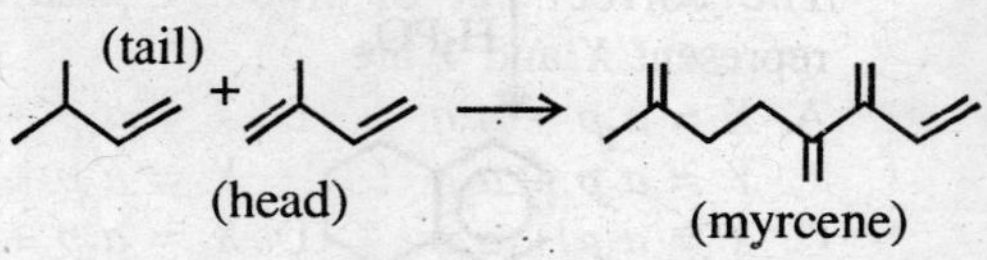

Therefore the structure c is myrcene.

Previous Paper (Solved)

IIT—JAM

JOINT ADMISSION TEST FOR M.SC. (CHEMISTRY)-2009

1. For an ideal gas, the plot that is NONLINEAR is
A. PV vs. T
B. PV vs. P, at constant T
C. P vs. V, at constant T
D. ln$P$ vs. ln$V$, at constant T

2. Consider two identical containers, one with 1 mole of H_2 and the other with 1 mole of He. If the root-mean-square (RMS) velocities of the two gases are the same, then the ratio of the temperatures, $T(H_2)/T(He)$ is
A. 1/2 B. 2
C. $1/\sqrt{2}$ D. $\sqrt{2}$

3. An electron moves around the nucleus in a circular orbit, according to the Bohr model. The radial vector $\vec{r}$ and the instantaneous linear momentum vector $\vec{p}$ are shown in the diagram below.

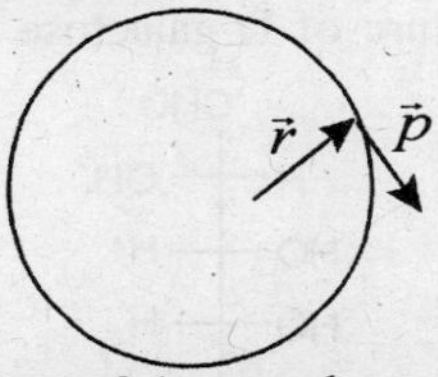

The direction of the angular momentum vector is
A. along $\vec{r}$
B. along $\vec{p}$
C. opposite to $\vec{p}$
D. perpendicular to both $\vec{r}$ and $\vec{p}$

4. X and Y are transformed co-ordinates obtained from p and q as follows:

$$\begin{pmatrix} X \\ Y \end{pmatrix} = \begin{pmatrix} a_1 & a_3 \\ a_2 & a_4 \end{pmatrix} \begin{pmatrix} p \\ q \end{pmatrix}$$

The correct set of linear equations that represent X and Y are
A. $X = a_1p + a_2q$, $Y = a_3p + a_4q$
B. $X = a_1p + a_3q$, $Y = a_2p + a_4q$
C. $X = a_2p + a_4q$, $Y = a_1p + a_3q$
D. $X = a_1p + a_4q$, $Y = a_2p + a_3q$

5. Which of the following is NOT a solution of the equation:

$$\frac{d^2x}{dt^2} + \omega^2 x = 0$$

A. $x = \cos \omega t$ B. $x = A \sin \omega t$
C. $x = At^2$ D. $x = A(e^{i\omega t} + e^{-i\omega t})$

6. An electron is found in an orbital with one radial node and two angular nodes. Which orbital the electron is in?
A. 1s B. 2p
C. 3d D. 4d

7. The acceptable valence shell electronic arrangement is:
A. 2s: [↑↓] 2p: [↑↓] [↑] [ ]
B. 2s: [↑↑] 2p: [↑] [↑] [↑]
C. 2s: [↑↓] 2p: [↑] [↑] [↑]
D. 2s: [↑↓] 2p: [↑] [↓] [↑]

8. If K_{sp} is the solubility product of a sparingly soluble salt A_3X_2, then its solubility is
A. $(K_{sp}/108)^{1/5}$ B. $(K_{sp})^{1/5}$
C. $(K_{sp}/72)^{1/5}$ D. $(K_{sp})^{1/2}$

9. For the formation of B from A, heat liberated is 20 kJ mol^{-1}, then the activation energy (in kJ mol^{-1}) for the reaction A → B is
A. 120 B. 100
C. 80 D. 60

10. For the reaction $A + B \rightarrow Z$, the concentration of Z at time t is given by
$[Z] = [A]_{t=0} (1 - e^{-kt}) + [Z]_{t=0}$, where k is the rate constant. The rate law is:
A. $-\frac{d[Z]}{dt} = k[A]$ B. $\frac{d[Z]}{dt} = k[A]$

C. $\frac{d[Z]}{dt} = k[Z]$ D. $\frac{d[Z]}{dt} = k[A][B]$

11. Identify the correct option:
In the Periodic Table, on moving from left to right along a period,
A. the atomic size of the element increases
B. the first ionization potential of the element decreases
C. the oxide of the element becomes less basic
D. the oxide of the element becomes more basic

12. Among the following, the INCORRECT statement is:
A. Diamond and graphite are two allotropes of carbon
B. In diamond, each carbon is sp^3 hybridized
C. In graphite, each carbon is sp^2 hybridized
D. Graphite shows high electrical conductivity in one direction only

13. The pH of a 1×10^{-8} M HCl solution is close to
A. 8.0   B. 7.1
C. 6.9   D. 6.0

14. The indicator phenophthalein changes colour at pH ~ 9. This indicator is NOT suitable for accurate determination of the end point in the titration of
A. CH_3COOH with NaOH
B. HCl with NH_4OH
C. HCl with NaOH
D. HCl with KOH

15. In the thermite process, iron oxide is reduced to molten iron by aluminium powder because
A. the melting point of iron is low
B. the reaction is highly endothermic
C. large amount of heat is liberated in the formation of Al_2O_3
D. aluminium is an amphoteric element

16. The number P = O bonds present in the tetrabasic acid $H_4P_2O_7$ is
A. three   B. two
C. one   D. none

17. Egyptian blue $CaCuSi_4O_{10}$ is an example of
A. sheet silicate   B. cyclic silicate
C. pyrosilicate   D. chain silicate

18. The formal charges on the nitrogen atom from left to right in the azide anion, $[N=N=N]^-$ are
A. +1, −1, −1   B. −1, +1, −1
C. −1, −1, +1   D. −2, +1, 0

19. The unit cell of diamond can be obtained from the unit cell of
A. ZnS   B. NaCl
C. CsCl   D. AgCl

20. Calgon used for water softening is $Na_2[Na_4(PO_3)_6]$ and it is prepared by heating microcosmic salt. The microcosmic salt is
A. Na_2HPO_3 B. NaH_2PO_4
C. Na_2HPO_4 D. $Na(NH_4)HOP_4$

21. The major product obtained in the following reaction

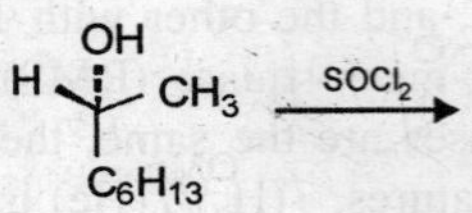

is

A. 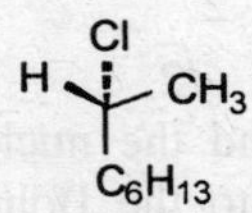

B. 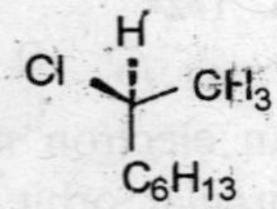

C. 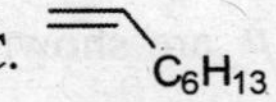

D. 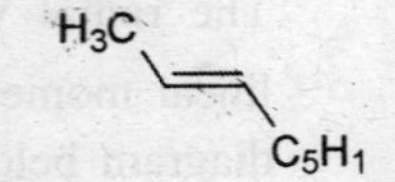

22. The structure of D-galactose is

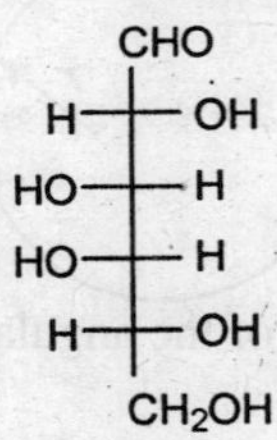

Which one of these structures is L-galactose?

A. 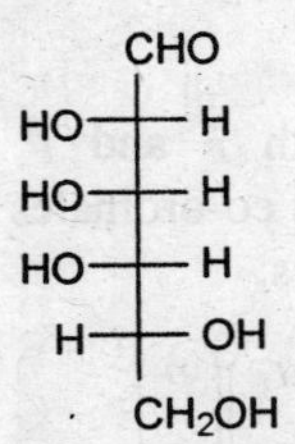

B. 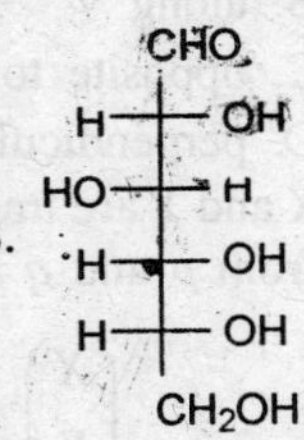

C. 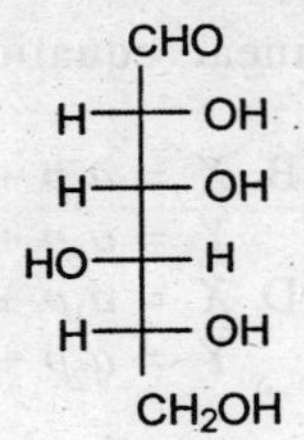

D. 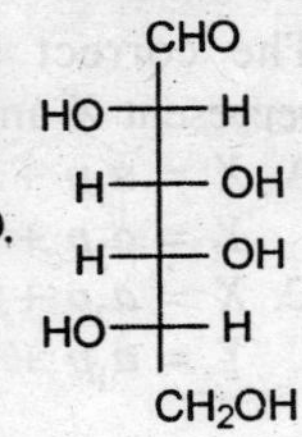

23. The maximum number of stereoisomers possible for 4-phenylbut-3-en-2-ol is

A. 1 B. 2

C. 3 D. 4

24. The major product of the reaction

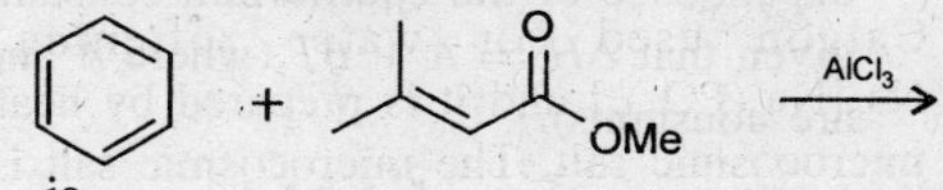

is

A. 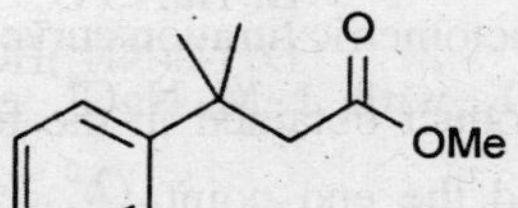

B. 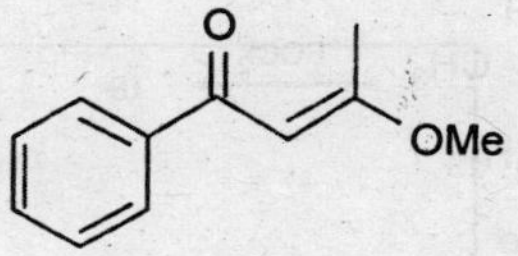

C. 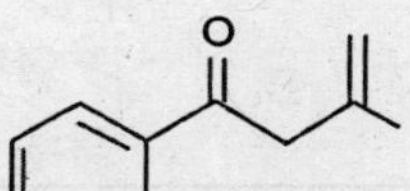

D. 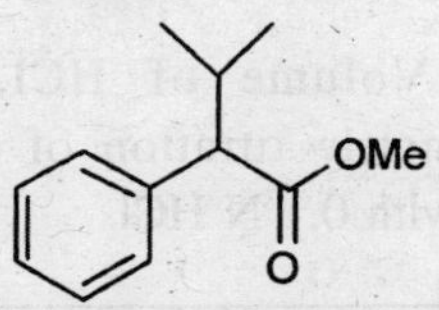

25. Which of the following is achiral?

A. alanine B. glycine

C. proline D. phenylalanine

26. The reactivity order of the indicated function groups towards a nucleophile

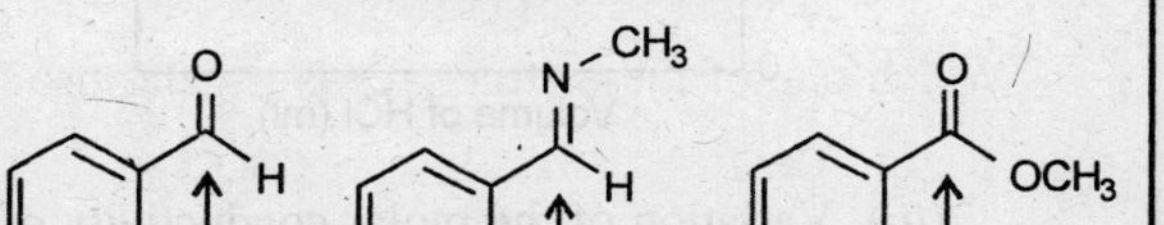

P Q R

is

A. P > Q > R B. Q > P > R

C. Q > R > P D. R > P > Q

27. The major product formed in the reaction

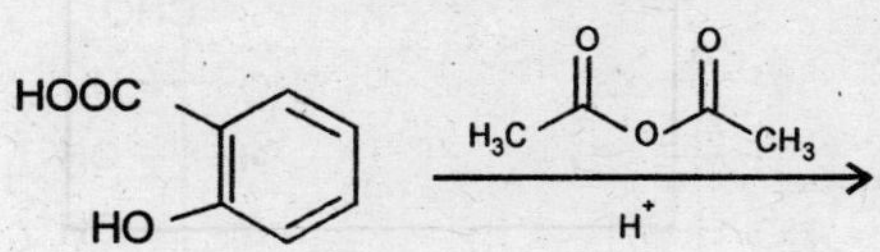

is

A. 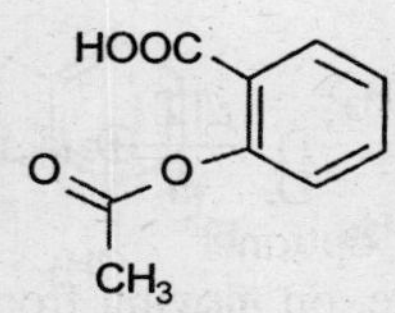

B. 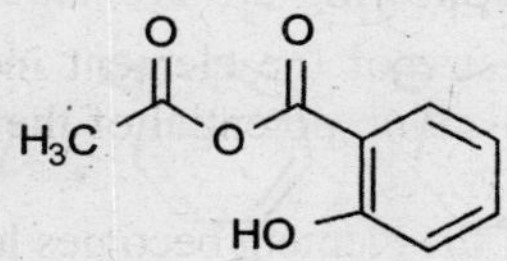

C. 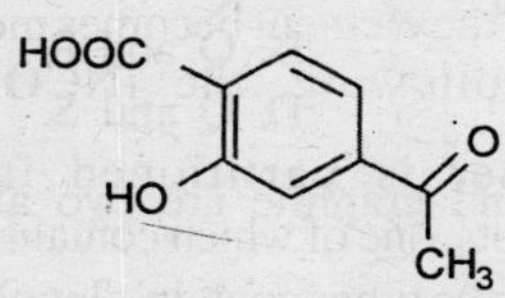

D. 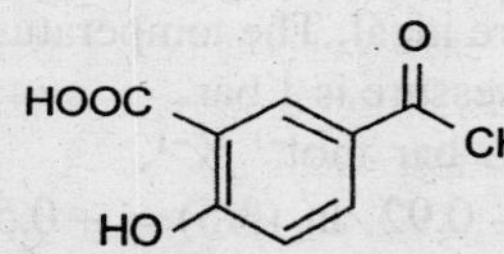

28. Arrange the following in the correct order of acidity of the hydrogen indicated in bold

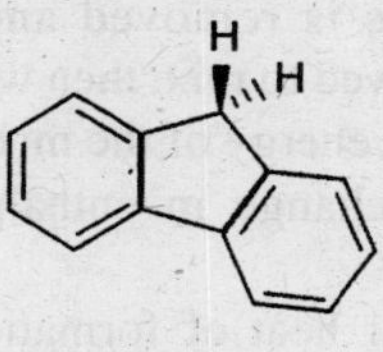

P

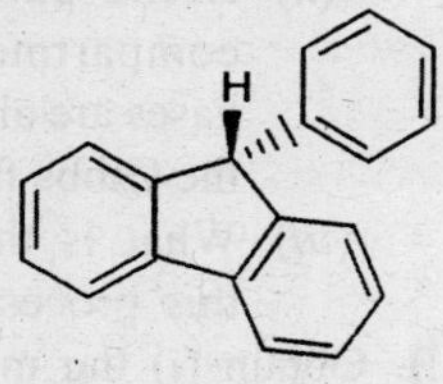

Q

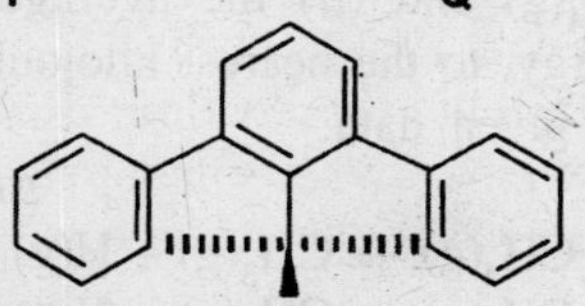

R

A. P > Q > R B. R > Q > P

C. Q > R > P D. P > R > Q

29. Among the following the major product obtained in the reaction below is

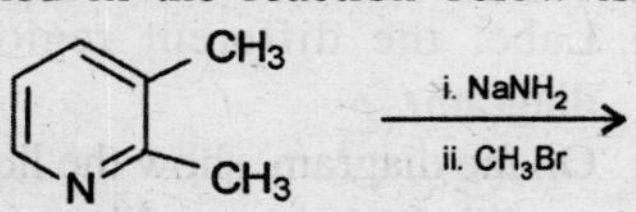

A. 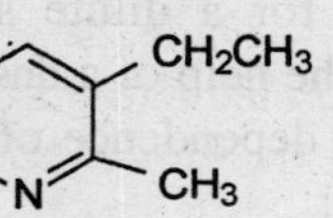

B. 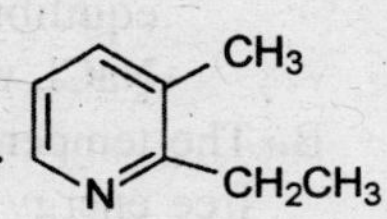

C. 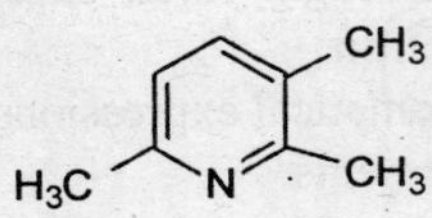
D. 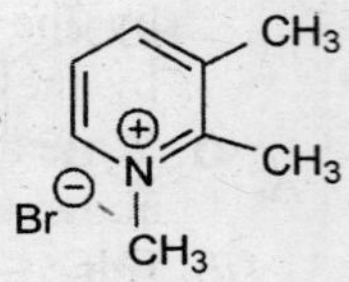

30. Which of the following are aromatic?

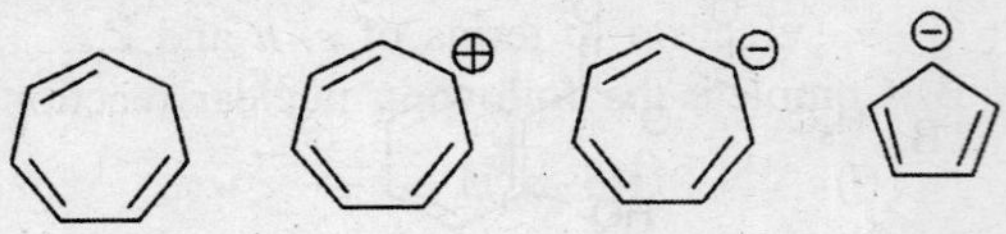

P Q R S

A. P and Q B. Q and R
C. R and S D. Q and S

31. A. A container is partitioned into two compartments, one of which contains 2 moles of He while the other contains 3 moles of Ar. The gases are ideal. The temperature is 300 K and the pressure is 1 bar.
$R = 0.083$ L bar mol^{-1} K^{-1},
$\ln(2/5) = -0.92$, $\ln(3/5) = -0.51$.

(*i*) What is the total *Gibbs free energy* of the two gases?

(*ii*) If the partition between the two compartments is removed and the gases are allowed to mix, then what is the Gibbs free energy of the mixture?

(*iii*) What is the change in enthalpy in this process?

B. Obtain (*i*) the molar heat of formation of CH_4(g) and (*ii*) the average C–H bond energy, to the nearest kilojoule (kJ), from the given data:

	ΔH(kJ mol^{-1})
(1) $CH_4(g) \rightarrow CH_3(g) + H(g)$	435
(2) $CH_3(g) \rightarrow CH_2(g) + H(g)$	444
(3) $CH_2(g) \rightarrow CH(g) + H(g)$	444
(4) $CH(g) \rightarrow C(g) + H(g)$	339
(5) C(graphite) $\rightarrow$ C(g)	717
(6) $C_2(g) \rightarrow 2H(g)$	436

32. A. (*i*) Draw the *P-T* phase diagram of water.

(*ii*) Label the different regions in this diagram.

(*iii*) On the diagram, show the liquid-vapour equilibrium for a dilute solution of NaCl, with the help of a dashed curve.

B. The temperature dependence of the Gibbs free energy *G* is:

$$\left(\frac{\partial(G/T)}{\partial T}\right)_P = -\frac{H}{T^2}$$

Obtain the expression for the temperature dependence of the equilibrium constant K given that $\Delta H^{\theta} = A + BT$ (where *A* and *B* are constants).

33. A. In the space provided, plot:

(*i*) Conductometric titration curve of 0.1M $AgNO_3$ with 1 M NaCl, extended beyond the end point $(\lambda^0_{Na^+} \approx \lambda^0_{Ag^+})$.

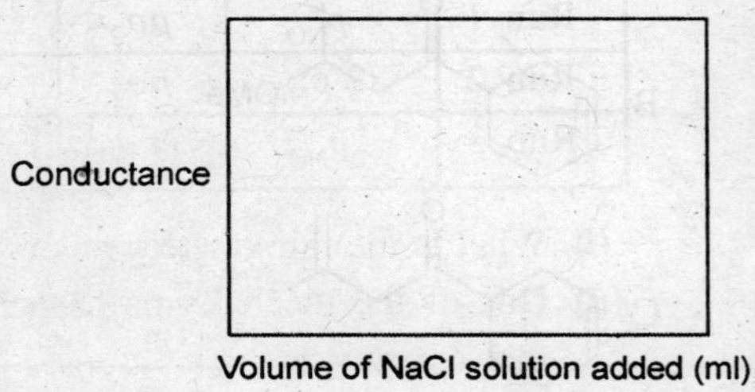

(*ii*) pH vs. Volume of HCl, for a potentiometric titration of 0.1 (N) NH_4OH with 0.1 N HCl.

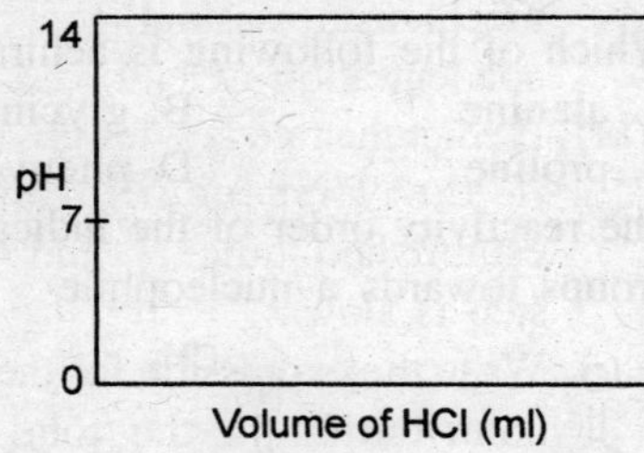

(*iii*) Variation of the molar conductivity of NaCl with the square root of its concentration.

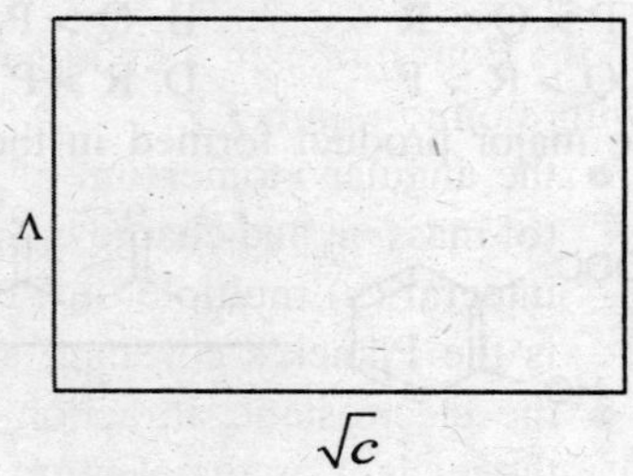

B. The $Zn^{2+} \mid Zn$ half cell ($E^\theta = -0.762$ V) is connected to a $Cu^{2+} \mid Cu$ half cell ($E^\theta = 0.340$ V). What is the value of E^θ_{cell} for spontaneous conversion of chemical energy to electrical energy? What is the value of $\log_{10} K$, where K is the equilibrium constant? Use (2.303 RT/F) = 0.06.

34. A. The following initial rate data were obtained for the reaction
$2NO(g) + O_2(g) \rightarrow 2NO_2(g)$

	Partial pressure of		Initial
	NO	O_2	rate
Run 1	p_{NO}	po_2	v
Run 2	$2\,p_{NO}$	po_2	$4v$
Run 3	p_{NO}	$2po_2$	$2v$

(*i*) What is the rate law for this reaction?

(*ii*) One of the mechanisms proposed for this reaction is

$$NO(g) + O_2(g) \underset{k_{-1}}{\overset{k_1}{\rightleftharpoons}} NO_3(g)$$

$$NO_3(g) + NO(g) \xrightarrow{k} 2NO_2(g)$$

Obtain the rate law predicted for this mechanism, assuming a steady state concentration of NO_3.

(*iii*) Predict the rate law for this mechanism, if the first equilibrium step is established quickly and the second step is slow.

B. (*i*) Write the expression for the vibrational contribution to the total energy of $CH_4(g)$ at 500 K. All the vibrational modes are active at this temperature.

(*ii*) Calculate the total internal energy of 1 mole of the gas at this temperature. $R = 8.314$ J mol^{-1} K^{-1}.

35. A. In the Bohr model of a hydrogen-like atom with atomic number Z.

- the angular momentum of an electron (of mass m_e and charge e) is a non-zero integral (n) multiple of $h/2\pi$, where h is the Planck's constant, and
- the electrostatic attraction exerted by the nucleus on the electron is balanced by the centrifugal force experienced by the electron.

(*i*) Write mathematical expressions for the above statements.

(*ii*) Hence obtain the expression for the radius r of the Bohr orbit of the electron in terms of e, n and Z.

B. Complete the following nuclear reactions:

(*i*) ${}^{14}_{7}N + {}^{4}_{2}He \rightarrow {}^{1}_{1}H + ---$

(*ii*) ${}^{7}_{8}Li + {}^{1}_{1}H \rightarrow ---$.

36. A. Highly pure nickel metal can be prepared from its sulphide ore *via* $Ni(CO)_4$. Write the chemical equations involved.

B. Addition of excess of aqueous NH_3 followed by ethanolic solution of dimethylglyoxime to a dilute aqueous solution of nickel sulphate changes the solution colour from green to blue to red. Write the structures of the metal complexes corresponding to green, blue and red colours.

37. The element **E** on burning in the presence of O_2 gives **F**. Compound **F** on heating with carbon in an electric furnace gives **G**. On passing nitrogen over a heated mixture of **F** and carbon produces **H**. Stream can decompose **H** to produce boric acid and a colourless gas that gives white fumes with HCl. Identify **F**, **G** and **H** and give balanced equations for their formation.

38. A. Provide IUPAC names for the following complexes:

(*i*) $[CoCl(NH_3)_5]$ (*ii*) $K_2[PdCl_4]$

B. The magnetic moment of $[Mn(H_2O)_6](NO_3)_2$ is approximately 6.0 μ_B. Find the number of unpaired electrons, show crystal field splitting and calculate the CFSE.

39. A metal salt on heating with a mixture of KCl and conc. H_2SO_4 yields a deep red vapour **J**. The vapour on passing through an aqueous solution of KOH gives a yellow solution of compound **K**. Passing SO_2 gas through acidified solution (with H_2SO_4) of **K** leads to green colouration of the solution due to the formation of **M**. Identify **J, K** and **M** giving balanced equations for the transformations, **J → K and K → M.**

40. A. **Identify E and F in the following reactions and suggest a suitable reason for their formation**

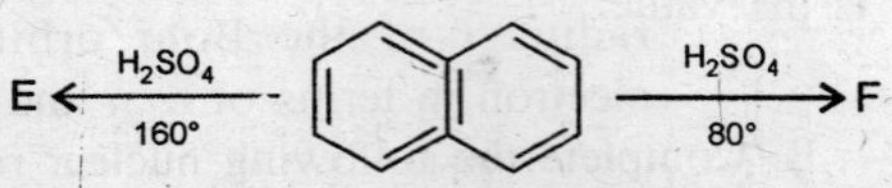

B. **Predict the products in each of the following reactions.**

(*i*)

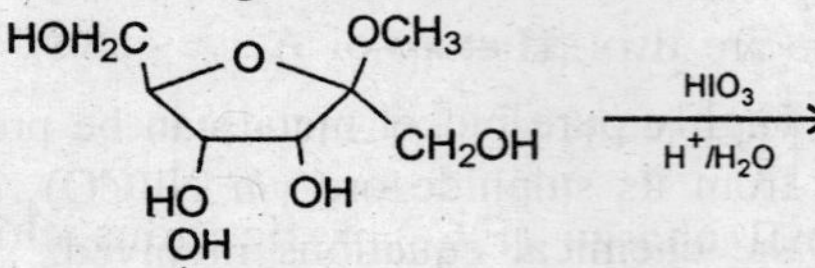

(*ii*)

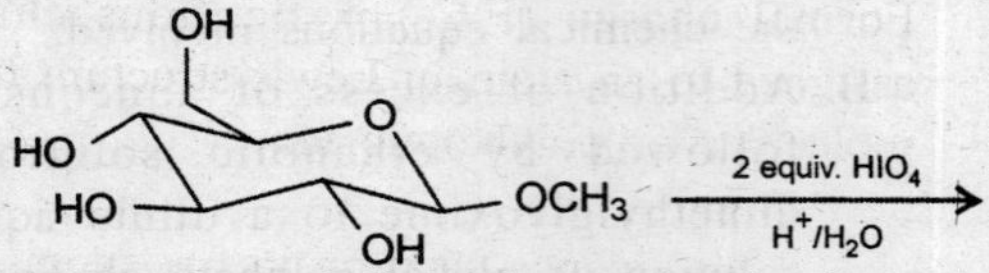

41. A. **A compound G having molecular formula C_6H_{12} decolourises both permanganate and bromine water. G on ozonolysis followed by reductive work-up (Zn/H_3O^+) produces equal amounts of H and J with identical molecular formula C_3H_6O. Both H and J from 2, 4-dinitrophenyl hydrazones, however, only J shows positive test with Tollens' reagent. Identify the compounds G, H and J.**

B. **Identify K and M in the following reaction sequence.**

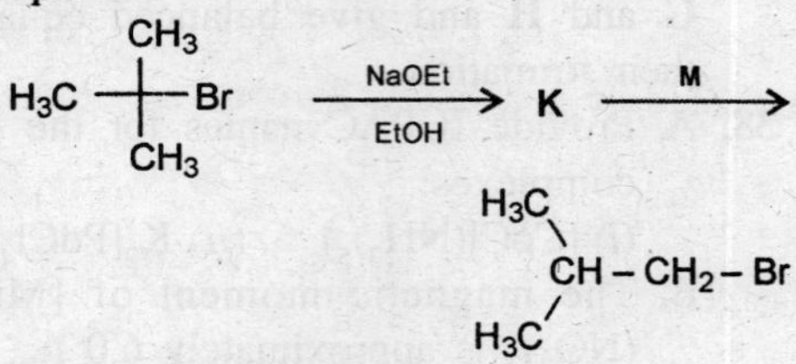

42. A. **Identify N, P and Q in the following synthetic transformation.**

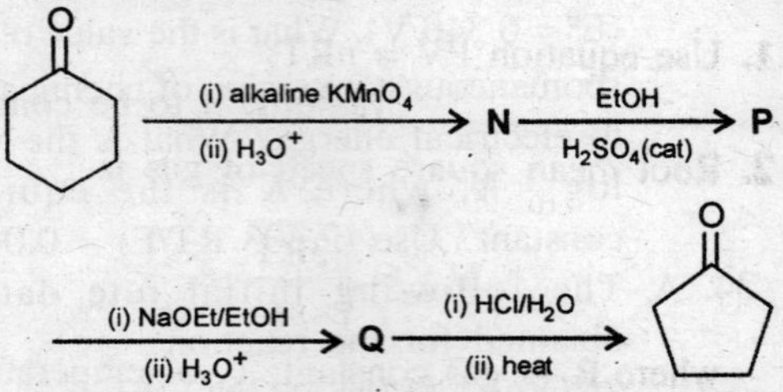

B. **Draw the most as well as the least stable chair conformation of *trans*-1-*tert*-butyl-4-methylcyclohexane.**

43. Identify R, S, T, X and Y in the following reaction sequences.

A.

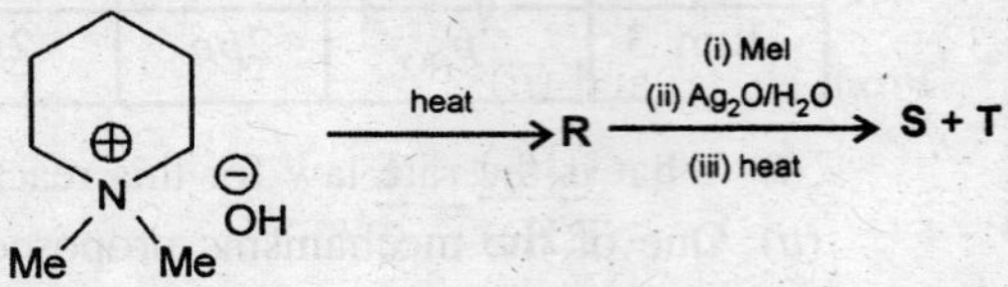

B.

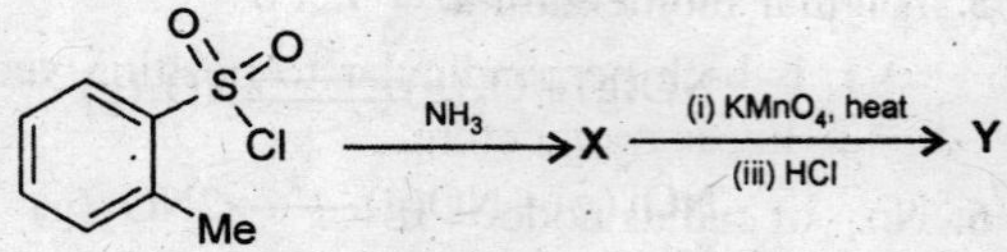

44. A. **Complete the following reaction sequences with the structures of X, Y, and Z.**

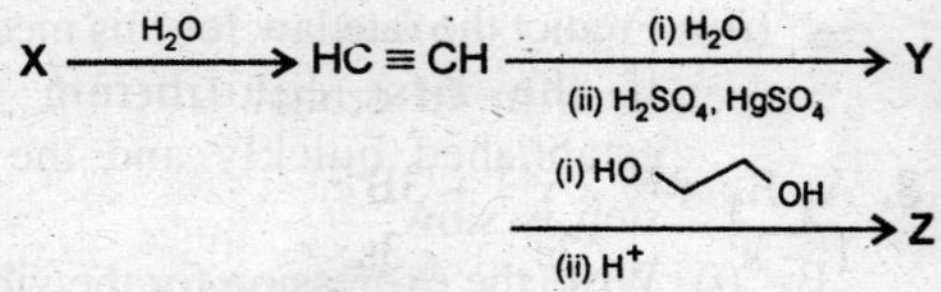

B. **Calculate the isoelectric point (*p*I) of lysine. given the *p*K_a of α-NH_3 is 8.95, *p*K_a of side chain NH_3 is 10.53 and *p*K_a of α-COOH is 2.18.**

ANSWERS

1	2	3	4	5	6	7	8	9	10
C	A	D	B	C	D	C	A	A	D
11	12	13	14	15	16	17	18	19	20
C	D	C	B	C	B	A	B	A	D
21	22	23	24	25	26	27	28	29	30
A	D	C	B	B	D	A	B	D	D

SOME SELECTED EXPLANATORY ANSWERS

1. Use equation PV = nRT (assume n to be constant).

2. Root mean square speed of gas is

$$V_{rms} = \sqrt{\frac{3RT}{m}}$$

where R → gas constant; T → temperature in Kelvin and m → molecular weight.

$$V_{rms}(H_2) = \sqrt{\frac{3RT(H_2)}{2}} \quad ...(i)$$

$$V_{rms}(He) = \sqrt{\frac{3RT(He)}{4}} \quad ...(ii)$$

From eq. (*i*) and (*ii*)

$$\frac{T(H_2)}{T(He)} = \frac{1}{2}$$

3. Angular momentum L = $\bar{r} \times \bar{p}$

⇒ L is both perpendicular to position vector & linear momentum.

6. No. of radial node = $n - l - 1$

angular node = l

∴ $n - l - 1$ and $l = 2$ (given)

∴ $n - 2 - 1 = 1$

⇒ $n = 4$

∴ electron is in 4d orbital.

8. $A_2B_3 \rightleftharpoons 2A^{+3} + 3B^{-2}$

1 – s 2s 3s

$K_{sp} = (2s)^2(3s)^3 = 108s^5$

$$\Rightarrow s = \left(\frac{K_{sp}}{108}\right)^{\frac{1}{5}}$$

13. HCl is strong acid so it dissociate in aqueous solution. Since pH = –log[H⁺] you need to fixed the concentration of H^+ + ([H^+]). Water normally dissociates

$H_2O \rightleftharpoons H^+ + OH^-$

The dissociation constant is $K_w = 10^{-7}$

So, you have 10^{-7} moles of H^+ in pure water. Add the 10^{-8} moles of HCl and the resulting concentration of H^+ is

$[H^+] = 1.1 \times 10^{-7}$

The negative log of 1.1×10^{-7} = 6.96 which is pH value.

16. 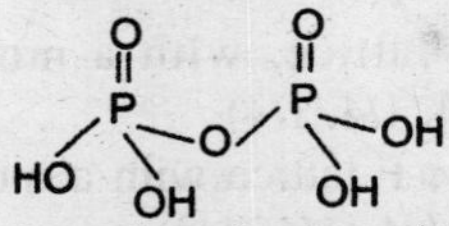

Pyrophosphoric acid ($H_4P_2O_7$)

18. There are two structure of Azide anion

$$\left[\ddot{N}_{0} \equiv N_{+1} - \ddot{N}:_{-2}\right]^- \quad \left[\ddot{N}_{-1} = N_{+1} = \ddot{N}_{-1}\right]^-$$

Formal charge (F.C.) = fictitious charge assigned to an atom in Lewis structure for a molecules or polyatomic ion

F.C. = F – A

F = Valance electron in free atom

A (Apparent valance electron owned by atom in structure) = number of electron in lone pair (L) + 1/2 of electrons shared with other atoms (B).

= 2 L + B

$$\left[\ddot{N}_{0} \equiv N_{+1} - \ddot{N}:_{-2}\right]^-$$

Left N appears to own

1 lone pair × 2 = 3

3 bond pairs = 3

A = 2 + 3 = 5

F = 5

F.C. = F – A = 5 – 5 = 0

Middle N appears to own

0 lone pair × 2 = 0

4 bond pairs = 4

A = 0 + 4 = 4

F = 5

F.C. = F – A = 5 – 4 = +1

Right N appears to own

3 lone pair × 2 = 6

1 bond pairs = 1

A = 6 + 1 = 7

F = 5

F.C. = F – A = 5 – 7 = –2

Similarly,

$$\left[\ddot{N}_{-1} \equiv N_{+1} = \ddot{N}_{-1}\right]^-$$

Formal charge on left nitrogen
$5 - 6 = -1$

Formal charge on middle nitrogen
$5 - 4 = 1$

Formal charge on right nitrogen
$5 - 6 = -1$

19. Diamond cubic-F lattice, with a motif of C(0, 0, 0) and C (1/4, 1/4, 1/4)
Zinc sulphide, cubic-F lattice with a motif of Zn (0, 0, 0) and S(1/4, 1/4, 1/4).

20. Hydrated sodium ammonium hydrogen phosphates is a microcosmic salt. It is found in urine.

21.

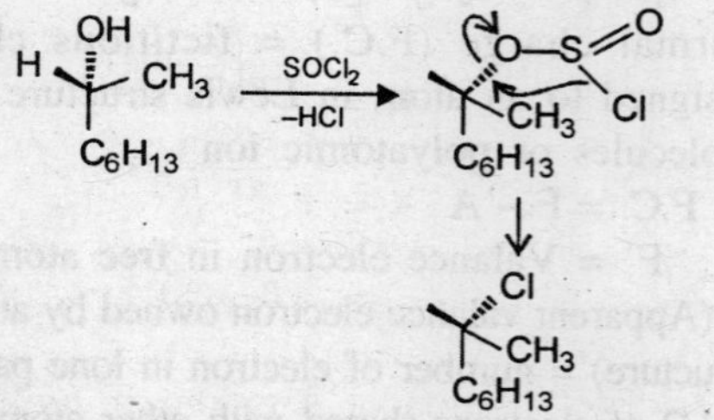

22.

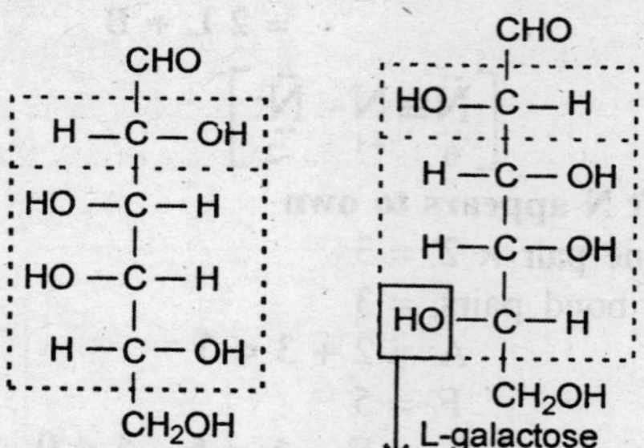

D-galactose — L-galactose — This determine D or L

23.

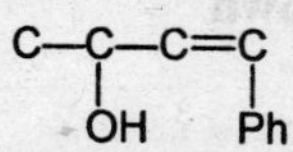

(4 phenyl but-3-on-2-ol)

It has chiral centre and can also show geometrical isomererism.

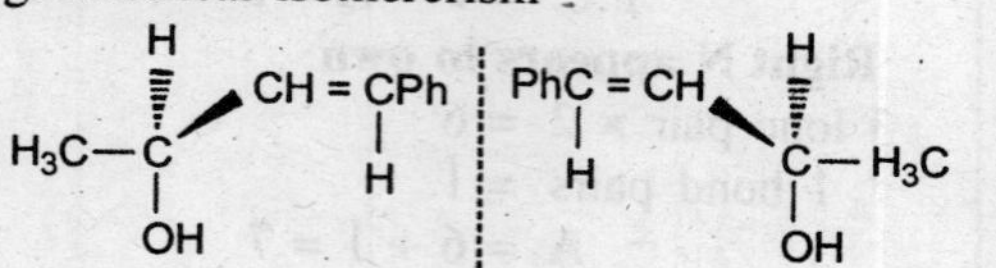

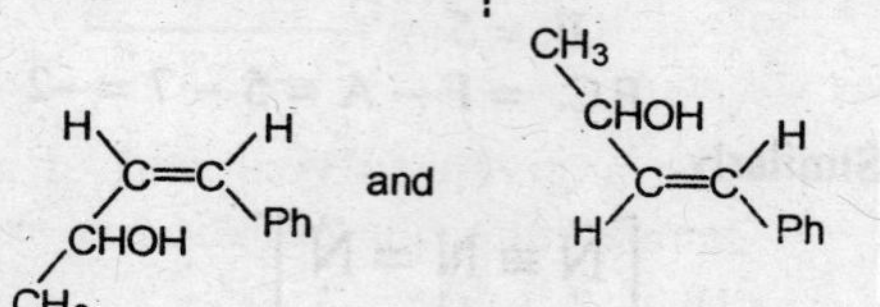

(cis) (trans)

25. The structure of glycine is

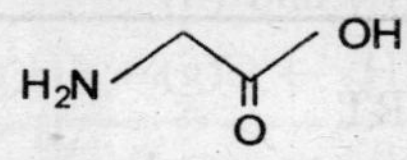

It has no chiral centre.

27.

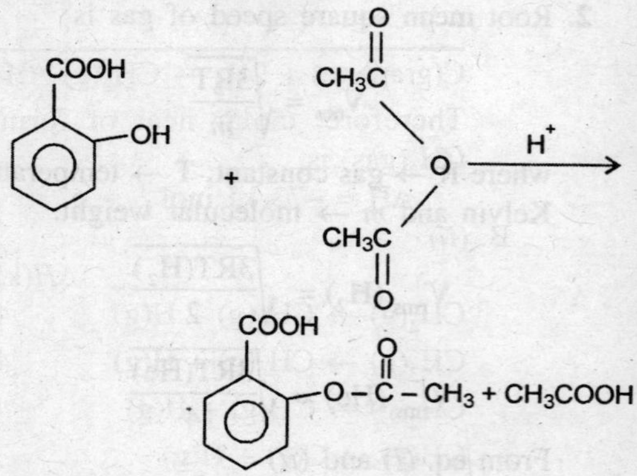

30. Use $4n + 2$ rule
Further electron should completely delocalised in ring.

Has 6 electron taking part in aromaticity of compound.

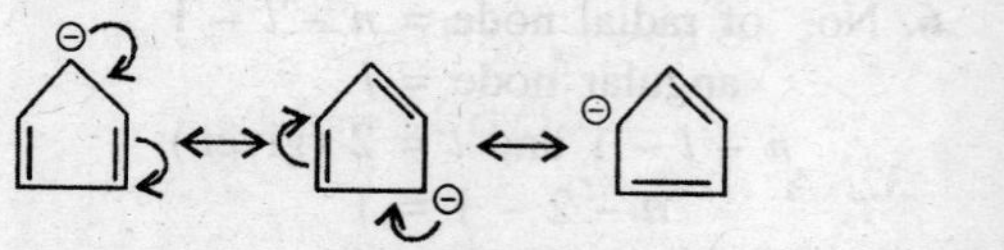

Above show complete delocalisation over the ring.

Similarly it could be shown for 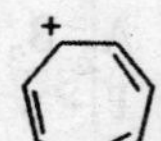

Here also 6 electron $(4 \times 1 + 2)$ take part in aromaticity. Structures are shown below:

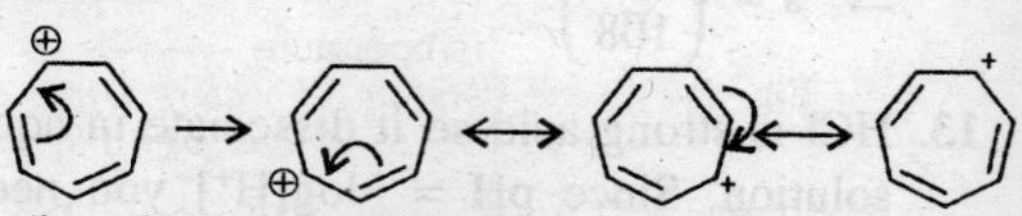

(i.e. electron is delocalised over complete ring)

31. B. (*i*)
Given in the question

C(graphite) → C(g)	ΔH = 717
H_2(g) → 2H(g)	ΔH = 436
C(graphite) + $2H_2$ → C(g) + 4H	ΔH = 1589

...(ii)

From equation (i) and (ii)

$C(graphite) + 2H_2 \rightarrow C(g) + 4H(g)$ $\quad \Delta H = 1589$

$CH_4(g) \rightarrow C(g) + 4H(g)$ $\quad \Delta H = 1662$

(–) (–) (–)

$C(graphite) + 2H_2 \rightarrow CH_4(g)$ $\Delta H = -73$

Therefore, molar heat of formation of CH_4(gas) is

$\Delta H = -73 \text{ kJ mol}^{-1}$

B. (*ii*)

	ΔH(kJ mol^{-1})
$CH_4(g) \rightarrow CH_3(g) + H(g)$	435
$CH_3(g) \rightarrow CH_2(g) + H(g)$	444
$CH_2(g) \rightarrow CH(g) + H(g)$	444
$CH(g) \rightarrow C(g) + H(g)$	339

Adding these equations

$CH_4(g) \rightarrow C(g) + 4H(g)$ ...(*i*)

$\Delta H = 435 + 444 + 444 + 339$

$= 1662 \text{ kJ mol}^{-1}$

The average bond energy of C–H bond is

$$\text{B.E.} = \frac{1}{4}(\Delta H) = \frac{1662}{4} \text{ kJ mol}^{-1}$$

$$= 415.5 \text{ kJ mol}^{-1}$$

32. A. (*i*) & (*ii*)

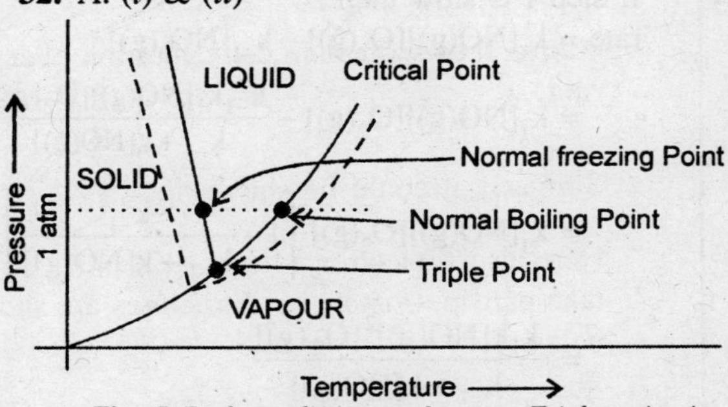

Fig. *P-T phase diagram of water. Triple point is lie at 273.16 K and 611 Pa.*

(iii) The boiling point of the solvent in a solution is higher than that of pure solvent and the freezing point (melting point) of the solvent in a solution is lower than that of pure solvent.

B. $$\left[\frac{\partial\left(G^\circ/_T\right)}{\partial T}\right]_P = -\frac{H^\circ}{T^2} = -\frac{(A+BT)}{T^2}$$

$$\Rightarrow \quad = -\frac{A}{T^2} - \frac{B}{T}$$

$$\therefore \quad d\left(\frac{G^\circ}{T}\right) = -\frac{A}{T^2}dT - \frac{B}{T}dT$$

(at constant P)

Integrating

$$\frac{G^\circ}{T} = \frac{A}{T} - B\ln T \quad \text{...(i)}$$

$$\Delta G^\circ = -RT \ln K$$

$$\Rightarrow \quad K = e^{-\frac{\Delta G^\circ}{RT}}$$

$$K = e^{-\frac{1}{R}\left(\frac{A}{T} - B\ln T\right)}$$

$$K = e^{-\frac{A}{RT} + \frac{B}{R}\ln T}$$

$$= T^{\frac{B}{R}} e^{-\frac{A}{RT}}$$

33. A. (*i*)

(*ii*) The solution of Ammonium hydroxide is basic in nature and therefore the pH of solution is greater than 7. On addition of HCl the solution turn acidic. As a result pH decreases. At equivalence point, the change is abrupt.

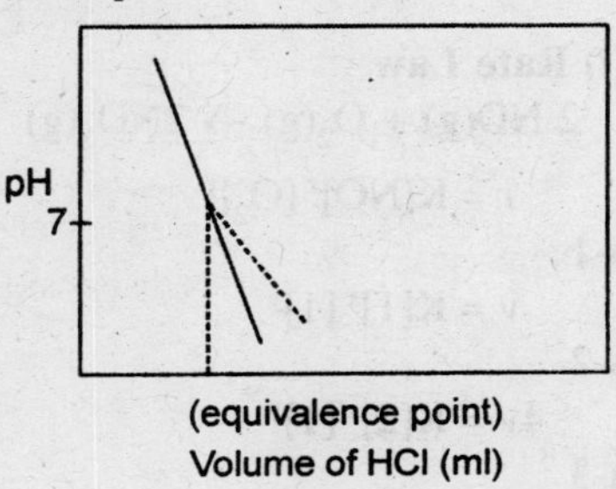

(*iii*)

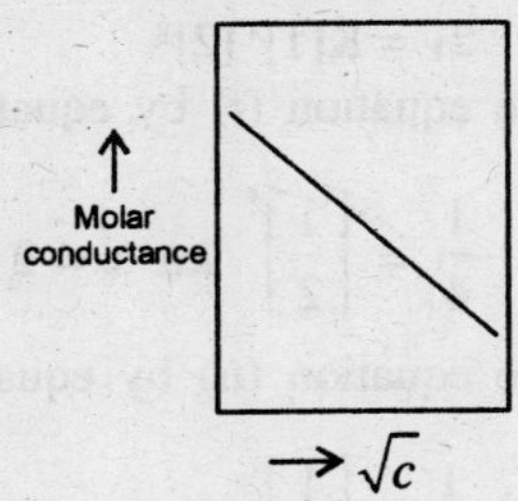

For a given solvent and at a given temperature, the equation is expressed as

$$\Lambda_m = \Lambda_m^0 - (A + B\Lambda_m^0)\sqrt{C}$$

B. $Zn \rightarrow Zn^{2+} + 2e^-$ (at anode)
$Cu^{2+} + 2e^- \rightarrow Cu$ (at cathode)

overall reaction $Zn + Cu^{2+} \rightarrow Cu + Zn^{2+}$

$$E^0_{cell} = E_{cathode} - E_{anode}$$
$$= .340 - (-.762)$$
$$= 1.104 \text{ V}$$

Nernst Equation

$$E_{cell} = E^0_{cell} - \frac{2.303RT}{nF} \frac{\log[Zn^{2+}][Cu(s)]}{[Cu^{2+}][Zn(s)]}$$

where n = 2

$$\therefore \quad E_{cell} = 1.104 - \frac{2.303RT}{F} \times \frac{1}{2} \log K$$

$$= 1.104 - .06 \times \frac{1}{2} \log K$$

$$\Rightarrow \log K = \frac{E_{cell} - 1.104}{.03}$$

At equillibrium $\Delta G = 0 \Rightarrow E_{cell} = 0$

$$\therefore \log K = \frac{1.104}{.03} = -36.8$$

34. A. (*i*) **Rate Law**

$$2\,NO(g) + O_2(g) \rightarrow 2NO_2(g)$$

$$r = K[NO]^x [O_2]^y$$

Run-1

$$v = K[1]^x [1]^y \quad ...(i)$$

Run-2

$$4v = K[2]^x [1]^y \quad ...(ii)$$

Run-3

$$2v = K[1]^x [2]^y \quad ...(iii)$$

Divide equation (*i*) by equation (*ii*)

$$\frac{1}{4} = \left[\frac{1}{2}\right]^x \text{ i.e. } x = 2$$

Divide equation (*ii*) by equation (*iii*)

$$\frac{1}{2} = \left[\frac{1}{2}\right]^y \text{ i.e. } y = 1$$

Therefore, rate law

$$r = K[NO]^2 [O_2]^1$$

(*ii*) $NO(g) + O_2(g) \underset{k_{-1}}{\overset{k_1}{\rightleftharpoons}} NO_3(g)$

$$NO_3(g) + NO(g) \xrightarrow{k} 2NO_2(g)$$

$$\frac{d[NO_3]}{dt} = k_1[NO(g)][O_2(g)] - k_{-1}[NO_3(g)] - k[NO_3(g)][NO(g)] \quad ...(i)$$

Steady state concentration of NO_3 implies that concentration of NO_3 does not changes with time i.e. $\frac{d[NO_3]}{dt} = 0$

$\therefore$ From (*i*) we have

$$[NO_3] = \frac{k_1[NO(g)][O_2(g)]}{k_{-1} + k[NO(g)]}$$

Assuming step II to be slow

$$\text{rate} = \frac{1}{2} k[NO_3(g)][NO(g)]$$

Putting steady state concentration of NO_3 we get

$$\text{rate} = \frac{k_1[NO(g)]^2[O_2(g)]}{k_{-1} + k[NO(g)]}$$

If step I is slow then
rate = $k_1[NO(g)][O_2(g)] - k_{-1}[NO_3(g)]$

$$= k_1[NO(g)][O_2(g)] - \frac{k_{-1}k_1[NO(g)][O_2(g)]}{k_{-1} + k[NO(g)]}$$

$$= k_1[NO(g)][O_2(g)]\left[1 - \frac{k_{-1}}{k_{-1} + k[NO(g)]}\right]$$

$$= \frac{k_1 k[NO(g)]^2[O_2(g)]}{k_{-1} + k[NO(g)]}$$

(*iii*) $NO + O_2 \overset{k_1}{\rightleftharpoons} NO_3(g)$ (fast)

$NO_3 + NO \xrightarrow{k_2} 2NO_2$ (slow)

Rate of Reaction is determined by the slowest step in the sequence. The slowest step is called rate determining step in the proposed mechanism.

$$\text{Rate law} = -\frac{dx}{dt} = k_2[NO_3]\,[NO]$$

35. A. $$mvr = \frac{nh}{2\pi} \quad ...(i)$$

$$\frac{q_1 q_2}{4\pi\varepsilon_0 r^2} = \frac{mv^2}{r} \quad ...(ii)$$

where m is mass of electron

From (*ii*)

$$mv^2 r = \frac{q_1 q_2}{4\pi\varepsilon_0} = \frac{ze^2}{4\pi\varepsilon_0}$$

$$(mvr)v = \frac{ze^2}{4\pi\varepsilon_0}$$

Putting value of mvr from (*i*)

$$\left(\frac{nh}{2\pi}\right)v = \frac{ze^2}{4\pi\varepsilon_0}$$

$$\Rightarrow \quad v = \frac{ze^2 2\pi}{nh \times 4\pi\varepsilon_0}$$

But $$r = \frac{nh}{2\pi} \times \frac{1}{mv} = \frac{nh}{2\pi} \times \frac{nh \times 4\pi\varepsilon_0}{m \times ze^2 \times 2\pi}$$

$$\boxed{r = \frac{n^2 h^2}{4\pi^2 zme^2} \times 4\pi\varepsilon_0}$$

B. $${}^{14}_{7}N + {}^{4}_{2}He \rightarrow {}^{1}_{1}H + {}^{17}_{8}O$$

$${}^{7}_{3}Li + {}^{1}_{1}H \rightarrow 2{}^{4}_{2}He + \Delta E$$

36. A. $$(Ni, Cu, Fe)S \xrightarrow{\text{Forth Flotation}} NiS, CuS, FeS$$

Pentalandite

$$(NiS, CuS, FeS) \xrightarrow{O_2/Si} (Ni, CuS) + FeSiO_2$$

$$(NiS, CuS) \xrightarrow{\text{Roasted}} (NiO, CuO) + SO_2$$

$$CuO, NiO + \text{water gas} \xrightarrow[520-620K]{\Delta} Cu + Ni$$

$$Cu + Ni \xrightarrow[330K]{CO} Ni(CO)_4\uparrow + Cu$$

$$Ni(CO)_4 \xrightarrow[450K]{Ni/\Delta} Ni + CO\uparrow$$

(Pure Metal)

B. $Ni^{+}(aq) + 2\ NH_3\ (aq) + 2H_2O\ (l)$

$$\rightleftharpoons \underset{\text{(green gelatinous)}}{Ni(OH)_2(s)} + 2NH_4(aq)$$

$Ni(OH)_2(s) + 6\ NH_3\ (aq)$

$$\rightleftharpoons \underset{\text{(blue complex)}}{[Ni(NH_3)_6(s)]^{2+}\ (aq)} + 2OH^{+}(aq)$$

$[Ni(NH_3)_6]^{2+}\ (aq) + 2(CH_3CNOH)_2\ (alc) \rightarrow$

$$\underset{\text{(Red)}}{Ni[ONC(CH_3)C(CH_3)NOH]_2(s)}$$

$$+ 2NH_4(aq) + 4NH_3(aq)$$

Structure of compounds

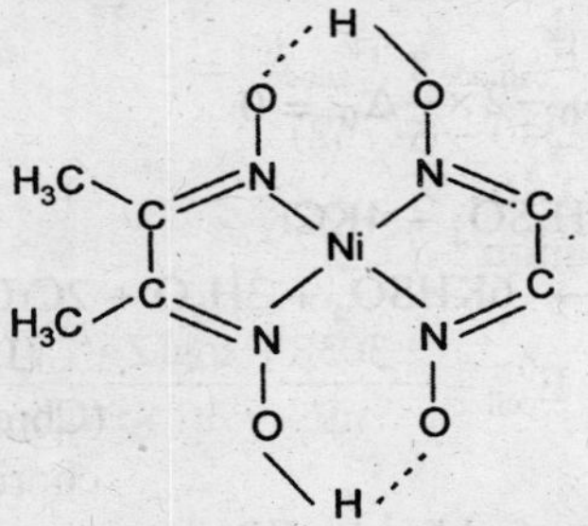

$Ni[ONC(CH_3)C(CH_3)NOH]_2$

Red Colour

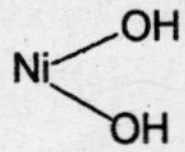

$Ni(OH_2)$

Green Colour

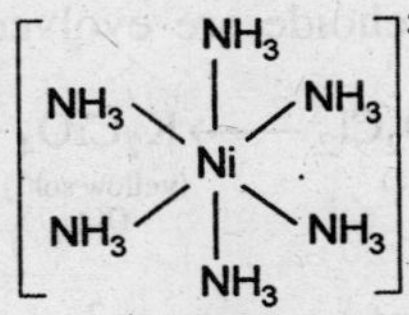

$[Ni(NH_3)_6]$

Blue Colour

37.

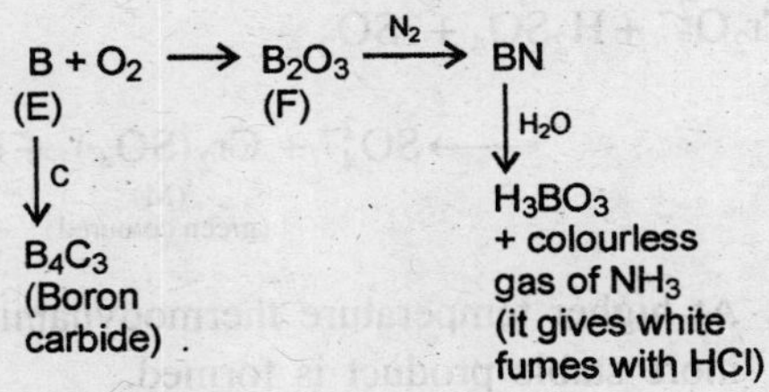

Reactions

$4B + 3O_2 \rightarrow 2B_2O_3$

$2BN + 3H_2O \rightarrow B_2O_3 + 2NH_3$

$B_2O_3 + H_2O \rightarrow HBO_2$

$HBO_2 + H_2O \rightarrow H_3BO_3$

38. A. (*i*) Pentaamminechlorocobalt (2) chloride

(*ii*) Potassium tetrachloridopalladate.

B. $[Mn(H_2O)_6]$

It is octahedral complex with 5 electrons in d orbital

↑ ↑ ↑   eg ($dx^2–y^2$, dz^2)

Δ_0 . . . .

↓ ↑ ↑ ↑ t_{2g} (dxy, dyz, dzx)

Since the ligand is weak, there is no pairing of electron.

$\therefore$ Magnetic moment $= \sqrt{5\times7} = \sqrt{35} \approx 6\mu_\beta$

Crystal field stabilization energy

$$= 3\times\frac{2}{5}\Delta_0 - 2\times\frac{3}{5}\Delta_0 = 0$$

39. $K_2Cr_2O_7 + 6H_2SO_4 + 4KCl \longrightarrow 6KHSO_4 + 3H_2O + \underset{\text{(J) (Chronyl choride)}}{2CrO_2Cl_2}$

This is a test of chloride. When a mixture of a metal chloride and potassium dichromate is heated with conc. H_2SO_4, orange red vapours or chromyl choide are evolved.

$$4KOH + \underset{(J)}{CrO_2Cl_2} \longrightarrow \underset{\substack{\text{(yellow sol}^n) \\ (K)}}{K_2CrO_4} + 2KCl + 2H_2O$$

$$\underset{(K)}{2CrO_4^{2-}} + 2H^+ \longrightarrow Cr_2O_7^{2-} + H_2O$$

$$Cr_2O_7^{2-} + H_2SO_4 + 3SO_2 \longrightarrow SO_4^{2-} + \underset{\substack{(M) \\ \text{(green coloured)}}}{Cr_2(SO_4)_3} + H_2O$$

40. A. At higher temperature thermodynamically more stable product is formed.

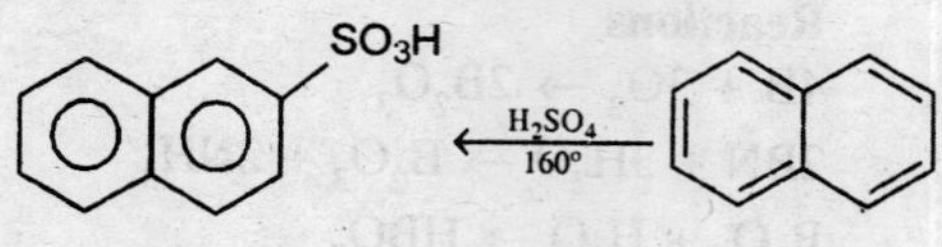

(E)

β-napthalenesulphonic acid

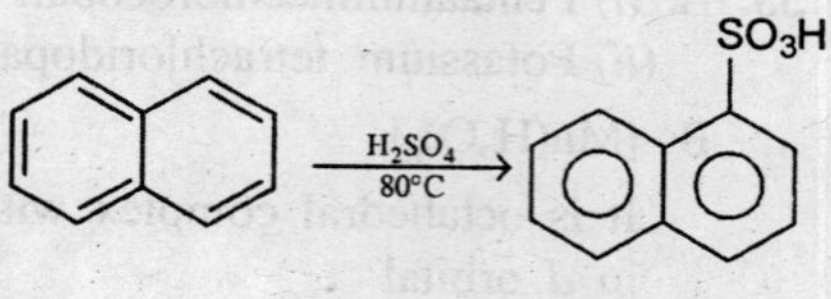

(F)

α-napthalenesulphonic acid

B. (*i*) HIO_3 react with –OH on two consecutive carbon.

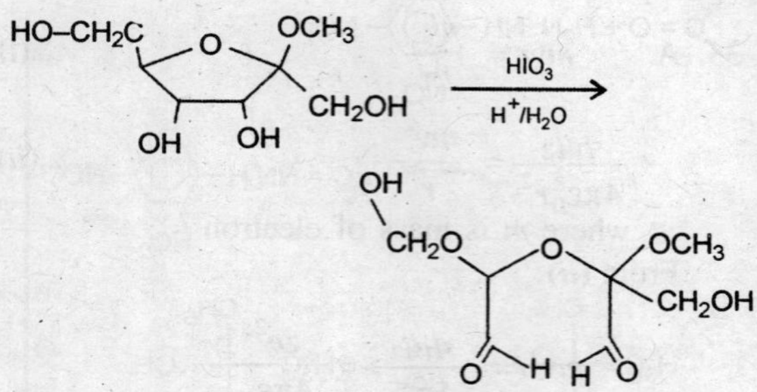

(*ii*)

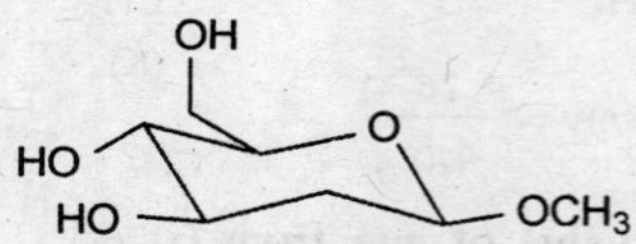

$$\xrightarrow[H^+/H_2O]{\text{2 equiv. } HIO_4} 5HCO_2H + 2CH_2O$$

41. A. C_6H_{12}

DBE = 7 – 6 = 1.

G on ozonolysis followed by reductive work gives C_3H_6O with identical molecular formula suggest alkene G is symmetrical.

$\therefore$ G is C—C—C=C—C—C or

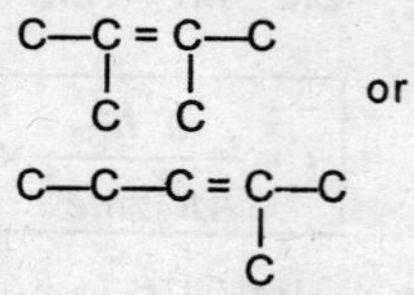

Only J shows positive

$$\Rightarrow \quad J = CH_3-CH_2-\overset{\overset{O}{||}}{C}-H$$

$$\text{and} \quad H = CH_3-\overset{\overset{O}{||}}{C}-CH_3$$

$$\underset{(G)}{CH_3-CH_2-CH=\underset{\underset{CH_3}{|}}{C}-CH_3} \xrightarrow{O_3} \xrightarrow{Zn/H_3O^+} \underset{\substack{(J) \\ \text{gives tollens test}}}{CH_3-CH_2-\overset{\overset{O}{||}}{C}-H} + \underset{\substack{(H) \\ \text{negative tollens test}}}{CH_3-\overset{\overset{O}{||}}{C}-CH_3}$$

Both (J) and (H) form 2, 4-dinitrophenyl hydrozones.

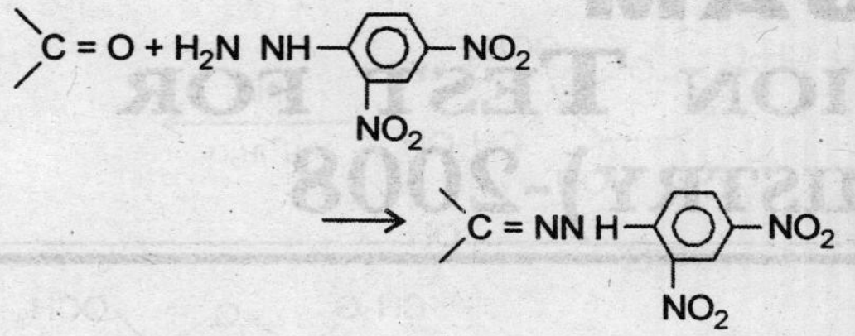

B.

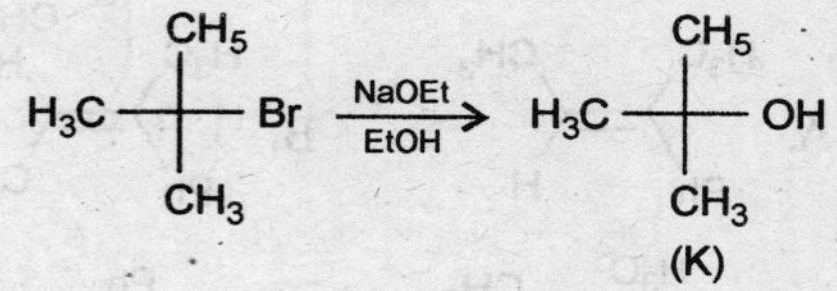

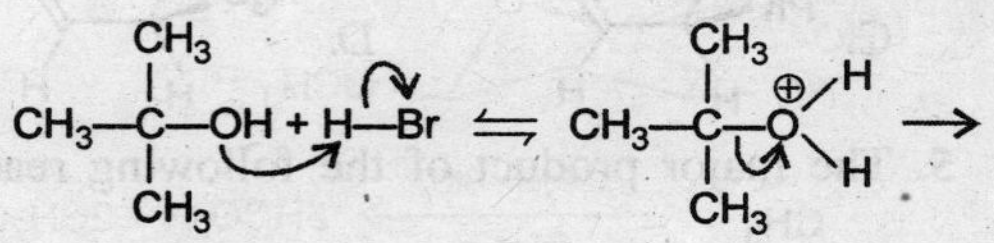

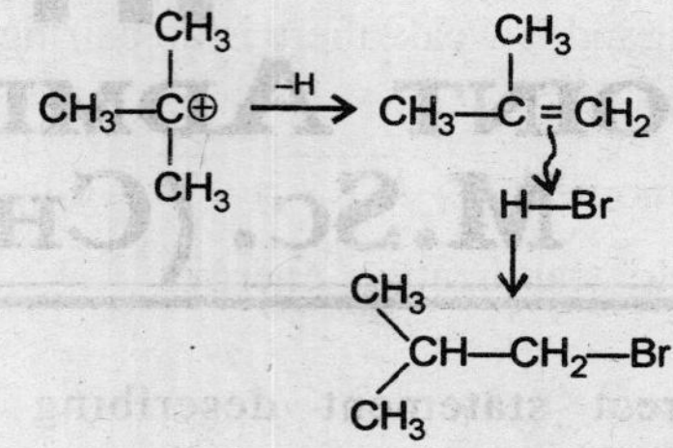

42. B.

(most stable conformation)

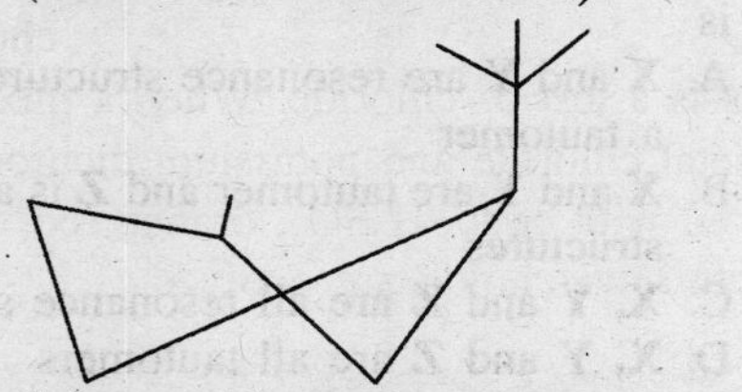

(Least stable conformation)

44. A.

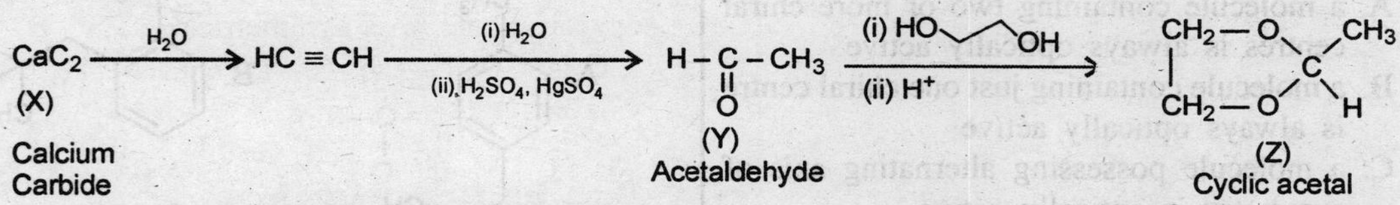

B.

$$pI = \frac{pK_a(NH_3) + pK_a(\text{side chain})}{2}$$

$$= \frac{8.95 + 10.53}{2} = 9.72$$

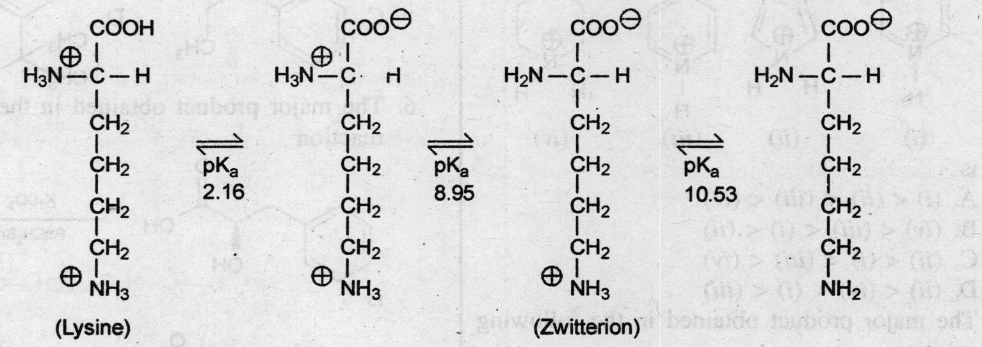

Previous Paper (Solved)

IIT—JAM

JOINT ADMISSION TEST FOR M.Sc. (CHEMISTRY)-2008

1. The correct statement describing the relationship between

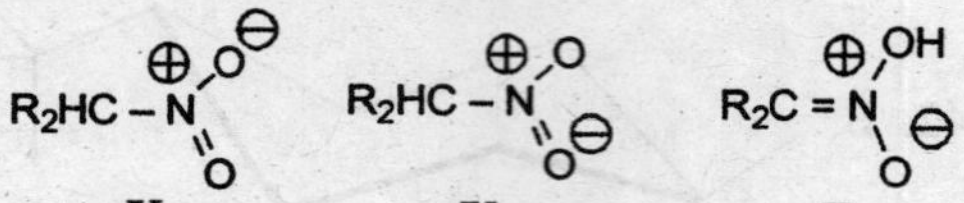

X Y Z

is

A. **X** and **Y** are resonance structures and **Z** is a tautomer

B. **X** and **Y** are tautomer and **Z** is a resonance structures

C. **X, Y** and **Z** are all resonance structures

D. **X, Y** and **Z** are all tautomers

2. Among the following, the correct statement concerning the optical activity is

A. a molecule containing two or more chiral centres is always optically active

B. a molecule containing just one chiral centre is always optically active

C. a molecule possessing alternating axis of symmetry is optically active

D. an optically active molecule should have at least one chiral centre

3. The correct order of acidity among

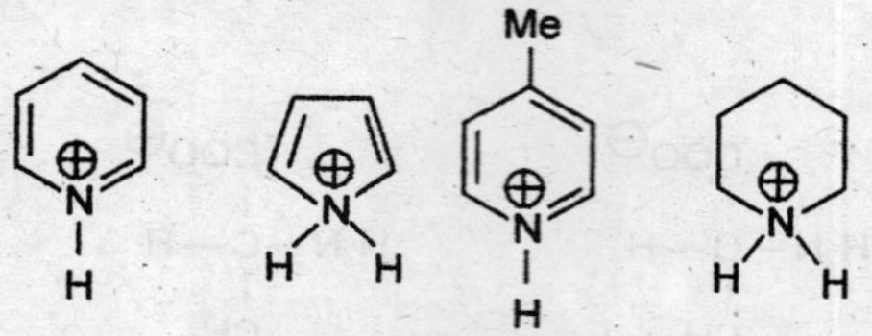

(*i*) (*ii*) (*iii*) (*iv*)

is

A. (*i*) < (*ii*) < (*iii*) < (*iv*)

B. (*iv*) < (*iii*) < (*i*) < (*ii*)

C. (*ii*) < (*i*) < (*iii*) < (*iv*)

D. (*ii*) < (*iv*) < (*i*) < (*iii*)

4. The major product obtained in the following reaction

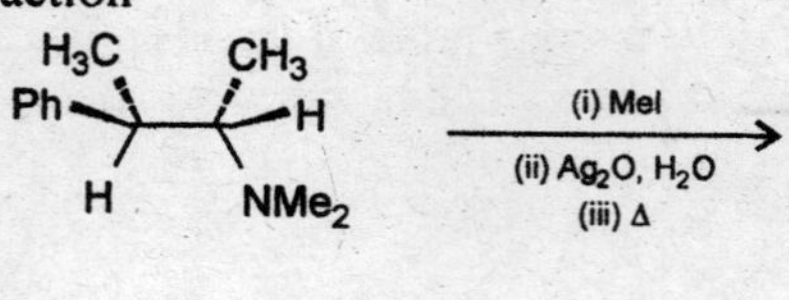

is

A. 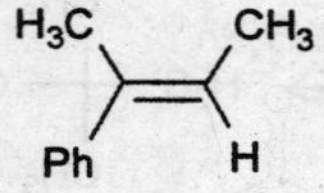 B. 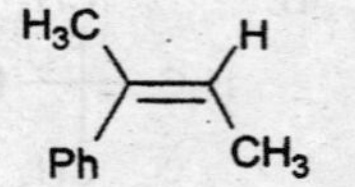

C. 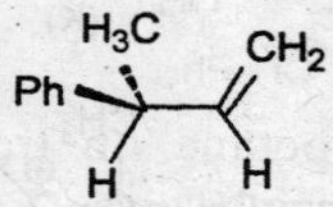 D. 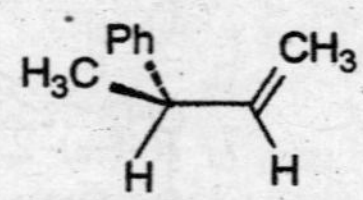

5. The major product of the following reaction

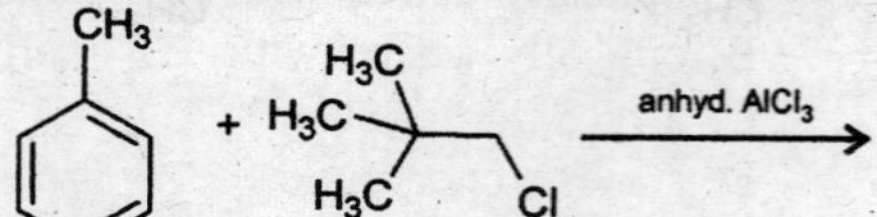

is

A. 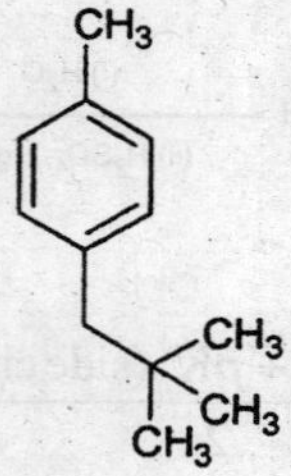 B. 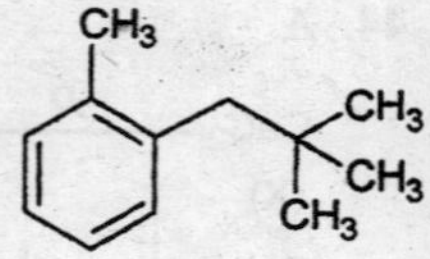

C. 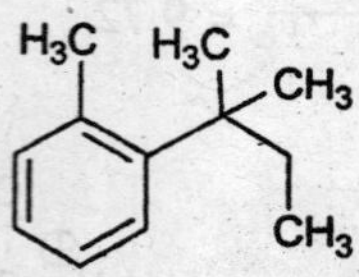 D. 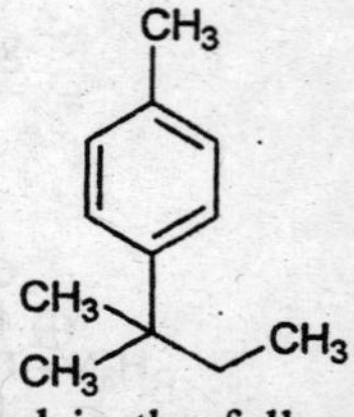

6. The major product obtained in the following reaction

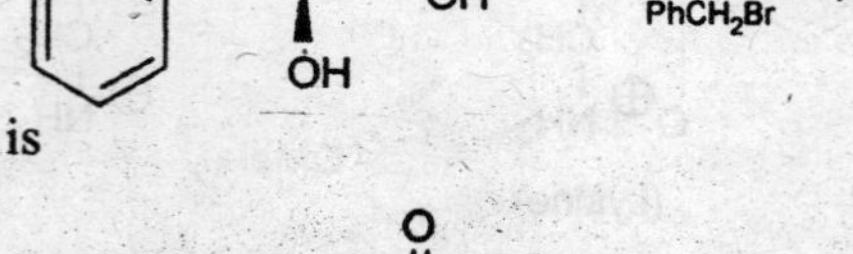

is

A. 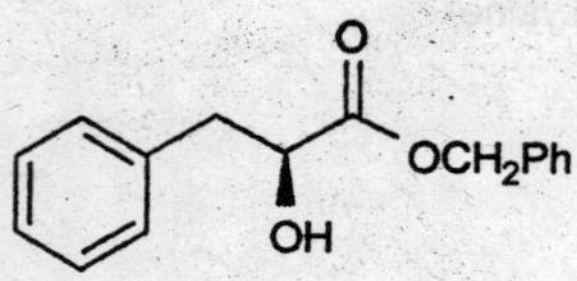

B. 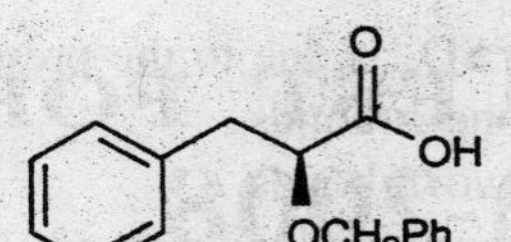

C. 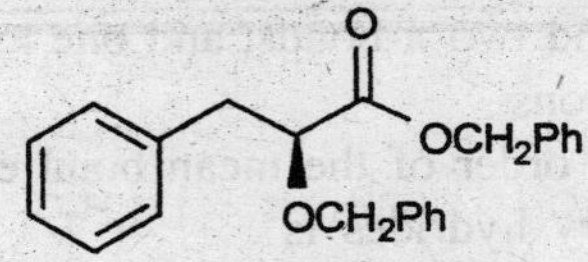

D. 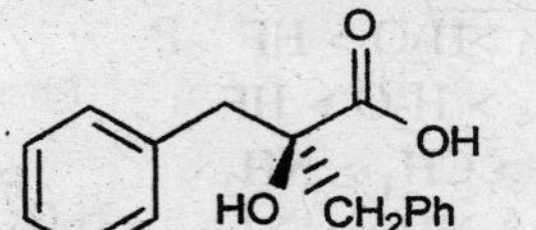

7. *R*-(–)-2-Bromooctane on treatment with aqueous KOH mainly gives 2-octanol that is
A. optically active with '*R*' configuration
B. optically active with '*S*' configuration
C. a racemic mixture
D. a meso compound

8. The major product obtained in the following reaction

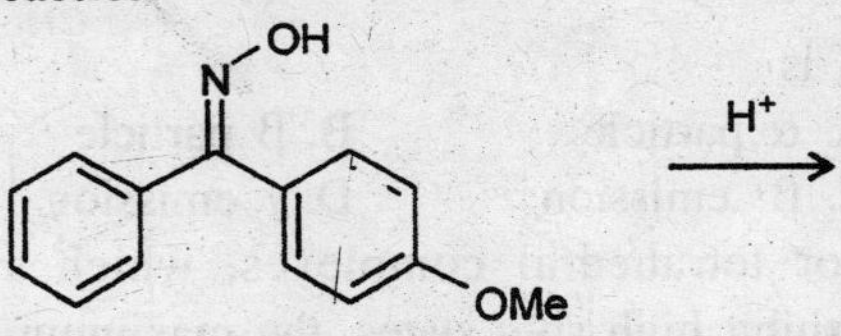

is

A. 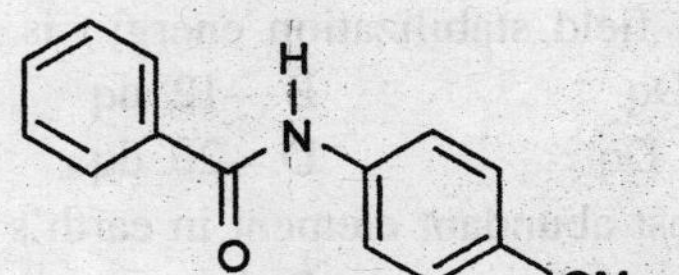

B. 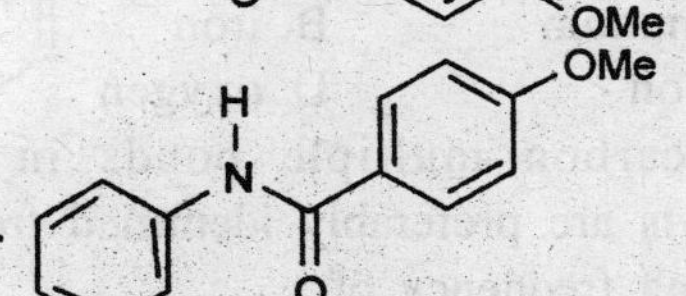

C. an equimolar mixture of

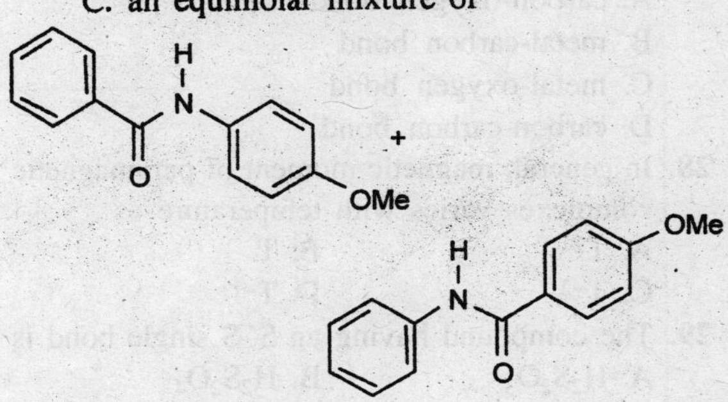

D. 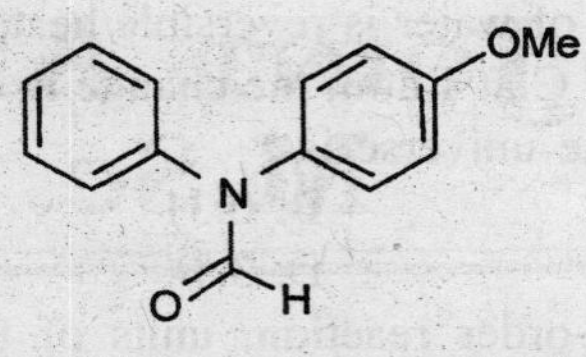

9. The major product obtained in the following reaction

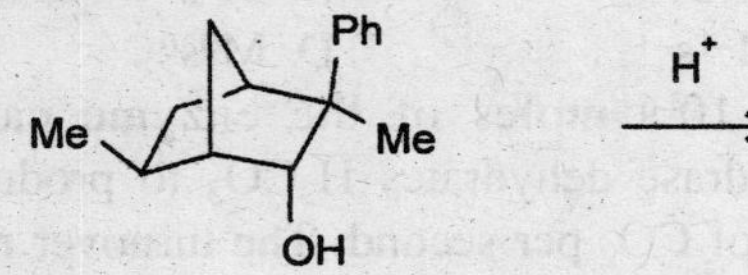

is

A. 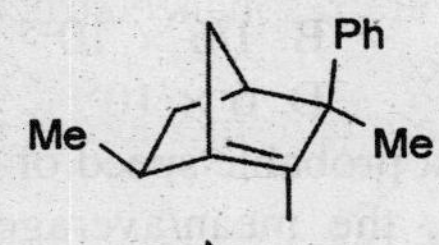 B. 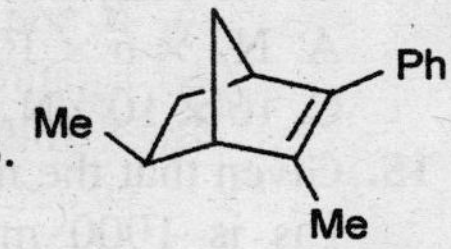

C. 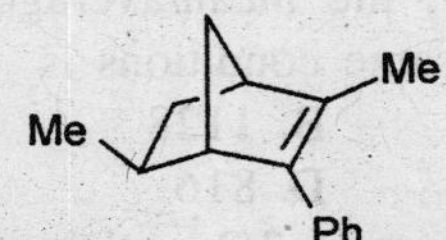 D. 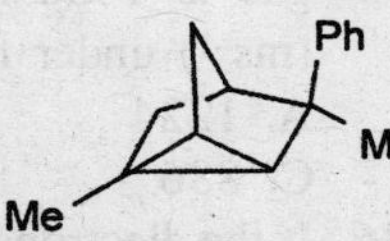

10. The product of the following reaction

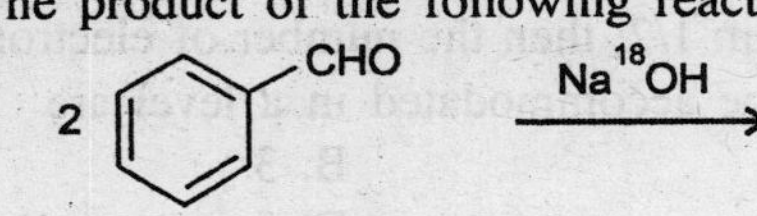

are

A. 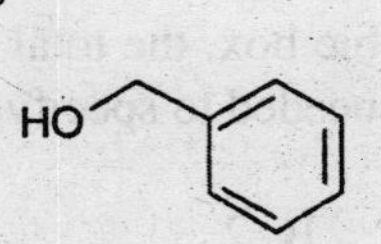 and 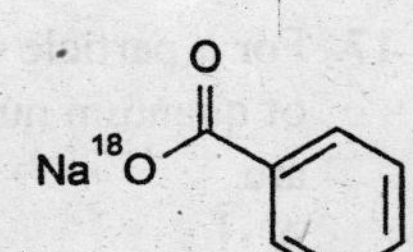

B. 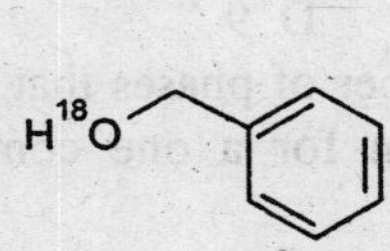 and 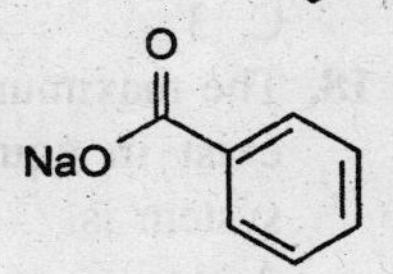

C. 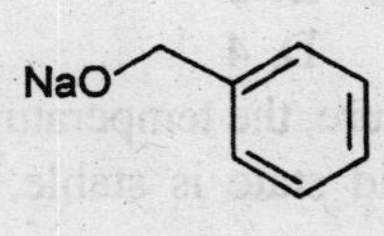 and 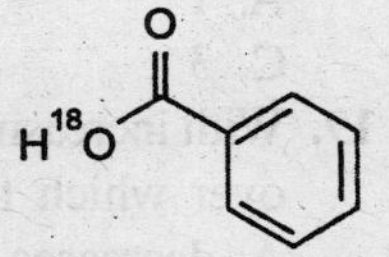

D. 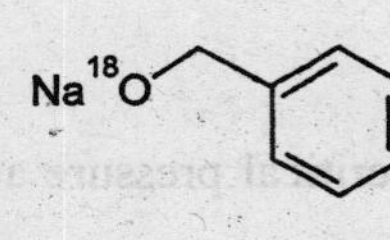 and 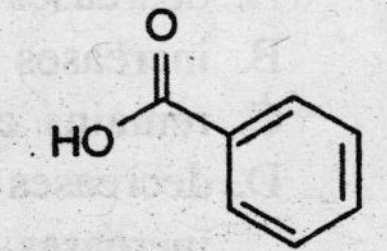

11. When one mole of ice is converted to water at 0°C and 1 atm, the work done (L atm) is
A. 1.1×10^{-4} B. 2.0×10^{-3}
C. 2.0×10^{-4} D. 1.1×10^{-5}

12. When 100g of water is reversible heated from 50°C to 75° C at 1 atm, the change in entropy (JK^{-1}) of the universe is

A. –2.31 B. 0.31
C. 0 D. 3.1

13. For a zero order reaction, units of the rate constant is expressed as

A. M^1s^{-1} B. M^0s^{-1}
C. $M^{-1}s^{-1}$ D. M^0s^0

14. 1×10^{-6} moles of the enzyme carbonic anhydrase dehydrates H_2CO_3 to produce 0.6 mol of CO_2 per second. The turnover number of the enzyme is

A. $N_A \times 6 \times 10^{-5}$ B. $1/6 \times 10^{-5}$
C. $(6 \times 10^5)/N_A$ D. 6×10^5

15. Given that the most probable speed of oxygen gas is 1000 ms^{-1}, the mean/average speed (ms^{-1}) under the same conditions is

A. 1224 B. 1128
C. 886 D. 816

16. If the electrons were spin 3/2 particles, instead of spin 1/2, then the number of electrons that can be accommodated in a level are

A. 2 B. 3
C. 4 D. 5

17. For a particle in a cubic box, the total number of quantum numbers needed to specify its state are

A. 1 B. 2
C. 3 D. 9

18. The maximum number of phases that can co-exist in equilibrium for a one component system is

A. 1 B. 2
C. 3 D. 4

19. With increasing pressure, the temperature range over which the liquid state is stable,

A. decreases
B. increases
C. remains constant
D. decreases till the critical pressure and then increases

20. The conductance at infinite dilution follows the order

A. $Li^+ > Na^+ > K^+$ B. $Na^+ > Li^+ > K^+$
C. $K^+ > Li^+ > Na^+$ D. $K^+ > Na^+ > Li^+$

21. The V-shape of SO_2 is due to the presence of

A. two σ-and one π-bonds
B. two σ-and two π-bonds
C. two σ-bond and one lone pair of electrons
D. two σ-and two π-bonds, and one lone pari of electrons

22. The correct order of the mean bond energies in the binary hydrides is

A. $CH_4 > NH_3 > H_2O > HF$
B. $NH_3 > CH_4 > H_2O > HF$
C. $HF > H_2O > CH_4 > NH_3$
D. $HF > H_2O > NH_3 > CH_4$

23. In CsCl structure, the number of Cs^+ ions that occupy second nearest neighbour locations of a Cs' ion is

A. 6 B. 8
C. 10 D. 12

24. In the process

$$^{234}_{92}U \longrightarrow {}^{230}_{90}Th + X\left({}^{4}_{2}He\right)$$

X is

A. α particle B. β particle
C. β^+ emission D. γ emission

25. For tetrahedral complexes, which always exhibit high spin states, the maximum CFSE (crystal field stabilization energy) is

A. –8 Dq B. –12 dq
C. –16 Dq D. –20 dq

26. The most abundant element in earth's crust is

A. aluminium B. iron
C. silicon D. oxygen

27. Metal-carbon multiple bonds in metal carbonyls are preferably identified from the stretching frequency of

A. carbon-oxygen bond
B. metal-carbon bond
C. metal-oxygen bond
D. carbon-carbon bond

28. In general, magnetic moment of paramagnetic complexes varies with temperature as

A. T^2 B. T
C. T^{-2} D. T^{-1}

29. The compound having an S–S single bond is

A. $H_2S_2O_3$ B. $H_2S_2O_4$
C. $H_2S_2O_7$ D. $H_2S_2O_8$

30. In a reaction, $Na_2S_2O_3$ is converted to $Na_2S_4O_6$. The equivalent weight of $Na_2S_2O_3$ for this reaction is (mol. wt. of $Na_2S_2O_3$ = M).

A. M B. M/4
C. M/2 D. M/3

31. A. Identify **A**, **B** and **C** in the following reaction sequence.

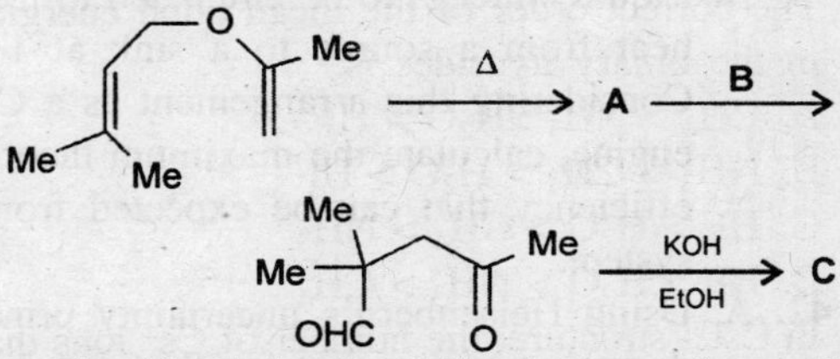

B. Identify **D** in the following reaction and suggest a suitable mechanism of its formation.

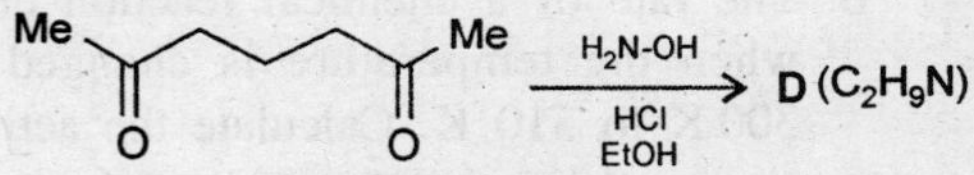

32. A. Explain with the help of mechanisms, the observed stereoselectivity in the following expoxide formation reactions.

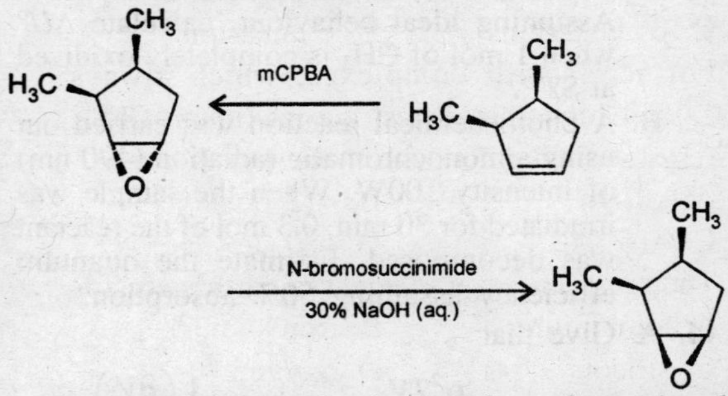

B. Explain on the basis of conformational analysis why (1*R*, 2*S*)-1,2-dimethyl-cyclohexane is optically inactive at room temperature.

33. A. Identify **E**, **F** and **G** in the following synthetic transformation.

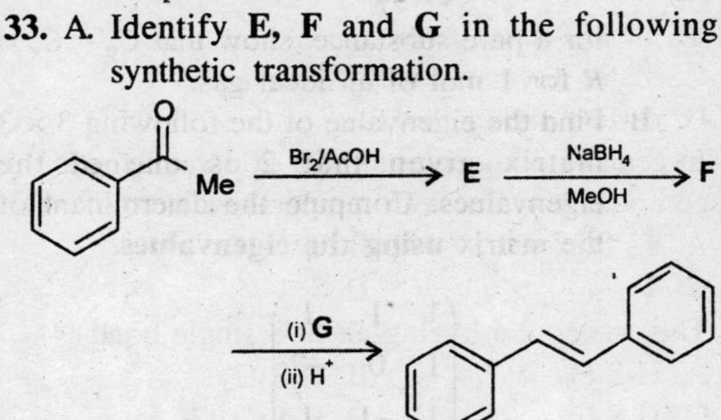

B. An optically active compound **H** (C_5H_6O) on treatment with H_2 in the presence of Lindlar's catalyst gave a compound **I** (C_5H_8O). Upon hydrogenation with H_2 and Pd/C, compound **H** gave **J**($C_5H_{12}O$). Both **I** and **J** were found to be optically inactive. Identify **H, I** and **J.**

34. A. A disaccharide **K** gives a silver mirror with Tollen's reagent. Treatment of **K** with MeOH/HCl gives a monomethyl derivative **L**, which does not react with Tollen's reagent. Methylation of **K** with Me_2SO_4 and NaOH affords an octamethyl derivative of **K**, which upon acidic hydrolysis gives a 1:1 mixture of 2,3,4,6-tetra-*O*-methyl-D-glucose and 2,3,4-tri-*O*-methyl-D-glucose. Disaccharide **K** is also hydrolysed by the enzyme maltase. Identify **K** and **L** with proper stereochemistry.

B. Identify **M** and **N** in the following reaction sequence.

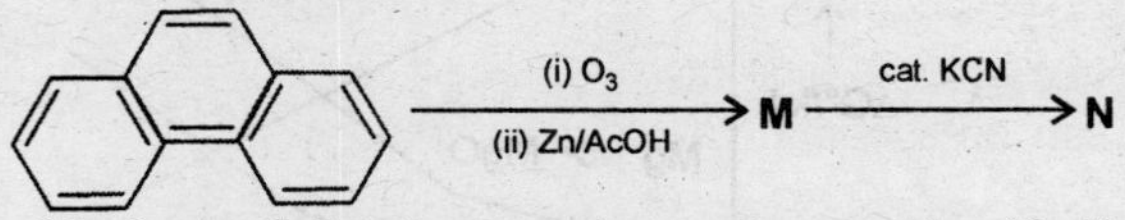

35. In the following reaction sequence, identify **P**, **R** and **S**. Suggest suitable mechanisms for the conversion of **P** → **Q** and **R** →**S.**

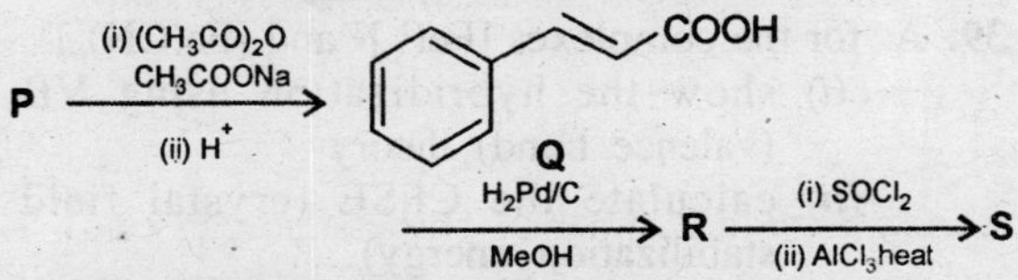

36. A. Consider the reaction

(I) $Cr_2O_7^{2-} + H_2O_2 \xrightarrow{A} \underset{\text{unstable}}{CrO(O_2)_2} \xrightarrow{\text{room temp.}} Cr^{3+}$

(II) $Cr^{3+} + H_2O_2 \xrightarrow{B} CrO_4^{2-}$

(*i*) Identify A and B.

(*ii*) What is the role of H_2O_2 in (I) and how does A favour the formation of Cr^{3+}?

(*iii*) What is the role of H_2O_2 in (II) and how does B favour the formation CrO_4^{2-}?

B. With the help of equations, illustrate the role of a *cis*-1,2-diol in the titration of boric acid with sodium hydroxide.

37. A. Draw the structure of anionic Ca(II)-EDTA chelate. How many rings are formed in the chelate and specify the number of atoms in each ring?

B. Based on VSEPR theory draw the most stable structure of ClF_3 and XeF_4.

38. A. Identify **A**, **B** and **C** in the following reaction scheme

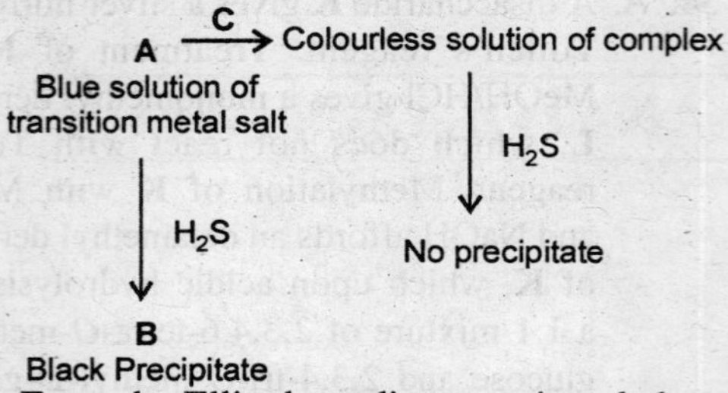

B. From the Ellingham diagram given below, identify the metal oxide that can be reduced at a lower temperature by carbon. Justify.

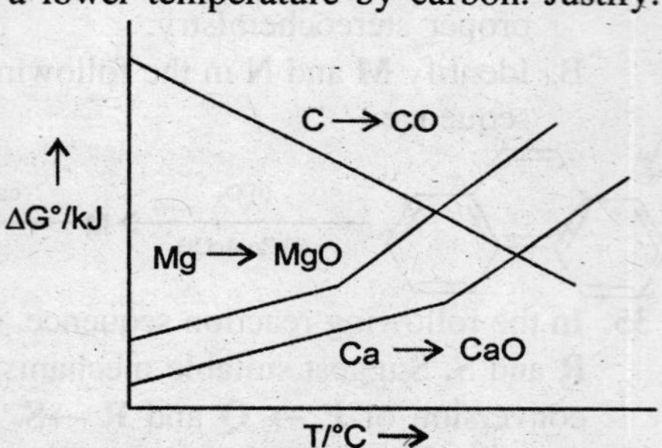

39. A. for the complexes $[FeF_6]^{3}$ and $[Fe(CN)_6]^{3-}$

(*i*) show the hybridization using VB (valence bond) theory

(*ii*) calculate the CFSE (crystal field stabilization energy)

B. Identify the dark blue complex formed when $[Fe(CN)_6]^{3-}$ is treated with $FeSO_4$ and account for the origin of its colour.

40. A. Consider the equilibrium

$$\text{A(g)} \rightleftharpoons \text{B(g)} + \text{C(g)}$$

At a constant pressure of 1 atm, **A** dissociates to the extent of 50% at 500 K. Calculate ΔG° (kJ mol^{-1}) for the reaction.

B. Consider the following redox system

$$\text{Q} + 2\text{H}^+ + 2e^- \rightleftharpoons \text{QH}_2 \quad E° = 0.699 \text{ V}$$

Calculate the pH of the solution at 298 K, if the redox potential of the system is 0.817 V.

41. A. A stream of oxygen molecules at 500 K exits from a pin-hole in an oven and strikes a slit that selects the molecules travelling in a specific direction. Given that the pressure outside the oven is 2.5×10^{-7} atm, estimate the maximum distance at which the slit must be placed from the pin-hole, in order to produce a collimated beam of oxygen. (Radius of O_2 = 1.8×10^{-10} m)

B. Liquid water is to be circulated to transfer heat from a source to a sink at 1 atm. Considering this arrangement as a Carnot engine, calculate the maximum theoretical efficiency that can be expected from the system.

42. A. Using Heisenberg's uncertainty principle, derive an expression for the approximate ground state energy of a particle of mass ***m*** in a one dimensional box of length ***L***.

B. The rate of a chemical reaction doubles when the temperature is changed from 300 K to 310 K. Calculate the activation energy (kJ mol^{-1}) for the reaction.

43. Consider the reaction

A. $CH_4(g) + 2O_2(g) \rightarrow CO_2(g) + 2H_2O(l)$

$$\Delta H° = -606.9 \text{ kJ mol}^{-1}$$

Assuming ideal behaviour, calculate $\Delta U°$ when 1 mol of CH_4 is completely oxidized at STP.

B. A photochemical reaction was carried out using a monochromatic radiation (490 nm) of intensity 100W. When the sample was irradiated for 30 min, 0.3 mol of the reactant was decomposed. Estimate the quantum efficiency assuming 50% absorption.

44. A. Give that

$$C_p - C_v = \frac{\alpha^2 TV}{k_T} \quad \text{where } \alpha = \frac{1}{V}\left(\frac{\partial V}{\partial T}\right)_p \text{ and}$$

$$k_T = -\frac{1}{V}\left(\frac{\partial V}{\partial P}\right)_T$$

for a pure substance, show that $C_p - C_v = R$ for 1 mol of an ideal gas.

B. Find the eigenvalue of the following 3 × 3 matrix given that 2 is one of the eigenvalues. Compute the determinant of the matrix **using the eigenvalues.**

$$\begin{pmatrix} 1 & 1 & 1 \\ 1 & 0 & -2 \\ 1 & -1 & 1 \end{pmatrix}$$

ANSWERS

1	2	3	4	5	6	7	8	9	10
A	D	B	A	D	B	C	A	B	D
11	**12**	**13**	**14**	**15**	**16**	**17**	**18**	**19**	**20**
*	C	A	B	A	B	C	C	B	D
21	**22**	**23**	**24**	**25**	**26**	**27**	**28**	**29**	**30**
D	A	A	A	C	C	A	D	B	A

SOME SELECTED EXPLANATORY ANSWERS

1. Tautomerism involved the movement of both electrons and atoms whereas resonance structures differ in respect of positions of electrons only.

3. 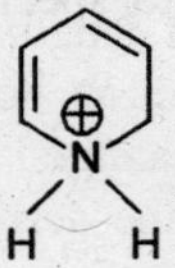

On loosing proton will become aromatic and therefore will most readily release H^+ to became stable.

In 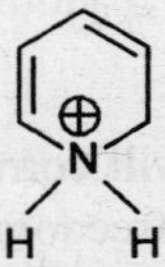

and 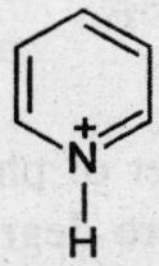

latter is most acidic hydrogen since in former the +I effect reduces positive charge on Nitrogen.

4. 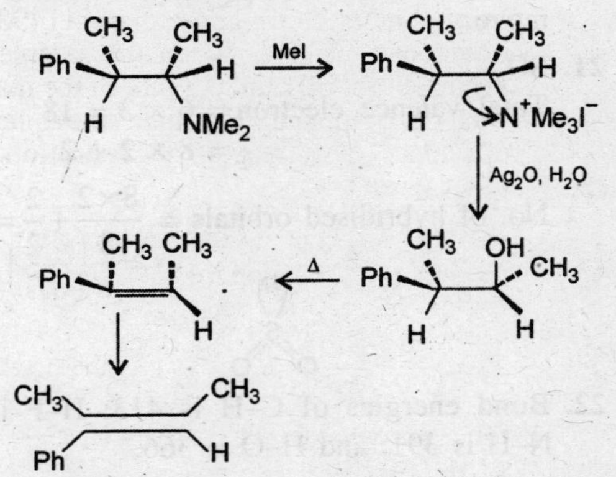

5. 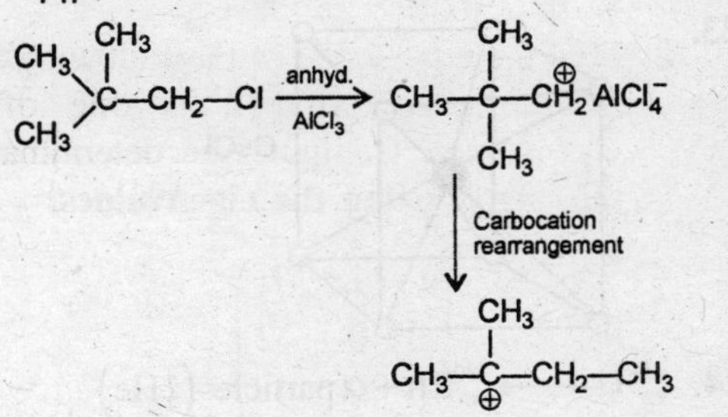

6. 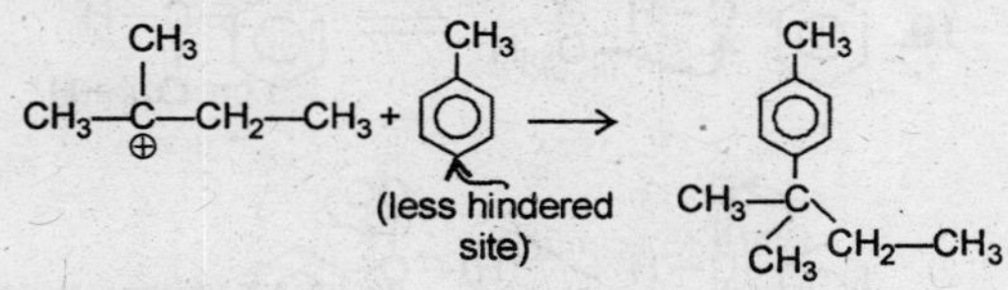

7. 2-Bromooctane

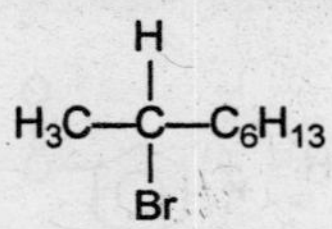

It will give $CH_3-\overset{\oplus}{C}(Br)-C_6H_{13}$ cation as solvent is polar. This planar carbocation can be attacked from both side giving both R and S configuration, thus producing racemic mixture.

8. 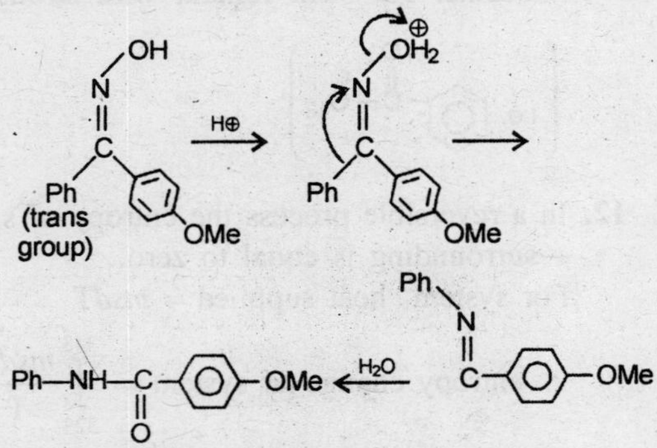

Trans group migrate preferably.

9. 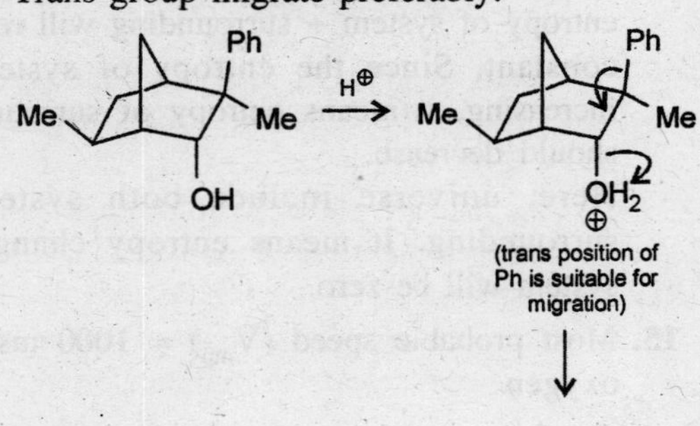

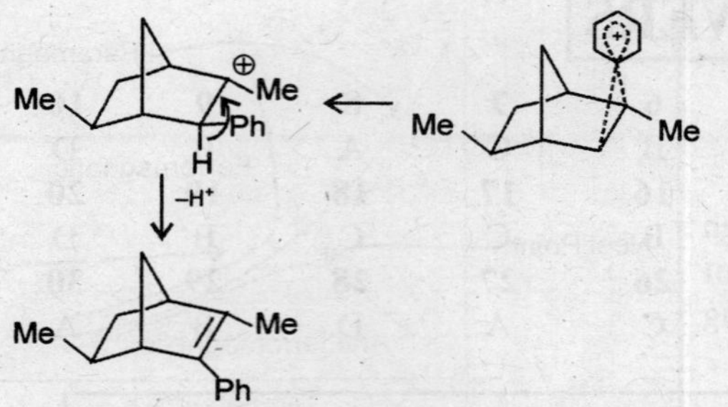

10. 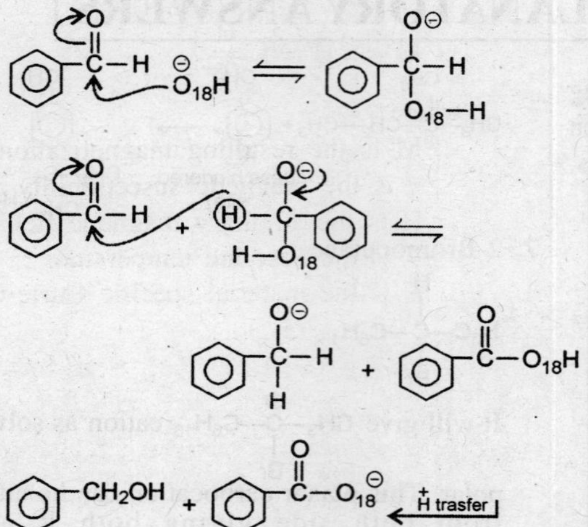

—Further Na^+ will remain with strong acid

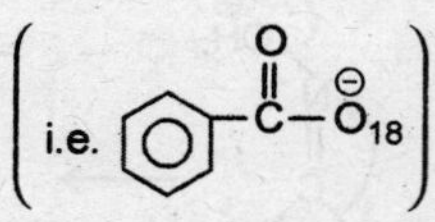

12. In a reversible process the entropy of system + surrounding is equal to zero.

For system heat supplied = msdT

$$\therefore \text{ entropy change of system} = \int_{323}^{348} \frac{msd\text{T}}{\text{T}}$$

Note: It is a reversible process and therefore entropy of system + surrounding will remain constant. Since the entropy of system is increasing, it means entropy of surrounding should decrease.

Here, universe include both system + surrounding. It means entropy change of system will be zero.

15. Most probable speed (V_{mp}) = 1000 ms^{-1} of oxygen

$$\left(\frac{2RT}{M}\right)^{1/2} = 1000 \text{ ms}^{-1} \qquad ...(i)$$

Mean/average speed of oxygen = x

$$\left(\frac{3RT}{M}\right)^{1/2} = x \qquad ...(ii)$$

From (*i*) and (*ii*)

$$\frac{1000}{(2)^{1/2}} = \frac{x}{(3)^{1/2}}$$

$$x = 1000 \times (1.5)^{1/2} = 1224 \text{ ms}^{-1}$$

17. The solution to Schrodinger equation for a particle in 3 dimensional box does not give spin quantum number. This means quantum number n, l, m are sufficient to specify the state.

18. $P + F = C + Z$

$\therefore \quad P = C - F + Z$

$= 3 - F \qquad (C = 1)$

$= 3.$

$\therefore$ Max. number of phases will correspond to a point where degree of freedom is zero.

20. The smaller the ion, the more it will be hydrated and more difficult will be for it to move.

21. SO_2

Total valence electron = 6 × 3 = 18

= 8 × 2 + 2

No. of hybridised orbitals = $\frac{8\times2}{8}+\frac{2}{2}=3.$

22. Bond energies of C–H is 413; H–F is 56; N–H is 391; and H–O is 366.

23. 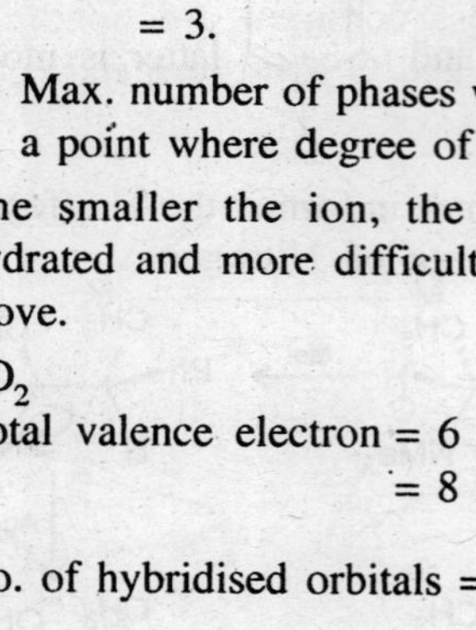

24. ${}^{234}_{92}U \longrightarrow {}^{230}_{90}Th + \alpha \text{ particles} \left({}^{4}_{2}He\right)$

25. Tetrahedral complex

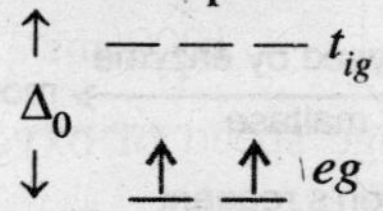

System with 2 electron will always show high spin state and above this number pairing of electron can take place in presence of strong ligand.

$$\therefore \text{ CFSE} = \frac{3}{5}\Delta_0 \times 2 = 16 \text{ Dq.}$$

27. Carbonyl ligand engaged in a range of bonding in metal carbonyl cluster chemistry. CO is often bridges between two (μ_2) or three (μ_3) metals.

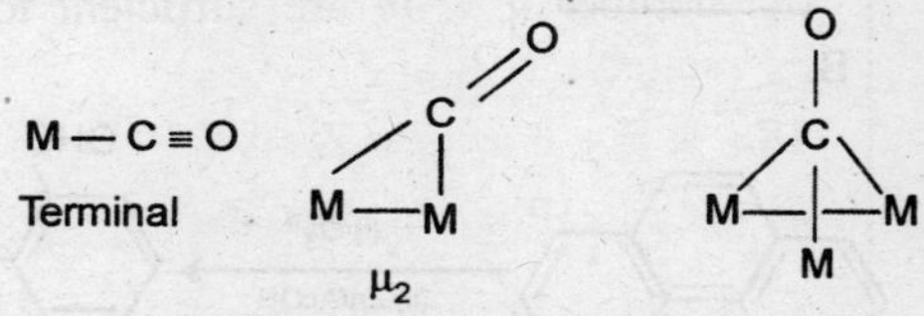

Much less common are bonding mode in which C and O bond to metal eq. $\mu_3 - \eta^2$

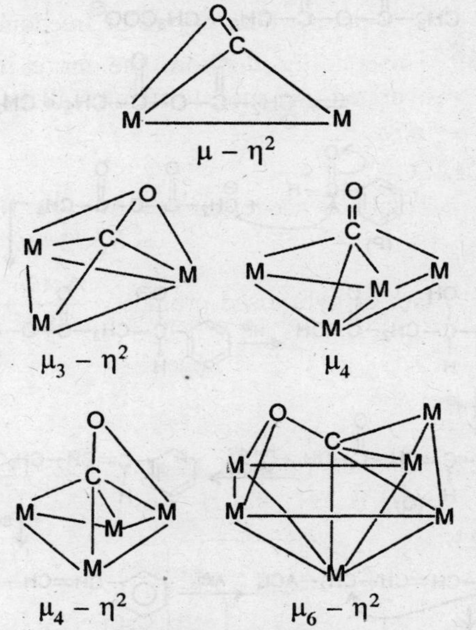

The increased π-bonding due to back donation from multiple metal centres results in further weakening of C–O bond.

28. The magnetic moment is dependent on both spin and orbital angular momentum

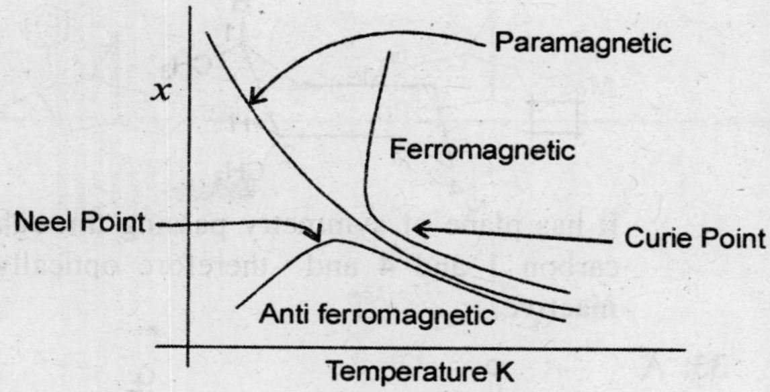

$$M = x.H = C.\frac{H}{T}$$

where

M is the resulting magnetization
x is the magnetic susceptibility
H is the auxiliary magnetic field
T is the absolute temperature
C is the material specific Curie Constant.

29.

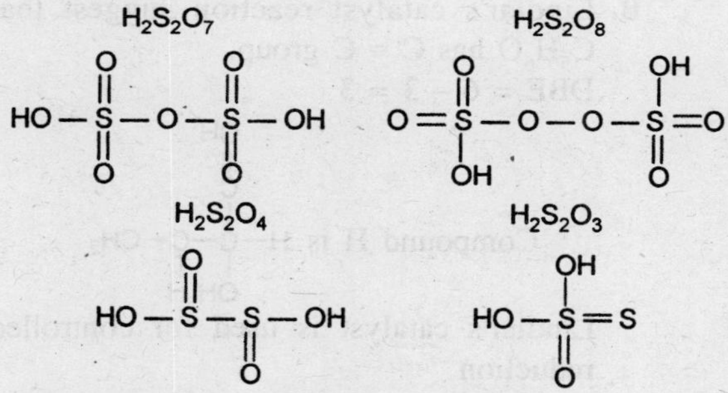

30. $2Na_2S_2O_3 \rightarrow Na_2S_4O_6 + 2\ Na$

Mol. wt. of $Na_2S_2O_3$ = M

For this reaction, oxidation state of 1 atom of sulphur on the left side is +2 and on the right hand side of the ignition, it is 2.5. So difference is 0.5 and we want to calculate equivalent weight of sulphur compound on the left hand side, thus the valance factor

= no of atoms × change in oxidation number
= 2 × 0.5 = 1

Therefore, equivalent weight is M.

32. B. The given compound is 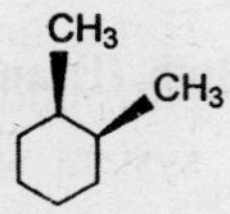

It has conformational structure as shown below

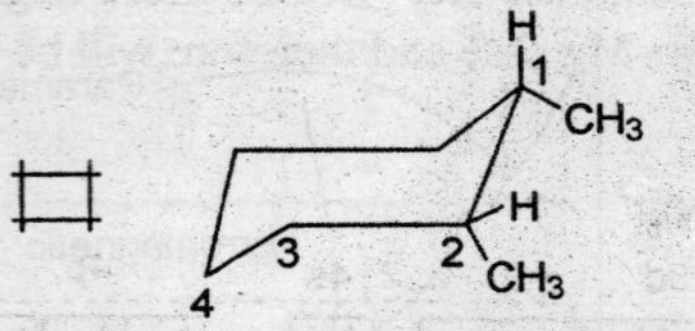

It has plane of symmetry passing through carbon 1 and 4 and therefore optically inactive.

33. A.

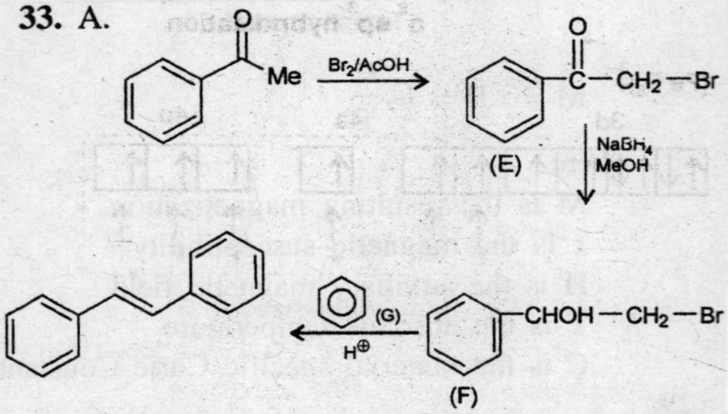

B. Lindlar's catalyst reaction suggest that C_5H_6O has $C \equiv C$ group.
DBE = 6 − 3 = 3

∴ Compound H is

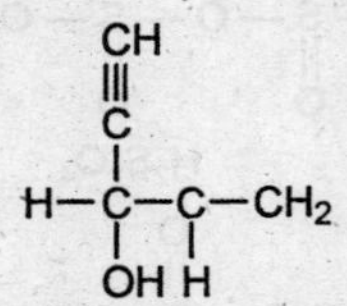

Lindlar's catalyst is used for controlled reduction

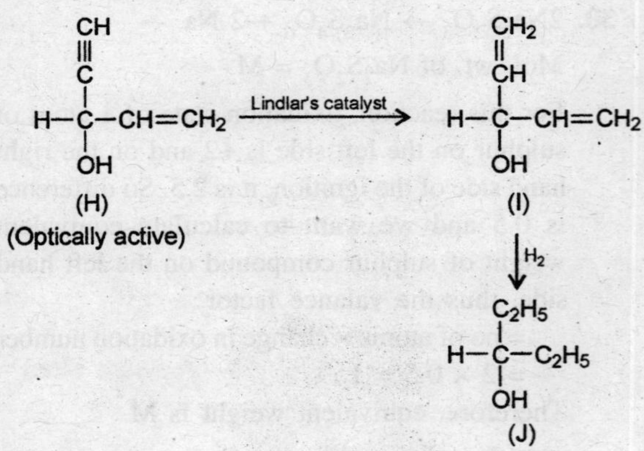

Both (I) and (J) are optically inactive.

34. A.

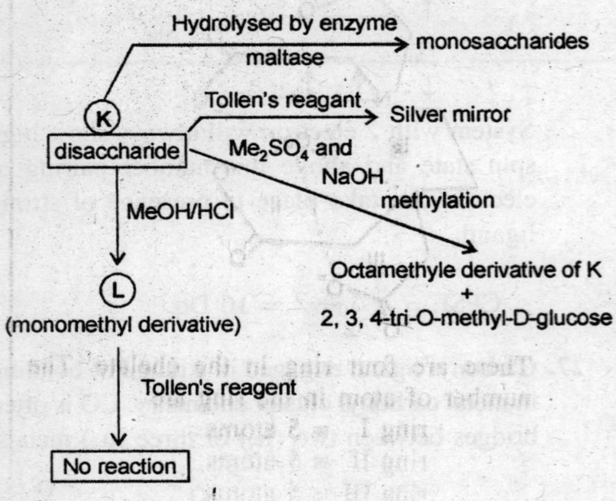

B.

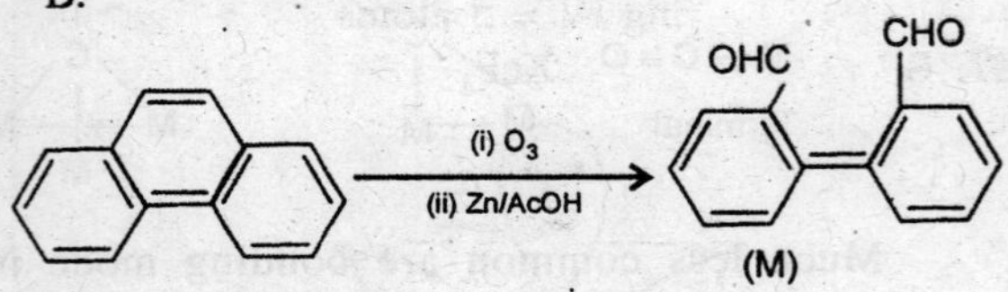

35.

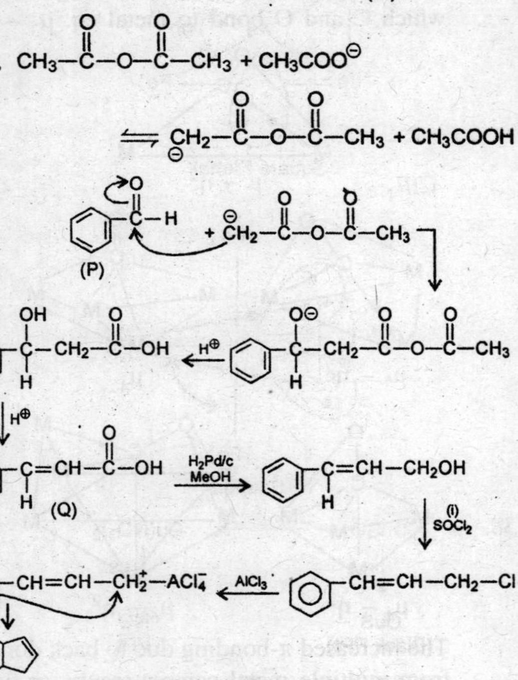

37. A.

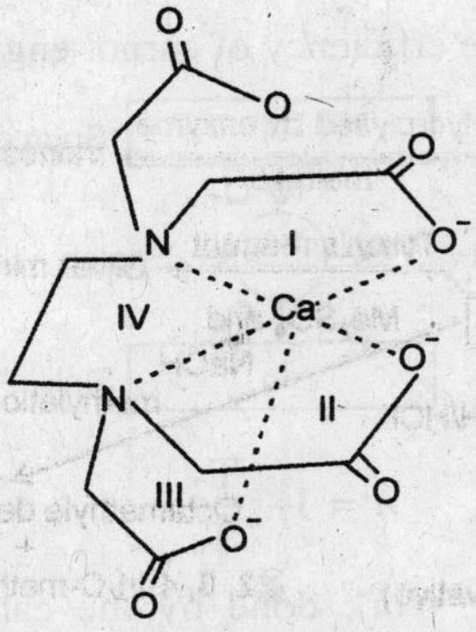

There are four ring in the chelate. The number of atom in the ring are

ring I = 5 atoms
ring II = 5 atoms
ring III = 5 atoms
ring IV = 5 atoms

37. B. XeF_4

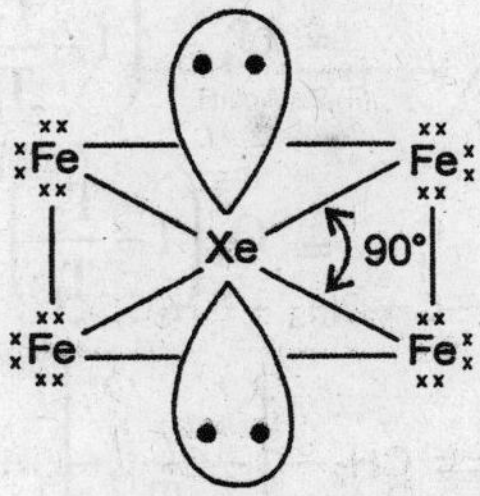

Square Planar

ClF_4

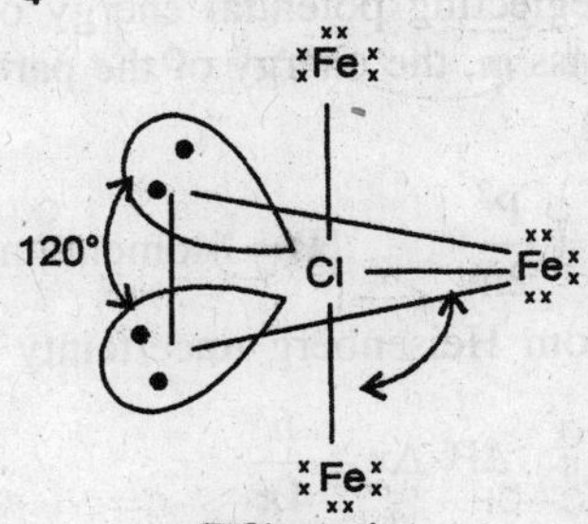

T-Shaped

38. A.

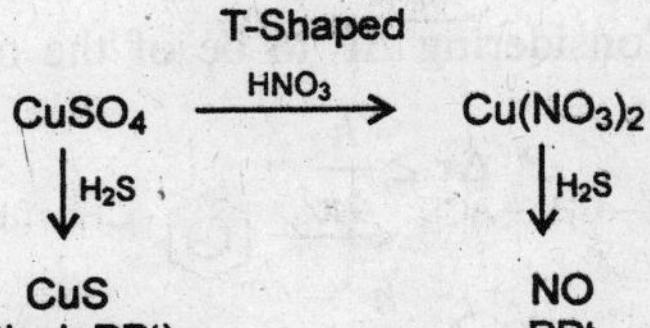

$CuSO_4$ is blue in colour in aqueous solution.

B. The more negative the Gibbs free energy for the reaction, more easily it will occur. In present case ΔG° will be more negative for $MgO \rightarrow Mg$ case and therefore will be reduced.

39. A. (*i*)

$[Fe(CN)_6]^{3-}$

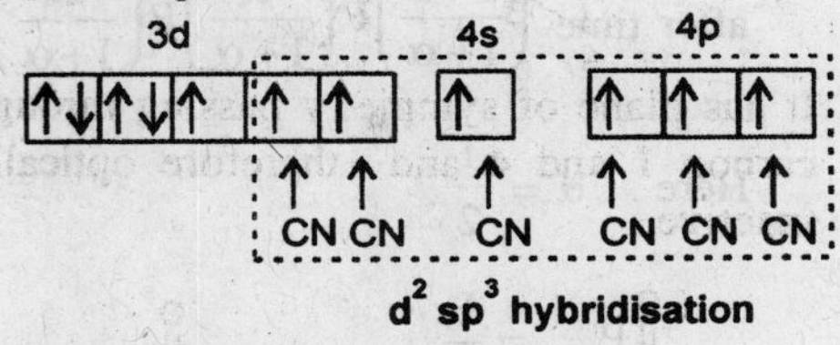

d^2sp^3 hybridisation

$[FeF_6]^{3-}$

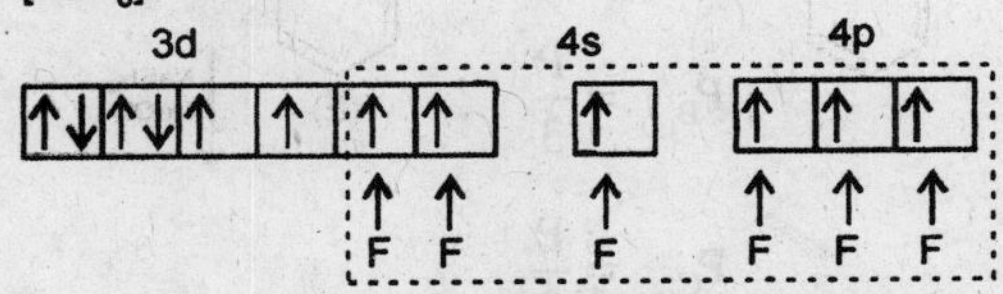

d^2sp^3 hybridisation

39. A. (*ii*) In $[Fe(CN)_6]^{3-}$, Fe^{3+} has $3d^5$ electronic configuration having five electrons

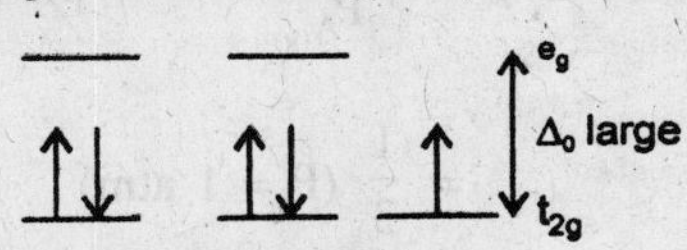

Low spin complex
(one unpaired electron)

$$CFSE = (-0.4_n(t_{2g}) + 0.6_n(e_g))\,\Delta_o + pP$$
$$= (-0.4 \times 5 + 0.6 \times 0)\Delta_o + pP$$
$$= -2\Delta_o + pP$$

In FeF_6^{3-}, F_e^{3-} has $3d^5$ electronic configuration having five electrons.

Low spin complex
(one unpaired electron)

$$CFSE = [-0.4_n(t_{2g}) + 0.6_n(e_g)]\,\Delta_o + pP$$
$$= (-0.4 \times 5 + 0.6 \times 0)\Delta_o + pP$$
$$= -2\Delta_o + pP$$

39. B. $Fe_4[Fe(CN)_6]_3$ is dark blue (Prussian blue) colour formed by following reaction

$$\underset{\text{Ferroussulphate}}{3FeSO_4} + \underset{\text{Ferrocyanids}}{2[Fe(CN)_6]^{3-}} \rightarrow \underset{\substack{\text{Ferresodiferric diletracyanids}\\ \text{(dark blue complex)}}}{Fe[Fe(CN)_6]_2} + 2SO_2^{2-}$$

40. A. $A_{(g)} \rightleftharpoons B_{(g)} + C_{(g)}$

initially P O O

after time $\left(\frac{1-\alpha}{1+\alpha}\right)P \left(\frac{\alpha}{1+\alpha}\right)P \left(\frac{\alpha}{1+\alpha}\right)P$

Here $\alpha = \frac{1}{2}$

$$\therefore \quad P_{A_{(g)}} = \frac{P}{3}$$

$$P_{B_{(g)}} = \frac{P}{3}$$

$$P_{C_{(g)}} = \frac{P}{3}$$

$$K_p = \frac{P_{C_{(g)}} P_{B_{(g)}}}{P_{A_{(g)}}} = \frac{(P/3)(P/3)}{P/3} = \frac{P}{3}$$

$$= \frac{1}{3} \quad (P = 1 \text{ atm})$$

$$\Delta G° = -RT \ln K_p$$

$$= -8.314 \times 500 \ln \frac{1}{3}$$

$$= 4.567 \times 10^3 \text{ Joules/mol}$$

B. $Q + 2H^+ + Le^- \rightleftharpoons QH_2 \quad E° = .699$

$$E = E°_{cell} - \frac{.0591}{2} \log \frac{1}{[H^+]^2}$$

$$= E°_{cell} - .0591 \text{ pH}$$

$\Rightarrow \quad .817 = .699 - .0591$ pH

or $\quad$ pH = –1.99

Instead of taking quinone and hydroquinone, a small amount of quinhydrone, which is an equimolecular compound of quinone (Q) and hydroquinone [QH_2] is taken. Since hydroquinone is a weak acid, its ionization is very small particularly if the pH value of solution is less than 7. Therefore, concentration of hydroquinone [QH_2] is the same as that of quinone [Q] i.e. the quantity [Q]/[QH_2] is unity.

41. B. The efficiency of carnot engine is given by

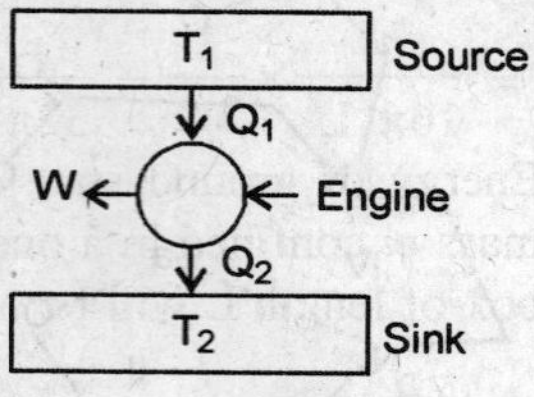

$$n = 1 - \frac{T_2}{T_1}$$

$\therefore$ Work done by the carnot engine is given by $\left(1 - \frac{T_2}{T_1}\right) \times Q_1$

and heat transfer from source to sink i.e. Q_2 will be

$$Q_2 = Q_1 - W$$

$$= Q_1 - \left(1 - \frac{T_2}{T_1}\right) \times Q_1$$

$$= Q_1 \left(1 - \frac{T_2}{T_1}\right)$$

42. A.

Neglecting potential energy of particle of mass *m*, the energy of the particle is given by

$$E = \frac{P^2}{2m} \quad \{P = \text{Momentum of Particle}\}$$

From Heisenberg uncertainty principle

$$\Delta P \cdot \Delta x \geq \frac{h}{4\pi}$$

Considering ΔP to be of the order of P.

$$P \cdot \Delta x \geq \frac{h}{4\pi}$$

$$\Rightarrow \quad \Delta x \geq \frac{h}{4\pi P}$$

But $\Delta x = L$

$$\therefore \quad P \geq \frac{h}{4\pi L}$$

$\therefore$ Energy of particle

$$= \frac{h^2}{16\pi^2L^2} \times \frac{1}{2m} = \frac{h^2}{32\pi^2 mL^2}$$

$\therefore$ Energy of ground state of particle of mass *m* confined in a one dimensional box of length L will be of the order of

$$\frac{h^2}{32\pi^2 mL^2}$$

B. Use $\log 10 \frac{k_2}{k_1} = \frac{E_a}{2.303R}\left[\frac{1}{T_1} - \frac{1}{T_2}\right]$

43. A. $\Delta H = \Delta E + \Delta nRT$

$CH_4(g) + 2O_2(g) \rightarrow CO_2(g) + 2H_2O(l)$

$\Delta n = -2$

$\Rightarrow \quad \Delta H = \Delta E - 2RT$

or $\quad \Delta E = \Delta H + 2RT$

B. Energy corresponding to 490 nm

$$= \frac{hc}{\lambda} = \frac{6.626 \times 10^{-34} \times 3 \times 10^8}{490 \times 10^{-9}}$$

$= 4.056 \times 10^{-19}$ Joules

$\therefore$ No. of particles emitted per second by the intensity source of 100 w

$$= \frac{100}{4.056 \times 10^{-19}} = 2.465 \times 10^{20}$$

$\therefore$ Total no. of particles emmitted during 30 min interval

$= 2.465 \times 10^{20} \times 60 \times 30$

$= 4.437 \times 10^{23}$

Only 50% of these get absorbed

i.e. $\frac{4.437 \times 10^{23}}{2} = 2.21 \times 10^{23}$

Quantum efficiency

$$= \frac{\text{No. of molecules of reactant decomposed}}{\text{Total no. of particle absorbed}}$$

$$= \frac{.3 \times 6.023 \times 10^{23}}{2.21 \times 10^{23}} = .817$$

44. A. For ideal gas PV = RT (1 mole of a gas) ... (*i*)

$$\therefore \quad P\left(\frac{\partial V}{\partial T}\right)_P = R$$

$$\Rightarrow \quad P\left(\frac{\partial V}{\partial T}\right)_P = \frac{R}{P}$$

$$\therefore \quad \alpha = \frac{1}{V}\left(\frac{\partial V}{\partial T}\right)_P = \frac{1}{V}\left(\frac{R}{P}\right) \quad ...(ii)$$

Again from equation (*i*) we have

$$P\left(\frac{\partial V}{\partial P}\right)_T + V = 0$$

$$\Rightarrow \quad \left(\frac{\partial V}{\partial P}\right)_T = \frac{-V}{P}$$

$$\Rightarrow \quad -\frac{1}{V}\left(\frac{\partial V}{\partial P}\right)_T = \frac{1}{P} = K_T \quad ...(iii)$$

$$C_P - C_V = \frac{\alpha^2 TV}{K_T} \quad \text{(given)}$$

$$= \frac{1}{V^2}\frac{R^2}{P^2} \times \frac{TV}{(1/P)}$$

$$= R^2 \frac{TV}{V^2 P} = R^2 \frac{T}{PV}$$

$$= R^2 \times \frac{1}{R} = R$$

$(\because PV = RT)$

B. $A = \begin{bmatrix} 1 & 1 & 1 \\ 1 & 0 & -2 \\ 1 & -1 & 1 \end{bmatrix}$

As product of eigen values = product of diagonal elements.

$\Rightarrow \quad \lambda_1\lambda_2\lambda_3 = 1.0.1 = 0$

i.e. one of the eigen value must be equal to zero.

or other way

Also $\lambda_1 + \lambda_2 + \lambda_3 = 1 + 0 + 1$

$\Rightarrow \quad \lambda_2 + \lambda_3 = 0$

Also one of λ is zero.

$\Rightarrow$ Both the eigen values of A is equal to zero.

$\Rightarrow$ Eigen value of A are 0, 0, 2.

IIT–JAM

JOINT ADMISSION TEST FOR M.SC. (CHEMISTRY)-2007

1. In the extraction of metals from their ores, which one of the following reduction methods can bring about an non-spontaneous reduction?

A. electrolytic reduction
B. reduction by carbon
C. reduction by another metal
D. reduction by hydrogen

2. The solid-liquid phase diagram for the Mg-Zn system is shown in the figure below where the vertical line at x(Mg) = 0.33 represents the formation of a congruent melting compound $MgZn_2$. The figure is divided into seven regions depending upon the physical state of the sytem. The composition of the region #6 represents

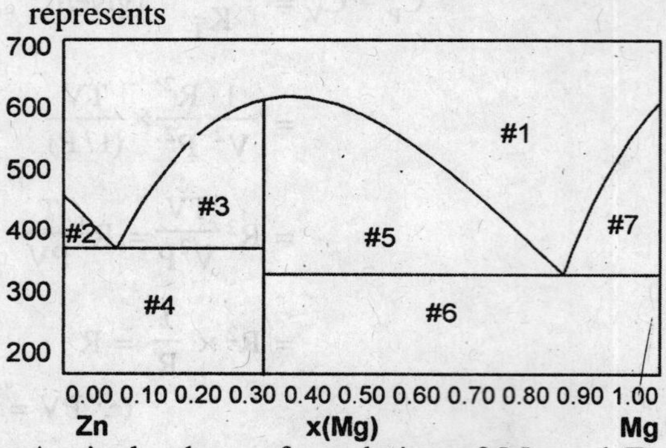

A. single phase of a solution of Mg and Zn
B. two phase region between the solid Zn and solid $MgZn_2$
C. two phase region between the liquid and solid $MgZn_2$
D. two phase region between solid Mg and solid $MgZn_2$

3. Which one of the following species is the conjugate base of HO^-?

A. H_2O B. O^{2-}
C. O_2^- D. O_2^{2-}

4. The plot of Gibb's free energy G and the extent of a reaction ξ is given below for the reaction $A \rightleftharpoons B$. If μ_A and μ_B are the chemical potentials of A and B respectively, the **incorrect** statements is

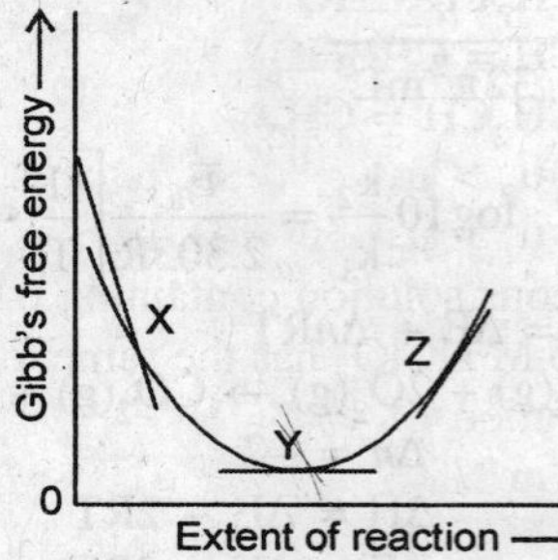

A. at point X, $\mu_A > \mu_B$
B. at point Y, $\Delta G = 0$
C. at point Z, $\mu_A > \mu_B$
B. at equilibrium, the composition of the reaction mixture can be identified

5. For a cyclic process performed by an ideal gas, changes in some thermodynamic functions are zero. Indicate the set in which all the functions are zero.

A. w, ΔE, ΔH, ΔG B. q, ΔS, ΔH, ΔA
C. q, ΔE, ΔS, ΔG D. ΔE, ΔS, ΔH, ΔA

6. For a reaction with rate equation $-dC/dt = kC^2$, C_0 and C are the concentrations of the reactant at time 0 and t respectively. If 10 minutes were required for C_0 to become $C_0/2$, the time required for C_0 to become $C_0/4$ is

A. 10 min B. 20 min
C. 30 min D. 40 min

7. Which of the following compounds is optically active?

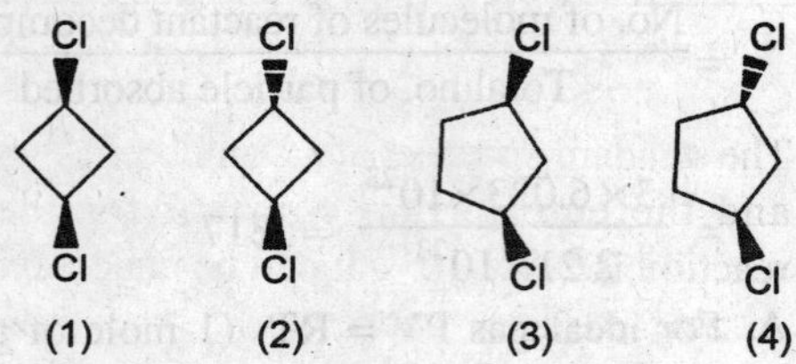

(1) (2) (3) (4)

A. 1 B. 2
C. 3 D. 4

8. Which one of the following compounds gives positive test for both nitrogen and halogen with its Lassaigne's extract?

A. $CH_3NH_2.HCl$ B. $NH_2OH.HCl$
C. NH_4Cl D. $H_2NNH_2.HCl$

9. The correct order of dipole moments (μ) of the following compounds is

1. $CH_3CH_2CH_2CHO$
2. $CH_3CH = CHCHO$
3. $CH_3CH_2CH = CH_2$

A. $\mu_1 > \mu_2 > \mu_3$ B. $\mu_2 > \mu_3 > \mu_1$
C. $\mu_3 > \mu_1 > \mu_2$ D. $\mu_2 > \mu_1 > \mu_3$

10. An aqueous solution containing 0.01 M $FeCl_3$ and 0.06 M $HClO_4$ has the same ionic strength as a solution of

A. 0.09 m NaCl B. 0.04 M Na_2SO_4
C. 0.06 M $CuSO_4$ D. 0.03 M H_3PO_4

11. Which one of the following figures, showing kinetic energy of the ejected electron *versus* the frequency (v) of the incident photon, represents the Einstein's photoelectric effect?

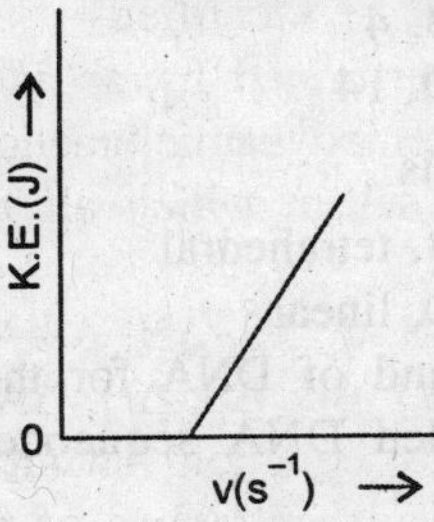

A.

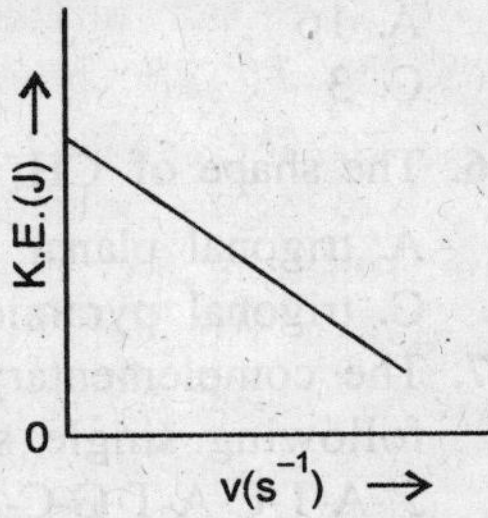

B.

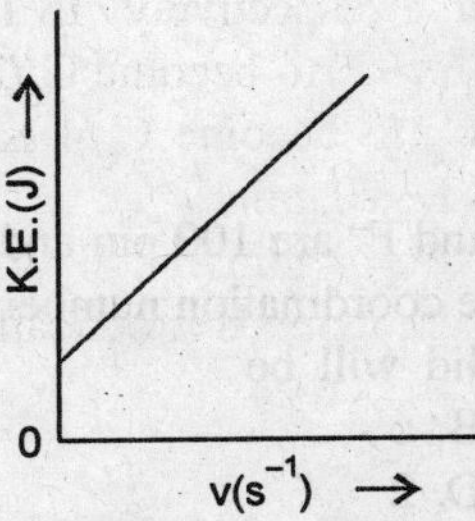

C.

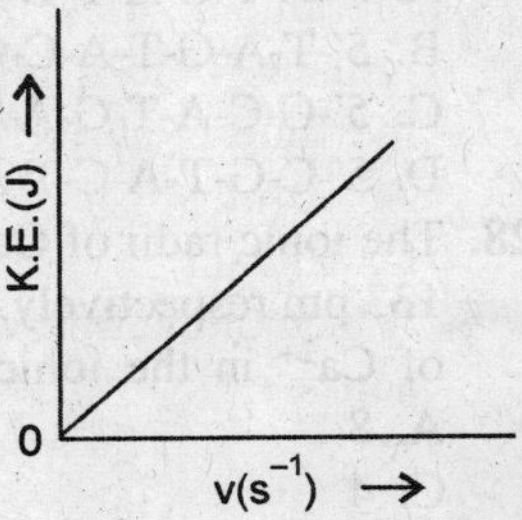

D.

12. The standard potential of a Daniel cell is + 1.10V and the equilibrium constant for the cell reaction is 1.5×10^{37}. It can be concluded that

A. zinc oxidises copper
B. displacement of copper by zinc goes to near completion
C. copper oxidises zinc
D. displacement of zinc by copper goes to completion

13. The main product obtained in the following reaction is

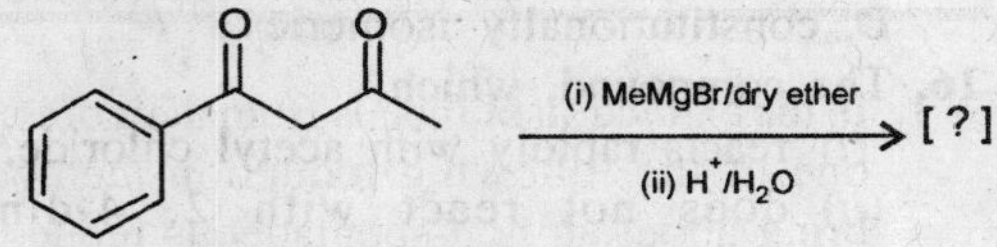

A. 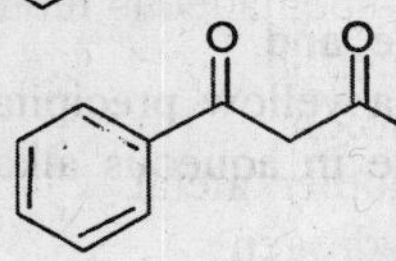

B. 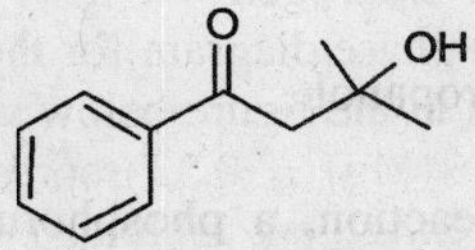

C. 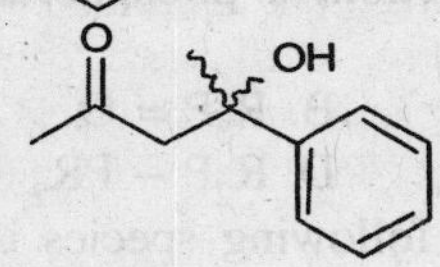

D. 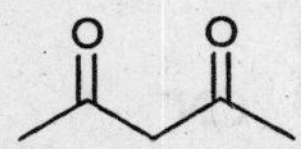

14. Which one of the following compounds reacts with nitrous acid to give the product [P]?

[P] = 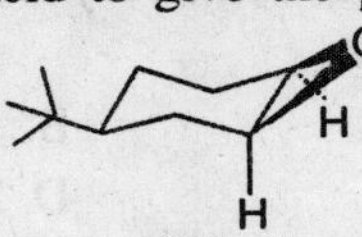

A. 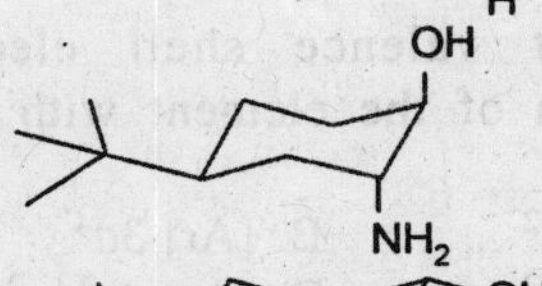

B. 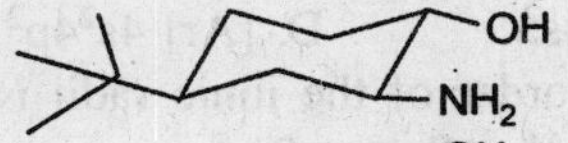

C. 

D. 

15.

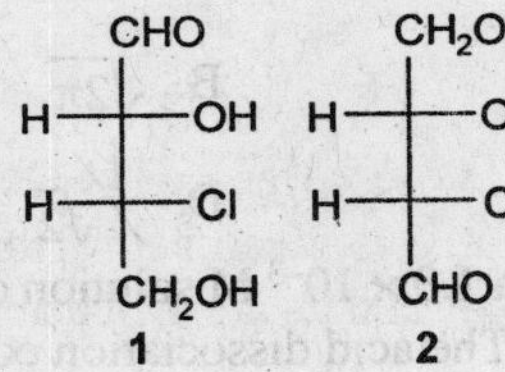

1 2

The given compounds 1 and 2 are
A. identical
B. diastereomeric
C. enantiomeric
D. constitutionally isomeric

16. The compound, which
(*i*) reacts rapidly with acetyl chloride,
(*ii*) does not react with 2, 4-dinitrophenylhydrazine and
(*iii*) does not form a yellow precipitate with excess of iodine in aqueous alkali is
A. acetone
B. diethyl ether
C. 2-methyl-2-propanol
D. ethanol

17. During Wittig reaction, a phosphorus ylide gets converted to
A. R_3P B. $R_3P = O$
C. $R_3P^+H\ OH^-$ D. $R_2P - PR_2$

18. Which one of the following species is NOT isoelectronic with CO?
A. N_2 B. CN^-
C. NO^+ D. O_2^+

19. The ligand with only sigma (σ) bonding character is
A. CN^- B. CH_3^-
C. CO D. NO

20. The correct valence shell electronic configuration of the element with atomic number 22 is
A. [Ar] $4s^2 3d^2$ B. [Ar] $3d^4$
C. [Ar] $3d^2 4s^2$ D. [Ar] $4s^2 4p^2$

21. The correct order of the ionic radii is
A. $In^{3+} > Sn^{4+} > Sr^{2+} > Rb^+$
B. $Sn^{4+} > In^{3+} > Sr^{2+} > Rb^+$
C. $Rb^+ > In^{3+} > Sr^{2+} > Sn^{4+}$
D. $Rb^+ > Sr^{2+} > In^{3+} > Sn^{4+}$

22. The normalisation constant 'A' for the wavefunction $\Psi(\phi) = Ae^{(im\phi)}$ where $0 \le \phi \le 2\pi$ is
A. $1/2\pi$ B. $\sqrt{2\pi}$
C. 2π D. $1/\sqrt{2}$

23. The pH of a 1.0×10^{-3} M solution of weak acid HA is 4.0. The acid dissociation constant K_a is
A. 1.0×10^{-3} B. 1.0×10^{-4}
C. 1.0×10^{-5} D. 2.0×10^{-5}

24. The overlap between the atomic orbitals sketched below is

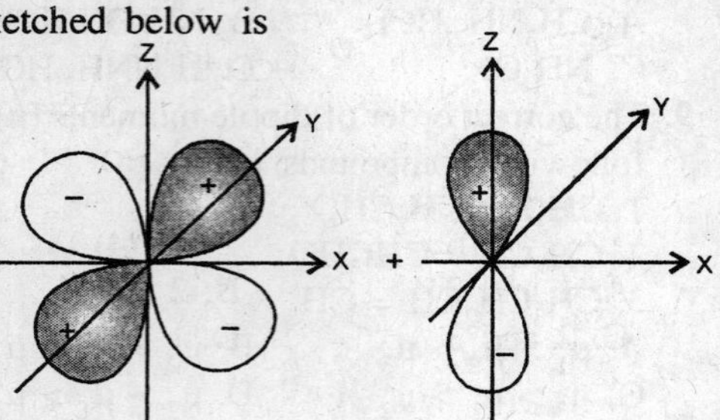

A. positive B. negative
C. zero D. no overlap

25. The value of 'n' for the following molecule according to Huckel's rule is

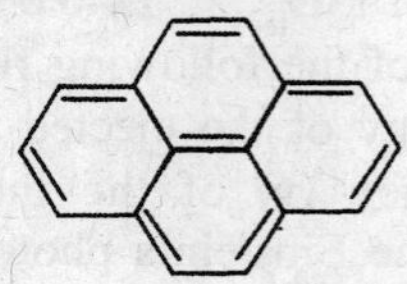

A. 16 B. 4
C. 3 D. 14

26. The shape of CH_3^- ion is
A. trigonal planar B. tetrahedral
C. trigonal pyramidal D. linear

27. The complementary strand of DNA for the following single stranded DNA sequence, 5′-A-T-C-A-T-G-C-3′ is
A. 5′-A-T-C-A-T-G-C-3′
B. 5′-T-A-G-T-A-C-G-3′
C. 5′-G-C-A-T-G-A-T-3′
D. 5′-C-G-T-A-C-T-A-3′

28. The ionic radii of Ca^{2+} and F^- are 100 pm and 133 pm respectively. The coordination number of Ca^{2+} in the ionic solid will be
A. 8 B. 6
C. 4 D. 2

29. The compounds that react with aqueous $NaHCO_3$ to release CO_2 are

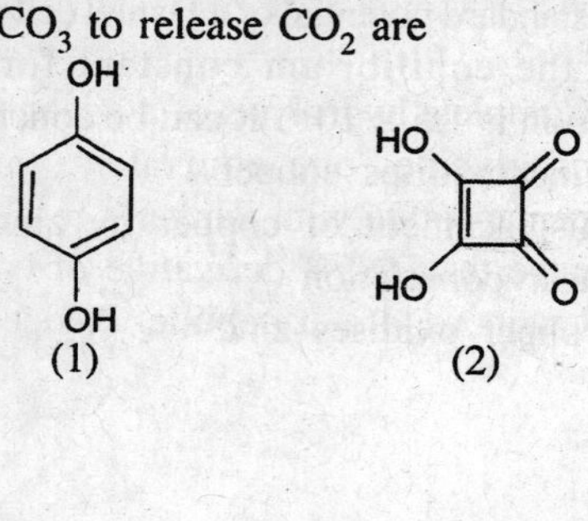

(1) (2)

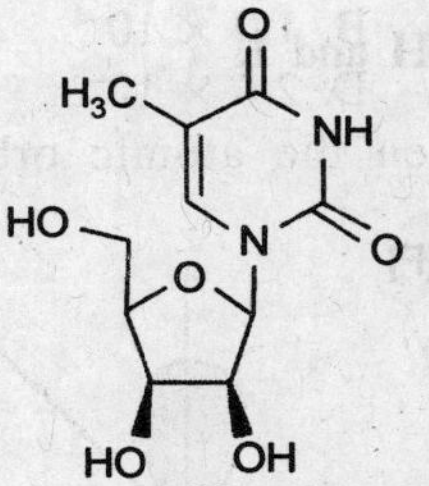

(3)

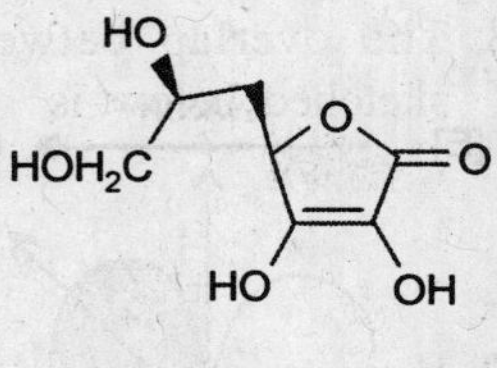

(4)

A. 1 and 3 B. 2 and 4
C. 2 and 3 D. 1 and 4

30. Which of the following reactions does NOT give H_3PO_4?

A. $Ca_3(PO_4)_2 + H_2SO_4 \longrightarrow$

B. $P_4O_6 + H_2O \longrightarrow$

C. $PCl_5 + H_2O \longrightarrow$

D. $P_4S_{10} + H_2O \longrightarrow$

31.

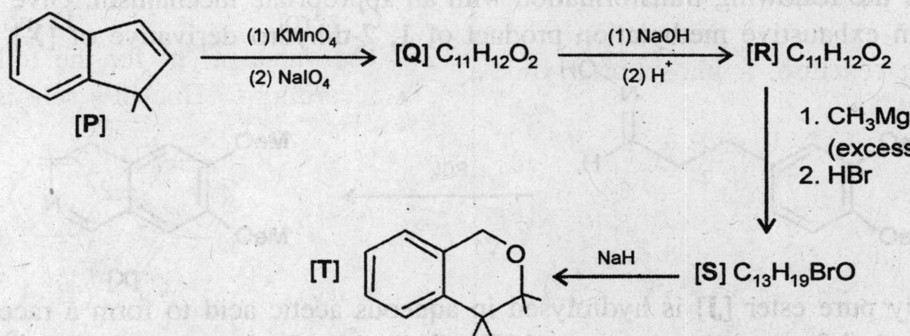

Identify the structures of the intermediate compounds **Q, R** and **S.** Show the transformation for each step.

32. A. For the following scheme of transformations, draw the structures of **A, B, C** and **D.**

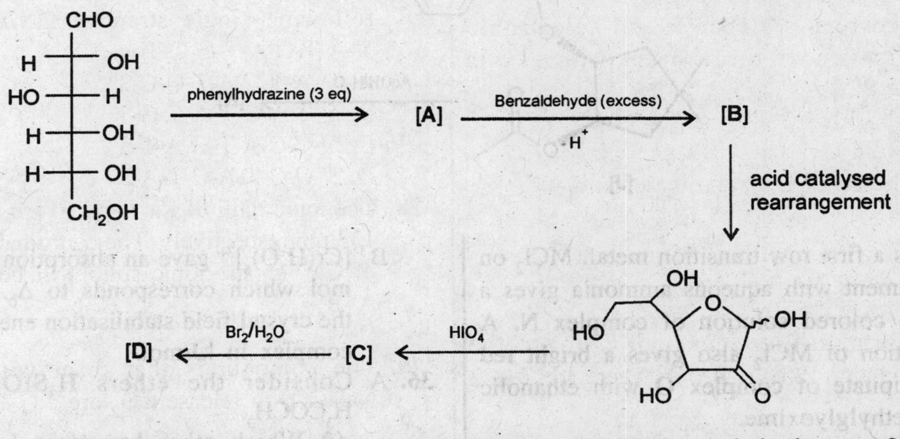

B. Complete hydrolysis of a pentapeptide with 6 N HCl at 110°C in a sealed tube gave 2 equivalents of glycine, one equivalent each of tyrosine, leucine and phenylalanine. Reaction of the pentapeptide with Sanger's reagent (2,4-dinitrofluorobenzene, DNFB) and subsequent hydrolysis gave the DNFB derivative of tyrosine. Chymotrypsin cleavage of this peptide yielded tyrosine, leucine and a tripeptide. Deduce the sequence of the pentapeptide.

33. Complete the following reactions with appropriate structures for **E, F, G, H** and **I.**

A.

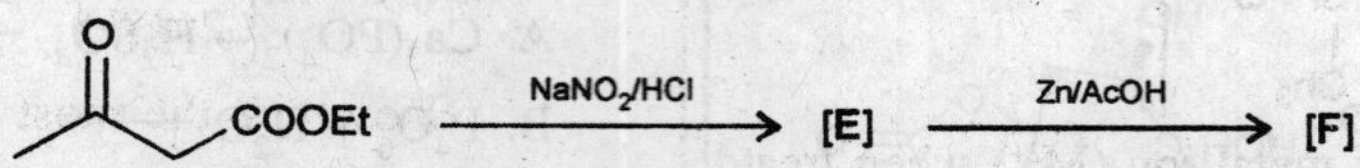

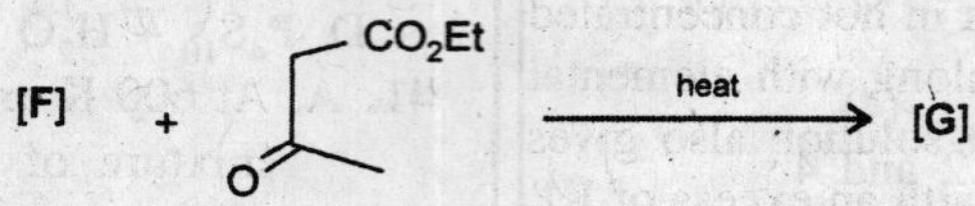

B.

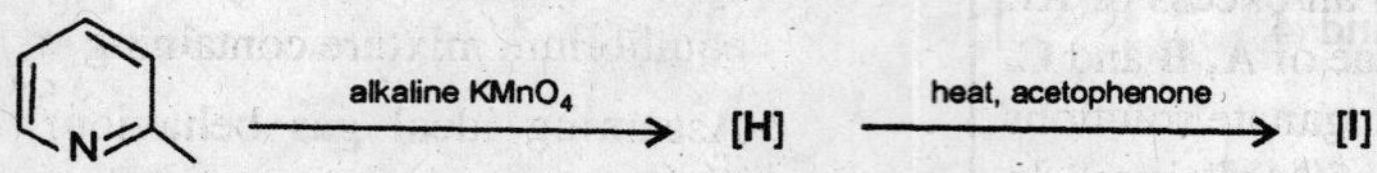

34. A. Account for the following transformation with an appropriate mechanism. Give the structure of the Hoffman exhaustive methylation product of 1, 2-dihydro derivative of **[X]**.

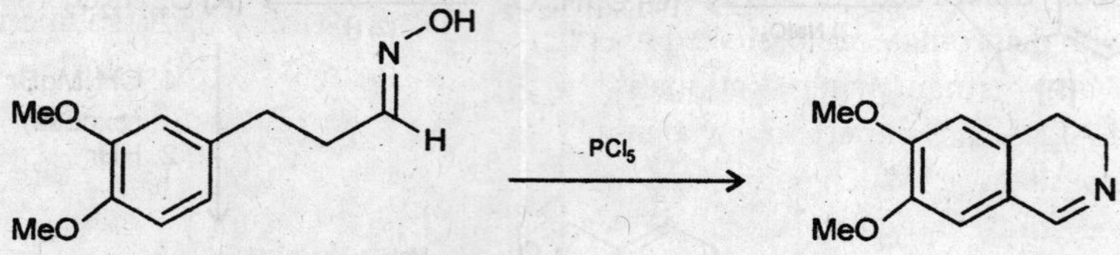

[X]

B. The optically pure ester **[J]** is hydrolysed in aqueous acetic acid to form a racemic mixture of *cis*-4, 4-dimethyl-2-acetoxycyclopentanol **[K]**. Give a mechanistic explanation to account for the formation of **[K]** and the observed change in the optical activity.

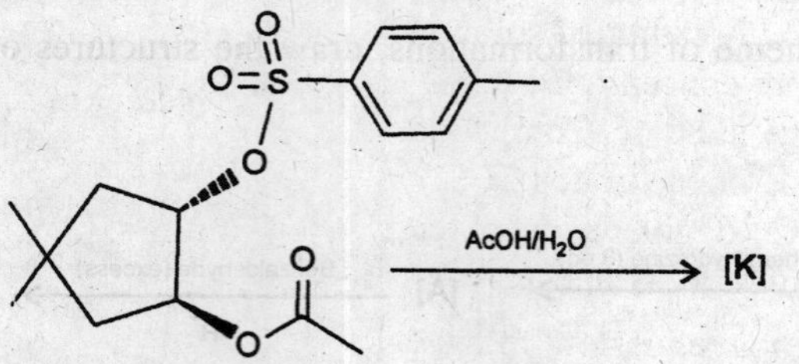

[J]

35. A. **M** is a first row transition metal. MCl_2 on treatment with aqueous ammonia gives a blue colored solution of complex **N.** A solution of MCl_2 also gives a bright red precipitate of complex **O** with ethanolic dimethylglyoxime.

(*i*) Identify **M** and draw the structure of **O.**

(*ii*) Determine the hybridisation of **M** in complex **N.**

(*iii*) Identify the paramagnetic complex.

B. $[Cr(H_2O)_6]^{3+}$ gave an absorption at 208 kJ/mol which corresponds to Δ_0. Calculate the crystal field stabilisation energy of this complex in kJ/mol.

36. A. Consider the ethers $H_3SiOSiH_3$ and H_3COCH_3.

(*i*) Which ether has more Lewis base character?

(*ii*) Which angle [Si-O-Si and C-O-C] is greater? Justify your answer.

B. Starting from SiO_2, show how the following polymer is prepared industrially?

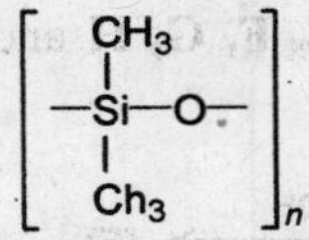

37. A. A solution of metal ion (M^{2+}) when treatd with H_2S gas gives a black precipitate **A.** Precipitate **A** dissolves in hot concentrated nitric acid to give **B** along with elemental sulfur. The metal iron solution also gives a white precipitate **C** with an excess of KI. Write the chemical formulae of **A, B** and **C.**

B. Why are potassium permanganate solutions unstable in the presence of Mn^{2+} ions? In the quantitative estimation of iron present in iron ores dissolved in dilute HCl, titrations with dichromate are preferred over titrations with permanganate. Rationalise.

38. A. Al_2Cl_6 and Al_2Me_6 are dimeric in gas phase. Draw their structures. Which compound has more Lewis acid character? Explain.

B. Arrange the halides $SnCl_2$, $PbCl_2$, $SiCl_2$ in increasing order of their stability. Give reasons for your answer.

39. A. Acidification of an aqueous solution of yellow sodium chromate gives an orange colored compound **A**. A saturated solution of **A** on treatment with concentrated H_2SO_4 gives a bright orange solid **B**. Compound **A** in the presence of concentrated H_2SO_4 reacts with anion **C** to give a deep red colored liquid. Identify **A, B** and **C.**

B. $^{215}_{84}Po$ undergoes an a emission to give element **X** followed by a β emission to give element **Y.**

(*i*) Write the valence shell electronic configuration of **Y.**

(*ii*) Indicate the groups of the periodic table to which **X** and **Y** belong.

40. A. When an ideal monoatomic gas is expanded from 1.5 bar, 24.8 L and 298 K into an evacuated container, the final volume becomes 49.6 L. Calculate ΔH, ΔS and ΔG for the process.

B. The Maxwell distribution function for the distribution of speeds of molecules in gaseous systems is given as,

$$f(c) = 4\pi\left(\frac{m}{2\pi kT}\right)^{3/2} c^2 \exp\left(\frac{-mc^2}{2kT}\right)$$

Show that the most probable speed, *cmps*

$$= \left(\frac{2kT}{m}\right)^{1/2}$$

41. A. At 600 K and 200 bar, a 1:3 (molar ratio) mixture of A_2 and B_2 react to form an equilibrium mixture containing $x_{AB_3} = 0.60$. Assuming ideal gas behaviour, calculate K_p for the reaction

$$A_2\ (g) + 3\ B_2\ (g) \rightleftharpoons 2AB_3\ (g)$$

B. A 50 mL 0.05 M solution of Fe(II) is titrated with 0.05 M solution of Ce(IV) in the presence of dilute H_2SO_4 at 25°C. Calculate the equivalence point potential and the equilibrium constant K in terms of log K.

[$E°(Fe^{3+}/Fe^{2+})$ = +0.75 V, $E°(Ce^{4+}/Ce^{3+})$ = +1.45 V]

42. A. The vapour pressure of D_2O at 20 °C is 745 mm Hg. When 15 g of a non-volatile compound is dissolved in 200 g of D_2O, the pressure changes to 730 mm Hg. Assuming the applicability of Raoult's law, calculate the molecular weight of the compound.

B. An enzyme following Michaelis-Menten kinetics was found to have highest activity at 37 °C and pH 7.0. If the maximum velocity V_{max} for this enzyme was 2.4×10^{-4} mol L^{-1} s^{-1} with an initial enzyme concentration $[E]_0$ = 2.4 nM, calculate the turnover frequency.

43. A. Consider the 4π electrons in cyclobutadiene to be free particles in a 2-dimensional square box of length 2 Å. Calculate the wavelength of the electronic transition from the highest occupied molecular orbital (HOMO) to the lowest unoccupied molecular orbital (LUMO). Also write down the normalised wavefunctions for the occupied degenerate states.

B. The reaction

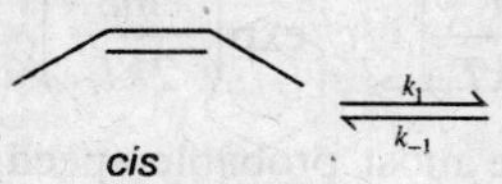

is first order in both directions. At 25°C, the equilibrium constant (K) of this reaction is 0.40. If 0.115 mol. dm^{-3} of *cis*-isomer is allowed to equilibrate, calculate the equilibrium concentration of each isomer.

44. A. With i, j and k as the unit vectors along X, Y and Z axes, express the vector $\overrightarrow{P_1P_2}$ in the given figure in terms of the coordinates of P_1 and P_2. Also determine the dot products of the unit vectors i, j, k.

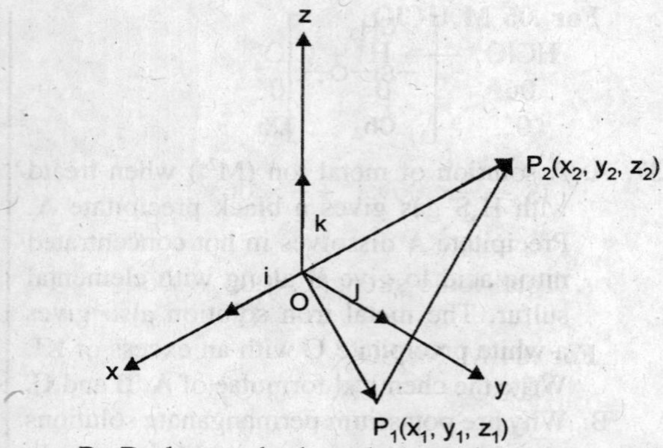

B. Deduce whether the matrices A and B commute or not.

$$A = \begin{pmatrix} 2 & 1 \\ 0 & 1 \end{pmatrix} \quad B = \begin{pmatrix} 1 & 1 \\ 0 & 1 \end{pmatrix}$$

ANSWERS

1	2	3	4	5	6	7	8	9	10
A	D	C	A	D	B	D	*	D	D
11	**12**	**13**	**14**	**15**	**16**	**17**	**18**	**19**	**20**
A	B	C	A	B	B	B	C	B	C
21	**22**	**23**	**24**	**25**	**26**	**27**	**28**	**29**	**30**
D	A	C	A	C	C	C	A	C	B

SOME SELECTED EXPLANATORY ANSWERS

5. Change is zero in a cyclic process for state functions.

6. For second order Reaction

$$t_1 \times a_1 = t_2 \times a_2$$

$$10 \text{ min} \times \frac{C_0}{2} = t_2 \times \frac{C_0}{4}$$

$$t_2 = 20 \text{ min}$$

7. Except (4), rest all have plane of symmetry.

9. 

Here charge separation will take place leading to increase in dipole moment.

Further in $CH_3—CH_2—CH_2—CHO$ and $CH_3—CH_2—CH = CH_2$, dipole moment will be more in former as oxygen accomodate –ve charge better because

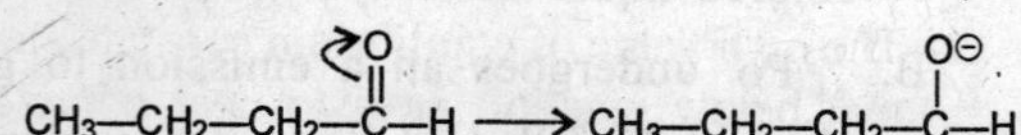

of its electronegativity.

10. Ionic strength of a solution is $\frac{1}{2} c_i Z_i^2$

where C_i is conc. of ions and Z is its valency.

For .01 M $FeCl_3$

$FeCl_3$	⟶	Fe^{3+}	+ $3Cl^-$
.01		0	0
0		.01	.03

$$\therefore \text{ IS} = \frac{1}{2} \times .01 \times 3^2 + \frac{1}{2} \times .03 \times 1^2$$

$$= .06$$

For .06 M $HClO_4$

$$HClO_3 \longrightarrow H^+ + ClO_4^-$$
$$\begin{matrix} .06 & 0 & 0 \\ 0 & .06 & .06 \end{matrix}$$

$$\therefore \text{ IS} = \frac{1}{2}\times.06\times1^2+\frac{1}{2}\times.06\times1^2$$
$$= .06$$

$\therefore$ Total ionic strength = .06 + .06 = .12

For .04 M Na_2SO_4

$$Na_2SO_4 \longrightarrow 2Na^+ + SO_4^{2-}$$
$$\begin{matrix} .04 & 0 & 0 \\ 0 & .08 & .04 \end{matrix}$$

$$\therefore \text{ IS} = \frac{1}{2}\times.08\times1^2+\frac{1}{2}\times.04\times2^2$$
$$= .12$$

11. The incident photon should have some energy, to be called work function. Below this energy no electron will be ejected.

$$KE = h\nu - h\nu_o$$

Here, $h\nu_o$ corresponds to work function

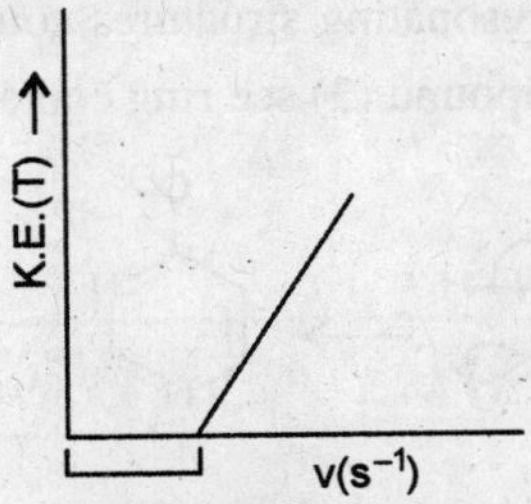

12. The high value of equilibrium constant suggest that below reaction goes to near completion

$$Zn_{(s)} + Cu^{2+}_{(aq)} \rightleftharpoons Zn^{2+}_{(aq)} + Cu_{(s)}$$

Further $\Delta G° = -RT \ln K = -nF\,E°_{cell}$

+ve value of $E°_{cell}$ indicate decrease in Gibbs free energy.

13. 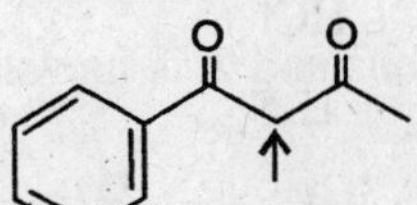

(two CO group make this methelene active)

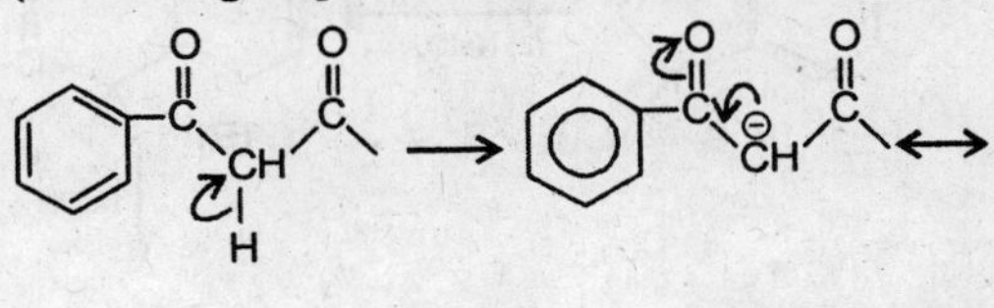

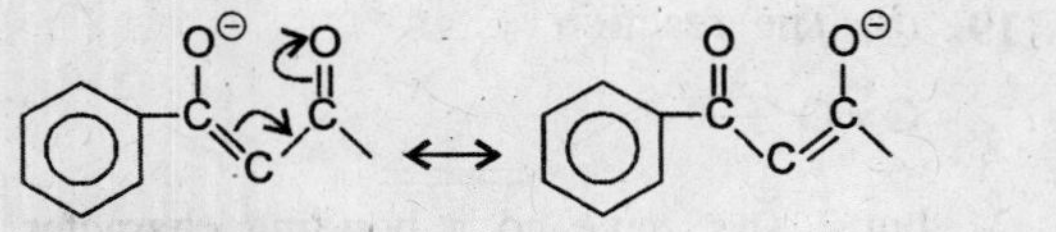

Now reaction

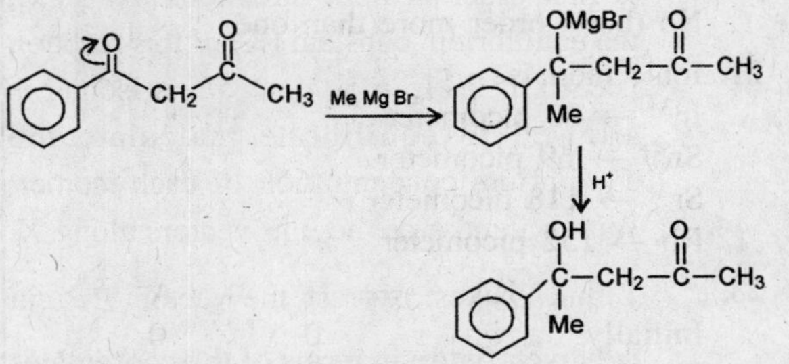

14. After reaction of compound in option A with nitrous acid we get

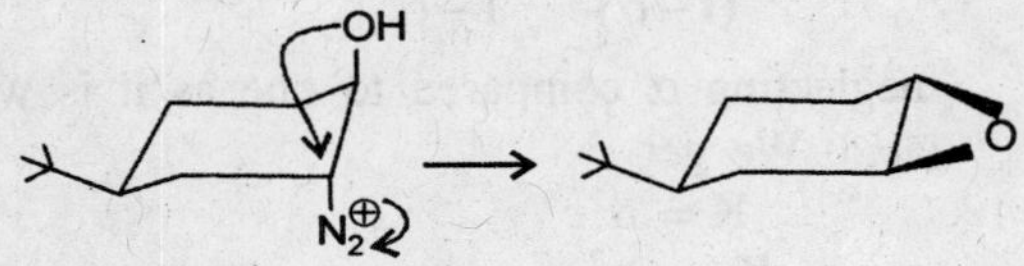

(trans configuration)

16. (*iii*) Suggest that compound cannot be have

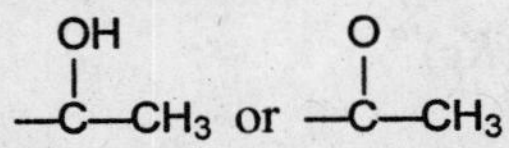 structure.

Further no reaction with 2,4-dinitro phenylhydrazine suggest that it does not have CO group. Thus option B.

i.e. diethyl ether is correct.

17. Witting Reactions (Ylide Reaction)

In case of Benzaldehyde, a phosphorous **'ylide'** ($C^-\ H_2PPh_3$) is added to form styrene as the final product

$$C_6H_5-\overset{H}{\overset{|}{C}}=O + \underset{\text{an Ylide}}{C^-H_2PPh_3} \longrightarrow C_6H_5\overset{H}{\overset{|}{C}}=CH_2 + O=PPh_3$$

18.
$$\left.\begin{matrix} CO = 14 \\ N_2 = 14 \\ CN^- = 14 \\ NO^+ = 14 \\ O_2^+ = 15 \end{matrix}\right\} \text{No. of electron}$$

19. $C \equiv N^-$

$C \overset{\leftarrow}{\equiv} O$

but 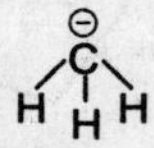 have no π bonding character.

No (bond order more than one)

21. Ionic radii is

$In^{3+} \rightarrow 80$ picometer

$Sn^{4+} \rightarrow 69$ picometer

$Sr^{2+} \rightarrow 118$ picometer

Rb $\rightarrow$ 152 picometer

23.

	HA	$\rightleftharpoons$	H^+	+	A^-
Initially	c		0		0
Finally	$(1-\alpha)c$		αc		αc

$$K = \frac{\alpha^2 c^2}{(1-\alpha)c} = \frac{\alpha^2 c}{1-\alpha}$$

neglecting α compared to one as it is weak acid. We get

$$K = \alpha^2 c$$

or $$Kc = \alpha^2 c^2$$

or $$\sqrt{Kc} = \alpha c$$

$$\therefore \quad [H]^+ = \sqrt{Kc}$$

$$-\log [H^+] = -\log (Kc)^{1/2}$$

$$4 = -\frac{1}{2}\log(K \times 10^{-3})$$

or $$8 = -\log K \times 10^{-3}$$

$$8 = -\log K \times 3$$

$$\Rightarrow \quad K = 10^{-5}$$

24. +ve & –ve lobe of Pz will overlap with corresponding lobe of d_{xz} resulting in development of bonding character.

25.

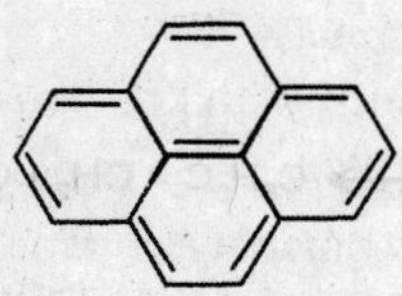

Huckel's rule: There must be a total of $(4n + 2)$ π electrons.

Total number of pi electron is 14

Therefore, $4n + 2 = 14$

$n = 3$

28. The Coordination number of a central atom in a molecule or crystal is the number of its neighbours the number is determined differently for molecules and crystal. In case of calcium fluorides (CaF_2); Ca^{2+} is surrounded by eight F^- anion neighbours and anion F^- is surrounded by four Ca^{2+}. Therefore, coordination number is (8, 4).

29. Strong acid will decompose $NaHCO_3$ to liberate CO_2.

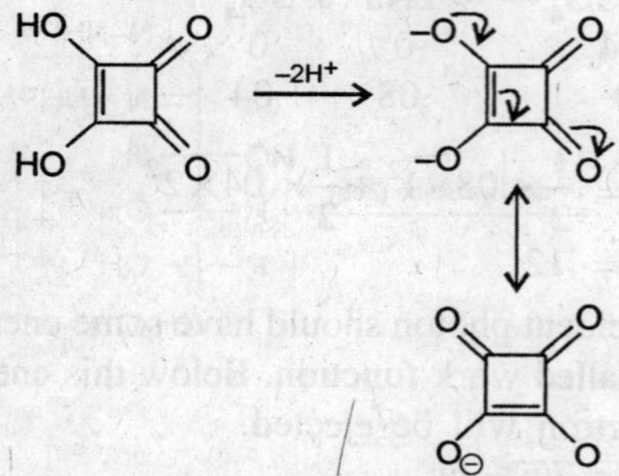

Above compound is aromatic and similarly other resonating structures could be obtained.

In compound (3) see ring containing Nitrogen.

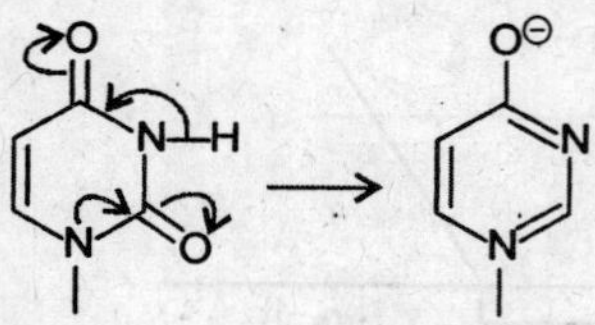

The compound obtained is also aromatic (with $4n + 2$ Huckel rule).

30. Reaction are

$Ca_3(PO_4)_2 + H_2SO_4 + H_2O \rightarrow$

$H_3PO_4 + 3CaSO_4\,2H_2O$

$P_4O_6 + H_2O \rightarrow H_3PO_3$

$PCl_5 + H_2O \rightarrow H_3PO_4 + HCl$

$P_4S_{10} + H_2O \rightarrow H_3PO_4 + H_2S$

31.

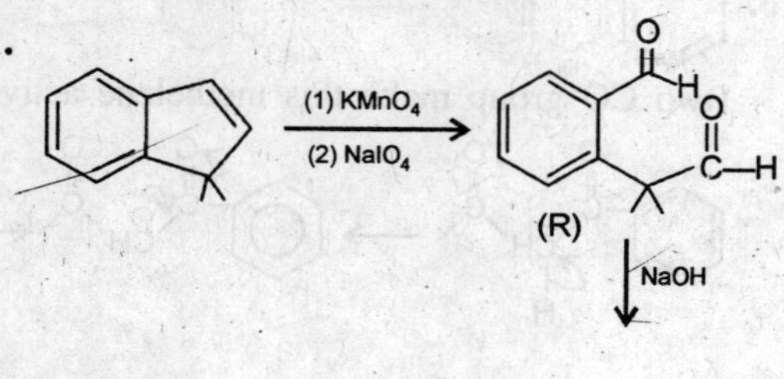

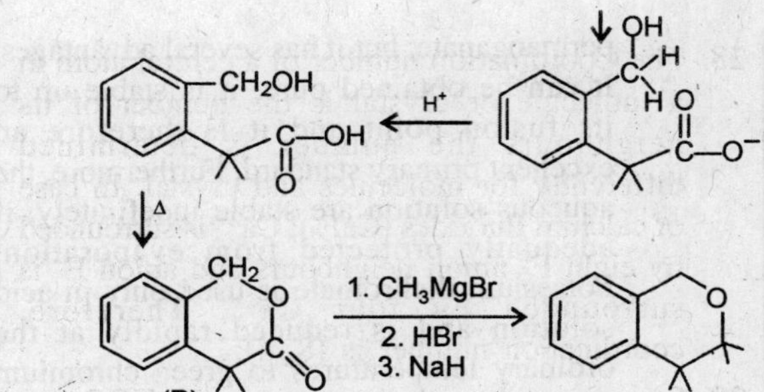

(R)

32. A.

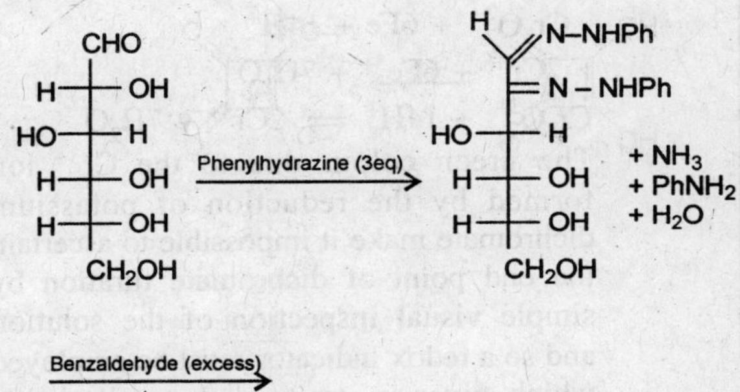

B.

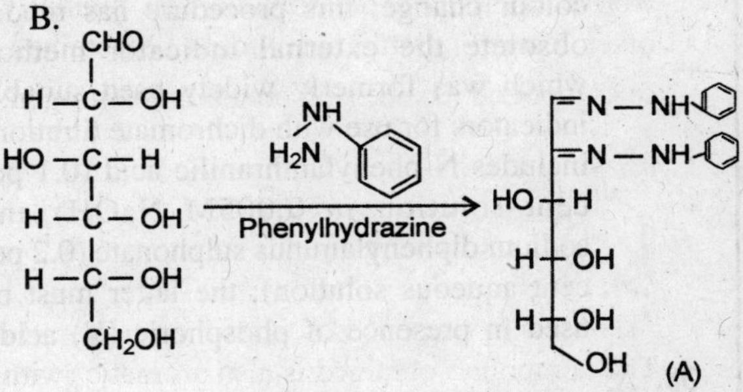

(A)

(Phenylosazone)

34. A.

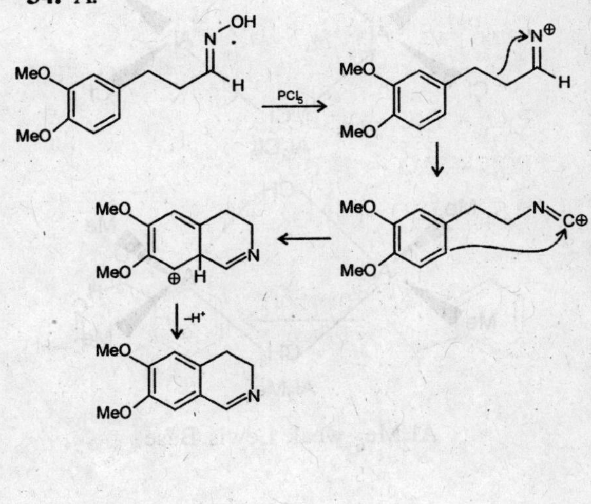

B.

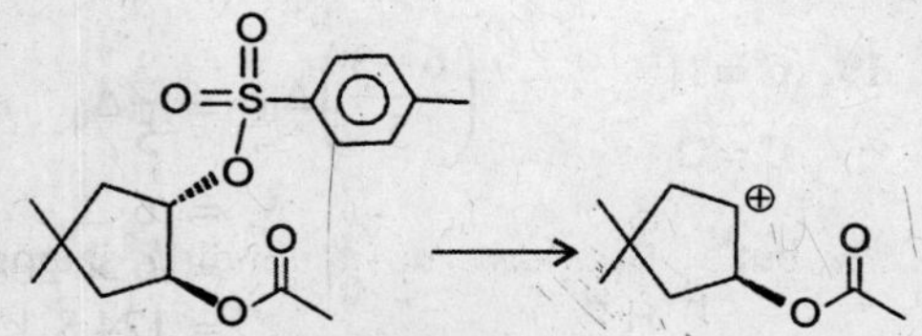

Above planar carbocation can be attacked from either side and therefore racemic mixture is obtained. The formation of carbocation is due to exceptionally stable

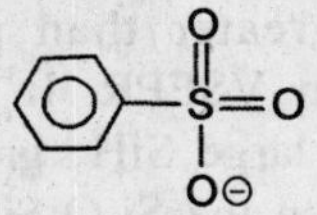 group which is resonance stabilized

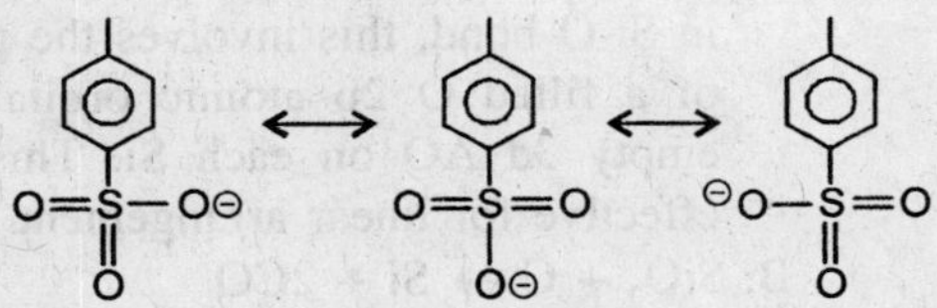

35. A. $NiCl_2 + 6NH_3\,(l) \longrightarrow [Ni(NH_3)_6]\,Cl_2$ (N)

$NiCl_2 + 2CH_3{-}C(=NOH){-}C(=NOH){-}CH_3 + 2NH_4OH$

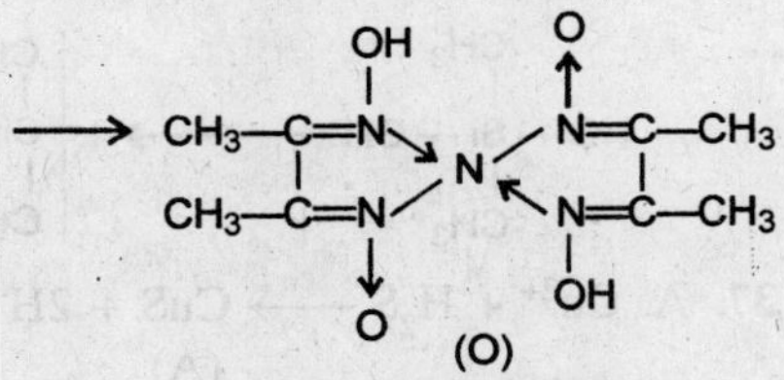

(O)

$+\ 2NH_4Cl + 2H_2O$

Ni^{2+} has 7 electron in its outermost orbit

⇅	⇅	1	1	1

(d orbital)

It is sp^3d^2 hybridised and is outer orbital (high Spin) complex.

B. $[Cr(H_2O)_6]^{3+}$ is octahedral complex. Its crystal field spliting is shown below.

1 — e_g

1 1 1 (t_{2g})

$$\text{CFSE} = \left(\frac{2}{5} \times 3 - \frac{3}{5} \times 1\right)\Delta_0$$

$$= \left(\frac{6-3}{5}\right)\Delta_0 = \frac{3}{5}\Delta_0$$
$$= .6\ \Delta_0$$
$$= .6 \times 208\ \text{kT/mol}$$
$$= 124.8\ \text{kT/mol.}$$

36. A. (*ii*) Solid state crystal structure (at low Temp.): Disiloxane $H_3SiOSiH_3$, Si-O-Si = 142.2(3)°C. These structure may well be close to linear in gas phase. Angle in the solid Phase is greater than predicted structure based on VSEPR. It is due to steric effect. The large SiH_3 group repel each other to widen the Si-O-Si bond.

There are pi-effects (double bond character) in Si-O bond, this involves the pi overlap of a filled O 2p atomic orbital with an empty 3d AO on each Si. This is more effective for linear arrangement.

B. $SiO_2 + C \rightarrow Si + 2CO$

$Si + CH_3Cl \rightarrow (CH_3)_2SiCl_2$

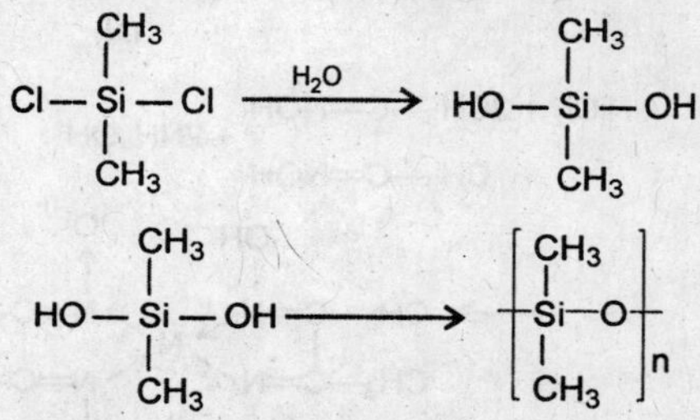

37. A. $Cu^{2+} + H_2S \longrightarrow CuS + 2H^+$
(A)

$3CuS + 8HNO_3 \longrightarrow 3Cu(NO_3)_2 + 2NO + 3S + 4H_2O$

$2Cu^{+2} + 4KI \longrightarrow Cu_2I_2 + 2K^+ + I_2 + 2I^-$

B. Potassium permanganate is auto-decomposed in presence of manganese dioxide.

$4MnO_4 + 2H_2O \rightleftharpoons 4MnO_4 + 3O_2 + 4OH^{\ominus}$

Permanganate is unstable in presence of Mn^{2+} ion

$2MnO_4 + 3Mn^{2+} + 2H_2O \rightleftharpoons 5MnO_4 + 4H^+$

The reaction is slow in acidic solution and is very rapid in neutral solution.

Potassium dichromate is not such a powerful Oxidising agent as potassium permanganate, but it has several advantages. It can be obtained pure, it is stable up to its fusion point and it is therefore an excellent primary standard. Furthermore, the aqueous solution are stable indefinitely, if adequatly protected from evaporation. Potassium dichromate is used only in acid solution and is reduced rapidly at the ordinary temperatures to green chromium (III) salt.

In acid Solution

$Cr_2O_7^{2-} + 6Fe + 14H^+$
$= 2Cr^{3+} + 6Fe^{3+} + 7H_2O$

$Cr_2O_7^{2-} + 14H^+ \rightleftharpoons 2Cr^{3+} + 7H_2O$

The green colour due to the Cr^{3+} ion formed by the reduction of potassium dichromate make it impossible to ascertain the end point of dichromate titration by simple visual inspection of the solution and so a redox indicator must be employed which gives a strong and unmistakable colour change; this procedure has render obsolete the external indicator method which was formerly widely used suitable indicators for use with dichromate titrations includes N-phenylanthranilic acid (0.1 per cent solution in 0.005M NaOH) and sodium diphenylaminus sulphonate (0.2 per cent aqueous solution); the latter must be used in presence of phosphoric (V) acid.

38. A.

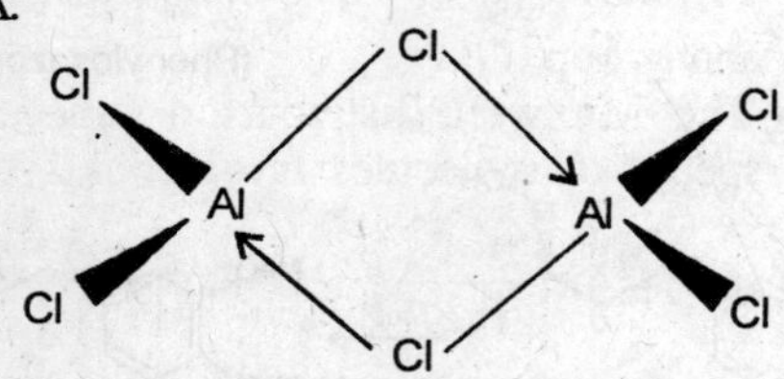

Al_2Cl_6

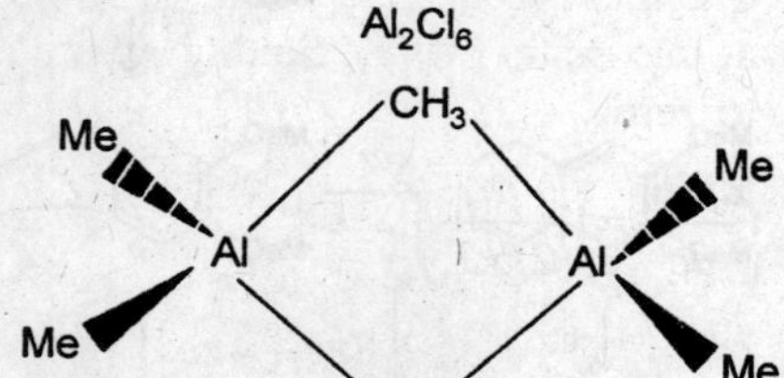

Al_2Me_6

Al_2Me_6 weak Lewis Base

B. When nS^2 electron of outermost shell do not participate in bonding it is called inert pair effect. The inert pair effect increases from Ge to Pb. This is because the electron are deep seated inside the d-orbitals and are not affected by external environment and therefore don't take part in reactions.

$PbCl_2 > SnCl_2 > SiCl_2$

$\xleftarrow{\text{stability increases}}$

39. A. $\underset{\text{(Yellow)}}{2CrO_4^{2-}} + 2H^+ \longrightarrow \underset{\underset{\text{(A)}}{\text{(Orange)}}}{Cr_2O_7^{2-}}$

$\therefore$ A is $Na_2Cr_2O_7$

$Na_2Cr_2O_7 + 2H_2SO_4 \rightarrow 2KHSO_4 + \underset{\text{(B)}}{2CrO_3} + H_2O$

$Na_2Cr_2O_7 + 2H_2SO_4 + NaCl$

$\rightarrow 6NaHSO_4 + \underset{\text{(C)}}{2CrO_2Cl_2} + 2H_2O$

CrO_3 is readily soluble in water giving a red solution which is highly acidic and contains a number of chromic acids.

B. ${}_{84}Po^{215} \xrightarrow{-\alpha} {}_{82}Pb^{211}(X)$

${}_{84}Po^{215} \xrightarrow{-\beta} {}_{85}At^{215}$ (Y)

(*i*) ${}_{85}At^{215} \rightarrow {}_{82}[Xe]4f^{14}5d^{10}6s^26p^5$

(*ii*) X (${}_{82}Pb^{211}$) belongs to period 6 and group 14, and Y (${}_{85}At^{215}$) belongs to period 6 and group 17.

40. B. The Maxwell distribution function for speeds of molecules in gaseous system

$$f(c) = 4\pi\left(\frac{m}{2\pi kT}\right)^{3/2} C^2 \exp\left(\frac{-mc^2}{2kT}\right)$$

The most probable speed C_{mps} is the speed at maximum of *f*(*c*). Setting *df*(*c*)/dc equal to zero.

$$\frac{df(c)}{dc} = \left(\frac{m}{2\pi kT}\right)^{3/2} e^{-mc^2/2kT} \left[8\pi c + 4\pi c^2\left(-\frac{mc}{kT}\right)\right] = 0$$

$$C_{mps} = \left(\frac{2kT}{m}\right)^{1/2}$$

41. A. $A_{2(g)} + 3B_{2(g)} \rightleftharpoons 2AB_{2(g)}$

Initially	n	$3n$	O
After time t	$n(1-x)$	$3n(1-x)$	$2nx$

$\therefore$ Total no. of mole $= n[1 - x + 3 - 3x + 2x]$

$= n[4 - 2x]$

Mole fraction $\frac{(1-x)}{4-2x} \cdot \frac{3(1-x)}{4-2x} \quad \frac{2x}{4-2x}$

But $x_{AB_3} = .6$

$\Rightarrow \frac{2x}{4-2x} = .6 \Rightarrow 2x = 2.4 - 1.2x$

$3.2x = 2.4$

or $x = \frac{2.4}{3.2} = .75$

$\therefore$ Mole fraction of $A_{2(g)}$, $B_{2(g)}$ and $AB_{3(g)}$ are .1, .3 and .6 respectively

$$K_p = \frac{\left[P_{AB_3(g)}\right]^2}{\left[P_{B_2(g)}\right]^3\left[P_{A_2(g)}\right]}$$

$$= \frac{(.6P)^2}{(.3P)^3(.1P)} = \frac{133.33}{P^2}$$

(where P= 200 base)

B. $Fe^{2+}(aq) + Ce^{4+}(aq) \rightarrow Fe^{3+}(aq) + Ce^{3+}(aq)$ Prior to addition of Ce^{4+} ions, the solution contains only the Fe^{2+} ions on adding small amount of Ce^{4+} ions to the solutions, a small amount of Fe^{2+} ions is oxidised to Fe^{3+} ions. With the presence of both the Fe^{2+} and Fe^{3+} ions, the electrode behaves as an oxidation-reduction electrode whose potential, according to the Nernst equation is given by

$$E_{el} = E_{el}^\circ - \frac{RT}{F}\ln\frac{[Fe^{2+}]}{[Fe^{3+}]}$$

$$= E_{el}^\circ + \frac{RT}{F}\ln\frac{[Fe^{3+}]}{[Fe^{2+}]}$$

$$= E_{el}^\circ + .0591 \log\frac{[Fe^{3+}]}{[Fe^{2+}]} \text{ at } 25^\circ C$$

Evidently the electrode potential is controlled by the ratio $[Fe^{3+}]/[Fe^{2+}]$ with addition of Ce^{4+} ions, the ratio $[Fe^{3+}]/[Fe^{2+}]$ changes, thereby changing the value of E_{el}.

At equivalence point $[Fe^{2+}] = [Ce^{4+}]$

and $[Fe^{3+}] = [Ce^{3+}]$

So that the electrode potential at the equivalence point E_{eq} is given by

$$E_{eq} = E_1^0 + .0591 \log \frac{[Fe^{3+}]}{[Fe^{2+}]}$$

$$= E_2^0 + .0591 \log \frac{[Ce^{4+}]}{[Ce^{3+}]}$$

The above equations may be written as

$$E_{eq} = E_1^0 + .0591 \log \frac{[Fe^{3+}]}{[Fe^{2+}]}$$

and $$E_{eq} = E_2^0 + .0591 \log \frac{[Ce^{4+}]}{[Ce^{3+}]}$$

Adding and simplifying we get

$$E_{eq} = \frac{(E_1^0 + E_2^0)}{2}$$

$$Fe^{3+}(aq) + e^- \rightleftharpoons Fe^{2+}(aq) \quad E_1^0 = .75V$$

$$Ce^{4+}(aq) + e^- \rightleftharpoons Ce^{3+}(aq) \quad E_2^0 = 1.45V$$

Beyond the equivalence point, $[Fe^{3+}] \approx 0$ as a result of which the electrode potential thereafter is controlled only by the $[Ce^{4+}][Ce^{3+}]$ ratio.

For potentiometric measurements, the oxidation reduction electrode (viz, Pt: Fe^{3+}, Fe^{2+}) is combined with a reference eg., a saturated calomel electrode, to form a galvanic cell which is represented as Hg, Hg_2Cl_2(s), KCl (sat. Solution)|| Fe^{2+}, Fe^{3+}; Pt in accordance with the positions of the electrodes in the electrochemical series.

Before equivalence point, the EMF of the cell would be given by

$$E = E_P - E_L = E_{el}^0 + .0591 \log \frac{[Fe^{3+}]}{[Fe^{2+}]} - E_{calomel}$$

$$= .75 + .0591 \log \frac{[Fe^{3+}]}{[Fe^{2+}]} - .2422$$

and after the equivalence point, the EMF of the cell is given by

$$E = 1.45 + .0591 \log \frac{[Ce^{4+}]}{[Ce^{2+}]} - .2422$$

At the equivalence point, the EMF of the cell would be given by

$$E = \frac{.75 + 1.45}{2} - .2422$$

42. A. Relative lowering of vapour pressure

$$\frac{P_1^0 - P_1}{P_1^0} = x_2$$

where x_2 is mole fraction of solute.

$$\therefore \quad \frac{745 - 730}{745} = \frac{\frac{15}{m}}{\frac{15}{m} + \frac{200}{20}}$$

(M_{wt} of D_2O = 20)

$$\frac{15}{745} = \frac{\frac{15}{m}}{\frac{15}{m} + 10}$$

$$\Rightarrow \quad 1 + \frac{10m}{15} = \frac{745}{15}$$

$$\frac{10m}{15} = 48.66$$

or $$m = 73 \text{ gm}$$

43. B.

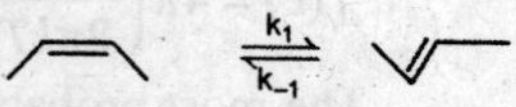

(cis) (trans)

Initially .115 0

At equillibrium $.115 - x$ x

$$K = .4 = \frac{x}{.115 - x}$$

$$.046 = 1.4\,x$$

$$\Rightarrow \quad x = .033$$

$\therefore$ euillibrium concentration of cis isomer is $.115 - x = .082$ and trans isomer is .033.

44. A.

$$\overrightarrow{OP_2} = \overrightarrow{OP_1} + \overrightarrow{P_1P_2}$$

$$\overrightarrow{P_1P_2} = \overrightarrow{OP_2} - \overrightarrow{OP_1}$$

$$= (x_2 - x_1)\bar{i} + (y_2 - y_1)\bar{j} + (z_2 - z_1)\bar{k}$$

Also,

$$\overrightarrow{B_1P_2} \cdot \vec{i} = x_2 - x_1$$

$$\overrightarrow{P_1P_2} \cdot \vec{j} = y_2 - y_1$$

$$\overrightarrow{P_1P_2} \cdot \vec{k} = z_2 - z_1 .$$

B. $A = \begin{pmatrix} 2 & 1 \\ 0 & 1 \end{pmatrix}$ $B = \begin{pmatrix} 1 & 1 \\ 0 & 1 \end{pmatrix}$

$$AB = \begin{pmatrix} 2 & 3 \\ 0 & 1 \end{pmatrix}$$

$$BA = \begin{pmatrix} 1 & 1 \\ 0 & 1 \end{pmatrix}\begin{pmatrix} 2 & 1 \\ 0 & 1 \end{pmatrix} = \begin{pmatrix} 2 & 2 \\ 0 & 1 \end{pmatrix}$$

$$[AB] = AB - BA \neq 0$$

⇒ They do not commute.

Previous Paper (Solved)

IIT—JAM

JOINT ADMISSION TEST FOR M.Sc. (CHEMISTRY)-2006

1. After the following interchanges of groups in the Fischer projection of 2-bromobutane, the configuration of (X) and (Y) will be

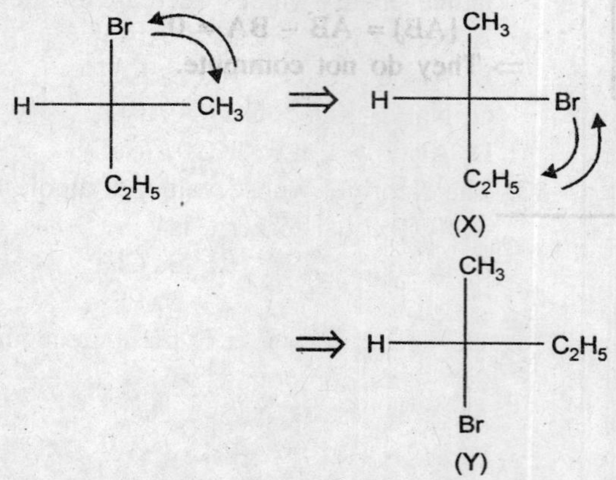

A. X = R; Y = S B. X = R; Y = R

C. X = S; Y = R D. X = S; Y = S

2. The major product of the reaction

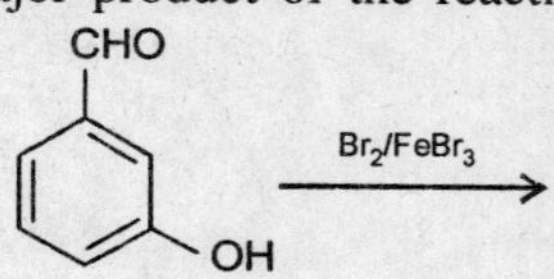

is

A. 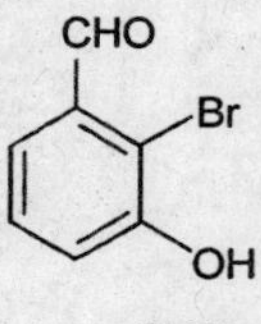

B. 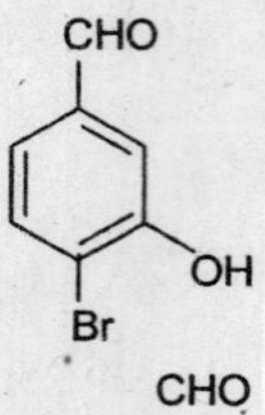

C. 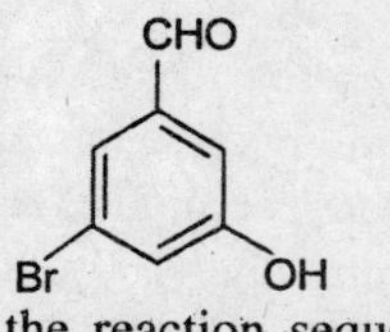

D. 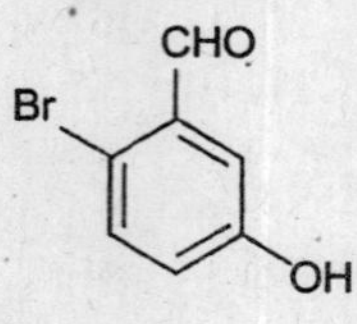

3. In the reaction sequence

$$CH_3COCH_2COOC_2H_5 \xrightarrow[CH_3Br]{C_2H_5ONa} (X)$$

$$\xrightarrow[(ii)H_2O/H^+]{(i)OH^-} (Y)$$

the product (Y) is

A. $CH_3COCH_2COOCH_3$

B. $CH_3COCH(CH_3)_2$

C. $CH_3COCHCOOH$ (with CH_3 on the CH)

D. $CH_3COC_2H_5$

4. The major product (X) in the reaction

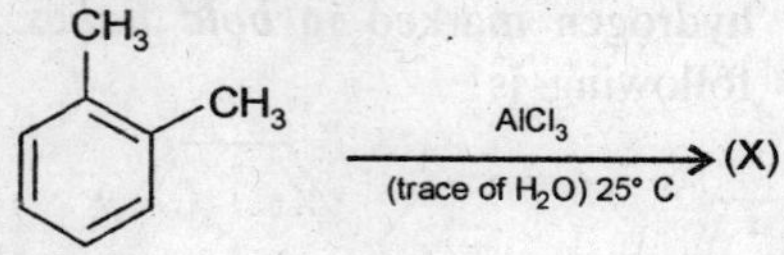

is

A. 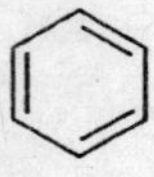

B. 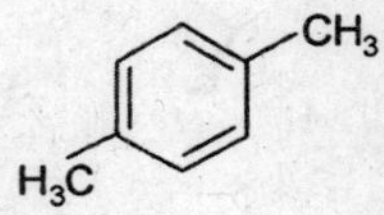

C. 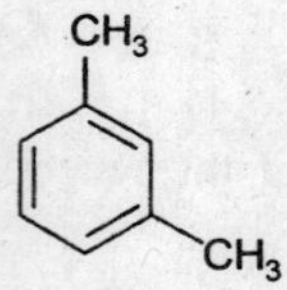

D. 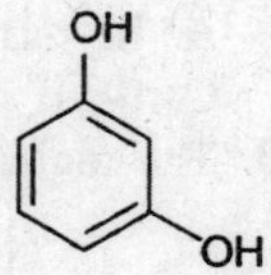

5. The product of the reaction

$$C_6H_6 + CO + HCl \xrightarrow[heat]{AlCl_3/Cu_2Cl_2}$$

gives positive test with Fehling's solution. The product is

A. C_6H_5OH B. $C_6H_4(Cl)CHO$

C. $C_6H_4(OH)CHO$ D. C_6H_5CHO

6. The compound (X) in the reaction sequence

$$\begin{array}{l} CH_2COONa \\ | \\ CH_2COONa \end{array} \xrightarrow[heat]{P_2S_3} (X)$$

$$\xrightarrow{Raney\ Ni} CH_3CH_2CH_2CH_3$$

is

A. 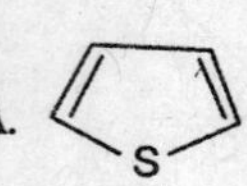

B. $\begin{array}{l} CH_2COOH \\ | \\ CH_2COOH \end{array}$

C. 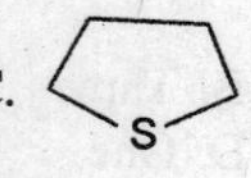

D. 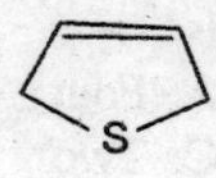

7. The major product of the reaction

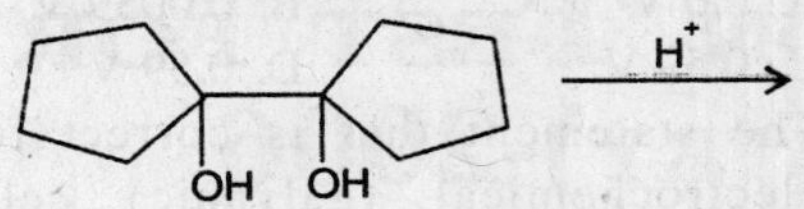

is

A. 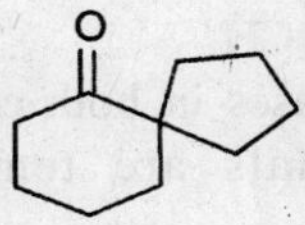 B. 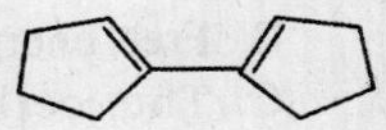

C. 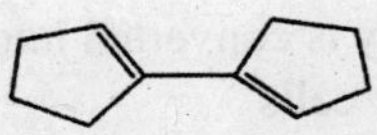 D. 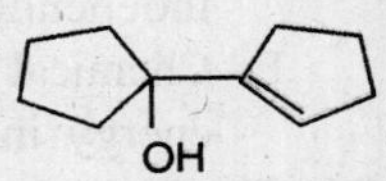

8. The increasing order of the acidity of the hydrogen marked in ***bold italics*** among the following is

I

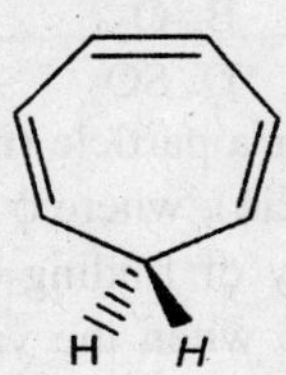

II

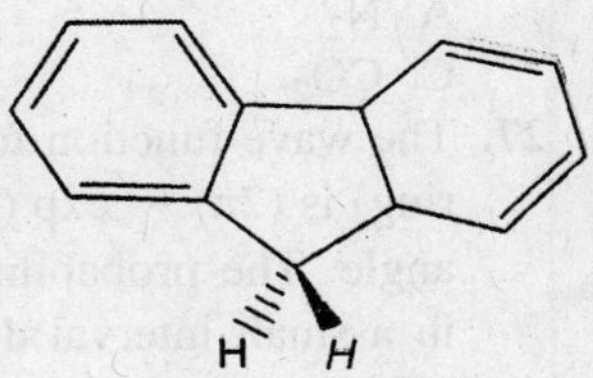

III

A. III < II < I B. II < I < III
C. I < II < III D. II < III < I

9. The major product of the reaction

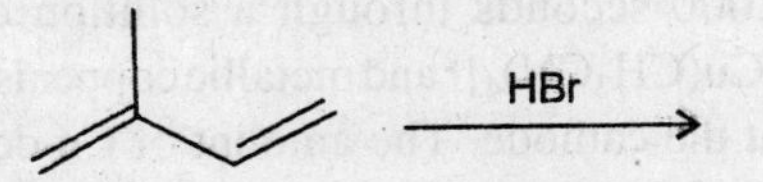

is

A. 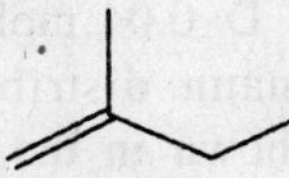 B. 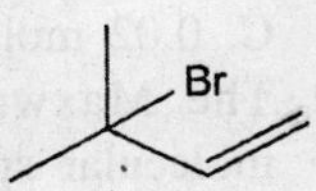

C. 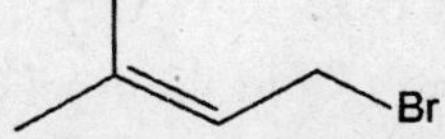 D. 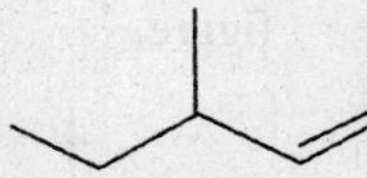

10. The number of enantiomers of camphor

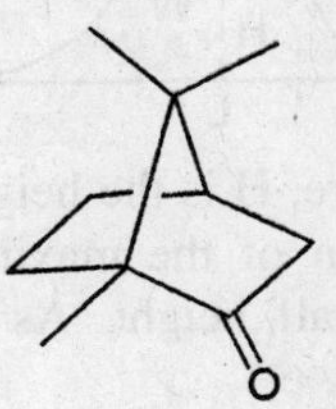

is

A. Four B. Three
C. Two D. One

11. The decreasing order of the first ionization energy of the following elements is
A. He > H > Be > B
B. Be > B > H > He
C. H > He > Be > B
D. B > Be > He > H

12. If the values of Madelung constants of the following compounds are equal, then their lattice energy values decrease in the order
A. KCl > NaF > CaO > Al_2O_3
B. Al_2O_3 > CaO > NaF > KCl
C. NaF > KCl > CaO > Al_2O_3
D. Al_2O_3 > CaO > KCl > NaF

13. The fluoride, whose value of dipole moment is NOT equal to zero, is
A. XeF_4 B. CF_4
C. SF_4 D. PF_5

14. The decreasing order of the ionic nature of the following compounds is
A. LiI > NaBr > KCl > CsF
B. LiI > KCl > NaBr > CsF
C. CsF > NaBr > KCl > LiI
D. CsF > KCl > NaBr > LiI

15. The atomicity and the total number of bond in the elemental white phosphorus molecule are, respectively,
A. 4 and 6 B. 6 and 4
C. 4 and 4 D. 6 and 6

16. The octahedral crystal field splitting (Δ_0) of *d* orbital energies of the following metal ions decreases in the order
A. Co^{2+} > Co^{3+} > Rh^{3+}
B. Rh^{3+} > Co^{3+} > Co^{2+}
C. Rh^{3+} > Co^{2+} > Co^{3+}
D. Co^{3+} > Co^{2+} > Rh^{3+}

17. The half-life of a radioactive nuclide is 20 years. If a sample of this nuclide has an activity of 6400 disintegrations per minute (dis/min) today, its activity (dis/min) after 100 years would be
A. 850 B. 1600
C. 200 D. 400

18. The average value of C-C bond order in graphite is
A. 1 B. 3/2
C. 3/4 D. 4/3

19. The optical absorption spectrum of $[Ti(H_2O)_6]^{3+}$ has its absorption maximum at 20300 cm^{-1}. The magnitude of crystal field stabilization energy in cm^{-1} is

A. 8120 B. 16240
C. 24360 D. 50750

20. In inorganic qualitative analysis, H_2S in acidic medium will NOT precipitate

A. HgS B. ZnS
C. CuS D. CdS

21. The phase diagram of a pure substance is sketched below.

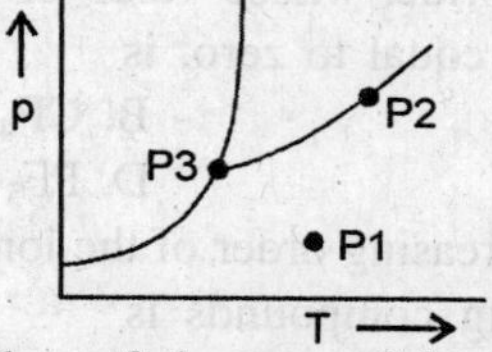

The number of degrees of freedom at points P1, P2 and P3, respectively, are

A. 2, 1 0, B. 1, 2, 0
C. 2, 0, 1 D. 0, 2, 1

22. The solubility products (K_{sp}) for three salts MX, MY_2 and MZ_3 are 1×10^{-8}, 4×10^{-9} and 27×10^{-8}, respectively. The solubilities of these salts follow the order

A. $MX > MY_2 > MZ_3$
B. $MZ_3 > MY_2 > MX$
C. $MZ_3 > MX > MY_2$
D. $MY_2 > MX > MZ_3$

23. The temperature (T) dependence of the equilibrium constant (K) of a chemical reaction is correctly described by the following statement:

A. For an endothermic reaction, the slope of ln K vs 1/T plot is positive
B. For an exothermic reaction, K is proportional to T
C. For an exothermic reaction, K at a higher temperature is lower than K at a lower temperature
D. If ΔH is independent of temperature, the change in K with T is smaller at lower temperatures.

24. When the concentration of K^+ across a cell membranes drops from 0.01 M to 0.001 M, the potential difference across the membrane is

A. 0.0 V B. 0.0059 V
C. 0.59 V D. 0.59 V

25. The statement that is correct for both electrochemical (galvanic) cells and electrolytic cells is

A. $\Delta G = -nFE$
B. Free energy decreases in both cells
C. The cell potentials are temperature independent
D. Chemical energy is converted into electrical energy in both cells

26. The molar heat capacity at constant volume of a colourless gas is found to be 25 J mol^{-1} K^{-1} at room temperature. The gas must be

A. N_2 B. O_2
C. CO_2 D. SO_2

27. The wave function for a particle (moving in a ring) is $(2\pi)^{-1/2} \exp(2i\phi)$, where ϕ is the polar angle. The probability of finding the particle in a small interval $d\phi$ when the value of $\phi = \pi/2$ is

A. $d\phi$ B. $d\phi/2\pi$
C. $d\phi \exp(i\pi)$ D. $d\phi \exp(i\pi)/2\pi$

28. An electric current of 0.965 ampere is passed for 2000 seconds through a solution containing $[Cu(CH_3CN)_4]^+$ and metallic copper is deposited at the cathode. The amount of Cu deposited is

A. 0.005 mol B. 0.01 mol
C. 0.02 mol D. 0.04 mol

29. The Maxwell-Boltzmann distribution for molecular speeds is shown in the following figure.

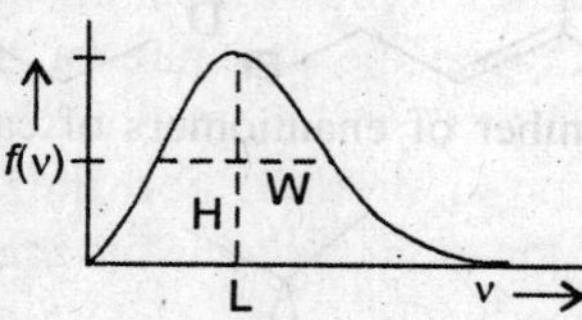

In the figure, H is the height of the peak, L is the location of the maximum and W is the width at half height. As the temperature is decreased,

A. H increases, L decreases and W increases
B. H increases, L decreases and W decreases
C. H decreases, L increases and W increases
D. H decreases, L decreases and W decreases

30. A system undergoes two cyclic processes 1 and 2. Process 1 is reversible and process 2 is irreversible. The correct statement relating to the two processes is

A. ΔS (for process 1) = 0, while ΔS (for process 2) $\neq 0$

B. $q_{cyclic} = 0$ for process 1 and $q_{cyclic} \neq 0$ for process 2

C. More heat can be converted to work in process 1 than in process 2

D. More work can be converted to heat in process 1 than in process 2

31. Identify reagent (P) and write the structure of products (Q, R, S and T) in the following series of reactions

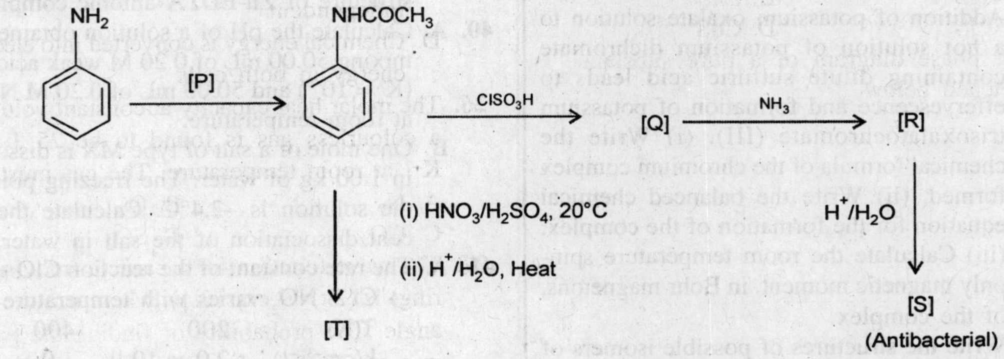

32. For the reaction

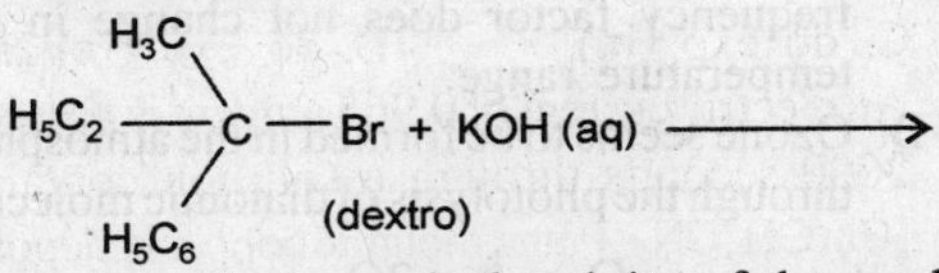

A. what is the optical activity of the product?

B. draw the energy profile for the reaction

C. write the structure of the intermediate

D. what is the effect of doubling the concentration of KOH on the rate of the reaction?

E. if aqueous KOH is replaced by alcoholic KOH, write the structure of the product formed

33. A. Suggest a method for the following transformation involving minimum number of steps.

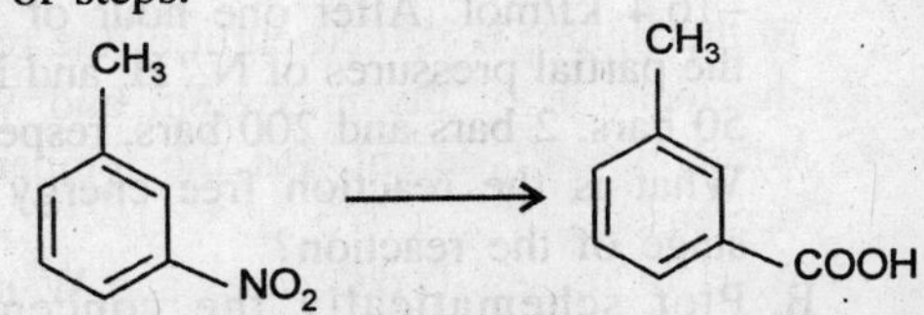

Indicate the reagents/reaction conditions required at each step clearly.

B. A dipeptide on hydrolysis gives two amino acids (X) and (Y). If the dipeptide is first treated with HNO_2 and then hydrolysis is carried out, (X) and lactic acid are obtained. (X) on heating gives 2, 5-diketopiperazine as shown below. Identify (X) and (Y), and write their sequence in the dipeptide.

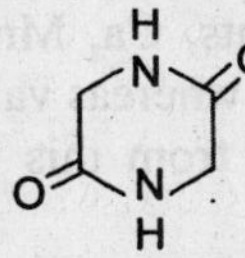

34. Identify the compounds A, B, C, D and E in the following reactions

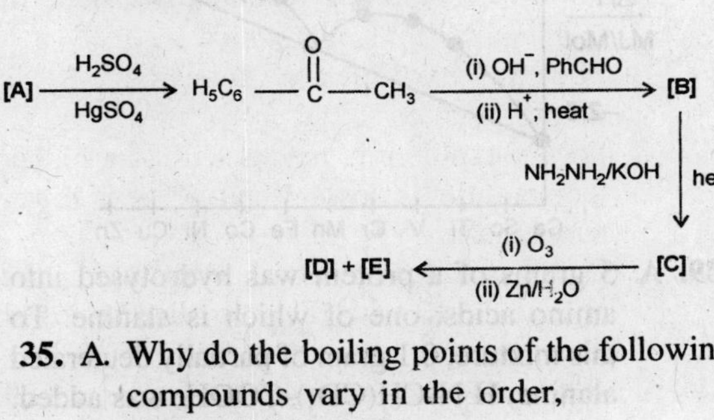

35. A. Why do the boiling points of the following compounds vary in the order, $H_2O > H_2Se > H_2S$?

B. Identify the products in the reaction of CCl_4 and $SiCl_4$ with water. Justify your answer.

36. A. Write the steps involved in the production of pure elemental silicon from silica.

B. Both the products A and B, in the following reactions, contain boron and nitrogen. Identify A and B.

$$3\ NH_4Cl + 3BCl_3 \xrightarrow[\text{heat}]{C_6H_5Cl} A \xrightarrow[\text{THF}]{LiAlH_4} B$$

37. A. Addition of potassium oxalate solution to a hot solution of potassium dichromate containing dilute sulfuric acid leads to effervescence and formation of potassium trisoxalatochromate (III). (i) Write the chemical formula of the chromium complex formed. (ii) Write the balanced chemical equation for the formation of the complex. (iii) Calculate the room temperature spin-only magnetic moment, in Bohr magnetons, of the complex.

B. Write the structures of possible isomers of $[CoCl_2(en)_2]\ Cl$

38. A. Draw the unit cell of CsCl lattice. Draw the (100) and (110) places separately and indicate the positions of cesium and chloride ions.

B. The hydration enthalpies of divalent metal ions of ten elements from calcium to zinc are plotted against their atomic numbers. Why do the hydration enthalpies of only three elements, Ca, Mn and Zn fall on a straight line, whereas values for other metal ions deviate from this line?

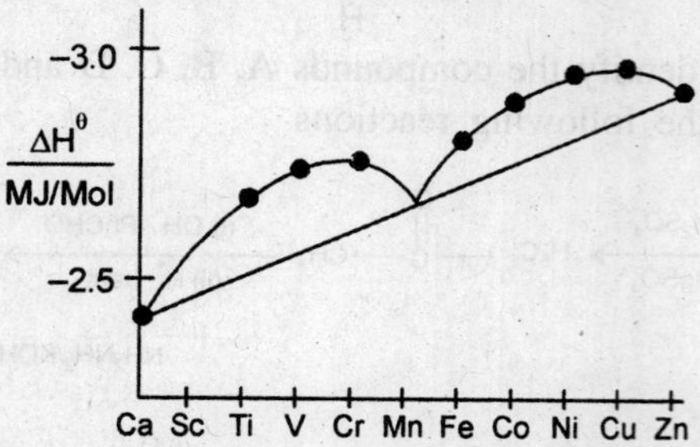

39. A. 5 grams of a protein was hydrolysed into amino acids, one of which is alanine. To this mixture, 0.1 gram of partially deuterated alanine, $H_2N\text{-}CH(CD_3)\text{-}COOH$, was added. After thorough mixing, some of the alanine was separated and purified by crystallization. The crystalline alanine contains 0.652 weight percent of D. How many grams of alanine were originally present in 5 grams of protein?

B. What is the role of ammoniacal buffer in the volumetric titration of zinc sulphate against EDTA, using Solochrome black (Eriochrome black T) indicator? Write the structure of Zn-EDTA anionic complex.

40. A. Calculate the pH of a solution obtained by mixing 50.00 mL of 0.20 M weak acid HA ($K_a = 10^{-5}$) and 50.00 mL of 0.20 M NaOH at room temperature.

B. One mole of a salt of type MX is dissolved in 1.00 kg of water. The freezing point of the solution is –2.4°C. Calculate the per cent dissociation of the salt in water.

41. A. The rate constant of the reaction $ClO + NO \rightarrow Cl + NO_2$ varies with temperature as:

T(K)	200	400
k($cm^{-3}s^{-1}$)	2.0×10^{-11}	1.0×10^{-11}

Determine the Arrhenius activation energy for the reaction, assuming that the frequency factor does not change in this temperature range.

B. Ozone seems to be formed in the atmosphere through the photolysis of diatomic molecule:

$$O_2 \xrightarrow[h\nu]{k_0} 2O$$

$$O + O_2 \xrightarrow{k_1} O_3$$

$$O_3 + O \xrightarrow{k_2} 2O_2$$

Applying steady-state approximation, determine the rate law for the formation of ozone. Show that the formation of ozone follows first order kinetics when the concentration of O_3 is extremely small.

42. A. The reaction $N_2 + 3H_2 \rightarrow 2NH_3$ is carried out at 300 K by mixing N_2 and H_2. The standard free energy of formation of NH_3 is –16.4 kJ/mol. After one hour of mixing, the partial pressures of N_2, H_2 and NH_3 are 50 bars, 2 bars and 200 bars, respectively. What is the reaction free energy at this stage of the reaction?

B. Plot schematically the concentration dependence of molar conductivity of a strong electrolyte and a weak electrolyte in the same figure. The limiting ionic molar conductivities of K^+ and Cl^- are 73.5 and 76.5 S cm^2 mol^{-1}, respectively. If the molar conductivity of 0.1 M KCl solution is 130.0 S cm^2 mol^{-1}, calculate the Kohlrausch's constant for KCl solution.

43. A. The electronic wave function (ψ) for hydrogen atom in the 2s state is given as

$$\psi \propto \left(2-\frac{r}{a_0}\right)\exp\left(\frac{-r}{2a_0}\right)$$

Determine the most probable radial distance for the electron in this state and also the position of the node (in terms of a_0).

B. Calculate the wavelength corresponding to the lowest energy excitation of an electron confined to a one-dimensional box of length 1 nm. (Energy levels for a particle-in-a-one-dimensional box are given by $E_n = n^2h^2/8ma^2$).

44. A. Solve the differential equation $y'' - 5y' + 6y = 0$ with the initial conditions $y(0) = -1$ and $y'(0) = 0$. Here y' and y'' refer to the first and the second derivatives, respectively, of y with respect to x. Verify your answer.

B. For a particle with position $\mathbf{r} = 2\mathbf{i} - 3\mathbf{j} + \mathbf{k}$ and momentum $\mathbf{p} = \mathbf{i} + 2\mathbf{j} - 2\mathbf{k}$ in m and kg. ms^{-1}, respectively, calculate the magnitude of the angular momentum $\mathbf{L} = \mathbf{r} \times \mathbf{p}$.

ANSWERS

1	2	3	4	5	6	7	8	9	10
A	B	C	B	D	C	A	D	C	C
11	12	13	14	15	16	17	18	19	20
A	B	C	D	A	B	C	D	A	B
21	22	23	24	25	26	27	28	29	30
A	B	C	C	A	*	B	B	C	A

SOME SELECTED EXPLANATORY ANSWERS

1. Specification of R (latin: rectus, right) *i.e.* clockwise and *S* (latin: sinister, left) *i.e.* counter clockwise is assigned to molecules with chiral center. Priority to the four atoms or groups of atoms attached to chiral centre is assigned depending upon atomic number. The atom of higher number having higher priority.

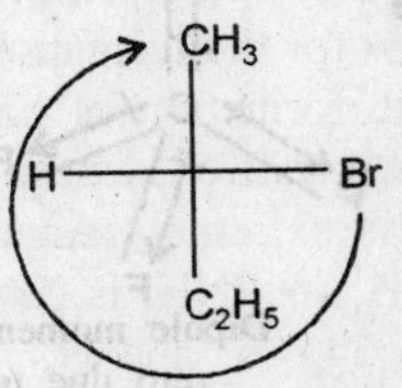

R

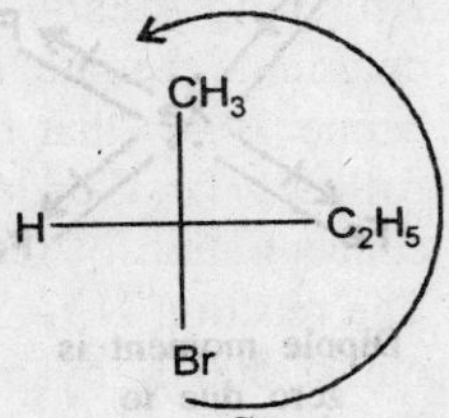

S

3.

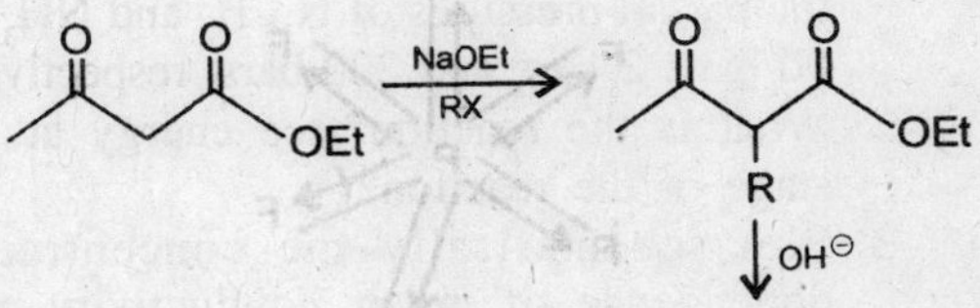

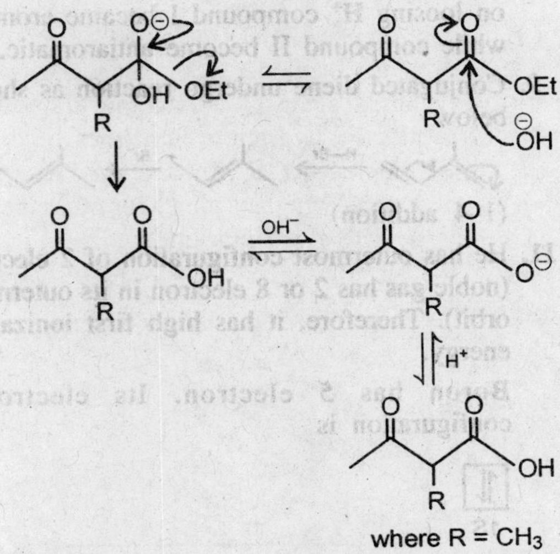

where R = CH_3

5. It is Gatterman – Koch synthesis of aldehyde. The reagent used also include Anhyd. $AlCl_3$/CuCl and Anhyd. $AlCl_3/Cu_2O$.

7. 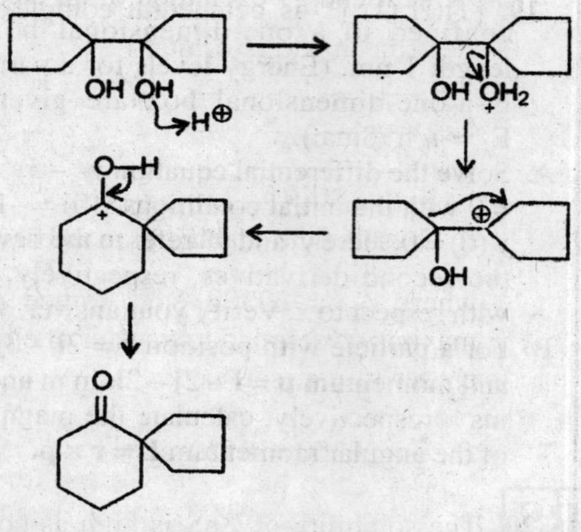

8. More stabilized the congugate base, A^- stronger is the acid, way to stabilise includes:
   (*i*) Having charge on electronegative element
   (*ii*) Delocalizing the negative charge over the carbon atoms, or even better, over more negative atoms.
   (*iii*) Spreading out charge over electron withdrawing group by polarisation of σ bonds.
   (*iv*) Having negative charge in an orbital with none S characters
   (*v*) becoming aromatic.

on loosing H^+ compound I became aromatic while compound II become antiaromatic.

9. Conjugated diene undergo reaction as shown below

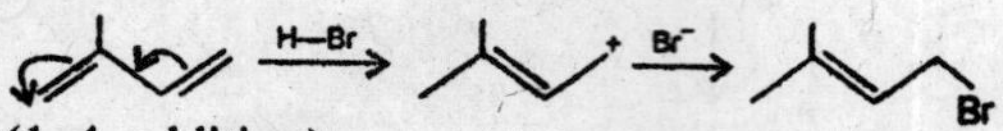

(1–4 addition)

11. He has outermost configuration of 2 electron (noble gas has 2 or 8 electron in its outermost orbit). Therefore, it has high first ionization energy.

Boron has 5 electron. Its electronic configuration is

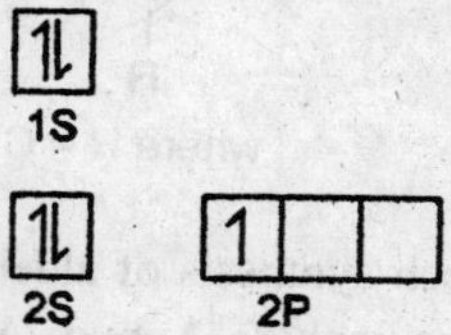

on loosing one electron it will have 2 electron in its outermost orbital, therefore its first ionization energy is least.

Further Be has electronic configuration.

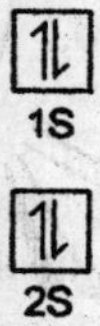

It has 2 electron in its outermost orbit. But these electrons are in orbit with $n = 2 \Rightarrow$ that they are away from nucleus as compared to He (which has $n = 1$). This mean less energy will be required to remove electron from Be as compared to He and therefore Be has lower first ionization energy as compared to helium.

12. Lattice energy could be derived from electrical potential of ionic lattice and repulsive potential energy term (Born and Larde, 1918)

$$E = -\frac{N_A M z^+ z^- e^2}{4\pi \epsilon_0 r_0}\left(1 - \frac{1}{n}\right)$$

where

N_A is the Avogadro constant

M is the madalung constant relating to geometry of the crystal

Z^+ is the charge number of cation

Z^- is the charge number of anion

e is the elementary charge (1.6022×10^{-19}C)

ϵ_0 is the permittivity of free space, ($8.8541 \times 10^{-12} C^2 j^{-1} m^{-1}$)

r_0 is the distance to closest ion and

n is the Born exponent

13. 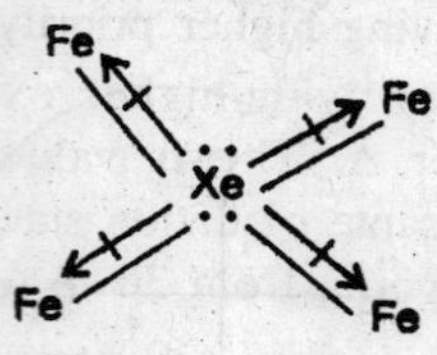

Dipole moment is zero due to symmetry

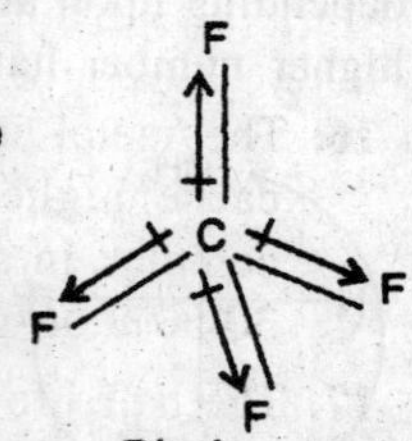

Dipole moment is zero due to symmetry

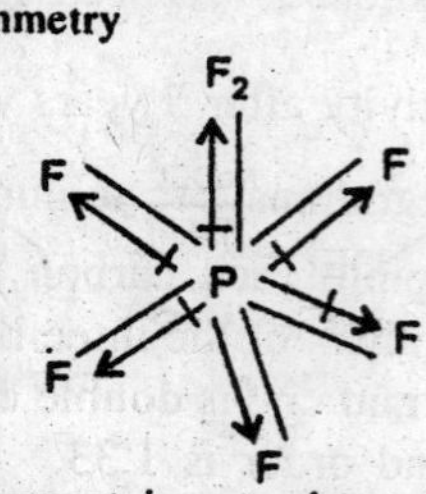

Dipole moment is zero due to symmetry

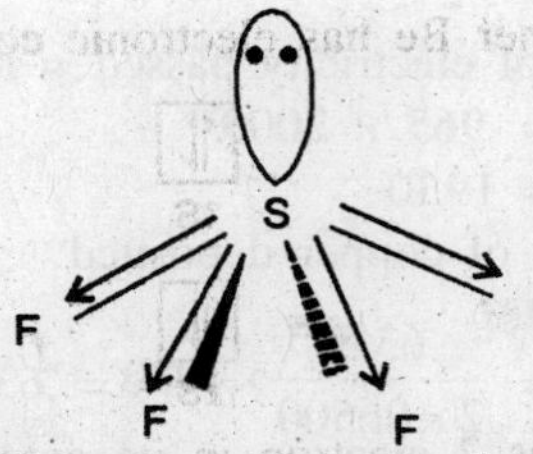

Dipole moment not equal to zero.

Dipole moment = 0.632 D.

14. The more the electronegativity difference between the constituent of compound the more will be the ionic character of compound. In present example CSF has maximum electronegativity difference while LiI has least. This could also be understand from concept of polarisation. In LiI, Li^+ has high polarising power due to its small size. While I^- due to large size (e^- are away from nucleus) could be polarised easily. This means it has high covalent character in the given compound and hence least ionic character.

15. White Phosphorus (P_4)

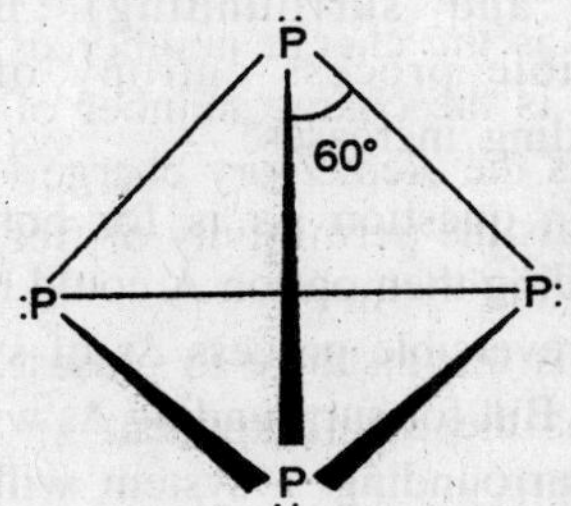

16. The metel ion with higher oxidation state cause higher Δ. The Δ value for similar complex in same oxidation state increase by 30-50% on going from 3d to 4d.

17. The half life is given (20 years)
100 years contain 5 half life time period. Since the readioactive process is first order reaction, the activity after 5 years will be $\frac{6400}{2^5} = 200$ disintegrations per minute.

18. In graphite each carbon atom is attached to three others of the three bonds, two are single bonds and one is double bond. Therefore over all bond order is 1.33.

19. $[Ti(H_2O)_6]^{3+}$ is octahedral complex with one electron in the *d* orbital.

∴ Crystal field stabilization energy is $\frac{2}{5}\Delta_0$, where $\Delta_0 = 20300\ cm^{-1}$ (since absorption maxima correspond to transfer of electron from t_{2g} set to e.g. set)

$$\therefore\ \frac{2}{5}\times 20300 = 8120\ cm^{-1}$$

20. The solubility of ZnS is high as compared to that of HgS and CuS. H_2S in acidic medium provide very less concentration of S^{2-} ions which is not sufficient to precipitate ZnS.

21. Phase rule

$$F = C - P + 2$$

At point P1

$$F = 1 - 1 + 2 = 2$$

At point P2

$$F = 1 - 2 + 2 = 1$$

At point P3

$$F = 1 - 3 + 2 = 0$$

22.

$$MX \longrightarrow \underset{s}{M^+} + \underset{s}{X^-}$$

$$K_{sp} = [M^+][B^-] = s^2$$

$$s = (K_{sp})^{1/2} \Rightarrow S = 10^{-4}$$

$$MY_2 \longrightarrow \underset{s}{M^{+2}} + \underset{2s}{2Y^-}$$

$$K_{sp} = [M^{+2}][Y^-]^2$$

$$= s \times 4s^2 = 4s^3$$

$$s = \left(\frac{K_{sp}}{4}\right)^{1/3} \Rightarrow S = 10^{-3}$$

$$MZ_3 \longrightarrow \underset{s}{M^{+3}} + \underset{3s}{3Z^-}$$

$$K_{sp} = [M^{+3}][Z^-]^3$$

$$= s \times 27s^3 = 27s^4$$

$$s = \left(\frac{K_{sp}}{27}\right)^{1/4} \Rightarrow S = 10^{-2}$$

23. $\log_{10}\left(\frac{K_2}{K_1}\right) = \frac{\Delta H^0}{2.303R}\left(\frac{1}{T_1}-\frac{1}{T_2}\right)$

or $\quad \ln K_P = \frac{-\Delta H^0}{RT} + C$

Now for exothermic reaction $\Delta H° = -ve$

$\Rightarrow$ Right hand side quantity is –ve

$\Rightarrow K_2 < K_1$

24. There is difference in concentration of K^+ across the cell membrane.

$\frac{.0591}{n}\log\frac{K_{+(I)}}{K_{+(II)}}$ part in the cell EMF took care of this. (as $E°_{cell}$ for K cancel each other)

$\therefore$ Potential difference $= \frac{.0591}{1}\log 10 = .0591$

26. $C_v = 25\ J\ mol^{-1}K^{-1}$

$\Rightarrow C_p = C_v + R = 25 + 8.314 = 33.314$

$\therefore\ y\frac{C_p}{C_v} = \frac{33.314}{25} = 1.33$

But $y = 1 + \frac{2}{f} = .33 \quad \Rightarrow f = 6$

(where f is degree of freedom)

$\Rightarrow SO_2$

27. $\psi = \frac{1}{\sqrt{2\pi}}e^{2i\phi}$

$\psi^* = \frac{1}{\sqrt{2\pi}}e^{-2i\phi}$

$\therefore \quad \psi\psi^* = \frac{1}{2\pi}$

$\therefore$ Probability of finding particle in a small interval $d\phi$ is $\psi\psi^*\ d\phi$

i.e. $\frac{1}{2\pi}d\phi$

28. $Cu^{2+} + 2e^- \longrightarrow Cu$

$\Rightarrow 2 \times 96500$ coloumb deposits 63.5 gms of copper.

Coloumb of electricity passed = it

$= .965 \times 2000$

$= 1930$

$\therefore$ amount of copper deposited

$= \frac{63.5}{2 \times 96500} \times 1930 = .635$ gm

or .01 mol

29.

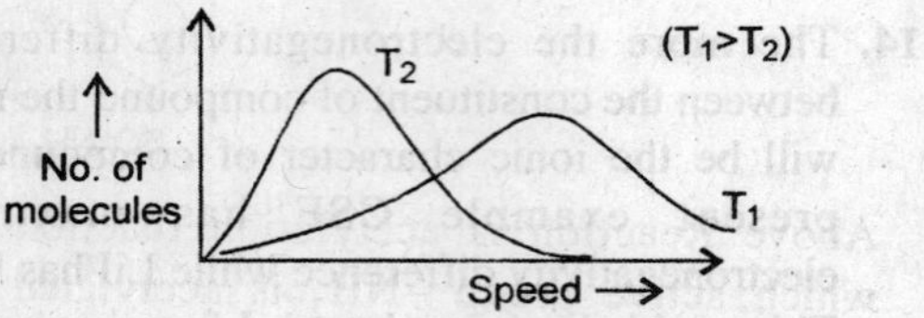

As temperature increases the speed occupied by maximum fraction of molecules of gas also increases.

30. According to third law of thermodynamics entropy (which is disorder associated with the system) is increasing. During reversible process the entropy change is zero (combining both system and surrounding). But during resversible process entropy of system + surrounding increases.

So, if in question Δs is for both system + surrounding then option A could be correct as during reversible process Δs of system could be zero. But for surrounding Δs will be > 0 ⇒ Δs of surrounding + system will be greater than zero.

However, if both process is performed between two temperature T_1 and T_2 then reversible process will have more efficiency ⇒ more heat can be converted to work in reversible process than in irreversible process. In this case option (c) will be correct.

31.

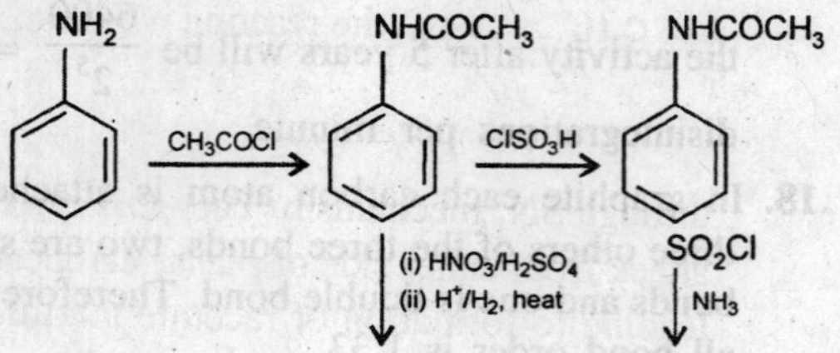

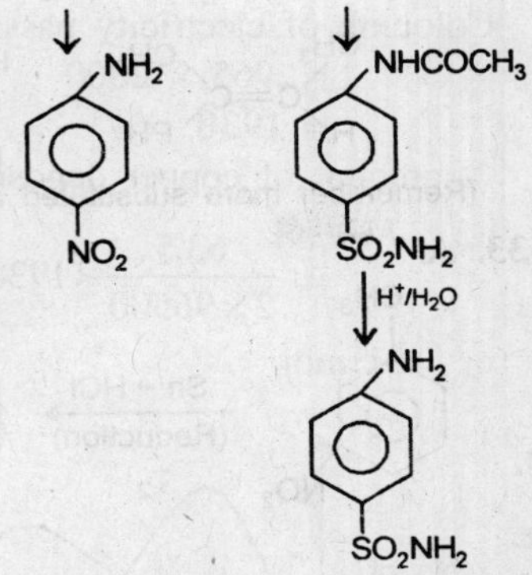

Above Reaction is acetylation reaction in which active group $-NH_2$ is acetylated to protect it. Otherwise $-NH_2$ group will react with the reactants. After completion of reaction, $NHCOCH_3$ group is again converted into $-NH_2$ group by acidic hydrolysis. The process is very useful in preparation of compounds. Further no where it is mentioned that the process is following carnot cycle. But any process can be considered as assembly of such cycle as shown below.

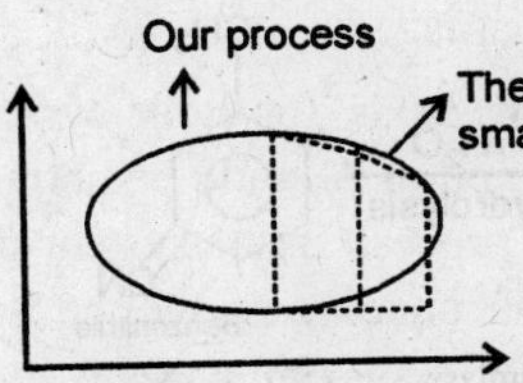

32. (*i*)

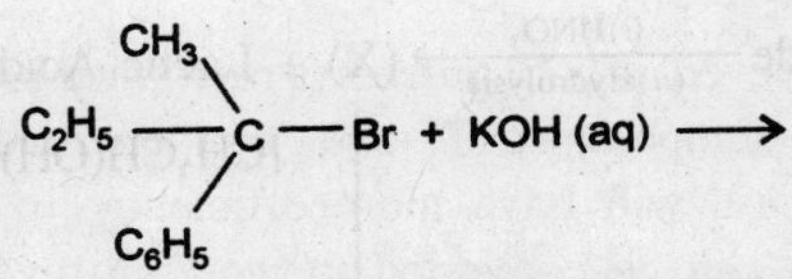

Since here stable carbocation is formed

i.e. 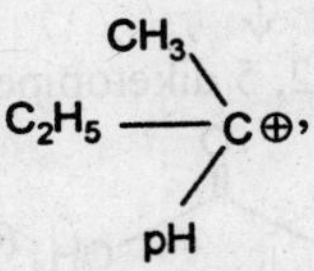 the reaction will proceeds through SN_1 mechanism. The –OH can than attack from either side of planar carbocation leading to formation of racemic mixture as shown below

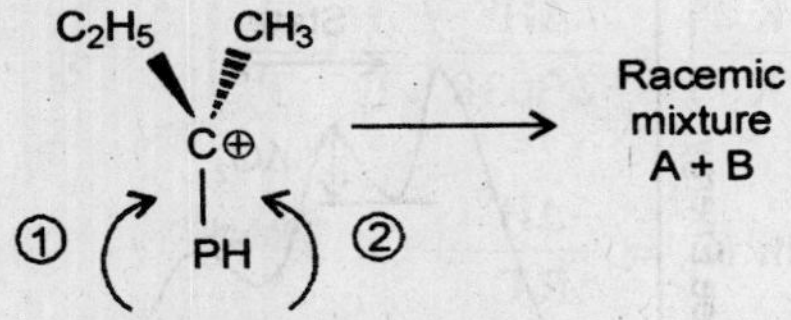

(Planar carbocation)

In case of attack shown in (1) the product A is formed

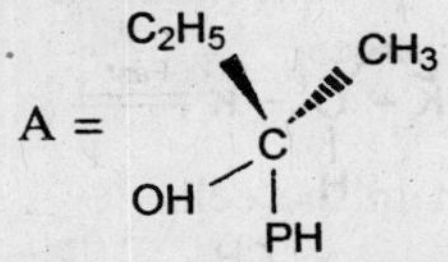

For attack on other side

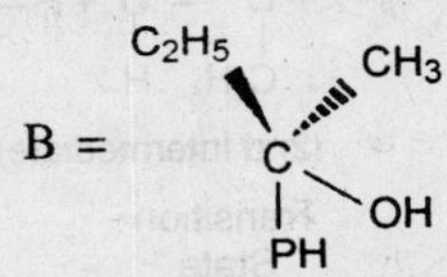

Since racemic mixture is formed then there will be no optical activity after some time.

(*ii*)

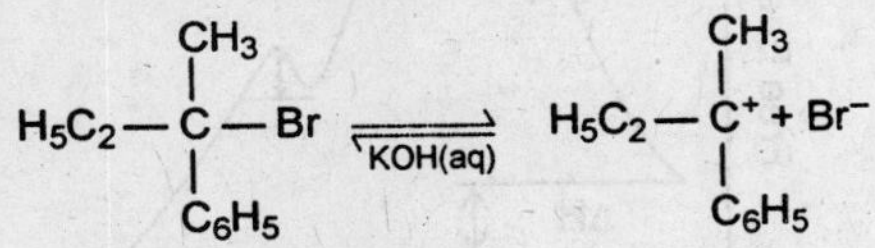

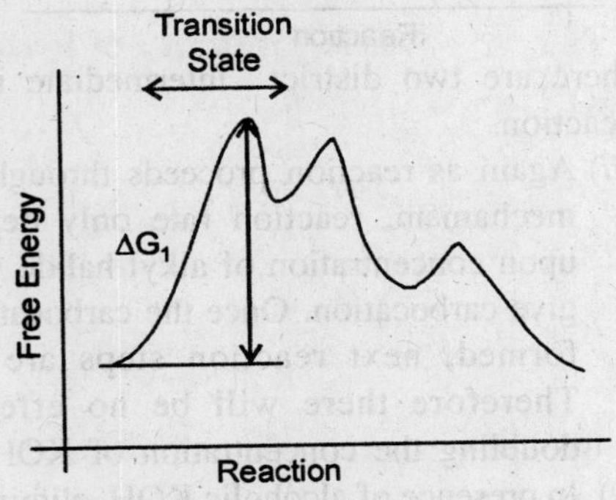

ΔG_1 is much larger than ΔG_2 or ΔG_3 hence this is the slowest step.

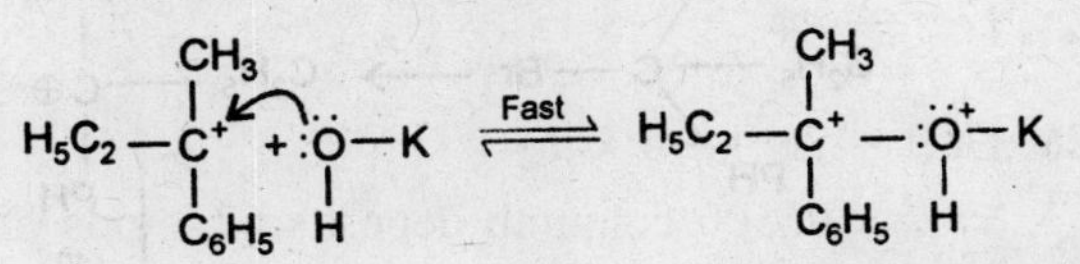

(1st Intermediate)

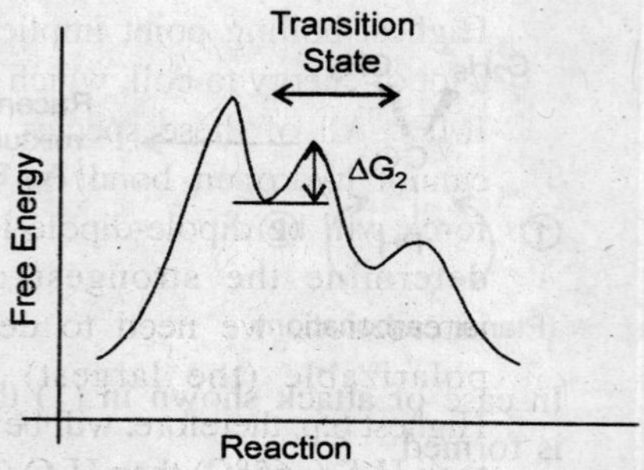

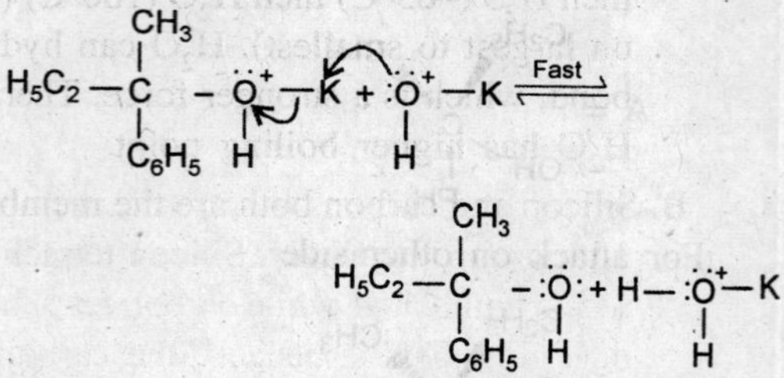

(2nd Intermediate)

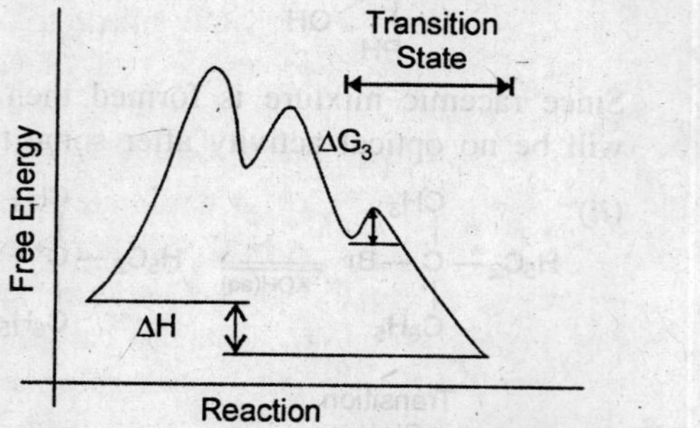

There are two district intermediate in the Reaction.

(*iii*) Again as reaction proceeds through SN_1 mechanism, reaction rate only depends upon concentration of alkyl halide which give carbocation. Once the carbocation is formed, next reaction steps are fast. Therefore there will be no effect of doubling the concentration of KOH.

(*iv*) In presence of alcoholic KOH, elimination reaction will occur as shown below.

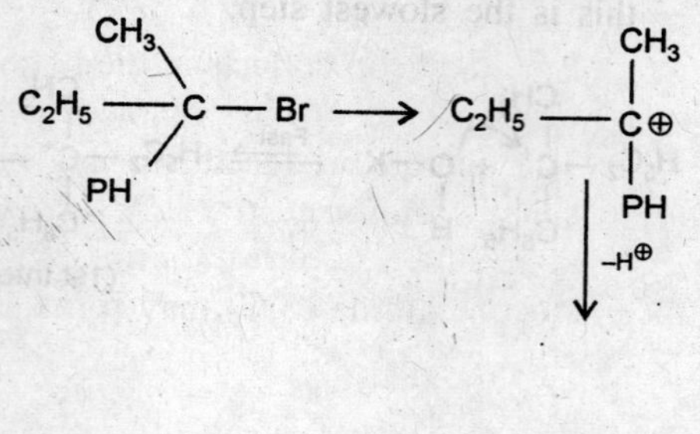

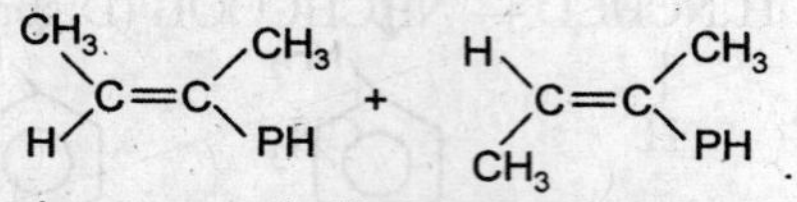

(Remember more substituted alkene is formed)

33. A.

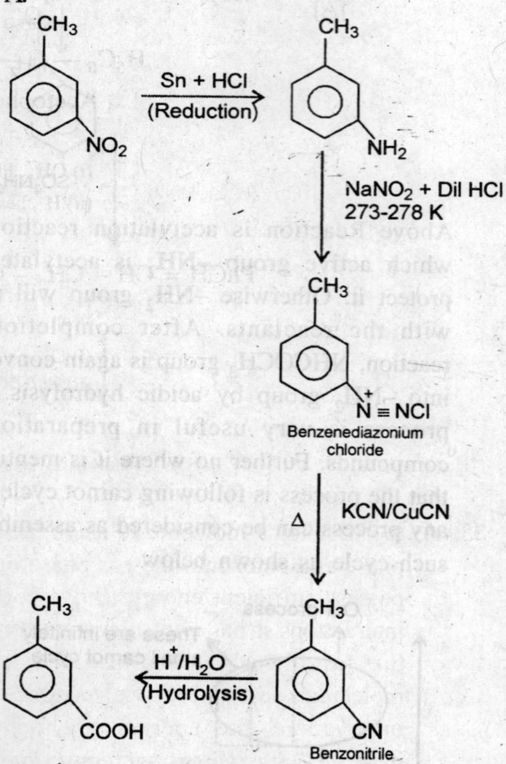

B. Dipeptide $\xrightarrow{\text{hydrolysis}}$ (X) + (Y)

Dipeptide $\xrightarrow[(ii)\text{Hydrolysis}]{(i)HNO_3}$ (X) + Lactic Acid

[$CH_3CH(OH)COOH$]

heating

2, 5 diketopiperazine

(X) ⟶ 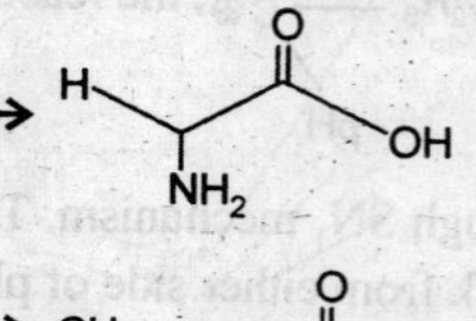 (Glycine)

(Y) ⟶ 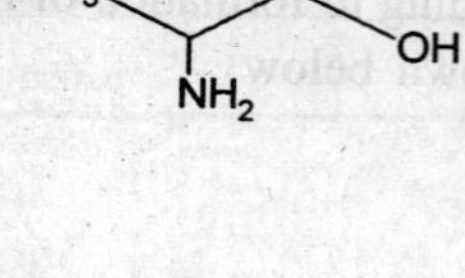 (Alanine)

$H_2N\underset{\underset{H}{|}}{C}HCO — NH\underset{\underset{CH_3}{|}}{C}HCOOH$ (Dipeptide)

34. B. $\underset{[A]}{H_5C_6 — C \equiv C — H} \xrightarrow{H_2SO_4/HgSO_4} H_5C_6 — \overset{\overset{O}{||}}{C} — CH_3$ Acetophenone

$\xrightarrow[\text{(ii) } H^+\text{, heat}]{\text{(i) } OH^-\text{, Ph CHO}} \underset{[C]}{PhCH = CH - CH_2 - C_6H_5} \xrightarrow[\text{(ii) } Zn/H_2O]{\text{(i) } O_3} \underset{[D]}{Ph\overset{\overset{O}{||}}{C}H} + \underset{[E]}{C_6H_5CH_2CHO}$

35. A. In order for a molecule to leave the liquid phase and enter into the gas phase, it must possess sufficient energy to overcome the interactions it has with other molecules in the liquid. Also recalling the kinetic molecular description, we recognize that, on average, the energies of molecules increase with increasing temperature. We can conclude from these two statements that a high boiling point implies that significant energy is required to overcome intermolecular interactions. Conversely, a substance with a low boiling point must have weak intermolecular interactions, surmountable even at low temperature.

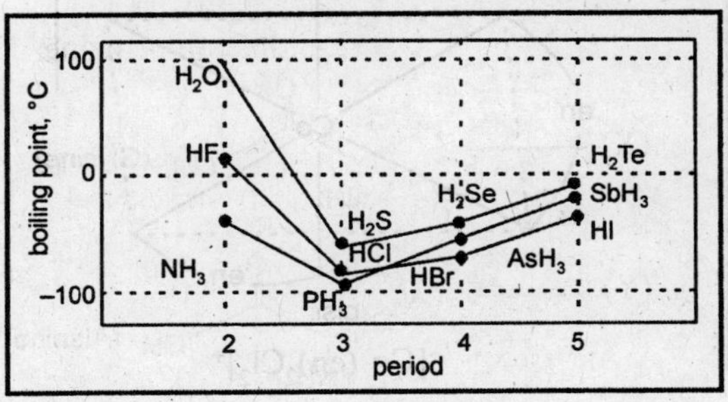

Highest boiling point implies that it takes a lot of energy to boil, which implies strong IMFs. All of these species are polar (but cannot hydrogen bond) so the dominant force will be dipole-dipole interaction. To determine the strongest dipole-dipole interaction, we need to determine most polarizable (the largest) species. The Highest b.p. therefore, will be H_2Se (–45°C), then H_2S (–65°C) then H_2O (100°C) (based on largest to smallest). H_2O can hydrogen bond, which is a stronger force. Therefore, H_2O has higher boiling point.

B. Silicon and carbon both are the members of 14th group. However, Silicon tetrachloride reacts with water while carbon tetrachloride does not. This is because the carbon does not have d-orbitals to accept lone pair of electron from water while silicon has vacant d-orbitals to accept lone pair of electron from water.

Silicon tetrachloride reacts readily with water, in contrast with carbon tetrachloride. The differing rates of hydrolysis are attributed to the greater atomic radius of the silicon atom, whereas carbon has a smaller atomic radius so the chlorine atoms effectively shield the carbon from attack. In water, the following reaction occurs:

$$SiCl_4 + 2H_2O \rightarrow SiO_2 + 4HCl$$

36. A. **Production:** Silicon is commercially prepared by the reaction of high-purity silica with wood, charcoal, and coal, in an electric arc furnace using carbon electrodes. At temperatures over 1,900 °C (3,450 °F), the carbon reduces the silica to silicon according to the chemical equations:

$$SiO_2 + C \rightarrow Si + CO_2$$
$$SiO_2 + 2C \rightarrow Si + 2CO$$

Liquid silicon collects in the bottom of the furnace, and is then drained and cooled. The silicon produced via this process is called *metallurgical grade silicon* and is at least 98% pure. Using this method, silicon carbide (SiC) may form. However, provided the concentration of SiO_2 is kept high, the silicon carbide can be eliminated:

$$2SiC + SiO_2 \rightarrow 3Si + 2CO$$

Pure silicon (>99.9%) can be extracted directly from solid silica or other silicon compounds by molten salt electrolysis. This method, known from 1854 has the potential to directly produce solar grade silicon without any CO_2 emission and at much lower energy consumption.

Purification: Today, silicon is purified by converting it to a silicon compound that can be more easily purified by distillation than in its original state, and then converting that silicon compound back into pure silicon. Trichlorosilane is the silicon compound most commonly used as the intermediate, although silicon tetrachloride and silane are also used. When these gases are blown over silicon at high temperature, they decompose to high-purity silicon.

At one time, DuPont produced ultra-pure silicon by reacting silicon tetrachloride with high-purity zinc vapors at 950°C, producing silicon:

$$SiCl_4 + 2\ Zn \rightarrow Si + 2\ ZnCl_2$$

However, this technique was plagued with practical problems (such as the zinc chloride byproduct solidifying and clogging lines) and was eventually abandoned in favour of the Siemens process.

In the **Siemens process,** high-purity silicon rods are exposed to trichlorosilane at 1150°C. The trichlorosilane gas decomposes and deposits additional silicon onto the rods, enlarging them:

$$2HSiCl_3 \rightarrow Si + 2HCl + SiCl_4$$

Silicon produced from this and similar processes is called *polycrystalline silicon.* Polycrystalline silicon typically has impurity levels of less than 10^{-9}.

In 2006 Renewable Energy Corporation (REC) announced construction of a plant based on fluidized bed technology using silane:

$$3SiCl_4 + Si + 2H_2 \rightarrow 4HSiCl_3$$

$$4HSiCl_3 \rightarrow 3HSiCl_4 + SiH_4$$

$$SiH_4 \rightarrow Si + H_2$$

36. B. $3NH_4Cl + 3BCl_3 \xrightarrow[\text{heat}]{C_6H_5Cl}$

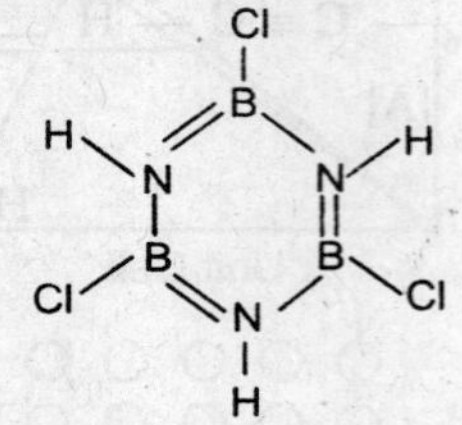

2, 4, 6-trichloroborazine

37. A. (*i*) Potassium trioxalatochromate $K_3[Cr(C_2O_4)_3]$

(*ii*) $K_2Cr_2O_7 + 7H_2C_2O_4 + 2K_2C_2O_4 \longrightarrow 2K_3[Cr(C_2O_4)_3]\ 3H_2O + 6CO_2 + H_2O$

(*iii*) Spin only magnetic moment

$$\sqrt{n(n+2)}$$

n (no. of unpaired electron in complex) = 3

$$\sqrt{3(3+2)} = \sqrt{15} = 3.87 \text{ BM.}$$

37. B. The octahedral complex $[Co(en)_2Cl_2]$ Cl exist as two isomers

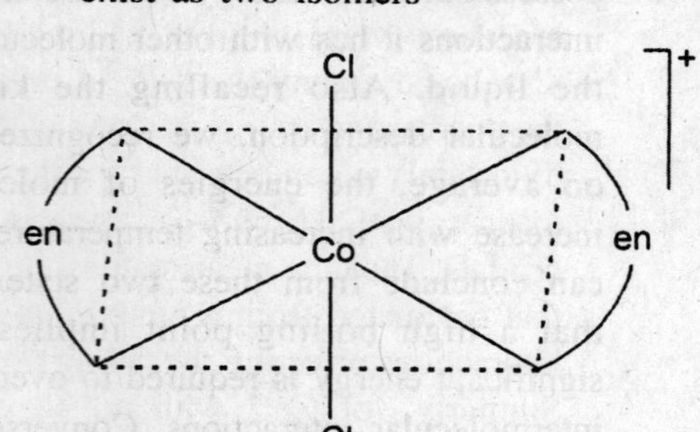

trans

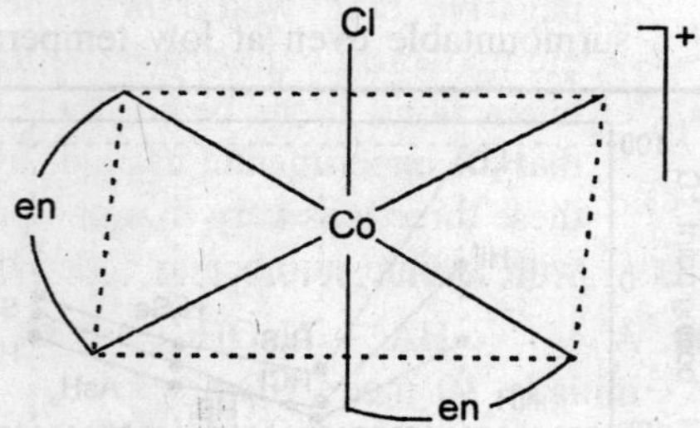

cis

$[Co\ (en)_2Cl_2]^+$

38. A.

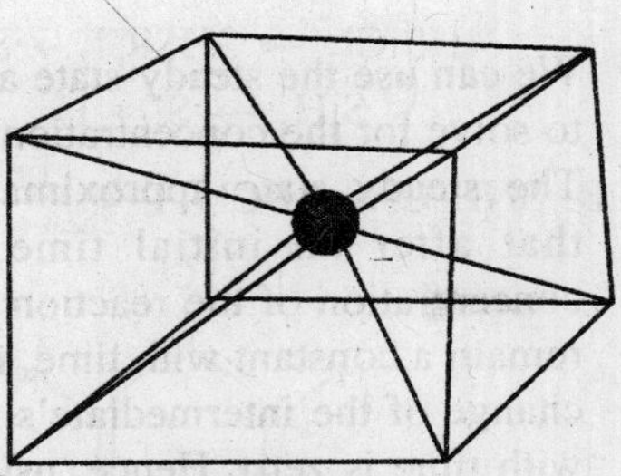

Unit Cell

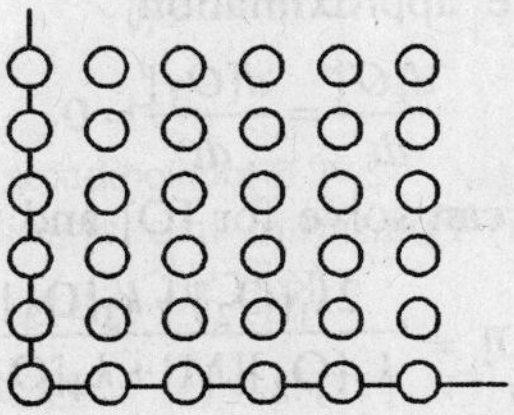

CsCl (100 Plane)

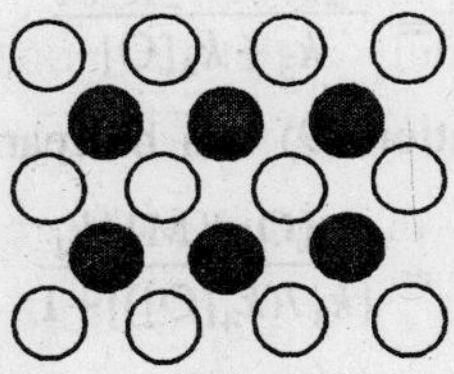

CsCl (110)

38. B. In case of hydrated divalent manganese ion, however, its five 3d electrons are distributed among the five 3d orbitals and the decrease in energy of three electrons in dv orbitals is compensated for the increase in energy of the two electrons in the d∈ orbitals. Thus the mean state is the same as that calculated from a model that neglects interactions affecting the filling of orbitals. Similarly, for Ca^{2+} with no 3d electrons and Zn with completely filled 3d shell, the heat of hydration does not become more negative than would be expected from electrostatic theory of ion-solvent interactions. It can be concluded, therefore that the experimental heats of hydration of these three ions vary in monotonic manner with atomic number as indeed they do.

40. A.

	HA	+ NaOH	⇌ NaA	+ H_2O
Initially	10 meq	10 meq	0	0
After some time	0	0	10 meq	10 meq

Now hydrolysis of salt of strong base and weak acid will give decide pH of solution. Since equal volume of HA and NaOH are mixed, molarity of given salt will be $\frac{.2}{2} = .1$

$$pH = 7 + \frac{1}{2}PKa + \frac{1}{2}\log C \quad \text{where } C = .1$$

$$= 7 + \frac{1}{2}(-\log 10^{-5}) + \frac{1}{2}\log .1$$

$$= 7 + \frac{5}{2} - \frac{1}{2}$$

$$= 7 + 2 = 9.$$

B. $\Delta T_f = iK_f \times$ molality

$\Delta T_f = 2.4$

One mole of salt in 1000 kg of water

⇒ molality is one (mol/kg)

K_f is 1.86 (K kg^{-1} mol^{-1})

$\therefore \quad 2.4 = i \times 1.86 \times 1$

$\Rightarrow \quad i = 1.3$

$$MX \longrightarrow M^+ + X^-$$
$$1-\alpha \qquad \alpha \qquad \alpha$$

$\therefore \quad i = 1 + \alpha$

$\Rightarrow \quad 1 + \alpha = 1.3$

or $\quad \alpha = .3$

Therefore 30% of salt dissociate in water.

41. A. The Arrhenius equation is

$$\log\frac{k_2}{k_1} = \frac{E_a}{2.303R}\left[\frac{1}{T_1} - \frac{T_1}{T_2}\right]$$

$k_1 = 2.0 \times 10^{-11}$ $\quad T_1 = 200$ K

$k_2 = 1.0 \times 10^{-11}$ $\quad T_2 = 400$ K

Substituting the values,

$$\log\frac{1.0\times10^{-11}}{2.0\times10^{-11}} = \frac{E_a}{2.303\times8.314}\left[\frac{1}{200} - \frac{1}{400}\right]$$

$$\log\frac{1}{2} = \frac{E_a}{19.147}\left[\frac{1}{400}\right]$$

$$E_\propto = 19.147 \times 400 \times -0.301$$

$$= -2305.29 \text{ J mol}^{-1}$$

$$= -2.30529 \text{ kJ mol}^{-1}$$

B. $O_2 + h\nu \rightarrow 2O \qquad k_1(s^{-1})$ (1)

$O + O_2 + M \rightarrow O_3 + M \qquad k_2(cm^6\ mol^{-2}\ s^{-1})$ (2)

$$O_3 + h\nu \rightarrow O + O_2 \qquad k_3(s^{-1}) \qquad (3)$$

$$O + O_3 \rightarrow 2O_2 \qquad k_4(cm^3\ mol^{-1}s^{-1}) \qquad (4)$$

M is any non-reactive species that can take up the energy released in reaction (2) to stabilize O_3. O_3 is not a very stable molecule and (without the presence of M) the O_3 formed by the collision of O_2 and O would immediately fall apart to give back O and O_2. Given that N_2 and O_2 are the major components in the atmosphere, M is either O_2 or N_2. The rate constants k_1 and k_3 depend on light intensity, which in this case is the light intensity of the sun.

Order of the Reactions

Looking at each elementary reaction, we would expect that reaction (1) follows first order kinetics, reaction (2) follows third order kinetics, reaction (3) follows first order kinetics and reaction (4) follows second order kinetics. Note that reaction (2) required three species to come together at the same time, i.e. it is an intermolecular reaction. If we look at the relative concentration of species in the atmosphere, O_2 and M (=O_2 + N_2) have much higher concentrations than O and O_3, and so they can be considered to be essentially constant over time. Thus, we might expect reaction (1) to obey zero order kinetics (a "pseudo" zero order reaction) and reaction (2) to obey first order kinetics ("pseudo" first order reaction).

Rate of formation of O and O_3

The concentration of ozone is found to be higher in the upper atmosphere (the stratosphere) when compared with the concentrations in the lower atmosphere (the troposphere). From reaction (1) to (4) the rates of formation of O and O_3 can be expressed as:

$$\frac{d[O]}{dt} = 2k_1[O_2] - k_2[O][O_2][M] + k_3[O_3] - k_4[O][O_3] \qquad (5)$$

$$\frac{d[O_3]}{dt} = k_2[O][O_2][M] - k_3[O_3] - k_4[O][O_3] \qquad (6)$$

We can use the steady-state approximation to solve for the concentration of O and O_3. The steady state approximation assumes that after an initial time period, the concentration of the reaction intermediates remain a constant with time, i.e. the rate of change of the intermediate's concentration with time is zero. Hence, using the steady state approximation

$$\frac{d[O]}{dt} = \frac{d[O_3]}{dt} = 0 \qquad (7)$$

we can solve for [O] and $[O_3]$

$$[O] = \frac{2k_1[O_2] + k_3[O_3]}{k_2[O_2][M] + k_4[O_3]} \qquad (8)$$

$$[O_3] = \frac{k_2[O][O_2][M]}{k_3 + k_4[O]} \qquad (9)$$

Equation (9) can be rearranged:

$$[O_3] = \frac{k_2[O_2][M]/k_4}{[k_3/(k_4[O])]+1} \qquad (10)$$

The reactions (1) to (4) have been very well studied and the rate constants for the reactions at different altitudes are known. For example, $k_1 \sim 10^{-12}s^{-1}$, $k_2 \sim 2\times10^{-33}$ cm^6 molecule^{-2}s^{-1}, $k_3 \sim 10^{-3}s^{-1}$, $k_4 \sim 10^{-15}$cm^3 molecule^{-1}s^{-1}. In addition, the concentrations of O, O_2 and O_3 in the atmosphere are known. If we assume that [O] ~ 10^7 molecule/cm^3 and $[O_3]$ ~ 10^{13} molecule/cm^3, using the values of the rate constants above we find that

$$\frac{k_3}{k_4[O]} >> 1$$

Hence equation (10) can be simplified to

$$[O_3] \approx \frac{k_2[O_2][M][O]}{k_3} \qquad (11)$$

Equation 11 indicates that the concentration of O_3 in the atmosphere depends proportionally on the rate of reaction 2 and inversely on k_3, the rate constant for the photolysis of ozone by the UV light from the sun.

42. A. $G = XG_{rnx} + RT \ln\left[\frac{(P_{NH_3})}{(P_{N_2})(P_{H_2})^3}\right]$

Given,

Partial pressure of $N_2 = 50$ bar

Partial pressure of $H_2 = 2$ bar

Partial pressure of $NH_3 = 200$ bar

Temperature = 300 K

Standard energy of formation of NH_3

$= -16.4\ \text{kJmol}^{-1}$

Now, put the values in equation

$-16.4\ \text{kJ mol}^{-1}$

$$= G_{rnx} + 8.3145 \times 300 \ln\left[\frac{(200)^2}{(50)(2)^3}\right]$$

$$-16.4\ \text{kJ mol}^{-1} = G_{rnx} + 2494.35 \ln 100\ \text{J mol}^{-1}$$

$$G_{rnx} = -16.4\ \text{kJ mol}^{-1} + 2494.35 \times 4.605\ \text{J mol}^{-1}$$

$$= -16.4\ \text{kJ mol}^{-1} + 11.486\ \text{kJ mol}^{-1}$$

$$= -27.886\ \text{kJ mol}^{-1}$$

B.

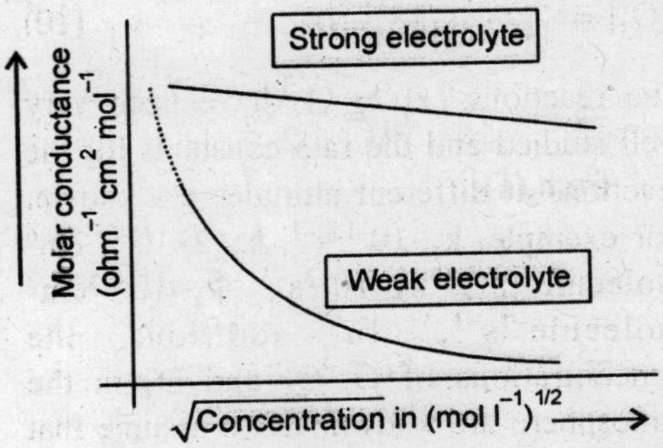

Variation of molar conductivity of strong electrolyte and weak electrolyte

Degree of Dissociation of KCl

$$\wedge^\circ(\text{KCl}) = \lambda^\circ(\text{K}) + \lambda^\circ(\text{Cl}^-)$$

$$= 73.5 \times 76.5$$

$$= 150\ \text{S cm}^2\ \text{mol}^{-1}$$

$$\propto = \frac{\wedge^c}{\wedge^\circ} = \frac{130}{150} = 0.8666$$

Dissociation Constant

	KCl ⇌	K^+ +	Cl^-
initial	c	o	o
Equilibrium	c(1–∝)	c∝	c∝

$$\text{Dissociation constant (K)} = \frac{[K^+][Cl^-]}{[KCl]}$$

$$= \frac{c \propto \times c \propto}{c(1-\propto)}$$

$$= \frac{c\propto^2}{1-\propto}$$

$$= \frac{0.1 \times (0.866)^2}{1-0.866}$$

$$= \frac{0.0749956}{0.134}$$

$$= 0.55962687$$

43. A. $\psi \propto \left(2 - \frac{r}{a_0}\right) e^{-\frac{r}{2a_0}}$

Probability of finding an electron is given by ψY^*

$$= \left(2 - \frac{r}{a_0}\right)^2 e^{-\frac{r}{a_0}}$$

The probability of finding an electron anywhere in space that is irrespective of direction, between radial distance r and $r + dr$ is obtained by multiplying the above by $4\pi r^2 dr$

$$P \propto r^2 \left(2 - \frac{r}{a_0}\right)^2 e^{-\frac{r}{a_0}}$$

$$\propto \left(2r - \frac{r^2}{a_0}\right)^2 e^{-\frac{r}{a_0}}$$

For max probability $\frac{dp}{dx} = 0$

$$\Rightarrow \quad 2\left(2r - \frac{r^2}{a_0}\right)\left(2 - \frac{2r}{a_0}\right) e^{-\frac{r}{a_0}} + \left(2r - \frac{r^2}{a_0}\right)^2 e^{-\frac{r}{a_0}}\left(\frac{-1}{a_0}\right) = 0$$

$$= e^{-\frac{r}{a_0}}\left(2r - \frac{r^2}{a_0}\right)\left[2\left(2 - \frac{2r}{a_0}\right) - \frac{1}{a_0}\left(2r - \frac{r^2}{a_0}\right)\right]$$

$$= e^{-\frac{r}{a_0}}\left(2r-\frac{r^2}{a_0}\right)\left[4-\frac{4r}{a_0}-\frac{2r}{a_0}+\frac{r^2}{a_0^{\,2}}\right]=0$$

$$= e^{-\frac{r}{a_0}}\left(2r-\frac{r^2}{a_0}\right)\left[4-\frac{6r}{a_0}+\frac{r^2}{a_0^{\,2}}\right]=0$$

$\Rightarrow$ either $\left(2r-\dfrac{r^2}{a_0}\right)=0$

or $r^2 - 6ra_0 + 4a_0^{\,2} = 0$ ...(i)

For $2r-\dfrac{r^2}{a_0}=0$

$\Rightarrow$ $r\left(2-\dfrac{r}{a_0}\right)=0$ i.e. $r = 0$

or $r = 2a_0$ ...(ii)

From equation (i) we have

$$r=\frac{6a_0\pm\sqrt{36a_0^2-16a_0^2}}{2}$$

$$=\frac{6a_0\pm a_0\sqrt{2}}{2}=3a_0\pm a_0\sqrt{5} \quad ...(iii)$$

Putting $r = 2a_0$ in probability function, it comes out to be zero $\Rightarrow$ node is at $r = 2a_0$ and maximum probability of finding the electron is in region where r

$$= 3a_0 \pm a_0\sqrt{5}.$$

B. $E_n = \dfrac{n^2h^2}{8ma^2}$

where, for lowest energy ($n = 1$)

$$E_1 = \frac{(1)^2(6.626\times10^{-34}\,Js)^2}{8(9.109\times10^{-31}\,kJ)(1\times10^{-9}\,m)^2}$$

wave length $= \dfrac{h}{P}=\dfrac{h}{\sqrt{2mE}}$

$$=\frac{6.626\times10^{-34}\,Js}{\sqrt{2\times9.109\times10^{-31}\,kg\times\dfrac{(6.626\times10^{-34}\,Js)^2}{8(9.109\times10^{-31}\,kg)(1\times10^{-9}\,m)^2}}}$$

$$=\frac{6.626\times10^{-34}\,Js}{\dfrac{1}{2}\times\dfrac{6.626\times10^{-34}}{1\times10^{-9}}}$$

$$=\frac{2\times1\times10^{-9}\,m}{1}=2\times10^{-9}m.$$

44. A. $y'' - 5y' + 6y = 0$

The auxiliary equation is

$$m^2 - 5m + 6 = 0$$

$\Rightarrow$ $m = 2, 3$

i.e. the complementary function is

$$y = c_1e^{2x} + c_2e^{3x}$$

Now $y(0) = 1$

$\Rightarrow$ $c_1 + c_2 = 1$ ...(1)

$y'(0) = 0$

$\Rightarrow$ $2c_1 + 3c_2 = 0$

$\Rightarrow$ $c_1 = -\dfrac{3}{2}c_2$

from (1)

$-\dfrac{3}{2}c_2 + c_2 = 1$ $\Rightarrow$ $c_2 = -2$

$\Rightarrow$ $c_1 = 3$

$\therefore$ $y = 3e^{2x} - 2e^{3x}$

B. $\bar{L} = \bar{r}\times\bar{p}$

$$=\begin{vmatrix}\hat{i} & \hat{j} & \hat{k}\\ 2 & -3 & 1\\ 1 & 2 & -2\end{vmatrix}$$

$$\hat{i}(6-2)+\hat{j}(1+4)+\hat{k}(4+3)$$

$$\bar{L} = 4\hat{i}+5\hat{j}+7\hat{k}$$

Previous Paper (Solved)

IIT—JAM

Joint Admission Test for M.Sc. (Chemistry)-2005

1. Arrange the following in the decreasing order of acidity of the hydrogen indicated in italics

(*i*) $CH_3COC\mathit{H}_3$

(*ii*) $CH_3COC\mathit{H}_2COCH_3$

(*iii*) $CH_3OOCC\mathit{H}_2COOCH_3$

(*iv*) $CH_3COC\mathit{H}_2NO_2$

A. (*ii*) > (*iii*) > (*i*) > (*iv*)

B. (*iv*) > (*ii*) > (*iii*) > (*i*)

C. (*iv*) > (*iii*) > (*ii*) > (*i*)

D. (*ii*) > (*iv*) > (*iii*) > (*i*)

2. For the reaction shown below if the concentration of KCN is increased four times, the rate of the reaction will be

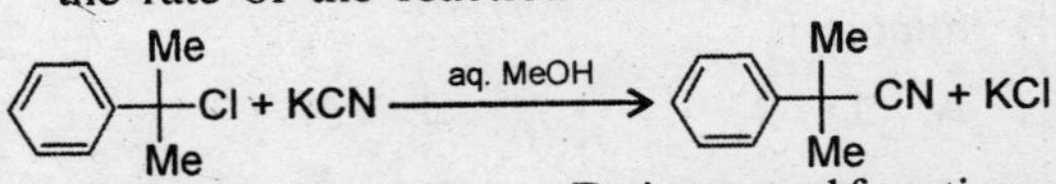

A. doubled B. increased four times

C. unaffected D. halved

3. Benzyl chloride is reacted with different nucleophiles shown below. Arrange them in the decreasing order of reactivity.

Nucleophiles: $HO^{\ominus}, CH_3COO^{\ominus}, PhO^{\ominus}, CH_3O^{\ominus}$

A. $CH_3O^{\ominus} > HO^{\ominus} > PhO^{\ominus} > CH_3COO^{\ominus}$

B. $HO^{\ominus} > CH_3O^{\ominus} > PhO^{\ominus} > CH_3COO^{\ominus}$

C. $HO^{\ominus} > PhO^{\ominus} > CH_3O^{\ominus} > CH_3COO^{\ominus}$

D. $CH_3COO^{\ominus} > CH_3O^{\ominus} > HO^{\ominus} > PhO^{\ominus}$

4. The rate of nitration of the following aromatic compounds decreases in the order

(*i*) benzene (*ii*) pyridine

(*iii*) thiophene (*iv*) toluene

A. (*iv*) > (*i*) > (*iii*) > (*ii*)

B. (*iii*) > (*iv*) > (*i*) > (*ii*)

C. (*iii*) > (*ii*) > (*i*) > (*iv*)

D. (*ii*) > (*i*) > (*iv*) > (*iii*)

5. The major product formed in the reaction on 1, 3-butadiene with bromine is

A. $BrCH_2CH(Br)CH = CH_2$

B. $CH_2 = CH—CH_2CH_2Br$

C. $CH_2 = C(Br)—C(Br)= CH_2$

D. $BrCH_2CH = CHCH_2Br$

6. The reaction of (+) 2-iodobutane and NaI* (I* is radioactive isotope iodine) in acetone was studied by measuring the rate of racemization (k_r) and the rate of incorporation of I* (k_i)

$(+)\ CH_3CH(I)CH_2CH_3 + NaI^* \rightarrow CH_3CH(I^*)\ CH_2CH_3 + NaI$

For this reaction, the relationship between k_r and k_i is

A. $k_i = 2 \times k_r$ B. $k_i = (1/2) \times k_r$

C. $k_i = k_r$ D. $k_i = (1/3) \times k_r$

7. DNA $\xrightarrow{Ba(OH)_2}$ (P)

DNA $\xrightarrow{MgO/\Delta}$ PO_4^{3-} + (Q) $\xrightarrow{HCl}$ (R) + (S) + sugar

In the scheme shown above (P), (Q), (R) and (S) are

A. (P) = purine bases, (Q) = pyrimidine bases, (R) = nucleotides, (S) = nucleosides

B. (P) = (Q) = nucleotides, (R) = pyrimidine bases, (S) = purine bases

C. (P) = nucleosides, (Q) = nucleotides, (R) = (S) = purine bases

D. (P) = nucleotides, (Q) = nucleosides, (R) = pyrimidine bases, (S) = purine bases

8. The products obtained from the following reaction are

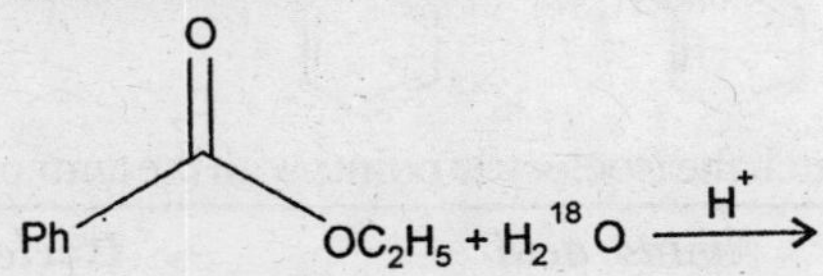

A.

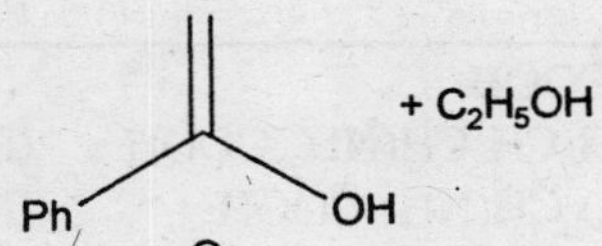

B.

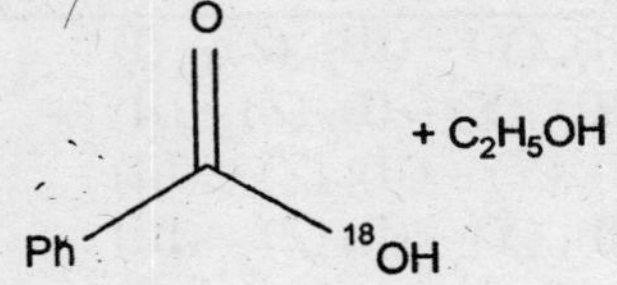

C. 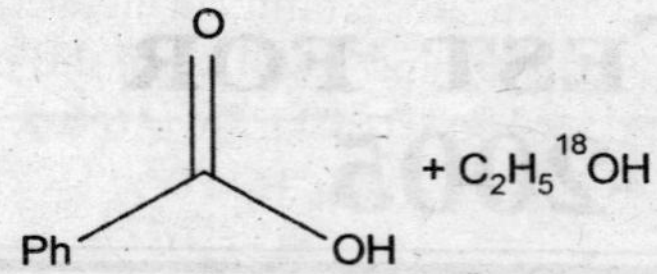

D. 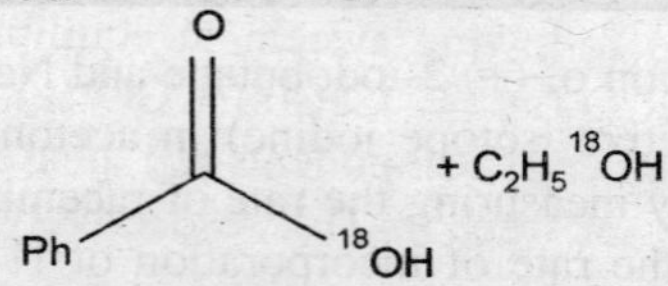

9. The product(s) obtained in the following reaction is (are)

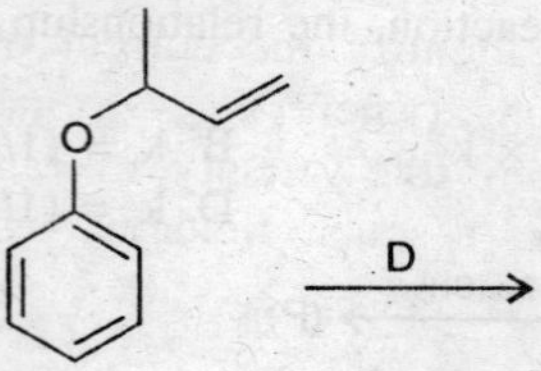

A. 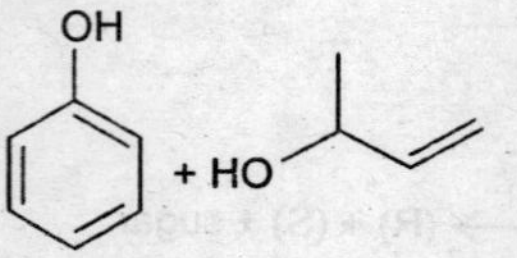

B. 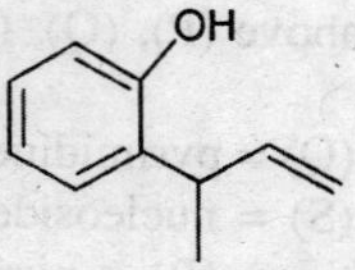

C. 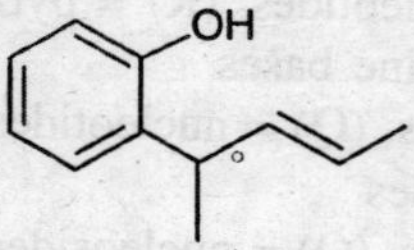

D. 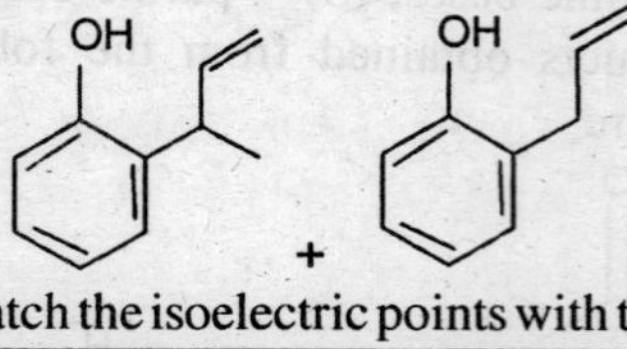

10. Match the isoelectric points with the amino acids

Amino acid	*Isoelectric point*
(X) H_2NCH_2COOH	(I) 9.5
(Y) $HOOCCH_2CH_2CH(NH_2)COOH$	(II) 6.0
(Z) $H_2N(CH_2)_4CH(NH_2)COOH$	(III) 3.1

A. (X) – (II), (Y) – (III), (Z) – (I)
B. (X) – (III), (Y) – (I), (Z) – (II)
C. (X) – (I), (Y) – (II), (Z) – (III)
D. (X) – (II), (Y) – (I), (Z) – (III)

11. The compound having the highest melting point is
A. LiCl B. LiF
C. LiI D. LiBr

12. The shape of SF_4 is
A. tetrahedral B. trigonal bipyramidal
C. square planar D. octahedral

13. The degree of hydration is expected to be maximum for
A. Mg^{2+} B. Na^+
C. Ba^{2+} D. K^-

14. The decreasing order of the first ionization energy of the following elements is
A. Xe > Be > As > Al
B. Xe > As > Al > Be
C. Xe > As > Be > Al
D. Xe > Be > Al > As

15. The radioactive isotope used to locate brain tumors is
A. ${}^{2}_{1}D$ B. ${}^{15}_{7}N$
C. ${}^{13}_{53}I$ D. ${}^{13}_{6}C$

16. The crystal field stabilization energy of high spin d^7 octrahedral complex is
A. $\frac{-4}{5}\Delta_0 + 2P$ B. $\frac{-4}{5}\Delta_0 + 3P$
C. $\frac{-9}{5}\Delta_0 + 2P$ D. $\frac{-9}{5}\Delta_0 + 3P$

17. The complex with the most intense colour among the following is
A. $[FeF_6]^{3-}$ B. $[MnCl_4]^{2-}$
C. $[CoCl_4]^{2-}$ D. $[CoF_6]^{3-}$

18. On addition of a solution of $AgNO_3$ to a solution of $Na_2S_2O_3$, it turns black on standing due to the formation of
A. Ag B. Ag_2S
C. $Ag_2S_2O_3$ D. Ag_2SO_4

19. Among the following complexes,
(*i*) $[Ru(bipyridyl)_3]^+$
(*ii*) $[Cr(EDTA)]^-$
(*iii*) *trans*–$[CrCl_2(oxalate)_2]^{3-}$
(*iv*) *cis*–$[CrCl_2(oxalate)_2]^{3-}$
the ones that show chirality are
A. (*i*), (*ii*), (*iv*) B. (*i*), (*ii*), (*iii*)
C. (*ii*), (*iii*), (*iv*) D. (*i*), (*iii*), (*iv*)

20. The electronic configurations that have orbital angular momentum contribution in an octahedral environment are
A. d^1 and high spin d^4
B. d^1 and d^2
C. d^2 and high spin d^6
D. high spin d^4 and high spin d^6

21. For an ideal solution formed by mixing of pure liquids A and B
A. $\Delta H_{mixing} = 0$ B. $\Delta H_{mixing} < 0$
C. $\Delta H_{mixing} > 0$ D. $\Delta S_{mixing} = 0$

22. The relationship between the equilibrium constant K_1 for the reaction:
$CO(g) + 1/2O_2(g) \rightleftharpoons CO_2(g)$
and the equilibrium constant K_2 for the reaction:
$2CO(g) + O_2(g) \rightleftharpoons 2CO_2(g)$ is
A. $2K_1 = K_2$ B. $K_1 = K_2^2$
C. $K_1 = K_2$ D. $K_1^2 = K_2$

23. For H-like atoms, the ground state energy is proportional to
A. $\frac{\mu}{Z^2}$ B. $\frac{Z^2}{\mu}$
C. μZ^2 D. $\frac{1}{\mu Z^2}$
where μ^* is the reduced mass and Z is the nuclear charge.

24. The value of the integral $\int e^{-x}x^2dx$ is
A. $x^2e^{-x} + 2xe^{-x} + 2e^{-x}$
B. $\frac{-1}{2}(x^2e^{-x} + 2xe^{-x} + 2e^{-x})$
C. $\frac{1}{2}(x^2e^{-x} + 2xe^{-x} + 2e^{-x})$
D. $-x^2e^{-x} - 2xe^{-x} - 2e^{-x}$

25. For the reaction $\alpha A \rightarrow$ *products*, the plot of $\frac{1}{[A]}$ versus time (t) gives a straight line. The order of the reaction is
A. 0 B. 1
C. 2 D. 3

26. The pH of the solution prepared from 0.005 mole of $Ba(OH)_2$ in 100 cc water is
A. 10 B. 12
C. 11 D. 13

27. For an electron whose x-positional uncertainty is 1×10^{-10}m, the uncertainty in the x-component of the velocity in ms^{-1} will be of the order of (Data: $m_e = 9 \times 10^{-31}$ kg, $h = 6.6 \times 10^{-34}$ Js)
A. 10^6 B. 10^9
C. 10^{12} D. 10^{15}

28. For the following system in equilibrium
$CaCO_3(s) \rightleftharpoons CaO(s) + CO_2(g)$
the number of components (C), phases (P) and degrees of freedom (F), respectively, are
A. 2, 2, 2 B. 1, 3, 0
C. 3, 3, 2 D. 2, 3, 1

29. For the distribution of molecular velocities of gases, identify the correct order from the following (where v_{mp}, v_{av} and v_{rms} are the most probable velocity, average velocity and root mean square velocity, respectively):
A. $v_{rms} > v_{av} > v_{mp}$ B. $v_{mp} > v_{rms} > v_{av}$
C. $v_{av} > v_{rms} > v_{mp}$ D. $v_{mp} > v_{av} > v_{rms}$

30. Given that $E^0_{Fe^{2+}/Fe} = -0.44$V and $E^0_{Fe^{3+}/Fe^{2+}} =$ 0.77V, the $E^0_{Fe^{3+}/Fe}$ is
A. 1.21 V B. 0.33 V
C. – 0.036 V D. 0.036 V

31. Identify the major product(s) formed in the following reactions ***Intermediate and reaction mechanisms need not be discussed.***

A. 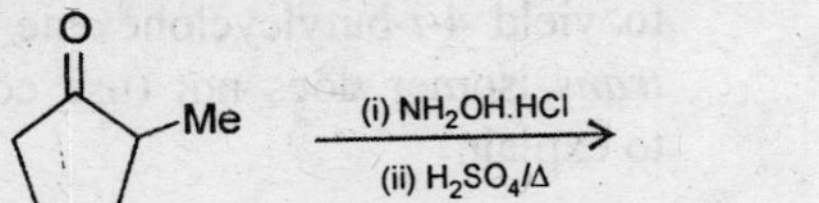

B. 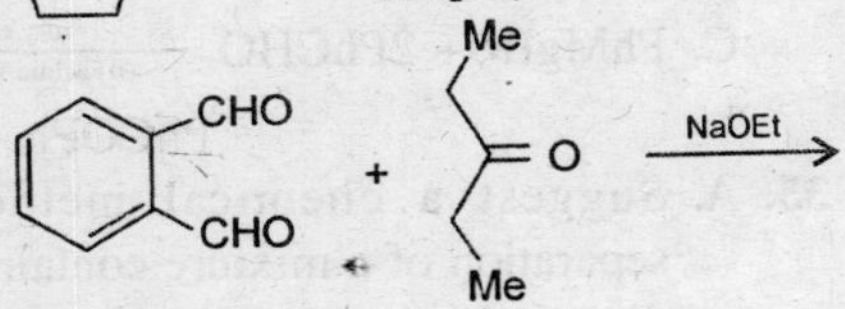

C. 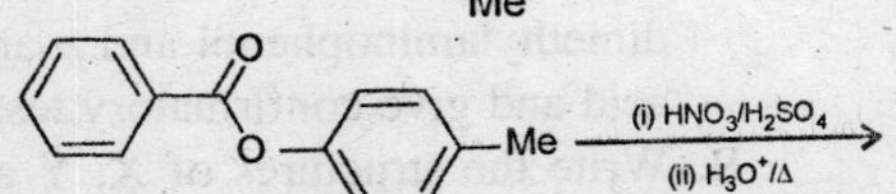

32. How may the following transformations be effected? Indicate the reagents/reaction conditions clearly in each step
A. (not involving any functional group transformation of the COOH group in the starting material)

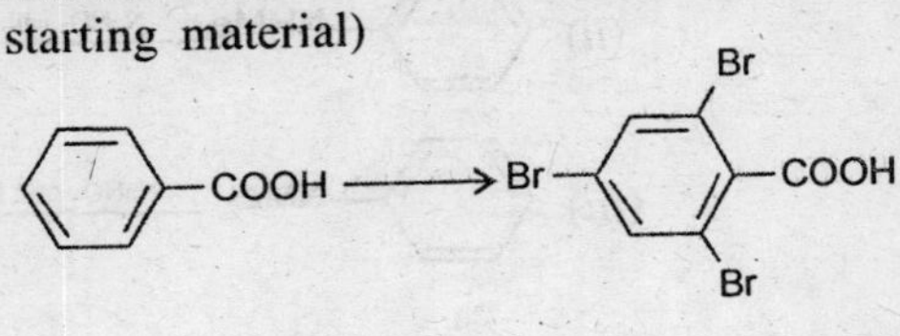

B. (using diethyl malonate as the only source of carbon)

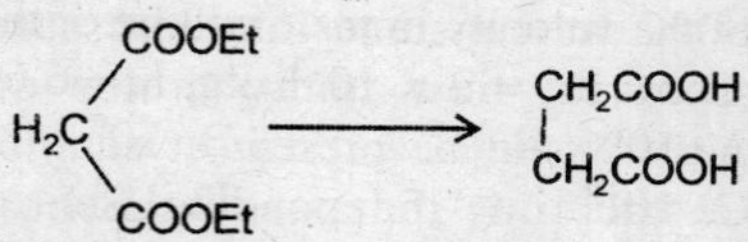

C. 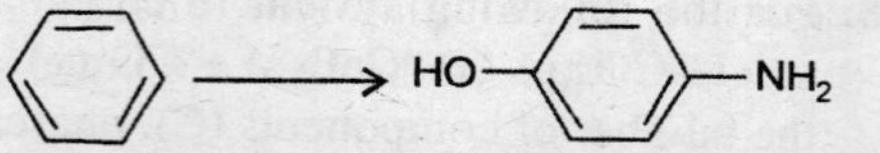

33. Suggest a suitable mechanism for each of the following reactions.

A. $PhCOCH_2CH_3 + Ph - C \equiv C - COOEt$

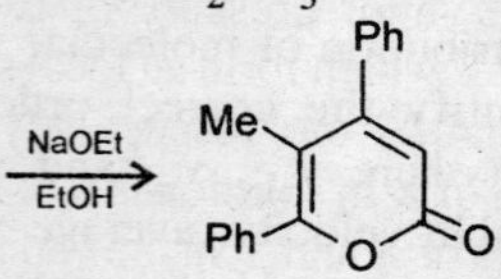

B. 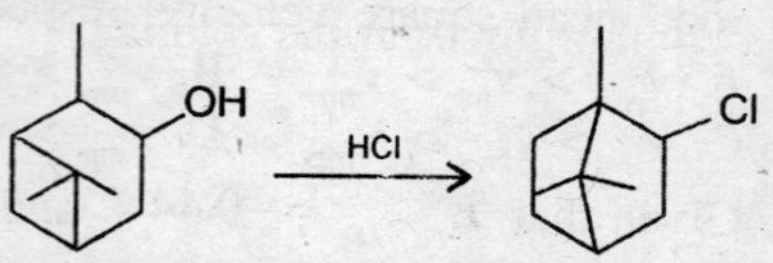

34. Rationalize the following observations using suitable machanisms.

A. Nitration of 4-*t*-butyltoluene gives 4-nitrotoluene as one of the products.

B. *cis*-4-*t*-Butylcyclohexyltrimethylammonium hydroxide undergoes Hoffman elimination to yield 4-*t*-butylcyclohexene whereas the *trans* isomer does not (use conformations to explain)

C. $PhMgBr + 2PhCHO \xrightarrow[\text{(ii) acidic workup}]{\text{(i) dry ether}} PhCOPh + PhCH_2OH$

35. A. Suggest a chemical method for the separation of a mixture containing *p*-N, N-dimethylaminophenol and *p*-aminobenzoic acid and give confirmatory test for phenol.

B. Write the structures of X, Y and Z in the following

(*i*) 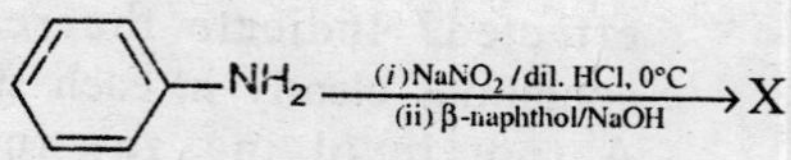

(*ii*) 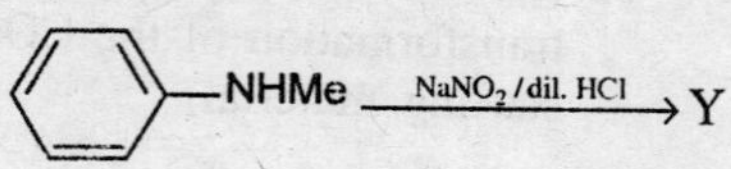

(*iii*) 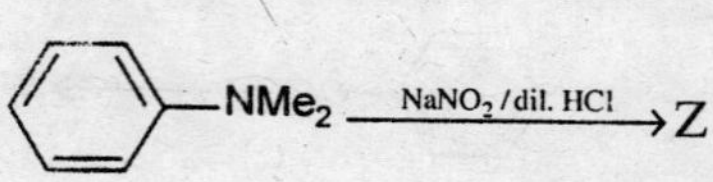

36. A. Predict the hybridization and draw the structure of the following molecules based on VSEPR theory:

(*i*) I_3^- (*ii*) SO_3^{-2} (*iii*) $P(CH_3)_3F_2$

B. Explain why PCl_5 exists and PH_5 does not.

37. A. Write balanced equations for the formation of

(*i*) $P_2O_7^{4-}$ from PO_4^{3-}

(*ii*) $[H_2O)_4\ Fe(OH)_2Fe(OH_2)_4]^{4+}$ from $[Fe(OH_2)_6]^{3+}$

B. Which one of the two solutions has lower pH? Justify your answer.

(*i*) 0.1 M $Fe(ClO_4)_2$ or 0.1 M $Fe(ClO_4)_3$

(*ii*) 0.1 M Hg $(NO_3)_2$ or 0.1 M $Zn(NO_3)_2$

38. A. Between $Cu(H_2O)_6^{2+}$ and $Co(H_2O)_6^{2+}$, which one has more distorted structure and why?

B. Calculate CFSE (in units of Δ_0) and spin only magnetic moment for the following complexes:

(*i*) $[CoF_6]^{3-}$ (*ii*) $[Fe(CN)_6]^{3-}$ (*iii*) $[NiCl_4]^{2-}$

39. A. The radioactive element Ra (Z=88) emits three alpha particles in succession. Deduce in which group the resulting element will be found?

B. A radioisotope sample has an initial activity of 23 dis/min. After $\frac{1}{2}$ h, the activity is 11.5 dis/min. How many atoms of the radioactive nuclide were present originally? $[\alpha t_{1/2}=0.69]$

40. A. Write the products of the following reactions:

(*i*) $CH_3I + HO^- \longrightarrow$

(*ii*) $CF_3I + HO^- \longrightarrow$

(*iii*) $2CF_3I + Na\ [Mn(CO)_5] \longrightarrow$

B. Arrange BF_3, BCl_3 and BBr_3 in the increasing order of Lewis acidity and justify.

41. Justify the following:

A. Considering CO_2 as an ideal gas, equipartition theorem predicts its total energy as 6.5 kT.

B. ΔS for a process is the same whether the process takes place reversibly or irreversibly.

C. The quantity ΔG equals the maxinum non-expansion work done by a system in a constant temperature-pressure process.

D. At constant temperature and pressure, $\Delta G = 0$ for a reversible phase change.

E. Transition states cannot be isolated as independent chemical species.

42. The rate constant k for a second order reaction $P + Q \rightarrow$ Products is expressed as $\log_{10} k = 20 - \frac{3000}{T}$, where the concentration is in mol lit^{-1}, T is in abosolute temperature and time is in minutes. The initial concentrations of both the reactants are 0.05 M. Calculate the activation energy and half life of the reaction at 27°C. ($R = 2$ cal K^{-1} mol^{-1}).

43. The equilibrium constant for the reaction

$$Fe_3O_4(s) + CO(g) \rightleftharpoons 3FeO(s) + CO_2(g)$$

at 600°C is 1.00. If a mixture initially consisting of 1 mole of Fe_3O_4, 2 moles of CO, 0.5 mole of FeO and 0.3 mole of CO_2 is heated to 600°C at constant total pressure of 5 atmospheres, how many moles of each substance would be present at equilibrium?

44. A. Use the time-independent Schrodinger equation to calculate the energy of a particle of Mass "m" with V = 0 in the state $\psi = \sqrt{\frac{8}{a^3}} \sin\frac{\pi x}{a} \sin\frac{\pi y}{a} \sin\frac{\pi z}{a}$ in a cubical box of length "a".

B. At 20°C, the vapor pressure of two pure liquids X and Y which form an ideal solution are 70 torr and 20 torr respectively. If the mole fraction of X in solution is 0.5, find the mole fractions of X and Y in the vapor phase in equilibrium with the solution.

ANSWERS

1	2	3	4	5	6	7	8	9	10
D	C	A	B	D	B	B	B	C	C
11	**12**	**13**	**14**	**15**	**16**	**17**	**18**	**19**	**20**
B	A	C	C	C	A	C	B	A	C
21	**22**	**23**	**24**	**25**	**26**	**27**	**28**	**29**	**30**
A	D	C	D	C	A	A	D	A	B

SOME SELECTED EXPLANATORY ANSWERS

1.

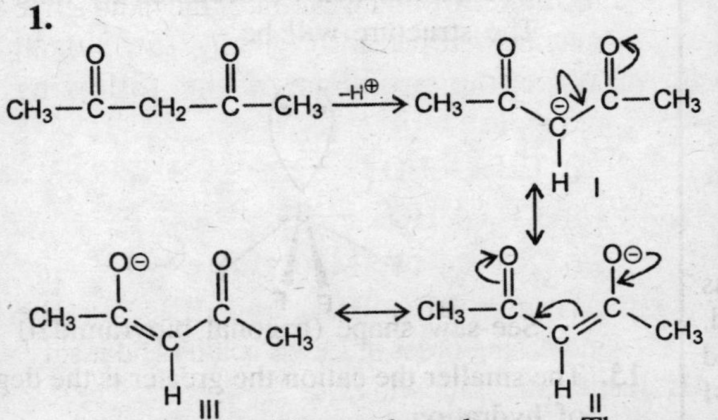

Structure II and III are of equal energy. The more the structure with same energy, the more stable the compound is.

Further structure II and III show hydrogen bonding. Six membered ring is stable.

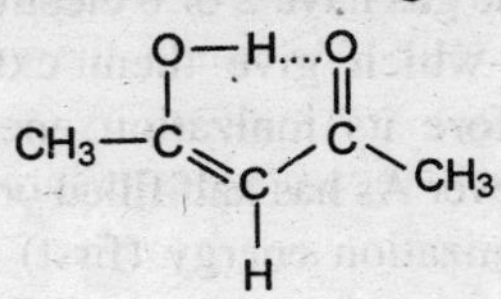

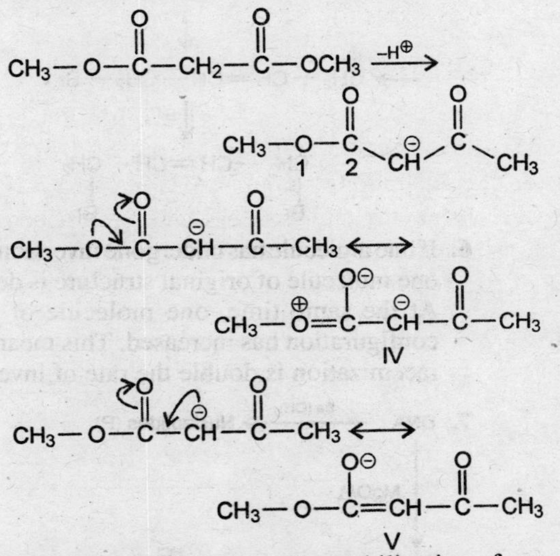

Formation of IV prevent the stabilization of –ve charge on carbon (attached to acidic hydrogen) and therefore is less stable.

In $CH_3—COCH_2NO_2$, $–NO_2$ group stabilizes the carbanion formed but the structure obtains are not of similar energy.

2. 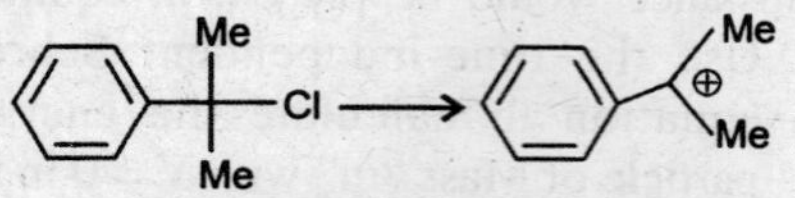

The ion is highly stable as it is tertiary and due to localization of postive charge in ring. Therefore, in presence of aqueous medium, reaction is expected to proceed by SN_1 mechanism.

Since the concentration of 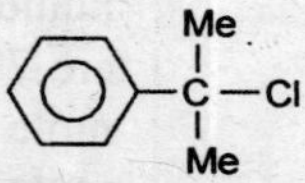 is constant, the rate of the reaction will no be affected.

3. $CH_3 \longrightarrow O^{\ominus}$

CH_3 will make available more –ve charge on oxygen as compared to –OH.

Further $CH_3—\overset{O}{\overset{\|}{C}}—O^{\ominus}$ is most stabilized because resonating structure obtain are of similar energy.

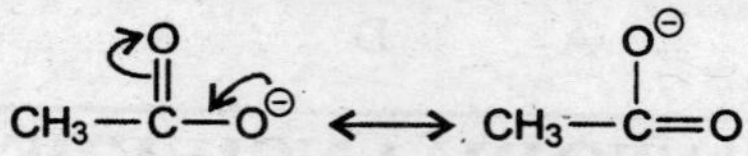

5. 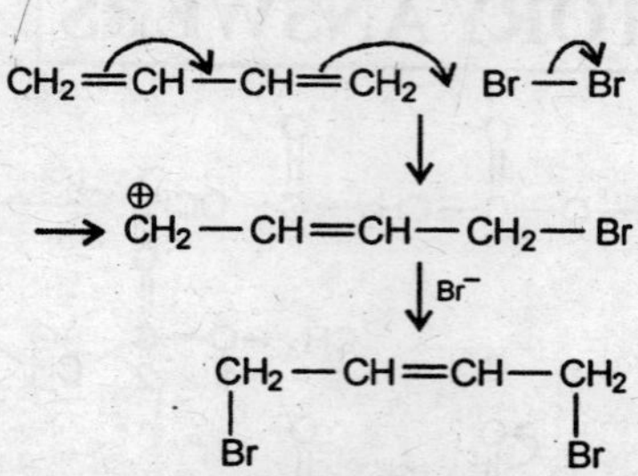

6. If one molecule has undergone inversion it means one molecule of original structure is decreased. At the same time, one molecule of inverted configuration has increased. This means rate of racemization is double the rate of inversion.

7. 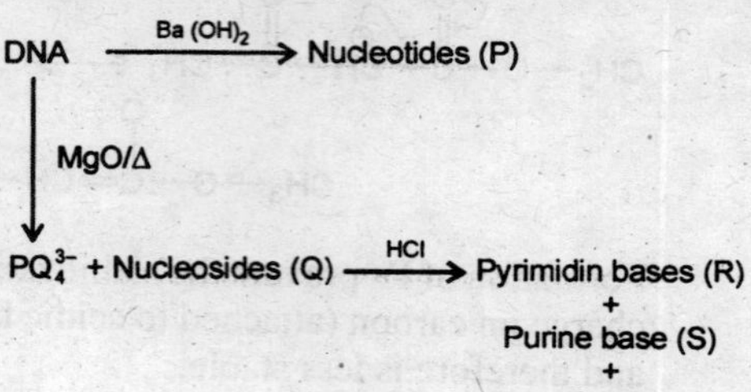

8. 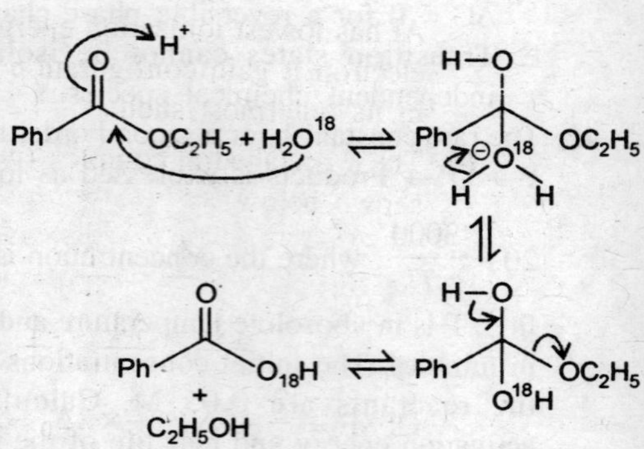

10.

Amino Acid	*Isoelectric Point*
Glycin	6.0
Glutamic acid	3.1
Lysine	9.5

11. Both Li^+ and F^- are small and are of comparable size. They will better fit into crystal structure formed by the two. There will be less distance between Li^+ and F^- and therefore more energy will be required to distort this structure.

12. SF_4

Total valence electron = 6 + 4 × 7 = 34

= 8 × 4 + 2

$\therefore$ Total orbital formed = $\frac{8 \times 4}{8} + \frac{2}{2} = 5$

One orbital will be occupied by lone pair The structure will be

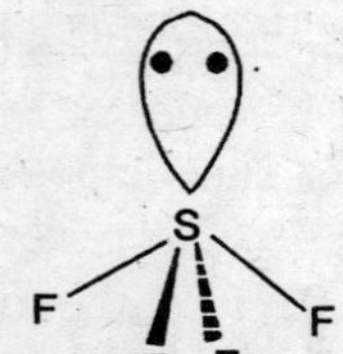

See-saw shape (trigonal bipyramidal)

13. The smaller the cation the greater is the degree of hydration.

14. Xe is noble gas therefore its first ionization energy is highest.

Be has two electron in its outermost orbit (Noble gas have 2 or 8 electron in its outermost orbit which give them extra stability) and therefore its ionization energy is also high. However As has half filled orbital and therefore its ionization energy (first) is more than Be.

Al has lowest ionization energy as on loosing electron it gain configuration with 2 electron in its outermost shell.

16. The d^7 octahedral complex (with high spin) is shown below

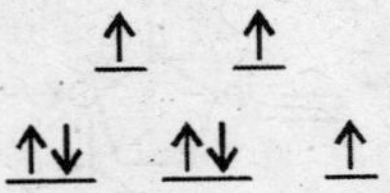

$$\text{CFSE} = \frac{2}{5}\times 5\Delta_0 - \frac{3}{5}\times 2\Delta_0 - 2P$$

$$= \frac{4}{5}\times \Delta_0 - 2P = -\left(-\frac{4\Delta_0}{5} + 2P\right)$$

18. $NO_2S_2O_3$ react with $AgNO_3$ to give $Ag_2S_2O_3$. The reaction is shown below

$$2AgNO_3 + Na_2S_2O_3 \longrightarrow Ag_2S_2O_3 + 2NaNO_3.$$

But $Ag_2S_2O_3$ on standing gives black colour due to formation of Ag_2S. The reaction is shown below

$$Ag_2S_2O_3 + H_2O \longrightarrow \underset{\text{(black)}}{Ag_2S} + H_2SO_4.$$

19.

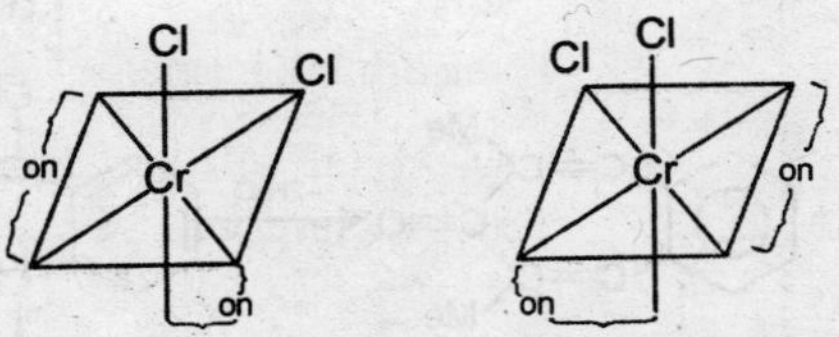

It is optically active and its mirror image is not superimposable

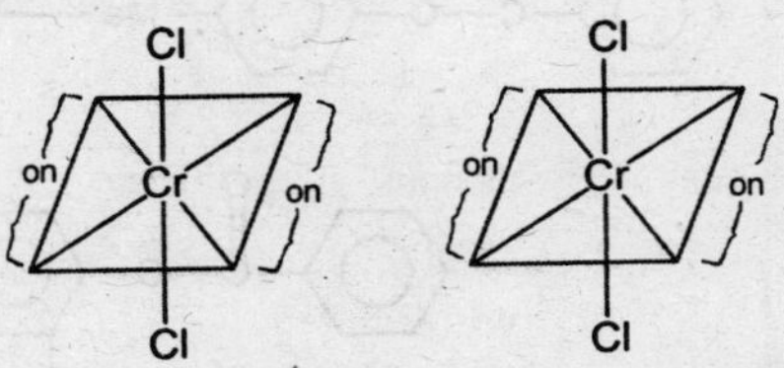

Its mirror image is superimposable on it. Further it has plane of symmetry making molecule optically inactive.

21. For an ideal solution formed by mixing of pure liquids A and B.

$$\Delta H_{\text{mixing}} = 0$$

$$\Delta V_{\text{mixing}} = 0$$

22. $CO(g) + \frac{1}{2}O_2(g) \rightleftharpoons CO_2(g)$

$$K_1 = \frac{[P(CO_2)g]}{[PCO(g)][PO_2(g)]^{\frac{1}{2}}}$$

$$2CO(g) + O_2(g) \rightleftharpoons 2CO_2(g)$$

$$K_2 = \frac{\left[PCO_{2(g)}\right]^2}{\left[PCO_{(g)}\right]^2\left[PO_{2(g)}\right]} = K_1^2$$

23. Energy in H-like atom is given by

$$E_n = \frac{-2\pi^2 z^2 \mu e^2}{(4\pi\varepsilon_0)^2 n^2 H^2}$$

24. $\int e^{-x} x^2 dx$

$$= x^2\int e^{-x}dx + \int 2x\int e^{-x}dx$$

$$= -x^2e^{-x} + 2\int x\, e^{-x}dx$$

$$= -x^2e^{-x} + 2\left[x\int e^{-x}dx + \int e^{-x}dx\right]$$

$$= -x^2e^{-x} - 2x\,e^{-x} - 2e^{-x}dx.$$

25.

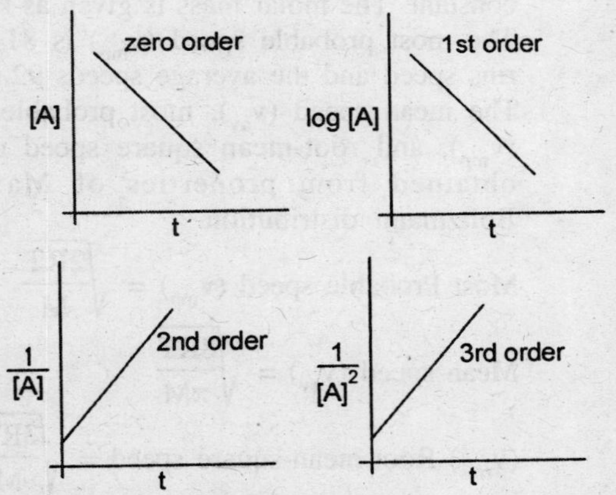

26. $Ba(OH)_2 \rightarrow Ba^{+2} + 2OH^-$

Concentration in molarity of Ba $(OH)_2$ is 5×10^{-5} M

$$[OH] = 2 \times 5 \times 10^{-5}\text{ M}$$

$$pOH = -\log[OH^-]$$

$$= -\log(1 \times 10^{-4}) = 4$$

$$pH + pOH = 14$$

$$\therefore \quad pH = 10$$

27. $\Delta x\,\Delta p \gtrsim \dfrac{h}{2\pi}$

$$\Delta v \gtrsim \frac{h}{2\pi}\Delta xm$$

$$\Delta v \gtrsim \frac{6.6\times10^{-34}\,Js}{2\times3.14}\times1\times10^{-10}\times9\times10^{-31}$$

$$\Delta v \gtrsim 1.1\times10^{6}\ ms^{-1}$$

28. Phase rule

$$P + F = C + 2$$

P → nos. of phase in equilibrium
F → nos. of degree of freedom
C → nos. of components

In equilibrium condition of the decomposition reaction of $CaCO_3$, there are two solid phases CaO and $CaCO_3$, these are physically seperable phase. The third phase is CO_2. Therefore, it has three phases (P = 3)

It has two components *i.e.* CaO and CO_2. The reason is that $CaCO_3$ and CO_2 are not seperate components that if we combine CaO with CO_2 and equilibrium will setup.

29. Root mean square speed of molecules

From kinetic formula it can be shown that

$$v_{rms} = \frac{3RT}{\text{molar mass}}$$

with v in m/s, T in kelvins, and R is the gas constant. The molar mass is given as kg/mol. The most probable speed (v_{mp}) is 81.6% of rms speed and the average speeds 92.1%. The mean speed (v_{av}), most probable speed (v_{mp}), and root-mean square speed can be obtained from properties of Maxwell-Boltzmann distribution.

Most Probable speed $(v_{mp}) = \sqrt{\dfrac{2RT}{M}}$

Mean speed $(v_{av}) = \sqrt{\dfrac{8RT}{\pi M}}$

(v_{rms}) Root-mean-square speed $= \sqrt{\dfrac{3RT}{M}}$

The typical speed are related as follows

$$v_{rms} > v_{av} > v_{mp}$$

30. $Fe^{2+} + 2e^- \longrightarrow Fe \qquad \Delta E = -.44V$

$Fe_0^{3+} + 3e^- \longrightarrow Fe \qquad \Delta E = ?$

$Fe^{3+} + e^- \longrightarrow Fe^{2+} \qquad \Delta E = .77V$

$Fe^{3+} + 3e^- \longrightarrow Fe \qquad \Delta E = .44 + .77V$

$\qquad\qquad\qquad\qquad\qquad = .331V.$

31. A.

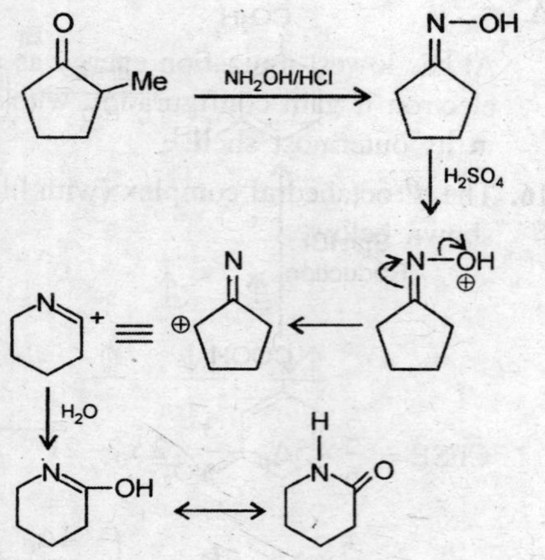

B.

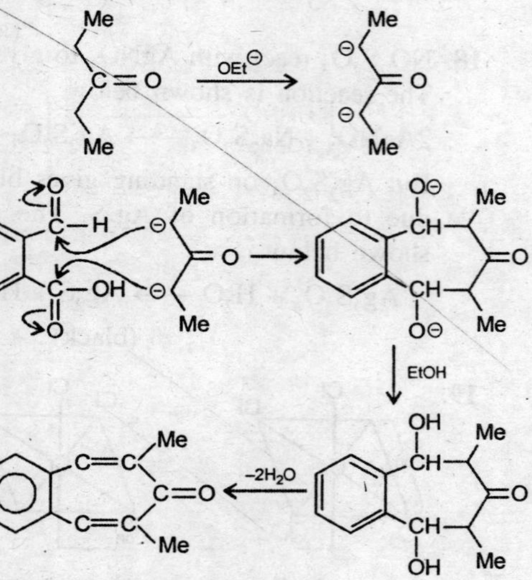

C.

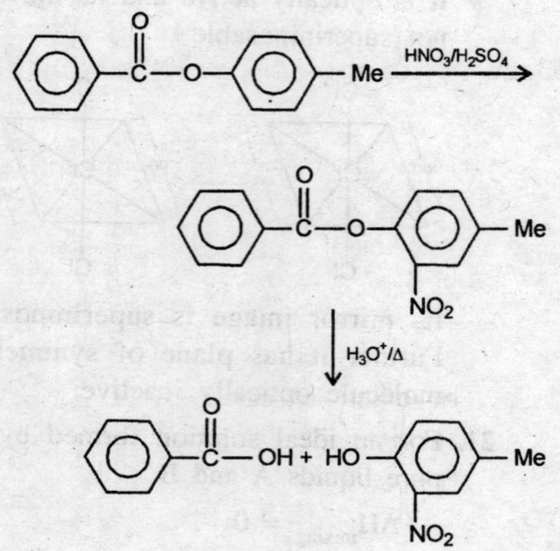

32. A.

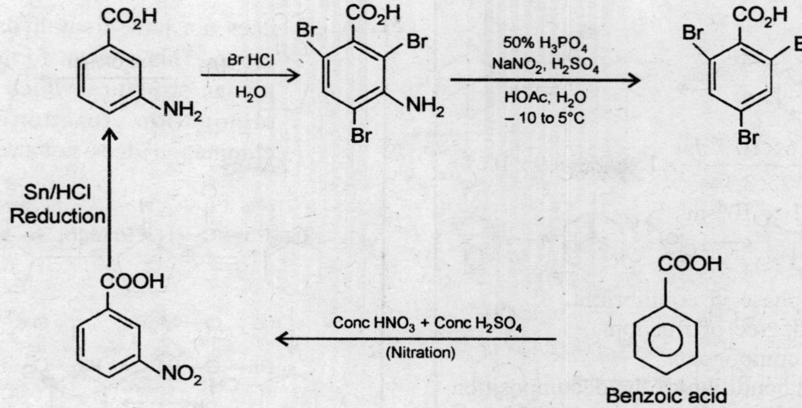
Br HCl
H₂O
50% H₃PO₄
NaNO₂, H₂SO₄
HOAc, H₂O
– 10 to 5°C
Sn/HCl
Reduction
Conc HNO₃ + Conc H₂SO₄
(Nitration)
Benzoic acid

C.

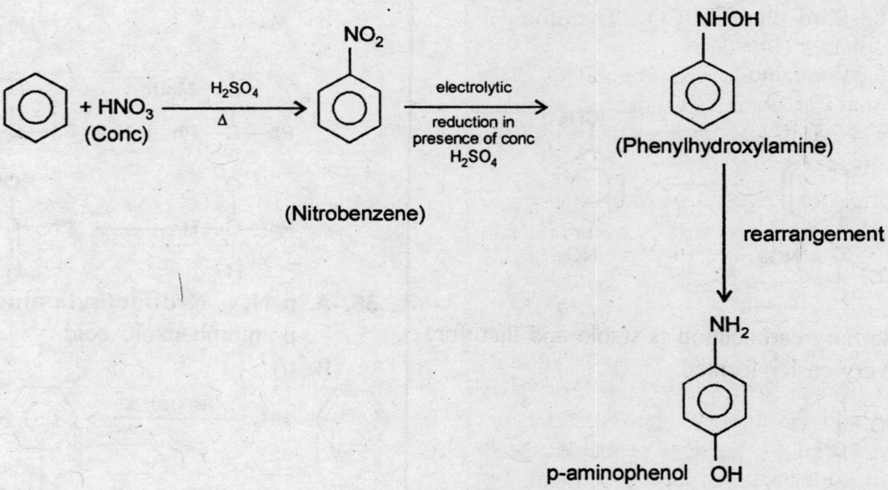
+ HNO₃
(Conc)
H₂SO₄
Δ
(Nitrobenzene)
electrolytic
reduction in
presence of conc
H₂SO₄
(Phenylhydroxylamine)
rearrangement
p-aminophenol

33. A.

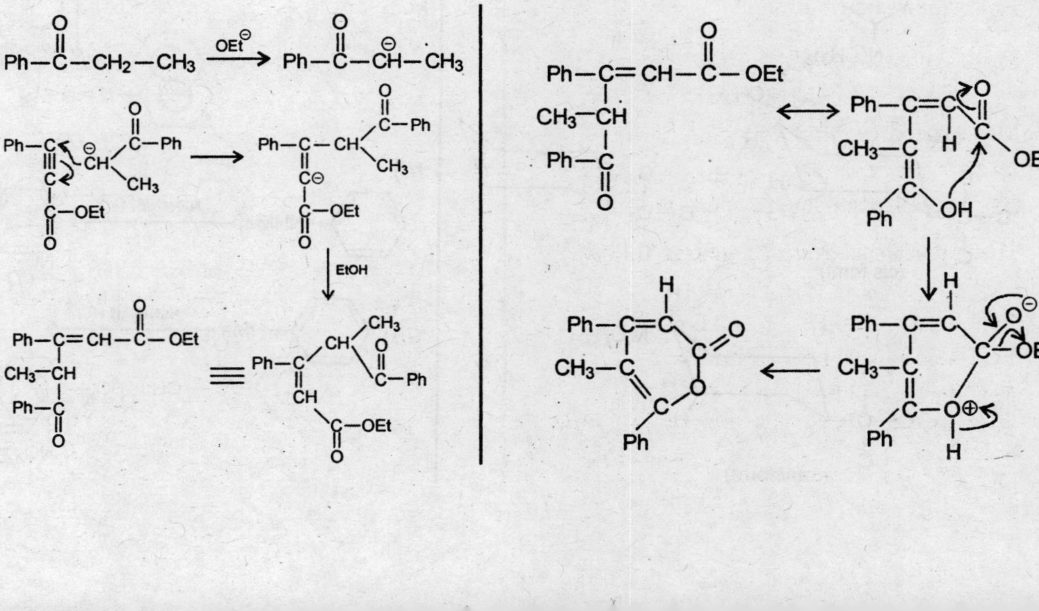
OEt⊖
EtOH

B.

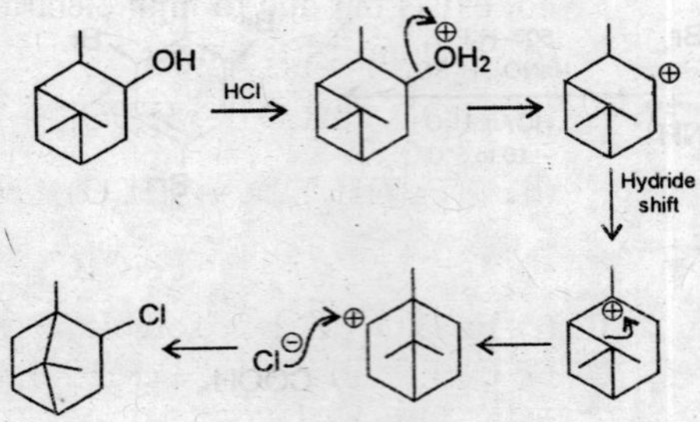

34. A.

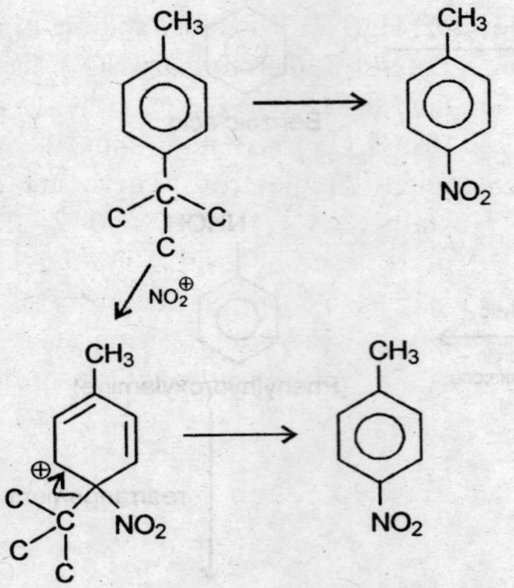

tertiary carbocation is stable and therefore very easily formed.

B. 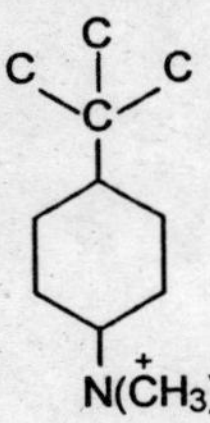 exist in both is and transform.

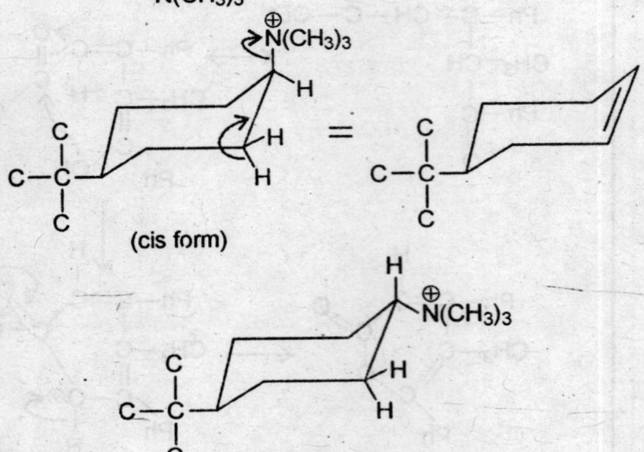

(cis form)

(transform)

does not have trans hydrogen to $\overset{+}{N}(CH_3)_3$ group. This prevent formation of anti peri planar structure which is essential for elimination reaction and therefore elimination does not take place.

C. 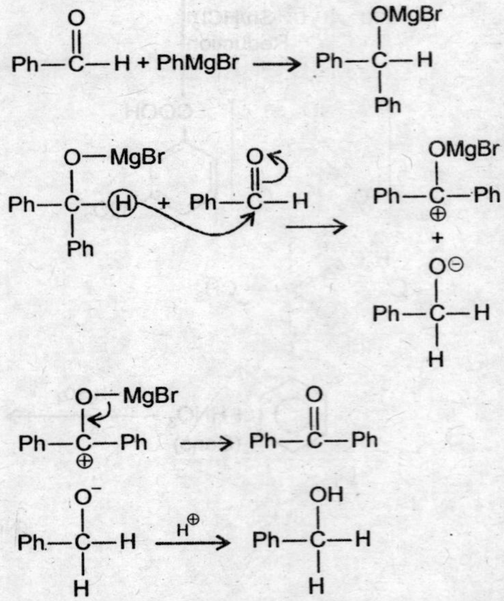

35. A. p-N, N-dimethylaminophenol and p-aminobenzoic acid

B. (*i*)

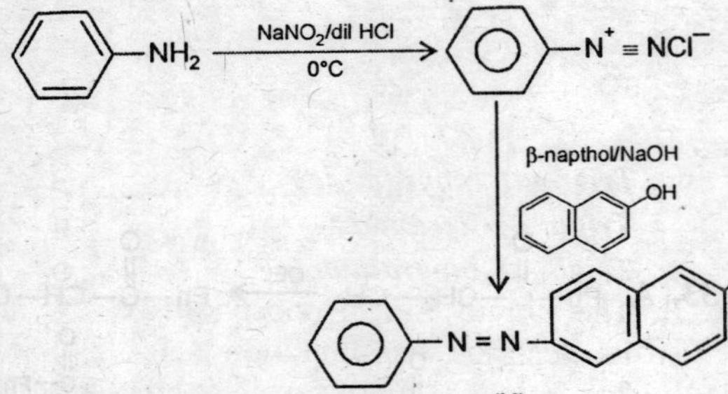

(X)

(*ii*)

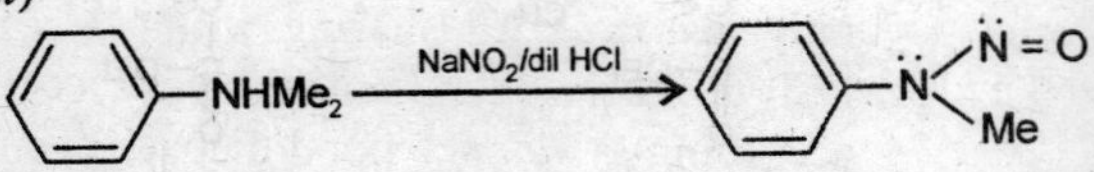

(Y)

(*iii*)

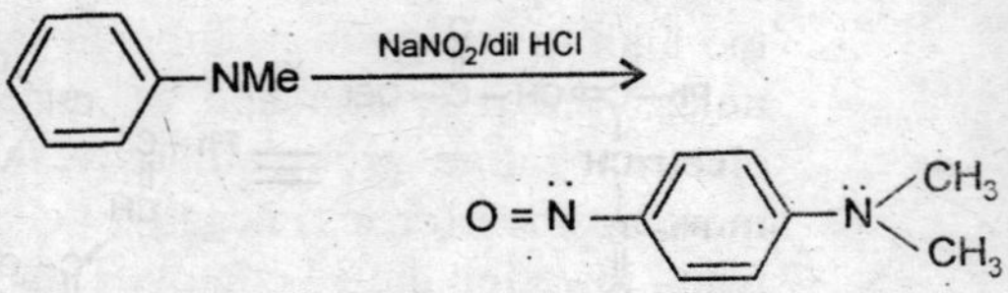

(Z)

36. A.

(i) I_3^-

(ii) SO_3^{2-} (iii) $P(CH_3)_3F_2$

(sp^3d hybridisation)

(sp^2 hybridisation)

(sp^2 hybridisation)

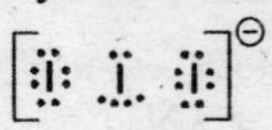

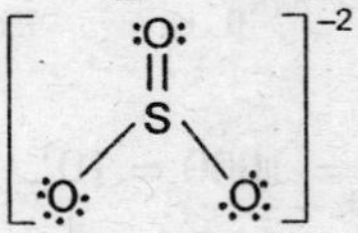

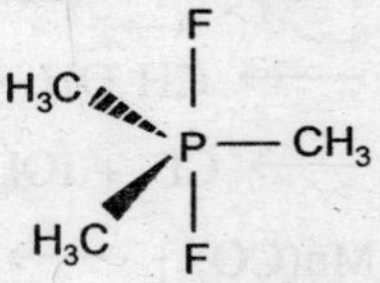

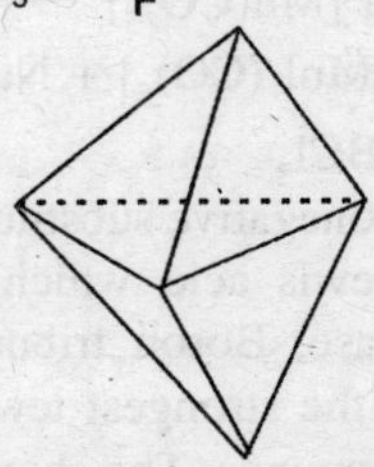

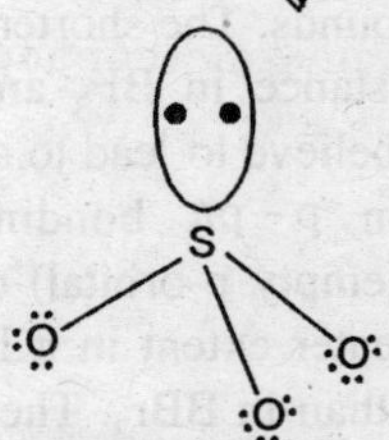

Trigonal bipyramidal

Trigonal Pyramidal

Trigonal bipyramidal

B. The atomic nos. of phosphorus is 15, and its electronic configuration is $1s^2, 2s^2, 2p^6, 3s^2, 3p^3$. PCl_3 forms covalent bond but PH_5 does not formed as first five of electron is only available for sharing with hydrogen. PCl_5 is either non existence or very reactive, according to valence bond theory. The PX_5 involves sp^3d hybridisation and the d is too high in energy to be brought into play unless the p is attached to sufficiently electronegative group, thereby inducing more positive (or less negative) charge on p and lowering the 3d energy. Thus, due to low electronegativity of H atom PH_5 does not exists but due to high electronegativity of Cl atom, PCl_5 exists.

37. A. (i) $4PO_4^{3-} + 8H_3O^+ \rightarrow H_4PO_{12}^{-4} + 12H_2O$

(ii) $2[Fe(OH_2)_6]^{3+} \rightarrow [(H_2O)_4Fe(OH)_2$

$Fe(OH_2)_4]^{4+} + 2H_3O$

B. *(i)* $Fe(ClO_4)$ is less soluble in water than $Fe(ClO_4)_2$, therefore, $Fe(ClO_4)_3$ has lower pH.

(ii) $Hg(NO_3)_2$ is more soluble in water than $Zn(NO_3)_2$, therefore $Zn(NO_3)_2$ has lower pH than $Hg(NO_3)_2$.

38. A. $[Co(H_2O)_6]^{2+}$ is high spin, d7, octahedral unpaired electron. There are 5e in the stabilized t_{2g} level and 2 electron in destabilised E_g level. The John-Teller effect is responsible for distortion of hexaaqua copper (II) complex ion $[Cu\ (H_2O)_6]^{2+}$, which might otherwise possess octahedral geometry.

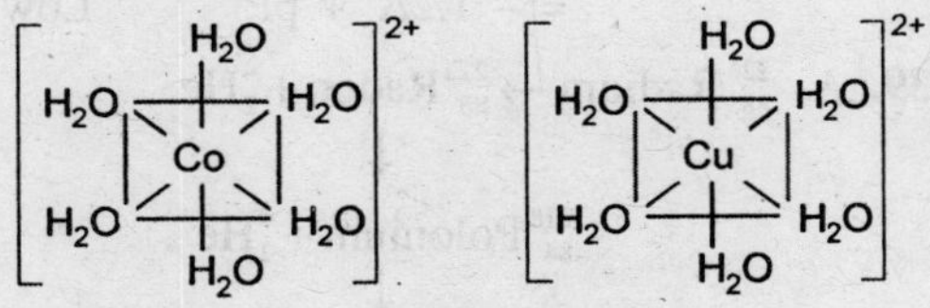

B. CFSE = $\Delta(0.4n(t_{2g}) - 0.6n\ (e_g))$

where, $n(t_{2g})$ and $n(e_g)$ are the numbers of electrons in the t_{2g} and e_g levels respectively.

CFSE = $(-0.4n_{t_{2g}} + 0.6n_{e_g})\Delta_o + pP$

where

$n_{t_{2g}}$ = nos. of electrons in t_{2g} orbitals

n_{e_g} = nos. of electorns in e_g orbitals

P = total nos. of electron pairs

p = mean pairing energy

(i) $[CoF_6]^{-3}$

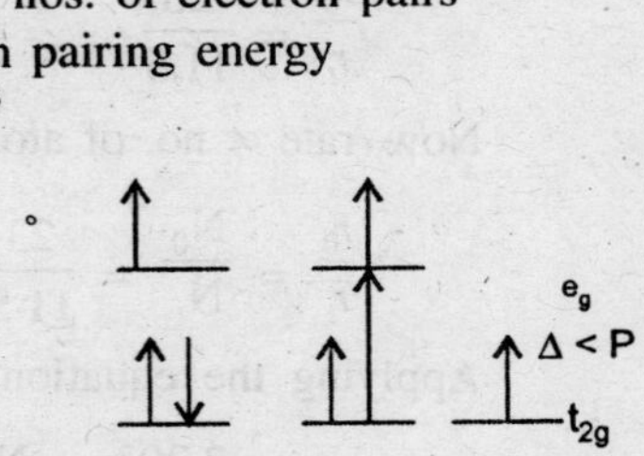

CFSE $= (-0.4 \times 4 + 0.6 \times 2)\Delta_o + pP$

$= (1.6 + 1.2)\Delta_o + pP$

$= -0.4\Delta_o + pP$ High spin

(ii) $[Fe(CN)_6]^{3-}$

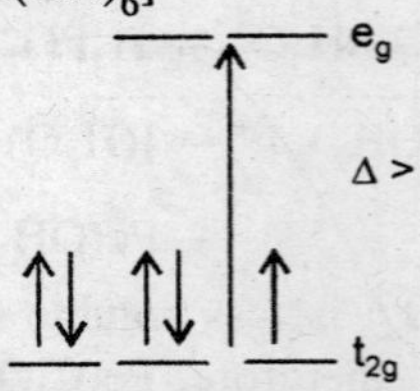

CFSE $= (1 - 0.4 \times 5 + 0.6 \times 0)\Delta_o + pP$
$= -2\Delta_o + pP$ Low spin

(iii) $[NiCl_4]^{2-}$

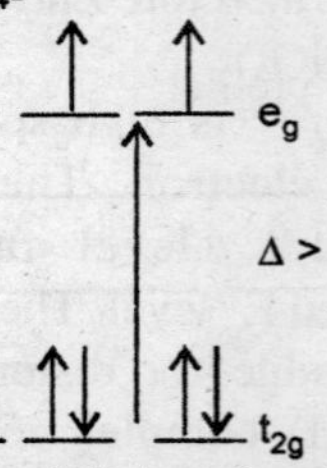

CFSE $= (-0.4 \times 6 + 0.6 \times 2)\Delta_o + pP$
$= (-2.4 + 1.2)\Delta_o + pP$
$= -1.2\Delta_o + pP$ Low spin

39. A. $^{226}_{88}\text{Radium} \rightarrow ^{222}_{86}\text{Radon} + ^{4}_{2}\text{He}$

$$\downarrow$$

$$^{218}_{84}\text{Polonium} + ^{4}_{2}\text{He}$$

$$\downarrow$$

$$^{212}_{82}\text{Lead} + ^{4}_{2}\text{He}$$

The position of lead in the periodic table is at period 6 and group 14.

B. Rate at t = 0 is

$r_0 = 23$ dis/min

Rate after 30 min,

$r_t = 11.5$ dis/min

$$\frac{r_0}{r_t} = \frac{23}{11.5}$$

Now, rate ∝ no. of atoms

$$\frac{r_0}{r_t} = \frac{N_0}{N_t} = \frac{23}{11.5}$$

Applying the equation

$$t = \frac{2.303}{k}\log\frac{N_0}{N_t}$$

$$k = \frac{2.303}{t}\log\frac{N_0}{N_t}$$

$$= \frac{2.303}{30}\log\frac{23}{11.5}$$

$$= \frac{2.303 \times 0.3010}{30} = 0.023$$

$$\text{rate} = -\frac{dN}{dt} = \lambda N_0$$

$$N_0 = \frac{23}{0.023} = 1000 = 10^3.$$

40. A. (i) $CH_3I + HO^- \longrightarrow CH_3OH + I^-$

(ii) $CF_3I + HO^- \longrightarrow CF_3 + IOH$

(iii) $2CF_3I + Na[Mn(CO)_5] \longrightarrow$
$[MnI(CO)_5] + NaI \rightarrow C_2F_6$

B. $BBr_3 > BF_3 > BCl_3$

The more electronegative substituents leads to a stronger lewis acid which does not work in this case, Boron triboronide. In observed to be the strongest lewis acid of these three compounds. The shorter boron-halogen bond distance in BF_3 and BCl_3 than in BBr_3 are believe to lead to stronger halogen to boron $p-p\pi$ bonding. The acceptor orbital (empty p-orbital) on born is involved to greater extent in π bonding in BF_3 and BCl_3 than in BBr_3. The acidity of BF_3 and BCl_3 are diminished relative to BBr_3.

41. A. ***Equipartition Energy***

Kind of Motion	CO_2
Translational	
No. of modes	3
Energy per mol	3/2 RT
Rotational	
No. of modes	2
Energy per mol	RT
Vibrational	
No. of modes	3N – 5
Energy per mol	(3N – 5) RT

$E_{Total} = 3/2\ RT + 2RT + (3N-5)\ RT$
$= 6.5\ RT$

There is significant deviation in the theoretical value from experimental value. It suggests that although not all vibrational degree of freedom are available, they can not be totally ignored. The bigger deviation is due to existence of low frequency bending vibration in carbon dioxide.

B. 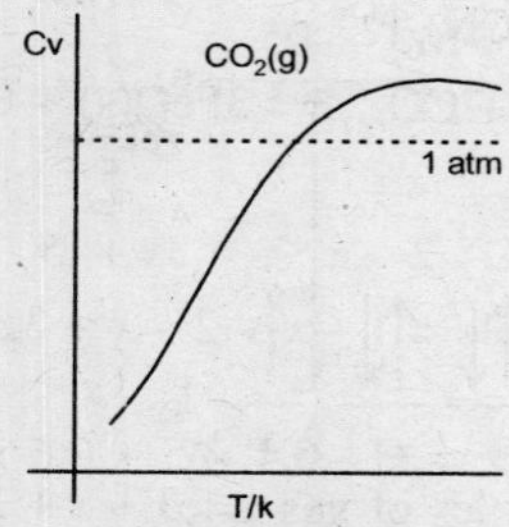

Total Energy
= (3N –(5/2)) RT

CO_2 considered as an ideal gas, the equipartition theorem predict
Cvm = [3(3) – 2.5] R = 6.5R independent of T.

CO_2	Translational	Rotational	Vibrational
A = 3		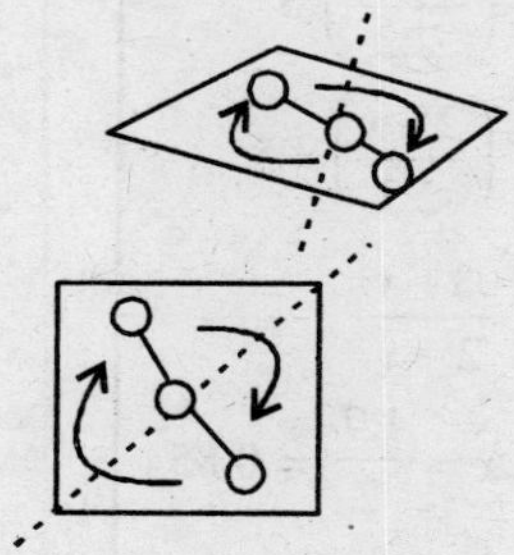	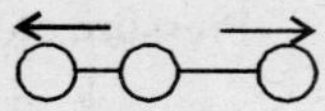 (Symmetric stretch)
3A = 9			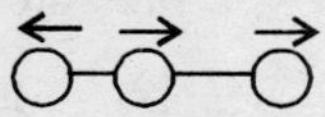 (Asymmetric stretch)
Linear			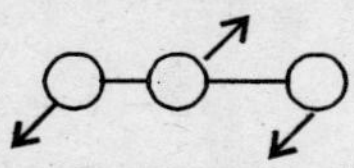 (Out of Plane bonding)

42. From Arhenics equation

$$k = Ae^{-\frac{Ea}{RT}}$$

$$\ln k = \ln A + \ln e^{-\frac{Ea}{RT}}$$

$$= \ln A - \frac{Ea}{RT}$$

$$2.303 \log k = 2.303 \log A - \frac{Ea}{RT}$$

$$\Rightarrow \quad \log k = \log A - \frac{Ea}{2.303\ RT}.$$

Comparing with $\log_{10} k = 20 - \frac{3000}{T}$

We get $\frac{Ea}{2.303\ RT} = \frac{3000}{T}$

$\Rightarrow$ $Ea = 2.303\ R \times 3000.$

	P +	Q $\longrightarrow$	Product
Initially	a	a	0
at time +	$a - x$	$a - x$	x

$$\frac{dx}{dt} = k(a-x)^2$$

On solving we get

$$k = \frac{1}{t}\ \frac{x}{a(a-x)}$$

Where a = .05 m.

$$\therefore \quad k = \frac{1}{t} \times \frac{x}{.05(.05-x)}$$

$$10^{\left(20-\frac{3000}{300}\right)} = \frac{1}{t} \times \frac{x}{.05(.05-x)}$$

$$10^{10} = \frac{1}{t} \times \frac{x}{.05(.05-x)}$$

at $x = \frac{.05}{2}$ $\quad t = t_{\frac{1}{2}}$

$$\therefore \quad 10^{10} = \frac{1}{t_{\frac{1}{2}}} \times \frac{\frac{.05}{2}}{.05 \times \frac{.05}{2}}$$

$$\Rightarrow \quad t_{\frac{1}{2}} = \frac{1}{10^{10} \times .05} = 2 \times 10^{-9}.$$

43. $Fe_3O_4(s) + CO_{(g)} \rightleftharpoons 3FeO(s) + CO_{2(g)}$

Initially	1	2	.5	.3
at equilibrium	$1 - x$	$2 - x$	$3x + .5$	$.3 + x$

Total no. of mole $= 1 - x + 2 - x + 3x + .5 + .3 + x$

$= 3.8 + 2x$

Total no. of moles of gas $= .3 + x + 2 - x = 2.3$

$$\therefore \text{ Mole fraction of } CO_{2(g)} = \frac{.3 + x}{2.3}$$

$$\text{Mole fraction of CO} = \frac{2 - x}{2.3}$$

$$\therefore \quad \text{Pressure of } CO_{2(g)} = \left(\frac{.3 + x}{2.3}\right) 5$$

$$\text{Pressure of CO} = \left(\frac{2 - x}{2.3}\right) \times 5$$

$$K_p = 1 = \frac{P(CO_2)}{P(CO)} = \frac{.3 + x}{2 - x}$$

$$\therefore \quad 2 - x = .3 + x \Rightarrow x = \frac{1.7}{2} = 0.85$$

$\therefore$ Mole of Fe_3O_4 $= .15$
Mole of CO $= 2 - x = 2 - .85 = 1.15$
Mole of FeO $= 3x + .5 = 3.05$
Mole of CO_2 $= 1.15.$

44. A. Consider the motion of a particle of mass m confined to three dimensional cubical box with edges of length a and volume equal to a^3. The potential is zero within the box and is infinite outside the box and at its boundaries. The time dependent Schrodinger equation for the particle is

$$\left[-\frac{\hbar^2}{2m}\left(\frac{\partial^2}{\partial x^2} + \frac{\partial^2}{\partial y^2} + \frac{\partial^2}{\partial z^2}\right)\right]\psi(x, y, z) = E\psi(x, y, z)$$

On rearranging

$$\frac{\partial^2\psi}{\partial x^2} + \frac{\partial^2\psi}{\partial y^2} + \frac{\partial^2\psi}{\partial z^2} + \frac{2mE}{\hbar^2}\psi = 0$$

Assuming that the wave function ψ is a product of three parts which separately depend on x, y and z we have

$$\psi(x, y, z) = X(x)\, Y(y)\, Z(z)$$

$$\frac{\partial^2\psi}{\partial x^2} = YZ\frac{\partial^2 X}{\partial x^2}$$

$$\frac{\partial^2\psi}{\partial y^2} = XZ\frac{\partial^2 Y}{\partial y^2}$$

$$\frac{\partial^2\psi}{\partial z^2} = XY\frac{\partial^2 Z}{\partial z^2}$$

$$\therefore \quad \frac{\hbar^2}{2m}\left(\frac{1}{X}\frac{\partial^2 X}{\partial x} + \frac{1}{Y}\frac{\partial^2 Y}{\partial y} + \frac{1}{Z}\frac{\partial^2 Z}{\partial z}\right) + E = 0$$

In above equation first term is function of x only and is independent of y and z. Similarly for second and third term. If the energy is written as the sum of three contributions associated with the three co-ordinates, then above equation can be separated into three equations.

$$-\frac{\hbar^2}{2m}\left(\frac{1}{X}\frac{\partial^2 X}{\partial x^2}\right) = E_x$$

$$-\frac{\hbar^2}{2m}\left(\frac{1}{Y}\frac{\partial^2 Y}{\partial y^2}\right) = E_y$$

$$-\frac{\hbar^2}{2m}\left(\frac{1}{Z}\frac{\partial^2 Z}{\partial z}\right) = E_z$$

Where $\qquad E = E_x + E_y + E_z$

The solution of above equation is

$$X(x) = \left(\frac{2}{a}\right)^{\frac{1}{2}} \sin\left(\frac{n_x \pi x}{a}\right) ; n_x = 1, 2, \ldots\ldots$$

and
$$E_x = \frac{n_x^2 h^2}{8ma^2}$$

$$\therefore \quad E = \left(n_{x^2} + n_{y^2} + n_{z^2}\right)\frac{h^2}{8ma^2}$$

B. $\quad P_x^\circ = 70$
$\quad P_y^\circ = 20$

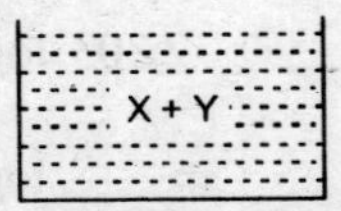

Total pressure of solution $= 70 \times .5 + 20 \times .5 = 45$ torr

Mole fraction of component X in vapour phase

$$Y_A = \frac{70 \times .5}{45} = .78$$

Mole fraction of component Y in vapour phase

$$Y_B = \frac{20 \times .5}{45} = .22$$

PRACTICE TEST PAPERS

(Solved)

IIT-JAM

JOINT ADMISSION TEST FOR M.Sc. CHEMISTRY

TEST PAPER-1

IMPORTANT INSTRUCTION FOR CANDIDATES

Questions 1-30 (Objective questions) carry three marks each and questions 31-44 (subjective questions) carry fifteen marks each.

1. Arrange the following with increasing basic characteristics

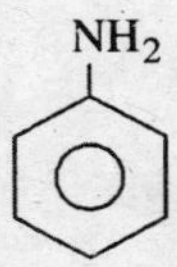

I

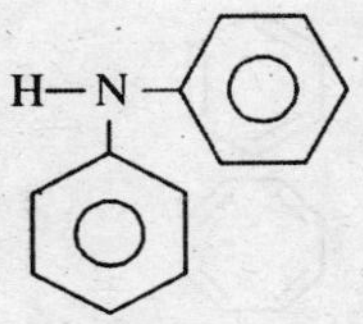

II

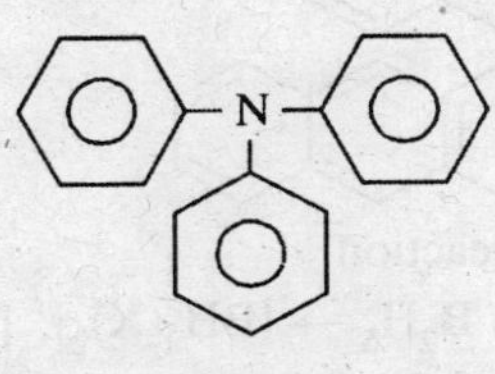

III

A. I > III > II B. III < II < I

C. III < I < II D. I < III < II

2. The major product of following reaction is

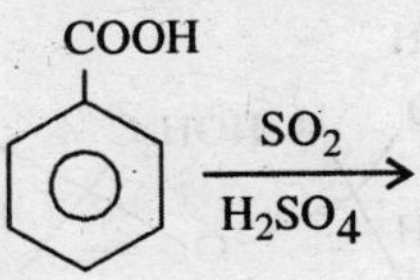

A. 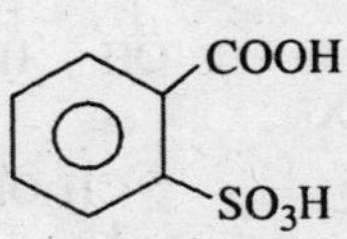

B. 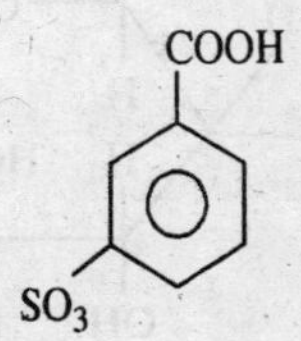

C. 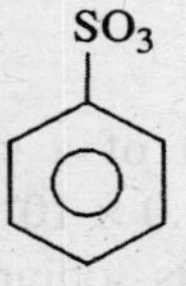

D. 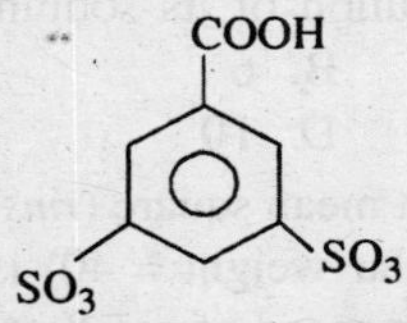

3. Calculate the work done during the process when one role of gas is allowed to expand freely into vacuum.

A. 1 B. 0

C. 3 D. 4

4. The enthalpy change for transition of liquid water is to 40.8 kJ mol^{-1} at 373 K. Calculate ΔS for the process.

A. 109.38 B. 209.38

C. 89.83 D. 88.83

5. 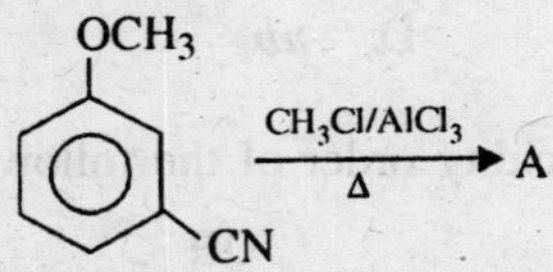

Here the product 'A' will be

A. 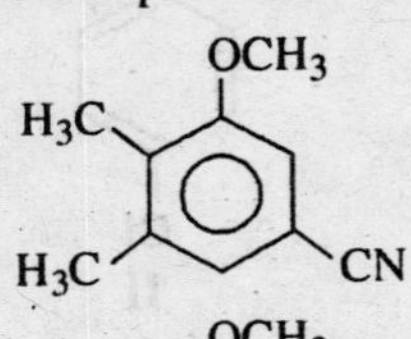

B. 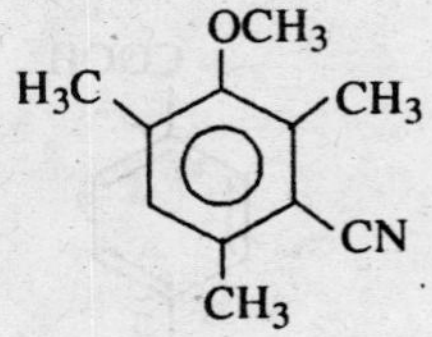

C. 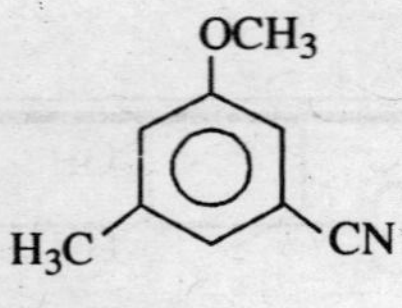

D. 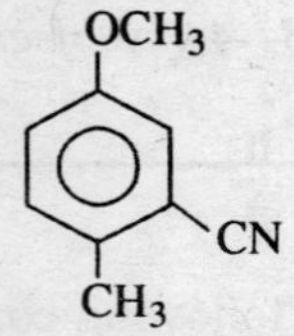

6. The dissociation constant of a substituted benzoic acid at 25° C is 1.0×10^{-4}. The pH of a 0.01 M solution of its sodium salt is

A. 8 B. 6
C. 7 D. 10

7. At 400K, the root mean square (*rms*) speed of a gas X (molecular weight = 40) is equal to the most probable speed of gas Y at 60K. The molecular weight of the gas Y is

A. 8 B. 3
C. 4 D. 9

8. The term that corrects for the attractive forces present in a real gas in the van der Waal's equation is

A. nb B. $\frac{an^2}{V^2}$
C. $-\frac{an^2}{V^2}$ D. $-nb$

9. The correct acidity order of the following is

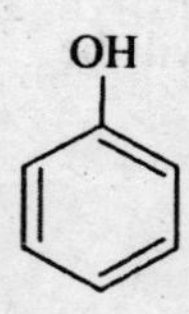

I

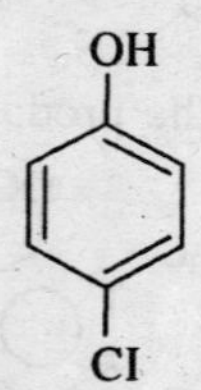

II

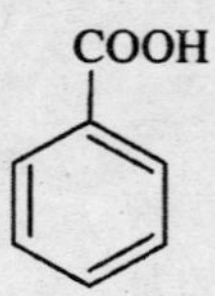

III

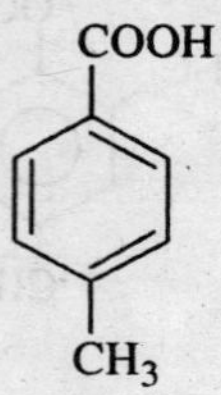

IV

A. III > IV > II > I
B. IV > III > I > II
C. III > II > I > IV
D. II > III > IV > I

10. The spin only magnetic moment value (in Bohr magneton units) of $Cr(CO)_6$ is

A. 0 B. 2.84
C. 4.90 D. 5.92

11. Which of the following will have lowest heat of hydrogenation per mole of compound

A. 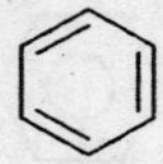

B. 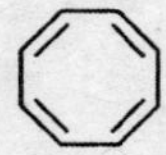

C. 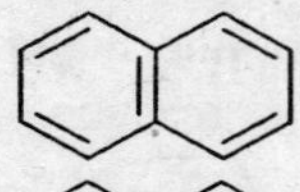

D. 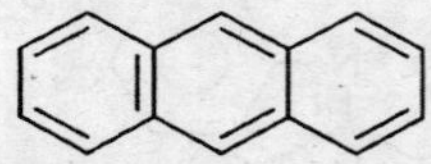

12. In the reaction

$$2X + B_2H_6 \rightarrow [BH_2(X)_2]^+ [BH_4]^-$$

Which of the following is not 'X'?

A. NH_3 B. CH_3NH_2
C. $(CH_3)_2NH$ D. $(CH_3)_3N$

13. The correct statement(s) about the following sugars X and Y is(are)

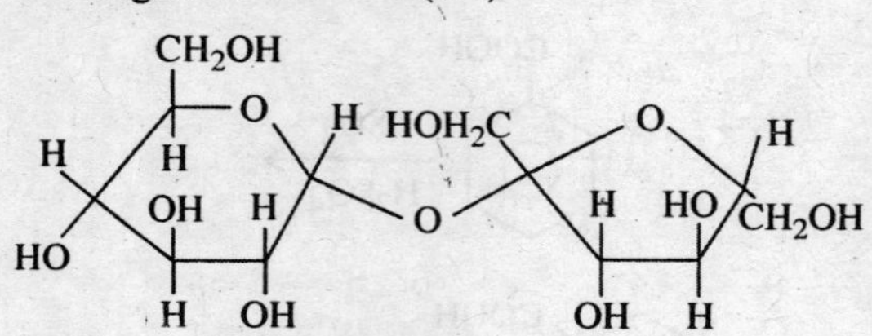

X

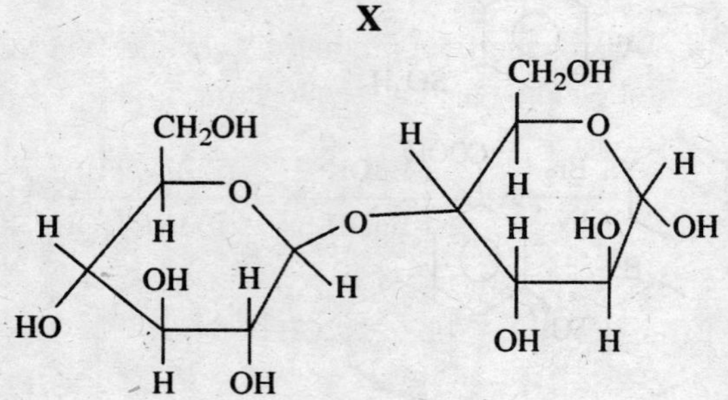

Y

A. X is a reducing sugar and Y is a non-reducing sugar

B. X is a non-reducing sugar and Y is a reducing sugar

C. The glucosidic linkages in X and Y are β and γ, respectively

D. The glucosidic linkages in X and Y are β and α, respectively

14. Which equation is an example of artificial transmutation?

A. ${}_{92}U^{238} \rightarrow {}_{2}He^{4} + {}_{90}Th^{234}$

B. ${}_{13}Al^{27} + {}_{2}He^{4} \rightarrow {}_{15}P^{30} + {}_{0}n^{1}$

C. ${}_{6}C^{14} \rightarrow {}_{7}N^{14} + {}_{-1}e^{0}$

D. ${}_{88}Ra^{226} \rightarrow {}_{2}He^{4} + {}_{86}Ra^{222}$

15. Select the structure of the major product formed in the following reaction.

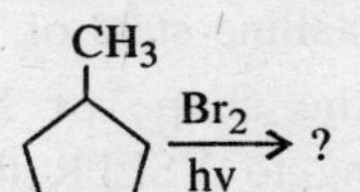

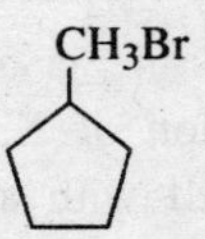

I

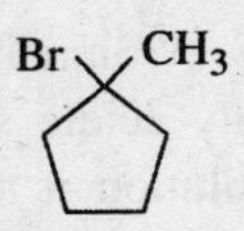

II

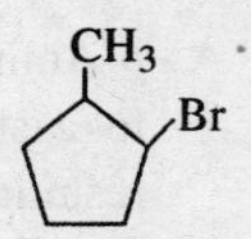

III

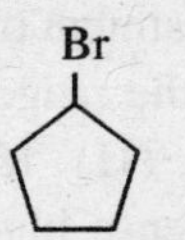

IV

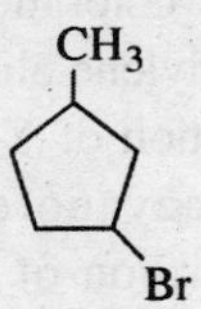

V

A. I B. II

C. III D. IV

16. What is the final product *C*, obtained via the following reaction sequence?

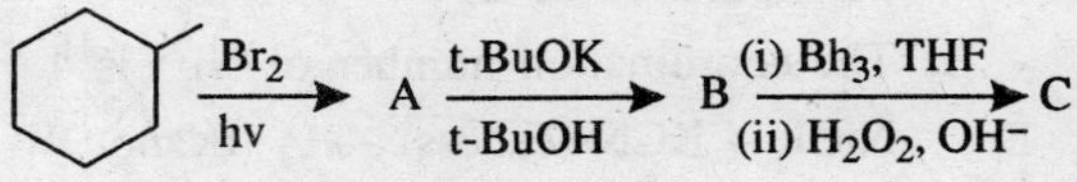

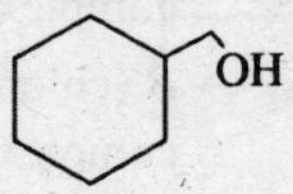

I

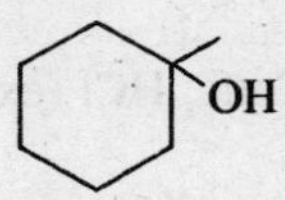

II

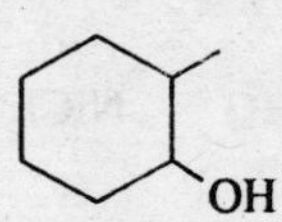

III

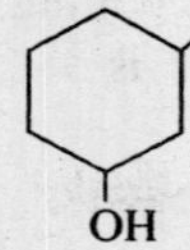

IV

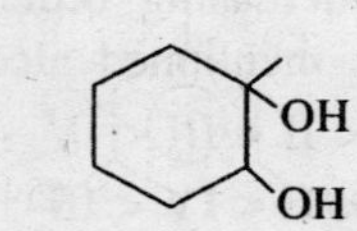

V

A. I B. II

C. III D. IV

17. The reagent(s) for the following conversion,

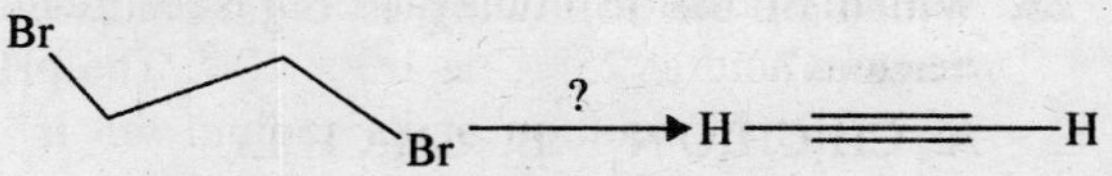

is/are

A. alcoholic KOH

B. alcoholic KOH followed by $NaNH_2$

C. aqueous KOH followed by $NaNH_2$

D. Zn/CH_3OH

18. The species having bond order different from that in CO is

A. NO^- B. NO^+

C. CN^- D. N_2

19. When benzene sulphonic acid and *p*-nitrophenol are treated with $NaHCO_3$, the gases released respectively are

A. SO_2, NO_2 B. SO_2, NO

C. SO_2, CO_2 D. CO_2, CO_2

20. A monatomic ideal gas undergoes a process in which the ratio of *P* to *V* at any instant is constant and equals to 1. What is the molar heat capacity of the gas?

A. $\frac{4R}{2}$ B. $\frac{3R}{2}$

C. $\frac{5R}{2}$ D. 0

21. I. 1,2-dihydroxy benzene

II. 1,3-dihydroxy benzene

III. 1,4-dihydroxy benzene

IV. Hydroxy benzene

The increasing order of boiling points of above mentioned alcohols is

A. I < II < III < IV

B. I < II < IV < III

C. IV < I < II < III

D. IV < II < I < III

22. ClO_4^- ion is

A. Tetrahedral B. Angular

C. Pyramidal D. None of these

23. Which of the following is organometallic reagents?

A. CH_3CH_2ONa B. CH_3CH_2Li

C. $CH_3CH_2BH_2$ D. $[Cr(NH_3)_4]SO_4$

24. Consider the following reactions I and II

I. 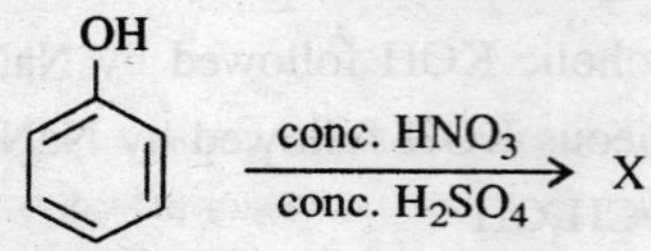

(Phenol)

II. 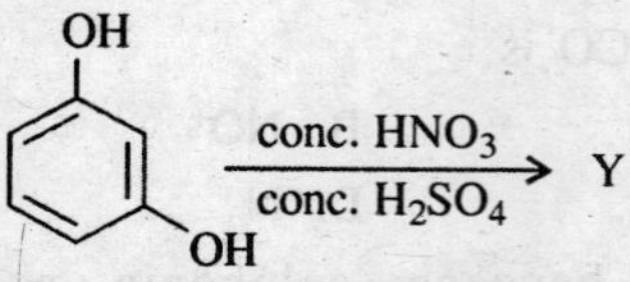

Products 'X' and 'Y' are respectively

A. Picric acid, styphnic acid

B. Styphnic acid, picric acid

C. Picric acid, benzoic acid

D. Picric acid, salicylic acid

25. The bond order of O_2^- is

A. 2 B. 1

C. 2.5 D. 1.5

26. Dipole moment is shown by

A. 1, 4-dichlorobenzene

B. Cis 1,2-dichloroethene

C. trans 1,2-dichloroethene

D. trans 2, 3-dichloro-2 butene

27. Which of the following is pure covalent?

A. H_2 B. CaS

C. KCl D. Na_2S

28. The K_{sp} of CuS, Ag_2S and HgS are 10^{-31}, 10^{-44} and 10^{-54}. The solubility to sulphides are in order of

A. $Ag_2S > CuS > HgS$

B. $Ag_2S > HgS > CuS$

C. $HgS > Ag_2S > CuS$

D. $CuS > Ag_2S > HgS$

29. Which of the following is Inorganic benzene (Borazole)?

A. B_2H_6 B. B_6H_{10}

C. $B_3N_3H_6$ D. BH_3O_3

30. How many isomers are possible in $[Co(en)_2Cl_2]$?

A. 2 B. 4

C. 6 D. 1

31. A. What is the total number of α and β particles emitted in the nuclear reaction $^{238}_{92}U \rightarrow ^{214}_{82}Pb$?

B. What is the coordination number of *Al* in the crystalline state of $AlCl_3$?

C. Draw the shape of XeF_4 and OSF_4 according to VSEPR theory. Show the lone pair of electrons on the central atom.

32. A. *p*-Amino-*N*, *N*-dimethylaniline is added to a strongly acidic solution of X. The resulting solution is treated with a few drops of aqueous solution of Y to yield blue coloration due to the formation of methylene blue. Treatment of the aqueous solution of Y with the reagent potassium hexacyanoferrate (II) leads to the formation of an intense blue precipitate. The precipitate dissolves on excess addition of the reagent. Similarly, treatment of the solution of Y with the solution of potassium hexacyanoferrate (III) leads to a brown coloration due to the formation of Z.

B. The coordination number of Ni^{2+} is 4.

$NiCl_2$ + KCN (excess) → *A* (cyano complex)

$NiCl_2$ + Conc. HCl (excess) → *B* (chloro complex)

What is the IUPAC name of *A* and *B*?

33. A. A carbonyl compound P, which gives positive iodoform test, undergoes reaction with MeMgBr followed by dehydration to give an olefin Q. Ozonolysis of Q leads to a dicarbonyl compound R, which undergoes intramolecular aldol reaction to give predominantly S.

$$P \xrightarrow[\text{2.}H^+,H_2O \;\; \text{3.}H_2SO_4,\Delta]{\text{1.MeMgBr}} Q \xrightarrow[\text{2.Zn},H_2O]{\text{1. }O_3} R \xrightarrow[\text{2.}\Delta]{\text{1. }OH^-} S$$

B. Fill in the blanks

(*i*) $^{235}U_{92} + {}_0n^1 \rightarrow {}^{137}A_{52} + {}^{97}B_{40} + ...$

(*ii*) $^{82}Se_{34} \rightarrow 2\,_{-1}e^0 + ...$

34. A. 75.2g of C_6H_5OH (phenol) is dissolved in a solvent of $K_f = 14$. If the depression in freezing point is $7K$ then find the of phenol that dimerises.

B. For the reaction, $2CO + O_2 \rightarrow 2CO_2$; $\Delta H = -560$ kJ. Two moles of CO and one mole of O_2 are taken in a container of volume 1 L. They completely form two moles of CO_2, the gases deviate appreciably from ideal behaviour. If the pressure in the vessel changes from 70 to 40 atm, find the magnitude (absolute value) of ΔU at 500 K. (1 L atm = 0.1kJ)

C. We have taken a saturated solution of AgBr. K_{sp} of AgBr is 12×10^{14}. If 10^{-7} mole of $AgNO_3$ are added to 1 litre of this solution find conductivity (specific conductance) of this solution in terms of $10^{-7}\ S\ m^{-1}$ units.

Given, $\lambda^0_{(Ag^+)} = 6\times10^{-3}\,Sm^2mol^{-1}$,

$\lambda^0_{(Br^-)} = 8\times10^{-3}\,Sm^2mol^{-1}$,

$\lambda^0_{(NO_3^-)} = 7\times10^{-3}\ Sm^2\ mol^{-1}$.

35. A. The edge length of unit cell of a metal having molecular weight 75 g/mol is 5 Å which crystallizes in cubic lattice. If the density is 2 g/cc then find the radius of metal atom. ($N_A = 6 \times 10^{23}$). Give the answer in pm.

B. An element crystallizes in fcc lattice having edge length 400 pm. Calculate the maximum diameter of atom which can be placed in interstitial site without distorting the structure.

36. A. Predict whether the following molecules are iso structural or not. Justify your answer.

(*i*) NMe_3 (*ii*) $N(SiMe_3)_3$

B.

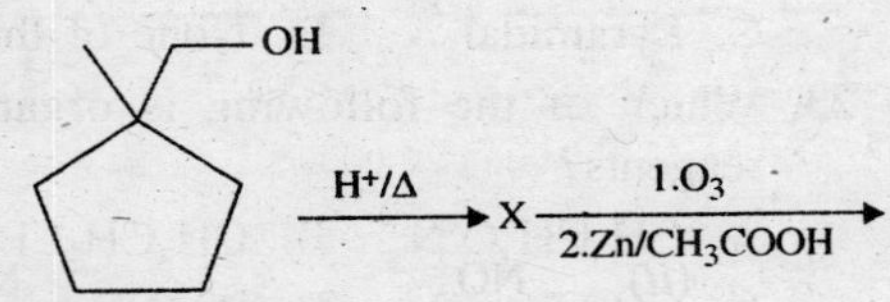

Identify X and Y.

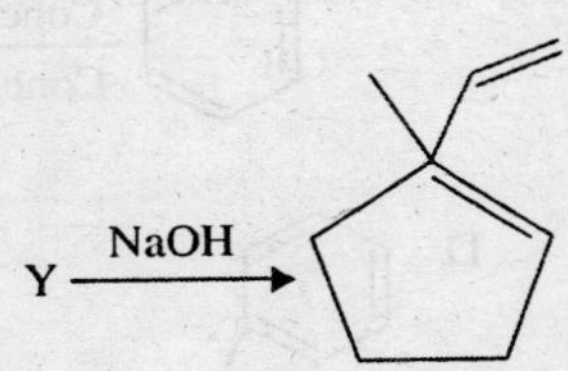

37. Give reasons:

A. (*i*)

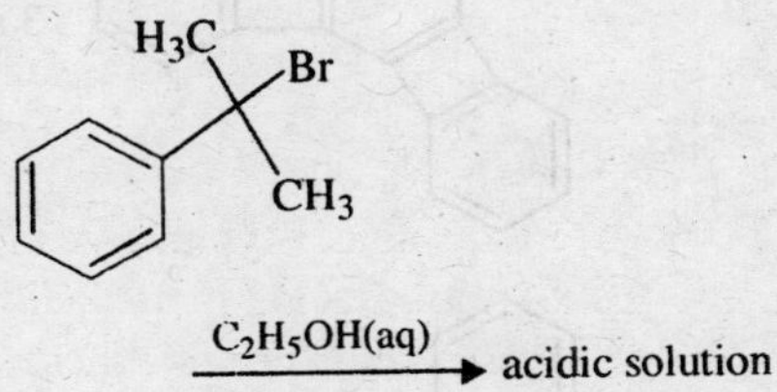

(*ii*)

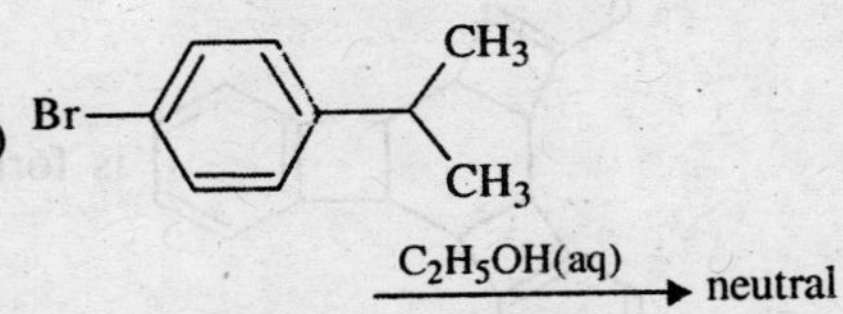

B. (*i*)

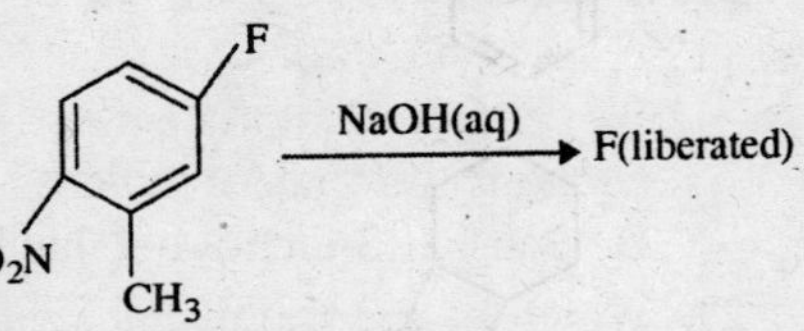

(*ii*)

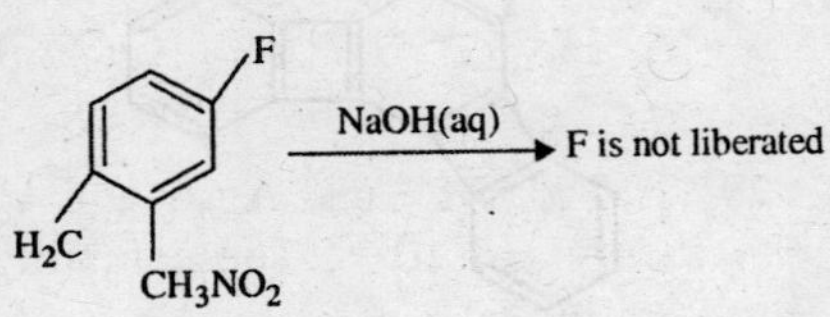

C. (i)

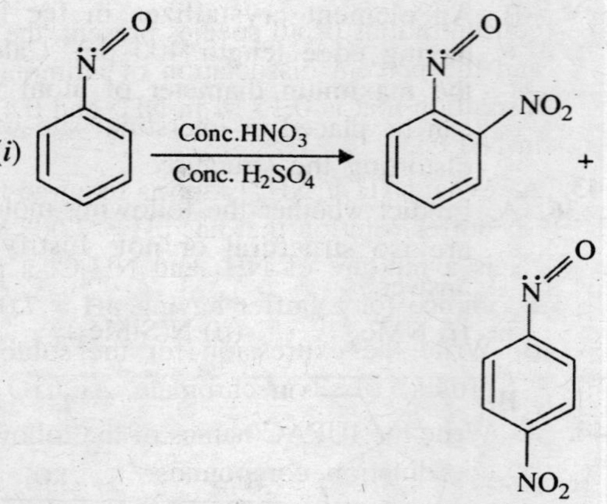

(ii)

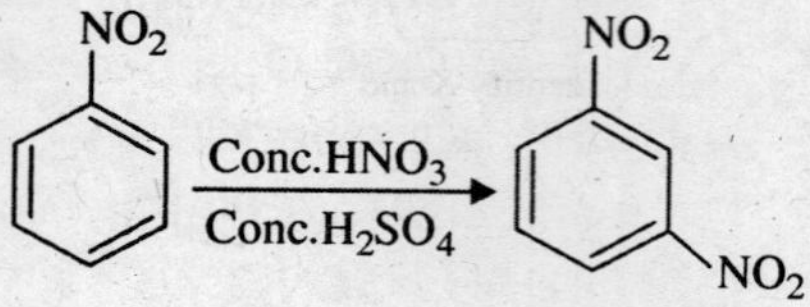

D.

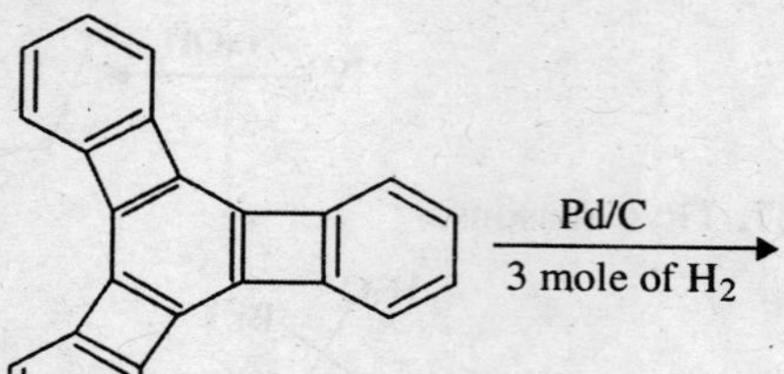

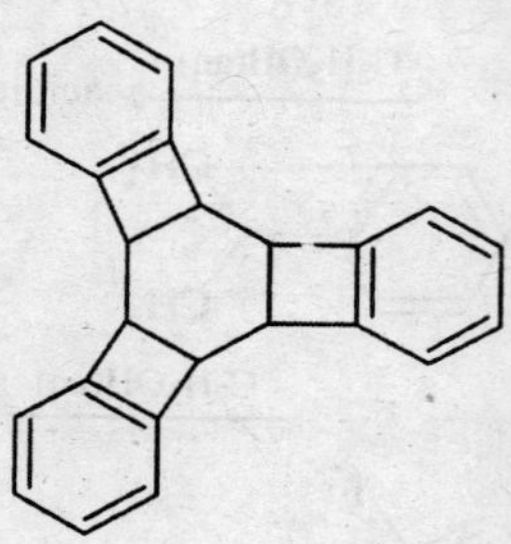

is formed but not

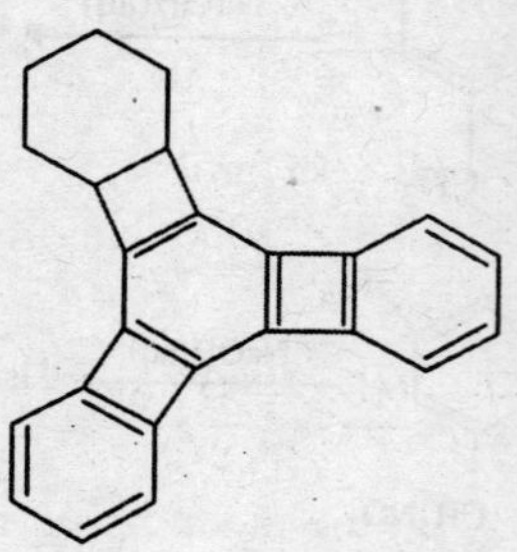

38. A. $2X_{(g)} \rightarrow 3Y_{(g)} + 2Z_{(g)}$

Time (in Min)	0	100	200
Parial pressure of *X* (in mm of Hg)	800	400	200

Assuming ideal gas condition. Calculate

(i) Order of reaction

(ii) Rate constant

(iii) Time taken for 75% completion of reaction.

(iv) Total pressure when $P_x = 700$ mm.

B. (i) Calculate velocity of electron in first Bohr orbit of hydrogen atom (Given $r = a_0$).

(ii) Find de-Broglie wavelength of the electron in first Bohr orbit.

(iii) Find the orbit angular momentum of 2p orbital in terms of $h/2\pi$ units.

39. A. Calculate ΔG_r^0 of the following reaction

$$Ag^+_{(aq)} + Cl^-_{(aq)} \rightarrow AgCl_{(s)}$$

Given

ΔG_f^0 (AgCl) = – 109 kJ/mole

ΔG_f^0 (Cl^-) = – 129 kJ/mole

ΔG_f^0 (Ag^+) = 77 kJ/mole

Represent the above reaction in form of a cell and calculate E° of the cell. Find $\log_{10}K_{sp}$ of AgCl.

B. 6.539×10^{-2} g of metallic Zn (amu = 65.39) was added to 100 ml of saturated solution of AgCl.

Calculate $\log_{10}\dfrac{[Zn^{2+}]}{[Ag^+]^2}$. Given that

$Ag^+ + e^- \rightarrow Ag$ $\quad E^0 = 0.80$ V

$Zn^{2+} + 2e^- \rightarrow Zn$ $\quad E^0 = -0.76$ V

Also find how many moles of *Ag* will be formed?

40. A. Convert 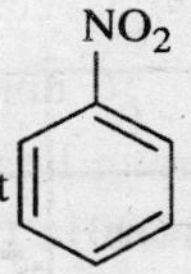 to 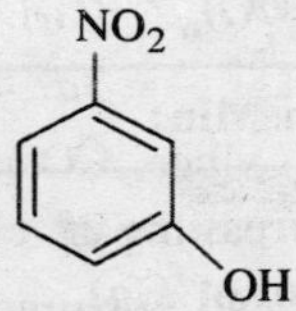 in not more than four steps. Also mention the temperature and reaction condition.

B. 7-bromo-1, 3, 5-cycloheptatriene exists as ionic species in aqueous solution while 5-bromo-1, 3 cyclopentadiene doesn't ionise even in presence of Ag^+ *(aq)*, Explain.

41. A. Write the chemical reactions involved in the extraction of metallic silver from argentite.

B. Write the balanced chemical equation for developing photographic films.

42. In 0.15 M NH_3, the pH is 11.21 and the pre cent dissociation is 1.1%. Calculate the concentrations of all species present, the pH, and the percent dissociation of ammonia in a solution that is 0.15 M in NH_3 and 0.45 M in NH_4Cl.

43. A. What $[NH_3]/[NH_4^+]$ ratio is required for a buffer solution that has pH = 7.00? Why is a mixture of NH_3 and NH_4Cl a poor choice for a buffer having pH = 7.00?

B. Write the expression for the solubility product of silver chromate, Ag_2CrO_4.

44. A. Write the IUPAC names of the following coordination compounds:

(*i*) $[Pt(NH_3)_2\ Cl(NO_2)]$

(*ii*) $K_3\ [Cr\ (C_2O_4)_3]$

(*iii*) $[CoCl_2\ (en)_2]Cl$

(*iv*) $[Co(NH_3)_5(CO_3)]Cl$

(*v*) $Hg[Co(SCN)_4]$

B. Draw structures of the geometrical isomers of $[Fe(NH_3)_2(CN)_4]^-$

ANSWERS

1	2	3	4	5	6	7	8	9	10
B	B	B	A	D	A	C	B	A	A
11	**12**	**13**	**14**	**15**	**16**	**17**	**18**	**19**	**20**
D	D	B	B	B	A	B	A	D	A
21	**22**	**23**	**24**	**25**	**26**	**27**	**28**	**29**	**30**
C	A	B	C	D	B	A	A	C	B

SOME SELECTED EXPLANATORY ANSWERS

1. Replacement of hydrogen atoms of amino group by electron withdrawing phenyl group decrease the basic character. Further steric effect of phenyl group also present other groups to come closer to lone pair of Nitrogen atom.

2. –COOH group is meta directing group for incoming electrophile.

3. Gas expands in vacuum *i.e.,* $P_{ext} = 0$

$\because \quad W = -P_{ext}\,\Delta V$

$\therefore \quad W = 0$

4. The entropy change for the vapourization of water is given by

$$\Delta S = \frac{\Delta H_{vap}}{T_{vap}}$$

Given, $\Delta H_{vap} = 40.8\ \text{kJ mol}^{-1}$

$= 40.8 \times 1000\ \text{J mol}^{-1}$

and $T = 373\ K$

$$\Delta S = \frac{40.8 \times 1000\, J\,\text{mol}^{-1}}{373 K}$$

$= 109.38\ \text{JK}^{-1}\ \text{mol}^{-1}$

5. —OCH_3 is ortho, para directing and activating group while —CN is meta directing and deactivating. Thus, electrophile substitution will take place at para-position with respect to —OCH_3 group. Ortho product will not be preferred due to steric hinderance.

6. Salt of weak acid and strong base

$$pH = 7+\frac{1}{2}(pK_a + \log_{10} C)$$

$$= 7+\frac{1}{2}(4+\log_{10} 0.01)$$

$$pH = 8$$

7. $$(C_{rms})_X = \sqrt{\frac{3RT}{M_X}} = \sqrt{\frac{3\times R\times 400}{40}} \quad ...(i)$$

$$(C_{MP})_Y = \sqrt{\frac{2RT}{M_Y}} = \sqrt{\frac{2\times R\times 60}{M_Y}} \quad ...(ii)$$

From (*i*) and (*ii*)

$$\Rightarrow \quad \sqrt{30R} = \sqrt{\frac{120R}{M_Y}}$$

$$\Rightarrow \quad M_Y = 4$$

8. The term for the attractive forces present in a real gas in van der Waal's equation is $\frac{an^2}{v^2}$

$$\left(P+\frac{an^2}{V^2}\right)(V-nb) = nRT$$

9. 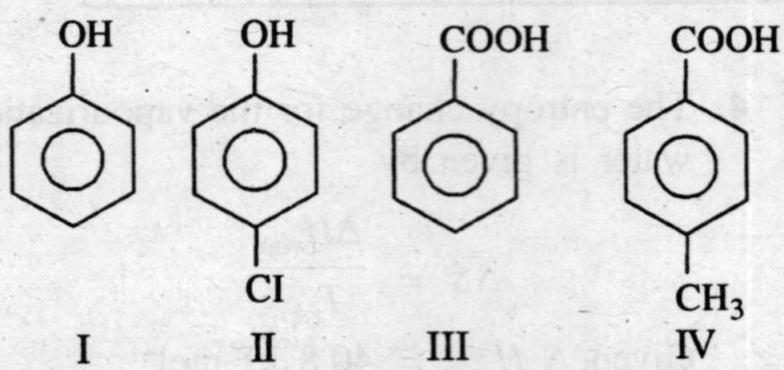

I, II, III, IV

II: $(-I, +M)$ ≈ Weak deactivating

IV: (+ *M* through Hyper conjugation)

–COOH is more acidic than phenols.

∴ III > IV > II > I

10. $Cr(CO)_6$

$Cr^{\circ}_{Z=24} \equiv 3d^5\, 4s^1$ [6 unpaired electrons

⇒ Since, CO is strong ligand it will cause pairing of electrons in Cr.

⇒ No unpaired electrons.

$$\mu = \sqrt{n(n+2)}\ B.M. = 0$$

11. Benzene has lowest heat of hydrogenation because it has least number of π-bond. The more the π-bond the more will be heat of hydrogenation.

12. $B_2H_6 + 2NH_3 \rightarrow [BH_2(NH_3)_2]^+ [BH_4]^-$

Similarly, CH_3NH_2 & $(CH_3)_2$ NH will also react.

13. *X* is sucrose & it is a non-reducing sugar. It has α-giucosidic linkage.

14. Transmutation means to change or transform atoms of one element into atoms of another element. Transmutation can be natural or artificial. In artificial transmutation nuclei in a special laboratory are bombarded by high energy particles: protons, neutrons, or alpha particles (a helium nuclei). If the nuclei becomes unstable, it can result in another form of the same element (isotope) or a different element. In case of $_{13}Al^{27}$ it is bombarded with $_2He^4$ in lab to convert into phosphorus.

15. $Br_2 \xrightarrow{hv} 2Br\cdot$

This will react with 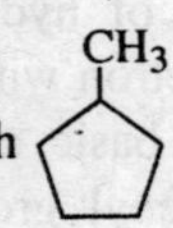 to give most stable radical. In this case, it will be tertiary free radical as shown below

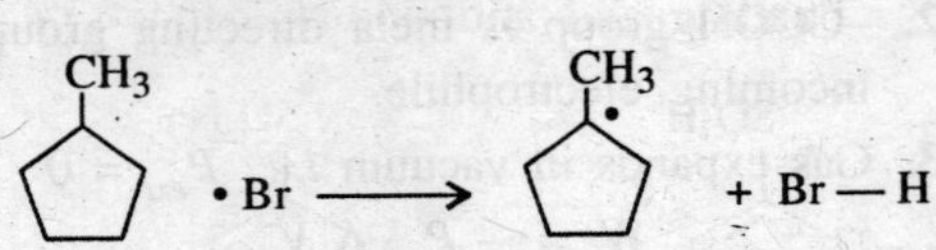

(tertiary & therefore stable)

16.

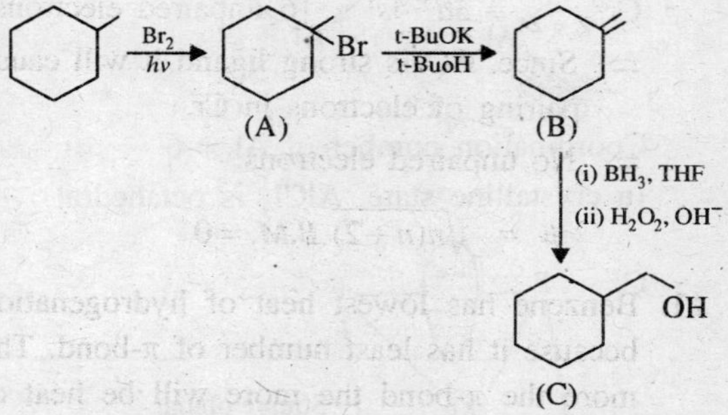

Since t-BuO⁻ is bulky group it will remove hydrogen from least sterically hindered site. This result in termation of B. Boron from BH_3 also react at less hindered site to give product (C).

17.

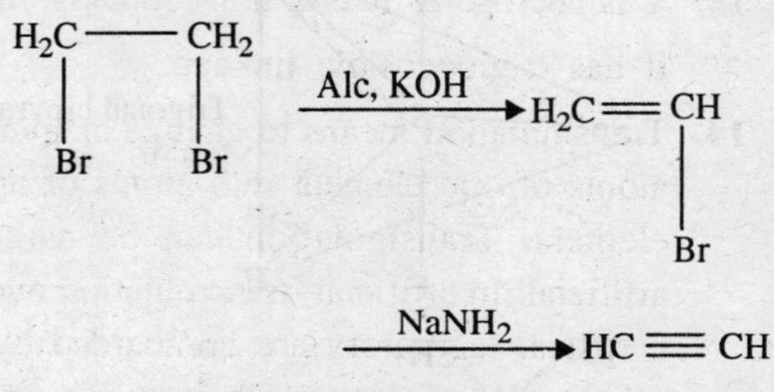

Because $CH_2 = CH - Br$ has partial C – Br double bond character, it requires more base to remove HBr.

18. NO^- (16 electron system)

Bond order = 2.

$NO^{\oplus}$, CN^- and N_2 are isoelectronic with CO therefore all have same bond order (= 3)

In case bond order is asked

$\sigma 1s, \sigma^* 1s, \sigma 2s, \sigma^* 2s, \sigma 2P_x, \pi 2P_y = \pi 2P_z,$

$\pi^* 2P_y = \pi^* 2P_z, \sigma^* 2P_x$

This could be used to get bond order where

bond order = $\frac{n_b - n_a}{2}$ where n_b & n_a are in bonding and antibonding orbitals

19.

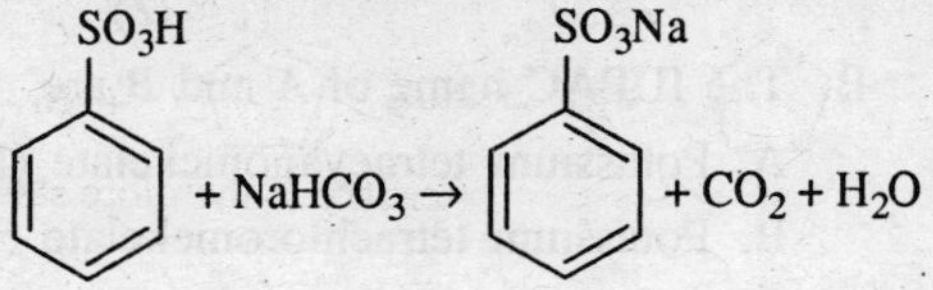

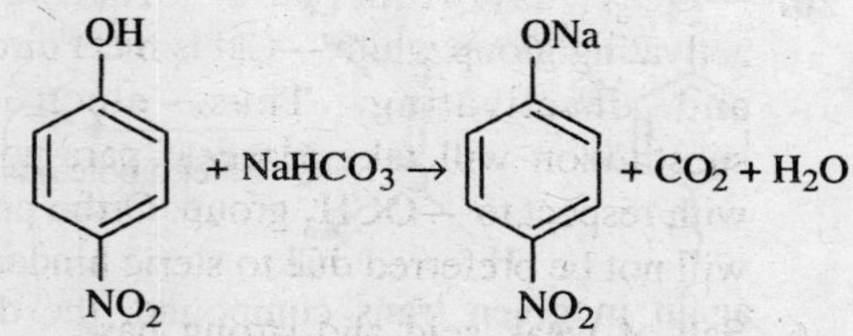

21. Intermolecular hydrogen bonding in 1, 2-dihydroxy benzene decreases its B.P. compared to 1, 3 and 1, 4 dihydroxy benzene.

22. ClO_4^-

Total electron = 7 + 6 × 4 + 1 = 32

$\frac{32}{8} = 4$

⇒ SP^3 hybridization or Cl atom. The above represent tetrahedral structure.

23. Organometallic compounds contain carbon metal bonds

24.

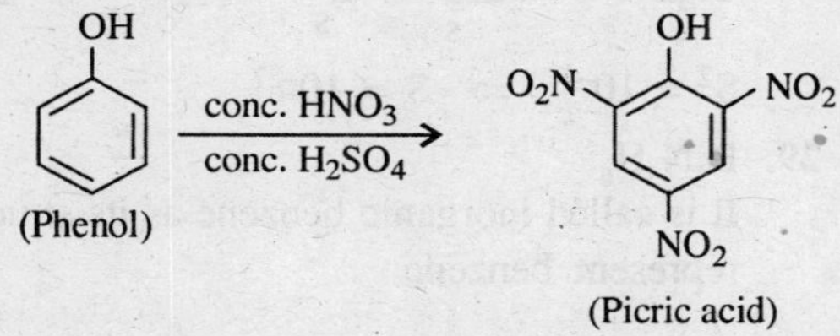

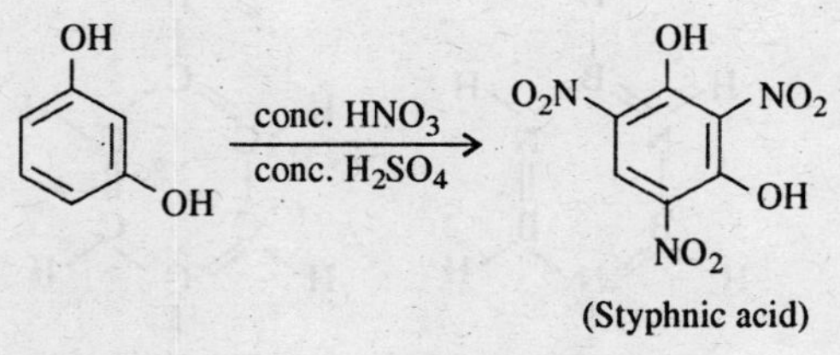

25. Total no. of electron in O_2^- is 17.

$$\underset{\sigma 1s,}{\uparrow\downarrow}\quad \underset{\sigma^* 1s,}{\uparrow\downarrow}\quad \underset{\sigma 2s,}{\uparrow\downarrow}\quad \underset{\sigma^* 2s,}{\uparrow\downarrow}\quad \underset{\sigma 2P_x,}{\uparrow\downarrow}$$

$$\underset{\pi 2P_x}{\uparrow\downarrow} = \underset{\pi 2P_y,}{\uparrow\downarrow}\quad \underset{\pi^* 2P_x}{\uparrow\downarrow} = \underset{\pi^* 2P_y}{1}$$

$$\therefore \text{BO} = \frac{\text{no. of bonding electron} - \text{no. of antibonding electron}}{2}$$

$$= \frac{10 - 7}{2} = 1.5.$$

26. 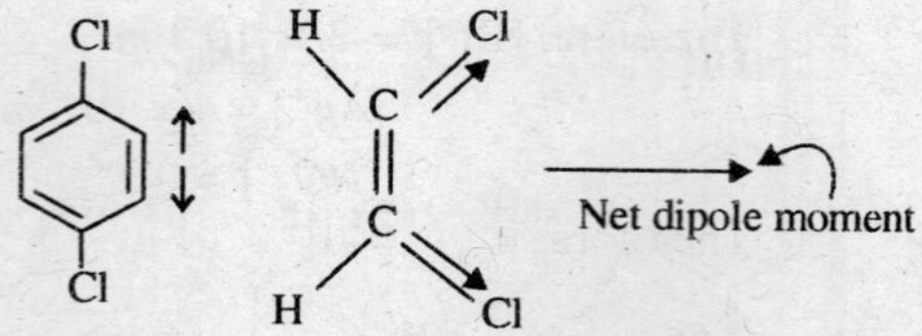

again in given trans compound, the dipole moment are in opposite direction and get cancelled.

27. H-H; electronegativity difference is zero so it is pure covalent bond.

28. $CuS \rightleftharpoons \underset{S}{Cu^{2+}} + \underset{S}{S^{2-}}$

$S^2 = 10^{-31} \Rightarrow S = 3.16 \times 10^{-16}$

$Ag_2S \rightleftharpoons \underset{2S}{2Ag^+} + \underset{S}{S^{2-}}$

$(2S)^2(S) = 4S^3 = 10^{-44}$

$\Rightarrow S = 1.357 \times 10^{15}$

$HgS \rightleftharpoons \underset{S}{Hg^{2+}} + \underset{S}{S^{2-}}$

$S^2 = 10^{-54} \Rightarrow S = 10^{-27}$.

29. $B_3N_3H_6$.

It is called inorganic benzene as its structure represent benzene

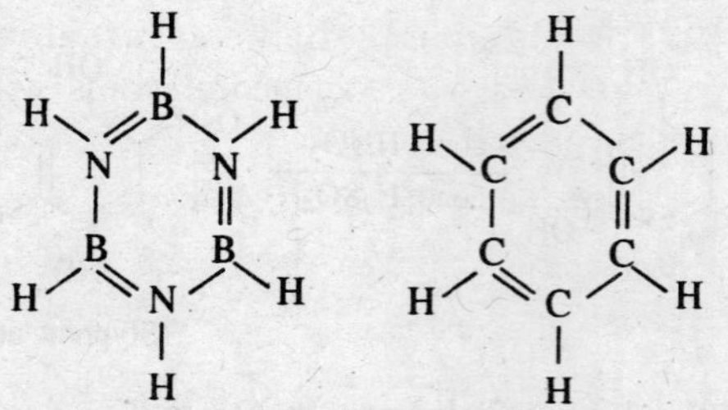

(Borazole)

Note: There is difference in length of BN bond in borazole.

31. A. ${}_{92}U^{238} \longrightarrow {}_{82}Pb^{214} + x\,{}_2He^4 + y\,{}_{-1}e^0$

Conservation of mass

$238 = 214 + 4x \Rightarrow x = 6$

Conservation of charge

$92 = 82 + 2x - y \Rightarrow y = 2$

B. 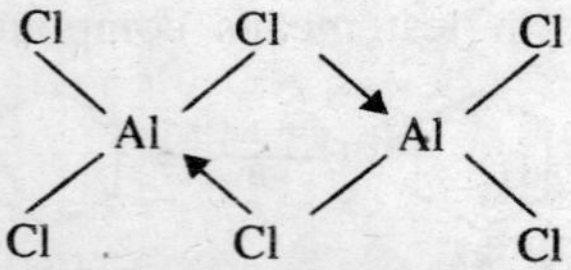

Coordination number of Al = 6

In crystalline state, $AlCl_3$ is octahedral

C. 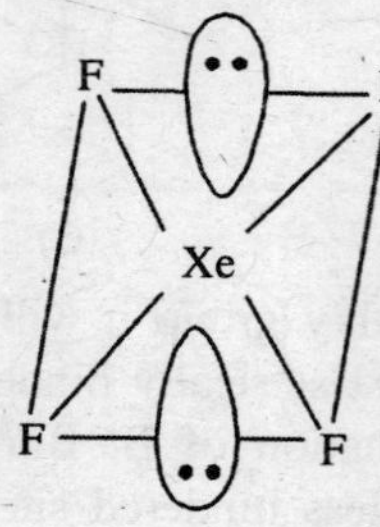

Square planar (sp^3d^2)

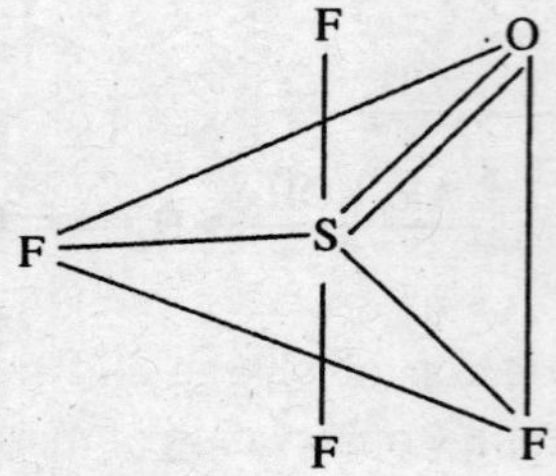

Trigonal bipyramidal (sp^3d)

32. A. 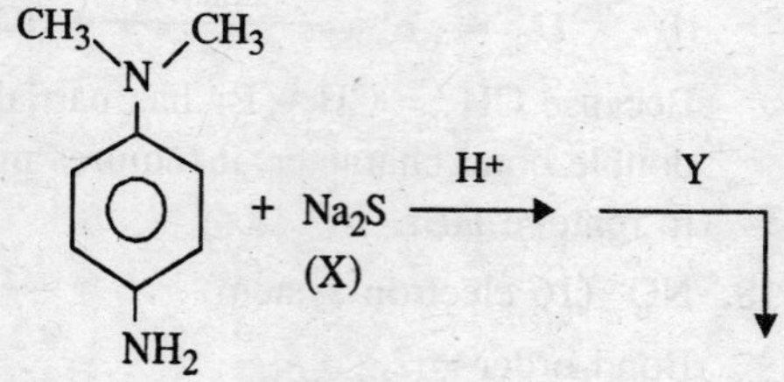

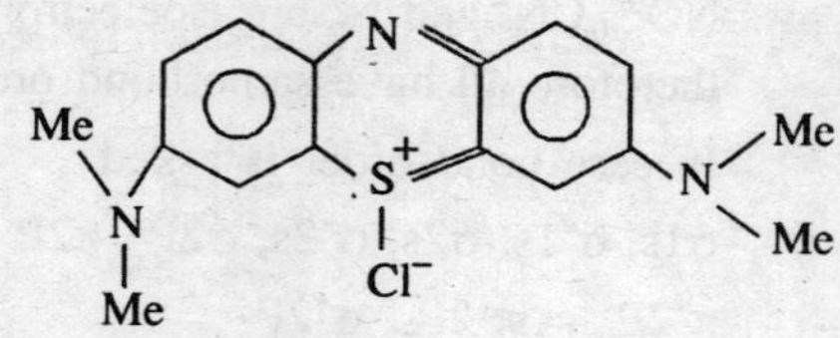

Methylene Blue

$\underset{(FeCl_3)}{Y} + \underset{(Excess)}{K_4[Fe(CN)_6]} \longrightarrow \underset{\text{Prussian Blue}}{Fe_4[Fe(CN)_6]_3}$

$Y + K_3[Fe(CN)_6] \longrightarrow \underset{(Z)}{Fe\,[Fe(CN)_6]}$

B. The IUPAC name of *A* and *B* are

A. Potassium tetracyanonickelate (II)

B. Potassium tetrachloronickelate (II)

33. A. Iodoform test means compounds have

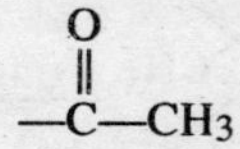

Structure

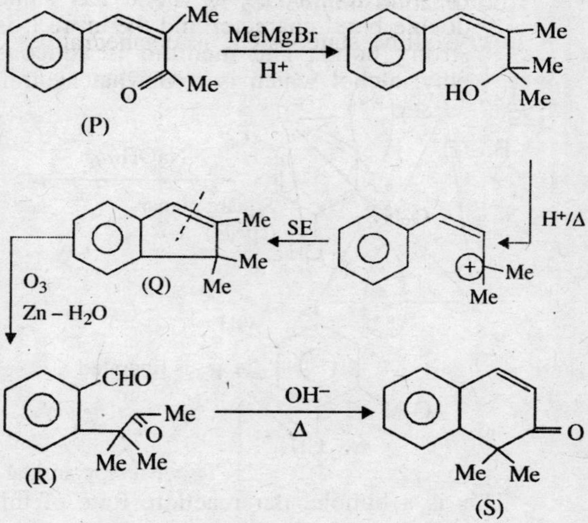

B. Apply conservation of charge and mass to get answer. Apply conservation of mass first.

(i) $^{235}U_{92} + {}_0n^1 \rightarrow {}^{137}A_{52} + {}^{97}B_{40} + 2\,{}_0n^1$

(ii) $^{82}Se_{34} \rightarrow 2\,{}_{-1}e^0 + {}^{82}Kr_{36}$

34. A. $\underset{C-C\alpha}{2C_6H_5OH} \rightleftharpoons \underset{\frac{C\alpha}{2}}{(C_6H_5OH)_2}$

$\Delta T = K_f \times$ molality

where ΔT_f is depression in freezing point.

$$7 = 14 \times 0.8\left(\frac{2-\alpha}{2}\right)$$

$\alpha = 0.75 = 75\%$

B. $\Delta H = \Delta U + \Delta(PV)$

$\Delta H = \Delta U + V\Delta P$ {since V is const.}

$\Delta U = \Delta H - V\Delta P$

$= -560 - 1 \times 30 \times 0.1$

$= -563$ kJ

Absolute value = 563 kJ

C. The solubility of AgBr in presence of 10^{-7} molar $AgNO_3$ is 3×10^{-7} *M*.

Therefore, $[Br^-] = 3 \times 10^{-4}\ m^3$,

$[Ag^+] = 4 \times 10^{-4}\ m^3$ and

$[NO_3^-] = 10^{-4}\ m^3$

Therefore, $\kappa_{total} =$

$\kappa_{Br^-} + \kappa_{Ag^+}\,\kappa_{NO_3^-}$

$= 55\ Sm^{-1}$

35. A. $\rho = \dfrac{ZA}{NV}$

$$Z = \frac{\rho NV}{A} = \frac{2 \times 6 \times 10^{23} \times (5 \times 10^{-8})^3}{75}$$

$n = 2$

$$r = \frac{\sqrt{3}}{4}a = \frac{\sqrt{3}}{4} \times 5 = 2.165\ \text{Å} = 216.5\ \text{pm}$$

B. In FCC, interstitial sites will be octahedral voids & tetrahedral voids.

For octahedral voids	For tetrahedral voids
$\dfrac{r_1}{r_2} = 0.414$	$\dfrac{r_1}{r_2} = 0.225$

Where r_1 = radius of atom in interstitial sites

r_2 = radius of atom arranged in FCC.

i.e., $4r_2 = \sqrt{2}a$,

For maximum diameter of atom in interstitial site, octahedral voids will be considered.

Diameter $= 2r_1 = 2(0.414\ r_2)$

$$= 2 \times 0.414 \times \frac{400}{2\sqrt{2}}$$

$= 117.1$ pm

36. A. $N(Me)_3$ & $N(SiMe_3)_3$ are not isostructural. $N(Me)_3$ is trigonal pyramidal while $N(SiMe_3)_3$ is trigonal planar due to back bonding. This is possible due to vacant *d*-orbital present in Si.

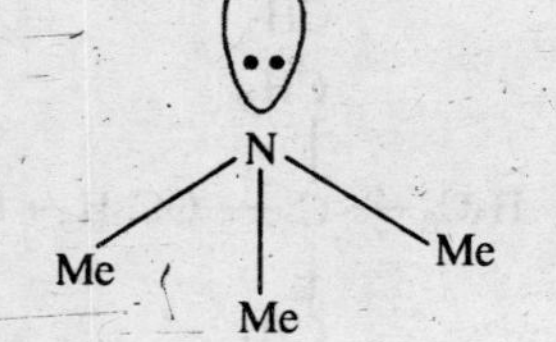

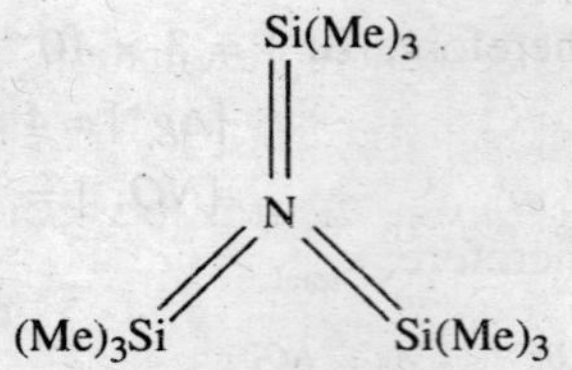

3.

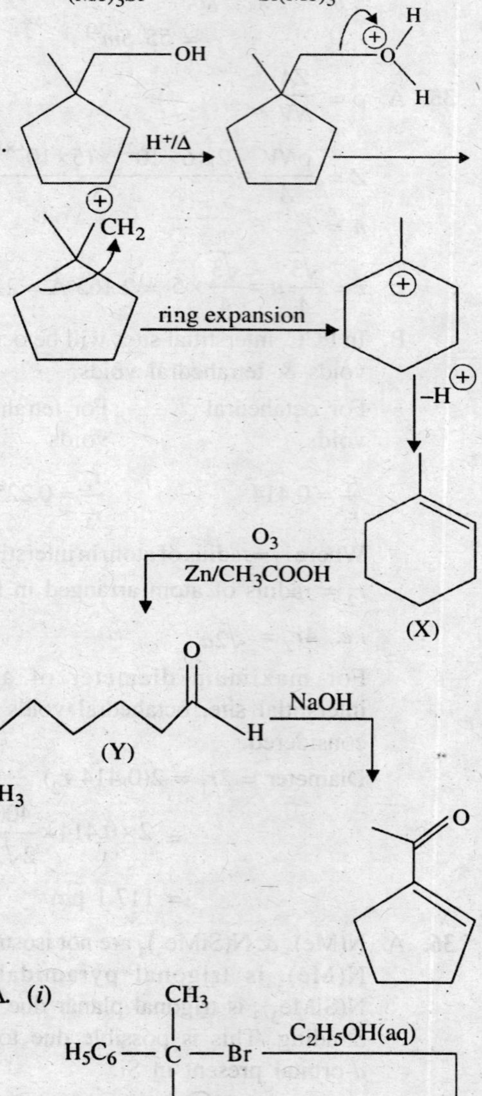

37. A. (*i*)

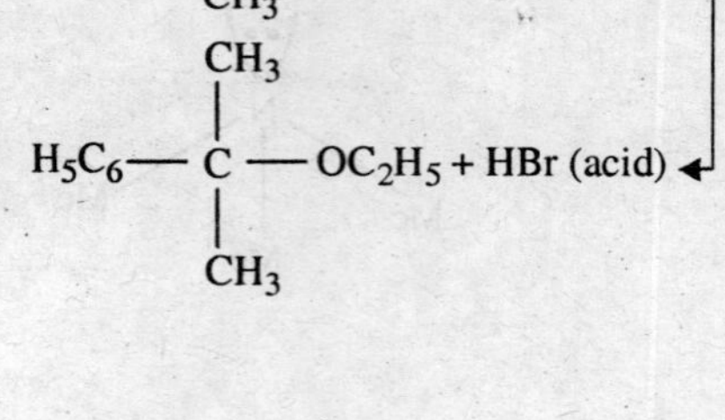

(*ii*)

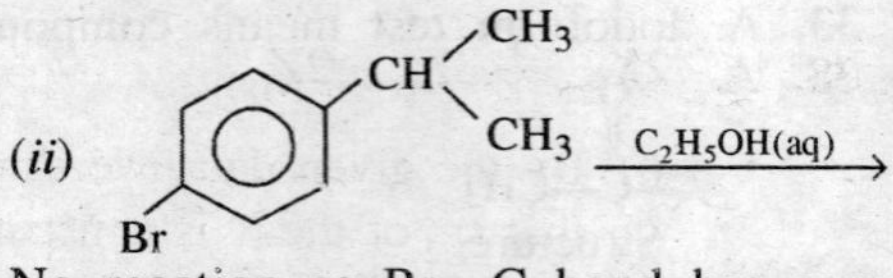

No reaction as Br—C bond has some double bond character and therefore it is strong bond. The medium is aqueous ethyl alchol which is somewhat neutral.

B. (*i*)

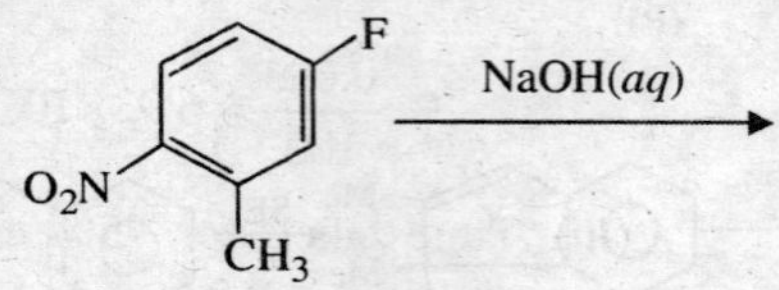

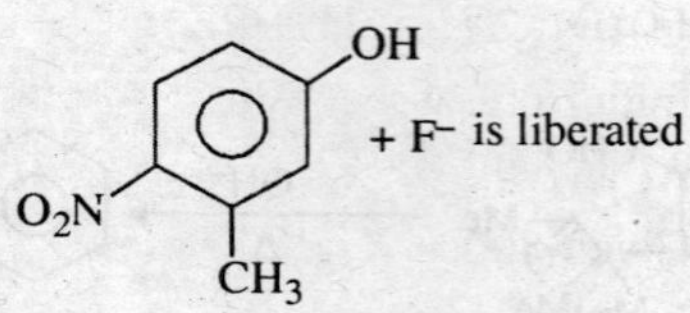

This is a bimolecular reaction. Rate of this reaction is being enhanced by presence of electron withdrawing groups at ortho and para positions. Since intermediate have –ve charge.

(*ii*)

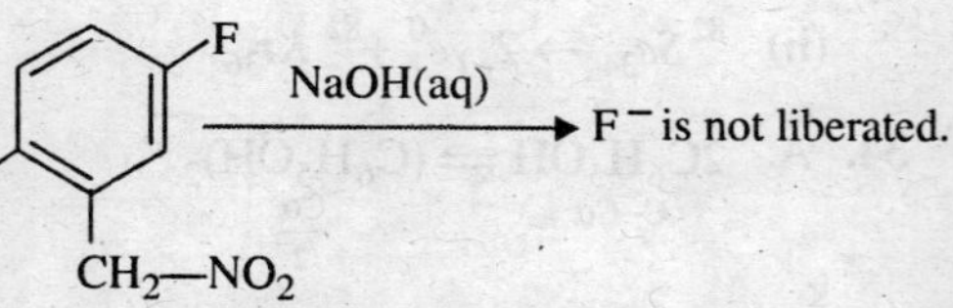

The reaction is not possible because $–NO_2$ group is not directly attached to benzene ring and therefore cannot stabilize the –ve charge of intermediate formed during the Reaction.

C. (*i*) Due to presence of lone pair on nitrogen atom NO group is electron donating and ortho, para directing.

(*ii*) NO_2 group is electron withdrawing and meta directing.

D. Due to reduction of central ring, three four membered antiaromatic rings become stable while on reduction of terminal ring only one antiaromatic ring can be stabilized.

38. A. $2X_{(g)} \rightarrow 3Y_{(g)} + 2Z_{(g)}$

(*i*) By the given data, we can observed that $t_{1/2}$ of the X is constant *i.e.*, 100 min. therefore order of reaction is one.

(*ii*) Rate constant $K = \dfrac{0.693}{t_{1/2}}$

$$= \frac{0.693}{100} = 6.93 \times 10^{-3} \text{ min}^{-1}$$

(*iii*) Time taken for 75% completion of reaction = 2 $t_{1/2}$

(*iv*) $2X \rightarrow 3Y + 2Z$

Initial pressure	800	0	0
At any time	800 – X	3/2 X	X

Given 800 – X = 700 mm

X = 100 mm

Total pressure = 700 + 150 + 100
= 950 mm

B. (*i*) $mvr = \dfrac{nh}{2\pi}$ $\quad r = a_0 = 0.529$ Å

$$v = \frac{nh}{2\pi mr} = 2.18 \times 10^6 \, m/\text{sec} \ (n = 1)$$

(*ii*) $\lambda = \dfrac{h}{mv} = \dfrac{6.63 \times 10^{-34}}{9.1 \times 10^{-31} \times 2.18 \times 10^6}$

$= 0.33 \times 10^{-9}$ m = 3.3 Å

(*iii*) For 2 p value of l = 1

Orbital angular momentum $= \sqrt{l(l+1)}\dfrac{h}{2\pi}$

$$= \sqrt{2}\frac{h}{2\pi}$$

39. A. Cell reactions are

$Ag + \frac{1}{2}Cl_2 \rightarrow AgCl$ ...(*i*)

$Ag \rightarrow Ag^+ + e^-$ ...(*ii*)

$\frac{1}{2}Cl_2 + e \rightarrow Cl^-$ ...(*iii*)

$Ag^+ + Cl^- \rightarrow AgCl$ (i – ii – iii)

Hence cell representation is

$Ag|Ag^+|\ AgCl|Cl^-|Cl_2,\ Pt$

$Ag^+(aq) + Cl^-(aq) \rightarrow AgCl(s);$

$$\sum \Delta G^\circ_P - \sum \Delta G^\circ_R$$

(*i*) $\Delta G^\circ = -109 - (-129 + 77)$
$= -109 + 129 - 77$
$= 20 - 77 = -57 = -1 \times F \times E^\circ$

$-57 = -1 \times 96500 \times E^\circ$

$$\Rightarrow \quad E^\circ = \frac{57000}{96500} = 0.59 \text{ Volts}$$

(*ii*) $-57 = -2.303\ RT \log K_0$

$$\log K_0 = \frac{57 \times 1000}{2.303 \times 8.314 \times 298}$$

$\log K_0 = 9.98 \approx 10$

$K_0 = 10^{10}$

$\therefore \quad K_{SP} = 1/K_0$

$\therefore \quad K_{SP} = 10^{-10}$

$\therefore \log K_{SP} = -10$

(*iii*) $10AgCl(s) \rightleftharpoons Ag^+(aq) + Cl^-(aq)$
$\qquad\qquad\qquad\qquad S \qquad\qquad S$

$10^{-10} = S^2$

$\therefore \quad S = 10^{-5}\ m/L$

B. When $\dfrac{65.39 \times 10^{-2}}{65.39} = 10^{-3}$ moles of Zn have been added,

$2Ag^+ + 2e \rightarrow 2Ag;$ $\quad E^0 = 0.80\ V$

$Zn \rightarrow Zn^{2+} + 2e;$ $\quad E^0 = 0.77V$

$2Ag^+_{(aq)} + Zn_{(s)} \rightarrow Zn^{2+}_{(aq)} + 2Ag_{(s)};$

$E^0 = 1.57V$

10^{-6} mole 10^{-3} moles

$\log_{10} K_{(eq)} = 52.8$

Therefore, this reaction will move in forward direction completely. Hence moles of Ag formed will be 10^{-6}

At equilibrium, (E_{cell} = 0)

$$E^0_{cell} = \frac{+0.0591}{2}\log_{10}\frac{[Zn^{2+}]}{[Ag^+]^2}$$

$$\therefore \frac{1.56\times 2}{0.0591} = \log\frac{[Zn^{+2}]}{[Ag^{+2}]^2} = 52.8$$

40. A.

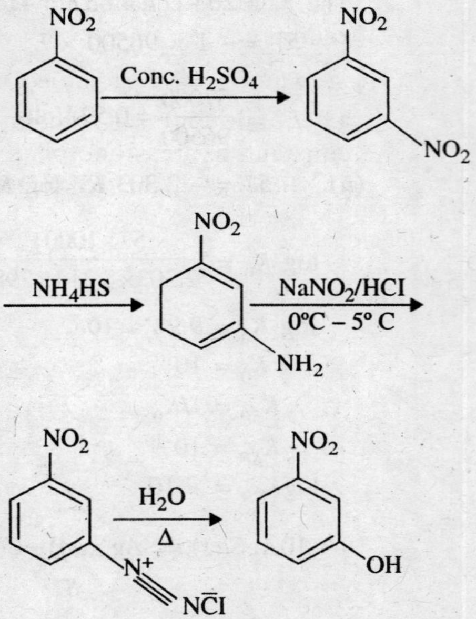

B.

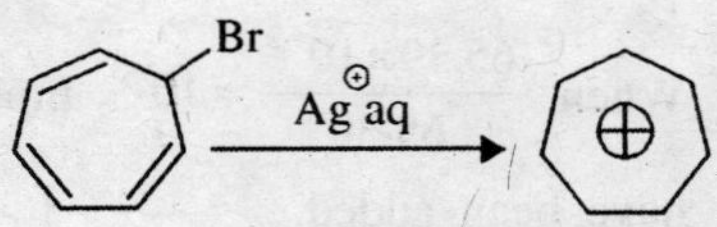

Aromatic ion (highly stable)
Satisfy $4n + 2$ rule with $n = 1$

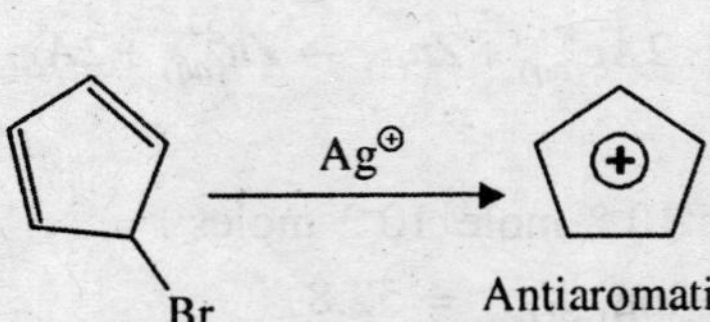

Antiaromatic ion (highly unstable) and therefore not formed

41. A. $Ag_2S + 4\,NaCN \rightarrow 2\,Na\,[Ag\,(CN)_2] + Na_2S$
Argentite — Sod. dicyanoargentate (I)

$$4Na_2S + 5O_2 + 2H_2O \rightarrow 2\,Na_2SO_4 + 4NaOH + 2S\downarrow$$

$$2Na\,[Ag\,(CN)_2] + Zn \rightarrow Na_2\,[Zn\,(CN)_4] + 2Ag\downarrow$$

Sod. tetracyanozincate (II)

41. B. (i) $C_6H_4(OH)_2 + 2AgBr \rightarrow 2Ag + C_6H_4O_2 + 2HBr$
Quinol — Quinone

(ii) $AgBr + 2Na_2S_2O_3 \rightarrow Na_3[Ag(S_2O_3)_2] + NaBr$
Sod. dithiosulphato-argentate (I)

42. The principal reaction is proton transfer to NH_3 from H_2O:

$$NH_3(aq) + H_2O(l) \rightleftharpoons NH_4^+(aq) + OH^-(aq)$$

Since NH_4^+ ions come both from the NH_4Cl present initially (0.45 M) and from the reaction of NH_3 with H_2O, the concentrations of the species involved in the principal reaction are as follows:

Principal reaction	$NH_3(aq)$ + $H_2O(l)$	⇌	$NH_4^+(aq)$ +	$OH^-(aq)$
Initial conc (M)	0.15		0.45	~ 0
Change (M)	− x		+ x	+ x
Equilibrium conc (M)	0.15 − x		0.45 + x	x

The equilibrium equation for the principal reaction is

$$K_b = 1.8\times 10^{-5} = \frac{[NH_4^+][OH^-]}{[NH_3]}$$

$$= \frac{(0.45+x)(x)}{0.15-x} \approx \frac{(0.45)(x)}{0.15}$$

We assume x is negligible compared to 0.45 and 0.15 because

(1) the equilibrium constant K_b is small and

(2) the equilibrium is shifted to the left by the common-ion effect. Therefore,

$$x = [OH^-] = \frac{(1.8\times10^{-5})(0.15)}{0.45}$$

$$= 6.0 \times 10^{-6} M$$

$$[NH_3] = 0.15 - x = 0.15 - (6.0 \times 10^{-6})$$

$$= 0.15\ M$$

$$[NH^+_4] = 0.45 + x = 0.45 + (6.0 \times 10^{-6})$$

$$= 0.45\ M$$

Thus, the assumption concerning the size of x is justified.

The H_3O^+ concentration and the pH are

$$[H_3O^+] = \frac{K_w}{[OH^-]} = \frac{1.0\times10^{-14}}{6.0\times10^{-6}}$$

$$= 1.7 \times 10^{-9}\ M$$

$$pH = -\log(1.7 \times 10^{-9}) = 8.77$$

The per cent dissociation of ammonia is

Per cent dissociation

$$= \frac{[NH_3]_{dissociated}}{[NH_3]_{initial}} \times 100\%$$

$$= \frac{6.0\times10^{-6}}{0.15} \times 100 = 0.0040\%$$

43. A. $$\log\frac{[NH_3]}{[NH_4^+]} = pH - pK_a$$

$$= 7.00 - 9.25 = -2.25$$

$$\frac{[NH_3]}{[NH_4^+]} = \text{antilog } (-2.25)$$

$$= 10^{-2.25} = 5.6 \times 10^{-3}$$

For a typical value of $[NH_4^+]$—say, 1.0 M—the NH_3 concentration would have to be very small (0.0056 M). Such a solution is a poor buffer because it has little capacity to absorb added acid. Also, because the $[NH_3]/[NH_4^+]$ ratio is far from unity, addition of a small amount of H_3O^+ or OH^- will result in a large change in pH.

B. The balanced equation for the solubility equilibrium:

$$Ag_2CrO_4(s) \rightleftharpoons 2Ag^+(aq) + CrO_4^{2-}(aq)$$

The exponents in the equilibrium constant expression for K_{sp} are the coefficients in the balanced equation. Therefore,

$$K_{sp} = [Ag^+]^2 [CrO_4^{2-}]$$

$$\therefore \quad K_{sp} = (2s)^2 s$$

$$= 4 s^3$$

where s is solubility of Ag_2CrO_4.

44. A. (*i*) Diaminchloridonitrito-*N*-platinum (II)

(*ii*) Potassium trioxalatochromate (III)

(*iii*) Dichloridobis (ethane- 1, 2-diamine) cobalt(III) chloride

(*iv*) Pentaaminecarbonatocobalt (III) chloride

(*v*) Mercury tetrathiocyanatocobaltate (III)

B.

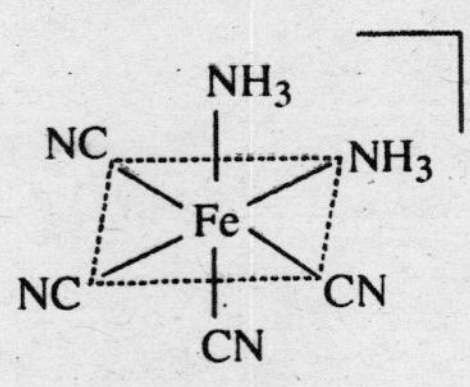

cis —

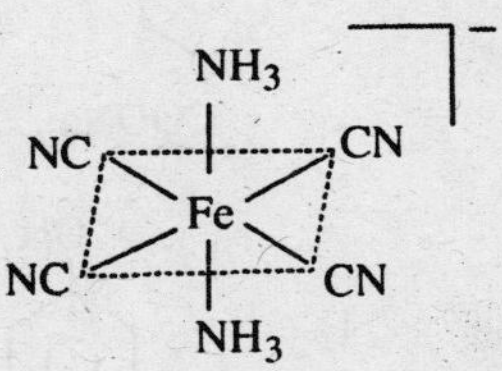

trans

(∵ NH_3 are on opposite side)

TEST PAPER-2

IMPORTANT INSTRUCTION FOR CANDIDATES

Questions 1-30 (Objective questions) carry three marks each and questions 31-44 (subjective questions) carry fifteen marks each.

1. The product obtained from the following reaction is:

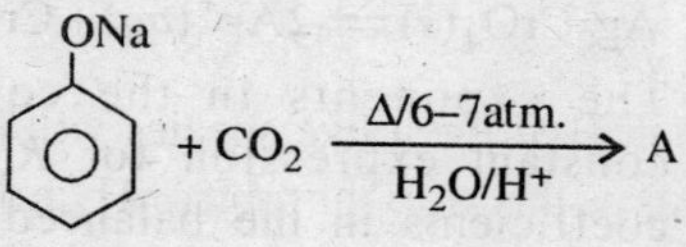

The product '*A*' is

A. 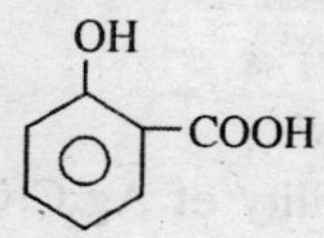

B. 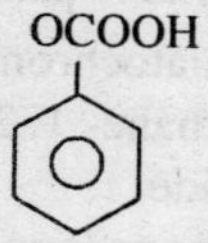

C. 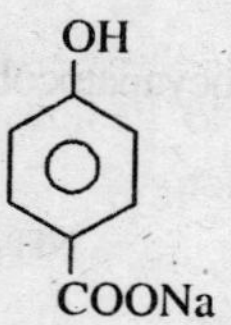

D. 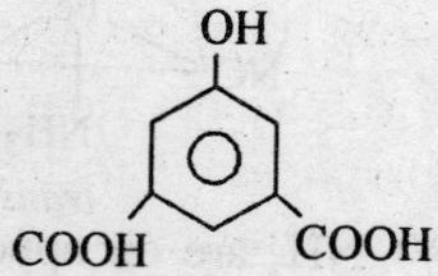

2. Benzamide on treatment with $POCl_3$ gives

A. Aniline

B. Benzonitrile

C. Chlorobenzene

D. Benzylamine

3. 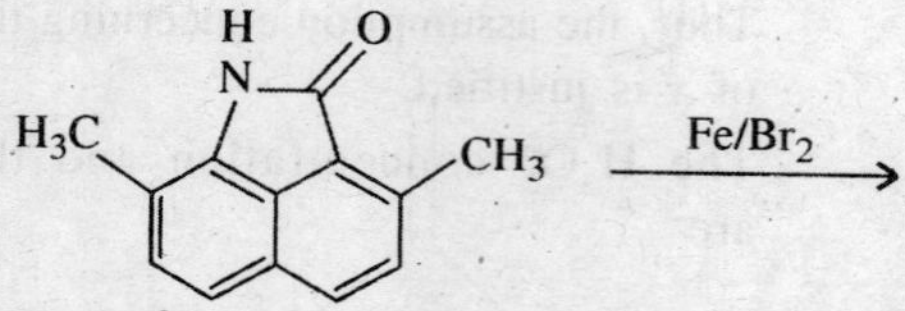

Product on monobromination of this compound is

A. 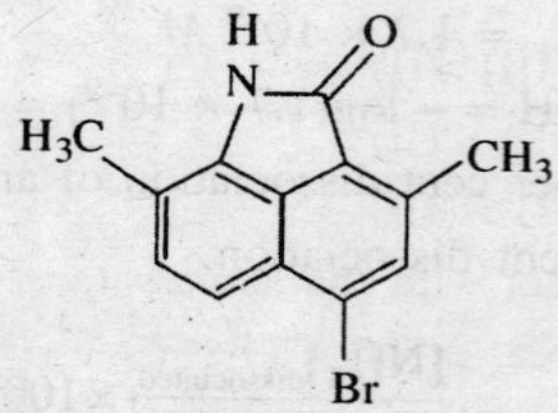

B. 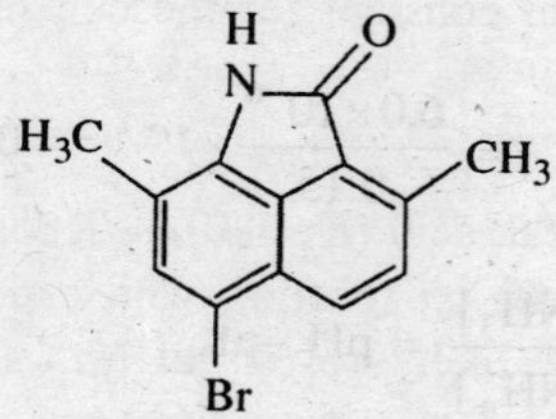

C. 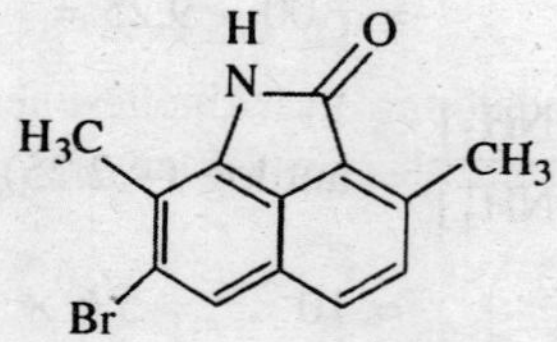

D. 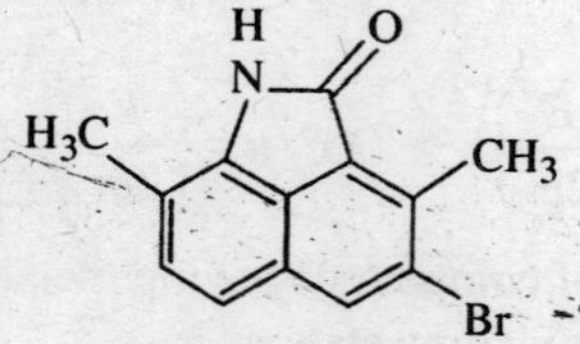

4. The order of reactivity of Phenyl Magnesium Bromide with the following compounds is

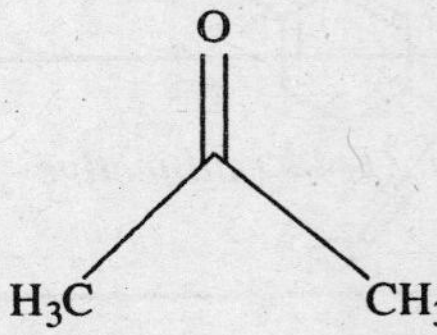
(I)

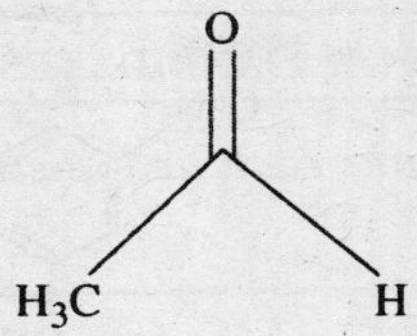
(II)

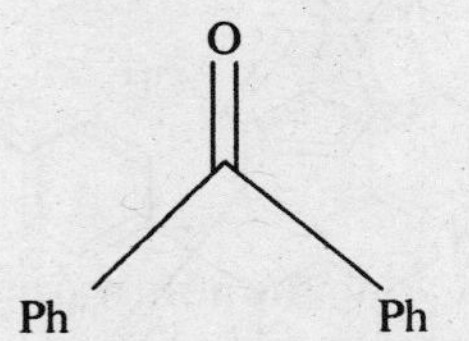
(III)

A. (II) > (III) > (I)
B. (I) > (III) > (II)
C. (II) > (I) > (III)
D. All react with the same rate

5. $Zn|Zn^{2+}$ $(a = 0.1M)$ || Fe^{2+} $(a = 0.01\ M)|Fe$. The emf of the above cell is 0.2905 V. Equilibrium constant for the cell reaction is

A. $10^{0.32/0.0591}$ B. $10^{0.32/0.0295}$
C. $10^{0.26/0.0295}$ D. $e^{0.32/0.295}$

6. HX is a weak acid ($K_a = 10^{-5}$). It forms a salt NaX (0.1 M) on reacting with caustic soda. The degree of hydrolysis of NaX is

A. 0.01% B. 0.0001%
C. 0.1% D. 0.5%

7. For a monoatomic gas kinetic energy = E. The relation with rms velocity is

A. $u = \left(\frac{2E}{m}\right)^{1/2}$ B. $u = \left(\frac{3E}{2m}\right)^{1/2}$

C. $u = \left(\frac{E}{2m}\right)^{1/2}$ D. $u = \left(\frac{E}{3m}\right)^{1/2}$

8. The pair of compounds having metals in their highest oxidation state is

A. MnO_2, $FeCl_3$
B. $[MnO_4]^-$, CrO_2Cl_2
C. $[Fe(CN)_6]^{3-}$, $[CoCN)_3]$
D. $[NiCl_4]^{2-}$, $[CoCl_4]^-$

9. The compound having tetrahedral geometry is

A. $[Ni(CN)_4]^{2-}$ B. $[Pd(CN)_4]^{2-}$
C. $[PdCl_4]^{2-}$ D. $[NiCl_4]^{2-}$

10. Spin only magnetic moment of the compound $Hg[Co(SCN)_4]$ is

A. $\sqrt{3}$ B. $\sqrt{15}$
C. $\sqrt{24}$ D. $\sqrt{8}$

11. Which Hydrogen like species will have same radius as that of Bohr orbit of Hydrogen atom?

A. $n = 2$, Li^{+2} B. $n = 2$, Be^{3+}
C. $n = 2$, He^+ D. $n = 3$, Li^{2+}

12.

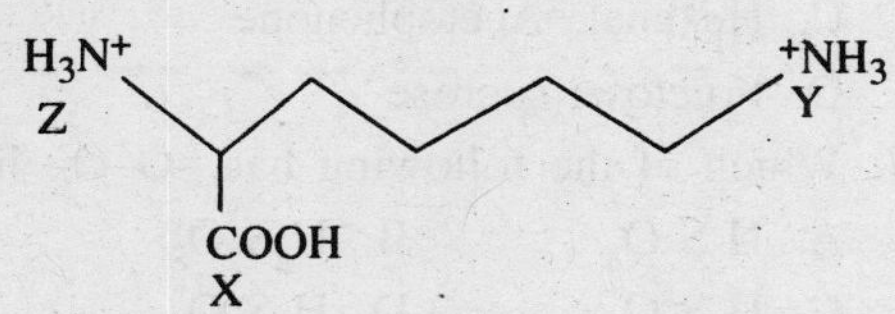

Arrange in order of increasing acidic strength

A. $X > Z > Y$ B. $Z < X > Y$
C. $X > Y > Z$ D. $Z > X > Y$

13. 2 mol of an ideal gas expanded isothermally and reversibly from 1 litre to 10 litres at 300 K. What is the enthalpy change?

A. 4.98 kJ B. 11.47 kJ
C. –11.47 kJ D. 0 kJ

14. (A) follows first order reaction. (A) → product Concentration of A, changes from 0.1 M to 0.025 M in 40 minutes. Find the rate of reaction of A when concentration of A is 0.01 M

A. $3.47 \times 10^{-4}\ M\ min^{-1}$
B. 3.47×10^{-5} , $M\ min^{-1}$
C. $1.73 \times 10^{-4}\ M\ min^{-1}$
D. $1.73 \times 10^{-5}\ M\ min^{-1}$

15. An aromatic compound $C_7H_6Cl_2$ (A), Gives AgCl on boiling with alcoholic $AgNO_2$ solution and yields C_7H_7OCl on treatment with sodium hydroxide. (A) on oxidation gives monochlorobenzoic acid. The compound (A) is

A. 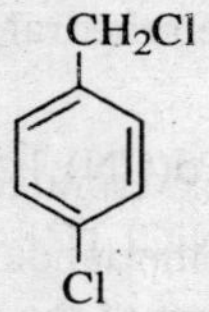 B. 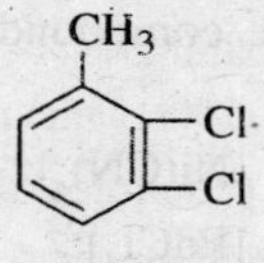

C. 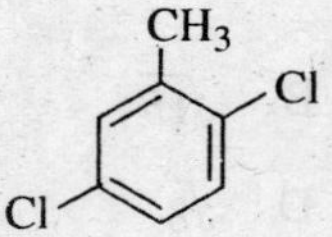 D. 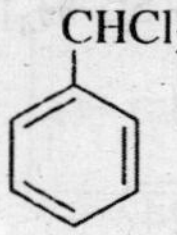

16. Which of the following pairs give positive Tollen's test?

A. Glucose, sucrose

B. Glucose, fructose

C. Hexanal, Acetophenone

D. Fructose, sucrose

17. Which of the following has –O–O– linkage

A. $H_2S_2O_6$ B. $H_2S_2O_8$

C. $H_2S_2O_3$ D. $H_2S_4O_6$

18. Among the following, the molecule with the highest dipole moment is:

A. CH_3Cl B. CH_2Cl_2

C. $CHCl_3$ D. CCl_4

19. 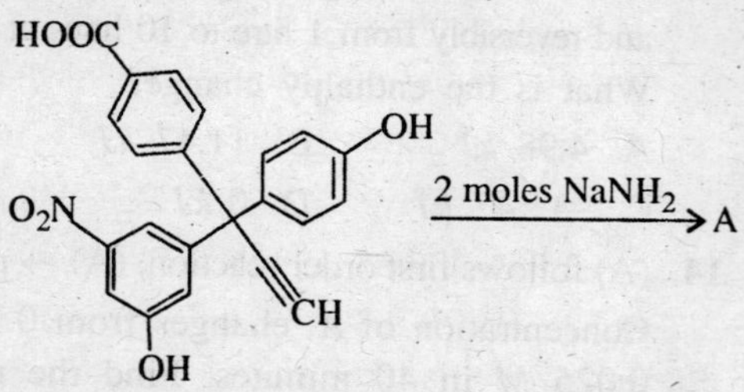

The product *A* will be

A. 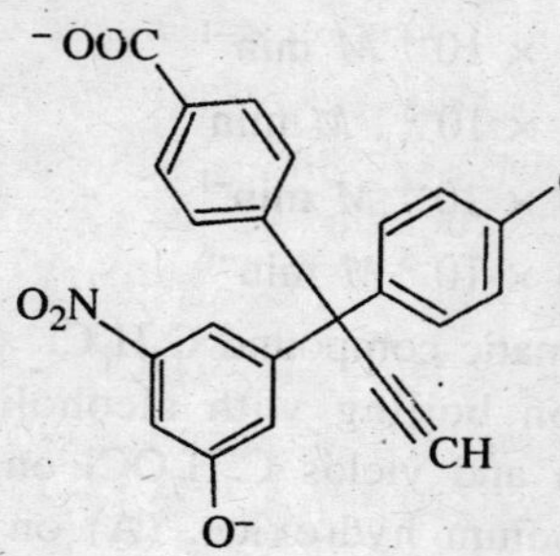

B. 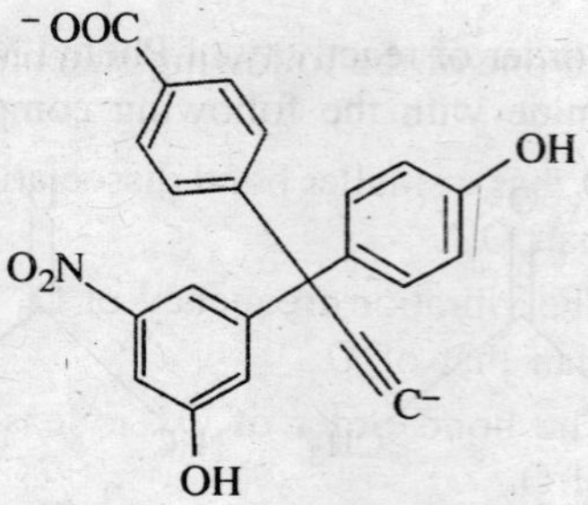

C. 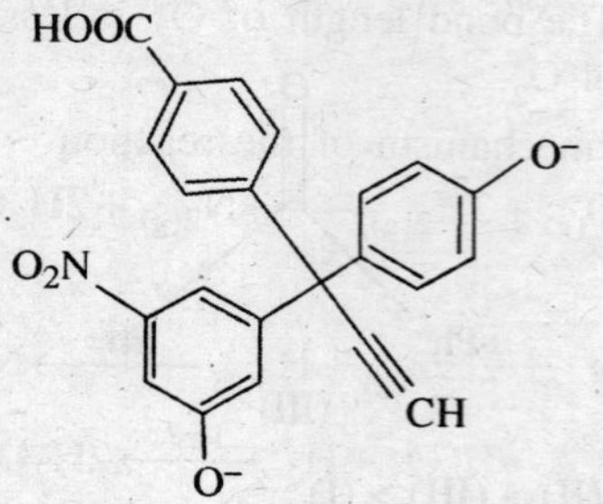

D. 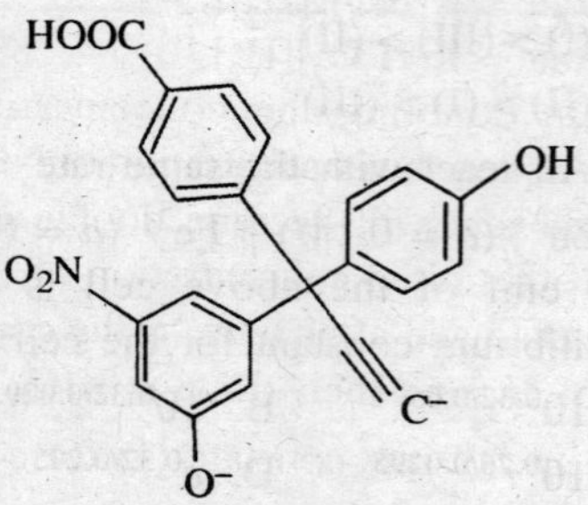

20. In a homogeneous catalytic reaction, 1.9 *M* of substrate and 1.0 μ*M* of a catalyst yields 1.0 *mM* of a product in 10 seconds. The turnover frequency (TOF) of the reaction (s^{-1}) is

A. 10^{-2} B. 10^{2}

C. 10^{3} D. 10^{-3}

21. Which of the following has lowest pKa value

A. 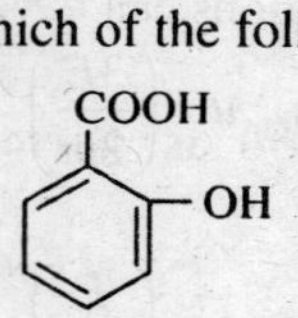 B. 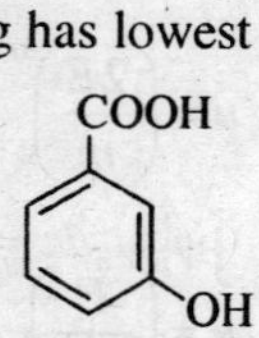

C. 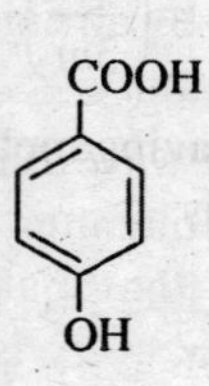 D. 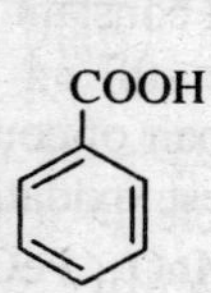

22. Which one of the following statements is not true?

A. O_2 has a smaller bond dissociation energy than O_2^+.

B. The vibration frequency of O_2^+ is greater than that of O_2.

C. The bond order of O_2^- is less than that of O_2.

D. The bond length of O_2^+ is less than that of O_2.

23. The mechanism of the reaction

$$2NO_{(g)} + 2H_{2(g)} \longrightarrow N_{2(g)} + 2H_2O_{(g)}$$

is

Step 1 : $2NO_{(g)} + H_{2(g)} \xrightarrow{\text{Slow}} N_2 + H_2O_2$

Step 2 : $H_2O_2 + H_2 \xrightarrow{\text{Fast}} 2H_2O$

A. Rate = $K[NO]^2[H_2]^2$

B. Rate = $K[H_2O_2][H_2]$

C. On doubling the concentration of H_2, keeping the concentration of NO constant, the rate will become double.

D. If the initial concentration of H_2 and NO is CO and after time '*t*' the concentration of N_2 is x then Rate = $K(C_0 - 2x)^x$

24. The unit of rate constant (k) for a zero-order reaction is

A. s^{-1} B. $L\ mol^{-1}\ s^{-1}$

C. s D. $mol\ L^{-1}\ s^{-1}$

25. Which of the following statements about the eigenfunctions is NOT true:

A. Eigenfunctions belonging to different eigenvalues are orthogonal.

B. No two eigenfunctions can have the same eigenvalue.

C. An eigenfunction is normalized if $\int \psi_n^* \psi_n d\tau = 1$.

D. A constant multiplied by an eigenfunction is still an eigenfunction.

26. If $\psi(x)$ is the normalised wave function of a particle in a particular quantum state, the probability of finding that particle at a position between x and $x + dx$ is:

A. $\psi(x)\ dx$

B. $\psi^*(x)dx$

C. $\psi^*(x).\psi(x)$

D. $\psi^*(x)\ \psi(x)\ dx$

(*denotes the complex conjugate)

27. Which one among the compounds A-D will have highest dipole moment?

1. 

2. 

3. 

4. 

A. 1 B. 2

C. 3 D. 4

28. The one among the compounds given below, with highest dipole moment is:

A. napthalene B. phenanthrene

C. anthracene D. azulene

29. The major products formed in the nitration (HNO_3 / H_2SO_4) of aniline and acetanilide are

A. *o*-nitroaniline and *o*-nitroacetanilide

B. *m*-nitroaniline and *p*-nitroacetanilide

C. *p*-nitroaniline and *m*-nitroacetanilide

D. *m*-nitroaniline and *m*-nitroacetanilide

30. An aromatic amine (X) was treated with alcoholic potash and another compound (Y) when a foul-smelling gas was formed with formula C_6H_5NC, (Y) was formed by reacting a compound (Z) with Cl_2 in presence of slaked lime. The comound (Z) is

A. $C_6H_5NH_2$ B. CH_3OH

C. CH_3COCH_3 D. $CHCl_3$

31. A. Write the IUPAC names of $HCO(CO)_3$ and $HRh(CO)(PPh_3)_2$ and mention the oxidation states of Co and Rh.

B. Why does KHF_2 exists but $KHCl_2$ does not?

C. AiF_3 is insoluble in liquid HF, but dissolves if NaF is present. When BF_3 is added to the solution, AlF_3 precipitates. Explain.

D. The conductivity of BrF_3 is increased by adding either AgF or SnF_4, Explain.

32. A. Draw the structure of S_4N_4.

B. Calculate the CFSE (Crystal Field Stabilization Energy) of $[TiCl_6]^{3-}$ if the λ_{max} is 770 *nm*.

33. A. Naphthalene has zero dipole moment whereas its isomer Azulene has a dipole moment of 0.8 Debye. Explain.

B. Which resonance structure among the following is more stable. Explain.

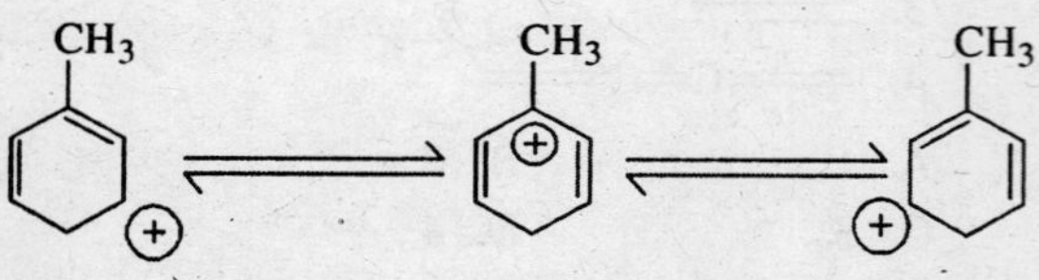

I II III

C. Although phenoxide ion has more number of resonating structures than benzoate ion, bonzoic acid is stronger acid than phenol. Why?

34. How do you convert benzene into following compounds?

A. 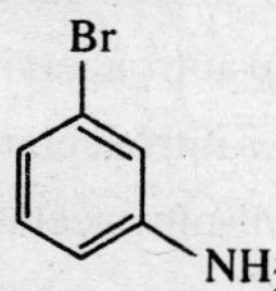 B. 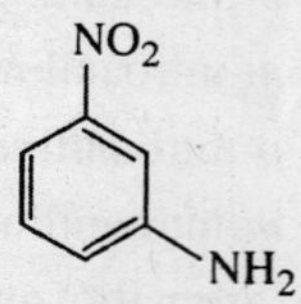

C. 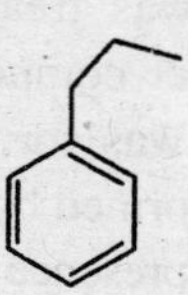 D. 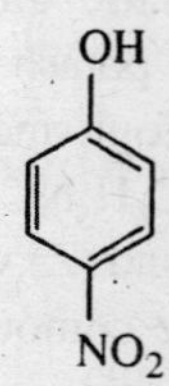

E. 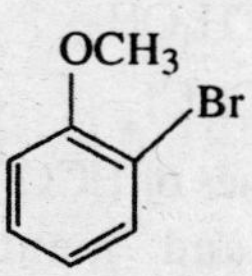 F. 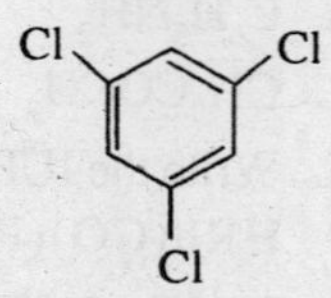

35. A. The Schrodinger wave equation for hydrogen atoms is

$$\Psi_{2s} = \frac{1}{4(2\pi)^{1/2}}\left(\frac{1}{a_0}\right)^{3/2}\left(2-\frac{r}{a_0}\right)e^{-r/a}$$

where a_0 is Bohr's radius. Let the radial node in 2*s* be at r_0. Then find *r* in terms of a_0.

B. A base ball having mass 100g moves with velocity 100 m/sec. Find out the value of wave length of base ball.

C. ${}_{92}X^{234} \xrightarrow[-6\beta]{-7\alpha} Y$. Find out atomic number, mass number of *Y* and identify it.

D. Prove that equilibrium constant for reaction $N_2O_4 \rightleftarrows 2NO_2$ is $4\alpha^2P/1 - \alpha^2$.

36. A. Find the heat of formation of ethyl alcohol.

$C(S) + O_2(g) = CO_2(g)\ \Delta H = -94\ k$ cal

$H_2(g) + \frac{1}{2}O_2(g) = H_2O(g)\ \Delta H = -68\ k$ cal

$C_2H_5OH(l) + 3O_2(g) = 2CO_2(g) + 3H_2O(l)$

$\Delta H = -327\ k$ cal

B. $\gamma = C_p/C_v$ for ozone is 1.15. Assuming ideal gas behaviour, is the molecule linear or nonlinear?

C. The gas-phase rearrangement reaction:

vinylallylether $\rightarrow$ allyl acetone

has a rate constant of 6.015×10^{-5} at 420 K and a rate constant of $2.971 \times 10^{-3}\ s^{-1}$ at 470 K. Calculate the values of a Arrhenius parameters A and E_a. Calculate the values of $\Delta H^{\neq}$ and $\Delta S^{\neq}$ at 420 K.

37. For the given reaction

$A + B \rightarrow$ Products

Following data were given

Initial conc. (m/L). [A]	Initial conc. (m/L) [*B*]	Initial rate [$mL^{-1}s^{-1}$]
0.1	0.1	0.05
0.2	0.1	0.1
0.1	0.2	0.05

A. Write the rate equation.

B. Calculate the rate constant.

C. 100 ml of a liquid contained in an isolated container at a pressure of 1 bar. The pressure is steeply increased to 100 bar. The volume of the liquid is decreased by 1 ml at this constant pressure. Find the ΔH and ΔU.

38. 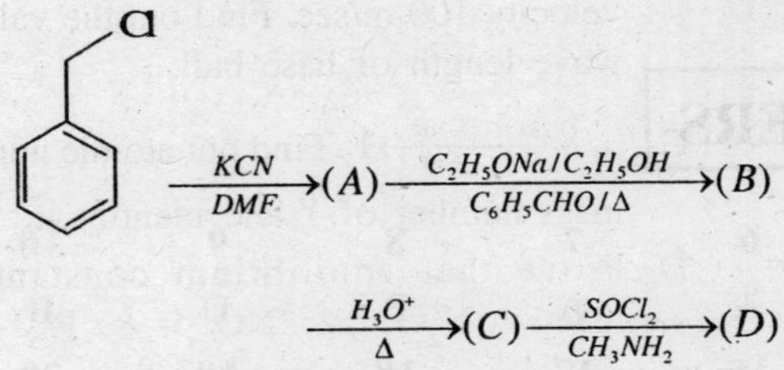

Identify A to D.

39. A_1 and A_2 are two ores of metal M. A_1 on calcination gives black precipitate, CO_2 and water.

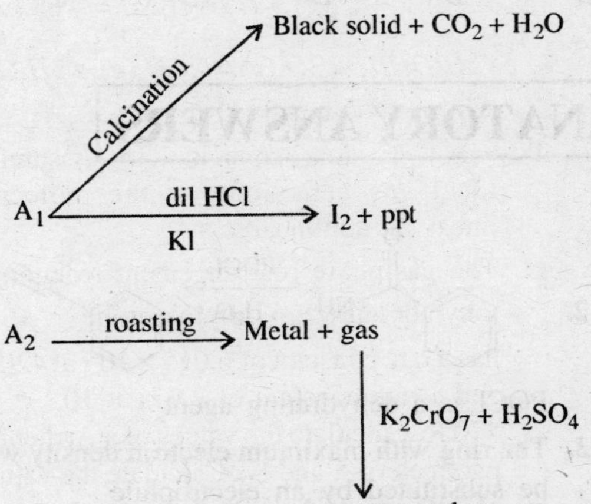

Identify A_1 and A_2.

40. A. Find the equilibrium constant for the reaction

$$Cu^{+2} + In^{+2} \rightleftharpoons Cu^{+} + In^{+3}$$

Given that

$$E^{\circ}_{Cu^{+2}/Cu^{+}} = 0.15\ V$$

$$E^{\circ}_{In^{+2}/In^{+}} = -0.4\ V$$

$$E^{\circ}_{In^{+3}/In^{+}} = -0.42\ V$$

B. An organic compound 'P' having the molecular formula $C_5H_{10}O$ treated with dil H_2SO_4 gives two compounds, Q and R both gives positive iodoform test. The reaction of $C_5H_{10}O$ with dil H_2SO_4 gives reaction 10^{15} times faster then ethylene. Identify organic compound of Q and R. Give the reason for the extra stability of P.

41. A. Convert Benzene to methyl orange.

B. An organic aromatic compound (A) on treatment with $CHCl_3$ and KOH gives (B) and (C), both of which, in turn, give the same compound (D) when distilled with zinc dust. Oxidation of (D) yields E of the formula $C_7H_6O_2$. The sodium salt of (E) on heating with soda lime gives F, which can also be obtained by distilling (A) with zinc dust. Identify (A), (B), (C), (D), (E) and (F).

C. Why mineral acid is added in excess in diazotisation of aryl amines.

42. A. What is the ground state energy for an electron. Which is confined to a potential well (one dimensional box) having a width of 0.2 nm?

B. Calculate ionic strength of a solution containing 0.1m KNO_3, 0.15m K_2SO_4 and 0.023 m $La_2(SO_4)_3$.

C. Calculate the free energy change when 2 moles of an ideal gas expand from an initial pressure of 700 mm to a final pressure of 70 mm at 27°C, R = 2 cal. $deg^{-1}\ mol^{-1}$.

43. Complete the following by identifying [*A*] to [*H*]

A. $CuSO_4.5H_2O \xrightarrow{100°C} [A] \xrightarrow{280°C} [B] \xrightarrow{800°C} [C] + [D]$

B. $AgNO_3 \xrightarrow{\text{red heat}} [E][F] + O_2$

C. $Na_2B_4O_7 \xrightarrow{740°C} [G] + [H]$

44. A. When a white crystalline compound X is heated with $K_2Cr_2O_7$ and concentrated H_2SO_4 a reddish brown gas A is evolved. On passing A into caustic soda solution, a yellow coloured solution of B is obtained. Neutralizing the solution B with acetic acid and on subsequent addition of lead acetate, a yellow precipitate C is obtained. When X is heated with NaOH solution, a colourless gas is evolved and on passing this gas into K_2HgI_4 solution, a reddish brown precipitate D is formed. Identify A, B, C, D and X. Write the equations of the reactions involved.

B. $HgCl_2$ and $SnCl_2$ cannot exist together in an aqueous solution. Why?

ANSWERS

1	2	3	4	5	6	7	8	9	10
A	B	B	C	B	A	A	B	D	B
11	**12**	**13**	**14**	**15**	**16**	**17**	**18**	**19**	**20**
B	A	D	A	A	B	B	A	A	A
21	**22**	**23**	**24**	**25**	**26**	**27**	**28**	**29**	**30**
A	D	C	D	B	D	B	D	B	C

SOME SELECTED EXPLANATORY ANSWERS

1. Kolbe's Schmidt Reaction

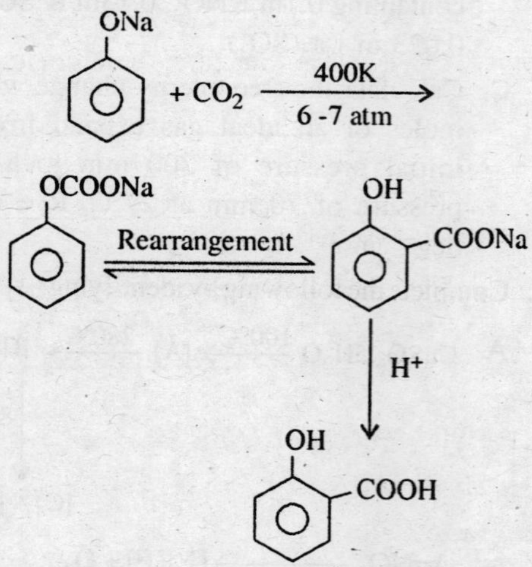

Salicylic Acid

2. 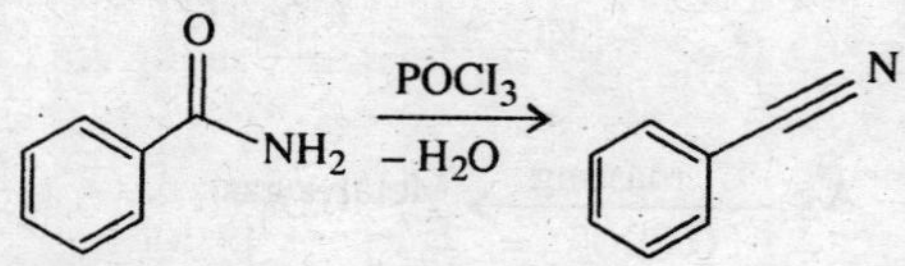

$POCl_3$ is a dehydrating agent

3. The ring with maximum electron density will be substituted by an electrophile

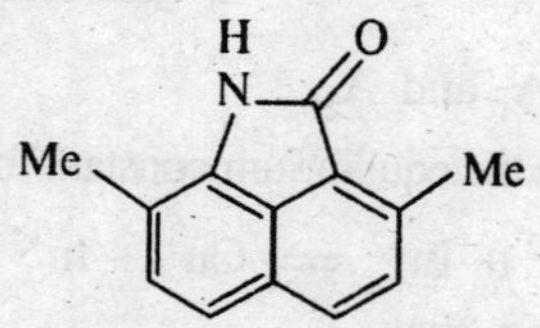

The ring attached with – NH will have rich electron density due to resonance. As ortho position is blocked, the electrophile attacks the para position.

4. Nucleophile attacks the most electrophilic site first. Among aldehyde and a ketone, aldehydes are more electrophilic as in ketones the δ + charge an carbonyl carbon is decreased by + I effect of both alkyl groups

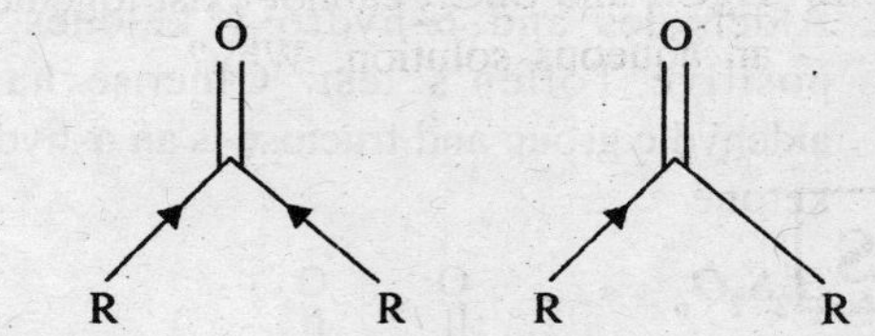

More over in the tetrahedral intermediate aldehydes have less steric repulsion than ketone and aldehydes increases the *–ve* charge on oxygen less in comparison to ketones

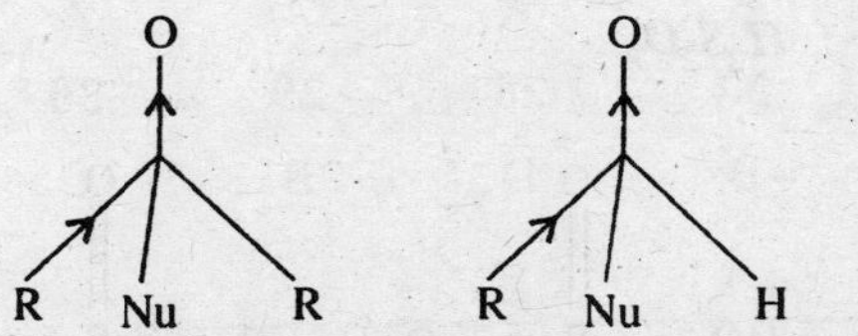

Based on the above the order of reactivity is (II) > (I) > (III)

5. $E = E° - \frac{0.0591}{n} \log Kc$

$0.2905 = E° - \frac{0.0591}{n} \log \frac{0.1}{0.01}$

$E° = 0.2905 + 0.0295 = 0.32$

$E° = \frac{0.0591}{n} \log K$

$0.32 = \frac{0.0591}{2} \log K$

$K = 10^{0.32/0.0295}$

6. $X^- + H_2O \rightarrow HX + OH^-$

$(1 - \alpha)C \quad\quad \alpha C \quad \alpha C$

$K_h = \frac{K_w}{K_a} = 10^{-9}$

$K_h = C\alpha^2 = 10^{-9}$

$\alpha^2 = 10^{-8} \Rightarrow \alpha = 10^{-4}$

% degree of dissociation $= 10^{-4} \times 100$

$= 0.01\%$

7. $P = \frac{1}{3} \times \frac{m}{v} \times c^2$ (c = rms velocity)

$\Rightarrow \sqrt{\frac{3PV}{m}} = c$

For 1 molecule $PV = kT \Rightarrow c = \sqrt{\frac{3kT}{m}}$

$\therefore KE = \frac{3}{2}kT \Rightarrow 2KE = 3kT$

$\Rightarrow c = \sqrt{\frac{2KE}{m}}$

8. $[MnO_4]^-$, $Mn = +7$

CrO_2Cl_2, $Cr = +6$

9. Ni^{2+},

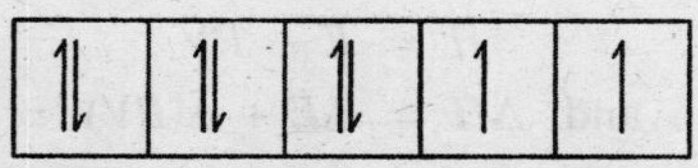

3d

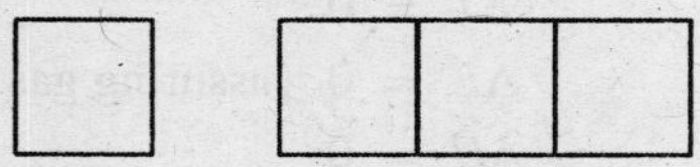

4s 4p

Since Cl^- is weak ligand it will not cause pairing

$[NiCl_4]^{2-}$

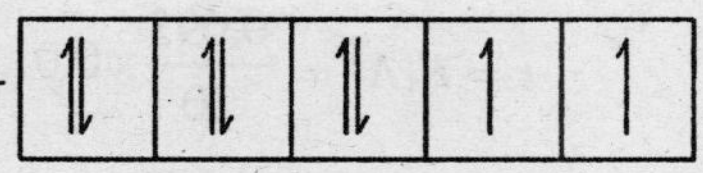

3d

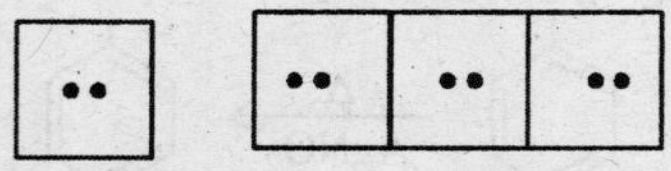

4s 4p

Hybridisation of $[NiCl_4]^{2-} = sp^3$

Shape of $[NiCl_4]^{2-}$ = Tetrahedral

10. $Hg[Co(SCN)_4]$

Co^{+2} =

3d

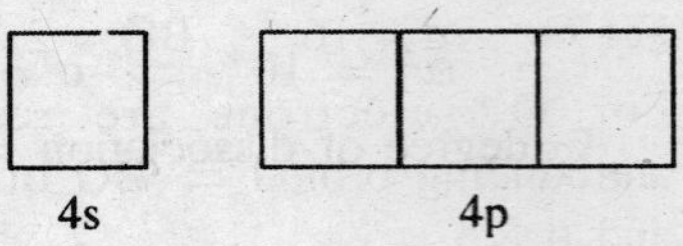

$n = 3$

$\mu_s = \sqrt{n(n+2)} = \sqrt{3\times5} = \sqrt{15}$

11. $r = \dfrac{n^2 r_{1(H^+)}}{z}$

$\because r = r_{(H^+)} \therefore n^2 = z$

$\therefore n = 2, z = 4$

so $r_{2(Be^{+3})} = r_{1(H^+)}$

12. *pKa* value of carboxylic group is less than *pKa* of $-N^+H_3$ (*Y*) in amino acid and $-\overset{+}{N}H_3(Z)$ will have comparatively less *pKa* than $-\overset{+}{N}H_3(Z)$ due to –I effect of carboxylate group.

13.

$$H = E + PV$$

and $\Delta H = \Delta E + \Delta(PV)$

or $\Delta H = \Delta E + nR\Delta T$

$\Delta T = 0$

$\Delta E = 0$ {assuring gas to be ideal}

$\therefore \Delta H = 0$

14. Concentration changes from 0.01 to 0.025 *M* in 40 minutes $\Rightarrow 2t_{1/2} = 40$ min $t_{1/2} = 20$ min

$$r = K[A] = \frac{0.693}{20}\times0.01 = 3.47\times10^{-4}$$

15.

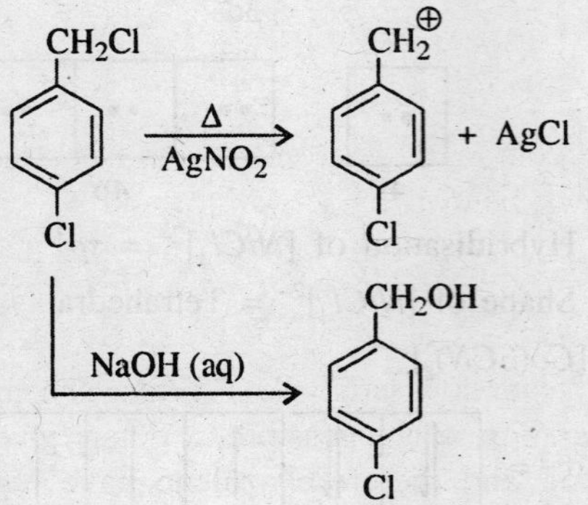

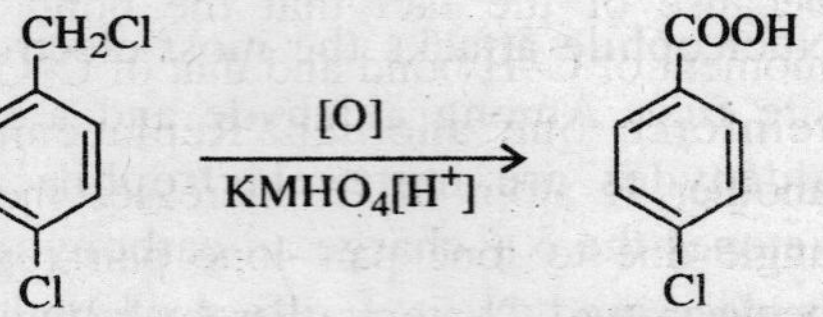

(Monochloro benzoic acid)

16. Aldehydes and α-hydroxy ketones give positive Tollen's test. Glucose has an aldehydic group and fructose is an α-hydroxy ketone

17. $H_2S_2O_6$

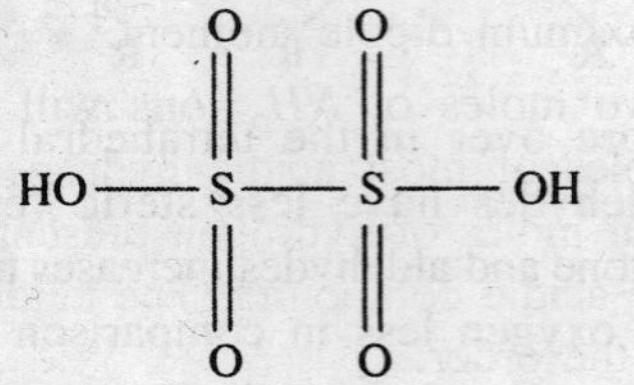

$H_2S_2O_8$

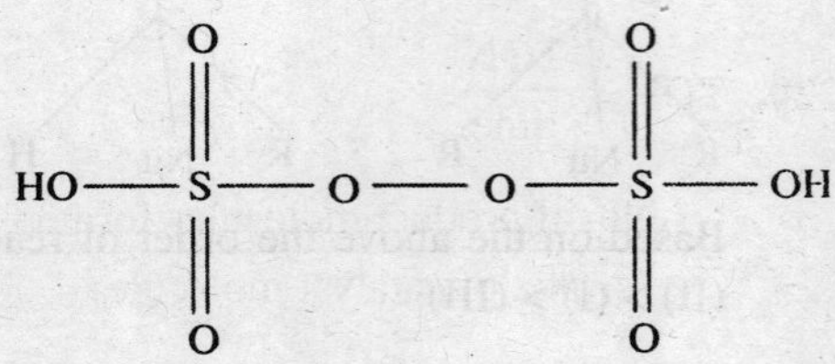

(peroxy linkage)

$H_2S_2O_3$

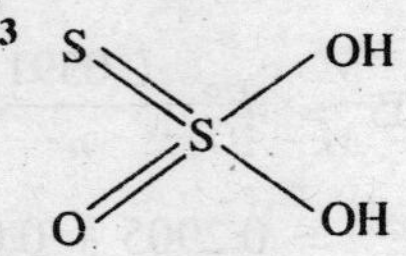

$H_2S_4O_6$

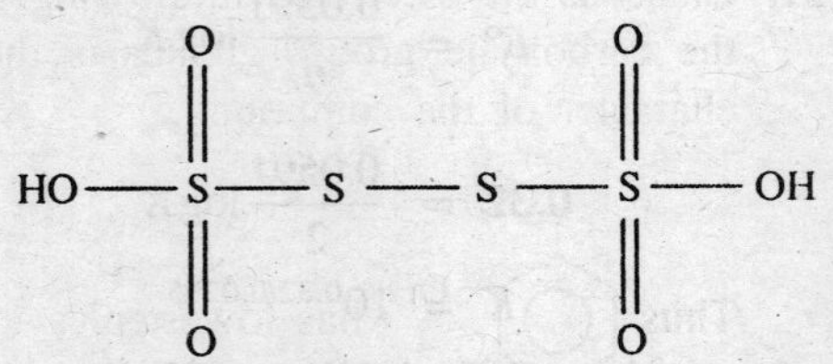

18. Methane molecule being symmetrical, has zero dipole moment. Replacement of one of the H– atoms by Cl atom increases the dipole moment. The increase in dipole moment is rather more than what can be expected because of the fact that the bond dipole moment of C–H bond and that of C–Cl bond reinforce one another. Replacement of another H atom of Cl increases the bond angle due to lone pair–lone pair repulsion between two Cl-atoms thereby reducing the dipole moment of the molecule. Increase in angle is again caused by the introduction of third Cl– atom. When the fourth Cl– atom is introduced, the molecule (CCl_4) again becomes symmetrical and dipole moment reduces to zero. So, CH_3Cl will have the maximum dipole moment.

19. Two moles of NH_2 ions will abstract two moles of most acidic hydrogen out of the four moles of hydrogen present per mole of the acidic compound. The acidic strength is in the order:

–COOH > –OH (phenolic deactivated by NO_2 group) > –OH (phenolic) > alkynic H.

20. $\text{TOF} = \dfrac{\text{TON}}{\text{time}}$

$$= \frac{\text{No. of product molecules formed}}{\text{No. of catalyst molecules}} \times \frac{1}{\text{time}}$$

$$= \frac{1.0mM}{1.0\mu M} \times \frac{1}{10\,\text{sec}}$$

$$= \frac{1.0 \times 10^{-3} M}{1.0 \times 10^{-6} M} \times \frac{1}{10\,\text{sec}}$$

$= 10^2\ \text{sec}^{-1}$

21. Closer is the electron withdrawing group to the carboxylic group, greater is the acidic character of the compound.

Thus 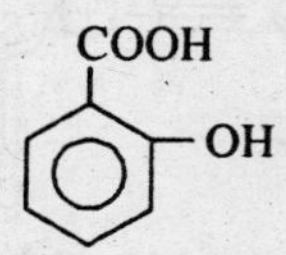 has lowest pKa value.

22. $\uparrow\downarrow$ $\sigma 1s$, $\uparrow\downarrow$ $\sigma^* 1s$, $\uparrow\downarrow$ $\sigma 2s$, $\uparrow\downarrow$ $\sigma^* 2s$, $\uparrow\downarrow$ $\sigma 2P_x$,

$\uparrow\downarrow$ $\pi 2P_y$ = $\uparrow\downarrow$ $\pi 2P_z$, $\uparrow\downarrow$ $\pi^* 2P_y$ = 1 $\pi^* 2P_z$

For O_2 $n = 16$ BO = 2

For O_2^+ electrons are removed from antibonding orbital $\Rightarrow$ BO of O_2^+ increases and it 2.5.

Now $\nu = \dfrac{1}{2\pi}\sqrt{\dfrac{k}{m}}$

for O_2^+ k is more and therefore its vibrational frequency is more.

23. Slowest step is rate determining

$\therefore$ Rate = $K[NO]^2[H_2]$

$\therefore$ on doubling the concentration of H_2 without changing the concentration of NO, the rate will become double.

24. In general, the unit of rate constant for n^{th} order reaction is given by

M^{1-n}. time^{-1} = (mol / L)$^{1-n}$. time^{-1}

= mol^{1-n}. L^{n-1}. time^{-1}

Hence for zero order reaction:

M^{1-0} sec^{-1} = mol. L^{-1}. sec^{-1}

27. 'B' can exist in the following stable resonance form in which the ring gets aromatic nature (Recall that the cyclopropenyl anion is aromatic as it has two π-electrons, which is a Huckel number). Hence it has the highest dipole moment among all.

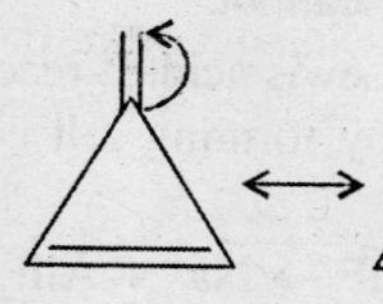

28. 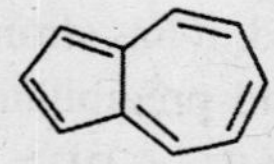

(azulene)

The compound is aromatic and has structure shown below:

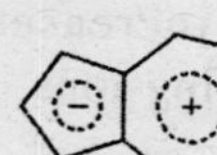

Both ring now satisfy $4x + 2$ rule. The charge separation is not possible in others given in option and therefore azulene have highest dipole moment.

29. In nitration mixture, aniline is protonated and anilinium ion is formed. As $-NH_3^+$ is a deactivating group, the orientation of the substitution is meta.
$-NH_2$ group is highly activating due to availability of lone pair on nitrogen to the ring.
Whereas, $-NH_3^+$ is highly deactivating as there is no lone pair available to the ring. It is now engaged with the proton added.
In case of acetanilide, the major product is para isomer. The other isomer possible is ortho but it is formed in minor quantity due to stearic factors.

30. 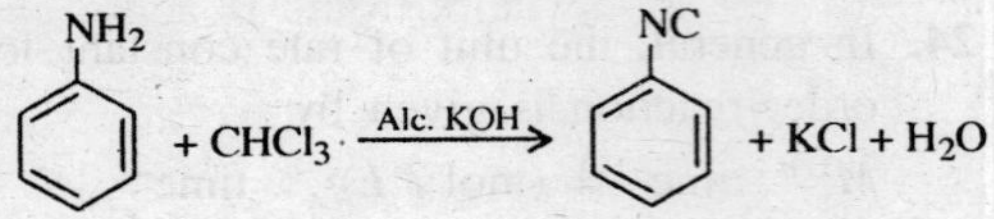

$$CH_3-\overset{\overset{O}{\|}}{C}-CH_3 + Cl_2 \xrightarrow{Ca(OH)_2} CHCl_3 + (CH_3COO)_2Ca.$$
(Z) (Y)

31. A. $HCo(CO)_3$ – Tricarbonylhydridocobalt (I)
$HRh(CO)(PPh_3)_2$ – Carbonylhydridobis (triphenylphosphine)rhodium (I)

B. HF can form strong hydrogen bonds where as HCl cannot. Hence HF_2^- ion can exist and HCl_2^- cannot.

C. AlF_3 is a Lewis acid. It reacts with F^- ion and thus by forming salt containing Na^+ and AlF_4^-

$AlF_3 + NaF \rightarrow Na^+ + AlF_4^-$

When BF_3 is added, it has stronger affinity for the F^- ions and precipitates out AlF_3

$AlF_4^- + BF_3 \rightarrow AlF_3 + BF_4^-$

Stronger acid replaces the weaker from its salt).

D. Conductivity is increased due to formation of following ions

$BrF_3 + AgF \leftrightarrow BrF_4^- + Ag^+$
(AgF is acting as a base)

$BrF_3 + SnF_4 \leftrightarrow BrF_2^+ + SnF_5^-$
(SnF_4 is acting as a acid)

$2BrF_3 + SnF \leftrightarrow 2\ BrF_4^+ + SnF_6^-$

32. A. 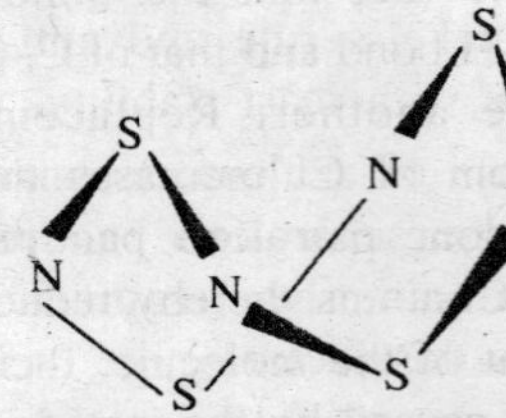

B. The energy corresponding to λ_{max} = 770 *nm* can be calculated as

$$E = \frac{hc}{\lambda_{max}}$$

$$= \frac{6.625\times10^{-34}\ J.sec\times3\times10^{8}\ m.sec^{-1}}{770\times10^{-9}\ m}$$

$= 2.58 \times 10^{-19} J$

$= 2.58 \times 10^{-22}\ kJ$ per one molecule

$= 2.58 \times 10^{-22}\ kJ \times 6.023 \times 10^{23}$

$= 155\ kJ$ per mole

This energy is equal to the magnitude of energy separation (Δ_o) between t_{2g} and e_g in the octahedral complex $[TiCl_6]^{3-}$.

E.C. of Ti^{3+} in the complex is $3d^1$ and the only electron occupies the t_{2g}.

Hence the CFSE = $1 \times -2/5\ \Delta_o$

$= -\ 2/5 \times 155$

$= 62$ kJ. $mole^{-1}$.

33. A. The resonance hybrid of Azulene is contributed by stable zwitter ionic resonance forms (II and III). Hence it has dipole moment. Resonance forms (II and III) are aromatic as they contain six π-electrons in both the rings and hence are stable.

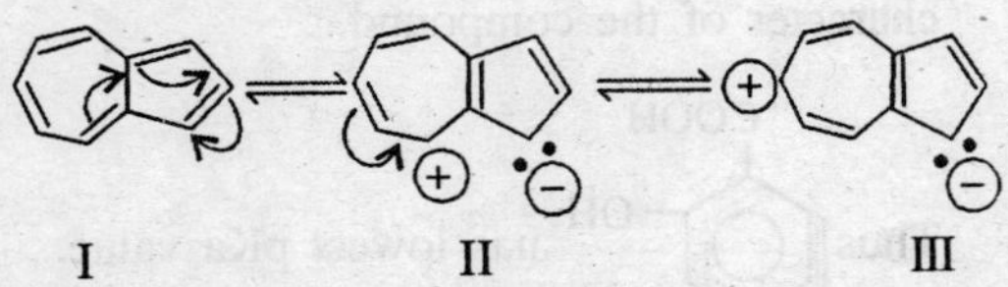

I II III

Whereas naphthalene cannot be stable in this type of zwitter ionic form with charge separation. Only non polar neutral forms are aromatic and stable. Hence it is non polar. The structure with charge separation is considered to be less stable.

In case of Naphthalene, this form will not satisfy Huckel's rule and anti-aromatic and hence with least stability.

But in case of azulene, resonance form with charge separation becomes more important as the aromatic nature outweighs this factor.

B. II is particularly stable as the positively charged carbon is directly attached to the methyl group, which stabilizes the positive charge by +I effect (electron releasing effect). I and III are equally stable.

C. The resonating structures are

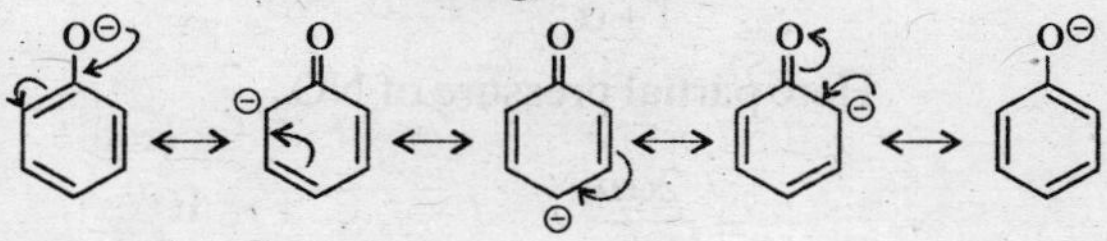

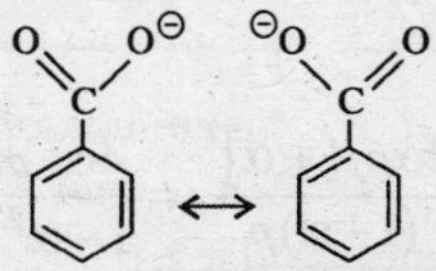

The benzoate ion is more stabilised because the negative charge is on the most electronegative oxygen atom, whereas in phenoxide ion, it is on the less electronegative carbon atoms. This causes benzoic acid to be a stronger acid than phenol.

34. A.

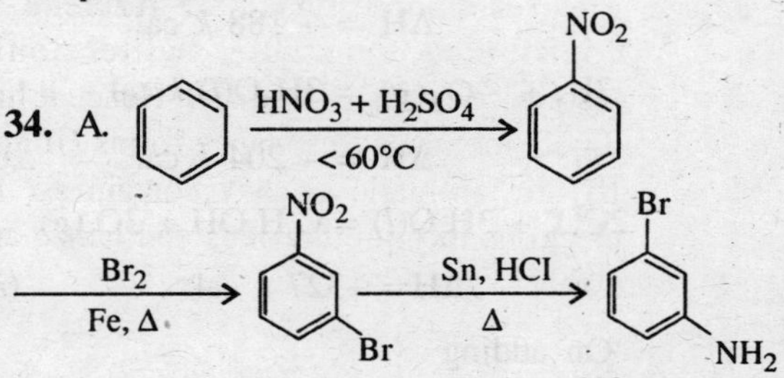

B.

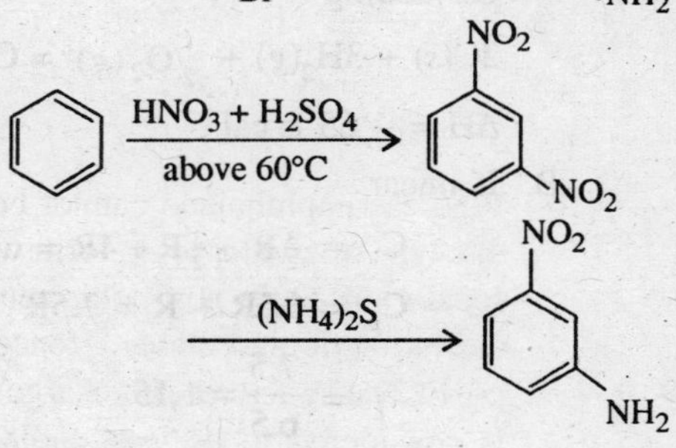

$(NH_4)_2S$ selectively reduce one nitro group in presence of other.

C.

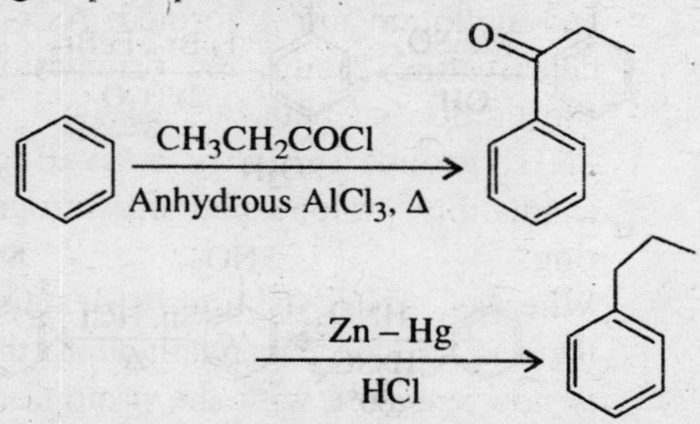

Friedel crafts alkylation with propyl halides give isopropyl benzene as major product due to rearrangement of propyl cation to more stable isopropyl cation. Hence acylation route is approached.

D.

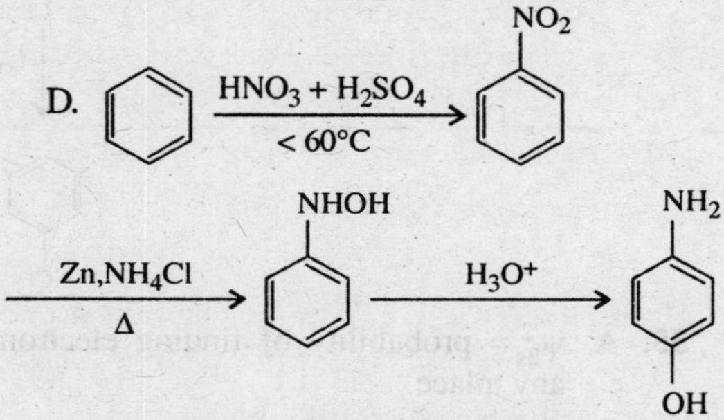

The acid catalyzed rearrangement of N-pheylhdroxylamine to 4-aminophenol is called Bamberger reaction. It's mechanism is given below.

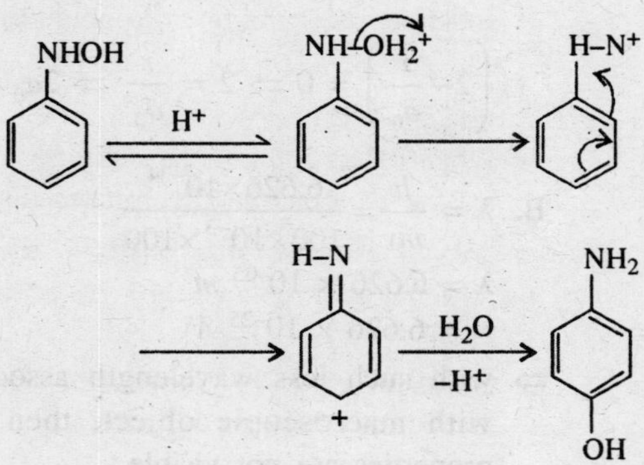

E.

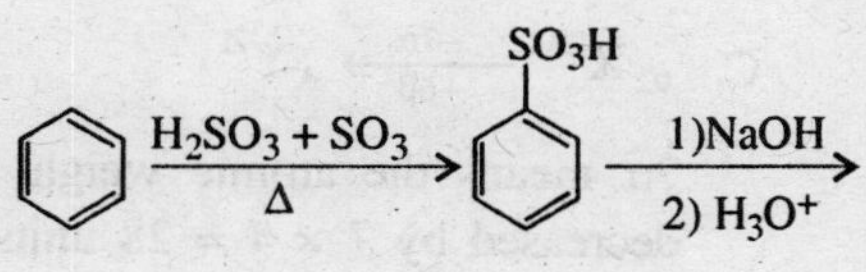

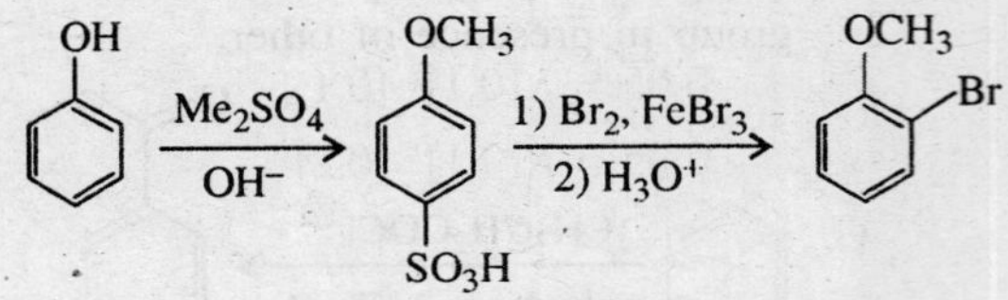

F. 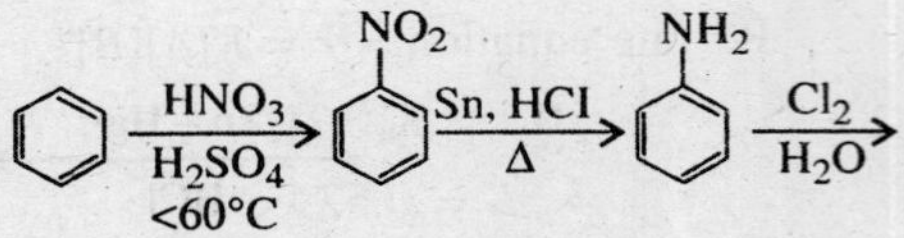

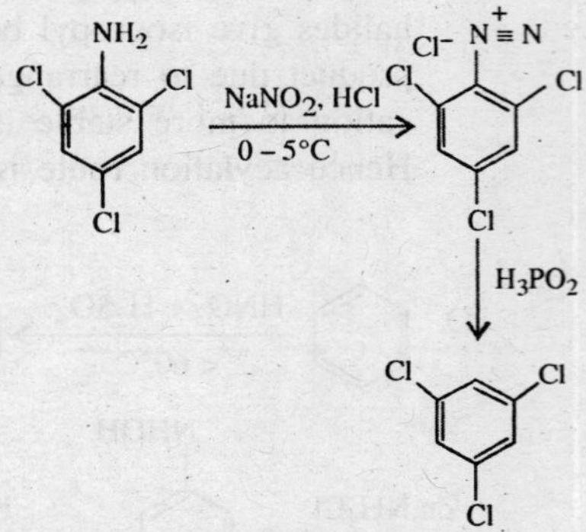

35. A. ψ_{2s}^2 = probability of finding electrons at any place

$\therefore \psi^2 = 0$ at node

$\therefore \psi^2 = 0$

$$= \frac{1}{4}\frac{1}{\sqrt{2\pi}}\left(\frac{1}{a^0}\right)^3\left(2-\frac{r}{a_0}\right)^2 \times e^{-r/a_0}$$

$$\left(2-\frac{r}{a_0}\right) = 0 \Rightarrow 2 = \frac{r}{a_0} \Rightarrow 2a_0 = r$$

B. $\lambda = \frac{h}{mv} = \frac{6.626\times10^{-34}}{100\times10^{-3}\times100}$

$\lambda = 6.626 \times 10^{-35}\ m$

$= 6.626 \times 10^{-25}\ A°$

$\Rightarrow$ with such less wavelength association with macroscopic object, then wave properties are not visible.

C. ${}_{92}X^{234} \xrightarrow[-6\beta]{-7\alpha} {}_{A}Y^{Z}$

7α means the atomic weight of Y has decreased by $7 \times 4 = 28$ units.

$\therefore Z = 234 - 28 = 206.$

Further 7α will reduce the atomic number by $7 \times 2 = 14$ units. But 6β will increase the charge by 6 unit.

$\therefore A = 92 - 14 + 6 = 84$

so element Y is ${}_{84}Pb^{106}$.

D. $N_2O_4 \rightleftharpoons 2NO_2$

$1-\alpha \qquad 2\alpha$

$\text{Total} = 1-\alpha+2\alpha = 1+\alpha$

Here partial pressure of N_2O_4

$$= \frac{(1-\alpha)}{1+\alpha}p$$

Here partial pressure of NO_2

$$= \frac{2\alpha p}{1+\alpha}$$

$$K_p = \frac{[NO_2]^2}{N_2O_4} = \frac{[2\alpha p/1+\alpha]^2}{\frac{(1-\alpha)p}{1+\alpha}} = \frac{4\alpha^2 p}{1-\alpha^2}$$

36. A. $2C(s) + 3H_2(g) + \frac{1}{2}O_2(g) = C_2H_5OH\ (l)$

$\Delta H_f = ?$

Given

$2C(s) + 2O_2(g) = 2CO_2(g)$

$\Delta H = -\ 188\ k\ \text{cal}$ ...(*i*)

$3H_2 + \frac{3}{2}O_2(g) = 3H_2O(l)\ k\ \text{cal}$

$\Delta H = -\ 204\ k\ \text{cal}$ ...(*ii*)

$2CO_2 + 3H_2O(l) = C_2H_5OH + 3O_2(g)$

$\Delta H = +327\ k\ \text{cal}$ ...(*iii*)

On adding

$2C(s) + 3H_2(g) + \frac{1}{2}O_2(g) = C_2H_5OH(l)$

$\Delta H = -\ 65\ k\ \text{cal}$

B. If linear

$C_v = \frac{3}{2}R + \frac{2}{2}R + 4R = 6.5R$

$C_p = 6.5R + R = 7.5R$

$\gamma = \frac{7.5}{6.5} = 1.15$

If nonlinear:

$$C_v = \frac{3}{2}R + \frac{3}{2}R + 3R = 6R$$

$$C_p = 6R + R = 7R$$

$$\gamma = \frac{7R}{6R} = 1.17$$

So, the molecule is linear.

C. We can write the Arrhenius equation for the two different temperatures and obtain:

$$E_a = R\left(\frac{T_1T_2}{T_1 - T_2}\right).\ln\frac{k_1}{k_2}$$

$$E_a = (8.315)\left[\frac{(420)(470)}{420-470}\right].\ln\frac{6.015\times10^{-5}}{2.97\times10^{-5}}$$

$= 128.0\ kJ\ mol^{-1}$

Using this value with the rate constant at 420K;

$$6.015 \times 10^{-5} = A\ .\exp -\left[\frac{128000}{(8.315)(420)}\right]$$

$$A = 5.01 \times 10^{11} s^{-1}$$

The reaction is unimolecular.

$$\Delta H^{\neq} = 128 - (8.315 \times 10^{-3})(420)$$

$= 124.5\ kJ.mol^{-1}$

Using the modified Eyring equation:

$$A = \frac{e^2 k_B T}{h}\exp(\Delta S^{\neq}/R)$$

$$\Delta S^{\neq} = (8.315)\ln\frac{(5.01\times10^{11})(6.27\times10^{-34})}{e^2(1.381\times10^{-23})(420)}$$

$= -40.4\ J\ .\ mol^{-1}.K^{-1}.$

37. A. Let the order w.r.t A and B are x and y respectively

$$r = K[A]^x[B]^y$$

$$0.005 = K[0.1]^x[0.1]^y$$

$$0.1 = K[0.2]^x[0.1]^y$$

or $\quad 2 = [2]^x$

$$x = 1$$

$$0.05 = K[0.1]^x[0.1]^y$$

$$0.05 = K[0.1]^x[0.2]^y$$

$$1 = [2]^y$$

$$y = 0$$

B. rate equation = $r = K[A][B]^0$

$$0.1 = K[0.2]$$

$$K = 0.5\ Sec^{-1}$$

C. $\Delta H = 0,\ \Delta q_p = \Delta U - W$

$W = PdV$

$= 100 \times 1$ atm mL

$= 10^{-2}\ KJ = \Delta U$

38. A.

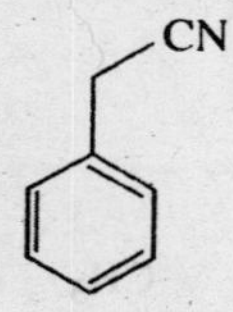

B.

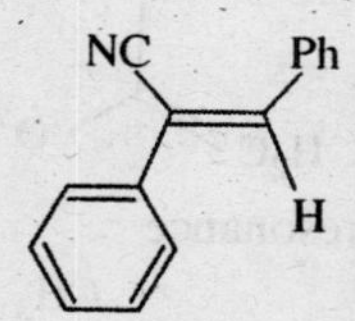

C.

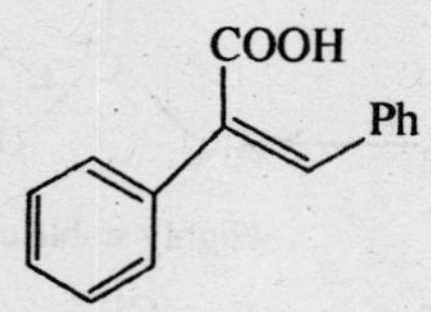

D.

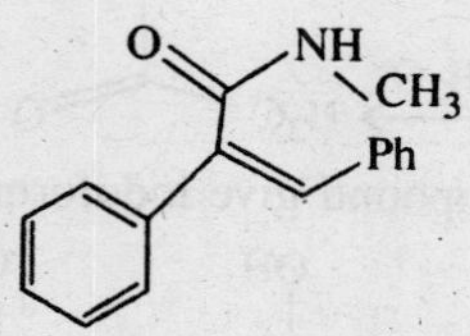

39. $A_1 = Cu(OH)_2\ CuCO_3$

$A_2 = Cu_2S$

$$\underset{(A_1)}{Cu(OH)_2CuCO_3} \xrightarrow{\text{Calcination}} \underset{\text{(Black Solid)}}{2CuO} + CO_2 + H_2O$$

$$Cu(OH)_2CuCO_3 \xrightarrow{\text{dilHCl}} CuCl_2 + CO_2 + 3H_2O$$

$$2CuCl_2 + 4KI \rightarrow Cu_2I_2 + I_2 + 4KCl$$

$$2Cu_2S + 3O_2 \rightarrow 2Cu_2O + 2SO_2$$
(A_2)

$$Cu_2S + 2Cu_2O \rightarrow 6Cu + SO_2$$

40. A. $Cu^{+2} + e^- \rightarrow Cu^+ \quad \Delta G_1^0 = -0.15\ F$

$In^{+2} + e^- \rightarrow In^+ + \quad \Delta G_2^0 = +0.4\ F$

$In^+ \rightarrow In^{+3} + 2e^- \quad \Delta G_3^0 = -0.84\ F$

$Cu^{+2} + In^{+2} \rightleftharpoons Cu^+ + In^{+3}\ \Delta G^0 = -0.59\ F$

$$-nFE^\circ = -0.59F$$
$$-E^0_{cell}F = -0.59F$$
$$E^0_{cell} = 0.59$$
$$E_{cell} = E^\circ - \frac{0.0591}{n}\log K_c$$
$$0.59 = \frac{0.0591}{1}\log K_c$$
$$K_c = 10^{10}$$

$C_5H_{10}O$ is

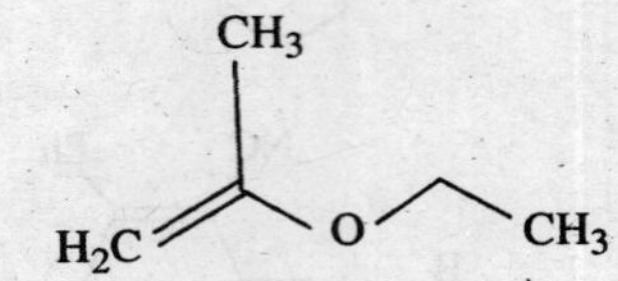

P is stabilized by resonance

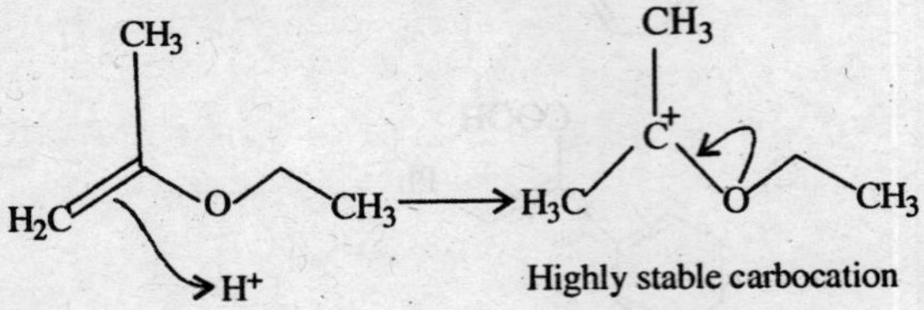

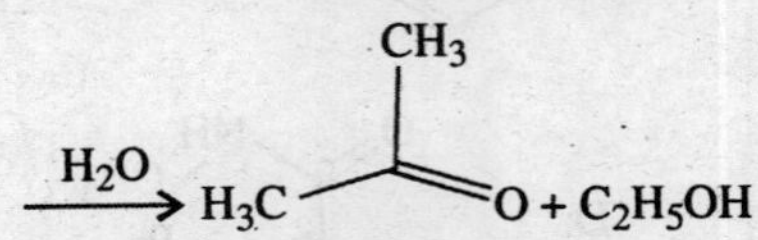

B. Since compound give iodoform test Q &

R should have $-\underset{|}{\overset{OH}{C}}-CH_3$ or $-\overset{O}{\overset{||}{C}}-CH_3$ in its structure.

41. A.

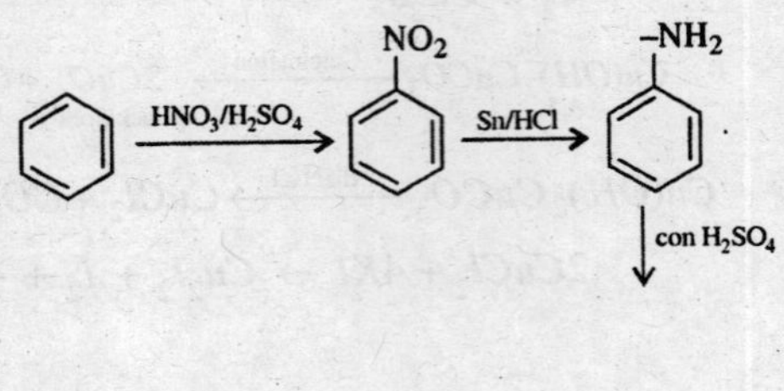

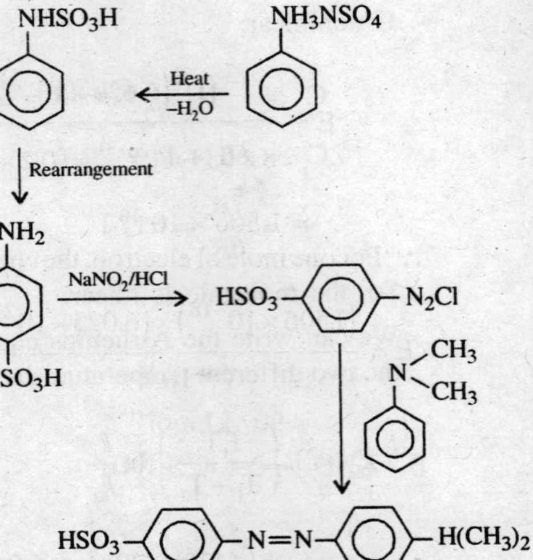

B.

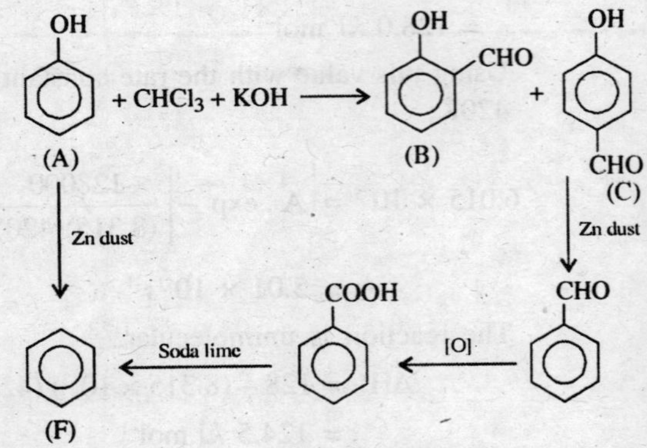

C. To keep the mixture strongly acidic which is necessary to prevent coupling of benzene diazonium chloride with excess of aryl amine.

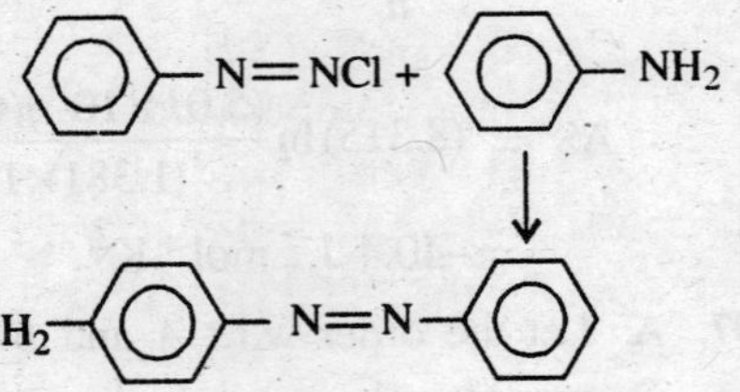

42. A. $E = \dfrac{n^2h^2}{8ma^2}$

Here $n = 1$, $m = 9.1 \times 10^{-31}$ kJ,
$a = 0.2 \times 10^{-9}$ m, $h = 6.626 \times 10^{-34}$ kgm^{2}s^{-1}

$$E = \frac{(1)^2(6.626\times10^{-34})^2}{8\times9.11\times10^{-31}\times(0.2\times10^{-9})^2}$$

$= 1.506 \times 10^{-18}$ J

$\therefore$ For one mole of electron, the energy will be

$$E = \frac{(1.506\times10^{-18})\times(6.023\times10^{23})}{10^3} \text{ kJ mol}^{-1}$$

$= 907$ kJ mol^{-1}

B. $KNO_3 \longrightarrow \underset{.1}{K^+} + \underset{.1}{NO_3^-}$

$$IS_1 = \frac{1}{2}C_iZ_i^2$$

$$= \frac{1}{2}[.1\times1^2 + .1\times1^2] = .1$$

$K_2SO_4 \longrightarrow \underset{.15\times2}{2K^+} + \underset{.15}{SO_4^{2-}}$

$$IS_2 = \frac{1}{2}[.3\times1^2 + .15\times2^2]$$

$= .45$

$La_2(SO_4)_3 \longrightarrow \underset{.023\times2}{2La^{3+}} + \underset{.023\times3}{3SO_4^{2-}}$

$$IS_3 = \frac{1}{2}[.046\times3^2 + .069\times2^2]$$

$$= \frac{1}{2}[.414 + .276] = .345$$

$\therefore$ Total ionic strength $= IS_1 + IS_2 + IS_3$
$= .895.$

C. $dG = Vdp - SdT$

Since temperature remains constant $dG = Vdp$

$$\therefore\ dG = nRT\frac{dp}{p}.$$

$$\therefore\ \Delta G = nRT\ln\left(\frac{p_2}{p_1}\right)$$

$$\Delta G = 2\times2\times300\times2.303\log\left(\frac{70}{700}\right)\text{cal}$$

$= -1200 \times 2.303$ cal $= -2764$ cal.

43. A. $CuSO_4.5H_2O \xrightarrow{100°C} \underset{[A]}{CuSO_4.H_2O}$

$\xrightarrow{280°C} \underset{[B]}{CuSO_4} \xrightarrow{800°C}$

$2\ \underset{[C]}{CuO} + 2\ \underset{[D]}{SO_2} + O_2$

B. $2AgNO_3 \xrightarrow{\text{red heat}} \underset{[E]}{2Ag} + \underset{[F]}{2NO_2} + O_2$

C. $Na_2B_4O_7 \xrightarrow{740°C} \underset{[G]}{2NaBO_2} + \underset{[H]}{B_2O_3}$

44. A. X = NH_4Cl, A = CrO_2Cl_2, B = Na_2CrO_4,

C = $PbCrO_4$, D = 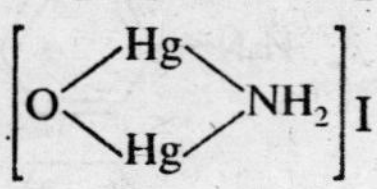

i.e., $NH_2HgO\ HgI$

The chemical reactions involved are as follows:

$4NH_4Cl + K_2Cr_2O_7 + 6H_2SO_4 \rightarrow$
$\underset{\text{Raddish brown}}{2CrO_2Cl_2} + 4NH_4HSO_4 + 2KHSO_4 + 3H_2O$

$CrO_2Cl_2 + 2NaOH \rightarrow \underset{\text{Yellow sol.}}{Na_2CrO_4} + 2HCl$

$Na_2CrO_4 + Pb(CH_3COO)_2$
$\rightarrow \underset{\text{Yellow ppt.}}{PbCrO_4} + 2CH_3COONa$

$NH_4Cl + NaOH \rightarrow NaCl + NH_3 + H_2O$

$2K_2HgI_4 + NH_3 + 3KOH \rightarrow$
$NH_2HgO\ HgI + 7KI + 2H_2O.$

B. $SnCl_2$ is a strong reducing agent and hence reduces $HgCl_2$ first to Hg_2Cl_2 (white) and then to Hg (black)

$SnCl_2 + 2HgCl_2 \rightarrow SnCl_4 + Hg_2Cl_2$

$SnCl_2 + Hg_2Cl_2 \rightarrow SnCl_4 + 2Hg$

TEST PAPER-3

IMPORTANT INSTRUCTION FOR CANDIDATES

Questions 1-30 (Objective questions) carry three marks each and questions 31-44 (subjective questions) carry fifteen marks each.

1. When propanoic acid is treated with aqueous $NaHCO_3$, CO_2 is liberated. The carbon of carbon dioxide comes from.

A. methyl group B. carboxylic group
C. methylene group D. bicarbonate

2. 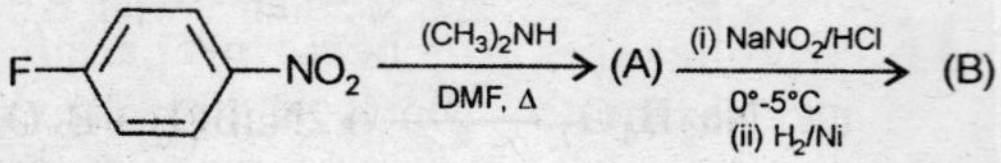

B is:

A. 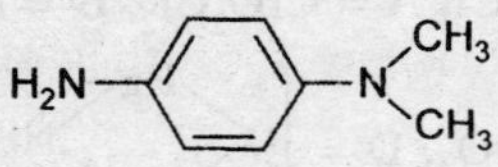

B. 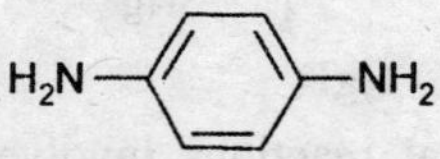

C. 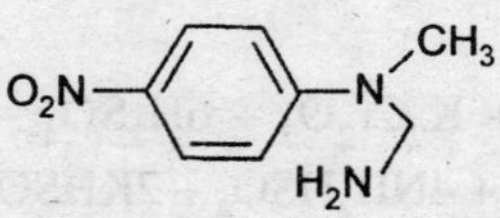

D. 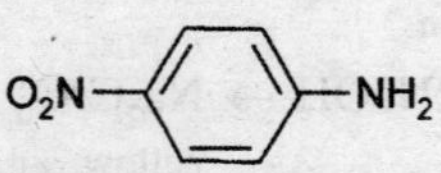

3. The product of acid hydrolysis of P and Q can be distinguished by

P = 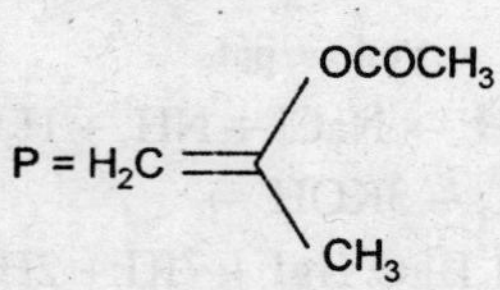

Q = 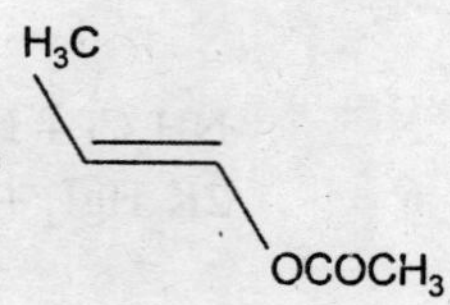

A. Lucas Reagent
B. 2, 4-DNP
C. Fehling's Solution
D. $NaHSO_3$

4. In constant volume calorimeter, 3.5 g of a gas with molecular weight 28 was burnt in excess oxygen at 298.0 K. The temperature of the calorimeter was found to increase from 298.0 K to 298.45 K due to the combustion process. Given that the heat capacity of the calorimeter is 2.5 kJ K^{-1}, the numerical value for the enthalpy of combustion of the gas in kJ mol^{-1} is

A. 10 B. 11
C. 8 D. 9

5. The correct statement(s) about the compound $H_3C(HO)HC - CH = CH - CH(OH)\ CH_3$(X) is (are)

A. The total number of stereoisomers possible for **X** is 6
B. The total number of diastereomers possible for **X** is 3
C. If the stereochemistry about the double bond in **X** is *trans*, the number of enantiomers possible for **X** is 4
D. If the stereochemistry about the double bond in **X** is *cis*, the number of enantiomers possible for **X** is 3.

6. Given that the abundances of isotopes ^{54}Fe, and ^{57}Fe are 5%, 90% and 5%, respectively, the atomic mass of Fe is

A. 55.85 B. 55.95
C. 55.75 D. 56.05

7. The term that corrects for the attractive forces present in a real gas in the van der Waal's equation is

A. nb B. $\frac{an^2}{V^2}$
C. $-\frac{an^2}{V^2}$ D. $-nb$

8. Among the electrolytes Na_2SO_4, $CaCl_2$, $Al_2(SO_4)_3$ and NH_4Cl, the most effective coagulating agent for Sb_2S_3 sol is

A. Na_2SO_4 B. $CaCl_2$
C. $Al_2(SO_4)_3$ D. NH_4Cl

9. Which of the following reactants on reaction with conc. NaOH followed by acidification gives the following lactone as the only product?

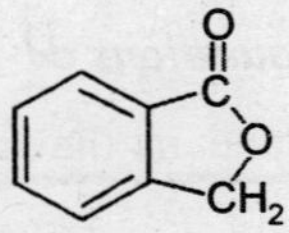

A. 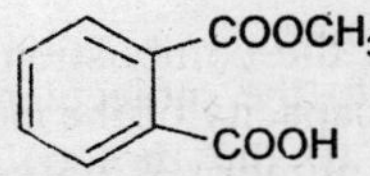

B. 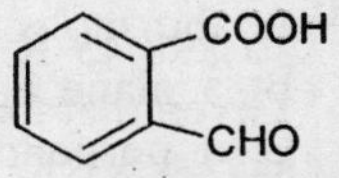

C. 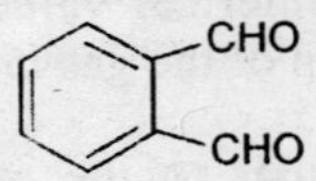

D. 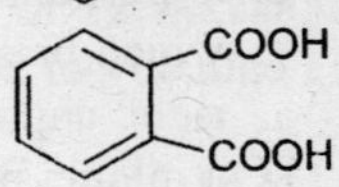

10.  $+ \; Cl-CH_2CH_2-CH_3 \xrightarrow{AlCl_3} P$

$\xrightarrow[(ii) H_3O^+]{(i) O_2/\Delta} Q$ + Phenol

The major products P and Q are

A. 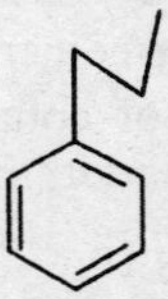 and CH_3CH_2CHO

B. 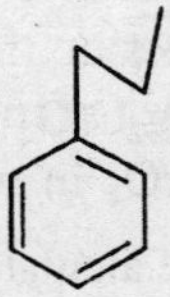 and CH_3COCH_3

C. 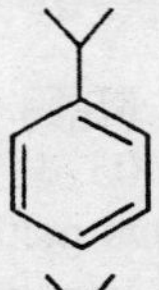 and CH_3COCH_3

D. 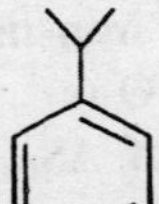 and CH_3CH_2CHO

11. The smallest ketone and its next homologue are reacted with NH_2OH to form oxime.
A. Two different oximes are formed
B. Three different oximes are formed
C. Two oximes are optically active
D. All oximes are optically active

12. 1-bromo-3-chlorocyclobutane when treated with two equivalents of Na, in the presence of ether which of the following will be formed?

A. 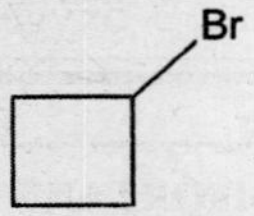
B. 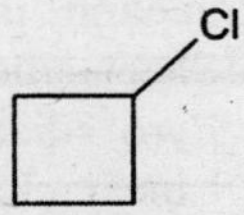
C. 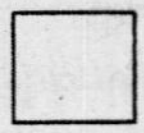
D. 

13. 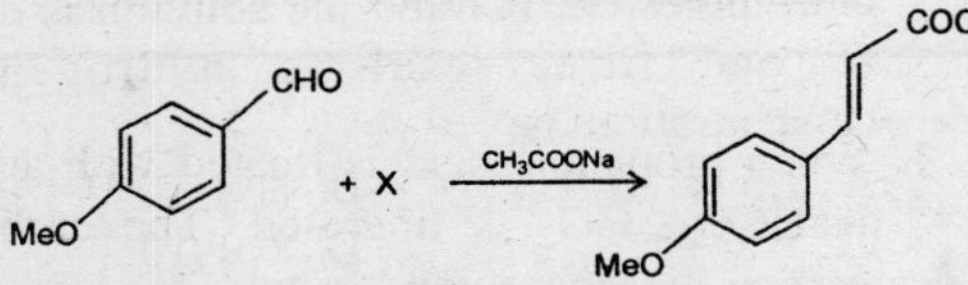

What is X?

A. CH_3COOH B. $BrCH_2.COOH$
C. $(CH_3CO)_2O$ D. CHO – COOH

14. Cyclohexene is best prepared from cyclohexanol by which of the following:
A. conc.H_3PO_4 B. conc. $HCl/ZnCl_2$
C. conc. HCl D. conc. HBr

15. The half cell reactions for rusting of iron are:

$$2H^+ + \frac{1}{2}O_2 + 2e^- \rightarrow H_2O; \; E^0 = +1.23V,$$

$$Fe^{2+} + 2e^- \rightarrow Fe_{(s)}; \; E^0 = -0.44V$$

ΔG^0 (in kJ) for the reaction is:
A. – 76 B. – 322
C. – 122 D. – 176

16. The number of radial nodes in 3*s* and 2*p* respectively are:
A. 2 and 0 B. 1 and 2
C. 0 and 2 D. 2 and 1

17. Which of the following are contains both Copper and Iron?
A. Cuprite B. Chalcocite
C. Chalcopyrite D. Malachite

18. Which of the following is obtained when 4-Methylbenzenesulphonic acid is hydrolysed with excess of sodium acetate?

A. 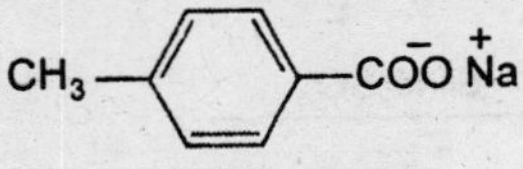

B. 

C. 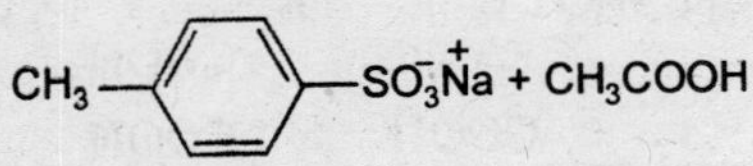

D. 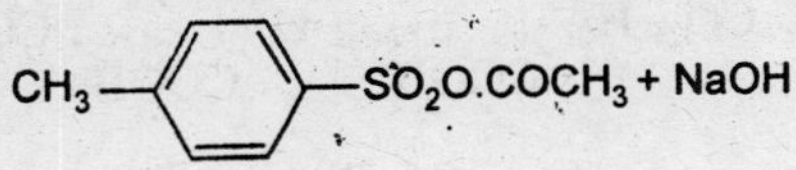

19. Which silicates is formed from $[SiO_4]^{4-}$, tetrahedral units by sharing 3 oxygen atoms?
A. Sheet silicates
B. Pyro silicates
C. Linear chain silicates
D. 3 dimensional silicates

20. $CH_3.NH_2$ (0.1 mole, $K_b = 5 \times 10^{-4}$) is added to 0.08 moles of HCl and the solution is diluted to one litre, resulting hydrogen ion concentration is:
A. 1.6×10^{-11} B. 8×10^{-11}
C. 5×10^{-5} D. 8×10^{-2}

21. Which one of the quantum numbers does not result from the solution of the Schroedinger's wave equation?
A. Magnetic B. Azimuthal
C. Principal D. Spin

22. Which of the following acid has the highest strength in aqueous solutions.
A. H_2SO_4 B. H_3AsO_4
C. $HMnO_4$ D. H_2SO_3

23. In the reaction : $Cl_2 + ClF + SbF_5 \rightarrow [Cl_3][SbF_6]$ the role of chlorine is to
A. stabilize Cl^+
B. function as Lewis acid
C. function as Lewis base
D. form the action

24. $B_{10}C_2H_{12}$ is isoelectronic with
A. $B_{12}H_{12}^{2-}$ B. $B_{12}H_{12}$
C. $B_{12}H_{12}^{+}$ D. $B_{12}H_{12}^{2+}$

25. Uranium exhibits several oxidation states because
A. It is an inner transition element
B. its atomic number is high
C. 5f orbitals participate in bonding
D. it forms strong bond with oxygen

26. 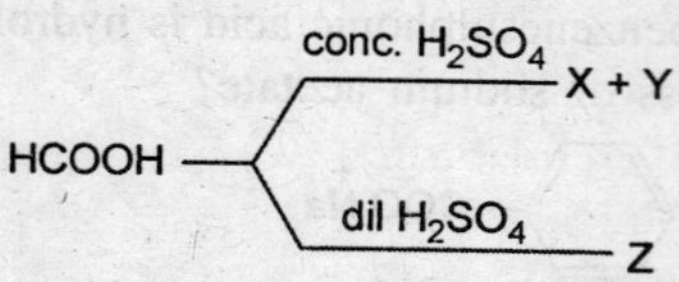

Products X, Y and Z are respectively
A. CO, H_2O, $\begin{matrix}COOH\\|\\COOH\end{matrix}$ B. $\begin{matrix}COOH\\|\\COOH\end{matrix}$, CO, H_2O
C. CO_2, H_2, $\begin{matrix}COOH\\|\\COOH\end{matrix}$ D. $\begin{matrix}COOH\\|\\COOH\end{matrix}$, CO_2, H_2

27. The solubility of AB_2 type of salt is
A. $\left(\frac{K_{sp}}{4}\right)^{1/3}$ B. $(K_{sp})^{1/2}$
C. $\left(\sqrt{\frac{K_{sp}}{4}}\right)^{1/3}$ D. None of the above

28. The nodal plane in the π-bond of ethene is located in
A. the molecular plane
B. a plane parallel to the molecular plane
C. a perpendicular to the molecular plane which bisects the carbon-carbon σ-bond at right angle
D. a plane perpendicular to the molecular plane which contains the carbon-carbon σ-bond.

29. The occurrence of the reaction is impossible if
A. ΔH is +ve, ΔS is also +ve
B. ΔH is –ve, ΔS is also –ve
C. ΔH is –ve, ΔS is also +ve
D. ΔH is +ve, ΔS is also –ve

30. The spin magnetic moment of cobalt in the compound $Hg[Co(SCN)_4]$ is
A. $\sqrt{3}$ B. $\sqrt{8}$
C. $\sqrt{15}$ D. $\sqrt{24}$

31. A. A saturated solution of Ag_2CrO_4 prepared by dissolving solid Ag_2CrO_4 in water has $[CrO_4^{2-}] = 6.5 \times 10^{-5}$ M. Calculate K_{sp} for Ag_2CrO_4.
B. Calculate the solubility of MgF_2 in water at 25°C in units of:
(*i*) Moles per liter (*ii*) Grams per liter

32. A. Consider the oxidation of iron metal:
$4\ Fe(s) + 3\ O_2(g) \rightarrow 2\ Fe_2O_3(s)$
By determining the sign of ΔS_{total}, show that the reaction is spontaneous at 25°C.
B. Iron metal can be produced by reducing iron (III) oxide with hydrogen:
$Fe_2O_3(s) + 3H_2(g) \rightarrow 2\ Fe(s) + 3H_2O(g)$
$\Delta H° = +98.8$ kJ; $\Delta S° = +141.5$ J/K
(*i*) Is this reaction spontaneous under standard-state conditions at 25°C?
(*ii*) At what temperature will the reaction become spontaneous?

33. A. The rate of a first order reaction is 0.8 mol L^{-1} after 10 min and 0.1 after 30 min from the start of the reaction. Find half time of the reaction.

B. The reaction 2A + B + C → D + 2E; is found to be first order in A; second order in B and zero order in C.

(*i*) Give the rate law for the above reaction in the form of a differential equation.

(*ii*) What is the effect on the rate of increasing the concentration of A, B and C two times?

C. At 27°C it was observed, during a reaction of hydrogenation that the pressure of H_2 gas decreases from 2 atm to 1.1 atm in 75 min. Calculate the rate of reaction (molarity/sec). Given (R = 0.082/litre atom K^{-1} $mole^{-1}$)

34. An element **G**, which is a liquid at 60°C, reacts with a limited amount of chlorine gas, giving a colourless liquid, **H** (b.p. 76°C, Cl 77.4%). **H** reacts with excess methanol in the presence of excess triethylamine to give a colourless liquid, **J**, and a colourless solid, **K**. The $^{31}P\{^{1}H\}$ NMR spectrum of **J** exhibits a singlet, whilst the proton coupled ^{31}P NMR shows a decet. Conductometry shows that **K** is a 1 : 1 electrolyte; its MS (ES+) shows a very intense peak at m/z 102.1.

H reacts with excess chlorine to give a pale yellow solid **L**, which has molecular trigonal bipyramidal structure in non-polar solvents, but conducts electricity well in polar solvents.

G reacts with a limited amount of oxygen to give a colourless solid **M** (O 43.6%). Dissolution of compound **M** in water gives an acidic solution of **N**. A solution of **N** (10 mmol) was neutralized by addition of 20 cm^3 of NaOH (1.00 mol dm^{-3}) to give compound **P**.

(*i*) Identify the element **G** and the compound **H** - **P**. Explain clearly how the data given allows you to arrive at your conclusions.

35. A. Draw the following molecules in their lowest energy chair conformations.

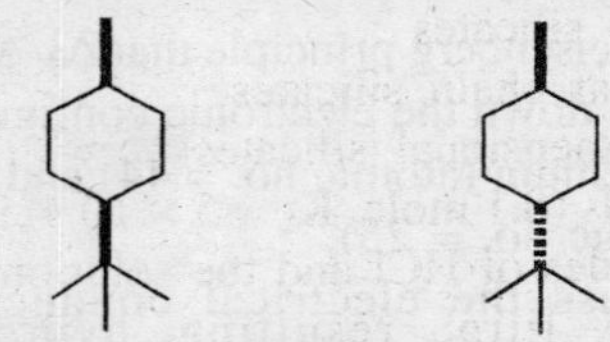

B. Write a structural formula for the most stable conformation of *cis*-1-*tert*-butyl 1-2-methyl-cyclohexane.

C. Explain using diagrams why *cis*-1, 3-dimethylcyclohexane is thermodynami-cally more stable than *trans*-1, 3-dimethyl-cyclohexane.

36. A. Lead can displace silver from solution:
Pb(*s*) + 2Ag^+ (*aq*) → Pb^2(*aq*) + 2Ag(*s*)
As a consequence, silver is a valuable by-product in the industrial extraction of lead from its ore. Calculate K and ΔG° at 298 K for this reaction.

B. A voltaic cell houses the reaction between aqueous bromine and zinc metal:
Br_2(*aq*) + Zn(*s*) → Zn^{2+} (*aq*) + $2Br^-$ (*aq*)
E°_{cell} = 1.83V
Calculate $E^\circ_{bromine}$ given E°_{zinc} = –0.76V

37. A. Assign R or S configuration to the chirality center in each of the following molecules:

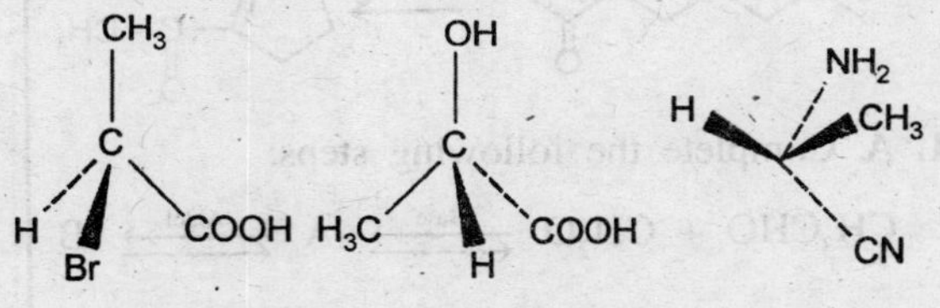

(*i*) (*ii*) (*iii*)

B. Out of the following two coordination entities which is chiral (optically active)? (*i*) *cis*-$[CrCl_2(OX)_2]^{3-}$ (*ii*) *trans*-$[CrCl_2(OX)_2]^{3-}$

C. The spin only magnetic moment of $[MnBr_4]^{2-}$ is 5.9 BM. Predict the geometry of the complex ion?

38. A. A particle is confined to one dimensional box of length L having infinitely high walls and is in its lowest quantum state. Calculate <x>, <x^2>, <p>, <p^2> using the definition

$\Delta A = \left[< A^2 > - (< A >)^2 \right]^{1/2}$, to define the uncertainty ΔA calculate Δx and Δp. Verify the Heisenberg principle that $\Delta x \, \Delta p \geq \hbar/2$.

B. Write down the electronic configuration of Ruthenium (atomic no. = 44) and Platinum (atomic no. = 78).

39. A. Discuss the electrical conductivity of Al_2Cl_6, and the changes which occur on heating it. Show the structure of compounds.

B. Draw the two isomers of $[Me_2Al(NMe_2)]_2$ and indicate which is likely to be more stable.

40. A. Write the mechanism.

(i) 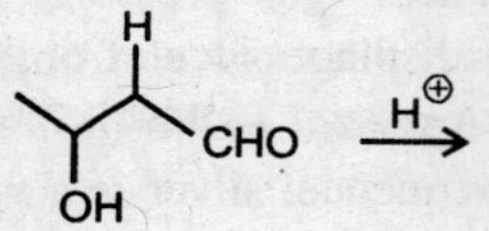

(ii) 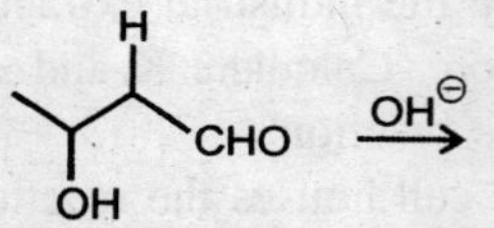

B. Carry out the following transformation.

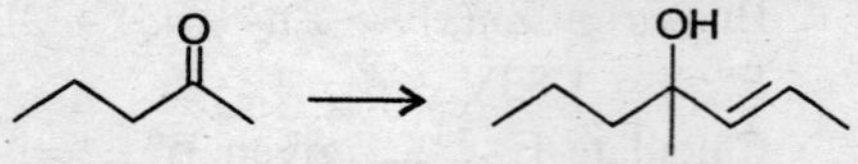

C. Carry out the following transformation.

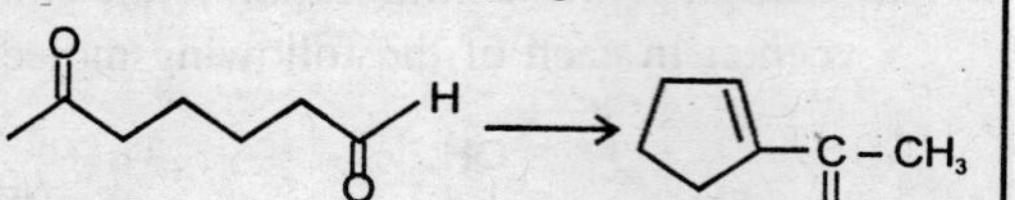

41. A. Complete the following steps:

$$CH_3CHO + CH_2O \xrightleftharpoons{\text{Base}} A \xrightleftharpoons{\text{Aldol}} B \xrightleftharpoons{\text{Aldol}} C \xrightleftharpoons[\text{Cannizaro}]{CH_2O} D + HCOOH$$

B. Complete the reaction 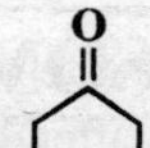 $+ CH_2O \xrightarrow{CaO,\ H_2O}$

42. A. What is A and B

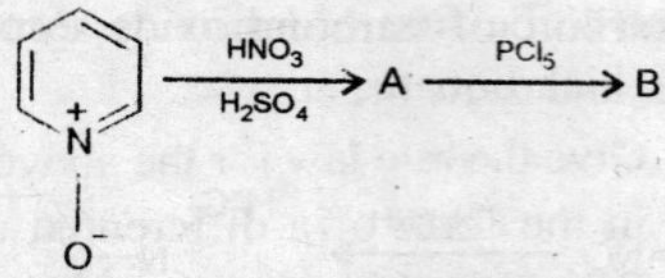

B. $(A) \xrightarrow[250°C]{Al_2O_3} (B) \xrightarrow[AgOH]{HI} (C) \xrightarrow[150°C]{Al_2O_3} (B) \xrightarrow{\text{(i) } B_2H_6 \text{ (ii) } H_2O_2,\ OH^-} (A)$

In the above reaction scheme (A) and (C) are isomers. (B) has a formula of C_5H_{10} which can also be obtained from the product of the reaction of CH_3CH_2MgBr and $(CH_3)_2CO$. Give structures of (A), (B) and (C).

43. In the following reactions

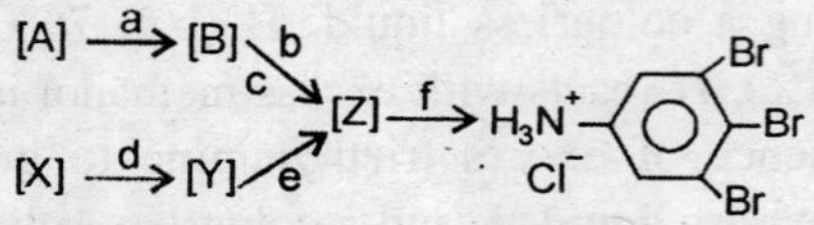

Identify [A], [B], [X], [Y] and [Z] in the above scheme of reactions if reagents a, b, c, d, e and f are Br/CH_3COOH, $NaNO_2/H_2SO_4$, CuBr, HNO_3/H_2SO_4, Br_2/Fe and Sn/HCl respectively.

44. A. How is 2, 4-dinitrophenylhydrazine prepared from chlorobenzene?

B. Complete the following reactions

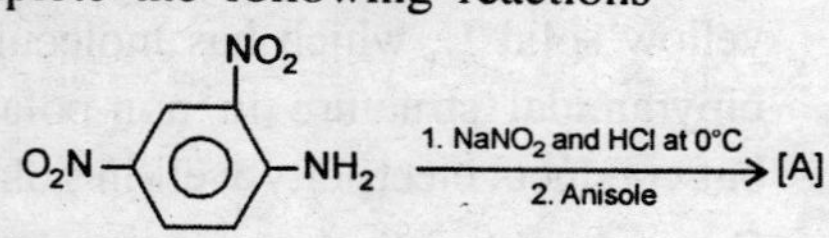

2, 4-dinitroaniline

ANSWERS

1	2	3	4	5	6	7	8	9	10
B	A	C	D	C	B	B	C	C	C
11	**12**	**13**	**14**	**15**	**16**	**17**	**18**	**19**	**20**
A	D	C	A	B	A	C	C	A	B
21	**22**	**23**	**24**	**25**	**26**	**27**	**28**	**29**	**30**
D	C	C	A	C	A	A	A	D	C

SOME SELECTED EXPLANATORY ANSWERS

1. $CH_3-CH_2-\overset{*}{C}OOH + NaHCO_3 \longrightarrow$

$CH_3CH_2\overset{*}{C}OONa + N_2O + CO_2$

Thus carbon of carbondioxide comes from sodium bicarbonate.

2.

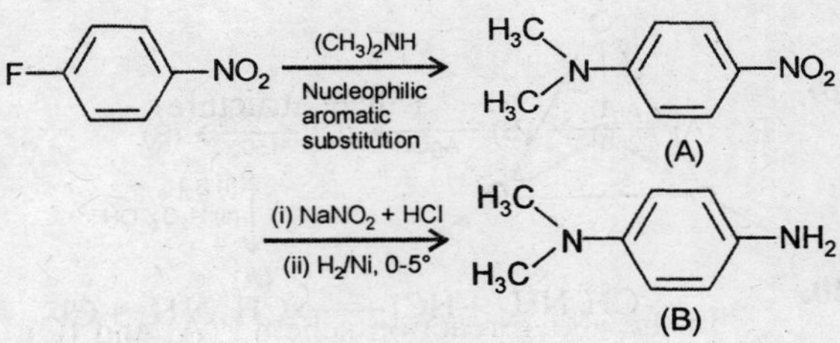

3.

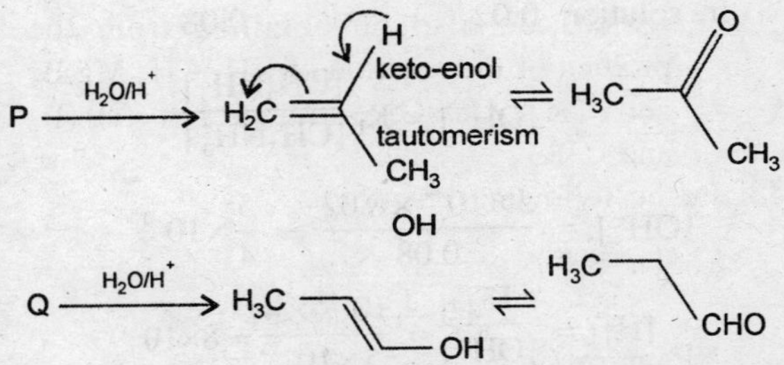

Ketone (non-reducing) and aldehyde (reducing) can be distinguished by Fehling solution.

4. Heat released (ΔU) = 2.5 × 0.45 kJ

$$\Rightarrow \quad \Delta U = \frac{2.5 \times 0.45}{3.5/28} \text{ kJ/mol}$$

$$= 9 \text{ kJ/mol}$$

5. $CH_3-\overset{*}{C}H(OH)-CH=CH-\overset{*}{C}H(OH)-CH_3$

(X)

Total number of chiral centres = 2

cis:

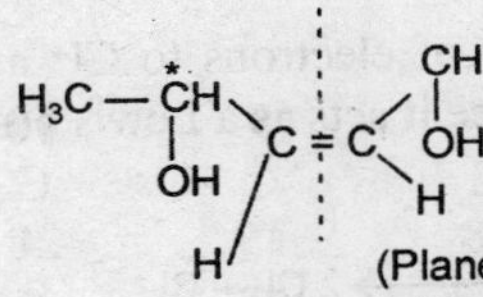

[3 stereoisomers]

(Plane of symmetry)
(Meso compound)

There are only two enantiomers for X.

Trans:

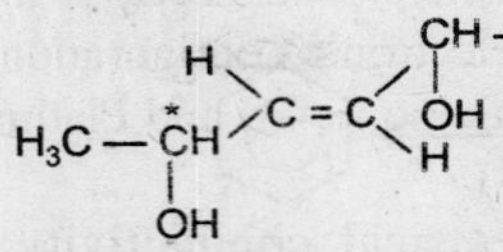

Four enantiomers & stereoisomers are possible

Total stereoisomers = 3 + 4 = 7

There will be lot of diastereomers.

6. Atomic mass = $\sum X_i.A_i$

= 54 × 0.05 + 56 × 0.9 + 57 × 0.05

= 55.95

7. $P_i v_i = nRT_i$

where P_i is ideal gas pressure. But due to attractive force, the molecules of gases are not able to exert pressure P_i which they otherwise in absence of attractive force should exert.

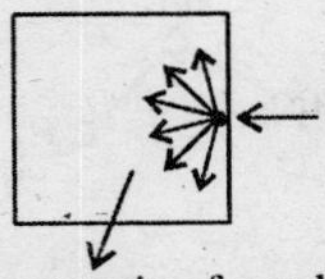

The pressure exerted by molecule is decrease

attractive force by molecules inside the vessel

P is observed pressure, it is less than P_i. So, a factor $\frac{an^2}{v^2}$ was added to it. Therefore, $\left(P + \frac{an^2}{v^2}\right)$ now satisfy ideal gas equation.

8. Sb_2S_3 is a negatively charged sol to coagulate it most effectively, charge on cation should be maximum. Thus, Al^{3+} in $Al_2(SO_4)$ will be most effective.

9. Canizaro Reaction

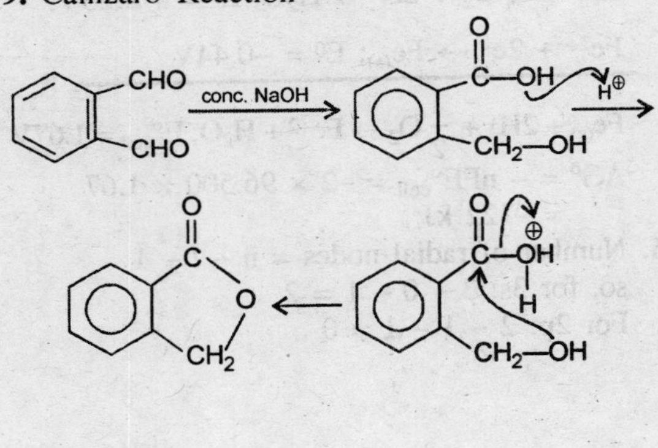

10. 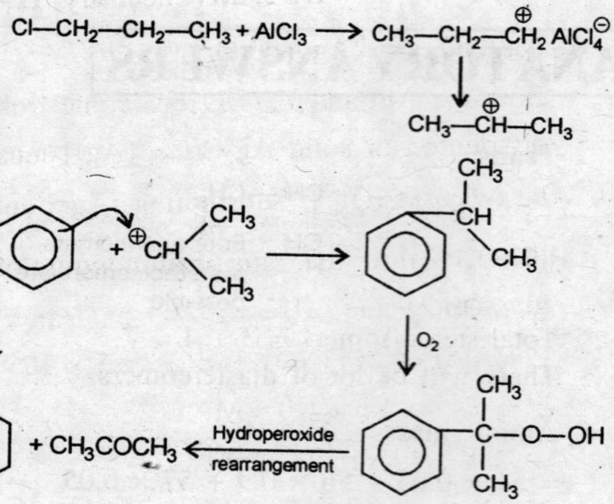

11. 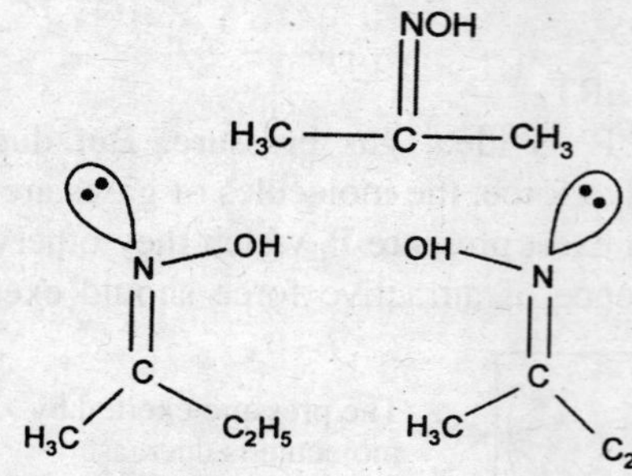

12. Na ⟶ $Na^+ + e^-$

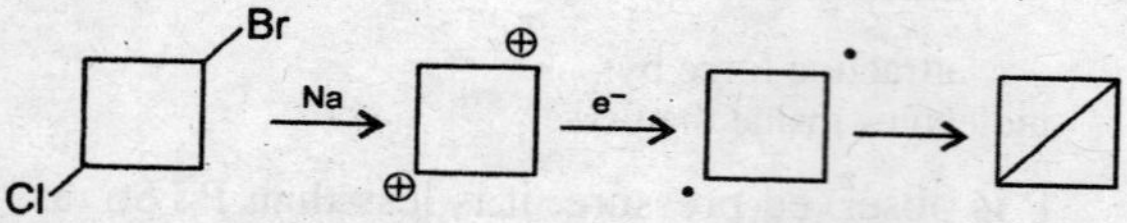

13. p – MeO – Ph – CHO + $(AcO)_2O$ (Perkin Reaction) $\xrightarrow{CH_3COONa}$

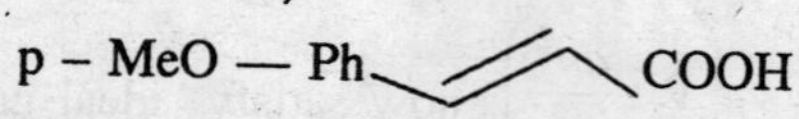

14. 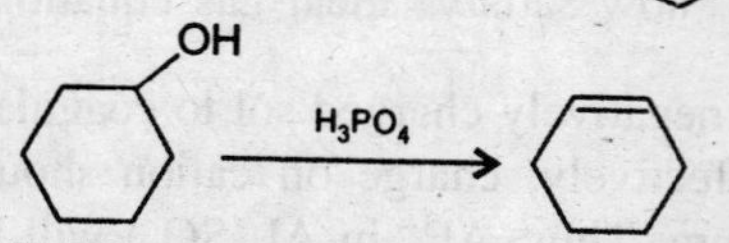

H_3PO_4 acts as dehydrating agent.

15. $2H^+ + \frac{1}{2}O_2 + 2e^- \rightarrow H_2O;\ E^0 = +1.23V,$

$Fe^{2+} + 2e^- \rightarrow Fe_{(s)};\ E^0 = -0.44V$

$Fe_{(s)} + 2H^+ + \frac{1}{2}O_2 \rightarrow Fe^{+2} + H_2O;\ E^\circ_{cell} = 1.67V$

$\Delta G^\circ = -nFE^\circ_{cell} = -2 \times 96.500 \times 1.67$

$= -322$ kJ

16. Number of radial nodes = n – l – 1

so, for 3s: 3 – 0 – 1 = 2

For 2p: 2 – 1 – 1 = 0

17. Chalcopyrite ($CuFeS_2$)

18. 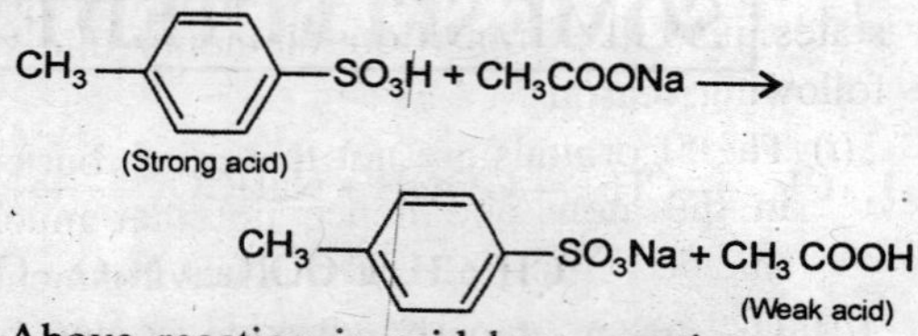

Above reaction is acid base reaction.

19. 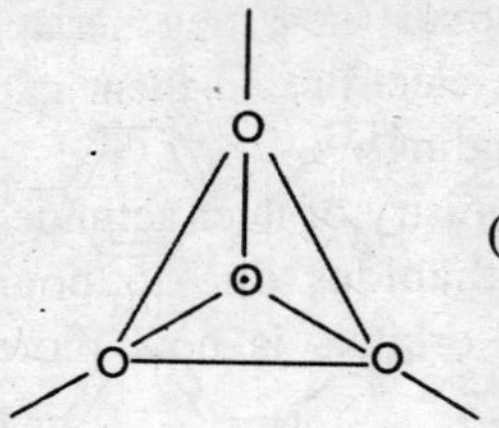 (Sheet structure)

20. $CH_3NH_2 + HCl \longrightarrow CH_3\overset{\oplus}{N}H_3 + Cl^-$

Initially	0.1	0.08	–
In solution	0.02	–	0.08

$$[OH^-] = K_b\frac{[CH_3NH_2]}{[CH_3NH_3^+]}$$

$$[OH^-] = \frac{5\times10^{-4}\times0.02}{0.08} = \frac{5}{4}\times10^{-4}$$

$$[H^+] = \frac{K_w}{[OH^-]} = \frac{10^{-14}\times4}{5\times10^{-4}} = 8\times10^{-11}$$

21. They ψ value is not dependent on spin quantum number. The electrons residing in one atomic orbital have same ψ value.

22. $H_3AsO_4 < H_3SO_3 < HMnO_4$

(*i*) Greater the oxidation number of the central atom, greater is the acidic strength.

(*ii*) Sulfur is a stronger non-metal than Arsenic.

(*iii*) Mn is a metal and metals usually form hydroxides (i.e., basic in nature). But due to high charge density on Mn^{7+} ion, $HMnO_4$ acts as acid (Mn-O bond is strongly covalent).

23. Cl_2 donates lone pair of electrons to Cl^+ and forms $[Cl_3]^+$ ion. Hence it acts as a Lewis base.

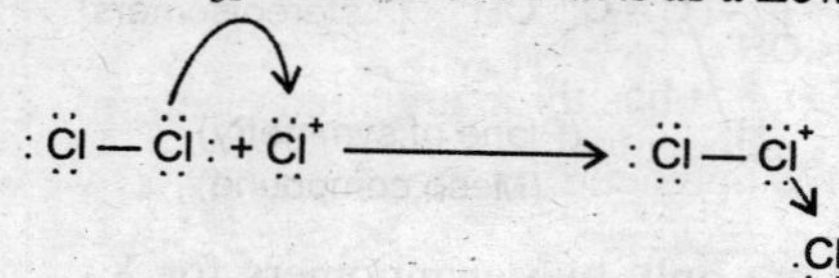

25. The early actinides show multiple oxidation states just like transition elements due to following reasons:

(*i*) The 5f orbitals are not that much buried in the atom and hence not that much shielded from the external environment.

(*ii*) The energy gap between 5f, 6d and 7s orbitals is very small (near degenerate) and hence all the electrons in them can participate in bonding.

But remember, the chemistry of later actinides resemble that of lanthanides due to poor shielding effect of 5f orbitals is now more pronounced.

26. $$HCOOH \xrightarrow{\text{conc. } H_2SO_4} CO_{(g)} + H_2O_{(g)}$$

$$2HCOOH + [O] \xrightarrow{\text{Dil. } H_2SO_4} \begin{matrix} COOH \\ | \\ COOH \end{matrix} + H_2O$$

27. $AB_2 \Rightarrow K_{sp} = 4s^3$

$$s = \left(\frac{K_{sp}}{4}\right)^{1/3}$$

28. Ethylene

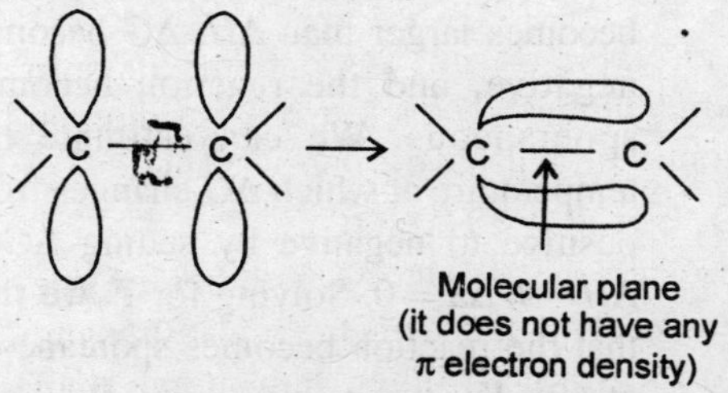

29. For reaction to be spontaneous ΔG should be the negative

$\Delta G = \Delta H - T\Delta S$

$\Rightarrow$ ΔH should be negative and ΔS should be positive.

Just reverse the condition for impossible reaction.

30. In the given complex, CO is in +2 state

${}_{27}Co = 3d^7\ 4s^2$,

$Co^{2+} = 3d^7$ *i.e.* it has three unpaired electron).

$\therefore$ Spin only magnetic moment $= \sqrt{n(n+2)}$

$= \sqrt{3(3+2)} = \sqrt{15}$ B.M.

31. A. $Ag_2CrO_4 \rightleftharpoons 2Ag + CrO_4^{2-}$

Both the Ag^+ and CrO_4^{2-} ions come from dissolution of solid Ag_2CrO_4, $[Ag^+]$ must be twice $[CrO_4^{2-}]$. Substituting $[Ag^+]$ and $[CrO_4^{2-}]$ into the equilibrium equation gives the value of K_{sp}.

$$[Ag^+] = (2)[CrO_4^{2-}] = (2)(6.5 \times 10^{-5})$$
$$= 1.3 \times 10^{-4}\ M$$
$$K_{sp} = [Ag^+]^2[CrO_4^{2-}]$$
$$= (1.3 \times 10^{-4})^2 (6.5 \times 10^{-5})$$
$$= 1.1 \times 10^{-12}$$

B. (*i*) $MgF_2(s) \rightleftharpoons Mg^{2+}(aq) + 2F^-(aq)$

$$K_{sp} = 7.4 \times 10^{-11}$$
$$K_{sp} = 7.4 \times 10^{-11} = [Mg^{2+}][F^-]^2$$
$$= (x)(2x)^2$$
$$4x^3 = 7.4 \times 10^{-11}$$
$$x^3 = 1.8 \times 10^{-11}$$
$$x = [Mg^{2+}] = \text{Molar solubility}$$
$$= 2.6 \times 10^{-4}\ \text{mol/L}$$

Thus, the molar solubility of MgF_2 in water at 25°C is 2.6×10^{-4} M. (Taking account of the side reaction that produces MgF^+ would increase the calculated solubility by about 6%).

Note that the number 2 appears twice in the expression $(x)(2x)^2$. The coefficient 2 in $2x$ is required because each mole of MgF_2 that disolves gives 2 mol of $F^-(aq)$

(*ii*) Solubility (in g/L)

$$= \frac{2.6 \times 10^{-4}\,\text{mol}}{L} \times \frac{62.3\,g}{\text{mol}} = 1.6 \times 10^{-2}\ g/L$$

Let's summarize our reasoning in a table under the balanced equation:

	$Ag^+(aq)$	+ $2NH_3(aq)$	$\rightleftharpoons$ $Ag(NH_3)_2^+(aq)$
Initial conc. (M)	0.10	3.0	0
After 100% reaction (M)	0	2.8	0.10
Equilibrium conc (M)	x	$2.8 + 2x$	$0.10 - x$

Substituting the equilibrium concentrations into the expression for K_f, and making the approximation that x is negligible compared to 0.10 (and to 2.8) gives

$$K_f = 1.7 \times 10^7 = \frac{[Ag(NH_3)_2^+]}{[Ag^+][NH_3]^2}$$

$$= \frac{0.10 - x}{(x)(2.8+2x)^2} \approx \frac{0.10}{(x)(2.8)^2}$$

$$[Ag^+] = x = \frac{0.10}{(1.7\times10^7)(2.8)^2}$$

$$= 7.5 \times 10^{-10}\ M$$

$$[Ag(NH_3)_2^+] = 0.10 - x = 0.10 - (7.5 \times 10^{-10})$$

$$= 0.10\ M$$

The concentration of $Ag(NH_3)^+$ can be calculated from either of the stepwise equilibria. Let's use the equilibrium equation for formation of $Ag(NH_3)^+$ from

$$Ag^+: K_1 = \frac{[Ag(NH_3)^+]}{[Ag^+][NH_3]} = 2.1 \times 10^3$$

$$[Ag(NH_3)^+] = K_2[Ag^+]\,[NH_3]$$

$$= (2.1 \times 10^3)\ (7.5 \times 10^{-10})\ (2.8)$$

$$= 4.4 \times 10^{-6}\ M$$

Thus, nearly all the Ag^+ is in the form of $Ag(NH_3)_2^+$.

32. A. $\Delta S_{sys} = \Delta S°$

$$= 2S°(Fe_2O_3) - [4S°(Fe) + 3S°(O_2)]$$

$$= (2\ mol)\left(87.4 \frac{J}{K.mol}\right) -$$

$$\left[(4mol)\left(27.3 \frac{1}{K.mol}\right) + (3mol)\left(205.0 \frac{J}{K.mol}\right)\right]$$

$$= -549.5\ J/K$$

$$\Delta H° = 2\Delta H°_f(Fe_2O_3) - [4\,\Delta H°_f(Fe) + 3\Delta H°_f(O_2)]$$

Because $\Delta H°_f = 0$ for elements and

$$\Delta H°_f = -824.2\ kJ/mol \text{ for } Fe_2O_3$$

$\Delta H°$ for the reaction is

$$\Delta H° = 2\Delta H°_f(Fe_2O_3)$$

$$= (2mol)(-824.2\ kJ/mol)$$

$$= -1647.4\ kJ$$

Therefore,

$$\Delta S_{surr} = \frac{-\Delta H°}{T} = \frac{-(-1{,}648{,}400J)}{298.15K}$$

$$= 5529\ J/K$$

$$\Delta S_{total} = \Delta S_{sys} + \Delta S_{surr}$$

$$= -549.5\ J/K + 5529\ J/K$$

$$= 4980\ J/K$$

Because the total entropy change is positive, the reaction is spontaneous under standard state conditions at 25°C.

B. (*i*) To determine whether the reaction is spontaneous at 25°C, we need to determine the sign of $\Delta G = \Delta H - T\Delta S$. At 25° C (298 K), ΔG for the reaction is

$$\Delta G = \Delta H - T\,\Delta S$$

$$= (98.8\ kJ) - (298\ K)\ (0.1415\ kJ/K)$$

$$= (98.9kJ) - (42.2\ kJ)$$

$$= 56.6\ kJ$$

Because the positive ΔH term is larger than the positive $T\Delta S$ term, ΔG is positive and the reaction is nonspontaneous at 298 K.

(*ii*) At sufficiently high temperatures, $T\Delta S$ becomes larger than ΔH, ΔG becomes negative, and the reaction becomes spontaneous. We can estimate the temperature at which ΔG changes from positive to negative by setting $\Delta G = \Delta H - T\,\Delta S = 0$. Solving for T, we find that the reaction becomes spontaneous at 698 K:

$$T = \frac{\Delta H}{\Delta S} = \frac{98.8\,kJ}{0.1415\,kJ/K} = 698\,K$$

This calculation assumes the values of ΔH and ΔS are unchanged on going from 298 K to 698 K. In general, the enthalpies and entropies of both reactants and products increase with increasing temperature, but the increases for the products tend to cancel the increases of the reactants. As a result, values of ΔH and ΔS for a reaction are relatively independent of temperature, at least over a relatively small temperature range. In this example, the temperature range is quite large (400 K), and so the calculated value of T is only an estimate.

33. A. Rate $\propto C^n$, where is the order of reaction for a first order reaction: N = 1 so

Rate $\propto$ C

$$\frac{C_1}{C_2} = \frac{r_1}{r_2} = \frac{0.8}{0.1} = 8$$

$$k = \frac{2.303}{t_2 - t_1}\log\frac{C_2}{C_1} = \frac{2.303}{20}\log 8$$

$$= 0.1036 \text{ min}^{-1}$$

$$t_{1/2} = \frac{0.693}{0.1036} = 6.689 \text{ min.}$$

B. (*i*) The rate law according to given information may be given as,

$$\frac{dx}{dt} = K[A]^1[B]^2[C]^0$$

(*ii*) When concentration of A, B and C are doubled then rate will be

$$\frac{dx}{dt} = K[2A][2B]^2[C]^0$$

$$= 8K\,[A][B]^2[C]^0$$

i.e., rate becomes 8 fold, the original rate.

C. $$\text{Rate} = \frac{\text{decrease in pressure}}{\text{Time duration}}$$

$$= \frac{2-1.1}{75} = 0.012 \text{ atm/min}$$

$$\text{Rate in atm/sec} = \frac{0.012}{60}$$

$$= 2 \times 10^{-4} \text{ atm/sec.}$$

Answer is required in molarity per second

$\therefore$ PV = nRT

$$\frac{P}{RT} = \frac{n}{V}$$

$$\frac{p/\text{sec}}{RT} = \left(\frac{n}{V}\right)/\text{sec}$$

$$\left(\frac{n}{V}\right)/\text{sec} = \text{molarity per second}$$

$$\frac{2\times10^{-4}}{0.0821\times300} = \left(\frac{n}{V}\right)/\text{sec}$$

8.12×10^{-6}. Rate in molarity/sec = (n/V)/sec

34. **G** must be phosphorus since its product with Cl_2 and then MeOH/Et_3N results in compound having signal in [13]P NMR. Further hint is that it is a liquid at 60°C. Also, given the Cl content in **H**, The atomic weight of **G** must the 10.3 if stoichiometry of **H** is 1 : 1 (nothing fits well, B 10.8 a.m.u.); or it must be 20.6 if **H** is 1 : 2 stoichiometry (nothing fits well); or it must be 31 if **H** is 1:3 stoichiometry, P fits well.

H is PCl_3 since this is the only chloride of P produced with limited amount of Cl_2, it is further hinted by stating that **H** is a liquid and by Cl content.

J is $(MeO)_3P$, this is hinted by giving its ^{31}P and $^{31}P\{^1H\}$ data. The decuplet stems from 9 magnetically identical H atoms. The reaction gives off HCl which is trapped by Et_3N, giving $Et_3N.HCl$ – compound **K.** This is hinted by 1:1 electrolyte composition, and cation's weight (Et_3NH^+, from ES + MS).

L is PCl_5, which is the highest chloride of P – therefore obtainable by the reaction with excess Cl_2, its tbp structure is another hint of its composition (ECl_5).

Reaction of **G** with a limited amount of oxygen can afford range of lower P oxides, however compound **M** must be P_4O_6 as can be easily deduced from P content given. The formula is P_4O_6 and not P_2O_3.

N is H_3PO_3 – acidic solution in water, produced by hydrolysis of P_4O_6.

P is Na_2HPO_3, this is hinted by giving the stoichiometry of the neutralization. The dibasicity of **N** is another help for confirming its identity as H_3PO_3.

35. A.

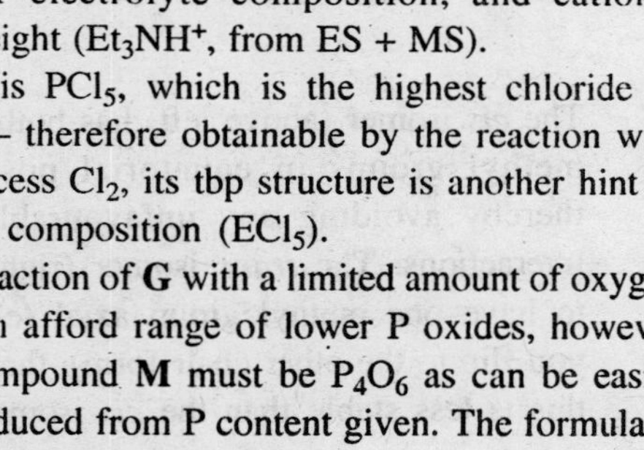

cis-1-*t*-butyl-4-methylcyclohexane *t*-Butyl group **has to be equatorial**. In axial position it will be sterically hindered by hydrogen.

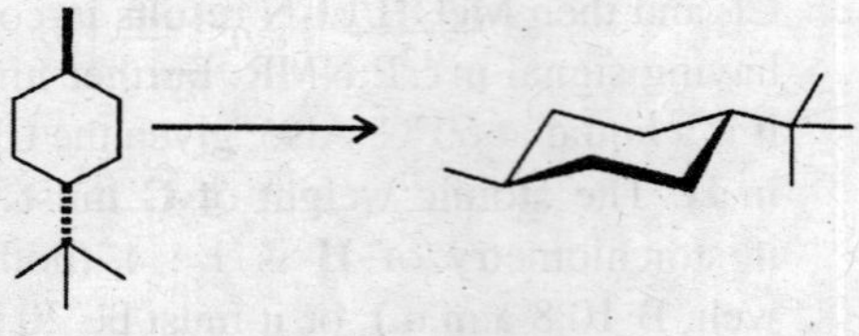

Trans-1-*t*-butyl-4-methylcyclohexane *t*-Butyl group **has to be equatorial**

B.

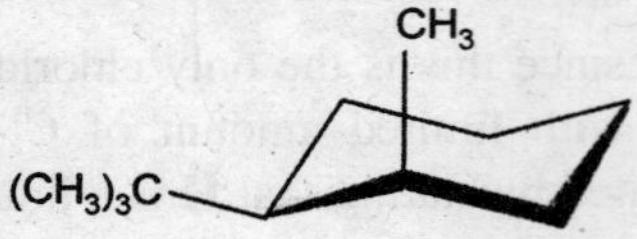

Both groups are pointing "up" from the ring, therefore they are cis, again the very bulky t-butyl group will be equatorial

C.

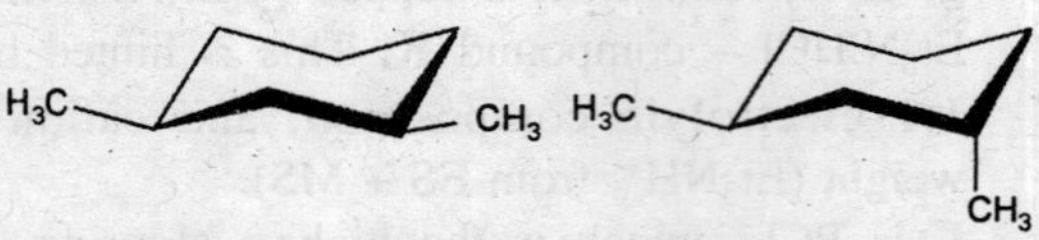

The *cis* isomer (above left) has both large methyl groups in equatorial positions thereby avoiding any unfavourable 1-3 interactions. The *trans* isomer (right) has to have one methyl group axial (even if you flip to the other chair form), therefore this is less stable than the *cis* isomer.

36. A. $Pb^{2}(aq) + 2e^- \rightarrow Pb(s)$ $E° = -0.13V$ $E° = 0.13V$

$Ag^+(aq) + e^- \rightarrow Ag(s)$ $E° = 0.80V$ $E° = 0.80V$

$Pb(s) \rightarrow Pb^{2+}(aq) + 2e^-$ $E°_{cell} = 0.93V$

$2 \times [Ag^+(aq) + e^- \rightarrow Ag(s)]$

$$E°_{cell} = \frac{0.025693V}{n} \ln K_{eq}$$

$$\Delta G° = -nFE°_{cell} = -(2)(96.5kJ/mol*V)(0.93V)$$

$$\ln K = \frac{n \times E^0_{cell}}{0.25693V} = \frac{(2)(0.93V)}{0.025693V} K$$

$$= 2.75 \times 10^{31}$$

$$\Delta G° = -1.8 \times 10^2 kJ$$

B. anode: $Zn(s) \rightarrow Zn^{2+}(aq) + 2e^-$ $E = +0.76$

$E°_{zn}$ as $Zn^{2+}(aq) + 2e^- \rightarrow Zn(s)$ is $-0.76V$

$E°_{cell} = E°_{cathode} - E°_{anode} = 1.83$

$= E°_{bromine} - (-0.76)$

$E°_{bromine} = 1.83 - 0.76 = +1.07\ V$

37. A.

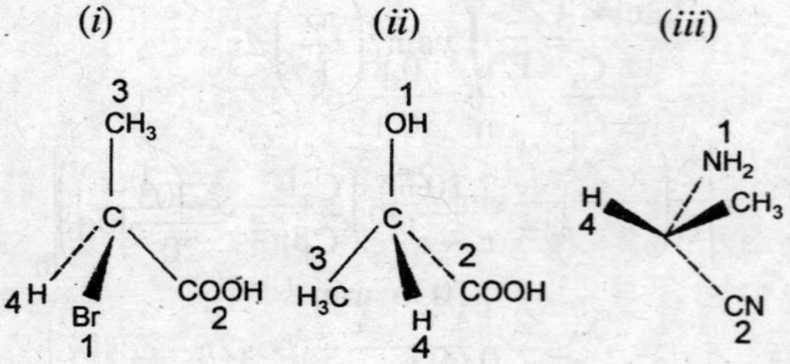

S S S

B.

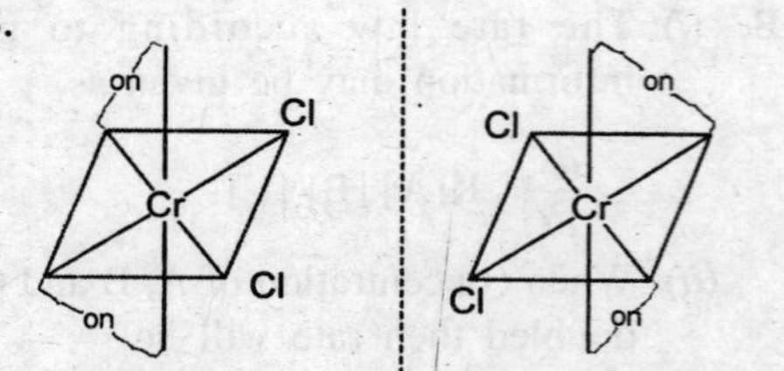

(cis form) (cis form)

The cis form is optically active and its mirror image is not superimposable.

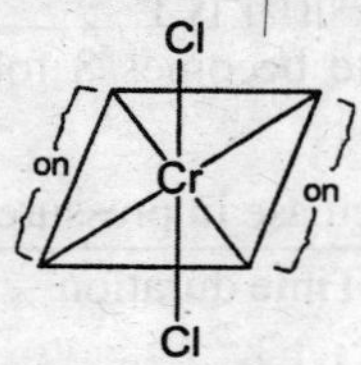

(Transform)

It has plane of symmetry and therefore optically inactive.

C. Since the coordination number of Mn^{2+} ion in the complex ion is 4, it will be either tetrahedral (sp^3 hybridisation) or square planar (dsp^2 hybridisation). But the fact that the magnetic moment of the complex ion is 5.9 BM, it should be tetrahedral in shape rather than square planner because of the presence of five unpaired electrons in the *d* orbitals.

38. A. For a particle in a box in its lowest quantum state

$$\psi = \sqrt{\frac{2}{L}} \sin\left(\frac{\pi x}{L}\right)$$

$$<x> = \int_0^L \psi^* x \psi \, dx$$

$$= \frac{2}{L} \int_0^L x \sin^2\left(\frac{\pi x}{L}\right) dx$$

$$= \left| \frac{2}{L}\left(\frac{x^2}{4} - \frac{xL}{4\pi}\sin\left(\frac{2\pi x}{L}\right) - \frac{L^2}{8\pi^2}\cos\left(\frac{2\pi x}{L}\right)\right) \right|_0^L$$

$$= \frac{2}{L}\left(\frac{L^2}{4} - \frac{L^2}{8\pi^2}(\cos 2\pi - \cos 0)\right)$$

$$= \frac{2}{L}\left(\frac{L^2}{4}\right) = L/2.$$

$$<x^2> = \int_0^L \psi^* x^2 \psi \, dx$$

$$= \frac{2}{L} \int_0^L x^2 \sin\left(\frac{\pi x}{L}\right) dx$$

$$= \frac{2}{L}\left(\frac{x^3}{6} - \left(\frac{x^2 L}{4\pi} - \frac{L^3}{8\pi^3}\right)\right) \sin \frac{2\pi x}{L}$$

$$- \frac{xL^2}{4\pi^2} \cos\left(\frac{2\pi x}{L}\right) \int_0^L$$

$$= \frac{L^2}{3} - \frac{L^2}{2\pi^2}$$

$$<p> = \int_0^L \psi^* p \psi \, dx$$

$$= \frac{2}{L} \int_0^L \sin\left(\frac{\pi x}{L}\right)\left(\hbar . \frac{d}{dx}\right) \sin\left(\frac{\pi x}{L}\right) dx$$

$$= \frac{2\hbar\pi}{L^2} \int_0^L \sin\left(\frac{\pi x}{L}\right) \cos\left(\frac{\pi x}{L}\right) dx$$

$$= 0$$

$$<p^2> = \int_0^L \psi^* p^2 \psi \, dx$$

$$= \frac{2}{L} \int_0^L \sin\left(\frac{\pi x}{L}\right)\left(-\hbar^2 . \frac{d^2}{dx^2}\right) \sin\left(\frac{\pi x}{L}\right) dx$$

$$= \frac{2\pi^2\hbar^2}{L^3} \int_0^L \sin^2\left(\frac{\pi x}{L}\right) dx$$

$$= \frac{2\pi^2\hbar^2}{L^2} \cdot \frac{\pi}{2} = \frac{\pi^2\hbar^2}{L^2}$$

$$\Delta x = \left[< x^2 > - [< x >]^2\right]^{1/2}$$

$$= \left[\frac{L^2}{3} - \frac{L^2}{2\pi^2} - \frac{L^2}{4}\right]^{1/2}$$

$$= L\left[\frac{1}{12} - \frac{1}{2\pi^2}\right]^{1/2}$$

$$\Delta p = \left[< p^2 > - [< p >]^2\right]$$

$$= \left[\frac{\pi^2\hbar^2}{L^2} - 0\right]^{1/2} = \frac{\pi\hbar}{L}$$

$$\Delta x \, \Delta p = \pi\hbar\left(\frac{1}{12} - \frac{1}{2\pi^2}\right)^{1/2}$$

$$= \frac{\hbar}{2}\left(\frac{4\pi^2}{12} - \frac{4}{2}\right)^{1/2} = \frac{\hbar}{2}\left(\frac{\pi^2}{3} - 2\right)^{1/2}$$

finally $\frac{\hbar}{2}\left(\frac{\pi^2}{3} - 2\right)^{1/2}$

$\therefore \Delta x \, \Delta p > \frac{\hbar}{2}$ because the factor $\frac{\pi^2}{3} - 2 = 7.87$ hence $\Delta x \, \Delta p = 7.87 \frac{\hbar}{2}$ which is greater than $\frac{\hbar}{2}$.

B. Ruthenium (44) : $[Kr]^{36}\ 4d^7\ 5s^1$
Platinum (78) : $[Xe]^{54}\ 4f^{14}\ 5d^9\ 6s^1$

39. A. $AlCl_3$ is on the ionic covalent borderline. It is ionic in the solid (hence conducting) but melts to covalent Al_2Cl_6. On heating it dissociates to $AlCl_3$

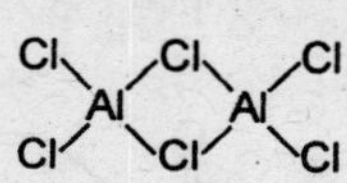

Al_2Cl_6

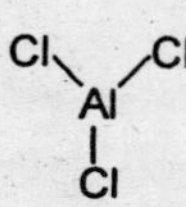

$AlCl_3$
(Trigonal)

B.

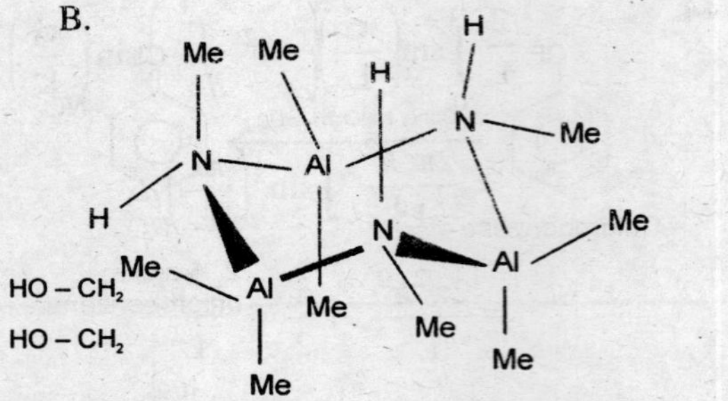

More stable because fewer axial Me group

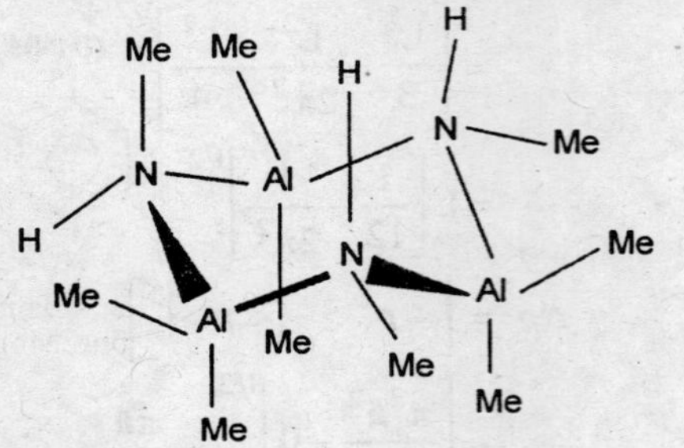

40. A. (*i*)

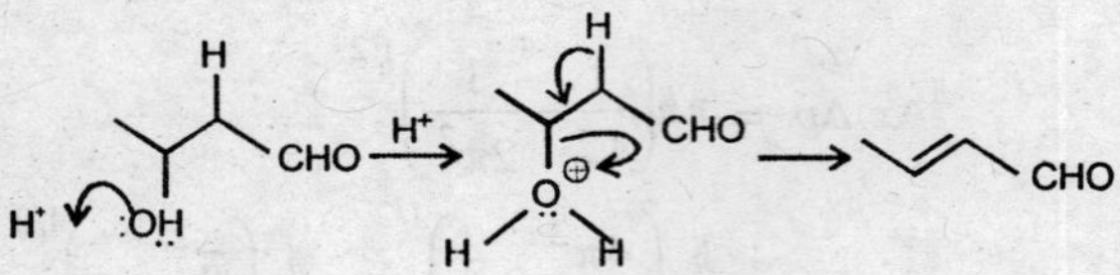

(*ii*)

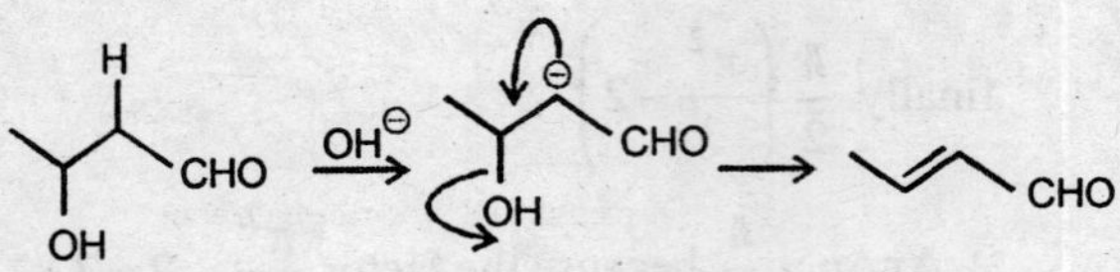

B.

$$CH \equiv C-CH_3 \xrightarrow{NH_2^{\ominus}} C^{\ominus} \equiv C-CH_3$$

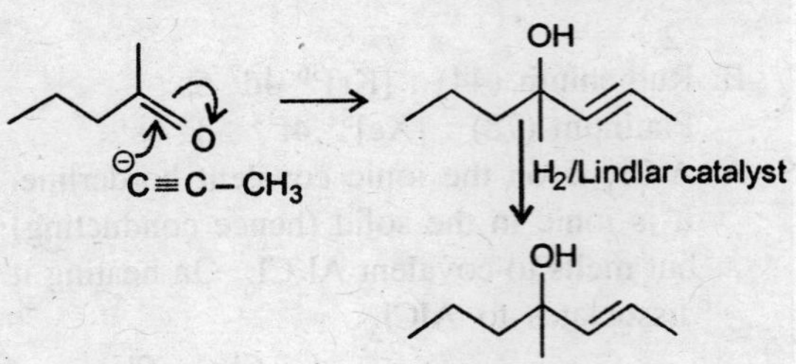

C.

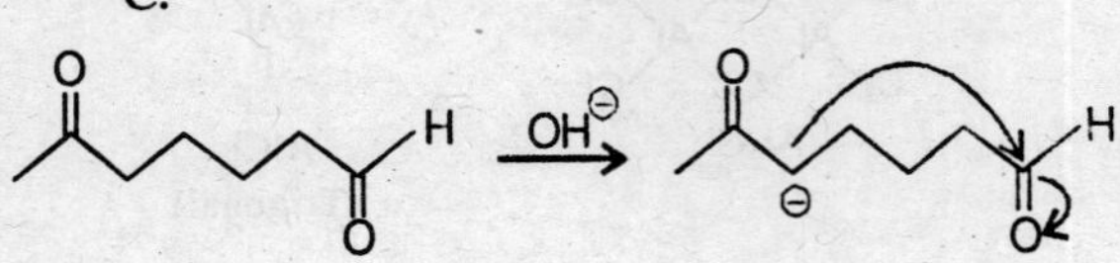

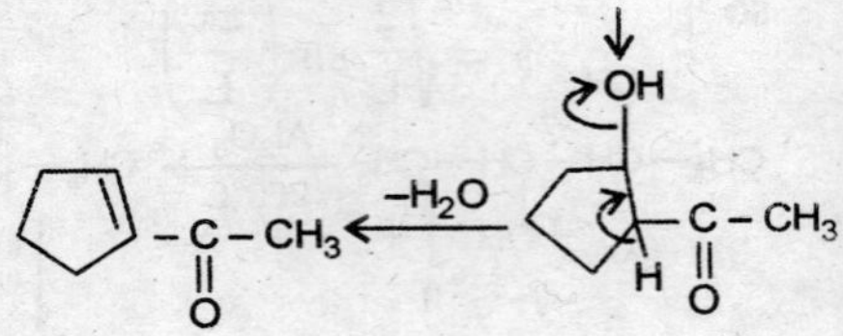

41. A. (*i*)

$$CH_3CHO + CH_2O \underset{}{\overset{Base}{\rightleftharpoons}} HOCH_2CH_2CHO$$

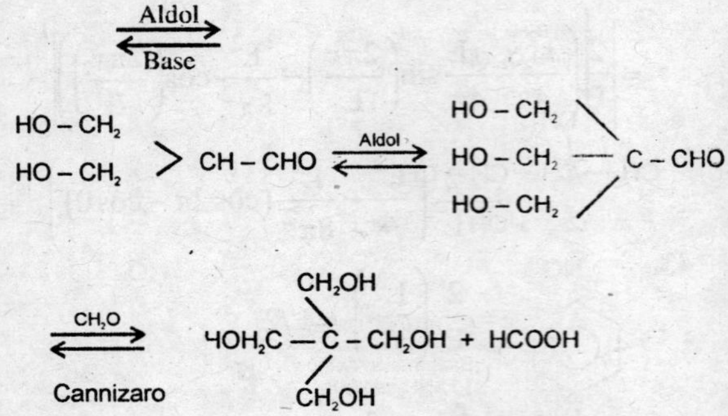

Pentaerythritol

This reaction is called as Tollen reaction. It is carried out in the presence of $Ca(OH)_2$.

B.

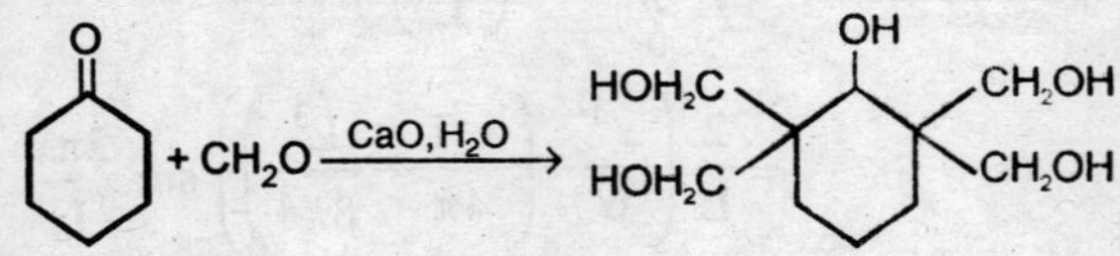

42. A.

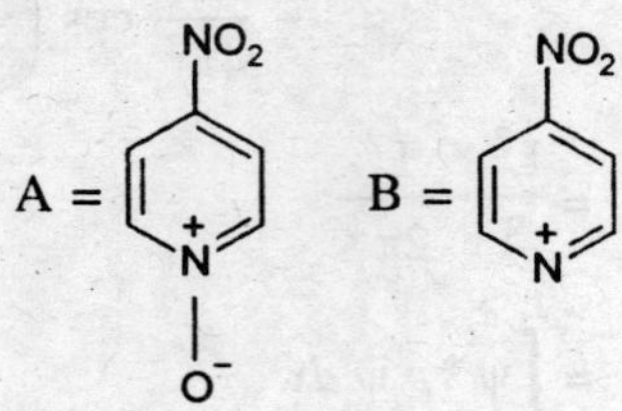

B.

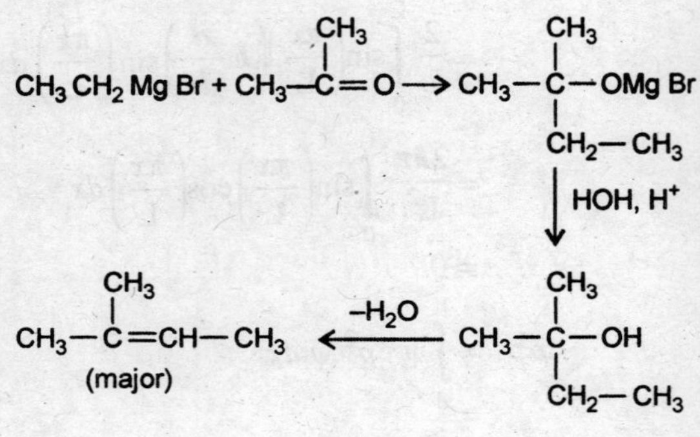

so

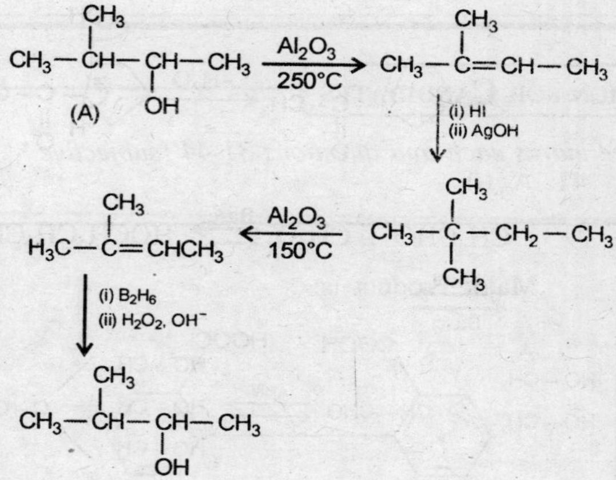
(A)
Al_2O_3
250°C
(i) HI
(ii) AgOH
Al_2O_3
150°C
(i) B_2H_6
(ii) H_2O_2, OH^-

43.

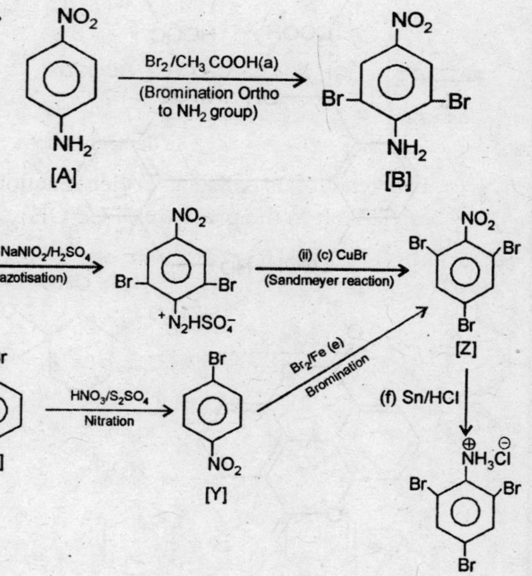
[A]
Br_2/CH_3COOH(a)
(Bromination Ortho to NH_2 group)
[B]
(i) (b) $NaNO_2/H_2SO_4$
(Diazotisation)
(ii) (c) CuBr
(Sandmeyer reaction)
[Z]
[X]
HNO_3/S_2SO_4
Nitration
[Y]
Br_2/Fe (e)
Bromination
(f) Sn/HCl

44. A.

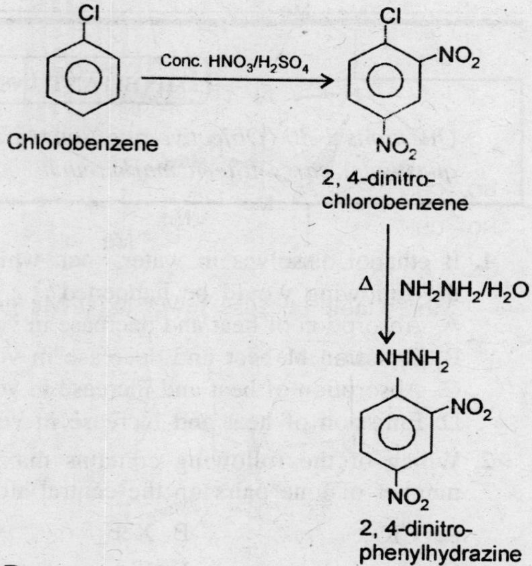
Chlorobenzene
Conc. HNO_3/H_2SO_4
2, 4-dinitro-chlorobenzene
Δ NH_2NH_2/H_2O
2, 4-dinitro-phenylhydrazine

B.

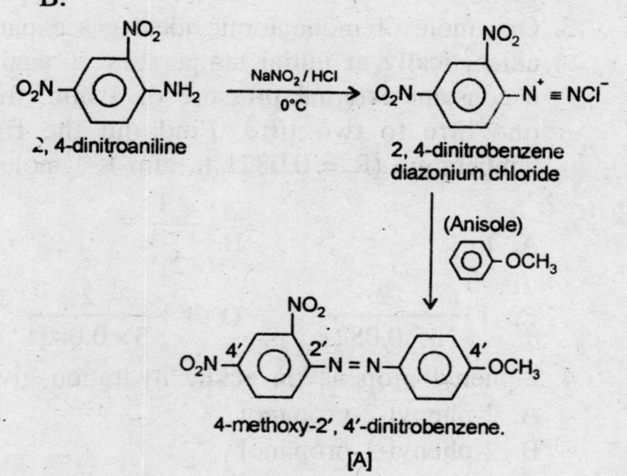
2, 4-dinitroaniline
$NaNO_2$ / HCl
0°C
2, 4-dinitrobenzene diazonium chloride
(Anisole)
4-methoxy-2′, 4′-dinitrobenzene.
[A]

TEST PAPER-4

IMPORTANT INSTRUCTION FOR CANDIDATES

Questions 1-30 (Objective questions) carry three marks each and questions 31-44 (subjective questions) carry fifteen marks each.

1. If ethanol dissolves in water, then which of the following would be happened?
A. Absorption of heat and decrease in volume
B. Emission of heat and decrease in volume
C. Absorption of heat and increase in volume
D. Emission of heat and increase in volume

2. Which of the following contains maximum number of lone pairs on the central atom?
A. ClO_3^- B. XeF_4
C. SF_4 D. I_3^-

3. One mole of monoatomic ideal gas expands adiabatically at initial temperature T against a constant external pressure of 1 atm. from one litre to two litre. Find out the final temperature (R = 0.0821 lt. atm K^{-1} $mole^{-1}$)

A. T B. $\frac{T}{(2)^{\frac{5}{3}-1}}$

C. $T-\frac{2}{3\times0.0821}$ D. $T+\frac{2}{3\times0.0821}$

4. 2-phenyl propene on acidic hydration gives
A. 2-phenyl-2-propanol
B. 2-phenyl-1-propanol
C. 3-phenyl-1-propanol
B. 1-phenyl-2-propanol

5.

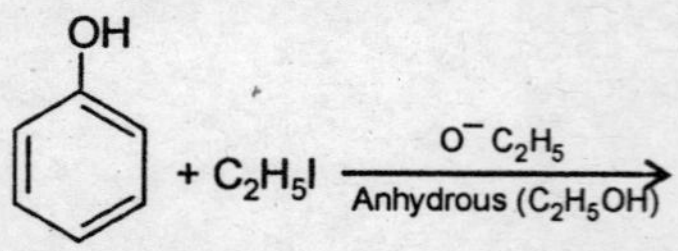

A. $C_6H_5OC_2H_5$ B. $C_2H_5OC_2H_5$
C. $C_6H_5OC_6H_5$ D. C_6H_5I

6.

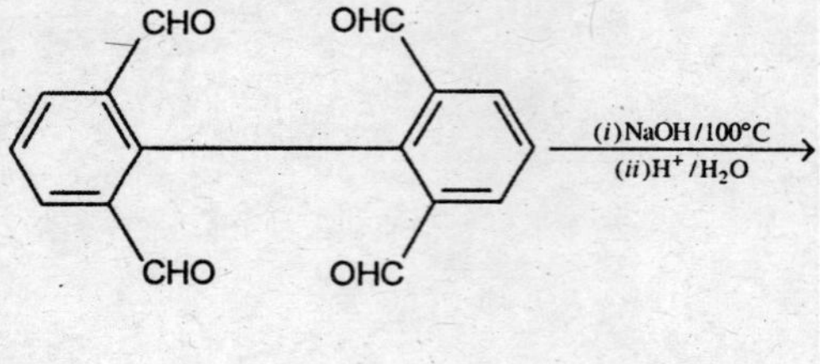

Major Product is:

A.

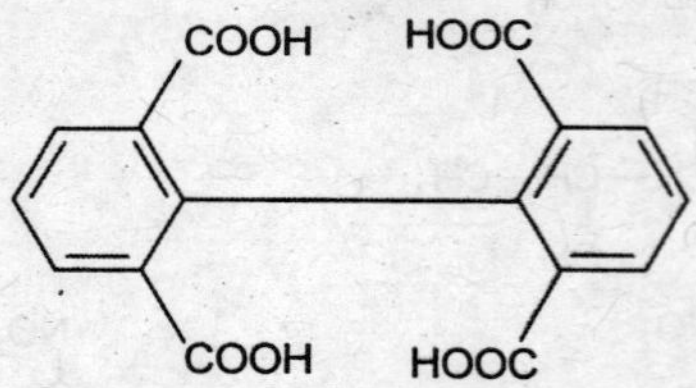

B.

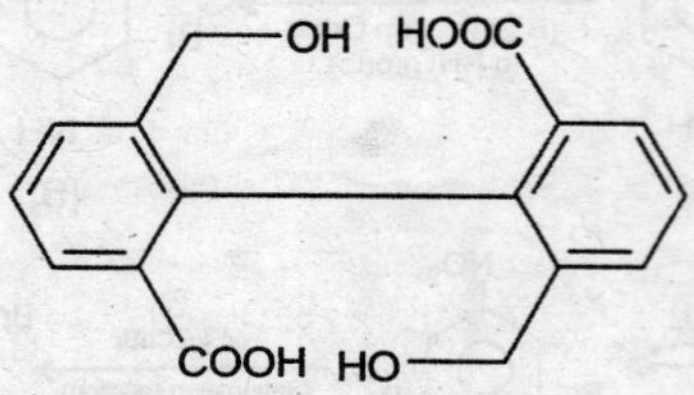

C.

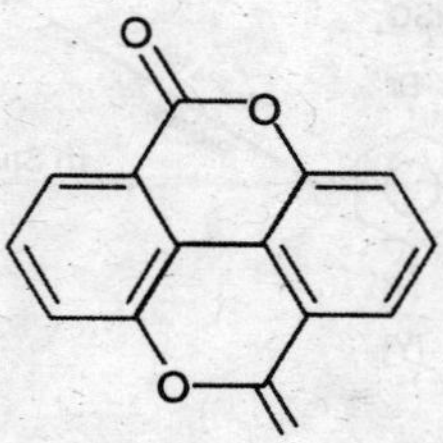

D.

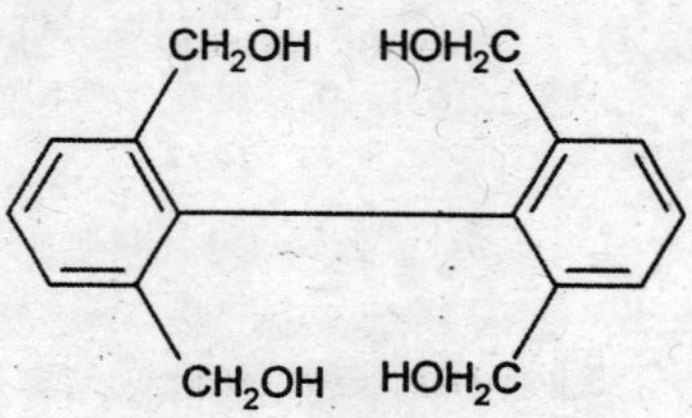

7. In a first order reaction the concentration of reactant decreases from 800 mol/dm³ to 50 mol/dm³ is 2×10^4 sec. The rate constant of reaction in sec^{-1} is:
A. 2×10^4 B. 3.45×10^{-5}
C. 1.386×10^{-4} D. 2×10^{-4}

8. $Ph-C\equiv C-CH_3 \xrightarrow{H_g^{2+}/H^+} [A.]$ The A is:

A. 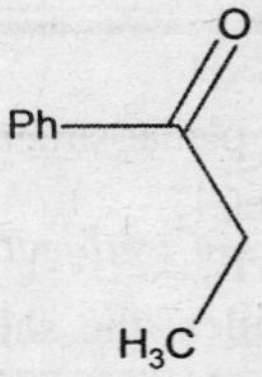 B. 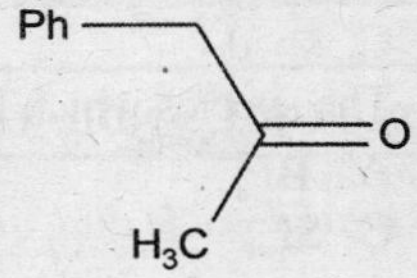

C. 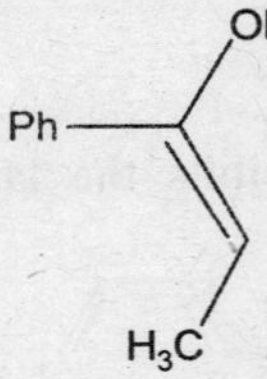 D. 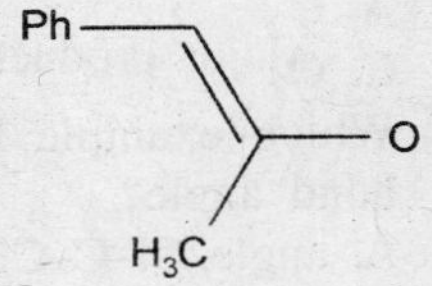

9. Ethyl ester $\xrightarrow[\text{excess}]{CH_3MgBr}$ P. The product P will be

A. 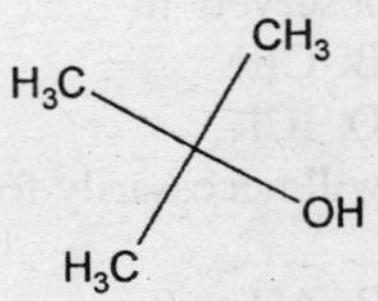 B. 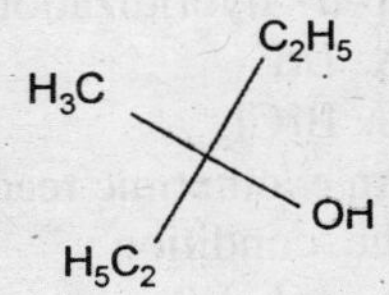

C. 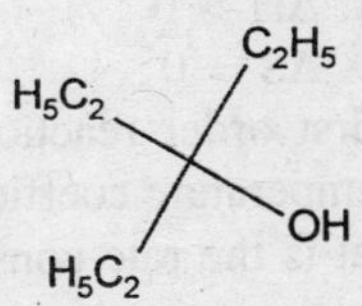 D. 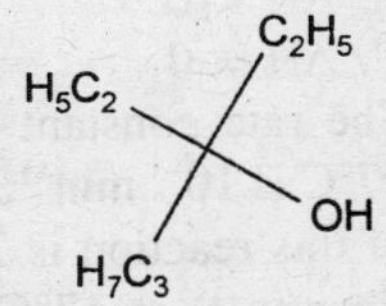

10. Which of the following will be major product when 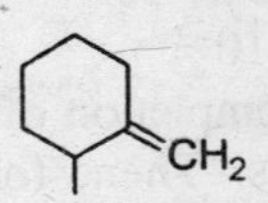 is treated with dil H_2SO_4 in presence of $HgSO_4$.

A. 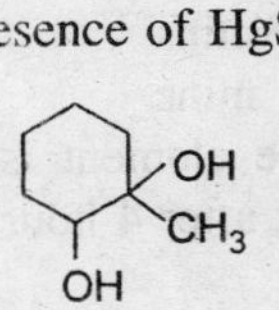 B. 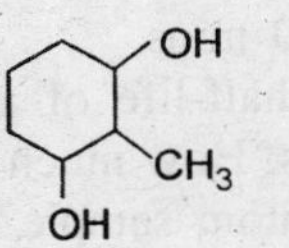

C. 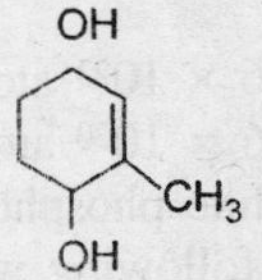 D. 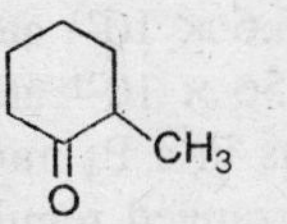

11. What configurations are found in the product(s) of the reaction below?

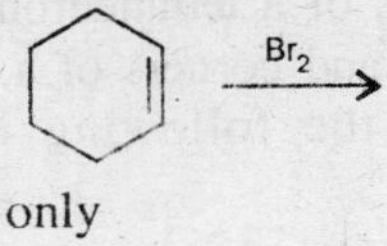

A. 1S, 2S only

B. 1R, 2S only

C. 1R, 2R only

D. an equal mixture of 1R, 2R and 1S, 2S

12. Which of the following compounds on reaction with CH_3MgBr will give a tertiary alcohol?

A. C_2H_5CHO

B. $C_2H_5COOCH_3$

C. C_2H_5COOH

D. $CH_3-\underset{\diagdown O \diagup}{CH-CH}-CH_3$

13. Select the structure of the major product formed from the following reaction

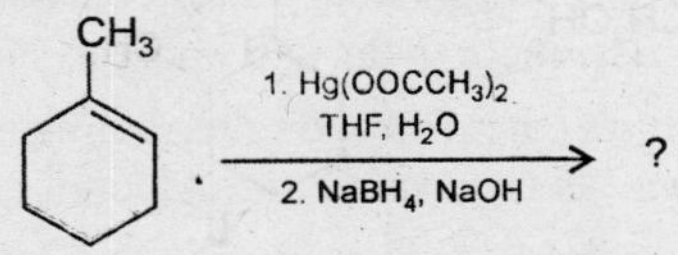

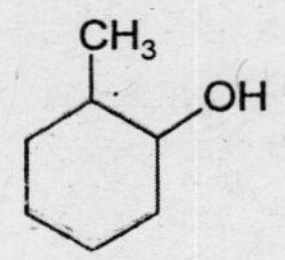

I

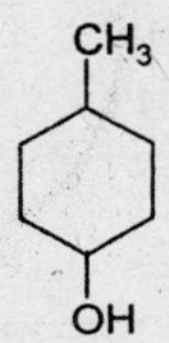

II

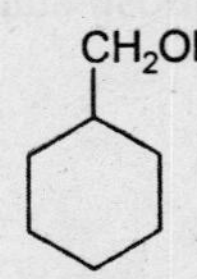

III

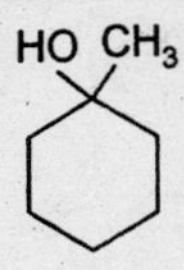

IV

A. I B. II

C. III D. IV

14. What would be the major product of the following reaction?

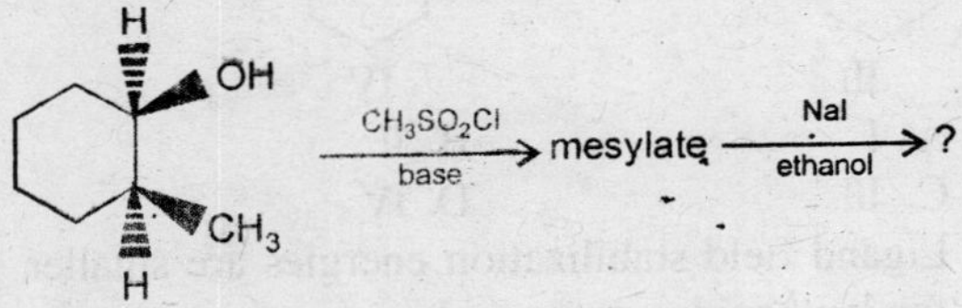

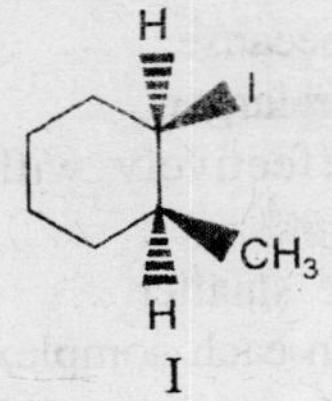

I

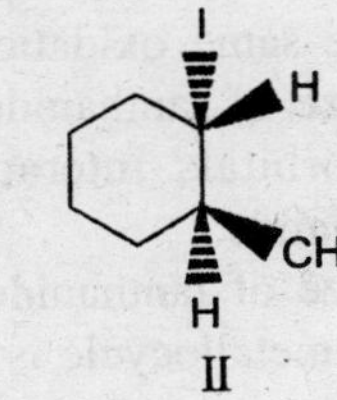

II

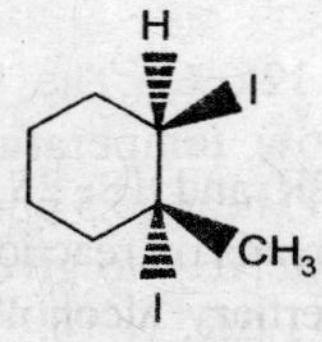

III

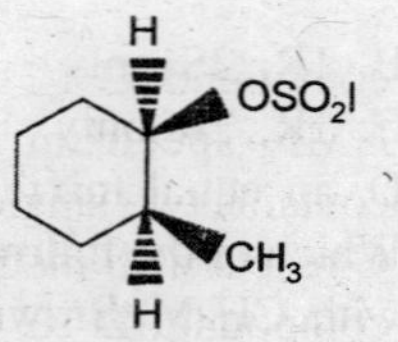

IV

A. I B. II

C. III D. IV

15. What is the major product of the following reaction?

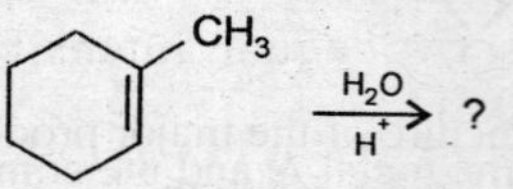

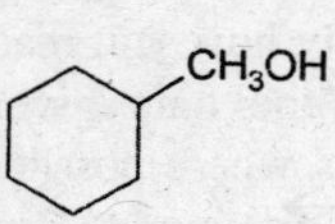

I

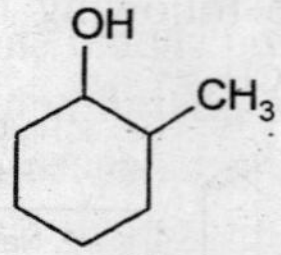

II

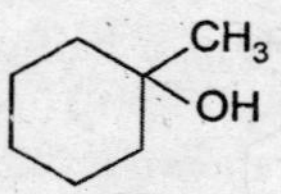

III

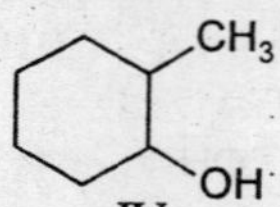

IV

A. I B. II

C. III D. IV

16. Which of the following is the most stable carbocation?

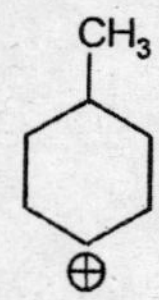

I

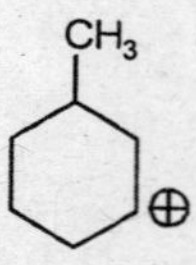

II

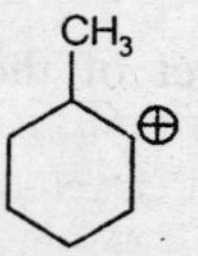

III

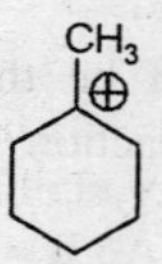

IV

A. I B. II

C. III D. IV

17. Ligand field stabilization energies are smaller for lanthanides compared to transition metals in the same oxidation state because:

A. Size of lanthanide ions are larger

B. f-orbitals interact less effectively with ligands

C. Size of lanthanide ions are smaller

D. A metallocycle is formed in each complex

18. The hybrid orbitals used by bromine atom in BrF_3 are

A. sp^2 B. sp^3

C. sp^3d D. sp^3d^3

19. The species which has a square planar structure is

A. BF_4^- B. $FeCl_4^-$

C. SF_4 D. XeF_4

20. Among the following molecules, the shortest bond length is to found in

A. C_2 B. N_2

C. O_2 D. F_2

21. Which example below exhibits the largest bond angle?

A. angle Cl–C–Cl in $CHCl_3$

B. angle F–B–F in BF_3

C. angle H–O–H in H_2O

D. angle F–Be–F in BeF_2

22. sp^3d^2 hybridization is observed in

A. BrF B. ClF_3

C. $BrCl_3$ D. ICl_5

23. An exothermic reaction will necessarily follow the condition

A. $\Delta H < 0$ B. $\Delta H > 0$

C. $\Delta H = 0$ D. $\Delta S = 0$

24. The rate constant of a first order reaction at 27°C is 10^{-3} min^{-1}. The temperature coefficient of this reaction is 2. What is the rate constant (in min^{-1}) at 17°C for this reaction?

A. 10^{-3} B. 5×10^{-4}

C. 2×10^{-3} D. 10^{-2}

25. The time taken for 10% completion of a first order reaction is 20 mins. Then, for 19% completion, the reaction will take

A. 40 mins B. 60 mins

C. 30 mins D. 50 mins

26. The half-life of a radioactive element is 10 hours. How much will be left after 4 hours in 1 g atom sample?

A. 45.6×10^{23} atoms B. 4.56×10^{23} atoms

C. 4.56×10^{21} atoms D. 4.56×10^{20} atoms

27. Atoms in a P_4 molecule of white phosphorus are arranged regularly in the following way:

A. at the corners of a cube

B. at the corners of a octahedron

C. at the corners of a tetrahedron

D. at the centre and corners of a tetrahedron

28. Which one of the following is called a carbylamine?

A. R CN B. R $CONH_2$
C. R – CH = NH D. R NC

29. What value of *n* in Huckel's rule applies to the aromatic compound shown below?

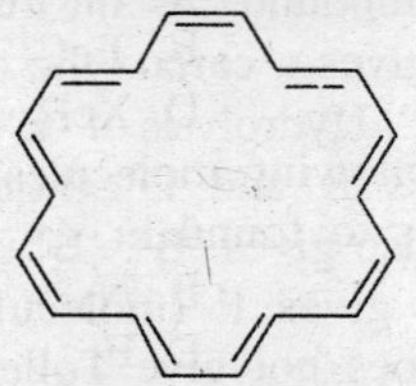

A. 3 B. 4
C. 5 D. 9

30. The increase in boiling points shown below is the result of an increase in which of the following from F_2 to I_2?

	°C
F_2	–187.9
Cl_2	–34.0
Br_2	+588
I_2	+184.5

A. Ionic bonding
B. Covalent bond strength
C. Electron affinity
D. van der Waal's forces

31. A. What are the concentrations of Ag^+, $Ag(NH_3)^+$, and $Ag(NH_3)_2^+$ in a solution prepared by adding 0.10 mol of $AgNO_3$ to 1.0 L of 3.0 M NH_3? $K_f = 1.7 \times 10^7$, $K_1 = 2.1 \times 10^3$, $K_2 = 8.1 \times 10^3$

B. The gas phase decomposition of dimethyl ether follows first order kinetics.
$CH_3OCH_{3(g)} \rightarrow CH_{4(g)} + H_{2(g)} + CO_{(g)}$
The reaction is carried out in a constant volume container at 500°C. Initially only dimethyl ether is present at a pressure of 0.40 atm. The total pressure of the gaseous reaction mixture after 12 minute is 0.75 atm. Calculate half-life of the reaction.

32. A silvery metal **A** reacts with chlorine to give a white crystalline solid, **B**, (Cl 79.8%), which conducts electricity. At its melting point (192°C), the electrical conductivity drops to zero. On further heating **B** vaporises, and the gas formed has M_r = 266.7 a.m.u., dropping to 133.3 a.m.u. at high temperature.
A reacts with Me_2Hg to give a liquid from which can be distilled a colourless pyrophoric compound **C** (C 50.0%, H 12.6%). The ^1H NMR spectrum of **C** at low temperature contains two singlets (ratio 2:1) near δ0.5 ppm. **C** reacts with methylamine ($MeNH_2$) to give a compound, **D** (C 41.4%, H 11.6%, N 16.1%, M_r = 261.3 a.m.u.) and with dimethylamine (Me_2NH) to give **E** (C 47.5%, H 12.0%, N 13.9%, M_r = 202.2 a.m.u.). In both cases, a gas, **F**, (M_r = 16) is evolved. **D** exists in two isomeric forms. The ^1H NMR spectrum of **E** contains two equal intensity singlets (δ 1.5 and 0.5).
Identify the metal **A** and the compounds **B**–**F**. You should show clearly how you reach these assignments from the data given, writing balanced equations where possible.

33. A. A concentration cell consists of two Ag/Ag^+ half-cells. In half-cell A, electrode A dips into 0.0100M $AgNO_3$, in half-cell B, electrode B dips into 4.0×10^{-4}M $AgNO_3$. What is the cell potential at 298 K? Which electrode has a positive charge?

B. In a test of a new reference electrode, a chemist constructs a voltaic cell consisting of a Zn/Zn^{2+} half-cell and an H_2/H^+ half-cell under the following conditions:
$[Zn^{2+}]$ = 0.010M
$[H^+]$ = 2.5M
P_{H_2} = 0.30atm
Calculate E_{cell} at 298 K.

34. A. Write the IUPAC name of following compounds
(*i*) $[CoCl(NO_2)(NH_3)_4]Cl$
(*ii*) $[PtCl(NH_2CH_3)(NH_3)_2]Cl$

B. (*i*) AB crystallises in a rock salt structure with A : B = 1 : 1. The shortest distance between A and B is $Y^{1/3}$ nm. The formula mass of AB is 6.023 Y a.m.u. where Y is an arbitrary constant. Find the density in kgm^{-3}
(*ii*) If measured density is 20 kg m^{-3}, identify the type of point defect.

35. A. Write the mechanism.

(i) 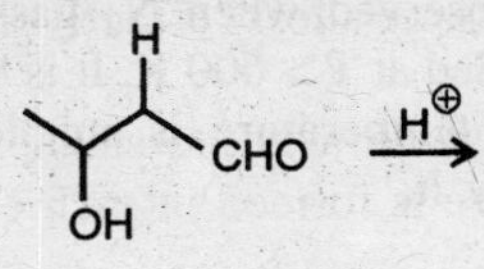

(ii) 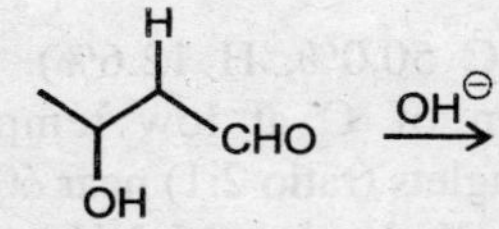

B. Carry out the following transformation.

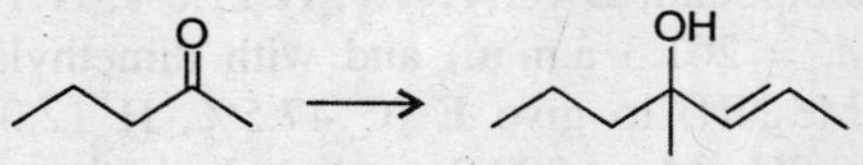

C. Carry out the following transformation.

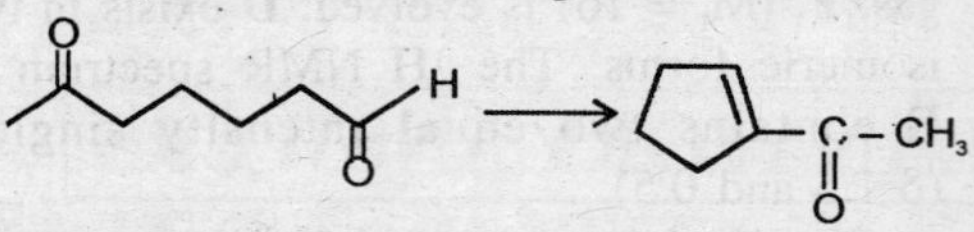

36. A. Calculate the freezing point of an aqueous solution of a non-electrolyte having an osmotic pressure of 2.0 atm at 300 K. (K_f = 1.86 K kg mol^{-1}, R = 0.082 L atm K^{-1} mol^{-1}).

B. A decimolar solution of potassium ferrocyanide is 50% dissociated at 300K. Calculate the osmotic pressure of the solution. (R = 8.314 JK^{-1} mol^{-1})

C. Calculate the molarity of water if its density is 1000 kg/m³.

37. What is the boiling temperature of pure water inside a pressure cooker? Let T_1 be the normal boiling temperature $T_{(boil)}$ of water (i.e. 100°C, 373 K, at $p^{\ominus}$) and let p_2 of 6 × $p^{\ominus}$ be the pressure inside the pan. The enthalpy of boiling water is 50.0 kJ mol^{-1}.

38. A. Calculate the CFSE (Crystal Field Stabilization Energy) of $[TiCl_6]^{3-}$ if the λ_{max} is 770 nm.

B. Crystal Field Stabilization Energies for Metal ions in Octahedral Complexes. By assigning a value of 0.4Δ_0 for each electron in a t_{2g} orbital, and –0.6 Δ_0 for each electron in an e_g orbital the crystal field stabilization energy of an octahedral complex can be calculated. Determine the CFSE for the following octahedral complexes:

(*i*) high spin d^4 (*ii*) low spin d^4
(*iii*) high spin d^7 (*iv*) low spin d^7

39. A. Heating is observed when N_2 gas at 200 atm is expanded at T > 600 K. It is because of inversion temperature is smaller than 600 k. Justify it.

B. Calculate the μ (dipole moment) of HCl? if bond distance is 1.34A°, charge = 4.8 × 10^{-10} esu and calculate % ionic character if experimental value of μ = 1.08 D?

40. An organic compound 'A' on treatment with ethyl alcohol gives a carboxylic acid 'B' and a compound 'C'. Hydrolysis of 'C' under acidic conditions gives 'B' and 'D'. Oxidation of 'D' with $KMnO_4$ also gives 'B'. 'B' upon heating with $Ca(OH)_2$ gives E (molecular formula, C_3H_6O). 'E' does not give Tollens' test and does not reduce Fehling solution but forms a 2, 4-dinitrophenylhydrazone. Identify A, B, C, D and E.

41. A. Explain briefly the formation of the product giving the structure of the intermediate

$$CH_2(COOC_2H_5)_2 \xrightarrow{NaOEt} \xrightarrow{CH_3CH(Br)COOC_2H_5} \xrightarrow[(ii)H^+]{(i)HO^-} \begin{array}{l} CH_3-CH-COOH \\ \qquad\;\;| \\ \qquad CH_2-COOH \end{array}$$

B. Write the structures of the products A and B.

$$CH_3-\overset{\overset{\Large O}{\|}}{C}-{}^{18}OC_2H_5 \xrightarrow{H_3O^+} A+B$$

42. Identify A, B, C, D and E in the following scheme and write their structures.

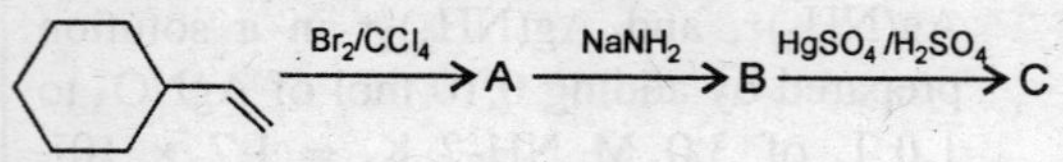

$$C \xrightarrow{NH_2NHCONH_2} D$$

$$C \xrightarrow{NaOD/D_2O\ (excess)} E$$

43. A. Predict the major product of the following reaction:

$$C_6H_6 + (CH_3)_2CHCH_2OH \xrightarrow{H_2SO_4}$$

B. 3, 3-Dimethylbutan-2-o1 loses a molecule of water in the presence of concentrated sulphuric acid to give tetramethylethylene as a major product. Suggest a suitable mechanism.

C. Give the structures of the major organic product when 3-ethylpent-2-ene is reacted with $Hg(OAc)_2$ / H_2O, $NaBH_4$.

44. A. Convert Ethylamine into methylamine.

B. Convert Isopropyl alcohol to *n*-propyl alcohol (2° alcohol to 1° alcohol).

C. Convert Benzaldehyde to cyanobenzene.

ANSWERS

1	2	3	4	5	6	7	8	9	10
C	D	C	A	A	B	C	A	A	D
11	**12**	**13**	**14**	**15**	**16**	**17**	**18**	**19**	**20**
D	D	D	B	C	D	B	C	D	B
21	**22**	**23**	**24**	**25**	**26**	**27**	**28**	**29**	**30**
D	D	A	D	A	B	C	D	B	D

SOME SELECTED EXPLANATORY ANSWERS

1. When ethanol is dissolved in water then the solution shows the positive deviation from Raoult's law.

$\therefore$ ΔH = +ve : (endothermic, heat absorbed)

ΔV = +ve : (increase of volume)

2.

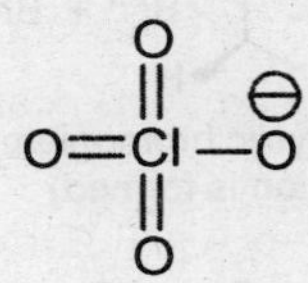

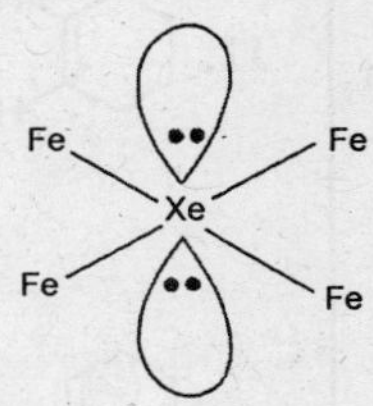

(Two lone pair)

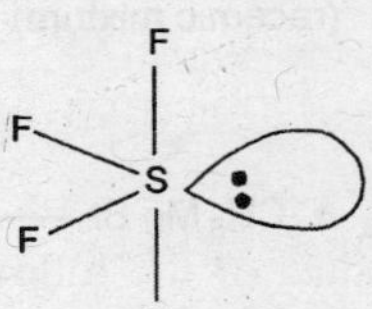

(One lone Pair)

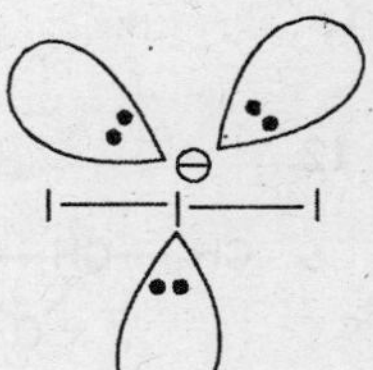

(Three lone pair)

3. Work done against constant external pressure $= P_{ext}\ (V_2 - V_1)$

In adiabatic condition $\Delta q = 0$ therefore $w = \Delta u$

$$\therefore -P_{ext}\ (V_2 - V_1) = \frac{3}{2} R\ (T_2 - T_1)$$

[Expansion work is negative]

On solving, $T_2 = T_1 - \dfrac{2}{3 \times 0.0821}$

4. More stable (here tertiary) carbocation will be formed

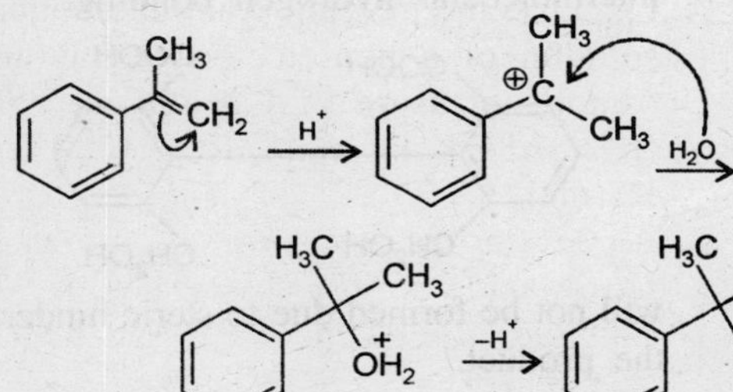

5. $C_2H_5O^-$ will abstract proton from phenol converting the latter into phenoxide ion. This would then make nucleophilic attack on the methylene carbon of alkyl iodide. But $C_2H_5O^-$ is in excess. $C_2H_5O^-$ is better nucleophile than $C_6H_5O^-$ (phenoxide) ion since while in the former the negative charge is localised over oxygen and in the latter it is delocalised over the whole molecular framework. So, it is $C_2H_5O^-$ ion that would make nucleophilic attack at ethyl iodide to give diethyl ether (Williamson's synthesis).

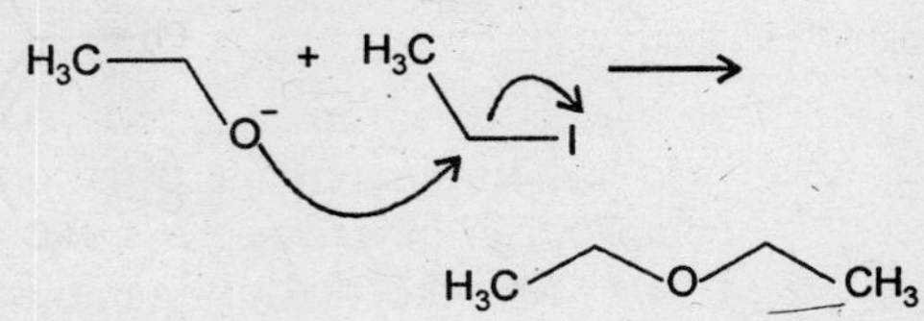

6.

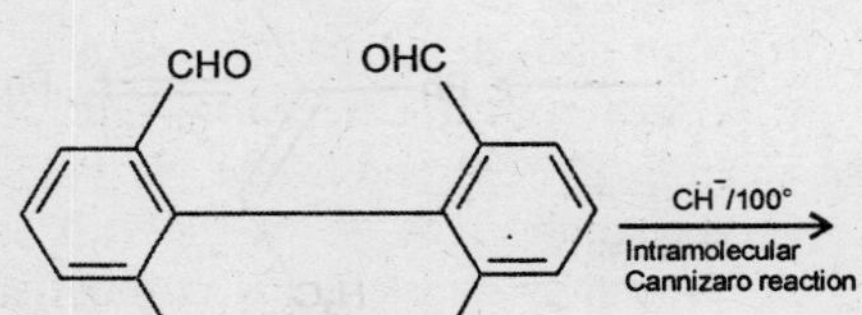

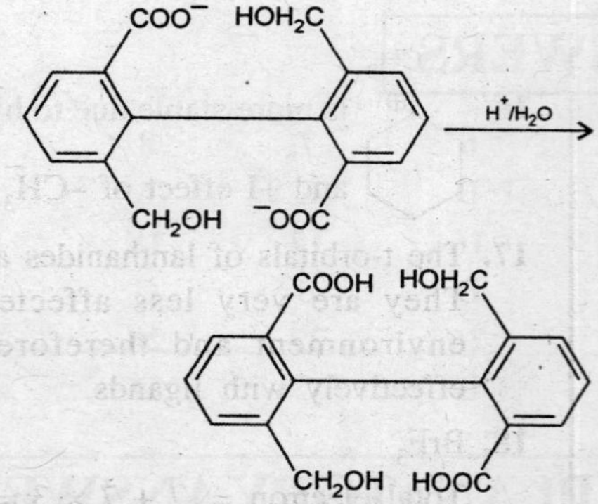

The product will be stable due to intermolecular hydrogen bonding.

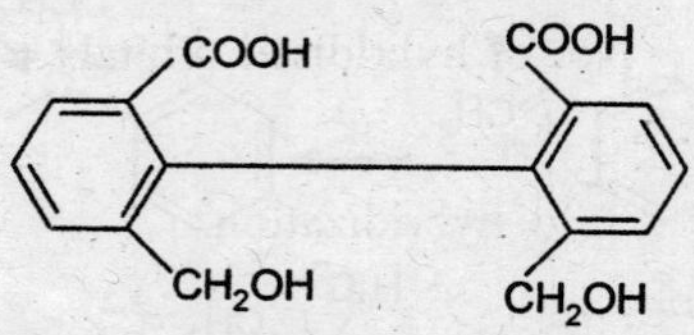

will not be formed due to steric hinderance in the product.

7. $K = \dfrac{2.303}{t}\log\dfrac{[A]_0}{[A]_t} = \dfrac{2.303}{2\times10^4}\log\dfrac{800}{50}$

$= 1.386 \times 10^4\ s^{-1}$

8.

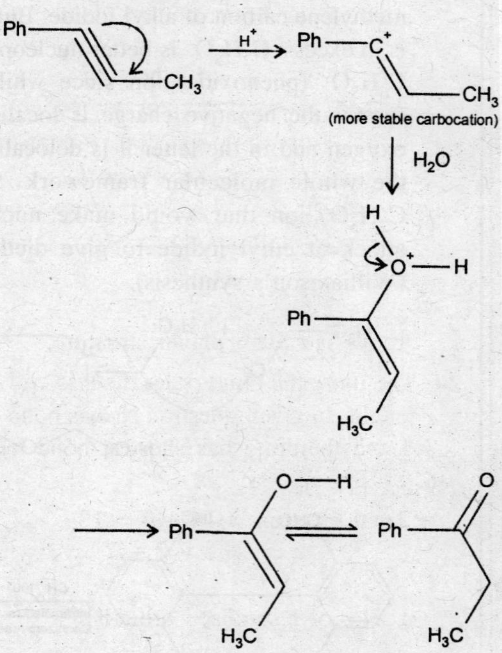

9.

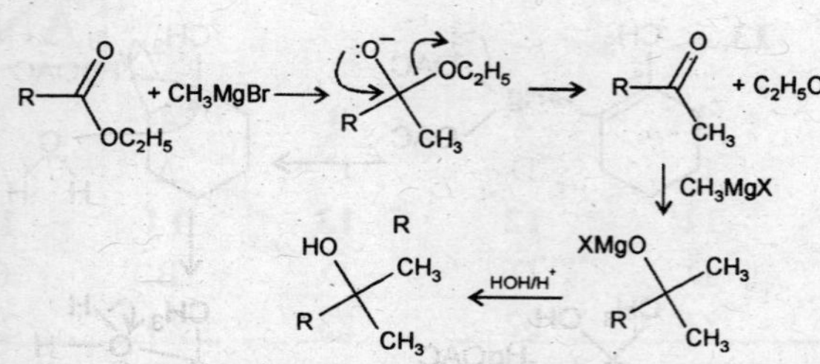

Thus, the choice with at least two methyl groups at the a carbon linked with –OH group will be the correct choice.

10.

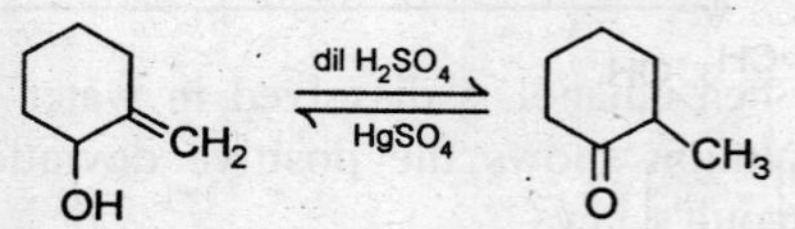

Above is keto-enol tautomerism.

11.

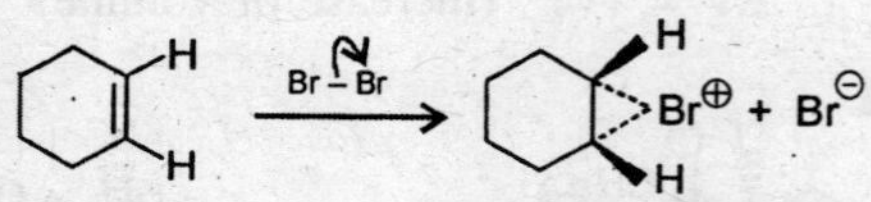

(Cyclic bromonium ion is formed)

∴

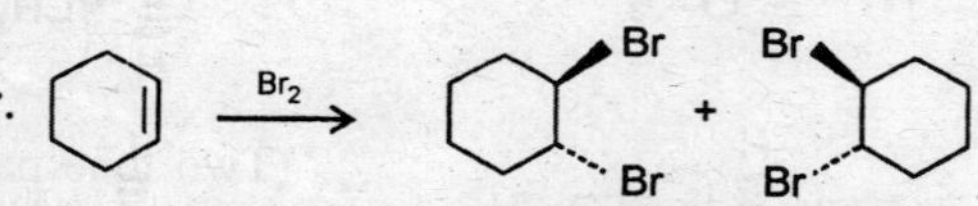

trans-1, 2-dibromocyclohexane (racemic mixture)

12.

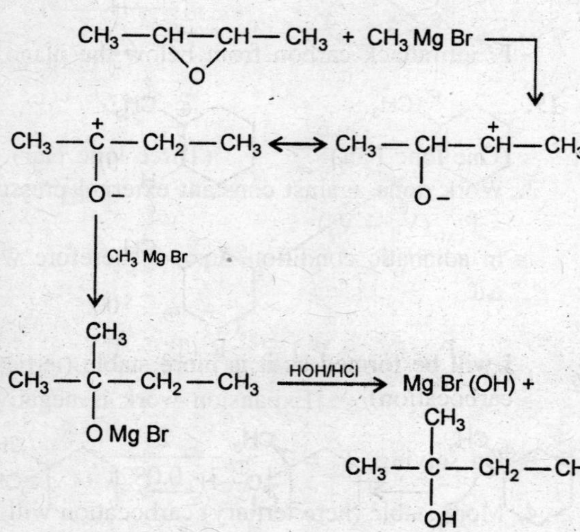

13. 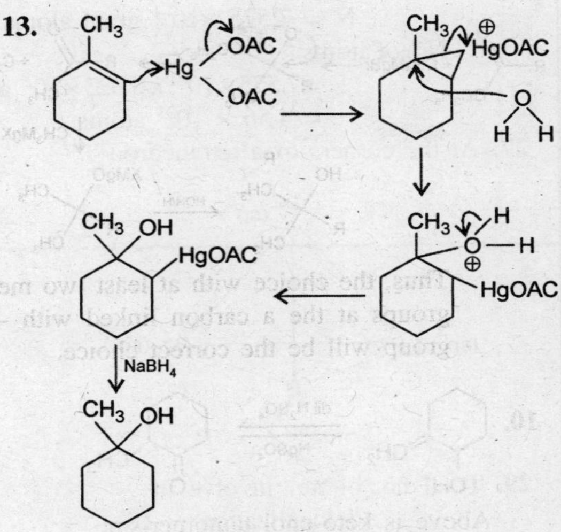

14.

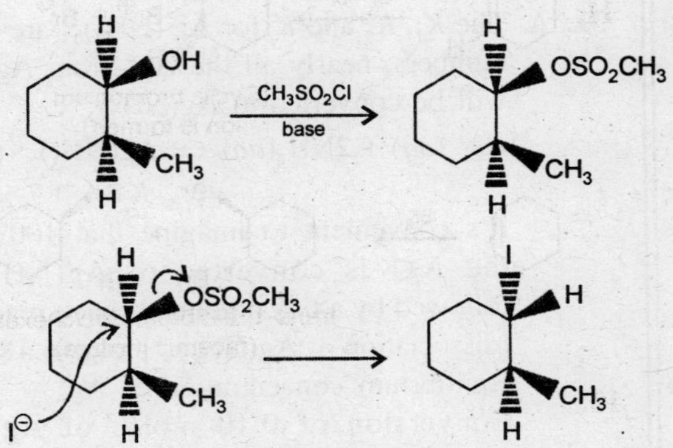

$I^{\ominus}$ ion attack carbon from below the plane.

15. 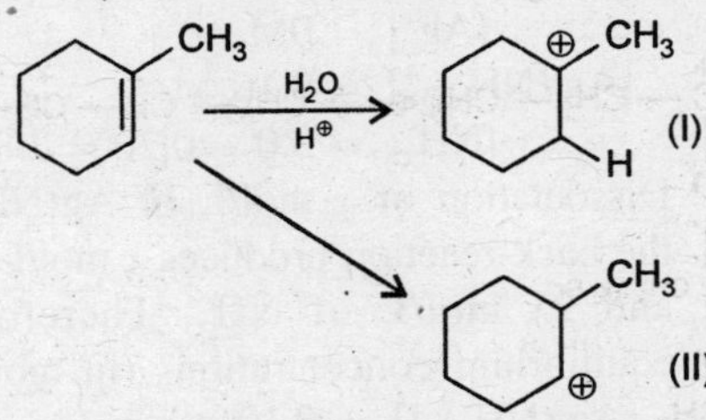

I will be formed as it is more stable (tertiary carbocation)

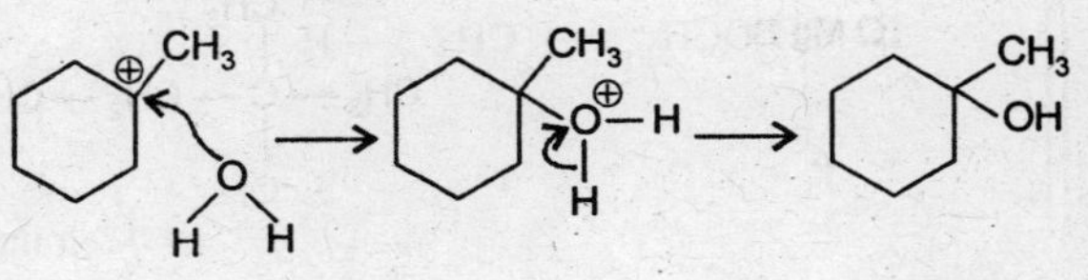

16. 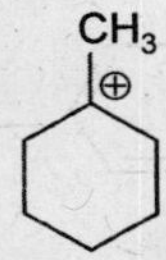 is more stable due to hyperconjugative and +I effect of $-CH_3$ group.

17. The t-orbitals of lanthanides are deep seated. They are very less affected by external environment and therefore interact less effectively with ligands.

18. BrF_3

Total electron = 7 + 7 × 3 = 28

28 = 8 × 3 + 4

$\therefore$ No. of hybridised orbitals = $\frac{8\times3}{8}+\frac{4}{2}$

= 3 + 2 = 5

$\Rightarrow$ sp^3d hybridization.

19. XeF_4

Total no. of electron = 8 + 7 × 4 = 36

= 8 × 4 + 4

$\therefore$ No. of hybridised orbitals = $\frac{8\times4}{8}+\frac{4}{2}$

= 4 + 2 = 6

Structure is shown below

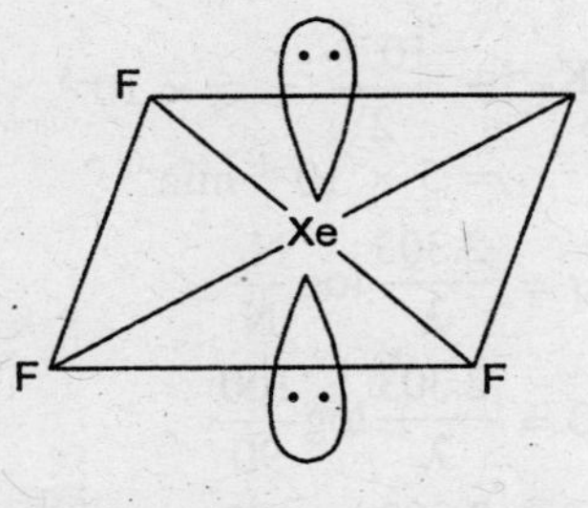

Above is square planar structure.

20. The more the bond order the less will be bond lenght. In given question N_2 has bond order of 3 and therefore has shortest bond length.

21. For F – Be – F

Total electron = 14 + 4 = 18

= 8 × 2 + 2

$\therefore$ No. of hybridised orbitals = $\frac{8\times2}{8}+\frac{2}{2}$

= 2 + 1 = 3

$\Rightarrow$ sp^2 hybridisation.

The bond angle will be about 120° effect of electronegativity difference for simplicity is neglected to arrive at 120° bond angle.

22. ICl_5

Total no. of electron = 7 × 6 = 42

= 8 × 5 + 2

∴ Total no. of hybridised orbitals

$$= \frac{8\times 5}{8} + \frac{2}{2}$$

= 5 + 2 = 7

$\Rightarrow$ Sp^3d^2.

23. In exothermic reaction the energy of product is less than reactant

$\Rightarrow$ $\Delta H < 0$.

24. $$\frac{K_{T_2}}{K_{T_1}} = (\mu)^{\Delta T/10}$$

$$\frac{10^{-3}}{K_{T_1}} = \mu^{10/10} = 2$$

$$K_{T_1} = \frac{10^{-3}}{2} = .5 \times 10^{-3}$$

$= 5 \times 10^{-4}$ min^{-1}.

25. $$t = \frac{2.303}{\lambda}\log\frac{N_0}{N}$$

$$20 = \frac{2.303}{\lambda}\log\frac{100}{90} \quad ...(i)$$

$$t = \frac{2.303}{\lambda}\log\frac{100}{81} \quad ...(ii)$$

equation (*i*)/(*ii*)

∴ t = 40 min.

26. $$t_{1/2} = 10 \text{ hr. } K = \frac{0.693}{10}$$

$$4 = \frac{2.303\times 10}{0.693}\log\frac{1}{N}$$

$$\log\frac{1}{N} = \frac{4\times 0.693}{2.303\times 10} = 1.12036$$

$\log N = -0.12036 = \bar{1}.87964$

$N = 7.575 \times 10^{-1}$ gram atoms

∴ No. of atoms

$= 7.575\times 10^{-1}\times 6.023\times 10^{23}$ atoms

$= 4.56 \times 10^{23}$ atoms.

27. At the corners of a tetrahedron

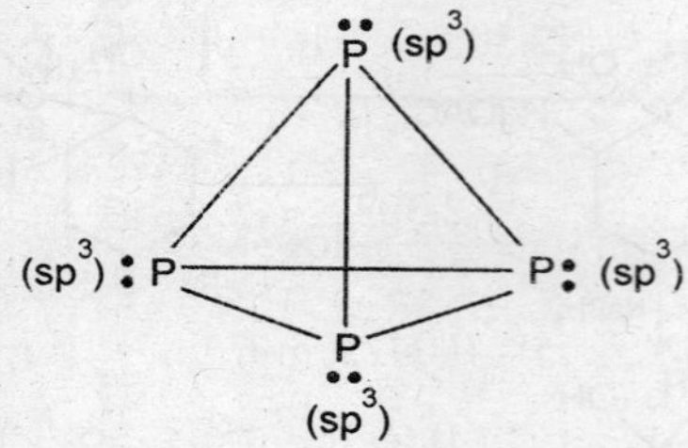

29. Total no. of πe^- involve in

delocalization = 18

$\Rightarrow$ $4n + 2 = 18$

or $n = 4$.

31. A. The K_1, K_2 and K_f for Ag $(NH_3)_2^+$ are large numbers, nearly all the Ag^+ from $AgNO_3$ will be converted to $Ag(NH_3)_2^+$:

$$Ag^+ (aq) + 2NH_3(aq) \rightleftharpoons Ag(NH_3)_2^+ (aq)$$

$$K_f = 1.7 \times 10^7$$

It's convenient to imagine that 100% of the Ag^+ is converted to $Ag(NH_3)_2^+$, followed by a tiny amount of back-reaction [dissociation of $Ag(NH_3)_2^+$] to give a small equilibrium concentration of Ag^+. Conversion of 0.10 mol/L of Ag^+ to $Ag(NH_3)_2^+$, the following concentration are obtained:

$[Ag^+]$ = 0M

$[Ag(NH_3)_2^+]$ = 0.10 M

$[NH_3]$ = 3.0 – 0.20 = 2.8 M

Dissociation of x mol/L of $Ag(NH_3)_2^+$ in the back-reaction produces x mol/L of Ag^+ and $2x$ mol/L of NH_3. Therefore, the equilibrium concentrations (in mol/L) are

$[Ag(NH_3)_2^+]$ = 0.10 – x

$[Ag^+]$ = x

$[NH_3]$ = 2.8 + 2x

B. $CH_3OCH_{3(g)} \rightarrow CH_{4(g)} + H_{2(g)} + CO_{(g)}$

P_0	0	0	0	...t = 0
$P_0 - x$	x	x	x	...t
				= 12 minute

From question $P_0 = 0.40$ atm
Total pressure after 12 minute

$$P_0 = x + x + x + x = 0.75 \text{ at},$$
$$\text{or } P_0 + 2x = 0.75$$
$$x = 0.175 \text{ atm}$$

At constant volume, mole ∝ pressure

$$\text{So, } k = \frac{2.303}{t}\log\frac{a}{a-x} = \frac{2.303}{t}\log\frac{P_0}{P_0 - x}$$
$$= \frac{2.303}{12}\log\frac{0.40}{0.40-0.175}$$
$$= 0.0475 \text{ min}^{-1}$$
$$t_{1/2} = \frac{0.693}{0.0475} = 14.58 \text{ min}$$

32. **A** if 1 Cl, 79.8/100 = 35.5/M_r so M_r = 44.5. Atomic mass of M would be 9. Nothing fits
If 2 Cl, 79.8/100 = 71/M_r so M_r = 89.0. Atomic mass of M would be 18. Nothing fits
If 3 Cl, 79.8/100 = 106/M_r so M_r = 135. Atomic mass of M would be 27. Fits for Al, which is trivalent. So A must be Al and B must be $AlCl_3$.
$2Al + 3Cl_2 \rightarrow 2AlCl_3$
C C 50%, H 12.5% C:H = 12.5/(50/12) = 3 so CH_3 must be present. Made from Al and Me_2Hg so may be $AlMe_3$. Microanalysis fits for this. NMR data shows two peaks so cannot be $AlMe_3$. It would fit for Al_2Me_6.

2 Signals ratio 2 (terminal : 1 bridging)
$2Al + 3Me_2Hg \rightarrow 2Al_2Me_6 + 3\ Hg$
D C 41.4%, H 11.5%, N 16.1%, gives C:H:N = 3.45:11.5:1.15 or 3:10:1. Made from Me_6Al_2 and $MeNH_2$ so C:N ratio suggests 2 Me and one amine. For 10 H must be $Me_2Al(NMeH)$, Microanalysis fits but M_r = 87 so must be a trimer $[Me_2Al(NMeH)]_3$
$3Me_6Al_2 + 6MeNH_2 \rightarrow 2[Me_2Al(NMeH)]_3 + 6CH_4$
F is methane

E C 47.5%, H 11.9%, N 13.9%, C:H:N = 3.95:11.9:0.99 or 4:12:1. Made from Me_6Al_2 and Me_2NH so C:N ratio suggests 2 Me and one amine. For 12 H must be $Me_2Al(NMe_2)$, Microanalysis fits but M_r = 101 so must be a dimer $[Me_2Al(NMe_2)]_2$
$Me_6Al_2 + 2Me_2NH \rightarrow [Me_2Al(NMe)_2]_2 + 2CH_4$

33. A. Ag^+(aq, 0.010M) half-cell A ⟶ Ag^+(aq, 4.0×10^{-4}M) half-cell B

$$E_{cell} = E^0_{cell} - \frac{0.0592V}{1}\log\frac{[Ag^+]_{dilute}}{[Ag^+]_{concentrated}}$$
$$E_{cell} = 0\ V - 0.0592 \log 4.0 \times 10^{-2}$$
$$= 0.0828\ V$$

Half-cell A is the cathode and has the positive electrode.

B. Determining E^0_{cell} :

$2H^+(aq) + 2e^- \rightarrow H_2(g) \quad E^0 = 0.00V$

$$Q = \frac{P_{H_2} \times [Zn^{2+}]}{[H^+]^2}$$

$Zn^{2+}(aq) + 2e^- \rightarrow Zn(s) \quad E^0 = -0.76V$

$$Q = \frac{(0.30)(0.010)}{(2.5)^2}$$

$Zn(s) \rightarrow Zn^{2+}(aq) + 2e^- \quad E^0 = +0.76V$

$Q = 4.8 \times 10^{-4}$

$$E_{cell} = E^0_{cell} - \frac{0.0592V}{n}\log Q$$
$$E_{cell} = 0.76 - (0.0592/2)\log(4.8 \times 10^{-4})$$
$$= 0.86V$$

34. A. (*i*) Tetraaminechloronitritocobalt (III) Chloride
(*ii*) Diaminechloro (methylamine) platinum (II) Chloride

B. (i) Edge of the unit cell (a) = 2 × $Y^{1/3}$ nm
Formula mass, M = 6.023 Y g mol^{-1}

$$= \frac{6.023Y}{1000} \text{ kg mol}^{-1}$$

For rock salt type structure, Z = 4

$$\therefore \text{Density } (\rho) = \frac{Z \times M}{a^3 \times N_0}$$

$$= \frac{4 \times (6.023 \times 10^{-3}\,\text{Y kg mol}^{-1})}{(2 \times \text{Y}^{1/3} \times 10^{-9}\,m)^3 \times (6.023 \times 10^{23}\,\text{mol}^{-1})}$$

$= 5\text{kgm}^{-3}$.

(ii) As the measure density is much higher than the calculated density, this means that some foreign species (impurity) or extra metal ions are present in the interstitial sites. Hence it is interstitial defect or metal excess defect.

35. A. (*i*)

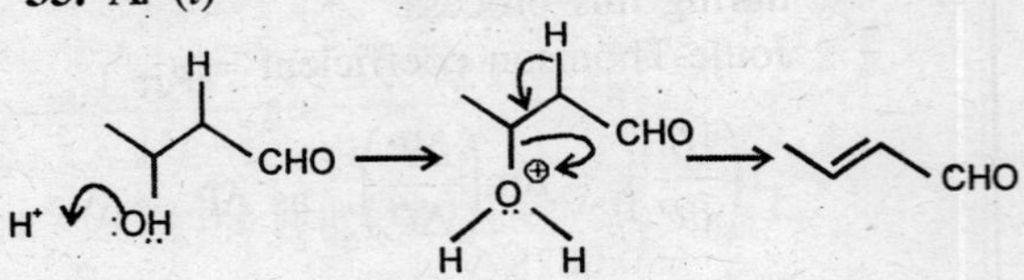

(*ii*)

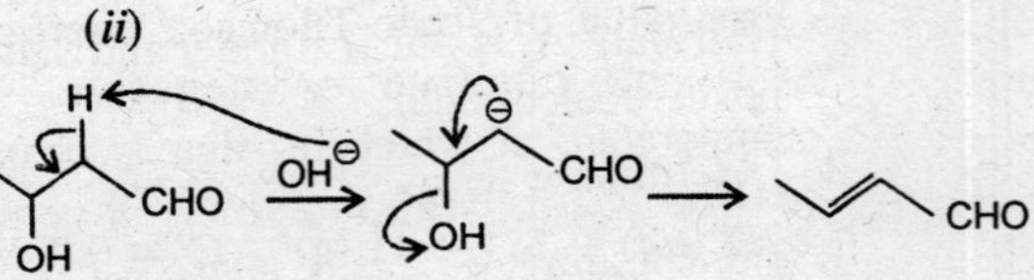

B. $CH \equiv C - CH_3 \xrightarrow{NH_2^{\ominus}} C^{\ominus} \equiv C - CH_3$

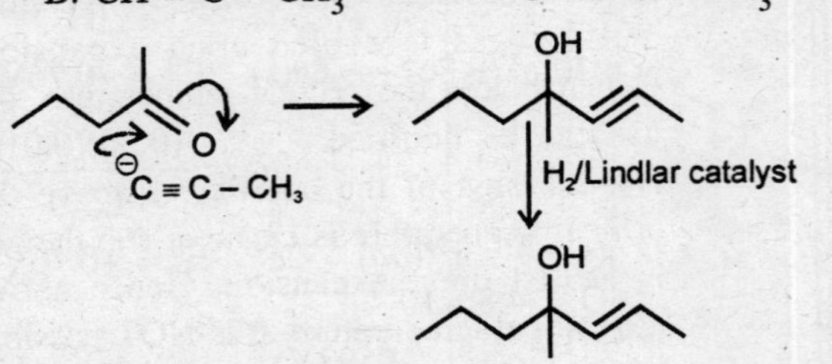

C.

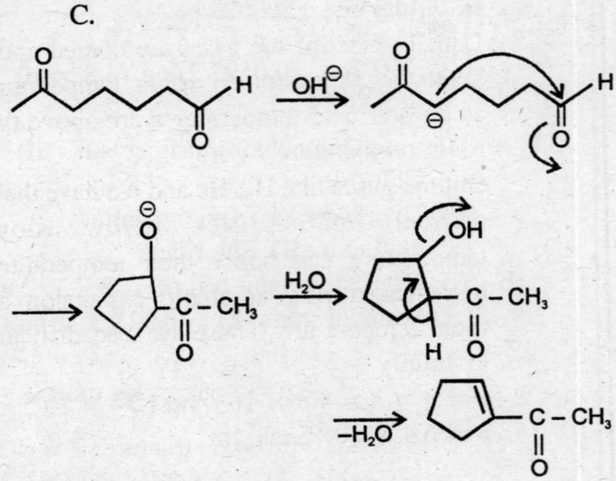

36. A. Apply P = CRT.

This gives C = 0.0812 M $\simeq$ 0.0812 m.

Then $\Delta T_f = K_f \times m$

$= 1.86 \times 0.0812 = 0.151°$

$\therefore$ Freezing point of the solution

$= -0.151°C$

B. Here $\alpha = 0.5$

	$K_4[Fe(CN)_6]$	$\rightleftharpoons$ $4K^+$	+ $[Fe(CN)_6]^{4-}$
Initial moles	1		
Moles after disso.	$1-\alpha$	4α	α

Total = $1 + 4\alpha$

$\therefore$ van't Hoff factor,

$$i = \frac{1+4\alpha}{1} = 1 + 4 \times 0.5 = 3$$

Osmotic pressure, P = *i*CRT

As R = 8.314 $JK^{-1}\,mol^{-1}$ *i.e.* it is in S.I. units.

$$C = 0.1\text{ M} = \frac{0.1}{10^{-3}}\text{ mol m}^{-3} = 10^2\text{ mol m}^{-3}.$$

Hence $P = 3 \times 10^2 \times 8.314 \times 300$

$= 7.483 \times 10^5\ Nm^{-2} = 7.483$ atm.

C. Molarity of water means number of moles of water in 1 litre of water

1 L of water = 1000 cm^3 = 1000 g

($\because d = 1\ kg/m^3 = 1 g/cm^3$)

$$1000g\ H_2O = \frac{1000}{18}\text{ moles} = 55.56\text{ moles}$$

Hence molarity = 55.56 M.

37. Insert the values into Equation and rearrange.

Inserting values gives

$$\ln\left(\frac{6 \times p^{\ominus}}{p^{\ominus}}\right) = \frac{-50000\,\text{J mol}^{-1}}{8.314\,\text{JK}^{-1}\,\text{mol}^{-1}} \times \left(\frac{1}{T_2} - \frac{1}{373\text{K}}\right)$$

We can omit the units of the two pressures on the left-hand side because the Equation is written as a ratio, so the units cancel: we require only a *relative* change in pressure.

$$\ln 6.0 = -6104\text{ K} \times \left(\frac{1}{T_2} - \frac{1}{373\text{K}}\right)$$

where ln 6.0 has a value of –1.79. Next, we rearrange slightly by dividing both sides by 6104 K, to yield:

$$\frac{-1.79}{6104\text{K}} = \frac{1}{T_2} - \frac{1}{373K}$$

so $$\frac{1}{T_2} = -2.98 \times 10^{-4}\ K^{-1} + \frac{1}{373K}$$

and $\frac{1}{T_2} = 2.38 \times 10^{-3}\ K^{-1}$

We obtain the temperature at which water boils by taking the reciprocal of both side. T_2 is 420 K, or 147°C at a pressure of $6 \times p^{\ominus}$, which is much higher than the normal boiling temperature of 100°C.

38. A. The energy corresponding to $\lambda_{max} = 770$ nm can be calculated as

$$E = \frac{hc}{\lambda_{max}} = \frac{6.625\times10^{-34}\ J.sec\times3\times10^{8}\ m.sec^{-1}}{770\times10^{-9}\ m}$$

$= 2.58 \times 10^{-19}$ J

$= 2.58 \times 10^{-22}$ kJ per one molecule

$= 2.58 \times 10^{-22}$ kJ $\times 6.023 \times 10^{23}$

$= 155$ per mole

This energy is equal to the magnitude of energy separation (Δ_o) between t_{2g} and e_g in the octahedral complex $[TiCl_6]^{3-}$.

E. C of Ti^{3+} in the complex is $3d^1$ and the only electron occupies the t_{2g}.

Hence the CFSE = $1 \times -2/5\Delta_o = -2/5 \times 155$ = 62 kJ. $mole^{-1}$.

B. (*i*) High spin d^4: In this case the d electrons experience a weak field and therefore are unpaired. Thus the electron distribution is $t_{2g}^3\ e_g^1$. Therefore if n_t and n_e respectively represent the number of electrons in the t_{2g} and e_g orbitals, then the crystal field stabilizing energy is given by:

CFSE $= n_t(0.4\Delta_o) + n_e(-0.6\Delta_o)$

$= (3)\ (0.4\Delta_o) + (1)\ (-0.6\Delta_o)$

$= 0.6\Delta_o$

(*ii*) Low spin d^4: Now all the electrons are paired and they reside only in the t_{2g} orbitals. Thus

CFSE $= (4)\ (0.4\Delta_o) + 0 = 0.6\Delta_o$

(*iii*) High spin d^7: The corresponding electron distribution is $t_{2g}^5 e_g^2$. Thus

CFSE $= (5)\ (0.4\Delta_o) + 2(-0.6\Delta_o)$

$= 0.8\Delta_o$

(*iv*) Low spin d^7: the electron distribution is $t_{2g}^6 e_g^1$. Accordingly

CFSE $= (6)\ (0.4\Delta_o) + 1(-0.6\Delta_o)$

$= 1.8\Delta_o$

39. A. ***Joule-Thomson Effect:*** The change in temperature of non-ideal gas when it is allowed to expand adiabatically from high pressure to low pressure is called Joule-Thomson effect.

The temperature may increase or decrease during this process.

Joule-Thomson coefficient = μ_{JT}

$$= \left(\frac{\partial T}{\partial P}\right)_H = \lim\left(\frac{\Delta T}{\Delta P}\right)_H \text{ as } \Delta P \to 0$$

The value of Joule-Thomson coefficient may be positive or negative. The temperature at which its sign is changed called Joule-Thompson inversion temperature.

The sign of the Joule-Thomson coefficient is positive below the critical temperature and the gas is cooled upon expansion. Hence below the critical temperature, the gas can be liquified.

But the sign of the coefficient above the critical temperature is negative and the gas is heated upon expansion. Hence above the critical temperature, it is NOT possible to liquify the gas.

Usually most of the gases are cooled upon adiabatic expansion at room temperature as their critical temperatures are above the room temperature.

But the gases like H_2, He and Ne have their critical temperatures below room temperature and hence their temperature increases during adiabatic expansion at room temperature. These are also difficult to liquify.

B. $\mu = q \times d = 4.8 \times 10^{-10} \times 1.34 \times 10^{-8}$

$\mu = 6.4 \times 10^{-18}$ esu cm

$$\%\ \text{Ionic character} = \frac{1.08}{6.4\times10^{-18}}\times100$$

$= 16.79\%$

40. The flow-sheet of the reactions involved in the question is

$$A \xrightarrow[\text{alcohol}]{\text{Ethyl}} \underset{\text{Carboxylic acid}}{B} + C$$

$$C \xrightarrow[\text{hydrolysis}]{H^+, H_2O} B + D$$

$$D \xrightarrow{\text{Oxidation}} B \xrightarrow[\Delta]{Ca(OH)_2} E(C_3H_6O)$$

$$\longrightarrow 2,\ 4\text{-Dinitrophenylhydrazone}$$

Step 1. To determine the structures of compounds (B), (D) and (E).

(*i*) Since compound E with M.F. C_3H_6O does not reduce Tollens' reagent and Fehling's solution but forms a 2, 4-dinitrophenylhydrazone; therefore, it must be a ketone, *i.e.*, acetone (CH_3COCH_3).

(*ii*) Since ketone E (acetone) is obtained from B by heating with $Ca(OH)_2$, therefore, B must be acetic acid (CH_3COOH).

(*iii*) Since B (acetic acid) is produced from D by oxidation, therefore, D must be ethyl alcohol.

All the above reactions can be explained as follows:

$$\underset{\text{Ethyl alcohol (D)}}{CH_3CH_2OH} \xrightarrow{[O]} \underset{\text{Acetic acid (B)}}{CH_3COOH} \xrightarrow[-CaCO_3]{Ca(OH)_2, \Delta}$$

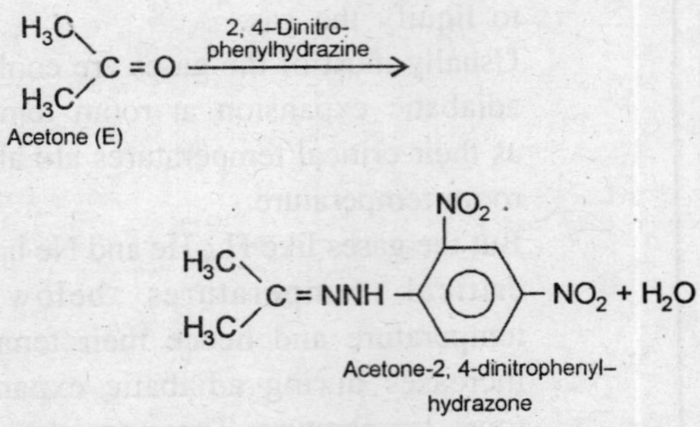

Step 2. To determine the structures of compounds (A) and (C).

(*i*) since compound (C) on acid hydrolysis gives B (acetic acid) and D (ethyl alcohol), therefore, C must be an ester, i.e. ethyl acetate ($CH_3COOC_2H_5$).

$$\underset{\text{Ethyl acetate (C)}}{CH_3COOC_2H_5} \xrightarrow[\text{Hydrolysis}]{H^+, H_2O}$$

$$\underset{\text{Acetic acid (B)}}{CH_3COOH} + \underset{\text{Ethyl alcohol (D)}}{C_2H_5OH}$$

(*ii*) Since carboxylic acid B (acetic acid) and ester C (ethyl acetate) are obtained by the treatment of compound A with ethyl alcohol, therefore, *A* must be an anhydride (acetic anhydride).

$$\underset{\text{Acetic anhydride (A)}}{(CH_3CO)_2O} + C_2H_5OH \longrightarrow$$

$$\underset{\text{Acetic acid (B)}}{CH_3COOH} + \underset{\text{Ethyl acetate (C)}}{CH_3COOC_2H_5}$$

41. A. The hydrogen atoms of the CH_2 group in malonic ester (I) are acidic due to the presence of two strongly electron-withdrawing $COOC_2H_5$ groups. Therefore, one of these can be easily abstracted by a strong base such as NaOEt to form carbanion (II). The bromo-ester (III) undergoes nucleophilic substitution reaction by the carbanion (II) giving product (IV) which upon alkaline hydrolysis followed by acidification gives (V). (V) being a malonic acid derivative on heating undergoes decarboxylation to give the product (VI).

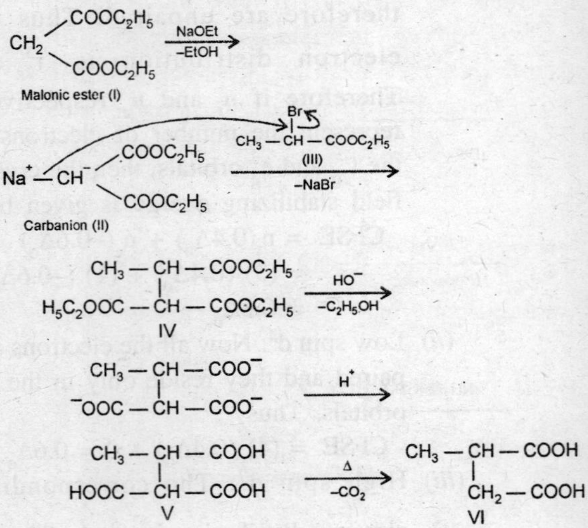

B. The acid-catalysed hydrolysis of esters occurs by the following mechanism:

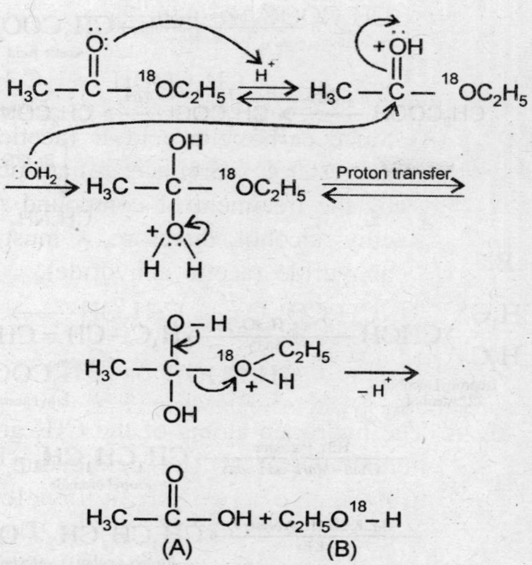

Thus, (A) = acetic acid and (B) = ^{18}O — ethyl alcohol.

42.

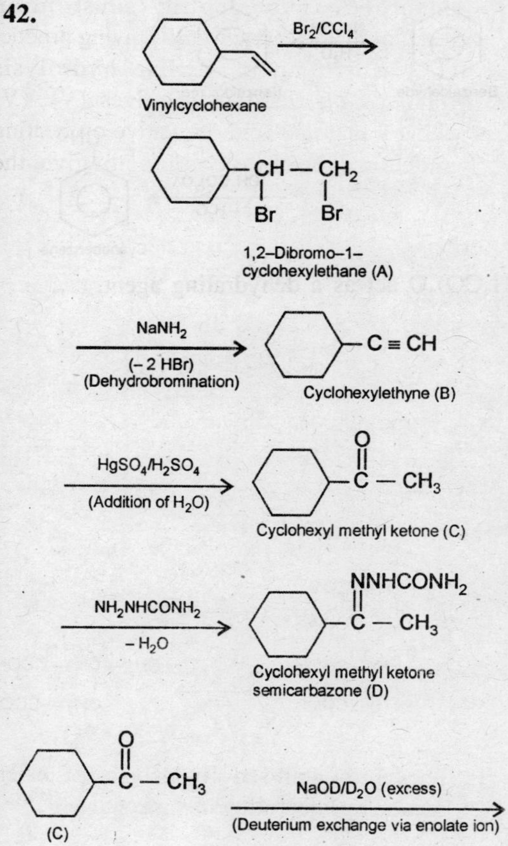

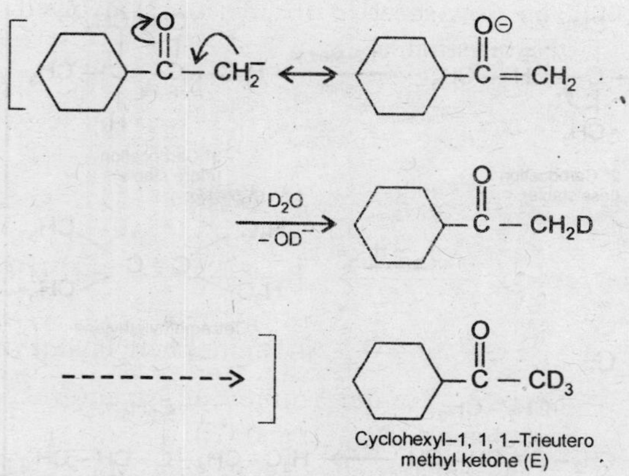

43. A. In presence of conc. H_2SO_4, isobutyl alcohol (I) first gives a 1° carbocation (II) which then rearranges to the more stable 3° carbocation (III) by a hydride ion shift. Carbocation (III), then reacts with benzene to form *tert*-butylbenzene.

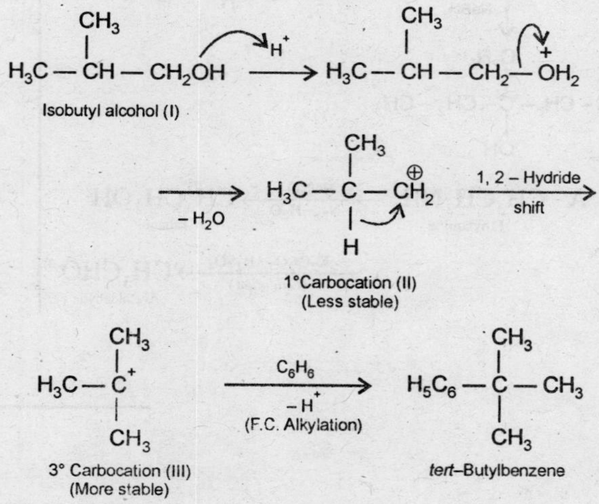

B.

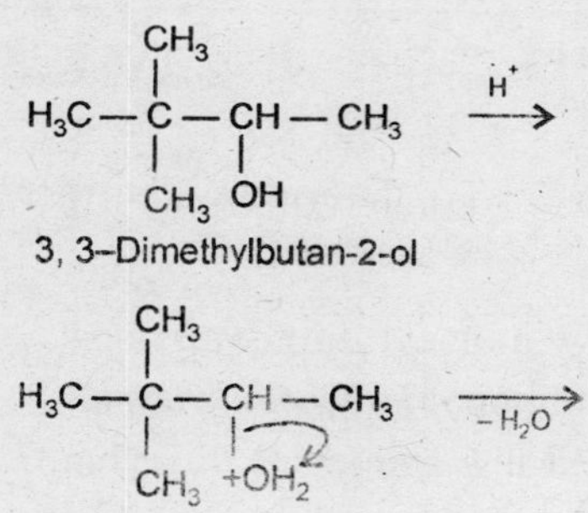

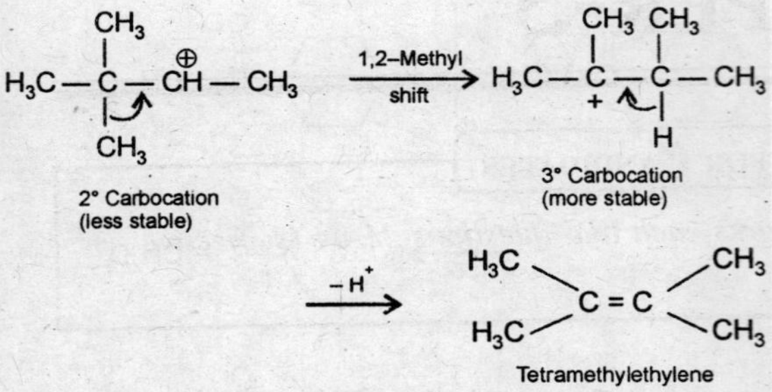

C.

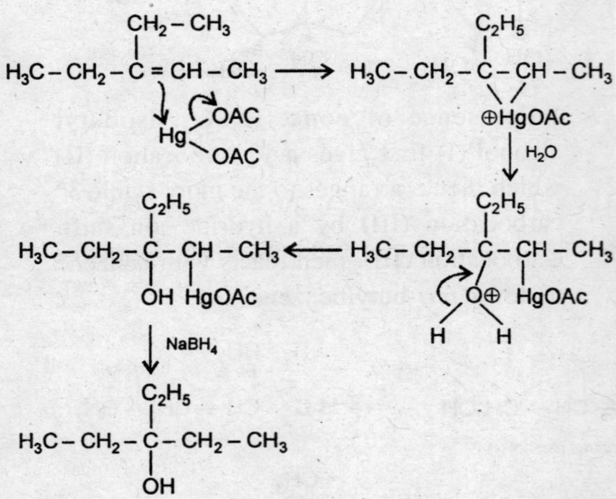

44. A. $CH_3CH_2NH_2 \xrightarrow[-N_2,\,-H_2O]{HONO} CH_3CH_2OH$
Ethylamine — Ethanol

$\xrightarrow[(Oxidation)]{K_2Cr_2O_7\,/\,H_2SO_4} CH_3CHO$
Acetaldehyde

$\xrightarrow[(Oxidation)]{K_2Cr_2O_7\,/\,H_2SO_4} CH_3COOH$
Acetic Acid

$CH_3COOH \xrightarrow{SOCl_2} CH_3COCl \xrightarrow{NH_3} CH_3CONH_2 \xrightarrow{Br_2/KOH} CH_3NH_2$

B.

$(H_3C)_2CHOH \xrightarrow[-H_2O]{Conc.\ H_2SO_4,\,\Delta} H_3C-CH=CH_2$
Isopropyl alcohol (2° Alcohol) — Propylene

$\xrightarrow[(Anti-Mark\ addition)]{HBr,\ Peroxide} CH_3CH_2CH_2-Br$
n-Propyl bromide

$\xrightarrow[-KBr]{Aq.\ KOH\ (Hydrolysis)} CH_3CH_2CH_2-OH$
n-Propyl alcohol (1° *Alcohol*)

C.

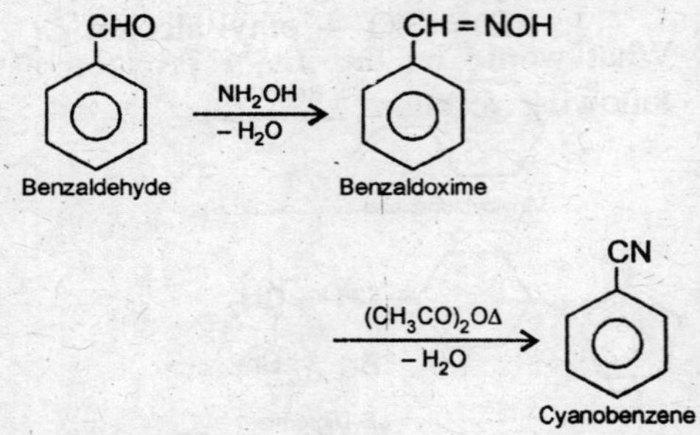

$(CH_3CO)_2O$ act as a dehydrating agent.

TEST PAPER-5

IMPORTANT INSTRUCTION FOR CANDIDATES

Questions 1-30 (Objective questions) carry three marks each and questions 31-44 (subjective questions) carry fifteen marks each.

1. Dehydro halogenation by strong base is slowest in

A. 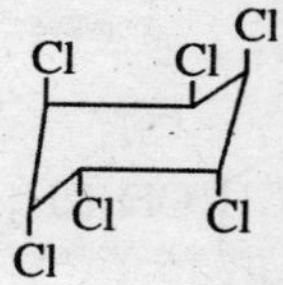

B. 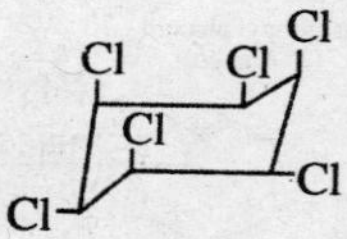

C. 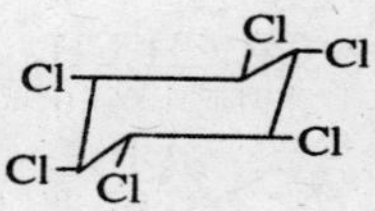

D. 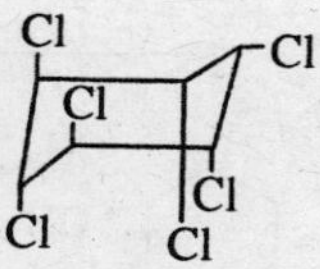

2. What would be the major product of the following reaction?

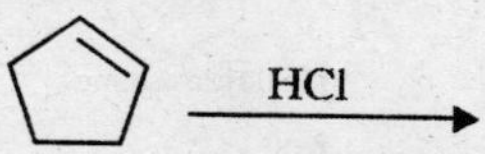

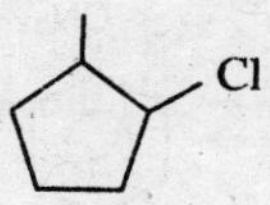

I

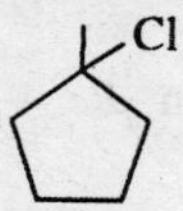

II

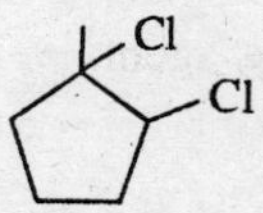

III

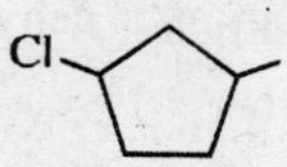

IV

A. I
B. II
C. III
D. IV

3. What product would result from the following reaction?

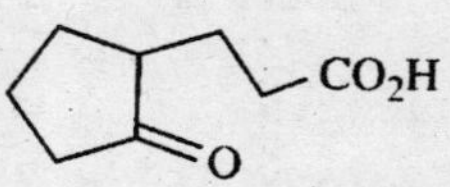

I

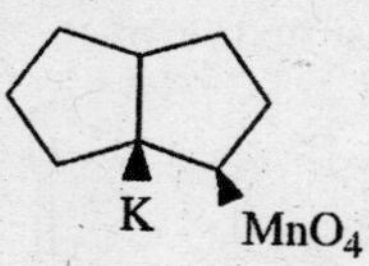

II

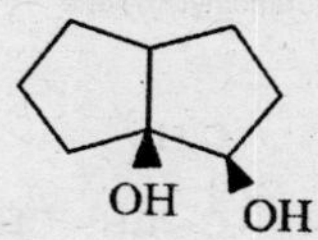

III

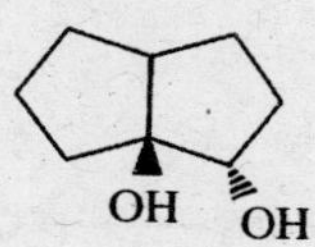

IV

A. I
B. II
C. III
D. IV

4. What is the major product of the following reaction?

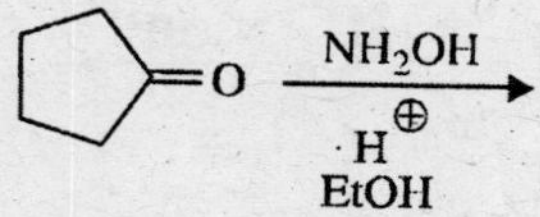

A. 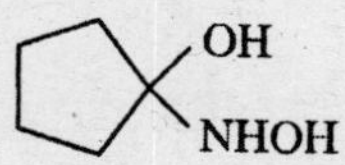

B. 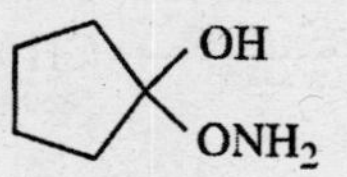

C. 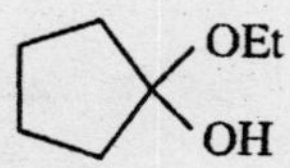

D. 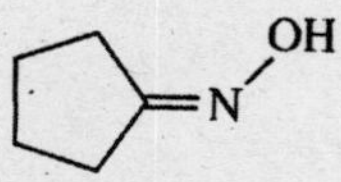

5. What is the major product of the following reaction?

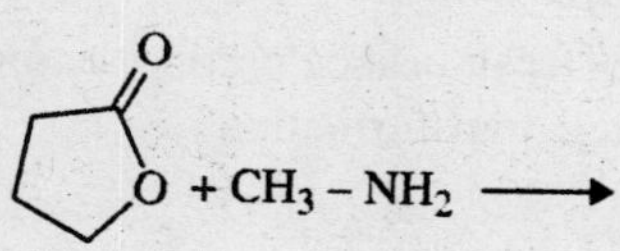

A. 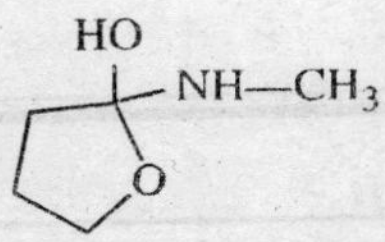

B. $HO-CH_2-CH_2-CH_2-\overset{O}{\overset{||}{C}}-NH-CH_3$

C. 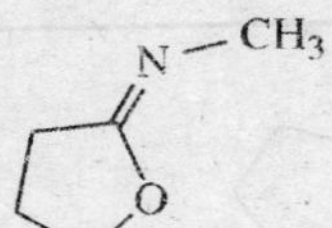

D. 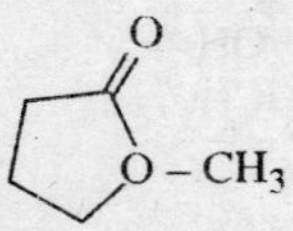

6. What is the major product of the following reaction?

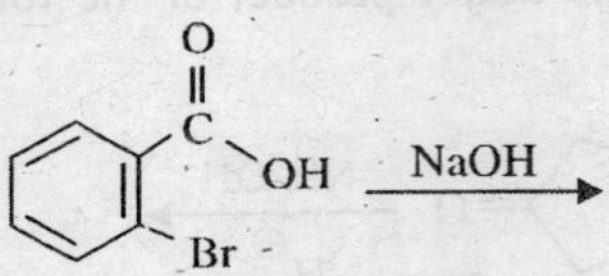

A. 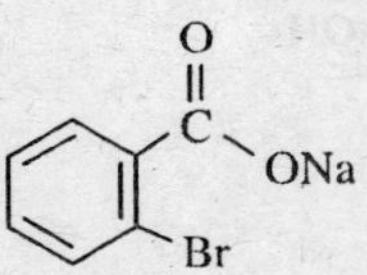

B. 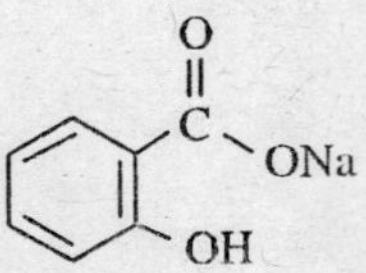

C. 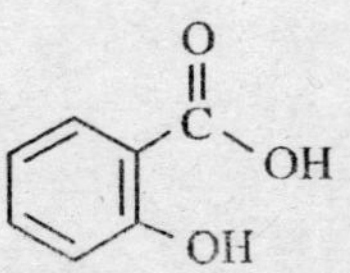

D. 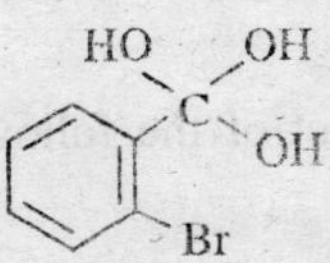

7. What reagents can best be used to accomplish the following transformation?

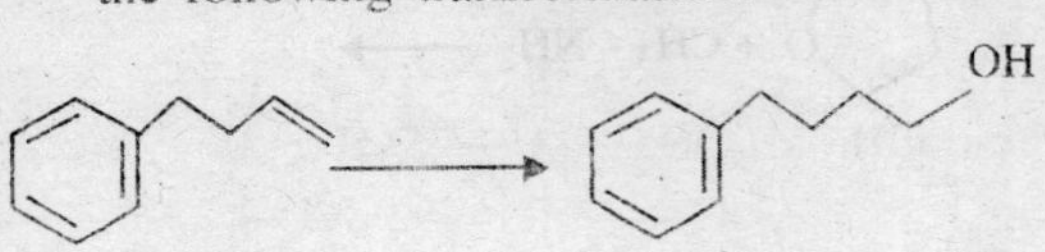

A. 2. BH3.THF 2. HO^-, H_2O_2

B. 1. $Hg(O_2CCF3)_2$, CH3OH 2. $NaBH_4$

C. 1. $Hg(OAc)_2$, H_2O/THF 2. $NaBH_4$

D. H^+, H_2O

8. What is the major product of the following reaction?

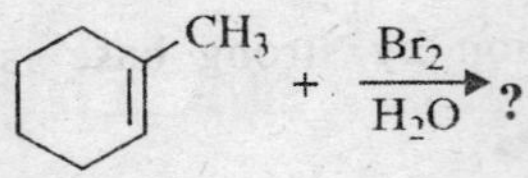

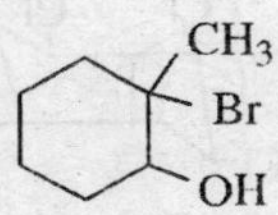

I

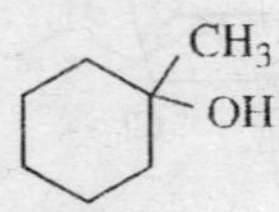

II

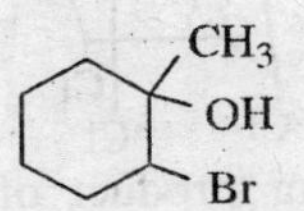

III

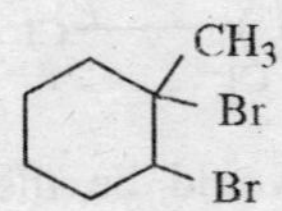

IV

A. I B. II

C. III D. IV

9. In the reaction ${}_4Be^9 + X \rightarrow {}_6C^{12} + {}_0n^1$, the X represents

A. an alpha particle

B. a beta particle

C. an electron

D. a proton

10. In the following reaction,

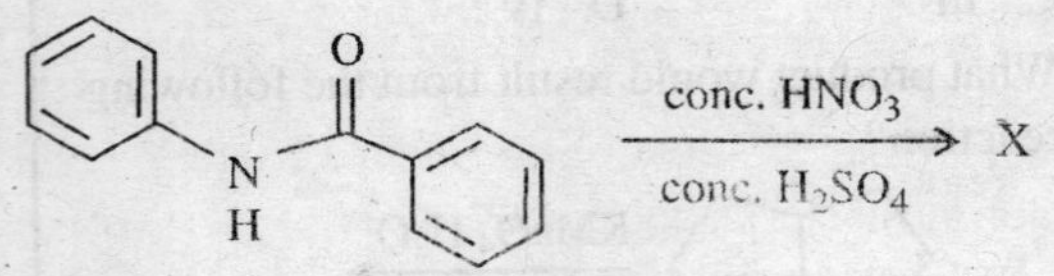

the structure of the major product 'X' is

A. 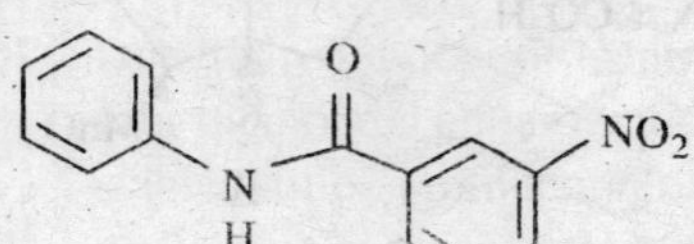

B. 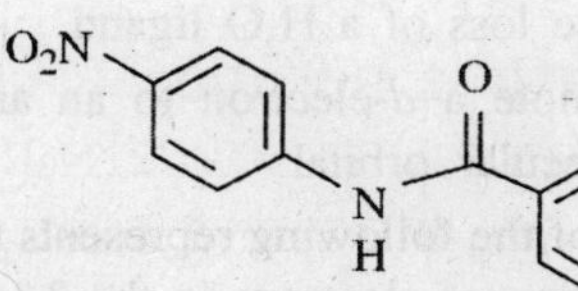

C. 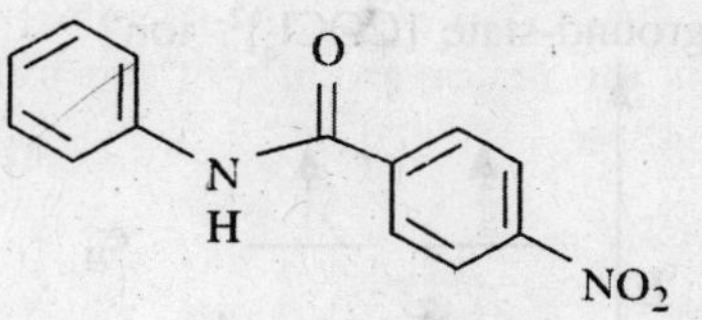

D. 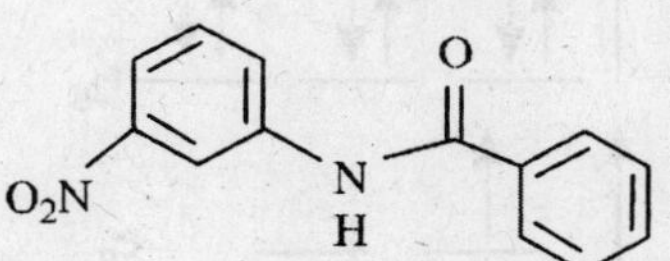

11. The major product formed in the reaction, given below, is

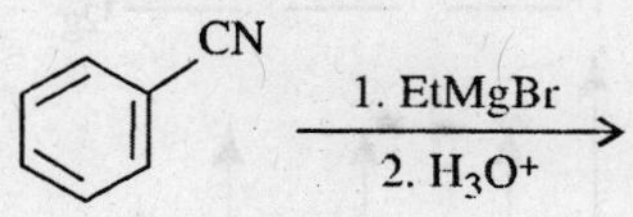

A. 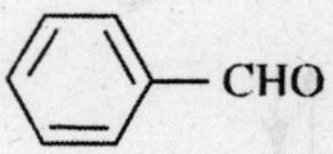

B. 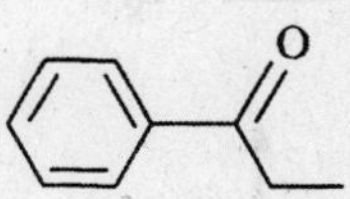

C. 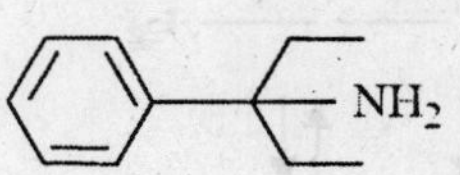

D. 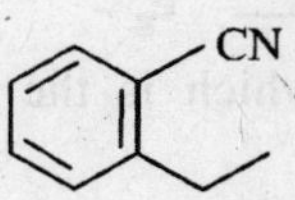

12. The major product formed when glucose is treated with methanol in the presence of acid

$$\text{D-Glucose} \xrightarrow[CH_3OH]{H^+}$$

A. 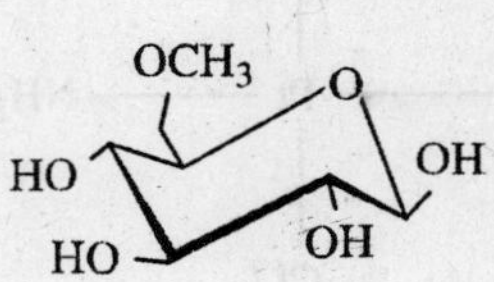

B. 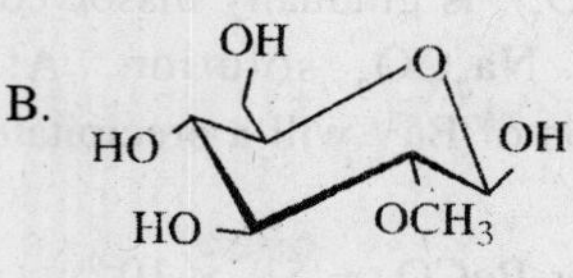

C. 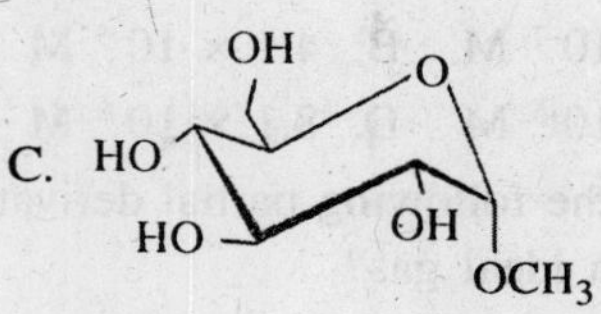

D. 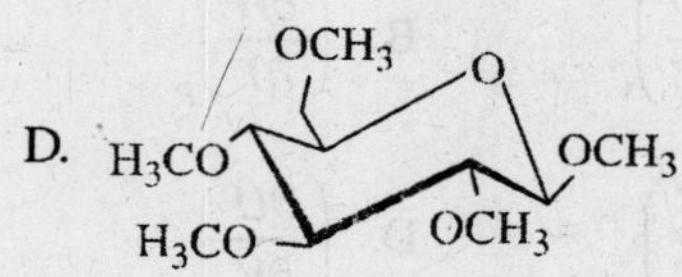

13. Sucrose is a disaccharide consisting of
A. glucose and glucose
B. glucose and galactose
C. glucose and fructose
D. glucose and mannose

14. Copper crystallises in fcc with a unit cell length of 361 pm. What is the radius of copper atom?
A. 181 pm B. 108 pm
C. 127 pm D. 157 pm

15. The set representing the correct order of ionic radius is:
A. $Mg^{2+} > Be^{2+} > Li^{+} > Na^{+}$
B. $Li^{+} > Be^{2+} > Na^{+} > Mg^{2+}$
C. $Na^{+} > Li^{+} > Mg^{2+} > Be^{2+}$
D. $Li^{+} > Na^{+} > Mg^{2+} > Be^{2+}$

16. The solubility product expression, K_{sp}, for the slightly soluble salt $Pb(IO_3)_2$ is equal to
A. $[Pb^{2+}]\,[IO_3^-]$ B. $[Pb^{2+}]^2\,[IO_3^-]$
C. $[Pb^{2+}]\,[IO_3^-]^2$ D. $[Pb^{2+}]^2\,[IO_3^-]^2$

17. The azide ion, N_3^-, is isoelectronic with which of the following?
A. NO_2^- B. NO_2
C. CO_2 D. SO_2

18. Solid $Ba(NO_3)_2$ is gradually dissolved in 1.0×10^{-4} M Na_2CO_3 solution. At what concentration of Ba^{2+} will a precipitate begin to form?

(K_{sp} for $BaCO_3 = 5.1 \times 10^{-9}$):

A. 8.1×10^{-7} M B. 4.1×10^{-5} M
C. 5.1×10^{-5} M D. 8.1×10^{-8} M

19. Which of the following partial derivatives is zero for an ideal gas?

A. $\left(\frac{\partial U}{\partial T}\right)_V$ B. $\left(\frac{\partial H}{\partial T}\right)_P$

C. $\left(\frac{\partial S}{\partial T}\right)_P$ D. $\left(\frac{\partial U}{\partial V}\right)_T$

20. A reaction is at equilibrium in a closed rigid vessel at constant temperature when

A. $\Delta S = 0$ B. $\Delta H = 0$
C. $\Delta U = 0$ D. $\Delta A = 0$

21. The quantity $T\Delta S$ may be expressed in units of

A. J B. K
C. J·K D. $J{\cdot}K^{-1}$

22. One mole of an ideal gas expands isothermally until its volume is doubled. What is the change in Gibbs energy, ΔG, for the process?

A. $R \ln \frac{1}{2}$ B. $R \ln 2$

C. $RT \ln \frac{1}{2}$ D. $RT \ln 2$

23. Of the following metal ions, which has the largest magnetic moment in its high-spin octahedral complex?

A. Fe^{3+} B. Co^{3+}
C. Co^{2+} D. Cr^{2+}

24. A Jahn-Teller distortion of $[Ti(H_2O)_6]^{3+}$ acts to

A. raise its symmetry
B. remove an electronic degeneracy
C. cause loss of a H_2O ligand
D. promote a *d*-electron to an antibonding molecular orbital

25. Which of the following represents the correct distribution of electrons in the 3*d* orbitals of a ground-state $[COCl_4]^{2-}$ ion?

A.
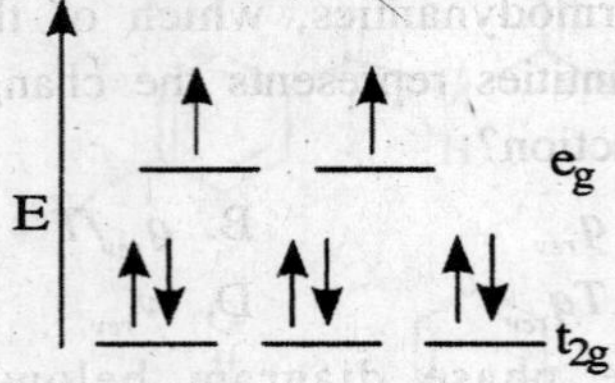

B.
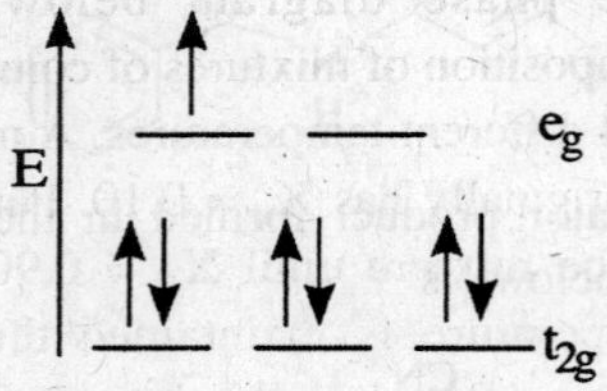

C.
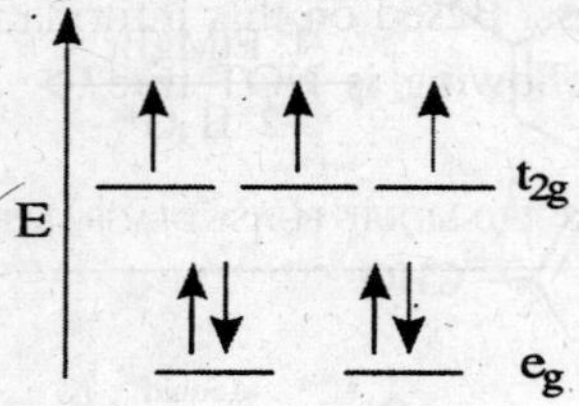

D.
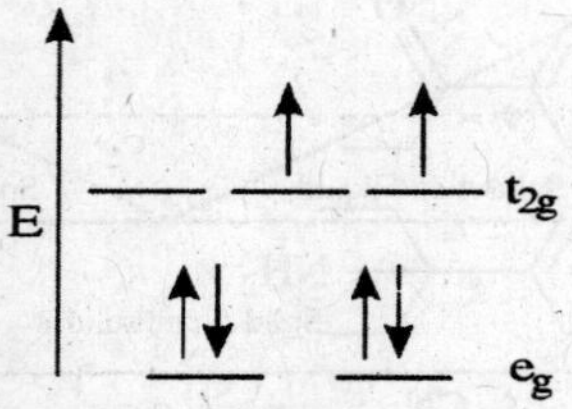

26. Of the following, which is the strongest oxidizing agent?

A. O_2^+ B. O_2
C. O_2^- D. O_2^{2-}

27. The systematic name of the compound shown below is

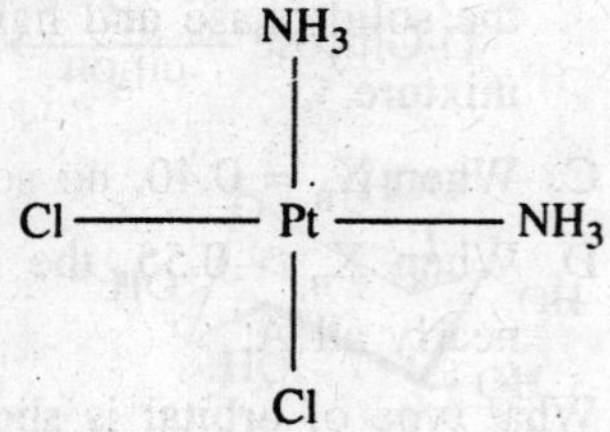

A. platinum *cis*-ammoniumchloride

B. *cis*-diammoniaplatinumdichloride

C. *cis*-diaminedichloroplatinum (II)

D. *cis*-dichlorodiamineplatinum (IV)

28. According to the second law of thermodynamics, which of the following quantities represents the change in a state function?

A. q_{rev} B. q_{rev}/T

C. Tq_{rev} D. w_{rev}

29. The phase diagram below shows the composition of mixtures of compounds *A* and B at different temperatures. A mixture at 310 K originally has X_B = 0.10. Pure B is added to the mixture until X_B = 0.90. A constant temperature is maintained throughout the process. Based on this information, which of the following is NOT true?

SOLID-LIQUID PHASE DIAGRAM FOR A AND B

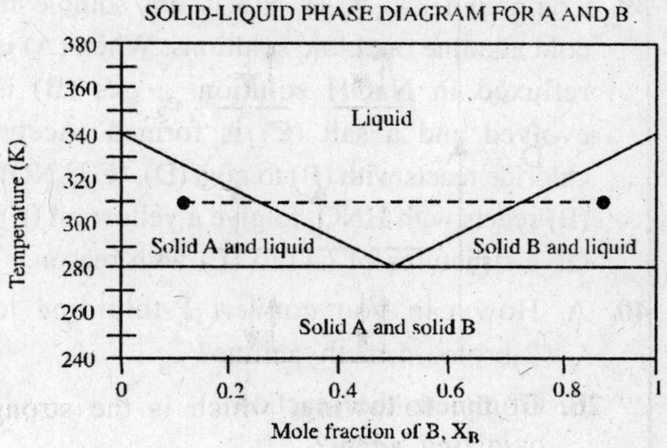

A. As B is initially added, it melts into the liquid phase.

B. When X_B = 0.10, about half of the A is in the solid phase and half is in the liquid mixture.

C. When X_B = 0.40, no solid exists.

D. When X_B > 0.55, the liquid solution is nearly all A.

30. What type of orbital is shown below?

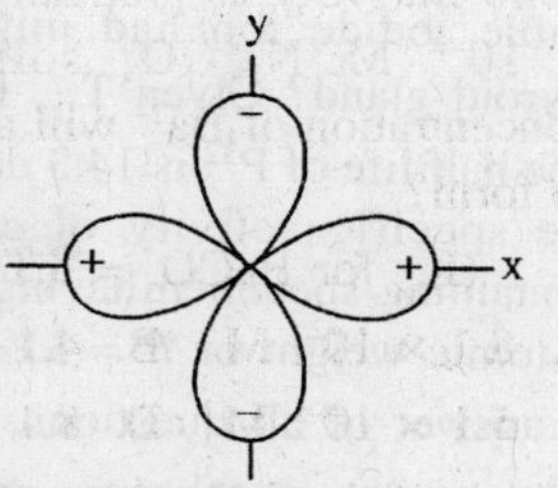

A. 3 p_x B. 3 p_y

C. 3 d_{xy} D. 3 $d_{x^2-y^2}$

31. Iron metal is produced commercially by reducing iron (III) oxide in iron ore with carbon monoxide:

$$Fe_2O_3(s) + 3\ CO(g) \rightarrow 2\ Fe(s) + 3\ CO_2(g)$$

A. Calculate the standard free-energy change for this reaction at 25°C.

B. Is the reaction spontaneous under standard-state conditions at 25°C?

C. Does the reverse reaction become spontaneous at higher temperatures? Explain.

32. In presence of an acid *N*-chloro acetanilide changes slowly into *p*-chloro acetanilide. Former substance liberated iodine from KI and not the later and hence progress of reaction can be measured by titrating iodine liberated with $Na_2S_2O_3$ solution, the results obtained were as follows:

Time (hours)	0	1	2	4	6	8
$(a - x)$ *i.e.*, hypo	45	32	22.5	11.3	3.7	2.9

show that reaction is unimolecular and find out the fraction of *N*-chloroacetanilide decomposed after three hours.

33. A. A sample of $_{53}I^{131}$, as iodide ion, was administered to a patient in a carrier consisting of 0.10 *mg* of stable iodide ion. After 4.00 days, 67.7% of the initial radioactivity was detected in the thyroid gland of the patient. What mass of the stable iodide ion had migrated to the thyroid gland? Given $T_{1/2}$ I^{131} = 8 days.

B. The half life of P^{32} is 14.3 days. Calculate the specific activity of a phosphorus containing specimen having 1.0 *ppm* P^{32} (Atomic weight of P = 31)

34. Give answer of all questions.

A. Discuss the syntheses, structures and reactivities of methyl compounds of beryllium and magnesium.

B. Discuss the uses of compounds of formula *ME*, where *M* may be one or a mixture of two elements from Group 12 and *E* is an element from Group 16 (not oxygen). How are thin films of these materials produced?

C. Discuss the composition and structures of the oxyacids of Group 17 elements. Indicate the uses of two of them or their salts.

35. A. The bonding of atoms *C*, *N* and *O* with themselves and with each other has certain unique features amongst *p*-block elements. Draw Lewis structures of common allotropes of *N* and *O* and their heavier congeners (*P* and *S*) and using these as examples explain its unique features.

B. Why do chiral amines racemise readily, while chiral phosphines do not?

36. Complete the reactions.

A.

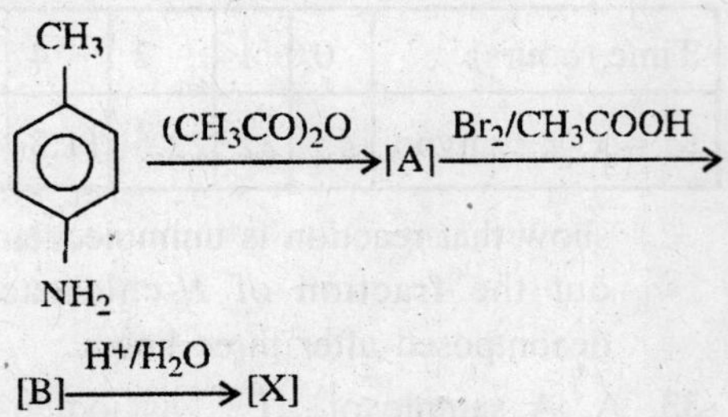

B. Convert the reaction.

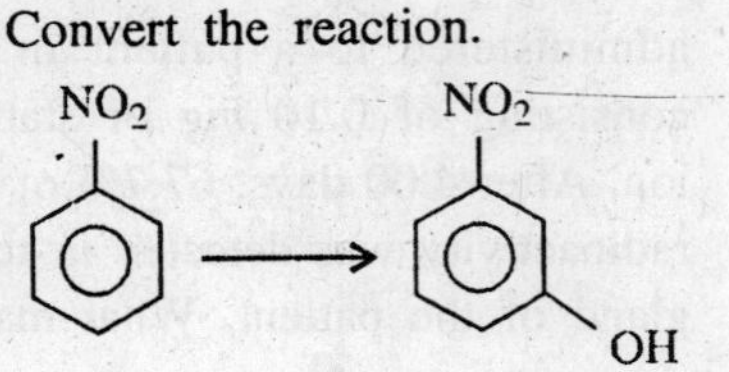

37. A colourless substance (A) is sparingly soluble in water and gives (B) on heating with mineral acids. Compound (B) on reaction with $CHCl_3$ and alcoholic potash produces an obnoxious smell of carbylamine due to the formation of (C). Compound (A) on reaction with chlorosulphonic acid gives (D) which on treatment with ammonia gives (E). Compound (E) on hydrolysis gives sulphanilamide; a well know drug. Give structures of (A) to (E) with proper reasoning.

38. An aqueous solution of a nitrogen and chlorine containing compound (A) is acidic to litmus. (A) on treatment with aqueous NaOH gives a compound (B) containing nitrogen, but not chlorine. Compound (B) on treatment with $C_6H_5SO_2Cl$ in the presence of NaOH gives an insoluble product (C), $C_{13}H_{13}HO_2S$. Give structures of (A) and (B).

39. Compound (A), $C_5H_{11}NO$ is not soluble in cold alkaline or acidic solutions. When (A) is refluxed in NaOH solution, a gas (B) is evolved and a salt (C) is formed. Acetyl chloride reacts with (B) to give (D), (C_4H_9NO). (B) reacts with HNO_2 to give a yellow oil (E). Give structures of (A) to (E) with reason.

40. A. How can you convert P-toluidine to 2-bromo-4-methyaniline?

B. Complete the reaction

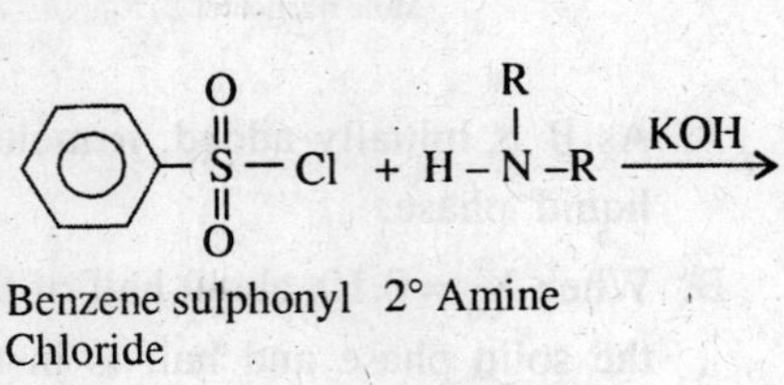

C. Complete the reaction

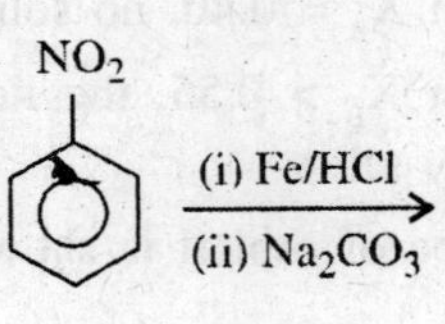

41. An organic compound *A*, $C_8H_4O_3$, in dry benzene in the presence of anhydrous $AlCl_3$ gives compound *B*, The compound *B* on treatment with PCl_5 followed by reaction with H_2/Pd ($BaSO_4$) gives compound *C*, which on reaction with hydrazine gives a cyclized compound *D* ($C_4H_{10}N_2$). Identify *A, B, C* and *D*. Explain the formation of *D* from *C*.

42. A. The rate constant for the first order decomposition of a certain reaction is described by the equation:

$$\log k(s^{-1}) = 14.34 - \frac{1.25\times10^4 K}{T}$$

(*i*) What is the energy of activation of this reaction?

(*ii*) At what temperature will its half life period be 256 minutes?

B. A hydrogenation reaction is carried out at 500 K. If the same reaction is carried out in the presence of a catalyst at the same rate, the temperature required is 400 K, calculate the activation energy of the reaction if the catalyst lowers the activation barrier by 20 kJ mol^{-1}.

C. The rate of a first order reaction is 0.04 mol litre^{-1} s^{-1} at 10 minutes and 0.03 mol litre^{-1} s^{-1} at 20 minutes. Find the half life period of the reaction.

43. A. The equilibrium constant K for a certain reaction is given by

$$\ln K = 4.800 - \frac{20.50}{T}$$

Derive an equation for $\Delta G°$ as a function of *T*.

B. In the above problem calculate $\Delta S°$ and $\Delta H°$ at 300 *K*.

C. One mole of an ideal gas is heated at constant pressure from 25°C to 300°C. Calculate the entropy change ΔS,

$$\text{if } m\ C_v = \frac{3}{2}R.$$

44. A. Molecular energy distribution is given by

$$n(\in)d\in = \frac{2\pi N}{(\pi KT)^{\frac{3}{2}}}\sqrt{\in e^{-\frac{\in}{KT}}}$$

Find average energy per molecule.

B. Treat the six π electron of benzene as particle force to move on a ring of radius 1.40Å. Calculate the energy of lowest transition.

C. For the ammonia equilibrium

$$\frac{3}{2}H_2(g)+\frac{1}{2}N_2(g) = NH_3(g)$$

at 900°C, the partial pressure of NH_3, N_2 and H_2 were 3.03, 6.75 and 20.22 atm. respectively. Calculate K_p and write its units.

ANSWERS

1	2	3	4	5	6	7	8	9	10
C	B	C	D	B	A	A	C	A	B
11	**12**	**13**	**14**	**15**	**16**	**17**	**18**	**19**	**20**
B	C	C	C	C	C	C	C	D	D
21	**22**	**23**	**24**	**25**	**26**	**27**	**28**	**29**	**30**
A	C	A	B	C	A	C	B	D	D

SOME SELECTED EXPLANATORY ANSWERS

1. Compound (C) has all equitorial substituent, hence, it is most stable and undergo elimination with slowest rate.

2.

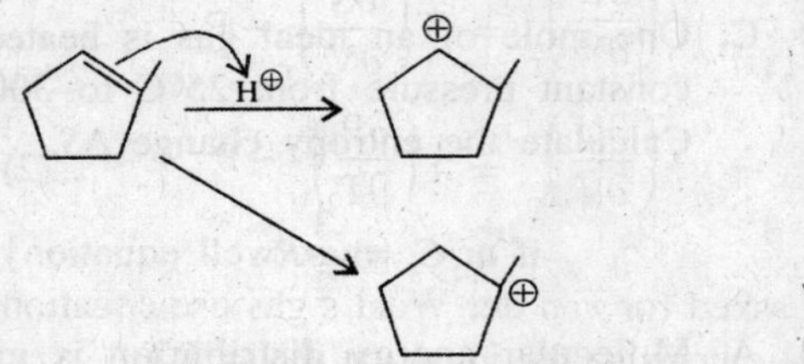

(more stable and therefore will be formed)

3. $KMnO_4$ gives syn addition. Therefore –OH group will be attached on the same side of C = C bond

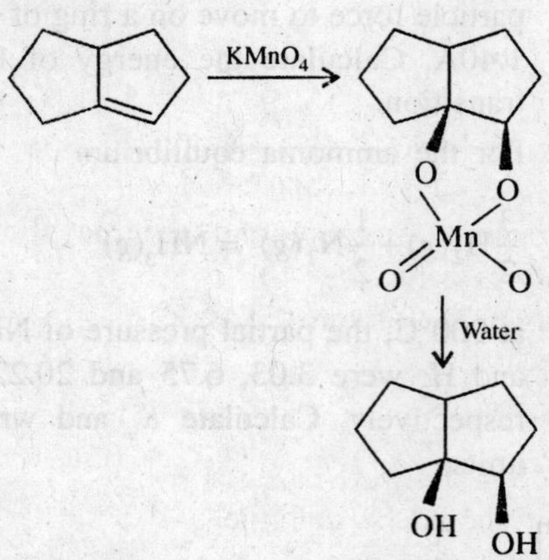

4. The nitrogen atom is the best nucleophile in this reaction mixture (the ethanol is the solvent) and the resulting imine is the more stable product.

5.

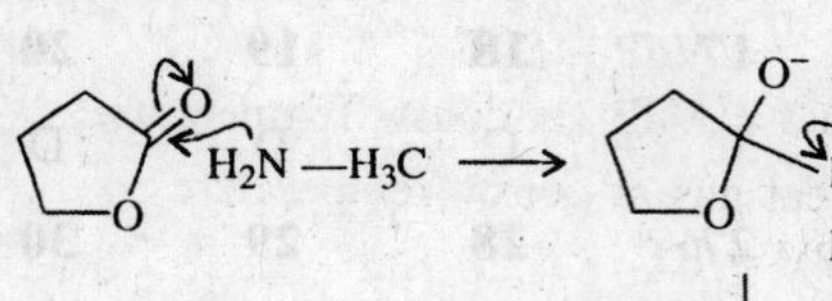

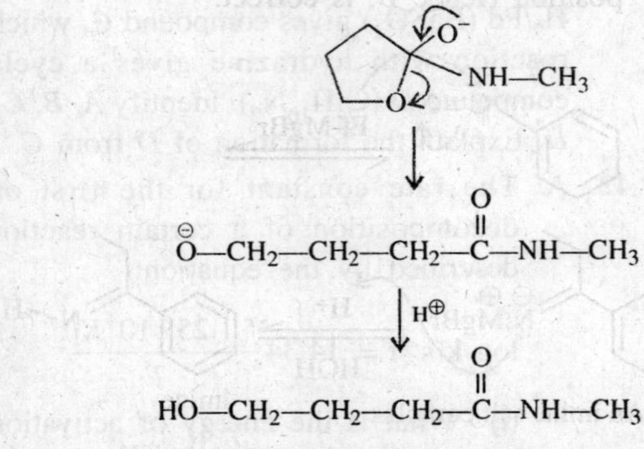

6. The carboxylic acid will react and form water and the carboxylate anion. This is a very favorable exothermic reaction. The bromine atom on the benzene ring will not react in a S_N2 reaction.

7. BH_3 alway attack less hindered site.

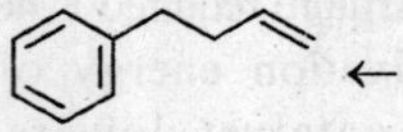 ← this site is sterically less hindered and therefore will be attacked by BH_3. $\bar{O}H$ treatment with H_2O_2. OH group will be attached to this site.

8.

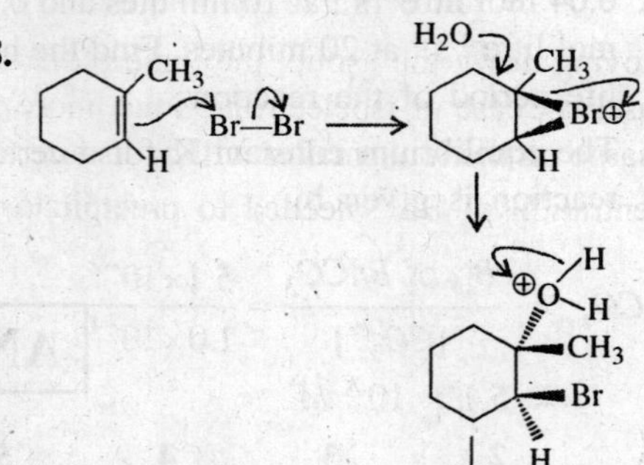

Product

10.

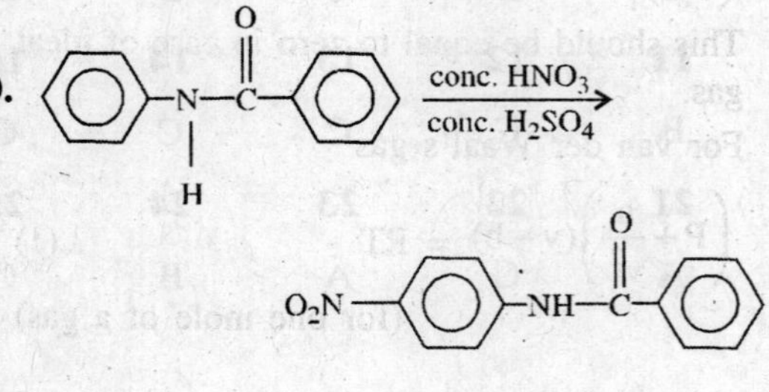

Due to presence of lone pair of electron on nitrogen atom, it will activate the ring and it will stabilize intermediate cation at *o* and *p* position Hence B. is correct.

11.

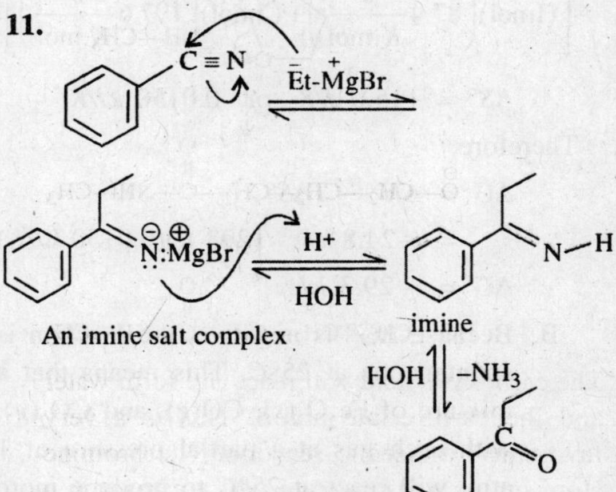

12. It is due to anomeric effect. All of the –OH groups are methylated with excess CH_3I in presence of Ag_2O or NEt_3.

14. For FCC, $4r = \sqrt{2}\ a$

or $r = \dfrac{a}{2\sqrt{2}} = \dfrac{361}{2\times1.414} = \dfrac{361}{2.828}$

$= 127.6$ pm.

15. On moving down the group, the ionic radius increases. In case of isoelectronic ions, more the charge on the ion, smaller will be its size.

18. Concentration of Ba^{2+} needed to precipitate

$$BaCO_3 = \frac{B_{sp} \text{ of } BaCO_3}{[CO_3^{2-}]} = \frac{5.1\times10^{-9}}{1.0\times10^{-4}}$$

$= 5.1 \times 10^{-5}$ *M*

19. $\left(\dfrac{\partial U}{\partial V}\right)_T$ represent internal pressure of a gas.

This should be equal to zero in case of ideal gas.

For van der Waal's gas

$$\left(P+\frac{a}{v^2}\right)(v-b) = RT \quad ...(1)$$

(for one mole of a gas)

$dQ = dU + Pdv$

(first law of thermodynamics)

$Tds = dU = Pdv$

$$T\left(\frac{\partial S}{\partial V}\right)_T = \left(\frac{\partial U}{\partial V}\right)_T + P$$

$$\Rightarrow \left(\frac{\partial U}{\partial V}\right)_T = T\left(\frac{\partial S}{\partial V}\right)_T - P$$

$$\left(\frac{\partial U}{\partial V}\right)_T = T\left(\frac{\partial P}{\partial T}\right)_V - P \quad ...(2)$$

{max well equation}

If asked for van der Waal's gas use equation (1) otherwise for ideal gas PU = RT

$$V\left(\frac{\partial P}{\partial T}\right)_V = R$$

Putting in (2)

$$\left(\frac{\partial U}{\partial V}\right)_T = \frac{TR}{V} - P = P - P = 0.$$

20.

$A = U - TS$

$dA = dU - Tds - SdT$

$= dU - dQ - SdT$

$= -(dQ - dU) - SdT$

$= -PdV - SdT$

For constant pressure and volume above quantity is zero.

$\Rightarrow$ $dA = 0$ (at const. T & V)

21. $\dfrac{dQ}{T} = ds$

$\Rightarrow$ $TdS = dQ$

$\therefore$ Unit should be in Joule.

22.

$G = H - TS$

$dG = dH - TdS - SdT$

$= d(V + PV) - TdS - SdT$

$= dV + PdV + VdP - TdS - SdT$

$= (dV + PdV - TdS) + VdP - SdT$

$= VdP - SdT$

$dG = VdP$ {at const. Temperature}

For ideal gas at const. Temperature

$PV = RT$

$PdV = VdP = 0$

$\Rightarrow$ $VdP = - PdV$

$$\therefore \quad dG = PdV$$
$$= -\frac{RT}{V} dV$$
$$\Delta G = -RT \int_{V}^{2V} \frac{dV}{V}$$
$$= -RT \ln 2$$
$$= RT \ln \frac{1}{2}$$

23. Cr^{2+} | ↿ | ↿ | ↿ | ↿ | |

Fe^{3+} | ↿ | ↿ | ↿ | ↿ | ↿ | ←Max unpaired electron

CO^{3+} | ⥮ | ↿ | ↿ | ↿ | ↿ |

CO^{2+} | ⥮ | ⥮ | ↿ | ↿ | ↿ |

24. Refer Jahn-Teller Distortion.
It remove an electronic degeneraly which results in distortion of shape of compound.

25. CO^{2+} have 7 electron in *d* orbital. Further in tetrahedral complex *e.g.* sets are at lower energy level then t_{2g}.

28. $\frac{q_{rev}}{T}$ = S which is state function.

31. A. The following values of ΔH°_f and S° are found in Appendix *B*:

	$Fe_2O_3(s)$	CO(g)	Fe(s)	$CO_2(g)$
ΔH°_f (kJ/mol)	–824.2	–110.5	0	–393.5
S°[J/K·mol)]	87.4	197.6	27.3	213.6

So we have

$$\Delta H^\circ = [2\,\Delta H^\circ_f(Fe) + 3\,\Delta H^\circ_f(CO_2)] - [\Delta H^\circ_f(Fe_2O_3) + 3\,\Delta H^\circ_f(CO)]$$
$$= [(2\text{ mol})\ (0\text{kJ/mol}) + (3\text{ mol})\ (-393.5\text{ kJ/mol})] - [(1\text{ mol})\ (-824.2\text{ kJ/mol}) + (3\text{ mol})\ (-110.5\text{ kJ/mol})]$$
$$\Delta H^\circ = -24.8\text{ kJ}$$

and $\Delta S^\circ = [2\,S^\circ(Fe) + 3S^\circ(CO_2)] - [S^\circ(Fe_2O_3) + 3S^\circ(CO)]$

$$= \left[(2\text{mol})\left(27.3\frac{J}{K\cdot mol}\right) + (3\text{mol})\left(213.6\frac{J}{K\cdot mol}\right)\right]$$
$$- \left[(1\text{mol})\left(87.4\frac{J}{K.mol}\right) + (3\text{mol})\left(197.6\frac{J}{K.mol}\right)\right]$$

$$\Delta S^\circ = +15.0\ J/K \quad \text{or} \quad 0.0150\ kJ/K$$

Therefore,

$$\Delta G^\circ = \Delta H^\circ - T\Delta S^\circ$$
$$= (-24.8\ kJ) - (298\ K)(0.0150\ kJ/K)$$
$$\Delta G^\circ = -29.3\ kJ$$

B. Because ΔG° is negative, the reaction is spontaneous at 25°*C*. This means that a mixture of $Fe_2O_3(s)$, $CO(g)$, and $CO_2(g)$, with each gas at a partial pressure of 1 atm, will react at 25°*C* to produce more iron metal.

C. Because ΔH° is negative and ΔS° is positive, ΔG° will be negative at all temperatures. The forward reaction is therefore spontaneous at all temperatures, and the reverse does not become spontaneous at higher temperatures.

32. The present reaction is –

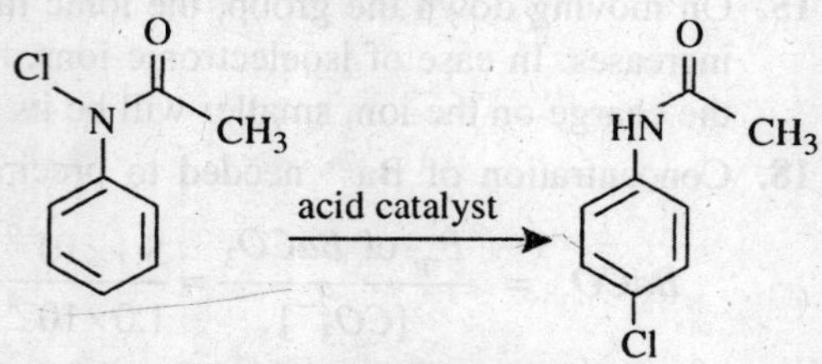

Let us apply the kinetics of first order reaction.

After 1 hours $K = \frac{2.303}{1}\log\left\{\frac{45}{32}\right\}$

$$= 0.34098\ \text{hour}^{-1}$$

After 2 hours $K = \frac{2.303}{2}\log\left\{\frac{45}{22.5}\right\}$

$$= 0.34660\ \text{hour}^{-1}$$

After 4 hours $K = \frac{2.303}{4}\log\left\{\frac{45}{11.3}\right\}$

$= 0.3455 \text{ hour}^{-1}$

After 6 hour $K = \frac{2.303}{6}\log\left\{\frac{45}{3.7}\right\}$

$= 0.4164 \text{ hour}^{-1}$

After 8 hours $K = \frac{2.303}{8}\log\left\{\frac{45}{2.9}\right\}$

$= 0.3428 \text{ hour}^{-1}$

Average value of constant $= 0.3584 \text{ hours}^{-1}$

Since, on applying first order kinetics, we get almost same values of rate constant after different time intervals, hence, the reaction is of first order.

Let us see the fraction decomposed after 3 hours.

$$K = \frac{2.303}{t}\log\left\{\frac{a}{a-x}\right\}$$

$$0.3584 = \frac{2.303}{3}\log\frac{a}{a-x}$$

$$\therefore \quad \frac{a}{a-x} = 2.98$$

$$\therefore \quad \frac{a-x}{a} = 0.3412$$

$$1-\frac{x}{a} = 0.3412$$

$$\therefore \quad \frac{x}{a} = 0.658 \text{ [fraction decomposed]}$$

33. A. We know,

$$\frac{0.693}{T_{1/2}} = \frac{2.303}{t}\log_{10}\left[\frac{N_0}{N}\right]$$

$$\frac{0.693}{8} = \frac{2.303}{4}\log_{10}\left[\frac{N_0}{N}\right]$$

$$\frac{N}{N_0} = 0.707$$

⇒ 70.7% of initial activity is present. Given that 67.7% activity is migrated to thyroid gland.

Thus, weight of I migrated to thyroid gland may be calculated as

$$\frac{67.7}{70.7}\times 100 = 95.75\%$$

$$i.e., \quad 0.1\times\frac{95.75}{100} = 0.09575 \ mg$$

B. Activity of 1g sample is the specific activity of the sample 10^6g contains 1g P^{32}

$\therefore$ 1g sample will contain 10^{-6} P^{32}

$$i.e., \quad \frac{10^{-6}}{31}\times 6.023\times 19^{23} \text{ atoms of } P^{32}$$

$$\lambda = \frac{0.693}{t_{1/2}} = \frac{0.693}{14.3\times 24\times 60\times 60}s^{-1}$$

$$-\frac{dN}{dt} = \lambda\cdot N$$

$$= \frac{0.693}{14.3\times 24\times 3600}\times\frac{10^{-6}}{31}\times 6.023\times 10^{23} \ dps$$

$$= 1.089 \times 10^{10} \ dps$$

Since this is activity *i.e.*, rate of decay of 1g sample

Specific activity = 1.089×10^{10} *dps* per gram

$$= \frac{1.089\times 10^{10}}{3.7\times 10^{10}} C_i \text{ per } g = 0.295 C_1 \text{ per } g$$

34. A. Synthesis $BeCl_2 + MeLi \rightarrow [Me_2Be]_n$

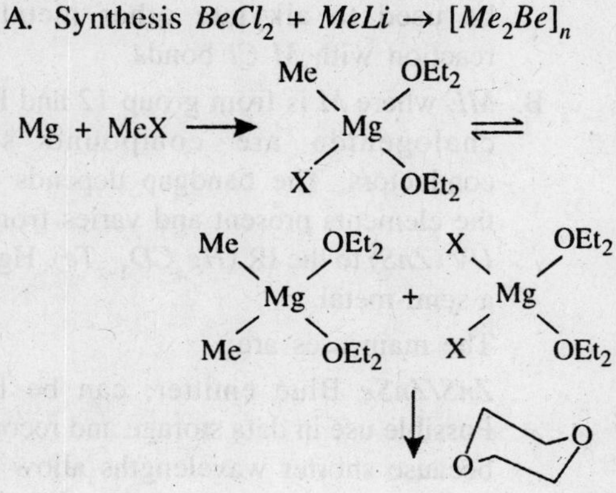

$$[Me_2Mg]_n \xleftarrow[\text{Heat}]{\text{Evaporate}} \underset{\text{soluble}}{Me_2Mg\ (\text{dioxan})} + \underset{\text{insoluble}}{MgI_2\ (\text{dioxan})}$$

Grignard reagents also contain such species as $[MeMg(OEt_2)_3][MgI_2\ Me(OEt_2)]$ and related ionic forms with *Me* and *I* exchanged, as well as dimeric species such as:

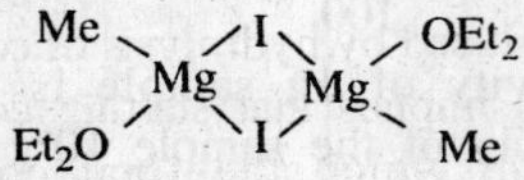

Structure of $BeMe_2$

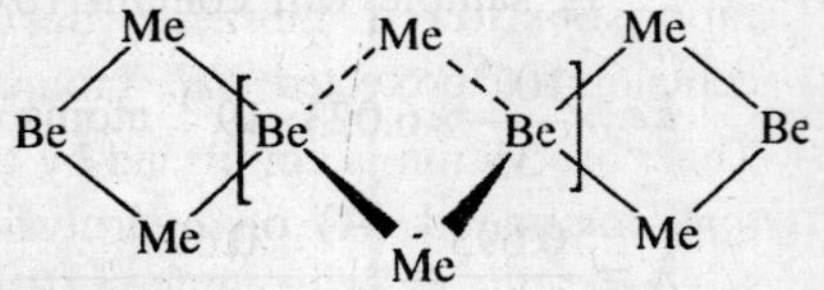

$3c\ 2e$ bonding

Me_2Mg is essentially an ionic solid.

Me_2Mg and Me_2Be both pyrophoric. Grignard solution is air sensitive.

Me_2Mg does not react with oxygen but inflames with water.

Me_2Mg and Me_2Be are both Lewis acids, reacting with *e.g.*, diethyl ether to give $Me_2M(OEt_2)_2$. They react with alcohols to give alkoxides and with primary or secondary amines to give amides.

All magnesium alkyls are good sources of *Me,* reacting with *e.g.*, aldehydes, ketones or acid chlorides. They can also be used to alkylate other metals by reaction with *M-Cl* bonds.

B. *ME* where *M* is from group 12 and E is a chalogenide are compound semi-conductors. The bandgap depends upon the elements present and varies from the *UV* (*ZnS*) to the IR ($Hg_xCD_{1-x}Te$). HgTe is a semi-metal.

The main uses are:

ZnS/ZnSe Blue emitter, can be laser. Possible use in data storage and recording because shorter wavelengths allow great storage density *CdSe* pigment and light emitting displays. For nanoparticles the bandgap can be varied from the *IR* (bulk material) right thought the visible to blue (small nanoparticles). This means that the one material can be used for emission of any colour of the rainbow.

$Hg_xCd_{1-x}Te$ is used in infrared lasers and detectors. The main uses of these detectors are in : Thermal Imaging (night vision, seeing through smoke screens, detecting people after earthquakes, medical applications, satellite weather maps)

Telecommuniucations: Using $Hg_xCd_{1-x}Te$/*CdTe* as a laser, *CdTe* as a detector and *ZBLAN* glass for the fibre, it is possible to increase the distance between repeater stations in fibre optic communications up to about 120 *km*.

Thin films can be made by *MOVPE*. Volatile organometallic compounds of group 12 such as Me_2Cd and *e.g.*, H_2Se are passed over a heated substrate, where they decompose give *e.g.*, *CdSe*.

C.

Acid	*X*	
HOX	*F, Cl, Br, I*	hypohalous
HXO_2	*Cl, Br*	halous
HXO_3	*Cl, Br, I*	halic
HXO_4	*Cl, Br, I*	perhalic

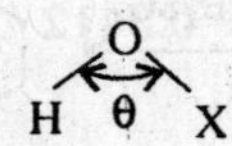

X	θ
Cl	103
F	97

O in H–O–F is very small may be H-bonding

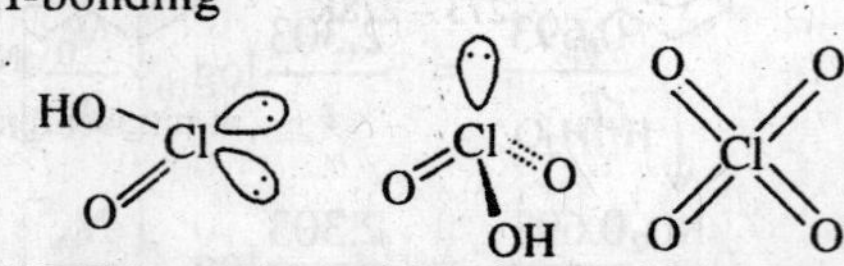

HOCl is used as a bleach, perchlorates are used as a solid rocket fuel with *Al*, also fireworks, background electrolyte, oxidizing agent.

35. A. *C, N* and *O* form particularly strong π bonds with themselves and with each other. This gives rise to allotropes (*e.g.*, *N* ≡ *N*, *O*=*O* and *O*=*O*–*O* denied to heavier elements (P_4 is tetrahedron with four single bonds around each *P* atom, S_8 has crown-like structure with *S-S* bonds throughout).

B. The inversion barrier needs to be above 100 *kJ* mol^{-1} if pure optical isomers are to be stable under normal conditions. Amines have inversion barrier well below this (≈ 30 *kJ* mol^{-1}), however tertiary phosphines (barrier for Me_3P ≈ 130 *kJ* mol^{-1}) are often readily resolvable.

36. A.

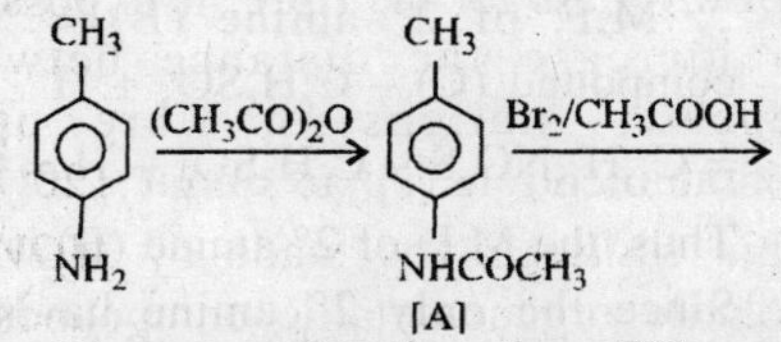

(more ortho para directing than CH_3 group)

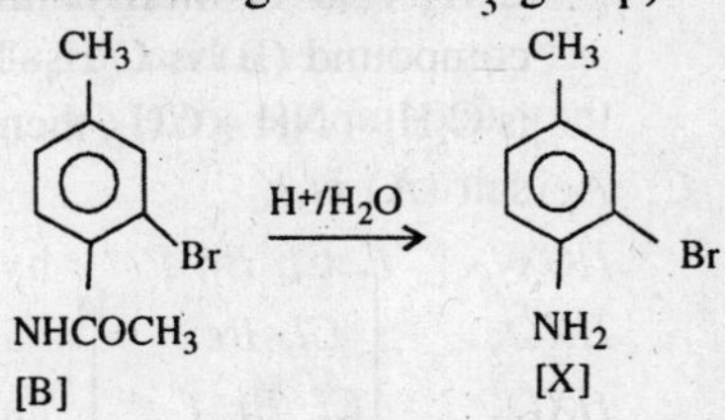

B.

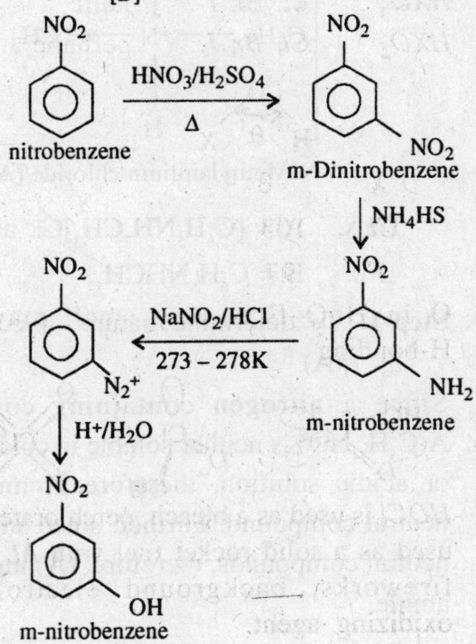

37. Step 1. *To determine the structures of compounds (A), (B) and (C).*

(*i*) The final compound, i.e., sulphanilamide is an aromatic compound containing —NH_2 and —SO_2 NH_2 at *p*-position of the benzene ring. Whereas SO_2NH_2 group has been introduced into the benzene ring *via* chlorosulphonation followed by treatment with NH_3, the NH_2 group has been produced by hydrolysis of compound (E). This implies that starting compound (*A*) (from which the final compound sulphanilamide has been prepared) is a monosubstituted benzene derivative containing a protected NH_2 group.

(*ii*) This observation is confirmed by the fact that compound (A) on hydrolysis with mineral acids gives compound (B) which on heating gives an obnoxious smell of carbylamine due to the formation of compound (B) must be a primary amine, *i.e.*, (B) is aniline and (C) is phenyl carbylamine.

(*iii*) Since a colourless substance (A) sparingly soluble in water on hydrolysis gives aniline (B), therefore, (A) must be acetanilide

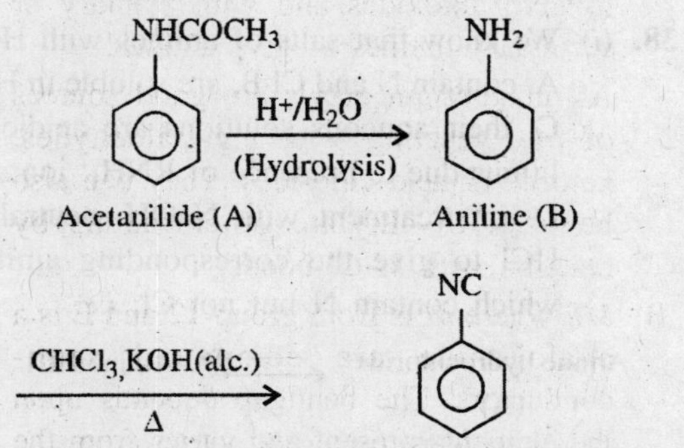

Step 2. To determine the structures of compounds (D) and (E).

If compound (A) is acetanilide, then structures of compounds (D) and (E) may be deduced as follows:

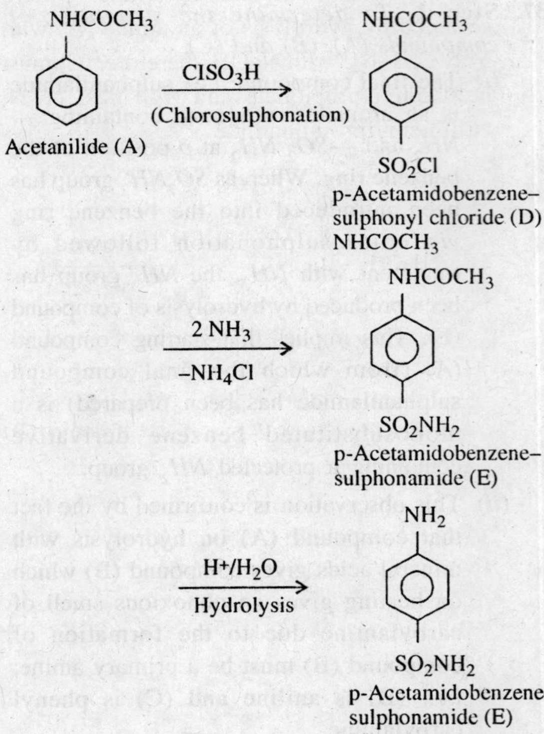

Thus, [A] = acetanilide, [B] = aniline, [C] = phenyl carbylamine, [D] = p-acetamidobenzene sulphonyl chloride and [E] = p-acetamidobenzenesulphonamide.

38. (*i*) We know that salts of amines with HCl: A. contain N and Cl B. are soluble in H_2O C. their aqueous solutions are acidic to litmus due to presence of RNH_3^+ ion and D. on treatment with NaOH, neutralize HCl to give the corresponding amines which contain N but not Cl, *i.e.*,

$$\underset{(A)}{\text{Amine hydrochloride}} \rightleftharpoons \text{Amine HCl} \xrightarrow{\text{NaOH}} \underset{(B)}{\text{Amine}} + H_2O + NaCl$$

Therefore (A) must be the hydrochloride salt of an amine and (B) must be the corresponding amine.

(*ii*) Since compound (B) on treatment with $C_6H_5SO_2Cl$ (Hinsberg's reagent) gives an insoluble product (C) with M.F. $C_{13}H_{13}NO_2S$, therefore (B) must be a 2° amine.

(*iii*) When a 2° amine is treated with $C_6H_5SO_2Cl$, the H-atom of 2° amine is replaced by $C_6H_5SO_2$ group, *i.e.*,

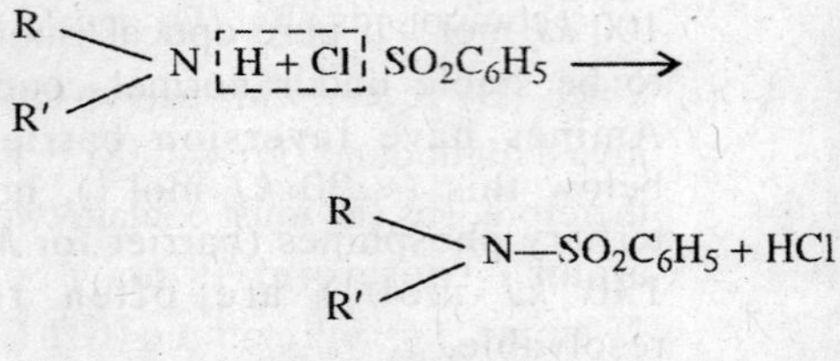

∴ M.F. of 2° amine (B) = M.F. of compound (C) – $C_6H_5SO_2$ + H

$= C_{13}H_{13}NO_2S - C_6H_5SO_2 + H = C_7H_9N$

Thus, the M.F. of 2° amine (B) is C_7H_9N. Since the only 2° amine having M.F. C_7H_9N is N-methylaniline, therefore, compound (B) is $C_6H_5-NH-CH_3$. If (B) is $C_6H_5-NH-CH_3$, then its hydrochloride salt (A) is

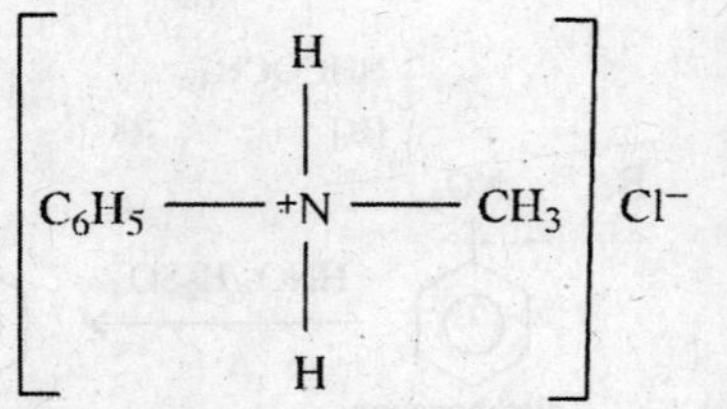

N-Methylanilium chloride (A)

Thus, $A = [C_6H_5NH_2CH_3]Cl^-$ and

$B = C_6H_5NHCH_3$

39. Step 1. To determine nature of compound (A).

Since a nitrogen containing compound $A(C_5H_{11}NO)$ is neither soluble in cold alkaline or acidic solution, therefore, it must be a neutral compound. Further, since amides are neutral compounds, therefore, (A) must be an amide.

Step 2. To determine nature of compound (B) and salt (C).

(*i*) Since an amide (A) when refluxed with NaOH solution, gives a salt (C) and a gas (B) therefore (C) must be sodium salt of an acid while (B) may be ammonia, a 1° or a 2° amine.

Step 3. To determine structures of compounds (B), (D) and (E).

(*i*) Since (B) reacts with acetyl chloride to give a compound (D) with M.F. C_4H_9HO, therefore, gas (B) must contain two carbon atoms. Therefore, it may be either 1° amine, *i.e.*, ethylamine ($CH_3CH_2NH_2$) or a 2° amine, *i.e.*, dimethylamine $(CH_3)_2NH$.

(*ii*) Further since (B) reacts with HNO_2 to form a yellow oily compound (E), therefore, (B) must be a 2° amine, *i.e.*, $(CH_3)_2NH$. If (B) is $(CH_3)_2NH$, then (D) must be N, N-dimethylacetamide and (E) must be N-nitroso-dimethylamine. Thus,

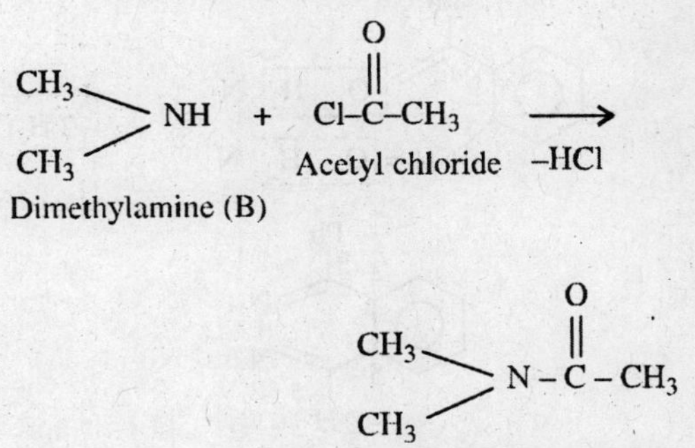

N, N–Dimethylamine (D)

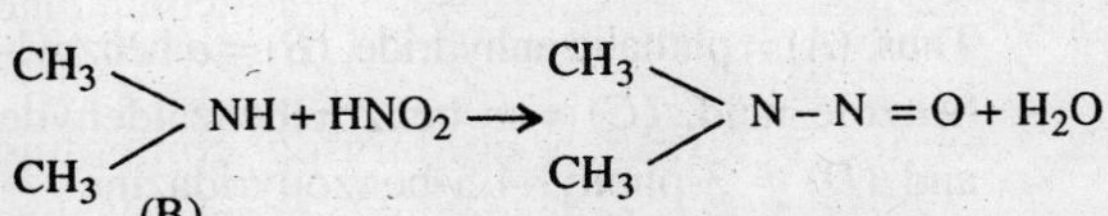

N, N–Dimethylamine (E)
(yellow oil)

Step 4. To determine the structures of compounds (A) and (C).

Since salt (C) and dimethylamine (B) are obtained by hydrolysis of an amide (A) with M.F. $C_5H_{11}NO$ with NaOH, therefore, (C) must be sodium propionate and (A) must be N, N-dimethylpropionamide.

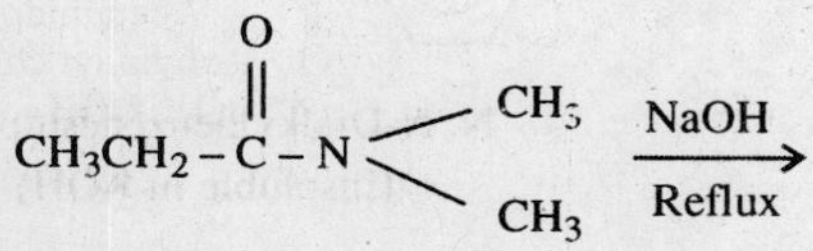

N, N–Dimethylpropionamide (A)
M.F. = $C_5H_{11}NO$

CH_3CH_2COONa + $(CH_3)_2NH$
Sod. propionate (C) Dimethylamine (B) (A gas)

Thus, $A = CH_3CH_2CON(CH_3)_2$,

$B = (CH_3)_2NH$,

$C = CH_3CH_2COONa$,

$D = CH_3CON(CH_3)_2$

and $E = (CH_3)_2N - N = O$.

40. A. Acetylation

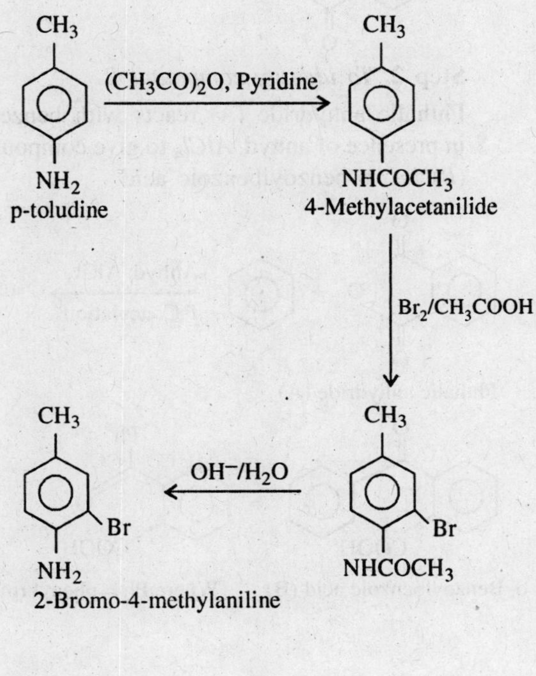

B. 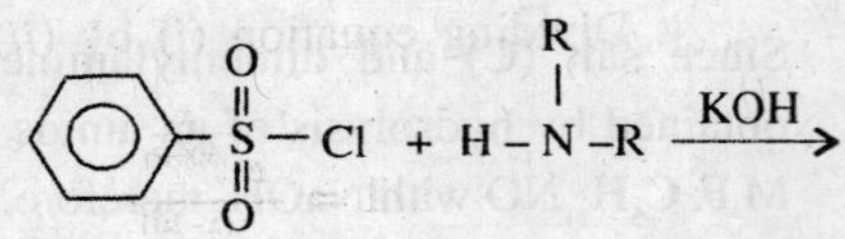

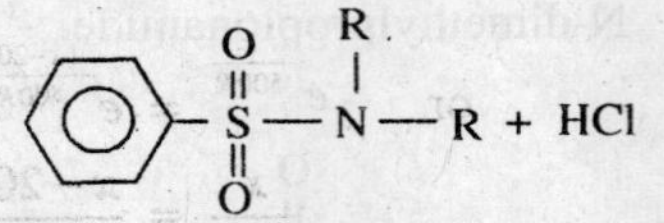

N, N-Dialkylbenzenesulphonamids
(Insoluble in KOH)

C.

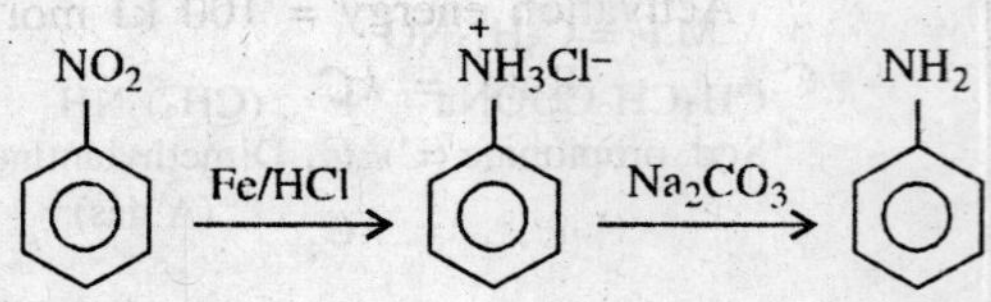

Nitrobenzene Aniline

41. Step 1. *To identify compound A.*

An important reactant with *M.E.* $C_8H_4O_3$ which readily undergoes *F.C.* reaction with benzene is phtahlic anhydride.

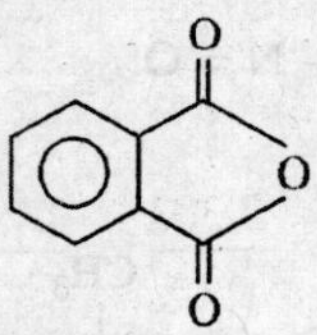

Phthalic anhydride (M.F. $C_8H_4O_3$)

Step 2. *To identify compound B*

Phthalic anhydride (*A*) reacts with benzene in presence of anhyd. $AlCl_3$ to give compound (*B*) *i.e., o*-benzoylbenzoic acid.

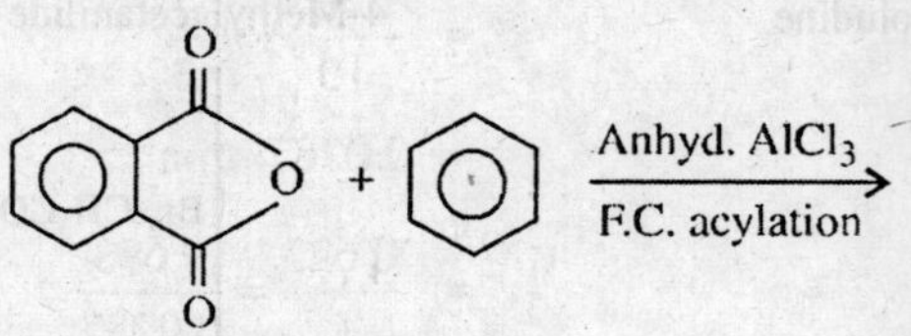

Phthalic anhydride (A)

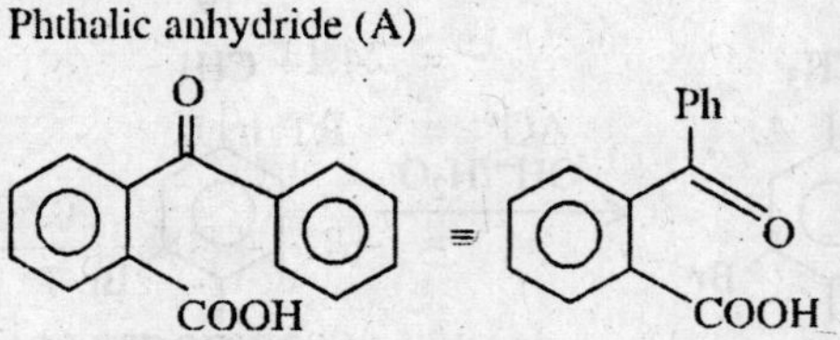

o–Benzoylbenzoic acid (B) (Where Ph = phenyl ring)

Step 3. *To identify compound (C).*

The compound (*B*) reacts with PCl_5 to give *o*-benzoylbenzoyl chloride which upon *Rosenmund's reduction* gives *o*-benzoylbenzaldehyde.

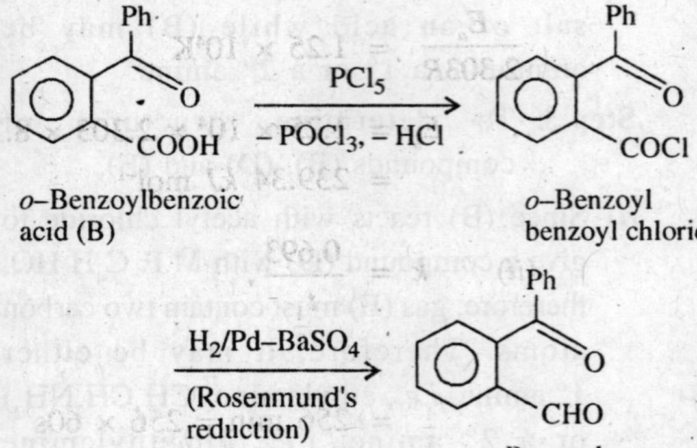

o–Benzoylbenzoic acid (B) → *o*–Benzoyl benzoyl chloride → *o*–Benzoyl–benzaldehyde (C)

Step 4. *To identify compound (D).*

The compound (*C*) being a 1, 4-dicarbonyl compound condenses with hydrazine (NH_2NH_2) to give pyridazine derivative (*D*)

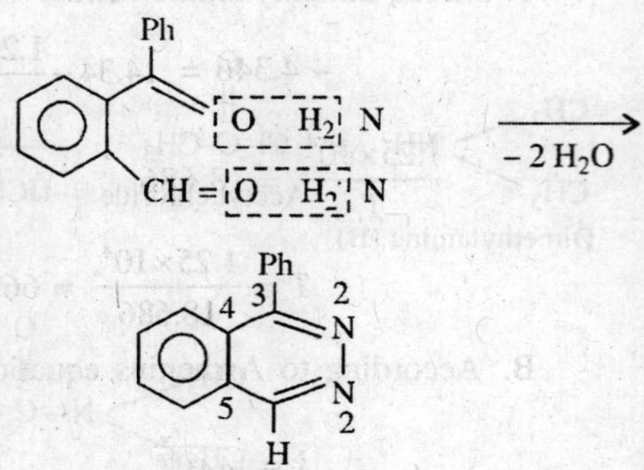

3–Phenyl–4, 5–benzopyridazine (D)

Thus, (*A*) = phthalic anhydride, (*B*) = *o* benzoylbenzoic acid, (*C*) = *o*-benzoylbenzaldehyde and (*D*) = 3-phenyl-4,5-benzopyridazine.

42. A. (*i*)

$$\log k(s^{-1}) = 14.34 - \frac{1.25 \times 10^4 K}{T} \quad ...(i)$$

Arrhenius equation may be written as

$$\log k = \log A - \frac{E_a}{2.303RT}$$

Comparing the equations we get,

$$\frac{E_a}{2.303R} = 1.25 \times 10^4 \text{K}$$

$$\therefore \quad E_a = 1.25 \times 10^4 \times 2.303 \times 8.314$$

$$= 239.34 \ kJ \ \text{mol}^{-1}$$

(*ii*) $$k = \frac{0.693}{t_{\frac{1}{2}}},$$

$$t_{\frac{1}{2}} = 256 \text{ min} = 256 \times 60\text{s}$$

$$\therefore \quad k = \frac{0.693}{256 \times 60} = 4.51 \times 10^{-5}\text{s}^{-1}$$

Substituting the value of k in equation (*i*), we get

$$\log(4.51 \times 10^{-5}) = 14.34 - \frac{1.25 \times 10^4 K}{T}$$

$$-4.346 = 14.34 - \frac{1.25 \times 10^4}{T}$$

$$\frac{1.25 \times 10^4}{T} = 18.686$$

$$\therefore \quad T = \frac{1.25 \times 10^4}{18.686} = 669\text{K}.$$

B. According to Arrhenius equation,

$$k = Ae^{-\frac{E_a}{RT}}$$

Let activation energy in the absence of catalyst = $x kJ$ mol^{-1}

and activation energy in the presence of catalyst = (x – 20) kJ mol^{-1}

At 500 K $$k = Ae^{-\frac{x}{500R}} \quad ...(i)$$

At 400 K $$k = Ae^{-\frac{(x-20)}{400R}} \quad ...(ii)$$

Dividing equation (*i*) by (*ii*),

$$1 = \frac{e^{-\frac{x}{500R}}}{e^{-\frac{(x-20)}{400R}}} \quad (k \text{ is same})$$

or $$e^{-\frac{x}{500R}} = e^{-\frac{(x-20)}{400R}}$$

$$\frac{x}{500} = \frac{x-20}{400}$$

$$100x = 10000$$

$$x = 100 \ kJ \ \text{mol}^{-1}$$

Activation energy = 100 kJ mol^{-1}

C. Rate = kC

or Rate, $r_1 = kC_1$

Rate, $r_2 = kC_2$

$$\therefore \quad \frac{r_1}{r_2} = \frac{C_1}{C_2}$$

$$\therefore \quad \frac{r_1(at 10 \text{ min})}{r_2(at 20 \text{ min})} = \frac{C_1}{C_2} = \frac{0.04}{0.03}$$

Now, $$t = \frac{2.303}{t} \log \frac{C_1}{C_2}$$

or $$k = \frac{2.303}{t} \log \frac{C_1}{C_2}$$

When $t = 10$ min

$$k = \frac{2.303}{10} \log \frac{0.04}{0.03}$$

$$k = \frac{2.303}{10} \log \frac{4}{3}$$

$$= 0.0287 \text{ min}^{-1}$$

$$t_{\frac{1}{2}} = \frac{0.693}{k} = \frac{0.693}{0.0287}$$

$$= 24.14 \text{ min.}$$

43. A. $$\Delta G° = -RT \ln k$$

$$= -RT\left(4.800 - \frac{20.50}{T}\right)$$

$$= 4.800RT + (20.50 \times R)$$

B. It is given that

$$\ln K = 4.800 - \frac{20.50}{T}$$

$$\therefore \quad \frac{\partial \ln K}{\partial T} = \frac{20.50}{T^2} = \frac{\Delta H^\circ}{RT^2}$$

$$\therefore \quad \Delta H^\circ = 20.50 \times R$$

Further $\left(\frac{\partial \Delta G^\circ}{\partial T}\right)_p = -\Delta S^\circ$

$$\Delta G^\circ = 20.50R - 4.800\ RT$$

$$\therefore \quad \frac{\partial \Delta G^\circ}{\partial T} = -4.800 \times R = -\Delta S^\circ$$

$$\therefore \quad \Delta S^\circ = 4.800 \times R = 4.8R$$

C. The relevant equation is

$$\Delta S = C_p \ln\left(\frac{T_2}{T_1}\right) - R\ln\left(\frac{p_2}{p_1}\right)$$

In the above case, pressure remains constant.

i.e., $p_2 = p_1$

$$\therefore \quad \Delta S = C_p \ln\frac{T_2}{T_1}$$

Further $C_p = C_p + R = \frac{3}{2}R + R = \frac{5}{2}R$

$T_1 = 25°C = 298K$ and

$T_2 = 300°C = 573$ K

$$\therefore \Delta S = \frac{5}{2}R \times 2.303 \times \log\frac{573}{298}\ \text{cal. deg}^{-1}$$

$$= \frac{5}{2} \times 1.987 \times 2.303 \times \log\frac{573}{298}$$

$$= 3.248 \text{ cal deg}^{-1}\text{ mol}^{-1}$$

44. A.

$$E_{Total} = \int_0^\infty \in n(\in) d\in$$

$$= \frac{2\pi N}{(\pi KT)^{\frac{3}{2}}} \int_0^\infty \in^{\frac{3}{2}} e^{-\frac{\in}{KT}} d\in$$

Making use of standard integrals

$$\int_0^\infty \in^{\frac{3}{2}} e^{-a\in} du = \frac{3}{4a^2}\sqrt{\frac{\pi}{a}}$$

$$= \frac{2\pi N}{(\pi KT)^{3/2}} \times \frac{3}{4}(KT)^2\sqrt{\pi KT}$$

$$\left(\therefore a = \frac{1}{KT}\right)$$

$$= \frac{3}{2}NKT$$

$$E_{Average} = \frac{E_{Total}}{N} = \frac{3}{2}KT$$

B.

$$\Delta E = \left(n^2_{excited} - n^2_{ground}\right)\frac{h^2}{2mr^2}$$

$$= \left(2^2 - 1^2\right)\frac{h^2}{2mr^2}$$

$$= 9.27 \times 10^{-12} \text{ erg.}$$

C. $\frac{3}{2}H_{2(g)} + \frac{1}{2}N_{2(g)} \rightleftharpoons NH_{3(g)}$

$$\Rightarrow \quad K_p = \frac{p_{NH_3}}{p_{N_2}^{\frac{1}{2}}\, p_{H_2}^{\frac{3}{2}}}$$

$$= \frac{3.03atm}{(6.75atm)^{\frac{1}{2}}(20.22atm)^{\frac{3}{2}}}$$

$$= \frac{3.03}{(6.75)^{\frac{1}{2}}(20.22)^{\frac{3}{2}}}\, atm^{-1}$$

$$= \frac{3.03}{2.60 \times 90.92}\, atm^{-1}$$

$$= 1.28 \times 10^{-2}\ atm^{-1}.$$